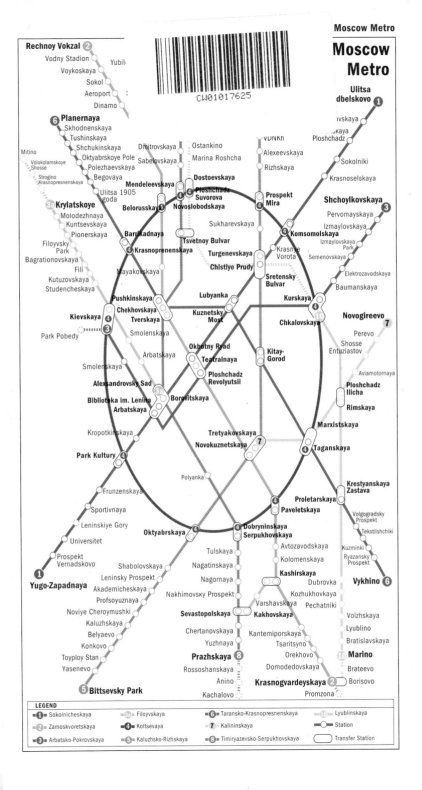

# Moscow Metro

## Moscow Metro

**LEGEND**

- ■■① Sokolnicheskaya
- ■■② Zamoskvoretskaya
- ■■③ Arbatsko-Pokrovskaya
- ③ₐ Filoyvskaya
- ■■④ Koltsevaya
- ■■⑤ Kaluzhsko-Rizhskaya
- ■■⑥ Taransko-Krasnopresnenskaya
- ⑦ Kalininskaya
- ■■⑧ Timiryazevsko-Serpukhovskaya
- ⑩ Lyublinskaya
- ■■ Station
- ⬭ Transfer Station

# Moscow

ZOO PARK

Khodynskaya

Presnensky Val

Tishinsky per.

Bolshaya Gruzinskaya ul.

Brestskaya ul.

Pervaya Tverskaya-Yamskaya

Oruzheyny p

Sadov.-Triu

ul. 1905 Goda

Sergeya Makeeva

Krasina

Yar. Gasheka

Zoologicheskaya

Sadovaya-Kudrin.

Malaya

Central Museum of the Revolution

PUS

TVERSKAYA

M ULTISA 1905 GODA

Krasnaya Presnya

M BARRIKADNAYA

Chekhov's House Museum

Bronnaya

Tverskoy bulvar

Leont

Shmitovsky pr.

Trekhgor. Val

KRASNOPRESNENSKAYA M

Kudrinskaya

Gorky's Apartment

Mantulinskaya

Rochdelskaya

KUDRINSKAYA PL.

ul. Gercena

NIKITSKIE VOROTA PL.

Nikitsky B-ul.

Merzlyakovsky

Mezhdnarodnaya Hotel

Konyushkovskaya

United States

Novinski bul.

Povarskaya

Trubnikovsky p.

Krasnopresnenskaya nab.

Tarasa Shevchenko

Novy Arbat

Novy Arbat

M ARBA

ARBATSKAYA P

Ukraina Hotel

ARBATSKAYA M

Zi

Protoch. per.

M SMOLENSKAYA

ul. Arbat

Starokonyushen. per.

Gogolevsky b.

Koly

Semashko

Kutuzovsky pr.

SMOLENSKAYA M

Kriv. p.

Foreign Ministry

Plotnikov per.

ul. Yesnina

ul. Shchukina

KROPOTKINSKAYA M

C.

th

KIEVSKAYA M

M

M

Rostovskaya nab.

Tolstoy Musuem

Pushkin Literary Museum

ul. Ostozhenka

Kievsky Station

ul. Plyuschikha

Smolensky bulvar

ul. Ryleeva

Prechinstenka

Prechistenska

Mosky-

Berezhkovskaya nab.

Moskva

Burdenko

Zubov. bul.

Krymsk

Savvinskaya nab.

Bolshoy Savvinsky

Pogodinskaya

Elanskovo

M PARK KULTURY

Frunzenskaya nab.

Pushkinskaya nab.

GORKY PARK

Novodev. pr.

Bolshaya Pirogovskaya ul.

Trubetskaya ul.

ul. Usacheva

FRUNZENSKAYA M

Frunzenskaya 1.

Novodevichy Monastery and Cemetary

SPORTIVNAYA M

Komsomolsky

Frunzenskaya 2.

SPORTIVNAYA M

Dovatora

Efremova

Frunzenskaya 3.

## Moscow

0        400 yards

0        400 meters

# Moscow

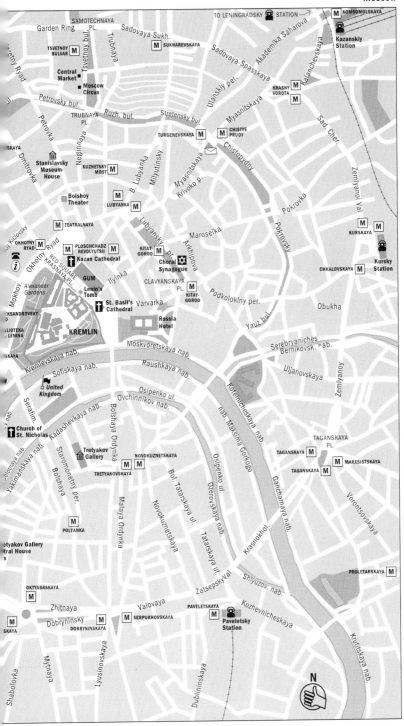

# Московское Метро

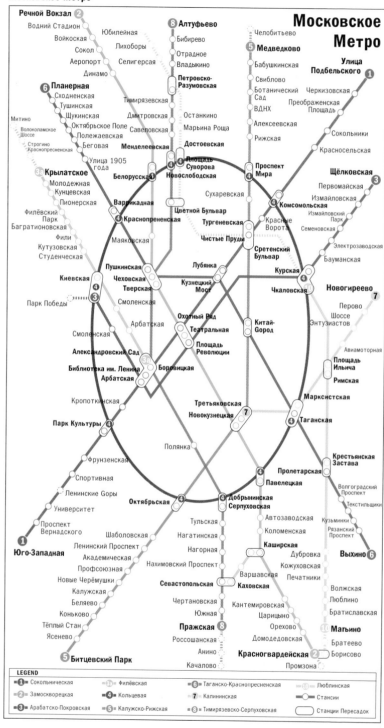

**Московское Метро**

Речной Вокзал ②
Водный Стадион
Войковская
Сокол
Аэропорт
Динамо
Юбилейная
Лихоборы
Селигерсая

⑥ Планерная
Сходненская
Тушинская
Щукинская
Октябрьское Поле
Полежаевская
Беговая
Митино
Волоколамское Шоссе
Строгино
Краснопресненская
Улица 1905 года

③а Крылатское
Молодежная
Кунцевская
Пионерская
Филёвский Парк
Багратионовская
Фили
Кутузовская
Студенческая

Киевская ④
Парк Победы ③

⑧ Алтуфьево
Бибирево
Отрадное
Владыкино
Петровско-Разумовское
Тимирязевская
Дмитровская
Савеловская
Менделеевская
Достоевская
Площадь Суворова ④
Новослободская ④
Сухаревская
Цветной Бульвар
Тургеневская
Чистые Пруды
Маяковская

Челобитьево
⑤ Медведково
Бабушкинская
Свиблово
Ботанический Сад
ВДНХ
Алексеевская
Рижская
Проспект Мира ④
Комсомольская ④
Красные Ворота
Сретенский Бульвар

Улица Подбельского ①
Черкизовская
Преображенская Площадь
Сокольники
Красносельская

Щёлковская ③
Первомайская
Измайловская
Измайловский Парк
Семеновская
Электрозаводская
Бауманская

Барракадная
④ Краснопрененская
Пушкинская
Чеховская
Тверская
Смоленская
Арбатская
Охотный Ряд
Театральная
Площадь Революции
Александровский Сад
Библиотека им. Ленина ③а
Арбатская
Боровицкая
Кропоткинская
Парк Культуры ④
Фрунзенская
Спортивная
Ленинские Горы
Университет
Проспект Вернадского
① Юго-Западная
Шаболовская
Ленинский Проспект
Академическая
Профсоюзная
Новые Черёмушки
Калужская
Беляево
Коньково
Тёплый Стан
Ясенево
⑤ Битцевский Парк

Менделеевская
Останкино
Марьина Роща

Лубянка
Кузнецкий Мост
Китай-Город
Третьяковская
Новокузнецкая ⑦
Полянка
Октябрьская ④
Добрынинская ④
Серпуховская
Тульская
Нагатинская
Нагорная
Нахимовский Проспект
Севастопольская
Чертановская
Южная
Пражская ⑧
Россошанская
Анино
Качалово

Курская ④
Чкаловская
Китай-Город
Площадь Ильича
Римская
Марксистская
Таганская ④
Крестьянская Застава
Пролетарская ④
Павелецкая
Автозаводская
Коломенская
Каширская
Варшавская
Каховская
Кантемировская
Царицыно
Орехово
Домодедовская
Красногвардейская ②

Новогиреево ⑦
Перово
Шоссе Энтузиастов
Авиамоторная

Волгоградский Проспект
Текстильщики
Кузьминки
Рязанский Проспект
Выхино ⑥
Дубровка
Кожуховская
Печатники
Волжская
Люблино
Братиславская
Марьино ⑩
Братеево
Борисово ②
Промзона

## LEGEND

- ① Сокольническая
- ② Замоскворецкая
- ③ Арбатско-Покровская
- ③а Филёвская
- ④ Кольцевая
- ⑤ Калужско-Рижская
- ⑥ Таганско-Краснопресненская
- ⑦ Калининская
- ⑧ Тимирязевско-Серпуховская
- ⑩ Люблинская
- Станции
- Станции Пересадок

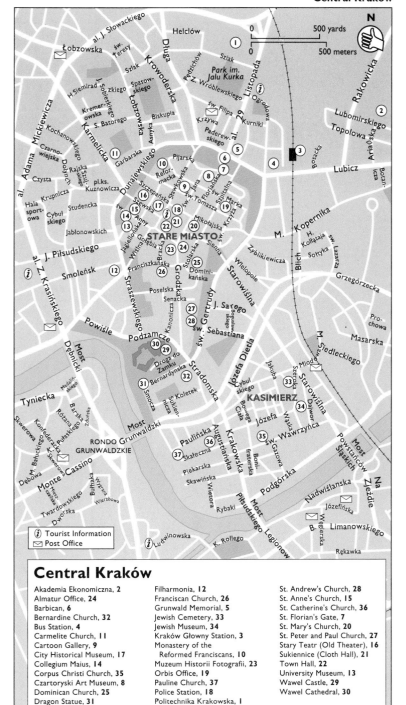

# Central Kraków

Akademia Ekonomiczna, **2**
Almatur Office, **24**
Barbican, **6**
Bernardine Church, **32**
Bus Station, **4**
Carmelite Church, **11**
Cartoon Gallery, **9**
City Historical Museum, **17**
Collegium Maius, **14**
Corpus Christi Church, **35**
Czartoryski Art Museum, **8**
Dominican Church, **25**
Dragon Statue, **31**

Filharmonia, **12**
Franciscan Church, **26**
Grunwald Memorial, **5**
Jewish Cemetery, **33**
Jewish Museum, **34**
Kraków Główny Station, **3**
Monastery of the
   Reformed Franciscans, **10**
Muzeum Historii Fotografii, **23**
Orbis Office, **19**
Pauline Church, **37**
Police Station, **18**
Politechnika Krakowska, **1**

St. Andrew's Church, **28**
St. Anne's Church, **15**
St. Catherine's Church, **36**
St. Florian's Gate, **7**
St. Mary's Church, **20**
St. Peter and Paul Church, **27**
Stary Teatr (Old Theater), **16**
Sukiennice (Cloth Hall), **21**
Town Hall, **22**
University Museum, **13**
Wawel Castle, **29**
Wawel Cathedral, **30**

(i) Tourist Information
✉ Post Office

Prague

## Prague

American Express, **23**
Anešský klášter, **22**
Basilica sv. Jiří (Basilica
of St. George), **5**
Canadian Embassy, **1**
Chrám sv. Mikuláše (St.
Nicholas Church), **8**
Chrám sv. Víta (St.
Vitus's Cathedral), **3**
Florenc bus station, **20**
Hlavní nádraží (Main train
station), **14**
Kafka's grave, **24**
Karlův most (Charles
Bridge), **11**
Lobkovický palác, **6**
Main post office, **21**
Masarykovo nádraží, **19**
Matka Boží před Týnem
(Týn Church), **17**
Národní divadlo
(National Theater), **12**
Národní galérie
(National Gallery), **2**
Národní muzeum
(National Museum), **13**
Panna Maria Sněžná
(Church of Our Lady
of the Snows), **15**
Panna Maria Vítězna
(Church of Our
Lady Victorious), **10**
Powder Tower, **18**
Staroměstská radnice
(Old Town Hall), **16**
Starý královský palác
(Old Royal Palace), **4**
U.K. Embassy, **7**
U.S. Embassy, **9**

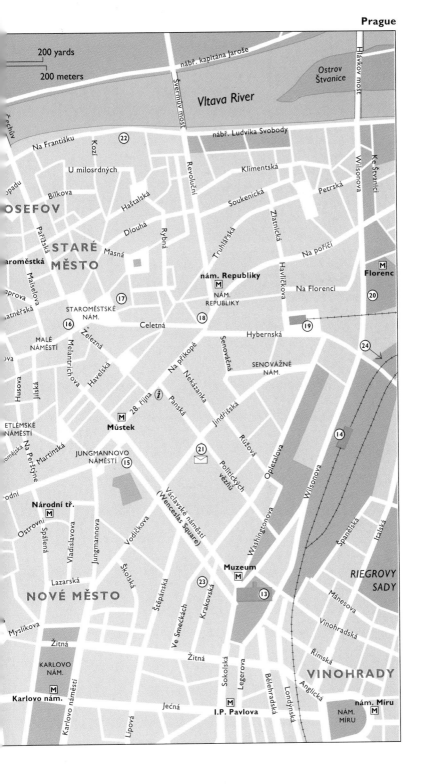

200 yards

200 meters

nábř. kapitána Jaroše

Švermuv most

Vltava River

Ostrov
Štvanice

Hlávkov most

r chův

Na Františku

Kozí

nábř. Ludvíka Svobody

Ke Štvanici

Wilsonova

U milosrdných

Klimentská

Petrská

²²

opadu

Bílkova

Revoluční

Soukenická

Zlatnická

Na poříčí

OSEFOV

Haštalská

Pařížská

Dlouhá

Rybná

Truhlářská

Havlíčkova

STARÉ

Masná

Na Florenci

Florenc

aroměstká

MĚSTO

nám. Republiky

Ⓜ

NÁM.
REPUBLIKY

M

²⁰

Maiselova

aprova

¹⁷

atnéřská

STAROMĚSTSKÉ
NÁM.

Celetná

¹⁸

Hybernská

¹⁹

SENOVÁŽNÉ
NÁM.

²⁴

MALÉ
NÁMĚSTÍ

¹⁶

Železná

Senovážná

va

Melantrichova

Havelská

Na příkopě

Nekázanka

ova

Husova

Jilská

28. října

ⓘ

Panská

Jindřišská

Ružová

ETLÉMSKÉ
NÁMĚSTÍ

Můstek

Ⓜ

Opletalova

¹⁴

omějská

Na Perštýně

Martinská

JUNGMANNOVO
NÁMĚSTÍ

¹⁵

²¹

✉

Politických
vězňů

Wilsonova

Národní tř.

Ⓜ

Jungmannova

Václavské náměstí
(Wenceslas Square)

Washingtonova

Španělská

Italská

Ostrovní

Spálená

Vladislavova

Vodičkova

RIEGROVY
SADY

NOVÉ MĚSTO

Lazarská

Školská

Štěpánská

Krakovská

Muzeum

Ⓜ

¹³

Mánesova

Vinohradská

Myslíkova

Ve Smečkách

Žitná

Sokolská

Legerova

Bělehradská

Londýnská

Anglická

Římská

KARLOVO
NÁM.

Žitná

VINOHRADY

Karlovo nám.

Ⓜ

Karlovo náměstí

Lipová

Ječná

I.P. Pavlova

Ⓜ

nám. Míru

Ⓜ

NÁM.
MÍRU

# Central Budapest

## Central Budapest

Hárfša u.

Erzsébet körút

Wesselényi u.

Kertész u.

Akácfa u.

Klauzál u.

Nagy

Diófa u.

Dohány u.

Kazinczy u.

Dob u.

Holló u.

Rumbach S. u.

Király u.

Andrássy út.

Lázár u.

BAJCSY-ZS. ÚT

**M1**

Bajcsy-Zsilinsky út.

DEÁK TÉR
DEÁK F. TÉR

**M123**

Tourinform **i**

José u.

Paulay Ede u.

**†** St. Stephen's Basilica

József A. u.

OKtóber 6.

Bécsi u.

City Hall

VÖRÖSMARTY TÉR **M1**

Deák F. u.

Nádor u.

Arany János u.

**i** Budapest Tourist

ROOSEVELT TÉR

Apáczai Csere J. u.

Belgrád rakpart

Vigadó tér Boat Station

Petőfi S. u.

Váci u.

**i** Non-stop Hotel Service

Szabad S.

Erzsébet híd

Széchenyi rakpart

Széchenyi lánchíd

TO PARLIAMENT

## Danube River (Duna)

Groza Péter rakpart

Apród u.

Döbrentei u.

DÖBRENTEI TÉR

Hadnagy u.

Attila út.

Kristina körút

Kereszt u.

Hegyalja út.

Lánchíd u.

Siklo u.

**†** National Gallery

Budapest History Museum

Ludwig Museum

**CASTLE HILL (VÁRHEGY)**

TO GELLÉRT HILL

Népszinház u.

BLAHA L. TÉR **M2**

BLAHA L. TÉR

Rákóczi út.

József körút

Gyulai P. u.

Vas u.

Szentkirályi u.

Mária u.

Horánszky u.

**☸** Great Synagogue and Hungarian Jewish Museum

Rákóczi út.

Puskin u.

Bródy Sándor u.

**†** Hungarian National Museum

Múzeum u.

Baross u.

Üllői út.

**M3** KÁLVIN TÉR

KÁLVIN TÉR

Semmelweis u.

Kossuth L. u.

Magyar u.

**†** Franciscan Church

Múzeum körút.

**M2** ASTORIA

Károly körút

Kecskeméti u.

Reáltanoda u.

Károlyi M. u.

Ferenczy I. u.

Veres Pálné

Váci u.

Molnár u.

Városház u.

FERENCIEK TÉR

**M3** FERENCIEK TERE

IBUSZ **i**

300 yards
300 meters

0
0

## 📎 Let's Go writers travel on your budget.

"Guides that penetrate the veneer of the holiday brochures and mine the grit of real life."

—*The Economist*

"The writers seem to have experienced every rooster-packed bus and lunar-surfaced mattress about which they write."

—*The New York Times*

"All the dirt, dirt cheap."

—*People*

## 📎 Great for independent travelers.

"The guides are aimed not only at young budget travelers but at the independent traveler; a sort of streetwise cookbook for traveling alone."

—*The New York Times*

"Flush with candor and irreverence, chock full of budget travel advice."

—*The Des Moines Register*

"An indispensible resource, *Let's Go*'s practical information can be used by every traveler."

—*The Chattanooga Free Press*

## 📎 Let's Go is completely revised each year.

"Only *Let's Go* has the zeal to annually update every title on its list."

—*The Boston Globe*

"Unbeatable: good sightseeing advice; up-to-date info on restaurants, hotels, and inns; a commitment to money-saving travel; and a wry style that brightens nearly every page."

—*The Washington Post*

## 📎 All the important information you need.

"*Let's Go* authors provide a comedic element while still providing concise information and thorough coverage of the country. Anything you need to know about budget traveling is detailed in this book."

—*The Chicago Sun-Times*

"Value-packed, unbeatable, accurate, and comprehensive."

—*Los Angeles Times*

# Let's Go Publications

Let's Go: Alaska & the Pacific Northwest 2001
Let's Go: Australia 2001
Let's Go: Austria & Switzerland 2001
Let's Go: Boston 2001 **New Title!**
Let's Go: Britain & Ireland 2001
Let's Go: California 2001
Let's Go: Central America 2001
Let's Go: China 2001
Let's Go: Eastern Europe 2001
Let's Go: Europe 2001
Let's Go: France 2001
Let's Go: Germany 2001
Let's Go: Greece 2001
Let's Go: India & Nepal 2001
Let's Go: Ireland 2001
Let's Go: Israel 2001
Let's Go: Italy 2001
Let's Go: London 2001
Let's Go: Mexico 2001
Let's Go: Middle East 2001
Let's Go: New York City 2001
Let's Go: New Zealand 2001
Let's Go: Paris 2001
Let's Go: Peru, Bolivia & Ecuador 2001 **New Title!**
Let's Go: Rome 2001
Let's Go: San Francisco 2001 **New Title!**
Let's Go: South Africa 2001
Let's Go: Southeast Asia 2001
Let's Go: Spain & Portugal 2001
Let's Go: Turkey 2001
Let's Go: USA 2001
Let's Go: Washington, D.C. 2001
Let's Go: Western Europe 2001 **New Title!**

## Let's Go *Map Guides*

| | |
|---|---|
| Amsterdam | New Orleans |
| Berlin | New York City |
| Boston | Paris |
| Chicago | Prague |
| Florence | Rome |
| Hong Kong | San Francisco |
| London | Seattle |
| Los Angeles | Sydney |
| Madrid | Washington, D.C. |

**Coming Soon:** *Dublin* and *Venice*

# EASTERN
# EUROPE
# 2001

**Andrea Volfová** editor
**Matthew DeTar Gibson** associate editor
**Xunhua Wong** associate editor

researcher-writers

| | |
|---|---|
| Taryn Arthur | Katie Heikkinen |
| Jessica Lucy Berenbeim | Kit Hodge |
| Kate Damon | Katharine Holt |
| David Egan | Maxfield Morange |
| Michal Engelman | Jennifer O'Brien |
| Kieran Fitzgerald | Nicholas Topjian |

**Filip Wojciechowski, John Fiore** map editors

**Macmillan**

## HELPING LET'S GO

If you want to share your discoveries, suggestions, or corrections, please drop us a line. We read every piece of correspondence, whether a postcard, a 10-page email, or a coconut. Please note that mail received after May 2001 may be too late for the 2002 book, but will be kept for future editions. **Address mail to:**

**Let's Go: Eastern Europe**
**67 Mount Auburn Street**
**Cambridge, MA 02138**
**USA**

Visit Let's Go at **http://www.letsgo.com,** or send email to:

**feedback@letsgo.com**
**Subject: "Let's Go: Eastern Europe"**

In addition to the invaluable travel advice our readers share with us, many are kind enough to offer their services as researchers or editors. Unfortunately, our charter enables us to employ only currently enrolled Harvard students.

Published in Great Britain 2001 by Macmillan, an imprint of Macmillan Publishers Ltd, 25 Eccleston Place, London, SW1W 9NF, Basingstoke and Oxford.
Associated companies throughout the world
www.macmillan.com

Maps by David Lindroth copyright © 2001, 2000, 1999, 1998, 1997, 1996, 1995, 1994, 1993, 1992, 1991, 1990, 1989, 1988 by St. Martin's Press.

Published in the United States of America by St. Martin's Press.

ISBN: 0-333-90122-3
First edition
10 9 8 7 6 5 4 3 2 1

**Let's Go: Eastern Europe** is written by Let's Go Publications, 67 Mount Auburn Street, Cambridge, MA 02138, USA.

**Let's Go®** and the thumb logo are trademarks of Let's Go, Inc.
Printed in the USA on recycled paper with biodegradable soy ink.

# ABOUT LET'S GO

## FORTY-ONE YEARS OF WISDOM

As a new millennium arrives, *Let's Go: Europe*, now in its 41st edition and translated into seven languages, reigns as the world's bestselling international travel guide. For over four decades, travelers criss-crossing the Continent have relied on *Let's Go* for inside information on the hippest backstreet cafes, the most pristine secluded beaches, and the best routes from border to border. In the last 20 years, our rugged researchers have stretched the frontiers of backpacking and expanded our coverage into Asia, Africa, Australia, and the Americas. This year, we've introduced a new city guide series with books on San Francisco and our hometown, Boston. Now, our seven city guides feature sharp photos, more maps, and an overall more user-friendly design. We've also returned to our roots with the inaugural edition of *Let's Go: Western Europe*.

It all started in 1960 when a handful of well-traveled students at Harvard University handed out a 20-page mimeographed pamphlet offering a collection of their tips on budget travel to passengers on student charter flights to Europe. The following year, in response to the instant popularity of the first volume, students traveling to Europe researched the first full-fledged edition of *Let's Go: Europe*, a pocket-sized book featuring honest, practical advice, witty writing, and a decidedly youthful slant on the world. Throughout the 60s and 70s, our guides reflected the times. In 1969 we taught travelers how to get from Paris to Prague on "no dollars a day" by singing in the street. In the 80s and 90s, we looked beyond Europe and North America and set off to all corners of the earth. Meanwhile, we focused in on the world's most exciting urban areas to produce in-depth, fold-out map guides. Our new guides bring the total number of titles to 51, each infused with the spirit of adventure and voice of opinion that travelers around the world have come to count on. But some things never change: our guides are still researched, written, and produced entirely by students who know first-hand how to see the world on the cheap.

## HOW WE DO IT

Each guide is completely revised and thoroughly updated every year by a well-traveled set of nearly 300 students. Every spring, we recruit over 200 researchers and 90 editors to overhaul every book. After several months of training, researcher-writers hit the road for seven weeks of exploration, from Anchorage to Adelaide, Estonia to El Salvador, Iceland to Indonesia. Hired for their rare combination of budget travel sense, writing ability, stamina, and courage, these adventurous travelers know that train strikes, stolen luggage, food poisoning, and marriage proposals are all part of a day's work. Back at our offices, editors work from spring to fall, massaging copy written on Himalayan bus rides into witty, informative prose. A student staff of typesetters, cartographers, publicists, and managers keeps our lively team together. In September, the collected efforts of the summer are delivered to our printer, who turns them into books in record time, so that you have the most up-to-date information available for your vacation. Even as you read this, work on next year's editions is well underway.

## WHY WE DO IT

We don't think of budget travel as the last recourse of the destitute; we believe that it's the only way to travel. Living cheaply and simply brings you closer to the people and places you've been saving up to visit. Our books will ease your anxieties and answer your questions about the basics—so you can get off the beaten track and explore. Once you learn the ropes, we encourage you to put *Let's Go* down now and then to strike out on your own. You know as well as we that the best discoveries are often those you make yourself. When you find something worth sharing, please drop us a line. We're Let's Go Publications, 67 Mount Auburn St., Cambridge, MA 02138, USA (email: feedback@letsgo.com). For more info, visit our website, www.letsgo.com.

# CONTENTS

| | | | |
|---|---|---|---|
| ✚ Hospital | ✈ Airport | 🏛 Museum | ▲ Mountain |
| Police | 🚌 Bus Station | Hotel/Hostel | |
| ✉ Post Office | 🚆 Train Station | ⛺ Camping | Park |
| ⓘ Tourist Office | M METRO STATION | Food & Drink | |
| 💲 Bank | ⚓ Ferry Landing | Shopping | Beach |
| Embassy/Consulate | ✝ Church | ♪ Arts & Entertainment | |
| ▪ Site or Point of Interest | Synagogue | Nightlife | Water |
| ☎ Telephone Office | Mosque | 🖥 Internet Café | |
| Theater | Castle | ⋯⋯ Pedestrian Zone | The Let's Go thumb always points NORTH. |

# MAPS

# RESEARCHER-WRITERS

**Taryn Arthur**                                                          *Moscow, St. Petersburg*

Not even the loss of her lone pair of pants—in 40° weather—could keep Taryn from pounding the pavements of Petersburg. Clad in a less-than-toasty skirt, she soldiered on, putting goth girls and museum *babushki* in their place when they gave her static. Margarita Alekseevna's generous hospitality (and hot tea) kept Taryn going through many a night of writing those Tolstoy-length copybatches. Smuggled into Moscow, she got down in the rowdiest of clubs and muttered a few choice expletives over Stalin's grave, all the while weaving through the crowded metro like a deer at an NRA convention.

**Jessica Lucy Berenbeim**                                                          *Hungary*

Always thoughtful and reflective, Jessica charmed us with prose so evocative we scrutinized art, tasted wine, and hit the waterpark right along with her. Despite annoying police and a certain demonic salad, Jessica had a splendid time. She fell head over heels for Budapest, exploring the city and squeezing in a little sunbathing on the roof of a Turkish bath in the meantime. We hope she enjoyed the exploits as much as we did.

**Kate Damon**                                                          *Bulgaria, Macedonia*

Not even the most trying disaster could stop our superwoman—not an earthquake (through which she successfully slept), or a goat on the bus, or a mad cow, or an attack by a grizzly bear, or the millionth icon, or even sickness and a hospital staff that mistakenly placed her on a midget ward. Always punctual, always thorough, always up for a new adventure, Kate is a star. She would like to thank Tsveti Traikova and Goce Bozinovski for invaluable help when mastering the Cyrillic alphabet and the nonexistent tourist infrastructure.

**David Egan**                                                          *Trans-Siberian Railroad*

We sent the ever-dapper Mr. Egan, a veteran of *Let's Go: Turkey 2000*, on one of the most challenging routes in the series, then spent the next few months wondering what time zone he was in. From Moscow, David got on the train and slept his way to the top of the Urals. Enduring such trials as Siberian prostitutes and video game-crazed Russian teens, he finally made it far enough to write the definitive coverage of Ulaanbaatar, a hipper city than anyone previously supposed, then forged onward to Beijing.

**Michal Engelman**                                                          *Moldova, Southeastern Poland, Ukraine*

Who could have known that one visit to her spiritual homeland would make Michal (a.k.a. Masha) a Ukrainian patriot? After only a few days in Kyiv (not Kiev!), Michal almost made us fall in love with Ukraine. She dazzled us with her sparkling prose and with the most thoughtful reflections we heard all summer. Her copious marginalia provided us with an insight into the Ukrainian psyche as well as with a social, political, and cultural analysis of the post-Soviet world.

**Kieran Fitzgerald**                                                          *Bosnia-Herzegovina, Croatia*

Our fearless running man took Croatia by storm, reassuring us that Dalmatia is indeed the most beautiful part of the world (ah, and the women!). Whether he was jamming with Croatian rock stars in the capital, lounging with NATO officers on the coast, or escaping bullets while exploring the biking options of Hvar (there aren't many), Kieran always made us laugh until we cried with witty remarks, poignant prose, and flawless research. By the end of the summer, we almost—almost—deciphered his cryptic cover letters.

**Katie Heikkinen** *Estonia*

After finishing research in Finland for *Let's Go: Europe 2001*, the trusty Katie worked her way through Estonia. Unfazed by belly-poking fourteen-year-olds and obscene amounts of sour cream, she bicycled wherever public transportation failed her. After she finally discovered that *kino* (cinema) was not in fact a game played by retirees in Vegas, she mastered Estonian and its funky "ö" with ease. From the university town of Tartu to the Estonian Islands, Katie kept us in stitches with her candid marginalia.

**Kit Hodge** *Romania*

What a trooper! Faced with more challenges on the road than any of our other researchers, Kit buckled down and worked like a madwoman even when times got tough, weathering wayward cockroaches and a flasher along the way. In the safety of our office, we were grateful for her Herculean efforts and conscientious research. She grew to love Romania, for better or worse, like no one else.

**Katharine Holt** *Poland*

Katie found a party in just about every city in Poland, exposing nightlife from Kraków to Łódz. Refusing to be unnerved by the staring Poles, who pounded on the phone booth during her calls to the office, she traveled an eight-week itinerary over most of the country. We always knew she was hard-core—Katie ran the Boston Marathon before our first meeting—but we never suspected she would manage to jog in Bialystok. We also never suspected that Poland was similar to the Midwest. She navigated flocks of nuns, who failed to shake her belief in karma...sort of...and searched *rynek* after *rynek* for basement student hangouts.

**Maxfield Morange** *The Carpathians, Slovakia, Slovenia*

Mighty Max took to the mountains with gusto, single-handedly supporting the Slovak and Slovenian dairy industries with the loads of ice cream and cheese he consumed. He had us so excited about tromping through the Tatras that we vowed to grow big red beards and take on nine-hour hikes as well. Adept at rolling with the punches and claiming it was "all part of the experience," he even slept on Ljubljana park benches when finances were unaccessible. When he finally returned and peeled off his boots, he worked some keyboard magic for us, typing up some of the cleanest copy we've ever laid eyes on. Max would like to thank Steve King.

**Jennifer O'Brien** *Belarus, Kaliningrad, Latvia, Lithuania*

Jenn never ceased to shock us with her capacity for dealing with disaster. Undeterred by the theft of her wallet in Riga, undiscouraged when her copy was held hostage, and unintimidated even by Belarus, Jenn didn't just peep behind the iron curtain—she destroyed it. She found the lighter side of any situation, especially in the Minsk McDonald's, where she saw two members of the local mafia fighting over a Happy Meal toy. She also learned more about amber than she wanted to know, kissed a sea lion, and crossed the Russian border on foot.

**Nicholas Topjian** *Czech Republic, Silesia*

With a guitar (later two!) in hand, our researcher-*cum*-street musician Nick explored the Czech Republic in depth. Even after suffering a laptop breakdown, Nick still finished the Prague itinerary on time and completed his copy with a diligence and energy all his own. He even found the time to critique some films in Karlovy Vary and to compare his talents with those of Pearl Jam (Eddie Vedder just don't compare). Just when he thought that Prague offered all that one could ever dream of, he discovered Czech Paradise. Always enthusiastic and committed, Nick had so much fun we thought he might never come back.

# HOW TO USE THIS BOOK

Welcome, comrades, to *Let's Go: Eastern Europe 2001*. We are a good fraternal socialist publication, but we have to change with the times, and this year is no exception. First off, the book is no longer free. We found that some comrades, having received the book without paying, were no longer completing their duties at the tractor factory. Also, Misha was selling copies on the black market. Second, it is smaller and lighter, as we are no longer evaluated based on tonnage sold. Although we continue to maintain that last year's lead-bound book built socialist character, after Vasily's back injury we decided to scale things back a bit. That was a joke. Laugh, comrades, laugh! You—Boris—not too enthusiastically, now. The western imperialist dogs may tell you that you can't take a true proletarian vacation in Europe these days, but we know the truth and we've put it in this book! Read, comrades, about beds so cheap the Americans don't want you to know about them! About trans-continental train rides for the price of one night in a bourgeois hotel! Take the wisdom of the Party to heart, comrades, and your vacation will be one long stretch of fraternal proletarian socialist ecstasy.

## THE ORGANIZATION OF THIS BOOK

**INTRODUCTORY MATERIAL.** The first chapter of this book, **Discover Eastern Europe,** provides an overview of travel in Eastern Europe, including **Suggested Itineraries** that give you an idea of what you shouldn't miss and how long it will take to see it. The **Eastern Europe: An Introduction** chapter provides a brief synopsis of the culture and history of the region. Meanwhile, the **Essentials** section outlines the practical information you will need to prepare and execute your trip.

**THE "MEAT".** Each chapter covers one country, except **Gateway Cities,** which covers several bases from which to explore Eastern Europe. When you are frustrated, beating your head against this portion of the book may help to relieve stress. You can also set fire to it to provide warmth in an emergency. Also included in each chapter is country-specific travel advice.

## A FEW NOTES ABOUT LET'S GO FORMAT

**RANKING ESTABLISHMENTS.** In each section (accommodations, food, etc.), we list establishments in order from best to worst. Our researchers' favorites are marked by the highest honor given out by Let's Go, the Let's Go thumbs-up (🌅).

**PHONE CODES AND TELEPHONE NUMBERS.** The **phone code** for each city or town appears opposite the name of that city or town, and is denoted by the ☎ icon. Dial the number in parentheses only when calling within the country.

**GRAYBOXES AND WHITEBOXES. Grayboxes** sometimes provide cultural insight; other times they just provide a healthy dose of crude humor. **Whiteboxes** provide important practical information, such as warnings (🔴) and helpful hints (🔵).

**GLOSSARIES.** We've provided a helpful table of words and phrases in the **Language** section of each chapter, complete with pronunciations.

---

**A NOTE TO OUR READERS** The information for this book was gathered by *Let's Go* researchers from May through August of 2000. Each listing is based on one researcher's opinion, formed during his or her visit at a particular time. Those traveling at other times may have different experiences since prices, dates, hours, and conditions are always subject to change. You are urged to check the facts presented in this book beforehand to avoid inconvenience and surprises.

# ACKNOWLEDGMENTS

**WE'D LIKE TO BESTOW THE ORDER OF LENIN UPON:** Our researchers, for devoting your blood and guts to this book; Jonathan, for your sharp tongue, critical eye, and cucumber dip; the Eurotrash discotheque, for the lovin' and for expanding our musical horizons; Melissa R., for being a goddess; John Fiore, for maps; Dan; Nick, for last-minute help; our typists—Joe, Lano, Max, Rich, & Rachel; David, Doina, Elena, Martin, Masha, & Zuzana, for native expertise; Ben, for the Clock; and God, for The Borscht.

**ANDREA THANKS:** Matt and Sunnypeg, *you* are the greatest. The kickball folks, for good times. Meredith, for making 6am fun. Becky, for commiserating. Anne C., for keeping me sane. Pam, for being my mentor and friend. Steve&Robin, for unconditional support. Rami, for staying. Megan, for not disappearing in Peru. The International Ladies of Mystery, for a hell of a year. My friends at home, for always taking me back. My family—mamince, tatíkovi, Megerce, babičce a dědečkovi Filipím. And Nicko, my soulmate, for Cali, flowers, for almost teaching me how to drive, for your love, and for being who you are.

**MATT THANKS:** Sunny, for refusing to get cynical and for being tolerant to a fault. The boss, Andrea, for being one fine taskmistress. Team WEUR: Kate-dawg for representing the West Side, Carla for keeping the economy going and her bourgeois influence, Karen for running and complete craziness, Dan for being a bastion of male sanity. Team EUR: Becky for Vivaldi and having a kind word handy, Amy and Vicky for being such stains, Craig for your interest in mullets. Bede, for knowing when to quit and head to the pub. Melissa R. for her skills and coffee. Mom and dad, for encouraging their wayward son to spend his summer so far off. Allison and Eric, for making the effort to stay in touch. Geoff and the Stevens family, for their hospitality. Mrs. Meredith Warren, for a wonderful day in Marblehead. Max, for an excellent bike ride.

**SUNNY THANKS:** Mom and Dad, for loving your delinquent daughter; Andrea, for being compassionate, totally wacky, and a žaňus of a boss; Matt, for being a walking encyclopedia and just plain awesome; the Eur and WEur ladies for street funk, ***** concerts, and downright silliness; Dan and Craig, for putting up with us; Alice, for gummy peach raids; Bede, for being the first friendly office face; Beth, for the block runs; reception, for smiles; 99 Marion St., for good times and insects; the Greenough crew, for being the Greenough crew; Lizard, for chats; Jess, for always being there; Laura, for emails I never answer; Madison friends, for the week *sniff* of fun, and Toscanini's, for vanilla lattes.

**Editor**
Andrea Filipí Volfová
**Associate Editors**
Matthew DeTar Gibson, Xunhua Wong
**Managing Editor**
Daryush Jonathan Dawid
**Map Editors**
Filip Wojciechowski, John Fiore

**Publishing Director**
Kaya Stone
**Editor-in-Chief**
Kate McCarthy
**Production Manager**
Melissa Rudolph
**Cartography Manager**
John Fiore
**Editorial Managers**
Alice Farmer, Ankur Ghosh, Aarup Kubal, Anup Kubal
**Financial Manager**
Bede Sheppard
**Low-Season Manager**
Melissa Gibson
**Marketing & Publicity Managers**
Olivia L. Cowley, Esti Iturralde
**New Media Manager**
Daryush Jonathan Dawid
**Personnel Manager**
Nicholas Grossman
**Photo Editor**
Dara Cho
**Production Associates**
Sanjay Mavinkurve, Nicholas Murphy, Rosalinda Rosalez, Matthew Daniels, Rachel Mason, Daniel Visel
**Some Design**
Matthew Daniels
**Office Coordinators**
Sarah Jacoby, Chris Russell

**Director of Advertising Sales**
Cindy Rodriguez
**Senior Advertising Associates**
Adam Grant, Rebecca Rendell
**Advertising Artwork Editor**
Palmer Truelson

**President**
Andrew M. Murphy
**General Manager**
Robert B. Rombauer
**Assistant General Manager**
Anne E. Chisholm

Eastern Europe

Railways of
Eastern Europe

XVII

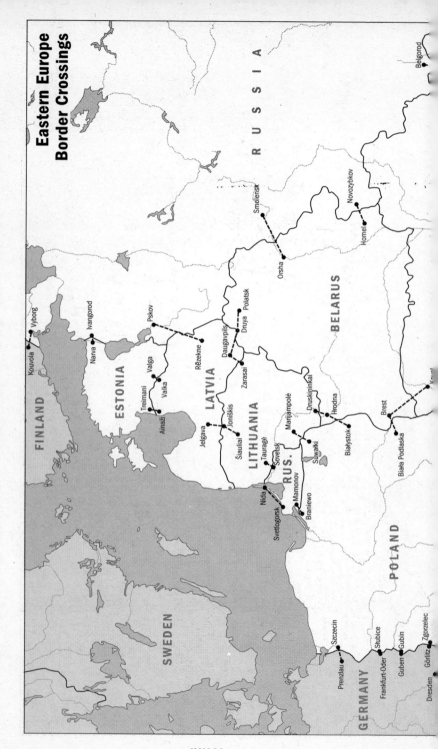

Eastern Europe
Border Crossings

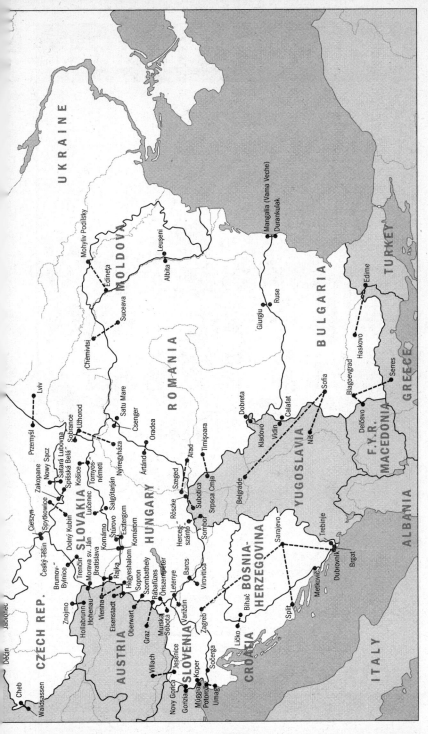

# DISCOVER EASTERN EUROPE

A decade after the fall of the Iron Curtain, Eastern Europe has become the darling of budget travelers. Undiscovered cities, pristine national parks, empty hostel beds, and ridiculously cheap beer are steadily luring in seekers of adventure, culture, and bargain. From hip, urban centers like Prague, St. Petersburg, and Budapest to the peaks of the Tatras and the Alps, from the shores of the Dalmatian Coast to the expanses of barren Siberia, the myriad wonders of Eastern Europe sprawl across 18 countries and two continents. While distances are great and transport connections unpredictable, it's all part of the Eastern European adventure. After all, where else in the world can a single train take you across seven time zones? Where else is a bottle of vodka a more effective visa than the visa itself? Where else is the most reliable transportation a weekly mail bus or, better yet, a yak? In the face of such dilapidated bureacracy, the most important thing to bring is flexibility; go ahead and make plans, but always be ready to scrap them.

Part of the unpredictability of the region is, of course, due to political and economic restructuring. You'll inevitably encounter frustrating delays, astronomical inflation, and mind-boggling bureaucracy. When the absurdity of the post-Soviet world is about to get you down, take a deep breath and know that for every stony border guard and badgering *babushka* (grandmotherly old women common throughout the region), there are countless locals willing to give you a bed, a shot of homemade liquor, and a ride to the next town. With a little patience and a lot of perseverence, you'll have an utterly rewarding jaunt through one of the most geographically varied, historically interesting, and culturally rich areas of the world.

## FACTS AND FIGURES

**TOTAL POPULATION:** 330 million Eastern Europeans, 50,000 American expats.

**OLDEST UNIVERSITY:** Charles University in Prague, Czech Republic.

**WORLD'S LARGEST BUST:** Of Lenin, in Ulan Ude, RUS.

**PER CAPITA BEER CONSUMPTION IN THE CZECH REPUBLIC:** 156L per year.

**NUMBER OF ISLANDS IN ST. PETERSBURG:** 101

**TALLEST BUILDING NEVER BUILT:** Stalin's proposed Palace of Soviets, with a 100m statue of Lenin on top, in Moscow, RUS.

**HOURS OF POLISH TECHNO BEFORE INSANITY SETS IN:** 6.5

**LITERS OF PEPSI CONSUMED IN RUSSIA EACH YEAR:** 450 million

**LITERS OF VODKA:** 2.3 billion

# WHEN TO GO

Summer is Eastern Europe's high season. What high season means, however, varies for each country and region. In Prague, Kraków, and Budapest, *everything* is swarmed with backpackers. In the countryside, high season simply means that hotels might actually have guests staying in them. In Croatia and along the Baltic and Black Sea Coasts, things fill up as soon as it is warm enough to lounge on the

beach, usually from June to September. In the Tatras, Julian Alps, and Transylvanian Alps, there is both a summer high season for hiking (usually July and August)
and a winter season for skiing (November to March). In the low season, you'll
often be the only tourist in town. While securing accommodations and walking
down the street will be easier in low season, high season brings with it an entire
subculture of young backpackers. You decide whether that's a good thing. For a
temperature chart, please see **Climate,** p. 747. Major national holidays are listed in
the introduction to each country, while festivals are detailed in city listings where
appropriate; major festivals in each country are summarized on p. 15.

# THINGS TO DO

Like a jumpsuit-clad mafioso on a Moscow streetcorner, Eastern Europe has got
what you need. Its vastness encompasses heavily-backpacked cities and sleepy
hamlets—perhaps the only constant is the generally good, though inordinately
strong, alcohol. For more specific regional attractions—from absinthe to
*zubrówka*—see the **If you're here for...** box at the start of each chapter.

## THE GREAT OUTDOORS

Leave the urban bustle behind to explore the wonders of the Eastern European
wilderness. From the rolling hills of Poland and the Czech Republic to Siberia, the
untamed corners are a thrill-seeker's Eden. The seven-day **Trail of Eagles' Nests** (p.
508) treks through the heart of Poland's green uplands past limestone eruptions
and castle ruins. Head to the **High Tatras, SLK** (p. 498, p. 721) for jagged peaks,
Olympic-quality skiing, and heart-stopping hang-gliding. Truly isolated adventure
awaits along the Trans-Siberian Railroad, RUS (p. 677). A few more days on the
train brings you to Lake Baikal (p. 685), the deepest, oldest, and largest freshwater
lake on earth and a playground for trekkers. Other wonderlands of outdoor adventure include: **Mazury, POL** (p. 546); **Julian Alps, SLN** (p. 749); **Southern Bohemia, CZK**
(p. 253); Białystok National Park, POL (p. 551); Transylvania, ROM (p. 570); Lahemaa National Reserve, EST (p. 291); Plitvice Lakes National Park, CRO (p. 163);
Mljet National Park, CRO (p. 202); and Woliński National Park, POL (p. 530).

## BEACH BUMMING

Most travelers don't come to Eastern Europe for its beaches, but they should: the
region boasts enough surf and sand to accommodate months of lounging and sunning, provided those months are in summer. The indisputable star of the Mediterranean is Croatia's fabled **Dalmatian Coast** (p. 176). From the karst-lined cliffs near
Dubrovnik to the isolated beaches of **Hvar** (p. 191) and **Vis** (p. 190), the azure
waters of the Adriatic lap at the feet of this coastal god. Spear-fishing and rock-
climbing are only a few of the diversions in **Crimea, UKR** (p. 780), the beauty of the
Black Sea. For more relaxed Crimean days, lounge with wealthy Russians on the
pebbled beaches around **Yalta, UKR** (p. 790). Chillier waters await to the north in
the Baltic Sea, where you can bike for days along the deserted roads of the **Estonian Islands** (p. 296) to reach equally deserted beaches. Isolated from the outside
world by 50 years of Soviet rule, the pristine archipelago shelters wind-swept look-
outs, sandy shores, and the occasional Soviet base. If you can't make it to the
coast, Hungary has the answer: **Lake Balaton** (p. 351) is like a slice of sea in the
middle of the Hungarian plain, complete with tanned masses, endless water
sports, and tacky discos. It's fun, we swear. Farther south, Macedonia's **Lake Ohrid**
(p. 444) is one of the most scenic parts of Eastern Europe. You can also play Beach
Blanket Bingo on the Black Sea coast in **Bulgaria** (p. 131); on the Baltic near Świ-
noujscie, POL (p. 531) and the **Tri-City Area, POL** (p. 531); and along the Curonian Spit
near **Kaliningrad, RUS** (p. 670) and **Klaipėda, LIT** (p. 428).

# THE LEGACY OF THE 20TH CENTURY

While most of the region is successfully rebuilding after the fall of communism, it can't quite shake off the devastating legacy of the past century. Certainly not the most uplifting of the region's highlights, the towns memorializing events of the past 100 years are some of the most powerful in Eastern Europe. The Resistance movement of Nazi-occupied **Odessa, UKR** (p. 790) hid itself underground during World War II; their headquarters are now one of Europe's most stirring war memorials. The most sobering memorials, however, are undoubtedly the numerous concentration camps; **Auschwitz-Birkenau, POL** (p. 489) was the largest and most infamous of the Nazi death camps and today houses a sobering museum on the Holocaust. After total destruction by German bombers in World War II, re-constructed **Warsaw, POL** (p. 460) is a testament to the region's admirable ability to regroup and rebuild, even in the face of utter ruin. **Sarajevo, BOS** (p. 92), however, is still ravaged by landmines and ethnic tensions from the recent war with Serbia, and is struggling to unravel itself from Balkan violence in order to enter the 21st century as a new city. Other places of historical significance include: **Brest, BLR** (p. 84); **Livadia, UKR** (p. 787); **Gdańsk, POL** (p. 532); **Cēsis, LAT** (p. 401); **Vis, CRO** (p. 190); **Schlisselburg, RUS** (p. 662); **Majdanek, POL** (p. 495); **Terezín, CZR** (p. 244); **Paneriai, LIT** (**p. 417**); **Kaunas, LIT** (p. 420); **Dārziņi, LAT** (p. 398); **Bucharest, ROM** (p. 561); **Zadar, CRO** (p. 176); **Kaliningrad, RUS** (p. 670); and **Moscow, RUS** (p. 605).

# ALCOHOLIC DELIGHTS

Mmm...beer. And vodka. Absinthe. Plum brandy. Kvas. Even wine. Eastern Europe is perhaps most loved for its endless shelves of locally produced, throat-burning liquors. Don't limit yourself to imported, far-away versions; drink these magic liquids straight from the source. The world's best hops are in the Czech Republic: the world-famous **Pilsner Urquell** is produced in Plzeň (p. 247) while České Budějovice (p. 253) brews the delectable Budvar (namesake of American Budweiser). The best beer in the Czech Republic, Krušovice, is produced right in Prague (p. 215); enjoy it alonside a fiery glass of absinthe. While it pales next to the Czechs, the Polish Żywiec is concocted just south of Bielsko-Biała (p. 502). The Ukrainian version of beer, kvas is sold from barrels on the streets of Kyiv (p. 766), even in pouring rain. In Karlovy Vary, CZR (p. 250), imbibe on Becherovka, an herb liquor purported to have "curative powers." For good vodka, head anywhere in Russia (p. 588). Better yet, head to the Latvian/Estonian (p. 386) or Belarussian/Polish borders (p. 85) where vodka smuggling makes for very cheap inebriation. Hungary has the monopoly on Eastern Europe's potable wines: don't miss Bull's Blood in Eger (p. 375), Aszú vintages in Tokaj (p. 381), and the Balaton-flavored wines of Badascony (p. 360). The wines of twin cities Mělník, CZR (p. 246) and Melnik, BUL (p. 127) are so good, Churchill had them shipped to England, even during World War II.

# COME FOR A WEEK, STAY FOR A YEAR

You've been on an Eastern European whirlwind tour, frantically climbing every mountain and touring every capital, determined to see it all before heading back to the real world. But then it happens: you encounter that one place, the city with the most enchanting alleys or the hostel that casts a spell over its guests, and you can't bring yourself to leave. Ever. Lucky for you, Eastern Europe is bursting with settlement-worthy towns. **Prague** (p. 215) is Eastern Europe's ex-pat capital; the number of Anglophone residents here today has elicted comparisons to 1920s Paris. If the hordes of Hemingway wannabes frequenting Prague's cafes frightens you, head south to **Český Krumlov** (p. 256), where mellower backpackers-*cum*-locals relish the tight-knit community of this medieval town. The Backpacker's Guesthouse (p. 325) is the home-base for **Budapest's** (p. 318) English-speaking denizens who spend their days lingering in Turkish baths and their nights dancing at Fat Mo's Speakeasy. And who can really blame **Dubrovnik's** (p. 195) recent converts? It *is* the most beautiful city on the Adriatic, after all. The most unlikely (and un-European) of the alluring locales is **Ulaanbaatar, MON** (p. 689), the capital of Mongolia. Sure, you'll sleep in *ger* and ride yaks, but there's an *English bookstore*. Other cities that should top the lingering list include: **St. Petersburg, RUS** (p. 637), **Kraków, POL** (p. 481), and **Vilnius, LIT** (p. 411).

## ▨ LET'S GO PICKS

**BEST BEACHES:** Croatia's Dalmatian Coast (p. 176).

**BEST BEDS:** Youth hostel in Bled, SLN (p. 749).

**BEST MONUMENT TO FORMER SOVIET GLORY:** The Exhibition of Soviet Economic Achievements in Moscow, RUS (p. 623).

**BEST BACCHANALIAN ORGIES:** The Hungry Duck in Moscow, RUS (p. 629).

**BEST PLACE FOR A RUBBER DUCKIE:** Turkish bath in Budapest, HUN (p. 318).

**MOST RANDOM MONUMENT:** The Frank Zappa Monument, in Vilnius, LIT (p. 417).

**BEST BIZARRE DESTINATION:** Ulaanbaatar, MON (p. 689).

**BEST PLACE TO FEEL LIKE JAMES BOND:** Red Square, in Moscow, RUS (p. 616).

**TASTIEST SCULPTURE:** The marzipan bust of Michael Jackson in Szentendre, HUN (p. 338). Don't let the kids near this one.

**MOST VIOLENT FOLK HERO:** Vlad "The Impaler," of Romania. Don't ask. (p. 572)

**BEST TRANS-CONTINENTAL ODYSSEY:** The Trans-Siberian Railroad, RUS (p. 677).

**BEST CHEESY TOURIST RESTAURANT:** Титаник (Titanic), in Kaliningrad, RUS (p. 673).

**STRANGEST PLACES TO SLEEP:** In a Mongolian *ger* hut (p. 689), in Ulaanbaatar, MON, or a monastic cell in Rila, BUL (p. 119).

**BEST PLACE TO SEE A GIANT CAMPBELL'S SOUP CAN:** The Andy Warhol Museum, in Medzilborce, SLO (p. 732).

**BEST CHEAP BREW:** *Pilsner Urquell*, in Prague, CZR (p. 215).

**WEIRDEST VODKA:** *Żubrówka*, made in Poland from bison grass (p. 459).

**BEST KITSCH:** Wooden sculptures in the Fairy Tale Meadow in Yalta, UKR (p. 786).

**BEST PLACE WHERE NO ONE IS:** Białowieski National Park, POL (p. 551).

**BEST PLACE TO FORGET YOU'RE IN EUROPE:** Lake Baikal, RUS (p. 685). It's in Asia.

**BEST FOOD THAT WON'T MOO AT YOU:** The horseburger, in Ljubljana, SLN (p. 743).

**PLACE TO SEEK DIAPERS OF JESUS:** The Cathedral of the Assumption of the Virgin Mary, in Dubrovnik, CRO (p. 199).

**MOST DANGEROUS ROCK CLIMBING:** Psycho Killer, Paklenica National Park, CRO (p. 179).

**BEST WAY TO EAT A GENIUS:** Copernicus gingerbread in Torun, POL (p. 521).

**BEST GAME OF "PIN THE MOLE ON THE BABUSHKA":** Old Town Hostel in Vilnius, LIT (p. 414).

**BEST PLACE TO BASK IN THE GLOW OF CULTURAL HEGEMONY:** McDonald's, in Moscow, RUS (p. 615).

**CREEPIEST RELICS:** St. Stephen's light-up hand, in Budapest, HUN (p. 332), and Lenin's embalmed body in Moscow, RUS (p. 619).

**BEST MACABRE SIGHT:** The ossuary in Kutná Hora, CZR (p. 245).

**BEST PARTY ON A NUCLEAR REACTOR:** The month-long rave in Kazantip, UKR (p. 783). If only Chernobyl hosted parties.

**BEST PLACE TO GET DOWN IN A BOMB SHELTER:** Griboyedov, in St. Petersburg, RUS (p. 659).

**BEST PLACE TO MEET BEAUTIFUL WOMEN:** Croatia (p. 146).

**BEST-PRESERVED ROMAN AMPITHEATER:** In Pula, CRO (p. 164).

**BEST PLACE TO GET SLOSHED:** The wine cellars of the Valley of the Beautiful Women, HUN (p. 378).

# SUGGESTED ITINERARIES

## HABSBURG'S LAST HURRAH (31 DAYS)

Start your trek in starlet **Prague, CZR** (p. 215; 4 days), the steeple-topped, tourist-filled gem of Bohemia. Český Krumlov, CZR (p. 256; 2 days) might be the most enchanting town in Central Europe. **Vienna, AUS** (p. 64; 3 days) is home to world-renowned museums and chain-smoking, Freud-reading hipsters. **Ljubljana, SLN** (p. 743; 2 days) might just make you forget you're in Eastern Europe. **Zagreb, CRO** (p. 156; 2 days) offers the pleasant mix of Mediterranean idleness and modest Westernization. **Pécs, HUN** (p. 361; 1-2 days) surprises with a happening modern art scene. Relax in a radioactive thermal bath in **Keszthely, HUN** (p. 357; 2 days), a serene spot in the glam playland of Lake Balaton. **Budapest, HUN** (p. 318; 4 days) might just surpass Prague as the region's hippest city. Experience the giddiness of Bull's Blood wine in **Eger's** (p. 375; 1-2 days) Valley of the Beautiful Women. The **Tatras** (p. 498 and p. 721; 3 days) tower over Slovakia and Poland with rocky hikes and snowy skiing; **Zakopane** (p. 498) and **Tatranská Lomnica** (p. 725) are the best bases. **Kraków** (p. 481; 4 days) is Poland's answer to Prague and Budapest, backpackers included. **Auschwitz** (p. 489) is a sobering daytrip from Kraków. From here, return to **Prague.**

## THE BEST OF CENTRAL EUROPE (41 DAYS)

Overwhelming and techno-paced, **Berlin, GER** (p. 804; 4 days) is a city of ruins, rubble, and piercings; **Prague, CZR** (p. 215; 5 days) is a more subdued follow-up, as long as you consider beer, absinthe, and ghosts subdued. Český Krumlov, CZR (p. 256; 2-3 days) is a great base for exploring the surrounding virgin forest, or to head down to Mozart's city of Salzburg, AUS (1 day) or to Vienna, AUS (p. 64, 3 days). Although it's often overlooked, Slovakia's capital, Bratislava, SLK (p. 701; 1-2 days), makes for a fascinating stop en route to the rest of the country. Ljubljana, SLN (p. 743; 2 days) is a lively capital overflowing with students and Josip Plečnik's creations. Pula, CRO (p. 164; 2 days) boasts more Roman ruins than many a town Italy; it comes as no surprise that Diocletian summered in Split, CRO (p. 184; 2 days) and George Bernard Shaw in Dubrovnik, CRO (p. 195; 3 days). To witness a rebirth of a city, visit Sarajevo, BOS (p. 92; 2 days). Zagreb, CRO (p. 156; 3 days) is a Central European

city plunged into hot Mediterranean air. The Ottoman invasion left Budapest, HUN (p. 318; 4 days) with thermal baths. The true gem of Poland is its UNESCO-protected Kraków, POL (p. 481; 2 days)—explore the dreamy city, not forgetting haunting Auschwitz, POL (p. 489). **Warsaw, POL** (p. 460; 2 days) is Poland's answer to Berlin: sprawling, hectic, and still struggling to recover from World War II.

## VIA BALTICA (34 DAYS)

Although not officially Baltic, **St. Petersburg, RUS** (p. 637; 6 days) is the alterego of the former Soviet Union: more cultured, friendlier, and much less overwhelming. Multicultural **Helsinki, FIN** (p. 810; 3 days) is the epitome of chill. **Tallinn, EST** (p. 285; 3 days) is surprisingly cosmopolitan. The island of **Saaremaa, EST** (p. 296; 3-4 days) is more Estonian than Estonia itself, complete with windmills, meteor craters, and undisturbed beaches. Get muddy in **Pärnu, EST** (p. 293; 1 day) at one of the town's infamous spas. **Tartu, EST** (p. 303; 1 day) is the oldest city in the Baltics. **Rīga, LAT** (p. 388; 3 days) is decidedly more Soviet than its neighbors. Lithuania's third-largest city, **Klaipéda, LIT** (p. 428; 2-3 days) is the gateway to the Curonian Spit; the best beaches are at **Nida, LIT** (p. 432). On your way to Vilnius, stop by **Kaunas, LIT** (p. 420; 1 day), Lithuania's second-largest city. **Vilnius, LIT** (p. 409; 3 days), long considered the "Jerusalem of Europe," is now touted as the "New Prague." While

there, hop to the totalitarian but beautiful **Minsk, BLR** (p. 79; 2 days). Missing Mother Russia? **Kaliningrad, RUS** (p. 670; 2 days), the birthplace of Immanuel Kant, is your place. The Polish port of **Gdansk, POL** (p. 532; 2 days), will take you back to the 21st century.

## NOT FOR THE FAINT OF HEART (30 DAYS)

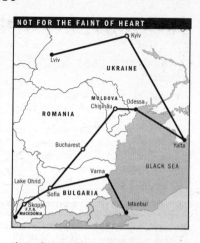

Start your adventure in **Istanbul, TUR** (p. 814; 5 days), the gateway to the Black Sea. Head north to **Sozopol, BUL** (p. 137; 2 days) for Bulgaria's warmest water. Continue lounging in **Balchik, BUL** (p. 134; 2 days), without hordes of Bulgarian teeny-boppers. Head inland to **Sofia, BUL** (p. 112; 4 days) and farther yet to Macedonia's capital **Skopje** (p. 439; 2 days) and the georgeous Lake Ohrid (p. 444; 4 days). **Bucharest, ROM** (p. 561; 4 days), once dubbed "Little Paris," now stands as a ghost of itself. The journey gets rougher as you head to Moldova's capital, **Chişinău** (p. 450; 2 days), which still considers itself Soviet. **Yalta, UKR** (p. 790; 3 days) is one of the least spoiled resorts in the Black Sea. Once the party town of the USSR, **Odessa, UKR** (p. 790; 3 days) still hums, just at a lower frequency. Gold-domed and poplar-crowned **Kyiv, UKR** (p. 763; 4 days) hasn't quite figured out how to become a thriving capitalist metropolis. **Lviv, UKR** (p. 797; 3 days), with uninterupted flow of hot water, is your gateway to Europe.

DISCOVER

## THE RUSSIAN OBSESSION (32 DAYS)

Start your monumental journey in **St. Petersburg** (p. 637; 6 days), then hit **Moscow** (p. 605; 6 days) to stock up on supplies and civilization. The first stop is **Yaroslavl** (p. 631; 4½hr.; 2 days), a leafy city offering the comforts of a capital. **Novosibirsk** (p. 680; 46hr.; 2 days) brings you to the heart of Central Asia. Continue on to **Irkutsk** (p. 683; 33hr.; 1-2 days), a former Siberian trading-post where you can rest up before trekking to **Lake Baikal** (p. 685; 4 days), the world's deepest freshwater lake. **Ulan Ude** (p. 687; 8hr.; 2 days), center of Russian Buddhism and home to the world's largest Lenin bust, is quite possibly Russia's most surreal city. Break up the final leg to **Beijing** (p. 820; 4 days) with a stop in **Ulaanbataar** (p. 689; 22hr., 2 days), Mongolia's sprawling desert oasis.

# EASTERN EUROPE: AN INTRODUCTION

During the Cold War, "Eastern Europe" was a name imposed by Westerners on the Soviet satellites east of the Berlin Wall. It has always been somewhat of a misnomer, capturing a political rather than geographical reality: Vienna lies farther east than Prague, Croatia sits on the Mediterranean, and most of Russia is, in fact, in Asia. But Eastern Europe is not merely a Western construction. The region is united by what it longs to leave behind—an arduous history of political upheaval and disillusionment—and by what it now confronts—a more optimistic but similarly uncertain future. To understand the remarkable complexity of Eastern Europe is to imagine a map of the region a little over a decade ago: in 1989, there were a total of seven countries behind the Iron Curtain; today, that same area is comprised of 19 independent states. In that time, the region has undergone an astounding political and cultural transformation. While communism has fallen throughout Europe and the Soviet Union no longer exists, Eastern Europe continues to be defined by its historical legacy. Forty years of the communist regime have left a deep scar not only on the economies and architectures of the countries, but also on the souls of their citizens. These citizens have, in the process, created another Europe, which some might consider backward, others more authentic. As the region unites under one common language—that of the market economy—and looks to shed its past in a the rush to the West, Eastern Europe stands at a unique and exciting point in its extraordinary history.

## HISTORY OF HALF THE WORLD IN FIVE PAGES

### SLAVS (BEFORE 800 AD)

With the exception of Austria, Hungary, Romania, and the Baltic countries, Eastern Europe is populated primarily by **Slavic** peoples who constitute the largest ethnic and linguistic group in Europe. Originally believed to come from the Caucasus, the Slavs migrated to the Dnieper region in today's Ukraine during the 2nd or 3rd millennium BC. The movement of ancient Germanic tribes westward in the 5th and 6th centuries AD sparked the **Great Migration,** during which Slavs penetrated deeply into Europe, displacing Celts in the Czech lands and Slovakia, Illyrians in the Balkans, Turks and Avars in Bulgaria, Vikings in Russia and Ukraine, and Germanic tribes in Hungary. In the 9th century, Poland was the last to be settled by Slavs. In mid-9th century AD, the Slavs in the Dnieper region established the first major civilization in Eastern Europe, **Kyivan Rus.** Unlike other migrating tribes at this time, the Slavs were cultivators and settlers rather than pillagers, which contributed to their lasting presence. From the 6th century up until 1945, however, there was virtually no unity among the Slavic peoples. The cultural and political history of the western Slavs is inextricably linked to Western Europe, whereas the southern and eastern Slavs were subjected to the rule of Mongols and Ottomans in the 11th century, and thus isolated from the rest of Europe.

The non-Slavic lands in Eastern Europe were inhabited by a vast array of settlers and invaders. Estonia was invaded by **Vikings** and **Finns** in the 9th and 11th centuries respectively, while Latvians and Lithuanians are of **Baltic** descent. All of the non-Slavic areas, including Romania, Hungary, and Bulgaria, intermingled and were strongly influenced by their Slavic neighbors and settlers. Romanians, who belong to indigenous **Dacian** tribes, assimilated the Slavic migrants of the 6th century while the **Magyars** who started invading Hungary from their homeland between the Baltics and the Ural Mountains in the 9th century subsumed the Slavs already settled there. The originally **Turkic** Bulgarians adopted slavic language and are now regarded as Slavs.

# OTTOMANS AND HABSBURGS (800-1914)

Beginning in the 8th century, several short-lasting kingdoms emerged in Eastern Europe, such as the **Empire of Great Moravia** in Bohemia, Moravia, Hungary and Slovakia in 830. One of the few Eastern European empires to actually achieve longevity and greatness was the **Hungarian Kingdom.** It first came to power in the late 9th century and kept growing for 700 years to include Polish Silesia, Croatian Pannonia, and as far east as Romanian Wallachia and Bessarabia. The Kingdom came to an end at the **Battle of Mohács in 1526** when Louis II, king of Hungary and Bohemia, lost to the Ottomans. By the 19th century, nearly all of Eastern Europe was controlled by either the Ottoman, Russian, or Austro-Hungarian Empires.

The **Ottoman Empire** firmly established itself in southeastern Europe when it crushed the **Serbs** on June 28, 1389 at the **Battle of Kosovo**. This victory confirmed its dominion over what are now Hungary, Romania, Bulgaria, Macedonia, Serbia, Montenegro, Bosnia and inland Croatia. The Ottoman infiltration of Europe was forever halted by defeat at the siege of **Vienna** in 1683, following which its decline was inevitable. It was sped along by a series of losses to Russia from the 17th to the 19th century. The **1878 Congress of Berlin** marked the end of the **Russo-Turkish Wars;** in Eastern Europe, only Bulgaria and Macedonia remained in the Ottoman sphere of influence. All other nations were either granted independence or ceded to the Russian and Austro-Hungarian Empires.

As the Ottoman Empire was declining, the **Russian Empire** was rapidly expanding east to the Pacific and westward into Poland and Ukraine. At the first partition of Poland in 1772, the Russians wrested the control of Estonia and Lithuania from Sweden and eventually dissolved the **Polish-Lithuanian Commonwealth,** then one of the largest realms in Europe. By 1801, the Russians controlled Lithuania, Estonia, Latvia, eastern Poland, Belarus, and Ukraine, but further expansion was halted in the 19th century. The Congress of Berlin denied Russia's vision of a large Bulgarian state and a pan-Slavic nation in Eastern Europe. Although it kept control of the entire region until the fall of communism in 1989, Russia's empire remained influential only in far Eastern Europe after this blow from the West.

The colossal **Austrian Empire** was the ultimate winner that swallowed most of Central and Eastern Europe. Although the Habsburgs' rule in Austria dates back to the early 13th century, they did not come to dominate Central Europe until after the Battle of Mohács, when the Hungarian kingdom was split between Turkish and Austrian control. The Austrians acquired Bohemia, Moravia, Slovakia, and parts of Croatia, including Zagreb and Rijeka. After a series of Hungarian uprisings in 1699, the Turks relinquished the rest of Hungary to the Habsburgs. The Hungarians remained restive subjects, however, and in 1867, the Austrians entered into a **dual monarchy** with the Hungarians, by which Hungary was granted internal independence while sharing various ministries with the Austrian government. From then on, the country was called the **Austro-Hungarian Empire.** From 1867 until 1918, Austria-Hungary controlled what is now the Czech Republic, Slovakia, Croatia, Slovenia, Bosnia, and parts of Romania, Poland, Belarus, and Ukraine. Following **Napoleon**'s brief dominion over Europe at the beginning of the 19th century and the 19th-century **Industrial Revolution,** a wave of **Pan-Slavism,** or a belief in the unity of Slavic people, swept across the subordinated nations. Although it was confined to intellectual circles, it contributed to Europe's emerging **nationalism.**

## DEATH OF THE GREAT EMPIRES (1914-1938)

**World War I** started with an attempt by the Serbs to free the South Slavs from the clutches of the Austro-Hungarian Empire. Serb nationalists in the illegal **Black Hand** organization, believed that their cause would best be served by the death of **Archduke Franz Ferdinand d'Este,** heir to the Austro-Hungarian throne. On June 28, 1914, Bosnian Serb nationalist **Gavrilo Princip** assassinated Ferdinand and his wife Sophia in Sarajevo. Exactly one month later, Austria-Hungary declared war on the Serbs. What started as an attempt to save the Empire snowballed during the ensuing month into continual war declarations that included France, Germany, Russia, Belgium, Great Britain, Montenegro, Serbia, and the Ottoman Empire. Because they were controlled by the Austro-Hungarian and Ottoman Empires, most Eastern European nations fought alongside the **Central Powers.** The Baltic nations were controlled by both Germans and Russians and remained divided in their alliances with the Allied and Central Powers. The only nations to wholeheartedly support the Allies were Russia, Serbia, Montenegro and Bosnia. Belarus and Ukraine became hotly contested battlegrounds between the Germans and the Russians and eventually fell to German war-time occupation.

As the war dragged on, Russia's participation became more tenuous. The Russians had entered the war because of their dual interests in the demise of the Ottoman and Austro-Hungarian Empires and the growth of strong, Russia-friendly Slavic nations throughout Eastern Europe. As catastrophic losses caused the death toll to skyrocket, the Russian people became increasingly frustrated with an inefficient government. Coupled with a crippled war-time economy, the tension finally erupted into the **Russian Revolution.** Riots began over food shortages in March 1917, leading to the Tsar's abdication. In November, the **Bolsheviks** ascended to power, establishing Russia's first communist government led by **Vladimir Ilyich Lenin.** Weakened by the revolution, Russia witnessed the crumbling of her empire. In all her territories, nationalist independence movements emerged on the heels of the March 1917 revolution. Their voices, calling for the creation of **nation states** (one nation, one country), were heard by American president Woodrow Wilson. His declaration **Fourteen Points,** which followed the 1919 **Treaty of Versailles** that ended World War I, argued for self-determination of all nations under the yoke of the great empires. With support from the West, Latvia, Estonia, and Ukraine declared independence from Russia, and Lithuania declared independence from Germany. Poland, which had been divided by Prussia, Austria, and Russia, became one state for the first time since 1772.

In the same year, the defeated Austria-Hungary was mercilessly dismantled. The Czechs and Slovaks united into **Czechoslovakia.** Romania's size doubled by the inclusion of Transylvania, Wallachia, and Bukovina. Finally, in keeping with the vision of South Slav nationalism which had sparked the war, 1918 saw the creation of the **Kingdom of Serbs, Croats and Slovenes,** later known as **Yugoslavia.** In the wake of both World War I and the Russian Revolution, the great empires in Eastern Europe came to an end as newly independent nations were born.

## "PEACE IN OUR TIME" (1938-1945)

**World War II** was essentially sparked by the continuation of many unresolved conflicts from World War I. Hitler was determined to reclaim the "Germanic" parts of Poland, Bohemia, and Moravia that Germany had lost after the Treaty of Versailles. He claimed that the three million Germans living in the Czechoslovak **Sudetenland** were being discriminated against by the government. Hoping to avoid another war, France and Britain ignored Hitler's glaringly aggressive moves against a sovereign country and adopted their infamous policy of **appeasement.** In one of the greatest betrayals of the 20th century, France and Britain sealed the fate of Czechoslovakia by signing the **Munich Agreement** with Germany on September 30, 1938, which ordered all non-German inhabitants of the Sudetenland to vacate their homes within 24 hours and allowed the German army to enter. Upon his return from Munich, Britain's Prime Minister Chamberlain foolishly believed he had secured "peace in our time." Hitler, however, ignored the stipulations of the agreement and proceeded to annex the remainder of Czechoslovakia, which he turned into the **Bohemian-Moravian Protectorate** in March 1939. The USSR helped Hitler invade his next victim, Poland, by entering the **Molotov-Ribbentrop Nonaggression Pact,** which stipulated that after an invasion, Germany would control the western third of Poland, while the USSR would keep the eastern two-thirds. In September 1939, Hitler annexed Poland. World War II erupted.

Hitler had no intention of maintaining the Nonaggression Pact, and in June 1941 launched an offensive against the Soviet Union. An unsuccessful attempt to capture Moscow marked the beginning of the end for the German army, and led the Soviets to join the **Allied forces.** The **Anglo-Soviet Agreement** of 1941 was a turning point in the war, as were the Allies' decisive wins in 1942. Total casualties from the war for both civilians and military personnel are estimated at 50-60 million. Of these, Eastern Europe suffered the most losses. The USSR lost 20 million of its citizens (10% of its population), more than any other nation involved in the war. Yugoslavia also lost over 10% of its population. Poland lost nearly 6 million people, a staggering 20% of its prewar population, only about 200,000 of which were military casualties. The majority of the remaining 5.5 million were exterminated in **Nazi concentration camps;** of the 6 million estimated Jews murdered by the Nazis, more than half were Polish. Before World War II, Eastern Europe had been the geographical center of the world's Jewish population but Hitler's **"final solution"** succeeded in almost entirely eliminating the Jewish communities of Poland, Slovakia, Hungary, Lithuania, Moldova, Odessa and the Czech Republic through both genocide and forced emigration.

# THE RUSSIANS ARE COMING! (1945-1989)

The military alliance between the Soviet Union and the West was an uneasy one. The West was opposed to the ideological expansion of communism, but Russia claimed it necessary in order to prevent another German threat to the Slavic nations. Plans for post-war division of power in Europe were sketched out as early as 1944, but sealed at the **Yalta Conference** in February 1945. Wary of Churchill's colonial nostalgia as well as of Soviet communism, the United States reluctantly agreed to recognize Eastern Europe as the Soviet sphere of influence. The institution of communist governments in Czechoslovakia, Poland, Hungary, Yugoslavia, Romania and Bulgaria from 1946 to 1949 established a ring of satellite People's Democracies in Eastern Europe. The **Cold War** had begun.

The **Iron Curtain** first descended with the founding of the **Council for Mutual Economic Assistance (COMECON)** in January 1949, an organization meant to facilitate and coordinate the economic growth of the Soviet Bloc and created in response to the 1948 **Marshall Plan,** which poured US dollars into the reconstruction of Western Europe. The West reacted to this new, formal alliance in April with the creation of the **North Atlantic Treaty Organization (NATO),** a military alliance meant to "keep the Americans in, the Russians out, and the Germans down." In typical Cold War fashion, the Eastern Bloc retaliated in 1955 with a similar alliance, the **Warsaw Pact.** The pact allowed for the maintenance of Soviet military bases throughout Eastern Europe, and tightened Russia's grip on its satellite countries. The only communist European country never to join the Warsaw Pact was **Yugoslavia.** Led by former partisan **Josip Broz Tito,** Yugoslavia broke away from Russia as early as 1948 and followed its own path combining communism with market economy.

After Stalin's death in 1953 and his denunciation by **Nikita Khrushchev,** the Soviet bloc was plagued by chaos. The 1950s saw the emergence of **national communism,** or the belief that the attainment of ultimate communist goals should be dictated internally rather than by orders from Moscow. The presence of Russian troops in Eastern Europe, however, enabled Moscow to respond to rising nationalist movements with military force. Such was the case in 1956, when the Soviets violently suppressed the Hungarian Revolution and workers' strikes in Poland. The **Prague Spring** of 1968 was a similarly violent crushing of an emerging Czechoslovak dissi-

INTRODUCTION

dence movement which demanded increased freedom and attention to human rights. Russia consistently used the Warsaw Pact to justify military occupation and the institution of martial law.

# BRAVE NEW WORLD (1989 ONWARD)

Political repression coupled with the economic and political stagnancy of the Leonid Brezhnev years from 1964-1982 increased unrest and disapproval for Moscow and its policies among the satellites. When ▧ **Mikhail Gorbachev** became Secretary General of the Communist Party in 1985, he began to dismantle the totalitarian aspects of the Communist regime through his policies of **glasnost** (openness) and **perestroika** (restructuring). The new freedom of political expression led to a snowballing of dissidence, which finally erupted in 1989 with a series of revolutions throughout Eastern Europe. The first occurred in Poland in June when the Poles voted the communists out of office. In their place, they elected **Lech Wałęsa** and the **Solidarity** party to create the new government. This Polish victory was swiftly followed by a new democratic constitution in **Hungary** in October, the crumbling of the **Berlin Wall** on November 9, the resignation of the **Bulgarian** communists on November 10, the **Velvet Revolution** in Czechoslovakia on November 17 and the execution of Romania's communist dictator **Nicolae Ceauşescu** on December 25. Almost all of the Warsaw Pact nations had successfully—and almost bloodlessly—broken away from the Soviet Union and begun the move toward democracy.

The **USSR** crumbled shortly after its empire. Within the first five months of 1990, **Lithuania, Estonia, Latvia,** and **Ukraine** all declared independence from Moscow. In an attempt to keep the Soviet Union together, Gorbachev condoned military force against the rebellious Baltic republics. A bloody conflict erupted in Vilnius in January, 1991. By September, the Soviet Union was dead and all of its constituent republics and satellite nations were fully independent.

Following Tito's death in 1980, Yugoslavia was slowly disintegrating. Economic inequality between its different republics led to the resurfacing of suppressed nationalist sentiments. Inspired by the developments in the rest of Eastern Europe, both **Slovenia** and **Croatia** declared independence on June 25, 1991, to which the Serbian-controlled government responded with military force. The conflict in Slovenia lasted only ten days, but Croatia's attempts to secede resulted in a war that involved Serbia, Croatia, Bosnia-Herzegovina, and Montenegro and continued until the signing of the US-negotiated **Dayton Peace Agreement** in November, 1995. The only republics remaining in Yugoslavia were Serbia and Montenegro. Four years later, the ultra-nationalist greed of Serbia's leader and a indicted war criminal **Slobodan Milosevic** erupted in another military conflict in the Serbian province of **Kosovo.** In an attempt to stop the ethnic cleansing of Kosovo's Albanian majority by the Serbian army, **NATO** launched an intensive air campaign, which ruined the country's economy and led to Serbia's withdrawal. As long as Milosevic remains in power, however, the security of the region remains threatened.

With the exception of tumultuous Balkans, the former Soviet satellites are progressing, with varying speed and success, towards democracy and market economy. In March 1999, Russia felt NATO move closer when Poland, Hungary and the Czech Republic joined the alliance. Lithuania, Latvia, Estonia, Slovenia and Slovakia are vying to become the next members. The EU's next round of member selection will draw these countries even further Westward, perhaps as early as 2003.

# CULTURE

## THE PEOPLE OF EASTERN EUROPE

Although the region is becoming increasingly diversified in light of its recent opening up to the world, the population still remains fairly homogeneous. Most Eastern European countries are inhabited by **Slavic people.** After the Great Migration (see

p. 8), the Slavs split into three relatively distinct divisions of **West Slavs** (Czechs, Poles, and Slovaks), **South Slavs** (Croats, Macedonians, Serbs, and Slovenes) and **East Slavs** (Belarussians, Russians and Ukrainians). **Bulgarians,** originally of Turkic origin, became completely Slavified when the Slavs swept across Europe.

The non-Slavic nations inhabiting Central and Eastern Europe include Austrians, Hungarians, Latvians, Lithuanians, and Estonians. **Austrians** are of Germanic descent and lived in the region long before the marauding Slavs came from the east. **Latvians** (a.k.a. Letts) and **Lithuanians** belong to the Baltic branch of the Indo-European family. They live along the shore of the Baltic Sea, from which they derive their name. The Balts originally included more ethnic groups that are now extinct, such as the Prussians, the Curonians, and the Selonians. **Estonians,** who also occupy the Baltic Coast, form a branch of the Baltic Finns, descendants of the Finno-Ugric family who have been strongly Germanized. **Hungarians** constitute the "Ugric" part of the Finno-Ugric family. They separated from other Ugric tribes in the Urals and migrated southwest to the Carpathian Basin, which they inhabit today, at the end of the 9th century. Today, large Hungarian minorities live in southern Slovakia and the Romanian Transylvania. **Romanians** are descendants of Dacians, the earliest known inhabitants of the Balkan Peninsula, together with Thracians and Illyrians.

There are significant **Jewish** communities living in Poland, the Czech Republic, Hungary, and Russia, although their numbers decreased dramatically after the Second World War as a result of Hitler's "final solution." Well integrated into the society in most countries, Jewish people still face severe anti-Semitism in Russia and Belarus. Nomadic **Roma,** or gypsies, live in small communities (or rather ghettos) across Eastern Europe, particularly in the Czech Republic, Slovakia, Hungary, Bulgaria, and Romania. Finally, American and British **Expats** flooded Eastern Europe after the fall of the Berlin Wall, creating distinct cultures in Prague, Budapest, St. Petersburg, and other parts of Eastern Europe. In fact, last time we checked, Prague boasted around 10,000 native English speakers.

**GYPSY KINGS.** The Roma migrated to Europe from their homeland in northern India sometime in the 14th and 15th century. Also known throughout Europe as gypsies, they refer to themselves as Roma, meaning *man* or *husband* in their native tongue, Romany. Most Roma speak their native language, as well as the language of the country in which they settled. Their nomadic nature and darker skin color prevented any integration with white Europeans. In the early years of their immigration, Roma were regarded as exotic. When they first came to France in the 15th century, the French referred to them as "Bohemians," meaning "coming from Bohemia." Later, the word Bohemian acquired the meaning as we know it today, designating anyone leading an unconventional lifestyle like the Roma. Despite (and perhaps due to) their exotic image, the Roma have always found themselves on the edge of the society. Today, the treatment of Roma in Eastern Europe is as poor as ever. In June 1998, the local government of Ústí nad Labem, in Northern Bohemia, built a wall through the center of town to separate the "good" Czech citizens from the "bad" Roma. Although the wall was later torn down in response to pressures from the international community, the situation of the Roma remains dismal. Faced with extreme discrimination and violent attacks by skinheads, thousands of Roma left the Czech Republic in 1998 and 1999 to seek refuge first in Great Britain, then in Canada. Nearly all of them were sent back.

# RELIGION

The majority of Eastern Europe had accepted **Christianity** by the 10th century, and it remains the principal religion on the continent till this day. The monks **Cyril and Methodius** brought Christianity to the Slavs (see **Languages** and **What's In a Name?,** below); Belarussians, Bulgarians, Macedonians, Romanians, Russians, Serbs, and Ukrainians subscribe to the **Eastern Orthodox** faith. With the exception of the Baltic states, which have been influenced by German **Protestantism,** all other nations of

Eastern Europe are predominantly **Roman Catholic.** Birthplace of the present Pope John Paul II, Poland is one of the world's most strongly Catholic countries. In the Czech Republic, which lies geographically on the boundary between Protestant and Catholic Europe, both Catholicism and Protestantism are represented. Religious dissent from Catholicism in the Czech lands has been apparent since the 14th century, when **Jan Hus** (see p. 205) preached church reform, preceding Luther's **Reformation** by a full century. Under the Habsburgs, the Czechs were subjected to massive re-Catholization, resulting in a confusion that later contributed to the nation's strong **atheism.** The hopelessness that followed the World Wars and more importantly, communism, spread atheism across Eastern Europe.

**Islam** was brought to Europe with the Ottoman Empire. Bosnians, who came to be called simply Muslims during the recent wars, are Islamicized Serbo-Croats. There are significant Muslim Albanian minorities in Macedonia and Bulgaria. **Judaism** constitutes another important minority religion, practised by the Jewish diaspora mainly in the Czech Republic, Poland, Russia and Hungary.

## LANGUAGES

With the exception of Estonian and Hungarian, which are **Finno-Ugric** (though not mutually intelligible), all nations in Eastern Europe speak languages of **Indo-European** origin. German, spoken in Austria, belongs to the **Germanic** branch of Indo-European languages, Romanian to the **Romance** branch (similar to Italian), and **Latvian** and **Lithuanian** to the Baltic branch. Belarussian, Bulgarian, Czech, Macedonian, Polish, Serbo-Croatian, Slovak, Slovene, Russian and Ukrainian are all **Slavic** languages. The **Cyrillic alphabet** is a script used in Bulgaria, Macedonia, Serbia, Russia, and throughout the former Soviet Union. On a mission to Great Moravia (part of modern-day Czech Republic and Slovakia), two 9th-century monks developed the alphabet's first form in order to translate the Bible into Slavic. The monks, Cyril and Methodius, were Greek (which is why many Cyrillic letters look Greek) and Orthodox (which is why all countries using the Cyrillic alphabet are predominantly Eastern Orthodox). When Catholic powers gained control of the region that the monks were proselytizing, their disciples fled to the shores of Lake Ohrid, Macedonia, where they founded the first Slavic university, and the script spread swiftly to other Slavic lands. For more information on Cyril and Methodius, see **What's In a Name?,** below.

For many centuries, Cyrillic was a source of unity for the Slavic nations who wrote in it, and its use (or non-use) still makes a political statement in some parts of the world. One of the major differences between the otherwise very similar Serb and Croat languages is that Croatian is written in the Latin alphabet, while Serbian is written in Cyrillic. Furthermore, as republics of the former Soviet Union are discovering their roots, they are learning their own scripts instead of Cyrillic, which for decades Moscow had made the empire's *scripta franca.*

---

**WHAT'S IN A NAME?** When Greek priest Constantine and his brother Methodius set off on a Christian mission to the Slavs in 863, they brought with them more than their religion. To succeed where others had failed, Constantine translated liturgical text into the language of the people, using an alphabet he invented based on Greek script. The new script, **Old Church Slavonic,** was a smashing success among the people, facilitating unions in the name of religion and language that made the great empires of the Bulgarians and the Kyivan Rus possible. Rome, however, was less than thrilled to hear that the Word of God was being spread in any language less dignified than Greek or Latin. The brothers were summoned to explain themselves before Pope Nicholas I, who died before they arrived in 868. And while his successor Adrian II gave their mission his full blessing, Constantine fell ill and died before he could return to preach. Before he passed away, he adopted the name Cyril, which has been immortalized as the name of the alphabet that evolved from his work.

The Russian Cyrillic transliteration index is given below. Other languages include some additional letters and pronounce certain letters differently. Each country's language section (in the respective chapters) outlines these distinctions.

| CYRILLIC | ENGLISH | PRONOUNCE | CYRILLIC | ENGLISH | PRONOUNCE |
|---|---|---|---|---|---|
| А а | a | Garden | Р р | r | Random |
| Б б | b | Mr. Burns | С с | s | Saucy |
| В в | v | Village People | Т т | t | Tantalize |
| Г г | g | Galina | У у | oo | Doodle |
| Д д | d | David | Ф ф | f | Absolutely Fab |
| Е е | ye or e | Yellow | Х х | kh | Chutzpah (hkh) |
| Ё ё | yo | Your | Ц ц | ts | Let's Go |
| Ж ж | zh | Persia | Ч ч | ch | Chinese |
| З з | z | Zany | Ш ш | sh | Champagne |
| И и | ee | Kathleen | Щ щ | shch | Khrushchev |
| Й й | y | (see * below) | ъ | (hard) | (no sound) |
| К к | k | Killjoy | ы | y | lit |
| Л л | l | Louis | ь | (soft) | (no sound) |
| М м | m | Meteor | Э э | eh | Alexander |
| Н н | n | Nikki | Ю ю | yoo | You |
| О о | o | Hole | Я я | yah | Yahoo! |
| П п | p | Peter the Great | | | |

* Й creates dipthongs, altering the sounds of the vowels it follows: ОЙ is pronounced "oy" (boy), АЙ is pronounced "aye" (bye), ИЙ is pronounced "ee" (baby), and ЕЙ is pronounced "ehy" (bay).

## FOOD...BUT MAINLY DRINK

Although food and drink specialities vary from region to region, Eastern Europe stands united in its love of sausage and alcohol, primarily beer and—in Poland, Russia, and Ukraine—vodka. Indeed, many say that politics in Eastern Europe is made in its pubs and wine cellars. Sausage comes in an endless amount of varieties, the spiciest ones being from Hungary, a mecca of spicy food itself. Central European cuisine is characterized by lots of meat floating in a sauce accompanied by cabbage and potatoes, whereas on the coasts, a lighter, sea-based cuisine predominates. Good luck finding **vegetarian** restaurants that serve more than spaghetti with ketchup or soy cubes. Delicious **breads** are baked throughout the region, and always provide a welcome substitute for the region's heavy dishes.

The Czechs most certainly win the prize for Eastern Europe's greatest beer-maniacs, in production and consumption alike. The Czech Republic's most famous brand of beer, *Pilsner Urquell*, is by no means its best—try gems such as *Velkopopovický kozel* or *Krušovice*. Lesser-known to the outside world but often better than its pricey Western counterparts, wine is grown *en masse* in the Hungarian and Austrian Danube basin, as well as in the warm Bulgaria, Croatia, and Romania. For a guide to Eastern Europe's mind-erasing highlights, see **Alcoholic Delights, p. 3**.

# FESTIVALS IN EASTERN EUROPE

The following list is by no means exhaustive; it is meant to suggest highlights of Eastern European merriments.

| COUNTRY | APR. – JUNE | JULY – AUG. | SEPT. – MAR. |
|---|---|---|---|
| AUSTRIA | **Vienna Festival** mid-May to mid-June, Vienna (p. 72) | **JazzFest Wien** July, Vienna (p. 72) | |
| BOSNIA | | **Baščaršija Noci** July, Sarajevo (p. 99) | **Sarajevo Film Festival** Sept., Sarajevo (p. 99) |

# 16 ■ FESTIVALS IN EASTERN EUROPE

INTRODUCTION

| COUNTRY | APR. – JUNE | JULY – AUG. | SEPT. – MAR. |
|---|---|---|---|
| BULGARIA | International Ballet Festivals<br>May-Oct., Varna (p. 134) | International Jazz Fest.<br>late Aug., Varna (p. 134) | Love is Folly Film Fest.,<br>Aug.-Sept., Varna (p. 134) |
| CROATIA | Animated Film Fest.<br>June, Zagreb (p. 162)<br>Ceci is d'Best<br>June, Zagreb (p. 162)<br>Eurokaz Theater Fest.<br>June, Zagreb (p. 162) | Festival of Sword Dances<br>July, Korčula (p. 192)<br>Dubrovnik Summer Fest.<br>July, Dubrovnik (p. 199)<br>Summer Festival<br>July-Aug., Split (p. 188) | International Puppet<br>Sept., Zagreb (p. 162)<br>Jazz Fair<br>Oct., Zagreb (p. 162)<br>Marco Polo Festival<br>Sept., Korčula (p. 192) |
| CZECH REPUBLIC | Prague Spring<br>May, Prague (p. 240)<br>Five-Petal Rose Fest.<br>June, Č. Krumlov (p. 260)<br>Smetana Opera Festival<br>June, Litomyšl (p. 266) | International Film Fest.<br>July, Karlovy Vary (p. 253)<br>International Music Fest.<br>Aug.,Č. Krumlov (p. 260) | Jazz Goes To Town<br>Oct., Hradec Králové (p. 266)<br>International Organ Festival<br>Sept., Olomouc (p. 274) |
| ESTONIA | Old Town Days<br>June, Tallinn (p. 288) | Beersummer<br>July, Tallinn (p. 288) | |
| HUNGARY | Sopron Festival Weeks<br>June, Sopron (p. 348)<br>Int'l Military Band<br>June, Debrecen (p. 367)<br>Szentivánéji Festivities<br>June, Szombath. (p. 351) | Béla Bartók Choir Fest.<br>July, Debrecen (p. 367)<br>Lipicai (Horse) Festival<br>July, Szilvásvárad (p. 380)<br>Baroque Festival<br>July, Eger (p. 379) | Haydn Festival<br>Sept., Fertőd (p. 349)<br>Hírős Food Festival<br>Sept., Kecskem. (p. 374)<br>Eger Vintage Days<br>Sept., Eger (p. 379) |
| LITHUANIA | Jazz Festival<br>June, Klaipeda (p. 432) | Thomas Mann Festival<br>July, Nida (p. 433). | |
| MACEDONIA | Skopje Summer Festival<br>mid-June to mid-July, Skopje (p. 443) | Ohrid Summer Festival<br>mid-July to mid-Aug., Ohrid (p. 445) | |
| POLAND | International Short Film<br>May, Kraków (p. 488)<br>Probaltica<br>May, Toruń (p. 522)<br>Music and Architecture<br>May, Toruń (p. 522)<br>Jazz nad Odrą<br>May, Wrocław (p. 512)<br>Fest. of Jewish Culture<br>June, Kraków (p. 488) | Street Theater<br>July, Kraków (p. 488)<br>Country Picnic Fest.<br>July-Aug., Mrąg. (p. 547)<br>Highlander Folklore<br>Aug., Zakopane (p. 502)<br>Rock and Pop Music<br>Aug., Sopot (p. 541) | Jazz Vocalists<br>Sept., Zamość (p. 497)<br>Kraków Jazz Festival<br>Oct., Kraków (p. 488)<br>National Blues Music<br>Nov., Toruń (p. 522) |
| ROMANIA | Sibiu Jazz Festival<br>May-June, Sibiu (p. 575) | | |
| RUSSIA | White Nights Festival<br>June, St. Pete. (p. 657) | | |
| SLOVAKIA | Ghosts and Spirits<br>May, Bojnice (p. 710) | | Bratislava Music Fest.<br>Sept.-Oct., Brati. (p. 707) |
| SLOVENIA | Slovene Music Days<br>Apr., Ljubljana (p. 748)<br>International Jazz Fest.<br>June, Ljubljana (p. 748) | Peasants' Wedding Day<br>July, Lake Bohinj (p. 753)<br>Int'l Summer Festival<br>July, Ljubljana (p. 748) | Cow Ball<br>Sept., L. Bohinj (p. 753) |
| UKRAINE | | Nuclear Reactor Rave<br>July, Kazantip (p. 783) | Kyiv Theater Festival<br>Mar., Kiev (p. 779) |

# GEOGRAPHY

## LAND AND WATER

The vast majority of Eastern Europe consists of several low altitude plains. The North and East European Plains span from Poland to the Baltic states, Belarus, Ukraine and European Russia. The Hungarian Plain covers southern Slovakia and most of Hungary, whereas the Romanian Plain dominates the south of Romania. Most of the Czech Republic sits on a plateau, the Bohemian Massif. The largest mountains in Central Europe are the **Carpathians** (which include the **Tatras**), running along the Polish-Slovak border and further east to northern Romania. South of the lowlands lie Europe's highest mountain ranges, the **Alps** in Austria and Slovenia and the **Balkan Mountains** of Croatia, Bosnia, Macedonia and Bulgaria.

Europe's longest river is the **Volga** in Russia. The **Danube**, which creates a natural border between Hungary and Slovakia and cuts through Austria, is the region's economically and historically most important river. Other rivers include the **Dnieper** in Ukraine, the **Elbe** in the Czech Republic, and the **Oder** and **Vistula** in Poland. Eastern European rivers dump their water (and waste) into three seas, the **Baltic,** the **Adriatic,** and the **Black Sea.** Whereas the Baltic coast is entirely composed of lowlands, the Adriatic is characterized by dramatic mountains, jagged peninsulas and miniature islands. **Lake Balaton** in Hungary is the largest (and most popular) lake in Europe west of Russia; **Lake Ladoga** in northwestern Russia is the largest in Europe (though not the largest *in* Russia—Lake Baikal, in Asia, is bigger), but definitely not the most popular.

## CLIMATE

| AVG TEMP (HI/LO) | JANUARY | | APRIL | | JULY | | OCTOBER | |
|---|---|---|---|---|---|---|---|---|
| | °C | °F | °C | °F | °C | °F | °C | °F |
| **Bratislava, SLK** | 01/-4 | 34/25 | 15/6 | 59/43 | 25/15 | 77/59 | 14/7 | 57/45 |
| **Bucharest, ROM** | 01/-7 | 34/19 | 18/05 | 64/41 | 30/16 | 86/61 | 18/6 | 64/43 |
| **Budapest, HUN** | 01/-4 | 34/25 | 17/7 | 63/45 | 28/16 | 82/61 | 16/7 | 61/45 |
| **Kiev, UKR** | -4/-10 | 25/14 | 14/5 | 57/41 | 25/15 | 77/59 | 13/6 | 55/43 |
| **Ljubljana, SLN** | 02/-4 | 36/25 | 15/4 | 59/39 | 27/14 | 81/57 | 15/6 | 59/43 |
| **Minsk, BEL** | -4/-8 | 25/18 | 10/7 | 50/45 | 19/17 | 66/63 | 12/8 | 54/46 |
| **Moscow, RUS** | -9/-16 | 16/3 | 10/1 | 50/34 | 23/13 | 73/55 | 09/3 | 48/37 |
| **Prague, CZ** | 0/-5 | 32/23 | 12/3 | 54/37 | 23/13 | 73/55 | 12/5 | 54/41 |
| **Riga, LAT** | -4/-10 | 25/14 | 10/1 | 50/34 | 22/11 | 72/52 | 11/4 | 52/39 |
| **Sarajevo, BOS** | 03/-3 | 37/27 | 18/7 | 64/45 | 28/17 | 82/63 | 18/8 | 64/46 |
| **Skopje, MAC** | 05/-2 | 41/26 | 11/1 | 52/34 | 31/15 | 87/59 | 19/8 | 66/46 |
| **Sofia, BUL** | 02/-3 | 36/27 | 16/5 | 61/41 | 27/16 | 81/61 | 17/8 | 63/46 |
| **Tallinn, EST** | -4/-10 | 25/14 | 10/1 | 50/34 | 22/11 | 72/52 | 11/4 | 52/39 |
| **Vienna, AUS** | 01/-4 | 34/25 | 15/6 | 59/43 | 25/15 | 77/59 | 14/7 | 57/45 |
| **Vilnius, LIT** | -4/-10 | 25/14 | 10/1 | 50/34 | 22/11 | 72/52 | 11/4 | 52/39 |
| **Warsaw, POL** | 0/-6 | 32/21 | 12/03 | 54/37 | 24/15 | 75/59 | 13/5 | 55/41 |
| **Zagreb, CRO** | 02/-4 | 36/25 | 15/4 | 59/43 | 27/14 | 81/57 | 15/6 | 59/43 |

The sun also shines on the Eastern Bloc, despite what Western propaganda against communism, flooding television with images of rainy Moscow and ice-cold Siberia, used to suggest. Eastern Europe is so vast that its climate is extremely varied. The **central regions,** such as Poland, the Czech Republic, or Slovakia, get warm summers (May-September) and bitingly cold winters (December-February). **South** of these countries, however, toward the Mediterranean Sea (Slovenia, Croatia), summers become extremely hot and winters pleasantly mild. It gets just as hot along the Bulgarian, Romanian and Ukrainian **Black Sea Coast.**

# ESSENTIALS

At times frustratingly bureaucratic, at times lawless, the one constant of travel in Kafkaesque Eastern Europe is that it's never predictable. Start planning well in advance: begin stalking consulates for visas the moment you decide to go, follow the news, plot every detail of your itinerary—and be prepared to scrap the whole thing once you arrive. Things change quickly in Eastern Europe: exchange rates, phone numbers, even borders. The most important thing to bring is flexibility.

## DOCUMENTS AND FORMALITIES

### EMBASSIES AND CONSULATES AT HOME
Unless otherwise noted, all diplomatic missions listed below are embassies.

**Austria: Australia:** 12 Talbot St., Forrest, Canberra ACT 2603 (☎(02) 6295 1533; austria@dynamite.com.au); **Canada:** 445 Wilbrod St., Ottawa, ON KIN 6M7 (☎(613) 789-1444; fax 789-3431; embassy@austro.org; www.austro.org); **Ireland:** 115 Ailesbury Court Apts., 93 Ailesbury Rd., Dublin 4 (☎(01) 269 4577 or 269 1451); **New Zealand:** Consular General, 22-4 Garrett St., Wellington (☎ (04) 801 9709; for visas or passports, contact Australian office); **UK:** 18 Belgrave Mews West, London SW1 X 8HU (☎(0207) 235 3731; embassy@austria.org.uk; www.austria.org.uk); **US:** 3524 International Court NW, Washington DC 20008-3035 (☎(202) 895-6700); **South Africa:** 1109 Duncan St., Momentum Office Park, 0011 Brooklyn, Pretoria; P.O. Box 95572, 0145 Waterkloof, Pretoria (☎(012) 462 483; saembvie@ins.at).

**Belarus: UK:** 6 Kensington Ct., London, W8 5DL (☎(020) 7937 3288; fax 7361 0005). **US:** 1619 New Hampshire Ave. NW, Washington, D.C. 20009 (☎(202) 986-1606; fax 986-1805).

**Bosnia-Herzegovina: Australia:** 27 State Circle, Forest, Canberra ACT 2603 (☎(02) 6239 5955; fax 6239 5793). **UK:** 320 Regent St., London W1R 5AB (☎(020) 7255 3758; fax 7255 3760; bosnia@embassy_london.ision.co.uk). **US Embassy:** 2109 E St. NW, Washington, D.C. 20037 (☎(202) 337-1500; fax 337-1502; info@bosnianembassy.org; www.bosnianembassy.org). **US Consulate:** 866 UN Plaza Suite 580, New York, NY 10017 (☎(212) 593-0264 or 593-1042; fax 751-9019).

**Bulgaria: Australia Consulate:** 4 Carlotta Rd., Double Bay, Sydney, NSW 2028; postal address P.O. Box 1000, Double Bay, NSW 1360 (☎(02) 9327 7581; fax 9327 8067; bgconsul@ihug.com.au). **Canada:** 325 Stewart St., Ottawa, ON K1N 6K5 (☎(613) 789-3215; fax 789-3524). **South Africa:** 1071 Church St., Hatfield, PRETORIA; P.O. Box 32569, ARCADIA (☎(012) 342 37 20; fax 342 37 21; embulgsa@iafrica.com). **UK:** 186-188 Queensgate, London SW7 5HL (☎(020) 7584 9400; fax 7584 4948). **US:** 1621 22nd St. NW, Washington, D.C. 20008 (☎(202) 387-0174 or 387-7969; fax 234-7973; office@bulgaria-embassy.org or bgconsul@wizard.net; www.bulgaria-embassy.org or http://bulgaria.wdn.net).

**Croatia: Australia:** 14 Jindalee Crescent, O'Malley, Canberra ACT 2606 (☎(06) 286 6988; fax 286 3544; croemb@dynamite.com.au or croemb_aust@tqs.com.au). **Canada:** 229 Chapel Street, Ottawa, ON K1N 7Y6 (☎(613) 562-7820; fax 562-7821; info@croatiaemb.net; www.croatiaemb.net). **New Zealand Consulate:** 131 Lincoln Rd., Henderson, P.O. Box 83200, Edmonton, Auckland (☎(09) 836 5581; fax 836 5481). **South Africa:** 1160 Church St., Colbyn, PRETORIA; P.O. Box 11335, HATFIELD 0028 (☎(012) 342 1206; fax 342 1819). **UK:** 21 Conway St., London W1P 5HL (☎(020) 7387 2022; fax 7387 0936). **US:** 2343 Massachusetts Ave. NW, Washington, D.C. 20008 (☎(202) 588-5899; fax 588-8936; www.croatiaemb.org).

**Czech Republic: Australia:** 8 Culgoa Circuit, O'Malley, Canberra, ACT 2606 (☎(02) 6290 1386; fax 6290 0006; canberra@embassy.mzv.cz). **Canada:** 541 Sussex Dr.,

Ottawa, ON K1N 6Z6 (☎(613) 562-3875; fax 562-3878; ottowa@embassy.mzv.cz). **Ireland:** 57 Northumberland Rd., Ballsbridge, Dublin 4 (☎ (01) 668 1135; fax 668 1660; dublin@embassy.mzv.cz). **New Zealand Honorary Consul:** 48 Hair St., Wainuiomata, Wellington (☎/fax (04) 564 6001). **South Africa:** 936 Pretorius St., Arcadia 0083, PRETORIA; P.O. Box 3326, PRETORIA 0001 (☎ (012) 342 3477; fax 430 2033; pretoria@embassy.mzv.cz; www.icon.co.za/Ìczmzv/). **UK:** 26 Kensington Palace Gardens, London W8 4QY (☎(020) 7243 1115; fax 7727 9654; london@embassy.mzv.cz). **US:** 3900 Spring of Freedom St. NW, Washington, D.C. 20008 (☎(202) 274-9100; fax 966-8540; www.czech.cz/washington/).

**Estonia: Australia Honorary Consul:** 86 Louisa Rd., Birchgrove NSW, 2041 (☎(02) 9810 7468; fax 98 18 17 79; eestikon@ozemail.com.au). **Canada Honorary Consul:** 958 Broadview Ave., Suite 202, Toronto, ON M4K 2R6 (☎(416) 461-0764; fax 461-0353; estconsu@inforamp.net). **Ireland:** Merlyn Park 24, Ballsbridge, Dublin 4 (☎(01) 269 1552; fax 260 5119). **South Africa Honorary Consul:** 16 Hofmeyer St., Welgemoed, BELVILLE, 7530 (☎(021) 913 3850; fax 913 2579). **UK:** 16 Hyde Park Gate, London SW7 5DG (☎(020) 7589 3428; fax 7589 3430; tvaravas@estonia.gov.uk; www.estonia.gov.uk). **US:** 2131 Massachusetts Ave. NW, Washington, D.C. 20008 (☎(202) 588-0101; fax 588-0108; info@estemb.org; www.estemb.org).

**Hungary: Australia Consulate:** Suite 405, Edgecliff Centre 203-233, New South Head Rd., Edgecliff, NSW 2027 (☎(02) 9328 7859; fax 9327 1829). **Canada:** 299 Waverley St., Ottawa, ON K2P 0V9 (☎(613) 230-2717; fax 230-7560; h2embott@docuweb.ca; www.docuweb.ca/Hungary). **Ireland:** 2 Fitzwilliam Pl., Dublin 2 (☎(01) 661 2903; fax 661 2880). **South Africa:** 959 Arcadia St., Hatfield, ARCADIA; P.O. Box 27077, SUNNYSIDE 0132 (☎(012) 43 30 20; fax 430 3029; hunem@cis.co.za). **New Zealand:** 151 Orangi Kaupapa Rd., Wellington, 6005 (☎(644) 938 0427; fax 938 0428; sztmay@attglobal.net; www.geocities.com/CapitolHill/Lobby/1958/ContentsEn.htm). **UK:** 35 Eaton Pl., London SW1X 8BY (☎(020) 7235 5218; fax 7823 1348; www.huemblon.org.uk). **US:** 3910 Shoemaker St. NW, Washington, D.C. 20008 (☎(202) 362-6730; fax 966-8135; office@huembwas.org; www.hungaryemb.org).

**Latvia: Australia Consulate:** P.O. Box 457, Strathfield NSW 2135 (☎(02) 9744 5981; fax 9747 6055). **Canada:** 280 Albert Street, Suite 300, Ottawa, ON K1P 5G8 (☎(613) 238-6014; fax 238-7044; latvia-embassy@magmacom.com; www.magmacom.com/~latemb/). **UK:** 45 Nottingham Pl., London W1M 3FE (☎(020) 7312 0040; fax 7312 0042). **US:** 4325 17th St. NW, Washington, D.C. 20011 (☎(202) 726-8213; fax 726-6785; embassy@latvia-usa.org, for visa info visa@latvia-usa.org; www.latvia-usa.org).

**Lithuania: Australia Honorary Consul:** 40B Fiddens Wharf Rd., Killara NSW 2071 (☎(02) 949 825 71). **Canada:** 130 Albert St., #204, Ottawa, ON K1P 5G4 (☎(613) 567-5458; fax 567-5458; ltemb@storm.ca). **New Zealand Honorary Consul:** 28 Heather St., Parnell Auckland, NEW ZEALAND (☎(09) 379 6639; fax 307 2911; saul@f1rst.co.nz). **South Africa Honorary Consul:** Killarney Mall, 1st Floor, Riviera Rd., Killarney JOHANNESBURG, Postal address: P.O. Box 1737, HOUGHTON, 2041 (☎(011) 486 3660; fax 486 3650; lietuvos@iafrica.com). **UK:** 84 Gloucester Pl., London W1H 3HN (☎(020) 7486 6401; fax 7486 6403). **US:** 2622 16th St. NW, Washington, D.C. 20009-4202 (☎(202) 234-5860; fax 328-0466; admin@ltembassyus.org; www.ltembassyus.org).

**Moldova:** www.moldova.org. **US:** 2101 S St. NW, Washington, D.C. 20008 (☎(202) 667-1130; fax 667-1204; moldova@dgs.dgsys.com).

**Poland: Australia:** 7 Turrana St., Yarralumla ACT 2600 Canberra (☎(06) 273 1208 or 273 1211; fax 273 3184; ambpol@clover.com.au). **Canada:** 443 Daly St., Ottawa, ON, K1N 6H3 (☎(613) 789-0468; fax 789-1218; polamb@hookup.com). **Ireland:** 5 Ailesbury Rd., Dublin 4 (☎(01) 283 0855; fax 283 7562). **New Zealand:** 17 Upland Rd., Kelburn, Wellington (☎(04) 712 456; fax 712 455; polishembassy@xtra.co.nz). **South Africa:** 14 Amos St., Colbyn, PRETORIA 0083 (☎(012) 432 631; fax 432 608; amb.pol@pixie.co.za). **UK:** 47 Portland Pl., London W1N 4JH (☎(020) 7580 4324; fax

7323 4018). **US:** 2640 16th St. NW, Washington, D.C. 20009 (☎(202) 234-3800; fax 328-6271; embpol@dgs.dgsys.com; www.polishworld.com/polemb).

**Romania: Canada:** 655 Rideau St., Ottawa, ON K1N 6A3 (☎(613) 789-5345; fax 789-4365; romania@cyberus.ca). **South Africa:** 117 Charles St., Brooklyn PRETORIA; P.O. Box 11295, BROOKLYN, 0011 (☎(012) 466 940; fax 466 947). **UK:** 4 Palace Green, Kensington, London W8 4QD (☎(020) 7937 9666; fax 7937 8069). **US:** 1607 23rd St. NW, Washington, D.C. 20008 (☎(202) 332-4848; fax 232-4748; consular@roembus.org; www.roembus.org).

**Russia: Australia:** 78 Canberra Ave., Griffith ACT 2603 Canberra (☎(06) 295 90 33, visa info 295 1847; fax 295 9474). **Canada:** 285 Charlotte St., Ottawa, ON K1N 8L5 (☎(613) 235-4341, visa info 236-0920; fax 236-6342). **Ireland:** 186 Orwell Rd., Rathgar, Dublin 14 (☎/fax (01) 492 3525, visa info 492 3492; russiane@indigo.ie). **New Zealand:** 57 Messines Rd., Karori, Wellington (☎(04) 476 6113, visa info 476 6742; fax 476 3843; eor@netlink.co.nz). **South Africa:** Butano Building, 316 Brooks St., Menlo Park 0081, PRETORIA; P.O. Box 6743, PRETORIA 0001 (☎(012) 362 1337, visa info 344 4812; fax 362 0116). **UK:** 13 Kensington Palace Gardens, London W8 4QX (☎(020) 7229 3628, visa info 7229 8027; fax 7727 8625; harhouse1@harhouse1.demon.co.uk). **US:** 2650 Wisconsin Ave., N.W., Washington, D.C. 20007 (☎(202) 298-5700; fax 298-5735).

**Slovakia: Australia:** 47 Culgoa Circuit, O'Malley, Canberra ACT 2606 (☎(06) 290 1516; fax 290 1755). **Canada:** 50 Rideau Terrace, Ottawa, ON K1M 2A1 (☎(613) 749-4442; fax 749-4989; slovakemb@sprint.ca.) **South Africa:** 930 Arcadia St., Arcadia, PRETORIA; P.O. Box 12736, HATFIELD, 0028 (☎(012) 342 2051; fax 342 3688). **UK:** 25 Kensington Palace Gardens, London W8 4QY (☎(020) 7243 0803; fax 7727 5824; mail@slovakembassy.co.uk; www.slovakembassy.co.uk). **US:** 2201 Wisconsin Ave. NW, Suite 250, Washington, D.C. 20007 (☎(202) 965-5160; fax 965-5166; svkem@concentric.net; www.slovakemb.com).

**Slovenia: Australia:** Level 6, Advance Bank Center, 60 Marcus Clarke St. 2608, Canberra ACT 2601 (☎(06) 243 4830; fax 243 4827). **Canada:** 150 Metcalfe St., #2101, Ottawa, ON K2P 1P1 (☎(613) 565-5781; fax 565-5783). **New Zealand Honorary Consul:** Eastern Hutt Rd., Pomare, Lower Hutt, Wellington (☎(04) 567 27; fax 567 24). **UK:** Cavendish Ct. 11-15, Wigmore St., London W1H 9LA (☎(020) 7495 7775; fax 7495 7776; www.embassy-slovenia.org.uk). **US:** 1525 New Hampshire Ave. NW, Washington, D.C. 20036 (☎ (202) 667-5363; fax 667-4563; www.embassy.org/slovenia).

**Ukraine: Australia Honorary Consul:** #3, Ground Floor, 902-912 Mt. Alexander Road, Essendon, Victoria 3040. **Canada:** 331 Metcalfe St. Ottawa., ON, K2P 0J9 (☎(613) 230-2961; fax 230-2400; ukremb@cyberus.ca). **South Africa:** 398 Marais Brooklyn, PRETORIA; PO Box 57291 ARCADIA, 0007 (☎(012) 461 946; fax 461 944). **UK:** 60 Holand Park Rd., London W11 3SJ (☎(020) 7727 6312; fax 7792 1708). **US:** 3350 M St. NW, Washington, D.C. 20007 (☎(202) 333-7507; fax 333-7510; www.ukremb.com).

# EMBASSIES AND CONSULATES IN EASTERN EUROPE

American, Australian, British, Canadian, Irish, New Zealand, and South African embassies and consulates in Eastern European countries have been listed in the **Orientation and Practical Information** section for the capitals of each country.

# PASSPORTS

**REQUIREMENTS.** Citizens of Australia, Canada, Ireland, New Zealand, South Africa, the UK, and the US need valid passports to enter any country in Eastern Europe and to re-enter their own. Many European countries will not allow you to enter if your passport expires within six months of your trip. Returning home with an expired passport is illegal and may result in a fine.

**PHOTOCOPIES.** Photocopy the page of your passport that contains your photograph and passport number, along with other important documents such as visas, travel insurance policies, airplane tickets, and traveler's check serial numbers, in case of loss or theft. Carry one set of copies in a safe place apart from the originals and leave another set at home. Carry an expired passport or an official copy of your birth certificate in a part of your baggage separate from other documents.

**LOST PASSPORTS.** If you lose your passport, immediately notify the local police and the nearest embassy or consulate of your home government. To expedite its replacement, you'll need to show identification and proof of citizenship. In some cases, a replacement may take weeks to process and it may be valid only for a limited time. Any visas stamped in your old passport will be irretrievably lost. Your passport is a public document belonging to your nation's government. You may have to surrender it to a foreign government official, but if you don't get it back in a reasonable amount of time, inform the nearest mission of your home country.

**NEW PASSPORTS.** All applications for new passports or renewals should be filed several weeks before your departure. Most passport offices do offer emergency passport services for an significant extra charge. Citizens residing abroad who need passport services should contact the nearest embassy or consulate.

## VISAS, INVITATIONS, AND WORK PERMITS

**VISAS.** Visas can be purchased from your destination country's consulate or embassy. In most cases, you will have to send a completed visa application (also obtained from the consulate), the required fee, and your passport. You may also want to check your country for organizations offering visa services. For more information on each country's visa requirements, see the Essentials section at the beginning of each country chapter.

**WORK PERMITS.** Admission as a visitor does not include the right to work, which is authorized only by a work permit, and entering to study requires a special visa. Many countries require both a work permit and a special "visa with work permit." The former is issued by the country's Labor Office, and the latter by the consulate. For more information, see Alternatives to Tourism, p. 55, and the Essentials section for the country to which you're traveling.

## IDENTIFICATION

When you travel, always carry two or more forms of identification with you, including at least one photo ID. A passport combined with a driver's license or birth certificate usually serves as adequate proof of your identity and citizenship. Many establishments, especially banks, require several IDs before cashing traveler's checks. Never carry all your forms of ID together.

**STUDENT AND TEACHER IDENTIFICATION.** The **International Student Identity Card (ISIC)** is the most widely accepted form of student identification. Flash this card to receive discounts on sights, theaters, museums, accommodations, meals, and transportation. Ask about discounts even when none are advertised. International identification cards are preferable to institution-specific cards. For Americans traveling abroad, the ISIC also provides limited insurance benefits and a toll-free emergency helpline. See **Insurance**, p. 33, for details.

Many student travel agencies issue ISICs, including STA Travel in Australia and New Zealand; Travel CUTS in Canada; USIT in Ireland and Northern Ireland; SASTS in South Africa; Campus Travel and STA Travel in the UK; Council Travel and STA Travel in the US. Council Travel will process applications by mail; the appropriate form is available for download at www.counciltravel.com/idcards/apply.asp. When you apply for the card, request a copy of the International Student Identity Card Handbook, which lists some of the available discounts by country. You can also write to Council for a copy. The card is valid from September of one year to December of the following and costs AUS$15, CDN$15, or US$22.

**ESSENTIALS**

**VISA REQUIREMENTS**

| | AUS | CAN | IRE | NZ | SA | UK | US |
|---|---|---|---|---|---|---|---|
| **BELARUS** | Y* | Y* | Y* | Y* | Y* | Y* | Y* |
| **BOSNIA** | Y | N | N | Y | Y | N | N |
| **BULGARIA** | N¹ | N¹ | N¹ | N¹ | Y | N¹ | N |
| **CROATIA** | N | N | N | N | Y° | N | N |
| **CZECH REPUBLIC** | Y | N | N | N | Y | N | N¹ |
| **ESTONIA** | N | Y | N | N | Y | N | N |
| **HUNGARY** | Y | N | N | Y | N¹ | N | N |
| **LATVIA** | Y‡ | Y | N | Y‡ | Y | N | N |
| **LITHUANIA** | N | N | N | Y | Y | N | N |
| **MOLDOVA** | Y* | Y* | Y* | Y* | Y* | Y | Y* |
| **POLAND** | Y | Y | N | Y | Y | N | N |
| **ROMANIA** | Y | Y | Y | Y | Y | Y | N¹ |
| **RUSSIA** | Y* | Y* | Y* | Y* | Y* | Y* | Y* |
| **SLOVAKIA** | Y | N | N | Y | N¹ | N | N¹ |
| **SLOVENIA** | N | N | N | N | Y | N | N |
| **UKRAINE** | Y* | Y* | Y* | Y* | Y* | Y* | Y* |
| **KEY** | | | | | | | |

| ° | proof of travel required | * | invitiation required |
|---|---|---|---|
| ‡ | tourists can stay visa-free for up to 10 days | ¹ | tourists can stay visa-free for up to 30 days |

Applicants must be at least 12 years old and degree-seeking students of a secondary or post-secondary school. Because of the proliferation of phony ISICs, many airlines and some other services require additional proof of student identity, such as a signed letter from the registrar attesting to your student status or your school ID. The **International Teacher Identity Card (ITIC)** offers the same insurance coverage, and similar but limited discounts. The fee is AUS$13, UK£6, or US$22. For more information on these cards, contact the **International Student Travel Confederation (ISTC),** Herengracht 479, 1017 BS Amsterdam, Netherlands (☎ (20) 421 28 00; fax 421 28 10; istcinfo@istc.org; www.istc.org).

**YOUTH IDENTIFICATION.** The International Student Travel Confederation also issues a discount card to travelers who are 25 years old or younger but not students. Known as the **International Youth Travel Card (IYTC;** formerly the GO25 Card), this one-year card offers many of the same benefits as the ISIC. Most organizations that sell the ISIC also sell the IYTC (US$22).

# CUSTOMS

Upon entering any country, you must declare certain items from abroad and pay a duty on the value of those articles that exceed the allowance established by that country's customs service. Keeping receipts for purchases made abroad will help establish values when you return. It is wise to make a list, including serial numbers, of any valuables that you carry with you from home; if you register this list with customs before your departure and have an official stamp it, you will avoid import duty charges and ensure an easy passage upon your return. Be especially careful to document items manufactured abroad.

Upon returning home, you must declare all articles acquired abroad and pay a **duty** on the value of articles that exceed the allowance established by your country's customs service. Goods and gifts purchased at **duty-free** shops abroad are not exempt from duty or sales tax at your point of return; you must declare these items as well. "Duty-free" merely means that you need not pay a tax in the country of purchase. For more specific information on customs requirements, contact the customs information center in your country.

# MONEY

The biggest single expense on your trip will probably be your round-trip airfare to Eastern Europe, which can be much more expensive than a ticket to Western Europe (see **Getting There**, p. 41). Before you go, spend some time calculating a reasonable per-day budget that will meet your needs. A threadbare day in Eastern Europe (camping or sleeping in hostels, buying food at supermarkets) runs US$10-20; a slightly more comfortable day (sleeping in hostels and the occasional budget hotel, eating one meal a day at a restaurant, going out at night) runs US$20-30; spending more than that, you'd be living like royalty. Prices vary throughout the region: expect to spend US$5-10 more per day in Slovenia and Croatia, while Poland and Bulgaria may cost US$5 less. Don't forget to factor reserve funds (at least US$200) into your budget in case of emergency. Carrying cash with you is risky but necessary; personal checks from home are never accepted and even traveler's checks may not be accepted in some locations, particularly Russia. Your safest bet for carrying money, checks, and your passport is a flat money pouch around worn around your waist and underneath your clothing.

## CURRENCY AND EXCHANGE

In the **Money** section of each country chapter, we list the currency abbreviation and the September 2000 exchange rates between local currency and US dollars (US$), Canadian dollars (CDN$), British pounds (UK£), Irish pounds (IR£), Australian dollars (AUS$), New Zealand dollars (NZ$), South African rand (SAR), and German marks (DM). Check the financial pages of a large newspaper or the web for the latest rates. As a general rule, it is more expensive to buy foreign currency than domestic. In other words, Czech koruny are cheaper in the Czech Republic than in the UK. Bring enough foreign currency to last for the first 24-72hr. of a trip to avoid being penniless after banking hours or on a holiday. Using a cash (ATM) card or a credit card (see p. 24) will get you the best exchange rates.

If an ATM isn't available, go to banks or *bureaux de change* that have at most a 5% margin between their buy and sell prices. Since you lose money with every transaction, convert large sums (unless the currency is depreciating rapidly), but no more than you'll need, since it may be difficult either to change it back into your home currency or into a new one. Some countries, such as the Czech Republic, Slovakia, and Russia, may require transaction receipts to reconvert local currency. A few will not allow you to convert local currency back at all. Many Eastern European currencies are not exchangeable outside of their respective countries. Slovak koruny, for example, can only be exchanged in Slovakia itself.

If you use traveler's checks or cash, carry some in small denominations (US$50 or less), especially for times when you are forced to exchange money at disadvantageous rates. It's good to carry a range of denominations since charges may be levied per check cashed. Carry your money in a variety of forms, e.g. some cash, some traveler's checks, and an ATM and/or credit card. Australians, New Zealanders, and South Africans should consider carrying some US dollars or Deutschmarks, as some local tellers will prefer a more recognizable currency.

In some parts of Eastern Europe—particularly in countries with unstable currencies or those with a heavy German tourist industry—Deutschmarks and occasionally US dollars will be preferred to local currency. Some establishments will insist that they don't accept anything else, but avoid using Western money when you can. Not only are prices quoted in dollars or marks generally more expensive than those in the local currency, but Western currency may also attract thieves.

# TRAVELER'S CHECKS

Traveler's checks are one of the safest and least troublesome means of carrying funds, since they can be refunded if stolen. Unfortunately, they can be a hassle—if not impossible—to cash in Russia, Belarus, and Bosnia. For country-specific information on traveler's checks, refer to the **Tourist Services and Money** section in the **Essentials** of each chapter.

Several agencies and banks sell them, usually for face value plus a small percentage commission. **American Express** and **Visa** are the most widely recognized. If you're ordering checks, do so well in advance, especially if you are requesting large sums. Each agency provides refunds if your checks are lost or stolen, and many provide additional services, such as toll-free refund hotlines in the countries you're visiting and stolen credit card assistance.

In order to collect a refund for **lost or stolen checks,** keep your check receipts separate from your checks and store them in a safe place or with a traveling companion. Record check numbers when you cash them, leave a list of check numbers with someone at home, and ask for a list of refund centers when you buy your checks. Never countersign your checks until you are ready to cash them, and always bring your passport with you when you plan to use the checks.

**American Express:** ☎1800 251 902 in Australia; ☎0800 441 068 in New Zealand; ☎0800 521 313 in the UK; ☎800-221-7282 in the US and Canada. Elsewhere, call US collect 801-964-6665; www.aexp.com. Purchase checks for a small fee (1-4%) at American Express Travel Service Offices, banks, and American Automobile Association offices. AAA members can buy checks commission-free. American Express offices cash their checks commission-free (except where prohibited by national governments), but often at slightly worse rates than banks. The booklet *Traveler's Companion* lists travel offices and stolen check hotlines for each country.

**Citicorp:** ☎800-645-6556 in the US and Canada; ☎0800 622 887 in the UK; call US collect 813-623-1709 collect from elsewhere. Traveler's checks in 7 currencies. Commission 1-2%. Guaranteed hand-delivery of traveler's checks when a refund location is not convenient. Call 24hr.

**Thomas Cook MasterCard:** ☎800-223-7373 in the US or Canada; ☎0800 622 101 in the UK; call UK (+44) 1733 31 89 50 collect from elsewhere. Checks available in 13 currencies. Commission 2%. Thomas Cook offices cash checks commission-free but are much less common in Eastern Europe than American Express.

# CREDIT CARDS

Where they are accepted, credit cards often offer superior exchange rates. They may also offer services like insurance or emergency help and are sometimes required to reserve hotel rooms or rental cards. Few, if any, budget establishments in Eastern Europe will accept credit cards. Aside from the occasional splurge, you will probably reserve use of your credit card for financial emergencies.

The other use to which you might put your credit card is to get a **cash advance** which allows you to extract local currency from associated banks and teller machines instantly. **MasterCard** and **Visa** are the most welcomed; **American Express** cards work at some ATMs, as well as at AmEx offices and major airports. Pricey transaction fees for all credit-card advances (up to US$10 per advance, plus 2-3% extra on foreign transactions after conversion to US$) typically make credit cards a more costly means of withdrawing cash than ATMs or traveler's checks. In order to be eligible for a cash advance, request a **Personal Identification Number (PIN)** from AmEx, MasterCard, or Visa. When memorizing your PIN, be sure to remember the number code as opposed to the lettered code; key pads in Eastern Europe are not labeled with letters. If you already have a PIN, check with the company to make sure it will work in Eastern Europe; many machines require four digits.

## CASH (ATM) CARDS

ATMs get the same wholesale exchange rate as credit cards. There's often a limit on the amount of money you can withdraw per day (usually about US$500 but it can be as low as US$200). Additionally, both your home bank as well as the bank from which you're withdrawing money will charge you transaction fees that can be as much as US$5 per bank, per transaction. Also, if your PIN is longer than four digits, ask your bank whether the first four digits will work, or whether you need a new, longer number.

To locate ATMs worldwide, call US 800-4-CIRRUS (424-7787) for ATMs that accept Cirrus cards, 800-843-7587 for ATMs that accept PLUS cards, use www.visa.com/pd/atm for Visa, Visa Electron, and PLUS ATMs, and www.mastercard.com/atm for MasterCard, Maestro, and Cirrus ATMS.

## GETTING MONEY FROM HOME

**AMERICAN EXPRESS.** Cardholders can withdraw cash from their checking accounts at any of AmEx's major offices and many of its representatives' offices—the overseas transaction fee is 5% and the minimum amount US$3. Green card holders may withdraw up to US$1000 in a seven day period. AmEx also offers Express Cash at any of their ATMs for optimal cardholders. AmEx ATMs are few and far between in Eastern Europe. To enroll in Express Cash, Cardmembers may call 800-CASH NOW (227-4669) in the US; outside the US call collect 336-668-5041.

**WESTERN UNION.** Travelers from the US, Canada, and the UK can wire money abroad through Western Union's international money transfer services. In the US, call 800-325-6000; in the UK, call 0800 833 833; in Canada, call 800-235-0000. The rates for sending cash are generally US$10-11 cheaper than with a credit card, and the money is usually available at the place you're sending it to within an hour. Western Union services are available only sporadically in Eastern Europe.

**US STATE DEPARTMENT (US CITIZENS ONLY).** In emergencies, US citizens can have money sent via the State Department. For US$15, they will forward money within hours to the nearest consular office, which will disburse it according to instructions. The office serves only Americans in the direst of straits abroad; non-American travelers should contact their embassies for information on wiring cash. Check with the State Department or the nearest US embassy or consulate for the quickest way to have the money sent. Contact the Overseas Citizens Service, American Citizens Services, Consular Affairs, Room 4811, US Department of State, Washington, D.C. 20520 (tel. 202-647-5225; nights, Sundays, and holidays 647-4000; fax (on demand only) 647-3000; travel.state.gov).

# SAFETY AND SECURITY

Eastern Europe is generally regarded as a safe region through which to travel. The Czech Republic and Poland, for example, are as safe as—if not safer than—the USA and are as far removed from the situations in the Balkans and Russia as

The US Department of State issues Travel Warnings against unnecessary travel to politically unstable or dangerous regions. In 2000, travel warnings were issued for Bosnia-Herzegovina and the Yugoslav provinces of Serbia and Montenegro. All of these warnings were at least indirectly related to the NATO bombings in Yugoslavia in the spring of 1999. Due to the bombings and at the advice of the State Department, *Let's Go* was unable to send researchers to these provinces and they are not included in this year's guide. In addition, travelers should avoid the Transdniester region of Moldova, Eastern Slavonia in Croatia, and the Chechnya province in Russia, due to less safe conditions. For more specific information on the travel warnings issued, consult both the country's chapter in this book as well as the State Department's web page at travel.state.gov/travel warnings.html.

France or Italy is. In most countries, crime is restricted primarily to pickpocketing on crowded streets and public transportation. However, minority travelers should be aware that discrimination exists throughout; though it is mostly directed against Roma (Gypsies).

**BLENDING IN.** To avoid unwanted attention, try to blend in as much as possible. Respecting local customs (in many cases, dressing more conservatively) may placate would-be hecklers. Consider dressing more like an Eastern European: for women, that means skirts rather than shorts, and for both men and women, avoiding baggy jeans, sneakers, and sandals. Backpacks also stand out as particularly touristy; courier or shoulder bags are less likely to draw attention. Familiarize yourself with your surroundings before setting out; if you must check a map on the street, duck into a cafe or shop. Most importantly, carry yourself with confidence, as an obviously bewildered bodybuilder is more likely to be harassed than a stern and confident 98-pound weakling. If you are traveling solo, be sure that someone at home knows your itinerary and **never admit that you're traveling alone.**

Learn at least a few phrases before you leave for any Eastern European country; "please" and "thank you" are the two most important. Many Eastern Europeans simply assume that all tourists are rude and ignorant and any attempt on your part to prove them wrong will win you respect and potential friends. The more of a language you can speak, the better off you will be.

**EXPLORING.** Extra vigilance is always wise, but there is no need for panic when exploring a new city or region. Find out about unsafe areas from tourist offices, from the manager of your hotel or hostel, or from a local you trust. You may want to carry a **whistle** to scare off attackers or attract attention; memorize the emergency number of the city or area.

As much as you may be tempted, do not "explore" in Bosnia and Croatia; the countryside is littered with landmines and unexploded ordnance (UXO). While de-mining is underway, it will be years, if ever, before all of the mines are removed. UXOs are not a danger on paved roads or in major cities. Road shoulders and abandoned buildings are particularly likely to harbor UXOs.

**GETTING AROUND.** Road quality in Eastern Europe varies widely from country to country. In general, roads are poor with very few traffic signs; many are poorly lit dirt roads full of potholes. Drunk driving is common as is a general disregard for traffic laws. As with everything else though, the more Westernized the country, the better the roads: while roads in Belarus are very dangerous, Czech roads are up to Western standards. If you are using a car, learn local driving signals and wear a seatbelt. Children under 40 lbs. should ride only in a specially-designed carseat, available for a small fee from most car rental agencies. Study route maps before you hit the road; some roads have poor (or nonexistent) shoulders, few gas stations, and inattentive pedestrians. In many regions, road conditions necessitate driving more slowly and more cautiously than you would at home. If you plan on spending a lot of time on the road, you may want to bring spare parts. Be sure to park your vehicle in a garage or well-traveled area, and use a steering wheel locking device in larger cities. **Sleeping in your car** is one of the most dangerous (and often illegal) ways to get your rest, and should be avoided.

**SELF DEFENSE.** There is no sure-fire set of precautions that will protect you from all of the situations you might encounter when you travel. A good self-defense course will give you more concrete ways to react to different types of aggression. **Impact, Prepare,** and **Model Mugging** can refer you to local self-defense courses in the United States (☎ 800-345-5425) and Vancouver, Canada (☎ 604-878-3838). 2-3hr. workshops start at US$50 and full courses run US$350-500. Both women and men are welcome.

**FURTHER INFORMATION** The following government offices provide travel information and advisories by telephone or on their websites:

**Australian Department of Foreign Affairs and Trade.** ☎ (02) 6261 1111. www.dfat.gov.au.

**Canadian Department of Foreign Affairs and International Trade (DFAIT).** ☎ 800-267-8376 or 613-944-4000 from Ottawa. www.dfait-maeci.gc.ca. Call for their free booklet, *Bon Voyage...But.*

**United Kingdom Foreign and Commonwealth Office.** ☎ (020) 7238 4503. www.fco.gov.uk.

**United States Department of State.** ☎ (202) 647-5225; http://travel.state.gov. For their publication *A Safe Trip Abroad,* call ☎ (202) 512-1800.

# FINANCIAL SECURITY

**PROTECTING YOUR VALUABLES.** The first rule of safe travel is to **bring as little with you as possible.** That means leaving expensive watches, jewelry, cameras, and electronic equipment at home. After you've stripped your belongings down to the bare essentials, buy a couple small combination **padlocks** to secure them either in your pack (when it's in your sight) or in a hostel locker. **Never leave your pack unattended,** especially in hostels or train stations. **Carry as little cash as possible** and carry the rest in traveler's checks and/or in the form of an ATM card. Leave your purse or wallet at home, and instead carry the bulk of your cash in a **money belt** along with your traveler's checks, your passport, and any credit/ATM/ID cards. **Don't put a wallet in your back pocket** and never count your money in public. **Keep at least one reserve separate from your primary stash.** This should entail about US$50 worth of cash (US dollars or German Deutschmarks are best) sewn into or stored in the depths of your pack, along with your traveler's check numbers and receipt and a photocopy of your passport.

**CON ARTISTS AND PICKPOCKETS.** Among the more colorful aspects of large cities are con artists. Con artists and hustlers often work in groups, and children are among the most effective. They possess an innumerable range of ruses. Be aware of certain classics: sob stories that require money, rolls of bills "found" on the street, mustard spilled (or saliva spat) onto your shoulder or babies thrown at you, both distracting you for enough time to snatch your bag. Don't ever hand over your passport to someone whose authority you question (ask to accompany them to a police station if they insist), and *never* let your passport out of your sight. In city crowds and especially on public transportation, **pickpockets** are amazingly deft at their craft. Rush hour is no excuse for strangers to press up against you on the metro. If someone stands uncomfortably close, move to another car.

**ACCOMMODATIONS AND TRANSPORTATION.** Never leave your belongings unattended; crime occurs in even the most demure-looking hostel or hotel. If you feel unsafe, look for places with either a curfew or a night attendant. Lockers are useful if you plan on sleeping outdoors or don't want to lug everything with you, but don't store valuables in them. Many hotels provide free lock boxes.

Be particularly careful on **buses,** carry your backpack in front of you where you can see it, don't check baggage on trains, and don't trust anyone to "watch your bag for a second." Thieves thrive on **trains;** professionals wait for tourists to fall asleep and then carry off everything they can. When traveling in pairs, sleep in alternating shifts; when alone, use good judgement in selecting a train compartment: never stay in an empty one. Use a lock to secure your pack to the luggage rack. Keep important documents and other valuables on your body and try to sleep on top bunks with your luggage stored above you (if not in bed with you). In **Russia,** however, try to sleep on bottom bunks where luggage is stored under you; the only way to lift it is by moving you. Theft occurs more often on international trains and those between major cities (e.g. Moscow-St. Petersburg, Prague-Warsaw, or Kiev-Moscow) than on local trains.

If you travel by **car,** try not to leave valuable possessions—such as radios or luggage—in it while you are away. If your tape deck or radio is removable, hide it in the trunk or take it with you. If it isn't, at least conceal it under something else.

## DRUGS AND ALCOHOL

Laws vary from country to country, but **illegal drugs** are best avoided altogether. Remember that you are subject to the laws of the country in which you travel, not to those of your home country. Throughout Eastern Europe, all recreational drugs—including marijuana—are illegal. For more specific information on the drug laws of Eastern European countries, the US State Department's Bureau for International Narcotics and Law Enforcement Affairs has a comprehensive web page detailing each country's laws (www.state.gov/www/global/narcotics_law). If you carry **prescription drugs** while you travel, bring a copy of the prescriptions themselves and a note from a doctor, both readily accessible at country borders.

# HEALTH

Common sense is the simplest prescription for good health while you travel. Travelers complain most often about their feet and their gut, so take precautionary measures: drink lots of fluids to prevent dehydration and constipation, wear sturdy, broken-in shoes and clean socks, and use talcum powder to keep your feet dry. To minimize the effects of jet lag, "reset" your body's clock by adopting the time of your destination as soon as you board the plane.

## BEFORE YOU GO

Preparation can help minimize the likelihood of contracting a disease and maximize the chances of receiving effective health care in the event of an emergency.

For minor health problems, bring a compact **first-aid kit,** including bandages, aspirin or other painkiller, antibiotic cream, a thermometer, a Swiss army knife with tweezers, moleskin, decongestant for colds, motion-sickness remedy, medicine for diarrhea or stomach problems (Pepto Bismol and Immodium), Ex-Lax for constipation, TUMS for heartburn, sunscreen, insect repellent, burn ointment, and anti-itch cream (get a letter of explanation from your doctor).

In your **passport,** write the names of any people you wish to be contacted in case of a medical emergency and also list any **allergies** or medical conditions you would want doctors to be aware of. Allergy sufferers might want to obtain a full supply of any necessary medication before the trip. Matching a prescription to a foreign equivalent is not always easy, safe, or possible. Carry up-to-date, legible prescriptions or a statement from your doctor stating the medication's trade name, manufacturer, chemical name, and dosage. While traveling, be sure to keep all medication with you in your carry-on luggage.

**IMMUNIZATIONS.** Take a look at your immunization records before you go. Travelers should be sure that the following vaccines are up to date: MMR (for measles, mumps, and rubella); DTaP or Td (for diptheria, tetanus, and pertussis); OPV (for polio); HbCV (for haemophilus influenza B); and HBV (for hepatitus B). Adults traveling to the Commonwealth of Independent States should consider an additional dose of Polio vaccine if they have not already had one during their adult years. Hepatitis A vaccine and/or immune globulin (IG) is recommended for all travelers to Eastern Europe. If you will be spending more than four weeks in the region, you will be required to vaccinate for typhoid. In addition, a rabies vaccine is recommended for anyone who might be exposed to wild animals. Check with a doctor for guidance through this maze of injections.

**USEFUL ORGANIZATIONS.** The US **Centers for Disease Control and Prevention (CDC)** (☎888-232-3299; www.cdc.gov) are an excellent source of information for travelers around the world and maintain an international fax information service for travelers. The CDC also publish the booklet "Health Information for International Travelers" (US$20), an annual global rundown of disease, immunization, and general health advice, including risks in particular countries. Purchase this book by sending a check or money order to the Superintendent of Documents, US Government Printing Office, P.O. Box 371954, Pittsburgh, PA, 15250-7954, or order by phone (☎(202) 512-1800) with a major credit card.

The **United States State Department** (travel.state.gov) compiles Consular Information Sheets on health, entry requirements, and other issues for all countries of the world. For quick information on travel warnings, call the **Overseas Citizens' Services** (☎202-647-5225; after-hours 647-4000). To receive the same Consular Information Sheets by fax, dial (202) 647-3000 directly from a fax machine and follow the recorded instructions. The State Department's regional passport agencies in the US, field offices of the US Chamber of Commerce, and US embassies and consulates abroad provide the same data. Alternatively, send a self-addressed, stamped envelope to the Overseas Citizens' Services, Bureau of Consular Affairs, #4811, US Department of State, Washington, D.C. 20520.

**MEDICAL ASSISTANCE ON THE ROAD.** The quality and availability of medical assistance varies greatly throughout Eastern Europe. In major cities such as Prague or Budapest, there are generally English-speaking medical centers or hospitals for foreigners; the care at these hospitals tends to be better than elsewhere in the region. In the countryside and in relatively untouristed countries such as Belarus or Latvia, English-speaking facilities are virtually impossible to find. Tourist offices may sometimes have names of local doctors who speak English. In general, the medical service in these regions is sporadic at best, with very few hospitals maintained at Western standards. While basic medical supplies are always available, specialized treatment is not. In these countries, private hospitals will generally have better facilities than the state-operated hospitals.

If you are concerned about being able to access medical support while traveling, contact one of these two services: **Global Emergency Medical Services (GEMS)** has products called *MedPass* that provide 24hr. international medical assistance and support coordinated through registered nurses who have online access to your medical information, your primary physician, and a worldwide network of screened, credentialed English-speaking doctors and hospitals. Subscribers also receive a personal medical record that contains vital information in case of emergencies, and GEMS will pay for medical evacuation if necessary. Prices start at about US$35 for a 30-day trip and run up to about $100 for annual services. For more information contact them at 2001 Westside Parkway, Suite 120, Alpharetta, GA 30004-7408 (☎800-860-1111 or (770) 475-1114; fax 475-0058; www.globalems.com). The **International Association for Medical Assistance to Travelers (IAMAT)** offers a directory of English-speaking doctors around the world who treat members for a set fee. It provides detailed charts on immunization requirements, various tropical diseases, climate, and sanitation. Chapters include: **US,** 417 Center St., Lewiston, NY 14092 (☎(716) 754-4883, 8am-4pm; fax 519-836-3412; iamat@sentex.net; www.sentex.net/iiamat); **Canada,** 40 Regal Road, Guelph, ON N1K 1B5 (☎(519) 836-0102) or 1287 St. Clair Avenue West, Toronto, ON M6E 1B8 (☎(416) 652-0137; fax (519) 836-3412); **New Zealand,** P.O. Box 5049, Christchurch 5 (fax (03) 352 4630; iamat@chch.planet.org.nz).

**MEDICAL CONDITIONS.** Those with medical conditions (e.g., diabetes, allergies to antibiotics, epilepsy, heart conditions) may want to obtain a stainless steel **Medic Alert** identification tag (US$35 the first year, and $15 annually thereafter), which identifies the condition and gives a 24hr. collect-call information number. Contact the Medic Alert Foundation, 2323 Colorado Ave., Turlock, CA 95382 (☎800-825-3785; www.medicalert.org). Belarus, Moldova, and Russia all require documentation verifying that you are HIV negative in order to issue visas for periods longer than three months.

# ENVIRONMENTAL HAZARDS

**Heat exhaustion and dehydration:** Heat exhaustion, characterized by dehydration and salt deficiency, can lead to fatigue, headaches, and wooziness. Avoid heat exhaustion by drinking plenty of clear fluids. Always drink enough liquids to keep your urine clear. Alcoholic beverages cause the body to lose water, as do coffee, strong tea, and caffeinated sodas. Wear a hat, sunglasses, and a lightweight longsleeve shirt in hot sun. Continuous heat stress can lead to heatstroke, characterized by rising body temperature, severe headache, and cessation of sweating. **Heatstroke** is rare but serious, and victims must be cooled off with wet towels and taken to a doctor as soon as possible.

**Sunburn:** If you are planning on spending time near water or in the snow, you are at risk of getting burned, even through clouds. If you get sunburned, drink more fluids than usual and apply Calamine or an aloe-based lotion.

**Hypothermia and frostbite:** A rapid drop in body temperature is the clearest warning sign of overexposure to cold. Victims may also shiver, feel exhausted, have poor coordination or slurred speech, hallucinate, or suffer amnesia. Seek medical help, and *do not let hypothermia victims fall asleep*—their body temperature will continue to drop and they may die. To avoid hypothermia, keep dry, wear layers, and stay out of the wind. In wet weather, wool and synthetics such as pile retain heat. Most other fabric, especially cotton, will make you colder. When the temperature is below freezing, watch for frostbite. If a region of skin turns white, waxy, and cold, do not rub the area. Drink warm beverages, get dry, and slowly warm the area with dry fabric or steady body contact.

**High altitude:** Travelers to high altitudes should allow their bodies a couple of days to adjust to lower oxygen levels in the air before exercising strenuously. Alcohol is more potent at high elevations. High altitudes mean that ultraviolet rays are stronger and the risk of sunburn is therefore greater, even in cold weather.

# PREVENTING DISEASE

**INSECT-BORNE DISEASES.** Many diseases are transmitted by insects—mainly mosquitoes, fleas, ticks, and lice. Be aware of insects in wet or forested areas, while hiking, and especially while camping. **Mosquitoes** are most active from dusk to dawn. Use insect repellents; few are available in Eastern Europe, so if you're planning on hiking, be sure to bring along a repellent with DEET. Wear long pants and long sleeves (fabric need not be thick or warm; tropic-weight cottons can keep you comfortable in the heat) as well as shoes and socks, and tuck long pants into socks. Soak or spray your gear with permethrin, which is licensed in the US for use on clothing. Natural repellents can be useful supplements: taking vitamin B-12 pills regularly can eventually make you smelly to insects, as can garlic pills. Calamine lotion or topical cortisones (like Cortaid) may stop insect bites from itching, as can a bath with half a cup of baking soda or oatmeal. **Ticks**—responsible for Lyme's and other diseases—can be particularly dangerous in rural and forested regions. Pause periodically while walking to brush off ticks using a fine-toothed comb on your neck and scalp. Do not try to remove ticks by burning them or coating them with nail polish remover or petroleum jelly. Instead, use a fine-point tweezers to grasp the tick just behind the point of attachment and pull slowly and steadily until the tick is dislodged. Wash the bite area, apply antiseptic, and cover with a band-aid.

**FOOD- AND WATER-BORNE DISEASES.** If you get sick at all while in Eastern Europe, it will most likely be from something you ate or drank. In fact, you're more likely to suffer from **constipation** caused by eating a lot of meat and few vegetables than any other ailment. With both constipation and actual diseases, prevention is the best cure: be sure that everything you eat is cooked properly and that the water you drink is clean. Since the risk of contracting traveler's diarrhea or other diseases is high throughout Eastern Europe, you should never drink unbottled water that you have not treated yourself. To purify your own water, bring it to a rolling boil or treat it with **iodine tablets,** available at any camping goods store. Don't brush your teeth with tap water or rinse your toothbrush under the faucet, and keep your mouth closed in the shower. **Ice cubes** are just as dangerous as impure water in liquid form. **Salads** and uncooked vegetables are full of untreated water. Other culprits are raw shellfish, unpasteurized milk, and sauces containing raw eggs. Peel all fruits and vegetables yourself, and beware of watermelon, which is often injected with impure water. Watch out for food from markets or street vendors that may have been washed in dirty water or fried in rancid cooking oil, such as juices and peeled fruits. Always wash your hands before eating, or bring a quick-drying purifying liquid hand cleaner like Purrell. Your bowels will thank you.

**Traveler's diarrhea** is usually an indication of your body's temporary reaction to the bacteria in unfamiliar food ingredients. It can last three to seven days. Symptoms include nausea, bloating, urgency, and malaise. If the nasties hit you, have quick-energy, non-sugary foods with protein and carbohydrates to keep your strength up. Over-the-counter remedies (such as Pepto-Bismol or Immodium) may counteract the problems, but they can mask serious infections. The most dangerous side effect of diarrhea is dehydration; the simplest anti-dehydration formula is 8oz. of (clean) water with a ½ tsp. of sugar or honey and a pinch of salt. If you develop a fever or your symptoms don't go away after four or five days, consult a doctor. You may have dysentery (see below). If children develop traveler's diarrhea, consult a doctor, as treatment is different.

**Dysentery** results from a serious intestinal infection caused by certain bacteria. The most common type is bacillary dysentery, also called **shigellosis.** Symptoms include bloody diarrhea or bloody stools mixed with mucus, fever, and abdominal pain and tenderness. Bacillary dysentery generally only lasts a week, but it is highly contagious. **Amoebic dysentery** develops more slowly. It is a more serious disease and may cause long-term damage if left untreated. A stool test can determine what kind you have, so you should seek medical help immediately. In an emergency, the drugs norfloxacin or ciprofloxacin (commonly known as Cipro) can be used. If you are traveling in high-risk regions (especially rural areas) consider obtaining a prescription before you leave home.

**Cholera** is an intestinal disease caused by a bacteria found in contaminated food. It is a serious risk in Moldova, Russia, and Ukraine. Symptoms include watery diarrhea, dehydration, vomiting, and muscle cramps. See a doctor immediately; untreated cholera can cause death very quickly. Antibiotics are available, but the most important treatment is rehydration. Consider getting a (50% effective) vaccine if you have stomach problems (e.g. ulcers), or if you will be camping a good deal or living where water is not reliable.

**Hepatitis A** (distinct from B and C, see below) is a moderate risk throughout Eastern Europe. Hep A is a viral infection of the liver acquired primarily through contaminated water, ice, shellfish, or unpeeled fruits, and vegetables, but also from sexual contact. Symptoms include fatigue, fever, loss of appetite, nausea, dark urine, jaundice, vomiting, aches and pains, and light stools. Ask your doctor about the vaccine called Havrix, or ask to get an injection of immuno globulin (IG; formerly called gamma globulin). Risk is highest in rural areas and the countryside, but is also present in urban areas.

**Parasites** such as microbes and tapeworms also hide in unsafe water and food. **Giardia,** for example, is acquired by drinking untreated water from streams or lakes all over the world. Symptoms of parasitic infections in general include swollen glands or lymph nodes, fever, rashes or itchiness, digestive problems, eye problems, and anemia. Boil your water, wear shoes, avoid bugs, and eat only cooked food.

ESSENTIALS

## OTHER INFECTIOUS DISEASES

**Rabies** is transmitted through the saliva of infected animals. It is fatal if untreated. Avoid contact with animals, especially strays. If you are bitten, wash the wound thoroughly and seek immediate medical care. Once you begin to show symptoms (thirst and muscle spasms), the disease is in its terminal stage. If possible, try to locate the animal that bit you to determine whether it does indeed have rabies. A rabies vaccine is available but is only semi-effective. Three shots must be administered over one year.

**Hepatitis B** is a viral infection of the liver transmitted through the transfer of bodily fluids, by sharing needles, or by having unprotected sex. Its incubation period varies and can be much longer than the 30-day incubation period of Hepatitis A. A person may not begin to show symptoms until many years after infection. The CDC recommends the Hepatitis B vaccination for health-care workers, sexually active travelers, and anyone planning to seek medical treatment abroad. Vaccination consists of a 3-shot series given over a period of time and should begin 6 months before traveling.

**Hepatitis C** is like Hepatitis B, but the modes of transmission are different. Intravenous drug users, those with occupational exposure to blood, hemodialysis patients, or recipients of blood transfusions are at the highest risk, but the disease can also be spread through sexual contact and sharing of items like razors and toothbrushes, which may have traces of blood on them.

**Tuberculosis** is an increasing problem in the former Soviet Union, with over 200,000 cases in Russia alone. Symptoms include fever, a persistent cough, and bloody phlegm. TB is transmitted via coughing; infectious droplets can hang in the air for hours. If untreated, the disease is fatal, but it normally responds to antibiotics. If you think you are infected, be sure to tell the doctor you have been to Eastern Europe recently, since you may have acquired a drug-resistant strain that requires special treatment.

## AIDS, HIV, STDS

Sexually active travelers should take along a supply of latex condoms, which are often difficult to find on the road. Some countries (including Lithuania, Luxembourg, Russia, Slovakia, and the Ukraine) screen incoming travelers for HIV, primarily those planning extended visits for work or study, and deny entrance to those who test HIV-positive. For detailed information on AIDS in Eastern Europe, call the **US Centers for Disease Control's** 24hr. hotline at 800-342-AIDS (2437), or contact the **Joint United Nations Programme on HIV/AIDS (UNAIDS),** 20 av. Appia 20, CH-1211 Geneva 27, Switzerland (☎ +41 (22) 791 36 66, fax 791 41 87). Council Travel's brochure, *Travel Safe: AIDS and International Travel,* is available at all Council Travel offices and on their web site (www.ciee.org/Isp/safety/travelsafe.htm).

**Sexually transmitted diseases** (STDs) such as gonorrhea, chlamydia, genital warts, syphilis, and herpes are easier to catch than HIV and can be just as deadly. **Hepatitis B** and **C** are also serious STDs (see **Other Infectious Diseases,** above). Though condoms may protect you from some STDs, oral or even tactile contact can lead to transmission. Warning signs include swelling, sores, bumps, or blisters on sex organs, the rectum, or the mouth; burning and pain during urination and bowel movements; itching around sex organs; swelling or redness of the throat; and flu-like symptoms. If these symptoms develop, see a doctor immediately.

## WOMEN'S HEALTH

Women traveling in unsanitary conditions are vulnerable to **urinary tract** and **bladder infections,** common and severely uncomfortable bacterial diseases that cause a burning sensation and painful and sometimes frequent urination. To avoid these infections, drink plenty of vitamin-C-rich juice and clean water, and urinate frequently, especially after intercourse. Untreated, these infections can lead to kidney infections, sterility, and even death. If symptoms persist, see a doctor.

Women are also susceptible to **vaginal yeast infections,** a treatable but uncomfortable illness likely to flare up in hot and humid climates. Wearing loosely fitting trousers or a skirt and cotton underwear will help. Yeast infections can be treated with an over-the-counter remedy like Monostat or Gynelotrimin. Bring supplies from home if you are prone to infection, as they may be difficult to find on the road. Some travelers opt for a natural alternative such as plain yogurt and lemon juice douche if other remedies are unavailable.

**Tampons** and **pads** are sometimes hard to find when traveling and your preferred brands may not be available, so it's advisable to take supplies along. In Eastern Europe, only non-applicator tampons are available. **Reliable contraceptive devices** may also be difficult to find. Women on the pill should bring enough to allow for possible loss or extended stays. Bring a prescription, since forms of the pill vary a good deal. Though condoms are increasingly available, you might want to bring your favorite brand before you go, as availability and quality vary.

# INSURANCE

Travel insurance generally covers four basic areas: medical/health problems, property loss, trip cancellation/interruption, and emergency evacuation. Although your regular insurance policies may well extend to travel-related accidents, you may consider purchasing travel insurance if the cost of potential trip cancellation/interruption or emergency medical evacuation is greater than you can absorb.

**Medical insurance** (especially university policies) often covers costs incurred abroad; check with your provider. **Medicare does not cover foreign travel.** Canadians are protected by their home province's health insurance plan for up to 90 days after leaving the country; check with the provincial Ministry of Health or Health Plan Headquarters for details. **Homeowners' insurance** (or your family's coverage) often covers theft during travel and loss of travel documents (passport, plane ticket, railpass, etc.) up to US$500.

If purchased in the US, **ISIC** and **ITIC** (see **Identification**, p. 21) provide basic insurance benefits, including US$100 per day of in-hospital sickness for a maximum of 60 days, US$3000 of accident-related medical reimbursement, and US$25,000 for emergency medical transport. Cardholders have access to a toll-free 24hr. helpline for medical, legal, and financial emergencies overseas (US and Canada ☎(877) 370-4742, elsewhere call US collect 1 (713) 342-4104). **American Express** (☎800-528-4800) grants most cardholders automatic car rental insurance (collision and theft, but not liability) and ground travel accident coverage of US$100,000 on flight purchases made with the card.

Prices for travel insurance purchased separately generally run about US$50 per week for full coverage, while trip cancellation/interruption may be purchased separately at a rate of about US$5.50 per US$100 of coverage.

**INSURANCE PROVIDERS. Council** and **STA** (see p. 43 for complete listings) offer a range of plans to supplement your basic coverage. Other insurance providers in the **US** and **Canada** include: **Access America** (☎800-284-8300; fax 804-673-1491); **Berkely Group/Carefree Travel Insurance** (☎800-323-3149 or 516-294-0220; fax 516-294-1095; info@berkely.com; www.berkely.com); **Globalcare Travel Insurance** (☎800-821-2488; fax 781-592-7720; www.globalcare-cocco.com); and **Travel Assistance International** (☎800-821-2828 or 202-828-5894; fax 202-828-5896; wassist@aol.com; www.worldwide-assistance.com). Providers in the **UK** include **Campus Travel** (☎(01865) 258 000; fax (01865) 792 378) and **Columbus Travel Insurance** (☎(020) 7375 0011; fax 7375 0022). In **Australia** try **CIC Insurance** (☎(09) 202 8000).

# PACKING

Pack according to the extremes of climate you may experience and the type of travel you'll be doing. **Pack light:** a good rule is to lay out only what you absolutely need, then take half the clothes and twice the money. Don't forget the obvious things: no matter when you're traveling, it's always a good idea to bring a rain

ESSENTIALS

jacket, a warm jacket or wool sweater, and sturdy shoes and thick socks. You may also want to add one outfit beyond the jeans-and-t-shirt uniform, and maybe a nicer pair of shoes if you have the room. Keep in mind that women in Eastern Europe rarely wear jeans and t-shirts, and no-one wears baggy or flared trousers. Khakis and skirts are a less conspicuous and equally comfortable option. If you plan on exploring the nightlife in Eastern Europe, consider bringing the *de rigeur* all-black clubbing uniform. Remember that wool will keep you warm even when soaked through, whereas wet cotton is colder than wearing nothing at all.

**LUGGAGE.** If you plan to cover most of your itinerary by foot, a sturdy **frame backpack** is unbeatable. **Internal-frame packs** mold better to your back, keep a lower center of gravity, and can flex adequately on difficult hikes that require a lot of bending and maneuvering. **External-frame packs** are more comfortable for long hikes over even terrain—like city streets—since they keep the weight higher and distribute it more evenly. Look for a pack with a strong, padded hip belt to transfer weight from your shoulders to your hips. Good packs cost anywhere from US$150 to US$500. Before you leave, pack your bag, strap it on, and imagine yourself walking uphill on hot asphalt for three hours; this should give you a sense of how important it is to pack lightly. Mail-order pack retailers are listed on p. 37.

Toting a **suitcase** or **trunk** is fine if you plan to live in one or two cities and explore from there, but a very bad idea if you're going to be moving around a lot. In addition to your main vessel, a small backpack, rucksack, or courier bag may be useful as a **daypack** for sight-seeing expeditions; it doubles as an airplane **carry-on.** An empty, lightweight **duffel bag** packed inside your luggage may also be useful.

**WASHING CLOTHES.** *Let's Go* provides information on laundromats in the **Practical Information** listings for larger cities, but sometimes it's cheaper and easier to use a sink. Bring a small bar or tube of detergent soap, a small rubber ball to stop up the sink, and a travel clothes line.

**ELECTRIC CURRENT.** In Eastern Europe, electricity is 220 volts AC, enough to fry any 110V North American appliance. 220V electrical appliances don't like 110V current, either. Visit a hardware store for an adapter (which changes the shape of the plug) and a converter (which changes the voltage). Don't make the mistake of using only an adapter (unless appliance instructions explicitly state otherwise).

**CONTACT LENSES.** Contact lens and glasses wearers should bring an extra pair of glasses and a copy of the prescription. In addition, contact lens wearers should bring an extra pair of lenses, extra solution, and eyedrops. Those who use heat disinfection might consider switching to chemical cleansers for the trip.

**FILM.** Airport security X-rays *can* fog film, so either buy a lead-lined pouch, sold at camera stores, or ask the security to hand inspect it. Always pack it in your carry-on luggage, since higher-intensity X-rays are used on checked luggage.

**OTHER USEFUL ITEMS.** No matter how you're traveling, it's always a good idea to carry a first-aid kit including sunscreen, insect repellent, and vitamins (see **Health,** p. 28). Other useful items include: an umbrella; sealable plastic bags (for damp clothes, soap, food, shampoo, and other spillables); alarm clock; waterproof matches; sun hat; moleskin (for blisters); needle and thread; safety pins; sunglasses; pocketknife; plastic water bottle; compass; string (makeshift clothesline and lashing material); towel; padlock; whistle; rubber bands; flashlight; cold-water soap; earplugs; electrical tape (for patching tears); tweezers; garbage bags; a small calculator for currency conversion; a pair of flip-flops for the shower; a money-belt for carrying valuables; deodorant; razors; tampons; and condoms.

# ACCOMMODATIONS

## HOSTELS

> **A HOSTELER'S BILL OF RIGHTS** There are certain standard features that we do not include in our hostel listings. Unless we state otherwise, you can expect that every hostel has: no lockout, no curfew, a kitchen, free hot showers, secure luggage storage, and no key deposit.

Hostels are generally dorm-style accommodations, often in single-sex large rooms with bunk beds. They sometimes have kitchens and utensils for your use, bike or moped rentals, storage areas, and laundry facilities. There can be drawbacks: some hostels close during certain daytime "lock-out" hours, have a curfew, don't accept reservations, or impose a maximum stay. In Eastern Europe, a bed in any sort of hostel will range from US$5-10.

For their various services and lower rates at member hostels, hostelling associations, especially **Hostelling International (HI),** can definitely be worth joining. HI hostels are scattered throughout Eastern Europe and many accept reservations via the International Booking Network. To prepay and reserve ahead for a nominal fee, call: ☎(02) 9261 1111 in Australia; ☎800-663-5777 in Canada; ☎(01629) 581 418 in England and Wales; ☎(01232) 324733 in Northern Ireland; ☎(01) 830 1766 in the Republic of Ireland; ☎(09) 303 9524 in New Zealand; ☎(0541) 553255 in Scotland; and ☎(202) 783-6161 in the US. HI hostels are by no means as prevalent as in Western Europe. The International Youth Hostelling Federation's web page lists the web addresses and phone numbers of all national associations and can be a great place to begin researching hostelling in a specific region (www.iyhf.org). Other comprehensive hostelling websites include www.hostels.com and www.eurotrip.com. To join HI, contact one of the following organizations in your home country:

**Australian Youth Hostels Association (AYHA),** 422 Kent St., Sydney NSW 2000 (☎(02) 9261 1111; fax 9261 1969; yha@yhansw.org.au; www.yha.org.au). One-year membership AUS$49, under 18 AUS$15.

**Hostelling International-Canada (HI-C),** 400-205 Catherine St., Ottawa, ON K2P 1C3 (☎800-663-5777 or (613) 237-7884; fax 237-7868; info@hostellingintl.ca; www.hostellingintl.ca). One-year membership CDN$25, under 18 CDN$12; 2-yr. CDN$35.

**An Óige (Irish Youth Hostel Association),** 61 Mountjoy St., Dublin 7 (☎(01) 830 4555; fax 830 5808; anoige@iol.ie; www.irelandyha.org). One-year membership IR£10, under 18 IR£4, families IR£20.

**Youth Hostels Association of New Zealand (YHANZ),** P.O. Box 436, 173 Cashel St., Christchurch 1 (☎(03) 379 9970; fax 365 4476; info@yha.org.nz; www.yha.org.nz). One-year membership NZ$40, ages 15-17 NZ$12, under 15 free.

**Hostels Association of South Africa,** 3rd fl. 73 St. George's St. Mall, P.O. Box 4402, Cape Town 8000 (☎(021) 424 2511; fax 424 4119; info@hisa.org.za; www.hisa.org.za). One-year membership SAR55, under 18 SAR30.

**Scottish Youth Hostels Association (SYHA),** 7 Glebe Crescent, Stirling FK8 2JA (☎(01786) 891 400; fax 891 333; info@syha.org.uk; www.syha.org.uk). Membership UK£6, 5-17 yrs. UK£2.50, under 18 free if parent is a member.

**Youth Hostels Association of England and Wales (YHA),** 8 St. Stephen's Hill, St. Albans, Hertfordshire AL1 2DY, England (☎0870 870 8808; fax (01727) 844 126; customerservices@yha.org.uk; www.yha.org.uk). One-year membership UK£12, under 18 UK£6, families UK£24.

**Hostelling International Northern Ireland (HINI),** 22-32 Donegall Rd., Belfast BT12 5JN, Northern Ireland (☎(01232) 324 733 or 315 435; fax 439 699; info@hini.org.uk; www.hini.org.uk). One-year membership UK£7, under 18 UK£3, families UK£14.

**Hostelling International-American Youth Hostels (HI-AYH),** 733 15th St. NW, Suite 840, Washington, D.C. 20005 (☎(202) 783-6161, ext. 136; fax 783-6171; hiayhserv@hiayh.org; www.hiayh.org). One-year membership US$25, over 54 US$15, under 18 free.

## PENSIONS

After hostels, pensions are the most common budget accommodation in Eastern Europe. A cross between a hostel and a hotel, pensions are generally intimate and run by a family or out of someone's home, similar to a bed and breakfast, and usually rent by the room, although they occasionally offer dorm-style accommodations. Pensions are often the cleanest, safest, and friendliest budget accommodation available, with the owners going out of their way to arrange private excursions and help with such daily chores as doing laundry, checking e-mail, and communicating with locals. In Eastern Europe, a single room in a pension runs US$10-20. A night's stay usually includes breakfast.

## UNIVERSITY DORMS

Many colleges and universities open their residence halls to travelers when school is not in session, usually only in July and August. These dorms are often close to student areas—good sources for information on things to do—and tend to be very clean. Getting a room may take several frustrated phone calls and eventually require a trek to the dorm itself, but rates are low and the guests and students are fun. *Let's Go* lists colleges that rent rooms among the accommodations for appropriate cities; when they're not listed, check at the tourist office for local options.

## PRIVATE HOMES

An increasingly popular option in nowhere-near-the-beaten-path locations is to rent a room in a private home. Families throughout Eastern Europe rent out spare bedrooms to weary backpackers. These are not hotels—they are private homes in which you will share the family's bathroom, kitchen, and living space. Although it may at first seem sketchy to a hyper-safety-concerned Westerner, going home with an old woman from the train station or knocking on doors with *Zimmer Frei* signs is absolutely legitimate, generally reliable, and often preferable to hostels. In small towns, private homes often rent the only tourist rooms and offer such added perks as immaculate rooms, laundry, home-cooked meals, and a native tour guide. Prices vary but tend to hover between hostel and pension prices. *Let's Go* does not list specific homes in each town; check with the local tourist office.

## HOME EXCHANGE AND RENTALS

Home exchange offers the opportunity to live like a native and cheaply—usually only an administration fee is paid to the matching service. Once you join or contact one of the exchange services listed below, it is then up to you to decide with whom you would like to exchange homes. Most companies have pictures of member's homes and information about the owners. Home rentals, as opposed to exchanges, are much more expensive. Both home exchanges and rentals are ideal for families with children and travelers with special dietary needs; you often get your own kitchen, maid service, TV, and telephones.

**Intervac International Home Exchange:** www.intervac.com. **Intervac Czech Republic,** Antonin and Lenka Machackovi, Pod stanici 25/603, 10200 Prague 10/CSFR, Czech Republic (☎(02) 7196 1647; fax 786 0061; **Intervac Poland,** Ewa and Stanislaw Krupscy, ul. Bursztynowa 22 (22), 31-213 Krakow, Poland (☎(012) 415 1818; fax 425 1414; york@kraknet.pl).

**The Invented City: International Home Exchange,** 41 Sutter St., Suite 1090, San Francisco, CA 94104 (☎800-788-2489 in the US or (415) 252-1141; fax 252-1171; info@invented-city.com; www.invented-city.com). For US$75, you get your offer listed in 1 catalog and unlimited access to a database of thousands of homes.

## FURTHER READING
*People to People: An Introduction to over a thousand Eastern Europeans who would like to meet travelers like you!,* edited by Jim Haybes (Zephyr Press, US $12).

# CAMPING AND THE OUTDOORS

Eastern Europe offers myriad opportunities for hiking, mountain climbing, trekking, camping, and biking. Camping is one of the most authentic ways to experience the vacation culture of the region: not only are Eastern Europeans mountain goats who explore the outdoors for every vacation, but camping is also often the only affordable accommodation for locals. Unfortunately, there is very little English-language information on Eastern European outdoor opportunities. Fortunately, the lack of info means once you're in the wilderness, it'll be you, the Eastern Europeans, and the mountains, with not another Anglophone tourist for miles.

Undiscovered as the Eastern European wilderness is, it's surprisingly difficult to truly rough it. In most countries it's illegal to camp within the boundaries of a national park. As a result, **chaty,** huts offering dorm-style rooms for US$5-10, running water (not always hot), and some sort of mess hall, dot the parks' interiors, and the borders are surrounded with crowded campsites. **Organized campgrounds** offer tent space and bungalows. All campgrounds have running water; a few have restaurants. Tent sites range from US$1-10 per person with a flat tent fee of US$5-10. Bungalows hover around US$10.

## USEFUL PUBLICATIONS AND WEB RESOURCES

For information about camping, hiking, and biking, write or call the publishers listed below to receive a free catalogue.

**Automobile Association,** A.A. Publishing. Orders and enquiries to TBS Frating Distribution Centre, Colchester, Essex, CO7 7DW, UK (☎(01206) 255678; www.theaa.co.uk). Publishes *Camping and Caravanning: Europe* (UK£9). They also offer Big Road Atlases for Europe (UK£11).

**The Mountaineers Books,** 1001 SW Klickitat Way, #201, Seattle, WA 98134 (☎800-553-4453 or (206) 223-6303; customer_service@mountaineers.org; www.mountaineersbooks.org). Over 400 titles on hiking (the *100 Hikes* series), biking, mountaineering, natural history, and conservation. Publishes *Trekking in Russia and Central Asia: A Traveler's Guide,* by Frith Maier (US$17).

**Bradt Publications,** www.omnimap.com. Publishes a series of hiking guides to unusual destinations including *Hiking Guide to Romania* (Bradt Publications, US$16) and *Hiking Guide to Poland and Ukraine* (Bradt Publications, US$16).

## CAMPING AND HIKING EQUIPMENT

Good camping equipment is both sturdy and light. Camping equipment is generally more expensive in Australia, New Zealand, and the UK than in North America.

**Sleeping Bag:** Most good sleeping bags are rated by "season," or the lowest outdoor temperature at which they will keep you warm ("summer" means 30-40°F at night and "four-season" or "winter" often means below 0°F). Sleeping bags are made either of down (warmer and lighter, but more expensive, and miserable when wet) or of synthetic material (heavier, more durable, and warmer when wet). Prices vary, but might range from US$80-210 for a summer synthetic to US$250-300 for a good down winter bag. **Sleeping-bag pads,** including foam pads (US$10-20) and air mattresses (US$15-50) cushion your back and neck and insulate you from the ground. **Therm-A-Rest** brand self-inflating sleeping pads, part foam and part air-mattress, partially inflate when you unroll them, but are costly at US$45-80. Bring a **"stuff sack"** or plastic bag to store your sleeping bag and keep it dry.

**Tent:** The best tents are free-standing, with their own frames and suspension systems; they set up quickly and only require staking in high winds. Low-profile dome tents are the best all-around. When pitched, their internal space is almost entirely usable, which means little unnecessary bulk. Tent sizes can be somewhat misleading: two people *can* fit in a two-person tent, but will find life more pleasant in a four-person. If you're traveling by car, go for the bigger tent, but if you're hiking, stick with a smaller tent that weighs no more than 5-6 lbs (2-3kg). Good two-person tents start at US$90, four-person tents at US$300. Seal the seams of your tent with waterproofer, and make sure it has a rain fly. Other tent accessories include a **battery-operated lantern**, a **plastic groundcloth**, and a **nylon tarp.**

**Backpack:** (See **Luggage,** p. 34.) Any serious backpacking requires a pack of at least 4000 cubic inches (16,000cc). Allow an additional 500 cubic inches for your sleeping bag in internal-frame packs. A **waterproof backpack cover** will prove invaluable. Otherwise, plan to store all of your belongings in plastic bags inside your backpack.

**Boots:** Be sure to wear hiking boots with good **ankle support** which are appropriate for the terrain you plan to hike. Your boots should fit snugly and comfortably over one or two wool socks and a thin liner sock. Breaking in boots properly before setting out requires wearing them for several weeks; doing so will spare you from painful blisters.

**Other Necessities: Raingear** in two pieces, a top and pants, is far superior to a poncho. **Synthetics,** like polypropylene tops, socks, and long underwear, along with a pile jacket, will keep you warm even when wet. When camping in autumn, winter, or spring, bring along a **"space blanket,"** which helps you to retain your body heat and doubles as a groundcloth (US$5-15). Plastic **canteens** or water bottles keep water cooler than metal ones do, and are virtually shatter- and leak-proof. Large, collapsible **water sacks** will improve your lot in primitive campgrounds and weigh very little when empty. Bring **water-purification tablets** for when you can't boil water. Though most campgrounds provide campfire sites, you may want to bring a small **metal grate** or **grill** of your own. For those places that forbid fires or the gathering of firewood, you'll need a **camp stove.** The classic Coleman stove starts at about US$40. You will need to purchase a **fuel bottle** and fill it with propane to operate it. Note that you cannot take propane-filled bottles on planes, so fill up when you arrive. A **first aid kit, swiss army knife, insect repellent, calamine lotion,** and **waterproof matches** or a **lighter** are also essential.

# WILDERNESS SAFETY

**Stay warm, stay dry, and stay hydrated.** The vast majority of life-threatening wilderness situations result from a breach of this simple dictum. On any hike, however brief, you should pack enough equipment to keep you alive should disaster occur. This includes **raingear, hat** and **mittens, first-aid kit, reflector, whistle, high energy food,** and extra **water.** Dress in warm layers of **synthetic materials** designed for the outdoors, or **wool.** Pile fleece jackets and Gore-Tex raingear are excellent choices. Never rely on **cotton** for warmth. This "death cloth" will be absolutely useless should it get wet. Be sure to check all equipment for any defects before setting out.

Check **weather forecasts** and pay attention to the skies when hiking. Weather patterns can change suddenly. Whenever possible, let someone know when and where you are going hiking: either a friend, your hostel, a park ranger, or a local hiking organization. Do not attempt a hike beyond your ability—you may be endangering your life. See **Health,** p. 28, for information about outdoor ailments such as heatstroke, hypothermia, giardia, rabies, and insects, as well as basic medical concerns and first-aid. To read up on wilderness safety, check out *How to Stay Alive in the Woods,* by Bradford Angier (Macmillan, US$8).

# KEEPING IN TOUCH

The ease of communicating varies widely from country to country. In Central Europe, postal and telephone systems are as reliable and efficient as in Western Europe. Even the Russian mail system now offers reliable and relatively speedy delivery to the West. In the Ukraine and Belarus, particularly outside the capital, you'll be lucky if mail ever leaves the post office. Phone cards can also be problematic throughout the region: double-check with your carrier before assuming you'll be able to call home. Like everything else in Eastern Europe, keeping in touch can be problematic, inefficient, and downright mind boggling. Have patience: like ET, you will eventually phone home. For country-specific information, refer to the **Essentials: Communication** section at the beginning of every chapter.

# MAIL

## SENDING MAIL TO AND RECEIVING MAIL IN EASTERN EUROPE

**Airmail** letters between North America and Eastern Europe generally take 5-7 days. From the **US** (www.usps.gov), postcards/aerograms cost US$0.55/0.60; letters under 1 oz. cost US$1; packages under one pound cost US$7.20, while larger packages sent by parcel post cost a variable amount (around US$15). From **Canada** (www.canadapost.ca/CPC2/common/rates/ratesgen.html#international), air mail postcards and letters up to 20g cost CDN$0.95; small packages up to 0.5kg cost CDN$8.50, while larger packages up to 2kg CDN$28.30.

Allow at least 4-7 days for airmail from **Australia** (postcards and letters up to 20 grams AUS$1; packages up to 0.5kg AUS$12, up to 2kg AUS$45; www.auspost.com.au/pac), 6-12 days from **New Zealand** (postcards NZ$1, letters up to 20g NZ$1.80-6; small parcels up to 0.5kg NZ$15, up to 2kg NZ$39; www.nzpost.co.nz/nzpost/inrates), and 3-7 days from the **UK** (letters up to 20g UK£0.30; packages up to 0.5kg UK£2.22, up to 2kg UK£8.22; www.royalmail.co.uk/calculator). Envelopes should be marked "air mail" or "par avion."

There are several ways to arrange pick-up of letters sent to you by friends and relatives while you are abroad.

**General Delivery:** Mail can be sent to Eastern Europe through **Poste Restante** (the international phrase for General Delivery) to almost any city or town with a post office. While Poste Restante is reliable in most countries, the likelihood of it ever arriving in Russia, Ukraine, Belarus, and Moldova is slim. Addressing conventions for Poste Restante vary by country; *Let's Go* gives instructions in each country introduction. Be sure to include the street address of the post office on the third line or mail may never reach the recipient. The mail will go to a special desk in the central post office. As a rule, it is best to use the largest post office in the area, as mail may be sent there regardless of what is written on the envelope. When possible, it is usually safer and quicker to send mail express or registered—this is actually one of the only ways to ensure that mail gets into Russia and other postally problematic countries. When picking up your mail, bring a form of photo ID, preferably a passport. There is often no surcharge; if there is a charge, it usually does not exceed the cost of domestic postage. If the clerks insist that there is nothing for you, have them check under your first name as well.

**American Express:** AmEx's travel offices will act as a mail service for cardholders if you contact them in advance. Under this free **Client Letter Service,** they will hold mail for up to 30 days and forward upon request. Address the letter in the same way shown above. Some offices will offer these services to non-cardholders (especially those who have purchased AmEx Travelers Cheques), but you must call ahead to make sure. Let's Go lists AmEx office locations in the **Practical Information** section of most large cities. A complete list is available free from AmEx (☎800-528-4800).

ESSENTIALS

If regular airmail is too slow, **Federal Express** (US ☎800-247-4747) can get a letter from New York to Moscow in two days for a whopping US$65; rates among non-US locations are prohibitively expensive. By **US Express Mail**, a letter from New York arrives within four days and starts at around US$20.

**Surface mail** is by far the cheapest and slowest way to send mail. It takes one to three months to cross the Atlantic and two to four to cross the Pacific—appropriate for sending large quantities of items you won't need to see for a while. When ordering books and materials from abroad, always include one or two **International Reply Coupons (IRCs)**—a way of providing the postage to cover delivery. IRCs should be available from your local post office and those abroad (US$1.05).

## SENDING MAIL HOME FROM EASTERN EUROPE

**Aerogrammes,** printed sheets that fold into envelopes and travel via airmail, are available at post offices. It helps to mark "airmail" in the local language if possible, though "par avion" is universally understood. Most post offices will charge exorbitant fees or refuse to send aerogrammes with enclosures. Airmail from Eastern Europe averages 10-15 days, longer from smaller towns. Additionally, mail from parts of Russia, Ukraine, Belarus, and Moldova can take up to a month to reach its destination, if it arrives at all. Postage rates vary but are generally extremely inexpensive; for exact prices and other valuable postal information, refer to the **Essentials: Keeping in Touch** section at the beginning of each chapter.

# TELEPHONES

## CALLING EASTERN EUROPE FROM HOME

To call Eastern Europe direct from home, dial:

1. The international access code of your home country. **International access codes** include: Australia 0011; Ireland 00; New Zealand 00; South Africa 09; UK 00; US 011. Country codes and city codes are sometimes listed with a zero in front (e.g., 033), but after dialing the international access code, drop successive zeros (i.e. with access code 011 and city code 033, dial 011 33).

2. The country code of your Eastern European country of choice (see **Facts and Figures** box on the first page of the country's chapter).

3. The city code (see the city's **Practical Information** section) and local number. Remember to dial zero before the city code when calling from within the country and to drop the zero before the city code when calling from outside the country.

## CALLING HOME FROM EASTERN EUROPE

A **calling card** is probably your best and cheapest bet. Calls are billed either collect or to your account. **MCI WorldPhone** also provides access to MCI's Traveler's Assist, which gives legal and medical advice, exchange rate information, and translation services. Other phone companies provide similar services to travelers. To obtain a calling card from your national telecommunications service before you leave home, contact the appropriate company below. Be warned, however, that not all calling card companies offer services in every Eastern European country. It can be particularly difficult to successfully use a calling card in Russia, Ukraine, Belarus, and—inexplicably—Slovenia.

**USA: AT&T** (☎888-288-4685); **Sprint** (☎800-877-4646); or **MCI** (☎800-444-4141; from abroad dial the country's MCI access number).

**Canada:** Bell Canada **Direct** (☎800-565-4708).

**UK:** British Telecom **BT Direct** (☎0800 345 144).

**Ireland:** Telecom Éireann **Ireland Direct** (☎800 250 250).

**Australia:** Telstra **Australia Direct** (☎13 22 00).

**New Zealand:** Telecom New Zealand (☎0800 000 000).

**South Africa:** Telkom South Africa (☎09 03).

**To call home with a calling card,** contact the local operator for your service provider by dialing the access numbers listed in the **Essentials: Keeping in Touch** section at the beginning of each country chapter. Not all of these numbers are toll-free; in many countries, phones will require a coin or card deposit to call the operator, which counts as a local call.

Wherever possible, use a calling card for international phone calls—the long-distance rates for national phone services are often exorbitant. You can usually make direct international calls from pay phones, but if you aren't using a calling card you may need to drop coins as quickly as words. Where available, **prepaid phone cards** can be used for direct international calls, but they are still less cost-efficient. Look for pay phones in public areas, especially train stations, as private pay phones are often more expensive. **In-room** hotel calls invariably include an arbitrary and sky-high surcharge (as much as US$10).

If you do dial direct, you must first insert the appropriate amount of money or a prepaid card, then dial the international access code for the country you're in (listed on the opening page of every country chapter), and then dial the country code and number of your home. **Country codes** include: Australia 61; Ireland 353; New Zealand 64; South Africa 27; UK 44; US and Canada 1.

The expensive alternative to dialing direct or using a calling card is using an international operator to place a **collect call.** You can reach an English-speaking operator from your home nation by dialing the appropriate service provider listed above; they will place a collect call even if you don't have one of their phone cards.

## CALLING WITHIN EASTERN EUROPE

The simplest way to call within the country is to use a coin-operated phone or to use a **prepaid phone cards,** which are slowly phasing out coins in most Eastern European countries. Phone cards carry a certain amount of phone time depending on the card's denomination; the time is measured in minutes or impulses. Phone cards can usually be purchased at tobacco stands, post offices, train stations, and magazine stands. Phone rates tend to be highest in the morning, lower in the evening, and lowest on Sunday and late at night.

## EMAIL AND INTERNET

The World Wide Web is slowly making its way into Eastern Europe. Every major city now has some sort of internet access, usually a cyber cafe, but access is also available in public libraries and in many hostels. Access is more difficult to find in smaller towns, but not impossible. Tourist offices and hotels are the best source for local internet access. Rates are extremely reasonable; one hour costs US$3 on average, although they do fluctuate from country to country.

Free, web-based email providers include Hotmail (www.hotmail.com), Rocket-Mail (www.juno.com), and Yahoo! Mail (www.yahoo.com). Many free email providers are funded by advertising and some require subscribers to fill out a questionnaire. Almost every search engine has an affiliated free email service.

# GETTING THERE

# BY PLANE

When finding airfare to Eastern Europe, a little effort can save you a bundle. If your plans are flexible enough to deal with the restrictions, courier fares are the cheapest. Tickets bought from consolidators and standby seating are also good deals, but last-minute specials, airfare wars, and charter flights often beat these fares. Hunt around and be flexible; students, seniors, and those under 26 should never pay full price for a ticket.

ESSENTIALS

ESSENTIALS

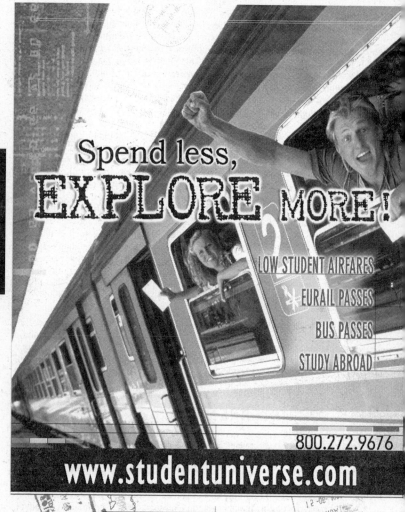

Spend less,
EXPLORE MORE!

LOW STUDENT AIRFARES
EURAIL PASSES
BUS PASSES
STUDY ABROAD

800.272.9676

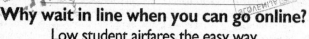
www.studentuniverse.com

**Why wait in line when you can go online?**
Low student airfares the easy way.
Go ahead... put your feet up and
plan your trip.

student universe.com
IT'S YOUR WORLD. EXPLORE IT

## DETAILS AND TIPS

**Timing:** Most airfares to Eastern Europe peak between mid-June and early Sep. (the high season); mid-Dec. to early Jan. can also be expensive. The cheapest times to travel are Nov. through mid-Dec. and early Jan. through Mar. Midweek (M-Th morning) round-trip flights run US$40-50 cheaper than weekend flights. Return-date flexibility is usually not an economical option for the budget traveler.

**Route:** Round-trip flights are by far the cheapest; "open-jaw" (arriving to and departing from different cities) and round-the-world (RTW) tickets are pricier but reasonable alternatives. If you are willing to make the extra effort, the least expensive route usually is to fly into London, Amsterdam, or Paris and reach your destination by train or bus; it will often be necessary to connect from one of these cities regardless.

**Boarding:** Pick up tickets for international flights well in advance of the departure date, and confirm by phone within 72hr. of departure. Most airlines require passengers to arrive at the airport at least two hours before departure. One carry-on item and two pieces of checked baggage is the norm for long-haul flights; weight allowances vary.

**Fares:** Round-trip commercial tickets to the larger, more touristed cities (Prague, Budapest, Warsaw) can usually be found, with some work, for US$500-600 in high season. Tickets to mid-range cities—including Moscow, Bucharest, Zagreb and Sofia—generally cost about US$100 more, while Bratislava, Kiev, Minsk and the Baltic capitals can cost anywhere from US$750-900. Prices drop US$100-200 the rest of the year.

> **SURFING AND READING** The following websites are online airfare databases: www.travelocity.com; www.thetrip.com; www.priceline.com; www.lowestfare.com. Many also offer discounted tickets.

# BUDGET AND STUDENT TRAVEL AGENCIES

A knowledgeable agent specializing in flights to Eastern Europe can make your life easy and help you save, but agents may not spend the time to find you the lowest possible fare, as they get paid on commission. Students and under-26ers holding **ISIC** or **IYTC** cards (see **Identification**, p. 21) can qualify for big discounts from student travel agencies. Most flights from budget agencies are on major airlines, but in peak season some may sell seats on less reliable chartered aircraft.

**Council Travel** (☎800-2-COUNCIL (226-8624); www.counciltravel.com). **US** offices include **Atlanta,** GA (☎(404) 377-9997); **Boston,** MA (☎(617) 266-1926); **Chicago,** IL (☎(312) 951-0585); **Los Angeles,** CA (☎(310) 208-3551); **New York,** NY (☎(212) 254-2525); **San Francisco,** CA (☎(415) 566-6222); **Seattle,** WA (☎(206) 329-4567); **Washington, D.C.** (☎(202) 337-6464); and many more. In the **UK,** 28A Poland St. (Oxford Circus), **London,** W1V 3DB (☎(020) 7437 7767; www.sta-travel.co.uk).

**STA Travel,** 6560 Scottsdale Rd. #F100, Scottsdale, AZ 85253 (☎(800) 777-0112 fax (602) 922-0793; www.sta-travel.com). **US** offices include: **Boston,** MA (☎(617) 266-6014); **Chicago,** IL 60605 (☎(312) 786-9050); **Los Angeles,** CA (☎(323) 934-8722); **New York,** NY (☎(212) 627-3111); **Seattle,** WA (☎(206) 633-5000); **Washington, D.C.** (☎(202) 887-0912); **San Francisco,** CA (☎(415) 391-8407); and many more. In the **UK, London** (☎(020) 7436 7779), and on most campuses. In New Zealand, **Auckland** (☎(09) 309 0458). In Australia, **Melbourne,** Vic (☎(03) 9349 4344).

**Travel CUTS** (Canadian Universities Travel Services Limited), 187 College St., **Toronto,** ON M5T 1P7 (☎(416) 979-2406; fax 979-8167; www.travelcuts.com). 40 offices across Canada. Also in **London,** UK (☎(020) 7255 1944).

**Wasteels,** Platform 2, Victoria Station, **London,** SW1V 1JT (☎(020) 7834 7066; fax 7630 7 28; www.wasteels.dk/uk). Huge European chain with 203 locations. Sells the Wasteels BIJ tickets, which are discounted (30-45% off regular fare), 2nd class international point-to-point train tickets with unlimited stopovers (must be under 26); sold only in Europe.

ESSENTIALS

# COMMERCIAL AIRLINES

The commercial airlines' lowest regular offer is the **APEX** (Advance Purchase Excursion) fare, which provides confirmed reservations and allows "open-jaw" tickets. Generally, reservations must be made 7 to 21 days in advance, with 7- to 14-day minimum and up to 90-day maximum-stay limits, and hefty cancellation and change penalties (fees rise in summer). Book peak-season APEX fares early, since by May you will have a hard time getting the departure date you want.

Although APEX fares are probably not the cheapest possible fares, they will give you a sense of the average commercial price against which to measure other bargains. Specials advertised in newspapers may be cheaper but have more restrictions and fewer available seats. Popular carriers to Eastern Europe include:

## FROM NORTH AMERICA

**Delta Air Lines** (☎ 800-221-1212; www.delta-air.com) flies more reliably to Eastern European cities than other US carriers, including Budapest, Moscow, and Warsaw.

**Continental Air Lines** (☎ 800-231-0856 in Canada; ☎ 800-525-0280 in the US; www.continental.com) offers flights to a number of destinations in Eastern Europe, including Prague and Bratislava.

**Lufthansa** (☎ (416) AIRPORT (247-7678) in Canada; ☎ 800-399-5838 in the US; www.lufthansa.com) has a wide variety of routes covering most of Eastern Europe.

**British Airways** (☎ 800-545-7644; www.british-airways.com) flies into most large cities in Eastern Europe via Heathrow.

**Air France** (☎ 800-237-2747; www.airfrance.com) covers much of Eastern Europe via several Western European cities.

**SAS** (☎ 800-221-2350; www.flysas.com) connects to Baltic cities from New York.

## FROM THE UNITED KINGDOM

**British Midland Airways** (☎ 0870 607 0555; www.iflybritishmidland.com) flies direct to many Eastern European cities.

**British Airways** (☎ 0345 222 111; www.british-airways.com) flies from Heathrow to a number of Eastern European hubs.

**KLM** (☎ 0870 507 4074; www.klmuk.com) connects to a number of cities in Eastern Europe via Amsterdam.

**Austrian Airways** (☎ (020) 7434 7380; www.aua.com) connects to many cities in Eastern Europe via Vienna.

## FROM AUSTRALIA AND NEW ZEALAND

**Qantas** (☎ 13 13 13; www.qantas.com) flies from a variety of departure cities in Australia and New Zealand to London, where connecting flights are easy to find.

**Air New Zealand** (☎ 0800 352 266; www.airnz.com) has reasonable fares from Auckland to London and often offers special sales at much lower prices.

## FROM SOUTH AFRICA

**Lufthansa** (☎ (011) 484 4711; www.lufthansa.com) offers reliable flights which connect to a number of cities throughout Eastern Europe.

**British Airways** (☎ (011) 441 8600 or 0860 011 747 within South Africa; www.british-airways.com) has flights from Johannesburg and Cape Town to places in Europe with easy connections.

# OTHER CHEAP ALTERNATIVES

**AIR COURIER FLIGHTS.** Couriers help transport cargo on international flights by guaranteeing delivery of the baggage claim slips from the company to a representative overseas. Generally, couriers must travel light (carry-ons only) and deal with complex restrictions on their flight. Most flights are round-trip only with short fixed-length stays (approximately one week) and a limit of a single ticket per

**AIRCRAFT SAFETY** In general, the international carriers listed comply with safety requirements, but some of the smaller airlines in post-communist countries have been known to use unreliable equipment. They are the only carriers available for certain routes; if you have any serious concerns, region-specific safety information can be obtained from the **International Airline Passengers Association** (☎800-821-4271 for the US and Canada; safety office open M-F 9-11am CST; iapausa@iapausa.com; UK ☎(020) 8681 6555; safety office open M-F 9am-5:30pm; info@iapa.co.uk; www.iapa.com). *The Official Airline Guide* (www.oag.com) and many travel agencies can tell you the type and age of aircraft on a particular route. The **Federal Aviation Administration** (www.faa.gov) reviews the airline authorities for countries whose airlines enter the US. **US State Department** (☎(202) 647-5225; travel.state.gov/travel_warnings.html) travel advisories sometimes involve foreign carriers.

issue. Most operate only out of the biggest cities, like New York. Usually, you must be over 21 (in some cases 18), have a valid passport, and procure your own visa, if necessary. Groups such as the **Air Courier Association**, 15000 West 6th Avenue, suite 203, Golden, Colorado 80401; larry@aircourier.org (☎800-282-1202; www.aircourier.org) and the **International Association of Air Travel Couriers**, 220 South Dixie Hwy. #3, P.O. Box 1349, Lake Worth, FL 33460 (☎(561) 582-8320; fax 582-1581; iaatc@courier.org; www.courier.org) provide their members with information on courier services worldwide for an annual fee. For more information, consult *Air Courier Bargains* by Kelly Monaghan (The Intrepid Traveler, US$15) or the *Courier Air Travel Handbook* by Mark Field (Perpetual Press, US$13).

**CHARTER FLIGHTS.** Charters are flights a tour operator contracts with an airline to fly extra loads of passengers during peak season. They can be cheaper than flights on scheduled airlines. Some operate nonstop, and restrictions on minimum advance-purchase and minimum stay are more lenient. However, charter flights fly less frequently than major airlines, make refunds particularly difficult, and are usually fully booked. Schedules and itineraries may also change or be cancelled at the last moment (as late as 48 hours before the trip, and without a full refund), and check-in, boarding, and baggage claim are often much slower. Pay with a credit card if you can, and consider traveler's insurance against trip interruption.

   **Discount clubs** and **fare brokers** offer members savings on last-minute charter and tour deals. Study their contracts closely; you don't want to end up with an unwanted overnight layover.

**STANDBY FLIGHTS.** To travel standby, you'll need considerable flexibility in the dates and cities of your arrival and departure. Companies that specialize in standby flights don't sell tickets but rather the promise that you will get to your destination (or near your destination) within a certain window of time (anywhere from 1-5 days). You may only receive a monetary refund if all available flights which depart within your date-range from the specified region are full, but future travel credit is always available. Read agreements with any company offering standby flights carefully, as tricky fine print can leave you in the lurch.

   To check on a company's service record, call the **Better Business Bureau of New York City** (☎(212) 533-6200). It's often difficult to obtain a refund and clients' vouchers will not be honored when an airline fails to receive payment in time.

**TICKET CONSOLIDATORS.** Ticket consolidators, or **"bucket shops,"** buy unsold tickets in bulk from commercial airlines and sell them at discounted rates. The best place to look is in the Sunday travel section of any major newspaper (among the best is the *New York Times*), where many bucket shops place tiny ads. Call quickly, as availability is typically extremely limited. Not all bucket shops are reliable establishments, so insist on a receipt that gives full details of restrictions, refunds, and tickets, and pay by credit card (in spite of the 2-5% fee) so you can stop payment if you never receive your tickets. For more information, check the web site **Consolidators FAQ** (www.travel-library.com/air-travel/consolidators.html) or the book *Consolidators: Air Travel's Bargain Basement*, by Kelly Monaghan (Intrepid Traveler, US$10).

From **North America, Travel Avenue** (☎ 800-333-3335; www.travelavenue.com) searches for best available published fares and then uses several consolidators to attempt to beat that fare. Also, **NOW Voyager**, 74 Varick St. #307, New York, NY 10013 (☎ (212) 431-1616; 219 1753; www.nowvoyagertravel.com), acts as a consolidator and books discounted flights, mostly from New York, as well as courier flights, for an annual registration fee of US$50. Other consolidators worth calling are **Interworld** (☎ (305) 443-4929; fax 443-0351); **Rebel** (☎ 800-227-3235; travel@rebeltours.com; www.rebeltours.com); **Cheap Tickets** (☎ 800-377-1000; www.cheaptickets.com); or **Travac** (☎ 800-872-8800; fax (212) 563-3631; www.travac.com). In **London**, the **Air Travel Advisory Bureau** (☎ (020) 7636 5000; www.atab.co.uk) provides names of reliable consolidators.

## OTHER OPTIONS FROM THE UK

**BY TRAIN.** Eurostar (☎ 0990 186 186; www.eurostar.com) runs a frequent train service from London to the continent. Ten to twenty-eight trains per day run to Paris (3hr., 2nd class US$75-159) and Brussels (3hr., 50min., 2nd class US$75-159).

**BY CAR.** If traveling by car, **Eurotunnel** (☎ 0800 969 992; www.eurotunnel.co.uk) shuttles cars and passengers through the Chunnel between Kent and Nord-Pas-de-Calais. Return fares for vehicle and all passengers range from UK£219-299 with car, UK£259-598 with campervan, and UK£119-299 for a trailer/caravan supplement. Same-day return costs UK£110-150, five-day return UK£139-195. Book online or by phone. Travelers with cars can also look into ferries (see below).

**BY BOAT. Seaview** (www.seaview.co.uk/Ferries.html) has a directory of ferries leaving from Britain and Ireland. **P&O Stena** (☎0870 600 0600 or (01304) 864003 from outside the UK; www.posl.com) runs ferries between Dover and Calais (1¼hr., 30 per day). Fares for foot passengers range from UK£5 (for a weekday daytrip) to UK£48 (for a 5-day stay); fares for cars range from UK£45 (for a daytrip, 5 passengers) to UK£315 (for a 5-day stay, 8 passengers). Same-day ticket purchases are more expensive (UK£2 per foot passenger; UK£20 per car). **Hoverspeed** (☎(0870) 240 8070; www.hoverspeed.co.uk) has frequent ferries from Dover to Calais (35-50min., 12 per day). Foot passengers are UK£24, with car UK£113-139. **Bikes** are usually free, although you may have to pay up to UK£10 in summer.

# GETTING AROUND

Fares on all modes of transportation are either "single" (one-way) or "return" (roundtrip). Unless stated otherwise *Let's Go* always lists single fares. Roundtrip fares on trains and buses in most of Europe are simply double the one-way fare.

# BY TRAIN

Trains are often the fastest and easiest way to travel. Second-class travel is pleasant, and compartments, which seat two to six, are excellent places to meet fellow travelers. Bring food and water; there are often no on-board cafes and train water is undrinkable. For long trips make sure you are in the correct car, as trains sometimes split at junctions. Towns listed in parentheses on Eastern European train schedules require a transfer at the town listed immediately before the parenthesis.

Many train stations have different counters for domestic and international tickets, seat reservations, and information; check before lining up. On major routes, reservations are always advisable, and often required, even with a railpass; you are not guaranteed a seat without one (US$3-5). Europeans often reserve far ahead of time; you should strongly consider reserving during peak holiday and tourist seasons (at the very latest a few hours ahead). It will be necessary to purchase a supplement (US$5-10) for trains like EuroCity, InterCity, and InterCityExpress.

You can either buy a **railpass**, which allows you unlimited travel within a particular region for a given period of time, or rely on buying individual **point-to-point** tickets as you go. Almost all countries give students or youths (under 26) direct discounts on regular domestic rail tickets, and many also sell a student or youth card that provides 20-50% off all fares for up to a year.

## RAILPASSES

It may be tough to make your railpass pay for itself in Eastern Europe, where train fares are ridiculously cheap and buses sometimes preferable. In general, it's better to travel on point-to-point tickets, which are almost always a better deal.

For those dead set on purchasing a multinational railpass, there are a few options. **Eurailpass,** however, is not one of them: it covers only Hungary in Eastern Europe. The **European East Pass** covers Austria, the Czech Republic, Hungary, Poland, and Slovakia (5 days in one month US$205). The **Central Europe Pass** provides unlimited rail travel through the Czech Republic, Germany, Poland, and Slovakia for any 5 days in one month (first-class only US$199; only available in US). The **Balkan Flexipass** is valid for travel in Bulgaria, Greece, the Former Yugoslavian Republic of Macedonia, Montenegro, Romania, Serbia, and Turkey (5 days in one month US$152, under 26 US$90). Available only in the UK are the **Baltic Rail Explorer Pass,** which allows ISIC holders and/or those under 26 unlimited rail travel in Estonia, Latvia, and Lithuania for 7 days (£25), 14 days (£37), or 21 days (£49); and the **Czech Republic/Slovakia Explorer Pass,** which allows unlimited travel in those countries for 7 consecutive days in first- or second-class (for both try Campus Travel, 52 Grosvenor Gardens, London SW1W 0AG, ☎(020) 7730 3402).

Purchase a pass before you arrive in Europe, as most passes are available only to non-Europeans and are consequently difficult to find in Europe. **Rail Europe,** 500 Mamaroneck Ave, Harrison, NY 10528 (☎(888) 382-7245, fax (800) 432-1329 in the US; ☎(800) 361-7245, fax (905) 602-4198 in Canada; ☎(0990) 848848 in the UK; www.raileurope.com) and **DER Travel Services,** 9501 W. Devon Ave Suite #301, Rosemont, IL 60018 (☎(888) 337-7350, fax (800) 282-7474 in the US; www.dertravel.com) provide information and offer a number of passes good in Eastern European countries.

For anyone who has lived in Europe for at least six months, **InterRail Passes** are an option. Of the 8 InterRail zones, 3 service Eastern European nations: D (Croatia, Czech Republic, Hungary, Poland, and Slovakia), G (Greece, Italy, Slovenia, and Turkey, including a Greece-Italy ferry), and H (Bulgaria, Romania, Yugoslavia, and Macedonia). If you buy a pass including the country in which you have claimed residence, you must pay 50% of all rail fares within that country. The **Under 26 InterRail Card** (UK£159-259) allows either 14 days or one month of unlimited travel within one, two, three, or all of the seven zones into which InterRail divides Europe; the cost is determined by the number of zones the pass covers. The **Over 26 InterRail Card** offers unlimited second-class travel in Bulgaria, Croatia, Czech Republic, Hungary, Poland, Romania, Slovakia, Slovenia, and Yugoslavia for 15 days or one month for UK£215 and UK£275, respectively.

**Bulgarian Flexipass, Polrail Pass, Czech Flexipass, Hungarian Flexipass,** and **Romanian Flexipass** are the only national passes available. These tend not to be as economical as point-to-point travel, but if you're spending a significant amount of time in one country, they can be worthwhile. Another type of regional pass covers a specific area within a country or a round-trip from any border to a particular destination and back. Examples include the **Prague Excursion Pass,** which covers travel from any Czech border to Prague and back out of the country (round-trip must be completed within 7 days; second-class US$35, under 26 US$30).

## DISCOUNT RAIL TICKETS

For travelers under 26, **BIJ** tickets (*Billets Internationals de Jeunesse;* sold under the names **Wasteels, Eurotrain,** and **Route 26**) are a great alternative to rail-passes. Available for international trips within Europe as well as most ferry services, they knock 25-40% off regular second-class fares. Tickets are good for 60 days after purchase and allow a number of stopovers along the normal direct route of the train journey. Issued for a specific international route between two points, they must be used in the direction and order of the designated route without side- or back-tracking and must be bought in Europe. They are available from European travel agents, at Wasteels or Eurotrain offices (usually in or near train stations), or occasionally at ticket counters. Contact **Wasteels** in London (see **Budget and Student Travel Agencies,** p. 43).

**FURTHER READING: TRAIN TRAVEL**

**Thomas Cook European Timetable** (US$28-39), includes a map of Europe highlighting all train and ferry routes. The timetable, updated annually, covers all major and most minor train, bus, and ferry routes in Europe. In Europe, find it at any Thomas Cook Money Exchange Center; elsewhere, call UK ☎(+44) 173 350 3571 or write Thomas Cook Publishing, PO Box 227, Thorpe Wood, Peterborough, PE3 6PU, UK.

**Hunter Publishing,** P.O. Box 7816, Edison, NJ 08818, USA (☎800-255-0343; fax 732-417-1744; hunterpub@emi.net; www.hunterpublishing.com), offers a catalogue of rail atlases and travel guides. Titles include *European Rail Atlas: Scandinavia & Eastern Europe* (US$16).

# BY BUS

All over Eastern Europe, short-haul buses reach rural areas inaccessible by train. In addition, long-distance bus networks may be more extensive, efficient, and occasionally even more comfortable than train services. In the Balkans, air-conditioned buses run by private companies are a godsend. **Eurolines,** 4 Cardiff Rd., Luton LU1 1PP (☎(01582) 404 511; fax 400 694), or in London, 52 Grosvenor Gardens, Victoria (☎(020) 7730 8235; welcome@eurolines.uk.com; www.eurolines.uk.com), is Europe's largest operator of coach services, offering passes (UK£159-249) for unlimited 30- or 60- day travel between 20 major tourist destinations, including spots in Eastern Europe and Russia.

# BY PLANE

Flying across Eastern Europe on regularly scheduled flights can devour your budget. London's **Air Travel Advisory Bureau** (☎(020) 7636 5000; www.atab.co.uk) can point the way to discount flights. It is possible to purchase **Europe by air** passes (US$99 each, airport taxes not included, reservations recommended) to travel between cities throughout Eastern Europe (US ☎(888) 387-2479, Australia ☎(02) 9285 6811, New Zealand ☎(09) 309 8094; www.europebyair.com). **Lufthansa** (US ☎800-399-5838; www.lufthansa-usa.com) offers "Discover Europe" to non-Europe residents, a package of three flight coupons which cost US$125-200 each depending on season and destination; up to six additional tickets cost US$105-175 each. **SAS** (US ☎800-221-2350) offers special airpasses for the Baltic region, ranging in price from US$75-155. Finally, **Austrian Airlines** (US ☎800-843-0002), **KLM/Northwest** (☎800-800-1504) and **Alitalia** (☎800-223-5730) all fly to many cities in Eastern Europe, and offer similarly priced package deals. Student travel agencies also sell cheap tickets. Consult budget travel agents and local newspapers and magazines for more information.

# BY BOAT

*Sometimes, yes, boats go to Yalta...but not today.*
*——Ferry ticket clerk in Odessa*

Ferries in the **North** and **Baltic Seas** are generally reliable and go everywhere. Those content with deck passage rarely need to book ahead. You should check in at least two hours early for a prime spot and allow plenty of time for getting to the port. Bring your own food and avoid the astronomically priced and gastronomically challenging cafeteria cuisine. Fares jump sharply in July and August. Always ask for discounts; **ISIC** holders often get student fares and **Eurail** passholders get many reductions and free trips. Advance planning and reserved tickets can spare you days of waiting in dreary ports. For complete listings of schedules and fares for ferries, steamers, and cruises throughout Europe, find a copy of the quarterly *Official Steamship Guide International* at your travel agent. **The Thomas Cook European Timetable** also lists complete ferry schedules (see **Further Reading: Train Travel**, p. 49). Links to some major European ferry companies can be found at www.youra.com/ferries/intnlferries.html.

# BY CAR

## DRIVING PERMITS AND CAR INSURANCE

**INTERNATIONAL DRIVING PERMIT (IDP).** If you plan to drive a car while in Eastern Europe, you must have an International Driving Permit (IDP), though certain countries allow travelers to drive with a valid American or Canadian license for a limited number of months. It may be a good idea to get an IDP anyway, in case you're in a situation (e.g. an accident or stranded in a smaller town) where the police do not know English.

Your IDP, valid for one year, must be issued in your own country before you depart; AAA affiliates cannot issue IDPs valid in their own country. You must be 18 years old and have a valid driver's license from your home country to accompany the IDP. An application for an IDP usually needs to include one or two photos, a current local license, an additional form of identification, and a fee.

**Australia:** Contact your local Royal Automobile Club (RAC) or the National Royal Motorist Association (NRMA) if in NSW or the ACT (☎(08) 94 21 42 98; www.rac.com.au/travel). Permits AUS$15.

**Canada:** Contact any Canadian Automobile Association (CAA) branch office in Canada, or write to CAA, 1145 Hunt Club Rd., Suite 200, K1V 0Y3 Canada. (☎(613) 247-0117; fax 247-0118). Permits CDN$10.

**Ireland:** Contact the nearest Automobile Association (AA) office or write: The Automobile Association, International Documents, Fanum House, Erskine, Renfrewshire PA8 6BW (☎0990 500 600). Permits IR£4.

**New Zealand:** Contact your local Automobile Association (AA) or their main office at Auckland Central, 99 Albert St. (☎(09) 377 46 60; fax 302 20 37; www.nzaa.co.nz.). Permits NZ$8.

**South Africa:** Contact your local Automobile Association of South Africa office or the head office at P.O. Box 596, 2000 Johannesburg (☎(011) 799 10 00; fax 799 10 10). Permits SAR28.50.

**UK:** Visit your local AA Shop. To find the location nearest you that issues the IDP, call (0990) 50 06 00. More information available at www.theaa.co.uk/motoring/idp.asp). Permits UK£4.

**US:** Visit any American Automobile Association (AAA) office or write to AAA Florida, Travel Related Services, 1000 AAA Drive (mail stop 100), Heathrow, FL 32746 (☎800-222-4357 and 407-444-7000; fax 444-7380). You do not have to be a member of AAA to receive an IDP. Permits US$10.

**CAR INSURANCE.** Most gold or platinum credit cards cover standard insurance. If you rent, lease, or borrow a car, you will need a **green card,** or **International Insurance Certificate,** to prove that you have liability insurance. Obtain it through the car rental agency; most include coverage in their prices. If you lease a car, you can obtain a green card from the dealer. Some travel agents offer the card and it may also be available at border crossings. Even if your auto insurance covers you abroad, you'll need a green card to certify this to foreign officials. If you have a collision abroad, the accident will show up on your domestic records if you report it to your insurance company. Rental agencies may require you to purchase theft insurance in countries that they consider to have a high risk of auto theft.

# BY THUMB

 *Let's Go* strongly urges you to seriously consider the risks of hitchhiking. We do not recommend hitching as a safe means of transportation, and none of the information presented here is intended to do so.

Hitchhiking involves serious risks. It means entrusting your life to a random person who happens to stop next to you on the road. You risk theft, assault, sexual harassment, and unsafe driving. In spite of this, many see benefits to hitching. Favorable hitching experiences allow hitchers to meet locals and get to places where public transportation is sketchy. If you decide to hitch, consider where you are. Hitching remains common in Eastern Europe, though Westerners are a definite target for theft. In Russia, the Baltics, and some other Eastern European countries, hitchhiking can be as ordinary as hailing a taxi, and drivers will likely expect to be paid a sum at least equivalent to a bus ticket to your destination.

# ADDITIONAL INFORMATION

## SPECIFIC CONCERNS

### WOMEN TRAVELERS

Solo female travelers are a novel phenomenon for Eastern Europe, particularly in public places like restaurants, as Eastern European women never eat out by themselves. As a result, most women traveling alone should expect more than a few quizzical stares and hushed comments as they eat. The attitudes that contribute to these surprised looks, when coupled with crime in urban areas, can make for dangerous situations. If you are concerned, you might consider staying in hostels which offer single rooms that lock from the inside or with religious organizations that offer rooms for women only. Communal showers in some hostels are safer than others; check them before settling in. Stick to centrally located accommodations and avoid solitary late-night treks or metro rides.

When traveling, always carry extra money for a phone call, bus, or taxi. **Hitchhiking** is never safe for lone women or even for women traveling together. Choose train compartments occupied by other women or couples. Ask the conductor to put together a women-only compartment. Look as if you know where you're going and consider approaching older women or couples for directions if you're lost.

Generally, the less you look like a tourist, the better off you'll be. Dress conservatively, especially in rural areas. Shorts and t-shirts, even if unrevealing by Western standards, may identify you as a foreigner and should be avoided. Wearing the shirts, long skirts and platform shoes that are fashionable among native women will cut down on those obnoxious stares, and a *babushka*-style kerchief is like kryptonite to even the most perceptive and tenacious of cat callers. Some travelers report that wearing a wedding band or carrying pictures of a "husband" or "children" is extremely useful to help document marriage status. Even a mention

**ESSENTIALS**

of a husband waiting back at the hotel may be enough in some places to discount your potentially vulnerable, unattached appearance.

In cities, you may be harassed no matter how you're dressed. Your best answer to verbal harassment is no answer at all; feigned deafness, sitting motionless and staring straight ahead at nothing in particular will do a world of good that reactions usually don't achieve. If need be, turn to an older woman for help; her stern rebukes should usually embarrass the most persistent harassers into silence.

Don't hesitate to seek out a police officer or a passerby if you are being harassed. *Let's Go* lists emergency numbers (including rape crisis lines) in the **Practical Information** listings of most cities. Memorize the emergency numbers in the places you visit. Carry a **whistle** or an airhorn on your keychain, and don't hesitate to use it in an emergency. A self-defense course will not only prepare you for a potential attack, but will also raise your level of awareness of your surroundings as well as your confidence (see **Self Defense**, p. 27). Women also face some specific health concerns when traveling (see **Women's Health**, p. 32).

### FURTHER READING

*Active Women Vacation Guide*, Evelyn Kaye. Blue Panda Publications (US$18).

*Adventures in Good Company: The Complete Guide to Women's Tours and Outdoor Trips*, Thalia Zepatos. Eighth Mountain Press (US$17).

*A Journey of One's Own: Uncommon Advice for the Independent Woman Traveler*, Thalia Zepatos. Eighth Mountain Press (US$17).

*Travelers' Tales: Gutsy Women, Travel Tips and Wisdom for the Road*, Marybeth Bond. Traveler's Tales. Travelers' Tales Inc. (US$8).

*A Foxy Old Woman's Guide to Traveling Alone*, Jay Ben-Lesser. Crossing Press (US$11).

## OLDER TRAVELERS

Discounts for senior citizens in Eastern Europe are few and far between. That having been said, it never hurts to ask. Agencies for senior group travel are growing in enrollment and popularity. These are only a few:

**ElderTreks,** 597 Markham St., Toronto, ON, Canada, M6G 2L7 (☎800-741-7956 or (416) 588-5000; fax 588-9839; eldertreks@eldertreks.com; www.eldertreks.com).

**Elderhostel,** 75 Federal St., Boston, MA 02110-1941, USA (☎(617) 426-7788 or (877) 426-8056; registration@elderhostel.org; www.elderhostel.org). Programs at colleges, universities, and other learning centers in Western Russia on varied subjects lasting 1-4 weeks. Must be 55+ (spouse can be of any age).

**The Mature Traveler,** P.O. Box 50400, Reno, NV 89513, USA (☎(775) 786-7419, credit card orders 800-460-6676; www.maturetraveler.com). Deals, discounts, and soft-adventure tours for the 50+ traveler. Subscription US$30.

**Walking the World,** P.O. Box 1186, Fort Collins, CO 80522, USA (☎800-340-9255 or (970) 498-0500; walktworld@aol.com; www.walkingtheworld.com). Organizes trips for 50Ğ travelers to the Czech Republic and Slovakia.

### FURTHER READING

*No Problem! Worldwise Tips for Mature Adventurers*, Janice Kenyon. Orca Book Publishers (US$16).

*A Senior's Guide to Healthy Travel*, Donald L. Sullivan. Career Press (US$15).

*Unbelievably Good Deals and Great Adventures That You Absolutely Can't Get Unless You're Over 50*, Joan Rattner Heilman. Contemporary Books (US$13).

## BISEXUAL, GAY, AND LESBIAN TRAVELERS

Homophobic views persist throughout much of Eastern Europe. Homosexuality remains illegal in Belarus and Bosnia and in other countries laws forbidding "scandalous homosexual activity" or public displays of homosexuality can give local authorities an excuse to be troublesome. Even within major cities, gay nightclubs and social centers are often clandestine and frequently change location. While *Let's Go* tries to list local gay and lesbian bars and clubs, word of mouth is often the best method for finding the latest hotspots. Listed below are contact organizations and publishers that offer materials addressing gay and lesbian concerns.

**Gay's the Word,** 66 Marchmont St., London WC1N 1AB (☎(020) 7278 7654; sales@gaystheword.co.uk; www.gaystheword.co.uk). The largest gay and lesbian bookshop in the UK, with both fiction and non-fiction titles. Mail-order service available.

**Giovanni's Room,** 345 S. 12th St., Philadelphia, PA 19107, USA (☎(215) 923-2960; fax 923-0813; www.queerbooks.com). An international lesbian/feminist and gay bookstore with mail-order service (carries many of the publications listed below).

**International Gay and Lesbian Travel Association,** 4331 N. Federal Hwy., #304, Fort Lauderdale, FL 33308, USA (☎(954) 776-2626; fax 776-3303; www.iglta.com). An organization of over 1350 companies serving gay and lesbian travelers worldwide.

**International Lesbian and Gay Association (ILGA),** 81 rue Marché-au-Charbon, B-1000 Brussels, Belgium (☎/fax +32 (2) 502 24 71; www.ilga.org). Not a travel service; provides political information, such as homosexuality laws of individual countries.

## FURTHER READING

*Damron Men's Guide, Damron's Accommodations, Damron's Amsterdam Guide,* and *The Women's Traveller.* Damron Publishing. Damron Company (US$10-19). For more info, call US ☎(415) 255-0404 or 800-462-6654 or check their web site (www.damron.com).

*Ferrari Guides' Gay Travel A to Z, Ferrari Guides' Men's Travel in Your Pocket, Ferrari Guides' Women's Travel in Your Pocket,* and *Ferrari Guides' Inn Places.* Ferrari International (Ferrari International Publishing, US$14-16. For more info, call 800-962-2912 or (602) 863-2408 or try www.q-net.com.

*The Gay Vacation Guide: The Best Trips and How to Plan Them,* Mark Chesnut Citadel Press (US$15).

*Spartacus International Gay Guide.* Bruno Gmunder Verlag (US$33).

# TRAVELERS WITH DISABILITIES

Unfortunately, compared to other travel destinations, Eastern Europe is largely inaccessible for disabled travelers. Handicap ramps and other such amenities are all but nonexistent in most countries. As a result, some extra planning before your trip will be necessary to ensure everything goes smoothly: contact your destination's consulate or tourist office for information, arrange transportation early, and inform airlines and hotels of any special accommodations required ahead of time. If you give notice, some major car rental agencies offer hand-controlled vehicles at select locations. Call ahead to restaurants, hotels, parks, and other facilities to find out about ramps, the widths of doors, the dimensions of elevators, etc. Guide-dog owners should inquire as to the specific quarantine policies of each destination.

## USEFUL ORGANIZATIONS

**Graphic Language Press,** P.O. Box 270, Cardiff by the Sea, CA 92007, USA (☎(760) 944-9594; niteowl@cts.com). Advice for wheelchair travelers, including accessible accommodations, transportation, and sightseeing for various European cities.

**Mobility International USA (MIUSA),** P.O. Box 10767, Eugene, OR 97440, USA (☎(541) 343-1284 voice and TDD; fax 343-6812; info@miusa.org; www.miusa.org). Sells *A World of Options: A Guide to International Educational Exchange, Community Service, and Travel for Persons with Disabilities* (US$35).

**Moss Rehab Hospital Travel Information Service,** 1200 West Tabor Rd., Philadelphia, PA 19141-3099, USA (☎(800) CALL-MOSS or (215) 456-9600; netstaff@mossresourcenet.org; www.mossresourcenet.org). An information resource center on travel-related concerns for those with disabilities.

ESSENTIALS

**Society for the Advancement of Travel for the Handicapped (SATH),** 347 Fifth Ave., #610, New York, NY 10016 (☎(212) 447-7284; fax 725-8253; sathtravel@aol.com; www.sath.org). An advocacy group that publishes the quarterly travel magazine OPEN WORLD (free for members, US$13 for nonmembers). Also publishes a wide range of info sheets on disability travel facilitation and destinations. Annual membership US$45, students and seniors US$30.

## MINORITY TRAVELERS

The minority that encounters the most hostility in Eastern Europe is Gypsies (Roma). Travelers with darker skin of any nationality might be mistaken for Gypsies and therefore face some of the same prejudice. Other minority travelers, especially those of African or Asian descent, will usually meet with more curiosity than hostility, especially outside of big cities. Travelers of Arab ethnicity may also be treated more suspiciously. The ranks of Skinheads are on the rise in Eastern Europe, and minority travelers, especially Jews and blacks, should regard them with caution. Anti-Semitism is still a problem in many countries, including Poland and the former Soviet Union; it is generally best to be discreet about your religion.

## DIETARY CONCERNS

**Vegetarian** and **kosher** travelers will have their work cut out for them in Eastern Europe. Most of the national cuisines tend to be meat and especially pork-heavy. Markets are often a good bet for fresh vegetables, fruit, cheese, and bread.

Travelers who keep kosher should contact synagogues in larger cities for information on kosher restaurants; your own synagogue or college Hillel should have access to lists of the abundant Jewish institutions across Eastern Europe. If you are strict in your observance, bring supplies to prepare your own food on the road. **The Jewish Travel Guide** lists synagogues, kosher restaurants, and Jewish institutions in over 80 countries. Available from Vallentine Mitchell Publishers, Newbury House 890-900, Eastern Ave., Newbury Park, Ilford, Essex IG2 7HH UK (☎(020) 8599 8866; fax 8599 0984). It is available in the US ($16.95 + $4 S&H) from ISBS, 5804 NE Hassallo St., Portland, OR 97213-3644 (☎800-944-6190).

# ALTERNATIVES TO TOURISM

## STUDY

Foreign study programs have multiplied rapidly in Eastern Europe. Most American undergraduates enroll in programs sponsored by US universities and many colleges staff offices that provide advice and information on study abroad. Local libraries and bookstores are also helpful sources for current information on study abroad, as are www.studyabroad.com and www.worldwide.edu. If your language skills are decent, you may want to consider enrolling directly in a foreign university. This route is usually less expensive and more immersive than programs run through American universities. The catch is that it may be harder to get credit for your adventures abroad. Contact the nearest consulate for a list of institutions in your country of choice. There are also several international and national fellowships available (e.g. Fulbright or Rotary) to fund stays abroad. In most Eastern European countries, studying requires a special study visa, issued for a duration longer than a tourist visa. Applying for such visa usually requires proof of admission in the University/program which you are planning to attend. Below are several organizations that run programs to Eastern European countries.

**American Field Service (AFS)**, 310 SW 4th Ave., #630, Portland, OR 97204-2608 (☎800-237-4636; fax (503) 241-1653; afsinfo@afs.org; www.afs.org/). Summer, semester, and year-long homestay international exchange programs for high school students and graduating high school seniors in Czech Republic, Hungary, Latvia, Russia, Slovakia. Financial aid available.

**American Institute for Foreign Study**, College Division, 102 Greenwich Ave., Greenwich, CT 06830 (☎800-727-2437, ext. 6084; www.aifs.com). Organizes programs for high school and college study in universities in Russia and the Czech Republic. Summer, fall, spring, and year-long programs available. Scholarships available. Contact Dana Maggio with questions at dmaggio@aifs.com.

**School for International Training, College Semester Abroad,** Admissions, Kipling Rd., P.O. Box 676, Brattleboro, VT 05302 (☎800-336-1616 or 802-258-3267; fax 258-3500; www.worldlearning.org). Runs semester- and year-long programs in Russia and the Czech Republic. Programs cost US$8200-10300, all expenses included. Financial aid available and US financial aid is transferable.

**Youth For Understanding International Exchange** (YFU), 3501 Newark St. NW, Washington, D.C. 20016 (☎(800) TEENAGE (833-6243) or (202) 966-6800; fax 895-1104; http://www.yfu.org). Places US high school students worldwide for a year, semester, or summer in the Czech & Slovak Republics (joint program), Estonia/Latvia, Hungary, Poland, Russia, and Ukraine. US$75 application fee.

## LANGUAGE SCHOOLS

Programs generally cost anywhere from US$2000-5000 and include your lodging, some meals, and daytrips to cultural centers and attractions. Some of the pricier ones include airfare to and from the program.

**ACTR/ACCELS**, 1776 Massachusetts Ave., NW, Suite 700, Washington, DC, 20036 (☎(202) 833-7522; fax (202) 833-7523; general@actr.org; www.actr.org). Offers college-level summer language study programs in Belarus, Czech and Slovak Republics (joint program), Hungary, Moldova, Russia and Ukraine. Prices range from US$2200-3400. $35 application fee.

**Russian and East European Partnerships,** Kenneth Fortune, President PO Box 227, Fineview, NY 14640 (☎888-USE-REEP; fax 800-910-1777; reep@fox.nstn.ca). Offers summer and term-time language and cultural immersion programs in Belarus, Bulgaria, Croatia, Czech Republic, Estonia, Hungary, Poland, Russia and Ukraine. Prices range from US$2995-4650.

**Debrecen Summer School at KLTE.** Offers cheap and extremely popular Hungarian language programs for students from around the world. The one- to four-week courses happen in January, May/June, July, August, and October/November. Contact **Debreceni Nyári Egyetem,** Egyetem tér 1, 4010 Debrecen Pf. 35, (☎/fax 489 117; nyariegy@tigris.klte.hu; http://summer06.sum.klte.hu) in June.

# WORK

Working in Eastern Europe, like studying there, forces one to jump through a whole new set of hoops involving visas in work permits. Both a work permit and a visa are required. In some countries, to make it all the more confusing, a particular visa called a "visa with work permit" is required, although, contrary to the name, this document does *not* include a work permit. These visas are issued from the nearest consulate or embassy, like any visa (see **Embassies and Consulates,** p. 18). Applying for it, however, will require that you present your work permit, which must be issued directly from the Labor Bureau in the country in question. There are often ways to make it easier. Friends living in the country can help expedite work permits or arrange work-for-accommodations swaps.

## TEACHING ENGLISH

**Central Bureau for Educational Visits & Exchanges,** 10 Spring Gardens, London SW1A 2BN, UK (☎(020) 7389 4419 fax 7389 4426). Places British undergraduates and teachers in teaching positions in Poland and Hungary. Also arranges study abroad in Hungary, Poland, Russia, and Slovenia.

**International Schools Services,** Educational Staffing Program, P.O. Box 5910, Princeton, NJ 08543 (☎(609) 452-0990; fax 452-2690; edustaffing@iss.edu; www.iss.edu). Recruits teachers and administrators for American and English schools throughout Eastern Europe and the world. All instruction in English. Applicants must have a bachelor's degree and two years of relevant experience. Nonrefundable US$100 application fee. Publishes *The ISS Directory of Overseas Schools* (US$35).

**Office of Overseas Schools,** A/OS Room 245, SA-29, Dept. of State, Washington, D.C. 20522-2902 (☎(703) 875-7800; fax 875-7979; overseas.school@state.gov; state.gov/www/about_state/schools/). Keeps a list of schools abroad and agencies that arrange placement for Americans to teach abroad.

# VOLUNTEER

Volunteer jobs are readily available throughout Eastern Europe. In some cases, you might receive room and board in exchange for your labor. You can sometimes avoid the high application fees charged by the organizations that arrange placement by contacting the individual workcamps directly.

**Peace Corps,** 1111 20th St. NW, Washington, D.C. 20526 (☎800-424-8580; www.peacecorps.gov). Write for their "blue" brochure, which details application requirements. Opportunities in agriculture, business, education, the environment, and health in Bulgaria, Estonia, Latvia, Lithuania, Moldova, Poland, Romania, Russia, Slovakia, and Ukraine. Volunteers must be US citizens, age 18 and over, and willing to make a 2-year commitment. A bachelor's degree is usually required.

**Service Civil International Voluntary Service (SCI-VS),** 814 NE 40th St., Seattle, WA 98105 (☎/fax (206) 545-6585; sciivsusa@igc.apc.org). Arranges placement in workcamps in Europe for those age 18 and over, including Belarus, Bosnia, Bulgaria, Croatia, Czech Republic, Estonia, Hungary, Latvia, Lithuania, Poland, Romania, Russia, Slovakia, Slovenia, and Ukraine. Local organizations sponsor groups for physical or social work. Registration fees US$50-250, depending on the camp location.

**Volunteers for Peace,** 1034 Tiffany Rd., Belmont, VT 05730 (☎(802) 259-2759; fax 259-2922; vfp@vfp.org; www.vfp.org). A nonprofit organization that arranges speedy placement in 2-3 week workcamps in more than a dozen Eastern European countries comprising 10-15 people. Most complete and up-to-date listings provided in the annual *International Workcamp Directory* (US$15). Registration fee US$195. Free newsletter.

# THE WORLD WIDE WEB

Many countries' embassies now maintain websites where you can check visa requirements and news related to your destination (see **Embassies and Consulates,** p. 18). Some highlights:

**Microsoft Expedia** (expedia.msn.com) has everything you'd ever need to make travel plans on the web: compare flight fares, look at maps, make reservations. FareTracker, a free service, sends you monthly mailings about the cheapest fares to any destination.

**The CIA World Factbook** (www.odci.gov/cia/publications/factbook/index.html) has tons of vital statistics on East Europeans nations. Check it out for an overview of the economy, and an explanation of its system of government.

**Foreign Language for Travelers** (www.travlang.com) can help you brush up on almost any language in Eastern Europe.

**Let's Go** (www.letsgo.com) is where you can find our newsletter, information about our books, up-to-the-minute links, and more.

ESSENTIALS

# AUSTRIA (ÖSTERREICH)

The mighty Austro-Hungarian Empire may have crumbled during World War I, but Austria remains a complex country. At the peak of Habsburg megalomania, one of the largest land empires in Europe was governed from Vienna, and much of the continent, from the Ukraine in the east to the Netherlands in the west, bears their mark. For so long the focal point of central Europe, Austria was a magnet for artistic and intellectual brilliance, and its denizens, from Mozart to Freud, occupy the pride of place in the Western canon with an indelible impact on art, literature, and life itself. The mention of Austria evokes images of onion-domed churches set against snow-capped Alpine peaks, lush meadows surrounding mighty castles, and 10th-century monasteries towering over the majestic Danube. Now, river cruises showcase their ruined castles as well as the thriving vineyards whose magic potion made the Middle Ages bearable. For more in-depth information on Austria's attractions, pick up a copy of *Let's Go: Austria & Switzerland 2001*.

## AUSTRIA AT A GLANCE

**OFFICIAL NAME:** Republic of Austria

**CAPITAL:** Vienna (pop. 1.5 million)

**POPULATION:** 8.2 million

**LANGUAGE:** German

**CURRENCY:** 1 schilling (AS) = 100 groschen

**RELIGION:** 80% Roman Catholic, 5% Protestant, 15% Other

**LAND AREA:** 83,858 km²

**GEOGRAPHY:** Rolling terrain by the Danube, otherwise mountainous.

**CLIMATE:** Cool summers, cold winters in the lowlands and snow in the mountains.

**BORDERS:** Czech Rep., Germany, Italy, Hungary, Slovakia, Slovenia, Switzerland

**ECONOMY:** 66% Services, 33% Industry, 1.5% Agriculture

**GDP:** US$22,700 per capita

**EMERGENCY PHONE NUMBERS:** Fire 122, Police 133, Ambulance 144

**COUNTRY CODE:** 43

**INTERNATIONAL DIALING PREFIX:** 00, 900 in Vienna only

# HISTORY

**THE BEGINNINGS.** Nomadic tribes roamed through what is now Austria for thousands of years when the **Celts** established the kingdom of **Noricum** around 500 BC. In 15BC, the kingdom was conquered by the **Romans** in to secure the Danube frontier against marauding Germanic tribes; Christianity came to Austria via the Roman soldiers. Even so, by the fifth century AD the Germans had overrun the area, and the future Austria was divided among three groups; the **Bavarians** in the north, the **Alemanni** in the south, and the non-Germanic **Slavs** in the southwest.

**THE HABSBURGS.** Austria had its second taste of imperialism in the mid-9th century when **Charlemagne,** founder of the Holy Roman Empire, turned his eyes east in hopes of heading off invaders on the frontiers of his empire. Holy Roman Emperor **Otto II** entrusted Margrave Liutpoldus (a.k.a. **Leopold of Babenberg**) with the defense of the Empire's eastern territories. The Babenberg dynasty concentrated both on stabilizing the frontiers and extending its protectorate. The last Babenberg died childless, which led to a bloody conflict from which **Rudolf von Habsburg** emerged as victor and lay the foundation for six centuries of Habsburg dynastic

rule in Austria. Gradually, the Habsburgs accumulated extensive territory all over central Europe, including present-day Hungary, the Czech Republic, Slovakia, as well as parts of Croatia, Poland, Ukraine, and Russia.

Despite the massive possessions and imperial veneer, the Habsburg ship hit rough waters in the 16th and 17th centuries as a result of Martin Luther's Protestant **Reformation** and the Catholic church's ensuing **Counter-Reformation.** Victories over Protestant forces during the **Thirty Years War** (1618-1648) restored Habsburg control over Bohemia, where they converted most of the peasants back to Catholicism. When, thanks to the **Pragmatic Sanction** passed by her father (which allowed succession through the female line), **Maria Theresia** ascended the throne in 1740, her neighbors were eager to see Habsburg power diminished. The arrival on the scene of **Napoleon Bonaparte** rapidly, if temporarily achieved this, and fear of Napoleon's own Imperial ambitions led **Franz II** in 1804 to dissolve the Holy Roman Empire—in name, if not in substance—to prevent the Frenchman from claiming the title for himself. Instead, he adopted the new title of Franz I, Emperor of Austria.

During the 1815 **Congress of Vienna,** which redrew the map of Europe after Napoleon's defeat, Austrian Chancellor **Clemens Wenzel Lothar von Metternich** tried to restore the old order while orchestrating the re-consolidation of Austrian power. His attempts were met with resistance (inspired by French revolutionary ideas), which was violently crushed in 1848. Austria's position in Europe continued to shift throughout the 68-year long reign of **Franz Joseph.** Burgeoning nationalist sentiments led to severe divisions within the multinational empire itself; the largest minority, the Magyars (Hungarians), were powerful enough to force the establishment of the dual **Austro-Hungarian** monarchy with the enfeebled Habsburgs in 1866.

**20TH CENTURY.** Brimming with ethnic tension and locked into a rigid system of alliances, the empire was a disaster waiting to happen. The spark that set off the explosion was the journey **Franz Ferdinand d'Este,** the heir to the imperial throne, took to Sarajevo in June 1914, where he was assassinated (see **Sarajevo: Sights,** p. 98). Austria's declaration of war against Serbia set off a chain reaction that pulled Europe into **World War I.** Proclamations of independence by the subjugated nations ensured the demise of the monarchy. On November 11, 1918, Emperor **Karl** achieved peace, but only after the **Republic of Austria** was established, ending the 640-year-old Habsburg dynasty. Between 1918 and 1938, Austria had its first, bitter taste of democracy as the shrunken state became the **First Republic.** The Republic suffered massive inflation, unemployment, and economic collapse, but was stabilized by the mid-1920s. Unfortunately, its stability did not last long—Hitler sealed the Republic's fate when he decided to **annex** (paradoxically called "Anschluss," or union in German) Austria on March 13, 1938. After Soviet troops brutally liberated Vienna in 1945, the country was temporarily occupied by Allied troops.

# POLITICS

The 1945 Federal Constitution provided for a president (head of state) who is elected for six-year terms, a chancellor (head of government), usually the leader of the strongest party, a bicameral parliament, and strong provincial governments. Until very recently the government has been dominated by two parties, the Social Democratic Party (SPÖ), and the People's Party (ÖVP). The two parties have built up one of the world's most successful industrial economies, with enviably low unemployment and inflation rates, as well as a generous welfare state. During the 1990s Austria has moved toward closer European integration. In 1994 **Thomas Klestil,** the current President, was elected on a platform of integration. In 1995 the people ratified membership of the European Union (EU) by referendum.

Austria has recently been plastered over front pages internationally thanks to the far-right **Freedom Party.** The party came second in the 1999 elections, effectively breaking up the traditional two-party lock. The Freedom Party is infamous for its leader **Jörg Haider,** who entered the public eye for his many remarks that have been seen as pro-Nazi. In leading his party to power Haider called the Nazi camps "punishment camps" rather than concentration camps, and has called for a complete ban on immigration, playing off Austrian fears of the influx of immigrants from the post-communist neighbors. In a compromise to allay international concerns about Haider, the SPÖ only entered a coalition with the Freedom Party after Haider had resigned as from the party leadership. Nonetheless, the other 14 EU members states immediately levied political sanctions against Austria. Small tensions prevail.

# CULTURE

| NATIONAL HOLIDAYS IN 2001 | |
|---|---|
| **January 1-2** New Year's Day | **June 14** Corpus Christi |
| **January 6** Epiphany | **August 15** Assumption Day |
| **April 13** Good Friday | **October 26** Austrian National Day |
| **April 15-16** Easter | **November 1** All Saint's Day |
| **May 1** Labor Day | **December 8** Immaculate Conception |
| **May 24** Ascension day | **December 25-26** Christmas |
| **June 3-4** Pentecost | |

# LITERATURE

In the Roman settlement Vindobona, Emperor **Marcus Aurelius** wrote his *Meditations*, starting a long tradition of Viennese immigrant (and *emigré*) artists. Born in Vienna in 1801, **Johann Nestroy** wrote biting comedies and satires such as *Der Talisman* and the *Tannhauser*. Around 1890, Austrian literature rapidly transformed in the heat of the "merry apocalypse" atmosphere that permeated society. The works of this era, known as **fin de siècle,** are legendary. **Sigmund Freud** diagnosed the crisis, **Karl Kraus** implacably unmasked it, **Arthur Schnitzler** dramatized it, **Hugo von Hofmannsthal** ventured a cautious eulogy, and **Georg Trakl** commented on the collapse in feverish verse. The cafe provided the backdrop for the *fin de siècle* literary landscape. Freud is best known for his theories of sexual repression, which he considered particularly applicable for bourgeois society, and his theories of the unconscious. Austrian literature today is still affected and informed by its literary tradition, but there is plenty of innovation as well. **Ingeborg Bachman's** stories and novels left an important legacy for Austrian feminism, while **Thomas Bernhard's** *Holzfäller* (Woodcutters) is a cogent critique of contemporary Austrian society.

## ART AND ARCHITECTURE

Landlocked in the middle of Europe with money to pave the streets with, the Habsburgs married into power and bought into art. **Gustav Klimt** (1862-1918) and his followers founded what is known as the **Secession** movement. **Oskar Kokoschka** and **Egon Schiele** revolted against "art *qua* art," seeking to present the energy formerly concealed behind the Secession's aesthetic surface. Schiele's paintings are controversial even today for their depictions of tortured figures seemingly destroyed by their own bodies or by debilitating sexuality.

In architecture, *fin de siècle* gave rise to the **Jugendstil (a.k.a. Art Nouveau),** which aimed to emphasize the ethic of function over form. It was embraced by Vienna's artistic elite, most notably by the guru of architectural modernism, **Otto Wagner.** These ideals later influenced the **Bauhaus** of Weimar Germany and paved the way for **Adolf Loos** who proclaimed, "Ornamentation is criminal."

## MUSIC

The first master musician of Viennese Classicism was **Josef Haydn,** but the work of **Wolfgang Amadeus Mozart** represents the pinnacle of the time period. He was the ideal child prodigy, playing violin and piano by age four, and produced such well-known operas as *The Marriage of Figaro*. Mozart's work has been proclaimed to be "the culmination of all beauty in music." **Franz Schubert** bridged the gap between Classicism and emerging Romanticism. While **Ludwig van Beethoven** and **Johannes Brahms** were both German by birth, both spent much of their lives in music-loving Vienna. **Anton Bruckner** is famous for his massively orchestrated symphonies and is recognized as one of the greatest symphonic masters of the 19th century. **Johann Strauss the Elder** (1804-1849), and his son **Johann Strauss the Younger** (1825-1899) kept Vienna on its toes for much of the 19th century. They created waltzes which offered a new exhilaration that broke free from older, more formal dances. Breaking into the modern era, **Arnold Schönberg** rejected tonal keys in favor of atonality which produced a highly abstracted sound from the melodic works of the classicists. **Anton von Webern** and **Alban Berg** were both students of Schönberg and both suffered under Nazi occupation for their creation of "degenerate art."

## FOOD AND DRINK

Loaded with fat, salt, and cholesterol, traditional Austrian cuisine is a cardiologist's nightmare but a delight to the palate. Staple foods include *Schweinefleisch* (pork), *Kalbsfleisch* (veal), *Wurst* (sausage), *Ei* (egg), *Käse* (cheese), *Brot* (bread), and *Kartoffeln* (potatoes). Austria's best known dish, *Wienerschnitzel,* is a meat cutlet (usually veal or pork) fried in butter with bread crumbs. Vegetarians should look for *Spätzle* (noodles), *Eierschwammerl* (tiny yellow mushrooms), or anything with the word "Vegi" in it. The best discount supermarkets are **Billa** and **Hofer,** where you can buy cheap bags of *Semmeln* (rolls) and fruits and veggies. Natives nurse their sweet tooths at *Café-Konditoreien* with *Kaffee und Kuchen* (coffee and cake). Try *Sacher Torte,* a rich chocolate cake layered with marmalade; *Linzer Torte,* a light yellow cake with currant jam embedded in it; *Apfelstrudel;* or just about any pastry. Austrian beers are outstanding—try *Stiegl Bier,* a Salzburg brew, *Zipfer Bier* from upper Austria, and *Gösser Bier* from Styria.

# LANGUAGE

Although German is the official language of Austria, borders with the Czech Republic, Slovakia, Hungary, Italy, Slovenia, Liechtenstein, and Switzerland make speaking more than one language imperative for most Austrians. In addition to foreign languages, however, the German spoken in Austria differentiates itself by accent and vocabulary from that of other German-speaking countries. As a result of the international connections of the Habsburg Empire, there are lots of French, Italian, Czech, Hebrew, and Hungarian words mixed in to the German, for example *Babuschka* for old woman.

# CUSTOMS AND ETIQUETTE

In Austria, menus will say whether service is included (*Preise inclusive* or *Bedienung inclusiv*); if it is, you don't have to tip. If it's not, leave a tip up to 10%. Austrian restaurants expect you to seat yourself, and servers will not bring the bill until you ask them to do so. Don't leave tips on the table. Say *Zahlen bitte* (TSAHL-en BIT-uh) to settle your accounts. Be aware that some restaurants charge for each piece of bread that you eat during your meal. Don't expect to bargain in shops or markets in Austria, except at flea markets in Vienna.

# ADDITIONAL READING

*Vienna: Its Musical Heritage* (1968). Egon Gartenberg.
*Fin-de-Siècle Vienna* (1961). Carl Schorske.
*The Fall of the House of Habsburg* (1963). Edward Crankshaw.
*The World of Yesterday* (*Die Welt von Gestern*; 1943). Stefan Zweig.

# TRAVELING ESSENTIALS

Citizens of the EU do not need a visa to visit, work, or study in Austria. Australians, Canadians, New Zealanders, and US citizens, do not need visas for stays of less than three months; visas are required to work or study. South Africans must have a visa and a valid passport for all stays. For more information, visit www.bmaa.gv.at/embassy/uk/index.html.en).

# TRANSPORTATION

**BY PLANE.** The only major international airport is **Vienna's** Schwechat Flughafen. European flights also land in Salzburg, Graz, Innsbruck, and Klagenfurt. From the UK, **buzz** flies to Vienna (☎ (0870) 240 70 70; www.buzzaway.com. UK$50-80.)

**BY TRAIN.** The **Österreichische Bundesbahn (ÖBB)**, Austria's train system, is frequent, fast, and comfortable. **Eurail, InterRail,** and **Europe East** passes are valid in Austria. The **Austrian Railpass** allows three days of travel within any 15-day period on all rail lines. The one-month **Bundesnetzkarte** (National Network Pass), sold only in Austria, allows unlimited domestic train travel. The **Kilometer Bank,** also sold only in Austria, involves prepurchasing a given number of kilometers' worth of travel, which can be used by one to six people traveling together on trips of over 70km one-way in first or second class. For **rail info,** dial 01717.

**BY BUS, FERRY, AND CAR.** The efficient bus system consists mainly of **Bundes-Buses,** which cover areas inaccessible by train. They usually cost about as much as trains. You can buy discounted tickets, valid for one week, for any particular route. For **bus info,** dial (0222) 71101 within Austria (from outside dial (1) 71101). Private **ferry** services are offered on most lakes, while the DDSG runs boats down the Danube between Vienna and Krems, Melk, Passau, and internationally to Bratislava and Budapest. If you bring a **car** into Austria, you must obtain a *vignette* sticker at the border to place on the windshield (70AS per week) or face a US$130 fine; if you rent a car in Austria this will be added to the rental cost.

**BY BIKE AND BY THUMB. Bicycling** is a great way to get around Austria; not only are the roads generally level (well, except in the Alps) and safe, but many private companies and train stations rent bikes (generally 150AS per day, 90AS with a rail-pass or valid train ticket from that day). If you get a bike at a train station, you can return it to any participating station. Look for the *Gepäckbeförderung* symbol (a little bicycle) on departure schedules to see if bikes are permitted in the baggage car. If your bike breaks down on the road, some auto clubs may rescue you; try the **Austrian Automobile, Motorcycle, and Touring Club (ÖAMTC)** (☎ 120) or **ARBÖ** (☎ 123).

Austria is a rough place to **hitchhike**—Austrians rarely stop, and many mountain roads are all but deserted. *Let's Go* does not recommend hitchhiking.

# TOURIST SERVICES AND MONEY

Virtually every town in Austria has a **tourist office**, most marked by a green **"i"** sign. You may run into language difficulties in the small-town offices, but most brochures are available in English. The website for Austrian tourism is www.experienceaustria.com.

**Currency exchange** is easiest at ATMs, train stations, and post offices, where rates are the same as or close to bank rates.

| CURRENCY | | |
|---|---|---|
| US$1=14.42 AS (AUSTRIAN SCHILLING) | 10AS=US$0.69 |
| CDN$1=9.80 AS | 10AS=CDN$1.02 |
| UK£1=21.87 AS | 10AS=UK£0.46 |
| IR£1=17.47 AS | 10AS=IR£0.57 |
| AUS$1=8.68 AS | 10AS=AUS$1.15 |
| NZ$1=6.85 AS | 10AS=NZ$1.46 |
| SAR1=2.09 AS | 10AS=SAR4.77 |

# ACCOMMODATIONS AND CAMPING

Rooms in Austria are usually spotless; even the least appealing of Austria's **youth hostels** *(Jugendherbergen)* are quite tolerable. Most hostels charge US$12-25 per night for dorms. Two independent organizations run the over 80 HI hostels in the country; the ÖJHV and the ÖJHW. **Hotels** are usually quite expensive. If you're on a tight budget, look instead for *Zimmer Frei* or *Privatzimmer* (Room available) signs; rooms are usually $10-25. Otherwise, smaller pensions and *Gästehäuser* are often within the budget traveler's range. **Camping** is a popular option; prices range from 50-70AS per person and 25-60AS per tent, with a tax of 8-10AS.

# KEEPING IN TOUCH

**Airmail** to North America takes 5-7 days, but up to 2 weeks to Australia and New Zealand. The cheapest option is to send **aerogrammes. Mail** can be received general delivery through *Postagernde Lagernde*. Address envelopes as follows: Bob (First name) DYLAN (LAST NAME), *Postagernde Lagernde Briefe*, A-1010 (Postal code) Vienna (City), AUSTRIA.

You can usually make **international calls** from a pay phone, but a better option is to buy **phone cards** *(Wertkarten)* at post offices, train stations, and *Tabak/Trafik* (50 or 100AS). The quickest and cheapest way to call abroad is to go to a post office and ask for *Zurückruf*, or "return call," and have your party call you back. **International direct dial** numbers include: **AT&T,** ☎ 022 90 30 11; **BT Direct,** ☎ 0800 20 02 09; **Canada Direct,** ☎ 0800 20 02 17; **MCI WorldPhone Direct,** ☎ 022 90 30 12; **Sprint Global One,** ☎ 0800 20 02 36; **Telkom South Africa Direct,** ☎ 022 90 30 27. Most towns in Austria have **internet** cafes, running 50-100AS per hr.

# VIENNA (WIEN)                    ☎ (0)222

It was not without reason that home-grown satirist Karl Kraus once dubbed Vienna—birthplace of psychoanalysis, atonal music, functionalist architecture, Zionism, and Nazism—a "laboratory for world destruction." Vienna has an important cultural heritage that rivals that of Paris and Berlin, thanks to its history of inspired musicians (including Mozart, Schubert, Strauss, and Schoenberg), imperial wealth, and impeccable taste in Baroque art and architecture. But the city's *fin de siècle* heyday carried the seeds of its decay—the Viennese self-mockingly called it the "merry apocalypse" as they stared down their own dissolution over coffee. The smooth veneer of waltz music and whipped cream concealed a darker reality expressed by Freud's theories and Mahler's music. As the last fringes of the Iron Curtain have been drawn back, Vienna has tried to revitalize its political, cultural, and economical life through connections with the former communist bloc, and to establish itself as the gateway to Eastern Europe.

## ⊞ ORIENTATION

Vienna is divided into 23 *Bezirke* (districts). The first district is the city center, *innere Stadt* or **Innenstadt** (inner city), bounded by the name-changing **Ringstrasse** (once the site of the old city fortifications) and the Danube. Many of Vienna's major attractions lie along **Opernring, Kärntner Ring,** and **Kärntner Strasse** in the southern section of the Ring, among them the **Kunsthistorisches Museum,** the **Rathaus,** and the **Burggarten.** At the intersection of the **Opernring, Kärntner Ring,** and **Kärntnerstrasse** stands the **Staatsoper** (Opera House), with the **tourist office** and the **Karlsplatz** U-Bahn (subway) stop. Districts two through nine radiate clockwise from the center between the Ring and the larger, concentric **Gürtel** ("belt"), beyond which further districts similarly radiate clockwise. Street signs indicate the district numbers in Roman or Arabic numerals. *Let's Go* includes district numbers before street addresses for establishments.

>  **VIENNESE CRIME.** Vienna is a metropolis with crime like any other. Be extra careful by the U-Bahn station in Karlspl., home to pushers and junkies. At night avoid the 5th, 10th, and, 14th districts, as well as Landstrasser Hauptstr., Prater Park, and sections of the Gürtel (Vienna's red-light district).

## ✈ INTERCITY TRANSPORTATION

**Flights: Wien-Schwechat Flughafen** (☎ 700 722 231), 18km from Vienna's center, is the home of **Austrian Airlines** (☎ 17 89; www.aua.com; open M-F 8am-7pm, Sa-Su 8am-5pm). The S-7 connects the airport (Flughafen/Wolfsthal; every 30min., 38AS) to U-3, 4: Wien Mitte/Landstr. **Vienna Airport Lines Shuttle Buses** run 24hr. from the airport to the City Air Terminal opposite Wien Mitte/Landstr. (every 20-30min.; 70AS)

**Trains:** Info ☎ 17 17 (24hr.); schedules online at www.bahn.at. Three main stations:

**Westbahnhof,** XV, Mariahilferstr. 132, primarily runs west. To: **Salzburg** (3hr., every hr., 430AS); **Innsbruck** (6hr., every 2hr., 660AS); **Budapest, HUN** (3-4hr., 6 per day, 420AS); **Munich, GER** (4½hr., 5 per day, 788AS); **Zurich, SWI** (9¼hr., 3 per day, 1122AS); **Berlin, GER** (11hr., 1 per day, 1678AS); **Amsterdam, NETH** (14hr., 1 per day, 2276AS); and **Paris, FRA** (14hr., 2 per day, 2096AS).

**Südbahnhof,** X, Wiedner Gürtel 1a, runs south and east. To: **Bratislava, SLK** (1hr., 3 per day, 166AS); **Prague, CZR** (4½hr., 3 per day, 550AS); **Kraków, POL** (7-8hr., 2 per day, 496AS); **Berlin, GER** (9¼hr., 1 per day, 1160AS); **Venice, ITA** (9-10hr., 3 per day, 880AS); **Rome, ITA** (13¾hr., 2 per day, 1352AS); and **Russia.**

**Franz-Josefs Bahnhof,** IX, Althamstr. 10, handles mostly commuter trains.

**Buses:** City **bus terminals** are located at Wien Mitte/Landstr., Hütteldorf, Heiligenstadt, Floridsdorf, Kagran, Erdberg, and Reumannpl. Domestic **BundesBuses** (info ☎ 71101) run from these stations to local and international destinations. Ticket counter open M-F

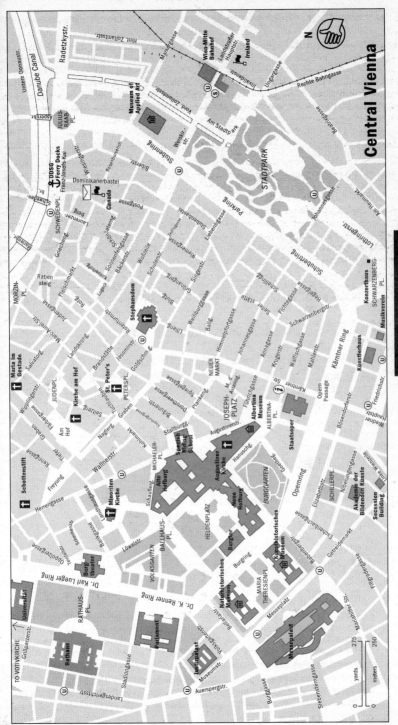

Central Vienna

AUSTRIA

6am-5:50pm, Sa-Su 6am-3:50pm. Many international bus lines also have agencies in the stations, each with different hours.

**Ferries: DDSG Donaureisen,** I, Friedrichstr. 7 (☎58 88 00; www.ddsg-blue-danube.at), offers Danube cruises for 130-690AS. In summer, ferries depart every Su from Reichbrücke (U-1). In summer they also send **hydrofoils** to **Bratislava, SLK** (1¾hr.; May-Sept. 9:30am; 240AS, round-trip 370AS) and **Budapest, HUN** (5-6hr.; June-July 8am, Aug. 9am and 1pm; 780AS, round-trip 1100AS). Eurail and ISIC holders get 20% off travel within Austria, children 10-15 travel at 50% off regular fare.

# ⊏ LOCAL TRANSPORTATION

**Public Transportation:** Info ☎580 00, ☎790 91 05 for point-to-point directions; www.wiennet.at/efa. Excellent **U-Bahn** (subway), **bus, Strassenbahn** (tram), and **S-Bahn** (elevated train) systems cover the city. Tickets 19AS per ride in ticket offices, *Tabak,* or U-Bahn station *Automaten* machines; 22AS on board. 1-day pass 60AS, 3-day "rover" 150AS, 7-day 155AS. The 3-day **Vienna Card** (210AS) includes unlimited transport as well as discounts at museums and sights. Trams and subways stop 12:30-5am, but **nightbuses** run every 30min. along most routes ("N" designates stops; 15AS; day passes not valid). **Maps** (15AS) and nightbus schedules are in U-Bahn stations.

**Taxis:** ☎313 00, 401 00, 601 60, 814 00, and 910 91. Stands at Westbahnhof, Süd-bahnhof, and Karlspl.

**Bike Rental:** At **Wien Nord** and the **Westbahnhof.** 150AS per day, 90AS with train ticket from day of arrival. **Pedal Power,** II, Ausstellungsstr. 3 (☎729 72 34). 60AS per hr., 300AS per half-day.

# 🄴 PRACTICAL INFORMATION

## TOURIST, FINANCIAL, AND LOCAL SERVICES

**Tourist Office: Main Office,** I, Am Albertinaplatz. 1 (www.info.wien.at), 1 block from the Opera House. Books rooms for a 40AS fee plus a deposit. Open daily 9am-7pm. **Branch** at the Westbahnhof train station. **Jugend-Info Wien** (Vienna Youth Information Service; ☎17 99; jiw@blackbox.at), in the underground Bellaria-Passage. Enter at Dr.-Karl-Renner-Ring/Bellaria (tram #1, 2, 46, 49, D, or J) or at the Volkstheater U-Bahn station. Gives out the indispensable *Jugend in Wien* brochure. Open M-Sa noon-7pm.

**Embassies: Australia,** IV, Mattiellistr. 2-4 (☎51 28 58 00), behind Karlskirche. Open M-Th 9am-1pm and 2-5pm, F 9am-1pm. **Canada,** I, Laurenzerburg 2, 3rd fl. (☎531 38, ext. 3000). Open M-F 8:30am-12:30pm and 1:30-3:30pm. **Ireland,** III, Hilton Center, Landstrasser Hauptstr. 21, 6th fl. (☎71 54 24 60; fax 713 60 04). Open M-F 9:30-11:30am and 1:30-4pm. **New Zealand,** XIX, Springsiedleg. 28 (☎318 85 05; fax 318 67 17). **South Africa,** XIX, Sandg. 33 (☎320 64 930). Open M-F 8:30am-noon. **UK,** III, Jauresg. 12 (☎71 61 30; fax 716 13 29 99), near Schloss Belvedere. Open M-F 9am-5pm. **US,** IX, Boltzmanng. 16 (☎313 39; staffed M-F 8:30am-noon and 1-5pm), off Währingerstr. Open M-F 8:30am-noon.

**Currency Exchange:** ATMs have best rates and typically accept Cirrus, Eurocard, MC, and Visa. **Banks** and **airport exchanges** offer official rates (commission on traveler's checks 65AS, cash 10AS). Most open M-W and F 8am-12:30pm and 1:30-3pm, Th until 5:30pm. The **main post office** has excellent rates and an 80AS fee.

**American Express:** I, Kärntnerstr. 21-23, P.O. Box 28, A-1015 (☎515 40), down the street from Stephanspl. Open M-F 9am-5:30pm, Sa 9am-noon. For 24hr. refund service, call 0800 20 68 40.

**Luggage Storage: Lockers** at all train stations 30-50AS per 24hr.

**Bisexual-Gay-Lesbian Services: Rosa Lila Villa,** VI, Linke Wienzeile 102 (☎586 81 50). Counseling, a library, nightlife info. Open M-F 5-8pm.

**Laundromat: Schnell und Sauber,** VII, Westbahnhofstr. 60 (☎524 64 60). U-6: Burgg. Stadthalle. Wash 60AS per 6kg, soap included. Spin-dry 10AS. Open 24hr.

# EMERGENCY AND COMMUNICATIONS

**Medical Assistance: Allgemeines Krankenhaus,** IX, Währinger Gürtel 18-20 (☎404 00 1964). **Emergency care** ☎141. Consulates provide lists of English-speaking physicians. **Fachärzte Lugeck** (☎512 1818) has English speaking doctors and nurses 24hr. Info on **24hr. pharmacies,** ☎15 50.

**Crisis Hotlines: 24hr. Rape Crisis Hotline,** ☎717 19. **Suicide Hotline,** ☎713 33 74.

**Internet Access: Amadeus Media Café,** I, Kärntnerstr. 19, 5th fl. of Steffl department store. Free. Open M-F 9:30am-7pm, Sa 9:30am-5pm. **Libro,** XXII, Donauzentrum (☎202 52 55). Free. Open Su-F 7am-7pm, Sa 9am-5pm.

**Post Office: Hauptpostamt,** I, Fleischmarkt 19. Open 24hr. **Branches** throughout the city and at the train stations; look for the yellow signs with the trumpet logo.

**Postal Codes:** In the 1st district A-1010, in the 2nd A-1020, in the 3rd A-1030, and so on, to the 23rd A-1230.

# ▛ ACCOMMODATIONS

In high-season (June-Sept.), reserve a room at least five days ahead, or before 9am for a shot at a same-day spot. If your choice is full, ask to be put on a waiting list. University dorms convert into hostels from July to September. One-star *Pensionen* in the districts VII, VIII, and IX offer singles from 350AS and doubles from 500AS.

## HOSTELS AND UNIVERSITY DORMS

▓ **Hostel Ruthensteiner (HI),** XV, Robert-Hamerlingg. 24 (☎893 42 02). Turn right as you exit the Westbahnhof, then right on Mariahilferstr, left on Haidmannsg., and right on Robert-Hammerlingg. A top notch hostel. Internet available. Breakfast 29AS. 4-night max. stay. Summer dorms 125AS, winter dorms 145-169AS; doubles 235AS.

▓ **Wombats City Hostel,** XV, Grangasse 6 (☎879 23 36). From Westbahnhof, turn right out of the Ausser Mariahilfer Strasse exit, take the 6th right on Rosinagasse, and take your 2nd left. Nice hostel with helpful staff. **Internet.** Breakfast 35AS. Laundry. 175-245AS.

▓ **Believe It Or Not,** VII, Myrtheng. 10, #14 (☎526 46 58). From Westbahnhof, take U-6 (dir. Heiligenstadt) to Burgg./Stadthalle, then bus #48A (dir. Ring) to Neubaug. Backtrack a block on Burgg. and turn right on Myrtheng. (15min.). Kitchen. Reception 8am-1pm. Lockout 10:30am-12:30pm. Dorms Easter-Oct. 160AS; Nov.-Easter 110AS.

**Myrthengasse (HI),** VII, Myrtheng. 7, opposite Believe It or Not, and **Neustiftgasse (HI),** VII, Neustiftg. 85 (☎523 63 16; hostel@chello.at). Simple Swedish hostels 20min. from the *Innenstadt.* Laundry. Reception at Myrtheng. 7am-11:30pm. Curfew 1am. Lockout 9am-2pm. Jan.-Mar. 18 and Oct. 29-Dec. dorms 170-200AS; rest of year dorms 185-215AS; nonmembers 40AS extra. Breakfast included.

**Hostel Panda,** VII, Kaiserstr. 77, 3rd fl. (☎522 53 53). From Westbahnhof, take tram #5 to Burgg. Fun and eclectic hostel in an old-fashioned Austrian apartment building. Kitchen and TVs. Easter-Oct. 160AS; Nov.-Easter 110AS; 50AS extra for 1 night only.

**Porzellaneum der Wiener Universität,** IX, Porzellang. 30 (☎31 77 28 20), 10min. from the Ring. From Westbahnhof, take tram #5 to Franz-Josefs Bahnhof, then tram D (dir: Südbahnhof) to Fürsteng. From Südbahnhof, take tram D (dir. Nussdorf) to Fürsteng. Open July-Sept. Singles 190AS; doubles 380AS; quads 760AS.

**Rudolfinum,** IV, Mayerhofg. 3 (☎505 53 84). U-1: Taubstummeng. Good location. Laundry 65AS. Open July-Sept. Singles 270AS; doubles 480AS; triples 600AS. Breakfast included.

**Gästehaus Pfeilgasse,** VIII, Pfeilg. 6 (☎401 74; acahot@academia-hotels.co.at). U-2: Lerchenfelderstr. Go right, another right on Lange Gasse, and left on Pfeilg. Open July-Sept. Singles 270AS; doubles 480AS; triples 600AS. Breakfast included.

**Studentenwohnheim der Hochschule für Musik,** I, Johannesg. 8 (☎514 84 48). Fabulous location, cheap meals. Open July-Sept. Singles 430AS, with bath 490AS; doubles 760AS, 940AS; triples 840AS; quads 1000AS; quints 1250AS. Breakfast included.

AUSTRIA

## PENSIONS AND CAMPING

■ **Lauria Apartments,** VII, Kaiserstr. 77, #8 (☎522 25 55). From Südbahnhof, take tram #18 to Westbahnhof, then tram 5 to Burgg. Close to city center. TVs and kitchens. 2-night min. for reservations. Sheets included. Dorms 160AS; singles 480AS; doubles 530-700AS; triples 700-800AS; quads 850-940AS.

**Pension Hargita,** VII, Andreasg. (☎526 1928). U-3: Zieglerg, then head down Mariahilferstr. away from the city center to Andreasg. Comfort in a prime location. Breakfast 40AS. Reception 8am-10pm. Singles 400AS, with shower 450AS; doubles 600AS, with shower 700AS, with bath 800-900AS.

**Wien-West,** Hüttelbergstr. 80 (☎914 23 14), 8km from the center. From U-4: Hütteldorf take bus #14B or #152 (dir. Campingpl.) to Wien West. Crowded, but grassy and pleasant. Laundry, store, and cooking facilities. Reception 7:30am-9:30pm. Closed Feb. July-Aug. 75AS per person, off-season 68AS; 40-45AS per tent, 63-70AS per camper. 2-person cabins 250AS; 4-person 400-440AS.

# ♻ FOOD

In a world full of uncertainty, the Viennese believe the least you can do is face things with a full stomach. Restaurants near **Kärntnerstr.** tend to be pricey—try north of the university near the Votivkirche (U-2: Schottentor), where **Universitätsstr.** and **Währingerstr.** meet, or the area around the **Rechte** and **Linke Wienzeile** near Naschmarkt (U-4: Kettenbrückeg.). The **Naschmarkt** is full of vendors selling delicacies to snack on while shopping at Vienna's premier flea market (Sa-Su only). Supermarkets **Billa, Hofer,** and **Spar** provide the building blocks for cheap, basic meals (most closed Su).

■ **Bizi Pizza,** I, Rotenturmstr. 4, by Stephanspl. Italy's best for a pittance. Pizza (60-75AS) or pasta (65-75AS) whipped up before your eyes. **Branches** at Franz-Josefs-Kai; Mariahilferstr. 22-24; and X, Favoritenstr. 105. All open daily 11am-11:30pm.

**OH Pot, OH Pot,** IX, Währingerstr. 22 (☎319 42 59). U-2: Schottentor. Adorable Spanish joint with amazingly good namesake "pots" (stew-like concoctions of veggie or meat varieties) 72-110AS. Open M-F 11am-midnight, Sa-Su 6pm-midnight.

**Brezelg'wölb,** I, Lederhof 9 (☎533 88 11), near Am Hof. Nestled in a tiny side street, this old-fashioned *Backstube* serves excellent, hearty Viennese cuisine. Lunch around 100AS. Open daily 11:30am-1am, hot food until midnight.

**Hungerkünstler,** VI, Gumpendorfstrasse 48 (☎587 9210). Exceptional food with mellow atmosphere. Main dishes around 90AS. Open daily 11am-2am.

**Zum Mogulhof,** VII, Burggasse 12. (☎526 28 64). Indian specialties with a sitar soundtrack. Main dishes around 90AS. Open daily 11:30am-2:30pm and 6-11:30pm.

**Tunnel,** VIII, Florianig. 39. U-2: Rathaus; with Rathaus behind you, head right on Landesgerichtstr. and left on Florianig. Funky decor, live music, and cheap Austrian, Italian, and Middle Eastern food. Lunch *Menüs* 45AS. 0.5L beer 27AS. Open 10am-2am.

**Rosenberger Markt,** I, Mayserderg. 2 (☎512 34 58), behind the Sacher Hotel. Large and chaotic subterranean buffet with a gargantuan selection of salad (29-64AS), fruit salad, waffles (55AS), antipasti, potatoes, and pasta bars. Open daily 10:30am-11pm.

# ◖ CAFES

The quintessential Viennese coffee is the *Melange;* you can order every kind of coffee as a *Kleiner* (small) or *Grosser* (large), *Brauner* (brown, with a little milk) or *Schwarzer* (black). Vienna's *Konditoreien,* as traditional as its coffee shops, focus on delectable pastries rather than coffee.

■ **Café Hawelka,** I, Dorotheerg. 6 (☎512 82 30), off Grabe, 3 blocks from the Stephansdom. With dusty wallpaper and dark wood, this legendary cafe is glorious. *Melange* 37AS. Open M and W-Sa 8am-2am, Su 4pm-2am.

**Café Central,** I (☎533 37 632), on the corner of Herreng. and Strauchg. inside Palais Ferstel. Theodor Herzl, Sigmund Freud, Vladimir Ilych Lenin, and Leon Trotsky hung out here. Piano 4-7pm. Open M-Sa 8am-8pm, Su 10am-6pm.

**Demel,** I, Kohlmarkt 14 (☎535 17 17), 5min. from the Stephansdom down Graben. The most luxurious *Konditorei*, Demel's was confectioner to the imperial court until the empire dissolved. Fresh chocolate made daily. Confections 40-50AS. Open 10am-7pm.

**Cafe Griensteidl,** I, Michaelerplatz 6 down the street from Café Central toward the Hofburg. Vienna's first literary cafe retains an intellectual flare. Open daily 8am-11:30pm.

# ◉ SIGHTS

Viennese streets are by turns startling, scuzzy, and grandiose; the best way to see the city is simply to get lost. To wander in a more organized manner, get the brochure *Vienna from A to Z* (50AS) or *Walks in Vienna* at the tourist office. **Vienna Bike,** IX, Wasag. (☎319 12 58), runs **cycling tours** (2-3hr.; 280AS). Another great way to see the city is to ride around the Ring on trams #1 or 2.

## THE RINGSTRASSE

In 1857, Emperor Franz Josef commissioned this boulevard, which defines the boundaries of the inner city, to replace the medieval city walls. Freud walked the 5½km circuit of the Ring every day during his lunch break; it took two hours. Extending south from the Danube Canal, **Schottenring** leads to the twin spires of the **Votivkirche,** a neo-Gothic wonder surrounded by rose gardens. The next stretch, **Karl-Lueger Ring,** runs from the **Universität Wien** to **Rathausplatz,** the inner city's largest square. The fluted arches of the Rathaus (town hall) and the Neoclassical, sculpture-adorned Parlament (Parliament) building mark **Dr. Karl-Renner Ring.** On **Burgring,** opposite the Hofberg, stand two of Vienna's largest museums, the **Kunsthistorisches Museum** (Museum of Art History) and the **Naturhistorisches Museum** (Museum of Natural History). From the Burggarten, **Opernring/Kärntnerring** heads to Schwarzenbergstr., marked by an equestrian statue. The **Staatsoper** (State Opera) dominates the Opernring. Former directors include Gustav Mahler and Richard Strauss. *(U-1, U-2, U-4, or tram #1, 2, J, or D: Karlsplatz. Tours July-Aug. 10, 11am, 1, 2, and 3pm; May-June and Sept.-Oct. 1, 2, and 3pm; Nov.-Apr. 2 and 3pm. 60AS, students 45AS.)*

## INSIDE THE RING

The **Innere Stadt** (Inner City), enclosed by the **Ringstrasse** and the **Danube Canal,** is Vienna's social and geographical center. With palaces, theaters, tenements, and toilet bowls designed by master architects, it's a gallery of the history of aesthetics.

### AROUND STEPHANSPLATZ

This active square lies in the shadow of the city's most treasured symbol, the Gothic **Stephan's Cathedral** (Stephansdom), whose smoothly tapered South Tower has become Vienna's emblem. Downstairs in the catacombs, skeletons of plague victims line the walls. The lovely Gruft (vault) stores the Habsburg's entrails. *(U-1 or U-3: Stephansplatz. English Cathedral tours M-Sa 10:30am and 3pm, Su 3pm; 40AS. Spectacular evening tour July-Sept. Sa 7pm; 100AS. South Tower open 9am-5:30pm; 30AS. Vault tours M-Sa 10, 11, 11:30am, 2, 2:30, 3:30, 4, and 4:30pm; Su 2, 2:30, 3:30, 4, and 4:30pm; 50AS.)* Head north up Tegetthoffstr. to the spectacular **New Market** (Neuer Markt), where a graceful fountain and the 17th-century **Church of the Capuchin Friars** (Kapuzinerkirche) await. This church also houses an imperial Vault (Gruft), a series of subterranean rooms containing the remains (minus heart and entrails) of all the Habsburg rulers since 1633. *(Open 9:30am-4pm. 30AS.)*

### FROM STEPHANSPLATZ TO HOHER MARKT

From Stephanspl., continue north up Rotenturmstr., bear left at Fleischmarkt onto Rabensteinerg. and turn left on Seitenstetteng. to reach the Jewish **Stadttempel,** the only one of Vienna's 94 synagogues to escape Nazi destruction during **Kri-**

---

## AUSTRIAN GRAFFITI

Scratched into the stones near the entrance of the Stephansdom is the mysterious abbreviation "O5." It's not a sign of hoodlums up to no good, but rather a reminder of a different kind of subversive activity. During World War II, "O5" was the secret symbol of Austria's resistance movement against the Nazis. The capital letter "O" and the number "5," for the fifth letter of the alphabet, form the first two letters of "Oesterreich"—meaning Austria. Recently the monogram has received new life. Every time alleged Nazi collaborator and ex-president of Austria Kurt Waldheim attends mass, the symbol is highlighted in chalk. Throughout the city, "O5"'s have also been appearing, drawn on the sides of buildings and on flyers, in protest against the Freedom Party of Jörg Haider's anti-immigrant policies.

---

**stallnacht** (Night of Broken Glass) on November 9-10, 1938. *(Seitenstetteng. 2-4. Bring your passport. Open Su-F. Free.)* Continue up Seitenstetteng. to the **Jew Lane** (Judengasse), a remnant of the old Jewish ghetto. Turn left to reach the **Hoher Markt,** the center of town, used as a market and execution site during the Middle Ages. The square's biggest draw is the magnificent *Jugendstil* **Clock** (Ankeruhr), which features 12 historical figures rotating past the old Viennese coat of arms; one 3m-tall figure appears every hour, but show up at noon to see all of them in succession. Peek under the bridge to see depictions of Adam, Eve, an angel, and the devil.

### FROM HOHER MARKT TO AM HOF

From Hoher Markt, follow Wipplingerstr. west (right) to the impressive Baroque facade of the **Bohemian Court Chancellery** (Böhmische Hofkanzlei), the seat of Austria's Constitutional Court. The **Old Town Hall** (Altes Rathaus), directly across the street, houses the **Austrian Resistance Museum** and various temporary exhibits. *(On Friedrich-Schmidt-Pl. ☎ 525 50. Open M, W, and Th 9am-5pm. Tours M, W, and F 1pm. Free.)* Turn left directly after the Chancellery to get to the **Jewish Square** (Judenplatz), the site of the city's first Jewish ghetto. On the other side of the square, Drahtg. opens into the grand courtyard **Am Hof,** a medieval jousting square that now houses the **Church of the Nine Choirs of Angels** (Kirche am Hof), built from 1386-1662.

### FROM AM HOF TO MICHAELERPLATZ

Head west from Am Hof to **Freyung,** an uneven square used for public executions in the Middle Ages. Freyung is linked to **Herrengasse,** home to Vienna's nobility during the Habsburg era, by the **Freyung-Passage.** Head left down Herreng. and turn right on Landhausg. to reach the peaceful **Minoritenplatz,** home of the 14th-century **Minoriten Church.** On the south side of the square stands the **Federal Chancery** (Bundeskanzleramt), where the Congress of Vienna met in 1815. Follow Schauflerg. to the left and you'll run into **Michaelerplatz,** named for the unassuming **Michaelerkirche.** *(Open May-Oct. M-Sa 10:30am-4:30pm, Su 1-5pm. 25AS.)* In the middle of Michaelerpl. are the excavated foundations of Roman Vienna, the military camp called **Vindobona** where Marcus Aurelius penned his *Meditations.* *(Open Sa-Su 11am-1pm. 25AS.)* The square is dominated by the green, neo-Baroque **Michaelertor,** the main gate of the Hofburg.

### THE HOFBURG

*Take tram #1 or 2 to Heldenplatz, or enter through the Michaelertor, in Michaelerplatz.*

The sprawling Hofburg was the Habsburgs' winter residence. Today, it houses the office of the Austrian President. Perhaps the best way to get an overview of the Hofburg is to walk around its perimeter. The **Palace Stables** (Stallburg), accessible via Josefspl., are home to the Royal Lipizzaner stallions of the Spanische Reitschule (Spanish Riding School). *(Mid-Feb. to June and Nov. to mid-Dec. Tu-F 10am-noon; early Feb. M-Sa 10am-noon. Tickets at Josefspl., Gate 2, from 8:30am. 100AS.)* Continue down Augustinerstr. to reach the 14th-century Gothic **Augustinerkirche,** where the hearts of the Habsburgs rest in the Little Heart Crypt. *(Herzgrüftel. Open M-Sa 10am-6pm, Su 1-6pm.)*

The **Albertina** has a film museum and the celebrated **Collection of Graphic Arts,** with an array of old political drawings by Michelangelo, da Vinci, Raphael, and Cézanne. *(Open Tu-Sa 10am-5pm. 70AS.)* In the fortress through the red-and-black-striped **Swiss Gate** (Schweizertor) and up the stairs to the right is the Gothic **Burgkapelle,** home of the heavenly **Vienna Boys' Treasury,** which displays the Habsburg jewels, the crowns of the Holy Roman and Austrian Empires, Imperial christening robes, and a tooth that reportedly belonged to John the Baptist. *(Open W-M 10am-6pm. 80AS, students 50AS. English tour 30AS.)* The passageway at the rear of the fortress opens up onto **Heroes' Square** (Heldenplatz). To the left is the vast **New Fortress** (Neue Burg).

# OUTSIDE THE RING

## KARLSPLATZ AND RESSELPARK

Karlsplatz, within the Resselpark, is home to Vienna's most impressive Baroque church. The **Karlskirche,** in the southeast corner of the park, combines a Neoclassical portico with a Baroque dome. *(Open M-Sa 9-11:30am and 1-5pm, Su 1-5pm. Free.)* The **Museum of the History of Vienna** (Historisches Museum der Stadt Wien), to the left of the Karlskirche, stands across the park from the **Kunsthalle.** Above one side of the park, a terrace links the *Jugendstil* **Karlsplatz Stadtbahn Pavilions,** designed in 1899 by Otto Wagner. Visible to the north across Lothringerstr., between Karlsplatz and the Ring, are the **Künstlerhaus,** the traditional home of Vienna's artistic community, from which the Secessionist artists seceded in 1897 and the **Musikverein,** home of the Vienna Philharmonic Orchestra. Northwest of the Resselpark across Friedrichstr. stands the nemesis of the Künstlerhaus, the **Secession Building,** whose restrained decoration and gilded dome were intended to clash with the Ringstrasse. The Secession exhibits of 1898-1903, which attracted cutting-edge artists, were led by Gustav Klimt. *(To get to Karlsplatz, take U-1, U-2, U-4, or any number of trams to Karlsplatz and exit toward Resselpark.)*

**BELVEDERE PALACE.** (Schloss Belvedere.) The landscaped gardens of the palace, originally the summer residence of Prince Eugene of Savoy, Austria's greatest military hero, lie southeast of the center. The Belvedere, originally only the Untere (Lower) Belvedere, was a gift from the emperor; Eugene later added the more opulent Obere (Upper) Belvedere. The grounds of the palace contain spectacular sphinx-filled gardens and excellent museums. *(Take tram D to Schwarzenberg, tram #71 1 stop past Schwarzenbergpl., or walk from the Südbahnhof.)*

**SCHÖNBRUNN PALACE.** (Schloss Schönbrunn.) Belvedere pales in comparison to the Schönbrunn, the former Imperial summer residence. The frescoes lining the Great Gallery once witnessed the Congress of Vienna. A six-year-old Mozart played in the Hall of Mirrors. The Millions Room wins the prize for excess, with Oriental miniatures covering its walls. Even more impressive than the palace are the classical gardens behind it. *(U-4: Schönbrunn. Open daily Apr.-Oct. 8:30am-5pm; Nov.-Mar. 8:30am-4:30pm. 22-room Imperial Tour 95AS, students 85AS; more worthwhile 44-room Grand Tour 125AS, 110AS. Audio guide included. Gardens open 6am-dusk; free.)*

**CEMETERY.** (Zentralfriedhof.) Life after death doesn't get any better than at this massive cemetery. It is the place to pay respects to your favorite Viennese decomposer: The **Second Gate** (Tor II) leads to Beethoven, Wolf, Strauss, Schönberg, Moser, and an honorary monument to Mozart. (His true resting place is an unmarked pauper's grave in the **Cemetery of St. Mark,** III, Leberstr. 6-8.) The **First Gate** (Tor I) leads to the **Jewish Cemetery** and Arthur Schnitzler's burial plot. Various structures throughout this portion of the burial grounds memorialize the millions slaughtered in Nazi death camps. *(XI, Simmeringer Hauptstr. 234. Take tram #71 from Schwarzenbergpl. or tram #72 from Schlachthausg. The tram stops at each of the 3 main gates; Tor II is the main entrance. Or, take S-7 to "Zentralfriedhof." Open May-Aug. 7am-7pm; Mar.-Apr. and Sept.-Oct. 7am-6pm; Nov.-Feb. 8am-5pm. 38AS.)*

AUSTRIA

# 🏛 MUSEUMS

Vienna owes its selection of masterpieces to the acquisitive Habsburgs, as well as the city's crop of art schools and world-class artists. All city-run museums are free Friday mornings; check out the tourist office's free *Museums* brochure. The **Messepalast**, Museumspl. 1/5, originally the imperial barracks, opens this year as the **MuseumsQuartier.** (☎523 58 81; www.mqw.at). The modern complex houses the **Leopold Museum** (which holds one of Austria's most significant collections, including a number of valuable Schieles), a **Museum of Modern Art**, and a new **Kunsthalle.**

⊠ **Österreichische Gallerie** (Austrian Gallery), III, Prinz-Eugen-Str. 27 (☎79 55 70), in the Belvedere Palace. Walk from the Südbahnhof or take tram D, #566, 567, 666, 668, or 766 to Prinz-Eugen-Str. 19th- to 20th-century Austrian art and famous Secessionist works by Schiele, Kokoschka, and Klimt (*The Kiss*) in the Upper Belvedere. The Lower Belvedere has the **Baroque Museum** and the **Museum of Medieval Austrian Art.** Both open Tu-Su 10am-6pm. Joint ticket 60AS, students 40AS. English tour 11am.

⊠ **Kunsthistorisches Museum** (Museum of Art History; ☎52 52 40), off the Burgring. U-2, 3: Volkstheater. The world's fourth-largest art collection oozes with 15th- to 18th-century Venetian and Flemish paintings as well as ancient art. Open Tu-Su 10am-6pm. 120AS, students 80AS. English tours in summer 11am and 3pm for 30AS.

⊠ **Museum für Völkerkunde,** I, in the Neue Burg on Heldenpl. U-2, 3: Volkstheater. Admire Benin bronzes, West African Dan heads, and Montezuma's feathered headdress, gathered by Habsburg agents during their travels. Art and artifacts from Africa, the Americas, the Middle East, and the Far East. Open W-M 10am-4pm. 50AS, students 30AS. Free May 16, Oct. 26, Dec. 10, and Dec. 24.

**Museum Moderner Kunst** (Museum of Modern Art; ☎317 69 00; www.mmkslw.or.at), has two locations. **Liechtenstein Palace,** IX, Fürsteng. 1, holds works by 20th-century masters—Magritte, Picasso, Miró, Kandinsky, Pollock, Warhol, and Klee. Take tram D (dir: Nussdorf) to Fürsteng. The **20er Haus,** III, Arsenalstr. 1, opposite the Südbahnhof, has influential 1960s and 1970s work and a great sculpture garden stocked with pieces by Giacometti, Moore, and others. Open Tu-W and F-Su 10am-6pm, Th 10am-8pm. Each museum 60AS, students 40AS; both 80AS, 60AS.

**Sigmund Freud Haus,** IX, Bergg. 19 (☎319 15 96), near the Votivkirche. U-2: Schottentor; walk up Währingerstr. to Bergg. Freud's home from 1891 until the *Anschluss.* Open July-Sept. 9am-6pm; Oct.-June 9am-4pm. 60AS, students 40AS. Tours 75AS.

**Secession Building,** I, Friedrichstr. 12 (☎587 53 07), on the western side of Karlspl. Originally built to give the pioneers of modern art space to hang artwork that didn't conform to *Künstlerhaus* standards. Substantial contemporary works are exhibited now. Open Tu-W and F-Su 10am-6pm, Th 10am-8pm. 60AS, students 40AS.

# 🎵 ENTERTAINMENT

**Bundestheaterkasse,** I, Hanuschg. 3, sells tickets for the world-class **Stadtopera.** (☎514 44 29 60. No shorts. ISIC not valid for student discounts. Open M-F 8am-6pm, Sa-Su 9am-noon. Advance tickets 120-2150AS go on sale a week ahead. Standing tickets 30-50AS; arrive 2-3hr. early in high season. Student tickets 30min. before curtain 100-150AS; line up to the left inside the main entrance at least 1hr. before curtain; ISIC not valid.) The world-famous **Wiener Philharmoniker** (Vienna Philharmonic Orchestra) has been directed by the world's finest conductors, including Gustav Mahler and Leonard Bernstein. Performances take place in the **Musikverein,** I, Dumbastr. 3, on the northeast side of Karlspl. (☎505 81 90. Box office open Sept.-June M-F 9am-7:30pm, Sa 9am-5pm. Standing-room tickets available; prices vary.)

Vienna hosts an array of annual **festivals,** mostly musical; check the tourist office's monthly calendar. The **Vienna Festival** (mid-May to mid-June) has a diverse program of exhibitions, plays, and concerts. (☎589 22 22; fax 589 22 49; www.festwochen.or.at.) The Staatsoper and Volkstheater host the annual **Jazzfest Wien** during the first weeks of July. (☎503 56 47; www.jazzfestwien.at.)

# ⚃ NIGHTLIFE

Vienna is a great place to party, whether you're looking for a quiet evening with a glass of wine or a wild night in a disco. U-1, 4: Schwedenplatz is just blocks from the **Bermuda Dreieck** (Triangle), so dubbed both for the three-block area it covers and for the tipsy revelers who lose their way here and never make it home. If your vision isn't foggy yet, head down **Rotenturmstrasse** toward the Stephansdom, or check out the cellar bars of smooth, dark **Bäckerstrasse**. Pick up a copy of the indispensable *Falter* (28AS) for entertainment listings.

⚃ **Cato,** I, Tiefer Graben 19. U-3: Herreng.; walk down to Strauchg., turn right, and continue on to Tiefer Graben. Laid-back, comfortable bar—you'll be singing songs with the friendly clientele before the end of the evening. Open Su-Th 6pm-2am, F-Sa 6pm-4am.

**Chelsea,** VIII, (☎407 93 09), Lerchenfeldergürtel under the U-Bahn between Thaliastr. and Josefstädterstr. The best place in Vienna for underground music, featuring live bands from across Europe. Cover 60-200AS. Open daily 7pm-4am.

**Flex Halle,** I, Donaulände/Augartenbrücke (☎533 7525), near the Schottenring U-Bahn station. Head towards the river and down a narrow staircase. Small, dark, on-the-water club with chemically enhanced dancing. Cover 70-150AS. Open 8pm-4am.

**Why Not,** I, Tiefer Graben 22 (☎535 11 58). Relaxed gay and lesbian bar/disco with both a chill chatting venue and a hip-hop-happening subterranean black-box dance floor. Sa drink specials (43AS). Cover 100AS. Open F-Sa 10pm-4am, Su 9pm-2am.

# ⚄ DAYTRIP FROM VIENNA

## BADEN BEI WIEN

*The Badener Bahn runs from Vienna's Karlspl., to Baden's Josefspl. (1hr., every 15min.); trains also connect Vienna's Südbahnhof and Josefspl. (Both 57AS).*

Only 26km from Vienna, Baden is a favorite weekend spot for Viennese and globe-trotters to rest their weary bones, thanks to the healing effects of its sulfur springs. Since the days of Roman rule, these naturally heated jets springing from the ground have been harnessed and used as therapeutic spas. Although the waters smell like rotten eggs, they're relaxing and healthy. The **Strandbad**, Helenenstr. 19-21, lets you simmer in the pool and cool off in normal chlorinated water. (☎486 70. Open M-F 8:30am-7:30pm, Sa-Su 8am-6:30pm. M-F 67AS, after 1pm 57AS; Sa-Su 79AS, 67AS.) The **Kurdirektion**, Brusattipl. 4 (☎445 31), is the center of all curative spa treatments, with an indoor thermal pool mainly for patients but also open to visitors (72AS). The spa has underwater massage therapy (295AS), sulfur mudbaths (305AS), and regular sport massages (310AS). Also be sure to smell the roses—all 20,000 of them—in Baden's **rosarium**, which extends from the center of town to the 90,000 sq. mile **Wienerwald** (Vienna Woods).

From the train station, walk toward the fountain, keep right, and follow Erzher-zog-Rainer-Ring to the second left (Brusattipl.) to the **tourist office**, Brusattipl. 3 (labeled "Leopoldsbad"). In summer, the office gives free **tours** of the *Altstadt* (1½hr.; M 2pm and Th 10am) and the wine region (2hr.; W 3pm) as well as guided **hiking** and **mountain-bike** tours. (☎418 33 ext. 57; fax 807 33; open May-Oct. M-Sa 9am-6pm, Su and holidays 9am-12:30pm.)

## EISENSTADT

*Trains run indirectly to Vienna Südbahnhof (1½hr., every hr., 76-95AS) via Neusiedl am See. There are direct buses to Wien Mitte (1½hr., every hr. 6am-8:45pm, 95AS).*

Where I wish to live and die.
—Josef Haydn

Haydn, *Heurigen,* and Huns are the three cultural pillars of Burgenland's tiny provincial capital (pop. 11,000). As court composer for the Hungarian Eszterházy princes, Josef Haydn composed some of his greatest melodies here. Built on the footings of a 14th-century fortress, the **Eszterházy Palace** acquired its cheerful hue when the family showed allegiance to Austria by painting the building *Marie Theresien gelb* (Maria Theresian yellow). More recently, the fabulously wealthy Eszterházys leased the family home to the Austrian provincial government, allowing the bureaucrats to occupy 40% of the castle while the family retrenched itself in the remaining 60%. In the **Haydn Hall** (Haydnsaal), the composer conducted the court orchestra from 1761 to 1790. Even today, more often than not the music of Haydn fills the hall. (At the end of Hauptstr. ☎ (02682) 719 3000. 50min. tours Easter-Oct. daily every hour on the hour 9am-5pm; Oct.-Easter M-F 60AS, students and seniors 40AS.) **Haydnmatinees** (☎ (02682) 719 300), held from May to October, feature four fine fellows, bewigged and bejeweled in Baroque costumes of imperial splendor. (Tu and F 11am in the palace. 95AS.) True Haydn enthusiasts can wait for the **Internationale Haydntage**, featuring concerts and operas outdoors near the *Schloss*. In 2001, the festival will begin the second week of September. (Festival office ☎ (02682) 618 660; fax 61805; office@hadynfestival.at. 200-1400AS.)

The **tourist office** is in the right wing of the palace. For a rural living experience, ask about *Beim Bauern Zur Gast*, which lists winegrowers who rent rooms in their houses. (☎ (02682) 67390; fax 67391; tve.info@bnet.at. Call for hours.) The **post office,** on the corner of Pfarrg. and Semmelweise, **exchanges currency** and has good rates for **traveler's checks** (☎ (02682) 62271; open M-F 7am-6pm, Sa 7am-1pm).

# GRAZ                                               ☎ (0)316

Since Charlemagne claimed this strategic gateway to Hungary and Slovenia for his empire in the 9th century, Graz has been fought over by Slavs, Frenchmen, and Russians. The ruins of Graz's own mini mountain, the Schlossberg, commemorate the turmoil. Wonderfully under-touristed, Graz's Old Town (Altstadt) rewards the traveller with every turn of its gently winding streets. This second largest of Austria's cities keeps an energetic nightlife thanks to its 45,000 students at Karl-Franzens-Universität, where the scientist of the stars, Johannes Kepler, hit the books.

**⌨ TRANSPORTATION AND PRACTICAL INFORMATION. Trains** run from the Hauptbahnhof, Europapl. to **Vienna** (3¾hr., 17 per day, 330AS); **Munich, GER** (6¼hr., 9 per day, 720AS); and **Zurich, SWI** (10hr., 4 per day, 1030AS). From the train station, go down Annenstr. and cross the Hauptbrücke (bridge) to reach central Hauptpl. Turn right on Herreng. to reach the **tourist office** at #16. (☎ 807 50; fax 807 55 15; www.graztourismus.at. Open in summer M-F 9am-7pm, Sa 9am-6pm, Su 10am-3pm; off-season M-F 9am-6pm, Sa 9am-3pm, Su 10am-3pm. Tours 2½hr., daily June-Sept. 2:30pm, Oct.-May Sa only, 75AS.) For **internet** access, stop by Cafe Zentral, Andreas-Hofer-Pl. 9, which charges 60AS for one hour. (☎ 83 24 68. Open M-Sa 6:30-10pm.) **Postal code:** A-8010.

**⌨ ACCOMMODATIONS AND FOOD.** The tourist office (see above) lists **private rooms** (150-300AS). From the train station, cross the street, head right on Eggenberger Gürtel, turn left at Josef-Huber-Gasse, and take the first right to reach the **Jugendgästehaus Graz (HI),** Idlhofg. 74. (☎ 71 48 76; fax 71 48 76 88. Laundry. Internet. Reception 7am-11pm. Dorms 220AS; singles 320AS; doubles 540AS. Overflow mattresses 155AS. Breakfast included.) To get to **Camping Central,** Martinhofstr. 3, from the train station, take tram #3 or 6 to Jakominipl. then take bus #32 to Badstrassgang (20min.), turn right at the Billa supermarket and walk up the road. (☎ (0676) 378 51 02. Laundry 70AS. Reception 8am-10pm. Open Apr.-Oct. 155AS includes tent site, shower and use of pool; additional adults 80AS.)

Cheap student hangouts line **Zinzendorfg.** near the university, while markets run along **Rösselmühlgass,** and **Jakoministr. Kebap Haus,** Jakoministr. 16, is a superior Turkish restaurant with delicious pitas and Mediterranean pizza. (☎ 81 10 06. Open M-Sa 11am-midnight.) **Mangolds,** Griesgasse 11, serves fresh vegetarian dishes, desserts, and has a salad bar. (☎ 718 002. Open M-F 11am-8pm, Sa 11am-4pm.)

**SIGHTS AND ENTERTAINMENT.** Napoleon didn't manage to capture Graz's **Schlossberg** (castle hill), which had already withstood substantial battering by Ottoman Turks, until *after* he conquered the rest of Austria—when he proceeded to raze it in. As you exit the tourist office, walk left up Herreng./Sackstr. to Schlossbergpl. and climb the **Schlossstiege,** zigzagging stone steps built by Russian prisoners during World War I, to the top of the Schlossberg (today a carefully tended park) for sweeping views of the vast plain surrounding Graz. The **Landhaus,** housing the tourist office below, is a sight in itself, remodeled by architect Domenico dell'Allio in 1557 in Lombard style. The **Provincial Arsenal** (Landeszeughaus) Herreng. 16, details the history of the arsenal and the Ottoman Turk attacks. (Open Apr.-Oct. M-F 9am-5pm, Sa-Su 9am-1pm. 70AS, students 50AS.) The solemn 17th-century Habsburg **Mausoleum,** on Burgg., is one of the finest examples of Austrian Mannerism. The domed tomb holds the remains of Ferdinand II in the underground chamber. (Open M-Sa 10am-noon and 1:30-3:30pm. 10AS.)

The hub of after-hours activity is the so-called **Bermuda Triangle,** an area of the old city behind Hauptpl. and bordered by Mehlpl., Färberg., and Prokopiag. **Tom's Bierklinik,** Färberg. 1, has the largest stock of international beers in Austria. (☎ 84 51 74. Open M-Sa 8pm-4am.)

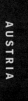

AUSTRIA

# BELARUS
# (БЕЛАРУСЬ)

Of the former Soviet Republics, Belarus has been the most willing to take refuge in the arms of Mother Russia. A collection of sprawling urban landscapes surrounded by unspoiled villages, the country has become the unwanted stepchild of its larger neighbor—while Belarus is heavily Russified, Russia is wary of taking on the burden of supporting its poorer neighbor. For those willing to endure the difficulties of travel in Belarus, the country presents a look at a people in transition; others should avoid its trials in favor of countries better prepared for tourists.

## BELARUS AT A GLANCE

**OFFICIAL NAME:** Republic of Belarus

**CAPITAL:** Minsk (pop. 1,666,000)

**POPULATION:** 10,400,000 (78% Belarussian, 13% Russian, 4% Polish, 3% Ukrainian, 2% other)

**LANGUAGE:** Belarussian, Russian

**CURRENCY:** Belarussian ruble (BR)

**RELIGION:** 80% Eastern Orthodox

**LAND AREA:** 207,600 km²

**CLIMATE:** Continental and maritime

**GEOGRAPHY:** Plains, marshes

**BORDERS:** Latvia, Lithuania, Poland, Russia, Ukraine

**ECONOMY:** 20% Agriculture, 43% Industry, 37% Services

**GDP:** $5,200 per capita

**EMERGENCY PHONE NUMBERS:** Fire 01, Police 02, Emergency 03

**COUNTRY CODE:** 375

**INTERNATIONAL DIALING PREFIX:** 810

## LANGUAGE

Most Belarussians speak mostly **Russian** and only very rarely Belarussian (see **The Cyrillic Alphabet,** p. 15, and the **Russian Glossary,** p. 597). In Hrodna and Brest, **Polish** is common. Some students will also speak **German** or **English.** Most street and place names have been converted into Belarussian since independence, but locals still use the old Russian versions, which is cause for much confusion. If you can handle substituting the Belarussian "i" for the Russian "и" and other minor spelling changes, you'll be fine. The only major difference is that the Cyrillic letter "г," which is pronounced "g" in Russian, is transliterated as "h" in Belarussian. *Let's Go* lists place names in Belarussian in deference to the official line, but in order to be understood, you'll have to replace "h" with "g" ("Hrodna" is more commonly pronounced "Grodno"). Common words in *Let's Go* include: *avtovakzal* (bus station; автовакзал), *gastsinitsa* (hotel; гасцініца), *sobor* (cathedral; собор), *vakzal* (station; вакзал), and *zamak* (castle; замак).

## NATIONAL HOLIDAYS IN 2001

**January 1** New Year

**January 7** Orthodox Christmas

**March 8** International Women's Day

**March 15** Constitution Day

**April 13** Good Friday

**April 15-16** Easter

**May 1** Labor Day

**May 9** Victory Day and Mother's day

**June 4** Radunitsa (Holy Trinity)

**July 3** Independence Day

**November 2** Remembrance Day

**November 7** October Revolution Day

**December 25** Catholic Christmas

# WORLDWIDE CALLING MADE EASY

## The MCI WorldCom Card, designed specifically to keep you in touch with the people that matter the most to you.

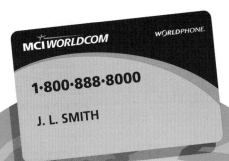

MCI WORLDCOM    WORLDPHONE.

1·800·888·8000

J. L. SMITH

**www.wcom.com/worldphone**

Please tear off this card and keep it in your wallet as a reference guide for convenient U.S. and worldwide calling with the MCI WorldCom Card.

---

## HOW TO MAKE CALLS USING YOUR MCI WORLDCOM CARD

> **When calling from the U.S., Puerto Rico, the U.S. Virgin Islands or Canada** to virtually anywhere in the world:
1. Dial 1-800-888-8000
2. Enter your card number + PIN, listen for the dial tone
3. Dial the number you are calling :
   **Domestic Calls:** Area Code + Phone number
   **International Calls:**
   011+ Country Code + City Code + Phone Number

> **When calling from outside the U.S.,** use WorldPhone from over 125 countries and places worldwide:
1. Dial the WorldPhone toll-free access number of the country you are calling from.
2. Follow the voice instructions or hold for a WorldPhone operator to complete the call.

> **For calls from your hotel:**
1. Obtain an outside line.
2. Follow the instructions above on how to place a call.
   **Note:** If your hotel blocks the use of your MCI WorldCom Card, you may have to use an alternative location to place your call.

### RECEIVING INTERNATIONAL COLLECT CALLS*
Have family and friends call you collect at home using WorldPhone Service and pay the same low rate as if you called them.
1. Provide them with the WorldPhone access number for the country they are calling from (In the U.S., 1-800-888-8000; for international access numbers see reverse side).
2. Have them dial that access number, wait for an operator, and ask to call you collect at your home number.

*\* For U.S. based customers only.*

## START USING YOUR MCI WORLDCOM CARD TODAY. MCI WORLDCOM STEPSAVERS℠
Get the same low rate per country as on calls from home, when you:

1. **Receive international collect calls to your home** using WorldPhone access numbers

2. **Make international calls with your MCI WorldCom Card** from the U.S.*

3. **Call back to anywhere in the U.S. from Abroad** using your MCI WorldCom Card and WorldPhone access numbers.

*\* An additional charge applies to calls from U.S. pay phones.*

**WorldPhone Overseas Laptop Connection Tips —**
Visit our website, www.wcom.com/worldphone, to learn how to access the Internet and email via your laptop when traveling abroad using the MCI WorldCom Card and WorldPhone access numbers.

**Travelers Assist®** — When you are overseas, get emergency interpretation assistance and local medical, legal, and entertainment referrals. Simply dial the country's toll-free access number.

**Planning a Trip?**—Call the WorldPhone customer service hotline at 1-800-736-1828 for new and updated country access availability or visit our website:

**www.wcom.com/worldphone**

## MCI WorldCom Worldphone Access Numbers

*Easy Worldwide Calling*

**MCI WORLDCOM.**

# The MCI WorldCom Card.
## The easy way to call
## when traveling worldwide.

## The MCI WorldCom Card gives you...

- Access to the US and other countries worldwide.
- Customer Service 24 hours a day
- Operators who speak your language
- Great MCI WorldCom rates and no sign-up fees

**For more information or
to apply for a Card call:**
## 1-800-955-0925

**Outside the U.S., call
MCI WorldCom collect
(reverse charge) at:**
## 1-712-943-6839

| COUNTRY | WORLDPHONE TOLL-FREE ACCESS # |
|---|---|
| Argentina (CC) | |
| Using Telefonica | 0800-222-6249 |
| Using Telecom | 0800-555-1002 |
| Australia (CC) ♦ | |
| Using OPTUS | 1-800-551-111 |
| Using TELSTRA | 1-800-881-100 |
| Austria (CC) ♦ | 0800-200-235 |
| Bahamas (CC) + | 1-800-888-8000 |
| Belgium (CC) ♦ | 0800-10012 |
| Bermuda (CC) + | 1-800-888-8000 |
| Bolivia (CC) ♦ | 0-800-2222 |
| Brazil (CC) | 000-8012 |
| British Virgin Islands + | 1-800-888-8000 |
| Canada (CC) ♦ | 1-800-888-8000 |
| Cayman Islands + | 1-800-888-8000 |
| Chile (CC) | |
| Using CTC | 800-207-300 |
| Using ENTEL | 800-360-180 |
| China ♦ | 108-12 |
| Mandarin Speaking Operator | 108-17 |
| Colombia (CC) ♦ | 980-9-16-0001 |
| Collect Access in Spanish | 980-9-16-1111 |
| Costa Rica ♦ | 0800-012-2222 |
| Czech Republic (CC) ♦ | 00-42-000112 |
| Denmark (CC ) ♦ | 8001-0022 |
| Dominica+ | 1-800-888-8000 |
| Dominican Republic (CC) + | |
| Collect Access | 1-800-888-8000 |
| Collect Access in Spanish | 1121 |

| COUNTRY | ACCESS # |
|---|---|
| Ecuador (CC) + | 999-170 |
| El Salvador (CC) | 800-1767 |
| Finland (CC) ♦ | 08001-102-80 |
| France (CC) ♦ | 0-800-99-0019 |
| French Guiana (CC) | 0-800-99-0019 |
| Germany (CC) | 0800-888-8000 |
| Greece (CC) ♦ | 00-800-1211 |
| Guam (CC) | 1-800-888-8000 |
| Guatemala (CC) ♦ | 99-99-189 |
| Haiti + | |
| Collect Access | 193 |
| Collect access in Creole | 190 |
| Honduras + | 8000-122 |
| Hong Kong (CC) | 800-96-1121 |
| Hungary (CC) ♦ | 06 * -800-01411 |
| India (CC) | 000-127 |
| Collect access | 000-126 |
| Ireland (CC) | 1-800-55-1001 |
| Israel (CC) | 1-800-920-2727 |
| Italy (CC) ♦ | 172-1022 |
| Jamaica + | |
| Collect Access | 1-800-888-8000 |
| From pay phones | #2 |
| Japan (CC) ♦ | |
| Using KDD | 00539-121 ♦ |
| Using IDC | 0066-55-121 |
| Using JT | 0044-11-121 |

| COUNTRY | ACCESS # |
|---|---|
| Korea (CC) | |
| To call using KT | 00729-14 |
| Using DACOM | 00309-12 |
| Phone Booths + | |
| Press red button ,03,then* | |
| Military Bases | 550-2255 |
| Luxembourg (CC) | 8002-0112 |
| Malaysia (CC) ♦ | 1-800-80-0012 |
| Mexico (CC) | 01-800-021-8000 |
| Monaco (CC) ♦ | 800-90-019 |
| Netherlands (CC) ♦ | 0800-022-91-22 |
| New Zealand (CC) | 000-912 |
| Nicaragua (CC) | 166 |
| Norway (CC) ♦ | 800-19912 |
| Panama | 00800-001-0108 |
| Philippines (CC) ♦ | |
| Using PLDT | 105-14 |
| Filipino speaking operator | 105-15 |
| Using Bayantel | 1237-14 |
| Using Bayantel (Filipino) | 1237-77 |
| Using ETPI (English) | 1066-14 |
| Poland (CC) + | 800-111-21-22 |
| Portugal (CC) + | 800-800-123 |
| Romania (CC) + | 01-800-1800 |
| Russia (CC) + ♦ | |
| Russian speaking operator | |
| | 747-3320 |
| Using Rostelcom | 747-3322 |
| Using Sovintel | 960-2222 |
| Saudi Arabia (CC) | 1-800-11 |

| COUNTRY | WORLDPHONE TOLL-FREE ACCESS # |
|---|---|
| Singapore (CC) | 8000-112-112 |
| Slovak Republic (CC) | 08000-00112 |
| South Africa (CC) | 0800-99-0011 |
| Spain (CC) | 900-99-0014 |
| St. Lucia + | 1-800-888-8000 |
| Sweden (CC) ♦ | 020-795-922 |
| Switzerland (CC) ♦ | 0800-89-0222 |
| Taiwan (CC) ♦ | 0080-13-4567 |
| Thailand (CC) | 001-999-1-2001 |
| Turkey (CC) ♦ | 00-8001-1177 |
| United Kingdom (CC) | |
| Using BT | 0800-89-0222 |
| Using C& W | 0500-89-0222 |
| Venezuela (CC) + ♦ | 800-1114-0 |
| Vietnam + ● | 1201-1022 |

**KEY**
**Note:** Automation available from most locations. Countries where automation is not yet available are shown in *Italic*

(CC) Country-to-country calling available.

♦ Limited availability.

★ Not available from public pay phones.

● Public phones may require deposit of coin or phone card for dial tone.

● Local service fee in U.S. currency required to complete call.

▶ Regulation does not permit Intra-Japan Calls.

✦ Wait for second dial tone.

■ Local surcharge may apply.

**Hint:** For Puerto Rico and Caribbean Islands not listed above, you can use 1-800-888-8000 as the WorldPhone access number.

# TRAVELING ESSENTIALS

To visit Belarus, you must secure an invitation and a visa—an expensive and head-spinning process. If you have an acquaintance in Belarus who can provide you with an official invitation, you may obtain a 90-day single-entry (5-day service US$50; next-day US$100) or multiple-entry (5-day processing US$170; next day $340) visa at an embassy or consulate (see **Embassies and Consulates,** p. 18). Together with the visa application and fee (by personal check or money order), you must submit your passport and one photograph. For mail orders include a self-addressed stamped envelope. Those without Belarussian friends can turn to **Russia House** (see **Russia Essentials,** p. 525), which will get you an invitation and visa in five business days (US$225; 3-day processing $275; next-day $325). **Host Families Association (HOFA)** provides invitations for its guests (see **Russia Essentials,** p. 600). You may also obtain an invitation by planning your trip through a **Belintourist** office. They will provide you with documentation after you have pre-paid all your hotel stays. Transit visas (US$20-30), valid for 48 hours, are issued at a consulate and theoretically at the border, but avoid the latter option anywhere other than Brest. Your train may leave while you're still outside getting your visa. At some Belarussian embassies and consulates, such as those in Daugavpils and Kiev, transit visas may be cheaper.

# TRANSPORTATION

**BY PLANE.** You can fly into Minsk on **Belavia,** Belarus's national airline (if you trust the old planes) from many European capitals. **LOT** also flies from Warsaw, and

**Lufthansa** has daily direct flights from Frankfurt. Leaving Belarus by air can be a nightmare, as customs officials are wont to rip through your bags.

**BY TRAIN.** Be aware that some international train tickets must be paid partly in US dollars and partly in Belarussian rubles. All immigration and customs are done on the trains. Tickets for same-day trains within Belarus are purchased at the station. Information booths in the stations charge 5BR per inquiry. It's better to ask a cashier (see p. 527 for more on post-Soviet train travel).

**BY BUS.** For city buses, buy tickets at a kiosk (or from the driver for a surcharge) and punch them on board.

# TOURIST SERVICES AND MONEY

**INFLATION** Inflation is rampant in Belarus, so we list many prices in US$. Posted prices in Belarus drop the final three zeros and all prices in this chapter follow that convention. Bills printed in 2000 and later also omit the zeros, however the old bills remain in circulation and are difficult to distinguish from the new ones. Try to find a local to help you tell the difference.

| CURRENCY | | |
|---|---|---|
| US$1 = 930BR (BELARUSSIAN RUBLES) | 1000BR = US$1.10 | |
| CDN$1 = 630BR | 1000BR = CDN$1.60 | |
| UK£1 = 1400BR | 1000BR = UK£0.71 | |
| IR£1 = 1000BR | 1000BR = IR£1 | |
| AUS$1 = 540BR | 1000BR = AUS$1.85 | |
| NZ$1 = 400BR | 1000BR = NZ$2.50 | |
| SAR 1 = 130BR | 1000BR = SAR 7.70 | |
| DM 1 = 420BR | 1000BR = DM 2.40 | |

**Belintourist** (Белінтуріст) is all that's left of the once omnipotent Intourist. It varies from mostly helpful to merely rubble, but is often the only resource. The staff hands out brochures and sometimes books train tickets, but does not cater to budget travelers. Hotel Belarus and Hotel Yubilyenaya in Minsk have **private travel agencies.** Be sure to carry plenty of hard **cash** when not in a potential bribe situation. US dollars, Deutschmarks, and Russian rubles are preferred; you'll have a great deal of trouble exchanging other currencies, even British pounds. Belarussian **inflation** is the highest in the former USSR at over 110%—expect exchange rates to change rapidly and prices quoted in Belarussian rubles to more than double over the next year. There are no **ATMs** aside from one or two that have recently popped up in Minsk, and most bank clerks leaf through their English dictionaries at the mention of "traveler's checks." Some hotels accept **credit cards,** mostly AmEx and Visa. Don't leave the country with Belarussian rubles; they're impossible to exchange abroad.

## STICKY FINGERS AND GREASY PALMS For

staid Westerners accustomed to price tags, Belarus's anything-goes bargaining practices can be tough to get used to. Among the most common practices is the *vzyat* (bribe). Do your best to avoid this: cross borders in the daytime, travel in train compartments with locals, and make sure your documents are in line before departing. Given enough time, though, even the most cautious will end up in a situation where cash is the only method of payment and receipts are not available. The uninitiated wonder how to price in such situations, but the answer is simple: supply and demand. The man with the semi-automatic weapon demands money and you supply all you have. The key is to limit the supply—as a rule, do not carry wads of cash. US$20 is usually plenty, since that's more than enough to buy a night's supply of beer.

BELARUS

# HEALTH AND SAFETY

Belarus was more affected by the 1986 **Chernobyl** accident than any other region. The faulty reactor was situated in Ukraine, just 12km south of the Belarussian border, and winds happened to blow north for the first six days after the explosion. An area of approximately 1200 sq. km just north of Chernobyl has been completely evacuated because of high concentrations of strontium-90, plutonium-239/240, and cesium-137. Today, more than 10 years after the tragedy, it is safe to travel through the formerly contaminated areas; experts say that a week's stay there is no worse than receiving an X-ray. None of the cities *Let's Go* covers are in affected regions. There's no need to panic, but it is important to be aware of a few safety considerations. Avoid inexpensive **dairy products,** which probably come from contaminated areas—opt instead for something German or Dutch—and stay away from **mushrooms** and **berries,** which tend to collect radioactivity. Drink only bottled water; **tap water,** especially in the southeast, may be contaminated. You will probably find plain old flat bottled water hard to come by, so get used to burping from the fizz.

Your embassy is a better bet than the police in an emergency—especially since some police have been known to deal with the mafia and may not be helpful to foreigners unless bribed. Although streets are usually safe and well lit, it is generally not a good idea to go out alone after dark. For children under 18 years old unaccompanied by an adult, there is a **mandatory 11pm curfew.** It's a good idea to stay clear of dodgy nightclubs, which are mostly run by the mafia, especially if you aren't dressed to the nines. **Toilet paper** is available in most supermarkets, making its absence from public toilets all the more befuddling. **Condoms** and **feminine hygiene** supplies from the West are becoming available.

# ACCOMMODATIONS AND CAMPING

Remember to keep all receipts from hotels; you just might have to show them to the authorities to avoid fines when leaving Belarus. **Hotels** have three rates—very cheap for Belarussians, outrageous for foreigners, and in-between for CIS member countries. The desk clerks will ask where you are from and request your passport, making it impossible to pass as a native. Some **private hotels** don't accept foreigners at all, but those that do are usually much cheaper and friendlier than the Soviet dinosaurs. To find a **private room,** look around for postings at train stations, or ask taxi drivers, who may know of a lead. The *babushki* at train stations might quote high prices, but they'll be willing to feed and house you for US$10 or less.

# KEEPING IN TOUCH

Avoid the **mail** system at all costs; almost everything is opened and read by the authorities. **Local calls** require tokens sold at kiosks or magnetic cards, available at the post office, train station, and some hotels (200-500BR). **International calls** must be placed at the telephone office and paid for in advance, in cash. Write down the number you're calling and say "Ya ha-tchoo po-ZVAH-neet" ("I'd like to call...") followed by the name of the country; pay with exact change. You will be told the number of a phone booth, which you then enter to make your call. Calls to the US and Western Europe US$1-3 per minute. Return to the kiosk to pick up change. International access numbers include: **AT&T,** ☎8, 80 01 01; **Australia Direct** ☎810; **BT Direct,** ☎88 00 44; **Canada Direct** ☎8, 10 80 01 11; **MCI,** ☎8, 80 01 03; **Sprint** ☎8, 80 01 02 from Grodna, Brest, Minsk, and Vitebsk; ☎8, 10 80 01 02 from Gomel and Mogilev.

# MINSK (MIHCK)                ☎(8)172

If you're looking for a true Soviet city, skip Moscow and head to Minsk (pop. 1.7 million), where the fall of communism has led to a reluctant shuffle, rather than an enthusiastic gallop west. A handful of streets have been renamed, but Lenin's statue still presides over Independence Square. With imaginary political reforms and con-

After years of telephone chaos, phone numbers in Minsk have finally been standardized. All numbers *should* have 7 digits and start with a "2," so if you come across a 6-digit number, add an initial "2." Some pay phones can still only handle 6-digits, however, so if you can't get through, drop the first "2."

crete everywhere, not to mention the omnipresent police, everyone is asking if the government is really giving Minsk a new face or just a new facade.

## ORIENTATION

The center of town lies in the 3km between northeast **pl. Peramohi** (Перамогі) and southwest **pl. Nezalezhnastsi** (Незалежнасці; Independence Square), with **pr. Frantsishka Skoriny** (Францішка Скорины) running between the two. **Pr. Masherava** (Машэрава), which turns into **vul. Lenina** (Леніна), runs perpendicular to pr. F. Skoriny. The **Svislac River** divides the city, with most of the attractions on the southwest bank. The **train station** sits behind **Privakzalnaya pl.** (Прівакзальная)—walk up vul. Leningradskaya and go left on Svyardlova (Свярдлова) to reach pl. Nezalezhnastsi. **Jaywalking** is illegal and carries a moderate fine, so always use the underpasses to cross major streets—it's best to avoid the Minsk police.

## TRANSPORTATION

**Flights:** The main airport, **Minsk II** (☎279 23 33), is 40km east of the city. Take bus #300 from Avtovakzal Vostochny (40min., every hr., 200BR). If you don't speak Russian, a taxi will cost US$25-40.

**Trains: Tsentralny Vakzal** (Центральны Вакзал; ☎220 99 89 and 596 54 10), Privakzalnaya pl. Same-day local tickets sold on 1st floor; international tickets on 2nd floor. For info, go to window #13 on the 2nd floor with the "даведка справка" *(davedka spravka)* sign. Purchase advance tickets at the Belintourist office next to Hotel Yubilaynaya (see **Tourist Offices,** below). Tickets through Poland must be paid for in both US dollars and BR. To: **Brest** (5hr., 3 per day, *coupé* US$1); **Vilnius, LIT** (4½hr., 3 per day, *coupé* US$5-14); **Warsaw, POL** (12hr., 3-5 per day, US$13 *and* 12,500BR); **Berlin, GER** (1 per day, US$40 *and* 22,000BR); **Kyiv, UKR** (14hr., 1-3 per day, *coupé* US$12); **Moscow, RUS** (14hr., 14-17 per day, *coupé* $20); **Prague, CZR** (1 per day, US$60 *and* 12,500BR); and **St. Petersburg, RUS** (3 per day, *coupé* US$14).

**Buses: Avtovakzal Tsentralni** (Автовакзал Центральны), vul. Babruyskaya 6 (Бабруйская; ☎227 78 20; advance booking ☎229 44 44; info ☎004). To the right of the train station. To: **Białystok, POL** (3 per day, US$11.50), **Prague, CZR** (6 per day, US$20); and **Vilnius, LIT** (4hr., 4 per day, US$11.50).

**Public Transportation:** The **Metro's** 2 lines cover downtown; they cross at Kastrychniskaya (Кастрычніская). Trains run 6am-1am (20BR). While the new stop names are announced and used on maps, many platforms still bear the old signs. Buses, trolleys, and trams run 5:35am-12:55am (20BR). Pick up a ticket and **map** at a kiosk.

**Taxis:** ☎061 and 081. Can be found at stands throughout the city. Generally safe and somewhat reasonable. Do not pay more than US$2 for a 10min. ride.

## PRACTICAL INFORMATION

**Tourist Office: Belintourist** (Белінтуріст), pr. Masherava 19 (☎226 94 85; fax 226 94 21; root@beltour.minsk.by). Next to Gastsinitsa Yubileynaya. Metro: Nemiga. A remnant of Intourist, but working hard to please. Visa registration and extension, sells plane and train tickets, and arranges tours of Minsk. English spoken. Open M-F 8am-5:30pm.

**Passport Office:** In theory, all foreigners visiting Minsk must **register** their passports at **OVIR** (ОВИР), pr. F. Skoriny 8, room 132 (☎220 29 82 and 220 15 05), although some short-term visitors (under 1 week) do not need to do so. Visa extensions are very hard to obtain; ask Belintourist (see above) for help if you're bent on trying.

0          200 yards
0          200 meters

N

**Svislac**

*Peramahi Park*

Kanatny

Krapotkina

Very Haruzay

Maksima Bagdanovica

Kulbysava

**Komarovski Market**

TO (2km)

**PLOSHCHA YAKUBA KOLASA**
**Philharmonic**

Varvaseni

Varvaseni

Kamunistycnaya

Starazouskaia

Zaslauskaya

Melnikayte

Pr. Masherava

**Jewish Memorial Stone**

**United States**

**Opera and Ballet**

Maksima Bagdanovica

Kulbysava

Kisyaleva

Kamunistyenaya

Pr. Franciska Skaryny

**Hall of Chamber Music**

**PLOSHCHA PERAMOHI**

**PL. PERAMOHI**

Tankavaya

**FRUZENSKAYA**

Spalernaya

**Cathedral of St. Peter and Paul**

Astrouskaha

**NYAMINA**

**Museum of the Great Patriotic War**

*Jonki Kupaly Park*

**Circus**

Haradski Val

Karalya

Kalektarnaya

Nyamiha

Revaliucinaya

Internacianalnaya

**Cathedral of the Holy Spirit**

Lenina

**PL. SVABODY**

**PL. KASTRYCNITSKAYA**

**KUPAALAUSKAYA/ KASTRYCHNITSKAYA (JUNCTION)**

Kirava

*Gorky Park*

Frunse

Persamayskaya

Syrvonaarmeyskaya

Pulihava

Nyamiha

Mrasnikova

Bersana

**Church of St. Simon**

**PL. NEZALEZNASCI**

**PLOSHCHA NEZALEZHNASTSI**

Leningradskaya

Pr. Frantsishka Skaryny

Karla Marxa

**Fine Arts Museum**

**United Kingdom**

Enfalsa

**National History and Culture Museum**

Kirava

*Stad. Dynamo*

**PERSHAMASKAYA**

Svislac

Ulyanaiskaya

Kastrysniskaya

**PRIVAKZALNAYA PL.**

Talstoia

Druznaya

Sverdlova

Babruskaya

Rabkorauskaya

**INSTITUT KULTURY**

Mahileuskaya

Partizansky

Oranskaya

## Central Minsk

🏠 ACCOMMODATIONS

Gostinitsa Druzhba, **1**
Gostinitsa Minsk, **2**
Gostinitsa Svisloch, **3**

BELARUS

**Embassies: Russia,** vul. Staravilenskaya 48 (Старавіленская; ☎250 36 65; fax 250 36 64). **UK,** vul. Karla Marxa 37 (Карла Маркса; ☎229 23 03; fax 229 23 06). Open M-F 9am-1pm. **Ukraine,** vul. Kirava 17, #306 (☎227 27 96; fax 227 28 61). **US,** vul. Staravilenskaya 46 (☎231 50 00; fax 284 78 53). Open M-F 9am-5:30pm.

**Currency Exchange:** Follow the "Абмен Валюты" signs, but do not be deceived by the posted hours or services—they're completely random. Most exchange kiosks along Masherava pr. now accept AmEx/Thomas Cook **traveler's checks.** The exchange office in **Gastsinitsa Yubileynaya** provides US$ advances on MC or Visa for a 4% commission and cashes Thomas Cook traveler's checks (open 24hr.), as does **Prior Bank** (Пріор Банк), vul. V. Kharyzhan 3a (Харыжан; ☎269 09 64). Open M-F 9am-6pm.

**Luggage Storage:** In the basement of the train station. Small bags 170BR. Large bags must be stored at an airplane hangar in the park 50m to the left of the station.

**Laundromat: Khimchistka Taidi** (Хімчістка Тайді), vul. Masherava 1 (Машерава; ☎226 99 56). US$0.50 per load. Open daily 10am-7pm.

**24hr. Pharmacy: Aptetsniykiosk** (Аптецнійкіоск; ☎220 99 89), train station, 2nd fl.

**Telephones:** Telephones take *zhetony* (жетоны; tokens; 80BR) and phone cards (200-500BR); both are sold at kiosks. **Central Telegraph Office,** to the left upon entering the post office. All international calls must be made here. Open daily 8am-11pm.

**Internet Access:** At the post office, to the right of the main entrance. By appointment before 4pm; long lines after 4pm. US$1 per hr. Open daily 8am-8pm.

**Post Office:** Pr. F. Skoriny 10 (☎227 15 67). Open daily 8am-8pm.

**Postal code:** 220 050.

## ACCOMMODATIONS AND FOOD

**Private rooms** are the best option; taxi drivers may know about them. Ask how far the room is from the center and agree on a price (approx. US$10) beforehand. **Gastsinitsa Svisloch** (Гасцініца Свіслочь), vul. Kirava 13, offers comfortable rooms in a good location. Bring your own toilet paper. From the train station, walk up vul. Kirava (the road 1 block to the right of McDonald's); the hotel is 3 blocks up on the left. (☎220 97 83. M-red: pl. Nezalezhnastsi. Singles 13,720BR, with shower 19,600BR.) **Gastsinitsa Druzhba** (Дружба), vul. Tolbukhina 3, has well-worn communal bathrooms without hot water, but there's no beating the price. Exiting the Metro station, take a right on the road in front of you that runs perpendicular to the main road. Reserve in advance. (☎266 24 81. M-red: Park Chelyuskintsev (Парк Челюскинцев). Bed in a triple US$8.) To satisfy that craving for Czech cuisine, head to **Restaran Novolune** (Рэстаран Новолуне), vul. Zakharava 31 (Захарава). Going up pr. Skaryny, take a right on vul. Zakharova at pl. Peramohi and walk 500m. (☎236 74 55. M-red: pl. Peramohi (пл. Перамогі). Meals US$3-8. Open daily noon-midnight.) **Patio Pizza** (Патіо-Пізза), pr. Skoriny 22, serves up the same great thin-crust pizza as its 2 Moscow cousins for 4-10,000BR. (☎227 17 91. M-red: pl. Peramohi. Open daily noon-midnight. AmEx/MC/Visa.) **Capriccio** (Каприччо), pr. F. Skoriny 23, is the hippest cafe in town. Students mingle with businessmen conducting deals over locally famous sweets. Don't forget to collect your cup-and-plate deposit before leaving. (Open M-Sa 9am-9pm, Su 9am-7pm.)

## SIGHTS

More than 80% of the buildings and 60% of the population—including almost all of Minsk's 300,000 Jews—were obliterated between 1941 and 1944. The city was rebuilt in grand Stalinist style, with gargantuan buildings and wide boulevards. Today the utter Sovietness emanating from both the architecture and people draws intrepid backpackers to Minsk, eager to catch a glimpse of the USSR in its prime.

**INDEPENDENCE SQUARE.** (пл. Незалежнасци; pl. Nezalezhnastsi.) This square was once pl. Lenina but now stands as the symbol of Belarussian independence. So too stands **Lenin,** a lasting and contradictory statue in front of government headquarters. *(M-red: pl. Nezalezhnastsi. Just north of the train station.)*

**THE OLD TOWN.** Minsk's restored Old Town, which preserves the feeling of pre-Soviet Minsk, sprawls between Nyamiha and pl. Nezaleshnastsi west of the Svislac. On a small island in the Svislac, a quadrangular monument honors Belarussians who died for the Soviet army. The powerful imagery is humbling, but the island also provides the most picturesque view in the city, making it a popular meeting place. *(M-red: pl. Nezalezhnastsi. North of pl. Nezaleshnastsi on the river, across the 1st small bridge.)*

**WORLD WAR II MEMORIALS. Victory Square** is "the holiest place in Minsk," according to the state tourism literature. A 40m-tall obelisk crowns the grand pr. Skoriny, celebrating the defeat of the German army in World War II. An eternal flame burns in honor of the 566 Belarussians honored as Heroes of the Soviet Union. *(M-red: pl. Peramohi (пл. Перамогі).)* Along the river on the south bank, the vast flatness of Minsk is painfully broken by the **Minsk Hero-City Monument.** Forty-five meters tall, the statue commemorates the spirit of the citizens of Minsk in the face of Nazi invasion. The **Jewish memorial stone** commemorates the more than 5000 Jews shot and buried by the Nazis on this site in 1941. *(M-blue: Nyamiha (Няміга). Exit the Metro onto pr. Masherava; the memorial stone is behind Gastsinitsa Yubileynaya, pr. Masherava 19. The Hero-City Monument is farther down Masherava.)*

**ST. SIMON'S CHURCH.** The city's churches have flourished over the past few years and many have been restored to their former beauty. A statue of **St. Simon** slays a dragon before the crimson church dedicated in his name, which looks startlingly out of place amid the surrounding architectural bombast. A few doors down, a statue of Lenin frowns disapprovingly at Simon, who has been dulled by the opiate of the masses. *(Savetskaya 15. M-blue: Frunzenskaya (Фрунзенская).)*

**MUSEUMS.** The 🏛**National Arts Museum** (Нацыянальны Мастацкі Музей Распублікі Беларусь; Natsyanalny Mastatski Muzey Raspubliki Belarus), pr. Lenina 20 (Леніна), exhibits breathtaking collections of Russian and Belarussian art across the centuries. *(☎227 56 72 and 227 71 63. Open W-M 11am-7pm. 250BR.)* The **Museum of the Great Patriotic War** (Музей Велікой Отечественной Войны; Muzey Velikoy Otechestvennoy Voyny), pr. Skoriny 25a, paints a suitably grim picture of the war in which Belarus lost 20% of its population. *(☎226 15 44. M-red: pl. Peramohi (пл. Перамогі). Open Tu-Su 10am-7pm. 250BR. English tours 800BR.)*

## 🎵 ENTERTAINMENT

**Opera and Ballet Theater,** vul. E. Pashkevich 23 (Пашкевіч; ☎234 06 66). M-blue: Nyamiha (Няміга). Exit the Metro onto Maksima Bagdanovica; the theater is in the park on your right. One of the best ballets in the former Soviet Union, but even the best seats in the house go for under US$5. Purchase advance tickets from the **Central Ticket Office,** pr. Skoriny 13 (☎220 25 70). Open M-Sa 9am-8pm, Su 11am-5pm.

**Belarussian Philharmonic,** pr. Skoriny 50 (☎233 35 80). M-red: pl. Yakuba Kolasa (пл. Якуба Коласа). Concerts at 7pm. Box office open Tu-Su 12:30-7:30pm.

**Hall of Chamber Music,** pr. Skoriny 44 (☎233 04 69), in St. Roch's Church. M-red: pl. Yakuba Kolasa. Organ music daily 7pm. *Kassa* open M-Sa 1-3pm and 3:45-7pm.

**Minsk Circus,** pr. Skoriny 32 (☎227 22 45; box office ☎227 78 42). M-red: pl. Peramohi (пл. Перамогі). Performs Aug.-June daily at 3 and 7pm. Under US$1.

# HRODNA (ГРОДНА) ☎(8)152

Hrodna's quick capture during World War II saved most of its Baroque buildings from destruction. Soviet planners had their way with the city's endless industrial outskirts, but the center is as good as it gets in Belarus.

**📧 TRANSPORTATION.** The train station, **Vakzal** (Вакзал), is on vul. Budonova (Будонова; ☎44 85 56). Pay for trains through Poland in US$ *and* BR. Buy international tickets at windows #13 and 14. Trains run to: **Minsk** (6-9hr., 2 per day, *coupé* US$1.30); **Vilnius, LIT** (4hr., 3 per day, US$5); **Białystok, POL** (5hr., 3 per day, US$3 and 1715BR); **Warsaw, POL** (5½hr., 4 per day, US$8 and 1700BR); and **Moscow, RUS** (12hr., 1 per day, *coupé* US$15). The bus station, **Avtovakzal** (Автовакзал), vul. Krasnoarmeyskaya 7a (Красноармейская; ☎ 72 37 24), is 1.5km from the center. Bus #15 and vul. Budonova connect the bus and train stations. Buses run to: **Minsk** (5½hr., 3 per day, US$2); **Brest** (7hr., 2 per day, US$1.75); **Druskininkai, LIT** (1½hr., 2 per day, US$1); **Białystok, POL** (3hr., 4 per day, US$1); **Vilnius, LIT** (5hr., 1 per day, US$2.50); **Warsaw, POL** (6hr., 3 per day, US$6); and **Kaliningrad, RUS** (10hr., 1 per day, US$5).

**🖪🖬 ORIENTATION AND PRACTICAL INFORMATION.** Hrodna straddles the **Neman River,** with its city center and sights on the north bank. The **train station** lies northeast of the center at the end of **vul. Azheshka** (Ажешка). Head away from the station on vul. Azheshka to reach **vul. Savetskaya** (Савецкая), the main pedestrian thoroughfare. This cobblestoned street winds away from the Lenin statue and empties into **pl. Stefana Batorya. Exchange currency** on the second floor of the train station's main hall. (Open M-F 9am-1pm and 2-6:30pm, Sa-Su 8am-1pm.) The lobby of **Hotel Turist** (see below) houses a currency exchange with good rates, but unpredictable hours. For MC/Visa **cash advances** for a 4% commission, head to **Prior Bank** (Пріор Банк), Mostovaya 37 (Мостовая), away from pl. Stefana Batorya and downhill toward the river. (☎ 72 31 37. Open daily 9am-3pm.) **Store luggage** in the train station's basement at the "камера храненія" (kamera khranenia) sign. (Open daily 8am-1pm, 2-7:30pm, and 8pm-7:30am. Small bags 35BR; large bags 60BR.) The same rates apply in the **bus station.** (Open daily 7am-1pm and 2-8pm.) The **post office** is at Vul. Karla Marksa 29 (Карла Маркса), between the bus station and pl. Stefana Batorya. (Open M-F 8am-8pm, Sa-Su 10am-4pm.) The **telephone office** is next door—make international calls here. Tell the attendant the number, pay, and make the call in the assigned booth. (☎ 96 75 15. Open 7:30am-11pm.) **Postal code:** 230 000.

**🖪🖬 ACCOMMODATIONS AND FOOD.** Consider taking a taxi (US$2) directly to **Gastsinitsa Turist** (Гасцініца Туріст), J. Kupala 64 (Купала), since other hotels will probably send you there as soon as they peg you as a Westerner. All rooms include bath and TV. (☎ 26 55 90. Doubles US$28 if paying in dollars, half price if paying in BR.) To reach **Gastsinitsa Belarus** (Гасцініца Беларусь), vul. Kalinovskaya 1 (Каліновская), take bus #15 from the train station and get off at "Кінотеатр Космос" (Kinoteatr Kosmos). Turn right onto the boulevard with a median strip. Rooms here are similar to those at Turist, all with bath. (☎ 44 16 74. Singles US$12; doubles US$24. MC/Visa.) Most hotels run restaurants that open at mealtimes; otherwise, wander vul. Savetskaya to find cafes and supermarkets.

**🖫 SIGHTS.** The city's best sights are its castles, which overlook the Neman river. From pl. Stefana Batorya (пл. Стефана Баторья), take vul. Zamkava (Замкава), the road to the right of the pillared building. At the intersection, with a tower on the right, go straight on the higher road. **Old Castle** (Стары Замак; Stary Zamak), on the right, was built in the 1570s on the foundations of an older structure. Walk up to the defensive wall for a gorgeous view of the river. Inside, 20 rooms cover Hrodna's history. (Open Tu-Su 10am-6pm; *kassa* closes at 5pm. 90BR.) On the opposite side of the hill, **New Castle** (Новы Замак; Novy Zamak), destroyed in World War II and rebuilt in 1951, exhibits Hrodna's history from its first written mention in 1128. (☎ 44 40 68. Open Tu-Su 10am-6pm; *kassa* closes at 5pm. 90BR.)

# BREST (БРЕСТ)                                    ☎ (8)162

From the windows of a train, Brest looks like a city comprised entirely of vast railroad yards. A stroll through the generic Soviet center won't change that impression, but a visit to the Brest Fortress, southwest of the city, will.

 Brest's phone numbers have finally been standardized. All numbers have 7 digits and start with a "2"; add a "2" to the front of old 6-digit numbers.

**🮮 TRANSPORTATION.** The **train station** (☎ 005), just north of vul. Ardzhanikidze, is the main border crossing for trains running between Moscow and Warsaw. Trains run to: **Minsk** (4½hr., 8-10 per day, 350BR); **Warsaw, POL** (5 per day, US$25);

Moscow, RUS (16hr., 8 per day, US$2.75, *coupé* US$4.10); Kyiv, UKR (16½hr., 1 per day, US$1.80, *coupé* US$3); and Prague, CZR (18hr., 1 per day, US$96). The bus station (☎ 225 51 36) towers over the corner of vul. Kuybyshava (Куйбышава) and vul. Mitskevicha (Міцкевіча), near the central market. (Open daily 6am-11pm.) Buses run to Hrodna (8hr., 2 per day, US$1) and Warsaw, POL (6hr., 1-3 per day, US$6.50).

■■ ORIENTATION AND PRACTICAL INFORMATION. The Mukhavets and Bug Rivers mark the south and west boundaries of the city; the Brest-Litovsk Fortress lies at their confluence. The Bug also marks the Polish border. At the train station, head toward the main overpass and take a right over the tracks. The first right leads to vul. Ardzhonikidze (Арджонікідзе). After two blocks, you'll reach vul. Lenina (Леніна). Head left to reach pl. Lenina, the main square; vul. Pushkinskaya (Пушкінская) runs to the left. Farther down is vul. Gogalya (Гогаля), the main east-west thoroughfare. The kiosk in the train station sells maps (266BR). The staff at Gastsinitsa Intourist speaks English and arranges English tours of the fortress if you call a week in advance. Prior Bank (Пріор Банк), vul. Pushkinskaya 16/1, gives MC/Visa cash advances and cashes AmEx and Thomas Cook travelers' checks for a 4% commission. (☎ 223 27 83. Open M-F 9am-3:30pm.) The entrance is in the back of the building. Store luggage in the train or bus stations. (Lockers 25BR.) The post office, with telephones and fax inside, is on vul. Pushkinskaya at pl. Lenina. (☎ 23 29 72. Open M-F 8:30am-8pm, Sa-Su 9am-4pm.) Postal code: 224 000.

■■ ACCOMMODATIONS AND FOOD. Gastsinitsa Vesta (Веста), vul. Krupskoi 16 (Крупской), is the best deal in town. Walk 200m behind the Lenin statue and take the first road on the left. Vesta offers clean bathrooms plus TVs and refrigerators. (☎ 223 71 69; fax 223 78 39. Singles US$14-16; doubles US$28. Reservation fee 50% of room price.) Restauran India (Рестаран Індіа), vul. Gogalya 29 (Гогаля), at vul. K. Marxa, revives your palate with super-spicy dishes. (☎ 26 63 25. Main dishes US$6-12. Open daily noon-midnight.) There's a grocery past the post office. (Open M-F 7:30am-9pm, Sa 8am-8pm, Su 8am-3pm.)

■ SIGHTS. ■Brest-Litovsk Fortress (Крэпасць Брэст-Літовск; Krepasts Brest-Litovsk) lies between the Bug and Mukhavets rivers. From the center, either take bus #17 down vul. Maskaiskaya and walk 15 minutes or take a taxi for US$1. After Napoleon's 1812 attack on Russia, several cities in Poland, Lithuania, and Belarus were heavily fortified; Brest was intended to be the central defense point. Brick walls 15m thick, moats, and encasements made this the most formidable battlement in Eastern Europe. The monumental Principal Entrance (Галоіны Іваход; Galoiny Ivakhod), at the end of vul. Maskaiskaya, welcomes visitors in grand Soviet style. Immediately to the right lies Eastern Fort (Усходны Форт; Uskhodni Fort), a complex where tenacious Soviets, cut off from their comrades, held their ground against the Nazis for three weeks. The worthwhile Museum of the Defense of the Brest Hero-Fortress (Музей Абароны Брэцкой Крэпасці-Героя; Muzey Abarony Brestskoi Krepastsi-Geroya), in the reconstructed barracks, recounts the siege. (Open M and W-Su 9:30am-6pm. Free.) Walk past the museum to the right to the Northern Gate (Паіночная Брама; Painochnaya Brama), the only fully intact gate.

**SCREWDRIVER** International trains are heavily taxed, so the cheapest way to get from Moscow or Minsk to Warsaw is to reach Brest or Hrodna, catch an *elektrichka* across the border, and take Polish trains from there. If you choose this most budget of all routes, you'll notice that as soon as the *elektrichka* embarks, quick-footed men with screwdrivers begin scaling walls and taking the train apart, hiding vodka of all shapes and sizes in the overhead compartments, the seats, and even, after unscrewing the lights, in the car ceiling. They then sit down and wait. You may be asked to hold a bottle of liquor: you are allowed one duty-free liter, so it's all right to take a bottle provided you don't already have your own. At the border, guards board the train and take it apart again, impounding roughly a third of the smuggled vodka. If you don't snitch on these hard-working folk, you might receive a little candy with some vodka in it.

BELARUS

# BOSNIA-HERZEGOVINA

The mountainous centerpiece of the former Yugoslavia, Bosnia-Herzegovina (herts-uh-goh-VIHN-ah) has defied the odds and the centuries to stand as an independent nation today. Bosnia's distinctiveness—and its troubles—spring from its self-proclaimed role as a mixing ground for Muslim Bosniaks, Catholic Croats, and Orthodox Serbs. In Sarajevo, its cosmopolitan capital, that ideal is at least verbally maintained, but ethnic problems continue in the countryside. Physically, the country is marked by rolling hills and sparkling rivers, though its lush valleys are now punctuated with abandoned houses and gaping rooftops. The past decade has been brutal, with a bloody war broadcast nightly to the world and much of the population displaced. Bosnia's future is uncertain, particularly with the imminent withdrawal of NATO troops, but its resilient people are optimistic. In this period of post-Dayton peace, rebuilding is underway.

BOSNIA

## BOSNIA-HERZEGOVINA AT A GLANCE

**OFFICIAL NAME:** Bosnia and Herzegovina

**ADMINISTRATIVE DIVISION:** 51% Muslim/Croat Federation, 49% Serb-led Republika Srpska

**CAPITAL:** Sarajevo (pop. 360,000)

**POPULATION:** 3,482,000 (40% Serbs, 38% Bosniaks, 22% Croats)

**LANGUAGES:** Bosnian

**CURRENCY:** 1 convertible mark (KM) = 100 convertible pfennigs

**RELIGION:** 40% Muslim, 31% Orthodox, 15% Catholic, 4% Protestant, 10% Other

**LAND AREA:** 51,233 km$^2$

**GEOGRAPHY:** Mountainous, plains in the north, 20km of shore

**CLIMATE:** Mild continental

**BORDERS:** Croatia, Yugoslavia

**ECONOMY:** 58% Services, 23% Industry, 19% Agriculture

**GDP:** US$ 1,720 per capita

**EMERGENCY PHONE NUMBERS:** Police 92, Fire 93, Emergency 94

**COUNTRY CODE:** 387

**INTERNATIONAL DIALING PREFIX:** 00

# HISTORY

**THE BEGINNINGS.** Bosnia belonged to the massive **Roman Empire** during the first centuries AD. After the fall of the Roman empire, Bosnia became a battleground between the Empire's Frankish and Byzantine successors. Bosnia first became an independent nation in 1180 when, after the death of the Byzantine emperor, neither

CROATIA
Glina
Slavonski
Brod
Novi Sad
Bosanski
Novi
Bosanski
Dubica
Bonsanska
Gradiška
Brčko
Bihać
Bosanski
Petrovac
Sanski
Most
Banja
Luka
Doboj
Graďanica
Bijeljina
Lukovac
Tuzla
REPUBLIKA
SRPSKA
Zavidovići
Zvornik
Jajce
Zenica
Bogojno
Travnik
Srebrenica
CROATIA
MUSLIM-CROAT
FEDERATION
Visoko
Livno
Jablanica
Sarajevo
Višegrad
Buška
jezero
Konjic
Gorazde
Split
Foča
Adriatic
Sea
Brač
Hvar
Mostar
YUGOSLAVIA
N
Korčula
Meďugorje
Pelješac
Neum
50 miles
Trebinje
50 kilometers
Bosnia-Herzegovina
Dubrovnik
Podgorica
Bosnia River

the Croatian or Serbian kingdoms could establish rule over the territory, and remained as such for more than 260 years. At that time, the population of Bosnia was almost entirely Christian.

**...AND THE ENDS.** Beginning in the late 14th century, the flourishing **Ottoman Empire** started invading the Balkans, and by 1463, had swallowed Bosnia. Largely due to the organizational weakness of the Church (both Catholic and Orthodox) in Bosnia, **Islam** gained more converts in Bosnia than in neighboring countries. During the 400-year period of Turkish rule, Bosnia developed into a prosperous and largely autonomous province of the Ottoman Empire, with a distinct Bosnian Muslim culture. Throughout the centuries that followed, Christians and Muslims lived in relative harmony and referred to themselves simply as Bosnians.

**YOU TOO WILL BE OURS.** In 1878, the Western European powers took advantage of the Ottoman Empire's increasing weakness, and transferred Bosnia to **Austria-Hungary** at the **Congress of Berlin.** Resentment of Austrian rule sparked nationalistic sentiments throughout Bosnia and led to the establishment of an illegal Bosnian Serb terrorist organization, the **Black Hand.** This caused Austria-Hungary to tighten its grip on Bosnia, and ultimately to **annex** the country in 1908. As in the rest of Balkans, the increased repression, coupled with ideology from Russia, contributed to the emergence of the idea of **South Slav** unity as the sole means of achieving sovereignty. On June 28, 1914, **Gavrilo Princip,** an eager member of the Black Hand, assassinated the Austrian heir to the throne **Archduke Franz Ferdinand** in Sarajevo, triggering the events that led to **World War I.**

**THE LAND OF SOUTH SLAVS.** After the war, the Pan-Slavic desires of the Balkan Slavs were given a concrete shape in the form of the **Kingdom of Serbs, Croats, and Slovenes** (later renamed Yugoslavia). As the name clearly indicated, Bosnians were reduced to nothing. It was during this era that either a Croat or a Serbian identity was imposed on the Muslim inhabitants of Bosnia. When Hitler put an end to the kingdom by invading Yugoslavia in 1941, he gave Bosnia as a present to his obedient satellite Croatia. The majority of Bosnians joined the ranks of pro-Allied Partisans led by **Josip Brož Tito** during **World War II.** In 1945, Bosnia joined its Slavic neighbors as one of the six constituent republics of **Yugoslavia.** In the 1960s Tito granted Bosnian Muslims status as a distinct ethnic group.

**THE ROAD TO HELL.** Nationalist sentiment was suppressed under Tito, but his death in 1980 triggered a nationalist revival. Tensions increased in 1986 with the rise to power of the Serb ultra-nationalist demagogue **Slobodan Milosevic,** who sought to abolish the federation and create a unitary state under Serbian control. The Federal Republic of Yugoslavia began its full collapse in 1990. Following the 1991 secession of Slovenia and Croatia from the federation, Bosnia held a referendum on **independence** in February 1992. Much to the outrage of Milosević and his aparatchiks in Belgrade, 70% of Bosnians, including a large section of the Serbian population, voted in favor of independence, which was subsequently announced on April 5th. Violence broke out as the federal army and Serb militias quickly took control of 70% of Bosnian territory. Sarajevo suffered a brutal siege that lasted from May 2, 1992 to February 26, 1996. A United Nations force sent to deliver humanitarian assistance, **UNPROFOR,** had little success in stopping the ethnic cleansing undertaken principally, although not exclusively, by Serb forces. Hoping to compensate for their lost territory at home, the Croats launched an operation in Herzegovina, cleansing its Muslim population.

**FINAL PEACE.** The international community remained largely ignorant of the conflict until footage of Serbian "ethnic cleansing" of **Srebrenica,** documenting the first genocide in Europe since World War II, was broadcast on television around the world. The atrocities continued until 1995, when American Richard Holbrooke negotiated the **Dayton Peace Accords.** Dayton brought a fragile peace to the region, which the UN peacekeeping forces have helped sustain until this day.

# POLITICS

Fighting in Bosnia among Serb, Bosnian, and Croatian forces continued until the signing of the 1995 **Dayton Peace Accords.** The area under dispute was divided into two loosely connected governing bodies, the Muslim/Croat **Federation of Bosnia-Herzegovina** and the Serbian **Republika Srpska (RS),** to segregate the warring ethnic groups. The country has a three-year rotating presidency. According to the constitution drafted in Dayton, the presidents must be a Croat, a Serb, and a Bosniak (Muslim), elected by a popular vote for four-year terms. The offices are presently held by a Serb **Zivko Radisić,** Croat **Ante Jelavić,** and Bosniak **Alija Izetbegović.** In summer 2000, Izetbegović announced that he was going to step down in the fall. The next elections are scheduled for 2002. The executive branch is headed by two co-chairmen, who appoint members of the cabinet.

Bosnia-Herzegovina has a bicameral parliament, in which all three ethnic groups are equally represented. Conflicts between the Federation and RS are diminishing slowly, but diminishing still. Today's Bosnia, however, resembles more of an international protectorate than an independent nation. High representative **Wolfgang Petritch,** a diplomat appointed by the UN Security Council to implement the Dayton Peace Accords, has the power to issue legal decrees and dismiss any member of the government—which he does with a passion. It is expected that Bosnia-Herzegovina will remain under direct international supervision for at least another 10 years.

The international community is optimistic about Bosnia's prospects for stability and peace—many claim that things have never been this calm. Refugees from the Kosovo conflict have been repatriated.

# CULTURE

| NATIONAL HOLIDAYS IN 2001 | |
|---|---|
| **January 1** New Year (Western/Gregorian) | **April 15** Easter (Orthodox and Catholic) |
| **January 7** Orthodox Christmas | **May 1** Labor day |
| **January 14** Old New Year (Julian) | **November 1-2** All Saints (Catholic) |
| **January 9** Republic Day | **November 25** National day |
| **March 1** Independence Day | **December 25** Catholic Christmas |

## LITERATURE AND ARTS

Bosnia's literary and artistic tradition dates back to the Middle Ages, but modern works dominate the heritage. One of the nation's only writers to receive international acclaim, Bosnian Serb **Ivo Andrić** won the Nobel Prize for Literature in 1961 for the "epic force" with which he handled his subjects and the sober compassion and beauty of his works. His novels, *The Bridge on the Drina* and *The Travnik Chronicles*, exemplify his contemplative prose and his treatment of delicate political issues. Bosnians celebrate **Mak Dizdar** as the nation's greatest poet. He revolutionized post-World War I Bosnian poetry with his stark modernist style and refusal to pander to Socialist Realism. Dizdar's poems inspired the 1992 creation of the Sarajevo War Theatre, a group of playwrights and actors who performed almost 2000 productions during the four-year siege of Sarajevo. In the wake of the fighting, most Bosnian authors have turned their energies to reflecting upon the war, particularly in memoirs and diaries. *Zlata's Diary*, by **Zlata Filipović**, a teenager during the siege of Sarajevo, is the *Anne Frank's Diary* of the conflict.

In 1993, several Bosnian artists organized the **Witnesses of Existence** exhibit in which language and national context were interpreted using shrapnel and bullets as media. The exhibit toured Italy and the US, but its creators were trapped in Sarajevo and unable to travel with it.

## RELIGION

Bosnia-Herzegovina's religious composition is the most complex in all of Eastern Europe. There are three large religious minorities, none of which is small enough to be subjugated or large enough to subjugate others. Bosnia-Herzegovina is a multi-ethnic state in which Orthodox Serbs, Catholic Croats, and Muslim Bosniaks try to coexist peacefully (for percentage breakdown, see **At a Glance** box on p. 86).

## CUSTOMS AND ETIQUETTE

Waitstaff expect **tips** only for excellent service; the amount is up to you. At restaurants and cafes, the bill is never split; instead, one person pays, and it is assumed that the other will pay next time. Don't be overly thankful or think the man is hitting on you—it's the norm. (So is hitting on women, though. On that note, it is acceptable to **stare** at people, take it or leave it.) The man, or the waiter, will open and pour the woman's drink. In **Muslim homes** and in **mosques,** it is customary to remove one's shoes at the door. **Smoking** is popular; most Sarajevans smoke the local *Drina* or *Aura*. **Bargaining** is a must, particularly in the clothing markets. Ask a Bosnian to accompany you; the price will be miraculously lower. **Fashion** was important even during the war, so stow away your grubby t-shirt. **Foreigners** are welcomed and regarded with great interest in Sarajevo. America, particularly, is beloved among Sarajevans, who were entertained during the war by such pirated American TV as *Beverly Hills 90210*. They tend to look to America as an ideal of the diversity they seek to achieve.

# LANGUAGE

When in Bosnia, speak Bosnian. When in Croatia, Croatian. When in Serbia, Serbian. The distinction is more in name than in substance, but never underestimate its importance, as languages in the former Yugoslavia have been co-opted by the governments as tools of nationalism. The languages do have certain distinctions. Take, for example, coffee. *Kava* is the Croatian term, *kafa* the Bosnian. So in the former Yugoslavia, mind your Ps and Qs—and Zs, Ks, Us, and Js. Foreigners who attempt to speak a little Bosnian are the exception, not the rule; an effort to pronounce even a few sentences will endear you to locals. See the Croatian Glossary for more words. English and German are widely spoken.

---

**STICKY TERMINOLOGY** Croat, Serb, and Bosnian refer to people of each ethnicity. Croatian, Serbian, and Bosnian are terms indicating the country. Thus, to say a Bosnian Serb denotes a Serb living in Bosnia (most often in the Republika Srpska (RS), the Serb-dominated entity in northeastern Bosnia). Likewise, a Bosnian Croat is a Croat living in Bosnia. Bosnian Muslims usually go by the term "Bosniak." Bosnians often refer to their Bosnian Serb enemies as "Četnik," or "Chetnik," a revived World War II ethnic slur. In other words, a Serb is different from a Chetnik—do not make this mistake. Another semantic caveat: the Bosnian Army is precisely that, and not the "Muslim Army."

---

## ADDITIONAL READING

A wealth of literature is available on Bosnia, especially documents on and memoirs of the recent war. Keep in mind that few books provide an objective account, as most authors have been directly involved in or affected by the conflict. Brian Hall's *Impossible Country is* a modern account of his travel in Bosnia. Hall, an American, journeyed through Yugoslavia in summer 1991, just as the "Impossible Country" began to fall apart. *Love Thy Neighbor* by Peter Maass is a more personal option, recounting stories from his days as a *Washington Post* war correspondent. Noel Malcolm's *Bosnia: A Short History* (1994) is a long-awaited historical overview of the lands that comprise present-day Bosnia-Herzegovina. American chief negotiator of the Dayton Agreement Richard Holbrooke wrote a brilliant personal account of the road to peace *To End a War* (1998), which mercilessly uncovers the intricacies of Milosević, Tudjman, and Izetbegović alike. This book is highly recommended by *Let's Go*.

# TRAVELING ESSENTIALS

Citizens of Canada, Ireland, the UK, and the US may visit Bosnia visa-free for up to one month; visas are required for citizens of Australia, New Zealand, and South Africa. Call your Bosnian consulate (see **Embassies and Consulates,** p. 18) for details. Applications take approximately two weeks to process; send your passport, one passport-sized photo, a copy of your round-trip ticket, a copy of your last bank statement as proof of sufficient funds to cover expenses during your stay, a letter of invitation, a voucher from your travel agency or hotel reservations if available, a completed visa application, a self-addressed, stamped envelope, and a money order for the proper fee (single-entry valid for one month and transit US$35; multiple-entry valid for 90 days US$65; multiple-entry valid for more than 90 days US$85). There are occasional police checkpoints within Bosnia; register with your embassy upon arrival, and keep your papers with you at all times. Visa extensions can be obtained in Bosnia at the Ministry of Foreign or Internal Affairs. Visitors are required to register with the police upon arrival—accommodations will usually do it for you.

Crossing the Bosnian border, with its congregation of trucks and army vehicles, is somewhat intimidating, but entering can be a fairly smooth procedure if the political climate allows. Bosnian visas are not available at the border. There is no fee for crossing a Bosnian border.

**ALTERNATIVES TO TOURISM** Many visitors to Bosnia are interested in helping the country to rebuild after its brutal war. The following organizations gladly accept volunteers and donations. All telephone numbers require the Sarajevo dialing prefix, (0)33.

**La Benevolencija,** Hamdije Krešavljakovicá 59, Sarajevo (☎66 34 72; fax 66 34 73; la_bene@soros.org.ba). In the Jewish community center across the river next to the old Sephardic synagogue. This humanitarian organization distributed free medicine to the elderly during the war. The center organizes local public service opportunities with children injured or orphaned during the conflict. Call at least one week in advance. Open M-F 9am-4pm.

**OXFAM,** Hiseta 2, Sarajevo (☎66 81 33).

**Save the Children,** Kotromanjćeva 48, Sarajevo (☎66 63 43 and 20 93 65).

**UNICEF,** Kolodvorska 6, Sarajevo (☎52 37 11; fax 64 29 70).

**UNHCR** (United Nations High Commission for Refugees; ☎66 61 60), will gladly provide advice on how and where to help.

# TRANSPORTATION

**BY PLANE.** Commercial plane service into Sarajevo is limited and expensive, but is the main recourse of the troops, journalists, and relief workers entering the country. Flights come from various European cities (see **Sarajevo: Airlines,** p. 94). **Croatia Airlines** has regular service from Zagreb. Travel agencies in Sarajevo can arrange and change flights, but to buy a ticket you must pay in cash.

**BY TRAIN.** Railways are barely functional and should not be considered an option.

**BY BUS.** Buses run daily between Sarajevo and Dubrovnik, Split and Zagreb, with the first one being the most popular route into the country. Buses are reliable, clean, and not very crowded, but brace yourself for Balkan driving.

# TOURIST SERVICES AND MONEY

| CURRENCY | |
|---|---|
| US$1 = 2.20KM (CONVERTIBLE MARKS, OR BAK) | 1KM = US$0.45 |
| CDN$1 = 1.50KM | 1KM = CDN$0.67 |
| UK£1 = 3.20KM | 1KM = UK£0.31 |
| IR£1 = 2.50KM | 1KM = IR£0.40 |
| AUS$1 = 1.30KM | 1KM = AUS$0.77 |
| NZ$1 = 0.94KM | 1KM = NZ$1.10 |
| SAR1 = 0.32KM | 1KM = SAR3.27 |
| DM1 = 1KM | 1KM = DM1 |
| HRV KUNA1 = 0.26KM | 1KM = KN3.90 |

In Sarajevo, travelers are welcomed by the excellent, polyglotic **tourist office.** Many Bosnians speak **English** or **German.** The **US Embassy** also has useful information. Several independent tourist agencies have sprung up, but most focus on arranging vacations for locals. Helpful Bosnians are often as good as a tourist office.

The new Bosnian currency, the **convertible mark (KM),** was introduced in summer 1998. It is fixed firmly to the Deutschmark at a 1:1 exchange rate. Deutschmarks can be changed directly into convertible marks for no commission at most Sarajevo banks. Beware store clerks trying to pass unsuspecting foreigners old Bosnian dinars: the dinar is no longer a valid currency. In addition, the **Croatian kuna** was named an official Bosnian currency in summer 1997. The kuna is not legal tender in Sarajevo, but it is accepted in the western (Croatian) area of divided Mostar. Make sure to change your money back to Deutschmarks when you leave, as convertible marks are inconvertible outside Bosnia. **Inflation** in Bosnia is almost non-existent. **Banks** are the best places to exchange money. **Traveler's checks** can be cashed at some Sarajevo banks. **ATMs in Bosnia remain non-existent. Western Union** in the capital has an extremely competent English-speaking staff. Most restaurants accept Visa, MC, and (to a lesser extent) AmEx, but Visa is best for getting **cash advances.** If your itinerary lies outside of Sarajevo, bring Deutschmarks with you.

# HEALTH AND SAFETY

Outside Sarajevo, **do not set foot off the pavement** under any circumstances. Even in Sarajevo, de-mining experts recommend staying on paved roads and hard-covered surfaces. Do not pick up any objects on the ground. Millions of **landmines** and **unexploded ordnance** (UXOs) cover the country. Mine injuries occur daily. 15% of landmine injuries occur on **road shoulders**—partly because farmers who find unexploded ordnance in their fields occasionally bring it to the roadsides for the troops to pick up. Should your car veer off the road, carefully retrace your tracks back to the pavement; if you want to take pictures, do so from your car while the car remains firmly on pavement. If you must go to the bathroom during a road trip, stop at a gas station. **Abandoned houses** are unsafe as well; many have been rigged with booby traps. Absolute caution is essential at all times. Estimates are that 30 years of intensive, full-time effort would be necessary to declare Bosnia "minefree"—and even de-mining is not 100% foolproof. See p. 95 for details on the Mine Action Center.

In Sarajevo, finding medical help and supplies is not a problem; your embassy is your best resource. Peacekeeping operations have brought English-speaking doctors, but not insurance; cash is the only method of payment. All drugs are sold at pharmacies, while basic hygiene products are sold at many drugstores. Condoms are available, but expensive. Bandages are even harder to come by.

# KEEPING IN TOUCH

Bosnia's **postal** system, operative since 1996, is gaining more functions. Yellow-and-white "PTT" signs indicate post offices. Sarajevo's post office can accommodate outgoing mail, but Poste Restante is unavailable; the only way to receive mail is to befriend a government employee and borrow their address. Few towns outside the capital are equipped with reasonable mail service. Mail to the US usually takes one to two weeks, somewhat less within Europe. **Postcards** cost KM1 to mail.

Telephone connections are troublesome and expensive; the best option is to call collect from the main Sarajevo post office just outside the center. To call **AT&T Direct,** dial ☎ 00 800 0010. Calling the UK is roughly 3.50KM per minute and the US 5KM, but prices vary significantly depending on where you are. **Faxes** can be sent from the post office; it's 3KM per page to Australia or the UK and 5KM to the US.

# SARAJEVO                                      ☎ (0)33

The posters at every bus stop in Sarajevo (pop. 360,000) read "Peace, Democracy, Prosperity and Hope are our goal," a sentiment often echoed in conversation with young Sarajevans. Although most of the classic tourist features of Sarajevo have been destroyed or are non-functional, the lively marketplace of the old Turkish Quarter, the burgeoning arts scene, and the nightlife are inspiring. Upon arrival in the city, newcomers find themselves among warm international company, sitting in cafes next to uniformed SFOR officers, camera-wielding journalists, and foreign aid workers. Perhaps wary of media stereotyping, the city remains largely aloof to the

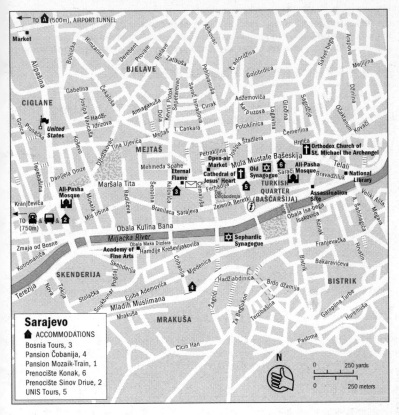

Sarajevo

 ACCOMMODATIONS

Bosnia Tours, 3
Pansion Čobanija, 4
Pansion Mozaik-Train, 1
Prenocište Konak, 6
Prenocište Sinov Driue, 2
UNIS Tours, 5

short-term visitor and tensions are on the rise as a result of the recent influx of refugees. It is just that sort of elusiveness, though, that makes finding the real Sarajevo—the city loved so passionately by its residents—all the more rewarding.

> The following outlying areas of Sarajevo were battlegrounds during the war and still contain landmines: Grbavica, Lukavica, Illidža, and Dobrinja. The Mine Action Center (see below), however, emphasizes that all parts of the city should be considered high-risk.

# ■ ORIENTATION

Sarajevo's center is easily navigable, a series of streets running parallel to the **Mili-jacka** river that can be traversed end-to-end in less than 30 minutes. **Maršala Tita** is the main street *(ulica)*, running from the yellow **Holiday Inn** to the **eternal flame,** a 1945 memorial that has been less than eternal due to gas shortages. Building numbers increase toward the flame. At the flame, Maršala Tita branches into **Ferhadija** and **Mula Mustafe Bašeskije,** the city's two pedestrian thoroughfares. Follow either of these for about 10 minutes to reach the cobblestoned streets of **Baščaršija** (Turkish Quarter). A walk in the opposite direction from the flame down Maršala Tita leads to the stark **Zmaja od Bosne** (Dragon of Bosnia), called **"Sniper's Alley"** during the war because of its proximity to the front lines. Between the Holiday Inn and the eternal flame, **Alipašina** bisects Maršala Tita. At their intersection (with the mosque on the corner), look toward the river—the sprawling strip mall built for the 1984 Olympic Games marks the **Skenderija Quarter.** Streets have changed names since the war, but street signs are up-to-date. You can purchase a **map** (10KM) at local bookstores, or get one free at the main tourist bureau (see below).

# ⊠ INTERCITY TRANSPORTATION

**Flights:** To: **Berlin, GER** (Lufthansa); **Istanbul, TUR** (Air Bosnia); **Ljubljana, SLN** (Adria Air); **Paris, FRA** (Croatia and Swiss Air); **Rome, ITA** (Swiss Air); and **Zagreb, CRO** (Croatia Air). Purchase tickets at **Centrotrans,** Ferhadija 16 (☎21 12 82 and 21 12 83; fax 20 54 81). Open M-F 8am-8pm, Sa 8am-3pm. See **Travel Agencies,** below, for other ticket providers. Taxi service to and from the airport 18KM.

**Trains:** Next to the bus station (see below). To **Mostar** (3hr., 1 per day, 7KM). Box office (☎65 53 30) open daily 5am-9pm. No international rail connections.

**Buses: Bus station,** Kranjčevića 9 (☎53 87 02; fax 53 22 81), behind the Holiday Inn at the corner with Halida Kajtaza. Ticket window (☎21 31 00) open daily 7am-7pm. Centrotrans (see **Flights,** above) services Sarajevo; purchase tickets at the Ferhadija office or at the bus station. To reach the center: with your back to the station, turn left, walk past the taxi stands and the train station, and continue straight through the 1st intersection. Continue on Kranjčevića for 20min. until the mosque appears at the large intersection. Go straight onto Maršala Tita, which branches at the eternal flame into Sarajevo's 2 walkways. To: **Dubrovnik, CRO** (7hr., 2 per day, 41KM); **Split, CRO** (8hr., 4 per day, 36KM); **Zagreb, CRO** (9hr., 4 per day, 51KM); **Vienna, AUS** (12hr., 2 per week, 81KM); and **Frankfurt, GER** (15hr., 1 per day, 190KM). 2KM extra per bag.

# LOCAL TRANSPORTATION

**Public Transportation:** Central Sarajevo is small and simple enough to allow you to avoid public transit altogether, but if you're in a rush, an excellent **tram** network loops west along Maršala Tita and back east along Obala Kulina Bana. Regular service runs 6am-10pm or midnight, depending on the route (1.2KM from kiosks; 1.5KM on board). **Buses** extend farther from the center, but operate mainly during commuter hours (M-F 6:45am-6pm). Monthly bus pass 12KM. A listing of the tram and bus lines and their working hours is inside the tourist information booklet available at the tourist office (see below). There are no exact schedules, but most transportation arrives every 5-15min. Ticket inspectors are often present and always vigilant; if you have no ticket or fail to punch it upon boarding, you risk a 15KM fine.

**Taxis:** Generally fair, with rates consistent among all the companies. Try **Radio Taxi** (☎970 and 65 21 31) or **Yellow Taxicab** (☎66 35 55 and 65 73 07). 2KM flat rate plus 1.30KM per km. If you call, you'll be charged for pickup. Fares 30% higher at night. Large bags 2KM per piece. Expect to pay 12KM from the bus station to the center.

# ⊡ PRACTICAL INFORMATION

## TOURIST AND FINANCIAL SERVICES

**Tourist Office: Turistička Zajednica,** Zelenih Beretki 22a (☎53 26 06 and 53 23 12; fax 53 22 81). From Maršala Tita, bear right at the eternal flame and continue until you see the Catholic church on the left; turn right down Strossmajerova, then left onto Zelenih Beretki; the tourist office is 1 block down. Staffed by friendly folks who provide extensive advice on accommodations. Free **map/city guide** and a smaller tourist info booklet. Open M-Sa 9am-5pm. The **Consular Department** (☎44 57 00; fax 65 97 22; www.usis.com) of the US Embassy (see below) is also helpful—ask for their weekly newsletter, *The Sarajevo Chronicle,* complete with consular news, English film listings, special events schedules, and classified ads. Open M-F 8:30am-noon and 2-4pm.

**Budget Travel: Air Bosnia,** Ferhadija 15 (☎20 31 67 and 21 48 72; fax 66 79 54). Arranges flights on all airlines. 25% off for under 26 to Germany. Open M-F 9am-5pm, Sa 9am-2pm. **Kompas Tours,** Maršala Tita 8 (☎20 80 14; fax 20 80 15), past the

**BOSNIA**

---

**SARAJEVO ROSES** All along Sarajevo's main thoroughfare, Maršala Tita, the pavement is littered with splash-shaped indentations. These distinctive marks were created by exploding grenades during the city's Serbian siege. Those marks filled in with red concrete are called "Sarajevo Roses," there to commemorate civilians killed on that spot by the exploding grenade. The roses are never stepped on out of respect for the deceased. Even in the most normalized and seamless of Sarajevo's neighborhoods, they are a constant reminder of the war and the thousands of Bosnians lost.

---

intersection with Alipašina toward the Holiday Inn. A Slovenian agency that books flights with a 25% student discounts on Austrian Airlines and Lufthansa. Can arrange car rentals. Open M-F 8:30am-5:30pm, Sa 9am-2pm.

**Embassies:** Citizens of **Australia** should contact their embassy in Austria, Mattiellistr. 2, 1040 Vienna (see **Austria: Embassies**, p. 66). **Canada**, Logavina 7 (☎44 79 00; fax 44 79 01). Open M-F 8:30am-noon and 1-5pm. **New Zealanders** should contact their embassy in Italy, Via Zara 28, 00 198 Rome (☎(6) 440 29 28; fax 440 29 84). **UK**, Tina Ujevica 8 (☎44 44 29; fax 66 61 31). Open M-F 8:30am-5pm. **US**, Alipašina 43 (☎44 57 00; fax 65 97 22). Open M-F 9am-1pm.

**Currency Exchange:** Among the largest and best of Sarajevo's many banks, **Central Profit Bank,** Zelenih Beretki 24 (☎53 36 88; fax 53 24 06 and 66 38 55), cashes AmEx **traveler's checks** for a 1.5% commission and **exchanges cash** for a 3% commission. Money can be wired here in 15min. using the new **MoneyGram** system. Open M-F 8am-7:30pm, Sa 8am-3pm. **Gospodarska Banka,** Maršala Tita 56 (☎44 29 59), is one of the few bureaus that will exchange Croatian kuna, but for a 3.75% commission (max. 500KM or US$300 per day). Open M-F 8:30am-7pm, Sa 9am-2pm.

**ATM:** There are no ATMs in anywhere in Bosnia. Bring lots of traveler's checks.

## LOCAL SERVICES AND COMMUNICATIONS

**Mine Action Center (MAC),** Zmaja od Bosne 8 (☎66 73 10 and 20 12 99; fax 66 73 11). Follow signs through the barracks on the right side of the street, 400m past the Holiday Inn from the center. Provides pamphlets and maps detailing the location of landmines—vital if you plan to travel beyond Sarajevo. Open M-F 8am-4pm.

**International Bookstore: Šahinpašić,** Mula Mustafe Bašeskije 1 (☎22 01 12), near the eternal flame. A small store with choice literary selection. English classics, dictionaries, guide books, maps, and international magazines. Open daily 9am-8pm.

**Ambulance:** ☎94 and 61 11 11.

**Hospital: Koševo University Medical Center,** Bolnicka 25 (☎66 66 20 and 44 48 00). **State Hospital,** Kranjčevića 12 (☎66 47 24; fax 47 24 98). Both English-speaking.

**24hr. Pharmacy: Baščaršija Apoteka,** Obala Kulina Bana 40 (☎23 67 00).

**Internet: Internet Club,** upstairs at Ferhadija 21 (☎53 41 16). The most central internet spot has fast connections. 3KM per hr. Open daily 8am-10:30pm.

**Telephones:** Inside and outside any post office. The most central one is behind the eternal flame on Ferhadija. Open M-F 7am-8pm. Phone cards sold at any post office. The main branch (see below) is the only place with phones that doesn't require a card (speak and pay afterward) and where you can call collect or use AT&T or MCI numbers. **Directory info:** ☎988. **International operator:** ☎900.

**Post Office: PTT Saobracaj** Sarajevo, Zmaja od Bosne 88 (☎65 43 65; fax 47 31 03), is well past the Holiday Inn in New Sarajevo. Take tram #3 west, get off at the 3rd stop after the Holiday Inn, and follow the tram 100m. Fax service available. Open M-Sa 7am-8pm. **Postal code:** 71000.

## ⸤ ACCOMMODATIONS

Until recently, housing in Sarajevo was absurdly expensive, but prices are stabilizing as competition works its capitalist magic. You can get a room in a **pension** for as little as 30KM, and with unemployment ravaging the economy, relatively cheap

**private rooms** (30-50KM) are available all over. Discounts are usually available for longer stays. If you arrive late at night without prior arrangements, ask a taxi driver at the station for help—they often make deals with local families offering private rooms. He might not speak English, but he'll understand "room" and "center" and will write down the price. The cost should be on par with those at agencies, but the fare to get you there will be upped for the service.

## PRIVATE ROOM AGENCIES

**Bosnia Tours,** Maršala Tita 54 (☎20 22 06 and 20 20 59; fax 20 46 11). Across from the eternal flame. Books rooms in family apartments along Maršala Tita and across the river. Bath, sheets, and laundry included. Breakfast 5-10KM. Open M-F 9am-7pm, Sa 9am-6pm. Call at least one day ahead. Singles 40KM; doubles 70KM.

**UNIS Tours,** Ferhadija 16 (☎/fax 20 90 89). Walk down Ferhadija to the right of the eternal flame; the office is upstairs across from the cathedral. A brusque staff finds central rooms with all the amenities, but they have fewer rooms than Bosnia Tours. Open M-F 9am-5pm, Sa 9am-3pm. Singles 40KM; doubles 70KM.

## PENSIONS

**Prenoćište "Konak,"** Mula Mustafe Bašeskije 48 (☎53 35 06). From Maršala Tita, go left at the eternal flame and past the market; it's on the right. Rustic but clean rooms smack in the center of town. The communal bathrooms are tiled and shiny. Reception daily 7am-midnight. Check-out noon. Call at least one day ahead. Singles 40KM, 30KM for stays over 3 nights; doubles 60KM.

☒ **Pansion "Čobanija,"** Čobanija 29 (☎44 17 49; fax 20 39 37). With your back to the eternal flame, take the 1st left onto Kulovica, which crosses the river and becomes Čobanija. The *pansion* is at the end of the street, 5min. from the center. Don't let the old building exterior fool you, the place is so modern that every bathroom has a telephone inside. If that doesn't spoil you, the satellite TV in every room, the sleek furniture, leather chairs, and the chandeliers surely will. Reception 24hr. Must reserve by fax or in person 7-10 days in advance. Singles 80KM; doubles 120KM. Breakfast included.

**Pansion Mozaik-Train,** Halida Kajtaza 11 (☎20 05 17; fax 20 05 22). With your back to the train station, take a left at the 1st intersection. At the 'El Tarik Oil' station, take a left and a quick right, then follow the train tracks on your left. After 100m you'll see a blue veranda tent stretching out from an old train to your left. If you like sleeping in train bunks but always hated the noise of travel, this is your place. The cars don't go anywhere, but do house a smoky restaurant and a few clean rooms. Reception 24hr. Singles 32KM; doubles 40KM. Breakfast included.

**Prenoćište Sinovi Drine,** Put Života bb. (☎44 56 51). Right across from the bus and train stations. If you arrive in Sarajevo and need to crash immediately, this place has clean sheets on hospital beds in doubles, triples, and quads. Grimy bathrooms and erratic electricity make this place a one-nighter. Reception 24hr. No reservations necessary. Dorms 31.60KM. Breakfast included.

# 🗗 FOOD

Sarajevan cuisine is quintessentially Balkan—meaty, cheesy, and greasy. For an authentic Bosnian meal, scour the Turkish Quarter for **čevabdžinica** (kebab) shops; 3KM buys a *čevapčiči* (nicknamed *čevaps*), lamb sausages encased in *somun*, Bosnia's tasty, elastic flatbread. Numerous **buregdžinica** shops stave off the McDonald's invasion with their namesake meat and potato pie. Vegetarians can munch on *sirnica* (cheese pie) and *zeljanica* (spinach pie). The burgeoning restaurant scene also includes a number of new eateries serving everything from Chinese to Indian. The depressed economy puts many restaurants beyond the reach of most Bosnians; SFOR troops, journalists, and businesspeople comprise the main clientele. There are no large grocery stores in the center, but the small **Max Market** at Mula Mustafe Bašeskije 3, near the eternal flame, is well-stocked and open 24hr. Two main **markets** provide fresh veggies and bakery. The more convenient one lies on Mula Mustafe Bašekija, a few blocks from the eternal flame. (Open M-Sa 8am-5pm, Su 8am-noon.) The larger one, under the Ciglane bridge on Alipašina, is five minutes from the US Embassy. (Open in summer M-Sa 8am-5pm, Su 8am-noon; off-season M-F 8am-dusk.) There's a **meat market** at Ferhadija 7. (Open M-Sa 6am-6pm).

☙ **Fnat Kuća (Despite House),** Veliki Alifakovac 1 (☎44 78 67). Walk past the Turkish Quarter along the river; at the National Library, cross onto Veliki Alifakovac. It once stood on the site now occupied by the National Library. When the city wanted to build the library there, the restaurant owner demanded they move his establishment stone by stone to its present location. Luckily, they did—it serves the best Bosnian food in town. Try *dolmes* (stuffed onions; 5KM). Main dishes 5-18KM. Open daily 9am-11pm.

☙ **Aščinica "ASDŽ,"** Bravadžiluk 24 (☎53 75 03), in the Turkish Quarter. Excellent national dishes buffet-style. Tell the staff how much you want to spend and let them serve up what they think is best. 8-10KM buys a satisfying meal. Open daily 8am-9pm.

**Čevabdžinica Željo,** Kundurdžiluk 19 (☎44 70 00), in the Turkish Quarter. Named after the local soccer team, this small restaurant brims with sporty patriotism and hordes of hungry locals. They only do one main course—*čevap* (4KM)—but they're damn good at it. Open daily 8am-10pm.

**Beijing,** Maršala Tita 38d (☎21 31 96), in a small alley. A kitschy interior tries to recreate China in the middle of Bosnia. More importantly, the food is excellent. Journalist/expat crowd. Chicken dishes 15-18KM; beef 12-14KM; vegetarian 10-25KM. Open daily 11:30am-11pm.

**Čevabdžinica Hodžić,** Bravadžiluk 34 (☎53 28 66), in the Turkish Quarter. Among the best *čevap* places for freshness and variety, in a pristine, white-arched building. All kinds of meat on display, but vegetarians can eat too—try *kaymak*, a melted cheese sandwich on *somun* (2KM). Main dishes 5-10KM. Open daily 8am-11pm.

# ◉ SIGHTS

The **eternal flame,** where Maršala Tita splits into Ferhadija and Mula Mustafe Bašeskije, was lit in 1945 as a memorial to all Sarajevans who died in World War II. Its dedication paying homage to South Slav unity now seem painfully ironic. Evidence of the city's recent four-year siege is increasingly difficult to detect within the center of the city, as buildings shake themselves free of scaffolding on a daily basis. Rubble and bullet holes are glaringly apparent only outside the center and in most of the rural towns that line the roads to Sarajevo.

**NATIONAL LIBRARY AND OTHER REMNANTS OF THE SIEGE.** The National Library, at the tip of the Turkish Quarter on Obala Kulina Bana, exemplifies Sarajevo's recent tragedy. The 1896 Moorish-style building was once regarded as the most beautiful in the city. It served as town hall until 1945, when it was converted into the university library. Now it's an open-air structure smothered in scaffolding

**BOSNIA**

**FIRED-UP NEWS** Some days the only newsprint was green, some days lavender, and all days in limited supply. But *Oslobodjenje*, Sarajevo's oldest and best independent newspaper, continued to print daily during the war. The *Oslobodjenje* offices were 50m from the front lines; by June 1992, they were destroyed. The printers, cloistered in a bunker below, were saved. The bunker gained some beds and became *Oslobodjenje*'s lightless wartime offices. Electricity to run the printers was totally cut off, so the paper turned to oil-operated generators. Oil also was in short supply, occasionally provided by the UN Protection Force (UNPROFOR) and occasionally snuck in via the makeshift airport tunnel, then the only route to Sarajevo. Generator power lasted two hours each day, a window during which the newspaper was frantically compiled. Wartime circulation reached about 200, or as many copies as possible, with four to eight pages the normal length. Today, *Oslobodjenje*'s circulation within Sarajevo approaches 10,000 and its page count is nearly 30. Internationally, some 25,000 copies circulate to Slovenia, Austria, Italy, and Germany.

both inside and out. The besieging Serbs, attempting to demoralize the city, targeted civilian institutions early on in the war—the library was firebombed on August 25, 1992, exactly 100 years after construction began. *(From Maršala Tita, walk toward the river to Obala Kulina Bana and turn left.)* The glaring **treeline** in the hills above the city serves as yet another reminder of the recent conflict, clearly demarcating the front lines. Bosnians trapped in Sarajevo cut down all the available wood for winter heat. During the siege, the city's defenders built a tunnel under the runway of Butmil airport to a nearby suburb. It became the city's lifeline, the only route by which food, arms, and medicine could be smuggled in and the President, the sick, and the wounded, out.

**CHURCHES, MOSQUES, AND SYNAGOGUES.** The structures of various religions huddling together in Central Sarajevo indicate the best and worst of what the city represents. The 16th-century **Gazi Husrev-Bey Mosque,** perhaps Sarajevo's most famous building, dominates the Turkish Quarter. The interior is closed to tourists for renovations, but it's still possible to visit the courtyard and its birdcage fountain. Prayer takes place on the outdoor terrace. *(12 Sarači. Facing the flame, walk right onto Ferhadija, which becomes Sarači after several blocks.)* The main Orthodox church, the **Saborna,** is closed for repairs as well, but the old Orthodox **St. Michael the Archangel** remains open. The dollhouse-sized church guards a trove of medieval iconography on its interior balcony. *(Mula Mustafe Bašeskije 59. ☎ 53 47 83. 10min. from the flame. Open daily 7am-6pm.)* The 1889 **Cathedral of Jesus' Heart** (Katedrala Srce Isusovo), on Ferhadija, is a mundane mix of Gothic and Romanesque styles, but its steps serve as a popular meeting place at night for the city's youth heading out to collect potential material for confession. *(Trg Grge Martica 2. ☎ 23 62 11 and 66 45 77. Mass daily at 8am and 6pm. Mass in English every Su at noon.)* The **old synagogue** preserved an art collection among sand bags during the war. Still closed in summer 2000, the synagogue plans to reopen as a museum. *(On Mula Mustafe Bašeskije, between the eternal flame and St. Michael's.)* The 1892 **Sephardic Synagogue,** serves as the base for *La Benevolencija*, the Jewish Community Center's service organization (see **Alternatives to Tourism,** p. 91). *(Hamdije Kreševljakovica 59. ☎ 66 34 72, fax 66 34 73. From the Cathedral, walk down to the river and cross over to the building directly opposite on the far bank.)*

**TURKISH QUARTER.** (Baščaršija.) The centerpiece of the mosque-flanked Turkish Quarter is a traditional Turkish-style Bazaar, with squares interlaced with tiny streets conducive to commerce. That commerce runs right out of your pocket at the highly overpriced shops and boutiques. Always bargain hard, and have someone who speaks Bosnian on your side if possible. The **Sebilj,** a wooden fountain in the Quarter's main square, is notable more for its dynamic surroundings than its own beauty. Legend has it that once you sip these waters you'll never leave the city behind. *(Walk a few minutes down Fehadija from the eternal flame.)*

**ASSASSINATION SITE.** It was here that Gavrilo Princip shot Austrian Archduke Franz Ferdinand and his wife Sofia on June 28, 1914, leading to Austria's declaration of war on Serbia and the subsequent maelstrom that spawned the First World War. Princip was a Serb from Belgrade and part of the *Black Hand* terrorist group that fought Austrian rule (see **History,** p. 87). He was actually the third in a string of rather pathetic assassins. The first, carrying a rifle, lost his nerve and didn't shoot. The second threw a grenade that overshot the Royal carriage and blew up the first assassin. Princip took no such chances and shot at near point-blank range. All of this happened in a matter of minutes. During the recent war, the plaque that formerly marked the historic spot with Princip's footprints was ripped out of the ground. *(The corner that made Sarajevo famous is at the intersection of Obala Kulina Bana and the second bridge when walking from the National Library toward the center.)*

# ⌂ MUSEUMS

Like its sights, Sarajevo's museums reflect the influence of war. Many are still closed for repair. To check on the status of any of the museums listed, contact the US Embassy or any tourist agency.

**National Museum (Zemaljski Muzej),** Zmaja od Bosne 3 (☎66 80 27). From the eternal flame, walk toward the bus station on Maršala Tita until it runs into Zmaja od Bosne; the museum is the large yellow building on the left. Among the Balkans' most famous museums, with botanical gardens, a large collection of Roman stonework from the 1st to 3rd centuries, and a superb ethnographic collection. Open Tu, Th, and Su 10am-2pm; W 11am-7pm. 5KM, students 1KM.

**History Museum (Historijski Muzej),** Zmaja od Bosne 5 (☎21 04 16). Next to the National Museum in a gray cubic building. Contemporary art donated by major European museums alongside work by local artists. Much of it reflects on the war. Open M-F 11am-2pm and 6-9pm, Sa-Su 9am-1pm. Free.

**Art Gallery of Bosnia and Herzegovina (Umjetnička Galerija Bosne i Hercegovine),** Zelenih Beretki 8 (☎66 75 32). Take the 1st right onto Ferhadija after the flame and follow Zelenih Beretki 2 blocks to the left. A collection of Bosnia's graphic art on the top floor. A permanent exhibit of contemporary art should be in place by summer 2001. Open M-Sa 10am-4pm. Free.

**Academy of Fine Arts,** Obala Maka Dizdara 3, in the yellow building, on the river near the Skenderija complex. There are no exhibits here, but if you're interested in the current Sarajevo art scene, this is mecca. The bottom floor houses a multimedia center and an office of the Sarajevo Film Festival (see below). Open M-F 10am-6pm.

**Jewish Museum** (☎53 56 88), inside the old synagogue on Mula Mustafe Bašekija. Built as a synagogue in 1580, when Jews fleeing the Spanish Inquisition arrived in Bosnia, it now traces the history of Jewish settlement in Bosnia until the Holocaust. Check at the Jewish Community Center to see if it will be open while you're in town.

# ❀ FESTIVALS

Sarajevo has a year-round roster of artistic events. Every summer in July, the Turkish Quarter hosts the **Baščaršija Noci** (Turkish Nights) featuring open-air music, theater, and film. The festival is coordinated by the Sarajevo Art Center at Dalmatinska 2/1. (☎20 79 21; fax 20 79 72.) In late August, the **Sarajevo Film Festival** gets rolling in theaters throughout the city: citizens turn up for eight days of movies that include American blockbusters, contemporary European productions, and local films. In the recent past, the festival has recruited the likes of Ingmar Bergman, Susan Sarandon, and Richard Gere for its "Honorary Board." It is organized by the Obala Art Center, 10 Obala Kulina Bana. (☎52 41 27; fax 66 45 47; www.sff.ba. Box office open in summer M-F 9am-6pm. 4-5KM per film.) For information during the winter, call the film festival office in the Academy building (see above; ☎66 81 86). Since 1984, Sarajevo has also held an annual **Sarajevska Zima** (Sarajevan Winter) from December to January, a celebration of culture and art that persisted even through the siege and continues to attract international performers. For more details, call the office at Maršala Tita 9. (☎20 79 48; fax 66 36 26.)

# ▼ NIGHTLIFE

Sarajevo's cafes are flourishing more than ever with the abolishment of the 11pm "police hour," after which people were not permitted to go outside. In the warmer months, it seems the entire city is on the streets with *pivo* (beer). Popular music fans will revel in the cafes along **Ferhadija** and **Maršala Tita,** which use their outdoor speakers to wage a non-stop battle for audio supremacy. The best nightlife, however, is found in basement bars and side-street cafes.

◪ **Jazz Bar "Clou,"** Mula Mustafe Bašeskije 5 (mobile ☎066 18 24 45), through the marked doorway near the eternal flame. By far the best music selection in town, playing rock, jazz, funk, drum'n'bass, and blues. Lounge in cushioned chairs on the open-air patio or descend to the moody basement, where local bands play live on F and Sa. Wet your lips with pints of beer (5KM). Open nightly 8:30pm-5am

BOSNIA

**The Bar,** Maršala Tita 5 (☎20 54 26). Draws a more sophisticated crowd. Basement doubles as a disco F-Sa. Beer 6KM. Happy hour (half-price beer, wine, and soda) M-F 5:30-6:30pm. Open M-Th and Su 11am-midnight, F-Sa 11am-2am.

**Cocktail Club,** Kranjćevića 1 (☎23 34 95), right behind The Bar (see above). Sit on the high terrace in a comfy chair while you sip on bottle of Heineken (0.33L 4KM) or the tasty Balkan liquor *Stock* (3KM). If you come in a group of more than 10 the drink prices are cut by 30%, so round'em up. A DJ inside spins rave and disco music F-Su. Open M-Th and Su 8am-midnight, F-Sa 8am-4am.

# MOSTAR                                                          ☎(0)88

The hub of Herzegovina and historically one of Bosnia's most important cities, Mostar spreads out on either side of the blue-green Neretva River that winds through the surrounding mountains. The 16th-century Turkish city takes its name from *Mostari*, the keepers of the famous *Stari Most* (Old Bridge). After the fall of the Ottoman Empire at the end of the 19th century, Mostar became increasingly defined by its capacity to harbor Catholic, Muslim, and Orthodox citizens alike in a peaceful, religiously tolerant environment. Recent civil war shattered much of that balance, as well as the Old Bridge. Today, as the bridge undergoes reconstruction, Mostar's citizens have begun to rebuild their own human bridges—slowly rekindling the magical mix that once was their city.

**▐ TRANSPORTATION. Buses** go to: **Sarajevo** (3hr., 3 per day, 11.50KM); **Dubrovnik, CRO** (3hr., 3 per day, 21KM); **Split, CRO** (4hr., 1 per day, 16KM); and **Zagreb, CRO** (9hr., 2 per day, 41KM).

**█▐ ORIENTATION AND PRACTICAL INFORMATION.** The **Neretva River** divides Mostar from north to south, paralleled on the east by the main street **Maršala Tita** and on the west by **Aleske Šantića.** The **Old Town** (Kujundžiluk) straddles both sides of the river toward the southern end of the two main streets. Unfortunately, you can only cross the river at two spots: the street near the bus station, **Deset Hercegivaške Brigade;** and the pedestrian crossing farther south, **Mostarskog Bataljona.** The bridges are 25 minutes and 15 minutes north of the Old Town, respectively. In general, Muslims live on the East side and Croats on the West side, though Muslims also inhabit the West river bank. The **bus station** (☎55 20 25) lies 50 meters from the river on the East bank in the northern part of the city. To get to the East side of the Old Town, face away from the bus station and turn left down **Maršala Tita** (25min.). To get to the Western side of the Old Town, with your back to the station, walk straight across the bridge on Deset Hercegivaške Brigade. At the Hotel Ero, just past the bridge, turn left down Aleske Šantića and walk for 15 minutes, turn left when it runs into Save Kovačevića, and walk for seven minutes. All major services—bank, post office, pharmacy—are clustered around the Hotel Ero. The best **tourist information** service in town is at the **Atlas Travel Agency,** Ante Starčevića bb, on one side of the Hotel Ero complex. The friendly staff speaks English, checks bus schedules, sells guidebooks, hands out makeshift maps, and can arrange private rooms. (☎/fax 31 87 71 and 32 66 31. Open M-F 8am-4pm, Sa 8am-noon.) Next door stands **Hrvatska Banka,** Kardinala Stepinca bb. Although you can deal in the Croatian Kuna in most places on the West side, it makes much more sense to carry Bosnian Convertible Marks (KM) which can be used everywhere in the city. The bank will **exchange currency** for a 1% commission and **traveler's checks** for 1.5% commission. (☎31 21 20. Open M-F 9:30am-4pm, Sa 8-11:30am.) Note that there are **no ATMs** in Mostar. Just across the traffic bridge from the bus station lies a **pharmacy,** Kardinala Stepinca 9. (☎32 82 86. Open M-F 7:30am-9pm, Sa 8am-7pm.) Next to Atlas stands the **post office,** Ante Starčevića bb. It **exchanges currency** for a 1% commission and holds **Poste Restante** for up to one month. An adjacent building houses **telephones.** (☎32 83 62. Open M-F 7am-8pm, Sa 7am-7pm.) **Postal Code:** 88000.

**▐▐** **ACCOMMODATIONS AND FOOD.** Unless you plan to spend a pretty penny in one of Mostar's modern hotels, lodging is fairly limited. Fortunately, so is tourism. **Pansions** are your best bet. A 5min. walk from the Old Town, **Villa Ossa,** Vukovića 40b, offers five spotless rooms with double beds, showers, and brand new furniture. With your back to the bus station, walk straight across the bridge and turn left just after Hotel Ero, at the Hrvatska Banka. Walk straight down Bulevar Hrvatskih Branitelja for 25 minutes, turn left onto Vukovića. Walk for three minutes; Villa is on the right. (☎57 83 22 and mobile ☎090 17 53 51. Cash only. Reserve 2-3 days in advance. Check-out 10am. Singles 30KM; doubles 40KM.) The **Pansion Zlatni Liljan,** Sehovina 6 (☎55 13 53), is a cheaper option. With your back to the bus station, turn left down Maršala Tita and walk about 30 minutes After passing through the Old Town, you'll see a mosque on the left side of the road. Turn left uphill in front the mosque and take the first left onto a narrow cobblestone street. Walk uphill for three minutes; the *pansion* will be on the right. Not the cleanest of establishments, but 20KM a night will do the trick. Watch your belongings, as most rooms do not lock. Try **Atlas** (see above) for **private rooms.** (Singles 25KM.)

The best places to dine are inside the Old Town. On the West side, try **Caffe Restaurant Šadrvan,** Jusovina 11, right before the ruins of Stari Most. It pleases with a quiet, shady courtyard around a bubbling Turkish fountain and Bosnian specialties like *Dulbastija* (beef cooked with onions, paprika, and special sauce; 10KM; barbecue dishes 3-12KM; ☎57 90 57; open M-Sa 8am-11pm). On the East side, **Terasa Labirint** overlooks the river and the remains of Stari Most. (Grilled dishes 5-10KM. ☎55 13 53. Open daily 8am-midnight.)

**▐▐** **SIGHTS AND NIGHTLIFE.** The world famous **Old Bridge** (Stari Most), though no longer existent, remains the symbol of Mostar. Built by the Turks in the 16th century, it survived the fall of the Ottoman Empire and two World Wars. On November 9, 1993—four years to the day after the Berlin Wall fell—Bosnian Croat artillery fire defied UNESCO protection and senselessly brought it down as the Bosnian government declared a day of mourning. Today, reconstruction of the bridge has begun, and is projected to end by 2005. The cobblestone **Kujundžiluk** (Old Town), lies on both sides of the bridge ruins. Locals sell Turkish-style souvenirs out of low medieval buildings; bargain hard. The most famous mosque in Mostar is the **Karadžozbeg Mosque,** built in 1557. From the Old Town, walk north up the river on Ulica Braće Fejića for 5 minutes. The mosque is open to visitors most of the day, but remember to take your shoes off. Though much of Mostar has been rebuilt since the 1992-1995 civil war, the **old front line** on the West side remains virtually untouched—if you're here to see what war did to Bosnia, this is your museum. Three kilometers of post-apocalyptic destruction start at the Hotel Ero, run down Aleske Santića for a block, then move West (away from the river) to the next street, Bulevar Hrvatskih Branitelja, and continue south. The line now divides the living areas of Muslims and Croats in Mostar.

If you've walked the front line, you'll need a drink. Head to the **Pavarotti Music Center,** on Maršala Tita bb, a 3 minute walk north on Maršala Tita from the Old Town. The brand new building houses a rock cafe with large Bob Marley and John Lennon posters, colorful seating, and draft beer for 3KM. (☎55 07 50. Open M-Sa 8am-11pm, Su noon-11pm.)

**BOSNIA**

# BULGARIA
# (БЪЛГАРИЯ)

**IF YOU'RE HERE FOR...**

**3-5 DAYS.** Spend a day in **Sofia** (p. 112); don't miss out on the magnificent **Rila Monastery** (p. 119), only 3hr. away. Then head to Bulgaria's cultural capital, **Plovdiv,** which shelters Roman ruins and remarkable art collections (p. 120).

**1-2 WEEKS.** Visit also the 5000-year old **Veliko Tarnovo** (p. 138) and the beachside city of **Varna** (p. 131).

**1 MONTH.** Bum around the **Black Sea** resorts (p. 136).

From the pine-clad slopes of the Rila, Pirin, and Rodop mountains in the southwest to the beaches of the Black Sea, Bulgaria is blessed with a lush countryside, rich in natural resources and ancient tradition. The history of the Bulgarian people, though, has not been congruous with the beauty of their nation: crumbling Greco-Thracian ruins and Soviet-style high-rises attest to centuries of oppression and struggle. Today, Bulgaria struggles with a flagging economy and a lack of Western attention, problems only heightened by the recent Balkan wars. As a result, the country has gone unnoticed by most travelers, and its people—only slowly crawling out from under the rubble of communism—are finding themselves too poor to package all they have to offer for Western consumption.

**BULGARIA AT A GLANCE**

**OFFICIAL NAME:** Republic of Bulgaria

**CAPITAL:** Sofia (pop. 1.2 million)

**POPULATION:** 8.2 million

**LANGUAGE:** Bulgarian

**CURRENCY:** 1 lev (lv) = 100 stotinki

**RELIGION:** 85% Orthodox Christian, 13% Muslim, 2% Other

**LAND AREA:** 110,550km²

**GEOGRAPHY:** Mountains to the west and plains to the east

**CLIMATE:** Maritime and continental

**BORDERS:** Yugoslavia, Romania, Turkey, Greece, Macedonia

**ECONOMY:** 46% Services, 29% Industry, 26% Agriculture

**GDP:** US$4100 per capita

**EMERGENCY PHONE NUMBERS:** Ambulance 150, Fire 160, Police 166

**COUNTRY CODE:** 359

**INTERNATIONAL DIALING PREFIX:** 00

# HISTORY

**BULGARIA IS BORN.** Although the ancient **Thracian tribes** occupying Bulgaria during the Bronze Age (circa 3500 BC) were gradually assimilated or expelled by Greek and Roman settlers, remnants of their civilization have been unearthed in several of Sofia's churches (see **Sights,** p. 116). By AD 46, the Thracian kingdom had fallen to the **Romans,** who divided present-day Bulgaria into Moesia and Thrace and used the land as a trade route to the Middle East. The Western Roman Empire crumbled in 476, and by the 6th and 7th centuries the Slavs invaded the Balkan Peninsula. The late 7th century also brought the **Bulgars,** as Bulgar khan **Asparukh** defeated the forces of Byzantine Emperor Constantine IV to win the region between the Balkans and the Danube. The year 681 marks the birth of the Bulgarian state (the third oldest in Europe), when Byzantium recognized Bulgar

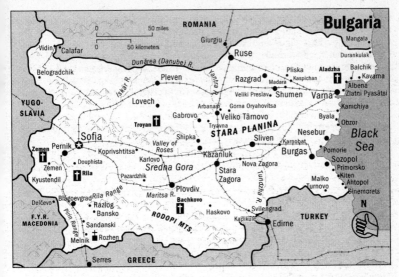

control of the disputed area. The Bulgars and the Slavs lived separately for the most part, with the Slavs paying tribute to the Bulgars.

**EXPANSION AND TURKISH RULE.** Over the next two centuries, the **First Bulgarian Empire** was slowly engulfed by Slavic culture. This process was abetted by the spread of Christianity: **Boris I** (852-899) was baptized in 865. The reign of **Simeon I** (893-927) brought greater awareness for the arts and an increase in the number of palaces and churches. He also expanded the borders of the state but exhausted Bulgaria by trying to take Constantinople just before his death. Soon Bulgaria fell to Emperor **Basil II** in 1014. Bulgaria was once again subject to Byzantine rule until 1185, when brothers **Ivan** and **Peter Asen** of Tarnovo forced Constantinople to recognize the independence of the **Second Bulgarian Empire.** During this period, Bulgaria was the leading power in the Balkans, extending from the Black Sea to the Aegean and, after 1204, the Adriatic. Internal upheaval, wars with the Serbian and Hungarian kingdoms, and attacks by Mongols from the north soon weakened the new nation, however, and by 1396 the last semblance of Bulgarian independence was lost to the Turks. For the next 500 years, Bulgaria suffered under the "Turkish yoke," during which the nobility was obliterated and the peasantry enserfed.

**REVOLUTIONARY RUMBLINGS.** During this period of repression, bandits known as **haiduks** kept the spirit of resistance alive. Their guerrilla tactics against the Turks gave nationalistic mythology its Robin Hood, even if their true intentions were far less lofty. At the same time, monasteries were busy preserving their culture through the transcription of liturgical writings into Bulgarian. These laid the groundwork for the **National Revival** of the 1870s, during which education developed and spread throughout the country. The establishment of the first independent Bulgarian church, a powerful revolt against Greek cultural and religious influence, proved equally important. Revolutionary fervor continued to build, and in 1866 **Lyuben Karavelov** and **Vasil Levsky** created the Bulgarian Secret Central Committee in Bucharest as a base for national uprising preparations. It sent "apostles" into Bulgaria to inform the people of their mission. Levsky, captured and hanged on one such trip, is considered the greatest hero of the revolutionary movement. The revolutionaries planned an uprising in 1876, but it erupted too soon and was brutally put down by the Turks. The suppression of the **April Uprising** was so violent that it fed the Bulgarian revolutionary fire, outraged the rest of Europe, and became known as the **Bulgarian Horrors.** A conference of European statesmen convened after the uprising and proposed reforms, which Turkey then refused to implement. Russia declared war in response.

**WAR.** The **Russo-Turkish War** (1877-78) ended with the **Treaty of San Stefano,** which fulfilled Bulgaria's territorial ambitions by granting it boundaries stretching from the Danube to the Aegean and from the Vardar and Morava valleys to the Black Sea. Austria-Hungary and Britain, however, were not pleased with such a large Slavic state in the Russian sphere of influence; at the 1878 **Congress of Berlin** they redrew the boundaries to create a much smaller state that included less of Macedonia. Simmering tensions over the new borders erupted in the **First** and **Second Balkan Wars** in the 1910s. These resulted in a further loss of territory for frustrated Bulgaria, which surrendered its neutrality in **World War I** and sided with the Central Powers in the hope of recovering its losses. Unsuccessful, Bulgaria lost land in the 1919 **Treaty of Neuilly** at the end of the war. Though neutral at the start of **World War II,** a lust for Greek and Yugoslav territories caused **Boris III** (1918-1943) to join the Axis in 1941, and in 1944 the Soviet Union declared war on Bulgaria. The Fatherland Front, an anti-German resistance group, led a successful *coup d'état* four days later, and the new prime minister sought an immediate armistice with the USSR. Elections in 1945 left Bulgaria a Communist republic.

**A NEW BULGARIA.** Bulgaria saw nationalization under Communist leader **Georgi Dimitrov** in the late 1940s, isolationism under **Vulko Chervenkov** in the 1950s, and rapid industrialization and alignment with the Soviet Union under **Todor Zhivkov** from 1962-89. Unpopular and much-ridiculed, Zhikov was retired by the Bulgarian Communist Party on November 10, 1989. The party was renamed the Bulgarian Socialist Party to symbolize a break from the past and the Union of Democratic Forces became the leading dissident party. The state adopted a new constitution in 1991 and held its first open presidential elections in 1992. With sociologist **Zhelyu Zhelev** as president and poet **Blaga Dimitrova** as vice president, the new government embraced openness and pluralism and ended repression of ethnic Turks.

# POLITICS

Bulgaria's **president** is elected for a five-year term as head of state. The **prime minister,** nominated by the largest parliamentary group in the National Assembly, serves as head of government and forms a Council of Ministers that oversees policy implementation. The **National Assembly,** or parliament, has 240 members elected to four-year terms. It retains the power to pass a motion of no confidence in the Council of Ministers or the prime minister, effectively forcing the individual's resignation.

The 1990s were not kind to Bulgaria. The country's first elections were won, perhaps fraudulently, by reform Communists of the **Bulgarian Socialist Party (BSP). Peter Mladenov,** the first post-totalitarian president, gained international praise for ending forced assimilation of ethnic Turks and Moslems. He experienced protests and political opposition, however, that rendered Prime Minister **Andrei Lukanov's** BSP cabinet impotent. A "government of national unity" took over to produce a new constitution, which parliament ratified in July 1991. Political scandal and currency troubles led to the resurgence of the BSP in 1994, but they only managed to drive the economy farther into the ground. Banks failed and the lev fell from 71lv to the US dollar in April 1996 to 3,000lv in February 1997. The **United Democratic Forces,** a coalition led by current Prime Minister **Ivan Kostov,** came to power and managed to stabilize the economy. Under public scrutiny for instituting reforms that have incurred such social costs as record unemployment, Kostov is continuing with his plans in the hopes that they will improve Bulgaria's chances of joining the EU. Though **President Petar Stojanov's** recent trips abroad have given the country a much-needed international-relations face-lift, **Alexander Bozhkov's** June 2000 resignation as chief negotiator with the EU indicates pressure from the west to combat corruption and poor governing in Bulgaria. Inflation remains high and economic growth is expected to slow further in the aftermath of the Kosovo crisis. While these setbacks do not seriously threaten the nation's stability, they do mean that Bulgaria will remain one of Europe's poorest countries.

# CULTURE

## LITERATURE AND ARTS

With Tsar Boris's conversion to Christianity came the first major epoch of Bulgarian literature, the aptly named **Old Bulgarian** period. Under the guidance of the first Slavic language school at court in Preslav, the translation of religious texts flourished. Bulgarian culture during this **Golden Age** was on pace to compete with that of the Byzantine capital of **Constantinople,** when conquest by the Byzantines stalled artistic progress until the 13th-century **Middle Bulgarian** period.

Art and literature went into hibernation during the 500 years of Ottoman rule, but monasteries such as Rila (see **Rila Monastery,** p. 124) managed to preserve manuscript writing and iconography until the coming of the **National Revival** (Vuzrazhdane) in 1762. The Revival coincided with **Paisy of Hilendar's** romanticized *Slavo-Bulgarian History (Istoria slavyanobulgarska),* which helped sow the first seeds of nationalism. Using their works as a tool toward liberation, realists **L. Karavelov** and **V. Drumev** depicted rural and small-town life, **Hristo Botev** wrote impassioned revolutionary poetry, and **Petko Slaveykov** and **Georgi Rakovski** drew on folklore to whip the populous into a revolutionary fervor. Meanwhile, brothers **Dimitar** and **Zahari Zograf** painted church walls and secular portraits (see **Plovdiv: Sights,** p. 123, **Bachkovo Monastery,** p. 124, **Rila Monastery,** p. 119, **Bansko: Sights,** and **Troyan Monastery,** p. 143). The works of national poet **Ivan Vazov** span the gap from subjugation to liberation, vividly describing the struggle against the Turks.

The 20th century marked a shift from socially-minded literature to a style akin to the Symbolism of the West. Such was the stance of the **Misul** (Thought) group, reflected in the musical and introspective verse of **Peyo Yavorov** and **Dimcho Debelyanov.** Realism persisted, however, as Bulgarian society was subjected to the cynical eye of **Anton Strashimirov** and the wit of **Elin Pelin.** Interwar composers **Lyubomir Pipkov** and **Petko Stainov** expanded the national repertoire from choral music to symphonies and ballets. After the 1944 Communist coup, **Socialist Realism** became the legally-mandated artistic standard, producing decades of uninspired works.

Several female poets have emerged in recent decades. **Petya Dubarova's** promising career was cut short by her early death in 1979; her collection *Here I Am, in Perfect Leaf Today* was recently published in English. Bulgaria's most important 20th-century poet, **Elisaveta Bagryana** skillfully fused the experimental and the traditional in her love poems. Bagryana's heir was the country's first post-Communism vice-president **Blaga Dimitrova.** Finally, although many consider her as French as the theory she expounds, literary critic **Julia Kristeva** is Bulgarian by birth.

## RELIGION

The state continued to encourage atheism after 1989, but religion is gradually more tolerated. Today the largest church is Bulgarian Orthodox, with Muslims, Jews, Bulgarian Catholics, Protestants, and Gregorian Armenians constituting minorities.

BULGARIA

# FOOD AND DRINK

Food from **kiosks** is cheap (0.60-2lv); **restaurants** average 6lv per meal. Kiosks sell *kebabcheta* (кебабчета; small sausage burgers), sandwiches, pizzas, and *banitsa sus sirene* (баница със сирене; cheese-filled pastries). Fruit and vegetables are sold in a *plod-zelenchuk* (плод-зеленчук; fruit store), *pazar* (пазар; market), or on the street. Try *shopska salata* (шопска салата), a mix of tomatoes, peppers, and cucumbers with feta cheese. *Tarator* (таратор), a cold soup made with yogurt, cucumber, garlic, and sometimes walnuts, is also tasty. You'll see "пържени" (fried; *purzheni*) used to describe many dishes. Bulgaria enjoys **meat.** Try *kavarma* (каварма), meat with onions, spices, and egg; *skara* (скара; grills) are cheaper. Vegetarian options with eggs (омлети; omelettes) and cheese are ubiquitous. Bulgarians are known for cheese and yogurt—the bacteria that makes yogurt from milk bears the scientific name *bacilicus bulgaricus.* Baklava and *sladoled* (сладолед; ice cream) are sold in *sladkarnitsy* (сладкарници).

Well-stirred *ayran* (айран; yogurt with water and ice cubes) and *boza* (боза; similar to beer, but sweet and thicker) are popular drinks that complement breakfast well. Bulgaria exports mineral water and locals swear by its healing qualities. Tap water is also safe to drink. Melnik produces famous red wine and the area around the old capitals in the northeast is known for excellent white wines. On the Black Sea Coast, Albenu is a good sparkling wine. Bulgarians begin meals with potent *rakiya*, a grape brandy. Good Bulgarian beers include Astika and Zagorka.

# CUSTOMS AND ETIQUETTE

**Businesses** open at 8 or 9am and take a one-hour lunch break between 11am and 2pm. Train and bus cashiers and post office attendants take occasional 15-minute coffee breaks, even while people wait in line—patience, planning, and asserting your place in line will help you get things done. Banks are usually open 8:30am to 4pm, but some close at 2pm. Tourist offices, post offices, and shops stay open until 6 or 8pm; in tourist areas and big cities, shops may close as late as 10pm. *Vseki den* (всеки ден; every day) usually means Monday through Friday, and "non-stop" doesn't necessarily guarantee a place will be open 24hr.

Seat yourself at restaurants and ask for the *smetka* (сметка; bill) when you're done. **Tipping** is not obligatory, as most people just round up to the nearset *leva*, but 10% doesn't hurt, especially in Sofia where waitstaff expect it. A 7-10% service charge will occasionally be added for you; always check the bill or the menu to see if it's listed and for other errors. Restaurants and *mehani* (механи; taverns) usually charge a small fee to use the restrooms. Tipping **taxi drivers** usually means rounding up to the nearest *leva* or half-*leva*. Bargaining for fares is not done too frequently, but be sure to agree on a price for the ride before getting in.

It is customary to share tables in restaurants and taverns. Наздраве! (Nazdrave!) means "Cheers!"—you're sure to hear this in bars. When clinking glasses (or beer mugs), make sure to look the person in the eye and call "Nazdrave!" loudly. It is respectful to buy a candle from the stand in front of churches and monasteries; place it high in honor of the living and low in remembrance of the dead.

 **YES AND NO** Bulgarians shake their heads to indicate "yes" and "no" in the opposite directions from Brits and Yanks. For the uncoordinated, it's easier to just hold your head still and say *dah* or *neh*.

# LANGUAGE

**Bulgarian** is a South Slavic language. A few words are borrowed from Turkish and Greek, but its vocabulary is most similar to Russian and other Slavic languages. **English** is increasingly spoken by young people and in tourist areas, although in the countryside you will find no English speakers. **German** is often understood. It's advisable, though not necessary, to learn the **Cyrillic alphabet** to sound out cognates. Street names are in the process of changing; you may need both old and new names. Bulgarian transliteration is much the same as Russian (see The Cyrillic Alphabet, p. 15) except that "x" is *h*, "щ" is *sht*, and "ъ" is either *a* or *u* (pronounced like the "u" in bug). *Let's Go* transliterates this letter with a *u*. Words frequently used in this chapter include *Stari Grad* (Стари Град; Old Town); *tsurkva* (църква; church); *hizha* (хижа; hut); and *kushta* (къща; house). See **Glossary**, p. 108, and **Phrasebook**, p. 109.

# ADDITIONAL READING

*A Concise History of Bulgaria*, by R.J. Crampton, delivers what it promises. Alternatively, opt for the slimmer *Bulgaria, History Retold in Brief* by Alexander Fol. For an in-depth study of one of Bulgaria's proudest moments of the 20th century, pick up Michael Bar Zohar's excellent *Beyond Hitler's Grasp: The Heroic Rescue of Bulgaria's Jews*. If you prefer poetry, try *Penelope of the 20th Century: Selected Poems of Elisiveta Bagryana*. It features an introduction by Blaga Dimitrova, whose own book, *The Last Rock Eagle*, has recently been published in English translation.

# TRAVELING ESSENTIALS

Citizens of Australia, Canada, the EU, New Zealand, and the US may visit Bulgaria visa-free for up to 30 days. Citizens of South Africa and anyone planning to stay more than 30 days must obtain a 90-day visa from their local embassy or consulate (see **Essentials: Embassies and Consulates**, p. 18). Single-entry visas are US$53 with issuance after ten business days, US$68 after five business days, and US$88 overnight (only available to US citizens). Multiple-entry visas cost US$123, transit (valid 24hr.) US$43, and double transit (valid 24hr.) US$63. Prices include a border tax of approximately US$20; those not needing visas are required to pay the tax upon entering the country. The application requires a passport valid more than six months after return from Bulgaria, one passport photograph, an invitation if not a US citizen, a copy of your green card (if applicable), payment by cash or money order, and a self-addressed, stamped envelope. There is no immediate service for multiple-entry visas. Visas are valid for three months after issue date and they may be extended at a police stations (in every major city) before the date of expiration, though likely at a high cost.

A Bulgarian border crossing can take several hours, as there are three different checkpoints: passport control, customs, and police.Visas cannot be purchased at the border. Tourists who don't need a visa and cross the border can expect to pay up to US$20. Walking across the border is not permitted. The border crossing into Turkey is particularly difficult. The easiest way to make it across is to be on an officially chartered bus, specifically a direct bus or train from Sofia to a neighboring capital; walking, driving, or hitching will hinder you.

# TRANSPORTATION

**BY PLANE. Balkan Bulgarian Airlines** (☎02 98 44 89; www.balkan.com) flies to several large cities worldwide.

**BY TRAIN.** Bulgarian trains run to **Hungary**, **Romania**, and **Turkey** and are better for transportation in the north; **Rila** is the main international train company. The train system is comprehensive but slow, crowded, and old. There are three types of trains: *ekspres* (express; експрес), *burz* (fast; бърз), and *putnicheski* (slow; пътнически). Avoid *putnicheski* like the plague—they stop at anything that looks

**BULGARIA**

## GLOSSARY

| ENGLISH | BULGARIAN | PRONOUNCE |
|---------|-----------|-----------|
| one | едно | ehd-NO |
| two | две | dveh |
| three | три | tree |
| four | четири | CHEH-tee-ree |
| five | пет | peht |
| six | шест | shesht |
| seven | седем | SEH-dehm |
| eight | осем | O-sehm |
| nine | девет | DEH-veht |
| ten | десет | DEH-seht |
| twenty | двадесет | DVAH-DEH-seht |
| thirty | òðèääñàò | TREE-deh-set |
| forty | четиридесет | TCHE-TEE-REE-deh-set |
| fifty | петдесет | peht-deh-SEHT |
| sixty | шестдесет | shest-deh-SEHT |
| seventy | седемдесет | se-dem-deh-SEHT |
| eighty | осем | OH-sem |
| ninety | деветдесет | de-vet-deh-SEHT |
| one hundred | сто | stoh |
| one thousand | хиляда | hi-LYA-da |
| Monday | понеделник | pa-ne-DYEL-nik |
| Tuesday | вторник | FTOR-nik |
| Wednesday | сряда | s-RYA-da |
| Thursday | четвъртък | chet-VUR-tuk |
| Friday | петьк | pe-TUK |
| Saturday | сьбота | su-BOH-ta |
| Sunday | неделя | ni-DYEL-ya |
| a day | ден | dyen |
| a few days | няколко дни | ni-KOL-ka dnee |
| a week | семица | syed-MEE-tsa |
| morning | сутрин | SOO-trin |
| afternoon | следобед | SLYE-dob-yed |
| evening | вечер | VEH-cher |
| today | днес | d-NYES |
| tomorrow | утре | OO-trye |
| spring | пролет | pro-LYET |
| summer | лято | LYA-ta |
| fall | есен | YE-sen |
| winter | зима | zee-MAH |
| hot | топло | tah-PLOH |
| cold | студено | stoo-DYEN-a |
| single room | единична | ye-din-EECH-nah |
| double room | двойна | dvoy-NAH |
| reservation | резевация | re-zer-VAH-tsee-yah |
| bakery | хлебарница | khleb-AR-nee-tsah |

| ENGLISH | BULGARIAN | PRONOUNCE |
|---------|-----------|-----------|
| post office | поща | POH-sha |
| stamp | марка | MAR-ka |
| airmail | въздушна поща | vooz-DOOSH-na POH-sha |
| departure | заминаващи | zaminavashti |
| arrival | пристигащи | pristigashti |
| one-way | отиване | o-TEE-vahn-eh |
| round-trip | отиване и Врьщане | o-TEE-van-e ee VRI-shtah-neh |
| luggage | багаж | ba-GAZH |
| reservation | резевация | re-zer-VAH-tsee-yah |
| train | влак | vlahk |
| bus | автобус | ahv-to-BOOS |
| airport | летище | LYET-i-shye |
| station | гара | gara |
| ticket | билет | bi-LYET |
| grocery | бакалия | bah-kah-LIH-ya |
| breakfast | закуска | za-KOO-ska |
| lunch | обяд | ah-BYAD |
| dinner | вечеря | veh-cher-YA |
| menu | меню | men-YOO |
| bread | хляб | hlyab |
| vegetables | зеленчуци | zelenchutzee |
| beef | телешко | teleshka |
| chicken | пиле | PEE-lye |
| pork | свинско | SVIN-ska |
| fish | риба | REE-ba |
| coffee | кафе | kah-FEH |
| milk | мляко | MLYAH-ko |
| beer | бира | BEE-rah |
| sugar | захар | ZAH-khar |
| eggs | яйца | yai-TSAH |
| holiday | ваканция | vah-KAHN-tsee-ya |
| open | отварят | ot-VAR-yaht |
| closed | затварят | zaht-VAR-yaht |
| bank | банка | BAHN-ka |
| police | полиция | pohl-EE-tsee-ya |
| exchange | обменно бюро | OB-myen-na byu-ROH |
| toilet | тоалетна | to-ah-LYET-na |
| square | площад | PLO-shad |
| monastery | манастир | mah-nah-STEER |
| church | цьрква | TSURK-ba |
| tower | кула | KOO-lah |
| market | пазар | pah-ZAR |
| passport | паспорт | pahs-PORT |
| left | отляво | ot-LYAH-vo |
| right | отдясно | ot-DYAHS-no |

# PHRASEBOOK

| ENGLISH | BULGARIAN | PRONOUNCIATION |
|---|---|---|
| Yes/no | Да/Не | dah/neh |
| Please/You're welcome | Извинете/jdsbfkdsf | eez-vi-NEH-teh/fdsjkhfdshf |
| Thank you | Благодаря | blahg-oh-dahr-YAH |
| Hello | Добър ден | DOH-bur den |
| Good-bye | Добиждане | doh-VIZH-dan-eh |
| Good morning | Добро утро | doh-BROH U-troh |
| Good evening | Добър Вечер | DOH-bur VEH-cher |
| Good night | Лека Нощ | LEH-ka nosht |
| Sorry/Excuse me | Извинете | iz-vi-NEE-tye |
| Help! | Помощ! | PO-mosht |
| When? | Кога? | ko-GA |
| Where is...? | Къде е? | kuh-DEH eh |
| How do I get to...? | Как да стигна...? | kak dah STEEG-na |
| How much does this cost? | Колко Струва? | KOHL-ko STROO-va |
| Do you have...? | Имате Ли...? | EEH-mah-teh lee |
| Do you speak English? | Говорите ли Английски? | go-VO-rih-te li an-GLIS-keeh |
| I don't understand | Не разбирам. | neh rahz-BIH-rahm |
| I don't speak Bulgarian | Не говоря по-български | ne gah-var-YA po-bul-GAR-ski |
| Please write it down. | Може лида ми го запишете | MAW-zhe LEE-dah mee gah za-pi-SHEE-tye |
| Speak a little slower, please. | Малко по-бавно, ако обичате. | MAHL-ka pah-BAHV-na, AH-ka ahb-i-CHAT-ye |
| I'd like to order... | Искам да порьчам... | EES-kahm da pah-ROO-cham |
| I'd like to pay/We'd like to pay. | Бих искал(а/и) да платя(им) | Bikh is-KAHL-(a/ee) da plat-YA-(yim) |
| I think you made a mistake in the bill. | Мисля че има трешка в сметката | mis-LYA che EE-mah TRESH-ka v smyet-KAH-ta |
| Do you have a vacancy? | Имате ли свободна стая? | ee-MAH-tye lee svah-BOHD-na-ya sta-YA |
| I'd like a room. | Искам стая | EES-kahm STAH-yah |
| May I see the room? | Може ли да видя стаята? | MOH-zhe lee da vid-YA sta-YA-ta |
| No, I don't like it. | Не, не ми харесва | nee, nee mee kha-RYES-va |
| Yes, I'll take it. | Да, ще я взема | dah, shi-YE ya b-ZYE-mah |
| Will you tell me when to get off? | Извинете, кода тряба да сляза? | eez-vee-NEH-teh ko-GAH TRYAHB-vah dah SLYAH-zah? |
| Is this the right train/bus to...? | Това ли е верният влак/рейс да...? | TOH-va lee ver-NYAT vlak/rehs dah |
| I want a ticket to... | Искам билет да... | is-KAHM beel-YET da |
| How long does the trip take? | Колка? | KOHL-ka? |
| When is the first/next/last train to... | Кога е последния влак да... | Ka-GAH ye pah-SLYED-nee-ya vlak dah |
| Where is the bathroom/nearest telelphone booth/center of town? | Къде е тоалетната/най-близкия телефон/центърът на града? | koo-DYE ye toh-ah-LYET-na-ta/nai-bliz-kee-ya te-ke-FOHN/TSENT-ur-ut na GRAD-ah |
| I've lost my... | Загубил(а) съм си... | zah-goo-BEEL-(a) soom see |
| Would you like to dance? | Искате ли да танцуваме | ees-KAH-tye lee dah tan-tsoo-VAHM-ye |
| Go away. | Махнете се/Оставете ме на мира | makh-NEE-tye seh/ah-sta-VEE-tye mye nah MEER-ah |

inhabited, even if only by goats. Arrive at the station well in advance if you want a seat. Stations are poorly marked, and often only in Cyrillic; know when you're reaching your destination, bring a map, and ask for help. *Ekspres* trains sometimes have cafes with snacks and alcohol. Be prepared not only for smoke-filled compartments and unaesthetic bathrooms but also for breathtaking views and friendly travelers. *Purva klasa* (първа класа; first-class seating) is very similar to *vtora klasa* (втора класа; second class), and probably not worth the extra money.

**BY BUS.** Buses head north from Ruse, and to Istanbul from anywhere on the Black Sea Coast, and are better for travel in eastern and western Bulgaria. Bus trips are more comfortable, quicker, and only slightly more expensive than trains. For long distances, **Group Travel** and **Etap** offer modern buses with air conditioning, bathrooms, and VCRs at prices 50% higher than trains. Some buses have set departure times; others leave when full. Grueling local buses stop everywhere—bring water and dress for a sweaty ride in summer. Due to the political situation in Yugoslavia, *Let's Go* does not recommend that travelers take direct buses from Bulgaria to Central and Western Europe. Instead, go up to Bucharest and begin your journey westward from there.

**BY BOAT.** There are ferries from Varna and Burgas to **Istanbul** and **Odessa**.

**BY CAR.** Major car rental companies such as **Hertz** and **EuroDollar** are in most large cities. The cheapest cars average US$70-80 per day. In Sofia, **Odysseia** rents reliable cars for US$15 per day.

**BY TAXI.** Yellow taxis are everywhere in cities. Refuse to pay in dollars and insist on *sus apparata* (a metered ride); ask the distance and price per kilometer to do your own calculations. Be sure the driver turns on the meter. Some Black Sea towns can only be reached by taxi.

# TOURIST SERVICES AND MONEY

| CURRENCY | | |
|---|---|---|
| US$1 = 2.20LV (LEVA, OR BGL) | | 1LV = US$0.46 |
| CDN$1 = 1.50LV | | 1LV = CDN$0.68 |
| UK£1 = 3.20LV | | 1LV = UK£0.32 |
| IR£1 = 2.50LV | | 1LV = IR£0.40 |
| AUS$1 = 1.20LV | | 1LV = AUS$0.80 |
| NZ$1 = 0.93LV | | 1LV = NZ$1.10 |
| SAR1 = 0.31LV | | 1LV = SAR3.20 |
| DM1 = 1LV | | 1LV = DM1 |

Tourist offices are fairly common, as are local travel agencies. Staff is helpful but usually does not speak English. A good resource is a big hotel, where you can often find an English-speaking receptionist and **maps** to purchase.

The **lev** (lv; plural *leva*) is the standard monetary unit. **Inflation** is around 3.5%, so prices and exchange rates should remain reasonably stable. Private banks and **exchange bureaus** are best for exchanging money. The latter tend to have extended hours and better rates, but may not change anything other than dollars. **Traveler's checks** can only be cashed at banks (with the exception of a few change bureaus). Banks also give Visa **cash advances. Credit cards** are rarely accepted. Don't be misled by credit card stickers in store windows; most are for show. **ATMs** are common and usually accept Cirrus, MC, and Visa. Don't deal with hawkers who approach you offering good exchange rates—it is illegal to exchange currency on the street. It is not possible to redeem discounts on your HI card in Bulgaria. Like other Eastern European countries with weak currencies, Bulgaria has recently tied its currency to the Deutschmark; 1 lev always equals 1 DM.

**BULGARIA**

**BATHROOM ETIQUETTE** Bathtubs are a rarity in Bulgaria; more often you'll find an inconspicuous shower nozzle sticking out of the wall. Just put the toilet seat down, set the trash can outside, and let the water flow. Most public bathrooms do not have toilet paper ("pay toilets," 0.20-0.30lv, generously issue about 4 meager squares). Bulgarian toilets don't use much water (a green idea?); avoid the wrath of angry hotel maids by using the provided brush to erase "skid marks."

## HEALTH AND SAFETY

Public **bathrooms** (Ж for women, M for men) are often holes in the ground; pack a small bar of soap and toilet paper, and expect to pay 0.05-0.20lv. The sign "Аптека" (apteka) denotes a **pharmacy**. There is always a night-duty pharmacy in larger towns; its address is posted on the doors of the others. *Analgin* is headache medicine; *analgin chinin* is for colds and flu; bandages are *sitoplast;* cotton wool is *pamuk.* Foreign brands of *prezervatifs* (condoms) are safer. Imported medications are popping up in larger cities. **Contact lens** wearers should bring supplies. **Tampons** are widely available. Emergency care is far better in Sofia than in the rest of the country; services at the Pirogov State Hospital are free, some doctors speak English, and the tourist office will send someone along to interpret for you.

Locals generally don't trust the police, and stories circulate of people being terrorized by the local mafia. Don't buy bottles of **alcohol** from street vendors, and be careful with homemade liquor—there have been cases of poisoning and contamination. Walking in the dark is generally more frightening than dangerous, but still inadvisable. It is generally fine for **women** to travel alone though usual precaution should be exercised. **Discrimination** in Bulgaria is focused on the **Roma** (gypsies), who are considered a nuisance at best and thieves at worst. Other minorities stand out but are not bothered. The Bulgarian government has recently recognized **homosexuality,** but general understanding and acceptance are slow in coming.

## ACCOMMODATIONS AND CAMPING

Upon crossing the border, citizens of South Africa may receive a **statistical card** to document where they sleep. If you don't get a card at all, don't worry. Ask hotels or private room bureaus to stamp your passport or a receipt-like paper that you can show upon border re-crossing, otherwise you stand to pay a fine. If you are staying with friends, you'll have to register with the **Bulgarian Registration Office.** See the consular section of your embassy for details.

Solo travelers should look for signs reading "частни квартири" (tschastnee kvartiri; private rooms). They can be arranged through Balkantourist or other tourist offices for US$5-15 per night; be sure to ask for a central location. It is also common for people to offer private accommodations in train and bus stations. Be careful if alone, and don't hand over any money until you've checked the place out. *Babushki* are the best; try to bargain them down. Bulgarian **hotels** are classed on a star system and licensed by the Government Committee on Tourism; rooms in one-star hotels are almost identical to those in two- and three-star hotels, but have no private bathrooms. Expect to pay US$15-50 per night, although foreigners are always charged higher prices. The majority of Bulgarian **youth hostels** are in the countryside. Outside major towns, most **campgrounds** provide spartan bungalows and tent space.

Hiking trails are marked by colored lines over a white background painted on rocks, trees, or anything else that won't walk away.

BULGARIA

# KEEPING IN TOUCH

Making international **telephone** calls from Bulgaria can be a challenge. Payphones are ludicrously expensive; opt for the telephones in a phones office. If you must make an **international call** from a payphone with a card, purchase the 400 unit, 20lv card. Units, however, run out quickly on international calls, so talk fast or have multiple cards ready. One minute costs 2.40lv to Australia, Canada, or the US, 1.80lv to the UK 1.80lv; and 3.60lv to New Zealand. International access numbers include: **AT&T Direct** (☎ 00 800 0010), **BT Direct** (☎ 00 800 99 44), **Canada Direct** (☎ 00 800 1359), **MCI** (☎ 00 800 001), and **Sprint** (☎ 00 800 1010). To **call collect,** dial ☎ 01 23 for an international operator or have the phone office or hotel receptionist order the call. The operator won't speak English, the staff may claim they can't make the call, and hotel receptionists are protective of phones, so good luck. The Bulgarian phrase for collect call is *za tyahna smetka* (за тяхна сметка).

For **local calls,** payphones will accept coins, but it's best to buy a phone card. There are two brands: **BulFon** (orange) and **Mobika** (blue), which work only at telephones of the same brand. Telephone booths, which are everywhere, are color-coded to match the card. Cards are sold everywhere. Prices are the same for both brands: 400 units=20lv; 200 units=12lv; 100 units=7.50lv; 50 units=4.90lv. You can also call from the post office, where a clerk assigns you a booth, a meter records your bill, and you pay when finished. Even here, connections are poor. **Faxes** are widely used; send and receive them from post offices.

**Internet** is widespread and definitely cheapest. "С въздушна поща" on letters indicates **airmail.** Sending a letter abroad costs 0.60lv for any European destination, 0.80lv for the US, and 0.80-1.00lv for Australia, New Zealand, or South Africa; note that a Bulgarian return address is required to do so. **Mail** can be received general delivery through Poste Restante, though it is unreliable at best. Address envelope as follows: Katherine (First name), DAMON (LAST NAME), POSTE RESTANTE, Gen. Gurko 6 (Post office street address), Sofia (City) 1000 (Postal code), BULGARIA. In Sofia as well as the rest of Bulgaria, mail and telephone system remain unreliable. Save your postcards.

# SOFIA (СОФИЯ)　　☎ (0)2

Contrary to popular opinion, Plovdiv is not the sole home of Bulgarian culture. It's in Sofia (pop. 1.4 million) as well, you just have to dig deeper to find it. That might mean sifting through pairs of fake Nikes to find handmade lace at a bazaar, or dodging trams and cars on the way to the theater, but it's well worth the effort. 1500 years of churches and cobblestones are not quite dwarfed by Soviet-era concrete blocks, and 19th-century elegance is weathering the fast food invasion more or less gracefully. If you get discouraged, Sofia's 1.4 million inhabitants, who navigate the capital with ease and composure, will inspire you to keep digging.

## ✠ ORIENTATION

The city's center, **pl. Sveta Nedelya** (пл. Света Неделя), is marked by the green roof of the Tsurkva (Church) Sv. Nedelya, the wide Sheraton Hotel, and Tsentralen Universalen Magazin (TSUM). **Bul. Knyaginya Maria Luiza** (Княгиня Мария Луиза) connects pl. Sveta Nedelya to the train station. Trams #1 and 7 run from the train station through pl. Sveta Nedelya to **bul. Vitosha** (Витоша), one of the main shopping and nightlife thoroughfares. Bul. Vitosha links pl. Sveta Nedelya to **pl. Bulgaria** and the huge, concrete **Natsionalen Dvorets Kultura** (Национален Дворец Култура; NDK; National Palace of Culture). Historical **bul. Tsar Osvoboditel** (бул. Цар Освободител; Tsar the Liberator) heads to the **university** and the hottest spots for dancing and drinking in Sofia. The monthly **Sofia City Guide** (free, available at the Sheraton Hotel) is a great English publication with loads of tourist information. **Maps** are also available in the lobby of the Sheraton Hotel and where books are sold—try Slaveikov Square (пл. Славйков) on Graf Ignatiev (Граф Игнатиев).

## Sofia

▲ ACCOMMODATIONS

Hostel in Sofia, 1
Hotel Niky, 2
Hotel Tsar Asen, 3

**BULGARIA**

San Stefano

Oborishte ul.
St. Methodius
& St. Cyril
National Library

Shipka ul.

University
of Sofia

ORLOV MOST
PL.

Vasil
Levski
Stadium

Tsar Osvoboditel bul.

Evlogi Georgiev bul.

N

200 yards
200 meters

V. Levski
Monument

Vasil Levski bul.

Yanko Sakazov bul.

Vrabcha

Moskovska ul.

Alexander
Nevsky
Cathedral

Parliament

NARODNO
SABRANIE
PL.

Vasil Levski bul.

Ljuben Karavelov

Graf Ignatiev

National
Opera House

St. Sofia

St. Nicholas
Russian Church

Royal Palace

Archaeological
Museum

Grand
Hotel Bulgaria

Aksakov

Slavianska

Tsar Shishman

Ivan Vazov

6th September

Gen. Gurko

Turt Venelin

Gen. Parensov

Church of
Seven Saints

Patriarch Evtimii bul.

United
Kingdom

Vasil Levski bul.

Ljuben Karavelov

Kniaz Dondukov bul.

Budapeshta

Moskovska ul.

Tsar Osvoboditel

Rakovski ul.

Han Krum

Presidency

Knjaz Alexander
Batenberg

Stefan Karadja

Rakovski ul.

Iskar

E. Josif

Serdika

Suborna

United
States

Lege

SLAVEIKOV
SQUARE

Racho
Dinchev

To (1.2km)

Banya
Bashi
Mosque

St. George's
Rotunda

Sheraton
Hotel

Knyaginya Maria
Luiza bul.

Alabin

Graf Ignatiev

Solunska

Parchevich

Angel Kanchev

BULGARIA
SQUARE

St. Nedelya

Denkoglu

Hristo Belchev

Synagogue
of Sofia

Lavele

Kniaz Boris I

Balkan
Tour

Pozitano

Karnigradska

Vitosha bul.

National Palace of Culture (NDK)

Gurguliat

Tsanov

Bratya Moladinovi

Tsar Samuil

Alexandar-Stamboliiski

Tri Ushi
POZITANO
PL.

Alabin

Kniaz Boris I

Uzundzhovska

Tsar Asen I

William Gladstone

Solunska

Neofit Rilski

Han Asparuh

Gen. M. Skobelev bul.

Shandor Petiofy

Pirotska

Naltcho

Hristo Botev bul.

Antim I

VAZRAZHDANE
PL.

MACEDONIA
PL.

Vladaiska

Damyan Guev

Hristo Botev bul.

Laroish koshut

Solunska

Tsar Samuil

RUSKI
PAMETNICK
PL.

Lyulin planina

Ivan Rilski

Strandja

Opalchenska

Pencho Slaveikov bul.

Konstantin Irechek

General Totleben bul.

BOIKO
PL.

# ✈ INTERCITY TRANSPORTATION

**Flights: Airport Sofia** (international info ☎ 79 80 35). Getting to the center from the airport can be very expensive. Bus #84 (to the left as you exit international arrivals; pay on board), has unreliable schedules, and taxis charge as much as 25lv. It's best to take *any* bus from the airport to anywhere in town and get a taxi to the center from there (2-5lv). **Balkan Airlines,** pl. Narodno Subranie 12 (Народно Субранье; ☎981 51 70), flies to **Moscow, RUS, Warsaw, POL, Prague, CZR,** and **Istanbul, TUR.** Open M-F 8am-7pm, Sa 8am-2pm. **Lufthansa,** Suborna 9 (Суборна; ☎980 41 41; fax 981 29 11). Open M-F 9am-5:30pm. **Air France,** Suborna 2 (☎981 78 30). Open M-F 9am-6pm. **British Airways,** Alibin 56 (Алибин; ☎981 70 00). Open M-F 9am-5pm.

**Trains: Tsentralna Gara** (Централна Гара; Central Train Station), Knyaginya Maria Luiza St. (Мария Луиза), north of the center. Trams #1 and 7 run to pl. Sv. Nedelya; #9 and 12 head down Hristo Botev (Христо Ботев). Buses #85, 213, 305, and 313 head to the station from different points in town. Info booth and tickets for northern Bulgaria are in the basement. To: **Ruse** (5 per day, 8.40lv); and **Varna** (6 per day, 11lv). Also in the basement, **Rila Travel Bureau** (Рила) sells tickets to: **Blagoevgrad** (2hr., 5 per day, 4.10lv); **Plovdiv** (2½hr., 15 per day, 3.80lv); **Varna** (7hr., 8 per day, 12.80lv, *couchette* 17.80lv); **Burgas** (7½hr., 6 per day, 8.50lv), and destinations abroad. Open daily 7am-11pm. It's cheaper, however, to buy international tickets at the **ticket office** (☎843 42 80), down the stairs in front of NDK. To: **Athens, GRE** (6 per day, 60lv); **Budapest, HUN** via **Yugoslavia** (1 per day, 85lv) and **Istanbul, TUR** (4 per day, 46lv). Due to the situation in Yugoslavia, west-bound tourists are strongly advised to travel through **Bucharest, ROM** (6 per day, 37lv). Duration of international trips is at the discretion of border officers. Open M-F 7am-3pm, Sa 7am-2pm.

**Buses: Ovcha Kupel** (Овча Купел), Tsar Boris III bul. (Цар Борис III). Take tram #5 or 19 heading away from Vitosha. Private buses, which leave from the parking lot across from the train station, are cheap and fast (though the length of the trip varies depending on which roads the bus chooses to take). One of them, **Group Travel** (☎320 122), sends buses to: **Burgas** (2 per day, 12.50lv); **Veliko Tarnovo** (1 per day, 8lv); **Varna** (5 per day, 13.50lv); **Athens, GRE** (3 per day, 66lv); and **Istanbul, TUR** (2 per day, 72lv). Buy tickets at kiosks labeled "Биллетни Център" (Billetni Tsentur) or on the bus. Pay in lv, US$, or DM. Open daily 7am-5:30pm and 6-7:30pm. Arrive 30-45min. early to be guaranteed a seat. **Matpu** (Матпу), ul. Damyan Gruev 23 (Дамян Груев; ☎ 52 50 04 and 51 92 01), also has buses to **Athens, GRE** (1 per day, 74lv, students 60lv) and **Istanbul, TUR** (6 per week, 50lv).

# ◰ LOCAL TRANSPORTATION

**Public Transportation:** Trams, trolleybuses, and buses cost 0.30lv per ride; day pass 1.50lv; 5-day pass 4.40lv. Buy tickets at kiosks labeled "билети" (bileti; tickets) or from the driver; punch them in the machines on board between windows to avoid a 10lv fine. Large backpacks may require an extra ticket. All transportation runs 5am-1am, but much less frequently after 9pm.

**Taxis: Softaxi** (☎ 12 84), **OK Taxi** (☎97 321 21), and **INEX** (☎919 19) are reliable options. Fares are 0.32-0.40lv per km, 0.45lv per km after 10pm—when it's really wise to take a cab. From the airport, don't pay more than 25lv to the center. Drivers are notorious for cheating everyone—don't be afraid to play hard-ball when bargaining for a low fare and agree on a price before the ride. A green light in the front window means the taxi is available.

**Car Rental: Hertz** and **Europcar,** at the airport. US$49-91 per day; 22% tax. **Odysseia-In** rents reliable cars for US$15 per day (see below).

# ⁊ PRACTICAL INFORMATION

## TOURIST AND FINANCIAL SERVICES

▓ **Tourist Office: Odysseia-In,** Stambolysky bul. 20-V (Страмболийски; ☎989 05 38 and 981 05 60; fax 980 32 00; odysseia@omega.bg; www.newtravel.com). From pl. Sv. Nedelya, head down Stambolysky and take the 2nd right on Lavele; Odysseia is half way down on the left, 2 floors up. The multilingual staff knows everything. They will tailor a trip for you, coordinate a wide variety of accommodations, transportation, and nation-wide tourist services. Consultation 5lv per 30min. Open M-F 9am-7pm, Sa 10am-4pm.

**Embassies:** Citizens of **Australia, Canada,** and **New Zealand** should contact the British Embassy. **South Africans** should contact their embassy in **Athens** (☎(30 01) 680 66 45). **UK,** bul. (*not* ul.) Vasil Levsky 38 (Васил Левски; ☎980 12 20 and 980 12 21), 3 blocks to the left of NDK when facing it. Open M-Th 8:30am-12:30pm and 1:30-5pm, F 8:30am-1pm. **US,** ul. Suborna 1a (Съборна; ☎980 52 41), 3 blocks from pl. Sv. Nedelya behind the Sheraton. Open M-F 8:30am-5pm. Consular section at Kapitan Andreev 1 (Капитан Андреев; ☎963 00 89), behind NDK. **Register** with the consular section upon arrival in Bulgaria, M-Th 2-4pm. Open for emergencies M-F 9am-5pm.

**Currency Exchange: Bulbank** (Булбанк), pl. Sv. Nedelya 7, cashes **traveler's checks** for a 0.5% commission and gives Visa cash advances for a 4% commission. Open M-F 8:30am-4pm. **Commercial Bank Biohim,** pl. Sv. Nedelya 19 (☎986 54 45, ext. 213), next to the Sheraton, cashes traveler's checks for a 1% commission and gives MC **cash advances** for a 6% commission. Open M-F 8:30am-3:30pm.

**ATMs:** Everywhere. All accept Cirrus/MC/Visa.

**American Express:** Aksakov 5 (Аксаков; ☎986 58 37). Open M-F 9am-6pm, Sa 9am-2:30pm.

## LOCAL AND EMERGENCY SERVICES

**Luggage Storage:** Downstairs at the central train station. Look for "гардероб" (*gard-erob*) signs. 0.50lv per piece. Open daily 5:30am-midnight.

**International Bookstore: USIS American Center,** Vitosha 18 (☎980 48 85), has a non-circulating English-language library. Open Tu-F 2-5pm. In addition, **Slaveikov Sq.** (Славейков) on Graf Ignatiev (Граф Игнатиев) is filled with vendors selling books and maps in many languages.

**Cultural Center: Euro-Bulgarian Cultural Centre** (ЕВСС; Евро-Булгарски Кулстурен Център), Al. Stambolysky bul. 17 (Ал. Стамболийски; ☎/fax 988 00 84; www.culture-link.nar.bg). Learn everything you ever wanted to know about Bulgaria (but were afraid to ask) from the English-speaking staff, bookstore, or website. **Internet access** 3lv per hr. Open M-F 9am-8pm, Sa 10am-7pm.

**24hr. Pharmacies: Purva Chastna Apteka** (Първа Частна Аптека), Tsar Asen 42, near Neofit Rilski. **Apteka #7,** pl. Sv. Nedelya 5 (☎986 54 53), near Stambolysky and Maria Luiza.

**Medical Assistance:** State-owned hospitals offer foreigners free 24hr. emergency aid. **Pirogov Emergency Hospital,** Gen. Totleben bul. 21 (Ген. Тотлебен; ☎515 31), across from Hotel Rodina. Take trolley #5 or 19 from the center. For **dog bites,** go to the **City Hospital** at Patriarch Evtimii bul. 37 (Патриарх Евтимий; ☎987 95 32 and 988 36 31). Open daily 7:30am-7:30pm.

**Telephones:** Ul. Stefan Karadzha 6 (Стефан Караджа), near the post office. Use 5lv coins for local calls. Bulgarian **phone cards** also sold here. Open 24hr.

**Internet Access: Club Cyberia,** Stephan Karadzha 18B (☎988 73 50). 2lv per hr. Open daily 10am-midnight. **ICN** (☎088 24 10 76), in NDK. 4lv per hr. Open daily 9am-10:30pm.

**Post Office:** Gen. Gurko 6 (Гурко). Go down Suborna behind pl. Sv. Nedelya, then turn right on Lege (Леге) and left on Gurko; entrance to the right on Vasil Levsky ul. (*not* bul.). **Poste Restante.** International mailing at window #7. Open M-F 7am-8:30pm.

**Postal code:** 1000.

BULGARIA

# ACCOMMODATIONS

Hotels are rarely worth the exorbitant price—if the hostel is full, private rooms are often the best option. Camping is another inexpensive choice; **Camping Vrana** (☎78 12 13) is 10km from the center on E-80, and **Cherniya Kos** (☎57 11 29) is 11km away on E-79. Check with Odysseia-In (see **Tourist Office**, p. 115) for both options. In most establishments, pay with either *leva* or US dollars and Deutschmarks.

**Hostel in Sofia (a.k.a Naska's Home for Weary Travelers),** Pozitano 16 (Позитано; ☎/ fax 989 15 04; hostelsofia@usa.net). From pl. St. Nedelya, walk down Vitosha. Turn right on Pozitano, just before the court. Walk 1 block; the hostel is on the right, above the Chinese restaurant. Great location and friendly staff with travel info. Homey atmosphere. Kitchen privileges, sunny balcony to dry your laundry, lounge with cable TV, shared hot shower and WC. Sheets and towel provided. Reception closed noon-5pm. Check-out noon. No curfew. US$10 per person. Breakfast included.

**Hotel Niky,** Neofit Rilski 16 (☎51 19 15; fax 951 60 91), off Vitosha. Old Bulgarian building with pleasant garden restaurant on ground floor. Shared toilets and showers; satellite TVs, sink, and closet in every room. Breakfast US$2. Reception 24hr. Check-out noon. Singles US$22; doubles US$40 per person. Students 10% off.

**Hotel Tsar Asen** (Цар Асен), Tsar Asen 68 (☎54 78 01 and 70 59 20; elenag@iterra.net). From the National Museum of History, walk toward the NDK on Tsar Asen I. It's on the right, just before Gen. M. Skobelev bul. (Ген. М. Скобелев). Ring the doorbell at the gate. Soft beds and thermostats in each room. Cable TV and private shower. Singles US$28; doubles US$34; triples US$45; quads US$50.

# FOOD

From fast food to Bulgarian specialties, cheap meals are easy to find. **24hr. supermarkets** abound on **Vitosha.** An **outdoor market** lines Graf Ignatiev (Граф Игнатиев) in the summer (past Slaveikov Square, near the Church of Seven Saints).

**Murphy's Irish Pub,** Karnigradska 6 (Кърниградска; ☎980 28 70). Run by 2 Irish blokes, Murphy's attracts an international crowd with its mouth-watering food and generous portions. Main dishes 4-9lv; a pint of *Murphy's* 4lv. Special "Irish breakfast" (2 meals in itself) comes with a drink. Open daily 10:30am-10:30pm.

**Trops House** (Тропс Къща), Saborna 11 (☎981 00 04). Convenient and quick, this great cafeteria-style restaurant is perfect for those puzzled by Cyrillic menus. Traditional Bulgarian costumes adorn the walls. Main dishes 1-2lv. Open daily 8am-9:30pm.

**Balbeck,** Vasil Levsky ul. 4 (☎987 09 07). Take advantage of the city's diversity while you can; outside Sofia non-Bulgarian meals are hard to find. Lebanese cooks excel at Middle Eastern cuisine and try their best with Bulgarian meals. Main dishes 2-6lv. Open M-F 10am-9pm, Sa-Su 10am-7pm.

**Jimmy's,** Angel Kunchev 11 (Ангел Кънчев). The local secret to surviving Sofia's summer heat waves, Jimmy's serves gourmet ice cream (0.50lv per scoop) in a shaded park.

**Luciano,** ul. Moskovska 29 (Московска; ☎981 97 77). At the corner of Rakovski and Moskovska, just up the street from the Opera House. The decor and live piano music top off desserts so lovely you're almost inclined not to eat them (2-4lv). Deserted non-smoking section. Open daily 10:30am-11pm.

# SIGHTS

**CATHEDRAL OF ST. NEDELYA.** (Катедрален Храм Св. Неделя; Katedralen Hram Sv. Nedelya.) The focal point of pl. Sveta Nedelya and all of Sofia, the cathedral is a reconstruction of the 14th-century original, which was destroyed by a bomb in a 1925 attempt on Boris III. The Tsar escaped, but the cupola buried 190 generals and politicians. The current frescoes date from 1975, but are already blackened with the soot of candles. *(At the center of pl. Sveta Nedelya. Open daily 7am-6:30pm.)*

**ST. GEORGE'S ROTUNDA.** (Св. Георги; Sv. Georgi.) The 4th-century St. George's stands near a former Roman bath and the remains of the ancient town of Serdica. St. George's itself is a brick structure covered in 11th- to 14th-century murals. After being converted from a bath to a church in the 5th century, it served as a house of worship under Bulgarians, Byzantines, and Turks, then as a museum, and now as a historical monument. *(In the courtyard enclosed by the Sheraton Hotel and the Presidency. Enter from Tsar Osvoboditel bul. Open daily 8am-6pm.)*

**CHURCH OF ST. PETYA SAMARDZHIYSKA.** (Църква Храм Св. Петя Самарджийска; Tsurkva Hram Sv. Petya Samardzhiyska.) The tiny, 14th-century St. Petya's contains layers of frescoes stretching across the walls and ceiling. The crypt and ruins date to Thracian times. The bones of Vasil Levsky (see **History,** p. 103), Bulgaria's national hero, are rumored to have been found inside. A museum during communist times, St. Petya's is again an operating church. *(In the underpass between pl. Sv. Nedelya and TSUM. Open Nov-Apr. M-Sa 9:30am-6pm; Su 9am-noon; May-Oct. M-Sa 8am-7pm, Su 9am-noon. 5lv, tours 10lv.)*

**SYNAGOGUE OF SOFIA.** (Софийска Синагога; Sofiiska sinagoga.) Sofia's only synagogue opened for services in 1909. Its foundation was built with stones from Sofia's Jewish cemetery. The interior is undergoing renovation to repair damage done by a stray Allied bomb from World War II, which miraculously did not explode. A museum upstairs (with captions in English) outlines the history of Jews in Bulgaria. *(On the corner of Tsar Simeon and George Washington. Walk to the gate on Tsar Simeon and ring the bell. Open Su-F 9am-5pm, Sa 10am-6:30pm. Weekly service Sa 6:30pm.)*

**ST. NICHOLAS RUSSIAN CHURCH.** (Св. Николай; Sv. Nikolai.) Named for the miracle-maker, this 1913 church has five traditional Russian Orthodox-style onion domes. *(Down Tsar Osvoboditel from sv. Nedelya. Open daily 8am-6pm, later if there's an evening service. Services Sa 9am and 6pm, Su 9am.)*

**ST. SOFIA CHURCH.** (Св. София; Sv. Sofia.) The city adopted the saint's name in the 14th century. During the 19th century, while the church was used as Sofia's main mosque, a series of earthquakes repeatedly destroyed the minarets. Amazingly, the 5th-century floor mosaic survived intact. The Ottoman rulers interpreted the catastrophes as a warning and gave up St. Sofia as their house of prayer. This church is unique in Sofia because of its white walls, adorned with fairly sparse frescoes. *(On pl. Alexander Nevsky. Open daily 8am-6pm. Donation requested.)*

**ST. ALEXANDER NEVSKY CATHEDRAL.** (Св. Александър Невски; Sv. Aleksandr Nevsky.) The gold-domed Byzantine-style cathedral, erected 1904-1912 in memory of the 200,000 Russians who died in the 1877-78 Russo-Turkish War, was named after the patron saint of the tsar-liberator. It is the largest Christian Orthodox Church on the Balkan Peninsula and one of the most artistic, housing over 400 frescoes by Russian and Bulgarian artists. In a separate entrance to the left of the main church, the **crypt** houses a spectacular array of painted icons and religious artifacts from the past 1000 years. *(In the center of pl. Alexander Nevsky. Cathedral open daily 7:30am-7pm; crypt open M and W-Su 10:30am-6:30pm. Cathedral free; crypt 3lv, students 1.50lv. Guided tours of the crypt for more than 10 people 15lv, less than 10 people 10lv. M free.)*

**BUL. TSAR OSVOBODITEL.** The imposing sculptures at the main entrance to the **University of Sofia** represent Evolgi and Hristo Georgiev, founders of the University. *(Tsar Osvoboditel 15, on the corner with Vasil Levsky ul.)* Behind the University, the **Bulgarian Artists' Union** (Съюз на Българските Художници; Suyuz na Bulgarskite Hudozhnitsi) has a four-floor gallery filled with the modern artwork of both professional and amateur Bulgarian artists. *(On Shipka (Шипка). Open M-Sa 11am-7pm. Free.)* As you stroll down bul. Tsar Osvoboditel, keep in mind that your boots are stepping on the first paved street in Sofia, weighted down on either end by the **House of Parliament** and the **Royal Palace.** The 1884 **National Assembly** provides a backdrop for a dramatic equestrian statue of the tsar *osvoboditel* (liberator) himself. Russian Tsar Alexander II towers astride his charger over pl. Narodno Subranie (Народно Събрание), with the Declaration of the War of Liberation (the Russo-Turkish War of 1877-78) in hand. **Rakovski** (Раковски) is Bulgaria's theater hub, with half a dozen

BULGARIA

theaters in a 1km stretch. A left on Rakovski leads to the columns of the **National Opera House,** built in 1950. *(Rakovski 59, main entrance at Vrabcha 1 (Врабча).* ☎ *987 70 11, 987 13 66, or 981 14 67; for group visits* ☎ *81 15 67. Shows Tu-Sa 9pm. Box office open M-F 9am-6:30pm and Sa-Su 11am-6pm. Tickets 15-50lv.)*

**NATIONAL PALACE OF CULTURE.** (Национален Дворец Култура; NDK, Natsionalen Dvorets Kultura.) Opened in 1981 to celebrate the 13th centennial of Bulgaria, the monstrous NDK is a barracks of culture, with restaurants, art displays, theaters, and movie halls, including the country's best cinema, which shows Bulgarian and subtitled American films. Buy tickets (approx. 5lv) from the ticket office (биллетни център; biletni centr) down the outside ramp to the left of the main entrance. Ask here about tickets for plays and concerts. *(In Yuzhen Park. From pl. Sv. Nedelya, walk down bul. Vitosha to bul. Patriarch Evtimy and enter the park. The Palace is at its far end. Open daily 10am-7pm. Box office open daily 8:30am-7pm.)*

# 🏛 MUSEUMS

**Museum of Archaeology** (Археологически Музей; Arheologicheski Muzey), on the corner of Lege and Tsar Osvoboditel. From Sv. Nedelya, head down Suborna and take the 1st left on Lege; the museum is on the right, at the corner of a busy intersection. Houses items from Thracian, Greek, Roman, and Turkish settlements, some 2000 years old. English captions. Open Tu-Su 10am-6pm. Free.

**National Museum of Ethnography** (Национален Етнографически Музей; Natsionalen Etnograficheski Muzey), in the Royal Palace on Tsar Osvoboditel bul. Take trolleybus #9 to Moskovska. Founded after the 1878 liberation (see **History,** p. 104), the museum covers the past 400 years. The upper floor exhibits a detailed photographic history, emphasizing the role of Armenians in Bulgaria. Open Tu-Su 10am-5pm. 3lv, students 1.50lv. Guided tour (for groups of more than 5) 5lv; individual tour or consultation 7lv.

**National Art Gallery** (Национална Художествена Галериа; Natsionalna Hudozhestvena Galeriya). In the Royal Palace on Tsar Osvoboditel. Possibly the best art museum in Bulgaria. Open Tu-Su 10am-6pm. 3lv, students 1.50lv. Guided tours in English up to 10 people 10lv, more than 10 people 15lv. Tu free.

# ◪ NIGHTLIFE

While nightlife in Sofia does not consume the entire city as in Plovdiv or Varna, the scene is getting wilder every year. Most nightlife centers around bul. Vitosha or, for the younger set, the University of Sofia at the intersection of **Vasil Levsky** and **Tsar Osvoboditel.** Young people often meet at **Popa,** the irreverent nickname for Patriarch Evtimy's monument, where bul. Patriarch Evtimy intersects with Vasil Levsky and **Graf Ignatiev.** Out on the town, be careful: the mafia often runs the show.

**Biraria Luchano** (Бирария Лучано), Slavekov 9 (Славеков; ☎ 980 30 50). Heading to NDK from Vitosha, take a left on Alabin (Алабин), then veer right onto Graf Ignatiev. When you reach pl. Slavekov (with McDonald's), take a left into the courtyard. Lively, well-lit pub with international beers (1-3lv). Open daily noon-11pm.

**Biblioteka** (Библиотека), in St. Cyril and Methodius Library. Enter from Oborishte. A crowd of mixed ages gathers to sing along phonetically to American cover songs. Karaoke in one room, live band in another. Cover 3lv. Open W-Sa 11pm-5am.

**Spartakus** (Спартакус), in the underpass past the pl. Narodno Subranie, leading toward Vasil Levsky. Keeps its gay and straight clientele happy with thumping techno and intense strobe lights. Cover 3lv. Open daily 11pm-late.

**Dali,** behind the University, on Krakra. The best Latin club in Sofia. Plenty of room to spin and swivel to the DJ's selections. Men 3lv. Open daily until 6am.

**Swinging Hall,** down Graf Ignatiev past the stadium, on the right. A laid-back jazz club featuring frequent live bands with character. Open daily 8:30pm-4am.

# NEAR SOFIA

## RILA MONASTERY        ☎ (0)7054

Holy Ivan of Rila built Rila Monastery (Рилски Манастир; Rilski Manastir) in the 10th century as a refuge from the lascivious, sexy outer world. It sheltered the arts of icon painting and manuscript copying during the Byzantine and Ottoman occupations, and remained an oasis of Bulgarian culture during five centuries of foreign rule. For the modern visitor, the monastery, perched atop verdant Rila Mountain, offers sanctuary from crowded buses and dirty cities.

**▐ TRANSPORTATION.** One **bus** leaves Sofia's Ovchu Kubel bus station for **Rila Town** (daily 10:15am, 4lv). Otherwise, take a bus from Sofia's Novotel Europa to **Blagoevgrad** (2hr., 8-10 per day, 3.80lv) and from Blagoevgrad to **Rila Town** (45min., every hr., 2lv). Then catch the bus up to the monastery (45min., 3 per day, 1.10lv; returns at 9am, 2, and 5pm). Don't trust the posted schedules in both Rila and Blagoevgrad, which are frequently incorrect; ask the ticket office for the correct time.

**▐ PRACTICAL INFORMATION.** **Balkantourist** arranges guided English-language **tours** of the monastery and the grounds (US$30 per person). There are **no currency exchanges** nearby. There is a single **telephone** behind the post office. Buy a magnetic phone card next to Restaurant Rila (see below).

**▐▐ ACCOMMODATIONS AND FOOD.** ▌Hotel Tsarev Vrukh (Царев Връх; ☎/fax 22 80) is a new hotel with sparkling rooms, private bathrooms and telephones, a fitness center, a sauna, and a fine restaurant and wine cellar. The reception also organizes sightseeing trips in the area and gives fishing advice. From behind the monastery, the hotel is 50m down the path that follows the river. At only US$14, plus US$2 for breakfast, the place is a steal. Inquire at room #170 in the monastery about staying in a heated **monastic cell** (30lv per person), but be prepared for bare rooms, cold water, and no shower. (☎ 22 08. Curfew midnight.) **Camping Bor** is tucked away at the base of the mountains with clean but bare campsites and bungalows. Walk down the road behind the monastery and take a right across the bridge at the triangular intersection. Then take a left and follow the signs. (Reception 24hr. 3lv per person, 2lv per tent; 2-bed bungalows 20lv. 3lv per car. Students 10% off.)

Behind the monastery are several cafes and a mini-market. Try some of the monks' homemade bread (0.30lv) or eat at **Restaurant Rila,** behind the monastery, where you can sit outside over the beautiful forest and rushing creek. (☎ 22 90. Main dishes 2-9lv. 7% service fee. Open daily 7:30am-11:30pm.)

**▣ SIGHTS.** Today's monastery was built between 1834 and 1837; only a brick tower remains from the 14th-century structure. The monastery's vibrant murals were painted by brothers Dimitar and Zahari Zograf—"Zograf" actually means "mural painter"—famous for their work at the Troyan and Bachkovo monasteries (see p. 105 and p. 124). The 1200 frescoes on the central chapel form a brilliantly colored outdoor art gallery. Inside lies the grave of Bulgaria's last tsar, Boris III. (Backpacks, cameras, shorts, and sleeveless shirts not permitted.) The **museum** displays weapons, embroidery, illuminated texts, and icons. The exhibit includes a wooden cross that took 12 years to carve and left its creator, the monk Rafail, blind. (Open daily 8:30am-4:30pm. 5lv, students 3lv. Sporadic English tours 15lv.)

**▟ HIKING.** **Maps** and suggested hiking routes through **Rila National Park** are on signs outside the monastery. Alternatively, look in the **Manastirski Padarutsi** (Манастирски Падаръци) alcove, just outside the monastery's back entry, for a Cyrillic map of all the paths (8lv). Don't miss the short hike (1hr.) to the **cave** where Holy Ivan lived and prayed for years. To reach it, walk down the road behind the monastery. After the triangular intersection, head left up the path through the field.

BULGARIA

Follow the signs for the grave (гроб; grob), which point the way to the church where Ivan was originally buried. Behind the church is the entrance to the cave.

> **!** The cave's upper exit is very narrow. Larger or claustrophobic travelers should think twice about attempting the trip through the cave.

It's believed that passing through will purify your soul. Enter at the bottom and crawl through the dark winding passages. A flashlight or lighter is helpful. According to legend, this part of the journey represents the journey out of the womb. Emerge at the top for a symbolic rebirth—unless you have sinned too much, in which case the legend has it that rocks will fall and crush you. Next, continue uphill 40m to the spring and cleanse yourself near the shrine to St. Ivan. You're now ready to enter the chapel guilt-free. If you'd like, write a question for the saint and leave it tucked in the wall. Incredible views—particularly at **Seventh Lake** (Седемте Езера; Sedemte Ezera) and **Malyovitsa** (Мальовица)—and welcoming huts *(hizhi)* await on other routes within the park. Expect to pay around US$2 for a spot (not necessarily a bed) to sleep. Follow the **yellow markings** to the **Hizha Sedemte Ezera** (Хижа Седемте Езера; Seventh Lake Hut; 6hr.). The **blue** trail leads to **Hizha Malyovitsa** (Мальовица; 7hr.). **Red** leads to the highest hut in the Balkans: **Ivan Vazov** (Иван Вазов; 6hr.).For more on hiking, see **Camping and the Outdoors**, p. 37.

# SOUTHERN MOUNTAINS

The Rila, Pirin, and Rodopi mountain ranges hid Bulgaria's cultural and political dissidents during 500 years of Turkish rule—monks copied manuscripts in remote monasteries while *haiduk* bandits struck from the highlands. Today, a visitor will find endless attractions, from hiking near Bansko to wine tasting in Melnik. The region is also rich in history dating back to the Roman settlement of Plovdiv.

## PLOVDIV (ПЛОВДИВ)                    ☎(0)32

Although second in size to Sofia, Plovdiv (pop. 376,000) is widely hailed as the cultural capital of Bulgaria. Founded around 600 BC as Philipopolis (for Philip II of Macedonia), the city now draws crowds to its trade fairs and arts festivals. A 10-minute stroll through the center invariably winds through its history—the cobblestone Stari Grad, overhung with lush oaks, church crosses, and 19th-century National Revival houses, gives way to the concrete Soviet highrises and finally pedestrian thoroughfares teeming with small vendors and Western ads.

### ORIENTATION

With no clearly defined center and poorly-marked streets, Plovdiv is difficult to navigate—basic knowledge of the main streets and an up-to-date **map** are essential. Street vendors sell good Cyrillic maps for 3lv. The east-west thoroughfare **bul. Hristo Botev** (Христо Ботев) marks the southern end of town, from which **bul. Ruski** (Руски) and **bul. Tsar Boris III Obedinitel** (Цар Борис III Обединител) run to the **Maritsa River** (Марица) at the northern end of **Stari Grad** (Стари Град; Old Town). In the middle of town, bul. Tsar Boris III Obedinitel runs along the east side of **pl. Tsentralen** (пл. Централен). From the northwest corner of pl. Tsentralen, **Knyaz Aleksandr** (Княз Александр), the main commercial street, runs north to **pl. Dzhumaya** (Джумая), where **bul. Suborna** (Съборна) rises to the east.

### TRANSPORTATION

**Trains:** The **train station** is at the corner of bul. Ruski and bul. Hristo Botev. To get from the train station to pl. Tsentralen, take bus #20 or 26 (buy 0.20lv tickets on the bus), or cross bul. Hristo Botev via the underpass and take **Ivan Vazov** (Иван Вазов) to the

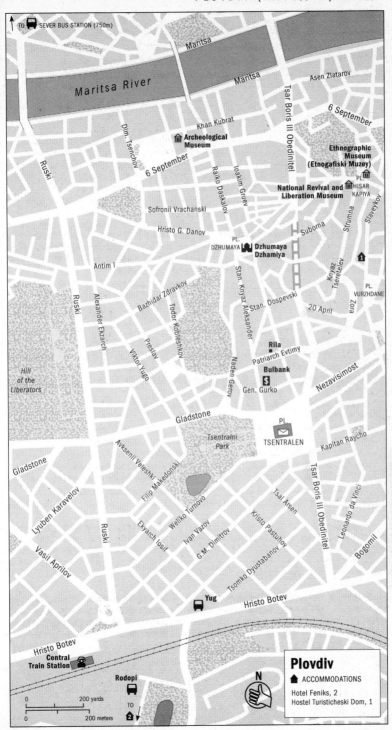

TO SEVER BUS STATION (750m)

Maritsa

Maritsa River

Maritsa

Asen Zlatarov

6 September

Dim. Tsenchov

Ruski

Khan Kubrat

Archeological Museum

6 September

Raiko Daskalov

Ioakim Gruev

Tsar Boris III Obedinitel

Ethnographic Museum (Etnografiski Muzey)

HISAR KAPIYA

National Revival and Liberation Museum

PL.

Slaveykov

Strumna

Sofronii Vrachanski

Hristo G. Danov

PL. DZHUMAYA

Dzhumaya Dzhamiya

Suboma

Knyaz Tseretelev

Zora

PL. VURZHDANE

1

Antim I

Bazhidar Zdravkov

Todor Kableshkov

Preslav

Viktor Yugo

Stan. Knyaz Aleksander

Stan. Dospevski

20 April

Nezavisimost

Ruski

Alexander Ekzarch

Hill of the Liberators

Naden Gerov

Rila

Patriarch Evtimy

Bulbank

Gen. Gurko

Gladstone

Tsentralni Park

PL TSENTRALEN

Kapitan Raycho

Gladstone

Lyuben Karavelov

Ruski

Avksenii Veleshki

Filip Makedonski

Weliko Turnovo

Ekvarch Iosif

Ivan Vazov

G.M. Dimitrov

Krsito Pastuhov

Tsomko Dyustabanov

Tsar Arsen

Tsar Boris III Obedinitel

Leonardo da Vinci

Bogomil

Vasil Aprilov

Yug

Hristo Botev

Hristo Botev

Central Train Station

Rodopi

TO

2

0    200 yards

0    200 meters

N

**Plovdiv**

⌂ ACCOMMODATIONS

Hotel Feniks, 2
Hostel Turisticheski Dom, 1

BULGARIA

square. To: **Karlovo** (2hr., 6 per day, 1.80lv); **Sofia** (2½hr., 14 per day, 3.90lv); **Burgas** (5hr., 7 per day, 6.20lv); and **Varna** (5½hr., 3 per day, 8.10lv). Most trains from Sofia to **Istanbul, TUR** or **Burgas** stop in Plovdiv. Only **Rila,** bul. Hristo Botev 31a (☎44 61 20), sells international train tickets. Open M-F 8am-7pm, Sa 8am-4pm.

**Buses: Matpu** (Матпу; ☎/fax 63 24 42), on bul. Tsar Boris III Obedinitel next to Hotel Trimondium (Тримондиум). Deals with all Balkan connections. To: **Istanbul, TUR** (daily 8pm, US$20); **Thessaloniki, GRE** (1-2 per day, US$25); **Skopje, MAC** (daily 8am and 4pm, US$15); and **Ohrid, MAC** (daily 8pm, US$18). Open daily 8am-6pm. In addition, 3 separate stations serve the areas indicated by their names:

**Sever** (Север; North; ☎55 37 05), north of bul. Bulgaria on Dimitur Stambolov (Димитър Стамболов) at its intersection with Pobeda (Победа). Ruski becomes Pobeda when it crosses the river. Take bus #2 from pl. Tsentralen.

**Yug** (Юг; South; ☎62 69 37), bul. Hristo Botev 47, on the other side of the street from the train station. Buses south and to **Sofia** (2hr., every hr., 5lv). **Traffic Express** (Трафик Экспрес), in the station (☎26 57 90 and 63 20 95), serves the **Black Sea** coast.

**Rodopi** (Родопи; ☎77 76 07), for the **Rodopi Mountains,** behind the train station through the underpasses beneath the trains. To **Smolyan** (9 per day, 1hr., 4.50lv).

**⚡ PRACTICAL INFORMATION**

**Tourist Office: Puldin Tours** (Пълдин), bul. Bulgaria 106 (☎55 38 48). Arranges tours of Plovdiv and the Valley of the Roses (see p. 128), exchanges money, and sells festival tickets. They will also find private rooms throughout Bulgaria (see **Accommodations,** below). From the train station, ride tram #2 or 102 (0.20lv) 9 stops to bul. Bulgaria and backtrack 1 block to the left. By foot, cross the river via bul. Tsar Boris III Obedinitel, pass Hotel Maritsa, and look for Puldin immediately after turning left on bul. Bulgaria (20min. walk). English spoken. Open M-F 9am-5:30pm, until 9pm during trade fairs.

**Currency Exchange: Bulbank** (Булбанк), Patriarch Evtimy 5 (Патриарх Евтимий; ☎26 02 70), off Knyaz Aleksandr in front of the large fountain. Cashes **traveler's checks** for US$1 per transaction. Open M-F 8:30am-4:30pm.

**ATM:** Cirrus/MC ATM in front of the Bulbank entrance. AmEx/Cirrus/MC ATM in the post office on pl. Tsentralen.

**Luggage Storage:** In the train station. Open daily 7am-6:20pm and 6:50pm-6:30am. 0.80lv per bag.

**24hr. Pharmacy: Apteka 47 Tunela** (Аптека 47 Тунела), bul. Tsar Boris III Obedinitel 64 (☎27 07 93). From pl. Tsentralen, follow bul. Tsar Boris III through the tunnel; the pharmacy is on the left. **Branch** on Knyaz Aleksandr.

**Internet access: VooDoo Net,** Knyaz Aleksandr 3, near the mosque, up 2 flights. 1lv per hr. for a slow connection. Open 24hr. **Internet Club** (Интернет Клуб), across from the post office on Tsar Boris III Obedinitel. 1.20 lv per hr. Open daily 10am-9pm.

**Telephones:** In the post office. Open daily 6am-11pm. **Faxes** (fax 493 00 44) open daily 8am-8pm.

**Post Office:** Pl. Tsentralen. Poste Restante in the room to the left of the west entrance. Open M-Sa 7am-7pm, Su 7-11am.

**Postal code:** 4000.

**🏠 ACCOMMODATIONS**

Prices triple during trade fairs during the first weeks of May and the end of September; at these times, stay in a **private room. Puldin Tours** (see above) arranges singles (US$13), doubles (US$16), and one-bedroom apartments (US$20). During summer months, especially July and August, budget hotels are often full; make reservations.

**Hostel Turisticheski Dom** (Туристически Дом), P.R. Slaveykov 5 (П.Р. Славейков; ☎63 32 11), in Stari Grad. From Knyaz Aleksandr, take Patriarch Evtimy (across from McDonald's) into Stari Grad, passing under bul. Tsar Boris III Obedinitel. Turn left on Slaveykov at pl. Vuzrazhdane (Възраждане), past the fruit market. Spacious 1-, 2-, and 5-bed dorms with sinks and shared bath in one of Plovdiv's National Revival buildings. Cafe and restaurant downstairs. Lockout 11pm. 22lv per person.

**Hotel Feniks** (Феникс), Silivria 18A (Силиврия; ☎77 48 51 and 77 49 51). From Rodopi bus station, head away from the train tracks on Dimitur Talev (Димитър Талев) for 15min. After crossing Nikola Vaptsarov (Никола Вапцаров), take the 2nd right; it's 200m down on the right. A variety of rooms with variable prices. Some have private bathrooms, others shared. Prices lower for longer stays. Around US$15 per person.

## 🗖 FOOD

Plovdiv offers a wide array of inexpensive Bulgarian restaurants, although cafes are the cheapest option. On the way to the Hostel Turisticheski Dom, the *ponedelnik pazar* (понеделник пазар; Monday market) in pl. Vuzrazhdane sells fruit and veggies for 1.50-2.50lv per kilo; get there early in the day for the freshest produce.

**Dreams,** next to Bulbank on Knyaz Aleksandr. Plenty of quick, simple meals (2-6lv) to enjoy on the shaded patio or eat on the run. The house specialty is the desserts, which are the dreamiest in Bulgaria (1.50-3lv). Open daily 8am-midnight.

**Cafe,** in the Philipopolis Stadium (see below). Serves traditional Bulgarian food on the different tiers of the stadium. Main dishes 2-8lv. Open daily 11am-midnight.

**Union Club** (Юниън Клуб), Mitropolit Paisy 6 (☎27 05 51). Take Suborna from pl. Dzhumaya, then make a sharp right where the street branches in front of the church; head up the steps through a forbidding wooden gate on the right. Features a high-walled garden where you can enjoy your brains-in-butter hors d'oeuvres. Also serves omelettes and chicken. Main dishes 1.50-6lv. Open daily 11am until the last customer leaves.

## 🗖 SIGHTS

Most of Plovdiv's historical and cultural treasures are concentrated among Stari Grad's **Trimondium,** or three hills.

**ROMAN RUINS.** A smaller version of Rome's Colosseum, the 2nd-century Roman **amphitheater** (Античен Театр; Antichen Teatr) looks out over the city from the heights, while busy Tsar Boris III Obedinitel now zooms through the tunnel below. It serves as a popular venue for concerts and shows, hosting the **Festival of the Arts** in the summer and early fall (contact **Puldin Tours** for details; see **Practical Information,** p. 17) and the annual **Opera Festival** in June. *(Take a right off Knyaz Aleksandr to Stanislav Dospevski (Станислав Доспевски), after the pink art gallery, and turn right at the end of the street. Take the steep stairs to the left. Open daily 8am-dark. 2lv.)* **Philipopolis Stadium** is a less well-preserved arena. The gladiator's entrance is still intact and locals claim that lion bones were found inside when the stadium was unearthed. *(Follow Knyaz Aleksandr to the end; the stadium is underneath pl. Dzhumaya.)*

**CHURCH OF ST. CONSTANTINE AND ELENA.** The oldest Orthodox church in Plovdiv, dating from the 4th century, it was renovated in 1832, complete with murals and icons by Bulgarian artist Zahari Zograf (see **Literature and Arts,** p. 105). *(On Suborna, before the Museum of Ethnography. Open daily 9am-6:30pm. Free.)*

**MUSEUMS.** The ⬛Museum of Ethnography (Етнографски Музей; Etnografski Muzey) displays artifacts from Bulgaria's past, including clothes, musical instruments, and tools. *(At the end of Suborna. Entrance in back. ☎96 56 54. Open Tu-Su 9am-noon and 2-5pm. 3lv, students 0.20lv.)* Each room in the **National Renaissance Museum** details a different stage in Bulgarian history through the 1800s. *(Tsanko Lavrenov 1 (Цанко Лавренов). Turn right at the end of Suborna and head through the Turkish Gate. ☎22 59 23. Open M-Sa 8:45am-noon and 2-5pm. 2lv, students 1lv. English brochure available.)*

**RUN FOR YOUR LIFE** You may notice that Bulgarian pedestrians faithfully obey crosswalk signs and that when they do cross the road they run like they're being chased by wild dogs. Cars, not pedestrians, have the right of way here and the motorists aren't about to let anyone forget it. In fact, the word for speed bump, "сприци полиция" (spritsi politsia), translates literally to "fallen policeman."

BULGARIA

**OTHER SIGHTS.** Enjoy the beautifully patterned mosaic walls of pl. Dzhumaya's namesake, **Dzhumaya Mosque** (Джумая Джамия; Dzhumaya Dzhamiya). *(Go past pl. Dzhumaya and turn right to reach the main entrance.)* If you grow tired of museums and relics, wander down the little **Strumna** (Стръмна) alley and watch the few remaining Plovdiv artisans pound and polish metal as their ancestors did. On a cool evening, head to the fountainside cafe in **Tsentralni Park** (Централни Парк), near pl. Tsentralen, where strobe lights illuminate the spring.

## ◪ DAYTRIP FROM PLOVDIV

### BACHKOVO MONASTERY

*Buses run from Plovdiv's Yug station to Asenovgrad (25min., 21 per day, 0.60lv), as do trains (25min., every hr., 0.80lv). From the Asenovgrad bus station, catch a bus to the monastery (20min., every 30min., 0.50lv). Get off at the 2nd stop (after the tunnel) and follow the cobblestones up the gradual rise.*

Twenty-eight kilometers south of Plovdiv, in the Rodopi mountains, stands Bulgaria's second-largest monastery, Bachkovo Monastery (Бачковски Манастир; Bachkovski Manastir). Built in 1083 by Georgian brothers Grigory and Abazy Bakuriani and almost entirely destroyed by the Turks in the early 14th century, it was rebuilt a century later. An oasis of Bulgarian culture, history, and literature during the 500 years of Turkish rule, Bachkovo today draws crowds to its phenomenal artwork. The main church is home to the **icon of the Virgin Mary and Child** (икона Света Богородица; ikona Sveta Bogoroditsa), which is said to have miraculous healing power. (Open daily 8am-dark.) Next door, the brightly colored paintings of famed Nation Revival artist Zahari Zograf (see **Literature and Arts**, p. 105) decorate the 12th-century **Church of Archangels.** Across the courtyard, ask to be let into the **Trapezaria** (old dining room). Inside the dark chamber sit the original 1601 table and frescoes featuring ancient Greek philosophers among the Biblical genealogies. Along either of the roads leading uphill from the monastery, there are other small shrines and paths that make for great day-hiking, with picnic areas and some of the most gorgeous mountain vistas in Bulgaria. Below, shops and cafes flank the road leading to the monastery. You can spend the night in one of the bare rooms above the monastery gate. (No shower, shared toilet. 2- to 20-bed rooms 10lv.) The **Vodapada Restaurant** (Водапада; Waterfall), is named for the cascade alongside its patio. (☎93 23 89. Main dishes 4-10lv. Open daily 9am-midnight.)

# BLAGOEVGRAD (БЛАГОЕВГРАД) ☎(0)73121

The epitome of Stalinist urban planning, much of Blagoevgrad (blah-GOY-ehv-grahd; pop. 78,000) was built in the 1950s, with big, open squares and orderly streets. The city is the transportation hub of Southwest Bulgaria, but its many parks and vibrant cafe culture provide plenty to do if you're staying longer than it takes to get from one bus to another. The American University of Bulgaria (AUB) enlivens the city center, one of the few in Bulgaria where Americans are not an anomaly.

⌷ **TRANSPORTATION.** Blagoevgrad's **bus** and **train stations** are 50m from each other on the southwest end of town along **Sv. Dimitur Solunski** (Св. Димитър Солунски) at the end of **Sv. Kiril i Metodii** (Св. Кирил и Методий). **Trains** head to **Sofia** (2hr., 6 per day, 3.10lv). **Buses** run to: **Rila Town** (50min., 3 per day, 1.50lv); **Sandanski** (1½hr., 7 per day, 1.80lv); **Sofia** (2hr., every hr., 3.50lv); and **Bansko** (3hr., 8 per day, 2.20lv).

◪◪ **ORIENTATION AND PRACTICAL INFORMATION.** To get to the center from the stations, take any bus (0.25lv) up Sv. Kiril i Metodii from the stop across the street from the train station. Three and four stops later is the **American University of Bulgaria** (AUB), a huge building that used to be the regional headquarters of the

Communist Party. For info, bus tickets, free **maps,** and private rooms (12-15lv per person), head to the **tourist office** in Hotel Alen Mak (Хотел Ален Мак), Sv. Kiril i Metodii 1. (☎232 18 and 230 31. Open M-F 9am-6:30pm.) **Bulbank** (Булбанк), Shishman 22 (Шишман), cashes **traveler's checks** into *leva* for a 0.2% commission or into US$ for a 1.4% commission (minimum US$3). They also give MC/Visa **cash advances** for a 4% commission. A Cirrus/MC/Plus/Visa **ATM** stands outside. (☎813 32. Open M-F 8:45am-4pm.) Access the **internet** at **Spider Net,** to the right of Hotel Alen Mak. Buy a time card, starting at 1.50lv for 45 minutes. (☎355 85. Open 24hr.) The **post office** is across the street from the AUB. (Open M-F 7:30am-noon and 1-6pm.) **Telephones** are inside. (Open daily 7:30am-6:15pm.) Fresh food can be found at the **Kooperativen Pazar** (Кооперативен Пазар), a market across the river. (Open daily dawn-dusk.) Otherwise, the restaurants and cafes on **Todor Aleksandrov** serve standard Bulgarian fare (1-4lv). At night, anglophone students crawl out to the many cafes and bars on the squares, like **Rock House** on the south side of pl. Bulgaria. **Postal code:** 2700.

# BANSKO (БАНСКО)　　　　☎(0)7443

At the base of the Pirin mountains, Bansko (pop. 91,700) is a gateway to 180 lakes and 100 steep peaks scattered across a sea of forget-me-nots and alpine poppies. The highest peak, Vihren, reaches 2914m. The mountain range offers hiking and skiing, while preserved stone houses and taverns line cobblestone streets below.

## ORIENTATION AND PRACTICAL INFORMATION

Take a **bus** from **Blagoevgrad** (1½hr., 10 per day, 2.20lv) or **Sofia's** Ovcha Kupel station (3½hr., 5 per day, 5.20lv). For a taxi, call ☎47 43. **Luggage storage** is available in the station at 0.40lv per piece. From Bansko's bus station, exit the parking lot and turn left on Patriarch Evtimy (Патриарх Евтимий). Take a right at the tiny pl. Makedonia (Македония), marked by the stairways leading under the street, and then veer left on **Todor Aleksandrov** (Тодор Александров), which leads to **pl. Vaptsarov** (Вапцаров), with its fountains. Continue on ul. Pirin (Пирин) to the second square, **pl. Vuzrazhdane** (Възраждане). You can get a **map** from a newsstand on pl. Vaptsarov (3lv) or from the **Tourist Information Center** (Туристически Информационен Центр; Turisticheski Informatsionen Tsentr), to the right as you enter pl. Vaptsarov. The helpful staff has bus schedules, as well as smaller maps and guides. (☎50 48. Open Dec.-Aug. M-Sa 10am-8pm.) **Bulgarian Post Bank,** Hristo Botev 1 (Христо Ботев) exchanges currency and gives Visa advances for a 4% commission. (☎21 86. Open M-F 8am-noon and 1-4:30pm.) A **pharmacy** is at Tsar Simeon 57, near the Todor Aleksandrov intersection. (☎23 43. Open M-F 7:30am-7:30pm, Sa-Su 8am-1pm and 2:30-7:30pm.) The **post office,** Tsar Simeon 69 (open M-F 7:30am-noon and 1-6pm), has **telephones.** (Open daily 7am-10pm.) **Postal code:** 2770.

## ACCOMMODATIONS AND FOOD

**Private rooms** can be arranged informally with locals (US$2-5 per person), but finding cheap accommodations is not a problem. Case in point: ◙ **Hotel Mir** (Мир), Neofit Rilski 28 (Неофит Рилски; ☎25 00, 21 60, and 30 26), offers spacious rooms, spotless bathrooms, 24hr. hot water, cable TV, and a shared sauna with massage available. (Half massage 8lv, full 16lv.) From pl. Vaptsarov, take a left on Tsar Simeon and turn right on ul. Bulgaria. Continue straight and turn left on Rilski just after the playground. (Singles in summer US$12; off-season US$15.)

With a *mehana* (механа; tavern) hiding in almost every house or courtyard, you'll never be at a loss for a meal in Bansko. **Dudo Pene** (Дъдо Пене), Aleksandr Buynov 1 (Александър Буйнов), is a rugged restaurant; they grow many of their own vegetables and even have their own slaughterhouse. Live folk music pipes up after 7:30pm on weekends. (☎50 71. Main dishes 2.20-15lv. Open daily 9am-late.)

BULGARIA

## 🔍 SIGHTS

**HOLY TRINITY CHURCH.** (Църква Света Троица; Tsurkva Sveta Troitsa.) The 1835 Holy Trinity is actually a product of Turkish rule, when Bulgarian Orthodox Churches were restricted to small buildings on the outskirts of town. In the early 19th century, the story goes, several of Bansko's resilient faithful hid an Orthodox icon under pl. Vuzrazhdane. Shortly thereafter, the local Turkish governor dreamt about this icon and when the people showed him it was actually there, they convinced him it was a sign from God that an Orthodox Church should be built on the spot. When finished, the church towered above the 5m-high fence built to conceal it. The villagers then worked out a deal with the Turkish officer to add an Islamic crescent to the cross on the church door, making the building a symbol of both faiths. It later served as a shelter during attacks on the city. *(On pl. Vuzrazhdane, at the corner of Neofit Rilski. Open daily 9am-noon and 2-6pm.)*

**◼NIKOLA VAPTSAROV HOUSE-MUSEUM.** (Къща-Музей Никола Вапцаров; Kushta-Muzey Nikola Vaptsarov.) This house-museum recalls the life and work of the 20th-century poet who gave his life in the struggle against Fascism. Connected to and included in the admission is the **House of Poetry and Art** (Дом Поези и Искуство; Dom Poezi i Iskustvo), which exhibits images of the National Revival movement, the liberation struggles of Southern Bulgaria at the outset of the century, and photographs of the region. *(On the corner of pl. Demokratsia and Vaptsarov. ☎ 30 38. Open daily 8am-noon and 2-6pm. 2lv, students 0.20lv. Taped tours available in English.)*

**VELIANOV HOUSE.** (Веляианова Къща; Velyaianova Kushta). Named after the painter from Debur (once in Bulgaria but now in FYR Macedonia) responsible for the interior of Holy Trinity Church (see above), the house is typically Revival. Its thick walls once protected the inhabitants from brigands. *(Left on Velian Ognev from pl. Vuzrazhdane. Open M-F 9am-noon and 2-5pm. 2lv, students 1lv. English tour 1lv.)*

**NEOFIT RILSKI HOUSE-MUSEUM.** (Къща-Музей Неофит Рилски; Kushta-Muzey Neofit Rilski.) Another National Revival structure, the house was home to one of the National Revival movement's forefathers; he later became Father Superior at Rila Monastery (see p. 124). A man of letters and founder of the Rila School of church singing, Rilski also taught painter Zahari Zograf. *(At the corner of Pirin and Rilski. ☎ 25 40. Open daily 9am-noon and 2-5pm. 2lv, students 1lv. Taped English tour 1lv.)*

**ICON EXHIBIT.** (Експозиция на икони; Ekspozitsiya na ikoni.) A nunnery when it was built in 1749, the house now shelters icons from Bansko, including one initially considered sacrilegious. Why? The angels portrayed were female. *(Down Yane Sandanski from pl. Vuzrazhdane. Open M-Sa 9am-noon and 2-5pm. 1lv.)*

## 🥾 HIKING

Hiking routes are marked with different-colored signs. The starting point for many trails is **hizha Vihren** (хижа Вихрен; Vihren Hut). From town, take any street leading to the Glazne (Глазне) River. At the river, follow the Glazne road upstream, out of town, and up to the entrance of **Pirin National Park** (Народен Парк Пирин). Hike (5hr. each way), drive, or take a taxi (10-14lv from Bansko) up the paved road. The route, marked with a yellow line on white background, runs past **hizhen Bunderitsa** (Бъндерица) and **baikushevata mura** (байкушевата мура), a fir tree that's as old as the Bulgarian state—1300 years. At Bunderitsa you'll find a place to sleep (US$5.50 per person) and a chef to cook a hot meal. Four trails begin at the hut and lead over a rocky peak. After 10 minutes, the red and green trails branch off and cross the river. The **red** leads up Vihren peak (2914m) to **hizha Yavorov** (Яворов; Javor's Hut; 1740m). Beware—not everyone can handle the beautiful but strenuous horse (кончето; koncheto) trail. The **green** trail scales Todorin peak (Тодорин) to **hizha Demyanitsa** (Демяница; 6hr.). **Hizha Bezbog** (Безбог), which is becoming increasingly popular as a ski resort, is another 8 hours away. A **lift** connects it to **hizha Gotse**

**Delchev** (Гоце Делчев), which is 2 hours by foot from the village of Dobrinishte (Добринище). **Buses** to **Bansko** or **Razlog** can be caught there, making this an excellent route for a three-day hike. The **blue trail** goes in the other direction and is much shorter, reaching **Sini vraha** in only 4 hours. You'll have plenty of time to turn back or to continue on the **yellow trail** to chalet **Yanel Sandanski** (5hr.) at the other side of the park. Mountain huts scattered throughout the park provide the barest of accommodations—floor space—for the barest of prices (US$4-5). Bring your own food.

## MELNIK (МЕЛНИК) ☎(0)997437

Bulgaria's smallest town, tiny Melnik (pop. 300+), and its exquisitely preserved National Revival houses sit in a sandstone gorge where life goes on as it has for centuries. While the houses' whitewashed walls attest to the town's uniqueness, Melnik is best known for what it keeps concealed in its cellars: barrels of delicious wine.

Winston Churchill had his favorite wine shipped all the way from Melnik even during World War II. Less bellicose travelers can see it in its original storage place at the 1754 ▧ **Kordopulova Kushta** (Кордопулова Къща), the biggest National Revival house in Bulgaria. It also contains the largest wine cellar in Melnik—the caves inside the sandstone hill took a full 12 years to carve and can store up to 300 tons of wine. To get there, follow the main road, take the right fork, and go left up the steep stone path. Alternatively, follow the signs pointing to "K.K." (Open 8am-9pm. 2lv, students 1lv.) Next door, Mitko Manolev's **wine-tasting cellar** (Изба за Дегустация на Вино; Izba za Degustatsiya na Vino) is a 200-year-old establishment that offers naturally cool caverns and some of the best Melnik wine. They serve straight from the barrel and provide info on winemaking in Melnik. (☎234. Open daily 9am-9pm. Glass 0.50lv, bottle 3lv.)

Melnik is an ideal base for several good day **hikes.** All paths are poorly marked by an orange-and-white line painted on trees and rocks. A plateau with a beautiful vista of Melnik and the surrounding hills awaits 15 minutes up the path to the left of Sv. Nikola church (the trail begins across the street from Hotel Vinarna). Part of the way up the trail, take a right to reach the ruins of the **Despot Slav Krepost** (Деспот Слав Крепост), a fortress built by Aleksy Slav in the Middle Ages to protect the townspeople. Two rings of walls surround a central **church** whose altar still stands. Turn off the trail halfway up to Sv. Nikola (at the sign) to reach the **Tsurkva Sveta Zona** (Света Зона; 10min.) where you'll find views of the sandstone gorges.

A 7km hike leads to the 13th-century **Rozhen Monastery** (Роженски Манастир; Rozhenski Manastir) and its impressive 16th-century murals, 17th-century stained glass, and magnificent views of the countryside. One bus leaves Melnik's main street daily at noon (15min., 0.70lv) and returns from the monastery at 12:30pm, so you'll have to hike at least one way (1½hr.). To walk, take a left at the sign that points to the monastery, midway up Melnik's main street.

Two buses per day leave Melnik for **Sandanski** (1hr., 1.30lv). One continues to **Sofia** (3½hr., 12lv) via **Blagoevgrad** (2hr., 3lv). From Sandanski, other buses run to **Blagoevgrad** (1hr., 5 per day, 2.20lv) and **Sofia** (2½hr., 1 per day, 10lv).

The **main street** curves around a dry river bed. A **map** isn't necessary but is available at some restaurants and hotels (1.50lv). The **post office** is farther up the main street. (Open M-F 7:30am-noon and 1-4:30pm.) The **telephone** outside is the only one in town; the restaurant next door sells phone cards. **Postal code:** 2820.

**Private rooms** run 7-14lv; signs advertising "rooms to sleep" are on houses and restaurants all over town. **Hotel-Vinarna MNO,** with a sign reading "Ресторант/Винарна" in front, is past the post office. Its 30 beds are divided among large doubles and triples with private baths. (☎249. 15lv per person.) **Uzunova Kushta** (Узунова Къща) is centered around a pleasant courtyard. Some rooms have fridges and all have private bath. (☎270. US$12 per person.) When it comes to culinary delights, Melnik's offerings belie its size. **Mencheva Kusta** (Мечева Куста) is a traditional restaurant with great atmosphere and tasty food. Don't forget to have a glass of Melnik's famous wine with your meal. It's just past the river, on the left side of the main street's right fork. (☎339. Main dishes 1.50-9lv. Open daily 9am-11pm.) A **mini-market** (мини маркет) is on the right side of the main street. (Open daily 6am-9pm.)

**BULGARIA**

# VALLEY OF ROSES (РОЗОВА ДОЛИНА)

Tourism in the Stryama and Tundzha valleys is tinted red—with roses and with the blood spilled in both the 1876 Uprising and the subsequent War of Liberation. The National Revival houses of Koprivshtitsa stand as memorials to the heroes of the fighting, while Shipka Town lies in the shadow of the famous battle fought in the pass above. Meanwhile, Kazanluk blooms with its spring rose harvest.

## KOPRIVSHTITSA (КОПРИВЩИЦА) ☎(0)7184

Todor Kableshkov's 1876 "letter of blood," urging rebellion against Ottoman rule, started its tour of the country in this little town, tucked away in the Sredna Gora mountains along the Topolka River. Today, Koprivshtitsa's revolutionaries are in the tourism business, hosting such events as the re-enactment of the uprising during the "Days of Koprivshtitsa" folk song and dance festival.

**TRANSPORTATION. Trains** stop at the Koprivshtitsa train station from **Sofia** (2hr., 5 per day, 2.40lv) and **Plovdiv** (3½hr., 3 per day, 2.30lv) via **Karlovo**. A **private bus** travels **Sofia** (2hr.; M-Sa 1 per day, Su 2 per day; 4lv). The Koprivshtitsa **bus station** posts bus and train schedules.

**ORIENTATION AND PRACTICAL INFORMATION.** A bus runs from the train station into town (15min., 0.70lv). To reach the **main square** from the bus station, backtrack along the river that bisects the town. The English-speaking **tourist office** is in the main square, 20 April (20 Април; ☎21 91; koprivshitza@hotmail.com; open daily 10:30am-6pm). Pick up an invaluable **map** (2lv) of the town with a guide. There is **no currency exchange** in town. Up the narrow street that intersects the main road between the bus station and the tourist office sits **pharmacy Apteka Ljusy** (Аптека Люси), Liuben Karavelov 2 (Любен Каравелов; ☎21 82; open M-Sa 9:30am-noon and 3-6pm). Across the street and one level up is a **clinic** (поликлиника), Liuben Karavelov 3. (☎21 12. Open M-Sa 9:30am-noon and 3-6pm.) The **post office**, Liuben Karavelov 14, sits behind the square farther along the river. (☎121. Open daily 7:30am-noon and 1:30-4:30pm.) **Telephones** are inside. (Open M-F 8:30am-noon and 1:30-4:30pm, Sa 8am-1pm.) **Postal code:** 2077.

**ACCOMMODATIONS AND FOOD.** In hopeful anticipation of tourists, the town has converted many old houses into hotels. Call ahead during festivals. In addition, many locals rent out **private rooms.** Bargained prices are as low as US$4. **Hotel Traianova Kashta** (Троянова Къща), ul. Gerenilogo 5 (Геренилого), on the same street as Oslekov House Museum, a bit farther from the town center, has homey rooms with shared bath. (☎22 50. BulFon available. US$10 per person. Breakfast included.) **Hotel Shuleva Kushta** (Шулева Къща), Hadzhi Nencho Palaveev 37 (Хаджи Ненчо Палавеев), is across the main bridge from the bus station. It has simpler doubles with shared hot-water baths. (Singles18lv; doubles 24lv.)

It is easy to find cheap food in one of the town's many *mehana* (механа; taverns). **National Restaurant "20 April"** (20 Април), in the central square, serves a wide variety of Bulgarian dishes, with upbeat background music and a bright front patio. (Main dishes 1-5lv. Beer 1-2lv. Open 7:30am-10:30pm.) **Mehana Chuchura** (Чучура), near the bus station on the way to the main square, serves an extensive, well-priced English menu under replicas of the town's famous wood ceilings. (☎27 12. Main dishes 1.40-6.50lv. Open daily 8am-midnight.)

**SIGHTS.** If you're not here for the folk festivals in early May and mid-August, see the wonderfully preserved **National Revival houses.** The low plank structures were once the homes of the town's first settlers. The sturdy, half-timbered dwellings, with open porches, high stone walls, and sparse ornamentation, are 19th-century additions. The most common type features enclosed verandas and delicate woodwork. Many homes of the leaders of the 1876 Uprising (see **History,** p. 103) have become **museums.** Tickets (3lv, students 1lv) are valid for all museums available at any of the houses or at the souvenir shop next to the tourist office.(Open daily 8am-noon and 1:30-5:30pm.) The 1845 **Todor Kableshkov Museum-House** (Къща-музей Тодор Каблешков; Kushta-muzey Todor Kableshkov) has an impressive facade and the hero's personal possessions to boot. (☎20 54. Open Tu-Su 8am-noon and 1:30-5:30pm. No English captions.) The 1831 **Georgi Benkovski Museum-House** (Георги Бенковски), away from town near the dominant statue of Benkovski, immortalizes the life of the leader of the "Flying Troop," a calvary unit, more symbolic than effective, in the April Uprising. (☎28 11. Open M and W-Su 8am-noon and 1:30-5:30pm.) The **Dimcho Debelyanov Museum-House** (Димчо Дебелянов) is the birthplace of one of Bulgaria's best lyric poets (see **Literature and Arts,** p. 105). Debelyanov died in World War I; inside, his work is mournfully recited while a statue of his mother waits in vain for his return in the yard. (☎20 77. Open Tu-Su 8am-noon and 1:30-5:30pm.) The house of the merchant **Lyutov** (Лютовата) preserves valuable examples of fine National Revival architecture. Besides ornate ceiling work, it houses a collection of fine carpets. (Open M and W-Su 8am-noon and 1:30-5:30pm.)

# KAZANLUK (КАЗАНЛЪК)          ☎(0)431

A typical concrete-block skyline and kiosked streets camouflage the center of Bulgaria's rose-growing world. In the first week of June, though, Kazanluk's (pop. 61,000) pride blossoms forth in the annual Rose Festival, celebrated with traditional song-and-dance troupes and comedians. Arrive after the festivities and you'll see nothing but a few struggling rose bushes amid the thorns of everyday life.

**⊟ TRANSPORTATION. Trains** go to: **Plovdiv** (3hr., 5 per day, 3.30lv) via **Karlovo** (1hr., 7 per day, 2lv); **Burgas** (3½hr., 5 per day, 5.10lv); and **Sofia** (3½hr., 3 per day, 5.10lv). **Buses** make their way to **Plovdiv** (2hr., 3 per day, 5lv).

**◪◪ ORIENTATION AND PRACTICAL INFORMATION.** From the train station, go left 100m and turn right on bul. Rozova Dolina (Розова Долина), which leads to the main square, **pl. Sevtopolis** (Севтополис). The main street, **23ti Pehoten Shipchenski Polk** (23ти Пехотен Шипченски Полк), runs perpendicular to ul. Rozova Dolina. Hotel Kazanluk, in the center, sells **maps** for 4lv. **Banka Biohim** (Банка Биохим), Rozova Dolina 4, **exchanges currency.** (☎215 20. Open daily 8:30-11:50am and 1-4pm.) An MC/Visa **ATM** stands on 23ti Pehoten Shipchenski near the post office. **Store luggage** at the train station. (Opens within 10min. of train arrivals or departures. 0.50lv.) A 24hr. **pharmacy** is located on 23ti Pehoten Shipchenski (facing away from the square, head right on 23rd; it's one block down on the right). **Internet** is available at **Orbital,** Skobelov 10 (Скобелов), one block from the square. (1.50lv per hr. Open M-Sa 9:30am-1am.) The **post office** is also on 23ti Pehoten Shipchenski. (Open M-F 8am-6:30pm, Sa 8am-12:30pm.) It houses **telephones** and **faxes.** (Fax 60 14 31. Open daily 7am-9:30pm.) **Postal code:** 6100.

**◪◪ ACCOMMODATIONS AND FOOD.** Inexpensive accommodations are limited. For a bed during the Rose Festival, call at least one month in advance. The best deal in Kazanluk is ◪**Hotel Arsenal,** (Арсенал). Head away from pl. Sevtopolis on the small road behind Hotel Kazanluk, take the first left onto Iskra (Искра), continue past the museum on the right, and take Oreshaka (Орешака) to the right when the road splits. Arsenal is 10 minutes past Hotel Vesta, inside the yellow and white sports complex on the left. Take a taxi after dark (2lv from the train station). Arsenal has spacious doubles with a refrigerator and phone in every room. (☎205 83. 25lv per person.) For luxurious but pricier rooms, try **Hotel Vesta** (Веста; ☎477 40), Chavdar Voivoda 3 (Чавдар Войвода), before Hotel Arsenal on Oreshaka. Rooms include private bath, huge beds, satellite TV, and refrigerator. (Singles US$30; doubles US$40. Breakfast included.)

The best Italian food in Bulgaria hides in the restaurant mysteriously called **Burger King,** in the main square. Use their picture menu to order some of their creative pizzas, such as the french-fry pizza or the one featuring your name written in cheese lumps. (Main dishes 2-6lv. Open daily 10am-10pm.)

🔲 **SIGHTS.** While best known for its roses, Kazanluk's sights maintain the town's spirit during the off-season and give a taste of what the festival is like. Kazanluk's foremost museum, the **Iskra Art Gallery and Historical Museum** (Художествена Галерия и Исторически Музей Искра; Hudozhestvena Galeriya i Istoricheski Muzey Iskra), St. Kiril i Metodii 9, features exhibits on ancient history, Thracian culture, and roses from Kazanluk. From pl. Svetopolis, go right on the small road behind the Hotel Kazanluk (Отец Паисий). Take a left onto St. Kiril and Metodii (Св. Кирил и Методий); the museum is on the right-hand corner with Iskra (Искра. Museum ☎281 04 and 364 29. Open daily mid-Mar. to late-Nov. 9am-noon and 2-5:30pm. US$1.) From the steps of the art gallery, head straight for one block and turn right on Stara Reka (Стара Река). Cross the bridge and head up the stone stairs to reach the **Thracian Tomb** (Тракийска Гробница; Trakiyska Grobnitsa), located inside a city park. The original resting place of the tomb, now sealed, dates from the third century BC. The interior has been re-created 20m away. The early Hellenistic frescoes in the corridor and dome chamber are original; those in the replica are from the more recent Soviet period. (☎247 50. Open daily Mar.-Oct. 8:30am-6pm. 2lv, students 1lv.) Facing the base of the steps to the tomb, head right on Tyulbenska (Тюлбенска), then take the first right onto the narrow cobblestone path, Knyaz Mirski (Княз Мирски). 40m down lies the oldest part of Kazanluk, **Kulata** (Кулата), a neighborhood that preserves the architecture of the National Revival. In the courtyard, the **Ethnographic Complex of Kulata** (Етнографски Комплекс Кулата; Etnografski Komplex Kulata) displays two buildings: a village house and a city dwelling from the Revival years. During the Rose Festival, they'll treat you to a shot of genuine rose brandy. The museum's highlight is a wonderfully sculpted garden courtyard in which a distillery shows how rose oil and liquor are traditionally made. (☎217 33. Open daily 9am-5pm. 2lv, students 1lv.)

To understand what this town is all about, visit the **Rose Museum and Gardens** (Музей на Розата; Muzey na Rozata), located 30 minutes from pl. Sevtopolis on bul. Osvobozhdenie (Освобождение). Either head out of the center on General Skobelev (Генерал Скобелев), opposite Hotel Kazanluk, to reach Osvobozhdenie or catch bus #5 or 6 across from Hotel Kazanluk (every 30min., 0.40lv) and ask to get off at "muzey." The museum displays centuries of rose oil production equipment. The souvenir shop sells such indispensable rose products as liquor, jam, and oil. To glimpse the flowers from which all this rosiness springs, head next door to the **Scientific Research Institute for Roses, Aromatic and Medicinal Plants,** home of experimental gardens that grow 250 varieties of roses. (☎251 70. Open May 15-Oct. 15 9am-5pm. No English captions. Free.) Ten kilometers south of Kazanluk, the man-made **Lake Koprinka** (Копринка) floods the remains of the Thracian city of Sevtopolis, making a good place for a swim. Take bus #3 from the train station (0.40lv) and head straight on the road for 15 minutes or take a bus directly to Lake Koprinka. (25min.; 8am, noon, 4, and 8pm; 0.50lv.)

# NEAR KAZANLUK: SHIPKA ☎(0)4324

*To get to Shipka Town from Kazanluk, take city bus #6, from the train station or opposite Hotel Kazanluk to the last stop (25min., every 30min., 0.75lv). To get to Shipka Pass and the monument, either take a bus between Kazanluk and Gabrovo and get off at the pass (30min., 6 per day, 1.50lv), or hike up the trail from behind St. Nicholas church in Shipka Town (1hr.).*

At the Rose Valley's north edge lies the small town of Shipka (Шипка), nestled in the shadow of the legendary **Shipchenski Prohod** (Шипченски Проход; ship-CHEN-skee pra-HOHD; Shipka Pass), site of the bloody and pivotal battle that lasted an entire winter and ultimately liberated Bulgaria from the Turks in 1878 (see **History,**

BULGARIA

p. 102). Shipka town's main attraction is the exquisite ■ **St. Nicholas Memorial Church,** built in honor of the Russian soldiers who lost their lives here. Walk up the road behind the building at the bus stop and follow it 10 minutes toward the gold domes. (Open daily 8:30am-5:30pm. 0.50lv.) Across from the bus stop in Shipka's center, a **grocery** hides under the remains of the old Hotel Shipka on the main square. (Open M-F 7:30am-9:30pm, Sa-Su 8am-9:30pm.) Next door, **Restaurant Asprobalta** (Аспровалта) serves cheap Bulgarian fare. (Main dishes 1.50-5lv. Open 10am-10pm.) From the center of Shipka Pass, follow the road toward the looming **Monument to Freedom** (Паметник на Свободата; Pametnik na Svobodata), and climb the 800 stone steps to the ridge above the pass. Views of the valley are breathtaking from the top of the monument, which has stood in memory of the Russian and Bulgarian dead since August 26, 1934. Many of the written fragments inside the monument are from Ivan Vazov's legendary poem "Shipka" (see **Literature and Arts,** p. 105), which most Bulgarian students learn by heart. (Open daily 8:30am-5pm. 2lv.) Be sure to try some water-buffalo yogurt (1.20lv), a treat found only at the cafes and restaurants at the pass, while you're there.

# BLACK SEA (ЧЕРНО МОРЕ)

Bulgaria's most popular destination for foreigners and native vacationers alike, the Black Sea Coast (Cherno More) is covered with centuries-old fishing villages with secluded bays, energetic seaside towns, and plastic resorts designed to suck in hard currency. The south is characterized by warm, sandy beaches, the north by rockier, white-cliffed shores. In Varna the past battles with the present, while in the quiet southern Sinemorets you're never far from a sand stroll through the Balchik cacti. Wherever you go, however, you're bound to run into more English speakers and higher prices than in any other region of Bulgaria.

## VARNA (ВАРНА)

☎ (0)52

In the 6th century BC, Varna (pop. 329,000), then the port of Odessos, was already crawling with sunburned Greek sailors. When the Romans arrived, the city was busy doing the things that cosmopolitan cultural centers do. It has remained the seaside commercial and cultural center of Bulgaria ever since. Thanks to a vibrant historical past of conquest and reconquest, the city's many museums house some of the country's best exhibits. Today, Varna's appeal centers around its extensive beaches and Mediterranean-esque climate.

**Black Sea Coast of Bulgaria**

ROMANIA — Kardam, Durankulak, General Toshevo, Krapets, Shabla, Dobrich, Tyulenovo, Kavarna, Kamen Bryag, Tuzlata, Balchik, Bulgarevo, Aladzha, Albena, Sveti Nikola, Varna, Kranevo, Golden Sands, Rusalka, Galata, Sveti Konstantin, Kamchiya, Novo Oryahovo, Shkorpilovtsi, Byala, Obzor, Saratovo, Emona, Sunny Beach, Nesebur, Ravda, Burgas, Pomorie, Chernomorets, Primorsko, Sozopol, Kiten, Kralmorie, Lozenets, Tsarevo, Varvara, Veleka, Ahtopol, Sinemorets, Malko Tarnovo, Rezovo, TURKEY

0    20 miles
0    20 kilometers

N

BULGARIA

## ⚜ ORIENTATION

Despite Varna's sprawl, its sights are all within a 30-minute walk of one another. To get to the central **pl. Nezavisimost** (пл. Независимост) from the train station, take **Tsar Simeon I** (Цар Симеон I). Varna's main pedestrian artery, **bul. Knyaz Boris I** (Княз Борис I), starts at pl. Nezavisimost. Preslav (Преслав) heads from pl. Nezavisimost to the **Sv. Bogoroditsa Cathedral.** To reach the beach and seaside gardens from the station, go right on Primorsky (Приморски)—*not* Osmi Primorski Polk.

## ▛ TRANSPORTATION

**Trains:** Near the commercial port by the sea. To: **Gorna Oryahovitza** (3hr., 6 per day, 5.55lv); **Ruse** (4hr., 2 per day, 5.10lv); **Plovdiv** (5½hr., 3 per day, 8lv); **Sofia** (7hr.; 7 per day; 12.10lv, couchette 17.90lv); and **Shumen** (11 per day, 2.74lv). **Rila**, ul. Preslav 13 (☎22 62 73), sells tickets to **Budapest, HUN** and **Istanbul, TUR.** Open M-F 8am-5:30pm, Sa 8am-3pm.

**Buses:** Ul. Vladislav Varenchik (Владислав Варенчик). To reach the bus station, take city bus #1, 22, 40, 41, or 409 from either the train station or the north side of the cathedral, across from the post office. Buses are the best way to and from **Burgas** (3hr., 6 per day, 5.50lv). You can also take a **minivan** from across from the bus station to Burgas. **Group Travel** (☎25 67 34 and 23 04 87), behind the bus station, sends buses to: **Sofia** (6½hr., 3 per day, 14lv); **Budapest, HUN** (M, Tu, and F; 80lv); and **Prague, CZR** (daily 10am, 85lv). Buy tickets in advance. Open daily 7am-11pm.

**Ferries:** At the passenger port (Морска Гора; ☎22 23 26). Bus #48 goes here from the cathedral. Ferries sail between resorts and are a pleasant alternative to crowded buses. Cashier open 1hr. before departure. Info kiosk open M-F 7:30am-6:30pm. Daily ferries (hydro-buses) depart from Varna at 8:30am for **Balchik** (2½hr., 8.10lv).

**Local Transportation: Buses** cost 0.35lv; pay on the bus. Bus stops are clearly marked with small black signs listing the bus number.

## ▟ PRACTICAL INFORMATION

**Tourist Office:** There is no official tourist office in Varna. The closest it comes to one is **Megatours,** Slivnitsa 33 (☎22 00 58; fax 22 00 61), in the Hotel Cherno More. Sells a **map** of Varna (US$3) and rents cars. Open June-Sept. M-F 9am-7pm, Sa 9am-2pm; Oct-May M-F 9am-6pm, Sa 9am-2pm. English spoken.

**Currency Exchange: Bulgarian Post Bank,** Zamenhoff 1 (☎60 33 16 07), in the main square. Cashes **traveler's checks** for a US$5 commission and gives Visa **cash advances** for a 4% commission. Open M-F 8:30am-5pm, Sa 8:30am-noon.

**ATM:** At the Valentina shopping complex next to Bulgarian Post Bank (above).

**American Express:** In Megatours (see Tourist Office, above).

**Luggage Storage:** At the train station, by the end of track #8. 0.5lv. Open daily 6-11:30am, noon-6pm, and 6:30-11pm.

**Hospital: Polyclinic Patanov** (Поликлиника "Патанов"), Saborni 16 (Съборни). ☎25 67 45.

**24hr. Pharmacy:** Bul. Knyaz Boris I 29 (☎60 71 97).

**Internet Access: The Game Club,** off pl. Nezavisimost on Musala (Мусала). 2lv per hr. Open 24hr.

**Telephones:** Around the side of the post office. Open daily 7am-11pm. **Faxes** (fax 60 00 81). Open daily 7am-9pm.

**Post Office:** Bul. Suborni (Съборни), behind the cathedral. **Poste Restante** to the left (0.20lv per item). Open M-F 7am-7pm, Sa 7:30am-7pm, Su 8am-noon.

**Postal code:** 9000.

BULGARIA

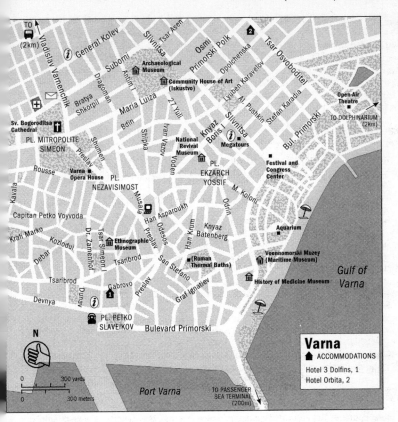

## ACCOMMODATIONS

**Solvex,** near track #4 at the train station, finds **private rooms** for US$6-10 per person. (☎60 58 61. Open summer daily 6am-10pm.) Plenty of locals approach backpackers at the train station offering lodging for US$3-7 per person.

**Hotel Trite Delfina** (Трите Делфина; Three Dolphins), ul. Gabrovo 27 (☎60 09 11 and 60 09 17). Close to the train station. Go up Simeon from the train station and take a right on Gabrovo. Well-kept, spacious rooms with large windows and well-lit desks. Singles US$20; doubles US$25.

**Hotel Orbita** (Орбита), bul. Tsar Osvoboditel 25 (☎22 51 62 and 22 13 04). A large hotel with generously furnished rooms (including some with TV) and exceptionally clean bathrooms. US$30 per person.

## FOOD

**Bul. Knyaz Boris I** and **Slivnitsa** swarm with cafes, kiosks, and vendors. Many restaurants along the beach have fresh seafood. Two chains, **"Happy" English Pub** and **Cafe Davidoff,** are everywhere. Happy serves American food in a hip sports bar atmosphere. (Main dishes 3-8lv. Open 24hr.) Davidoff is also trendy, but specializes in desserts and fresh fruit concoctions. (Main dishes 3-8lv. Open daily 7am-11:30pm.)

■ **Mexican Club Rico,** at the intersection of Simeon and pl. Nezavisimost, serves scrumptious Mexican food to spice up your Bulgarian diet. Look for the fluorescent tables and the flashing cactus at night. Main dishes 2.50-7.80lv. Open daily 11am-midnight.

**Godzila's Pizzeria** (Годзила; ☎ 60 44), Knyaz Boris 66. The monster himself stands ready to pluck you off the sidewalk. The Italian menu features extra-large "Godzila" specialties. Main dishes 1.50-5lv. Open daily 11am-2am.

## ■ SIGHTS

The well-preserved ■ **Roman Thermal Baths** (Римски Терми; Rimski Termi), the largest ancient building complex in Bulgaria, stand on San Stefano in the city's old quarter, **Grutska Makhala.** (Гръцка Махала. Open Tu-Su 10am-5pm. 1lv.)

Two sights maintain displays of 19th-century folk crafts in well-preserved buildings from Bulgaria's historic National Revival Period. The **Ethnographic Museum** (Етнографски Музей; Etnografski Muzey) is at Sofronii Vrachanski 22. (Софроний Врачански. ☎ 63 05 88. Open Tu-Sa 10am-5pm.) The **National Revival Museum** sits just off pl. Ekzarkh Yossif. (Екзарх Йосиф. Open Tu-Su 10am-5pm. 1.50lv.) The ■ **Archaeological Museum** (Археологически Музей; Arheologicheski Muzey), in the park behind Maria Luiza, traces the country's history from the Early Stone Age, with artifacts from the past 100,000 years. (Open Tu-Sa 10am-5pm. English guide 5lv. English booklet 6hv. 2lv, students 1lv.)

## ■■ ENTERTAINMENT AND FESTIVALS

Varna is home to many special arts events; for a complete seasonal schedule and tickets, check the **International Advertisement Office** (☎ 23 72 84), two floors below the main entrance of the Community House of Art (see below). Take the elevator and go down the hall to the left. Hidden among the fountains and trees in the seaside gardens is a vine-covered **open-air theater,** home of **international ballet festivals** (May-Oct.). Buy tickets at the gate or at the festival ticket office (see below). The big red **Opera House** on the main square has daily performances from Sept.-June and a reduced summer schedule. (☎ 22 33 88. Open M-F 10:30am-1pm and 2-7:30pm. Approx. 20lv.) The tall glass building in the park on Maria Luiza, the **Varna Community House of Art** (Община Варна Дом на Искуство; Obshtina Varna Dom na Iskustvo), hosts chamber music concerts.

In late August, Varna holds an **International Jazz Festival.** The chamber music festival **Varna Summer** (Варненско Лято; Varnensko Lyato) runs for six weeks starting in mid-June. The **Festivalen Complex,** with a cinema (4lv) and cafes, is popular with younger crowds and is another source for tickets and cultural info. From late August to early September, a film festival, **"Love is Folly,"** runs in the complex.

The family-dominated **beaches** are cramped in summer, but still make for an enjoyable afternoon. The sands stretch north from the train station and are separated from bul. Primorsky by the seaside gardens. In summer, a good number of discos and bars open by the beach. **Spartakus** (Спартакус), a self-advertised "private mixed club welcoming all sexual orientations," is in the Opera House. (Cover 1lv. Open nightly after 7:30pm.)

## ■ DAYTRIPS FROM VARNA

### BALCHIK (БАЛЧИК)☎(0)579

*Buses run from Varna (1hr., 14 per day, 2.20lv), but minivans waiting behind the station make the bumpy trip much more pleasant (2.50lv; leave when full). From Balchik's bus station, walk downhill on the main street, Cherno More (Черно Море), to pl. Nezavisimost. Continue to the left until pl. Ribarski. Ul. Primorska (Приморска) runs along the shore.*

If the mystical reputation of the Black Sea seems dulled by crowded boardwalks and the endless drone of Ricky Martin, Balchik (BAHL-chik) is the place to get re-enchanted. Life in this fishing village, with houses carved into the chalky cliffs, moves at a slower pace than in Varna. The result is a picture-perfect destination that has the conveniences of a resort without resort prices and crowds. The **public beach** is small but clean, with showers, changing rooms, bars, volleyballs, umbrellas, and paddleboat rentals (4lv per 30min.). The best sands lie sheltered by Romanian Queen Marie's **summer palace** and surrounded by restaurants. To reach the palace from pl. Ribarski (Рибарски), turn right and walk along Primorska (Приморска), or along the beach boardwalk (15min.). Once there, you can sit in her marble throne and explore the varied garden and the largest cactus collection in the Balkans. (Open daily 8am-7pm. 4lv.)

For an epidermal treat, visit the mud baths of **Tuzlata**, 7km north. Take a **bus** from the Balchik station (15min., 2 per day, 0.40lv) or a **taxi** (☎ 171) from pl. Ribarski (4lv; ask for the sanatoria). Although the spa has seen better, muddier days, you can still get a great *grazni banya* (грязни баня; grand bath). Go in the right side for women, the left for men; get naked and take a preparatory dip in the water, then rub mud all over yourself and sit in the sun while it dries. It's supposedly good for skin problems and rheumatism—or just for fun. (Open daily in summer 8am-4pm. 1lv.) From Cherno More, walk past the fruit market and to the left, up P. Yavorov (П. Яворов). Work up an appetite by climbing the overgrown stairs at pl. Ribarski to **Emona** (Емона), Emona 14 (☎722 69). The delicious fish dishes are enhanced by an unparalleled view. (Main dishes 1-6lv. Open daily 6-11:30pm.) **Bris Travel,** Zaimov 4, on the right off Ribarski as you head down Cherno More, provides info, arranges excursions, and books **hotels** and **private rooms.** (☎764 34. Open daily June-Sept. 8:30am-12:30pm and 1:30-8:30pm.) At night, relax or dance at one of the many beachside cafes or discos.

## ALADZHA MONASTERY (АЛАДЖА МАНАСТИР)

*Take bus #9 or 409 from Varna to Zlatny Pyascy (Златни Пясъци; Golden Sands; 30min., every 15min., 1lv). The bus passes the heavily populated resort area, then takes a left into a forested area. Get off at the next stop, at the intersection with the mountain road, near the sign for "Club Amazonia." Walk up the mountain road (3km, 45min.) or take a taxi from the bus stop (5lv). Monastery ☎ 35 54 60. Chapel open daily May-Oct. 9am-6pm, Nov.-Apr. Tu-Su 10am-5pm. 2lv, students 1lv.*

Known as the rock *(skalen)* monastery, Aladzha, 14km from Varna, was carved out of the side of a mountain during the 13th and 14th centuries. No written records of the monastery exist, and its original name remains a mystery ("*aladzha*" is Turkish for "patterned"). Now devoted entirely to life as a tourist attraction, the monastery rises two levels in the 40m white limestone cliff. The **chapel** on its second level preserves frescoes of the Madonna and child and other scenes. The view of the sea from the open cells is fantastic. A **museum,** to the left as you enter the premises, exhibits medieval paintings and gives background on the monastery and the **Golden Sands National Park** (Народен Парк "Златни Пясъци;" Naroden park Zlatni Pyastsi) that surrounds the monastery. An excellent guidebook in English is available at the museum, as is a book of legends (4lv). 800m northeast along the forest trail, past the museum, the **catacombs,** a group of three-level caves once inhabited by hermits, offer a stark look into the life of 14th-century monks.

# BURGAS (БУРГАС)                                    ☎(0)56

Upon arriving in Burgas (BOOR-gahs; pop. 210,000), one notices the contrast between the hulking black freight ships and the otherwise pristine bay. The city is less touristed and less pleasant than Varna; Burgas is best enjoyed with a stroll along the beach as you wait for transport elsewhere on the coast.

**▐ TRANSPORTATION. Trains** run to **Varna** (4½hr., 6 per day, 5lv) via **Karnobat;** and **Sofia** (7hr., 7 per day, 9.50lv) via **Plovdiv** or **Karlovo. Buses** serve the **Black Sea Coast,** including **Varna** (2½hr., 6 per day, 5.50lv). Quicker, cheaper **minibuses** run to the resorts from the end of the bus station farther from the train station.

**⌸ PRACTICAL INFORMATION.** Head to bigger and better places from the Burgas **train and bus stations,** near the port at **Garov pl.** (пл. Гаров). **Aleksandrovska** (Александровска), the main pedestrian drag, begins across the street. **Bulbank,** across the street from Hotel Bulgaria on Aleksandrovska, cashes **traveler's checks** for a 1% commission and has a Cirrus/MC/Visa **ATM.** (Open M-F 8:30-4pm.) Find **internet access** at **"The Gate,"** Alexsandrovska 24, past Hotel Bulgaria on the right. (1.20lv per hr. Open 24hr.) To get to the **post office,** walk to the end of Alexsandrovska and turn right on San Stefano (Сан Стефано), the busy street. It's one block down on the left. **Telephones** are inside. For overnight stays, **private rooms** are most convenient, running US$6-10. You can secure private rooms at the change bureau at Bogoridi 14, on the corner of Lermontov. (Лермонтов. ☎71 42. Open M-F 8am-8pm, Sa 9am-8pm.) Otherwise, put yourself up at the **Hotel Mirage** (Мираж), Lermontov 18. From the station, go up Alexsandrovska, take a right on Bogoridi, pass the Hotel Bulgaria, and take the first left onto Lermontov. (☎92 10 19. Doubles US$25, with TV US$28; triples US$33.) There are plenty of seaside vendors hawking cheap food; for dining with a table, there's **Biraria Stefani** (Стефани), Bogoridi 62, near the seaside gardens, which serves Bulgarian fare. (Main dishes 2-6lv. Open daily 8am-12:30am.) Evenings are as unexciting as the rest of the day in Burgas; try keeping yourself entertained at the open-air **Dance Club Strena,** right by Taverna Neptune, a few hundred meters north of Hotel Primorets in the Seaside Gardens. (Open daily 11pm-4am. 1lv.) **Postal code:** 8000.

# RESORTS NEAR BURGAS

Although ugly, Burgas is an ideal base from which to explore the southern coast. From the look of this weedy and industrial hole, a visitor might never guess that resorts on the Bulgarian Black Sea Coast could be appealing. Heading south from Burgas, one comes across a surprising array of seaside beauties, from the pristine hamlets of Kiten and Sinemorets to the thriving artistic and cultural centers of Sozopol and Nesebur. Even Bulgaria's biggest youth center lies only a short bus ride away from Burgas in Primorsko. All of these make good daytrips from Burgas, though many locals in the small resorts rent private rooms—just look around.

## NESEBUR (НЕСЕБЪР)                                            ☎(0)554

*Buses from Burgas (40min., every 40min. 6am-9pm, 2lv) stop at the Old Nesebur port and the gate leading to town. Minibuses also make the trip from Burgas (30min., leave when full, 2lv) but only stop in New Nesebur; take a city bus (10min., every 10min., 0.40lv.) from there to the Old Town (Stari Grad).*

Nesebur (neh-SEH-bur; pop. 10,000) is a museum town atop the peninsula at the south end of Sunny Beach. Don't expect a respite from the summer crowds, however; this might be the most touristed town in Bulgaria. That said, Nesebur has done a good job of preserving a charm that its resort neighbors sacrificed at the altar of commerce long ago. A walk through its ancient **Stari Grad** (Old Town) begins with the 3rd-century stone **fortress walls.** The Byzantine **gate** and **port** date from the 5th century. The **Archaeological Museum** (Археологически Музей; Arheologicheski Muzey), to the right of the town gate, exhibits ancient ceramics. (☎460 18 and 460 19. Open daily May-Oct. 9am-1:30pm and 2-7:30pm; Nov.-Apr. M-F 9am-9pm. English tour 4lv per group. 2.10lv, students 0.85lv.) The museum also sells a map of Old Nesebur's sights (0.50lv). The 13th-century **Church of Christ the Almighty** (Христос Пантократор; Hristos Pantokrator), in the main square, doubles as an art gallery in summer. (☎450 00. Open daily 9am-9pm.) The UNESCO-protected **Temple of John the Baptist** (Йоан Кръстител; Yoan Krustitel), now an art gallery, has been around since the 10th century. To reach it, walk down Mitropolitska from the center; the church is on the left. (Open daily June to mid-Sept. 10am-10pm.) The 11th-century **New Metropolitan Church of St. Stephen** (Църквата Свети Стефан; Tsurkvata Sveti Stefan) is plastered in 16th-century frescoes. It now serves as a museum. From the center, continue down Mesembria and take a right on Ribarska; the church is on the right. (Open daily June-Sept. 7am-7:30pm. 1.70lv, students 0.85lv.)

If you choose to stay overnight, private rooms are the best option. **Hotel Rony** (Хотел Рони), just past the Archaeological Museum, is fully equipped with A/C, cable TV, minibars, and very modern private bathrooms, but is consequently expensive. (Doubles 60lv. Breakfast included.) Along the harbor, street kiosks sell fruit and nuts or small meals (fish with fries and *shopska* salad 4lv). **Restaurant Avera,** Mitropolitska 13, has some great sea views. (☎453 39. Main dishes 3-10lv. Open daily 10am-midnight.)

# SOZOPOL (СОЗОПОЛ)   ☎(0)5514

*Buses arrive from Burgas (45min., every 30min. 6am-9pm, 1.70lv). Turn left on Apolonia (Аполония) to reach the Old Town. To get to the New Town, go right through the park and turn left onto Republikanska (Републиканска).*

Thirty-four kilometers south of Burgas, Sozopol (soh-ZO-pohl), settled in 610 BC, is Bulgaria's oldest Black Sea town. It was once the resort of choice for Bulgaria's artistic community and still caters to a more creative set than its neighbors. Take a **boat cruise** around Sozopol (15lv per boat) from the seaport (behind the bus station) to get a closer look at the two adjacent islands, **St. Peter** and **St. Ivan.** The best time to go is at sunset. To explore some of Sozopol's less popular beaches, rent a **motorbike** near the bus station and cruise along the shoreline (10lv per hr.). One of the most popular night spots is the misleadingly named ▨ **Country Club Saloon,** on the far end of the second beach in Novi Grad (New Town). Every night is a rave night. (Open daily 10pm-sunrise. Free.) During the first 10 days of September, artists take over the town for the **Arts Festival Apolonia.** At the bus station, **Lotos** arranges **private rooms** (US$7 per person), organizes trips to Istanbul, and distributes free **maps** of the town. (☎22 82; fax 24 29. Open daily 8am-8pm.) For a Sozopol experience, visit its famous restaurant, **Vyaturna Melnitsa** (Вятърна Мелница; Windmill), Morski Skali 27a (Морски Скали), on the street running along the tip of the old town's end of the peninsula; look for a little windmill. (☎28 44. Main dishes 3-10lv. Open daily 10am-midnight. Summer folk shows Th and Sa 9pm.)

# PRIMORSKO (ПРИМОРСКО)   ☎(0)5561

*Most southbound coastal buses and minibuses heading from Burgas to Tsavero, Ahtopol, or Sinemorets stop in Primorsko; check with the driver. The bus (1½hr., 1 per day, 3lv) and minibuses (1hr., every 1-2hr., 2.80lv) stop at Primorsko's main street, Cherno More (Черно Море). To reach the main complex of the ММЦ (International Youth Center) from the Primorsko bus station, take a right facing away from the station and head out of town. Turn left at the open intersection. Cross the bridge over Dyavolka Reka (Дяволка Река; Devil's River) and continue for 15min. A cab to the complex costs less than 3lv.*

Young Bulgarians know Primorsko (pree-MOR-sko) as the site of the **International Youth Center** (ММЦ, or Международни Младежки Център; Mezhdugarodni Mladezhki Tsentur), where the best Pioneers were sent to strengthen global comraderie. Today, Zhivkov would blush at this rocking, inexpensive resort and its scantily clad youths. When open (June-Oct.), the complex and its five hotels offer everything a tourist could need or want. (July-Aug. US$14 per person; June and Sept. US$10.) Slightly cheaper hotels lie near **ul. Cherno More** (Черно Море), a 20-minute walk from the complex. At the manicured **beach,** you can lie under an umbrella (2lv) or rent a paddleboat (*vodna koleva*; 15lv per hr.). In the oak forest, between the beach and the complex, you can play tennis, volleyball, basketball, handball, or table tennis. (US$2 or 5lv per hr.) If you're feeling more adventurous, rent a **bike** (3lv per hr.) and explore the area. In the far corner (away from downtown) is an open-air **theatre** and a **cinema.** The theatre hosts intermittent concerts by popular Bulgarian bands and folk groups while the cinema shows American films (with Bulgarian subtitles) nightly at 9 and 11pm (3-5lv). There are five **discos** in town, all located in one complex, **Stop,** which also has a **medical center, post office,** and **grocery store.** For info on any of the activities and a free **map,** head to the **information office** in room #1 of the building to the right of Hotel Druzhba, labeled "ММЦ Direction." (☎21 01. Open daily Apr-Oct 8am-5pm.)

**BULGARIA**

## KITEN (КИТЕН)
☎(0)5561

*Buses from Burgas stop in Kiten (1¾hr., 4 per day, 2.50lv) on their way to Ahtopol or Tsarevo, or from Primorsko (15min., 5 per day, 0.50lv). Minivans are cheaper and faster; they leave when full. Kiosks along the street sell bus tickets to Sofia (at least 5 per day, 18lv) and Plovdiv (at least 3 per day, 12lv). Luggage storage at the bus station (1lv per piece) is open when buses arrive and depart. To reach the main beach from the bus station, turn left onto Strandzha (facing the bus station, it's the street on the right) and follow it for 10min. Turn right after the supermarket and go down the stairs; there you'll find sand, volleyball, and paddleboats (5lv per hr.).*

Just south of Primorsko, Kiten has also been discovered by an ever-growing crowd of international tourists. Since its founding in 1932, the town has managed to shake off concrete apartment towers, providing a rare respite from the Soviet haze that seems to hang over much of Bulgaria. One of the more notable restaurants in town is **Mehana Kukeri** (Механа Кукери), on Altipan, whose decor resembles a pirate-themed mini-golf course. Traditional Bulgarian dishes (complete with coastal fish specialties) run 1-7lv. (Open daily 9am-1am.)

## SINEMORETS (СИНЕМОРЕЦ)
☎(0)55

*Buses run from Ahtopol (15min., 2 per day at 9:30am and 4:20pm, 0.50lv), which offer connections to Burgas (5 per day). Buses stop outside the town—facing away from the stop, turn left and take the middle fork in the road to reach the "center," where the minibuses stop. Coastal minibuses go directly to and from Burgas, stopping at coastal towns along the route. 2 per day Burgas to Sinemorets; 4 per day Sinemorets to Burgas; 3.50lv. Turn right at the 1st street after a trio of cafes, then take the 1st left. This street leads to the beach; turn right at the field when you see the sand (10min.).*

Sinemorets, a tiny village of 400 inhabitants only 10km north of Turkey, shelters the most beautiful beach in Bulgaria (nestled between high grassy bluffs)—and nothing else. No post office, no pharmacy, no bank, no street names. While you won't be alone, you certainly won't be overwhelmed by crowds of tourists. The best hotel and restaurant are at ■ **Domingo's** (Доминго) on the road to the beach; signs point the way from the center. The new, bright rooms have balconies with distant seaside views and every convenience this picture-perfect town could offer. (☎63 21 93. 18lv per person. Breakfast included.) Domingo's patio restaurant has an international cook who makes food to fit customers' tastes. Enjoy the fresh, seafood under a ceiling of cascading grapevines. (Main dishes 1-5lv. Open 7:30am-midnight.)

# NORTHERN BULGARIA

From the ancient ruins of Bulgaria's first capitals at Pliska and Veliki Preslav to the war memorial in Pleven, the region between the Danube and the Balkan Mountains is most notable for its historic relics. Veliko Tarnovo stands as a virtual microcosm of Bulgaria over the past 5000 years and Madara boasts prehistoric caves. In the midst of it all, Ruse bobs along with whatever trade makes it down the Danube.

## VELIKO TARNOVO (ВЕЛИКО ТЪРНОВО) ☎(0)62

Perched on steep hills above the twisting Yantra River, Veliko Tarnovo (veh-LEEK-uh TARV-no; 74,800) has watched over Bulgaria for 5000 years. The town has blessed the country with revolutionaries, kings, and—following the overthrow of the Turks—the first Bulgarian constitution. An air of historical import hovers over Bulgaria's biggest trove of ancient ruins, the "second" Bulgarian capital from 1185-1393, but Veliko Tarnovo's cozy balconies, rolling hills, and young population add levity to delight even the most jaded traveler.

## ✦ ORIENTATION

Veliko Tarnovo is spread along a loop in the river, with its center, **pl. Maika Bulgaria** (Майка България), on the outside bank. From the center, the main drag follows the river east, changing its name as it goes: it begins as **Nezavisimost** (Независимост), becomes **Stefan Stambolov** (Стефан Стамболов) and **Nikola Pikolo** (Никола Пиколо), and, as it reaches the ruins, **Tsarevets Krepost** (Царевец Крепост). The other key street, **Hristo Botev** (Христо Ботев), intersects the main drag near the center, at the corner with the post office. From the **bus station,** take bus #7 or 10 (0.30lv) five stops to the center. From the **train station,** go along the river toward the center and then cross the bridge, which leads to **Aleksandr Stamboliysky** (Александър Стамболийски). Turn right onto the large **Hristo Botev** (Христо Ботев) to reach the center. You can also take almost any of the buses (0.30lv; timed to meet trains) from the train station; ask *"za tsentur?"* ("to the center?"). The book and paper stores along Rakovski, the small street two minutes from Hotel Trapezitsa on the way to Hotel Comfort, have good **maps** (3lv).

## ▣ TRANSPORTATION

**Trains:** All trains north stop at nearby **Gorna Oryahovitsa** (Горна Оряховица), 7km northeast, where connecting trains are scheduled to meet them. (30min., 0.50lv). You can also take a **bus** from the Gorna train station (see **Buses,** below). Trains from Veliko Tarnovo run to **Gabrovo** (1½hr., 4 per day, 1.50lv). From Gorna Oryahovitsa to: **Pleven** (1½hr., 14 per day, 2.40lv); **Ruse** (2½hr., 12 per day, 2.80lv); **Varna** (4hr., 5 per day, 5.50lv); **Sofia** (5hr., 10 per day, 6.10lv); and **Burgas** (5½hr., 6 per day, 5.80lv).

**Buses:** On Nikola Gabrovsky (Никола Габровски), 5 stops from the center on bus #7 or 10 (0.30lv), heading away from the post office. Sends buses to **Gabrovo** (40min., every 90min. from 7:30am, 2.50lv) and **Stara Zagora** (2hr., 2 per day, 3lv). Minibuses and buses connect V. Tarnovo with Gorna: **minibuses** leave from across the street from Gorna's train station (30min., 1lv), while **bus #10** goes from the street corner 1 block up the street directly in front of Gorna's train station (40min., every 15min., 1lv). **Group Travel** (☎62 82 92), in Hotel Etur (walk down Hristo Botev and turn left on Alexander Stamboliyski; it's a tall tower about 40m down), runs a bus to: **Sofia** (3hr.; 5 per day; 7lv, students 5.30lv) and **Varna** (3hr.; 2 per day; 6.80lv, students 6.10lv). Open M-F 8:30am-7pm, Sa-Su 10am-noon and 3:30-6:30pm.

## ⁊ PRACTICAL INFORMATION

**Tourist Office: Rila Travel Bureau,** Hristo Botev, on the left across from the pizzeria with the bright red awning. English-speaking staff has info about planes, trains, and automobiles. Open M-F 9am-5:30pm.

**Currency Exchange: Biohim Bank** (Биохим), Rafael Mihailov 4 (Рафаел Михайлов). Facing away from the post office, walk right on Nezavisimost; it's the 1st left. Cashes **traveler's checks** into US$ or *leva* for a US$2 commission. Open M-F 8:30am-4pm.

**Hospital: St. Cherkezov Regional Hospital** (Св. Черкезов; ☎418 12), Nish 1 (Ниш), off Nikola Gabrovski.

**Pharmacy:** ul. Vasil Levsky 23 (Васил Левски). Open daily 7:30am-7pm.

**Luggage Storage:** At the train station. 0.50lv per day. Luggage must be claimed at least 30min. prior to departure of train.

**Internet Access:** At **La Scalla, Pizzeria Italiana.** From the center, walk down Hristo Botev and go up the stairs to the right of the restaurant entrance. 2lv per hr. Open 24hr.

**Telephones:** At the post office. *BulFon* and *Betkom* cards sold. Open daily 7am-10pm. **Fax office** (fax 62 98 77) open M-Sa 7am-8pm.

**Post Office:** pl. Maika Bulgaria (Майка България). **Poste Restante** in the building 30m left of main entrance. Open M-F 7am-7pm, Sa 8am-noon and 1-4:30pm.

**Postal code:** 5000.

## ACCOMMODATIONS

Rooms in Veliko Tarnovo are plentiful, and if you wear a backpack for more than five seconds in public you'll be approached by locals offering private rooms (US$7-12). Bargain and don't be afraid to say no; hotels are also feasible.

■ **Hotel Trapezitsa (HI)** (Хотел Трапезица), Stefan Stambolov 79 (☎220 61). From the center, walk down Nezavismost toward the post office and follow the street to the right (5min.). An excellent hostel with a view of the river. Clean rooms with private, hot-water bathrooms. Reception 24hr. Check-out noon. 14lv per person, nonmembers 18lv.

■ **Hotel Comfort,** Panayot Tipografov 5 (Панайот Типографов; ☎287 28). From Stambolov, turn left onto Rakovski. Turn left at the small square and continue straight; the hotel is on the left. Clean rooms, beautiful bathrooms, and amazing views of Tsarevets. Friendly owner speaks English. US$15 per person, students US$11. The top-floor apartment ($45) sleeps 4 and affords great views of the evening light shows.

## FOOD

A large **outdoor market** sells fresh fruit and veggies (1.20-3lv per kg) daily from dawn to dusk at the corner of Bulgaria and Nikola Gabrovsky, while multiple *mehana* (механа; taverns) make use of the balconies overlooking the river.

■ **Samovodska Sresha** (Самоводска Среша), Rakovski 33 (☎62 39 10), on the way to Hotel Comfort. Extensive menu of traditional and unusual Bulgarian food. Break free of the *shopska salat* dependency by trying their fried pumpkin slices. Main dishes 3-8lv. Open daily 11am-11pm.

**Pizzeria Gustoso** (Густозо), at pl. Velocha Zavera (Велоча Завера). The best of the town's disproportionate number of pizza joints. Pizzas 1.50-3.50lv. Open 24hr.

**Cafe Aqua,** Nezivisimost 3, next to Hotel Trapezitsa. Mounds of scrumptious desserts (starting at 1lv), *real* coffee, techno music, and funky decor. Open daily 8am-midnight.

## SIGHTS

The ruins of **Tsarevets** (Царевец), a fortress that once housed the royal palace and a cathedral, stretch across an overgrown hilltop outside the city. Nikola Pikolo leads to the gates, where the *kasa* (каса) stands. Inside the ruins to the far right is **Baldwin's Tower** (Балдвинова кула; Baldvinova kula), where the imprisoned Latin Emperor Baldwin of Flanders spent his last days after an unsuccessful attempt in 1205 to conquer Bulgaria. (Open daily Apr.-Sept. 8am-7pm, Oct. 8am-6pm, Nov.-Mar 9am-5pm. 4lv, students 2lv.) Climb uphill to the beautiful **Church of the Ascension** (Църква Възнесениегосподне; Tsurkva Vuznes-eniegospodne), restored in 1981 for the 1300th anniversary of Bulgaria. There's a free **puppet show** (15min.) shown just inside the gates. It's given in Bulgarian, English, German, Russian, and French throughout the day. ■ **The National Revival Museum** (Музей на Възраждането; Muzey na Vuzrazhdaneto) exhibits many relics from the National Revival, including the first Bulgarian Parliament chamber (see **History,** p. 103), and the first Bulgarian constitution. From the center, follow Nezavisimost until it becomes Nikola Pikolo, then veer right onto ul. Ivan Vazov (Иван Вазов). It's a light blue building, set off the street. (Open daily 8am-noon and 1-5:30pm. 4lv, students 2lv. English tours 3lv.) Go down the stairs to the left and around to the back to reach the **Museum of the Second Bulgarian Kingdom** (Музей Второто Българско Царство; Muzey Vtoroto Bulgarsko Tsarstvo), a.k.a the Archaeological Museum, which traces the region's history from the Stone Age to the Middle Ages with Thracian pottery, medieval crafts from Tarnovo, and religious frescoes. (Open Tu-Su 8am-noon and 1-6pm. 4lv, students 2lv. English tours 3lv.) The **Monument to the Founders of the Second Bulgarian Kingdom** sits surrounded by the sweeping hairpin turn in the Yantra River.

## 🎵 ENTERTAINMENT

On summer evenings there's often a 📷 **sound and light show** above Tsarevets Hill—multi-colored lasers play out Bulgaria's history symbolically on the fortress ruins. (30min. show starts between 9:45 and 10pm.) Check at **Interhotel Veliko Tarnovo** (☎630 571 or 630 578), off Hristo Botev, for dates, although they may not know if the show will go on until two hours before. The building with the big "БАР ПОЛТАВА" (**Bar Poltava**) sign, which shines blue above the main square, houses a disco (open daily until 6am, dead except on weekends; cover 0.50lv), with three tiers of balconies overlooking a classic black-lit disco hall, and a **movie theater.** (Th-F 0.50lv.) The **Spider Club,** one block down at Hristo Botev 15, pulls dancers into its web for theme nights, posted on the door. (Open M-Sa 9pm-3am. Cover 0.50lv.)

## 🏛 DAYTRIP FROM VELIKO TARNOVO

### ETURA (ЕТЪРА)
*Buses from Veliko Tarnovo (40min., every 90min., 2.50lv) and Kazanluk (40min., 5 per day, 1.40lv) stop in Gabrovo. From the Gabrovo bus station, turn left and continue to the end of the street, then turn right to reach the center. Take trolley #32 or bus #1 from the center away from the bus station to the last stop, Bolshevik (20min., 0.30lv), then take bus #7 or 8 and ask to be dropped off at Etura (10min., 0.30lv). Buses are rare on weekends, when it's better to approach the museum on foot (45min.) or by taxi (☎128, 5lv from the bus station). All buses stop by Hotel/Restaurant Etura, a white building with dark wood on the front and top, convenient for quick meals. (☎421 91. Open daily 10am-10pm.) The steps to the right of the restaurant go down to the Ethnographic Complex; follow the path across the bridge and to the right.*

Midway between Kazanluk and Veliko Tarnovo sits a small village where blacksmiths still pound goatbells by hand and nothing is a lost art. At least, that's the way it seems at Etura's (EH-tu-rah) Ethnographic Complex, an outdoor museum of some 20 National Revival buildings, workshops, and mills. Climb through tiny doors and up narrow staircases into workshops, with artisans making woodcarvings, metalwork, jewelry, icons, musical instruments, herbal medicines, and pottery just as they've done for centuries. The candy store sells sweet, sticky sesame-and-honey bars for 0.50lv, while the bakery pleases with fresh breads and pastries for 0.30-0.60lv. (Open daily Apr.-Oct. 8:30am-noon, 12:30-6pm; Nov.-Mar. 8am-4:30pm. 5.30lv, students 3.50lv. English tours 5.40lv, students 4.50lv.)

# PLEVEN (ПЛЕВЕН) ☎(0)64

Pleven (pop. 138,500) offers an odd mix of history and modernity in its drab residential neighborhoods and exciting central areas. With dozens of memorials to the Battle of Pleven, it's a living monument to the Russo-Turkish War of 1877-78, yet also a youthful cafe town. A fountain fans over flower-covered parks in the lively town center, a testament to the rejuvenating waters still found in this town's stones.

📩 **TRANSPORTATION. Trains** go to **Sofia** (3hr., 11 per day, 3.70lv); **Ruse** (3½hr., 4 per day, 4.10lv); and **Gorna Oryahovitsa** outside **Veliko Tarnovo** (1½hr., 16 per day, 2lv). **Buses** run to **Sofia** (2½hr., 1 per day, 6lv) and **Ruse** (3hr., 1 per day, 3.40lv).

📌 **ORIENTATION.** The focal points of Pleven are its Siamese twin squares—**pl. Svoboda** (Свобода; Freedom) and **pl. Vazrazhdane** (Възраждане)—connected by a short stretch of the pedestrian **Vasil Levsky** (Васил Левски), which continues to the train station. From the train station, go through the park in front and then walk down **Danail Popov** (Данаил Попов), which runs perpendicular to the front of the train station and turns into **Osvobozhdenie** (Освобождение) and eventually hits pl. Svoboda (10 min. walk). **Maps** of the city aren't entirely necessary, but some kiosks on Vasil Levsky sell an excellent English map of Pleven's sights.

BULGARIA

**◪ PRACTICAL INFORMATION.** There is no tourist office in town. Store **luggage** at the train station. (0.50lv. Open 24hr., with breaks 8:15-8:45am and pm.) The lobby of **Hotel Plevin,** next to the bus station, **exchanges currency** (open 8:30am-6pm), as does the **Bulgarian Post Bank** (Българска Пощенска Банка) on Vasil Levsky pedestrian way. (Open M-F 8am-5pm.) **Gradska Poliklinika** (Градска Поликлиника), San Stephano 1 (Сан Стесфано; ☎ 335 80 and 335 76), provides **medical assistance.** There are pharmacies in every square; **Pharmacy 7** (Аптека 7; ☎ 281 04) sits next to the Gradska Poliklinika. The **post office** at pl. Svobodata has **telephones** inside. (Open M-F 7:30am-7pm, Sa 8am-7pm. Telephones open M-F 7am-10pm, Sa 8am-7pm.) **Postal code:** 5800.

**◪ ACCOMMODATIONS AND FOOD. Rostov na Don** (Ростов на Дон), Osvobozhdenie 2, on the left as you enter pl. Svoboda, is a standard tower hotel with clean private baths, TVs, and phones. (☎ 80 18 92. Check-out noon. Singles 60lv; doubles 92lv. US$ accepted. MC/Visa 5% surcharge.) **Hotel Pleven,** pl. Republika 2 (Република), is to the right when you're facing the bus station and offers bare-bones amenities. (☎ 301 81, 363 20, and 363 22. Singles 42lv; doubles 44lv.)

Vendors sell veggies at the **outdoor market** on Osvobozhdenie before Rostov na Don. The famous **Peshterata** (Пещерата) restaurant is 3km from town in Kailuka Park. Built in a sandstone cave, it has chairs made of drained wooden kegs and a large cool outdoor patio completely surrounded by cascading greenery and fountains. Take tram #3 or 7 from San Stefano (0.25lv) heading away from the train station. From the end of the tram line, follow the sidewalk in the park for 15 minutes until you pass the pond. Cross the bridge to the left and head for the cave. (☎ 41 53 47. Main dishes 1-4lv. Open daily 10am-midnight.) The streets in the center are filled with trendy cafes, somewhat classier restaurants, and heaps of proud bars.

**◪ SIGHTS.** The granddaddy of Pleven's sights, the **Panorama** (Панорама) depicts the third Russo-Turkish Battle of Pleven and the liberation of Bulgaria (see **History,** p. 102). Among its attractions are a series of huge murals and one 360° panorama. From the center, take bus #1, 9, or 12 away from the train and bus stations (ask for the Panorama), then go left and follow the windy road to the top of the hill. (☎ 300 80. Open daily 9am-noon and 12:30-5:30pm. 3lv. Useful English booklet 5lv.) Down the path from the main entrance of the Panorama is the old battlefield, now **Park Skobelev** (Парк Скобелев). Wild greenery, guns, and an ossuary lying within make for an enjoyable walk. Built in 1834, St. Nicholas (Св. Николай; Sv. Nikolai) was sunk 2m into the ground to comply with Ottoman laws that no church be higher than local mosques. It sits between the Museum of the Liberation of Pleven (see below) and the train station. (☎ 372 08. Open daily 8:30am-6:30pm.)

**◪ MUSEUMS.** The nicest house in Pleven 120 years ago, the **Museum of the Liberation of Pleven** (Музей Освобождението на Плевен; Muzey Osvobozhdenieto na Pleven), in the fenced-in park on the right as you walk down Vasil Levsky toward the train station, witnessed visits from Russian Tsar Alexander II. (Open Tu-Sa 9am-noon and 1-6pm. 1lv.) The **Historical Museum** (Исторически Музей; Istoricheski Muzey) complex, minutes from the center of town at Sv. Zaimov 3 (Св. Заимов), stretches across two floors in several buildings and takes you through archaeology, ethnography, and National Revival exhibits, ending with the Russo-Turkish War and early 20th-century history. To get there, go through the park at the end of pl. Vuzrazhdane to the far right corner and cross the street. (☎ 230 69. Open Tu-Sa 9am-noon and 1-5pm. Helpful English brochure 0.50lv. 3lv, 2.40lv with ISIC.) Named after a famous Bulgarian caricaturist, the **Iliya Beshkov Art Gallery** (Художествена Галерия "Илия Бешков"; Hudozhestvena Galeria "Iliya Beshkov"), boasts a surprisingly good 5000-piece collection. Temporary exhibits have included the likes of Picasso and Rembrandt. The gallery sits at bul. Skobolev 1, across the street from the Historical Museum. (☎80 20 58 or 80 20 39. Open Tu-Sa 9am-5pm. Knock if door is locked. Some English. Free.) Now an **art gallery,** the Turkish Bathhouse (Дойран), at Doiran 75, offers a melange of Bulgarian and international painting. Coming from the train station, it lies midway between the two main squares on the right. (☎383 42. Open M-F 10:30am-6pm. Free.)

# NEAR PLEVEN: TROYAN MONASTERY

*The monastery is a 30min. city bus ride from Troyan. Buses run from Pleven to Troyan (1½ hr., 1 per day, 2lv). Troyan can also be reached from Pleven (45min., every hr., 2.20lv) via Lovech. From Lovech, take a bus to Troyan (50min., every hr., 1.70lv). In Troyan, catch the bus to the monastery outside the station (25min., every hr., 0.70lv.); get off when you see the monastery.*

Located in the tiny village of Oreshka (Орешка) in the picturesque Balkan mountain range near Pleven, the Troyan Monastery (Троянски Манастир; Troyansky Monastir) is the country's third largest. It is said to have been built by a lone 14th-century monk shortly after the area came under Turkish control. It attracted a large order of monks in the late 1600s, then became an active participant in the 19th-century independence movement, hiding revolutionary leader Vasil Levsky from his oppressors (see **History,** p. 102). Today it's the largest monastery in the Balkan Range. It contains a wide range of murals by master artist **Zahari Zograf** (see **Literature and Arts,** p. 105). Zograf's brother, Dimitev, contributed a number of icon paintings, most of which are in the main church. Look for the crafty, miracle-working **Three-handed Holy Virgin,** the monastery's oldest icon, dated to the 17th century. The **iconostasis** is also noteworthy for its ornate woodcarving, featuring plumed birds and twisting grape vines. Small shops sell replicas of the icons (starting at 1lv) and other Balkan crafts. The **Chapel of St. Nikolai the Miracle Worker** (Св. Никола) is the monastery's oldest, best-preserved building, but may be a disappointment after seeing the monastery itself. It's a 30-minute hike from the main complex—cross the bridge across the road from the monastery, head right, and take the first left onto a path that soon turns into an unpaved trail. Take a right at the trail's junction, marked by an old sign and continue straight to the chapel. The monastery is open daily 6am-midnight. The church is open daily 7:30am-7:30pm.

You can sleep in a monastic **cell,** complete with lumpy beds (12lv in the new building, with private bathrooms; 10lv in the old building), and eat across the street at the **Manastirska Bara Restaurant** (Манастирска Бара). The balcony serves standard Bulgarian fare above a bubbling brook. (☎69 52 31 05. Main dishes 4-8lv. Open daily 8:30am-midnight.)

# SHUMEN (ШУМЕН) ☎(0)54

Shumen (pop. 106,400) is notable only for its proximity to archaeological sites at Preslav, Pliska, and Madara, which date from the beginning of the Bulgarian state. The city itself is mainly industrial, with little to offer tourists other than worn buildings well on their way to becoming archaeological relics themselves.

**⊏ TRANSPORTATION.** Shumen can be reached by **train** from: **Varna** (1½ hr., 11 per day, 2.70lv); **Ruse** (3hr., 1 per day, 3.70lv); **Sofia** (6hr., 5 per day, 8.80lv); and elsewhere via **Gorna Oryahovitsa** (2hr., 8 per day, 4lv), just outside **Veliko Tarnovo. Group Travel** (☎627 13), in a kiosk next to the **bus station** and directly across from the train station, sends **buses** to: **Varna** (1hr., 2 per day, 5lv); **Veliko Tarnovo** (2½ hr., 5 per day, 7lv); and **Sofia** (6hr., 4 per day, 11lv, students 9lv).

**⊓ PRACTICAL INFORMATION.** To get to the center, take bus #1, 4, or 10 (0.30lv) from behind the bus station and get off at Hotel Shumen. The **tourist office** inside the hotel arranges **private rooms** (single US$10; double US$16), sells **maps**

BULGARIA

(3lv), and provides info. (Open M-F 8:30am-5:30pm, Sa 9am-1:30pm.) **BulBank** cashes **traveler's checks.** (☎572 89. Open M-F 8:45am-4:30pm.) There's an **ATM** between the Halts (Халц) and the United Bulgarian Bank on Tsar Osvoboditel, the cobblestone street off Hristo Botev and near the central pl. Oborishte. **Hotel Orbita** in Kyoshkovete Park (Кьошковете Парк), at the western end of town near the Shumen Brewery. Take bus #6 to its last stop from the train and bus stations. Enter the park and walk down the paved path; the hotel is on the right. Recently renovated rooms boast showers and shaded terraces. (☎523 98. Singles 30lv; doubles 40lv.) **Bul. Slavyansky** is lined with restaurants while fruit and vegetable stands dot Hristo Botev. The *mehana* inside Hotel Shumen serves the best food in town. (English menu. Main dishes 3-8lv. Open daily 10am-midnight.)

# DAYTRIPS FROM SHUMEN

Pliska (PLEE-ska) and Veliki Preslav (Veh-LEEK-ee PRES-lav), the first and second capitals of the Bulgarian Kingdom (681-893 and 893-972, respectively), now archaeological sites, stand as testaments to Bulgaria's Golden Age. They also reflect the present; their neglect is a sign of a country too poor to take care of its treasures.

## PLISKA (ПЛИСКА)

*23km northeast of Shumen, Pliska can be reached by bus (1hr., 4 per day, 1.40lv). Buses returning to Shumen are few and far between; the last one leaves around 5pm. Museum open M-F 9am-5pm. 2lv, students 1lv.*

The antithesis of a tourist trap, the tiny village of Pliska offers nothing but local hospitality. The real attraction is the huge archaeological excavation 3km away, which has unearthed parts of palaces, 31 churches, and fortifications. Although the ruins are essentially unmarked, it is easy enough to let your imagination guide you through the partially reconstructed **King's Palace.** Unfortunately, no public transportation serves the ruins. To get there from Pliska's bus station, cross the big, white-tiled area behind the cafe, head left on Han Krum (Хан Крум), and settle in for the long haul among the sunflowers (30min.). You'll enter through the large Eastern Gate in the second of the ruins' three main fortified rings. The path straight ahead leads to the palace; the path to the right brings you to the museum.

## VELIKI PRESLAV (ВЕЛИКИ ПРЕСЛАВ)

*Buses run to Preslav, 18km south of Shumen (30min., 11 per day, 1.10lv). Facing the bus station, walk to the left up the main street, then take a left on the road just before the plaza with big stone statues and a church. Pass the food market (пазар; pazar) to reach the ruins. To get to the museum, enter the park, walk straight past the statue, and bear right at the next intersection. Walk to the cafe, then take a sharp left onto a paved path to the museum (20min.). ☎ 32 43. Open daily Apr.-Sept. 9am-6pm; Oct.-May 9am-5pm. 2lv, students 1lv. Film 1.50lv. English guide by request and free.*

Preslav is home to Veliki Preslav, one of the more informative archaeological reserves. The first white-clay icons in Europe were made here; making white-clay ceramics is still the town's popular pastime. The museum sells a map and guide to the ruins for 1lv. The **Archaelogical Museum** (Археологически Музей; Arheologicheski Muzey) exhibits artifacts found in the area and shows three short films in English on the town's history. The ruins are down the road from the museum through a stone gate. Be sure to see the remains of the AD 908 **Golden Temple** and its well-preserved floor mosaic. The **King's Palace** is marked by a column and parts of the city's fortress wall still stand.

## MADARA (МАДАРА)

*To get to Madara, 16km east of Shumen, take a bus (20min., 3 per day, 0.90lv) or any putnicheski (slow train; 20min., 5 per day, 3 stops, 0.50lv) to Varna. Walk past the bus station, toward the back, but continue straight for several blocks. Take a right when you see the tracks; cross them at the main road (near the post office) and head straight up the road to the horseman (30min.). From the train station, face the tracks and go left on the small path toward town. Turn left at the 1st paved street, which crosses the tracks next to the post office, and follow the winding road uphill (30min.). Take the stairs on the right up to the horseman, then take the small path to the left at the top of the stairs to the fortress.*

Madara (mah-DAH-rah) is home to the famous **Madara Horseman** (Мадарски Конник; madarski konnik) stone relief. On a 25m vertical cliff, the life-size figure features a horse with a rider, lion, and dog—an ensemble so legendary it graces the backs of all *leva* coins and the labels of Shumen beer. It was created in the 8th century and supposedly symbolizes the victories of Bulgarian ruler Han Tervel over the Byzantine Empire. A path leads methodically through the **caves** (3500 BC). The largest one served as the **Temple of Three Thracian Nymphs** (Тракически Светилище; Trakicheski Svetilishchte; 1st-4th century BC) and now in June hosts the annual festival **Madara Music Days** (Мадарски Музикални Дни; Madarski Musikalni Dni). There's a **hostel** on the paved mountain road, 20m past the souvenir stands, with spacious balconies on every floor and a large kitchen available to guests. (☎ (05) 313 20 91. 12lv.) There are also **camp-sites** to the right of the mountain road, past the restaurant and before the stairs to the horseman. (0.50lv per site.)

BULGARIA

# CROATIA (HRVATSKA)

**IF YOU'RE HERE FOR...**

**1-3 DAYS.** See **Dubrovnik,** the pearl of the Adriatic, with your own eyes (p. 195).

**1 WEEK.** Up the coast from Dubrovnik, stop in **Split** to understand why Roman Emperor Diocletian summered here. Don't miss **Pula's** (p. 164) breathtaking amphitheater.

**2-3 WEEKS.** Venture from Split to the nearby **Trogir** (p. 183) and to the islands of **Hvar** (p. 191) and **Korčula** (p. 193). Abandon the coast and explore the country's capital city of **Zagreb** (p. 156) to see the contrast between Habsburg splendor and Mediterranean idleness. En route to Zagreb, visit the **Plitvice Lakes National Park** (p. 163)

**1 MONTH.** Cruise up and down the coast and see everything covered in this chapter.

Croatia is a land of unearthly beauty. Traced with thick forests, dramatic barren mountains, and the translucent sea, it has served for centuries as a summer playground for residents of countries less scenically endowed. Positioned where the Mediterranean, the Alps, and the Pannonian plain converge, it has also been situated on dangerous divides—between the Frankish and Byzantine empires in the 9th century, the Catholic and Orthodox Churches beginning in the 11th century, Christian Europe and Islamic Turkey from the 15th to the 19th centuries, and its own fractious ethnic groups in the past decade. Today, dancing in nightclubs in Dubrovnik and lounging on the sunny beaches, locals try to forget the tensions that have played out here in the past. Experiencing independence for the first time in 800 years, Croatians are finally free to enjoy the extraordinary landscape in peace.

**CROATIA AT A GLANCE**

**OFFICIAL NAME:** Republic of Croatia

**CAPITAL:** Zagreb (pop. 1 million)

**POPULATION:** 4,677,000 (78% Croats, 12% Serbs, 1% Bosniaks, 9% others)

**LANGUAGES:** Croatian (Latin script)

**CURRENCY:** 1 kuna (kn) = 100 lipas

**RELIGION:** 77% Catholic, 11% Orthodox, 1% Muslim, 11% other

**LAND AREA:** 56,538 km²

**CLIMATE:** Mediterranean

**GEOGRAPHY:** Mountainous coast with numerous islands; lowlands in the north

**BORDERS:** Bosnia-Herzegovina, Hungary, Slovenia, Yugoslavia

**ECONOMY:** 64% Tourism and Services, 24% Industry, 12% Agriculture

**GDP PER CAPITA:** US$5,100

**EMERGENCY PHONE NUMBERS:** Police 92, Fire 93, Ambulance 94

**COUNTRY CODE:** 385

**INTERNATIONAL DIALING PREFIX:** 00

# HISTORY

**WHEN IN ROME...** Just across the Adriatic Sea from Italy, the lands of present-day Croatia—Dalmatia, Istria and Pannonia—were among the first territories conquered by the expansive **Roman Empire** between the 2nd century BC to the 4th century AD; Roman ruins still litter the country. After the fall of the Roman Empire in the 4th century, Croatia became a battlefield between the empire's Eastern successor, **Byzantium,** and the western **Frankish** invaders. To this day, Croatia is marked as a crossroads between West and East, between Catholicism and Orthodoxy, and between Christianity and Islam.

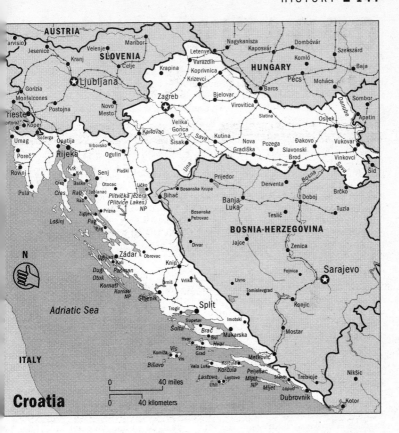

**Croatia**

0     40 miles

0     40 kilometers

**SLAVS!** The Slavic ancestors of Croatia's present inhabitants settled the region in the 6th and 7th centuries, partly expelling and partly assimilating the indigenous Illyrian (Latin) population. They followed a largely unknown native religion until **Catholicism** arrived slowly over the next two centuries. In the 9th century, an independent Croatian state emerged, uniting Dalmatia, Pannonia, and Slavonia. **King Tomislav** (910-28BC) consolidated the state by earning papal recognition for his country, which facilitated resistance against Charlemagne's attempts to gain control of the area. King Zvonimir was crowned by Pope Gregory in 1076, decisively strengthening Croatia's orientation toward Catholic Europe.

**UNDER THE HUNGARIAN YOKE.** In 1102, the **Kingdom of Croatia-Slavonia** entered into a dynastic union with Hungary. At first, it seemed as though the kingdom retained its independence through the Sabor (an assembly of Croatian nobles) and the ban (viceroy), but in fact this move literally erased Croatia from the map of Europe for the next 800 years. The kingdom was stripped not only of its independence, but also of its territory; in 1420, Dalmatia was lost to the **Venetian Empire,** and after the defeat of Hungary at the **Battle of Mohaćs** in 1526, the area that comprises present-day Bosnia-Herzegovina was ceded to the **Ottoman Empire.** Following Hungary's defeat in 1526, Austrian Habsburgs took over what remained of Croatia and turned most of it into a **Military Frontier** (Vojna Krajina), which served as a bumper against Ottomans. Orthodox Christians from the Ottoman-controlled area migrated to the Krajina, laying foundation for the Serbian minority in Croatia. In 1797, the Habsburgs incorporated Dalmatia and Istria into their kingdom. Seeking protection from growing Austrian centralism, the Croats turned to Hungary, but gained little; Hungarian nationalism grew like mushrooms after rain and soon led to the imposition of Hungarian as the official language in Croatia in the 1830s. Desperate to carve out some autonomy, the Croats once again looked to the Habsburgs for help; when Hungary revolted against Austria in 1848, the Croats, led by **ban Josip Jelačić,** sided with the Austrians, convening a diet in Zagreb to demand self-government. Disillusionment with Austrians and Hungarians alike found its expression in the **Illyrian movement.** Led by **Ljudevit Gaj,** the Illyrianists called for the unification of South Slavs as the sole means of achieving sovereignty.

**BITTERSWEET INDEPENDENCE.** As part of Austria-Hungary, Croatian troops fought on the side of the Germans during **World War I.** Meanwhile, political exiles strove to create a union of Serb, Croat, and Slovene nations, but failed to agree on its form. After the defeat of Austria-Hungary, the Croatian Sabor declared **independence** on December 1, 1918, and announced the incorporation of Croatia into the **Kingdom of the Serbs, Croats, and Slovenes** (the original name for Yugoslavia), with Serbian King Alexander I as its formal head. The Croats desired a federation, but the government soon became centralized in Belgrade. In 1934, Alexander was assassinated by Croatian nationalists from the illegal **Ustaše (Insurgents).** The Ustaše terrorist organization was a pro-fascist organization, and demanded the complete independence of Croatia.

**FASCISM.** The Ustaše finally achieved Croatia's "independence" in 1941 in the form of a fascist puppet state. The ruthless regime sought to eliminate the country's Jewish and Serbian populations, killing more than 350,000 people in massacres and concentration camps. Croatia's support of the Axis powers during **World War II** (while Serbia supported the Allies) was the principal reason behind the reluctance of the international community to support its quest for independence in the 1990s. The majority of Croats, however, joined communist-led **partisan** resistance early on in the war. Rather than complete independence, the Partisans, led by **Josip Brož Tito,** demanded the creation of a federal Yugoslav state. In 1945, the **Socialist Federal Republic of Yugoslavia** declared its independence.

**TITO AND NOTHING ELSE.** Tito, who became Yugoslavia's first president, placed all industry and natural resources under state control. Under his unchallenged rule Yugoslavia broke with Russia in 1948 and walked down its own communist path, which allowed economic trade with the West. Under Tito, ethnic rivalries were suppressed, giving Yugoslavia the appearance of a tolerant, prosperous state. But underneath the pretense, disgruntlement was brewing. For the Croats, the major points of dispute were the growing numbers of Serbian nationals in the government, and the fact that as the most prosperous republic in Yugoslavia, Croatia sponsored other parts of the union. In 1971 Croatian communist leadership demanded a greater autonomy within Yugoslavia, which led to its dismissal and replacement with more obedient Communists. After Tito's death in 1980, Yugoslavia descended into confusion.

**A COSTLY FREEDOM.** A failure to find Tito's successor led to the establishment of a rotating presidency, which was ineffective in curbing the resurfaced nationalist sentiments. In April 1990 Croatian nationalist **Franjo Tudjman** was elected President of Croatia, and on June 25, 1991, the people of Croatia declared **independence.** Tensions began to arise between the Croats and its large Serbian minority, which soon escalated into violence. Claiming to protect Serbian nationals, the Serb-controlled **Yugoslav National Army** invaded Croatia. In a few months, it expelled hundreds of thousands of Croatians from Eastern Slavonia and shelled Vukovar and Osijek in Slavonia, Zagreb, and Dubrovnik. Meanwhile, the Serbian minority declared their own independent republic, the **Serbian Krajina,** around Knin in central Croatia. The Serbian Krajina spanned across central Dalmatia, and practically severed any communication between Zagreb and southern Dalmatia.

Not until art lovers worldwide watched the senseless destruction of Dubrovnik did the international political leadership realize that Croatia was not a fascist secessionist republic as the Serbian propaganda suggested and that it was indeed occupied. On January 15, 1992, Croatia's independence was recognized by the EU, largely thanks to Germany's lobby. A UN military presence kept further fighting at bay. In May 1995, Croatia, frustrated with its lack of control over more than half its territory, began an operation in Western Slavonia and seized the Serb-controlled Krajina in August, expelling over 150,000 Serbs. Sadly, occupation of its own territory did not stop Croatian leadership from making claims on Bosnia-Herzegovina, sending its troops and participating in the massacres of Bosnian Serbs and initially, Muslims. The **Dayton Peace Agreement** of 1995, negotiated by American Richard Holbrooke, brought a cease-fire in Bosnia-Herzegovina, and stabilized the situation in the disputed areas of Croatia.

# POLITICS

Croatia is a parliamentary democracy with extensive executive powers invested in the President, who is elected in a popular vote for a 5-year term. It has a bicameral parliament, the **Sabor**; deputies are elected for four years. The Prime Minister, currently **Ivica Račan,** is appointed by the President. For better or worse, **Franjo Tudjman** led Croatia as its President from 1991 until his death from cancer in December 1999. During eight years in power, Tudjman and his nationalist **Democratic Party** (Hrvatska demokraticka zajednica; HDZ) managed to establish Croatia as a sovereign state, but their abuse of power, corruption, and censorship of the media also led to the country's isolation from the West. The elections in 2000 transferred power to the democratically-thinking left, headed by a reformed communist **Social Democratic Party (SDP).** A pro-Western liberal, **Stipe Mesić,** became President. The new government immediately began accession talks with the EU and NATO.

With an economy founded on tourism, Croatia suffered severely from the war. Its hopes for a recovery were halted by the Kosovo crisis in 1999, which once again discouraged Western tourists from coming. Croatia's unemployment skyrocketed to nearly 20%. In January 1998, fulfilling a long-delayed stipulation of the Dayton Peace Agreement, Zagreb took over Serb-held **Eastern Slavonia** after two years of U.N. control. The biggest challenge has been the exchange of refugees, with tensions between returning refugees and the still-displaced refugees occupying their former homes. Ethnic violence ranges from rare to nonexistent, but only because the majority of Serbs have been expelled and do not want to come back. What remains of the pre-1991 Serbian population, however, suffers from stigmatization and unemployment.

# CULTURE

## NATIONAL HOLIDAYS IN 2001

| | |
|---|---|
| **January 1** New Year | **June 22** Anti-Fascist Struggle Day |
| **January 6** Epiphany | **August 5** National Thanksgiving Day |
| **April 15-16** Easter | **August 15** Assumption |
| **May 1** May Day | **November 1** All Saints' Day |
| **May 30** Independence Day | **December 25-26** Christmas |

# LITERATURE AND ARTS

The first Croatian texts date from the 9th century, but for the next 600 years Croatian literature consisted almost entirely of translations of Europe's greatest literary hits. In southern Dalmatia, Dubrovnik (Roman Ragusa) was the only independent part of Croatia after 1102, and became the center of **Renaissance,** producing literature that had a lasting impact on Croatian language. After the city's 1667 devasta-

CROATIA

tion by an earthquake, the focus of Croatian literature shifted north. The 16th century dramatist **Martin Držić** and the 17th century poet **Ivan Gundulić,** both from Dubrovnik, raided Italy for models (of the literary type), combining them with traditions from back home. During Austrian and Hungarian repressions of the Croatian language, **Ljudevit Gaj** led the movement to reform and codify the vernacular. **August Šenoa,** Croatia's dominant 19th-century literary figure, played a key part in the formation of a literary public and in completing the work that Gaj had begun.

Croatian prose sparkled in the 20th century, inspired in the 1930s by the novels of **Miroslav Krleža.** More recently, **Dubravka Ugresić's** personal, reflective novels took on political overtones during the recent war, when she publicly opposed Croatian President Tudjman. Her works, which discuss nostalgia and the revision of history, are instant best-sellers in Croatia, much to the chagrin of the state media apparatus. **Slavenka Drakulić,** another novelist and feminist, is more popular abroad than at home. Let's Go recommends her *How We Survived Communism and Even Laughed,* which offers humorous insight into everyday lives of Eastern European women under communism and provides commentary on the civil war of 1991.

In the 20th century, Croatian visual arts increased in importance. Characterized by the rejection of conventional and "civilized" depictions of subjects, **naïve art** presides as the most popular painting style. Highly influenced by folk traditions, it eliminates perspective and uses only brilliant and vivid colors. **Ivan Meštrović** (see **Zagreb: Sights,** p. 160 and **Split: Sights,** p. 187), Croatia's most famous modern sculptor and architect, was mentored by French sculptor Auguste Rodin and immigrated to the United States in the 1950s. Outside Croatia, his wooden religious sculptures can be seen at London's Tate Gallery and the Metropolitan Museum of Art in New York City. **Vinko Bresan** is Croatia's recent contribution to the international film scene. His 1996 comedy, *How the War Started on My Island (Kako je poceo rat na mom otoku),* won multiple awards at the 1996 Croatian Film Festival, including the Golden Arena for Best Director and the Golden Arc for Audience Approval.

# RELIGION

Like Poland, Croatia is one of the **Catholic** bastions of Eastern Europe, with nearly 100% of the ethnically Croat population subscribing to the faith. Serbian nationals remaining in the country after the massive exodus of 1995 belong to the **Serbian Orthodox** church. **Islam** is practiced by the Bosnian minority.

# FOOD AND DRINK

Cuisine *à la* Hrvatska is defined by the country's varied geography; in continental Croatia around and east of Zagreb, typically heavy Slavic meals predominate (think meat and sauces). On the coast, however, seafood blends with Italian pasta dishes. After years of wartime drought, restaurants are eagerly preparing for the return of guests. *Purica s mlincima* (turkey with pasta) is the regional dish near Zagreb. The spicy *Slavonian kulen,* available everywhere, is considered one of the world's best sausages by the panel of fat German men who decide such things. Along the coast, don't miss out on *lignje* (squid) or *Dalmatinski pršut* (Dalmatian smoked ham). The oysters from Ston Bay have received a number of awards at international competitions. If your budget does not allow for such treats, *slane sardele* (salted sardines) are a tasty substitute. *Grešak varivo* (green bean stew), *tikvice va lešo* (steamed zucchini in olive oil), and *grah salata* (beans and onion salad) are meatless favorites. The eclectic nature of Croatian culture is most apparent with desserts; if you always ask for a regional specialty, you'll never eat the same sweet twice. *Zagorski štrukli* (dumplings with a cottage cheese filling) in Zagreb and *fritule* (thin baked pastry) in Dalmatia are just two examples.

Croatia offers excellent wines; price is usually the best indicator of quality. Mix red wine with tap water to get the popular *bevanda,* and white with carbonated water to get *gemišt.* Reds famous on the coast include *Teran, Merlot,* and *Cabanetia Istria.* Farther south, they include *Plavac, Opolo, Dingac,* and *Pos-*

*tup.* Coastal white wines of renown include *Malvazija, Zlahtina, Posip, Kujundzusa,* and *Grk. Karlovačko* and *Ožujsko* are the two most popular beers, especially among fishermen.

# CUSTOMS AND ETIQUETTE

**Tipping** is not expected, but you may round up to the nearest whole figure; in some cases, the establishment will do it for you—check your change. In the beach-oriented south, beauty is most definitely skin deep; the darker your tan, the trendier you'll be with the locals. This land of skin and shorts is also predominantly Catholic, but you'll only notice the contradiction if you try to jump from the beach to the cathedral without a change of clothes. Croats have few qualms about drinking and smoking, and prove it again and again just about everywhere. In such a heavily Catholic country, **homosexuals** may be subjected to disapproving looks.

# ADDITIONAL READING

The most objective book available on Croatian history is Stephen Gazi's *A History of Croatia;* unfortunately, the book only covers the country prior to 1939. It is difficult to find any book on Croatian history after the outbreak of WWII that is not rejected by either Serbs or Croats as a piece of nationalist propaganda or as media lies. The safest option, therefore, is to read the nationalist propaganda from both sides. Two opposing books about WWII and its aftermath in Yugoslavia are John Prcela and Stanko Guldescu's *Operation Slaughterhouse,* a detailed account of the persecution and murdering of Croats by Serbs, and *The Yugoslav Auschwitz and the Vatican: the Croatian Massacre of the Serbs During World War II,* by Vladimir Dedijer and Harvey Kendall. Fair texts dealing with the recent wars in Croatia are as difficult to find; an exception Dubravka Ugresić, who rejects all forms of nationalist propaganda in her recent collection of controversial political essays, *The Culture of Lies: Antipolitical Essays.* A more personal perspective on the Balkan situation is offered in *The Suitcase: Refugee Voices from Bosnia and Croatia,* edited by American Cornel West. Well-written and researched, if slightly pro-Croat, is *Croatia: A Nation Forged in War,* by a British journalist Marcus Tanner. US peace negotiator Richard Holbrooke captures the spirit of 1990s wartime Balkans in *To End a War,* his personal account of the rocky path to Dayton Peace Agreement. For an incredible (and incredibly long—over 800 pages) but pro-Serbian travelogue, grab Rebecca West's *Black Lamb and Gray Falcon: A Journey Through Yugoslavia.*

# SPORTS

The most popular sport in the country is **soccer,** or football. As in most of Eastern Europe, the local teams have suffered from the migration of its best players to better-paying teams in the West. Such is the case with **Zvonimir Boban** who, in addition to running a restaurant in Zagreb cryptically called Boban, is also a star of kicking ball in AC Milan. The best local teams are Dinamo Zagreb and Hajduk Split. Although not a part of Croatian national identity like soccer is, **basketball** and **handball** are also widely played. And of course, along the coast, **water sports** abound.

# LANGUAGE

Croats speak a South Slavic language and write in Roman characters. Only a few expressions differ from Serbian, but be careful not to use the Serbian ones in Croatia—you'd make few friends. Words are pronounced exactly as they are written; "č" and "ć" are both "ch" (only a Croat can tell them apart), "š" is "sh," and "ž" is "zh." The letter "r" is rolled, except in the absence of a vowel, in which case it makes an "er" sound as in "Brrrr!" The letter "j" is equivalent to "y," so *jučer* (yesterday) is pronounced "yuchur." In Zagreb and most tourist offices, some people know **English,** but the most common language on the coast is **Italian.** Street desig-nations on maps often differ from those on signs by "-va" or "-a" because of gram-matical declensions (see p. 156). Helpful phrases include *dobar dan* (good day), *do videnja* (good bye), *hvala* (thank you), and the multi-purpose *molim* (you're welcome/please/excuse me). See **Bosnia: Language** (p. 92) for the differences between Bosnian, Croatian, and Serbian. Words that appear frequently in this chap-ter include: *crkva* (church); *hram* (temple); *kolodvor* (station); *ljekarna* (phar-macy); *most* (bridge); *novi grad* (new town); *stari grad* (old town); *šetalište* (promenade); and *trg* (square). See **Glossary,** p. 154, and **Phrasebook,** p. 155.

# TRAVELING ESSENTIALS

Citizens of Australia, Canada, Ireland, New Zealand, the UK, and the US do not need visas for stays of up to 90 days. Visas are required of South African citizens; send your passport, a visa application, two passport-sized photos, a document proving your intent of tourism (i.e. invitation, voucher, or receipt of business arrangements), and a personal check or money order (US$29 for single-entry, US$37 for double-entry, or $59 for multiple entry) to the nearest embassy or consu-late (see **Essentials: Embassies and Consulates,** p. 18). Visas either take two business days or four to six weeks to process, depending on the country. Only transit visas, valid for seven days, can be purchased at the border, and at wildly varying prices. Citizens of countries that don't require visas who wish to stay more than 90 days should fill out an "extension of stay" form at a local police station. All visitors must register with the police within two days of arrival, regardless of their length of stay. Hotels, campsites, and accommodation agencies should automatically register you, but those staying with friends or in private rooms must do so themselves to avoid fines or expulsion. Police may check foreigners' passports anywhere. There is no entry fee required at the border. As always, the most direct way of entering or exit-ing Croatia is to take a direct bus or train to or from Zagreb to a neighboring capital.

# TRANSPORTATION

Whether by plane, train, or bus, Zagreb is Croatia's main entry point.

**BY PLANE. Croatia Airlines** flies from many cities, including Chicago, Frankfurt, London, New York, Paris, and Toronto, and often continues on to Dubrovnik and Split. Rijeka, Zadar, and Pula also have tiny international airports.

**BY TRAIN.** Trains travel to Zagreb from Budapest, Ljubljana, and Vienna, continu-ing on to other destinations throughout Croatia. Due to the destruction of railways during the recent war, train connections are *very* slow, and nonexistent south of Split. *Odlazak* means departures, *dolazak* arrivals.

**BY BUS.** For domestic travel, buses are by far the best option, running faster than their railed counterparts for comparable prices. Tickets are actually cheaper if you buy them on board, as you bypass the 2kn "service charge" at the station kiosks. In theory, luggage must be stowed (3kn), but this is only enforced on the most crowded of lines.

**BY CAR.** You can **rent a car** in larger cities, but downtown parking can be expen-sive, roads in the country are in atrocious condition, and those traveling through the Krajina region and other conflict areas should be wary of off-road land mines. Traveling by car can get especially expensive when island-hopping—Jadrolinija charges obscene amounts for decking your wheels.

**BY BOAT.** If you're on the coast, take one of the **ferries** run by **Jadrolinija.** Boats sail the Rijeka-Split-Dubrovnik route, stopping at islands along the way. Ferries also float from Split to Ancona, Italy, and from Dubrovnik to Bari, Italy. Although slower than buses and trains, they're more comfortable. A basic ticket provides only a place on the deck. Cheap beds sell out fast, so purchase tickets in advance. If the agency will only offer a basic ticket, you'll need to *run* to get a bed.

**BY THUMB.** *Let's Go* does not recommend hitchhiking. No, really. Don't hitchhike in Croatia, it's a bad idea.

**BY TAXI.** Unlike in other parts of Eastern Europe, taxi drivers will generally not want to rip you off. Prices are set; there is no haggling.

# TOURIST SERVICES AND MONEY

| CURRENCY | | |
|---|---|---|
| US$1 = 8.40KN (KUNA OR HRK) | 10KN = US$1.20 |
| CDN$1 = 5.70KN | 10KN = CDN$1.80 |
| UK£1 = 12KN | 10KN = UK£0.81 |
| IR£1 = 9.60KN | 10KN = IR£1.00 |
| AUS$1 = 4.85KN | 10KN = AUS$2.10 |
| NZ$1 = 3.60KN | 10KN = NZ$2.80 |
| SAR 1 = 1.20KN | 10KN = SAR 8.30 |
| DM1 = 3.90KN | 10KN = DM 2.60 |

Even the smallest of towns have a branch of the excellent and resourceful **state-run tourist board** (turistička zajednica). The staff speak great English, almost always Italian, and sometimes German and gives out amazing free maps and booklets. Private accommodations are handled by private tourist agencies (turistička/putnička agencija), the largest of which is the ubiquitous **Atlas** with branches in every major city. Smaller local outfits are generally cheaper. Agencies exchange money and arrange excursions, including infamous fish picnics on the coast. Tourist offices are typically open M-F 8am-6pm and Sa 9am-2pm; on the coast, they like to take a midday "break" between noon and 5pm and then stay open until 10pm.

# HEALTH AND SAFETY

The **climate** is mild and continental around Zagreb and Mediterranean along the coast. Although Croatia is no longer at war, travel to the Slavonia and Krajina regions remains dangerous due to **unexploded mines. Crime** is rare. **Pharmacies** are generally well-stocked with Western products, including condoms, but apart from major cities they tend to close at night.

Croatians are friendly toward foreigners and sometimes a little too friendly to female travelers; going out in public with a companion will help to ward off unwanted displays of machismo. Establishments are very receptive to travelers with young children, and discounts abound. Croatians are just beginning to accept **homosexuality,** so be discrete. The official age limit for alcohol consumption is 18, but—as far as natives are concerned—what's a couple of years between friends? Nonetheless, *Let's Go* does not recommend or condone underage drinking.

# ACCOMMODATIONS AND CAMPING

Two words: **private rooms.** Apart from the country's five **youth hostels** (in Zagreb, Pula, Zadar, Dubrovnik, and Punat) and **camping** (bring your own tent), they are the only affordable option. Look for *sobe* signs, especially near transportation stations. Agencies generally charge 30-50% more if you stay under three nights. All accommodations are subject to a **tourist tax** of 5-10kn (another reason the police require foreigners to register). If you opt for a hotel, calling a few days in advance is imperative, especially during the summer on the coast when there isn't a war going on somewhere nearby. For info on HI hostels around Croatia, contact the **Croatian Youth Hostel Association** in Zagreb (☎ 482 92 94; fax 482 92 96; hfhs@alf.tel.hr). In private lodging, hot water is often heated in a barrel and then fed into the house's pipes. Shower fast or shower cold.

CROATIA

# GLOSSARY

| ENGLISH | CROATIAN | PRONOUNCE | ENGLISH | CROATIAN | PRONOUNCE |
|---------|----------|-----------|---------|----------|-----------|
| one | jedan | ehd-NO | pharmacy | ljekarna | lye-KHA-rna |
| two | dva | dveh | post office | pošta | POSH-ta |
| three | tri | tree | stamp | markica | MA-rki-tsa |
| four | četiri | CHEH-tee-ree | airmail | zrakoplovom | ZRA-ko-plo-vom |
| five | pet | peht | departure | odlažak | OD-lazh-ak |
| six | šest | shesht | arrival | polažak | PO-lazh-ak |
| seven | sedam | SEH-dahm | one-way | u jednom smjerna | oo YEH-dnom smee-YEH-roo |
| eight | osam | O-sehm | round-trip | povratna karta | POV-rat-na KAR-ta |
| nine | devet | DEH-veht | reservation | rezervacija | re-ze-RVAH-ci-ya |
| ten | deset | DEH-seht | bus | avtobus | av-TOH-bus |
| twenty | dvadeset | DVAH-deseht | airport | zračna luka | ZRA-chna lu-kah |
| thirty | trideset | TRI-deseht | station | kolodvor | KO-lo-dvor |
| forty | četrdeset | CHETR-deseht | grocery | trgovina | TR-goh-vi-na |
| fifty | pedeset | peh-DEH-seht | breakfast | doručak | DO-ruh-chak |
| sixty | šestdeset | shest-DEH-seht | lunch | ručak | ru-chak |
| seventy | sedamdeset | sedam-DEH-seht | dinner | večera | VE-che-ra |
| eighty | osamdeset | osam-DEH-seht | menu | karta | KA-rta |
| ninety | devedeset | de-vet-DEH-seht | bread | kruh | krooh |
| one hundred | sto | sto | vegetables | povrče | POH-ver-chay |
| one thousand | tisuća | TEE-soo-chah | beef | kravji | kra-vlyi |
| Monday | ponedeljak | POH-nye-del-yak | chicken | živina | ZHI-vi-nah |
| Tuesday | utorak | UH-to-rak | pork | svinja | SVI-nya |
| Wednesday | srijeda | SREE-yeda | fish | riba | REE-bah |
| Thursday | četvrtak | CHE-trh-tak | coffee | kava | KAH-vah |
| Friday | petak | PE-tak | milk | mlijeko | mli-YE-koh |
| Saturday | subota | suh-BO-tah | beer | pivo | PEE-voh |
| Sunday | nedjelja | nedje-LYA | eggs | jajce | YA-ytse |
| a day | dan | dan | holiday | sadovnik | |
| a week | sedmica | SED-mi-tsah | open | otprto | OT-pr-toh |
| morning | ujutro | uh-YU-troh | closed | zaprto | ZA-pr-toh |
| afternoon | popodne | poh-POH-dne | police | policia | po-LEE-tsee-ya |
| evening | večer | VYE-cher | bank | banka | BAN-kah |
| today | danas | DAH-nas | exchange | menjalnica | men-YAL-ni-tsa |
| tomorrow | sutra | SUH-tra | toilet | WC | WC |
| spring | proljece | proh-LYE-cheh | square | trg | trg |
| summer | ljeto | LYE-toh | castle | grad | grad |
| fall | jesen | YE-sen | church | crkva | TSR-kvah |
| winter | zima | ZI-ma | sugar | cukor | tsu-KOR |
| hot | vruče | vRUH-che | market | trg | trg |
| cold | zima | ZI-ma | left | lijevo | leeyehvo |
| passport | pasovnica | PA-so-vnee-tsa | right | desno | dehtsno |

CROATIA

## PHRASEBOOK

| ENGLISH | CROATIAN | PRONOUNCIATION |
|---|---|---|
| Yes/no | Da/Ne | Da/Neh |
| Please/You're welcome | Molim | MO-leem |
| Thank you | Hvala lijepa | HVAH-la leepa |
| Hello/*HI* | Zdravo/*Bog* | ZDRAH-vo/*bog* |
| Good-bye | Doviđenja | do-vee-JEHN-ya |
| Good morning | Dobro jutro | DO-bro YOO-tro |
| Good evening | Dobra večer | DO-bra VE-Cher |
| Good night | Laku noć | LA-koo noch |
| Sorry/Excuse me | Oprostite | o-PRO-sti-teh |
| Help! | U pomoć! | OO pomoch |
| When? | Kada? | KA-da |
| Where is...? | Gdje je? | GDYE je |
| How do I get to...? | Kako mogu doći do ...? | KAH-ko MO-goo DO-chee do... |
| How much does this cost? | Koliko to košta? | KO-li-koh toh KOH-shta |
| Do you have...? | Imate li...? | EEM-a-teh lee |
| Do you speak English? | Govorite li engleski? | GO-vor-i-teh lee eng-LEH-ski |
| I don't understand. | Ne razumijem. | neh ra-ZOO-mi-yem |
| I don't speak Croatian. | Ne govorim hrvatski. | Nye GOH-voh-rim KHR-va-tskee |
| Speak a little slower, please. | Govorite polako, molim. | go-VOR-iteh PO-la-koh MOH-leem |
| I'd like to order... | Želio bih naručiti... | Jelim na-ROO-chiti |
| *Check, please.* | *Račun, molim.* | *RACH-un mo-leem* |
| Do you have a vacancy? | Imate li slobodne sobe? | IMA-te li SLO-bo-dneh SOH-beh? |
| I'd like a room. | Želio bih sobu. | ZHEL-i-o bih SO-bu |
| Will you tell me when to get off? | Hoćete li mi reći kada tebam sići | ho-CHEH-teh lee mee REH-cheh KAH-dah TREH-bahm SEE-chee |
| I want a ticket to... | Htio bih kartu za... | HTEE-o beeh KAHR-too zah... |
| When is the *first*/next/*last* train to... | Kada je slijedenći vlak za... | KAH-dah yeh ZAH-dnyee vlahk za ... |
| Where is the bathroom/nearest public phone/center of town? | Gdje je kadom/nalazi najbliža telefonska govornica/centar grada? | gdyeh yeh KAH-dom/NAH-lahzee nahy-BLEE-zhah tehleh-FON-skah govor-NEE-tsah/TSEN-tahr GRAH-dah? |
| I've lost my... | Jaz sam izgubil(a) | YA SAM eez-GU-bee-lah |
| Go away. | Bježi/Idi odavde. | BYEH-zhee/EE-dee |

# KEEPING IN TOUCH

Most banks, tourist offices, hotels, and transportation stations exchange currency and traveler's checks. Banks usually have the best rates. Croatia's monetary unit, the **kuna** (kn)—divided into 100 lipa—is pretty much impossible to exchange abroad, except in Hungary and Slovenia. Neither South African rand nor Irish pounds are exchangeable in Croatia. **ATMs** *(bankomat)* are everywhere. Most banks give MC/Visa **cash advances,** and credit cards are widely accepted.

   **Mail** from the US arrives in 7 day or less; if addressed to *Poste Restante*, it will be held for 90 days at the main (not always the most central) post office. Address envelope as follows: Kieran (First name), FITZGERALD (LAST NAME), POSTE RESTANTE, Put republike bb (Post office street address), Dubrovnik (City) 200 00 (Postal code), CROATIA. *Avionski* and *zrakoplovom* both mean "air mail" in Croatian. **Post offices** usually have **public phones;** pay after you talk. All phones on

CROATIA

the street require *telekartas* (phone cards), sold at all newsstands and post offices. 50 "impulses" cost 23kn (1 impulse equals 3min. domestic, 36 seconds international; 50% discount 10pm-7am and Sundays and holidays). International access numbers include: **AT&T Direct** (☎ 0800 22 01 11); **BT Direct** (☎ 0800 22 00 44); **Canada Direct** (☎ 0800 22 0101); **MCI WorldPhone** (☎ 0800 22 0112); **Sprint** (☎ 0800 220 113). Technically, this operator assistance is free, but some phones demand a telekarta card. Calls to the US are expensive (20kn per min.). **Internet access** is available in the smallest towns, making email a viable and cheap method of keeping in touch.

# ZAGREB ☎ (0)1

Not as many tourists flock to Zagreb (pop. 1,000,000) as to other European capitals, but they should. In the time of the Austro-Hungarian Empire, Zagreb played the role of little sister to Vienna and Budapest. Beware the charm of the 900-year-old little sister, though—this city has an aura of its own, stemming from its glamorous architecture as well as its lively street scene. Spacious Austro-Hungarian boulevards and extensive parks blend with the historic Old Town as easily as the locals chain-smoke and sip coffee in the city's numerous outdoor hangouts. Though mostly Central European in its build, Zagreb is filled with sleepy Mediterranean air that is bound to relax your mind. Come nightfall, the object of the city's trendy youth is to see or to be seen—and it should be yours, too.

The recent civil war has left many scars on Zagreb's streets, but rapid renovations have turned the city into a modern metropolis. Though political instability in the Balkan region delayed its integration into Europe, Zagreb is slowly—but surely—catching up. With first-class museums and a plethora of international festivals, it has more to offer than many of its neighbors in the West.

## ✈ ORIENTATION

Zagreb is 30km south of the Slovene border; Austria and Hungary are about 100km north; Bosnia lies about 75km to the southeast. The **Sava** river separates the historical **Gornji Grad** (Upper Town) comprised of the **Kaptol** and **Gradec** hills—and the central **Donji Grad** (Lower Town) from the modern residential area **Novi Zagreb** (New Zagreb). Nothing ever happens in Novi Zagreb, but both Gornji and Donji Grad are bustling centers of activity, day or night. Most shopping occurs around the city's central square, **Trg bana Josipa Jelačića** (Ban Josip Jelačić Square) and on **Ilica,** the commercial artery that runs through it.

> **THE NAME GAME** Many street names in Zagreb appear differently on street signs than on maps and in addresses because of grammatical declensions. The root of the name remains the same, but the ending changes, often dramatically. For example, on a street sign, you might find ul. kralja Držislava; addresses and maps, however, will usually list the street as Držislavova. In general, the case declension from proper street name to an address or map changes the ending from -a to -ova or from -e to -ina. Also, "bb" after a street name indicates that buildings on the street are not numbered.

## ✈ INTERCITY TRANSPORTATION

**Flights:** The international airport (☎ 626 52 22) is about 20km away. **Buses** (☎ 615 79 92) run between the bus station and the airport (every ½hr. M-F 7am-8pm, after 8pm following flight arrivals; 20kn). **Taxis** cost 150-200kn. No luggage yet? Lost and found ☎ 456 22 29. **Croatia Airlines,** Zrinjevac 17 (☎ 481 96 33; booking ☎ 487 27 27; www.ctn.tel.hr/ctn). Inquire here to book flights on other airlines. Open M-F 8am-8pm, Sa 9am-noon.

## Zagreb

**ACCOMMODATIONS**
Hotel Astoria, 5
Hotel Ilica, 1
Hotel Sjedan Radić, 3
Omladunski Turistički
Centar (HI), 4
Student Hotel Cvjetno, 2

CROATIA

**Trains: Glavni kolodvor** (main station), Trg kralja Tomislava 12 (domestic travel info ☎98 30; international travel info ☎457 32 38). To: **Split** (9hr., 2 per day, 69kn); **Ljubljana, SLN** (2½hr., 5 per day, 87kn); **Vienna, AUS** (6½hr., 2 per day, 347kn); **Budapest, HUN** (7hr., 4 per day, 210kn); **Venice, ITA** (7hr., 2 per day, 332kn, students 266kn); and **Zurich, SWI** (8hr., 1 per day, 680kn). No trains to **Sarajevo, BOS** or **Dubrovnik**. Within Croatia, stick to the bus.

**Buses: Autobusni kolodvor** (bus station), Držićeva bb (☎060 31 33 33; domestic travel info ☎615 79 86; international travel info ☎615 79 83). To reach the train station, take tram #2, 3 or 6 and get off at the 3rd stop. Information, tickets, and luggage storage are on the 2nd floor. To: **Split** (6½-9hr., 32 per day, 95-116kn); **Dubrovnik** (11hr., 8 per day 139-165kn); **Ljubljana, SLN** (2hr., 3 per day, 70kn); **Vienna, AUS** (8hr., 2 per day, 180-190kn); **Sarajevo, BOS** (9hr., 5 per day, 207kn); **Frankfurt, GER** (12hr., 5 per day, 590kn) and **Berlin, GER** (15hr., 2 per day, 720kn).

**Ferries: Jadrolinija**, Zrinjevac 20, (☎487 33 07; fax 487 31 41; www.jadrolinija.tel.hr/jadrolinija), reserves tickets for travel along the Dalmatian coast to Split and Dubrovnik and to Ancona, Italy. Open M-F 9am-5pm, Sa 9am-1pm.

# ⊟ LOCAL TRANSPORTATION

**Trams:** Trams are sweaty in the summer but cover the entire city. Buy tickets at any newsstand (5.50kn) or from the driver (6kn); they are valid 1½hr. 1-day pass 15kn. Punch them in the boxes near the doors. 100kn fine for riding ticketless. Trams are less frequent midnight-4am, when tickets cost 20% more. Be wary of altered routes.

**Taxis:** Rates are generally fair, averaging 15kn to start plus 6kn per km, but prices rise 20% from 10pm-5am and Su. Large companies like **Radio Taxi** (☎668 25 05) are the most reliable. Cabs congregate at the stand on Gajeva and at the corner of Trg b. Jelačića and Bakačeva.

# ⃞ PRACTICAL INFORMATION

## TOURIST AND FINANCIAL SERVICES

**Tourist Office: Tourist Information Center (TIC),** Trg b. Jelačića 11 (☎481 40 51, 481 40 52, and 481 40 54; fax 481 40 56; info@zagreb-touristinfo.hr; www.zagreb-touristinfo.hr), in the southeast corner of the square. Friendly, resourceful staff distributes free maps and pamphlets, and can call hotels and hostels to check availability, but doesn't make reservations. Open M-F 8:30am-8pm, Sa 9am-5pm, Su 10am-2pm.

**Embassies: Australia,** Inside Hotel Inter-Continental, (☎483 66 00, emergency ☎098 41 47 29). Open M-F 10am-2pm. **Canada,** Prilaz Đure Deželića 4 (☎488 12 00; fax 488 12 30). Open M-F 10am-noon. **UK,** Vlaška 121 (☎455 53 10; fax 455 16 85). Open M-Th 8:30am-5pm, F 8:30am-2pm. **US,** Hebrangova 2 (☎455 55 00; after hours ☎455 52 81, Consular services ext. 2276; fax 455 85 85). Open M-F 8am-4:45pm.

**Currency Exchange: Zagrebačka Banka** has branches throughout the city. The one at Trg b. Jelačića 10 (☎480 82 18) is open M-F 7:30am-7pm, Sa 7:30am-noon. Cashes **traveler's checks** for a 1.5% commission.

**ATM:** ATMs (*bankomat*) are all over the center and at the bus station; the train station has a 24hr. AmEx machine.

**American Express: Atlas,** Lastovska 23 (☎612 44 22). Mail held, cards replaced, and traveler's checks cashed for no commission. Open M-F 8am-7pm, Sa 8am-noon.

## LOCAL SERVICES AND COMMUNICATIONS

**Luggage Storage:** At the **train** station: 10kn per piece per day. Open 24hr. At the **bus** station: 1.20kn per bag per hour. 2.30kn for bags over 15kg. Open M-Sa 5am-10pm, Su 6am-10pm.

**Lost Property: Lost and Found Office,** Petrova 152 (š21 87 03). Open daily 8am-2pm.

**International Bookstore: Algoritam,** Gajeva 1 (☎481 88 72; fax 481 74 97) next to Hotel Dubrovnik carries international newspapers, magazines and music on the ground floor, while the basement offers Croatian phrase books and a choice selection of English classics. Open M-F 8:30am-9pm and Sa 8:30am-3pm. MC/Visa.

**Laundromat: PREDOM,** Draškovićeva 31 (☎461 29 90). 2-20kn per item, next day pickup. No English spoken. Open M and F-Sa 8am-noon, Tu-Th 7:30am-7pm.

**Police: Department for Foreign Visitors,** Petrinjska 30 (☎456 31 11). Room 101 on the 2nd floor of the police station. To **register,** use Form #14. Open M-F 8am-2pm.

**Pharmacy: Gradska Ljekarna Zagreb,** Zrinjevac 20 (☎487 38 73). Open M-Sa 7am-8pm, Su 7am-2:30pm. **Night service** at Ilica 43 (☎484 84 50) Open 8pm-7am.

**Medical Assistance: Hospital REBRO,** Kišpatićeva 12 (☎238 88 88). Open 24hr.

Internet Access:

**Art Net Club,** Preradovićeva 25 (☎455 84 71). Drop down into a creative underworld: photo exhibits, live music Sept.-Nov., sports TV, bar, and fast connections. 20kn per hr. Open M-Su 9am-11pm.

**Aquariusnet,** Držislavova 4 (☎461 88 73). Friendly staff can connect you *and* pour you beer. 16kn per 30min. or 85kn for 30hr. card. Open M-Sa 10am-2am, Su 3-11pm.

**Sublink Cyber Cafe,** Teslina 12 (☎481 13 29), through the courtyard, up the stairs, and to the left. 19kn per hr. Open M-Sa 10am-10pm and Su 1-10pm.

**Telephones:** Call from the post office and pay afterwards. Open 24hr.

**Post Office:** Branimirova 4 (☎484 03 45), next to the train station. **Poste Restante** on 2nd floor (desk #3); enter from the side facing Branimirova and turn left up the stairs. Mail held for one month. Desk #1 exchanges cash and traveler's checks for 1.5% commission (open 24hr.). Open M-F 7am-8pm, Sa 7am-2pm.

**Postal Code:** 10000.

# ▐ ACCOMMODATIONS

Cheap accommodations are scarce in Zagreb; fortunately, so are the young and the penniless. Going directly to the hostel will most likely be your best bet. If the masses do invade (which is most likely during festivals—see **Festivals,** p. 160), head straight to **Evistas,** Šenoina 28. From the train station, take a right on Branimirova, a quick left onto Petrinjska, and then a right onto Šenoina. This friendly husband and wife travel agency can register you, or reserve a bed. (☎483 95 46; fax 483 95 43; evistas@zg.tel.hr. Singles 175kn; doubles 240kn; apartments 140-180kn per person. Min. stay 3 days; 20% more for 1 night only, 30% more during festivals; under 25 15% off. Tax 7kn. Open M-F 9am-1:30pm and 3-8pm, Sa 9:30am-5pm.) All foreigners coming to Croatia through Zagreb and staying in private accommodations must **register** at the Police Station (see above) within 2 days of arrival. Hostels and hotels will register you automatically.

**Omladinski Turistički Centar (HI),** Petrinjska 77 (☎484 12 61; fax 484 12 69). With your back to the train station, walk right on Branimirova and Petrinjska will be on your left. Nothing beats the hostel's central location. Hot water, clean sheets, and abundant graffitti. Reception 24hr. Check-in 2pm-1am. Check-out 9am. No reservations necessary. 6-bed dorm 67kn, non-members 72kn; singles 149kn, with bath 202kn; doubles 204kn, with bath 274kn.

**Hotel Ilica,** Ilica 102 (☎377 75 22 and 377 76 22; fax 377 77 22; info@hotel-ilica.hr; www.hotel-ilica.hr). From the train station, take tram #6 toward Črnomerec and get off the 2nd time it stops on Ilica. Walk back about 20m. Satellite TV and telephones grace every room in this small private hotel. The marble floored lobby doubles as a bar and breakfast cafe. Reception 24hr. Check-in before midnight. Check-out noon. Reservations necessary. Singles 299kn; doubles 399kn; 3-person apartments 639kn, 4-person 779kn. Breakfast and parking included.

**Hotel Astoria,** Petrinjska 71 (☎484 12 22; fax 484 12 12). Just a few steps past the youth hostel on Petrinjska (see above). Enter through the Chinese restaurant. This super-clean, dimly lit hotel is blessed with an excellent location. TV and phone in every room. Very little English spoken. 120 rooms. Reception 24hr. Check-out noon. Singles 300kn; doubles 500kn; triples 600kn. Breakfast included.

# ◌ FOOD

*Zagrebčani* adore meat, and restaurant menus reflect it. Pasta and seafood are the best available options for leaf-eaters. Along with endless bars and cafes, *slastičarne* (pastry shops)—famous for their exquisite ice cream—play an important part in the Zagreb culinary experience. Across from the train station, an escalator leads to a huge underground **mall,** replete with inexpensive cafes, bakeries, sandwich shops and pizzerias. Behind Trg b. Jelačića in Gornji Grad sprawls Zagreb's cheapest and liveliest open-air market, **Dolac**—a hectic sea of canopied fruit, vegetable, and fish vendors. (Open M-F 7am-3pm, Sa 6am-2pm, Su 6am-1pm.) There are grocery stores throughout the city, including **Konzum** at Britanski Trg 12. (Open M-F 7am-8pm, Sa 7am-9pm, Su 8am-1pm.) If you need a late-night snack to absorb some of that *Tomislav* (Croatia's fine dark brew), head to **Hamby,** Ilica 1, for a hot ham sandwich. (10kn; open 24hr.) For a complete list of the best restaurants and pubs, pick up a free *Zagreb-Gastro* at the tourist office.

▨ **Baltazar,** Nova Ves 4 (☎ 43 41 27). Follow Kaptol till it turns into Nova Ves. Scrounge up your kunas, whistle on the street, or play dead—do whatever necessary to save up for this gastronomic orgasm. On the patio with grape vines, or inside the family farmhouse-style restaurant, join throngs of locals in devouring homemade sausages (35kn), throwing back house wine (1L, 50kn), and indulging in the local specialties like *puenjeni lungic,* pork fillet stuffed with ham and cheese (65kn). Main dishes 30kn-70kn. Cover 5kn. Open daily 1pm-midnight. AmEx/MC/Visa.

**Boban,** Gajeva 9 (☎ 481 15 49). Italian eatery owned by well-known soccer player Zvonimir Boban. On your lucky day, he'll be there. Cafe upstairs, restaurant downstairs, and—of course—a TV for watching soccer. Main dishes 23-40kn. Cafe open M-Th and Su 7am-midnight, F-Sa 7am-1am; restaurant open daily 10am-midnight.

**Korčula,** Teslina 17 (☎ 487 21 59). From Trg b. Jelačića, walk down Gajeva to Teslina. Named after the Adriatic island, Korčula brings a taste of the sea to inland Zagreb with its Dalmatian specialties, as well as fishnets and anchors. If you can eat a kilo of fish, try the *Jadranske ribe* (Adriatic fish; 160kn), but mind you—that's a lot of fish. Main dishes 36-65kn. Buffet open daily 10am-11pm, bar open 8am-11pm.

**Grill Rubelj,** Mala terasa Dolac 2/2 (☎ 481 87 77), between the Dolac market and Trg b. Jelačića, the 2nd restaurant in the row of three. Locals laud the inexpensive grilled meat specialties, and so will you if you can decide whether to use hands or cutlery with the awkward buns that contain *ćevapi* (11-20kn), or the spicy *šiš-ćevapi* (10-30kn) Open daily 8am-11pm.

# ◉ SIGHTS

The best way to see Zagreb is on foot. A short walk up any of the streets behind Trg b. Jelačića leads to **Gornji Grad,** where you can wander through winding cobblestone streets—most of them free of traffic—and visit most sights in a single day. If the sun's getting you down, ride up in the **funicular** (*uspinjača*; 2kn) on Tomićeva, which connects Donji Grad and Gornji Grad. From Trg b. Jelačića, walk down Ilica; Tomićeva is on your right. The **Strossmayerovo šetalište** on top of the funicular provides a view of the city. Carry a copy of *Zagreb: City Walks,* available at the TIC (see **Tourist and Financial Services,** p. 158) for an organized route.

▨ **MIROGOJ CEMETERY.** Once you've walked through Mirogoj, you will never feel so alive in a cemetery again. The most profoundly humbling sight in Zagreb, the cemetery is a labyrinth of cyprus trees, wide avenues and sleek gravestones. Among the newest additions to the cemetery is the massive grave of Croatia's first president Franjo Tudjman, who died of cancer in the fall of 1999. Don't take pictures. *(From Kaptol, take a bus. (8min., every 15min.) Open M-F 6am-8pm, Su 7:30am-6pm.)*

**THE CATHEDRAL OF THE ASSUMPTION OF VIRGIN MARY AND ST. STEPHEN.** Although the foundations of this cathedral date back to the 11th century, renovations and additions of the later centuries make it a veritable visual history book. Its most striking features, two slim neo-gothic bell-towers, were erected at the start of the 20th century. *(On Kaptol Hill. Open M-Sa 10am-5pm, Su and holy days 1-5pm.)*

**ST. MARK'S CHURCH.** (Crkva Sv. Marka.) Though it looks more like an oversized gingerbread house than a 13th-century church, St. Mark's is actually not edible. The dazzling 19th-century roof depicts the coat of arms of Croatia, Dalmatia, and Slavonia on the left side and that of Zagreb on the right. If you're wondering about the elongated black cat on the Slavonian coat of arms, wonder no more—its a marten. The church also houses stone figures by Croatia's most famous sculptor, Ivan Meštrović (see **Literature and Arts,** p. 149). *(In Markog trg. From the top of the funicular, take a left onto Ćirilometodska.)*

**LOTRŠČAK TOWER.** (Kula Lotršćak.) This 13th century tower, constructed to guard against southern attacks on the city, is marked by a 19th century addition—a peculiar staircase that winds halfway on the outside, and halfway on the inside. The tower walls themselves, though, are no flimsy, romantic period reconstructions. Good old medieval quantity-over-quality logic produced walls that are 195cm thick (that's about the width of a Volkswagen Beetle). So climb the whitewashed tower for a splendid view of Zagreb, and rest easy—unlike its feeble Italian counterpart, this tower is not leaning anywhere. *(At the corner of Strossmayerovo and Ćirilometodska. Go right at the top of the funicular. Open June and July, M-Sa 11am-7pm).*

**STONE GATE.** (Kamenita Vrata.) This 1761 sacred gate is wide enough to qualify as a tunnel. It remains the only structure of Gradec's original city walls. While fire consumed the entire gate in 1731, legend has it that a painting of the Blessed Virgin and Child (today enshrined in the gate) was left untouched by the flames. Locals come to worship before the painting and light candles, while tourists come to get out of the sun. *(Head up Radićeva from Trg b. Jelačića and take a left on Zmaja.)*

**ST. CATHERINE'S CHURCH.** Built between 1620 and 1632, St. Catherine's exudes a quiet elegance both inside and out. Sculptures touched with gold leaf and delicate pink designs across the church's ceiling decorate the interior. *(From top of funicular, take a right. Open M-F and Su 7am-11pm, Sa 7am-6:30pm.)*

**BLOOD BRIDGE.** (Krvavi Most.) This border street between Kaptol and Gradec once served to span the Medveščak brook that powered the mills of Zagreb's textile industry. For hundreds of years after Gradec was proclaimed a free city in 1242, its burgher citizens engaged in periodic conflict with their ecclesiastical neighbors from Kaptol. This bridge provided a battle ground until the two hills united in 1850 to create modern Zagreb. After the unification, Medveščak brook was covered by asphalt and Tkalčićeva street was born. Today, no sign of the bridge remains, but Kravi Most does provide safe passage from the bars on Tkalčićeva to the bars on Radićeva. *(From Trg b. Jelačića, head up Radićeva.)*

# 🏛 MUSEUMS

Zagreb takes pride in its many well-stocked museums, which eagerly await visitors after a brief wartime hiatus. A complete list of the museums can be found in the free *Zagreb: Events and Performances*, published monthly and available at Tourist Office (see p. 158). It also lists galleries, plays, festivals, concerts and sporting events. Many of the museums lie in Donji Grad below Ilica.

**Gallery of Modern Art** (Moderna galerija), Hebrangova 1 (☎492 23 68), across from the US embassy. Features Croatia's best artists, including late 19th and early 20th century painters Babić, Bečić, and Uzdać. Well worth the trip. Open M-Sa 10am-6pm, Su 10am-1pm. 20kn, students 10kn.

**Ivan Meštrović Foundation** (Meštrović Atelier), Mletačka 8 (☎485 11 23). Walk past St. Mark's church on the left side, go left on Brezovačkog, then right on Mletačka. Small collection of some of Meštrović's best work housed in a delightful building in Gornji Grad. Ask the curator about the sculptor—she knows it all. Open Tu-F 9am-2pm, Sa 10am-6pm. 10kn, students 5kn.

**Mimara Museum** (Muzej Mimara), Rooseveltov trg 5 (☎482 81 00). A vast and varied collection, from Egyptian art to Raphael, Velasquez, Rubens, and Rembrandt. Open Tu, W and F-Sa 10am-5pm, Th 10am-7pm, Su 10am-2pm. 20kn, students 15kn. Groups of 20 or more 15kn, students 10kn.

**Museum of Arts and Crafts** (Muzej za Umjetnost i Obrt), Trg Maršala Tita 10 (☎482 69 22). Judaica collection is one of the biggest and most renowned in the world. Open Tu-F 10am-6pm, Sa-Su 10am-1pm. 20kn, students 10kn. English booklet 30kn.

**Ethnographic Museum** (Etnografski muzej), Trg Mažuranića 14 (☎482 62 20). Tools of the trade from African spears to samurai swords. The best section features traditional folk robes from all parts of Croatia. Tours in English and most Euro-tongues 100kn. Open Tu-Th 10am-6pm, F-Su 10am-1pm. 10kn, students 5kn. English booklet 50kn.

# ✳ FESTIVALS

Zagreb is a city of festivals. The season opens with a concert by the **Vienna Symphony Orchestra** in April 2001. Streets fill with performances of all kinds in the 2nd week in June for the annual Zagreb street festival **Cest is d'Best** ("the streets are the best," see **Graybox** below). In mid-June of even-numbered years, Zagreb hosts the biannual **World Festival of Animated Film,** with offerings ranging from the best of Disney to high-tech Japanese *anime*, in Vatroslav Lisinski Concert Hall (Trg S. Radica 4. ☎612 11 66.) **Eurokaz,** a festival of avant-garde European theater, takes place annually at the end of June throughout Zagreb. Folklore fetishists will flock to Zagreb in July 2001 for the **International Folklore Festival,** the premier gathering of European folk dancers and singing groups. The **Zagreb Summer Festival** hosts open-air concerts and theatrical performances during July and August; some of the best concerts take place in the Muzejski Prostor Atrium. (Jezuitski trg 4. ☎27 89 57.) There is also a huge (and again annual) **International Puppet Festival** at the beginning of September. The **Zagreb Jazz Fair** at the **BP Club** (see **Nightlife,** below) hosts Croatia's best jazz artists, October 2 to 22. **Zagreb Fest,** a pop festival, in November, attracts rock bands from across Europe. A local favorite, the **Portugizac** wine festival at the end of October brings out revelers regardless of age to end the festival season. For up-to-date information and schedules contact the **Zagreb Convention Bureau** (☎481 43 43; fax 481 49 49; zagreb.convention@ccb.hr; www.zagreb-convention.hr.)

# ◪ NIGHTLIFE

The numerous sidewalk **cafes** along **Tkalčićeva,** in Gornji Grad, beckon to an older, classier crowd, while **Opatovina,** a parallel street, hosts a slightly younger and more budget-minded group. Many **discos** are open all week; the best ones lie outside the center. For a complete listing of all discos and nightclubs in Zagreb, consult the free *Zagreb: Events and Performances* available at TIC. You can fill your own bottles with homemade wine at **Vinarija Kaptol,** Kaptol 14, a drive-thru fast-food joint for wine lovers. (Under the courtyard on the left side of the street. ☎481 46 75. 7-20kn per 1L. Open M-F 8am-2pm and 4pm-7pm, Sa 8am-2pm, Su 9am-1pm.)

**CROATIA**

## WOODSTOCK WHERE?
Yes, Jimmy, Janice, and Creedence are back—with Croatian accents—at Zagreb's reconstructed Woodstock during the **Cest is d'Best** street festival in June. When famed Croatian street musicians Zlatko Petrović (Pajo) and Miran Hadži-Vekyković (Hadži) first organized the gathering 6 years ago, they molded its easygoing, hippy philosophy on the saying '*izaotit van da biste bili doma*' (get out of your houses to be at home in the streets). Today, *Zagrebčani* of all ages flock to the call in a movement that epitomizes Zagreb's emerging light-hearted attitude. Standing in the streets during the festival is a doorframe and swinging door, postered with newspaper articles about the civil war, economic trouble, and other national traumas—when you walk through the door, you leave it all behind.

■ **Aquarius,** ☎364 02 31, on Lake Jarun. Take Tram 17 from the center and get off on Sred-njaci at the 3rd unmarked stop (15min.). Turn around, cross the street, and follow any one of the dirt paths—they all lead to the lake. At the lake, walk along the boardwalk to the left; Aquarius is the last building. This lakeside cafe and nightclub offers something for everyone. Live jazz Tu (Sept.-Nov. and Apr.-June), funk W, latin Th, house Su, and grab-bag of everything on weekends. Boogie inside and out, or frolic in the waters of the lake. Drinks 15-35kn. Cover 30kn. Club open W-Su 10pm-4am. Cafe open daily 9am-9pm.

**Tolkien's House,** Vsanicanijeva 8, (☎485 20 50) From St. Mark's, go down Ćirilometod-ska, take a right on Vsanicanijeva. Quirky Irish pub festooned with memorabilia from JRR Tolkien's fantasy books. The Tolkienmania decorations may seem a bit cheesy at first, but the Irish music and the pints of Guinness (25kn) make this a great place to chill. Drinks 11-25kn. Open daily 9am-11pm.

**Bulldog,** Bogovićeva 6 (☎481 73 93). An energized outdoor bar that pulls in young locals all week long. Come weekends, it takes over most of the street. *Ožujsko* 10kn. Drinks 10-25kn. Open M-Th and Su 9pm-1am, F-Sa 9pm-2am.

**Pivnica Medvedgrad,** Savska cesta 56 (☎617 71 19). Take tram #13, 14, or 17 from Trg b. Jelačića to the corner of Avenija Vukovar and Savska cesta. Long wooden tables and dim lights attract crowds of students and businesspeople. Brews its own beer; try the dark *Crna kraljica* (15kn). Open M-Sa 10am-midnight, Su noon-midnight.

**BP Club,** Teslina 7 (☎481 44 44). Head for the right side of the courtyard, then down-stairs. *The* venue for jazz in Zagreb only has live music during festivals in September and April (see **Entertainment,** p. 162) but keeps the cool tunes going year-round. BP coffee (with Irish cream) 23kn. 0.5L Heineken 25kn. Open daily 10am-2am.

# ▶ DAYTRIPS FROM ZAGREB

Defining the crests of Zagreb's surrounding hilltops, the mysterious **castles** of Hrvatsko Zagorje (the region north of Zagreb) are ripe for conquering—this time with Canons instead of cannons. The following three are the most popular; for a more comprehensive listing consult the free *Zagreb and Surroundings*, available at TIC in Zagreb.

## TRAKOŠĆAN                ☎(0)42

*From the Zagreb bus station, take a bus to Varaždin (1¾hr., 20 per day, 40kn), and change to a local bus—call ahead to check times to Trakošćan (Varaždin bus station ☎23 19 40; 1¾hr., 11 on weekdays, 7 on weekends, 19kn.) ☎79 62 81. Open daily 9am-6pm. 20kn, students 10kn. English booklet 20kn. Free guided tours in English available, reservations necessary.*

Trakošćan's magical white walls, its high seat above deep forests and quiet lake, impresses the wonder of another realm. Built as a defense tower in the 13th century, it passed to the Drašković nobility in 1584, who enlarged its structures, refurbished its rooms, and retained the castle until World War II. Today suits of armor, family portraits, tapestries, and a collection of fire arms are on display. After the visit, head to **Goning Trakošćan** for the 45kn local beefsteak specialty *trakoščanski odrezak* (☎79 62 14. Open daily 9am-11pm.)

## MEDVEDGRAD

*From Trg b. Jelačića, take tram #14 to Mihaljevac; change to #15 to Gračani. From here, follow the well-marked path up the hill for 1½hr. to Medvedgrad.*

Officially still part of Zagreb city district, Medvedgrad is a royal fortress that has guarded Mount Medvednica since the 13th century. You'll hardly get a better view of the city than from this stone beauty. It is free and open to the public except on national holidays, when the president lays flowers on the **Altar of the Homeland,** a monument to all who have died for Croatia.

## PLITVICE LAKES NATIONAL PARK                ☎(0)53

*Buses run from Zagreb (2½hr., every 30min., 39kn) and Zadar (3hr., every 30min., 50kn); ask the driver to drop you at one of the park entrances. Tourist office ☎75 10 15 and 75*

CROATIA

*10 14; fax 75 10 13; np-plitvice@np-plitvice.tel.hr; www.np-pltvice.tel.hr/np-pltivice. Park open daily 7 am-7 pm. July-Aug. 60kn, students 40kn. May-June and Sept.-Oct. 50kn, 30kn. Jan.-Apr. and Nov.-Dec. 40kn, 20kn. There is a tourist center at each of the 3 park entrances with maps and a comprehensive guide. You can store your luggage with the center while you explore the lakes.*

 Plitvice Lakes National Park lies in the Krajina region, where Croatia's bloody war of independence began. Throughout the conflict (1991-95), the area was held by the Serbs, who planted landmines in the ground. Although the park is safe and accessible, there are over a million landmines in the surrounding area. Under no circumstances should you leave the road and marked paths. Don't let this warning stop you from visiting the natural wonder of the Plitvice lakes; just be intelligent about where you walk.

Though a little farther away from Zagreb, the Plitvice Lakes National Park (Nacionalni park Plitvička jezera) is definitely worth any transportation hassles. If you crushed all the Smurfs together with a mortar and pestle, the resulting pigment would not touch the incredible blue hue of the lakes. Some 30,000 hectares of forested hills, dappled with 16 lakes and more waterfalls than you can imagine comprise this pocket of paradise. Declared a national park in 1949, Plitvice was then added to the UNESCO World Heritage list in 1979 for the unique evolution of its lakes and waterfalls, which formed through the interaction of water and petrified vegetation. Modes of transportation around the park include two bus routes (buses every 20min), one boat (every 30min.), and walking. While most tourists circulate around the four lower lakes (Donja Jezera) to snap pictures of Plitvice's famous 78m waterfall, **Veliki Slap** (2-3 hr.), the true wanderer takes to the hidden falls of the 12 upper lakes, Gornja Jezera. (4 hours.)

# ISTRIA

The Istrian peninsula lies on the northern part of the Adriatic Coast, where the Mediterranean laps at the foot of the Alps. The region—in language, tradition, and culture—seems almost more Italian than Croatian. Perhaps this has always been the case: ancient fishing ports, countless craggy coves, and the deep blue-green hues of the sea led a Roman chronicler almost 2000 years ago to remark, "In Istria, Roman patricians feel like gods." Today, Roman Pula, UNESCO-protected Poreč, and 19th-century Rovinj may worship the false idol of tourism, but the intrepid can still find two millennia of history—without a tour guide.

# PULA                                                         ☎(0)52

At the threshold of Pula's Old Town an enormous billboard welcomes visitors to a "3000 year-old town," which has seen governance from Romans to Venetians. Vespasian's amphitheater, second largest in the world, has witnessed bloodshed from gladiators to Napoleon and entertainment from Italian opera to Brian Adams. Yet after all these years Pula remains a town, fit for lazy strolls through winding medieval corridors and jaunts out to the Brijuni Archipelago, where Tito built mansions worthy of an emperor. Pula's amicable residents, formidable Roman ruins, and appealing cafes glow not with the impersonal grandeur of a stately metropolis, but with the warmth of a small town.

## ✴ ORIENTATION

**Sergijevaca,** Pula's main street, circles around the central hill in **Stari Grad** (Old Town) and turns into **Kandlerova** after **Trg Forum. Castropola,** a parallel street higher up, also circles the hilltop. To get to Sergijevaca from the **train station,** walk on Kolodvorska for five minutes, keeping the sea to your right. Turn right onto **Istar-**

ska at the **amphitheater.** Follow Istarska though its name change to **Giardini,** passing the inter-city and local **bus stations** on your right. A right through the **Slavoluk Sergijevaca** (Arch of the Sergians) leads to Sergijevaca.

# ⊏ TRANSPORTATION

**Trains:** Kolodvorska 5 (☎54 17 33 and 54 19 82). To: **Rijeka** (2½hr., 4 per day, 36kn); **Zagreb** (7hr., 4 per day, 88-120kn); and **Ljubljana, SLN** (7½hr., 1 per day, 130kn).

**Buses:** Matta Balotta 6 (☎21 89 28). Ticket office open M-Sa 5am-9pm, Su 5:30am-9pm, but all tickets can be purchased on the bus. To: **Poreč** (1½hr., 12 per day, 32kn); **Opatija** (2hr., 16 per day, 43kn); **Rijeka** (2½hr., 18 per day, 47-60kn); **Zagreb** (5-6hr., 15 per day, 112kn); **Šibenik** (9hr., 3 per day, 170kn); and **Trieste, ITA** (3¾hr., 4 per day, 100kn).

**Ferries:** Jadroagent Riva 14 (☎21 04 31; fax 21 17 99; jadroagent-pula@pu.tel.hr). Open M-Sa 8am-4pm, Su 9am-3pm. Ferries go to: **Zadar** (8hr., 4 per week, 80kn); **Trieste, ITA** (5hr., 1 per day, 160kn); and **Venice, ITA** (6hr., 2 per week, 240kn).

**Local Transportation:** Purchase tickets on the bus for 10kn or at any newspaper stand for 8kn. Most local buses pass by the garden on Giardini, next to the international and regional bus station (see above) and stop running around 10:30pm.

**Taxis:** Call ☎22 32 28 or catch one across from the bus station on Via Carrara. Average fare 15kn plus 7kn per km and 2kn per piece of luggage.

# ◪ PRACTICAL INFORMATION

**Tourist Office: Tourism Office Pula,** Forum 3 (☎212 987 and 219 197; fax 211 855; tz-pula@pu.tel.hr; www.gradpula.com). Friendly English-speaking staff provides maps and information about hotels, apartments, private rooms, and ferry and bus schedules. Open M-Su 9am-8pm.

**Currency Exchange: Zagrebačka Banka** (☎21 47 44), at the corner of Giardini and Flanatička, exchanges cash and travelers checks for 1.5% commission. Open M-Sa 7:30am-9pm. There is a currency exchange machine outside **Kaptol Banka,** Istarska 5, next to the bus station.

**ATM:** 24hr. Cirrus/MC outside Zagrebačka Banka (see above). AmEx/Visa outside Atlas (see below).

**American Express: Atlas Travel Agency,** Starih Statuta 1 (☎21 41 72; fax 21 40 94; atl.pula@atlas.tel.hr; www.atlas-croatia.com). Open M-Sa 8am-8pm, Su 9am-12:30pm and 6-8pm.

**Luggage Storage:** At the bus station. 7kn per hr., over 15kg 13kn per hr. Open M-F 4am-11pm, Sa 5am-11pm, Su 5:30am-11pm, closed daily 9:30-10am and 6-6:30pm.

**English Bookstore: Istarske Knjižare,** Giardini 9 (☎21 81 85). A sparse selection of books from Agatha Christie to John Grisham, plus maps of Croatia and historical books on Pula. Open M-Sa 8am-noon and 6-9pm.

**Pharmacy:** Ljekarna Centar, Giardini 15 (☎22 25 44). Open M-F 24hr., Sa-Su 7:30am-8pm.

**Police:** Trg Republike (☎53 26 29 and 53 26 28). With your back to the Arch of the Sergians, go straight up Flanatička, then right onto Trg Republike. Open 24hr.

**Hospital: Clinical Hospital Center,** Zagrebačka 34 (☎21 44 33). With your back to the garden on Giardini, go straight up Zagrebačka.

**Internet Access: Sveučilištna Knjižnica** (University Library), Herkulov Prolaz 1 (☎21 38 88). Up the stairs behind the Arch of the Sergians. Free. Open M-F 7:30am-8pm, Sa 7:30am-1pm.

**Post Office:** Danteov Trg 4 (☎22 22 50 or 22 24 21; fax 21 89 11), to the left to send mail, to the right for **Poste Restante** and telephones. Open M-F 7am-8pm, Sa 7am-2pm, Su 8am-noon.

**Postal Code:** 521 00.

# ACCOMMODATIONS

Several **travel agencies** help tourists find overpriced hotels, expensive apartments, and reasonably priced private rooms. **Arenaturist,** Giardini 4, may seem a bit brusque, but their rooms have the best locations. (☎21 86 96; fax 21 22 77; arenaturist1@pu.tel.hr; www.gradpula.com/comp/arenatours. July-Aug. singles 68kn; doubles 56kn per person; June and Sept. 52kn, 44kn. 50% more for 1 night, 25% for 2-3 nights. Registration 8kn. Open M-Sa 8am-8pm, Su 8am-1pm.)

**Omladinski Hostel (HI),** Zaljev Valsaline 4 (☎39 11 33; fax 39 11 06; hfhs-pula@pu.tel.hr; www.nncomp.com/hfhs). Exit the bus station onto Istarska, turn right and follow the street to a small park on Giardini where local buses stop. From the park, take bus #2 to "Veruda," exit at the last stop, and follow the signs downhill to the hostel. On the outskirts of Pula, this hostel has clean rooms and its own beach and bar. Reception 24hr. Reservations not necessary, but call ahead to be sure. July-Aug. 80kn; June and Sept. 72kn; May and Oct. 66kn; Nov. and Apr. 63kn. Breakfast included.

**Stoja Camping** (☎241 44; fax 24 74 48). From Giardini (see directions to the hostel above), take bus #1 toward Stoja to the end. On the tip of Pula's western peninsula called the "Premantura." July-Aug. 28kn, off-season 14kn. Registration 8kn.

# FOOD

**Puljanka grocery Store** has several branches throughout the town, including one on Sergijevaca 4. (Open M 6am-1:30pm, Tu-F 6am-10pm, Sa 6:30am-10pm, Su 7am-noon.) Buffets and fast-food restaurants line **Sergijevaca.** There is an open-air fruit and vegetable **market** at Narodni trg, off of Flanatička. (Open daily 6am-noon).

**Galija,** Epulonova 3 (☎21 44 68). Hidden away from the primary tourist arteries, this local terrace eatery offers the best samples of Pula's traditional, if slightly upscale, cuisine. Fresh fish (40-70kn) and meat dishes (35-60kn) including the tasty specialty Galija Veal (65kn). Open M-Sa 10am-11pm, Su noon-11pm.

**Pizzeria Orfej,** Istriana 1 (☎317 84). In Pula's medieval quarter, Orfej's outside tables fill the street. Excellent thin-crust pizza (15-40kn). Open daily 7am-midnight.

**Restaurant Delfin,** Trg sv. Tome 1 (☎222 89), across from the 4th-century cathedral. Provides cheap, excellent seafood amid fish-themed decor or on a patio facing the cathedral. Main dishes 33-52kn. Open daily 11am-10pm.

# SIGHTS

**AMPHITHEATER.** The must-see sight of Pula is the amphitheater, a wonder of ancient Roman architecture built in the first century AD during the reign of the Roman Emperor Vespasian. It was used solely for gladiatorial combat until the sport-killing was outlawed in the 4th century. Though it suffered through centuries of neglect, the amphitheater still stands in astoundingly complete condition and houses Pula's best concerts. An underground system of passages originally constructed as a drainage system now serves as a **museum** of local viticulture. *(From the bus station, take a left on Istarska. Amphitheater open daily 7:30am-9pm. 16kn, students 8kn. English booklet 30kn. Museum open daily 8am-8pm. 12kn, students 6kn.)*

**ARCH OF THE SERGIANS.** (Slavoluk obitelji Sergii.) It was built in 29BC for three members of the Sergii family from Pula, one of whom commanded a Roman battalion at the famous battle of Actium between Mark Antony and Octavian Augustus in 31 BC. *(From the bus station, follow Istarska as it turns into Giardini; the arch is on the right.)*

**THE FORUM.** The Forum, at the end of Sergijevaca, served as the central gathering place for political, religious, and economic debate. Today the original cobblestones lie buried safely 1.2m beneath the ground.

**TEMPLE OF AUGUSTUS.** (Augustov hram.) This remarkably preserved temple, constructed between 2 BC and AD 14, was dedicated to Roman Emperor Augustus. There were originally two similar temples nearby—the larger one was destroyed but the rear wall of the smaller one, the Temple of Diana, now serves as the facade of the City Hall. *(At the Forum.)*

**OTHER SIGHTS.** Up the street from Sergijevaca, the **Citadel** has guarded Pula since Roman times. On the nearby hilltop stand the remains of a **Roman Theater,** and, farther down, the **Twin Gate** (Dvojna vrata). The **Archaeological Museum of Istria** (Arheološki Muzej Istre), Carrera 3, offers an overview of Istria's history, with an emphasis on Roman stone artifacts. *(☎21 86 03 and 21 86 09. Open May-Sept. M-Sa 9am-8pm, Su 10am-3pm; Oct.-Apr. M-F 9am-2pm. 12kn, students 6kn.)*

##  FESTIVALS AND BEACHES

Amphitheater shows are not to be missed: Carmen, Andrea Bocelli, Sting, and Don Quijote Ballet have all performed here. Buy tickets there, or from the bookings agency **Lira Intersound.** (☎21 78 01. Open daily 8am-8pm. Prices vary.) The agency also sells tickets to the popular **Biker Days** festival during the last few days of July (150kn). Shows at this chrome and leather orgy have included female mud wrestling. The **Croatian Film Festival** during the last week of July and the **Art and Music Festival** during the first week of August offer fun for fewer *kunas* (30-60kn).

Looking from Stari Grad to the shipyards, you wouldn't guess that Pula had **beaches** at all, but there are plenty of private coves. Take bus #1 to the Stoja campground. Facing the sea, walk left down the coastline. For quieter, less crowded beaches head to **Fažana** (see the **Brijuni Archipelago** below for bus directions), where walking either direction along the coast leads to white stone beaches.

## 🍸 NIGHTLIFE

**Lungo Mare,** Cortanova Ujula bb (☎39 10 84). Take bus #2 or 7 from Giardini, get off at Veruda, and walk right on Verudela to the Hotel Pula; then go down to the sea. Cafe by day, raging club by night, this outdoor chameleon blasts music over its own cove. 1L *Favorit* 25 kn; coffee 4kn. No cover. Open M-Su 10am-4am.

**Rock Cafe,** Scallerova 5 (☎21 09 75). Not to be confused with a "harder" worldwide chain, this sturdy oak bar with pool tables and pictures of Hendrix and Morrison will transport you back a few decades—and so will the beer. 0.5L *Favorit* 10kn; coffee 4k. Open M-Sa 9am-midnight, Su 10am-midnight.

**Serenca,** Trg Forum 12 (☎22 34 07). Outdoor seating with an unobstructed view of the Temple of Augustus. 0.5L *Favorit* 10kn; coffee 4-10kn. Open daily 6am-midnight.

## 📷 DAYRTIP FROM PULA

### BRIJUNI ARCHIPELAGO

*Unless you're staying at the Brijuni Hotel, the only way to see the island is with a guided tour. The* ■*Brijuni Agency, Brijunska 10, in Fazana, has the lowest rates. Tours daily 11:30am; call the day before to reserve a spot. Round-trip ferry and a 4hr. tour 160kn. ☎52 58 83 and 52 58 82; fax 52 11 24 and 52 13 57; np-brijuni@pu.tel.hr; www.np.bri-juni.hr. Open daily 8am-8pm. To get to Fazana, take a local bus from the station on Istar-ske Divizije in Pula (20min., 1 per hr., 10kn).*

The Brijuni Archipelago, just a short bus and a lovely ferry ride away from Pula, is perhaps Croatia's most culturally and historically diversified piece of land. Even if you're only spending a few days in Istria, make sure to reserve one for Brijuni. It's got something for everyone—animals for the kids, ruins for the historians, politics for the bold, medical history for the doctors, and a general sense of mystery, enforced by the armed guards outside private residences still used by the government. The archipelago's largest island, **Veli Brijun,** was once home to a Roman resort, a Venetian colony, the discovery of a cure for malaria, and finally, the residence of former Yugoslav president Josip Brož Tito—if you can call the opulent complex that Tito erected on the island a "residence." The guided tour includes a miniature train ride through a safari park inhabited by such curiosities as a camel given to Tito by Colonel Kaddafi. The walking part of the tour leads through a picture gallery, full of such rarities as photos of Tito with Sophia Loren.

# POREČ ☎(0)52

Brightly colored Gothic and Baroque houses, distinctive 6th-century Byzantine mosaics in the UNESCO-protected St. Euphrasius's Basilica, polished cobblestone streets that turn and duck just enough to get the traveler pleasantly lost—this is Poreč (PO-retch) by day. By night the dreamy seaside town, situated on the ruins of a 2000 year-old Roman colony, succeeds in living up to the party ethic of its boisterous Roman ancestors—it offers enough clubs and discos to attract local throngs and dilute the daytime tourist influx.

**▛ TRANSPORTATION.** Buses link Poreč with the rest of Croatia, Slovenia, and Italy, including: **Pula** (1hr., 13 per day, 29kn); **Trieste, ITA** (2hr., 2 per day, 51kn); **Rijeka** (3½hr., 8 per day, 45kn); **Ljubljana, SLN** (5hr.; July-Aug. 2 per day, off-season 1 per day; 88kn); and **Zagreb** (6hr., 7 per day, 120kn).

**▛ PRACTICAL INFORMATION.** The **bus station** is on Rade Končara 1 (☎43 21 53); **luggage storage** is available there. (5kn. Open M-F 6-9am, 9:30am-5:30pm, and 6-8pm.) To reach the central **Trg Slobode,** turn left out of the bus station, walk down the street, and take a right onto the pedestrian Milanovića. The **tourist office,** Zagrebačka 9, won't find accommodations, but they'll tell you how to do so yourself. (☎45 12 93; fax 45 16 65. Open daily in summer 8am-3:30pm and 5-10pm; off-season 9am-4pm.) **Zagrebačka banka,** Obala M. Tita bb, by the sea, **exchanges cash** for no commission and cashes **traveler's checks** for a 1.5% commission. (☎45 11 66. Open M-F 8am-6pm, Sa 8am-noon.) There is a Cirrus/MC **ATM** and a currency exchange machine outside; a MC/Visa ATM is available at Negrija 2. There's a **pharmacy** at Trg. Slobode 13. (☎43 23 62. Open daily 7:30am-9pm.) The **post office,** Pino Brudičin 1, is equipped with **telephones** inside. (☎43 18 08. Open M-F 8am-noon and 6-9pm, Sa 9am-1pm.) **Postal code:** 524 41.

**▛▚ ACCOMMODATIONS AND FOOD.** For **private rooms,** go to **Sol Avis,** Zagrebačka 17, near the tourist office. (☎43 40 00; fax 45 33 77; rex-porec@pu.tel.hr. Singles 71-87kn; doubles 111-134kn; apartments 90-128kn per person. 30% more for stays under 4 nights. Open Mar.-Oct. 8am-10pm, Nov.-Feb. 8am-1pm.) **Hotel Poreč,** R. Končara 1, has modern and clean rooms, with TVs, fridges, and telephones. (☎45 18 11; fax 45 17 30; hp-duga@pu.tel.hr; www.tel.hr/duga. Singles 144-258kn; doubles 182-315kn; 20% more for stays under 3 nights.) **Camping** is by far your pocket's best friend: the large **Lanternacamp** is 13km to the north and has clean facilities. (☎40 45 00. 24kn per person; tents 30kn. Open Apr.-Oct.) The nudist camp and apartment-village **Solaris** is next door. (☎44 34 00. 24kn per person; no tents rented; apartments 95-106kn per person.) Both camps are accessible by the same bus from the bus station (25min., 9 per day, 12kn).

**Barilla,** Eufrazijeva bb, near the tip of the peninsula, serves up local pasta specialties such as *Spaghetti Ubriache* (drunk spaghetti, with cognac and vodka) and pizza (27-40kn; ☎45 27 42; open daily noon-midnight). **Sofora,** Obala M. Tita 13, by the sea, offers pizza (23-45kn), seafood dishes (40-100kn), and tasty pastas like spaghetti with mussels (21kn; ☎43 20 53; open daily Apr.-Oct. 11am-11pm). **Grill Sarajevo,** on M. Vlačića off Dekumana, offers Bosnian and Croatian specialties like *pljeskavica* (beef patty with french fries; 30kn) and fish dishes (30-80kn; ☎43 19 04; open daily Apr.-Oct. 9am-11pm). There is a **supermarket** at Zagrebačka 2, next to the bus station. (Open M-Sa 7am-9pm, Su 7am-1pm.)

**▛ SIGHTS.** The main pedestrian walkway, **Decumanus,** runs through Stari Grad (Old Town) and is lined with shops, cafes, and restaurants. From Trg Slobode,

> **THE FLASHY AND THE FLESHY** Part of the coastline from Poreč south to Rovinj holds the title of the world's longest stretch of naturist, or nude, beaches, many of which are owned privately by naturist camps. Anyone interesting in getting naked should take off their clothes. Anyone interested in getting naked with other people should ask at any of the naturist camps to apply for a naturist membership card, as entrance to the camps is not permitted without one. No special attributes or equipment are necessary to obtain the card, though men are not allowed into the camps alone, even with membership.

walk past—or even climb up—the 15th-century Gothic **Pentagonal Tower** (Peterokutna kula). The remains of the Roman **Temple of Neptune** (Veliki hram i Neptunov hram), from the first century AD, await at the end of Decumanus. **St. Euphrasius's Basilica** (Eufrazijeva bazilika) on Eufrazijeva, one block to the right when facing the tip of the peninsula, is the city's most important monument. Composed of 6th-century foundations, late Gothic choir stalls, and a Renaissance belltower, the basilica houses Venetian painter Giacomo Palma Jr.'s *The Last Supper* and golden mosaics that surround the altar. To the left of the basilica entrance stand the remains of the **chapel** of the first bishop of Poreč, St. Mauro, a 4th-century martyr. The relics include astounding mosaics from the original chapel floor. In December 1997, UNESCO classified the entire complex a national and historical heritage monument for the uniqueness and fragility of the mosaics therein. *(Chapel 10kn, basilica free. Both open M-Sa 7:30am-7pm, Su 11am-8pm. Services held Su 11am and 7pm.)* From Trg Slobode, head down A. Negrija to Narodni Trg, site of the **Round Tower**, a 15th-century defensive structure. Climb free to the top where you can pay 5kn for a cappuccino at the Kula cafe bar. *(Open M-Su 10am-2pm and 4pm-2am.)*

☑ **BEACHES.** Beaches in Poreč—and along most of the Istrian coast—are steep and rocky, but offer convenient tanning shelves cut into the shoreline. The best ones are south of the Marina. Facing the sea on Obala M. Tita, turn left and head along the coast for about 7 minutes to reach the **Blue Lagoon** (Plava Laguna) and for another 10 minutes to get to the **Green Lagoon** (Zelena Laguna). Both keep their customers coming with water slides, ping-pong, minigolf, tennis, and select "naturist" (nudist) areas. The only real way to escape the crowds and the aesthetically turbulent nudity is to continue past the Green Lagoon, but it's a good 30-minute walk. A **ferry** leaves from the Marina for the less popular, quieter beaches on **Saint Nicholas Island** (Sveti Nikola; every 30min. 7am-midnight; round-trip 14kn). A d **bike map** is available for free from the tourist office (see above). Its two marked trails take you through more than 50km of olive groves, forests, vineyards, and medieval villages.

◪ **NIGHTLIFE.** Any area on the coast that has a name also has a hotel complex and **disco**, frequented by tourists of all ages. (Generally open nightly 10pm-4am.) Facing the sea to the left, take a 5-minute walk down the beach to dance with a more local crowd at the seaside, open-air, Roman-columned **Colonia Ivlia Parentium.** (Open daily June-Oct. 10pm-4am.) In the Old Town, ◪ **Capitol**, Vladimira Nazora 9, attracts large crowds and good times. (☎41 51 51. Cover 15kn. Open nightly 10pm-5am.) **Club No. 1,** Marafor 10, has a higher bar-to-dance floor ratio. (0.3L *Favorit* 8kn. Open nightly 6pm-4am.) Bar **Casablanca**, Eufrazijeva 4, draws customers with friendly service. (☎45 31 31. Open daily 9am-1am.) **Bar Ulixes,** Dekumana 2, hides in a narrow alley off Dekumana. Drink whiskey-cola (20kn), *Guinness* (0.3L 18kn), or coffee (4kn) in the cellar or outside under a crumbly stone arch and the neighbors' drying laundry. (☎45 11 32. Open daily 9pm-3am.)

# ROVINJ ☎(0)52

At the beginning of the 19th century, a seaside sanatorium called "Maria Theresia" opened in Rovinj (ro-VEEN), and the town and island became a favorite summer resort for the Austro-Hungarian emperors and their friends. Today it remains oriented toward travelers with money to burn; shopkeepers and entertainment providers are more aggressive here than elsewhere in the country. Some believe Rovinj has sold its soul to the tourist-pleasing Man, but if you avoid the crowds you'll still find laundry hanging from windows, roosters crowing, and crystal-clear waves breaking against the walls of buildings built long before the days of travel agencies.

**⌸ TRANSPORTATION.** With no train station, Rovinj depends on **buses** from: **Poreč** (1hr., 7 per day, 21kn); **Pula** (1hr., every 30min., 19kn); **Trieste, ITA** (2½hr., 2 per day, 64-82kn); **Rijeka** (3½hr., 8 per day, 66kn); **Zagreb** (5-6hr., 9 per day, 126kn); and **Ljubljana, SLN** (5hr., 1 per day, 102kn).

**⍰ PRACTICAL INFORMATION.** The **bus station** is on M. Benussi and offers **luggage storage.** (☎81 14 53. 6kn for small bags, 10kn for large—distinction between small and large made at the attendant's discretion, so haggle.) Turn left out of the bus station and walk down Nazora toward the Marina, or walk up on Karera to the Stari Grad. Orientation can be tricky at first, as street signs are often difficult to find or non-existent and some streets do not have numbers. Tourist agencies offer free miniscule **maps,** but they're impossible to read. Buy a large map for 10kn at any agency and save your eyesight. The official tourist office, **Turistička Zajednica Rovinj** is at Pino Budičin 12. (☎81 15 66 and 81 34 69; fax 81 60 17 and 81 60 07; tzg-rovinj@pu.tel.hr; www.istra.com/rovinj. Open M-Su 8am-8pm.) To get there from the bus station, walk down Nazora to the sea and follow the waterfront to your right for about 10min. **Istarska Banka,** on Aldo Negri on the way to the tourist office, charges no commission on **traveler's checks** or **currency exchange.** (☎81 32 33. Open M-F 7:30am-8pm, Sa 7:30am-noon.) There is a Cirrus/MC **ATM** at Zagrebačka Banka, Karera 21, an AmEx/Visa ATM outside of the **Atlas** tourist agency on Trg Pignaton 1., and an AmEx/Cirrus/MC/Visa ATM outside the bus station. With your back to the bus station, turn right on M. Benussi to reach the **pharmacy.** (☎81 35 89. Open M-F 8am-9pm, Sa 8am-4pm, Su 8am-noon.) **Bikes** are available at **Bike Planet,** Trg na Lokvi 3, across the street from the bus station. (☎81 33 96 and 81 11 61. 20kn per hr., 70kn per day. Open M-Sa 8:30am-12:30pm and 5-8pm.) The tourist office (see above) has **maps** for suggested bike routes 22-60km in length. The **post office** across from the bus station, next to the pharmacy, has **telephones** inside and out. (☎81 14 66. Open M-Sa 7am-8pm, Su 7am-2pm.) **Postal code:** 522 10.

**⌂⍰ ACCOMMODATIONS AND FOOD.** With a tourist industry that might well be on steroids, Rovinj has bulked up on accommodations—and on prices. Shop around for **private rooms.** Across the street from the bus station, **Natale,** Carducci 4, offers decent prices, but call ahead in the summer. (☎81 33 65; fax 83 02 39; natale@pu.tel.hr; www.cel.hr/natale. Singles 80-108kn; doubles 112-160kn; 2-person apartments 192-212kn; 100% more for only 1 night, 50% for 2, 30% for 3. Tax 7kn. Registration 8kn.) For those with tents, **Camping Polari,** 2.5km east of town, also has a supermarket and several bars. (☎80 15 01; fax 81 13 95. June 74kn, July-Aug. 87kn. Closed Oct.-Mar.) To get there, take one of the frequent buses from the bus station (6min., 9kn).

A **grocery store** stands at Nazora 6, between the bus station and the sea. (Open M-Sa 6:30am-9pm, Su 7am-noon.) There is an **open-air market** on Trg Valdibora. (Open M-Su 6am-10pm.) Don't miss the local seafood hot spot ▨ **Veli Jože,** at the end of the Marina heading toward the tip of the peninsula on Svetog Križa 3. Furnished with funky maritime artifacts, including a primitive deep-sea diving suit, this bustling eatery grills up monk fish (220kn per kg), scorpion fish (240kn per kg), and meat dishes (35-80kn; ☎81 63 37; open M-Su noon-2am). **Gostionica Cisterna,** Trg Matteotti 3, in the heart of the medieval quarter, dishes up meat, pasta, and fish (30-90kn; ☎81 13 34; open M-Su noon-3pm and 6-11:30pm).

**▨ SIGHTS.** By the 7th century Rovinj was surrounded by town walls, which were later buttressed by towers. Three of the original seven gates that led into the

Old Town have survived—**St. Benedict's Gate, Holy Cross Gate,** and **the Portico.** The
Baroque archway called **Balbijer Arch** (Balbijer luk), which now serves as the principal threshold of the Old Town, was built on the site of the 17th-century outer
gate. Perhaps the best view of town is from a distance: old houses packed on the
tiny peninsula lead up to the 18th-century **St. Euphemia's Church** (Crkva sv. Eufem-
ije). Most people trek here to see the 6th-century Byzantine **sarcophagus** containing
the remains of St. Euphemia, the 3rd-century patron of Rovinj. During Roman
Emperor Diocletian's reign, Euphemia and other Christians were imprisoned and
tortured for refusing to deny their faith. The 15-year-old martyr survived the
wheel, but not the pack of lions. Amazingly, the beasts left her body intact and her
fellow Christians then encapsulated it in a sarcophagus. The vessel made its way
to Constantinople but disappeared from there in AD 800 to arrive the same year at
Rovinj—floating near the shoreline. Today it lies behind the right-hand altar, visited often by locals, particularly on Sept. 16, St. Euphemia's Day. Make the precarious climb up the **bell tower** for a majestic view of the city and coastline. (Church
and bell tower open M-Su 10am-9pm, services Su at 10:30am and 7pm. 10kn.) In
summer, the lawn outside hosts many classical music performances.

The **Museum of National Heritage,** Trg Maršala Tita 11, contains the works of local
masters spanning nearly three millennia. (Open M 9am-12:30pm, Tu-Sa 9am-
12:30pm and 6-9:30pm. 10kn.) There are boats anchored in the harbor raring to take
off on trips to the 22 nearby **islands** (around 50kn) or to the **Lim Fjord** (approx. 80kn),
a sea inlet that separates Rovinj from Poreč. You can buy tickets at the tourist
office but it's more fun to barter with the owners of the boat. If you try, you can usually get a student discount of some sort.

■ **FESTIVALS.** August 18-19, Rovinj takes to the sky for **Rovinjska noć** (Rovinj
Night), its famous annual night of fireworks. Every second Sunday in August, the
traditional open-air art festival **Grisia** takes place on the street of the same name and
international artists come to display their work.

■ **BEACHES.** For the prettiest **beaches** in the area, take a ferry to **Red Island.**
(Crveni Otok; 17 per day, 20kn.) On the mainland, natural rock shelves can be
reached by walking past the marina for 30 minutes (facing the sea, go left) and cutting through **Golden Cape** (Zlatni vrt). Alternatively, try the man-made patios cut
into the tip of the peninsula, where locals gather for glorious sunset seating. Ferries
from the Marina also go to beaches on **Katarina Island.** (1 per hr., 10kn.)

■ **NIGHTLIFE.** At night, Rovinj is not nearly as boisterous as Poreč or Pula. **Cay-
enne Disco Club,** Ob. Aldorizmondo bb., is a moored ferry boat-cum-party house on
the Marina that offers drinks upstairs and grooving in the hull. (☎81 73 67. Open
nightly Apr.-Sept. 6pm-5am. 20kn.) Join the locals at **Riviera Caffe Bar,** Santa Croce
4, at the end of the Marina. The bar features a loud crowd and *Favorit* (0.5L 10kn;
☎81 61 26; open M-Su 8am-3pm and 8pm-1am). **Bar Sax Caffe,** Ribarski Prolaz 4, has
a bar but no sax. Try *Bambus* (red wine and coca-cola; 11kn; open daily 8am-3am).

# GULF OF KVARNER

Blessed by long summers and gentle sea breezes, the islands just off the coast of
mainland Croatia are natural good-weather draws. Larger Krk bears the brunt of
the tourist infestation. Farther south and away from the mainland, Rab is less visited, less disturbed, and well worth the longer trip.

# RIJEKA                                                            ☎ (0)51

The sprawling port town of Rijeka (ri-YE-kah) is not the cleanest or prettiest stop
on the Croatian coast. It does, however, provide access to the islands in the Gulf of
Kvarner and much of the Dalmatian coast—places that warrant a trip through as
many Rijekas as necessary.

CROATIA

**⊡ TRANSPORTATION.** Escape by **train** to: **Zagreb** (3½hr., 5 per day, 55kn); **Split** via **Ogulin** (7hr., 2 per day, 73kn); **Ljubljana, SLN** (2½hr., 4 per day, 83kn); **Budapest, HUN** (9hr., 1 per day, 240kn); **Vienna, AUS** (9hr., 1 per day, 400kn); and **Berlin, GER** (11¾hr., 3 per day, 1003kn). The information desk, (☎98 30) is open daily 7am-6:45pm. The **bus station**, which consists of an **Autotrans office**, Žabica 1, is five minutes down Trpimirova from the train station. (☎33 88 11 and 21 12 22. Open daily 5:30am-9pm.) Buses to: **Krk** town (1½hr., 13 per day, 31kn); **Pula** (2½hr., every hr., 35kn); **Zagreb** (4hr., every hr., 85kn); **Split** (8hr., 12 per day, 167kn); **Dubrovnik** (12hr., 3 per day, 265kn); **Trieste, ITA** (2hr., 4 per day, 58kn); **Ljubljana, SLN** (3hr., 2 per day, 90kn); **Sarajevo, BOS** (13hr., 2 per week, 240kn). For **ferry** tickets, face the sea from the bus station and go left down the waterfront to **Jadrolinija**, Riva 16. (☎66 61 00. Open M-F 7am-6pm, Sa 7am-8pm, Su 7am-1pm.) To: **Zadar** (6hr., 4 per week, 86kn); **Hvar-Stari Grad** (10-15hr., 9 per week, 142kn); **Split** (12hr., 7 per week, 128kn); **Korčula** (15-18hr., 8 per week, 156kn); **Dubrovnik** (18-24hr., June-Sept. 5 per week, off-season 2 per week, 173kn); and **Sobra** (21hr., 2 per week, 173kn). All prices listed are for July and August; off-season 20% less.

**⊉ PRACTICAL INFORMATION. Luggage storage** in the train station is open 24hr. and costs 10kn for 24hr. of storage time. It's also available at the bus station. (9kn, 10kn for backpacks. Open 5:30am-10:30pm. If you need to spend the night in Rijeka, the closest and cheapest hotel to the train and bus stations is **Prenoćište Rijeka**, 1. maja 34/1. With your back to the train station, turn right on Trpimirova and left on 1. maja. Walk uphill for about five minutes; a sign on the right directs you through an archway to the hotel. A concrete monster from the outside, it provides clean rooms with balconies. (☎55 12 46. Reception 24hr. Singles 101kn; doubles 202kn.) For food, try the grilled specialties (22-33kn) and pizza (13-23kn) at **Viktorija**, Manzzon 1a, a cheap modern place next to the hotel. (☎33 74 16. Open M-Sa 7am-11pm, Su noon-11pm.) There's a **bank** in the train station, which exchanges **cash** and **traveler's checks** for no commission. (☎21 33 18. Open M-Sa 8am-8pm, Su 8am-12:30pm.) The train station has an AmEx/Cirrus/MC/Visa **ATM**.

# OPATIJA ☎(0)51

Set against steep, forested hills, Opatija ("abbey" in Croatian; pop. 9000) overlooks the Gulf of Kvarner and the impressive mountains that divide Istria from the rest of Croatia. The sharp majesty of its location and vistas has always made the city a delightful hideaway resort. Opatija's magnificent hotels, exotic gardens, and vibrant cafe life retain the same enchantment that attracted such artists as Anton Chekhov to stroll along its seaside promenade. Still, Opatija's best sights are natural ones. Head through the entrance to the Kvarner hotel off M. Tita to **Park Sv. Jakov** and **Park Angiolina**, both of which are filled with red camelia, the symbol of Opatija. For excellent **hiking**, the tourist office organizes free **guided walks** led by the president of Opatija's mountaineering society. Alternatively, ascend the steep **Učka Hill** behind the city with a little less effort by renting a **scooter** at the Palace Hotel, M. Tita 144. (☎25 98 29; half-day 141kn or 225kn per day. Open M-Sa 8am-4pm and 6-8pm, Su 9am-noon.) A nice sandy **beach** stretches out from the Kvarner Hotel.

The **AutoTrans** travel agency, M. Tita 200 at the main square, serves as the **bus station**. There is **no luggage storage.** (☎27 16 17 and 27 15 53; fax 27 14 30. Open M-Sa 7:30am-1pm and 1:30-7pm, Su 7:30am-2pm.) **Buses** connect Opatija to: **Rijeka** (20min., every ½hr., 11kn); **Pula** (2hr., 11 per day, 44kn); **Trieste, ITA** (3hr., 1 per day, 51kn); and **Zagreb** (5hr., 9 per day, 89kn). To reach the tourist office, banks, post office, and pharmacy, face the sea and turn left on **Maršala Tita**. At the **tourist office** on M. Tita, the staff gives out **maps**, organizes island excursions, and deciphers bus schedules. (☎27 13 10; fax 27 16 99 and 71 22 90; tzgr.op@ri.tel.hr. Open M-F 8am-3pm, Sa 8am-2pm.) **Privredna Banka Zagreb**, M. Tita bb., **exchanges currency** and cashes **traveler's checks** for no commission. (☎27 18 42. Open M-F 8am-9pm, Sa 8am-12:30pm.) There's a Cirrus/MC **ATM** outside the bank and an AmEx/Visa ATM outside the **Atlas/American Express Agency**, M. Tita 116/2. (☎27 10 32 and 27 11 55;

# Here's your ticket to freedom, baby!

**Wherever you want to go...
priceline.com can get you there for less.**

- Save up to 40% or more off the lowest published airfares every day!

- Major airlines serving virtually every corner of the globe.

- Special fares to Europe!

If you haven't already tried priceline.com, you're missing out on the best way to save. **Visit us online today at www.priceline.com.**

fax 27 15 62. Open M-Sa 8am-8pm, Su 4-8pm.) Follow Vjekoslava from M. Tita uphill to the **post office,** Eugena Kumičića 4. (☎27 19 05. Open M-F 7am-8pm, Sa 7am-2pm.) The cheapest bed is in a **private room.** For centrally located rooms, try **Dariva Tourist Agency,** M. Tita 162. Facing the sea at the bus station, head right, uphill on M. Tita. (☎27 24 82 and 27 29 90; fax 27 24 82; da-riva@iridis.com; www.iridis.com/da-riva/. July-Aug. doubles 80-100kn, 2-person apartments 260kn; June and Sept. 60-80kn, 220kn. Registration 8kn. Tourist tax 7kn. 50% more for singles. 30% more for stays of under 3 nights.) Restaurants line **M. Tita.** There is a **supermarket** at M. Tita 126. (☎71 11 95. Open daily 7am-9pm.) A night town by nature, Opatija offers a number of discos. **Quorum,** M. Tita bb., is a house music favorite. (Open Sa and Su 11pm-6am. 25kn.) For techno and disco on a beach, head to **Madona,** M. Tita 112. (☎27 22 40. Open Th-Sa midnight-5am, Aug. daily midnight-5am. 20kn.) The bar scene offers excellent rock pubs like **Hobboton,** M. Tita, 136/2. This underground, Batcave-esque pub hosts rock and blues concerts twice a month and sturdy drinkers every night. (☎71 22 11. 0.5L *Ožujsko* 15kn; coffee 5kn. Open nightly 9pm-5am.) **Postal code:** 514 10.

# KRK ISLAND ☎(0)51

Croatia's largest island, Krk is only a short ride across the Krk Bridge from the mainland. Its mountains and valleys are most stunning toward the southern end, in the town of Baška. While both Krk town and Baška reel in a large catch of tourists, their small streets, scuba diving, hiking trails, and hidden coves give the island a wild, undiscovered feel. Krk is a worthwhile getaway from the mainland and a great starting point for a cruise of the more alluring Dalmatian Coast.

**⊏ TRANSPORTATION. Buses** run from Rijeka to **Krk Town** (1½hr., 13 per day, 31kn); most continue to **Baška** (1hr., 10 per day, 11kn). **Jadrolinija** operates a **ferry** between Baška and Lopar on the northern tip of **Rab Island.** (1hr., 4 per day, 22.30kn, car 130kn, bike 24.10kn. June-Aug. only.)

## KRK TOWN

Krk Island's gateway to the rest of Croatia and the main intra-island transport hub, Krk Town is a well located base for visiting the rest of the island. The town's primary attraction is the 14th-century fortification, still visible today at the **South Town Gate** (Mala Vrata), the entrance to the Old Town right on the Marina. The waters around Krk Town have more excitement to offer than the town itself. **Fun Diving Krk,** Lukobran 8, leads a variety of underwater expeditions throughout the year. (☎/fax 22 25 63. Dive 148kn; full day trip with 2 dives 300kn; novice dive 320kn; night dive 172kn; snorkel trip 100kn. Equipment rental 24-40kn. Open daily 8am-7pm.) The town's only **beach** is next to the diving center. Less populated beaches are farther away in Autocamp Ježevac (see below).

The **bus station** is on Šetalište sv. Bernardina 1 (☎22 11 11). With your back to the station, a short walk to the left along the sea leads to Old Town and its main square, **Vela placa. Autotrans** tourist and travel agency, Šetalište sv. Bernardina 3, next to the bus station, **exchanges currency** and cashes **traveler's checks** for no commission. (☎22 26 61; fax 22 21 10; Open M-Sa 8am-9pm, Su 9am-1:30pm.) **Riječka Banka** has a Visa **ATM;** a Cirrus/MC ATM stands outside the **supermarket** on Šetalište sv. Bernardina bb, behind the bus station. (Open daily 7am-9pm.) There's a **pharmacy** at Vela pl. 3. (☎22 11 33. Open M-F 7:30am-9pm, Sa 7am-1pm and 6-8pm, Su 9-noon.) The **post office,** Trg b. Josipa Jelačića bb, gives MC **cash advances** and has **telephones** both inside and out. (☎22 11 25. Open M-F 7am-8pm, Sa 7am-2pm.) Autotrans (see above) also books **private rooms** (singles July-Aug. 128-144kn, doubles 160-200kn; off-season 20% cheaper; 30% surcharge for less than 3 days; tourist tax 7kn; registration 8kn), but it's cheaper to look for a room yourself. *Sobe* and *apartman* signs line Slavka Nikoliča (the road to the bus station from Rijeka) and Plavnička. **Autocamp Ježevac,** Plavnička bb, is a 5-minute walk from the bus station away from the Old Town. (☎/fax 22 10 81. Registration 8kn. Open April-Oct. July-Aug. 24kn per person; April-June and Sept.-Oct. 19kn. Tent 16kn. Car 14kn. Daily tax 7kn.) **Galeb,** Obala hrvatske mornarice bb, serves Adriatic standards on a terrace overlooking the marina. (Main dishes 25-65kn, vegetarian 25kn. Open daily 9am-midnight.) At the far end of the old town, The town's only club, **Trezor,** Put Halvdova 1, attracts dancers of all ages. (Open nightly Aug. 11pm-5am, Sept.-July Th-Su 11pm-5am. Cover Th and Su 10kn, F-Sa 20kn.) **Postal code:** 51500.

## BAŠKA

A narrow road winding through mountain valleys and green forests descends into the town of Baška on Krk's southern coast. Baška's famous pebbled beach, **Vela Plaža,** coils around 2km of barren coastal mountains. Packed with bodies during the day, it lights up after dark to become the romantic center of the town's nightlife. Home only to sheep and seagulls, the white rock mountains surrounding the town appear an unearthly land. To scale their heights, pick up a trail map at the tourist office (see below). While the trails are clearly blazed, it is advisable to have a map and to hike on sunny days. Much of the terrain is above treeline, on sharp sliding rocks, so wear appropriate footwear. A 2-hour hike along the coast (red trail #1 on the map) leads to **Škuljica,** the tip of Baška's southern peninsula. Venture off the trail down the coastline to find secluded, pebbly coves. The tourist office (see below) sells replicas of the **Baška tablet**—the town's historical claim to fame. The tablet is a white limestone piece, dated around 1100, on which the first known use of the Croatian language is inscribed. Originally built into the Church of St. Lucy near Baška, the tablet now sits in the Croatian Academy of Sciences and Arts in Zagreb, but the simple 9th century church houses a worthy replica. Take any Rijeka-bound bus to **Jurandvor** (5min., 10 per day, 10kn); the church is on the right off the main street. (5kn, 2.5kn for groups.)

The **tourist office** is at Zvonimirova 14. (☎/fax 85 65 44; tz-baska@ri.tel.hr.) To get there from the bus station, walk down Kralja Tomislava (the road to the right when facing the sea) and go right on Zvonimirova. Outside the bank across from the tourist office is a Amex/Cirrus/MC/Visa **ATM.** There is a **pharmacy** at Zvonimirova 114, behind the tourist office. (☎85 69 00. Open M-Sa 7:30am-9pm, Su 7:30am-7pm.) The **post office,** on the corner of Prilaz Kupalištu and Zdenke Čermakove, gives MC **cash advances** and has **telephones** inside and outside. (Open M-F 7am-7pm, Sa 7am-2pm.) **Kompas,** Frankopanska bb, in Hotel Corinthia (☎85 64 60; fax 85 65 20; kompas-baska@ri.tel.hr; www.corinthiatours.hr; open daily 8am-9pm), and **Primaturist,** Zvonimirova 98 (☎85 61 32; fax 85 69 71; primaturist@ri.tel.hr; open daily 8am-10pm) arrange **private rooms.** (July-Aug. singles 92-134kn; doubles 134-177kn; cheaper off-season. 30% surcharge for stays under 3 nights. Daily tax 8kn. Registration 8kn. Ecological tax 1.2kn.) Many *sobe* and *apartman* signs line Stari Dvori. To reach **Camping Zablaće** at Emila Geistlicha 38 from the bus station, walk to Zvonimirova and turn right, then take a left on Prilaz Kupalištu beyond the tourist office. The campground rents the cheapest sleep in town, but only if you carry your bed on your back. (☎85 69 09 and 85 66 04; fax 85 65 04. Open May-Sept. Reception 24hr. July and Aug. 26kn per person; tents 13kn; cheaper off-season. Registration 8kn. Daily tax 8kn. Ecological tax 1.2kn.) **Franica,** Ribarska 39, serves delightful pastas, pizzas, and fish. (Main dishes 22-50kn. ☎86 00 23. Open daily 10am-2am.) To get there, walk left facing the sea to the end of the marina. At the opposite end of the marina, you can dine to live music at **Tamaris,** Zarok bb, which offers patio tables heaped with fish (25-80kn) and local sausages for 25kn. (☎85 65 75. Open M-Su 8am-11pm.) For night excitement, walk past Tamaris to ▓ **Condor,** Zarok 6. This pizzeria/club carries on into the wee hours with popular dance music and a lively local crowd. (☎85 62 24. Cocktails 25kn. 20kn cover from 11pm. Open M-Su 8am-4am.) There's a **grocery store** at Zvonimirova 60. (Open daily 7am-9pm.) **Postal code:** 51523.

# RAB ISLAND: RAB TOWN ☎(0)51

With whitewashed stone houses jutting like whitecaps above the sea, Rab seduces its visitors. Perhaps it was this charm that persuaded the town's numerous rulers to preserve the town's architectural magnificence. Having survived Byzantine, Venetian, Hungarian, and Croatian rulers, Rab still boasts ruins from the original Roman municipality constructed under Emperor Augustus in the first century BC. If the buildings don't seduce you, the beaches will. Unlike rocky-shored Krk, Rab is blessed with long stretches of sandy coastline, making it a worthwhile trek from both the coast and Zagreb.

**E TRANSPORTATION.** Getting to and from Rab is inexplicably more difficult than traveling to other islands, so be prepared for frustrations. **Buses** connect Rab Town with **Rijeka** (3hr., 3 per day, 79kn) and **Zagreb** (5½hr., 3 per day, 121kn). To head south along the coast, you can catch a Zagreb- or Rijeka-bound bus to **Jablanac** (20min., 4 per day, 29kn). Tell the driver your ultimate destination, and he'll drop you off on the *magistrala* (highway) where southbound buses stop. Before jumping on the bus, you should explain to someone at the ticket office in Rab where you're trying to go to be sure that a southbound bus to your destination will indeed pick you up off the highway. Still, regardless of what the ticket office says, the only buses that are sure to come are those serving major cities such as Zadar or Split. (Ticket office open daily 5:40am-1am.) Between June and August, a **ferry** runs between **Baška** on Krk and Lopar on the northern tip of Rab Island. (1hr., 4 per day, 22.30kn.) From the ferry drop-off, walk five minutes down the road to the bus stop to catch the bus to Rab Town. (20min., 9 per day, 10kn.)

**■ ⃝ ORIENTATION AND PRACTICAL INFORMATION.** Stretching along Rab's southwestern coast, Rab Town is the island's largest. The peninsular Old Town is organized around three parallel streets: **Gornja** (Upper), **Srednja** (Middle), and **Donja** (Lower). To reach them from the bus station on Mali Palit (☎72 41 89), with your back to the station turn left and walk downhill until you reach the sea. The friendly staff at the **tourist office, Turistička zajednica,** on the other side of the bus station at Mali Palit, hands out free **maps** of the town and island and can decipher the ferry schedules. (☎77 11 11; fax 77 11 10. Open daily 8am-10pm.) **Riječka Banka,** on Mali Palit just a few steps from the tourist office, **exchanges currency** for no commission. (Open M-F 8-11:30am and 5:30-8pm, Sa 8am-noon.) There is a AmEx/Cirrus/MC/Visa **ATM** outside the bank and another one off Trg sv. Kristofora on the waterfront. A **pharmacy** sits next to the bus station. (☎/fax 72 54 01. Open M-Sa 8am-9:30pm, Su 9-11:30am.) **Internet access** is available at **Break,** Donja bb. (☎72 40 58. 40kn per hr. Open daily 11am-3pm and 7pm-2am.) Head 20m toward the water from the tourist office to reach the **post office,** Palit bb, which gives MC **cash advances. Telephones** are located inside. (Open M-Sa 7am-9pm.) **Postal code:** 51280.

**◫⃝ ACCOMMODATIONS AND FOOD.** The tourist agency **Katurbo,** M. de Dominisa, between the bus station and the center, arranges **private rooms.** (☎/fax 72 44 95; katurbo-tourist-agency@ri.tel.hr. Open daily 7:30am-10pm. Singles July-Aug. 80kn, June and Sept. 64kn, Oct.-May. 50kn; doubles 360kn, 300kn, 260kn. 30% more for stays under 3 nights. Tourist tax 4.50-7.60kn.) **Camping Padova** boasts its own sand beach. (☎72 43 55; fax 72 45 31. 22kn per person; 20kn per tent. Registration 4kn. Daily tax 7kn.) Get there via the bus that heads to **Barbat** (10min., 7 per day, 8kn) or, facing the sea, walk left along the shore for 2km.

Restaurant **St. Maria,** Dinka Dokule 6, on a street that is a continuation of Srednja, specializes in such Hungarian pleasures as *vinski gulaš* (goulash; 45kn) and *punjena paprika* (stuffed bell pepper; 45kn), served in a medieval courtyard. (☎72 41 96. Main dishes 45-85kn. Open daily 11am-2pm and 4pm-midnight.) **Buffet Harpun,** Donja bb., treats you to friendly service and tasty fish specialties (25-55kn) or pasta and risotto for 30-35kn. (☎82 27 43. Open daily 10am-midnight.) Eat cheap at **Pizzeria Mare,** Srednja 8. (☎77 13 15. Pizza 25-35kn; pasta 20-35kn. Open daily 7am-midnight.) A **supermarket** is in the basement of Merkur, Palit 71, across from the tourist office. (Open M-Sa 6:30am-9pm, Su 6:30-11am.)

**◉⃝ SIGHTS AND ENTERTAINMENT.** A stroll along Gornja takes you from the remains of **St. John's Church** (Crkva sv. Jvana), a Roman basilica, to the ruins of the

CROATIA

**Church of the Holy Cross** (Crkva Sv. Križa), where, according to legend, the figure of Jesus once wept on the cross. Farther down, Gornja leads to Trg. Slobode, dominated by **St. Justine's Church** (Crkva sv. Justine), which houses a **museum** dedicated to Christian art. (Open daily 9am-noon and 7:30-10pm. 7kn.) Sunsets from atop of the Bell Tower **St. Mary's Church**, built in the beginning of the 13th century, are truly astonishing. (Open daily 10am-1pm and 7:30-10pm.) The 12th-century **Virgin Mary Cathedral** (Katedrala Djevice Marije) and the nearby 14th-century **St. Anthony's Monastery** (Samostan sv. Antuna), farther down Gornja, complete the tour of this history-laden quarter. For more information, pick up a free pamphlet from the tourist office (see above). **Komrčar,** one of the most beautiful parks in the Mediterranean, lies at the base of the Old Town peninsula and offers shade as well as a **beach.** There are sandy beaches around the town, but the nicest ones are scattered all over the island. To reach a local favorite named "Sahara," take a bus to San Marino (25min., 9 per day, 11kn) and follow signs to the Sahara trail (20min.). Other choices include Supetarska Draga, Kampor, and Barbat, can all be reached by bus and a 20- to 30-minute walk (ask at the tourist office).

Cafes abound in Rab. The most popular spot among local youth is **Le Journal,** at Donja just off Kristofor Trg. Scenesters gather here to hear the latest in underground music, and throw back a few heavy-hitting "Le Journal" cocktails for 30kn. (0.33L Heineken 15kn. Open nightly 10pm-5am.) Closer to the waterfront, **San Antonio,** Trg Municipium Arbae, tends a fine fiesta with a bar outside for the loungers and a bar inside for the dancers. (☎72 11 45. Coffee 4kn. Open daily 8am-4am.)

# DALMATIAN COAST

After his last visit to Dalmatia, George Bernard Shaw wrote: "The gods wanted to crown their creation and on the last day they turned tears, stars and the sea breeze into the isles of Kornati." Though he was referring to specific islands, Shaw's words speak to the entire Dalmatian Coast—a stunning seascape of hospitable locals and unfathomable beauty. With more than 1100 islands (only 66 of which are inhabited), Dalmatia boasts not only the largest archipelago, but also the cleanest and clearest waters in the Mediterranean. Zadar and its preserved environs are excellent starting points for exploring smaller wonders: Pag's remarkable lace-making tradition, Brač's astounding beach, Hvar, one of the most beautiful islands in the world, and the UNESCO-protected town of Trogir. Farther south, the nightlife of Split and vibrant culture on Korčula are preludes to the country's gem, Dubrovnik.

## ZADAR ☎(0)23

The modern center of northern Dalmatia, Zadar hides its many scars well. Allied attacks destroyed most of the city during the World War II, and the Serbs ruined much of what had been rebuilt between 1991 and 1995. Its residents have rebuilt again and today the city stands as beautiful as the shoreline road leading to it, coiling between a blue-green sea and white mountain peaks. With the extraordinary national parks nearby and a history preserved well enough to afford Roman ruins as benches and playgrounds, Zadar is a quintessentially Dalmatian city.

### ■ ORIENTATION

Most of the city's businesses and sights are scattered along the main street of the Old Town, **Široka**. The **bus** and **train stations** are on Ante Starčevića. To get to Široka from them, take a left at the large crossroad to the right of the stations, then take another left. Follow Zrinsko-Frankopanska (and the signs to the "Centar'") all the way to the water, then walk along the left side of the harbor to the gate of the Old Town. Pass through the gate and Široka shoots off of **Narodni trg** on the right.

## Dalmatian Coast

Adriatic Sea

**CROATIA**

**BOSNIA AND HERZEGOVINA**

TO BARI, ITALY
(ferry from Dubrovnik)

Dubrovnik
Zaton
Šipanska Luka
Šipan
Lopud
Lokrum

Ston
Sobra
Blato
Soline
Mljet
Mljet National Park
Polače
Govedari
Pelješac

Mostar

Metković

Tijpanj
Drvenik
Sučuraj

Korčula
Korčula
Lastovo
Lastovo
Ubli

Makarska

Sumartin

Hvar

Vela Luka

Bol
Stari Grad
Sv. Nedjelja

Supetar
Brač
Hvar

Vis
Vis
Komiža

Split
Rogač
Šolta

BišEvo

Paklemi Očci

Sinj

**CROATIA**

Trogir

Primošten

Šibenik

Vodice

Knin

Krka National Park

Murter
Biograd na moru

Benkovac

Kornat
Kornati National Park

Zadar
Kali
Ugljan
Zaglav
Dugi Otok
Telašćica Natural Park
Pašman

Paklenica National Park

TO ZAGREB
(road from Zadar)

TO RIJEKA
(Road from Zadar)

TO RIJEKA
(ferry line)

TO ANCONA, ITALY
(ferries from Vis and Split)

20 miles

20 kilometers

0

0

## TRANSPORTATION

**Trains:** Ante Starčevića bb (☎43 05 99). Much less convenient than buses; avoid them.

**Buses:** Ante Starčevića bb (☎21 19 38). To: **Split** (3hr., 2 per hr., 60kn); **Rijeka** (4½hr., 1 per hr., 85kn); **Zagreb** (5hr., 1 per hr., 85kn); **Dubrovnik** (8hr., 9 per day, 130kn); **Trieste, ITA** (7hr., 2 per day, 95kn); and **Ljubljana, SLN** (8hr., 1 per day, 137kn).

**Ferries:** Depart from **Liburnska Obala,** where 2 **Jadrolinija** stands provide information and sell tickets. The one on the tip of the peninsula handles ferries operating outside the local islands of **Ugljan** and **Dugi Otok.** (☎21 20 03; fax 31 11 51). To: **Split** (6hr., 4 per week, 62kn); **Rijeka** (7hr., 4 per week, 72kn); **Korčula** (12hr., 4 per week, 107kn); and **Dubrovnik** (16hr., 3 per week, 118kn). Open M-F 7am-8pm and 11pm-1am, Sa 7am-8pm, Su 7am-noon, 5-10pm, and 11:30pm-1am.

**Public Transportation:** Often has neither schedules nor stop names; use it cautiously and ask for help whenever possible.

## PRACTICAL INFORMATION

**Tourist Office:** Ilija Smiljanica bb. (☎21 22 22; fax 21 17 81; tzg-zadar@zd.tel.hr). Turn left inside the main gate of the Old Town onto Don Ive Prodana, then left at the street's end. The office offers good, detailed **maps** of Zadar, but little more.

**Currency Exchange: Dalmatinska banka,** Trg sv. Stošije 3 on Široka (☎31 13 11), exchanges currency for no commission and traveler's checks for a 1.5% commission. Open M-F 8am-8pm, Sa 8am-noon.

**ATMs:** All over the city; one outside the bank and 2 at the bus station.

**Luggage storage:** At the train station. 10kn for 24hr. Open 24hr. Safer at the bus station. 1.2kn per hr. Open daily 7am-9pm. Follow the *Garderoba* signs to both.

**Pharmacy:** Barakovića 2 (☎21 33 74), next to Narodni trg. Open M-F 7am-8pm, Sa 8am-noon.

**Internet Access:** In the brand new **Gradska Knjižnica Zadar** (Zadar City Library), Stjepana Radića 116 (☎31 57 72). Free. Open M-F 8am-noon and 6-8pm, Sa 8am-1pm.

**Post office:** Nikole Matafara 1 (☎21 16 84), off Široka, has **telephones** inside and gives MC **cash advances.** Open M-Sa 7am-9pm. **Poste Restante** at the main post office, Kralja Držislava 1 (☎31 60 23). Open M-Sa 7am-9pm.

**Postal code:** 23000.

## ACCOMMODATIONS

Zadar is blessed with a youth hostel, but it's a long trek to the Old Town. For the party types, **private rooms** in the center of town might be the best option. There are occasional *sobe* (room) signs on the waterfront, or try **Aquarius Travel Agency,** inside the main gate at Nova Vrata bb. (☎/fax 21 29 19; jureska@zd.tel.hr. Open daily 7am-10pm. Singles 100kn; 2-person apartments 200-250kn. Tourist tax 5kn.)

**Omladinski Hostel Zadar,** Obala kneza Trpimira 76 (☎33 11 45; fax 33 11 90), on the waterfront near the outskirts of town. From the station, take a bus heading to Puntamika or Diklo (15min., 6kn); plan to get off at the last stop, but ask someone to let you know when your stop comes. From the bus stop, walk 50m left down the waterfront to the hostel. Large, clean bathrooms make up for cramped bunks. Reception 24hr. Check-out 10am. Call ahead in the summer; it's often booked by large school groups. July 15-Aug. 20 80kn per person; June 1-July 14 and Aug. 21-Sept. 16 72kn; May and Sept. 16-Oct. 30 65kn; Jan.-April and Nov.-Dec. 58kn. Daily tax 4.50-7kn. Breakfast included.

**Autocamp Borik,** Gustavo Matoša bb (☎33 20 74; fax 33 20 65), on the beach. Take a bus to Puntamika or Diklo. After about 12min., look for signs to the camp on the right. July-Aug. 23kn per person; tents 20kn; cars 39kn. Tourist tax 7kn. May-June and Sept. 16kn per person; tents 16kn; cars 31.50kn; tourist tax 5.50kn.

##  FOOD

**Restaurant Dva Ribara** ("Two Fishermen"), Blaža Jurjeva 3, off of Plemića Borelli, lays out heaps of pasta (32-46kn), pizza (27-35), and even fish (37-70). For the tree-huggers, they have a vegetarian platter for 27kn. (☎21 34 45, Open daily 10am-1am.) Just outside the city walls, **Foša**, Kralja Dmitra Zvonimira 2, grills up sizeable portions of fish (30-90kn) and meat (55-75kn) on a patio overlooking the bay. (☎31 44 21. Open M-Sa 11am-midnight, Su 7pm-midnight.) **Gostionica Zlati Vrtič**, Borelli 12, parallel with Široka, serves meat dishes (35-55kn) and fish (45-90kn) in a pebble courtyard, accompanied by traditional Croatian music. (☎21 30 76. Open daily 7:30am-11:30pm.) The **Zadranka supermarket** has branches around town, including one at Široka 10 and at J. Štrossmayerova 6. (Both open daily 6:30am-10pm.)

## ■ ♪ SIGHTS AND ENTERTAINMENT

On the maps distributed by the tourist office you'll find the numbered locations and matching snapshots of all major sights. Guidebooks (20-60kn) in several languages are available at the Aquarius Travel Agency (see above) and any *Tisak* store. The most historically laden part of town is the ancient **Forum,** on Široka in the center of the peninsula. **St. Donat's Church** (Crkva sv. Donata), dominates the square. Built at the beginning of the 9th century in Byzantine style, it sits on the site of an ancient Roman temple, still visible inside, and remains one of only three Catholic churches in the world constructed in such a circular fashion. (Open daily 9am-1pm and 5-9pm. 5kn.) **St. Mary's Church** (Sv. Marija), Trg Opatice Čike 1, is just across the square from St. Donat's and houses the fabulous **Permanent Exhibition of Religious Art** (Stalna Izložba Crkvene Umjetnosti). The display of **gold and silver** busts, reliquaries, and crosses kept here stand as Croatia's most precious collection; shrewd nuns keep a close watch on things. Buy tickets to the left of the church. (☎21 15 45. Open M-Sa 10am-12:30pm and 6-7:30pm, Su 10am-12:30pm. 20kn, students 10kn.) Next to St. Mary's stands the **Archeological Museum** (Arheološki Muzej), with extensive collections documenting the history of Zadar: artifacts from the Middle Ages on the ground floor, Roman period on the first floor, and prehistoric times on the 2nd floor. (☎21 18 37 and 21 24 47. Open M-Sa 9am-1pm and 6-8pm. 15kn.) Though it may strain your pocketbook, consider taking a guided boat tour of the **Kornati National Park.** For 160-240kn (depending on whether you want lunch and cocktails) venture out into the only European park of its kind—365 islands, all completely uninhabited, home of the famous salt-water Silver Lake. You'll find plenty of eager trip vendors at the waterfront next to the main gate, and across the pedestrian harbor bridge. Shop around and bargain down.

The trendiest and liveliest place to party is **Central Kavana** on Široka 3, a kaleidoscope of funky lights and decorations that include hanging blue bicycles, orange TVs, and sewing machines. Live music on weekends ranges from jazz to reggae. (0.5L *Tuborg* 17.50kn. ☎21 10 41. Open daily 7:30am-1am.) **Caffe bar Forum,** on Široka at the Forum, has comfortable chairs and fantastic outdoor seating overlooking the ruins. (0.5L *Karlovačko* 10kn. Open daily 7am-midnight.)

## ■ DAYTRIP FROM ZADAR

### PAKLENICA NATIONAL PARK

*Buses run from Zadar (1hr., 2 per hr., 20kn). Ask the driver to let you off at the road to the park entrance. Tourist office ☎/fax 36 92 02; np-paklenica@zd.tel.hr; www.tel.hr/paklenica. Open M-F 8am-3pm. Park open daily Apr.-Oct. 7am-9pm; Nov.-March. 8am-4pm. 25kn, students 15kn. Cave tours M, W and F-Sa 10am-1pm. Tunnel tours Tu 9am-1pm, Th 4-8pm, and Su 9am-1pm. Both tours 10kn.*

The craggy peaks of the Velebit Massif mountain range rule most of Paklenica's 3657 hectares. The mountains are a playground for a wide range of activities—from

CROATIA

There are still **landmines** around the park; stay on the marked paths. It is a good idea to bring water, as temperatures in summer get high. And don't forget your hiking boots. For more info on hiking, see **Hiking and Outdoors,** p. 37.

casual strolls and cave-crawling to challenging hikes and advanced rock-climbing routes with self-explanatory names like *Psycho Killer*. For any visitor, **Mala Paklenica** (Small Canyon) and **Velika Paklenica** (Big Canyon) are the must-see attractions; both can be visited in under two hours. Mala Paklenica is the less-touristed of the two, as the trail tends to be slippery from descending streams in spring and fall. The actual park entrance is about 1km off the main road, but there is a **tourist office,** across the street from the bus stop and two minutes toward the lake, that offers a wealth of camping, rock climbing, hiking, and weather information. For park tickets and cave tours, walk or drive up to the park entrance.

# PAG ISLAND: PAG TOWN      ☎(0)23

The low white buildings of Pag Town are set on one side of an artificial isthmus on the southern end of Pag Island. Mountains rise up on either side of the sleepy town, visual reminders of the isolation from crowds and tourism Pag enjoys. Come here to find local traditions unaltered for the sake of tourist business—*Paška čipka*, the famous local lace, still sells straight from the hands of its makers. While Pag boasts no outstanding architecture and many of its original 15th-century houses stand beside modern structures, the town belongs solely to its people.

**▐ TRANSPORTATION.** There is only a **bus stop** in Pag Town, no station. The best way to get to Pag is to take a bus from **Zadar** (1hr., 2 per day, 24kn). Buses also come from **Zagreb** (6hr., 5 per day, 120kn) and **Rijeka** (4hr., 1 per day, 100kn). If you're on a southbound bus along the coast, you'll need to ask the driver to drop you off at **Prizna.** Walk 2km down to the water, where **ferries** run to **Žigljen** on Pag Island. Buses to Pag Town meet the incoming ferries.

**▐▊ ORIENTATION AND PRACTICAL INFORMATION.** To get to the center from the bus stop, face the sea and walk left along the waterfront. Turn left onto Vela Ulica to reach the main square, **Trg. Kralja Krešimira IV.** The center of Pag is miniscule, so getting around should be easy. For those less in touch with their internal compass, there are **maps** available at the official **tourist office,** Katine bb, on the waterfront. (☎/fax 61 13 01. Open daily 7am-9pm.) **Riječka Banka** is on the way to the main square at Vela Ulica bb and has an **ATM** outside. (Open M-F 8-11:30am and 6-8:30pm, Sa 8am-noon.) There's a **pharmacy** on the waterfront just beyond the tourist office, S. Radića bb. (☎61 10 43. Open M-Sa 7:30am-1pm and 5-9pm, Su 8am-noon.) The **post office** stands two streets behind the bus stop at A. B. Šimića and **exchanges cash** and cashes **travelers checks** for no commission. There are **telephones** inside. (☎61 10 04. Open M-Sa 7am-9pm). **Postal code:** 23250.

**▐▊ ACCOMMODATIONS AND FOOD.** The luxurious lack of commercial tourism in Pag means low prices for **private rooms.** Try **Meridijan 15 Travel Agency,** A. Starčevića 1, conveniently located next to the bus stop in the same building complex as Hotel Pagus. (☎61 21 62 and 61 21 65; fax 61 21 61; meridijan-15@zd.tel.hr. Singles 30-60kn; doubles 100-200kn. 30% more for stays under 3 nights. Tax 5.50-7kn. Open daily May-Oct. 8am-9pm.) Those with tents can head down to **Autocamp Šimuni.** The camp offers some of the best beaches on the island. (☎69 82 08. Open May-Sept. and July-Aug. 96kn per person; May-June and Sept. 56kn. Tax 4kn.) To get there from the town, grab one of the buses heading to Zagreb and ask the driver to let you off at Šimuni (20min., 5 per day), then follow the signs downhill.

Follow the locals to **Na Tale,** S. Radića 2, to eat well outside amid boisterous Croatian families and plates of pasta (22-35kn), pizza (24-35kn), calamari (48kn) and *Kotlet sa žara* (grilled cutlet, 34kn; ☎61 11 94; open daily 8am-11pm). Behind the main square, the terrace restaurant **Tamaris,** Križevaćka bb., serves up pizza (25-

**LACED LABOUR LOST** Four hundred years ago, nuns from the Venetian island of Burano arrived in Pag and founded the industry that now puts the island town on Croatia's cultural and historical maps—*Paška čipka* (lace from Pag). In Croatia, handmade lace is produced only in the town of Pag. Though many of the designs and patterns have developed over the centuries, the Pag women still use the same methods as their pious predecessors from Burano, now taught in a school for lacemaking. The process is a supreme act of patience; producing a piece of lace the size of a frisbee can take up to 6 months. The results are beautifully intricate and dauntingly costly; that same frisbee will go for anywhere from 800-2000kn. Fortunately, you needn't worry about shopkeepers overpricing the goods, as all lace is only sold out of private homes or from the Lace Gallery near the main square, Kralja Zvonimira 1. (Open every evening 7:30-11pm. Free.) For more information on *Paška čipka*, contact Pag's Cultural Center at Franijevački Trg. (☎61 10 25. Open M-F 8am-3pm.)

33kn), pasta (25-30kn), and house specialties (30-70kn) such as the local favorite *Pileći Batak* (chicken leg with bacon and cheese, 30kn; ☎61 22 77; open daily 6:30am-midnight). There is an open-air **fruit and vegetable market** in front of Tamaris. (Open daily 6am-10pm.)

🎵📷 **ENTERTAINMENT AND NIGHTLIFE.** On the last weekend in July, Pag's main square hosts the town's **summer carnival.** Locals dress up in traditional garb called *Paška Naškja* to perform the traditional dance *Paška Kolo.* On the last day, the ceremonial "Burning of Marco"—the burning of a sealed coffin meant to symbolize the year's sins takes place. If you can find any **beach** between the bodies, try the sandy Gradska Plaža, right across the bridge from the Old Town. For less-peopled tanning options, walk past the crowds and continue down the coast. Alternatively, facing the sea in the Old Town, walk right along the waterfront past Hotel Pagus to reach beaches on the opposite bank of the bay.

Bars and cafes line the waterfront between the bus stop and the tourist office. To join the younger crowd, grab a seat at ■ **Kamercengo,** Jadrulićeva Br. 1. Soothing green lighting, light dance music, and the self-proclaimed "most comfortable chairs in Croatia" mix nicely with a 10kn pint of *Karlovačko* or *Ožujsko.* (Open daily 8am-1am.) Cafes all close around 1am—but fear not, the party marches on right across the bridge at Pag's mainstay of youth and dance, **Disco V Magazin,** Proska bb. This 500-year-old building-turned-party-warehouse comes complete with high wooden rafters, ancient stone walls, disco balls, and *all* of the late-nighters of Pag Island. (Cocktails 25kn. Open W-Su 11pm-6am. Sa 10kn cover.)

# ŠIBENIK ☎(0)22

Facing the magnificent bay of Šibenika Luka at the mouth of the Krka river, Šibenik (pop. 40, 000) seems to have missed a spot on the average tourist itinerary. The few who come here are rewarded with a town of proud, nightlife-loving locals, steep medieval streets devoid of tourist shops, and one of the most beautiful cathedrals on the Adriatic. Much enlarged since its establishment as the Diocese of Šibenik in 1298, this town has kept itself a hidden delight well worth the finding.

📧 **TRANSPORTATION.** The **bus station** is at Drage bb. (Info ☎21 20 87. Open daily 6:30am-9pm.) Buses go to: **Split** (1½hr., 20 per day, 31kn); **Zadar** (1½hr., 20 per day, 31kn); **Zagreb** (6hr., 10 per day, 100kn); **Dubrovnik** (6hr., 10 per day, 100kn); and **Ljubljana, SLN** (7hr., 1 per day, 140kn). From the bus station, face the water and walk right for 10 minutes along the waterfront to reach the Old Town.

🏛📷 **ORIENTATION AND PRACTICAL INFORMATION.** While much of newer Šibenik spreads out across the hills rising from the harbor, the **Gorica Grad** (Old Town) is packed tightly on a steep face against the water. A nice respite from the many alleyways, the Old Town's main street, **Kralja Tomislava,** runs diagonally up the

# 182 ■ DALMATIAN COAST

hill from the waterfront **Cathedral of St. Jacob**. It leads to the main traffic artery, **Kralja Zvonimira**, that serves as a border between the Old and New Towns. The **tourist office**, Fausta Vrančića 18, is just above Trg Palih šibenskih boraca, one of the squares traversed by Kralja Tomislava. The enthusiastic staff hands out **maps**. (☎21 20 75; fax 21 90 73; tzg-sibenika@si.tel.hr; www.summernet.hr. Open in summer M-F 8am-9pm, Sa-Su 8-11am and 7-8pm, off-season M-F 8am-3pm.) **Jadranska Banka**, at Trg Kralja Držislava, **exchanges currency** and cashes **traveler's checks** for no commission. (☎33 33 88. Open M-F 7:30am-9pm, Sa 7am-1pm.) There is an **ATM** across from the bank. **Luggage storage** is available at the bus station. (3.70kn per day. Open daily 6:30am-9pm.) The **pharmacy, Ljekarna Varoš**, stands at Kralja Zvonimira 2. (☎21 22 49. Open M-F 7am-8pm, Sa 7am-1pm.) Just above the bus station is the **post office**, Vladimira Nazora 5, with **telephones** inside. (☎21 49 90. Open M-Sa 7am-9pm, Su 7am-2pm.) **Postal code: 22000.**

**▐▐▐ ACCOMMODATIONS AND FOOD.** **Private rooms** are the best option for horizontal repose. To find one, try **Mihovil Tours**, Trg Pavla Šubića 1, 50m back from the waterfront in Gorica Grad. (☎21 66 66; fax 21 48 41; mihoviltours@si.tel.hr. Singles 80kn; doubles 160kn. Open M-F 8am-2pm and 5-8pm, Sa 8am-noon.) Tent folk should make their way to **Autocamp Solaris** on the Zablaće peninsula across the bay from Šibenik, where **beaches** abound. Take a local bus from the station to Zablaće (10min., 1 per hr., 7kn) and ask the driver to drop you off at the camp.(☎36 39 99 and 35 40 15; fax 36 18 00; solaris.hotels@si.tel.hr; www.dalmacija.net/solaris/solaris.htm. July-Aug. 20kn per person, 36kn with tent or car. Tax 8kn. May-June and Sept.-Oct. 12kn, 32kn, 6kn.)

Getting good food is a serious problem in Šibenik. Locals cook at home and eat well, but unless you can talk your way into someone's kitchen, you'll be stuck with pizza. **Pizzeria Kike**, Durija Sižgorića 3, whips them up in quiet courtyard off Kralja Tomislava. (☎33 01 41. Pizza 23-35kn. Open daily 6:30am-1:30am.) **Pizzeria Zora** does it by the sea at Oslobodenja 4. For something really special, try the 23-40kn pizza. (☎21 58 41. Dirt cheap 0.5L *Karlovačko* 8kn. Open M-F 7am-11pm, Sa-Su 7am-midnight.) The expensive option is to try a country restaurant outside town—a favorite local excursion. Inquire at the tourist office (see above) for directions to **Zlatna Ribica** and **Barun**. The hungry go to the **supermarket** at Poljana 3, at the top of Vladimira Nazora. (Open daily 6:30am-10pm.)

**▐▐ SIGHTS AND ENTERTAINMENT.** Šibenik's pride is the Gothic-Renaissance **Cathedral of St. Jacob** (Katedrala Sveti Jakova). This massive, white stone masterpiece by Croatian sculptor Juraj Dalmatinac commands a view of the Old Town. A native of Zadar, Dalmatinac took over construction of the cathedral in 1432, but it wasn't completed until 1536 by his pupil and architect of the cathedral at Trogir, Nikola Firentinac. Both the intricate dome designed by Firentinac and the frieze of 71 heads on the exterior walls of the apses—all stone portraits of 15th century commoners—are striking. (Open daily May-Oct. 8am-noon and 6-8pm. Services daily at 9am, on Su also at 9:30am, 11am, and 7:30pm.) For an incredible view of the town, harbor, outlying islands, and the distant Kornat, climb up to the **St. Ana Fortress** above the Old Town. (Open 24hr. Free.)

Šibenik has no beaches to speak of, but a short bus ride out to Zablaće (10min., 1 per hr., 7kn) across the harbor takes you to a number of **pebble beach** options. The cultural event of the year is the **Children's Festival** held in the Old Town during the last week of June and the first week of July. The first week invites international performers, while the second is designated for dancers and local comedians.

**▌ NIGHTLIFE.** Welcome to one of the best nightspots on the Dalmatian Coast. Every night of the week is a party in Šibenik and the party happens at **Dolac**. Facing the water from the Old Town, walk right along the harbor straight into the crowds and the beats. People pack into the many bars along the water and spill out into the street. For techno, try **Domald**, Obala Prvoboraca 3. (0.5L *Guinness* 40kn. Live music Tu, DJs Th-Sa. Open daily 7am-1am.) For a quieter sit-down scene and Croatian tunes, head to **Pescharia** at Dolac. (Open daily 7am-1am.)

# TROGIR
☎ (0)21

With medieval buildings packed tightly into winding streets and a surrounding sea lapping and crashing against pristine parks, Trogir (pop. 1500) is a stone beauty that seems to deserve more space than its tiny island locale affords. Its miniature scale has always enhanced the town's appeal, attracting Gothic and Renaissance artists to grace it with countless churches from the 13th to the 15th centuries and earning it a coveted place on the UNESCO World Heritage List in 1997.

**TRANSPORTATION.** The **bus station** is on the mainland. **Buses** from **Zadar** to **Split** stop in Trogir (2½hr., 2 per hr., 64kn from Zadar). Local buses also go from Trogir to **Split** (30min., 3 per hr., 15kn) and **Šibenik** (30min., 2 per hr., 29kn). There are **no ferries** to or from Trogir. To check up on **ferry and bus schedules**, head across the Čiovo bridge to **Atlas**, Obala kralja Zvonimira 10. The friendly staff will clear up any confusion from the bus station and can sell ferry tickets for boats from Split. (☎ 88 42 79 and 88 13 74; fax 88 47 44. Open M-Sa 8am-9pm, Su 6-9pm.)

**ORIENTATION AND PRACTICAL INFORMATION.** The town spills from the mainland onto two islands, both connected by short bridges. The **Stari Grad** (Old Town) is on the small island of Trogir; behind it lies Čiovo Island, which has the town's best beaches, reachable by the Čiovski bridge. The main street, **Kohl-Genscher,** is a short walk from the bus station across the tiny bridge and through the stone **North Gate.** It leads past the central square, **Trg Ivana Pavla,** to the Čiovski bridge. The **tourist office, Turistička Zajednica Grada Trogir,** Obala b. Berislavića 12 at the end of Kohl-Genscher, sells **maps** of the city (2kn) and English guidebooks (80kn; ☎/fax 88 14 12; open M-Sa 8am-noon and 4-10pm). **Zagrebačka banka,** Gradska vrata 4, just past the North Gate, **exchanges cash** for no commission and cashes **traveler's checks** for a 1.5% commission. (Open M-F 8:30am-2:30pm, Sa 8:30am-12:30pm.) There is a Cirrus/MC **ATM** outside the bank and an AmEx/Visa **ATM** at Kohl-Genscher 15, near the tourist office. The **pharmacy** is at Kohl-Genscher 23. (☎ 88 15 35. Open M-F 7am-8pm, Sa 7am-2pm.) Log on to the **Internet** at **Vodoo,** Maja Čarija Monarska 7. (5kn per 5min. 25kn per hr. Open M-Sa 10am-2pm and 7-11pm, Su 7-11pm.) The **post office,** B. Jurjeva Trogiranina 1, gives MC **cash advances,** exchanges cash for a 1.5% commission and cashes **traveler's checks** for no commission. (☎ 88 14 52 and 88 14 70. Open M-Sa 7am-9pm.) **Telephones** are at the post office. **Postal code:** 21220.

**ACCOMMODATIONS AND FOOD.** The best deals in town are **private rooms,** arranged by **ČIPIKO,** Kohl-Genscher 41, across from the cathedral and through an archway. (☎/fax 88 15 54. Open daily 8am-8pm. July-Aug. singles 96-112kn; doubles 240-284kn; tourist tax 6kn. May-June and Sept. 80-96kn; 208-256kn; 4.50kn.) Beachside **Prenoćište Saldun,** Sv. Andrije 1, puts you up in small rooms with clean hall bathrooms. Half the rooms have balconies overlooking the harbor. Cross the Čiovski bridge and go straight onto Put Balana, which winds up the hill; signs for Saldun will be at the top. (☎ 88 20 53 and 88 20 85. Reception 24hr. Breakfast 28kn. 70kn per person.) **Vila Sikaa,** Obala Kralja Zvonimira 13, sits on the waterfront just across the Čiovski Bridge. It's well worth the extra cash to bask in this lap of luxury—modern rooms with baths, telephones, internet, A/C, and satellite TV. (☎ 88 12 23 and 88 56 60; fax 88 51 49; stjepan.runtic@st.tel.hr. Reception 24hr. Reserve at least 10 days ahead. Singles 280kn; doubles 320-400kn. Breakfast included.)

**SIGHTS AND ENTERTAINMENT.** A statue of Trogir's patron, St. Ivan Orsini, tops the **North Gate,** a beautiful Renaissance arch that forms the entrance to the Old Town. Most sights, including the **Cathedral of St. Lawrence** (Crkva sv. Lovre), are in **Trg Ivana Pavla,** at the center of the Old Town. Begun in 1213 as a Romanesque basilica, it was not completed until 1598. Its famous portal was chiseled by the Croatian Master Radovan in 1240. Inside the cathedral is the Renaissance **Chapel of St. John of Trogir**—a work from 1461-1497 guided chiefly by Florentine architect Nikola Firentinac. The 47m **bell tower** *(campanile)* has four bells, once proclaimed

CROATIA

"the most harmonious in Dalmatia," but if you climb up the scary stairs on the hour, you'll be cheated: the bells ring without moving. Tank-tops, shorts, and gum-chewing are not permitted inside. (Open daily 9am-noon and 4:30-7:30pm. Mass M-Sa 7:30am; Su 8, 9, 10:30am, and 7:30pm. Bell tower 10kn, students 5kn.) The 15th-century Venetian **Kamerlengo Fortress** on the tip of the island, once the sight of a 1941 mass execution by Italian fascists, now houses a summer movie theater.

The rocky **beach** starts at Hotel Saldun and winds around the larger island. Cafes of similar atmosphere, prices, and menus line Kohl-Genscher and the waterfront, but there's only one named **Big Daddy**, Obala b. Berislavića 14. It will fill you with 0.33L bottles of *Karlovačko* for 11kn. (Open daily 7am-5am.) For a view of the cathedral, try **Radovan**, Trg Ivana Pavla 2, with seating on a quiet terrace. (☎88 23 80. 0.5L *Karlovačko* 12kn; coffee 5kn. Open daily 7am-midnight.)

# SPLIT                                                          ☎(0)21

Metropolitan, busy and dusty, Split (pop. 200, 000) is by no means a typical Dalmatian town. More a cultural mecca than a picturesque beach town, it boasts a wider variety of activities and nightlife than any of its neighbors. More women holding the title of Miss Croatia have come from Split than from anywhere else in the country; the aesthetic appeal of its female population is rivaled only by the architecture of this palace-city by the sea. The Old Town, wedged between a high mountain range and a palm-lined waterfront, is framed by a luxurious palace where Roman Emperor Diocletian used to summer. In the 7th century, the local Ilyrian population fled inside the palace to escape the attacks of marauding Slavs, building a town within and creating perhaps the most puzzling piece of architecture in Europe.

## ORIENTATION

The **train** and **bus stations** lie across from the **ferry** terminal on **Obala kneza Domagoja**. Leaving the stations, follow Obala kneza Domagoja to the waterside mouthful **Obala hrvatskog narodnog preporoda**, which runs roughly east to west. To the north lies **Stari Grad** (Old Town), packed inside the walls of **Diocletian's Palace** (Dioklecijanova Palača). To get to Stari Grad from the **local bus station** (where buses from nearby Trogir arrive), turn right on Domovinskog Rata with the station behind you. Domovinskog Rata turns into Livanjska and then Zagrebačka. Turn right onto Kralja Zvonimira at the end of Zagrebačka and follow it to the harbor.

## TRANSPORTATION

**Trains:** Obala kneza Domagoja 10 (info ☎33 85 35). Due to the destruction of railways during the recent war, trains are inefficient; use buses. There are no trains running south of Split. To: **Zadar** via **Knin** (6½hr., 1 per day, 57kn); **Zagreb** (7½hr., 4 per day, 65kn); **Rijeka** via **Oguli** (12hr., 2 per day, 70-79kn); **Ljubljana, SLN** (12hr., 2 per week, 152kn); and **Budapest, HUN** (16hr., 1 per night, 225kn). Ticket booth open daily 6-10am, 10:30am-4:30pm, and 5-10pm.

**Buses:** Obala kneza Domagoja 12 (info ☎33 84 83 and 33 84 86). Domestic tickets sold outside, international (međunarodni karte) inside. To: **Zadar** (3½hr., every 30min., 53-68kn); **Dubrovnik** (4½hr., 15 per day, 65-84kn); **Rijeka** (7hr., 13 per day, 167kn); **Zagreb** (8hr., every 30min., 86-113kn); **Sarajevo, BOS** (7½hr., 6 per day, 143kn); **Ljubljana, SLN** (11hr., 1 per day, 193kn); and **Prague, CZR** (19hr., 1 per week, 360kn). Open daily 5am-11pm. Buses to **Trogir** (30min., 3 per hr., 15kn, round-trip 23.50kn) leave from the **local bus station** on Domovinskog rata.

**Ferries:** Obala kneza Domagoja bb (☎33 83 33; fax 33 82 22). To: **Korčula** (6hr., 5 per week, 125kn); **Dubrovnik** (8hr., 5 per week, 139kn); **Rijeka** (10½hr., 5 per week, 102kn); **Ancona, ITA** (10hr., 4 per week, 311kn); and **Bari, ITA** (25hr., 3 per week, 345kn) via **Dubrovnik**.

**Local Transportation:** Most buses run every 30min. 5kn per ride; buy tickets from the driver and punch them on board.

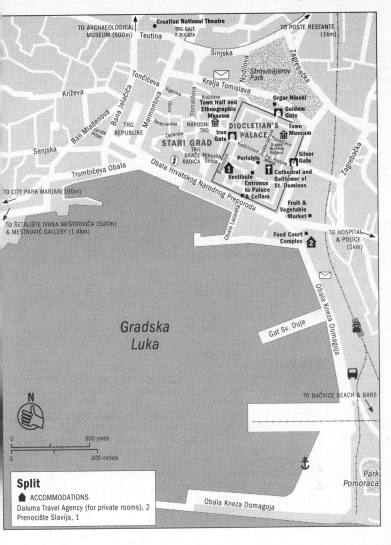

**Split**

⬆ ACCOMMODATIONS
Daluma Travel Agency (for private rooms), 2
Prenocište Slavija, 1

**Taxis:** ☎ 34 77 77. Many stand in front of Diocletian's Palace on Obala hrvatskog narodnog preporoda. Average fare 18kn plus 9kn per km.

## 🔢 PRACTICAL INFORMATION

### TOURIST AND FINANCIAL SERVICES

**Tourist Office: Turistički Biro,** Obala hrvatskog narodnog preporoda 12 (☎/fax 34 21 42), hands out detailed **maps** and booklets. Open M-F 7:30am-8pm, Sa 8am-3pm.

**Budget Travel: Croatia Express,** Obala kneza Domagoja 9 (☎33 85 25; fax 33 84 70; croatia-express@st.tel.hr). Sells bus, train, and plane tickets and offers student discounts for train tickets. Open daily 7am-10pm.

**Consulates: UK** (☎24 14 64), **Italy,** and **Germany** share a building at Obala hrvatskog narodnog preporoda 10, above Zagrebačka bank. There is no US consulate in Split.

CROATIA

**Currency Exchange: Zagrebačka banka,** Obala hrvatskog narodnog preporoda 10 (☎34 78 10), exchanges currency for no commission and cashes traveler's checks for a 1.5% commission. Open M-F 8:30am-2:30pm, Sa 8:30am-12:30pm.

**ATM:** Cirrus/MC outside Zagrebačka banka (see above). AmEx/Visa outside Croatia Express (see above).

**American Express: Atlas Travel Agency,** Nepotova (☎34 30 55; fax 36 20 12). Open M-Sa 8am-8pm, Su 8am-noon.

## LOCAL AND EMERGENCY SERVICES

**Luggage Storage:** At the bus station: 2.50kn per hr. Open daily 6am-10pm. At the train station: 10kn per day. Open daily 5:30-10:30am, 11am-4:30pm, and 5-10pm.

**Pharmacy:** Marmontova 2 (☎488 40). Open M-F 7am-8pm and Sa 7am-1pm.

**Police:** Trg hrvatske bratske zajednice 9 (☎30 71 11). From Stari Grad, take Kralja Zvonimira and bear right onto Pojišanka; the station is on the right.

**Hospital: Clinical Hospital Center,** Spinčiceva 1 (☎55 61 11). From Stari Grad, follow Kralja Zvonimira until it runs into Pozjička Cesta. Then turn right onto Put Iza Nove Bolnice; the hospital is on the right.

**International Press:** Obala hrvatskog narodnog preporoda 21 (☎34 16 26). Good international magazines. Open M-Sa 8am-8pm, Su 8am-1pm.

**Internet Access: Cyber Caffe Mriža,** Kružićeva 3 (☎36 08 26). 20kn per hr. Open M-F 9am-9pm, Sa 9am-2pm.

**Post Office:** Ul. Kralja Tomislava 9 (☎36 14 21). Go in the main doors to send mail, and through the left-hand doors for **telephones** and **fax.** Open M-Sa 7am-9pm. **Poste restante** is on the outskirts of town at Hercegovačka 1 (☎38 33 65). To get there, take Zagrebačka from Stari Grad to Domovinskog Rata. Walk for 25min, then turn left onto Put Stinica, and right onto Hercegovačka. **Poste restante** is on the ground floor.

**Postal code:** 21000.

# ▐ ACCOMMODATIONS

For a city its size, Split has a paltry selection of budget accommodations. **Daluma Travel Agency,** Obala kneza domagoja 1, can help find **private rooms** in the center of town. (☎33 84 84; ☎/fax 33 84 39; daluma-st@st.tel.hr; www.tel.hr/daluma-travel. Open M-F 8am-8pm, Sa 8am-12:30pm. May-Oct. singles 100kn; doubles 200kn. Nov.-Apr. 80kn; 160kn.) People at the bus station and ferry landing offer rooms; some at lower prices. **Prenoćište Slavija,** Buvinova 2, recently renovated after a stint housing refugees, has 70 beds in high-ceilinged, clean rooms right in the middle of Stari Grad. Follow Obala hrvatskog narodnog preporoda, then turn right onto Trg Braće Radića. Turn right onto Mihovilova Širina and follow signs up the stairs in the left-hand corner. (☎34 70 53; fax 59 15 58. Reception 24hr. Check-out 11am. Singles 180kn, with shower 220kn; doubles 210kn, 260kn; triples 250kn, 300kn; quads 280kn, 360kn. Breakfast included.)

# ◖ FOOD

There is a **supermarket** inside the Jadrolinija complex across from the bus station (open M-Sa 6am-9pm, Su 7am-9pm), and another at Svačićeva 4 (open daily 7am-10pm). At Obala kneza Domagoja 1, between Stari Grad and the stations, is a super-cheap **food court.** (Pizza 8kn; sandwiches 10kn.) Across Kralja Zvonimira from the food court is an **open-air market** that sells everything from fruit and vegetables to smuggled clothing and cigarettes. (Open daily 6am-8pm.)

▨ **Konoba Varoš,** Ban Mladenova 7 (☎39 61 38). Facing the water on Obala hrvatskog narodnog preporoda, head right onto Varoški Prilaz, then right onto Ban Mladenova. A true Dalmatian feast, prepared and served in a local den adorned with fishing nets and wine racks. Prepare your taste buds for something different—frogs with prosciutto (*žabe na žaru s pršutom,* 215kn per kg) and calves' brains (*mozak pohani,* 53kn). Or stick with the basics: pasta and omelettes 30-44kn. Open M-F 9am-1am, Sa-Su noon-1am.

**Ponoćno Sunce,** Teutina 15 (☎36 10 11). From the waterfront, follow Marmontova to Trg Gaje Bulata, then left onto Teutina. A small basement eatery, where the quality of the pasta (25-45kn) makes up for the cheesy music and the tacky modern art on the walls. Grilled meat dishes 35-60kn. Open M-F 10am-midnight, Sa-Su 1pm-midnight.

**Restaurant Sarajevo,** Domaldova 6 (☎474 54). From the waterfront, turn into Stari Grad at Trg Braće Radića and follow Marunlićeva to Narodni trg. Turn right onto Domaldova in the farthest corner of Narodni trg. Eat well under brick archways in this quiet cellar restaurant. Go royal with steak "Lord Charles" (55kn) or pasta and omelettes (25-35kn). Open daily 9:30am-midnight.

**Restaurant Libar,** Svačićeva 10 (☎34 57 66). Follow Marmontova from the waterfront to Trg Gaje Bulata. Turn left onto Teutina and then right onto Svačićeva. As cheap as it gets—a soup, grilled meat dish, french fries, and salad for 33kn. That is, however, the only option on the menu. Open daily 7am-8pm.

##  SIGHTS

### DIOCLETIAN'S PALACE (DIOKLECIJANOVA PALAČA)

*Across from the taxis on Obala hrvatskog narodnog preporoda. 6kn, students 3kn. Cellars open daily 9am-1pm and 6-8pm.*

The eastern half of Split's Old Town (Stari Grad) inhabits the one-time fortress and summer residence of the Roman Emperor Diocletian. The palace once served as a sanctuary for Roman royalty. Galla Placidia, daughter of Byzantine Emperor Theodosius, and her son Valentinius III escaped the blades of usurpers within these walls a century later. In the 7th century, local residents were forced into the fortress to protect themselves from raids by the Slavs and later built their city within its walls. Today, it's a living museum of classical and medieval architecture.

**CELLARS.** The cellars of the city are located near the entrance to the palace; turn through either gate to wander around this haunting labyrinth. The dark stone passages originally constituted a flat floor for the emperor's apartments. The 1700 years of trash stored here have gained some archaeological significance. The hall on the left also houses a brand-new computer that calls up a wealth of history about the palace and city while entertaining you with Renaissance music. Some of the finds are displayed in hallways to the left of the entrance, which also hold a complex of dripping domes. The airier right side is used as a space for art displays.

**PERISTYLE.** The open-air peristyle of the palace is a colonaded square used for outdoor operas and ballets. The open-domed **vestibule** becomes the backstage during the Summer Festival. You can explore it freely during the day. *(Straight through the cellars and up the stairs.)*

**CATHEDRAL.** The cathedral on the right side of the peristyle is one of architecture's great ironies—it was originally the mausoleum of Diocletian, who was known for his violent persecution of Christians. Its later conversion to a Catholic cathedral makes it the world's oldest. The small circular interior, with intricately wrought stonework, leaves almost no room for tourists who come to wonder at the magnificent inner door and altar. The cathedral **treasury,** including 15th-century ecclesiastic garments, delicate 13th-century books, and a mass of silver busts and goblets lies up the stairs to the right. The adjoining **Belltower of St. Domnius** (Zvonik Sv. Duje), begun in the 13th century, took 300 years to complete. The stairs are unnerving, but the view is incredible. *(Cathedral and tower open daily 7am-noon and 4-7pm. Tower and treasury 5kn.)*

### OTHER SIGHTS IN THE OLD TOWN

The Old Town is framed on the eastern side by the **Silver Gate** (Srebrna Vrata), which leads to the main open-air **market** (see above). Outside the north **Golden Gate** (Zlatna Vrata) stands Ivan Meštrović's rendering of **Gregorius of Nin** (Grgur Ninski), the 10th-century Slavic champion of commoners' rights. The western **Iron Gate** (Željezna Vrata) leads onto Narodni trg. Although this side of town

CROATIA

lacks any excavations, medieval architecture dominates. Even if you don't find history, it just might find you—many of the houses are crumbling with age and drop an occasional stone here and there.

## 🏛 MUSEUMS

**Meštrović Gallery** (Galerija Ivana Meštrovića), Šetaliste Ivana Meštrovića 46 (☎35 84 50), is a 25min. walk along the waterfront from the center. Don't miss its comprehensive collection of works by Ivan Meštrović (see **Literature & Arts,** p. 150). The entrance fee gets you into both the gallery, housed in a stately villa with fabulous ocean views that the artist built for himself, and the Kaštelet, decorated with wood carvings that depict the life of Jesus. Meštrović once proclaimed that the crucifix in the Kaštelet was the best work he would ever do. Open in summer Tu-Sa 10am-6pm, Su 10am-3pm; off-season T-Sa 10am-4pm, Su 10am-2pm. 15kn, students 10kn. English booklet 5kn.

**Archeological Museum** (Arheološki muzej), Zrinsko-Frankopanska 25 (☎31 87 21 and 31 87 62). From the waterfront, follow Marmontova to Trg Gaje Bulata, turn onto Frankopanska. Meander through headless statues in its beautiful garden. Open M-Sa 9am-1pm and 5-8pm. 10kn, students 5kn.

**City Museum** (Muzej Grada Splita), Papalićeva 1 (☎34 12 40). From the Golden Gate, enter Stari Grad and turn left onto Papalićeva. Houses a minimal selection of artifacts but tells the history of Split in detail with English placards. The building itself is particularly notable—it's a 15th-century construction by the architect of Šibenik's cathedral, Juraj Dalmatinac (see **Šibenik,** p. 181). Open Tu-F 9am-noon and 6-9pm, Sa-Su 10am-noon. 10kn, students 5kn.

**Ethnographic Museum** (Etnografski muzej), on the north side of Narodni trg, rests inside the 15th-century former Venetian town hall in Stari Grad. Open Tu-F 10am-noon and 5-9pm, Sa-Su 10am-1pm, M 10am-noon. Free.

## 🏖🎵 BEACHES AND ENTERTAINMENT

The rocky cliffs, green hills, and sandy beaches on the west end of Split's peninsula make up **City Park Marjan** and serve as a reminder that Diocletian once vacationed here. Facing the water, turn left on Obala kneza Domagoja and follow it to the beach for 10 minutes. Paths are indicated on the map; you can find your own, but watch for signs indicating that a trail leads to private lands—the dogs bite. The closest beach to downtown Split is sandy **Bačvice,** a nighttime favorite for local skinny dippers and the starting point of an excellent strip of bars along the waterfront.

From mid-July to mid-August, Stari Grad hosts an annual **Summer Festival,** when the city's best artists join international guests in performing ballets, operas, plays, and classical concerts among the town's churches and ruins.

## 🍸 NIGHTLIFE

**Tropic Club Equador,** Kupalište Bačvice bb. Just past Bačvice beach (see above). A Latin terrace bar overlooking the sea that plays the rumba. Sip on not-so-subtly named cocktails—go see for yourself (30kn). Open daily 9am-1am.

**Shakespeare,** Cvetna 1 (☎51 94 92). Follow the waterfront past Tropic Club Equador for another 20min. The bard might turn over in his grave now that 2 floors of raging techno bear his name. 30kn cover. Open Th-Su 11pm until you drop.

**Jazz planet,** Grgura Ninskoga 3 (☎34 76 99). Hidden on a tiny back street across from the City Museum, the soothing blue lighting inside mixes well with jazz and beer. (0.5L *Guinness* 25kn, 0.5L *Bavaria* 15kn.) Open M-Th and Su 8am-midnight, F-Sa 8am-2am.

**Obojena svjetlost** (Colored Light), Uvala Zvončac. Walk along Šetalište Ivana Meštrovića to Meštrović Gallery, and then go down to the beach. The outdoor patio is home to card-playing students during the day and concerts at night. DJs take the stage on weekends. Pint of beer 10kn. Concerts 25kn. Open M-Th and Su 9am-2am, F-Sa 9am-4am.

# BRAČ ISLAND: BOL                                      ☎ (0)21

Central Dalmatia's largest island, Brač (BRAtch; pop. 1500), and particularly the town of Bol on its southern coast, is a tourist's paradise. Most visitors come here for Zlatni rat, arguably the most beautiful beach on the Adriatic. Just a short walk from the town center, its white pebbles roll from the surrounding pine forest into the sea. Brač has more to offer than location, though: churches, galleries, and lively nightlife will keep you busy for as long as you choose to stay.

**☐ TRANSPORTATION.** The **ferry** from **Split** docks at **Supetar** (45min., July-Aug. 13 per day, Sept.-June 8 per day, 15kn, round-trip 38kn). From there, take a **bus** to Bol (45min., M-Sa 6 per day, Su 4 per day, 10kn). The last bus back to the ferry leaves at 5:50pm and the last ferry to Split leaves at 8:30pm. Alternatively, a **catamaran** runs directly to Bol from Split (1½hr., departs Bol M-Sa 7am, Split 3pm, 45kn, round-trip 70kn). Buy tickets on board.

**▦▨ ORIENTATION AND PRACTICAL INFORMATION.** The town is organized around the many-named waterfront: at the bus stop and marina, it's called **Obala Vladimira Nazora;** to the left of the bus station (facing the water) it becomes **Riva,** then **Frane Radića,** then **Porat Bolskih Pomorca;** and to the right it's called **Put Zlatnograta.** The **tourist office,** Porad bolskich pomorca bb, is a 5-minute walk to the left facing the sea of the bus station. It dispenses a Bol guide and large **maps.** (☎63 56 38; fax 63 59 72; tzo-bol@st.tel.hr.) **Zagrebačka banka,** Uz pjacu 4, uphill from Frane Radića, **exchanges currency** for no commission and cashes **traveler's checks** for a 1.5% commission. (☎/fax 63 56 11. Open M-F 8:30am-2:30pm, Sa 8:30am-12:30pm.) **Bol Tours,** Obala Vladimira Nazora 18, **rents bikes** (70kn per day, 45kn per half-day; ☎63 56 93 and 63 56 94; fax 63 56 95; bol-tours@st.tel.hr; open daily 8am-9pm). There's a **pharmacy** and **ambulance** on Porat bolskih pomorca bb. (☎63 51 12. Open M-F 8am-1pm and 6-8pm, Sa 8am-noon.) **Hotel Elaphusa,** on Put zlatnog rata right before the beach, boasts the first **internet cafe** on Brač, consisting of one computer. (15kn plus 50kn per hr. Open daily 6am-midnight.) The **post office,** Uz pjacu 5, has **telephones.** (☎63 52 35; fax 63 52 53. Open M-Sa 7am-9pm.) **Postal code:** 21420.

**▣☐ ACCOMMODATIONS AND FOOD.** Your cheapest bet is to call one of the local residence numbers listed in the tourist office's booklet *Bol,* and arrange a **private room.** This method generally saves you 10-20% by bypassing agency prices. If the locals are all at the beach, **Bol Tours** (see above) will find you a room. (Singles 65-100kn; doubles 102-142kn. Tax 5.50kn. Prices depend on season. 20% surcharge for stays under 3 nights.) There are five **campsites** around Bol; the largest is **Kito,** Bračka cesta bb, on the road into town. (☎63 54 24 and 63 55 51. Open May 1-Sept. 30. 38kn per person; tent included.)

 **Konoba Gušt,** Frane Radića 14, offers shady respite among hanging fishing gear and local diners, not to mention the Dalmatian specialties *Dalmtinska Paštičada* (meat with macaroni; 45kn) and *Dalmatinski Brodet* (tomato and fish gulash; 45kn; main dishes 30-65kn. ☎63 59 11. Open daily noon-2am). Restaurant **Plaža Borak,** Put Zlatnog rata bb., on the beach just before Zlatni rat, attracts topless customers of both sexes interested in tanning on the patio while munching on frog's legs (60kn). Live Dalmatian music kicks off every night at 9:30pm. (Pasta and omelettes 25-40kn; grilled meat dishes 40-80kn. Open daily 8am-1am.) **Pizzeria Topolino,** A. Radića, on the waterfront in the center of town, has good pizza and pasta for 25-40kn. (Open daily 8am-2am.) Tourists have driven food prices up, but **supermarket Vrtić,** on Uz pjatu up the hill from the post office, can slice up a sandwich for around 10kn. (Open daily 6:30am-9pm.)

**▣☐ SIGHTS AND ENTERTAINMENT.** The free **map** distributed by the tourist office (see above) shows all the town's sights, the most important of which is the **Dominican Monastery,** built in 1475. Facing the water, walk left for 15 minutes. It resides at the eastern tip of Bol and has an adjacent **museum,** which houses a collection of prehistoric artifacts, ecclesiastic robes, and town archives. (Open daily

CROATIA

10am-noon and 5-7pm. 10kn.) **Dešković Gallery,** on Porat bolskih pomoraca next to the bus station, exhibits contemporary Croatian art in a small 17th-century Renaissance-Baroque mansion. (Open daily 5-10pm. 5kn.) More art comes to town during **Bol Cultural Summer** (Bolsko Kulturno Ljeto; June-Sept.). Inquire at the tourist office about particular events and look out for posted signs with festival schedules throughout town. **Big Blue Sport,** Podan glavice 2, organizes scuba diving and wind-surfing. (☎/fax 63 56 14; www.tel.hr/big-blue-sport. Open daily 8:30-11:30am and 6-10pm. One day dive or night dive with equipment rental 200kn. 8hr. course of wind-surfing for beginners 707kn; rentals 300kn per day, 160kn per half-day. )

# VIS ISLAND: KOMIŽA ☎(0)21

The island of Vis, the farthest from mainland Croatia, spent nearly 50 years in geographical and political isolation after having been taken by the Yugoslav People's Army after World War II. In 1985, the inhabitants initiated the first civil action against their oppressors, signing a petition demanding that their island be opened to foreigners. When their dreams finally came true in 1990, however, the islanders found themselves embroiled in a civil war. Since the war's end in 1995, the people of Vis have been struggling to attract tourists, all the while fishing, growing olives, and making wine as they always have. Their location does have an upside: today, Vis is the most virginal island in the Adriatic, and has a true end of the world feel.

**E TRANSPORTATION.** A **catamaran** from Hvar Town runs daily (1½hr., 1 per day, 100kn, round-trip 170kn). Jadrolinija runs a **ferry** to Vis Town from Split (2½hr., 1-2 per day, 22kn). **Buses** to Komiža meet the ferry (30min., 7 per day, 12kn). During the summer, the ferry between **Rijeka** and **Dubrovnik** stops in Vis once a week—inquire at any tourist agency in Komiža or at Jadrolinija offices on the mainland.

**■ ⁊ ORIENTATION AND PRACTICAL INFORMATION.** The town of Komiža is tiny enough that you can't get lost. The bus stops on **Hrvatskih mučenika,** and Riva (the waterfront) is just a few steps down. A right turn onto Riva leads to **Ribarska** street and to the beach, while a left turn leads to most services and sights. To get to the **tourist office,** Riva 1, face the water and walk left along the waterfront until the end of the harbor. No maps or booklets, but great staff that knows a wealth of local folklore. (☎/fax 71 34 55. Open M-Sa 8am-nooon and 6-9pm, Su 9am-noon.) Closer to the bus station, the **tourist agency Darlić & Darlić** sits at Riva 13. Mother Darlić, brother Darlić, or sister Darlić will let you check **email** on their fast computer (free), arrange accommodations (see below), and **exchange currency** for a 1% commission. (☎/fax 71 34 66; ines.darlic@st.tel.hr; www.pl-print.tel.hr/darlic. Open daily 7am-9pm.) **Splitska banka,** Trg kralja Tomislava 10, on the waterfront, exchanges cash for no commission and **traveler's checks** for a 2% commission. (☎71 82 88. Open M-F 8am-2pm, Sa 8-11:30am.) There are **no ATMs** on the island. The **pharmacy,** San Pedro 11, is the only tricky place to find; from the waterfront, turn onto Hrvatskih mučenika, then take the 2nd left. When the street curves to the left, walk straight and up the stairs onto the complex patio. (☎71 34 45. Open M-F 8am-1pm and 7-8pm, Sa 8:30-10:30am.) The **post office,** Hrvatskih mučenika 8, next to the bus station, **exchanges currency** for a 1.5% commission, cashes **traveler's checks** at no commission, and gives MC **cash advances.** There are **telephones** inside. (☎71 30 20; fax 71 35 98. Open M-Sa 8am-1pm and 6-9pm). **Postal Code:** 21485.

**⌐⌐ ACCOMMODATIONS AND FOOD.** With no camping, the only budget option is a **private room** arranged by Darlić & Darlić (see above). They will find you a bed at all costs—even in their own home. (July 15-Aug. 19 singles 90-130kn; doubles 130-180kn. July 1-10 and Aug. 19-Sept. 10 65-105kn, 90-150kn. June and Sept. 60-80kn, 75-105kn. Tourist tax 3.50-6kn. 30% surcharge for under 3 nights.)

Restaurants are scarce and pricey but excellent. Don't miss the local favorite ▩ **Konoba Bako,** Gundulićeva 1. The benches and tables are set right on the beach. (☎71 37 42. Pasta 25-40kn; meat dishes 55-65kn. Open daily 11am-1am.) For a more central location, head to **Riblji restoran** (Fish Restaurant), on the waterfront next to

Darlić & Darlić. Cephalopods are the name of the game here, from the eminently affordable octopus salad (25kn) to the speciality *crno rižoto* (risotto with squid) for 40kn. (Pasta and omelettes 22-30kn. Open daily 7am-11pm.) There's a **supermarket** right in the center on Riva. (Open M-Sa 6:30am-9pm.)

**◉ SIGHTS. St. Nicholas Church** (Crkva sv. Nikole), called Muster (monastery) by the locals, overlooks Komiža. Built as part of a Benedictine monastery in the 12th century, it now holds regular services and stays open for visitors during the morning and evening. To get there, follow any side street uphill from the waterfront. Right on the beach sits the **Pirates' Church** (Gusarica). According to legend, pirates stole a Madonna from this church, but were soon caught in a storm; only the Blessed Virgin made it back to shore. (Open daily morning and evening.) Several agencies organize daytrips to the neighboring **island**; try the ones by Darlić and Darlić (see above). Trips include the **Green Cave** on Ravnik Island (daily, 85kn), the incredible **Blue Cave** on Biševo Island (2 per day, 65kn), and **St. Andrew** (1 per week, 85kn). According to legend, the Illyrian queen Teutha was banished to the island of St. Andrew for murdering her lover. She brought with her a royal stash of gold—treasure that has yet to be found. If you'd rather spend a few days digging than a couple hours with the tour boat, ask at the tourist office about traveling there with local fishermen; they stay three to four days on the island on fishing excursions. A small permanent **exhibit** at Riva 31 houses intriguing recent finds from Palagruža—the Island of Diomedes. Placards in English explain how the shards of pottery prove that this barren rock of an island was the site of a much disputed temple to Diomedes, a Greek hero of the Trojan War. (Open daily 10am-1pm and 6-10pm. 5kn. Locals free, so sharpen your fisherman's brogue.) **The Fisherman's Museum** (Ribarski muzej), on Riva next to the tourist office has the same fishing gear you can see by the waterfront, but does offer a splendid view of the town from its rooftop. (Open M-Sa 10am-noon and 7pm-10pm, Su 7pm-10pm.)

**🎵 ENTERTAINMENT.** Komiža's **beach** is short and crowded, but that makes no difference when you're floating in water so clear you can see your toes. The most popular cafe-bar is **Speed**, Škor 12, though the name betrays the town's lazy, easygoing nightlife. The only speedy one here is the waiter, who delivers pints of *Kaltenberg* for 12kn. (Open daily 6am-1am.) For an energy boost, hit the **Voga Disco Bar**, Trup 9, right on the water between the hotel and the center; ask a local to tell you which side street to walk down. This 800-year-old building became the first disco in Croatia in 1969. It's packed every night, but not until around 1am. (0.5L *Točeno* 15kn. 0.33L *Heineken* 12kn. Open daily summer 8am-4am. Closed in the winter.)

# HVAR ISLAND: HVAR TOWN    ☎(0)21

In 1997, *Traveller* magazine named Hvar (KH-vaar) one of the ten most beautiful islands in the world. Visitors, who have been having a love affair with the island for the past 150 years, are bound to agree. The skinny 88km island affords breathtaking views of the mainland mountains from high rugged hills smothered in the scent of lavender. In the town of Hvar, the island's pride, you can buy the lavender in bouquets from street vendors.

**▐ TRANSPORTATION. Ferries** make the trip from **Split** to Hvar's **Stari Grad** (2hr., M-F 3 per day, Sa-Su 2 per day, 28kn, 180kn with car). From there, **buses** scheduled around the ferry take passengers to **Hvar Town** (15min., 11kn). Alternatively, take a **ferry** from **Split** directly to Hvar Town: there's a fast boat in the morning (1hr., 1 per day, 28kn) in addition to a regular ferry (2hr., 2 per day, 21kn). Pelegrini Tours (see below) runs a **catamaran** between Hvar and **Komiža** on Vis island during summer (1½hr., 1 per day, 100kn, round-trip 170kn).

**▰▱ ORIENTATION AND PRACTICAL INFORMATION.** Hvar Town has virtually no street names and even fewer signs, which would make navigating tricky if it were not so small. The main square, **Trg sv. Stjepana,** directly below the bus station by the waterfront (Riva), is the one place graced with a name. Facing the sea from the main square, a left along the waterfront leads to the tourist agency, post office, bank, and ferry terminal; a right leads to the major hotels and beaches. **Jadrolinija,** Riva bb on the left tip of the waterfront, sells **ferry** tickets. (☎74 11 32; fax 74 10 36. Open M-Sa 5:30am-12:30pm and 2-9pm, Su 5:30-6:30am, 10am-noon, and 2-9pm. Opening hours may vary according to ferry schedule). During the summer **Pelegrini Tours,** on Riva bb., **rents cars** (350kn per day, unlimited mileage) and bikes (50kn per day) for exploring the rest of the island. (☎/fax 74 22 50. Open M-Sa 8:30am-12:30pm and 6-9pm, Su 6-8pm.) The **tourist office, Turistička Zajednica,** Trg sv. Stjepana 21, is in the corner of the main square closest to the water. Smiling staff has detailed **maps** and bus schedules. (☎/fax 74 10 59; tz-hvar@st.tel.hr; www.hvar.hr. Open M-Sa 8am-2pm and 4-10pm, Su 9am-noon and 6-9pm.) **Splitska Banka,** Riva 4, **exchanges currency** for no commission and cashes **traveler's checks** for a 2% commission. (Open M-F 7:30am-1pm and 2-8pm, Sa 8-11:30am.) There's a Visa **ATM** outside the bank and a AmEx/Cirrus/MC **ATM** across the harbor in front of Zagrebačka Banka. A **pharmacy** sits at Trg Sv. Stjepana bb. (☎74 10 02. Open M-F 8am-9pm, Sa 8am-1pm and 5:30-8:30pm, Su 9am-noon.) The **post office,** Riva 5, has **telephones** inside and **Poste Restante.** (☎74 24 13. Open M-Sa 7am-10pm.) **Postal code:** 21450.

▓▓ **ACCOMMODATIONS AND FOOD.** As in other Croatian resort towns, the only budget accommodations are **private rooms,** and even those are expensive; Pelegrini Tours (see above) can arrange them. (May 1-June 26 and Sept. 25-Oct. 23 singles 97kn; doubles 124kn. June 26-July 24 and Aug. 28-Sept. 25 113kn; 156kn. July 24-Aug. 29 125kn; 170kn. 30% surcharge for stays under 3 nights.) Many locals hang around the bus station offering rooms for less. If all else fails, try your luck finding *sobe* (room) signs down the waterfront from the main square.

Overpriced restaurants line the waterfront and the square. Eat away from other tourists under hanging lanterns and grapevines at **Alviz,** across from the bus station. (Crepes 15-25kn, pizza 28-43kn. Open daily 6pm-1am.) Tucked back from the main square on the street ascending to the fortress, **Macondo** devastates the travel budget but leaves you most content. (*Big Mama* (steak stuffed with cheese, ham, and olives) 65kn; shellfish and mussels 40-80kn; pasta 30-35kn. Open daily noon-2pm and 6:30pm-midnight.) There's a cheap **open-air market** between the bus station and the main square. (Open daily 7am-8pm.) The **supermarket,** Trg sv. Stjepana bb, is small but well-stocked. (Open M-Sa 6am-10pm, Su 6am-noon.)

▣ **SIGHTS.** The best way to see town is from above. Facing the sea, a side street to the right of the square leads up to the 13th-century **Venetian fortress.** In the past the fortress suffered severe blows from Turks, but the lightning that once struck the powder-room was more devastating. (Open daily 9am-11pm. 10kn.) Inside, you'll find a **marine archaeological collection** (*hidroarheološka zbirka*), consisting primarily of Greek and Byzantine amphorae. (Open daily 10am-1pm. Free.) Also in the fortress is a patio where soft dance hits play in the early evening, and rages as a popular **disco** late into the night. (Open nightly 10pm-5am.) Any remaining museum-going thirst can be quenched at the central **Gallery Arsenal** (open daily 10am-noon and 8-11pm; 10kn, students free), or at the **Last Supper Collection** in the **Franciscan monastery,** which includes the *other* famous *Last Supper*, painted in oil by Matteo Ignoli. (Open daily 10am-noon and 5-6pm. 10kn.)

▓▓ **FESTIVALS AND NIGHTLIFE.** The Franciscan monastery hosts many outdoor performances of the **Hvar Summer Festival.** Some of the indoor performances take place above the Arsenal in one of Europe's oldest **community theaters,** dating from 1612. (Festival performances 30-50kn.) For 10 days every summer in either July or August, Hvar hosts the **Shakespeare Days** festival. An celebration of the bard's work by international actors and directors, including performances and workshops at the monastery. Inquire at the tourist office (see above) for more information. The most crowded bars are along the waterfront. For something smaller and more intimate, head to ▧ **The Café,** Burak bb., on a side street uphill

**TO HELL AND BACK** If you make the trip out to one of the Hellish islands (Pakleni Otoci), you will no doubt ask yourself why on earth such lush green beauties deserve their dark title. The answer is an exercise in word play. The singular form of 'pakleni' is 'paklina,' which means tar—the black tar used by fishermen to seal the hulls of their boats. 'Paklina' is similar in pronunciation to the word 'pakao,' which means hell. So what should translate literally as the 'Tar Islands' has been damned forever by a slip of the tongue. But if the name succeeds at all in warding off the tourist masses for the rest of us, we should be grateful to go to hell and back.

from the post office. Friendly owners serve fresh-squeezed juice (melon juice 13kn, orange juice 17kn) and hot sandwiches (12kn). If the green interior touches your Irish side, have a pint of *Guinness* (30kn). A computer inside offers fast **Internet** connections (0.50kn per min., 5min. minimum. Open daily 9:30am-1am).

◨▨ **BEACHES AND ISLANDS.** Some of the Adriatic's clearest waters surround Hvar, but to enjoy them you'll have to brave the loud, crowded, gravel **beaches** and fearsome aquatic hedgehogs. The less crowded ones are a 15-20 minutes walk to the left down the waterfront. You may instead choose to head out to the nearby **Hellish Islands** (Pakleni otoci): Jevolim, Ždrilca, and Palmižana. The latter is home to the sandy **Palmižana beach.** Boats in the harbor run a **taxi service** between them. (Boats run every 30min. starting at 10am, last boats back to Hvar around 6:30pm; round-trip 20-25kn.) The **diving center** in Hotel Amfora, on the beach, offers **diving** and rentals. (☎/fax 74 24 90. Open daily 10am-6pm. Shore dives including equipment 133-150kn; 1 boat dive with equipment 122kn; 2 for 245kn. Bike rental 54kn per day; motorboats 200kn per day; snorkel equipment 31kn per day; kayaks 30kn per hr.)

# KORČULA ISLAND: KORČULA TOWN ☎(0)20

Like Corfu, Korčula (KOR-chu-lah) got its name from the Greek words *korkyra melaina* (black), because of the macchia thickets, woods, and preponderance of slender cypress trees cloaking the island. The Korčula Town (pop. 3000) faces the stunning mountains of the Croatian mainland, just a short ferry trip away. The island's proximity to the mainland makes it an ideal trip *en route* from Split to Dubrovnik, but more attractive than its location is its distinctive personality. Weekly sword dances in the summer, local musicians, and the friendliness of the natives combine to make a small town rich in culture and unique in Croatia.

▐ **TRANSPORTATION.** Korčula is one of the few islands served by buses; they board a ferry to the island. The **bus station** is at Porat bb. (☎71 12 16. Ticket and info window open M-Sa 6:30-9am, 9:30am-4pm, and 4:30-7pm and Su 2-7pm). **Buses** run to: **Dubrovnik** (3½hr., 1 per day, 58kn); **Split** (5hr., 1 per day, 90kn); **Zagreb** (11-13hr., 1 per day, 190kn); and **Sarajevo, BOS** (6½hr., 4 per week, 145kn). For **ferry information** and **tickets,** check the **Jadrolinija** office, 20m toward the Old Town from the ferry landing. (☎71 54 10; fax 71 11 01. Open M-W and F 7:30am-8pm, Th 7:30am-3pm, Sa 7:30am-6pm, Su 8am-1pm.) **Ferries** run to **Vis** (3hr., 1 per week, 54kn); **Dubrovnik** (3½hr., 5 per week, 64kn); and **Split** (4½hr., 1 per day, 74kn). Ferries from other destinations arrive in **Vela Luka** on the opposite side of the island. A bus connects Vela Luka to Korčula Town (1hr., 5 per day, 20kn). For a **taxi,** call ☎71 54 52 or 71 11 95.

▟▨ **ORIENTATION AND PRACTICAL INFORMATION.** The town is situated beside the sea on the northeast end of the island. **Stari Grad** (Old Town) was built on a small oval peninsula, its streets drawn up in a herringbone pattern. Outside the city walls, medieval, Baroque, and modern houses mix together, eventually tapering off into resort hotels farther down along the coastline. Street addresses are scarce, but the town is small and easily navigable. The **tourist office, Turistička zajednica,** is on the opposite side of the peninsula from the bus and ferry terminals. To

CROATIA

get there, face the water and walk left around the peninsula to Hotel Korčula; the office is next door. A well-staffed office hands out schedules for the Sword Festival (see below) and books accommodations. (Open M-Sa 8am-3pm and 4-9pm, Su 9am-1pm.) **Splitska Banka,** in front of the stairs leading to Stari Grad, **exchanges currency** for no commission, cashes **traveler's checks** for a 2% commission, gives Visa **cash advances,** and offers **Western Union** services. (☎71 10 52. Open M-F 7:30am-7:30pm, Sa 7:30-11am.) There are two Visa **ATMs** in Korčula, one outside Splitska Banka and one across the square outside Dubrovačka Banka. The **pharmacy,** Trg kralja Tomislava bb, is at the foot of the Stari Grad stairs. (☎71 10 57. Open M-F 7am-8pm, Sa 7am-noon and 6-8pm, Su 9-11am.) For **Internet access,** head to **PC Centar Artina.** Facing the water, walk right along the street that follows the coastline for 10 minutes; Artina is in front of Hotel Park. (☎71 10 57. 10kn per 15min., 25kn per hr. Open daily 8:30am-12:30pm and 5-8pm.) The **post office,** Trg Kralja Tomislava 1, hidden behind the palms next to the pharmacy, has **telephones** inside and out and **exchanges currency** and **traveler's checks** for 1.5% commission. (☎71 11 32. Open M-F 7am-9pm, Sa 8am-8pm.) **Postal code:** 20260.

**⌐⌐☐ ACCOMMODATIONS AND FOOD. Private rooms** are the only budget accommodations available. **Marko Polo,** Biline 5, will arrange one for you with a smile. They're right on the waterfront where the ferry docks. (☎71 54 00; fax 71 58 00; marko-polo-tours@du.tel.hr. Open daily 8am-10pm. Singles 76-160kn; doubles 100-212kn; triples 140-272kn. Prices depend on season. Tourist tax 4.50-7kn.) If they have no available rooms, head to the tourist office (see above) to see if they can bed you down. Alternatively, head uphill from the bus station away from Stari Grad and look for *sobe* (room) signs. If you're packing a tent, you can pitch it at **Autocamp Kalac.** (☎71 11 82 and 72 63 36; fax 71 17 46. Reception open daily 7am-10pm. 24kn per person; 12kn per car; 7kn tourist tax. No rented tents.) A bus runs directly to the camp from the station. (10min., every hr., 4kn.)

Eating out in Korčula is expensive. For the frugal, there's a **supermarket** next to Marko Polo (open M-Sa 6:30am-9pm, Su 7am-9pm) and a **market** to the right of the stairs up to Stari Grad (open daily 6am-9pm). For gourmets, ■ **Adio Mare,** Marka Pola bb, next to Marco Polo's house, is hands down the best restaurants in Croatia. This popular cellar eatery spoils the stomach with sumptious *Korčulanska Pasticada* (Korčula beef stewed in vegetables, onions and plum sauce with Dalmatian dumplings) for 60kn or *Ražnjic Adio Mare* (mixed meats skewered with apples, onions, and bacon) for 55kn. (Main dishes 40-70kn. Open M-Sa 1-11pm, Su 6-11pm.) Up the double staircase by the Hotel Korčula, **Pizzeria Agava,** Cvit. Bokšic 6, serves cheap pizzas (22-35kn) and jumbo pizzas (53-66kn; open daily 8am-midnight).

**◎ SIGHTS.** Korčula's grandest tribute to its patron, **St. Mark's Cathedral** (Katedrala Sv. Marka), stands at the highest point of the Stari Grad peninsula. Planning began in the 14th century, inspired by the founding of the Korčula Bishopric and the confidence of a strong economy, but construction wasn't completed until 1525. The large blocks of limestone came from the island. The Gothic-Renaissance cathedral is complimented by the adjacent, older **bell tower.** (Services daily at 6:30pm and Su at 7am, 9:30am, and 6:30pm.) The **Abbey Treasury of St. Mark** (Opatska Riznica Sv. Marka), next to the cathedral, contains collections of 12th-century manuscripts, Renaissance and Baroque drawings, contemporary paintings and sculptures, and coins ranging from 3rd-century BC Greek pieces to a 1972 American penny. (Open M-Sa 9am-1pm and 5-6:30pm, Su 11pm-1am. 8kn.) The **Town Museum** (Gradski Muzej) sits opposite the treasury in the Renaissance Gabrielis Palace. Four floors display multiple faces of Korčula's history and culture; highlights include 5000-year-old knives from Badija, a 3rd-century BC Greek tablet listing some of the city's first colonists, and a 19th-century wedding dress. (Open M-Sa 9am-1pm and 7-9pm. 10kn, students free.) **Marco Polo's House,** supposedly where the famed explorer was born in 1254 (though the history remains vague), is a late-Gothic ruin to the left of the cathedral. No Polo artifacts await in the house tower, but it does offer great views of the city and cathedral. (Open daily 9am-1pm and 5-9pm. 5kn.)

**EN GARDE** The Moreška sword dance, first recorded in Korčula in the 17th century, may have started after the Turkish siege in 1571. Over the next few centuries it was performed all over the Mediterranean, but it has been preserved only in Korčula. It is characterized by simple, fluid movements, swordsmanship, and a folk drama symbolizing a battle between Christians and Muslims. The dance is performed by two groups of young men called *moreškanti.* They are led by kings and fight for Bula, the Christian king's fiancée, who was kidnapped by the Muslim King Moro. After a dialogue between the kings and Bula's subsequent refusal of Moro, the armies collide; the wind orchestra accompanying the dance quickens its tempo as the clashing of the swords grows fiercer. Predictably, the Christians win and Bula is returned. Today, you can catch the dance (updated, with dancers flying the Croatian flag above their heads), during the Sword Dance Festival.

**FESTIVALS AND NIGHTLIFE. Carnival celebrations,** including weekly masked balls (maškare), are held from Epiphany to Ash Wednesday. All events are free. The **Festival of Sword Dances** (Festival Viteških Igara) takes place every summer from July 5 to August 23. The Moreška, Moštra, and Kumpanija sword dances are performed throughout the island. In the city of Korčula, you can catch a performance of the Moreška at least once a week. Tickets are available at any major tourist agency (40kn), but to save money, plan to come for the free shows on July 28 and 29. The first two weeks of September liven up for the **Marco Polo Festival.** Events include folk entertainment and a grand reconstruction of the famous 1298 naval battle in the Pelješac channel between Korčula and the mainland. (All events free.) The September 7 battle, reenacted on the same day, brought Signore Polo and the forces of Venetian Korčula into combat with the navy from Genoa. The Genoese won and Polo was imprisoned. All the spare time inspired him to dictate the memoirs that made him famous.

For a taste of Latin nightlife, head right down the waterfront to ■ **Dos Locos,** Borak 90. Cocktails like *Kiss me Loco* (30kn) and *Watermelon Man* (30kn) fuel sweaty, happy salsa dancers. (Open daily 9am-2am.) The techno crowd gathers near the bus station at **Amadeus,** Put Brodograditelja bb. (Draft beer 10kn. Open M-Sa 6am-2am, Su 7am-2am.)

# DUBROVNIK                                                        (0)20

Those who seek Paradise on Earth should come to Dubrovnik.
   —George Bernard Shaw

Endless epithets have been given to Dubrovnik, including "the pearl of the Adriatic" and "the city made of stone and light," but words fail to grasp the majesty of this walled city, wedged between the Adriatic Sea and the Dinaric Alps. Ravaged by war and Serbian shells in 1991 and 1992, Dubrovnik is miraculously almost scarless; only close inspection reveals bullet holes and crumbled buildings. Instead, as the 30,000 fiercely proud residents will attest, Dubrovnik is defined by its Mediterranean grace and its uncanny resemblance to paradise. The azure waters, copper sunsets from atop the 14th-century city walls, and glistening Italian marble of the central plaza are almost as enchanting as the cadence of the local dialect. If you make it as far south as Dubrovnik—and you must—you just might never leave.

**ORIENTATION**

The walled **Stari Grad** (Old Town) is the city's cultural, historical, and commercial center. Its main street, called both **Placa** and **Stradun,** runs from the **Pile Gate,** the official entrance of Stari Grad, to the **Old Port** at the tip of the peninsula. The main traffic arteries, **Put Republike** and **Ante Starčevića,** embrace the **bus station** (from the front and rear, respectively), merge into Ante Starčevića, and end at the Pile Gate.

CROATIA

To the west of Stari Grad, two hilly peninsulas—**Babin Kuk** and **Lapad**—jut out from the mainland. Both are home to modern settlements, sand beaches, and numerous hotels. Dubrovnik has **no train station.**

While it may be tempting to explore the beautiful bare mountains rising above Dubrovnik, don't—the city was shelled from atop these very peaks, which may still hide landmines.

# ▐■ TRANSPORTATION

**Buses:** Put Republike 38 (☎35 70 88). To get to Stari Grad, face the bus station, walk around to the other side of the building, and turn left onto Ante Starčevića. Follow this road uphill; the street numbers decrease as you approach Stari Grad. Ante Starčevića runs straight to the Pile Gate (30min.). Local buses (see below) running to Stari Grad stop at a number of places along Ante Starčevića. To: **Split** (4½hr., 14 per day, 47-85kn); **Zadar** (8hr., 6 per day, 142kn); **Zagreb** (11hr., 8 per day, 135-173kn); **Rijeka** (12hr., 4 per day, 242kn); **Mostar, BOS** (3hr., 3 per day, 54-85kn); **Sarajevo, BOS** (6hr., 2 per day, 163kn); **Ljubljana, SLN** (14hr., 1 per day, 154kn); **Trieste, ITA** (15hr., 1 per day, 225kn); and **Frankfurt, GER** (27hr., 1 per day, 740kn).

**Ferries: Jadrolinija,** Obala S. Radića 40 (☎41 80 00; ☎/fax 41 81 11). Open M, Tu and Th 8am-8pm; W and F 8am-8pm and 9-11pm; Sa 8am-2pm and 7-8pm; Su 8-10am and 7-8:30pm. The ferry terminal is across from the Jadrolinija office. To reach the terminal, face away from the bus station and head left; when the road forks, go right; it's a 5min. walk. To: **Split** (8hr., 1 per day, 80kn); **Zadar** (16hr., 1 per week, 140kn); **Rijeka** (22hr., 1 per day, 180kn); and **Bari, ITA** (9hr., 2 per week, 270kn).

**Public Transportation:** All buses except #5, 7, and 8 go to Stari Grad's Pile Gate. Tickets 7kn at newsstands, 10kn from the driver. Exact change required except on buses 1a and 1b. No cheating the system here, the driver checks everyone's ticket.

**Taxis:** ☎35 70 44. In front of the bus station, the ferry terminal, and the Pile Gate. 25kn plus 8kn per km. 50kn from the bus station to Stari Grad.

# ▐? PRACTICAL INFORMATION

## TOURIST AND FINANCIAL SERVICES

**Tourist Office: Turistička Zajednica Grada Dubrovnika,** Cvijete Zuzoric 1/2 (☎42 63 03 and 42 63 04; fax 42 24 80; tzgd@du.del.hr; www.laus.hr/dubrovnik). Walk to the end of Placa, turn right between **St. Blasius' Church** and cafe Gradska Kavana, and take the 1st right; the office is on the 2nd floor. Friendly English-speaking staff answers questions, and hands out the invaluable *City Guide,* complete with listings of hotels and restaurants, local bus schedules, ferry schedules, and concert dates. Open M-F 8am-3pm, Sa 9am-1pm, Su 9am-noon. **Turistički Informativni Centar (TIC),** Placa bb (☎42 63 54 and 42 63 56; fax 42 63 55). Right next to the fountain at the head of Placa. Arranges private rooms, dispenses info, **exchanges currency** for 1.5% commission, develops photos, sells film, **maps** (10kn), posters, and stamps. Open daily in summer 9am-9pm, off-season 9am-8pm.

**Budget Travel: Atlas,** Lučarica 1 (☎44 25 28; fax 42 02 05; atlas@atlas.tel.hr; www.atlas-croatia.com). Next to St. Blasius's Church at the end of Placa. Arranges accommodations, sells plane and ferry tickets (student discounts with Euro 26), **exchanges currency** for a 1% commission, and cashes and sells AmEx traveler's cheques. Organizes tours to: **Neretva River Delta** (1 per week, 315kn with lunch); **Mljet National Park** (3 per week, 280kn); **Mostar** (2 per week, 200kn); and the **Elafiti Islands** (2 per week, 390kn). Other branches at sv. Durda 1 (☎44 25 74; fax 44 25 70), near the Pile Gate, and at Grušla Obala (☎41 80 01; fax 41 83 30) near the ferry terminal. All open in summer M-Sa 8am-9pm, Su 9am-1pm; off-season M-Sa 8am-7pm.

CROATIA

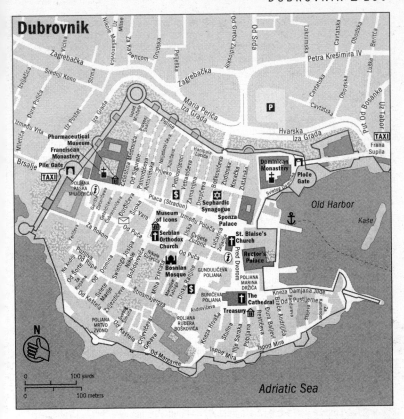

**Currency Exchange: Dubrovačka Banka,** Placa 16 (☎41 29 67). Exchanges currency and cashes traveler's checks for no commission. Open M-F 7:30am-1pm and 2-9pm, Sa 7:30am-1pm and 2-8pm, Su 8am-noon. Also next to the bus station, Put Republike 9. Open M-F 7:30am-1pm and 2-9pm, Sa 7:30am-1pm. Also at **Atlas** (see above).

**ATM:** Cirrus/MC at Brsalje 9, outside Croatia Airlines, and at Placa 4, on the corner with Zlatarska. 24hr. AmEx/Visa at the ferry terminal and on Lučarica bb, next to Atlas and St. Blasius's Church.

## LOCAL AND EMERGENCY SERVICES

**Luggage Storage:** At the bus station. 1kn per hr. for bags under 15kg, 2kn per hr. for bags over 15kg. Open daily 4:50am-9pm.

**International Bookstore: Algoritam,** Placa 8 (☎/fax 42 64 31). Loads of English-language paperbacks, the best international magazine selection in town, and guidebooks in 9 languages. Open daily 9am-10:30pm.

**Pharmacy:** Ljekarna Mala Braća, Placa 2 (☎42 63 72), inside the Franciscan monastery just within the Pile gate—the oldest working pharmacy in Europe. Open daily 8am-2pm. **Night service** (8pm-8am) either at Ljekarna Gruž, Gruška Obala bb. (☎41 89 90), at the ferry terminal, or Ljekarna Kod Zvonika Placa 1 (☎42 86 56).

**Internet Acces: Cyber Club DuNet,** Put Republike 7, room 112 (☎35 68 94). With your back to the bus station, walk right past Dubrovačka Banka to the black glass building next to it; it's upstairs. 5kn per 10min., students 4kn. Open daily 8am-midnight.

**Post Office,** Put Republike 28 (☎41 39 68). With your back to the bus station, walk right for 100m. Turn left at the "ginekološka ordinacija" sign and walk right around the

construction site. The post office is on the left side of the large stone building. **Poste Restante.** Open M-F 8am-9pm, Sa 8am-7pm, Su 8am-noon. The post office in Stari Grad, on Široka, has **telephones** inside and is much more conveniently located than the main branch. Open M-F 8am-9pm, Sa 9am-1pm and 6-9pm.
**Postal code:** 20 000.

# ACCOMMODATIONS

Dubrovnik offers accommodations in a wide range of locales: city center, beachside in Lapad, or close to the ferry terminal. For two people, a **private room** is the cheapest option; arrange one through the TIC or Atlas (see **Tourist and Financial Services,** above). Both offer singles (100-150kn) and doubles (120-180kn) in and around Stari Grad. For cheaper rooms, try your luck with the women who spend their days spotting backpackers around the bus and ferry terminals. Shrewd haggling tactics can win you singles for 60kn (doubles 100kn), but make sure you're sleeping legally (see **But it's so cheap...,** below). There are campgrounds 20km from town.

■ **Youth Hostel (HI),** B. Josipa Jelačića 15/17 (☎ 42 32 41; ☎/fax 41 25 92; hfhs-du@du.hinet.hr). From the bus station, walk 10min. up ul. Ante Starčevića, turn right at the lights, and right again after 40m onto b. Josipa Jelačića. Look for a well-concealed HI sign on your left immediately before #17. Climb up all the stairs to reach the steps to the hostel. From the ferries, take bus #12 toward "Pile" and get off at the stop after the bus station, at the aforementioned traffic lights. A 15min. walk from the city center, and hands down Croatia's best hostel. Clean doubles, quads, and 6-person dorms. Hall bathrooms with spotless blue tiled floors, an outdoor terrace, and a TV/dining room. Check-out 10am. Curfew 2am. July 15-Aug. 20 87kn, June 1-July 14 and Aug. 21-Sept. 15 79kn, May and Sept. 16-Oct. 30 73kn; Nov.-Dec. 65kn. Breakfast included.

■ **Begović Boarding House,** Primorska 17 (☎ 43 51 91; fax 45 27 52). From the bus station, take bus #6 toward Dubrava and tell the driver you want to get off at post office Lapad. Facing the walkway, turn right at the intersection. Go left at the fork, and take the 1st right onto Primorska. #17 is near the top of the hill on the left. Call ahead and the delightfully hospitable owner, Sado, will pick you up at the bus or ferry terminal. 10min. by bus to the center, but the sandy beach is just a staircase away. A cozy villa of 10 airy rooms with double beds, kitchenettes and a spectacular terrace view. Shared bath. Reserve at least 10 days ahead. July-Aug. 85kn per person, Sept.-June 75kn.

**Hotel Zagreb,** Šetalište Kralja Zvonimira 31 (☎ 43 61 46; fax 43 60 06). From the bus station, take bus #6 toward Dubrava and tell the driver you want to get off at post office Lapad. Walk through the 1st intersection and proceed onto the pedestrian Šetalište Kralja Zvonimira. #31 is on the left. Beautiful location close to the beach. Clean rooms with hardwood floors, bath, TV, phone, and large windows. Reception 24hr. Check-out noon. July 9-Sept. 2 singles 265kn; doubles 430kn. June 11-July 8 and Sept. 3-Sept. 30 230kn; 360kn. May 1-June 10 and Oct. 190kn; 290kn. Jan.-Apr. and Nov.-Dec. 150kn; 240kn. Tax 4.50-7kn. Breakfast included.

# FOOD

If you're coming from Split, you'll be pleasantly surprised by the abundance of restaurants in Dubrovnik, but disappointed by higher prices and limited variety. Most places feature seafood-oriented menus, risotto, and some pasta. **Prijeko,** the first street parallel to Placa on the left when coming from the Pile Gate, is packed with cookie-cutter *konobi* (pubs), competing obnoxiously for patrons—stay away if you like your money and good food. The **outdoor market,** on Gundulićeva Poljana, sits behind St. Blasius' Church. **Supermarket Mediator,** Od puča 4, faces the market. (Open M-Sa 6:30am-9pm, Su 7am-9pm.)

■ **Marco Polo,** Lučarica 6 (☎ 42 23 04). While many of Dubrovnik's restaurants have lowered their standards for the 'easy-to-please' tourist appetite, this place puts food quality first. In a quiet alley off of Lučarica, with fantastic meals at reasonable prices. Meats 45-76kn, calamari and prawns 45kn, pastas 35-40kn. Open daily 10am-midnight.

**BUT IT'S SO CHEAP...** Descending wearily from the ferry or bus in Dubrovnik, you will hear chants of *sobe!*, *rooms!*, and *zimmer!* from the throngs of ladies done up in their Sunday best to lure the traveler to their rooms for rent. While the prospect of a place to lie down and an appealing price may seem ideal at the time, there are a few considerations to keep in mind before you tramp off with the lady of your choice. Most importantly, if Dubrovnik is your first stop in Croatia, you must **register** with the police (see **Croatia Essentials**, p. 152). If the rooms you see are sanctioned by the tourist office (if a stamped, signed document with the price listed is posted in the room), then you're good to go: the lady will file your passport number with the proper authorities. Otherwise, keep out. Large and unnecessary fines ensue if for any reason the police find you unregistered. Besides, rooms that have not been inspected by the tourist office may not necessarily meet its requirements, which include hot water and clean sheets. So pick your women wisely and well.

🗷 **Buffet Škola,** Antuninska 1 (☎41 67 90), just off Placa. The best little sandwich shop in Croatia. Local *sir iz ulje* (cheese in oil) and the famous *dalmatinski pršut* (Dalmatian ham) layered between thick slices of homemade bread (14-19kn per sandwich). Unbeatable prices keep customers coming back for more. Open daily 9am-midnight.

**Buffet Kamenice,** Gundulićeva Poljana 8 (☎42 14 99), behind the market. One of the shortest and cheapest menus in town. Good food served under outdoor umbrellas. Bees from the market can and will make advances, so protect your food. Pasta and mussels 30kn. Main dishes 15-45kn. Open daily 7am-2am.

**Chinese Restaurant Shanghai,** Ante Starčevića 25 (☎42 57 54). With your back to Pile Gate, walk 200m uphill. The Chinese owners cook good semi-authentic Chinese food, but the terrace is right on noisy Starčevića. Largest selection of vegetarian dishes in town (18-29kn). Main dishes 30-70kn. Open Tu-Su noon-midnight.

## 👁 SIGHTS

Stari Grad is a condensed zone of churches, museums, monasteries, palaces, and fortresses—every angle is an eyeful. The most obvious sights are those along the broad Placa, but much of Dubrovnik's fascinating history is found off the beaten path. Side streets reveal a broad diversity of religious practice: a mosque on one corner neighbors an orthodox church on the next.

**CITY WALLS.** (Gradske zidine.) 1940 uninterrupted meters of limestone with an average thickness of 1.5m—reaching 25m high in places—join together four round towers, two corner towers, three fortresses, 12 quadrilateral forts, five bastions, two land gates, two ports gates, and a partridge in a pear tree; one need not wonder why they're world-famous. Walls enclosed the entire city as early as the 13th century. Extensive work was carried out toward the end of the 14th century, when Dubrovnik was liberated from Venetian rule, to protect against potential Turk attackers after the fall of Constantinople in 1453. Once you've seen the sunset from the top of the walls, you'll feel like G.B. Shaw. Take our friendly advice: give yourself at least an hour and a roll of film. *(Entrances to the walk on the walls are at Pile gate and the old port. 10kn. Open daily 8am-sunset, about 7-8pm in summer.)*

**CATHEDRAL OF THE ASSUMPTION OF THE VIRGIN MARY AND TREASURY.** (Riznica Katedrale.) The present-day Baroque structure was erected after the previous Romanesque cathedral (built from the 12th to 14th centuries) was destroyed in a massive earthquake in 1667. In 1981, the foundations of a 7th-century Byzantine cathedral were found beneath the cathedral floor; this discovery led to considerable revision of Dubrovnik's history. The cathedral treasury houses religious relics collected by Richard the Lionheart, refugees from the Roman town of Epidaurium, and a few centuries of fishermen. Crusaders in the 12th century brought back a silver casket from Jerusalem that contains 2000-year-old cloth material

CROATIA

alledgedly worn by Jesus—don't miss the 'Diapers of Jesus' in the treasury. *(Kneza Damjana Jude 1. From Pile gate, follow Placa to the Bell Tower and turn right to Poljana Marina Džića. Cathedral open daily 9am-8pm. Treasury open daily 9am-5pm. 5kn.)*

**CHURCH OF ST. BLASIUS.** (Crkva Sv. Vlaha.) Named for Dubrovnik's patron saint in 1715, this church was built on the site of a structure that was damaged in the 1667 earthquake and then obliterated in a 1706 fire. The city senate hired Venetian architect Marino Gropelli to design the present Baroque church. The high altar boasts a 15th-century gilt silver statue of St. Blasius—the only surviving relic of the fire and a symbol of the saint's miraculous powers. Statues of Blasius abound along the city walls, and a feast in his honor takes place every February 3. *(At the Bell Tower end of Placa, on the right. Open 9am-noon and 6-9pm.)*

**SPONZA PALACE AND CITY ARCHIVES.** (Palača Sponza i Arhiv.) From its successful rebellion against Venetian rule in 1358 until its occupation by Napoleon in 1808, Dubrovnik was a free republic (Respublica Ragusina) and its heart was the Sponza Palace. The Gothic-Renaissance structure housed the customs office, the mint, the bank, the treasury, the armory, and most of the state offices. When the palace miraculously survived the 1667 earthquake, the Republic survived with it. Historical documents from the 12th century to the present are kept here in the city archives. *(At the Bell Tower end of Placa on the left. Open daily 10am-2pm and 7-11pm. 5kn.)*

**FRANCISCAN MONASTERY AND PHARMACEUTICAL MUSEUM.** (Franjevački samostan.) Stunning stonework marks this 14th-century monastery. The southern portal that opens onto Placa includes a Pietà relief by the Petrović brothers—it stands as the only element left from the original Franciscan church. The cloister was built in 1360 by Mihoje Brajkov; no two capitals of the colonnade are the same. The monastery also houses the oldest working pharmacy in Europe, established in 1317, while the small museum displays elegant medicinal containers and historical tools along with a collection of gold and silver jewelry. *(Placa 2. On the left side of Placa, just inside Pile gate. Monastery and museum open daily 9am-6pm. Museum 5kn.)*

**RECTOR'S PALACE AND CULTURAL-HISTORICAL MUSEUM.** (Knežev dvor i Kulturno-Povijesni Muzej.) A fortress stood at this site during the early Middle Ages, but in the 14th century, documents began to refer to the building as a *palatium* (palace). Renaissance, Gothic, and Baroque restorations and additions followed through the centuries as the palace saw repeated damage from fires, earthquakes, and gunpowder explosions. Upstairs houses an elegant 18th-century furniture exhibit, a 16th-century firearms display, and a collection of royal seals. *(Pred Dvorom 3. Across from the Church of St. Blasius at the end of Placa. Open daily in summer 9am-7pm, off-season M-Sa 9am-1pm. 10kn, students 5kn.)*

**DOMINICAN MONASTERY AND MUSEUM.** (Muzej Dominikanskog Samostana.) Dominicans established the monastery in 1225, but construction went on until the 15th century. The massive Dominican church is one the largest on the east Adriatic coast, but is simple in design and decoration. The museum exhibits a good stock of standard church art, as well as some nonstandard gold jewelry. *(Sv. Dominika 4. From Pile gate, walk all the down Placa and continue straight through the arch under the Bell Tower. The monastery is up the stairs on the left after the arch. Open daily 9am-6pm. 5kn.)*

**ORTHODOX CHURCH AND MUSEUM OF ICONS.** (Pravoslavna Crkva i Muzej Ikona.) Around 2000 Serbs live in Dubrovnik—approximately a third of the population that existed here before the 1991-1995 civil war—and their church stands as a symbol of Dubrovnik's continued ethnic and religious tolerance. The museum houses a wide variety of 15th- to 19th-century icons gathered by local families. Traditionally each Serb household is protected by a specific Saint and any member of the family traveling abroad collects icons to that Saint. Also on display is a permanent exhibit of paintings by the Croatian master Vlaho Bukovać (1855-1922). *(Od Puča 8. From Pile gate, walk 100m down Placa and turn right onto Široka, the widest side street. Turn left down Od Puča and the church and museum are on the left. Church open daily 8am-noon and 5-7pm. Museum open M-Sa 9am-1pm, 10kn.)*

**MOSQUE.** (Džamija.) This apartment-turned-mosque serves Dubrovnik's 4000 Bosnian Muslims. The beautifully carpeted room is divided in two: one half contains an Islamic school for children and the other is used for prayer. A small antechamber serves as a social center for members of the Bosnian community, who aren't used to many tourist visits but will be glad to let you in as long as you take off your shoes. *(Miha Pracata 3. From Pile gate, walk down Placa and take the 8th street on the right, M. Pracata. The mosque is marked only by a small door sign on the left side of the street. Open daily 10am-1pm and 8-9pm.)*

**SEPHARDIC SYNAGOGUE.** (Sinagoga.) Round off your tour of the religious world with a visit to the 2nd-oldest existing (but no longer functional) Sephardic synagogue in Europe (the oldest one is the Old-New Synagogue in Prague). The city's 46 Jews have their offices inside. Most of the Jewish archives from Dubrovnik were lost under Nazi occupation, but a number of families risked their lives to hide much of the synagogue's interior in their own homes. *(Žudioska 5. From the Bell Tower, walk toward Pile gate and take the 3rd right onto Žudioska. Open M, Th, and F 11am-1pm.)*

#  BEACHES AND FESTIVALS

There aren't any beaches in the center of town, but the water is clear enough to allow bathing almost anywhere. For sand, palms, and crowds, hop on bus #6 toward Dubrava and ask to get off at post office Lapad. Head straight through the intersection onto the pedestrian boulevard and follow the bikinis. The most popular option, however, is the nearby island of **Lokrum,** which features a **nude beach** for the brave (or the anxious). Ferries go there daily from the Old Port. (15min., every 30min. 9am-8pm, 20kn round-trip.) Once there, take a break from the sun to stroll through the botanical garden. If you have an entire day to spare, go straight to the fantastic sands of the Elafiti Archipelago (see **Lopud,** p. 202).

From July 10 to August 15, the ▨ **Dubrovnik Summer Festival** (Dubrovački Ljetni Festival) transforms the city into a cultural mecca and a crazy party scene. The country's most prominent artists in theater, ballet, opera, classical music, jazz, and rock all perform. Three or four times in July, Hamlet (or another Shakespearean classic) is performed at the towering Lovrjenac Fortress just outside Pile gate. Summer 2001 will see Croatian 'ER' star Goran Višnjić brooding as the prince, but tickets will sell out at least a month in advance. The Festival office on Placa hands out schedules, sells tickets (50-300kn), and raves about Goran. (☎42 88 64; fax 42 79 44. Open during the festival daily for info 8:30am-9pm, for tickets 9am-2pm and 3-7pm.) Provided the show isn't sold out, you can buy tickets at the entrance one hour before it starts. For information and ticket reservations during the off-season, contact the head office at Poljana Oaska Miličevica 1, across from Pile Gate. (☎41 22 88; fax 42 63 51; program@dubrovnik-fesitval.hr; www.dubrovnik-festival.hr.)

#  NIGHTLIFE

Among Croatian cities, Dubrovnik is by far the liveliest at night. Crowds congregate in a few areas: often, they'll overflow from **Stari Grad** and the cafes on **Buničeva Poljana.** Another great center of nightlife lies on **B. Josipa Jelačića,** also known as "Bourbon Street, " near the Youth Hostel.

▨ **Divinae Follie,** Put Vatroslava Lisinskog 56, Babin Kuk (☎43 56 77). From Stari Grad, take bus #6 and ask the driver to let you off near the disco, then follow the beats uphill. The bus stops running at 1:45am, but cabs gather in front of the disco (60kn to Stari Grad). A massive tent covers crazy crowds of techno fans, 2 bars, and outdoor seating. Aside from the scantily-clad hip-shakers, hordes of locals gather around this fantastic disco to socialize, stroll through the surrounding woods, and slam draft beer (15kn). 50kn cover. Open June-July and Sept. F-Sa 11pm-5am, nightly in August.

**Troubadour,** Buničeva Poljana 2 (☎41 21 54). The sprawling outdoor tables at this cathedral-side cafe offer a place to hear nightly jazz and a place to throw back pints of draft *Tuborg* (25kn). Open daily 9am until the last guest leaves.

CROATIA

**Be Bop Caffe Bar,** Kneza Damjana Jude 6. Walk down the narrow side street opposite the cathedral entrance. A mini rock museum, every inch of the walls inside is covered with holy relics: posters signed by Santana, Hendrix, and Pink Floyd, Gibson guitars, and gold records. Plays the best selection of rock and blues in town. 0.5L *Heineken* 22kn, 0.5L *Guinness* 27kn, coffee 4kn. Open daily 9am-2pm and 6pm-4am.

**Club Roxy,** B. Josipa Jelačića 11. Here begins the Bourbon Street scene: loud music from rock to techno, tables that invade the street, and a whole lot of skin. Only a few steps away from the hostel for easy access to a midnight drink. 0.5L domestic draft 15kn, 0.33L *Guinness* 18kn, coffee 5kn. Open daily 8am until you pass out.

**Galerie,** Kunićeva 5. If you come in early, don't be deceived. This tiny side-street bar explodes with locals around 10pm. They sit on the street, hang from windows, and talk it up over bottles of *Ožjusko* (0.33L, 10kn). Open daily 9am until people start falling down the stairs.

# ▓ DAYTRIPS FROM DUBROVNIK

## LOPUD ISLAND

*A ferry runs from Dubrovnik to Lopud and the Elafiti islands (50min., 2 per day, off-season 1 per day, round-trip 25kn). The beach is on the opposite side of the island from the village. On the road between the high wall and the palm park, look for the "Konoba Barbara" sign and turn off the road onto a large path. Ignore small paths branching off; when the path forks, keep right.*

 Beautiful as it is, parts of Lopud are still rife with landmines. Stick to the paved paths and beach, and do not traipse off into the wilderness.

Less than an hour from Dubrovnik, Lopud is an enchanting island of the Elafiti Archipelago. The tiny village, dotted with white buildings, chapels, and parks, stretches along the island's waterfront *(obala)*. Currently under renovation, **Dorđić Mayneri** remains among the most beautiful parks in Croatia. Signs from Kavana Dubrava on the waterfront point to the **museum,** which is the meeting place for tours of the church, museum, and monastery. (Th 9am.) A 15-minute stroll along the waterfront leads to a gazebo with a breathtaking view of the white cliffs and dark blue sea. The island's absolute highlight, however, is its **beach,** Plaza Šunj. Arguably the best beach in Croatia, it has all the qualities that most places on the Dalmatian Coast lack: sand, waves, and a secluded cove.

## MLJET NATIONAL PARK

*The easiest way to visit Mljet is on an organized Atlas tour (see **Dubrovnik: Practical Information,** p. 196) from Korčula (130kn) or Dubrovnik (285kn). This is the only way to visit Mljet in one day because Atlas operates its hydrofoil just for customers. The Jadrolinija ferry from Dubrovnik drops passengers in Sobra, on the eastern side of the island (2¼hr., 2 per day, 29kn). The bus that meets the ferry in Sobra travels to its western end, Pomona (1hr., 12kn), stopping at villages along the way. The bus ride itself is an exciting tour of the park. Entrances to the park are in Polače and Pomona. 50kn with boat ticket to the island of St. Maria, 25kn without, students 25kn. Park 50kn.*

Mljet's relative isolation and correspondingly small population made it an ideal location for a national park. Sure enough, the Croatian government preserved the westernmost third of the island in 1960. Difficult access and scarce transport have kept tourism at bay and the island's mystery intact: it has been featured in literature since the *Odyssey* and the writings of St. Paul. The saltwater **Large** and **Small Lakes** (Veliko and Malo Jezero), created by the rising sea level 10,000 years ago, are the most unique formations on the island. They are connected to each other by a narrow passage, and to the sea by **Solin Bay.** Every six hours the direction of waterflow between the lakes switches with the tides, so they are constantly cleaned and pristine. In the center of Veliko Jezero sits the **Island of St. Maria** (Sv. Marija) with a beautiful, white-stone **Benedictine monastery,** built in the 12th century and aban-doned by the church 700 years later when Napoleon conquered the area. Today it houses a restaurant and its church is used for wedding ceremonies.

The tour organized by Atlas from either Dubrovnik or Korčula includes a park ticket with a boat trip to the Island of St. Maria and a few speeches by tour guides, in five different languages, relating information you could get from the free park brochure. Unless you have only one day, save your cash and go on your own. In you are traveling alone, **Polače** is worth a bus stop for its Roman ruins and Christian basilica, once part of the 2nd largest Roman city in Croatia (largest being Dio-cletian's palace in Split). Unfortunately, most of the city is now under water. Get off at Polače (which also has a tourist office), walk 2km to Pristanište, where the park's info center is located, and jump on the boat to St. Maria (5min., every hr.). To return, take the boat to Mali Most (2min.), and walk another 3km to Pomona. When you get tired, a minivan run by park management will give you a ride, otherwise catch one of the Atlas-operated buses. If you want to cheat the park out of 50kn, ask the driver to drop you off at Pristanište—no tickets are sold there but no one seems to care.

# CZECH REPUBLIC (ČESKÁ REPUBLIKA)

## IF YOU'RE HERE FOR...

**3-5 DAYS.** Visit the capital city of **Prague**, the starlet of Central Europe (p. 215).

**1-2 WEEKS.** Take advantage of the numerous daytrips that can be made from Prague, particularly to the **Terezín** (p. 244) concentration camp and to the **Karlštejn Castle** (p. 245), Charles IV's weekend residence. UNESCO-protected **Český Krumlov** and its medieval midsummer festival await in the south of the country (p. 256).

**1 MONTH.** Give yourself about a week to get lost in Prague, then spend some time hiking in **Czech Paradise** (p. 262). Don't miss **Kutná Hora's** (p. 245) creepy church-cum-ossuary, **Karlovy Vary's** (p. 250) healing mineral springs, Becherovka liquor, and summer film festival, **Olomouc's** (p. 273) wine-growing surroundings.

From the Holy Roman Empire through the Nazis and Soviets, foreigners have long driven the Czechs' internal affairs. Unlike many of their neighbors, the citizens of this small, landlocked country in the heart of Europe have rarely fought back as armies marched across their borders, often choosing to resist with words instead of weapons; as a result, Czech towns and cities are among the best-preserved in Europe. Today, the Czechs are facing a different kind of invasion, as enamored tourists sweep in to savor the magnificent capital, welcoming locals, and the world's best beers.

## CZECH REPUBLIC AT A GLANCE

**OFFICIAL NAME:** Czech Republic

**CAPITAL:** Prague (pop. 1.2 million)

**POPULATION:** 10.3 million

**LANGUAGES:** Czech

**CURRENCY:** 1 Czech crown (Kc) = 100 halers

**RELIGION:** 39% Catholic, 4% Protestant

**LAND AREA:** 78,864km²

**GEOGRAPHY:** Plateaus and mountains

**BORDERS:** Austria, Germany, Hungary, Poland, Slovakia

**ECONOMY:** 61% Services, 34% Industry, 5% Agriculture

**GDP:** US$11,300 per capita

**EMERGENCY PHONE NUMBERS:** Ambulance 155, Fire150, Police 158

**COUNTRY CODE:** 420

**INTERNATIONAL DIALING PREFIX:** 00

# HISTORY

**FROM BARBARIANS TO KINGS.** The mythological inception of the Czech state is attributed to **Father Čech** (Czech) who is said to have climbed the Říp mountain near what is now Prague and declare the land around him his. Factually, the civilization's birth is rooted in the first century settlement of the **Boii**, a Celtic tribe, in what is now **Bohemia.** Slavs arrived in the 6th century—Moravians in the east and Czechs in the west—displacing the Celts.

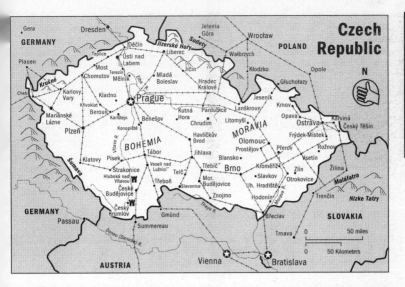

The Slavs of the Czech lands (Bohemia, Moravia, and Silesia) were first united under the **Empire of Great Moravia,** which dominated Central Europe in the first half of the 9th century. At the end of the 10th century, however, as the Moravian Empire was disintegrating, the **Přemyslid Dynasty** united the Czechs and created a strong autonomous state. The legendary patron saint of Bohemia, **Václav** (Wenceslas) was one of the dynasty's earliest rulers. In 1114, the Holy Roman Empire invited the Czech kings to join as electors. With the coronation of Vladislav II as king in 1140, the region became a hereditary kingdom.

**THE GOLDEN AND THE DARK AGES.** The reign of Holy Roman Emperor **Charles (Karel) IV** (1346-1378) was indisputably a Golden Era for the Czechs. Thanks to cunning alliances and numerous marriages, Karel governed a territory larger than he could have ever traveled through at that time, but he made Bohemia the center of his empire. He not only elevated Prague to an Archbishopric, but also gave it the first university in Central Europe (now named Charles University), founded a new city quarter (New Town), and constructed or renovated hundreds of buildings. Charles's son Václav "the Lazy" was, as his name suggests, less productive. During his reign, **Jan Hus** (1369-1415), a Rector at the university, spoke out against the corruption of the Catholic hierarchy and was subsequently burned to death as a heretic. The **Hussite movement,** a proto-Protestant revolt that originated in the Czech lands in response to Jan Hus's execution, led to the **First Defenestration of Prague** in 1419, in which Hussite protestors threw the royalist mayor and several of his councillors out of the window of the Council House. The **Second Defenestration of Prague** set off the **Thirty Years' War** (1618-1648). The Czech Protestants' defeat was sealed when they suffered an early, harsh blow in the **Battle of White Mountain** (Bílá Hora), fought just outside Prague on November 8, 1620. The war led to the absorption of Czech territory into the **Austrian Empire** and three centuries of oppressive rule.

**CZECHOSLOVAKIA.** The spirit of nationalism that swept across Europe from west to east during the nineteenth century penetrated even to Bohemia. During the **1848 revolutions,** however, this new trend was violently crushed by imperial conservatism. While **World War I** did nothing to increase harmony among the nationalities of the Habsburg Empire, it did help unite the Czechs and Slovaks. In the post-war confusion, **Edvard Beneš** and **Tomáš Garrigue Masaryk** convinced the victorious Allies to legitimize a new state that united Bohemia, Moravia, and Slovakia into **Czechoslovakia.** On October 28th, 1918, Masaryk became the new country's first president.

Between the two worlds war, the **First Republic** brought another golden era for the Czechs. Czechoslovakia not only maintained a parliamentary democracy (rare in Eastern Europe), but also enjoyed remarkable economic prosperity, only to be torn apart as Hitler exploited the Allies' **appeasement** policy. The infamous 1938 **Munich Agreement** handed a Czech border region, the Sudetenland, over to Germany, ignoring the Czechoslovak government's pleas that such a drastic measure would destroy the country. The following year, Hitler brutally annexed the entire territory. He proclaimed the **Protectorate Bohemia-Moravia** over the Czech lands, and turned Slovakia into an independent fascist state under Hungarian control. Most of Czechoslovakia's Jews were murdered by the Nazis during the five-year occupation. On May 8, 1945, the Soviets and Americans liberated the country.

**COMMUNISM.** Immediately following liberation, Germans were expelled from the Sudetenland and nationalization of the Czechoslovak industry and economy began. The Communists, under **Klement Gottwald,** won 38% of the vote in the 1946 elections and instituted a government, seizing permanent power in 1948. In 1968, Communist Party Secretary **Alexander Dubček** sought to implement "socialism with a human face," dramatically reforming the country's economy and easing political oppression during the **Prague Spring.** Displeased, the Soviets violently suppressed Dubček's counter-revolution by invading the country together with other armies of the Warsaw Pact. Slovak leader **Gustáv Husák,** who became president in 1971, introduced an even more repressive regime that lasted for the next 18 years.

Czech intellectuals protested Husák's violation of human rights throughout the 70s with **Charter 77,** a nonviolent protest movement. Most of its leaders were imprisoned and persecuted, but they nonetheless fostered increasing dissidence among Czechs and Slovaks. After the demise of the Communists in Hungary and Poland and the fall of the Berlin Wall in 1989, the **Velvet Revolution,** named as such for the almost entirely bloodless transition from Communism to multi-party state system, rippled into Czechoslovakia. On November 17th, 1989, students and the leaders of Charter 77 organized a peaceful demonstration in the center of Prague. Its violent suppression by the police outraged the nation, which immediately went on strike. Within a few days the Communist government had resigned. **Václav Havel,** the long-imprisoned playwright and leader of both Charter 77 and the Velvet Revolution, became president soon thereafter. After three years of debate, the Czech and Slovak nations parted ways on January 1, 1993.

# POLITICS

The Czech Republic is a parliamentary democracy. The president, who is elected by Parliament for a 5-year term, is the official head of state. His powers, however, are as symbolic as those of the British Queen, extending little beyond the power to veto (which can be overridden by the Parliament), to grant amnesty, and to represent the country outside its borders. The Prime Minister, who chooses members of the cabinet, has greater political power. Appointed by the President, the Prime Minister is typically a leader of the majority political party. An upper chamber of the Parliament, the Senate, was recently introduced into the constitution, but its inactivity (and the money it costs taxpayers) has led many to doubt its necessity.

The country has enjoyed its status as the ex-communist pet of Western investors and politicians, but recent economic stagnation, massive political corruption, and rising unemployment are beginning to abate Western investors' enthusiasm. In May 1997, the poorly conceived economic policies of Prime Minister **Václav Klaus** (whose idol was Britain's hard-line conservative ex-Prime Minister Margaret Thatcher) resulted in a tremendous depreciation of the koruna's value. In June 1998, new elections allowed **Miloš Zeman,** leader of the **Social Democrats,** to form the first left-wing government since 1989. Klaus' **ODS (Civic Democratic Party)** went into opposition, but to retain at least some power, it signed an oxymoronic **Oppositional Treaty** with Zeman's party, agreeing to vote in favor of bills proposed by the government provided that certain conditions of the ODS are met. This "innovative" move has put the country's democracy into coma. Zeman needed only two years in power

**ENFANT TERRIBLE** During the Cold War era, **Václav Havel** (VAA-tslav HA-vel) outraged party functionaries with his plays and essays that openly opposed the communist establishment. In 1977, he became a leader of Charter 77, a political-intellectual protest against the violation of human rights in Czechoslovakia. Even repeated incarceration did not silence Havel; after leading the Velvet Revolution in 1989, he was elected President. But his years as an *enfant terrible* were not yet over. During eleven years of presidency, he exhibited few of the characteristics of a well-behaved statesman. Today politicians, the media, and the public alike indulge in criticizing him for anything he says or does. A marriage to younger actress Dagmar Veškrnová less than a year after his first wife's death, outraged the public. Likewise, Havel's New Year's speech of 1998, in which he expressed disgust with the political and moral climate of the country, earned him an all-time low in popularity polls. Yet Havel does nothing but maintain the qualities that made him famous: saying what others don't want to hear, and doing what others do not brave.

to prove that his party is utterly incapable of running a country, but the scandal-ridden ODS does not seem to be viable alternative. Playwright and former dissident ▨ **Václav Havel** was re-elected as President in 1998 by only one vote. His re-election was probably due to the lack of a more attractive candidate rather than public approval of his politics. It remains unclear who will fill Havel's shoes in the 2003 election, but the President made the headlines of newspapers worldwide in spring 2000 when he expressed his interest in having Czech-born US Secretary of State **Madeleine Albright** as his successor. Albright quickly denied any possibility of running for such a position, and the Presidential office reacted by stating that Albright's name was only mentioned as an example of an ideal leader.

The uncertain economic and political future of the Czech Republic has provoked skepticism from the EU, although the country has managed to meet the standards necessary to be invited to join in 2003. The Czechs have also joined the other bastion of organized Western power, NATO—in March 1999, the Czech Republic, along with Hungary and Poland, was inducted into the military organization just in time for NATO's 50th anniversary and the air raids on Yugoslavia. NATO membership has complicated economic dealings with Russia.

# CULTURE

### NATIONAL HOLIDAYS IN 2001

| | |
|---|---|
| **January 1** New Year | **September 28** St. Wenceslas Day |
| **April 15-16** Easter | **October 28** Republic (Independence) Day |
| **May 1** May Day | |
| **May 8** Liberation Day | **November 17** Student Day; Day of Fight for Freedom and Democracy |
| **July 5** Cyril and Methodius Day | **December 24-25** Christmas |
| **July 6** Jan Hus Day | |

# LITERATURE

The Czech Republic is a literature-obsessed country in which writers hold a privileged position as social and political commentators. From the first Czechoslovak president, **T.G. Masaryk,** to current incumbent **Václav Havel,** literary figures have been revered as the nation's most powerful citizens and most subversive political figures. Through the 18th century, Czech literature was marked by the Habsburgs' oppressive insistence that texts be written only in German and always praise the empire. The 19th century, however, saw a nationalist literary renaissance coinciding with the 1848 revolutions against the Austrian empire. Fueled by **Josef Dobrovský** and **Josef Jungmann's** endeavors to revitalize and codify the Czech language, **Karel Hynek Mácha** penned his celebrated epic *May* (*Máj*; 1836), considered the lyric masterpiece of 19th century Czech literature. The founding of the literary journal *Máj* in 1856—named after Mácha's poem—marked the beginning of the **National Revival,** an explosion of nationalist literary output. One of its brightest stars was **Božena Němcová,** who introduced the novel to modern Czech literature and repopularized the folk tale with *Granny* (*Babička;* 1855). Poet and fiction writer **Jan Neruda,** another prominent figure of the National Revival, inspired the Chilean poet Pablo Neruda to take on his famous pseudonym.

The 20th century has proved an extraordinarily fruitful time for the Czech arts. In literature, **Jaroslav Hašek's** epic satire, *The Good Soldier Švejk* (*Dobrý voják Švejk;* 1921-23), which recounts the adventures of the bumbling Švejk during WWI, has become a classic Bohemian commentary on life under Habsburg rule. **Karel Čapek's** play *R.U.R.* (1920), another classic of the period, presented a frightening look at a world overrun by robots (a word he coined). While he wrote in German, **Franz Kafka's** work is pervaded by the literary traditions and dark circumstances of his native Prague under Habsburg rule. His existentialist works, such as *Metamorphosis* or *The Castle*, were shaped by his upbringing as a member of a "minority within a minority"—a German-speaking Jew in a predominantly Czech city. **Jaroslav Seifert** and **Vítězslav Nezval** explored Poetism and Surrealism, producing ecstatic and image-rich meditations on the city and nationality. In 1984, Seifert became the first Czech author to receive the Nobel Prize.

After World War II, the novels of **Milan Kundera** (now in France), **Josef Škvorecký** (now in Canada), and **Bohumil Hrabal** (now dead; see p. 232) created an international following for not only Czech art and literature, but also for the support of Czechoslovakia's struggle against the Russian bear. The dramas of prisoner-turned-president **Václav Havel** remain part of the Czech Republic's daily life. Although Kundera's *Unbearable Lightness of Being* (*Nesnesitelná lehkost bytí;* 1984) may be the best-known among English speakers, *Let's Go* recommends the author's first novel, *The Joke* (*Žert;* 1965).

# VISUAL ARTS, MUSIC AND FILM

Playwright Karel Čapek's brother **Jozef** was an important Cubist and charicaturist best known for his satire of Hitler's ascent to power. Another prominent Cubist and post-Impressionist was **Jan Zrzavý.** Other artists, such as surrealist **Marie Čerminová Toyen,** worked as expatriates, who immigrated to Paris in the 1920s and worked closely with André Breton. One of the most important Czech artists of the early 20th century, **Alfons Mucha,** also worked in Paris for most of his career and helped develop the **art nouveau** style of graphic design and painting.

The National Revival during the 19th century also affected Czech music. The nation's most celebrated composers, **Antonín Dvořák, Leoš Janáček** and **Bedřich Smetana,** are renowned for transforming Czech folk tunes and tales into 19th-century Wagnerian symphonies and operas. Dvořák's *Symphony No. 9, "From the New World,"* which combines Czech folk tradition with the author's experience of America, is probably the most famous Czech masterpiece. Among Czechs, Smetana's collection of symphonic poems *My Country (Má vlast)*, especially *Vltava*, remains the most popular.

For such a small country, the Czech Republic has also been quite successful in the film industry. In 1966, director **Jiří Menzel's** *Closely Watched Trains (Ostře sledované vlaky)*, based on a novel by Hrabal, won the Academy Award for Best Foreign Film. Another Oscar traveled to the Czech Republic in 1997 with Jan Svěrák for his film *Kolya* (1996). Director **Miloš Forman** immigrated to the US in 1968 and exploded into the American film industry with his critically acclaimed film *One Flew Over the Cuckoo's Nest* (1975). Additionally, the films of **Ivan Vojnar,** particularly his 1997 *The Way Through the Bleak Woods (Cesta pustým lesem)*, are celebrated for their treatment of delicate historical issues and the legacy of a rural, landlocked nation in the modern world.

# RELIGION

Communists had a relatively easy time convincing most Czechs that atheism was the way of life. Dating back to Jan Hus' preaching of church reform in the late 14th century, Czech scepticism toward religion was well-grounded following the Habsburgs' violent imposition of Catholicism on predominantly Protestant populace. Today, a vast majority of the population is atheist or non-religious, thanks in part to communist propaganda, but largely due to the trend away from religion after the two world wars. Recently, though, the previously suppressed voices of the religious community, mostly Catholic but also Protestant and Jewish, have been regaining a place in the Czech society.

# FOOD AND DRINK

Anyone in the mood for true Czech cuisine should start learning to pronounce *knedlíky* (KNED-lee-kee). These thick, pasty loaves of dough, feebly known in English as dumplings, serve as staples of Czech meals, soaking up *zelí* (sauerkraut) juice and other sauces. The Czech **national meal** is *vepřové* (roast pork), *knedlíky*, and *zelí* (known as *vepřo-knedlo-zelo*), but *guláš* (stew) runs a close second. The main food groups seem to be *hovězí* (beef), *sekaná pečeně* (meatloaf), *klobása* (sausage), and *brambory* (potatoes). If you're in a hurry, grab a pair of *párky* (frankfurters) or some *sýr* (cheese) at a *bufet, samoobsluha,* or *občerstvení,* all variations on a food stand. **Vegetarian** restaurants serve *šopský salát* (mixed salad with feta cheese) and other *bez masa* (meatless) specialties; at most restaurants, however, vegetarians will be limited to *smažený sýr* (fried cheese). Ask for *káva espresso* rather than just *káva* to avoid the mud Czechs call coffee. *Koblihy* (doughnuts), *jablkový závin* (apple strudel), and *ovocné knedlíky* (fruit dumplings) are favorite sweets, but the most beloved is *koláč*—a tart filled with poppyseed jam or sweet cheese. *Zmrzlina* is closer to *gelati* than American ice cream.

Moravian **wines** are worth a try. *Rulandské,* from Znojmo in South Moravia, is good, but the quality of *Müller-Thurgau* varies. Any *Welschriesling* or *Frankovka* is drinkable. Wine is typically drunk at a *vinárna* (wine bar) that also serves a variety of hard spirits, including *slivovice* (plum brandy) and *becherovka* (herbal bitter), the national drink. The most prominent beer is *Plzeňský Prazdroj* (Pilsner Urquell), although many Czechs are loyal to *Budvar* or *Krušovice*.

# CUSTOMS AND ETIQUETTE

Although discrimination against individuals because of age, race, or sexual orientation is illegal in the Czech Republic, as in the rest of Europe; a neo-Nazi skinhead community has repeatedly assaulted **ethnic minorities. Gay** and **lesbian** travelers who publicly display affection might be subject to stares and remarks by pubescent Czech boys in cities or confused *babičky* in small towns.

Nearly all **museums** and **galleries** close on Mondays, and **theaters** rarely perform regular shows in December and from late June to early September.

Czech eating and drinking is governed by firmly established customs. When beer is served, wait until all raise the common *"na zdraví"* ("to your health") toast, then drink. Always look into the eyes of the individual with whom you are toasting, otheriwse your gesture may seem rude. Similarly, before biting into a sauce-drowned *knedlík,* wish everyone *"dobrou chut"* ("to your health"). **Tip** by rounding up your bill, and not by calculating 10-15%.

Another facet of Czech life governed by etiquette is **public transport.** *Babičky* are allowed to cut lines and evict anyone with a seat with tales of woe, hardship, and aching legs. Most younger Czechs give in to the mighty power of age, but as a result scamper over each other for seats. When it comes to public transport, there is no such thing as a line; crowds just push and lunge to get on the bus, tram, or train first, which is understandable, considering that most routes are overbooked and there's a good chance you'll have to stand for four hours. Go ahead and push, but don't push the *babičky,* because they'll clobber you with their canes.

## SPORTS

Sports have always been an important element of Czech world renown. Although they now hold US citizenship, **Ivan Lendl** and **Martina Navrátilová** learned to play tennis in their Czech homeland. **Jaromír Jágr** and **Dominik Hašek** are possibly the world's best ice-hockey players. The national ice-hockey team has won the World Hockey Championship a total of nine times, most recently in St. Petersburg in 2000. The defeat of Russia in the final game of the 1998 Winter Olympic Games quite literally caused an uprising in the Czech Republic: the nation flooded the streets and celebrated for more than a week, welcoming the victorious players with slogans such as "Hašek to the Castle." The craze went so far that during last year's deliberations in the parliament about a revision of the country's days off, some deputies proposed that the 1998 Nagano victory be added to the list of Czech national holidays. Among Czechs, soccer (fotbal in Czech) and skiing are highly popular sports, both on TV and in real life; on weekends from December to March, don't expect to find any families at home—they are all skiing in the Krkonoše mountains.

## LANGUAGE

**Russian** *was* every student's mandatory second language, but these days, **English** will earn you more friends. A few **German** phrases go further, especially in the western spas, but might gain you some enemies. An English-Czech dictionary is indispensable and should be on anyone's packing list. *"Zaplatíme"* (ZAH-plah-tee-meh—we're ready to pay; *"zaplatím"* if you're dining by yourself) is a handy phrase. Ask *"Kolik stojí?"* to find out how much something costs, and *"V kolik hodin?"* to find out when your bus is leaving. When all else fails, a polite *"Dobrý den"* ("good day"), *"prosím"* ("please," or "that's okay"), and a smile will win you more Czech friends than you'll know what to do with. If you've learned Czech abroad, beware the Prague cockney—or just allow for some imaginative "mispronunciations."

The trick to good pronunciation is to pronounce every letter. Stress is always placed on the first syllable. However, don't confuse stress with elongation. When there is a diacritical over a vowel—such as á, é, í, ó, ú, ů, and ý—this simply means you hold the vowel sound for longer; do not place the emphasis on the vowel. In other words, *dobrý* is pronounced DOH-bree-ee and not doh-BREE. C is pronounced "ts"; g is always hard, as in *g*od; ch, which is considered one letter, is a cross between "h" and "k" and actually comes from the back of your throat (imagine Arabic), but "h" is a comprehensible approximation; j is "y"; r is slightly rolled; and w is "v." The letter ě softens the preceding consonant: dě (also written ď) becomes "dy," as in *děkuji* (DYEH-koo-yee-ee, not DEH-koo-yee-ee); mě is "mnye," as in *město* (MNYEH-stoh, not MEH-stoh); ně (also written ň) is "ny," as in *něco* (NYEH-tsoh, not NEH-tso); and tě (also written ť) is "ty," as *tělo* (TYEH-loh, not TEH-loh). All other diacritics soften the consonant: č is "ch," ř is "rzh" (see "The World's Most Difficult Sound," below), š is "sh," and ž is "zh."

For a list of common words and phrases, see **Glossary**, p. 212, and **Phrasebook**, p. 213.

**THE WORLD'S MOST DIFFICULT SOUND** Not quite a Spanish "r" and simply not the Polish "rz," Czech's own linguistic blue note, the letter "ř" lies excruciatingly in between. Although many of Prague's ex-pats would sacrifice a month of Saturdays at Jo's Bar to utter the elusive sound just once, few manage more than a strangely trilled whistle. Most foreigners resign themselves to using the "ž" in its place, but what we consider a subtle difference often confuses Czechs. For all those linguistic daredevils in the audience, here's a sure-fire method of tackling the randy Mr. Ř: roll your tongue and quickly follow with a "ž," then repeat.

# ADDITIONAL READING

For a comprehensive and accessible treatment of Czech history, turn to Derek Sayer's *The Coasts of Bohemia*. Peter Demetz offers a more focused historical account in *Prague in Black and Gold*. Of the many travelogues written about adventures in the Czech Republic, Douglas Lytle's *Pink Tanks and Velvet Hangovers: An American in Prague* is particularly engaging; *Kafka's Prague: A Travel Companion*, by Klaus Wagenbach, leads the reader through the haunted streets of Kafka's life. President Havel's *The Art of the Impossible: Politics as Morality in Practice* meditates on the confluence of literature and politics and the role of the intellectual in Czech culture. An entirely different take on Czech cultural and political life is explored in *Allskin and Other Tales by Contemporary Czech Women*, the first collection of Czech women's fiction to be published or translated.

# TRAVELING ESSENTIALS

Americans may visit visa-free for up to 30 days, Irish and New Zealand citizens for up to 90 days, and Canadian and UK citizens for up to 180 days. Australians and South Africans must obtain 30-day tourist visas. Visas are available at embassies or consulates (see **Embassies and Consulates**, p. 18), but not at the border. Processing takes seven to ten days when materials are submitted by mail, five days when they are submitted in person. With the application, you must submit your passport, one photograph (two if applying to the Czech consulate in Los Angeles) glued—not stapled—to the application, a self-addressed, stamped envelope (certified or overnight mail) and a cashier's check or money order for the price of the visa. Single-entry visas cost US$28 for Australians, US$22 for citizens of most countries, while 90-day multiple-entry visas cost US$28 for Australians, US$84 for citizens of most other countries. Prices for single- and double-entry transit visas are the same as those for other single-entry visas. A multiple-entry transit visa costs US$84. The maximum stay in the Czech republic is five days per transit and all transit visas are valid for 90 days. Visas are available at three border crossings: Rozvadov, Dolní Dvořiště, or Hatě for an additional US$50 fee. Travelers on a visa to the Czech Republic must register with the Czech Immigration Police within three days of arrival; guests in hotels are registered automatically.

There is no fee for crossing a Czech border by train or bus; if you're driving, there is an 800Kč entrance charge. If heading to Austria or Hungary, it's cheapest to buy a Czech ticket to the border; once inside the country, buy a separate ticket to your destination. When coming from Poland, it's cheapest to walk across the border at Cieszyn/Český Těšín. Czech border patrol is fast and efficient; crossing delays are uncommon. It is best to enter or leave the Czech Republic via Prague or Brno.

# TRANSPORTATION

**BY PLANE. Air France, British Airways, ČSA, Delta, KLM, Lufthansa,** and **Swissair** are among the major carriers with flights into Prague.

**BY TRAIN.** The most economical way to enter the country is by train. **Eastrail** is accepted in the Czech Republic, but **Eurail** is valid only with a special supplement. The fastest trains are *EuroCity* and *InterCity* (*expresní*, marked in blue on schedules). *Rychlík* trains, also known as *zrychlený vlak*, are fast domestic trains, marked in red on schedules. Avoid slow *osobní* trains, marked in white. **ČSD,** the national transportation company, publishes the monster *Jízdní řád* train schedule (74Kč), which has a two-page English explanation. *Odjezdy* (departures) are printed in train stations on yellow posters, *příjezdy* (arrivals) on white. Seat reservations (*místenka;* 10Kč) are recommended on express and international trains and for all first-class seating; snag them at the counter with a boxed "R."

# GLOSSARY

| ENGLISH | CZECH | PRONOUNCE |
|---|---|---|
| one | jeden | YEH-den |
| two | dva | dv-YEH |
| three | tři | tr-ZHIH |
| four | čtyři | SHTEER-zhee |
| five | pět | p-YEHT |
| six | šest | shest |
| seven | sedm | SEH-duhm |
| eight | osm | OSS-uhm |
| nine | devět | dehv-YEHT |
| ten | deset | des-SEHT |
| twenty | dvacet | dvah-TSEHT |
| thirty | třicet | tr-zhih-TSEHT |
| forty | čtyřicet | SHTEEh-ri-TSETH |
| fifty | padesát | PA-des-aath |
| sixty | šedesát | shest-des-aath |
| seventy | sedmdesát | SEH-duhm-des-aath |
| eighty | osmdesát | OSS-uhm-des-aath |
| ninety | devadesát | DE-va-des-aath |
| one hundred | sto | STO |
| one thousand | tisíc | TI-seets |
| Monday | pondělí | PO-ndeh-lee |
| Tuesday | úterý | UH-te-reeh |
| Wednesday | středa | STRHE-dah |
| Thursday | čtvrtek | CZ-tvr-tekh |
| Friday | pátek | PAA-tekh |
| Saturday | sobota | SO-bo-tah |
| Sunday | neděle | NEH-dyeh-leh |
| a day | den | DEN |
| a few days | několik dní | NYE-ko-lik DNEEH |
| a week | týden | TYH-den |
| morning | ráno | RAH-no |
| afternoon | odpoledne | OT-pol-ed-ne |
| evening | večer | VE-cher |
| today | dnes | d-NEHS |
| tomorrow | zítra | ZEE-trah |
| spring | jaro | YA-ro |
| summer | léto | LEE-to |
| fall | podzim | POD-zim |
| winter | zima | ZI-ma |
| hot | teplý | TEP-leeh |
| cold | studený | STU-de-neeh |
| single room | jednolůžkový pokoj | YED-noh-luu-zhko-veeh PO-koy |
| double room | dvoulůžkový pokoj | DVOU-luu-zhko-veeh PO-koy |
| reservation | rezervace | RE-zer-va-tse |
| with shower | se sprchou | SE SPR-khou |
| pharmacy | lékárna | LEE-khaar-nah |

| ENGLISH | CZECH | PRONOUNCE |
|---|---|---|
| post office | pošta | POSH-ta |
| stamps | známka | ZNAHM-ka |
| airmail | letecky | LE-tets-ky |
| departure | odjezd | OD-yezd |
| arrival | příjezd | PREE-yezd |
| one-way | jen tam | yen tam |
| round-trip | zpáteční | SPAH-tech-nyee |
| luggage | | |
| reservation | místenka | mis-TEN-kah |
| train | vlak | vlahk |
| bus | autobus | OUT-oh-boos |
| airport | letiště | LEH-tish-tyeh |
| station | nádraží | NA-drah-zhee |
| ticket | lístek | LIS-tek |
| grocery | potraviny | PO-tra-vee-nee |
| breakfast | snídaně | SNEE-dan-ye |
| lunch | oběd | OB-yed |
| dinner | večeře | VE-cher-zhe |
| menu | listek | LIS-tek |
| bread | chléb | khleb |
| vegetables | zelenina | ZE-le-nee-na |
| beef | hovězí | HO-vye-zee |
| chicken | kuře | KOO-rzheh |
| pork | vep | VEPRZH |
| fish | ryba | RY-bah |
| coffee | káva | KAH-va |
| milk | mléko | MLEH-koh |
| beer | pivo | PEE-voh |
| sugar | cukr | TSOO-kur |
| eggs | vejce | VEY-tse |
| holiday | prázdniny | PRAHZ-dni-nee |
| open | otevřeno | O-te-zheno |
| closed | zavřeno | ZAV-rzhen-o |
| bank | banka | BAN-ka |
| police | policie | PO-lits-iye |
| exchange | směnárna | smyeh-NAR-na |
| toilet | WC | VEE-TSEE |
| square | náměstí | NAH-mye-stee |
| castle | hrad | KHRAD |
| church | kostel | KO-stel |
| tower | vě | VYEZH |
| market | trh | TH-rh |
| passport | cestovní pas | TSE-stov-neeh |
| bakery | pekařství | PE-karzh-stvee |
| left | vlevo | VLE-voh |
| right | vpravo | VPRA-voh |

# PHRASEBOOK

| ENGLISH | CZECH | PRONOUNCE |
|---|---|---|
| Yes/no | Ano/ne | AH-no/neh |
| Please/You're welcome | Prosím | PROH-seem |
| Thank you | Děkuji | DYEH-koo-yih |
| Hello | Dobrý den (formal), Ahoj | DO-bree den |
| Good-bye | Nashedanou | NAH sleh-dah-noh-oo |
| Good morning | Dobré ráno | DO-breh RAH-no |
| Good evening | Dobrý večer | DO-breh VE-tcher |
| Good night | Dobrou noc | DO-broh NOTS |
| Sorry/excuse me | Promiňte | PROH-mihn-teh |
| Help! | Pomoc! | POH-mots |
| When? | Kdy? | k-DEE |
| Where is...? | Kde je...? | k-DEH |
| How do I get to...? | Jak se dostanu do...? | YAK seh dohs-TAH-noo doh |
| How much does this cost? | Kolik to stojí? | KOH-lihk STOH-yee |
| Do you have...? | Máte...? | MAH-teh |
| Do you speak English? | Mluvíte anglicky? | MLOO-vit-eh ahng-GLIT-ski |
| I don't understand. | Nerozumím. | NEH-rohz-oo-meem |
| I don't speak Czech. | Nemluvím česky. | NEH-mloo-veem CHESS-kee |
| Please write it down. | Napište to, prosím. | PRO-seem nah-PEESH-tye |
| Speak a little slower, please. | Mluvte pomaleji, prosím. | MLUV-te PO-ma-le-yi PRO-seem |
| I'd like to order... | Prosím... | khtyel bikh |
| I'd like to pay/We'd like to pay. | Zaplatím/Zaplatíme. | ZAH-plah-teem/ZAH-plah-tee-meh |
| I think you made a mistake in the bill. | Myslím, že máte chybu v účtu. | MYS-leem zhe MAH-te khybuh v UHCH-tuh |
| Do you have a vacancy? | Máte volný pokoj? | MAA-teh VOL-nee PO-koy? |
| I'd like a room. | Prosím pokoj. | pro-SEEM PO-koy |
| May I see the room? | Mohl(a) bych se podívat na ten pokoj? | MO-hul (MO-hla) bikh se PO-dyeh-vat na ten PO-koy |
| No, I don't like it. | Promiňte, nelíbí se mi. | RZHEK-nete mi gdy mahm VI-stohpit |
| Yes, I'll take it. | Ano, vezmu si ho. | yeh TOH-leh vlahk DO... |
| Will you tell me when to get off? | Řekněte mi, kde mám vys-toupit? | RE-kne-te MI PRO-seem khde MAAM VYS-tou-pit? |
| Is this the right train/bus to...? | Je tohle vlak/autobus do...? | Ye TOH-le AUTO-bus do |
| I want a ticket to... | Prosím jízdenku do... | khytel a bikh YEEZ-denkoo DO... |
| How long does the trip take? | Jak dlouho trvá ta cesta? | YAK DLOU-ho TRH-vaa TSE-stah |
| When is the first/next/last train to... | Kdy jede první/další/poslední vlak do... | gdi YE-de ... vlak DO-pulznye |
| Where is the bathroom/nearest telephone booth/center of town? | Kde je koupelna/nejbližší telefonní budka/centrum města? | gde ye TO-aleti/TA-di NE-yblish-nee TE-le-fo-nee BOOT-ka/MNE-HST-skeh TSEN-troom |
| I've lost my... | Ztratil(a) jsem... | ZTRA-til(a) YSEM |
| Would you like to dance? | Chtěl(a) byste si zatancovat? | khtyehl(a) BI-ste si ZA-tan-chit |
| Go away. | Prosím odejděte. | pro-SEEM ODEY-dhe-te |

**BY BUS.** Buses are the preferred means of domestic travel, but are inefficient for crossing borders. **ČSAD** runs national and international bus lines. Consult the time-tables posted at stations or buy your own bus schedule (25Kč) from kiosks.

**BY THUMB. Hitchhikers** report that it still remains popular in the Czech Republic. Although it is a common means of transport among young Czechs, *Let's Go* does not recommend hitchhiking.

# TOURIST SERVICES AND MONEY

| CURRENCY | |
|---|---|
| US$1 = 39KČ (KORUNA,OR CSK) | 10KČ = US$0.25 |
| CDN$1 = 27KČ | 10KČ = CDN$0.37 |
| UK£1 = 58KČ | 10KČ = UK£0.17 |
| IR£1 = 45KČ | 10KČ = IR£0.22 |
| AUS$1 = 23KČ | 10KČ = AUS$0.44 |
| NZ$1 = 17KČ | 10KČ = NZ$0.59 |
| SAR 1 = 5.70KČ | 10KČ = SAR 0.18 |
| DM 1 = 18KČ | 10KČ = DM 0.55 |

**CKM,** junior affiliate of communist dinosaur Čedok, is helpful for the budget and student traveler, serving as a clearinghouse for youth hostel beds and issuing ISICs and HI cards. **Municipal tourist offices** in major cities provide printed matter on sights and cultural events, as well as lists of hostels and hotels. If they're nice, they might even book you a room. German is most widely spoken, but English is also common in touristed regions. Most bookstores sell a fine national hiking map collection, *Soubor turistických map*, with an English key.

The Czech unit of currency is the **koruna** (crown; Kč), plural *koruny*. **Inflation** is around 3.5%, meaning prices and exchange rates should be relatively stable. **ATMs** are everywhere—look for the red and black "Bankomat" signs—and offer the best exchange rates available. **Traveler's checks** can be exchanged almost everywhere, if at times for an obscene commission. **Komerční banka** operates wherever a human being earns cash; its many branches accept all sorts of checks. **Česká spořitelna** is another common chain. Banks are generally open Monday to Friday 8am to 4pm. MC and Visa are accepted at most expensive places, but rarely at hostels.

# HEALTH AND SAFETY

The greatest risk of ill-feeling comes from food—unacclimatized bodies tend to rebel against mass quantities of sausage and sauerkraut. What vegetables and fruits you do happen upon should be washed thoroughly. If you fall ill, medical services are quite good, and major foreign insurance policies are accepted. If you're not covered, pay in cash. Prague has a separate hospital for foreign patients. *Lékárna* (pharmacies) and supermarkets carry international brands of *náplast* (bandages), *tampóny* (tampons), and *kondomy* (condoms). **Petty crime** has increased dramatically since 1989; beware pickpockets prowling among the crowds in Prague's main squares, on the way to the Castle, and on tram #22. In an **emergency,** notify your consulate—police may not be well versed in English.

# ACCOMMODATIONS AND CAMPING

Hostels, particularly in **university dorms,** are the cheapest option in July and August; two- to four-bed rooms are 200-300Kč per person. CKM's **Junior Hotels** (year-round hostels giving discounts to ISIC and HI cardholders) are comfortable but often full. Private hostels have broken the CKM monopoly, but not always surpassing its reliability. Showers and bedding are included. **Pensions** are the next most affordable option; expect to pay 600Kč, including breakfast. Reserve at least one week ahead from June to September in Prague, Český Krumlov, and Brno. If you can't keep a reservation, call to cancel so that some weary backpacker won't be sleeping on the street—at some point, that weary backpacker might be you.

**Private homes** are not nearly as popular (or as cheap) as in the rest of Eastern Europe. Scan train stations for *Zimmer frei* (rooms available) signs. Quality varies; do not pay in advance. In Prague, reject anything not easily accessible by public transport. Outside Prague, **local tourist offices** and **CKM/GTS** book rooms, with private agencies burgeoning around train and bus stations. **Campgrounds,** strewn throughout the countryside, run 60-100Kč per person and 50-90Kč per tent. Most are only open mid-May to September. *Ubytování v ČSR*, in decodable Czech, lists all the hotels, hostels, huts, and campgrounds in Bohemia and Moravia.

# KEEPING IN TOUCH

The Czech Republic's **postal system** has embraced capitalist efficiency; letters reach the US in less than 10 days. A postcard to the US costs 8Kč, to Australia 7Kč. When sending by air mail, stress that you want it to go on a plane *(letecky)*. Go to the customs office to send packages heavier than 2kg abroad.

To make a call, seek out the blue cardphones (150Kč per 50 units) rather than playing Sisyphus to a coinphone's giant boulder. Calls run 31Kč per minute to the **UK;** 63Kč per minute to **Australia, Canada,** or the **US;** and 94Kč per minute to **New Zealand.** The international operator is at 013 15; International access numbers are: **AT&T Direct,** ☎ 00 42 00 01 01; **BT Direct,** ☎ 00 42 00 44 01; **MCI WorldPhone,** ☎ 00 42 00 01 12; **Canada Direct,** ☎ 00 42 00 01 51; and **Sprint,** ☎ 00 42 08 71 87. **Mail** can be received general delivery through Poste Restante. Address envelope as follows: Nicholas (First name), TOPJIAN (LAST NAME), POSTE RESTANTE, Jindřišská 14 (Post office street address), Praha (City) 110 00 (Postal code), CZECH REPUBLIC.

The **internet** has spread its spindly wires to most towns. Internet cafes are the easiest to use if you're just passing through; the computers are fast and cheap, with rates around 2Kč per minute. Most public libraries also have internet access, but computers tend to be slower and require a membership card (100-500Kč).

# PRAGUE (PRAHA)   ☎ (0)2

"I see a grand city whose glory will touch the stars."
  —Countess Libuše

From Countess Libuše's mythological prophecy to the present, benefactors have placed Prague (pop. 1,500,000) on the cusp of the divine. Envisioning a royal seat worthy of his rank, King of Bohemia and Holy Roman Emperor Charles IV refashioned Prague into a city of soaring cathedrals and lavish palaces. The city's maze of shady alleys, along with the legends of demons haunting its houses, lent Prague a dark side and provided frightening fodder for Franz Kafka's 20th-century paranoia. Benevolent or evil, a dreamy magic hangs over the city, where the clocks run backwards or not at all.

The magic has been well-tested in recent years. After the fall of the Iron Curtain, hordes of Euro-trotting foreigners flooded the Czech Republic's venerable capital. In summer, most of Prague's citizens leave for the country and the foreigner-to-resident ratio soars above nine-to-one; masses pack some streets so tightly that crowd-surfing could become a summer pastime. Yet the fact that Czech beer is cheaper than water is not what retains Prague's magic. Walk a few blocks from any of the major sights and you'll be lost in a maze of cobblestone alleys, looming churches, and dark cellars. Head to an outlying Metro stop and you'll find haggling *babičky*, supermodel-esque natives, and not a backpack in sight. Even in the hyper-touristed Old Town, Prague is still majestic: the Charles Bridge—packed so tightly on a summer's day the only way off is to jump—is still breathtaking at sunrise and eerie in a fog. The spell might be fading, but if you look closely enough, there's still plenty of stardust left in the cobblestone cracks.

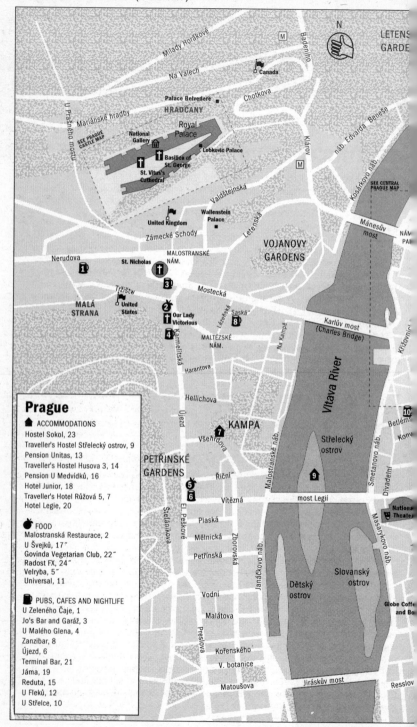

N

LETENS
GARDE

Milady Horákové

Na Valech

Canada

Na Valech

Badeniho

Chotkova

Palace Belvedere
HRADČANY

National
Gallery

Royal
Palace

Lobkovic Palace

Basilica of
St. George

St. Vitus's
Cathedral

Klárov

nábř. Edvarda Beneše

Kosářkovo náb.

SEE PRAGUE
CASTLE MAP

U Prašného mostu

Mariánské hradby

SEE CENTRAL
PRAGUE MAP

Valdštejnská

United Kingdom

Wallenstein
Palace

Letenská

Mánesův
most

NÁM
PAI

Zámecké Schody

VOJANOVY
GARDENS

Nerudova

St. Nicholas

MALOSTRANSKÉ
NÁM.

**1**

**3**

Mostecká

Tržištw

United
States

**2**

Our Lady
Victorious

Lázeňská

Saská

**8**

Karlův most
(Charles Bridge)

Křižovníc

MALÁ
STRANA

**4**

Karmelitská

MALTÉZSKÉ
NÁM.

Na Kampě

Harantova

Hellichova

KAMPA

Vltava River

Betlém

**10**

Kon

Všehrdova

**7**

Malostranské náb.

Střelecký
ostrov

PETŘINSKÉ
GARDENS

Říční

Smetanovo náb.

Divadelní

Újezd

Vítězná

**5**
**6**

most Legií

**9**

Štefánikova

Plaská

Mělnická

Petřínská

Zborovská

Janáčkovo náb.

Dětský
ostrov

Slovanský
ostrov

Masarykovo náb.

Nationa
Theater

El. Peškové

Vodní

Malátova

Preslova

Kořenského

V. botanice

Globe Coffe
and Bo

Matoušova

Jiráskův most

Resslov

## Prague

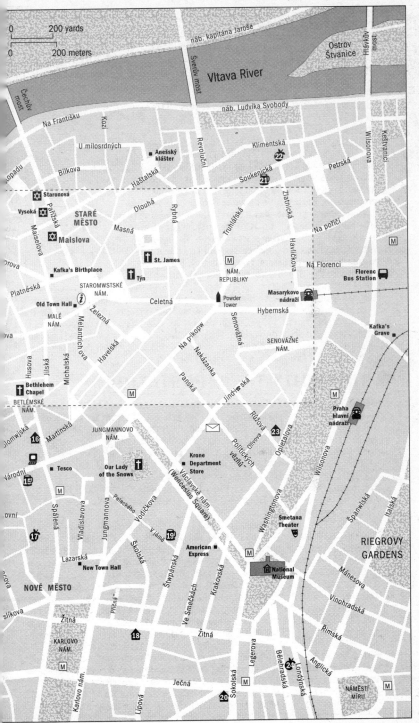

0 | 200 yards
0 | 200 meters

Vltava River

náb. kapitána Jaroše

Ostrov Štvanice

Hlávkův most

Svedů most

Čechův most

náb. Ludvíka Svobody

Na Františku

Kozí

U milosrdných

Klimentská

Petrská

Keřkvanice

Wilsonova

Revoluční

Soukenická

22

Anežský klášter

Bílkova

Haštalská

Zlatnická

Na poříčí

Staronová

Dlouhá

Rybná

21

STARÉ MĚSTO

Pařížská

Vysoká

Masná

Truhlářská

Havlíčkova

Maiselova

Maislova

St. James

Ná Florenci

M

Kafka's Birthplace

Týn

M

Florenc Bus Station

STAROMĚSTSKÉ NÁM.

NÁM. REPUBLIKY

Masarykovo nádraží

Platnéřská

Celetná

Kafka's Grave

Old Town Hall

Železná

Powder Tower

Hybernská

MALÉ NÁM.

Melantrichova

Havelská

Na příkopě

Senovážná

SENOVÁŽNÉ NÁM.

Husova

Jilská

Michalská

Nekázanka

Panská

Jindřišská

Bethlehem Chapel

M

BETLÉMSKÉ NÁM.

Růžová

Olivova

Opletalova

Praha hlavní nádraží

M

JUNGMANNOVO NÁM.

23

Politických vězňů

16

Martinská

Wilsonova

Olomoucká

Národní

15

Tesco

Our Lady of the Snows

Krone Department Store

Washingtonova

M

Vladislavova

Spálená

Jungmannova

Palackého

Vodičkova

Václavské nám. (Wenceslas Square)

Smetana Theater

RIEGROVY GARDENS

Španělská

Italská

17

V jámě

19

American Express

Lazarská

Štěpánská

Ve Smečkách

Krakovská

M

National Museum

Mánesova

New Town Hall

NOVÉ MĚSTO

Příčná

Vinohradská

Žitná

Žitná

Legerova

Římská

Anglická

slíkova

KARLOVO NÁM.

18

Ječná

Sokolská

Bělehradská

Londýnská

24

NÁMĚSTÍ MÍRU

M

Karlovo nám.

Lipová

20

M

M

# ■ ORIENTATION

Straddling the river **Vltava,** Prague is a gigantic mess of suburbs and labyrinthine medieval streets. Fortunately, nearly everything of interest lies within the compact, walkable downtown. The river Vltava runs south-northeast through central Prague and separates the **Staré Město** (Old Town) and the **Nové Město** (New Town) from **Malá Strana** (Lesser Side). On the right bank of the river, the Old Town's **Staroměstské náměstí** (Old Town Square) is the focal point of the city. From the square, the elegant **Pařížská ulice** (Paris Street) leads north into **Josefov,** the old Jewish ghetto; unfortunately, all that remains are six synagogues and the Old Jewish Cemetery. In the opposite direction from Pařížská lies **Nové Město.** It houses **Václavské náměstí** (Wenceslas Square), the administrative and commercial heart of the city. West of Staroměstské nám., **Karlův most** (Charles Bridge) traverses the Vltava and connects the Old Town with **Malostranské náměstí** (Lesser Town Square). **Pražský Hrad** (Prague Castle) sits on the **Hradčany** hilltop above Malostranské nám.

## Central Prague

**♠ ACCOMMODATIONS**
Dům u krále Jiřího, 4
Pension Týn, 14
Traveller's Hostel Dlouhá 33, 16
Traveller's Hostel Křižovnická 7, 2
U Lilie, 3

**🍴 FOOD**
Pizza Express, 13
U Špirků, 10
Country Life, 9
Klub architektů, 5
Shalom, 6

**🍺 PUBS, CAFES AND NIGHTLIFE**
Cafe Marquis De Sade, 17
Roxy, 15
Jazz Club Železna, 12
Blatouch, 11
U Staré Pani, 8
Žiznivý Pes (Thirsty Dog), 7
Lávka, 1

Prague's main train station, **Hlavní nádraží,** and **Florenc bus station** sit in the northeastern corner of Václavské nám. All train and bus terminals are on or near the excellent **Metro** system. To get to Staroměstské nám., take the Metro A line to Staroměstská and walk down Kaprova away from the river. *Tabák* stands and bookstores sell the indexed *plán města* (map); this, along with the English-language weekly *The Prague Post,* is essential for visitors.

# ■ INTERCITY TRANSPORTATION

**Flights: Ruzyně Airport** (☎20 11 11 11), 20km northwest of the city. Local bus #119 operates between the airport and Metro A: Dejvická. Tickets sold in kiosks or machines but not on board. (Daily 5am-midnight; 12Kč; 6Kč more per luggage.) An **airport bus** (☎20 11 42 96; every 30min.) collects travelers right outside the Metro stations at Nám. Republiky (90Kč) and Dejvická (60Kč). **Taxis** to the airport are extremely expensive but may be the only option at night. Many major carriers, including **Air France,** Václavské nám. 57 (☎24 22 71 64), **British Airways,** Ovocný trh 8 (☎22 11 44 44), **Czech Airlines** (ČSA), V celnici 5 (☎20 10 41 10), **Delta,** Národní třída 32 (☎24 94 73 32), **KLM,** Na Příkopě 13 (☎33 09 09 33), **Lufthansa,** Pařížská 28 (☎24 81 10 07), and **Swissair,** Pařížská 11 (☎24 81 21 11).

**Trains:** ☎24 22 42 00; international info ☎24 61 52 49. Some English spoken. Prague has four main terminals. **Praha Hlavní nádraží** (☎24 22 42 00; Metro C: Hlavní nádraží) is the largest, but most international service runs out of **Nádraží Holešovice** (☎24 61 72 65; Metro C: Nádraží Holešovice). To: **Bratislava, SLK** (5½hr., 7 per day, 300Kč); **Berlin, GER** (5hr., 5 per day, 1580Kč); **Budapest, HUN** (10hr., 5 per day, 1290Kč, Wasteels 1050Kč); **Kraków, POL** (8½hr., 3 per day, 1000Kč); **Moscow, RUS** (30¼hr., 1 per day, 2500Kč); **Munich, GER** (6hr., 3 per day, 2450Kč, Wasteels 1900Kč); **Vienna, AUS** (4½hr., 3 per day, 780Kč) and **Warsaw, POL** (9½hr., 3 per day, 670Kč). Domestic trains go from **Masarykovo nádraží** (☎24 61 72 60; Metro B: Náměstí Republiky), on the corner of Hybernská and Havlíčkova, or from **Smíchovské nádraží** (☎24 61 72 55; Metro B: Smíchovské nádraží). **B.I.J. Wasteels** (☎24 61 74 54; fax 24 22 18 72), on the 2nd floor of Hlavní nádraží, to the right of the stairs, sells discounted international tickets to those under 26 and books couchettes. Open summer M-F 7:30am-8pm, Sa 8-11:30am and 12:30-3pm; off-season M-F 8:30am-6pm. Wasteels tickets are also available from the **Czech Railways Travel Agency** (☎800 805; fax 806 948) at Nádraží Holešovice. Open M-F 9am-5pm, Sa-Su 8am-4pm.

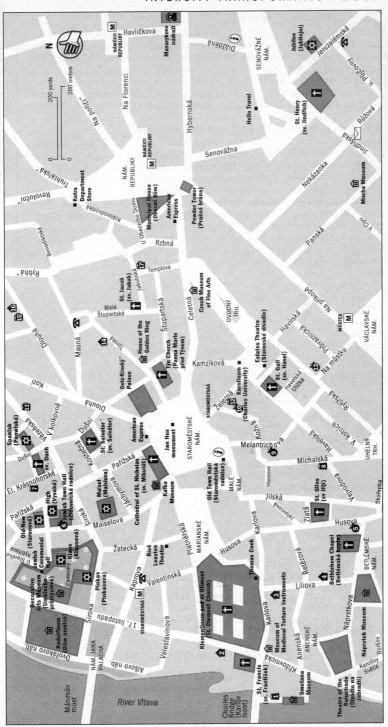

N

0    200 yards
0    200 meters

**Havlíčkova**

NÁMĚSTÍ REPUBLIKY Ⓜ

Masarykovo nádraží

Dlážděná

SENOVÁŽNÉ NÁM.

Na Florenci

Hybernská

ℹ Hello Travel

Jeruzalémská

Jubilee (Jubilejní)

u. Půjčovny

Růžová

Jindřišská

St. Henry (sv. Jindřich)

Senovážná

NÁMĚSTÍ REPUBLIKY Ⓜ

NÁM. REPUBLIKY

U Obecního Domu

Municipal House (Obecní dům)

American Express

Powder Tower (Prašná brána)

Mucha Museum

Nekázanka

V Cípu

Panská

Truhlářská

Na poříčí

Kotra Department Store

Králodvorská

Revoluční

Rzbná

Benediktská

Rybná

Templova

Jakubská

St. Jacob (sv. Jakub)

Malá Štupartská

House of the Golden Ring

Štupartská

Celetná

Czech Museum of Fine Arts

OVOCNÝ TRH.

Dlouhá

Masná

Týnská

Týn Church (Panna Marie před Týnem)

Golz-Kinský Palace

Kamzíková

Estates Theatre (Stavovské divadlo)

St. Gall (sv. Havel)

Havelská Ulička

Na můstku

MŮSTEK Ⓜ

VÁCLAVSKÉ NÁM.

Na příkopě

Havířská

Kozí

Kozná

Zelená

STAROMĚSTSKÁ

Karolinum (Charles University)

Rytířská

Kožná

V kotcích

Rytířská

Jánský

Haštalská

V kolkovně

Dlouhá

Spanish (Panvíská)

U Vězeňská

Dušní

St. Salvator (sv. Salvátor)

American Express

Jan Hus monument

STAROMĚSTSKÉ NÁM.

Melantrichova

Michalská

Hlasova

V kotcích

UHELNÝ TRH.

Skořepka

Kostečná

sv. Duch

High (Vysoká)

Jewish Town Hall (Židovnická radnice)

Maisel (Maislova)

Kafka Museum

Cathedral of St. Nicholas (sv. Mikuláš)

Old Town Hall (Staroměstská radnice) ℹ

MALÉ NÁM.

St. Giles (sv. Jiljí)

Jilská

Zlatá

Husova

El. Krásnohorské

Dušní

Pařížská

Jáchymova

Vězeňská

Maiselova

Široká

Pařížská

Old-New (Staronová)

Žatecká

Maiselova

Řásě Loustek Theater

Platnéřská

MARIÁNSKÉ NÁM.

Bethlehem Chapel (Betlémská kaple)

BETLÉMSKÉ NÁM.

U Starého hřbitova

Decorative Arts Museum (Uměleckoprůmyslové)

Jewish Ceremonial Hall

Klaus (Klausová)

Pinkas (Pinkasova)

Kaprova

Valentinská

STAROMĚSTSKÁ Ⓜ

Thomas Cook

Retězová

Liliova

Náprstkova

Kaprova

Řetězová

Anenská

ANENSKÉ NÁM.

Náprstek Museum

Karoliny Světlé

Boršov

Rudolfinum (Dům umělců)

NÁM. JANA PALACHA

Alšovo nábř.

17. listopadu

Veleslavínova

Klementinum and sv. Kliment (St. Clement Church)

Husova

Karlova

Museum of Medieval Torture Instruments

Mariánské

Mánesův most

Dvořákovo nábř.

River Vltava

Charles Bridge (Karlův most)

St. Francis (sv. František)

Smetana Museum

Theatre at the Balustrade (Divadlo na zábradlí)

Křižovnická

**Buses:** The state-run **ČSAD** (Česká státní automobilová doprava; Czech national bus transport) has several bus terminals. The biggest is **Florenc,** Křižíkova 4 (☎24 21 49 90 and 24 21 10 60; Metro B, C: Florenc). Timetables can be initially confusing; start by looking up bus stop numbers for your destination. Info office open M-F 6am-9pm, Sa 6am-6pm, Su 8am-8pm. Buy tickets in advance. To: **Berlin, GER** (6hr., 1 per day, 1038Kč); **Vienna, AUS** (8½hr., 1 per day, 870Kč); and **Sofia, BUL** (26hr., 4 per day, 1850Kč). Students may get 10% discount. The **Tourbus** office upstairs (☎24 21 02 21) sells tickets for **Eurolines** and airport buses. Open M-F 8am-8pm, Sa-Su 9am-8pm.

# ▛ LOCAL TRANSPORTATION

**Public Transportation:** The **Metro, tram,** and **bus** services are excellent and share the same ticket system. Buy tickets from newsstands and *tabák* kiosks, machines in stations, or DP (*Dopravní podnik;* transport authority) kiosks. From the machines, select the ticket price, then insert your coins. The basic 8Kč ticket is good for one 15min. ride (or four stops on the Metro); the 12Kč ticket is valid for 1hr. (90min. 8pm-5am) anywhere in the city with unlimited connections between bus, tram, and Metro, as long as you keep heading in the same direction. Large bags 6Kč each (buy an extra 6Kč ticket and punch it as well), as are bikes and baby carriages without babies in them (*with* babies free). Validate your ticket in the machines above the escalators, as plainclothes DP inspectors roam Prague's transport lines (most frequently the Metro) issuing 200Kč spot fines. If you're nabbed, make sure you see their official badge, and get a receipt. The **Metro's** three lines run daily 5am-midnight: A is green on the maps, B is yellow, C is red. **Night trams** #51-58 and **buses** run all night after the last Metro; look for the dark blue signs with white letters at bus stops. All night tram lines wait for one another in Lazarská, two stops from Václavské nám. away from the center. DP office by the Jungmannovo nám. exit of Metro A, B: Můstek (☎24 22 51 35; open daily 7am-9pm) and tourist office in Old Town Hall also sell **multi-day passes** valid for the entire network. (24hr. 70Kč, 3 days 200Kč, 1 week 250Kč.)

**Taxis: Taxi Praha** (☎8577 or 1087) or **AAA** (☎24 32 24 32). Prague has finally instituted set rates: 25Kč flat rate plus 13Kč per km. Hail a cab anywhere on the street, but calling one of the above numbers is a better protection against getting ripped off.

**TAXI A LA PRAHA** Prague's taxi drivers are notorious scam artists who could drain your wallet faster than you can say *"To je zlodějina!"* (It's a rip-off!) Before getting in, check that the meter is set to zero and ask the driver to start it by saying *"Zapněte prosím taximetr."* For longer trips, agree on a price before setting off and get it in writing. Make sure the driver knows exactly where he's taking you; a common trick is to charge higher than the set price by feigning ignorance of exactly how far your destination was. Always ask for a receipt (*"Prosím, dejte mi účet"*) with distance traveled, price paid, and the driver's signature. If the driver doesn't write the receipt, it's your legal right not to pay.

**Car Rental: Hertz,** at the airport (☎312 07 17; fax 20 56 34 72; open M-F 8am-10pm, Sa-Su 8am-8pm) and at Karlovo nám. 28 (☎22 23 10 10; fax 22 23 10 15; open daily 8am-8pm). Cars start at 1006Kč per day for the first 4 days with unlimited mileage. Specials on weekends (Th-Su) 700Kč per day. Rentals require a valid 3-year-old driver's license, a major credit card, and an over-21 renter.

# ▟ PRACTICAL INFORMATION

## TOURIST AND FINANCIAL SERVICES

**Tourist Office:** The green "i"s around Prague mark the multitude of tourist agencies that book rooms and sell maps, bus tickets, postcards, and guidebooks. **Pražská informační služba** (PIS; Prague Information Service), in the Old Town Hall (☎24 48 25

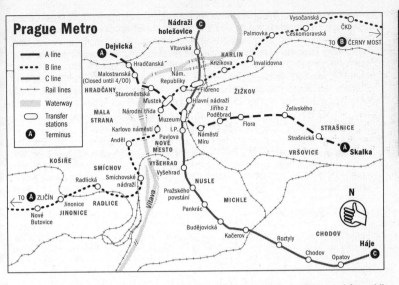

Prague Metro

— A line
···· B line
≈≈≈ C line
+·+· Rail lines
≋ Waterway
⬭ Transfer stations
Ⓐ Terminus

62; English ☎54 44 44). Sells **maps** (39-49Kč) and tickets to shows and for public transport. Open summer M-F 9am-7pm, Sa-Su 9am-6pm; off-season M-F 9am-6pm, Sa-Su 9am-5pm. Other offices at Na příkopě 20, at Hlavní nádraží, and in the tower on the Malá Strana side of the Charles Bridge all have the same hours. **Budget Travel: CKM,** Jindřišská 28 (☎24 23 02 18; fax 26 86 23; ckmprg@mbox.vol.cz). Metro A, B: Můstek. Sells budget air tickets to those under 26. Also books accommodations in Prague from 350Kč. Open M-Th 10am-6pm, F 10am-4pm. **KMC,** Karoliny Světlé 30 (☎/fax 22 22 03 47). Metro B: Národní třída. Books HI hostels. Open M-Th 9am-noon and 2:30-5pm, F 9am-noon and 2:30-3:30pm. **GTS,** Ve smečkách 27 (☎54 34 55). Metro A, C: Muzeum. Offers student discounts on airfares. Open M-F 8am-6pm, Sa 9am-4pm. **STA Travel,** Široká 15 (no phone). Metro A: Staroměstská. From the Metro, walk down Kaprova, turn left onto Valentinská, then right onto Široká. Also has great student deals. Open M-F 8:30am-5:30pm. Visa/MC/AmEx.

**Passport Office:** Foreigner police headquarters at Olšanská 2 (☎683 17 39). Metro A: Flora. From the Metro, turn right onto Jičínská with the cemetery on your right, and right again onto Olšanská. Or take tram #9 from Václavské nám. toward Spojovací and get off at Olšanská. To obtain a **visa extension,** get a 90Kč stamp inside, line up in front of doors #2-12, and prepare to wait up to 2hr. Little English spoken. Open M-Tu and Th 7:30-11:30am and 12:30-2:30pm, W 7:30-11:30am and 12:30-5pm, F 7:30am-noon.

**Embassies: Canada,** Mickiewiczova 6 (☎24 31 11 08). Metro A: Hradčanská. Open M-F 8am-noon and 2-4pm. **France,** Velkopřerovské nám. 2 (☎24 51 04 02). Metro A: Malostranská. **Germany,** Vlašská 19 (☎57 32 01 90). Metro A: Malostranská. **Hungary,** Badeniho 1 (☎36 50 41). Metro A: Hradčanská. Open M-W and F 9am-noon. **Ireland,** Tržiště 13 (☎530 911). Metro A: Malostranská. Open M-F 9:30am-12:30pm and 2:30-4:30pm. **Poland,** Valdštejnské nám. 8 (☎57 32 06 78). Metro A: Malostranská. Open M-F 7am-noon. **Russia,** Pod Kaštany 1 (☎38 19 40). Metro A: Hradčanská. Open M, W, and F 9am-1pm. **Slovakia,** Pod Hradební 1 (☎32 05 21). Metro A: Dejvická. Open M-F 8:30am-noon. **South Africa,** Ruská 65 (☎67 31 11 14). Metro A: Flora. Open M-F 9am-noon. **UK,** Thunovská 14 (☎57 32 03 55). Metro A: Malostranská. Open M-F 9am-noon. **US,** Tržiště 15 (☎57 53 06 63; emergency after-hours ☎53 12 00). Metro A: Malostranská. From Malostranské nám., head down Karmelitská and take a right onto Tržiště. Open M-F 8am-1pm and 2-4:30pm. **Australia** (☎24 31 00 71) and **New Zealand** (☎25 41 98) have consuls, but citizens should contact the UK embassy in an emergency.

**Currency Exchange:** Exchange counters are everywhere, with wildly varying rates. Don't bother with the expensive hotels, and don't even think about changing money on the streets. **Chequepoints** are conveniently open till late hours, but charge unpredictable commission and may try to rip you off, so know your math. Try bargaining. **Komerční banka,** Na příkopě 33 (☎22 43 21 11), buys notes and checks for a 2% commission. Open M-F 8am-5pm. **Thomas Cook:** Národní třída 28 (☎21 10 52 76; fax 94 90 04). MC/Visa cash advances. Open M-F 9am-7pm, Sa 9am-6pm, Su 10am-6pm. Branch on Karlova 3 (☎22 22 10 55; fax 22 22 00 68). Open daily 10am-10pm.

**ATMs:** All over the place; look for the green and orange "*Bankomat*" signs. The one at **Krone supermarket,** Václavské nám. 21, accepts Cirrus/Plus/MC/Visa.

**American Express:** Václavské nám. 56 (☎22 80 02 37; fax 22 21 11 31). Metro A, C: Muzeum. The **ATM** outside takes AmEx cards. Grants MC/Visa **cash advances** for a 3% commission. Open open daily 9am-7pm. Branches on Mostecká 12 (☎57 31 36 38; open daily 9:30am-7:30pm), Celetná 17 (☎/fax 24 81 82 74), and Staroměstské nám. 5 (☎ 24 81 83 88; fax 24 81 83 89).

## LOCAL SERVICES

**Luggage Storage:** Lockers in all train and bus stations take two 5Kč coins. If you forget the locker number or combination, you'll be charged 20Kč. For storage longer than 24hr., use the luggage offices to the left in the basement of **Hlavní nádraží** (under 15kg 15Kč per day; larger bags 30Kč per day; open 24hr.) and halfway up the stairs at **Florenc** (up to 15kg 10Kč per day; larger bags 25Kč per day; 100Kč if you lose ticket; open daily 5am-11pm).

**International Bookstores: The Globe Bookstore,** Pštrossova 6 (☎24 91 62 64). Metro B: Národní třída. Exit Metro left onto Spálená, make first right onto Ostrovní, then turn left to Pštrossova. New and used books and periodicals, a coffeehouse, and free **Internet** access. A legendary (pick-up) center of anglophone Prague. Open Su-Th 10am-midnight, F-Sa 10-1am. **Anagram Bookshop,** Týn 4 (☎24 89 57 37; fax 24 89 57 38; anagram@terminal.cz; www.anagram.cz). Metro A: Staroměstské. Behind Týn Church in the Ungelt passageway. Open M-Sa 10am-8pm, Su 10am-6pm. **Big Ben Bookshop,** Malá Štupartská 5 (☎231 80 21; fax 231 98 48; bigben@terminal.cz). Metro A: Nám. Republiky. Turn onto U obecního domů, right behind the Powder Tower. Turn right onto Rybná, left onto Jakubská, then right onto Štupartská. Open M-F 9am-6:30pm, Sa-Su 10am-5pm. For a more upscale spot, head to **U Knihomola International Bookshop,** Mánesova 79 (☎627 77 67; fax 627 77 82). Metro A: Jiřího z Poděbrad. Open M-F 9am-9pm, Sa 2-9pm.

**Laundromat: Laundry Kings,** Dejvická 16 (☎312 37 43), one block from Metro A: Hradčanská. Cross the tram *and* railroad tracks, then turn left onto Dejvická. As much a social center as a laundromat, in the evenings the place is filled with thirsty travelers who watch CNN and try to pick each other up. Bulletin board for apartment seekers, English teachers, and potential "friends." Wash 60Kč per 6kg; dry 15Kč per 8min. (usually takes 45min.; use the spinner to save on drying). Soap 10-20Kč. Full-service 30Kč more and takes 24hr. Beer 17Kč.Open M-F 6am-10pm, Sa-Su 8am-10pm.

## EMERGENCY AND COMMUNICATIONS

Don't be fooled by the different lengths of telephone numbers ranging from 4 to 8 digits. Prague is continuously updating its phone system, often giving businesses extremely short notice. Some numbers listed here are likely to be obsolete by the time you read this—but then again, nothing is sacred.

**Emergency: Na Homolce** (Hospital for Foreigners), Roentgenova 2 (☎52 92 21 74; after-hours ☎57 21 11 11). Doctor on call M-F 8am-4pm, emergency service 24hr. Major insurance plans and credit cards accepted. **American Medical Center,** Janovského 48 (☎807 756). Major foreign insurance policies accepted. **Canadian Medical Centre,** Veleslavínska 30 (☎316 55 19). BUPA and MEDEX insurance accepted.

**24hr. Pharmacies: U Anděla,** Štefánikova 6 (☎57 32 09 18). Metro B: Anděl. Exit Metro toward Anděl and follow Nádražní until it becomes Štefánikova.

**Telephones:** Everywhere, including the post office. Cardphones are most common and convenient. Phonecards sell for 175Kč per 50 units and 320Kč per 100 units at kiosks, post offices, and some exchange places: don't let kiosks rip you off.

**Internet Access:** Prague is Internet nirvana. Access is everywhere: in libraries, hostels, posh cafes, and trendy bars. Národní is home to several computer-lab-like cyber cafes.

**Terminal Bar,** see **Beerhalls & Pubs,** p. 241.

**Globe Bookstore,** see **International Bookstores,** p. 172.

**Cafe Electra,** Rašínovo nábřeží 62 (☎297 038). Metro B: Karlovo nám. Exit on the Palackého nám. side. 25 computers and extensive menu. Cheapest at 80Kč per hr. Open M-F 9am-midnight, Sa-Su 11am-midnight.

**Internet Cafe,** Národní třída 25 (☎21 08 52 84; internetcafe@highland.cz; www.internetcafe.cz). Metro B: Národní třída. Across from Tesco in Pasáž paláce METRO. 17 speedy PCs and 4 Macs 120Kč per hr. and virtually no wait. Open M-Th 9am-11pm, Sa-Su 10am-11pm.

**Cafe.com,** Na Poříčí 36 (☎24 81 94 35). Metro B: Florenc. Cyber cellar with a hip blue tile bar. 50Kč per 30min. Open M-F 9am-midnight, Sa-Su 11am-midnight.

**Laundromat/Internet Cafe,** Korunní 14 (☎ 22 51 01 80). Metro A: Nám. Míru. Kill two birds with one stone. Washer 65Kč, dryer 65Kč per load. Soap 20Kč. Internet 30Kč per 15min. Open daily 8am-8pm.

**Post Office:** Jindřišská 14. Metro A, B: Můstek (☎21 13 15 20). Stamps at window #11; letters and small parcels at #12-14; info at window labeled "i"; #17 is **Poste Restante.** Airmail to the US takes 7-10 days. For sizeable packages, go to booths #3-9 (boxes available). Open daily 7am-8pm.

**Postal Code:** 110 00.

# ACCOMMODATIONS

While hotel prices have risen beyond your worst nightmare, the hostel market is glutted; prices have stabilized around 270-420Kč per night. Smaller hostels with a home-away-from-home atmosphere tend to be cheaper than the larger hostels in the center of town. Rooms must be reserved at least two days in advance, and even earlier in July and August. The Strahov complex and other student dorms bear the brunt of the summer's backpacking crowds. Most accommodations have 24-hour reception and require that you check in after 2pm and check out by 10am. Though the practice is far less common than in other parts of Eastern Europe, a growing number of Prague residents are renting affordable rooms.

## ACCOMMODATION AGENCIES

Many of the hawkers who besiege visitors at the train station are agents hired by other people. Many of them will offer legitimate deals, but others just want to rip you off. The going rates for **apartments** hover around 600-1200Kč per day, depending on proximity to the city center; haggling is possible. If you're wary of bargaining on the street, try a private agency. Staying outside the center can be fine if you're near public transport, so ask where the nearest tram, bus, or Metro stop is. Don't pay until you know what you're getting—if in doubt, ask for details in writing. You can often pay in US dollars or Deutschmarks, but prices are lower if you pay in Kč.

**Hello Travel Ltd.,** Senovážné nám. 3 (☎24 21 26 47; fax 24 21 28 24; hello@hello.cz). Metro B: Náměstí Republiky. Walk down Revoluční toward the Powder Tower, turn left to Senovážná at the tower, then another left to Senovážné nám. Arranges every sort of housing imaginable. Accommodation rates 500-1500Kč per person in summer, off-season 400-1200Kč. Open M-F 8am-7pm.

**Ave.,** Hlavní nádraží (☎24 22 35 21 and 51 55 52 32; fax 51 55 51 56), on the 2nd floor of the train station next to the leftmost stairs. Burgeoning firm offers hundreds of rooms (shared and private) starting at 800Kč per person. Books hostels from 300Kč. Open daily 6am-11pm. AmEx/MC/Visa.

# HOSTELS

If you're schlepping a backpack in Hlavní nádraží or Holešovice, you *will* be bombarded by hostel runners. Many are university dorms that free up for travelers from June to August, and often you'll be offered free transport. These rooms are the easiest option for those arriving in the middle of the night without a reservation. For those who prefer hostels that offer more than just a place to sleep, there are smaller, friendlier alternatives. Unfortunately, not all places accept reservations, so it's best to phone the night before you arrive or at 10am. Like everywhere else in Prague, the staff typically speaks English. Curfews are distant memories.

## STARÉ MĚSTO

**Traveller's Hostels** (hostel@terminal.cz). These summertime big-dorm specialists round up travelers at bus and train stations around the city and herd them into one of their city-center hostels for lots of beds and beer. Price varies with proximity to the center of town. At all hostels, breakfast is included and internet access available (27Kč per 15 min.).

**Husova 3** (☎24 21 53 26). Metro B: Národní třída. Turn right onto Spálená (which turns into Na Perštýně after Národní), and then Husova. Right in the middle of the Old Town. Satellite TV. Still the classiest, with dorms for 400Kč.

**Dlouhá 33** (☎24 82 66 62; fax 24 82 66 65). Metro B: Nám. Republiky. From the Metro, follow Revoluční toward the river. Turn left on Dlouhá; the hostel will be on your right. Unbeatable location right off Staroměstské nám. In the same building as the Roxy club, but with good soundproofing. The only one of Traveller's hostels that stays open year-round. Laundry 150Kč per load. 6-bed dorms 380Kč; 10-bed 350Kč; doubles 550Kč per person; triples 430Kč per person.

**Křížovnická 7** (☎232 09 87). Metro A: Staroměstská. Exit the Metro toward the river; Křížovnická runs along it. Outdoor picnic area and an indoor pub. Dorms 230Kč.

**Střelecký ostrov** (☎24 91 01 88). An island off Most Legií. Metro B: Národní třída. A tennis court available. Dorms 300Kč.

**Růžová 5** (☎24 21 69 71). Metro C: Hlavní nádraží. Bar and sauna are definite highlights. 220Kč.

**Pension Týn**, Týnská 19 (☎/fax 24 80 83 33; backpacker@razdva.cz). Metro A: Staroměstská. From Staroměstské nám., head down Dlouhá, bear right at Masná, and another right onto Týnská. A quiet getaway conveniently located in the center of the Old Town. No common room, but immaculate facilities. Dorms 400Kč; singles 1000Kč; doubles 1200Kč.

## NOVÉ MĚSTO

**Hostel U melounu** (At the Watermelon), Ke Karlovu 7 (☎/fax 24 91 83 22; pus@cz.com.cz). Metro C: I.P. Pavlova. Follow Sokolská to Na Bojišti and turn left at the street's end onto Ke Karlovu. In a historic building with great facilities 5min. from Nové Město. Dorms 380Kč; singles 450Kč; doubles 420Kč. 100Kč off with ISIC. Breakfast included.

**Prague Lion**, Na Bojišti 26 (☎/fax 96 18 00 18; praguelion@mbox.vol.cz). Metro C: I.P. Pavlova. Follow Sokolská to Na Bojišti. Good location, clean rooms, but a little pricey. Breakfast 50Kč. Internet 3Kč per min. No singles. Doubles 1050Kč; quads 1700Kč.

**Hotel Junior**, Senovážné nám. 21 (☎24 23 17 54 and 22 10 55 36; fax 24 22 15 79; euroagentur@euroagentur.cz). Metro B: Náměstí Republiky. See directions to Hello Travel (p. 223). 1970s revival decor, but rooms are neat and central. Check-in 2pm. Dorms 550Kč, 450Kč with ISIC/HI card. Breakfast included.

**Hostel SPUS**, Dittrichova 15 (☎/fax 24 91 53 80). Metro B: Karlovo nám. Head down Resslova toward the river and turn left on Dittrichova. Rooms escape the otherwise institutional feel in this July-Aug. only dorm. Closed for renovation during summer 2000, but should reopen in 2001. In 1999, the prices were: 2- to 4-bed dorms 380Kč; 6-bed dorms 320Kč; doubles with bath 450Kč per person. 30Kč off with ISIC, GO-25, or Euro26.

## MALÁ STRANA

**Hostel Sokol**, Všehrdova 10 (☎57 00 73 97; fax 57 00 73 40). Metro A: Malostranská. From the Metro, take tram #12 or 22 toward Hlubočepy or Nádraží Hostivař to Hellichova; walk down Újezd to Všehrdova. 10- to 12-person dorms in the Malá Strana sports club. Communal kitchen. Safes and lockers. Check-in/check-out 11am. Reception 24hr. 270Kč.

## VINOHRADY

**Domov Mládeže,** Dykova 20 (☎/fax 22 51 25 97 and 22 51 17 77). From Metro A: Jiřího z Poděbrad, follow Nitranská and turn left on Dykova; it's two blocks down on your right. Great view of the city from the patio-roof. 80 beds in the tree-lined Vinohrady district; so peaceful you might forget you're in Prague. Clean 2- to 7-person dorms 430Kč; lone double 650Kč. Breakfast included. If they're full, they might have space in a sister hostel: **Amadeus,** Slavojova 108/8. Metro C: Vyšehrad. From the Metro, descend the bridge to Čiklova, turn left, and the hostel is on the left. **Máchova,** Máchova 11. Metro A: Nám. Míru. From the Metro, walk down Ruská and turn right onto Máchova. **Košická,** Košická 12. Metro A: Nám. Míru. All hostels use the same telephone and prices.

## OUTSIDE THE CENTER

🏠 **Hostel Boathouse,** Lodnická 1 (☎/fax 402 10 76). Take tram #3 from Hlavní nádraží or #17 from Nádraží Holešovice south toward Sídliště and get off at Černý Kůň (20min.). From the tram stop, follow the yellow Boathouse signs down to the Vltava. If coming from the airport, don't pay more than 500Kč for taxi. As Věra, the owner, says, "This isn't a hostel; it's a crazy house." A young, energetic crowd, and 70 beds worth of Anglophones make this hostel the perfect fusion of nurturing home and summer camp. Also serves meals (breakfast 50Kč, dinner 70Kč) and offers board games, internet access, satellite TV, and laundry service (100Kč per load). 2 nights minimum. Call ahead; if they're full, Věra or Helena might let you sleep in the hall. Beds in 3- to 5-bed dorms perched above a working boathouse 290Kč.

🏠 **Penzion v podzámčí,** V podzámčí 27 (☎/fax 41 44 46 09; evacib@yahoo.com). From Metro C: Budějovická, take bus #192 to the 3rd stop—ask the driver to stop at Nad Rybníky. Eva and other staff make this the homiest hostel in Prague, from extraordinary laundry service (they *iron* your socks! 100Kč per load) to daily clothes-folding and bed-making. They make great hot chocolate and have a communal kitchen, satellite TV, comfy beds, umbrellas, friendly cats, and great stories. Internet access 25Kč per 15 min. Dorms 280Kč; doubles 320Kč; triples 300Kč.

**Welcome Hostel,** Zíkova 13 (☎24 32 02 02; fax 24 32 34 89; welcome@welcome.cz; www.welcome.cz). Metro A: Dejvická. From the escalators, follow Šolinova to Zíkova. A free beer welcomes weary travelers. Great if you're arriving from the airport late at night. Very institutional, but improvements to come in 2001. Check-in 2pm. Check-out 9:30am. Open June-Sept. Singles 350Kč; doubles 230Kč per person.

**Strahov Complex,** Vaníčkova 5 (☎52 71 90). Take bus #217 or 143 from Metro A: Dejvická to Koleje Strahov. Known as a "hostel ghetto," Strahov is 10 concrete blocks next to the enormous stadium that opens June-Aug. to accommodate the hordes (some beds available all year). Not very convenient, but there's always space, and you can catch the Strahov concerts from the comfort of your cubicle. Singles 300Kč; doubles 220Kč; students 180Kč with ID.

**Hotel Standart,** Přístavní 2 (☎875 258 and 875 674; fax 806 752). From Metro C: Vltavská, take tram #1 toward Spojovací, #3 toward Lehovec, #14 toward Vozovna Kobylisy, or #25 toward Střelničná; get off at Přístavní. Continue along the street, then turn left onto Přístavní. Very quiet neighborhood far, far away. Singles 620Kč; doubles 800Kč; triples 1100Kč; quads 1400Kč. Breakfast included.

# HOTELS AND PENSIONS

With so many tourists colonizing Prague, hotels are upgrading service, appearance, and prices; budget hotels are now scarce. Beware that hotels may try to bill you for a more expensive room than the one you in which you stayed; arm yourself with receipts. The good, cheap ones require reservations up to a month in advance, but too many backpacker no-shows have forced many businesses to refuse reservations altogether. Call first, then confirm by fax with a credit card.

## STARÉ MĚSTO

**Pension Unitas/Cloister Inn,** Bartolomějská 9 (☎24 21 10 20; fax 232 77 09; unitas@cloister-inn.cz). Metro B: Národní třída. Cross Národní and head down Na Perštýně away from Tesco. Turn left on Bartolomějská. An old monastery where Beethoven once performed, later a Communist jail where Havel was incarcerated; but no worries—it's been renovated. Comfortable rooms with communal bathrooms. Singles 1020Kč; doubles 1200Kč; triples 1650Kč. Breakfast included.

**Dům U krále Jiřího,** Liliová 10 (☎22 22 09 25; fax 22 22 17 07; kral.jiri@telecom.cz). Metro A: Staroměstská. Exit the Metro onto Nám. Jana Palacha. Walk down Křížovnická toward the Charles Bridge and turn left onto Karlova; Liliová is the 1st street on the right. Gorgeous rooms with private bath. Singles 1700Kč, off-season 1500Kč; doubles 2900Kč, off-season 2700Kč. Buffet breakfast included.

**U Lilie,** Liliová 15 (☎22 22 04 32; fax 22 22 06 41). Metro A: Staroměstská. See the directions to U krále Jiřího (above). Enjoy satellite TV in the rooms and a cozy courtyard. Singles with shower 1700Kč; doubles 1700Kč, with bath 2300Kč. Breakfast included.

## NOVÉ MĚSTO

**Hotel Legie,** Sokolská 33 (☎24 92 02 54; fax 24 91 44 41; legie@netforce.cz). Metro C: I.P. Pavlova. From the Metro, turn left onto Ječná; the hotel is across the steet on the corner. Rather grim exterior, but rooms are newly renovated with private showers, phone, and cable TV. June-Sept. and Jan. doubles 2600Kč; triples 3500Kč. Feb.-May and Oct.-Dec. doubles 2200Kč; triples 3100Kč. Breakfast included.

### OUTSIDE THE CENTER

**Hotel Kafka,** Cimburkova 24 (☎/fax 22 78 04 31), in Žižkov near the TV tower. From Metro C: Hlavní nádraží, take tram #5 toward Harfa, #9 toward Spojovací, or #26 toward Nádraží Hostivař, and get off at Husinecká. Go uphill along Seifertova three blocks and turn left onto Cimburkova. Brand-new hotel amid 19th-century buildings, near plenty of restaurants and beerhalls. Breakfast and parking 100Kč. Mar. 15-July 31 singles 1650Kč; doubles 2450Kč; triples 2550Kč; quads 2800Kč. Aug. and New Year's 1900Kč; 2950Kč; 3050Kč; 3400Kč. Sept.-Dec. and Jan. 1-Mar. 14 1100Kč; 1600Kč; 1750Kč; 1950Kč. MC/Visa (5% commission).

**B&B U Oty (Ota's House),** Radlická 188 (☎/fax 57 21 53 23; mb@bbuoty.cz; www.bbuoty.cz). 400m from Metro B: Radlická, up the slope. Exit the Metro to the left and go right on the road. In what could be Prague's best neighborhood, Ota is a charming Anglophone who strives to take the kinks out of your stay in Prague. Kitchen facilities and, after 3 nights, laundry free. Free parking, provided you're not using the car while in Prague. Lone doubles 700Kč; doubles 770Kč; triples 990Kč; quads 1300Kč. 100Kč extra per person if staying only one night.

# CAMPING

Campsites have taken over both the outskirts and the centrally located Vltava islands. Bungalows must be reserved in advance, but tent space is generally available without prior notice. Tourist offices sell a guide to sites near the city (15Kč).

**Císařská louka,** on a peninsula on the Vltava. Metro B: Smíchovské nádraží, then tram #12 toward Hlubočepy to Lihovar. Walk toward the river and onto the shaded path. Alternatively, take the ferry service from Smíchovské nádraží. **Caravan Park** (☎54 50 64; fax 543 305) sits near the ferry. 90-140Kč per tent, plus 95Kč per person. Singles 365Kč; doubles 630Kč; triples 945Kč. **Caravan Camping** (☎/fax 540 129) is near the tram. 90-120Kč per tent, plus 110Kč per person.

**Sokol Troja,** Trojská 171 (☎/fax 83 85 04 86). Prague's largest campground, north of the center in the Troja district. From Metro C: Nádraží Holešovice, take bus #112 to Kazanka, the 4th stop. If full (or if you're frightened by the deer heads, bear skins, and hunting apparel), at least 4 nearly identical places line the same road. Tents 105-130Kč plus 100Kč per person. Dorms 250Kč; bungalow 230Kč per person.

**Na Vlachovce,** Zenklova 217 (☎/fax 688 04 28). Take bus #102 or 175 from Nádraží Holešovice toward Okrouhlická, get off, and continue in the same direction. Great view of Prague. Reserve a week ahead. If you've ever felt like crawling into a barrel of *Budvar*, this bungalow city provides romantic 2-person barrels at 200Kč per bed. The *pension* attached has doubles with bath for 975Kč. Breakfast included.

# ◻ FOOD

The basic rule is that the nearer you are to the center, the more you'll pay; in the less touristed areas, you can have pork, cabbage, dumplings, and a half-liter of beer for 50Kč. Check your bill carefully—you'll pay for anything the waiter brings, including ketchup and bread, and restaurants have been known to massage bills higher than they ought to. In Czech lunch spots, *hotová jídla* (prepared meals) are cheapest. Vegetarian eateries are quickly multiplying, but often the options are still limited to fried cheese and cabbage. Outlying Metro stops become impromptu marketplaces in the summer; look for the **daily market** at the intersection of Havelská and Melantrichova in Staré Město.

## RESTAURANTS

### STARÉ MĚSTO

**▨ U Špirků,** Kožná ulička 12 (☎ 24 23 84 20). Metro A: Staroměstská. With your back to the astronomical clock on Staroměstské náměstí, go down Melantrichova and take the first left onto Kožná. The restaurant is a few steps away from the armory store. This Czech lunch favorite serves some of the city's best and cheapest food in a spacious pub. Salads 20-35Kč; main dishes 89-138Kč. Open daily 11am-midnight.

**Lotos,** Platnéřská 13 (☎ 232 23 90). Metro A: Staroměstská. Exit the Metro onto the corner of Kaprova and Valentinská. Turn left down Valentinská away from the Jewish cemetery, then right onto Platnéřská. Vegetarian (and non-smoking!) restaurant that deserves applause for its Czech soups (23-28Kč) and unique organic menu (60-140Kč). 0.5L Pilsner 33Kč. Open daily 11am-10pm.

**Klub architektů,** Betlémské nám. 52 (☎ 24 40 12 14). Metro B: Národní třída. Take Spálená through its name change to Na Perštýně, then turn left onto Betlémské nám. Walk through the gate on your right and descend below the ground. A 12th-century cellar thrust into the 20th century with sleek table settings and copper pulley lamps. Plenty of veggie options 80-90Kč; meat dishes 120-150Kč. Open daily 11:30am-midnight.

**Shalom,** Maiselova 18 (☎ 231 90 02). Metro A: Staroměstská. Walk down Kaprova away from the river and go left on Maiselova; the restaurant is inside the synagogue on the right. Fine kosher lunches in the old Jewish Quarter. Set menu 220-520Kč. You'll need to buy tickets beforehand at Legacy Tours, the travel agent across the road (☎ 232 19 51; open M-F and Su 9am-6pm). Order tickets in advance for Jewish holidays. Open M-Sa 11:30am-2pm.

**Country Life,** Melantrichova 15 (☎ 24 21 33 66). Metro B: Staroměstská. See the directions to U Špirků (above). For the ultimate healthnut, Country Life serves a variety of dishes (120Kč) all cooked without eggs, milk, cheese or butter. Sandwiches and salad bar. Open M-Th 9am-8:30pm, Su 11am-8:30pm.

### NOVÉ MĚSTO

**▨ Universal,** V jirchářích 6 (☎ 24 91 81 82). Metro B: Národní třída. Cross the tram tracks and follow the narrow Ostrovní. Take a left onto Opatovická, then a quick right around the church to V jirchářích. A transplanted California-style eatery prepares the biggest and freshest salads in Prague (97-143Kč) for an international crowd of hipsters. Stoplights and a mix of rock n' jazz keep this place pumping at night. Open daily 11:30am-1am.

**▨ Velryba** (The Whale), Opatovická 24 (☎ 24 91 23 91). Metro B: Národní třída. See directions to Universal (above). Across from the church on Opatovická. Relaxed with a bit of chic, this cafe-restaurant houses a gallery in the back. A truly diverse crowd of locals, American ex-pats, business types, and tourists enjoys inexpensive international and Czech dishes (38-155Kč) and adventurous vegetarian platters (lentils with eggs and pickles 38Kč). Can *you* see the whale on the sea-green wall? Open daily 11am-2am.

**Góvinda Vegetarian Club,** Soukenická 27 (☎ 24 81 66 31). Metro B: Nám. Republiky. The restaurant is upstairs at the back of the building. Rama and Krishna gaze upon diners and delicious vegetarian stews. A plate with the works 70Kč. Daily menu. Lectures on the *Bhagavadgítá* Wednesdays at 6:30pm. Open M-Sa 11am-5:30pm.

**Radost FX,** see **Late Night Eating,** p. 179.

**Restaurace U Pravdů,** Žitná 15 (☎29 95 92). Metro B: Karlovo nám. A deservedly popular Czech lunch spot, where spillover from the dining room is seated in the beer garden. Main dishes 80-149Kč. Open M-F 10am-11pm, Sa-Su 11am-11pm.

**Pizzeria Kmotra,** V jirchářích 12 (☎24 91 58 09). Metro B: Národní třída. Same directions as to Universal (above). One of the first pizza restaurants in Prague, this cellar eatery still has lines spilling onto the street at dinner time. Huge salads and pizzas (69-149Kč). Open daily 11am-midnight.

## MALÁ STRANA

🖾 **Bar bar,** Všehrdova 17 (☎53 29 41). Metro A: Malostranská. Follow the tram tracks from the Metro station down Letenská, through Malostranské nám., and down Karmelitská. Turn left on Všehrdova after the museum. A jungle jungle of salads salads with meat meat, fish fish, cheese cheese or just veggies veggies (30-90Kč). The other choice is, shockingly, not fried pork with french fries, but pancakes pancakes—sweet sweet (20-60Kč) or savory savory (80-230Kč). The stuttering eatery has a good vibe, good music, and 40 varieties of good whiskey (from 55Kč). Open daily noon-midnight.

**Malostranská restaurace,** Karmelitská 25 (☎57 53 14 18). Metro A: Malostranská. From the Metro, go down Klárov, then right onto Letenská. Traverse Malostranské nám. and continue on Karmelitská. Chairs spill out onto the street from the vaulted interior. The usual long table in the corner surrounded by beer and *Becherovka* fans is made up of women; the men are usually too drunk to notice. Bacon dumplings and other Czech yummies (70-80Kč). Open M-F 10am-midnight, Sa 11am-midnight.

**U Švejků,** Újezd 22 (☎53 56 29). Metro A: Malostranská. Follow directions from Malostranská restaurace (above), but follow Karmelitská until it becomes Újezd. Aggressively touristy, complete with nightly accordionist (6-11pm), but prices are low and portions large. The place has a picture of Emperor Franz Josef on the wall—fans of Hašek's novel may wonder about its condition. Good soldiers should partake of beef in cream sauce (89Kč), dumplings (10Kč), or garlic soup (19Kč). Open daily 11am-midnight.

## LATE-NIGHT EATING

4:45am. Charles Bridge. Lavka's house disco beat is still pumping ferociously, but all you can hear is your stomach growling. Rather than catching the night bus home and going to bed hungry, grab a *párek v rohlíku* (hot dog) or a *smažený sýr* (fried cheese sandwich) from a vendor on Václavské nám. or a gyros from a stand on Spálená or Vodičkova. Or, even better, make a morning of it and uncover Prague's developing late-night eating scene.

**Radost FX,** Bělehradská 120 (☎24 25 47 76). Metro C: I.P. Pavlova. The late-night veggie cafe satisfies the appetites of sweaty, starving dancers from the club below with a highly imaginative menu (karma chameleon wrap 150Kč). Gallery in back. Open M-Sa 11am till late (at least 3am on weekdays and 5am on weekends).

**Iron Door,** Michalská 13 (no phone). Metro B: Národní třída. From the Metro, go down Spálená, turn right onto Národní, then left onto Perlová. Follow Perlová through the intersection until it becomes Michalská. A trendy nightspot that serves everything from Czech favorites to Japanese sushi. Large, comfy couches and a mesmerizing fish tank. Beer 30Kč. Kitchen open daily till 3am.

**Pizza Express,** Na mustku 1. Metro A, B: Mustek. 24 hours of nothing but pizza, sandwiches, and pastries (30-40Kč). Open daily.

## SUPERMARKETS

Go to the basement of Czech department stores for food halls and supermarkets. Small *potraviny* (delis) and vegetable stands can be found on most street corners.

**Tesco,** Národní třída 26 (☎22 00 36 14). Right next to Metro B: Národní třída. Open M-F 7am-8pm, Sa 8am-7pm, Su 9am-7pm.

**Krone department store** (☎24 23 04 77), on Václavské nám. at the intersection with Jindřišská. Metro A, B: Můstek. Open M-F 8am-8pm, Sa 8am–6pm, Su 10am-6pm.

**Kotva department store** (☎24 21 54 62), at the corner of Revoluční and Nám. Republiky. Metro B: Nám. Republiky. Open M-F 7am-8pm, Sa 8am-6pm, Su 10am-6pm.

# ⌗ CAFES

When Prague journalists are bored, they churn out yet another "Whatever happened to cafe life?" feature. The answer: it turned into *čajovna* (teahouse) culture. Tea is all the rage, and many teahouses double as bars or clubs in the evening.

▨ **U malého Glena,** Karmelitská 23 (☎ 535 81 15). From Metro A: Malostranská, take tram #12 to Malostranské nám. With their motto "Eat, Drink, Drink Some More," they've got consumption down to a science. The "light entree" menu has veggie plates (80-150Kč) and *croques-monsieur* 85Kč. Killer margaritas (80Kč). Mixed crowd of locals and foreigners descend to the Maker's Mark basement bar for nightly jazz or blues at 9pm. Cover 60-120Kč. Open daily 10am-2am; Su brunch 10am-3pm.

**Dobrá čajovna U čajovníka** (Good Tearoom), Boršov 2. Metro A: Staroměstská. Walk along Křížovnická past the Charles Bridge, then bear left onto Karoliny Světlé. Boršov is a tiny street on the left. Locals relax their minds at this mysterious tea house where you'll have to ring a bell to be let in and to be served. With over 90 teas from all over the world (12-150Kč) and complementary snacks (eggplant dip 55Kč), U čajovníka will leave you in a pleasant daze. Open M-Sa 10am-midnight, Su noon-midnight.

**Jazz Cafe 14,** Opatovická 14 (☎ 24 92 00 39). Metro B: Národní třída. Usually filled with smoke and satisfied 20-somethings. There's no live jazz music, but photos of Louis, Miles, and others line the walls. Cheap snacks (30Kč). Open daily noon-11pm.

**The Globe Coffeehouse,** Pštrossova 6 (☎ 24 91 62 64). See directions to the Globe Bookstore, p. 222. Tasty black coffee (20Kč), gazpacho (35Kč), and fresh fruit smoothies (60Kč), as well as plenty of English speakers trying to make a love connection. Open Su-Th 10am-midnight, F-Sa 10am-1am.

**Kavárna Medúza,** Belgická 17 (☎ 25 85 34). Metro A: Nám. Míru. Walk down Rumunská and turn left at Belgická. Antique shop masquerading as a cafe. Fluffed-up Victorian seats and lots of coffee (19-30Kč). Open M-F 11am-1am.

**Blatouch,** Vězeňská 4 (☎ 232 86 43). Metro A: Staroměstská. From Staroměstské nám., walk down Dlouhá at the far northeast corner of the square and follow it as it changes into Kozí. When the street becomes U obecního dvora, turn left on Vězeňská. A scoping bar with a Europop feel. Cocktails (50-70Kč) and pleasantly large *Velvet* beer (25Kč). Open M-Th noon-midnight, F-Su noon-1am.

**U zeleného čaje,** Nerudova 19 (☎57 53 00 27). Metro A: Malostranská. Follow Letenská to Malostranské nám.; in the square, stay right of the church and walk onto Nerudova. One of the only *čajovny* that feels more like a cafe than a zen-den. Sandwiches (20Kč), apple strudel (25Kč), and tons of teas (29-58Kč). Open daily 11am-10pm.

# ⌖ SIGHTS

The only Central European city left unscathed by either natural disaster or World War II, central Prague is a well-preserved combination of labyrinthine alleys and Baroque buildings. Don't be disheartened by the hordes of tourists: you can easily leave the umbrella-following packs by venturing off Staroměstské nám., the Charles Bridge, and Václavské nám. Prague is best explored on foot; central Prague—Staré Město, Nové Město, Malá Strana, and Hradčany—is extremely compact and can be traversed in one day (but give yourself more). You can't leave Prague without wandering the back alleys of Josefov, exploring the heights of Vyšehrad, and getting lost in the maze of Malá Strana's uphill streets.

## NOVÉ MĚSTO

Established in 1348 by Charles IV (see **History,** p. 204) as a separate municipality, Nové Město is not exactly new. Its age, however, is not readily apparent; its wide boulevards and sprawling squares seem hundreds of years ahead of their time. Today, Nové Město has grown into the commercial core of Prague, and—with the exception of Wenceslas Square—is spared the city's infamous throngs of tourists.

**WENCESLAS SQUARE.** (Václavské náměstí.) Not so much a square as a broad boulevard running through the center of Nové Město, **Wenceslas Square** owes its name to the equestrian statue of a 10th century Czech ruler and patron saint Wenceslas (Václav) in front of the National Museum. He is cherished as a patriot who was tragically murdered by his brother. Kneeling beneath him in solemn prayer are smaller statues of the country's four other patron saints: St. Ludmila (his grandmother), St. Agnes, St. Prokop, and St. Adalbert (Vojtěch). Wenceslas has presided over a century of turmoil and triumph, witnessing no fewer than five revolutions from his pedestal. The perfectionist sculptor Myslbek completed the statue after 25 years of deliberation; as others gasped at its 1912 unveiling, poor Myslbek just mumbled, "It could have been bigger." The inscription under St. Wenceslas declares, "Do not let us and our descendants perish." Czechs have taken this seriously: a new Czechoslovak state was proclaimed here in 1918, Jan Palach set himself on fire here to protest the 1968 Soviet invasion, and it was from atop this statue that major proclamations against the communist regime were made in 1989. The square sweeps down from the statue and the **National Museum** (Národní muzeum) past department stores, overpriced discos, posh hotels, sausage stands, and trashy casinos. The view of the St. Wenceslas in front of the museum from Můstek's base is hypnotic at full moon. At the lower end of Wenceslas Square near the Můstek Metro station, Art Nouveau, expressed in everything from lampposts to windowsills, dominates the square. A prime example is the 1903 **Hotel Evropa** at #25. *(Metro A, B: Můstek serves the bottom of the square; Metro A, C: Muzeum serves the top of the square by the statue and museum.)*

**FRANCISCAN GARDEN.** (Františkánská zahrada.) No one is quite sure how the Franciscans who keep this rose garden have managed to maintain such a bastion of serenity in the heart of Prague's bustling commercial district. The garden provides a perfect spot to relax, read the paper, or eat food from the nearby kiosks. *(Metro A, B: Můstek. Enter through the arch at the intersection of Jungmannova and Národní. Open daily Apr. 15-Sept. 14 7am-10pm; Sept. 15-Oct. 14 7am-8pm; Oct. 15-Apr. 14 8am-7pm. Free.)*

**CHURCH OF OUR LADY OF THE SNOWS.** (Kostel Panny Marie Sněžné.) Founded by Charles IV in 1347, this church was meant to be the largest in Prague. The Gothic walls are, indeed, higher than those of any other house of worship, but the rest of the structure is still unfinished—there was only enough cash to finish the choir. *(Metro A, B: Můstek. From the bottom of Wenceslas Square, turn left onto 28. října to reach Jungmannovo nám.; the entrance will be to your back left behind the statue of Jungmann.)*

**VELVET REVOLUTION MEMORIAL.** Under the arcades halfway down Národní stands a memorial to the hundreds of Prague's citizens beaten on November 17, 1989. A march, organized by students at the Film Faculty of Charles University (FAMU) to mourn the 50th anniversary of the Nazi execution of nine Czech students, was savagely attacked by the police, sparking further mass protests against the police and the regime that led to the total collapse of communism in Czechoslovakia. The simple, yet moving structure depicts a wall of hands—*Máme holé ruce* (Our hands are empty) was the protesters' slogan as they were being beaten by the police. President Havel was one of the primary leaders of the Velvet Revolution; his Civic Forum was based at the **Magic Lantern Theater** (Laterna magika divadlo), Národní 4. *(Metro B: Národní třída. Exit the Metro and head down Spálená until you hit Národní. The memorial is in the arcade on left side of the street.)*

**MUNICIPAL HOUSE.** (Obecní dům.) By far the most impressive Art Nouveau building in the city, the Municipal House captures the opulence of Prague's 19th-century cafe culture. Originally conceived as a Czech cultural center in Habsburg-controlled Prague, the Municipal House is the National Revival's proudest architectural achievement. Appropriately, the new Czechoslovak state proclaimed its independence here on October 28, 1918. The interior was designed by celebrated Czech artist Alfons Mucha and is adorned with his posters and paintings. Today, it serves as an exhibition site. *(Nám. Republiky 5. Metro B: Nám. Republiky. Open daily 10am-6pm. Guided tours available.)*

**THE DANCING HOUSE.** (Tančící dům.) Built by American architect Frank Gehry of Guggenheim-Bilbao fame in cooperation with Slovene architect Milunić, the building—called Fred and Ginger by Anglophones and the Dancing House by Czechs—is quite possibly Prague's most controversial landmark. It opened in 1996, next to President Havel's former apartment building. On the embankment of the Vltava amid a stretch of remarkable Art Nouveau buildings, it is considered by many to be an eyesore and an irreverent disruption of Prague's renowned architecture, while others find it a shining example of post-modern design. Its undulating glass wall and windows and its paired cone and cube evoke a dancing couple that gave the building its name. *(Metro B: Karlovo nám. Exit on the Karlovo nám. side of the Metro and head down Resslova toward the river. It's at the corner of Resslova and Rašínovo nábřeží.)*

# STARÉ MĚSTO

Settled in the 10th century, Staré Město remains a labyrinth of narrow roads and alleys. It's easy to get lost, but doing so is the best way to appreciate the neighborhood's charm. The heart of Staré Město is **Old Town Square** (Staroměstské nám.), surrounded by eight magnificent towers. It is because of its Old Town that Prague is called *Praha stověžatá*, or "a city of hundred spires." The vast stone plaza is filled with blacksmiths, carriages, and ice cream vendors in summer.

**OLD TOWN HALL.** (Staroměstská radnice.) Next to the grassy knoll in Old Town Square, Old Town Hall is the multi-facaded building with the bit blown off the front. The building was partially demolished by the Nazis in the final week of World War II. You can see what's left of the pink facade jutting out from the tower. Prague's Town Hall has long been a witness to violence—crosses on the ground in front of it mark the spot where 27 Protestant leaders were executed on June 21, 1621 for staging a rebellion against the Catholic Habsburgs. The tourist office inside offers tours of the interior. The Old Senate boasts a Baroque stove with a figure of Justice and a sculpture of Christ. The inscription reads, "Judge justly, sons of Man." Crowds gather on the hour to watch the wonderful astronomical clock *(orloj)* chime with its procession of apostles, a skeleton, and a thwarted Turk. They say the clockmaker Hanuš's eyes were put out so he couldn't design another—but they say that about the man who built St. Basil's in Moscow, too. The clock's animation is turned off nightly at 9pm. *(Metro A: Staroměstská; Metro A, B: Můstek. In Staroměstské nám. Town hall open summer daily 9am-5:30pm. 30Kč, students 15Kč.)*

**JAN HUS STATUE.** The Czech Republic's most famous martyred theologian, Jan Hus hovers over Old Town Square in bronze effigy. Anguished figures bow in reverence beneath his commanding grandeur. In summer, masses of travelers sit at the base of his robes, drinking, smoking, sucking face, and performing a hundred other deeds upon which he can only frown. *(In the center of Staroměstské nám.)*

**TÝN CHURCH.** (Chrám Matky Boží před Týnem.) Across from Old Town Hall, the spires of the Gothic Týn Church rise above a mass of medieval homes. Alas, only the right spire is original; the left one is a barely distinguishable copy. The famous astronomer Tycho Brahe is buried inside. He overindulged at one of Emperor Rudolf's lavish dinner parties, where it was unacceptable to leave the table unless the Emperor himself did so. When poor Tycho needed to go to the bathroom, he was forced to stay seated, and his bladder burst. Although the church is under restoration, you can catch a glimpse of its gold and black interior from the entrance. *(In Staroměstské nám.)*

**GOLTZ-KINSKÝ PALACE.** The flowery 14th-century Goltz-Kinský Palace is the finest of Prague's Roccoco buildings. It is also the official birthplace of Soviet Communism in the Czech Republic: on February 21, 1948, Klement Gottwald declared communism victorious from its balcony. *(At the corner of Staroměstské nám. and Dlouhá, next to Týn Church. Open Tu-F 10am-5pm; closes early in summer for daily concerts.)*

**ST. JACOB'S CHURCH.** (Kostel sv. Jakuba.) A thief's arm has dangled from the entrance to St. Jacob's for 500 years. Legend has it that a thief tried to pilfer a gem from the Virgin Mary of Suffering, whereupon the figure came to life, seized the thief's arm, and wrenched it off. The monks took pity on the profusely bleeding soul and invited him to join their order. He accepted and remained pious; the arm hangs as a reminder to the faithful that Mary is not averse to the occasional steel-cage maneuver. *(Metro B: Staroměstská. On Malá Štupartská, off Staroměstské nám. behind Týn Church.)*

**A ROOM WITHOUT A VIEW** At decisive points in European history, unlucky men tend to fall from Prague's window ledges. The Hussite wars began on July 30, 1419, after Catholic councillors were thrown to the mob from the New Town Hall on Karlovo nám. The Thirty Years' War devastated Europe after Habsburg officials were tossed from the windows of Prague Castle's Bohemian Chancellery into a heap of steaming manure on May 23, 1618. These first and second defenestrations echo down the ages, but two more falls this century have continued the macabre tradition. On March 10, 1948, liberal foreign minister Jan Masaryk fell to his death from the top floor of his ministry just two weeks after the Communist takeover; murder was always suspected, but never proven. On Feb. 3, 1997, Bohumil Hrabal, age 82, popular author of *I Served the King of England* and *Closely-Observed Trains*, fell from the 5th floor of his hospital window and died in his pajamas. Nothing unusual here, except that two of his books describe people committing suicide—by jumping out of 5th-floor windows.

**BETHLEHEM CHAPEL.** (Betlémská kaple.) Although the current Bethlehem Chapel dates from the 1950s, it is a surprisingly accurate reconstruction of the medieval chapel made famous by Jan Hus. Today, the students of Charles University in Prague graduate here. *(Metro A, B: Můstek. From the Metro, walk down Národní třída toward the river and turn right on Na Perštýně; the Chapel is in Betlémské nám., which will appear on your left. Open daily 9am-6pm. 30Kč, students 20Kč.)*

**JAN PALACH SQUARE.** (Náměstí Jana Palacha.) This rather uninspiring square is bordered by inspiring sites. Standing right by the river is the **Rudolfinum,** a famous concert hall with lions adorning its entrance that hosts the annual festival of classical music *Pražské jaro* (Prague Spring; see **Entertainment,** p. 240). Across tram tracks from the Rudolfinum is the main building of the **Faculty of Arts** of Charles University (*Filozofická fakulta Univerzity Karlovy*) with a *post-mortem* mask of Jan Palach flanked by its outside wall. The stunning view of the Prague Castle from the classrooms of the Faculty keeps many a student awake during boring lectures on medieval English syntax. The area was originally called Red Army Square in honor of the Russians who liberated Prague in 1945. During popular unrest in 1969 and then again in November 1989, students renamed the square in honor of the late Jan Palach, who studied at Charles University before burning himself to death on Václavské nám. to protest the 1968 Soviet invasion. The square permanently changed names in 1990. *(Metro A: Staroměstská. Just off the Metro exit on Křížovnická.)*

**CHARLES BRIDGE.** (Karlův most.) Thronged with tourists and the hawkers who prey on them, the Charles Bridge is Prague's most recognizable landmark. Charles IV built this 520m bridge to replace the wooden Judith, the only bridge crossing the Vltava, which washed away in a 1342 flood. The bridge is bordered by a defense tower on each side; the smaller *Malostranská mostecká věž* (Malá Strana Bridge Tower) dates from the 12th century as part of Judith's original fortification, while the taller *Staroměstská mostecká věž* (Old Town Bridge Tower) was erected in the 15th century. You can climb both towers for a splendid view of the river and Prague's most precious sites. It is said that people from all over the country contributed materials to build the bridge—at that time "materials" stood for eggs and flour. Legend has it that overzealous inhabitants of a village in East Bohemia sent the eggs boiled so that they would not break on the way. Over the years, the bridge acquired 16 Baroque statues that became its hallmark feature—but don't be fooled—all the ones on the bridge are replicas, while the originals are safe in local museums, tucked away from tourists and pigeons.

When darkness falls, the street musicians emerge, but the penalty for requesting "Wish You Were Here" is being tied up in goatskin and thrown into the Vltava. This happened to St. Jan Nepomuk, although for a different reason: at the center of the bridge, the 8th statue from the right is a depiction of hapless Jan being tossed over the side of the Charles for faithfully guarding his queen's extramarital secrets from a suspicious King Wenceslas IV. Torture by hot irons and other devices failed to loosen Jan's lips, so the King ordered that he be drowned. A halo of five gold stars appeared as Jan plunged into the icy water. The right-hand rail, from which Jan was supposedly ejected, is now marked with a cross and five stars between the 5th and 6th statues. Place one finger on each star and make a wish: it is guaranteed to come true. *(The best way to reach Charles Bridge is of course on foot. The nearest Metro stops are A: Malostranská on the Malá Strana side, and A: Staroměstská on the Old Town side.)*

**POWDER TOWER.** (Prašná brána.) The gothic Powder Tower looms at the edge of Nám. Republiky as the entrance to Staré Město. After its stint as royal fortification of the city, it was used primarily for gunpowder storage. A small history exhibit is inside, but forego it for a climb to the top. *(Metro B: Nám. Republiky. Open daily Apr.-Sept. 10am-6pm.)*

## JOSEFOV

*Metro A: Staroměstská. From the Metro, walk down Maiselova, which is parallel to Kaprova. ☎231 71 91. Synagogues and museum open M-F and Su 9am-6pm. Closed Jewish holidays. Admission to all sights except Staronová Synagogue 450Kč, students 330Kč. Staronová Synagogue 200Kč, students 140Kč. Admission to museum only 280Kč, students 200Kč.*

Prague's historic Jewish neighborhood and the oldest Jewish settlement in Central Europe, Josefov is north of Staromětstské nám., along Maiselova and several side streets. Its cultural wealth lies in five well-preserved synagogues. In 1179, the Pope decreed that all good Christians should avoid contact with Jews; a year later, Prague's citizens complied with a 12-foot wall. The gates were opened in 1784, and the walls came down in 1848, when the Jews were granted limited civil rights. The closed city bred exotic legends, many focusing on **Rabbi Loew ben Bezalel** (1512-1609), whose legendary *golem*—a creature made from mud that supposedly came to life to protect Prague's Jews—predates Frankenstein's monster by 200 years. Rabbi Loew lived at Široká 90, now a private residence. The century following 1848 was not a happy one for Prague's Jews. The open quarter rapidly became a disease-racked slum, and many old buildings were demolished due to a massive rebuilding project which was to turn Prague into a small Paris (evident in today's Pařížská). Finally, the Nazis deported the Jewish people to Terezín and then to death camps. Hitler's decision to create a "museum of an extinct race" resulted in the preservation of Josefov's old Jewish cemetery and five of the synagogues.

**MAISEL SYNAGOGUE.** (Maiselova synagoga.) This synagogue exhibits treasures from the extensive collections of the Jewish Museum—returned to the city's Jewish community only in 1994. The introductory section serves as a good primer on the history of Czech Jews and their status in the medieval state; it makes a logical starting point for a tour of Josefov. *(On Maiselova, between Široká and Jáchymova.)*

**PINKAS SYNAGOGUE.** (Pinkasova synagoga.) Built in the 1530s for the wealthy Pinkas family, the Pinkas Synagogue was converted in 1958 into a sobering memorial to the 77,000 Czech Jews killed in the Holocaust. After a period of Communist neglect, the synagogue reopened as a memorial in 1991, its walls once again listing the names of victims of Nazi persecution; the memorial is the longest epitaph in the world. *(On Široká, between Žatecká and 17. listopadu.)*

**OLD JEWISH CEMETERY.** (Starý židovský hřbitov.) This cemetery remains Josefov's most popular attraction. Between the 14th and 18th centuries, 20,000 graves were laid in 12 layers. The striking clusters of tombstones result from a process in which the older stones were lifted up from underneath. Rabbi Loew is buried by the wall directly opposite the entrance—you will recognize his grave by the piles of stones with wishes placed on his tomb. *(At the corner of Široká and Žatecká.)*

**OLD-NEW SYNAGOGUE.** (Staronová synagoga.) The oldest operating synagogue in Europe and the earliest Gothic structure in Prague, the 700-year-old Old-New Synagogue is still the religious center for Prague's Orthodox Jewish community. Behind the iron gates of the *bimah* flies a tattered remnant of the original Star of David flag flown by the congregation in 1357 when Charles IV allowed them to display their own municipal standard; Prague's Jews were the first to adopt the Star of David as their official symbol. *(On the corner of Maiselova and Pařížská.)*

**CEREMONY HALL.** (Obřadní dům.) Originally a ceremonial hall for the Jewish Burial Society, Ceremony Hall now houses two permanent exhibits. The first is devoted to the themes of illness and medicine in the ghetto, Jewish cemeteries in Bohemia and Moravia, and the activities of the Prague Burial Society. The second is the world-renowned exhibit, "Children's Drawings from Terezín: 1942-44"; most of the artists died at Auschwitz. *(On Červená, just off Maiselova.)*

**KLAUS SYNAGOGUE.** (Klausová synagoga.) Built in the 1690s in a notorious red-light district, Klaus now displays rotating exhibits on Judaica and has in-depth explanations of Jewish traditions. *(Next to Ceremony Hall on Červená, just off Maiselova.)*

**JEWISH TOWN HALL.** (Židovská radnice.) Once the administrative control center of Josefov, the Jewish Town Hall is one of the few Jewish administrative centers in Europe to survive World War II. The Hebrew clock in the pink Rococo exterior of the town hall runs counterclockwise. On the other side of the building, a statue of Moses by František Bílek (himself a Protestant) was hidden from the Nazis during the war. *(Next to the Old-New Synagogue, on the corner of Maiselova and Červená.)*

**HIGH SYNAGOGUE.** (Vysoká synagoga.) Now a working synagogue closed to the public, this 16th-century synagogue housed massive collections of textiles and Judaica during the war for Hitler's "museum of an extinct race." *(On Červená.)*

**SPANISH SYNAGOGUE.** (Španělská synagoga.) The most ornate synagogue, the Moorish interior of the Spanish Synagogue was modeled after the Alhambra. It displays a history of Czech Jews since World War II. *(On the corner of Široká and Dušní.)*

# MALÁ STRANA

The seedy hangout of criminals and counter-revolutionaries for nearly a century, the cobblestoned streets of Malá Strana have become the most prized real estate on either side of the Vltava. Yuppies now dream of a flat with a view of St. Nicholas's Cathedral, and affluent foreigners sip beer where Jaroslav Hašek and his bumbling soldier Švejk once guzzled suds (see **Literature and Arts**, p. 207). The current trend seems to fit the plans of the original designer, King Přemysl Otakar II, who in the 13th century dreamed of creating a powerful economic quarter. This was not to occur until the 15th century, when Austrian nobility erected grand churches and palaces. As nationalism mounted, however, the quarter became known as a rat's den of surly sailors, rotten dealers, and drunken brawls. The 1989 revolution brought a new appreciation for the district's architecture, and careful restorations have made it one of the most enjoyable sections of Prague to visit.

**ST. NICHOLAS'S CATHEDRAL.** (Chrám sv. Mikuláše.) Malá Strana is centered around **Malostranské nám.** and its centerpiece, the Baroque St. Nicholas's Cathedral, whose towering dome is one of Prague's most notable landmarks. The father-son team of Kristof and Kilian Ignaz Dienzenhofer, creators of the small Church of St. Nicholas in Staré Město and the Břevnov Monastery (see **Outer Prague,** p. 238) near Hradčany, built St. Nicholas's Cathedral as their crowning glory. Expensive classical music concerts take place nightly. *(Metro A: Malostranská. Follow Letenská from the Metro to Malostranské nám. ☎53 69 83. Open daily 9am-4pm. 45Kč, students 15Kč. Concert tickets an unholy 400Kč, students 290Kč.)*

**WALLENSTEIN GARDEN.** (Valdštejnská zahrada.) A simple wooden gate opens through a 10m wall into the Wallenstein Garden, one of Prague's best-kept secrets. This tranquil, 17th-century Baroque garden is enclosed by old buildings that glow golden on sunny afternoons. General Albrecht Wallenstein, owner of the palace of the same name and hero of Schiller's grim plays (the *Wallenstein* cycle), held parties here among Vredeman de Vries's classical bronze statues. When the works were plundered by Swedish troops in the waning hours of the Thirty Years' War, Wallenstein replaced the original casts with facsimiles. Frescoes inside the arcaded loggia depict episodes from Virgil's *Aeneid*. *(Letenská 10. Metro A: Malostranská. Open May-Sept. daily 9am-7pm; Mar. 21-Apr. 30 and Oct. daily 10am-6pm.)*

**CHAROUSKOVÁ MEMORIAL.** Across the street from the Malostranská Metro station, a plaque hidden in a lawn constitutes the Charousková Memorial, the sole monument to those slain in the 1968 Prague Spring. It commemorates **Marie Charousková,** a graduate student who was machine-gunned by a Soviet soldier for refusing to remove a black ribbon protesting the invasion.

**JOHN LENNON WALL.** Hidden on Hroznová, a tiny street on Kampa Island, is a 1990s version of the infamous John Lennon Wall. Until summer 1998, the mural was a crumbling memorial to John Lennon and the 1960s global peace movement. Once interesting when the authorities kept trying to suppress it, it had fallen into disrepair and was plagued by unimaginative graffiti. In summer 1998, the wall was whitewashed, and is now covered with a pre-fab portrait of John Lennon and even less imaginative tourist graffiti. Still, the wall is a positive landmark that continues to remind people that "all you need is love." *(Metro A: Malostranská From the Metro, walk down U Lužického semináře to the Charles Bridge. Once on the bridge, descend the stairs leading to Na Kampě and make first right onto Hroznová. Stay close to the wall and bear right over the bridge onto Velkopřerovské nám.)*

**CHURCH OF OUR LADY VICTORIOUS.** (Kostel Panny Marie Vítězné.) The modest Church of Our Lady Victorious is not notable for its exterior. Instead, the famous polished-wax statue of the **Infant Jesus of Prague,** said to bestow miracles on the faithful, draws visitors inside. The figurine has a wardrobe of more than 380 outfits; every sunrise, he's swaddled anew by the nuns of a nearby convent. The statue first arrived in town in the arms of a 16th-century Spanish noblewoman who married into the Bohemian royalty; mysteriously, the plague bypassed Prague shortly thereafter. In 1628, the Carmelite abbey gained custody of the Infant and allowed pilgrims to pray to the statue; the public has been infatuated ever since. *(Metro A: Malostranská. Follow Letecká from the Metro through Malostranské nám., and continue onto Karmelitská; it's on your right. Open M-F 8:30am-6:30pm, Sa 7:30am-8pm, Su 9am-9pm.)*

**PETŘÍN HILL AND GARDENS.** (Petřínské sady.) Petřín Gardens provide some of the most spectacular views of the city. A cable car runs to the top (8Kč; look for *lanová dráha* signs), leaving from just above the intersection of Vítězná and Újezd. It stops once along the way to deposit visitors at **Nebozízek,** Prague's most scenically endowed cafe. *(Open daily 11am-6pm and 7-11pm.)* A bag of goodies stands at the summit: a small Eiffel tower, the city's observatory, the **church of St. Lawrence,** and the wacky labyrinth of mirrors at **Bludiště.** *(☎53 13 62. Open Tu-Su 10am-7pm. 20Kč, students 10Kč.)* Just east of the park is Strahov Stadium, the world's largest, covering the space of 10 soccer fields.

# PRAGUE CASTLE (PRAŽSKÝ HRAD)

*Metro A: Hradčanská. There are three ways to enter the castle complex. The more comfortable way is to take trams #22 or 23 from the center and get off at "Pražský Hrad." Alternately, you may hike up the steep but picturesque Nerudova street from Malostranské nám., or climb the Staré zámecké schody (Old Castle Stairs) from Malostranská. ☎24 37 11 11. Open daily Apr.-Oct. 9am-5pm; Nov.-May 9am-4pm. Ticket office across from St. Vitus' Cathedral, inside the castle walls. Ticket—valid for 3 days—good for admission to the Royal Crypt, Cathedral Tower, Old Royal Palace, Powder Tower, and Basilica of St. George. 120Kč, students 60Kč.*

Founded 1000 years ago, Prague Castle has always been the seat of the Bohemian government and the center of its politics. For centuries, conflicts between medieval dynasties, Czechs and Germans, or Protestants and Catholics have played out within—and sometimes plummeted down beside—its walls. In this century, liberal presidents, Nazi despots, and communist apparatchiks have all held court here. The most recent ideological struggle saw the socialists replaced by playwright Václav Havel. The complex saw major renovations after the creation of independent Czechoslovakia in 1918. First President Tomáš Garrigue Masaryk invited renowned

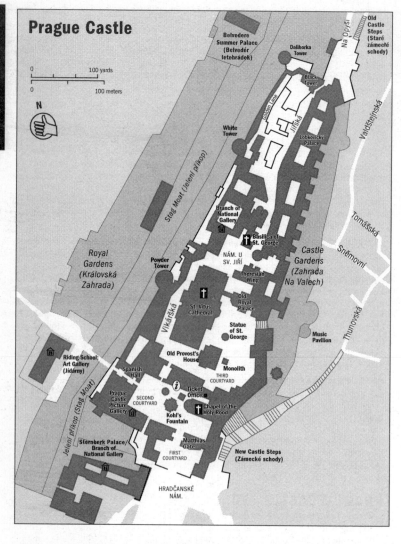

# Prague Castle

0 _____ 100 yards

0 _____ 100 meters

N

Belvedere
Summer Palace
(Belvedér
letohrádek)

Old
Castle
Steps
(Staré
zámecké
schody)

Daliborka
Tower

Na Opyši

Black
Tower

Golden Lane

Jiřská

White
Tower

Lobkovický
Palace

Valdštejnská

Branch of
National
Gallery

Stag Moat (Jelení příkop)

Basilica of
St. George

Tomášská

NÁM. U
SV. JIŘÍ

Powder
Tower

Sněmovní

Theresian
Wing

Castle
Gardens
(Zahrada
Na Valech)

Royal
Gardens
(Královská
Zahrada)

Old
Royal
Palace

St. Vitus
Cathedral

Vikářská

Statue
of St.
George

Music
Pavilion

Thunovská

Riding School;
Art Gallery
(Jídárny)

Old Provost's
House

Spanish
Hall

Monolith

THIRD
COURTYARD

Prague
Castle
Picture
Gallery

SECOND
COURTYARD

Ticket
Office

Chapel of the
Holy Rood

Jelení příkop (Stag Moat)

Kohl's
Fountain

Šternberk Palace/
Branch of
National Gallery

Matthias
Gate

FIRST
COURTYARD

New Castle Steps
(Zámecké schody)

HRADČANSKÉ
NÁM.

Slovene architect Josip Plečnik to rebuild his new residence, which had crumbled into ruins after centuries of Habsburg neglect. Plečnik not only restored all the castle's buildings and redesigned its gardens, but also added fountains, columns and embellishments, characteristic of his style. Next to the historic center of his native Ljubljana, the Prague Castle is the best example of Plečnik's architectural genius.

**ROYAL GARDEN.** (Královská zahrada.) Recently opened to the public after years as a private paradise for the eyes of the highest communist functionaries, the Royal Garden hides many of the castle's most beautiful buildings. Its serenity in the middle of one of the city's main tourist attractions is astounding. The **Ball-Game House** (Míčovna) was used for just that since its construction in the 16th century, but today it serves as a concert hall. Further down the green lawns is the glorious and newly renovated **Royal Summer Palace** (Královský letohrádek,

# Hmm, call home or eat lunch?
## With  you can do both.

Nathan Lane for YOU[SM].

No doubt, traveling on a budget is tough. So tear out this wallet guide and keep it with you during your travels. With YOU, calling home from overseas is affordable and easy.

If the wallet guide is missing, call collect 913-624-5336 or visit www.youcallhome.com for YOU country numbers.

**Dialing instructions:** Dial the access number for the country you're in.
*Need help with access numbers while overseas? Call collect, 913-624-5336.* Dial 04 or follow the English prompts.
Enter your credit card information to place your call.

| Country | Access Number | Country | Access Number | Country | Access Number |
|---|---|---|---|---|---|
| Australia v | 1-800-551-110 | Israel v | 1-800-949-4102 | Spain v | 900-99-0013 |
| Bahamas ✚ | 1-800-389-2111 | Italy ✚ v | 172-1877 | Switzerland v | 0800-899-777 |
| Brazil v | 000-8016 | Japan ✚ v | 00539-131 | Taiwan v | 0080-14-0877 |
| China ✚ ▲ v | 108-13 | Mexico u v | 001-800-877-8000 | United Kingdom v | 0800-890-877 |
| France v | 0800-99-0087 | Netherlands ✚ v | 0800-022-9119 | | |
| Germany ✚ v | 0800-888-0013 | New Zealand ▲ v | 000-999 | | |
| Hong Kong v | 800-96-1877 | Philippines T v | 105-16 | | |
| India v | 000-137 | Singapore v | 8000-177-177 | | |
| Ireland v | 1-800-552-001 | South Korea ✚ v | 00729-16 | | |

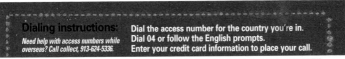

*Service provided by Sprint*

**v** Call answered by automated Voice Response Unit. ✚ Public phones may require coin or card.
▲ May not be available from all payphones. u Use phones marked with "LADATEL" and no coin or card is required.
T If talk button is available, push it before talking.

# Pack the Wallet Guide
## and save 25% or more* on calls home to the U.S.

It's lightweight and carries heavy savings of 25% or more*
over AT&T USA Direct and MCI WorldPhone rates. So take this
YOU wallet guide and carry it wherever you go.

### To save with YOU:
- Dial the access number of the country you're in (see reverse)
- Dial 04 or follow the English voice prompts
- Enter your credit card info for easy billing

Service provided by Sprint

usually called Belveder by the Czechs), the purest example of southern Renaissance architecture outside Italy. In front of the palace stands the **Singing Fountain.** Follow the hordes of schoolchildren and put your head under the fountain to hear the chiming water. The garden also houses an **Orangery** and a **Fig Garden** (both closed to the public). *(The garden entrance is on U Prašného mostu, between the Second Castle Courtyard and the tram #22 and 23 tracks.)*

**HRADČANY SQUARE AND FIRST CASTLE COURTYARD.** Outside the Castle gates at Hradčany Sq. (Hradčanské nám.) is the **Šternberk Palace,** home of the National Gallery's European art collection (not to be confused with the Šternberk Palace on Malostranské nám.). The gems include an 1815 Goya and three Rubens, including a fine *Visitation.* Willem Droost's *Annunciation* was formerly attributed to Rembrandt on the not unreasonable grounds that it bore his signature; a genuine Rembrandt is in the next room. *(☎ 20 51 46 34. Open Tu-Su 10am-6pm. 90Kč, students 40Kč.)* The Baroque **Matthias Gate** (Matyášská brána) on the First Castle Courtyard marks the official entrance to the castle complex. Next to it rise two wooden flagpoles, designed by Josip Plečnik.

**SECOND CASTLE COURTYARD.** When entering through Matthias Gate, the **Spanish Hall** marks the Second Castle Courtyard's left boundary. On the right hand side are the presidential offices, which President Havel supposedly cruises on his scooter. The Castle Information Center and ticket booth may be found in this courtyard.

**THIRD CASTLE COURTYARD.** In the Third Castle Courtyard stands Prague Castle's centerpiece, the colossal **St. Vitus' Cathedral** (Katedrála sv. Víta or Svatovítská katedrála), which may look Gothic but in fact was only finished in 1929—600 years after construction began. The cathedral's stained-glass windows were created by some of the most gifted Czech artists—Alphonse Mucha's brilliant depiction of Sts. Ludmila and Wenceslas is the most recognizable. To the right of the high altar stands the **tomb of St. Jan Nepomuc,** 3m of solid, glistening silver, weighing in at 1800kg. Look for an angel holding a silvered tongue—Jan was allegedly tied in a goatskin and chucked into the Vltava for refusing to betray the Queen's confidences (see **Charles Bridge,** p. 232). His tongue was somehow recovered and eventually silvered. The story was declared false in 1961, but the tongue is still on display. Emperor Charles IV has his own bridge, university, and fortress (at Karlštejn)—but his tomb is in the **Royal Crypt** below the church along with a handful of other Czech kings and all four of his wives, who are tactfully buried in the same grave to his left. Back up the stairs in the main church, the walls of **St. Wenceslas's Chapel** (Svatováclavská kaple) are lined with precious stones and a painting cycle depicting the legend of this saint. In an adjoining but inaccessible room, the real crown jewels of the kings of Bohemia are stored. More superstition claims that people who try them on inappropriately meet sticky ends. The last to do so was Hitler's *Reichs-Protektor* Reinhard Heydrich, later assassinated by the Czech resistance. Finally, if you have mountain goat thighs, climb the 287 steps of the **Cathedral Tower** to the city's best view. The **Old Royal Palace** (Starý královský palác), to the right of the cathedral behind the Old Provost's House and the statue of St. George, houses the lengthy expanse of the **Vladislav Hall,** which once hosted jousting competitions; upstairs is the **Chancellery of Bohemia,** the site of the Second Defenestration of Prague (see **A Room Without a View,** p. 232). On May 23, 1618, angry Protestants flung two Habsburg officials through the windows and into a steaming dung heap that broke their fall, triggering the Thirty Years' War.

**ST. GEORGE'S SQUARE.** Behind the cathedral and across the courtyard from the Old Royal Palace stand the Romanesque **St. George's Basilica** (Bazilika sv. Jiří) and its adjacent convent. The basilica was built in 921; in its right-hand corner you'll find the tomb of St. Ludmila, with skeleton on display. A mason who stole the thighbone supposedly activated a vicious curse that killed three before the mason's son restored the bone to the grave. The convent houses the **National Gallery of Bohemian Art,** with art ranging from Gothic to Baroque. In the medieval galleries, Master Theodorik's ecclesiastical portraits, the relief from *Matka Boží* *před Týnem*, and the so-called Kapucínský cycle of Christ and the apostles stand out; upstairs, paintings by Michael Leopold Willmann (1630-1706) warrant scrutiny. *(Open Tu-Su 10am-6pm. 90Kč, students 40Kč.)*

**ALONG JIŘSKÁ STREET.** Jiřská begins to the right of the basilica. Halfway down, the tiny and colorful **Golden Lane** (Zlatá ulička) heads off to the right. Alchemists once worked here, and their attempts to create gold inspired the street's name. Kafka later lived at #22, and today there is a small forest of cramped souvenir shops for tourists to squeeze in and out of. Above the souvenir shops is a hallway displaying replicas of the Bohemian court's armory; at its end, you can take three shots with a crossbow for 50Kč. Back on Jiřská, the **Lobkovický Palace** contains a replica of Bohemia's coronation jewels and a history of the Czech lands. *(Open Tu-Su 9am-5pm. 40Kč, students 20Kč.)* At the end of the street is the **Museum of Toys.** *(Muzeum hraček.* ☎ *24 37 22 94. Open daily 9:30am-5pm. 40Kč, students 30Kč.)* The **Old Castle Steps** (Staré zámecké schody) at the end of the street descend down to Malostranská.

# OUTER PRAGUE

If you have more than two days in Prague, explore the city's outskirts to find greenery, nifty churches, and panoramic vistas, all hidden from the tourist hordes.

**BŘEVNOV MONASTERY.** Břevnov Monastery was founded in 993 by King Boleslav II and St. Adalbert (also a founder of Bohemia's oldest Benedictine order), each independently guided by a divine dream to create a monastery atop a bubbling stream. **St. Margaret's Church** (Kostel sv. Markéty), a Benedictine chapel, waits inside the complex. Beneath the altar rests the tomb of St. Vintíř, who, even in Bohemia, vowed to forego all forms of meat. Czechs claim that on one particular diplomatic excursion, St. Vintíř met and dined with a German king who was a fanatical hunter; the main course was an enormous pheasant slain that morning by the monarch's own hand. The saint prayed for deliverance from the myriad *faux pas* possibilities, whereupon the main course sprang to life and flew out the window. The green belltower and red tile roof of the monastery building are all that remain of the original Romanesque construction; the complex was redesigned in high Baroque by the Dienzenhofers. During the Soviet occupation, the monastery was used to store truckloads of secret police files. *(From Mariánské hradby, the street beside the Royal Summer Palace, take tram #22 away from the river toward Bílá Hora to Břevnovský klášter. Guided tours set off Sa 9am, Sa-Su 10:30am, 1pm, 2:30pm, and 4pm. 50Kč.)*

**TROJA.** Troja is the site of French architect J. B. Mathey's masterful **château.** The pleasure palace, overlooking the Vltava from north of the U-shaped bend, includes a terraced garden, an oval staircase, and a collection of 19th-century Czech artwork. The tourist office carries schedules of **free concerts** in the château's great hall. *(Bus #112 winds from Metro C: Nádraží Holešovice. Open Tu-Su 9am-5pm.)*

**VYŠEHRAD.** The former haunt of Prague's 19th-century Romantics, Vyšehrad is a storehouse of nationalistic myths and imperial legends. It was here that Countess Libuše prophesied the founding of Prague and embarked on her search for the first king of Bohemia. The 20th century has passed the castle by, and Vyšehrad's elevated pathways now escape the throngs of Staré Město. Quiet walkways still wind between crumbling stone walls to a magnificent **church,** a black Romanesque rotunda, and one of the Czech Republic's most celebrated sites—**Vyšehrad Cemetery** (home to the remains of **Dvořák** and Božena Němcová of the 500Kč bill). Even the Metro C: Vyšehrad subway stop has a movie-sweep vista of Prague. *(Metro C: Vyšehrad. Exit Metro and look for a large congress building—it's behind. Open 24hr.)*

**VÍTKOV.** For a magnificent view of Staré Město and the castle, stroll up forested Vítkov Hill, topped by the world's largest equestrian monument. One-eyed Hussite leader Jan Žižka scans the terrain for Crusaders, whom he stomped out on this spot in 1420. *(From Metro B: Křižíkova, walk down Thámova, through the tunnel, and up the hill.)*

**NEW JEWISH CEMETERY.** Although less a pilgrimage destination than the Old Jewish Cemetery, the New Jewish Cemetery, far to the southeast, is one of Central

Europe's largest burial grounds. **Kafka** is interred here; obtain a map and, if you're male, a mandatory head covering from the attendant before you start hunting for the tombstone. *(Enter at Metro A: Želivského. Open summer Su-Th 9am-4:30pm, F 9am-1:30pm; off-season Su-Th 9am-3:30pm, F 9am-12:30pm. Free.)*

# 🏛 MUSEUMS

Prague's magnificence is not harbored in her museums, which often have striking facades and mediocre collections; if the weather's good, stick to the streets. The city is victim to many rainy days, though, and does have quite a few museums sheltering interesting and quirky collections. Additionally, private galleries along the side streets off Národní třída and Staroměstské nám. exhibit the works of Czech artists. Almost all museums are closed on Mondays and exhibits do change occasionally, so keep your eyes open.

**House of the Golden Ring** (Dům u zlatého prstenu), Týnská 6 (☎24 82 80 04). Metro A: Staroměstská. Behind Týn Church. An astounding collection of 20th-century Czech art, curated by a refreshingly liberal gallery that emphasizes installations and technological art. Four floors, each with a separate theme; the 2nd floor exhibit, "In the Distorted Mirror and Behind the Mirror," might sound like the most interesting exhibit, but the basement collection of 1990s Czech art is the museum's must-see. Open Tu-Su 10am-6pm. 60Kč, students 30Kč; free first Tu of the month.

**National Gallery** (Národní galerie; ☎20 51 46 34). Spread around nine different locations; the notable **Šternberský palác** and **Klášter sv. Jiří** are described above in the **Prague Castle** section (see p. 235). All museums carry a pamphlet describing the collections of the other galleries, which are in suburban Prague and not worth the trek. **Trade Fair Palace and the Gallery of Modern Art** (Veletržní palác a Galerie moderního umění), Dukelských hrdinů 47 (☎24 30 11 11). Metro C: Vltavská. Displays the National Gallery's impressive collection of 20th-century Czech art. The seven-story functionalist building is almost as stunning as the art inside; even Le Corbusier approved. Open Tu-W and F-Su 10am-6pm, Th 10am-9pm. 90Kč, students 40Kč.

**Mucha Museum,** Panská 7. Metro A, B: Můstek. From the Metro, walk up Václavské nám. toward the St. Wenceslas statue. Turn left onto Jindřišská, then left onto Panská. Boasts the only collection devoted entirely to the work of Alfons Mucha, the Czech Republic's most celebrated artist. Collection includes his Paris works as well as his sketchbooks and furniture. Open daily 10am-6pm. 120Kč, students 60Kč.

**Czech Museum of Fine Arts** (České muzeum výtvarných umění), Celetná 34 (☎24 21 17 31). Metro A: Nám. Republiky. The building itself, the House of the Black Madonna (Dům u Černé matky boží), is one of Prague's finest examples of Cubist architecture. The collection continues with the theme, devoting two floors to a comprehensive collection of Czech Cubism. The downstairs gallery hosts rotating exhibits of Western European Modernists. Open Tu-Su 10am-6pm. 40Kč, students 10Kč.

**Municipal Museum of Prague** (Muzeum Hlavního města Prahy), Na poříčí 52 (☎24 81 67 72). Metro B, C: Florenc. In the park. Holds the original calendar board from the town hall's astronomical clock and a 1:480 scale model of old Prague, exact to the last window pane of more than 2000 houses and all of Prague's monuments. See what your hostel looked like in 1834. Borrow an English guidebook to walk through the fine historical galleries. Open Tu-Su 9am-6pm. 30Kč, students 15Kč.

**Huť Rudolfa II.,** Břehová 4 (☎231 61 22; glasspo@mbox.vol.cz). Metro A: Staroměstská. The most interactive of Prague's museums. Witness the mind-blowing glassworks of Czech professionals, help create a souvenir, then take a tour of the gallery above to explore the world of glassmaking. Open daily 10am-9pm. Glass making exhibitions close at 5pm. 50Kč.

**Monument to National Literature** (Památník národního písemnictví), Strahovské nádvoří 1 (☎20 51 66 95). Metro A: Hradčanská. From the Metro, take tram #8 toward Bílá Hora to Malovanka. Turn around, follow the tram tracks, then turn right onto Strahovská. The museum is inside the monastery on the left. The star attraction here is the **Strahov library** with its magnificent **Theological and Philosophical Halls.** The frescoed, vaulted ceilings of the two Baroque reading rooms were intended to spur monks to the loftiest peaks of erudition. Great pagan thinkers of antiquity oversee their progress from the ceiling in the Philosophical Hall. Open Tu-Su 10am-5pm. 20Kč, students 10Kč.

**Rudolfinum,** Alšovo náb. 12 (☎24 89 32 05). Metro A: Staroměstská. The entrance faces the river. The Czech Philharmonic shares the building with one of Prague's oldest galleries. Rotating art exhibits in a huge Art Nouveau interior. The cafe at the end seems too elegant to be self-serve. Open July-May Tu-Su 10am-6pm. 50Kč, students 25Kč.

**Bertramka Mozart muzeum,** Mozartova 169 (☎543 893). Metro B: Anděl. Take a left on Plzeňská, and look for a green sign pointing up the slope to the 3rd street on the left. Mozart, a guest at Villa Bertramka, dashed off the overture to *Don Giovanni* here the day before it opened in 1787. Open Tu-Su 9:30am-6pm; Nov-Mar. 9:30am-5pm. 90Kč, students 50Kč. Concerts vary with seasons, see schedule.

**Museum of Medieval Torture Instruments,** Karlova 2, across the street from the Charles Bridge. Metro A: Staroměstská. Exit Metro and follow Křížovnická along the river, then turn left onto Karlova. The museum is on the right. Not for the weak of stomach. Collection highlights include: the Head Crusher, thumbscrews, iron gag, Spanish tickle torture, and the Masks of Shame and Infamy. All accompanied by highly-detailed explanations guaranteed to nauseate. Open daily 10am-10pm. 100Kč, students 80Kč.

# 🎵 ENTERTAINMENT

For a list of current concerts and performances, consult *The Prague Post*, *Threshold*, or *Do města-Downtown* (the latter two are free and distributed at many cafes and restaurants). Most performances begin at 7pm; unsold tickets are sometimes available 30min. before showtime. Most of Prague's theaters shut down in July and August. The selection is more varied the rest of the year, peaking between mid-May and early June when the **Prague Spring Festival** draws musicians from around the world. Tickets (400-3500Kč) may sell out as much as a year in advance; try **Bohemia Ticket International,** Malé nám. 13 (☎24 22 78 32; fax 21 61 21 26), next to Čedok. (Open M-F 9am-5pm, Sa 9am-2pm.) **Národní divadlo, Stavovské divadlo,** and **Státní opera** all stage operas; while performances rarely scintillate, the staggeringly low prices do. **Cinemas** abound, showing English-language blockbusters three months to a year after US release. Prices depend on the movie's popularity; ask at a tourist office for a list of current films. The **Kino Cafe-bar,** Karlovo nám. 19 (entry on Odborů; ☎24 91 57 65), shows Czech films with English subtitles, as do many theaters in the center of town—look for a sign posted on the ticket booth. (Tickets around 100Kč.)

**Národní divadlo** (National Theater), Národní třída 2/4 (☎24 90 14 19). Metro B: Národní třída. Features theater, opera, and ballet. Tickets 100-1000Kč. Box office open M-F 10am-6pm, Sa-Su 10am-12:30pm and 3-6pm, and 30min. before performances.

**Stavovské divadlo** (Estates Theater), Ovocný trh 1 (☎24 91 34 37). Metro A, B: Můstek. Left from the pedestrian Na Příkopě. This is where *Don Giovanni* premiered all those years ago; it features mostly classic theater now. Some opera and ballet. Use the Národní divadlo box office, above, or turn up 30min. before the show to try your luck.

**Státní opera** (State Opera), Wilsonova 4 (☎265 353). Metro A, C: Muzeum. Tickets 50-600Kč. Box office open M-F 10am-4pm, Sa-Su 10am-noon and 1-4pm.

**Říše loutek** (Marionette Theater), Žatecká 1 (☎232 34 29 and 232 25 36). Metro A: Staroměstská. On the corner of Žalecká and Mariánské nám. Puppetry is taken seriously in the Czech Republic and isn't just for kids (see also **Not Just for Kids,** below). The touristy-but-amusing version of *Don Giovanni* has become a Prague stand-by. Tickets 490Kč, students 390Kč. June and July performances Su-Tu and Th-Sa 8pm. Box office open daily 10am-8pm.

**Image Theater,** Pařížská 4 (☎232 91 91). Metro A: Staroměstská. Exit Metro and walk down Křížovnická toward Josefov. Turn right onto Široká and continue straight until you hit Pařížská. Features silent, black light performances guaranteed to entertain through dance and pantomime. Shows daily 8pm. Box office open daily 9am-8am. 350Kč.

**NOT JUST FOR KIDS** So you're in Prague and wondering, as every good ol' traveler should, what to bring back home. Perhaps a portrait of your own beautiful self by one of the Old Town Square artisans? The oh-so-original Russian army hats and babushkas-cum-Soviet premiers? Or one of the ubiquitous "KGB: Still Watching You" T-shirts? Despite the preponderance of kitsch in Prague's streets, there are actually real pieces of art to be found that make better souvenirs. Woodcrafting and puppetry have a long history in the Czech lands, and many young artists struggle to survive in the kitch-ridden economy. One store with traditional wooden and textile toys, **Hračky Trnka,** sits at Ostrovní 21, just around the corner from the Velryba restaurant (p. 227). Its wide selection of works by over 200 Czech artists, ranging from balloons to games and pillows, is bound to satisfy friends and family members of all ages. (☎24 93 08 58; www.shopdrive.cz/kid. 50-2000Kč. Open M-F 10am-7pm, Sa 11am-5pm.)

# ◪ NIGHTLIFE

The most authentic way to experience Prague at night is through an alcoholic fog. With some of the best beers in the world on tap, pubs, and beer halls are understandably the city's favorite form of nighttime entertainment. These days, however, authentic pub experiences are often restricted to the suburbs and outlying Metro stops; in central Prague, nearly everything has been overtaken by tourists. Irish pubs and American sports bars are cropping up everywhere, with appropriately high prices for their foreign beers (but who comes to Prague to drink Guinness?). There are a few trusty Czech pubs scattered throughout Staré Město and Malá Strana to ease the offensive sting of T.G.I. Friday's.

Prague is not a clubbing city, although there are enough dance clubs pumping out techno to sweaty hordes to satisfy Eurotrash club scene cravings. More popular among Czechs are the city's many jazz and rock clubs, hosting excellent local and international acts. Otherwise, you can always retreat to the Charles Bridge to sing along with aspiring Brit-pop guitarists. Whichever way you indulge in Prague nightlife, swig down a few pints of *pivo*, grab some 4am snacks (see **Late Night Eating,** p. 228), and at least once, forego the night bus for the morning Metro, joining bleary-eyed Czech students in their scandalization of the city's hard-working adults.

## BEERHALLS AND WINE CELLARS

◪ **U Fleků,** Křemencova 11 (☎24 91 51 18). Metro B: Národní třída. Turn right onto Spálená, away from Národní, then right onto Myslíkova and right again onto Křemencova; the beer hall is on the left. Founded in 1491, this is the oldest surviving brewhouse in Prague. The bands play "Roll out the Barrel" nightly. 50Kč per 0.4L of homebrewed beer. Open daily 9am-11pm.

**Vinárna U Sudu,** Vodičkova 10 (☎22 23 22 07). Metro A: Můstek. Cross over Václavské nám. to Vodičkova, and follow it as it curves left. The bar is on your left. Virtually undiscovered by tourists, this Moravian wine bar looks rather quotidian from its entrance and first floor, but beneath the veneer sprawls an infinite labyrinth of cavernous cellars, each with its own mood lighting. A liter of smooth red (110Kč) goes down frighteningly fast. Open M-F 11am-midnight, Sa-Su 2pm-midnight.

**Pivnice u Sv. Tomáše,** Letenská 12 (☎57 32 01 01). Metro A: Malostranská. The mighty dungeons echo with boisterous beer songs and slobbering toasts. The homemade brew is 30Kč. Live brass band plays nightly 7pm. Open daily 11:30am-midnight.

## BARS

◪ **Kozička,** Kozí 1 (☎24 81 83 08). Metro A: Staroměstská. Take Dlouhá from the square's northeast corner; the street becomes Kozí after veering to the left. Giant cellar bar is always packed, and you'll know why after your 1st *Krušovice* (25Kč). 20-something Czechs come early and stay all night. Open M-F noon-4am, Sa-Su 4pm-4am.

■ **Iron Door,** Michalská 13. See **Late Night Eating,** p. 228.

**Le Chateau,** Jakubská 2 (☎232 62 42). Metro B: Náměstí Republiky. From the Metro, walk through the Powder Tower to Celetná, then take a right onto Templová. On the corner of Templová and Jakubská. The Châpeau recharges the tired souls of travelers by fulfilling all of their vicarious needs. Non-stop techno-rock keeps the place pumpin' till the wee hours. Open M-Th noon-3am, F noon-4am, Sa 4pm-4am, Su 4am-2am.

**Újezd,** Újezd 18 (☎53 83 62). Metro B: Národní třída. Exit the Metro onto Národní and turn left toward the river. Cross the Legíí bridge, continue straight on Vítězná, and turn right onto Újezd; the bar is on your right. A mid-20s Czech crowd smokes the night away at this mecca of mellowness. 3 floors of acid jazz. 0.5L *Budvar* a mere 22Kč. Open daily 11am-4am.

**Terminal Bar,** Soukenická 6 (☎21 87 119 99). Metro B: Nám. Republiky. Head toward the river on Revoluční and turn right onto Soukenická. A multimedia bar with style, this bar/cafe features superfast computers (1.5Kč per min.), a downstairs bookstore, live music on weekends, a new sushi bar, and electronic music. You might even forget you came to check email. Open M-Th and Su 11am-1am, F-Sa 11am-3am.

**Cafe Marquis de Sade,** Templová 8 (☎24 81 75 05). Metro B: Nám. Republiky. See directions to Le Châpeau Rouge above. Might not live up to its name, but this brothel-turned-bar is full of fresh air and red velvet couches. Don't forget to check out the fine modern artwork as you get drunk on (how appropriate!) *Velvet* beer (35Kč). Live music on Th. Happy hour M-F 4-6pm. Open daily 11am-2am.

**Žíznlvý pes** (Thirsty Dog), El. Krásnohorské 1. Metro A: Staroměstská. Walk up Pařížská, the street next to St. Nicholas's Church. Go right on Široká, then left on Krásnohorské. The inspiration for the Nick Cave song, this bar is the watering hole for crazy ex-pats and a few artsy Czech regulars. Open M-F 11am-2am, Sa-Su 2pm-2am.

**Molly Malone's,** U obecního dvora 4 (☎53 47 93). Metro A: Staroměstská. Turn right onto Křižonvická, away from the Charles Bridge. After Nám. Jana Palacha, turn right onto Široká, which becomes Vězeňská; at its end, turn left. The Irish prove they're the most fun at this cozy bar, where overturned beds and sewing machines double as tables. A pint of Guinness is cheaper than in Ireland at 70Kč. Open Su-Th noon-1am, F-Sa noon-2am.

**Zanzibar,** Saská 6 (cellular ☎0602 75 24 74). Metro A: Malostranská. From the square, head down Nostecká toward the Charles Bridge, turn right on Lázeňská, and another left on Saská. The classiest place to see and be seen among Czech cocktail lovers. The tastiest, priciest, and most extensive cocktails this side of the Vltava (120-150Kč). Cuban cigars (?!) 600-1200 Kč. Reserve on weekends. Open daily 5pm-3am.

**Jo's Bar and Garáž,** Malostranské nám. 7 (cellular ☎0602 97 14 78). Metro A: Malostranská. If you can't bear the idea that the people at the next table might not speak English, all-Anglophone Jo's Bar is the perfect spot for you. With new ownership, the bar is getting better. DJ and dance floor downstairs. *Staropramen* 25Kč. Long Island iced tea 110Kč. Open daily 11am-2am.

**Jáma** (The Hollow), V jámě 7 (☎24 22 23 83). Metro A, C: Muzeum. Hidden off Vodičkova. The closest thing Prague has to a real sports bar, Jáma attracts a diverse but largely foreign crowd. Watch American sporting events live via satellite with *Kelt* (32Kč) in hand. Brand new garden in back and in-house internet access (1.5 Kč per min.) Open daily 11am-1am.

## CLUBS AND DISCOS

■ **Roxy,** Dlouhá 33 (cellular ☎0603 56 99 27). Metro B: Nám. Republiky. Walk up Revoluční to the river; go left on Dlouhá. Hip locals and in-the-know tourists come here for experimental DJs, theme nights, and endless dancing. Cover 150-200Kč. Open Sept.-June Tu-Su 9pm-late; July-Aug. daily 9pm-late.

**Radost FX,** Bělehradská 120 (☎25 69 98). Metro C: I.P. Pavlova. Heavily touristed, but still plays bad-ass techno, jungle, and house music. Hi-tech laser lights, Nintendo and twistedly creative drinks (sex with an alien 140Kč) *will* expand your clubbing horizons. Cover 80-150Kč. Open M-Sa 10pm-dawn.

**Palác Akropolis,** Kubelíkova 27 (☎697 64 11). Metro A: Jiřího z Poděbrad, then down Slavíkova and right onto Kubelíkova. Live bands several times a week. Top Czech act Psí vojáci are occasional visitors. Open daily 10pm-5am.

## ABSINTHE MAKES THE HEART GROW FONDER
Shrouded in Bohemian mystique and taboo, this translucent turquoise fire water is a force to be reckoned with. Despite being banned in all but three countries this century due to allegations of opium-lacing and fatal hallucinations, Czechs have had a long love affair with absinthe. It has been the mainstay spirit of the Prague intelligentsia since Kafka's days, and during WWII every Czech adult was rationed a half-liter of it per month. Today, backpackers (who apparently will drink anything) have discovered the liquor, which at its strongest can be 160 proof. The bravest and most seasoned ex-pats sip it on the rocks, but for the most snapshot-worthy ritual douse a spoonful of sugar in the alcohol, torch it with a match until the sugar caramelizes and the alcohol burns off, and dump the residue into your glass.

**Lávka,** Novotného lávka 1 (☎22 22 21 56). The irresistible location under the Charles Bridge draws crowds of tourists to this trashy club, even though it's devoid of character. The fluorescent disco downstairs pops eyeballs. Cover 50Kč. Open nightly 10pm-late.

## JAZZ CLUBS

■ **U staré paní,** Michalská 9 (☎/fax 26 72 67). Metro A, B: Můstek. Walk down Na můstku at the end of Václavské nám. through its name change to Melantrichova. Turn left on Havelská and right on Michalská. "The Old Lady's Place" showcases some of the finest jazz vocalists in Prague in a tiny, dark, and classy upstairs venue. Shows nightly 9pm-midnight. Cover 160Kč, includes a free drink. Open daily 7pm-1am.

**U malého Glena II,** Karmelitská 23 (☎535 81 15), the basement club of "U malého Glena" (see **Cafes,** p. 229). This small bar hosts bouncy jazz or white blues from Stan the Man nightly at 9pm. Beer 25Kč. Cover 50-70Kč. Open daily 8pm-2am.

**Jazz Club Železná,** Železná 16 (☎24 23 96 97). Metro A, B: Můstek. Walk down Na Můstku away from Václavské nám.; go right on Havelská, then left on Železná. Club is on the left at the back of the building. Dark cellar bar showcases live jazz. Beer 30Kč. Cover 90-120Kč. Shows daily 9-11:30pm. Open daily 3pm-12:30am.

**Reduta,** Národní 20. Metro A: Národní třída. Favorite haunt of Presidents Clinton and Havel, as the photos won't let you forget. Cover 120Kč. Open daily 9am-midnight.

**Agharta,** Krakovská 5 (☎22 21 12 75), just up Krakovská from Václavské nám. Metro B, C: Muzeum. Nightly live jazz ensembles starting at 9pm. Cover 100Kč, beer 40Kč, but the music is great and the vibe chill. Open M-F 5pm-1am, Sa-Su 7pm-1am.

## THE FAGUE AND THE DRAGUE OF PRAGUE

If Prague had a desert, *Priscilla II* could be shot here. The scene is developing fast and in many directions: transvestite shows, stripteases, discos, bars, cafes, restaurants, and hotels aimed at gay and lesbian travelers can be found easily. At any of the places listed below, you can pick up a copy of the monthly *Amigo* (39Kč), the most thorough guide to gay life in the Czech Republic and Slovakia, with a lot in English, or *Gaycko* (59Kč), a glossier piece of work mostly in Czech.

■ **U střelce,** Karolíny Světlé 12 (☎24 23 82 78). Metro B: Národní třída. Exit Metro right, go down Spálená until it becomes Na Perštýně. Turn left onto Bartolomějská, then right to Karolíny Světlé. Under the arch on the right. Gay club pulls a diverse crowd for its F and Sa cabarets, when magnificent female impersonators take the stage, occasionally sitting on unprepared audience members. Cover 80Kč. Open W, F and Sa 9:30pm-5am.

**A Club,** Milíčova 25 (☎22 78 16 23). Metro C: Hlavní Nádraží. Take tram #5 toward Harfa, #9 toward Spojovací, or #26 toward Nádraží Hostivař, and get off at Lipanská. Walk back down Seifertova and turn right on Milíčova. A nightspot for lesbians, but men are welcome. All class, with wire sculptures, soft light, and comfy couches near the bar. Disco in the back starts at 10pm, but don't come before midnight. Beer 20Kč. Open nightly 7pm-sunrise.

**Drake's,** Petřinská 5 (☎53 49 09). Tram #9 or 12. 24hr. gay complex, both adored and hated by Prague's gay community. Come here to dance, cruise, or make a love connection. Nightly strip shows and private video rooms. Very pricey.

**Tom's Bar,** Pernerova 4 (☎232 11 70). Metro B, C: Florenc. Walk down Křižíkova, pass under the tracks, and go right on Prvního pluků, which curves to the left and becomes Pernerova. Video screening rooms. Men only. Open M-Sa 7:30am-3am.

# ⚡ DAYTRIPS FROM PRAGUE

Even if you're only spending a few days in the capital, take the time to explore the towns and sights in the Bohemian hills around Prague. When you're in the city, it's easy to believe that Prague is the only place worth visiting in the Czech Republic. One trip to the magnificent castles of Karlštejn, Konopiště, or Křivoklát; one jaunt through the wine cellars of Mělník or the motorcycles at Kámen; or one sobering day at Terezín or Kutná Hora, however, will begin to expose the wealth of historically, aesthetically, and hedonistically significant towns in the Czech Republic.

## TEREZÍN (THERESIENSTADT)                              ☎(0)416

*The bus from Prague-Florenc (1hr., 7 per day, 59Kč) stops by the central square, where the tourist office sells maps (29Kč; open daily until 6pm).*

The fortress town of Terezín (Theresienstadt) was built in the 1780s on Habsburg Emperor Josef II's orders to safeguard the northern frontier with the German states. In 1940, Hitler's Gestapo set up a huge prison in the Small Fortress, and in 1941 the town itself became a concentration camp for Jews—by 1942, the entire pre-war civilian population had been evacuated. 140,000 Jews were deported to the ghetto, at first just from the Bohemia-Moravia Protectorate, but later from all over the *Reich*. Twice Terezín was beautified in order to receive delegations from the Red Cross, who were wholly deceived about the true purpose of the place: Nazi propaganda films touted the area as an almost idyllic spa resort where Jews were "allowed" to educate their young, partake in arts and recreation, and live a "fulfilling" life. Terezín was one of Hitler's most successful propaganda ploys.

In reality, 35,000 died here, some of starvation and disease, others at the hands of brutal guards. 85,000 others were transported to death camps, primarily Auschwitz. More than 30,000 prisoners (mostly political) were held in the Small Fortress, and many Czech resistance fighters and Communists were shot here. After the Red Army liberated Terezín, the Czechoslovak regime used the camp to hold Sudeten Germans awaiting deportation: the Czech and German governments recently exchanged apologies for the ethnic cleansing both countries attempted during this ghastly time. Terezín has been repopulated since the war and the town's life goes on in the midst of the one time concentration camp; families live in the former barracks and supermarkets occupy Nazi offices. The population, however, has never approached its pre-war levels, when the town was inhabited by over 4,000 Czechs and Germans—the last census counted fewer than 2,000 residents.

**THE GHETTO MUSEUM.** The museum, on Komenského in town, displays mountains of documents, helpfully setting Terezín in the wider Nazi context. It also displays children's art from the ghetto alongside staggering adult work, all with English explanations. *(☎782 577; fax 782 245; manager@pamatnik-terezin.cz. Open daily Apr.-Sept. 9am-6pm; Oct.-Mar. 9am-5:30pm. Closed Dec. 24-26 and Jan. 1. 130Kč, students 100Kč; including Small Fortress 150Kč, 110Kč. English tour 240Kč.)*

**SMALL FORTRESS.** (Malá pevnost.) East of the town and across the river sits the Small Fortress. Much of it is left bare and untouched for visitors to explore freely. Permanent exhibitions chart the town's development from 1780-1939, and, in the museum, the story of the fortress during WWII. Upon entrance to the Small Fortress, the words *"Arbeit macht frei"* ("Work makes you free") leap off the left gate leading to the first courtyard. This cruelly ironic inscription was typical of most Nazi concentration camps, but not of a Gestapo prison. Beyond the blocks of the first courtyard is the entrance to the underground passage, a dimly lit pathway with barred airholes that winds around the length of the camp to the excavation area. *(Open daily Apr.-Sept. 8am-6pm; Oct.-Mar. 8am-4:30pm. Closed Dec. 24-26 and Jan. 1.)*

Don't leave Terezín without seeing the **Jewish cemetery** and **crematorium**. The furnaces and autopsy lab are as they were 50 years ago, with the addition of flowers, cards, and photos left as tributes by the victims' descendants. Men must cover their heads. *(Open Mar.-Nov. M-F and Su 10am-5pm. Free.)*

# KONOPIŠTĚ ☎(0)301

*Buses run from Prague-Florenc to Benešov (1hr., 7 per day, 59Kč). From the bus station, turn left on Nádražní and go left over the bridge. Continue straight along Konopištská, then bear left at the fork and follow the road to the castle. Trains also run from Hlavní nádraží (45min.-1hr., every 30min., 36Kč). ☎213 66. konopiste@pusc.cz. Open May-Aug. Tu-Su 9am-12:30pm and 1-5pm; Sept. and March Tu-F 9am-12:30pm and 1-4pm, Sa-Su until 5pm; Sept.-Oct. Tu-F 9am-12:30pm, 1-3pm, Sa-Su until 4pm. 70Kč, students 35Kč; tours 120Kč, 70Kč; tours of the Archduke's private rooms 130Kč, 250Kč.*

The mighty castle Konopiště (KOH-no-peesh-tyeh), south of Prague in Benešov, boasts more than 300,000 taxidermied animals, an eternal tribute to the shooting prowess of Archduke Franz Ferdinand. His collection of ivory pistols and armor used in 16th-century Italian theater astounds, as well.

# KARLŠTEJN ☎(0)311

*Trains run from Hlavní nádraží or Praha-Smíchov (45min., 1 per hr., 27Kč). Turn right out of the train station, cross the Berounka river over the absurdly modern bridge, turn right, and walk through the shop-lined village to the castle. ☎681 617. Open Tu-Su July-Aug. 9am-6pm; May-June and Sept. 9am-5pm; Apr. and Oct. 9am-4pm; Nov.-Dec. 9am-3pm. Czech tour 70Kč, students 40Kč; 50min. English tour 200Kč, students 100Kč, 7-8 per day.*

Bohemia's patriotic gem, Karlštejn is a walled and turreted fortress built by Charles IV as his personal *dacha* and to house his crown jewels and holy relics. Charles originally banned women from entering the castle, but soon changed his mind when his wife snuck inside cross-dressed as a castle guard and managed to spend the night—or so the legend says. The castle has been immortalized in a popular Czech musical *Noc na Karlštejně* (Night at Karlštejn). Most of the interior decorations were stolen during one war or another over the centuries, but the **Chapel of the Holy Cross** is decorated with more than 2,000 inlaid precious stones and 128 apocalyptic paintings by medieval artist Master Theodorik. *(Open Tu-Su 9am-5pm. Mandatory tours 200Kč, in English 600Kč.)*

The castle's surroundings are just as (if not more) impressive as the castle itself, so take your time to stroll through the forests. Stay on the marked paths, though, as the area is part of the state-protected Nature Reservation Český Kras.

# KUTNÁ HORA

*Buses run from Prague-Florenc (1½hr., 6 per day, 46Kč). The chapel is about 2km from the bus station. Take a local bus to Sedlec Tabák (every 20min.). If walking, exit the station and turn left onto Benešova. Follow the road until it becomes Vítězná; the ossuary will be in front of you. Open daily Apr.-Oct. 8am-6pm; Nov.-Mar. 9am-noon and 1-4pm. 30Kč, students 15Kč. Cameras 30Kč, video 60Kč.*

1½hr. east of Prague, the former mining town of Kutná Hora (Mining Mountain) has a history as morbid as the bone church that made the city famous. Founded in the latter half of the 13th-century when lucky miners hit a vein, the city boomed with 100,000 gold diggers. Unfortunately, the Black Plague halted the fortune-seekers dead in their tracks. A few years later, a local monk sprinkled soil from the biblical Golgotha Cemetery on Kutná Hora's cemetery; this religious infusion made the rich and superstitious quite keen to be buried there and the graveyard quickly became over-crowded. Neighbors started to complain about the stench by the 15th-century, so the Cistercian Order built a chapel and started cramming in bodies. In a fit of whimsy (or possibly insanity), the monk in charge began design-

CZECH REPUBLIC

ing flowers out of pelvi and crania. He never finished the ossuary, but the artist František Rint eventually completed the project in 1870 with flying butt-bones, femur crosses, and a grotesque chandelier made from every bone in the human body. Some lucky corpse even got to spell out the artist's name, in addition to an amazing rendering of the Schwarzenberg family crest.

# MĚLNÍK ☎(0)206

*Buses run from Prague-Florenc (45min., 6 per day, 51Kč). From the bus station, make a right onto Bezručova and bear left at the road split onto Kpt. Jaroše; this brings you to the town center. Head in the direction of the big clock tower; the onion-domed St. Peter and Paul Cathedral is directly behind it.*

Dramatically perched atop a hill above the confluence of the Vltava and Elbe rivers, wine-making Mělník is an ideal daytrip. In one day, you can visit the ossuary, tour the stately Renaissance château, sample the castle's homemade wines, and savor your favorite vintage over lunch in the old schoolhouse overlooking the Říp Valley. The town's vinticulture was honed about 1000 years ago, when Princess Ludmila—later St. Ludmila—planted the first vineyards for communion wine. Her grandson, St. Wenceslas, the patron saint of Bohemian wine-makers, was supposedly introduced to the secrets of wine-making in the vineyards of Mělník. Both the castle and the vineyards were abandoned during the Thirty Years' War, but recent restorations by the Lobkowicz family have revived the town's former glory.

The **castle** tour winds through the absurdly fancy color-themed château rooms and ends in the Gothic wine cellars, where you'll walk on a floor composed entirely of upside-down wine bottles. Wine tasting (110Kč) is available with a reservation. (☎62 21 21 25. Open daily Mar. 1-Nov. 20 10am-5pm. Tours 50Kč, students 30Kč.) Directly across from the *château* is the 15th-century **St. Peter and Paul Cathedral**, whose crypt houses the bones of 10,000 medieval plague victims. (Open Tu-Su 10am-4pm. 20-30Kč.)

# KŘIVOKLÁT ☎(0)313

*Take a train from Hlavní nádraží or Praha-Smíchov in Prague to Beroun and switch trains to Křivoklát (1¾hr. total, every 90min., 48Kč). From the train station, follow Hradní toward the castle. ☎55 84 40. Open June-Aug. 9am-5pm; May Tu-Su 9am-4pm; Sept.-Apr. 9am-3pm. Closed noon-1pm. Last tour at closing time. Czech tours 60Kč, students 30Kč; English tours 120Kč, 60Kč.*

Much less touristed (and some might argue more magnificent) than Konopiště, Křivoklát (KRZIIEE-voh-klaht) is a 13th-century royal hunting lodge nestled in a UNESCO-protected nature reserve. The obligatory tour covers the castle chapel (in which the pews are adorned with malevolent animal carvings signifying "evil forces"), an amazing collection of hand-carved sleds, and the starvation chambers.

# KÁMEN ☎(0)36

*Reach Kámen from Prague via Tábor (2hr., 7 per day, 70Kč). From the Tábor bus station, catch a local bus to Kámen (30min., 30Kč). Try to avoid visiting on the weekend as bus connections are infrequent.*

If the sights closer to Prague haven't satiated you, head farther south to the **Kámen Castle and Motorcycle Museum** for some refreshingly different historical exhibits. Reopened to the public in 1974, the Kámen Castle is named after the stone (*kámen* in Czech) on which it was founded. Owned for 200 years by the Malovec family, it now pays homage to the Czech motorcycle industry. See a bike made out of agricultural equipment, or examine the Czech *Devil* moped. Additionally, there are four rooms of valuable 16th-19th century books and maps of the Czech Republic. Besides the museum, the castle has a prison-turned-wedding-altar, complete with a hidden trap door leading to a torture room—sure to cure even the worst case of cold feet. (☎543 66 19. Open May-Sept. Tu-Su 9am-noon and 1-5pm; Apr. and Oct. Sa-Su 9am-noon and 1-4pm. Tours 30Kč, students 15Kč.)

# WEST BOHEMIA

Bursting at the seams with curative springs of all sorts, West Bohemia is the Czech mecca for those in search of a good bath or a good beer. Over the centuries, emperors and intellectuals have soaked in the waters of Karlovy Vary (Carlsbad in German), while Plzeň (Pilsen in German) gave birth to one of the world's most famous beers, the original Pilsner Urquell.

## PLZEŇ ☎(0)19

Tell a Czech you're going to Plzeň (PIL-zenh; pop. 175,000), and they might say *"to je škoda"* ("what a pity"). The unfortunate pun on "Škoda" alludes to the notorious arms factory-*cum*-auto plant that made Plzeň one of Bohemia's most polluted cities. Whatever pollution does exist here, however, is shadowed by the beautiful architecture and layout of the city. Plzeň offers an intriguing center, thriving youth culture, and its hometown brew, the famed Pilsner Urquell. If it's chic you're after, hit Prague; come here for hard rock, flowing pints, and a pinch of soot.

### ✈ ORIENTATION

**Nám. Republiky** (Republic Sq.), the main square, lies amid a grid of streets surrounded by parks. Restaurants and cafes cluster outside the square. The city's sights are spread all over, but the happening nightlife is concentrated on **Americká** street. From the **train station**, turn right onto **Sirková** and enter the pedestrian underpass. Turn left onto **Pražská** and follow it when it bears right and you'll end up in Nám. Republiky. From the bus, turn left onto **Husova.** Follow it as it becomes **Smetanovy sady,** then turn onto **Bedřicha Smetany** and follow it to the square.

### ⌷ TRANSPORTATION

**Trains:** ☎701 46 90. On Sirková between Americká and Koterovská. To **Prague** (1¾hr., 12 per day, 78Kč) and **Český Krumlov** (4hr., 2 per day, 114Kč) via **České Budějovice.** Domestic tickets on the 1st fl.; international tickets and info office on the 2nd fl. Open M-F 6am-10pm, Sa-Su 6am-7pm.

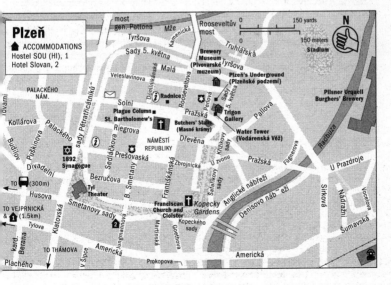

**Buses:** Husova 58 (☎22 37 04; info ☎1034). Many Eurolines buses pass through *en route* to **Prague** (2hr., at least 1 per hr., 60Kč) from **France, Switzerland,** or **Germany.** To **Karlovy Vary** (1¾hr., 17 per day, 72Kč). Open M-Sa 5am-10:30pm, Su 5am-8pm.

**Local Transportation: Tram** #2 goes to the train and bus stations, Nám. Republiky, and the hostel. Tram #4 runs north-south along Sady Pětatřicátníků. Get tickets from any *tabák* and punch them on board (8Kč; backpacks 4Kč). 200Kč fine for riding ticketless. Trams stop running at 11:45pm. Identically numbered **buses** replace trams at night.

# 🛈 PRACTICAL INFORMATION

**Tourist Office: Městské informační středisko (MIS),** Nám. Republiky 41 (☎703 27 50; fax 703 27 52; infocenter@mmp.plzen-city.cz). Sells **maps** (50Kč) and phone cards (175Kč); also books rooms from 200Kč. English spoken. Open daily Apr.-Sept. 9am-6pm; Oct.-Mar. M-F 10am-5pm, Sa-Su 10am-3:30pm. The town hall nearby sells the helpful *Plzeň Open Town* (28Kč).

**Currency Exchange: Komerční Banka,** Zbrojnická 4 (☎721 42 11), off Nám. Republiky's southeast corner. Cashes **traveler's checks** for a 2% commission (50Kč minimum). Open M-F 8am-5pm. A **currency exchange machine** sits outside **Československá obchodní banka,** Americká 60, near the train station. Open 24hr.

**International Press: American Center Plzeň,** Dominikánská 9 (☎723 77 22).

**Luggage Storage:** At the train station. 10Kč per bag; 20Kč over 15kg. Lockers 5Kč per day. Open 24hr.

**Pharmacy: Lékárna Martinská,** Martinská 4 (☎723 55 15). From Nám. Republiky, turn right onto Františkánská, which becomes Martinská. Open M-Sa 10am-8pm.

**Internet Access: Alien Club,** Dominikánská 3 (mobile ☎0604 568 911). Park your UFO and go to the 3rd floor for a fast connection. 1Kč per min. Extra-terrestrials free. Open M-F 11am-11pm, Su 2-11pm.

**Post Office:** Solní 20 (☎721 11 11). **Poste Restante.** Wheelchair accessible. Open M-F 7am-7pm, Sa 8am-1pm, Su 8am-noon.

**Postal code:** 301 00.

# 🏠 ACCOMMODATIONS

There aren't many budget accommodations in Plzeň. **MIS** (see above) and **CKM,** Dominikánská 1 (☎723 63 93) both book rooms; *pension* prices start at 350Kč.

**Hotel Slovan,** Smetanovy sady 1 (☎722 72 56; fax 722 70 12). From the bus station, turn left onto Husova and follow it to Smetanovy sady. Clean rooms with breakfast in a Hollywood-esque building 5min. from the center. Breakfast 120Kč. Reception 24hr. Singles 500Kč; doubles 750Kč. Extra bed 350Kč.

**Hostel SOU (HI),** Vejprnická 58, pavilion #8 (☎28 20 12). Take tram #2 to Internáty, walk back 50m, and turn left into the fenced compound. This former Škoda workers' hostel is institutional and far from the center, but cheap. Check-out 10am. 189Kč.

# 🍴 FOOD

Every meal in Plzeň should include a glass of *Pilsner Urquell* (Plzeňský Prazdroj) or its dark brother, *Purkmistr.* If you can't decide between them, have a *řezané,* a Czech black and tan. For groceries, head to **Tesco,** Americká 47, near the train station. (Open M-W 7am-7pm, Th-F 7am-8pm, Sa-Su 8am-6pm.)

**U Bílého Lva** (At the White Lion), Pražská 15 (☎722 69 98) could pass as a hunter's cabin with its animal skins and savory meat dishes (37-144Kč). Good daily soup (12.80Kč). Open daily 10am-11pm.

**U Salzmannů,** Pražská 8 (☎723 58 55). Dishes out hearty Czech pub food to compliment your *Pilsner.* Main dishes 69-125Kč. Open M-Sa 11am-11pm, Su 11am-10pm. Kitchen open until 10pm.

**S&S Grill,** Sedláčkova 7 (☎22 66 05). From Nám. Republiky's southwest corner, take Riegrova toward Sady Pětatřicátníků. Go left onto Sedláčková; S&S is on the right after Prešovská. True Bohemian fast food. Locals sit at the grill's tiny tables and eat turkey goulash (28Kč). Open M-F 8:30am-7pm, Sa 9am-3pm, Su 10am-2pm.

# ⚫ SIGHTS

Aside from the Pilsner Brewery, the town's attractions all lie within or around Nám. Republiky, which is a convenient place to start a tour.

**REPUBLIC SQUARE.** (Náměstí Republiky.) Imperial dwellings loom over this marketplace, but none overshadow the belfry of the **Church of St. Bartholomew** (Kostel sv. Bartoloměje). Inside, a rich collection of Gothic statues and altars bows to the stunning 14th-century polychrome statue **Plzeňská Madona,** recalling Bohemia's glory days under Charles IV. It's free to look from the entrance, but you have to pay to walk around. *(Open W-F 10am-4pm, Sa 10am-5pm, Su noon-4pm. 20Kč.)* For a vertiginous view of the town, tourists climb 60 of the 103m to the observation deck, where they can read sad stories about why the town no longer has an outsized bell called Bartholomew (Bárta to its friends). Bárta was cracked, removed, smelted in a fire, shot at, and cracked again before being melted down to make bullets during World War II. Now no one has the heart or the money to forge another. The **Plague Column** (Morový sloup) seems to be working: residents may suffer from industrial diseases and liver complaints, but the plague hasn't been here for a while. Plzeň's Renaissance **town hall,** topped with a golden clock, connects on the inside to the 1607 **Kaiser House** (Císařský dům). *(Nám. Republiky 39.)*

**▨ PILSNER URQUELL BREWERY.** (Měšťanský Pivovar Plzeňský Prazdroj.) The building that best epitomizes the essence of Plzeň lies outside of the city center. In 1840, over 30 independent brewers plied their trade in the beer cellars of Plzeň. Some of the suds were good, some were awful, so the burgher brewers formed a union with the goal of creating the best beer in the world. Many would agree that the Pilsner Urquell Burghers' Brewery succeeded with its legendary *Pilsner Urquell.* A huge neo-Renaissance gate welcomes visitors to this pastel palace of the brewing arts. After the stimulating "kaleidoscope" film (with English subtitles) about Prazdroj's past and present, the group divides into Czech, German, English, and French subgroups led by knowledgeable guides. *(The entrance to the complex lies 300m from Staré Město over the Radbuza River, where Pražská becomes U Prazdroje. ☎706 28 88. 1hr. tours M-F 12:30pm. 75Kč.)*

**BREWERY MUSEUM.** This underground labyrinthine museum exhibits beer paraphernalia from medieval taps to a coaster collection. The original malt-house room displays the top-secret Pilsner process. The last room, labeled "the room of curiosities," is the zaniest, with gigantic steins, wacky Pilsner signs, and a statue of Shakespeare's most famous drunk, Sir John Falstaff. You can even buy a glass and sample the beer to enhance the exhibit's effect. *(Veleslavínova 6. Perlová ends at Veleslavínova. ☎722 49 55; fax 723 55 74. Open daily 10am-6pm. 40Kč, students 10Kč. Beer 30Kč. English tour extra 20Kč by reservation.)*

**WATER TOWER COMPLEX.** Bear left from the tourist office to reach the **water tower** (vodárenská věž), which once stored the crystal-clear water needed for fine beer. *(Pražská 19.)* The well's dried up, so the **Trigon Gallery** next door doesn't have to worry about water damage to its mostly modern art collection. *(Pražská 19. ☎732 54 71. Open M-Th 10am-6pm, F 10am-5pm, Sa 10am-noon. 10Kč, students 5Kč. 1st floor free.)* The tower and **Plzeň's underground** (Plzeňské podzemí) can be visited in a 40-minute tour that leads through the cellars, which were once used for the covert guzzling of beer. *(Perlová 4. ☎722 52 14. Open June-Sept. Tu-Su 9am-5pm, Apr.-May and Oct.-Nov. W-Sa 9am-5pm. Tours every 30min., last 4:20pm. 35Kč, students 25Kč.)*

**OTHER SIGHTS.** The black iron gate of the **Franciscan Church and Cloister** (Františkánský kostel a klášter) leads through a wooden door into a quiet cloister garden with statues striking despairing Gothic poses. The church also houses the renowned **Black Madonna of Hájek,** an 18th-century sculpture protected by a gate except during services. *(Across from the corner of Františkánská and Bezručova, south of Nám. Republiky. Open Tu-Su 10am-6pm. 30Kč, students 15Kč.)* The 1892 **synagogue** is an impressive monument to Plzeň's one-time Jewish community of 3,200. Today only 70 Jews live in Plzeň. The interior has been damaged, but the hallways exhibit early 20th-century Czech photos sure to please. *(From the south end of Nám. Republiky, walk down Prešovská to Sady Pětatřicátníků and turn left; the synagogue is on the right. Open Su-F 11am-5pm. English info book 3Kč. 30Kč, students 20Kč.)* People stroll and relax in the **Kopecký gardens** (Kopeckého sady) in the shade of the trees as brass bands perform polkas, waltzes, and folk tunes. *(Františkánská runs into the park south of Nám. Republiky.)*

 ## NIGHTLIFE

Thanks to students from the University of West Bohemia, Plzeň booms with bars and late-night clubs. The young English-speaking summer staff at the tourist office eagerly gives suggestions. The best bars sit just outside the square and a flock of energetic nightclubs can be found at the intersection between Jungmannova and Americká. Things get hoppin' around 9:30pm.

**Zach's Pub,** Palackého nám. 2 (☎722 31 76). From Nám. Republiky, turn left onto Solní, which becomes Přemyslova after intersecting Pětatřicátníků. Palackého nám. lies just past Přemyslova's intersection with Jízdecká; the pub is on the left. The hottest spot in Plzeň to down a pint of Guinness (50Kč). Beer from 15Kč. Live music F-Sa. Occasional cover 50Kč. Open M-Th 1pm-1am, F 1pm-2am, Sa 5pm-2am, Su 5pm-midnight.

**U Dominika,** Dominikánská 3 (☎22 32 26), off Nám. Republiky's northwest corner. With a bonfire in the beer garden and Pearl Jam in the bar, this boisterous pub is the ultimate student hangout. Beer (19Kč) and sludge-like coffee (16Kč) are the drinks of choice. Open M-Th 11am-midnight, F 11am-2am, Sa 3pm-2am, Su 2pm-midnight.

**Club Alfa,** on Americká at the intersection with Jungmannova. From the square, take B. Smetany until it becomes Jungmannova; turn right onto Americká. A renaissance-looking ballroom with plenty of techno and pop to keep you sweating it out on the dance floor. No cover. Open M-Th and Su 7:30pm-5am, F-Sa 7:30pm-6am.

**Jazz/Rock Cafe,** Sedláčova 18 (mobile ☎0603 47 66 74), hosts a diverse crowd in its underground music loft. Pictures of the world's best musicians cover the walls and live music comes to town on Tu or W (40Kč cover). Beer (24Kč) and pizza toast all night (33Kč). Open M-F 10am-4pm, Sa-Su 9pm-4am.

# KARLOVY VARY (CARLSBAD)    ☎(0)17

From the bus station, Karlovy Vary (pop. 60,000) doesn't look like much more than a dingy Bohemian town. A stroll into the spa district or up into the hills, however, reveals why this town developed into one of the great salons of Europe, frequented by Johann Sebastian Bach, Peter the Great, Sigmund Freud, and Karl Marx. Along the Teplá, the town is peaceful and beautiful—swans, ducks, and fish populate the gurgling river, while ornate pastel buildings and sweeping willows line its banks. Once a vacation spot for Charles IV, the town now hosts mostly older Germans and Russians seeking the therapeutic powers of the springs—except in early July, when the excellent International Film Festival brings students from around the country and film stars from around the world.

## ✳ ORIENTATION

Karlovy Vary straddles the **Teplá River** (Warm River). **T.G. Masaryka,** one of the main streets, leads to **Hotel Thermal,** from which **I.P. Pavlova** (followed by several name changes) begins the journey through the town's hot springs, called **Kolonáda** (Colonade). To get to the center from the **bus station, Dolní nádraží,** turn left onto Západní, continue past the Becher building, and bear right onto T. G. Masaryka, which runs parallel to the other main thoroughfare, **Bechera**. From the **train station, Horní nádraží,** take bus #11 or 13 (8Kč) to the last stop. By foot, it's a 15-minute walk downhill. Facing away from the station, cross the street and turn right onto Nákladní. Take the first left, which will leave you on Nákladní, and upon reaching the highway cross Ostrovský most. Follow the road along the Teplá to T.G. Masaryka. *Promenáda,* a part-English monthly, has a handy **map** of the town in the middle (40Kč; available at every kiosk).

# ⌸ TRANSPORTATION

**Trains: Horní nádraží,** northwest of town. Train connections are extremely inconvenient; save your time and take a bus. To **Chomutov** (4½hr. plus 1-2hr. layover in Chomutov, 4-5 per day, 152Kč) and **Berlin, GER** (6-8hr., 1 per day, 1600Kč).

**Buses: Dolní nádraží,** on Západní. To **Plzeň** (1½hr., 12 per day, 82Kč) and **Prague** (2½hr., 25 per day, 89-130Kč). Buy tickets on board or at the **ČSAD office,** Dr. Engla 6 (☎322 43 59), 5min. away from the terminals. Open M 6am-6pm, Tu-F 8am-6pm, Sa 8am-noon, Su 12:30-6pm.

**Public Transportation:** All local buses pass through the main stop on Varšavská (8Kč).

**Taxi:** 24hr. service at Zeyerova 9 (☎322 29 98), but taxis wait outside the main local bus stop on Varšavská and in front of the train station.

# ⍰ PRACTICAL INFORMATION

**Tourist Office: Kur-info,** in Sprudel Colonnade (☎322 40 97 or 322 93 12), sells **maps** (20-45Kč) and theater tickets (60-400Kč). It also books accommodations. Open M-F 7am-5pm, Sa-Su 10am-4pm.

**Currency Exchange: Komerční banka,** Tržiště 11 (☎322 22 05), exchanges currency for a 2% commission and has an **ATM** outside. Open M-F 9am-5pm.

**Luggage Storage:** In the train station. 5Kč per day; lockers also 5Kč per day.

**Telephones:** At the junction of Masaryka and Bechera.

**Post Office:** Masaryka 1 (☎316 11 01). Open M-F 7:30am-7pm, Sa 8am-1pm, Su 8am-noon.

**Postal code:** 360 01.

# ⌸ ACCOMMODATIONS

Budget accommodations are scarce. **Karlovarský Autorent,** the kiosk at Nám. Dr. Horákové 18, will book you a double in a private house for 1000Kč. (☎322 28 33. Open M-F 9am-5pm, Sa-Su 9am-1pm.) **Kur-Info** (see above) also books rooms. While accommodations for the festival get booked up months in advance, **Kawex Travel Agency,** Zeyerova 15 (also inside Hotel Thermal) may be able to hook you up. (☎322 45 94; travel@kawex.cz. Triples 570Kč; doubles with bath 700Kč. Open M-Th 8-5:30pm, F 8am-4pm. Lunch break 11:30am-12:30pm.)

**Pension Kosmos,** Zahradní 39 (☎323 04 73; fax 322 31 68). In the center of the spa district, down the street from the post office. Follow the directions from the bus and train stations to T.G. Masaryka and bear right at the post office. Simply furnished rooms with giant down comforters. Singles 440Kč, with bath 750Kč; doubles 720Kč, 1340Kč. Oct.-Apr. 100Kč off.

**Pension Hestia,** Stará Kysibelská 45 (☎322 59 85; fax 322 04 82). Take bus #6 from the main stop on Západní and get off after Vítězná becomes Stará Kysibelská; the *pension* is on the left. Outside town, but cheap. Two baths per floor, common room with TV. Reception 24hr. 320Kč 1st night, 290Kč 2nd, 250Kč thereafter.

**Pension Romania,** Zahradní 49 (☎322 28 22). Next to the post office at the corner of Zahradní and T.G. Masaryka. Luxurious singles, doubles, and triples with bath, TV, and fridge. 850-930Kč, students 680-745Kč. Breakfast included.

## FOOD

Karlovy Vary is known for its sweet *oplatky* (wafers), which are to be enjoyed with its therapeutic spa waters. Many vendors sell them on the street (5Kč). If you have a sweet tooth, check out the **crepe shop** on Zeyerova where you can design your own dessert for 13-23Kč. (Open M-F 9am-7pm, Sa 9am-noon.) A **supermarket,** Horova 1, occupies the large building with the "Městská tržnice" sign near the local bus station; it also **exchanges currency** and has a sandwich shop and bakery. (Open M-F 6am-7pm, Sa 7am-5pm, Su 9am-5pm. MC/Visa.)

**Vegetarian Restaurant,** I.P. Pavlova 25 (☎322 90 21). Combines (mostly) veggie cooking with a traditional Czech interior suitable for serious beer drinking. Fruit kebab 45Kč; spicy veggie (or sausage) *guláš* 40Kč. Open daily 11am-midnight.

**Bistro Pupík** (Belly Button), Horova 4 (☎322 34 50). Just across from the main bus stop on Západní. Delicious meals (50-75Kč) and quick service, with little damage to the wallet. Open M-F 7:30am-7pm, Sa-Su 8am-5pm.

**E&T,** Zeyerova 3 (☎322 60 22). Between Bechera and T.G. Masaryka. A more expensive eatery with faithful regulars. A diverse list of dishes (75-197Kč) and starters (20-40Kč) is sure to satiate. Open daily 9:30am-2am.

## SIGHTS

The real beauty of Karlovy Vary is that one must indulge in relaxation in order to sightsee. The spa district officially begins with the Victorian **Bath 5** (Lázně 5), Smetanovy Sady 1, across the street from the post office, marked by flowers displaying the date. You may have to enter in the back. Thermal baths (300Kč) and underwater massages (420Kč) are among the blessed services offered. (☎322 25 36. Open M-F 8am-9pm, Sa 8am-6pm, Su 10am-6pm. Massages M-F 3-9pm, Sa-Su 10am-6pm.) Cross the bridge from T.G. Masaryka, turn right and continue along the river. You'll notice the Victorian **Garden Colonnade** (Sadová kolonáda) along the south rim of the **Dvořák gardens.** Here you can sip the curative waters of Karlovy Vary's 12th spring, **Garden Spring** (Sadový pramen), from a marble fountain shaped like a peasant woman. The pedestrian **Mlýnské nábř.** meanders alongside the Teplá under the cool protection of shady trees, peppered with folk singers and portrait artists who prey on tourists. **Bath 3,** Mlýnské nábř. 5, lies to the right, just before **Freedom Spring** (Pramen svobody) and also offers massages. (☎322 56 41. Neck and shoulders 325Kč; full body 525Kč. Open M-F 7am-2pm and 3-7pm, Sa-Su 7am-11am.) Bring your own drinking vessel to the springs or buy souvenir porcelain cups from the kiosks (75-220Kč). The good news for the budget traveler is that the spring waters are free to drink, although you may be able to manage only a few sips of the extremely metallic stuff—it's *much* stronger and warmer than the so-called mineral water served in a restaurant. The bad news is water bottles are banned, as they "break the hygienic conditions of the drinking cure." Next door, the imposing **Mill Colonnade** (Mlýnská kolonáda) shelters five different springs. Farther along the spa area, the former **market** (tržiště) appears with the delicate white **Market Colonnade** (Tržní kolonáda), where two more springs bubble to the surface. The **Zawojski House,** now the Živnostenská Banka, a gorgeous cream-and-gold Art Nouveau building from the turn of the century, sits at Tržiště 9. The **Vřídlo spring** inside the **Vřídlo Collonade** (Vřídelní kolonáda), spouts 30L of water each second at 72° Celsius. This is Karlovy Vary's hottest and highest-shooting spring. (Open daily 6am-6:30pm.)

At the end of Stará Louka sits **Grandhotel Pupp.** Founded in 1774 by Johann Georg Pupp, the Grandhotel was the largest hotel in 19th-century Bohemia. The intricate facade is the work of the Viennese Helmer-Fellner duo. The interior features luxurious suites, a concert hall, and multiple ballrooms. Paths, with monuments to famous spa visitors, cut through the sloping woods above Stará Louka. Follow the narrow walkway on the right side of the hotel to the **funicular,** which leads up to the 555m high **Diana Observatory** (Rozhledna) and a magnificent panorama of the city. (Funicular runs every 15min. 9am-7pm, 25Kč, round-trip 40Kč. Tower open daily 9am-7pm. 10Kč. English guide 20Kč.) Descend back to the town along **Petra Velikého** to see a statue of **Karl Marx** commemorating his visits to the decidedly bourgeois spa between 1874 and 1876. He apparently needed to experience the fruits of wealth before he could stir up revolution against it in good conscience.

## ENTERTAINMENT AND OUTDOORS

If seeing a monument to Comrade Marx distresses your inner bourgeois, escape for an afternoon to the 12th-century **Loket Castle,** inside an elbow in the Ohře river 12km to the west. Used as a prison until 1947, the castle now displays dungeons and porcelain manufactured in nearby Loket nad Ohří. (Open Apr.-Oct. Tu-Su 9-noon and 1-5pm. 50Kč, 100Kč with guide.) **Buses** go from Karlovy Vary (30min., every 25min., 26Kč), but the **hike** is half the fun. Follow the 17km **blue trail** from the steps of Diana Rozhleda Observatory entrance in Karlovy Vary. Two-thirds of the way into the trail you'll find the magnificent rocks of **Svatošské skály,** a supposed source of inspiration for Goethe and the Brothers Grimm.

*Promenáda* (see **Orientation,** p. 250) lists the month's concerts and performances. Karlovy Vary's **International Film Festival,** which screens independent films from all over the globe, guarantees a splendid time and is not to be missed. The event is held in the first couple of weeks of July (exact dates vary from year to year) and attracts some of the world's biggest stars. It you are planning on seeing many films, buy an accreditation inside **Hotel Thermal,** the festival's center. (Student 3-day 200Kč, full-festival 500Kč; film professional accreditation is double the price, but gives more access.) While the accreditation allows you to see five films per day, tickets sell out quickly so get to the box office as early as possible.

Like its restaurants, Karlovy Vary's nightlife is geared toward its older tourists. Nightclubs and pubs are sparse, while expensive cafes reproduce like fruit flies. **Propaganda,** Jaltská 5, off Bechera, understandably attracts Karlovy Vary's hippest and youngest crowd with live music and a trendy blue steel interior. (☎323 37 92. Mixed drinks 40-100Kč. Beer from 11Kč. Pool table. Open daily 5pm-late.)

# SOUTH BOHEMIA

Truly a rustic Bohemian Eden, South Bohemia is a scenic ensemble of scattered villages, unspoiled brooks, virgin forests, and castle ruins. Low hills and plentiful attractions have made the region a favorite of Czech bicyclists and hikers, who ply the countryside wildlife-watching, castle-traipsing, and *Budvar*-guzzling.

# ČESKÉ BUDĚJOVICE ☎(0)38

No amount of beer will help you correctly pronounce České Budějovice (CHESS-kay BOOD-yeh-yoh-vee-tsay). In the heart of the Bohemian countryside, this city's countless bus and train connections make it a great base from which to visit the region's many wonders. Mill streams, the Malše, and the Vltava wrap around the city center, a fusion of Gothic, Renaissance, and Baroque houses. While convenient, České Budějovice— blemished by fast food, department stores, and shampoo billboards—lacks the charm of Český Krumlov, its smaller neighbor to the south. On the other hand, the city does have the forever-famous *Budvar* Brewery.

## ORIENTATION

**Staré Město** (Old Town) centers around **Nám. Přemysla Otakara II.** Cheap rooms, generally beyond Staré Město's walls, are reachable by **buses** and **trolleybuses.** The **train station** is 10 minutes by foot from Staré Město. From the station, turn right onto **Nádražní.** Go left at the first crosswalk to the pedestrian **Lannova třída,** which becomes **Kanovnická** after the moat and pours out into the northeast corner of the gigantic **Nám. Otakara II.** The **bus station** is on Žižkova, around the corner from the train station. To get to the center, go down Žižkova, turn right onto Jeronýmova, and then left onto Lannova třída. The street then becomes Kanovická as it leads into Nám. Otakara II.

**CZECH REPUBLIC**

## TRANSPORTATION

**Trains:** Nádražní 12 (☎635 33 33). To: **Plzeň** (1½hr., 11 per day, 90Kč); **Prague** (2½hr., 12 per day, 114Kč); and **Brno** (4½hr., 2 per day, 152Kč). Info office open in summer M-F 9am-6pm, Sa 9am-4pm; off-season M-F 9am-5pm.
**Buses:** ☎7312701. Around the corner from the train station. To: **Prague** (2½hr., 8 per day, 96Kč); **Plzeň** (3hr., 2 per day, 92Kč); and **Brno** (4½hr., 6 per day, 136Kč).
**Public Transportation: Buses** and **trolleys.** 6Kč per ride. Buy tickets at kiosks; punch them on board.
**Taxi:** ☎477 44.

## PRACTICAL INFORMATION

**Tourist Office: Turistické Informační Centrum (TIC),** Nám. Otakara II 26 (☎/fax 635 25 89). English-speaking staff books private rooms (230Kč in the center, cheaper farther out) and organizes castle, museum, and brewery tours. Open May-Sept. M-F 8am-6:30pm, Sa 8am-4:30pm, Su 9am-4:30pm; Oct.-Apr. M-F 8am-6pm, Sa 8am-4:30pm.
**Currency Exchange: Komerční banka,** Krajinská 15 (☎774 11 47). Off Nám. Otakara II. Cashes **traveler's checks** for a 2% commission. Open M-F 8am-5pm.
**ATMs:** Cirrus/MC along Lannova and opposite the train station. Also in Nám. Otakara II.
**Luggage Storage:** In the train station, on the right wall of the main level. 10Kč per day.
**Pharmacy:** Nám. Otakara II 26 (☎635 30 63). Open M-F 7am-6pm, Sa 8am-noon.
**Internet Access: X-Files@Internet Cafe,** Senovážné nám. 6 (☎635 04 04). Agent Mulder connects you at 1Kč per min. Open M-F 10am-10pm, Sa-Su 4-10pm.
**Post Office:** Senovážné nám. 1 (☎773 41 29). South of Lannova as it enters Staré Město. Open M-F 7am-7pm, Sa 8am-noon.
**Postal code:** 370 01.

## ACCOMMODATIONS

**Private rooms** are the best option in town (see **Tourist Office,** above).

**Penzion U Výstaviště,** U Výstaviště 17 (☎724 01 48; mobile ☎0602 84 09 06). Take bus #1, 14, or 17 from the bus station 5 stops to "U parku" and continue 150m along the street that branches off to the right behind the bus stop. If you call from the station, the English-speaking staff may offer a free lift in their red minivan. This hostel-like accommodation is the friendliest sleep in town. Call ahead to reserve; only 12 beds. 250Kč 1st night, 200Kč thereafter.
**University of South Bohemia,** Studentská 19 (☎777 44 00). Take tram #1 from in front of the bus station 5 stops to "U parku." Turn around and head back down Husova, then turn right on Studentská. Go to the end of the street and the dorms are in the 4 large complex buildings. Open July-Sept. Doubles 260Kč, 300Kč with bath.

## FOOD

The small streets around the town center shelter an abundance of tiny *restaurace*, many with terraces and most with hearty fare. The **Večerka** grocery sits at Palackého 10. (Entrance on Hroznova. Open M-F 7am-8pm, Sa 7am-1pm, Su 8am-8pm.)

**Petit Restaurant,** Hradební 14 (☎6353 146). Right off ul. Černé věže. Wooden booths create an atmosphere perfect for garlic soup with cheese and fried croutons. Main dishes 70-130Kč. Open M-Th 11am-11pm, F 11am-midnight, Sa 6pm-midnight.
**Restaurace U paní Emy,** Široká 25 (☎731 28 46), near the main square. Fine Czech cooking. Aid your digestion of Tábor steak (95Kč) or veggie dishes (50-70Kč) with a tall *Budvar* (0.5L 20Kč). Open M-Th 10:30am-1am, F-Sa 10:30am-3am, Sa noon-11pm.
**Restaurace Ameno,** Riegrova 8 (☎636 07 33). Satisfies your pasta (55-105Kč) and chimichanga craving. Chocolate fondue 55-65Kč. Open M-Sa 11am-midnight.

**THIS BUD'S FOR EU** Many Yankees, having tasted the malty goodness of *Budvar* brew, return home to find that the beer from Budweis is conspicuously unavailable. The fact that *Budvar* is the Czech Republic's largest exported beer, beating out even *Pilsner Urquell* in 1995, makes its absence from American store shelves stranger still. About the only way to sip and authentic *Budvar* on a porch in New York is to sneak a few bottles in your pack and pray they don't shatter in transit.

So where's the *Budvar*? The answer lies in a tale of trademarks and town names. České Budějovice (Budweis in German) had been brewing its own style of lager for centuries when the Anheuser-Busch brewery in St. Louis, Missouri came out with its Budweiser-style beer in 1876. Not until the 1890s, however, did the Budějovice Brewery begin producing beer labeled "Budweiser." International trademark conflicts ensued, and in 1911 the companies signed a non-competition agreement: Budějovice Brewery got markets in Europe, and Anheuser-Busch took North America. But the story continues. A few years ago, Anheuser-Busch tried to end the confusion by buying a controlling interest in the makers of *Budvar,* but the Czech government refused. Coincidentally, Anheuser-Busch didn't order its usual one-third of the Czech hop crop the following year. Anheuser-Busch then sued for trademark infringement in Finland, while Budějovice Brewery petitioned to the EU to make the moniker "Budweiser" as exclusive as "Champagne," meaning that any brand sold in the EU under that name would have to come from the Budweiser region. As long as the battle continues, there's little chance that *Budvar* in America will be anything but an illegal alien, so fill up while you can (and take a few for the road).

## 👁 SIGHTS

Surrounded by Renaissance and Baroque architecture, cobblestone **Nám. Otakara II** is the largest square in the Czech Republic, measuring exactly 133x133 ft. **Samson's Fountain** (Samsonova kašna; 1726) towers over the center of the square and serves as a good orientation point for the town. Behind Samson and to the left, the square's ornate 1727-1730 Baroque **town hall** *(radnice)* stands a full story above the other buildings on the square. The town hall was built during a time of economic prosperity by the Schwarzenbergs' architect Antonius Martinelli. Samson's right eye looks to the **Black Tower** (Černá věž). To climb the 72m tower and see all the pretty bells costs nothing, but to get to the 360° balcony after the climb costs 10Kč. Beware: the stairs are treacherous even for the sober. (☎635 25 08. Open daily July-Aug. 10am-6pm; Apr.-June Tu-Su 10am-6pm; Sept.-Oct. Tu-Su 10am-6pm.) The tower once served as a belfry for the neighboring 13th-century **Cathedral of St. Nicholas** (Chrám sv. Mikuláše), which became a cathedral when the town became a bishopric in the 18th century. The altar is from 1791; the Stations of the Cross date back to the 1920s. (Open daily 7am-6pm.)

The city's most famous attraction, the **Budvar Brewery,** Karoliny Světlé 4, is connected to the center by buses #2 and 4. In theory, tours for groups of six or more ought to be booked weeks in advance; in practice, travelers who turn up early often manage to get inside. The English leaflets make joining non-English groups easier. Contrary to popular belief, there's no free beer at the end of this brewery tour. (☎770 51 11. Tours can be booked from 8am-4pm. 100Kč per person.)

## 🍸 NIGHTLIFE

The lakes around Budějovice host open-air disco concerts in the summer—check the posters on buses and lampposts. Later in the evening, a younger, livelier crowd—some leather, a bit of facial hair, and plenty of piercings—drinks *Velvet* (25Kč) under metal skeleton lampshades at the **MotorCycle Legend Pub,** Radniční 9. (☎635 49 45. Open M-Th 11am-midnight, F-Su 5pm-3am.) For late night munching and *Budvar* merriment, head to the funky **Restaurant Heaven Club Zeppelin,** on the third floor of Nám. Otakara II 38. (Open M-Sa 11am-1am.) Quieter types can opt for a cup of tea at **Dobrá čajovna,** Hroznova 16, directly behind the Black Tower, where regulars take off their shoes to sip sweet herbal brews and whisper in deference to the thrumming sitar. (☎ 635 30 40. 80 different teas. Open daily 3-11pm).

## 🔁 DAYTRIPS FROM ČESKÉ BUDĚJOVICE

### HLUBOKÁ NAD VLTAVOU

*Buses run from České Budějovice to Hluboká nad Vltavou (25 min., 12Kč) frequently, although there are fewer on weekends—look for buses with Týn nad Vltavou as their final destination. The most pleasant way to here is by bike (30min.). You can also hike from České Budějovice (2hr.). From the bus stop, head left on Nad parkovištěm, the main bus route. Turn left onto Zborovská, then right onto Bezručova at the street's end. From there, hike up the hill and bear left at the fork in the path. The castle will be on the right. Castle open daily May-Oct. 9am-5pm. Gallery open daily 9:30-11:30am, noon-6pm. English tours 130Kč, students 65č. Armory tours 100Kč, students 50Kč. Gallery 30Kč, students 15Kč.*

Hluboká is an ordinary town blessed with an extraordinary castle. This structure owes its success to Eleonora Schwarzenberg, who transformed the original Renaissance-Baroque castle into a Windsor-style fairy-tale stronghold in the mid-19th century. The 45-minute tour takes in 20 of the castle's 141 rooms. *En route*, there are more Schwarzenberg portraits than you could shake a stick at, as well as tapestries, paintings (including copies of Raphael and da Vinci), and absurdly ornate wooden furniture. A tour is compulsory, and English tours only happen once or twice per day, depending on demand and the whim of the tour guide. If there is one, it costs an exorbitant amount. Czech tours are cheaper and more frequent. Tours of the **armory,** the second largest in Bohemia, are also available. If you aren't whipped by this time, check out the **gallery** across from the castle entrance. The religious paintings and sculptures are worth the time.

### TŘEBOŇ                                                  ☎ (0)333

*Buses run from České Budějovice (40min., every 30min., less frequently on weekends, 20Kč). From the bus station, turn left on Sportovní and right onto Svobody, which curves to the right. At Palackého nám., turn left and follow Sokolská out of the square, past the gardens and through the pedestrian underpass. Sokolská becomes Husova within the town walls; turn right onto Březinova, the 1st street on the right, which leads to the castle courtyard. The ticket booth is around the corner on the right, directly under the clock. Estate ☎72 11 93. Tour A (45min.; 80Kč, students 40Kč); tour B (45min.; 100Kč, students 50Kč); tour C (30min.; 40Kč, students 20Kč). All tours daily 9am-5pm. Last tour 4:15pm. Reservations 10Kč extra per person.*

Yet another Rožmberk-Schwarzenberg dream house dotting the South Bohemian hills, the **Třeboň Estate** is ideally placed in a town graced by a colorful center, shady parks, and a refreshing lake. The castle itself is notable as the final home of Petr Vok, the last of the Rožmberk family. After being evicted from his Český Krumlov estate in 1602 (see **Český Krumlov: Sights,** p. 259), Vok moved his court to Třeboň, which he constantly redecorated until his death in 1611. His additions to the chateau can be seen only with a guided tour *(trasa A)* that takes you through the Rožmberk armory, the picture gallery, the women's waiting room, and the gallery of shooting targets, marked by authentic gunshot holes. *Trasa B* leads through the 19th-century Schwarzenberg rooms. There's even a *trasa C*, which uncovers the dog's kitchen and underground corridors. Call at least two days ahead to reserve an English-speaking guide for a group, or join a Czech tour and read along in the English pamphlets, in which case tickets are half the price.

## ČESKÝ KRUMLOV                                          ☎ (0)337

The worst part about Český Krumlov (TSCHes-kee KRUM-lov) is leaving. Maybe it's the medieval cobblestone streets that lead through stone courtyards; maybe it's the Vltava, the winding river that darts in and around the town center and on into the South Bohemian countryside; or maybe it's the 13th-century castle that hovers over it all. Whatever it is, this UNESCO-protected town lures visitors in and doesn't let them go. Weeks could (and should) be spent hiking through the surrounding hills, kayaking down the Vltava, horseback riding through the gardens, and exploring the meandering center.

 ## ORIENTATION

The **Vltava** river squiggles, forming a pocket that contains the central square, **Náměstí Svornosti.** The **main bus terminal** lies to the southeast. To get to Nám. Svornosti from here, head to the upper street where stops #20-25 are located. Facing away from the station, turn right and follow the small dirt path that veers to the left and heads uphill. Turn right at the path's intersection with Kaplická. At the light, cross the highway and head straight onto Horní, which leads into the square. If you get off at the small **Špičák** stop on the northern outskirts of town, it's an easy march downhill to the medieval center. From Špičák, pass through **Budějovice gate** and follow **Latrán** past the castle and over the Vltava. The street becomes Radniční as it enters Staré Město and leads into Nám. Svornosti.

 ## TRANSPORTATION

**Trains:** Nádražní 31 (☎71 14 77), 2km uphill from the center. Trains to **České Budějovice** (1hr., 9 per day, 27Kč). Bus goes to the center (5Kč).

**Buses:** Kaplická 439 (☎34 14). To **České Budějovice** (30-45min., M-F 31 per day, Sa-Su 7 per day, 22-24Kč.)

**Taxis: Krumlov Taxi** (☎71 27 12) or **Taxi Růže** (☎71 17 11). Taxis are easy to find in Nám. Svornosti.

## PRACTICAL INFORMATION

**Tourist Office:** Nám. Svornosti 1 (☎71 16 50; fax 71 11 83; infocentrum@ckrf.ckrumlov.cz). Books *pensions* (starting at 600Kč) or private rooms, which can be a bit cheaper (doubles 800Kč). Also sells **maps** for cycling and hiking trips (69Kč). Hi-tech audioguides available for rental (2hr. 150Kč, students 100Kč; 3hr. 180Kč, 120Kč. 500Kč or passport deposit.) Open daily 9am-6pm.

**Rentals: Globtour Vltava,** Kájovská 62 (☎/fax 71 19 78). Rents boats Apr.-Sept.: **kayaks** from 250Kč per day, **canoes** from 300Kč per day, and **rafts** from 650Kč per day. **Mountain bikes** with lock and helmet 200Kč per 6 hr., 300Kč per day, outrageous 3000Kč deposit. Cheaper off-season. Open daily 8am-8pm. AmEx/MC/Visa.

**Currency Exchange: Bank SMW,** Panská 22 (☎712221) cashes **traveler's checks** for a 0.75% commission. 100Kč minimum.

**ATM:** On the left side of Horní just before it merges into Nám. Svornosti.

**Luggage storage:** At the train station, across from the ticket booths (15Kč per day).

**Pharmacy:** Nám. Svornosti 16 (☎71 17 87). Open M-F 8am-5pm.

**Internet Access:** 10Kč per 10min. at the **tourist office** (see above). The **Internet Café** (☎71 22 19) in the castle courtyard offers more computers. 30Kč per 15min., 90Kč per hr. Open daily in summer 9am-10pm; off-season 10am-10pm.

**Post office:** Latrán 193 (☎71 66 10). **Poste Restante** at window #2. Card-operated **phones** outside. Open M-F 7am-6pm, Sa 7-11am.

**Postal code:** 381 01.

 ## ACCOMMODATIONS

Krumlov's stellar hostels undoubtedly offer the best beds in town, but they fill up quickly in the summer so make reservations days in advance. **Private rooms** (*Zimmer frei* or *ubytování*) also abound; look for signs on ul. Parkán.

**CZECH REPUBLIC**

■ **U vodníka,** Po vodě 55 (☎71 19 35; vodnik@ck.bohem-net.cz; www.krumlovhostels.com). Follow the directions to Nám. Svornosti, turn left onto Rooseveltova after the traffic lights (the last street before the bridge), and follow the signs. This 13th-century hostel has a name that translates roughly as "the place of the river troll," but it is more like the place of the river god. American ex-pats Carolyn, Cal, and baby Aidan have lovingly turned their home into one of the best hostels in Europe. There's a garden out back where you can grill sausages on a spit or sit in a hand-carved seat and serenade the passing fish with the hostel's guitar. You can even borrow an inner tube to cruise down the Vltava. The staff will do your laundry (100Kč per 5kg), rent you a mountain bike (200Kč per day), lend you books from their fine library, and arrange boat rentals. Dorms 200Kč; doubles 250Kč per person.

■ **Krumlov House,** Rooseveltova 68 (☎ as for U vodníka), on your right before the highway, with beautiful dragon doors. This former bakery immediately became a legend when it transformed into a hostel in 1996. The same rates and services apply here as in U vodníka, but Krumlov House hosts a livelier crowd. Sleep in hand-carved birch bunks, socialize with Australians in a huge kitchen (stereos and guitars included), and drink into the wee hours of the morning.

**Hostel Skippy,** Plešivecká 123 (☎72 83 80). Follow the directions from the main bus station to Nám. Svornosti, but at the light turn left onto the highway, which intersects Plešivecká after it crosses the river; the hostel is on the right. Rooms are a hodge-podge of crazy rugs, comforters with big beds, and beautiful views of the Vltava below. Communal kitchen. Bike rental 180Kč per day. Laundry 80Kč per 5kg. Manager Zdeňka (a.k.a. 'Skippy') will serve you a made-to-order breakfast (30-50Kč). Dorms 175Kč; doubles 200Kč per person.

**Traveller's Hostel,** Soukenická (☎71 13 45). From the main square, go down Panská and you'll run into it on Soukenická. A cousin of the Prague hostel chain, Traveller's offers its own late-night bar with ocassional live music and a social crowd of English speakers. There's a barbecue in back, a kitchen, and a TV/common room. Lockers 100Kč. Laundry 100Kč. Reception 24hr. Dorms 190Kč, nonmembers 220Kč; off-season 170Kč, 200Kč. Breakfast included.

**Ryba Hostel** (Fish), Rybářská 5 (☎71 18 01). Overlooking the Vltava across from the town center. Set out from the right-hand corner of Nám. Svornosti, across from the tourist office, drift left onto Kájovská, then head over the bridge and down Rybářská; you'll see it from the bridge. Dorms with huge comforters and superb views of the town. 17 beds. 200Kč; doubles 250Kč. 7th night free.

**Hostel U Šneka,** Panská 19 (mobile ☎0606 92 07 49; snail_hostel@email.cz). Follow the directions from the main bus station to Nám. Svornosti. Facing away from Horní, go to the right corner of the square, then head straight down Panská; the "Snail" hostel is 50m down on the right. Immaculate and centrally located. Houses a bar and rock club. Laundry 100Kč. Dorms 200Kč; doubles with bath 250Kč per person.

# ◖ FOOD

The most central supermarket in town is **SPAR**, Linecká 49. (Open M-Sa 7am-6pm, Su 9am-6pm.) For fresh fruit and veggies, head to **Ovoce Zelenina**, Latrán 45; the shop is on the left through the hallway.

■ **Na louži,** Kájovská 66 (☎71 12 80). Sizeable portions of great Czech cooking. Be prepared to wait; it's well worth it. Incredible fruit dumplings 49Kč. Main dishes 85-118Kč. Veggies options 45-68Kč. Open daily 10am-10pm.

■ **Barbakán,** Kuplická 26 (☎71 26 79) is not the cheapest option in town, but has some of the best meat selections. Sit outside on the patio which overlooks the river, or in the elegant dining room. Salads 18-39Kč. Main dishes 69-192Kč. Open daily in summer noon-midnight; off-season 3pm-midnight.

**Vegetarian Restaurant Laibon,** Parkán 105 (☎71 25 08). Facing away from Horní in Nám. Svornosti, turn right onto Radniční. Take the 2nd right onto Parkán; the restaurant is on the right. Heaping portions of vegetarian dishes from countries around the world

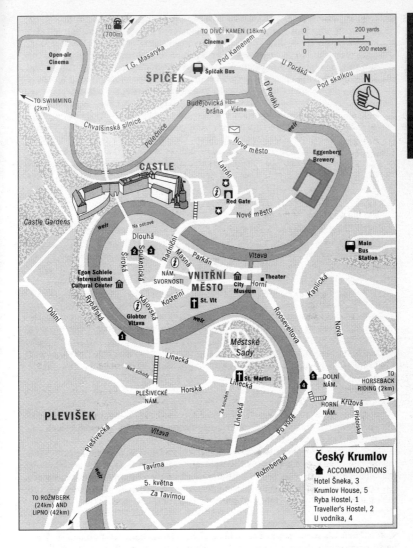

**Český Krumlov**

▲ ACCOMMODATIONS

Hotel Šneka, 3
Krumlov House, 5
Ryba Hostel, 1
Traveller's Hostel, 2
U vodníka, 4

on a stone porch overlooking the Vltava. Appetizers 25-48Kč. Main dishes 60-105Kč. Open daily 11am-11pm.

**Cikánská jizba** (Gypsy Room), Dlouhá 31 (☎ 71 15 85). Follow Radniční out of the main square and turn left down Dlouhá. Fire it up with spicy gypsy goulash (53Kč). The *halušky*, a gnocchi-like pasta, is not to be missed (55Kč). Open M-Sa 3pm-midnight.

**Nonna Gina Pizzeria,** Klášterní ul. 52 (☎ 71 71 87), right off Latrán. It's *amore:* pizza (65-120Kč), pasta (60-120Kč), and a radical tiramisu (30Kč). Quiet, almost romantic ambiance. Open daily 11am-11pm.

## 🔥 SIGHTS

Perversely, pollution may have been Český Krumlov's biggest boon. In the early 20th century, an upstream paper mill putrefied the river and most citizens moved to the town's outskirts. Thanks to such benign neglect, the medieval inner city escaped "development." Originally a 13th-century fortress, the **castle** was later home to a number of wealthy families. The main entrance to the castle is on Latrán. Take Radniční out of the town center, cross the river, and go up the stairs on the left; the gate is at the top of the stairs. The **stone courtyards** are free and open to the public. Don't miss the three depressed bears lurking in the moat. Two tours cover the castle—the first visits the older wing, taking in the **Chapel of St. George,** passing through the Baroque **Schwarzenberg chambers,** the **Eggenberg room,** and finally the Baroque theater's **Masquerade Hall.** The second tour explores the older, Renaissance-style rooms before moving into the 19th-century areas of the castle and ending with the splendid **Schwarzenberg Gallery.** Czech tours are only 70Kč, but to understand anything more than "Blah, blah, Schwarzenberg, blah," take the hourlong English tour. (☎71 16 87. Open June-Aug. Tu-Su 9am-6pm; May and Sept. Tu-Su 9am-5pm; Apr. and Oct. Tu-Su 9am-4pm. Last tour 1hr. before closing. Enter ticket office through the 3rd stone courtyard, just after the moat with the bears. English tour 130Kč, students 65Kč.) A tour of the **Mansion Baroque Theater** covers the rest of the impressive structure. (English tour 150Kč, students 75Kč; Czech tour 100Kč, 50Kč.) You can also visit the castle **tower** for a fine view of the town. (Open daily May-Sept. 9am-6pm, last admission 5:35pm; Oct. and Apr. 11am-3pm. 30Kč, students 20Kč.) Wander the **galleries of the crypt** where local artists' works are displayed. (Open May-Oct. Tu-Su 10am-5pm; July-Aug. also M 10am-5pm. 30Kč, students 20Kč.) A stroll through the **gardens,** which house a riding school and a summer palace, completes a tour of the castle. (Open daily Apr.-Oct. 9am-7pm.)

The Austrian painter Egon Schiele (1890-1918) found Český Krumlov so enchanting that he decided to set up shop here in 1911. Sadly, the citizens ran him out after he started painting burghers' daughters in the nude. Decades later, less Puritan citizens founded the 🖼 **Egon Schiele International Cultural Center,** Široká 70-72, with a wide variety of browsing material. Schiele's works, including the infamous nudes, share wall space with paintings by other 20th-century central-European artists, including Haher Fronius's excellent Kafka illustrations. (☎70 40 11. Open daily 10am-6pm. 120Kč, students 60Kč.)

# 🎵 ENTERTAINMENT

Hike into the hills for a pleasant afternoon of **horseback riding** at **Jezdecký klub Slupenec,** Slupenec 1. Rides take you through trails high above Český Krumlov. From the town center, take Horní to its intersection with the highway. At the second light, turn left onto Křížová and follow the red trail to Slupenec. It's about a 25-minute walk. The horses are hung over after the weekend of partying, so there are no rides on Mondays. (☎71 10 53. Open Tu-Sa 9am-6pm. 220Kč per hr. Full-day trip with refreshments 2500Kč. Call ahead.) Summer in Krumlov gets hot; if you're not up for a swim in the Vltava, check out the town's **indoor pool** and **steambaths.** For only 18Kč per hour you can plunge into icy-cold waters with Krumlov moms and sweat off your beers in a steamy sauna. From the town square, take Radniční to Latrán. Walk past the castle and the post office, take a left on the highway *Chvalšinská,* then a right on Fialková. The pool is two minutes up on the left. (Pool open M-Sa 7am-10pm, Su 1-9pm. Steambaths open W and F 7-9pm, Sa 6-9pm. 20Kč per hr. 20Kč lock deposit.) To fully enjoy the waters of the Vltava, ask at your hostel about innertubes and spend a day lazing down the river. Jump out next to **Pepo's Pub** (or you'll float to Budějovice) and repeat the circuit. You can also cruise the river in a canoe or kayak, which can be rented from **Maleček Boat Rental,** Rooseveltova 28. (☎71 25 08. Open daily 8:30am-7:30pm.) Maleček offers various river trips: 2-person boat (200-870Kč), 4-person raft (300-1390Kč), and 6-8-person raft (350-1590Kč). For the most scenic route, start in Krumlov and head to Zlatá Koruna.

The castle's **Revolving South Bohemia Theater** (Jihočeské divadlo) hosts opera, Shakespeare, and classic comedies. Performances are in Czech, but watching the set revolve around the audience more than makes up for it. (Open June-early Sept. Check at the tourist office for current showings and to purchase tickets, 260-

390Kč.) If you'd rather see something in English, **cinemas** abound in Český Krumlov, usually in English with Czech subtitles. **Kino J&K,** Highway 159 next to the
Špičák bus stop, is open year-round and shows all of the latest Hollywood blockbusters. (Open M-F 6:30pm, Sa 6pm. 50Kč.) Ask your hostel owner about the town's
**open-air cinema** in the summer—it's like a drive-in, but without the cars. The **Five-
petal Rose Festival,** Krumlov's hip medieval gig the third weekend of June, is a great
excuse to wear tights and joust with the locals. Krumlov also hosts two world-class
music festivals—the **Early Music Festival** (the second week of July) with live appearances by Basso di Gamba and other cool old instruments, and the **International
Music Fest** (mid-August), which attracts hordes of major Czech acts.

## ■ NIGHTLIFE

Party animals in Český Krumlov enjoy the city's full array of bars and cafes. People
tend to go out early (around 8pm).

**U Hada** (Snake Bar), Rybářská 37. There are live snakes, but that's only half the reason
this place is so hip. 0.5L beer 20Kč. Open daily 7pm-3am.

**U baby,** Rooseveltova 66 (☎71 23 00). An authentic Czech bar that pours hefty steins
of beer (12-22Kč) in a refurbished medieval building next door to Krumlov House (see
**Accommodations,** p. 258). Enjoy *horké víno* (mulled wine; 25Kč) and chat with local
characters. Open daily 6pm-late.

**Babylon,** Rybářská 6. Next to Ryba Hostel (see **Accommodations,** p. 258). Krumlov's
attempt at a biker bar, with AC/DC blaring inside and men in leather dominating the riverside terrace. Occasional live music in the evening and on weekends. Kitchen open
until 10pm. Open daily noon-late.

**Dobrá Čajovna,** Latrán 6 (☎712594), has a worldwide selection which runs 30-130Kč
per pot. Open daily noon-11pm.

**Rumyší díra** (Mouse hole, a.k.a. The Boat Bar). Continue down the steps to the river from
Barbakán (see **Food,** p. 258), to this notorious summer-only midnight spot that makes
the river a little more interesting by supplying booze to canoers and kayakers who stop
as they drift by. *Budvar* 16Kč. Open M-Th 10am-10pm, F-Su 10am-late.

## ■ OVER THE RIVER AND THROUGH THE WOODS

Local firms and hostels rent out mountain bikes. There are a couple of routes that
begin in Český Krumlov itself. The first is a 70km loop along the banks of the
Vltava, the second a much shorter, hillier trip to a couple of local sites. Check the
weather before you go. (See **Camping and the Outdoors,** p. 37.)

**LONG ROUTE (70KM).** For a ride along the Vltava, turn right onto the bridge from
Globtour/Vltava Travel (which rents bikes for 300Kč per day). Cross the river, turn
left onto Linecká, then turn right when it crosses the river again and intersects with
Po vodě. At the intersection with the highway, turn right onto Května, cross the
river, and follow the signs to **Rožmberk** (24km), which boasts the first real sight
along the way. The route leads through the towns **Vetřní** and **Zátoň.** Vetřní hosts a
paper mill largely responsible for the polluted condition of the river, while Zátoň is
so small it would be unnoticeable except for a lovely church perched atop a hill
200m to the left of the road. Carry on along the banks of the river until you see a
pale fortress tower up on the left. Rožmberk is around the next bend. You can stop
here and see **Rožmberk Castle,** the seat of the mighty Rožmberks. (Rosenbergs; ☎74
98 38. Open June-Aug. Tu-Su 9am-5pm; May and Sept. Tu-Su 9am-4pm; Apr. and
Oct. Sa-Su 9am-4pm. Tours every hr., but call about specific times and availability
in English. 100Kč, students 50Kč.)

**Lipno** lies another 18km upstream, and the "up" makes itself particularly evident
here. Before you reach it, look for the ancient Cistercian monastery at **Vyšší Brod.
Frýmburk** sits along the lake shore 8km west. Complete with a waterside church, it
smacks of Swiss quaintness and is a better rest spot than Lipno. From Frýmburk, a
road leads back to Český Krumlov, mostly downhill for 22km, to close the 70km

loop. If you can't make it this far, you must retreat the way you came: there's no alternate route. If biking up the hills seems daunting, you can take a **bus** to Rožmberk or Lipno—two of the best towns in southern Bohemia.

**SHORTER ROUTE (40KM).** Unlike the road that curves around the Vltava, this route north heads through hillside meadows. From the town center, take Horní across the river to its intersection with the highway. Turn left at the light and follow the highway as it veers left and crosses the river. Turn right at the sign toward Budějovice. Head up the giant hill and turn toward Srnín; two gas stations and a supermarket point the way. Be careful crossing railway tracks without a crossing guard. When the road splits near a factory, turn right and head up into the meadow. From here, you'll whiz through Srnín and follow the signs to **Zlatá Koruna.** The long descent ends at the gate of the 1263 **monastery.** A tour winds through the massive complex's courts, halls, library (the second largest in the Czech Republic), convent, chapel, and church. Over the course of its tumultuous history, the local order of monks was almost abolished several times and was stripped of its property before finally being sent into the lay world in 1785. Since then, the building has been a pencil factory and an under-appreciated tourist attraction. (☎74 31 26. Open June-Aug. Tu-Su 8am-noon and 1-5pm; Apr.-May and Sept.-Oct. Tu-Su 9am-noon and 1-4pm. Last tour 45min. before closing. Minimum 5 people; available in English. 35Kč per person, students 20Kč.) From here, walk your bike back uphill. At the T-junction, go straight toward **Křemže** (left leads back the way you came).

After entering **Třísov,** take the second right (by the village notice board) and cross the railway line just below the tiny station. Continue down this stone path toward the river. After about 10 minutes you'll reach a few houses and the river bank. Here the stone path becomes a sidewalk, passes left of an abandoned building, and comes to a metal bridge. Chain your bike and head over the bridge and to the left. Be sure not to cross the second metal bridge; trot up the steps to the right to get to the 1349 ruins of the castle **Dívčí kámen.** Climb to the top of the ruins for a gorgeous panorama of the Šumava region—it's a great spot for meditating or picnicking. Getting out of Dívčí kámen, unfortunately, is rather brutal. Once you've climbed back out of Třísov, though, it's downhill (almost) all the way home.

**SHORTEST ROUTE (17KM).** A third option is to catch a train with your bike from Český Krumlov to Horní Planá (1hr., every 2-3hr., approx. 30Kč) and enjoy the downhill 17km coast with a gorgeous vista of the countryside. Facing away from the train station, turn right on the dirt path, left on the first road, then right at the intersection with the highway. Signs point the way back to Český Krumlov.

# ČESKÝ RÁJ (CZECH PARADISE)

Czechs horded most of their country's gems in the capital city, but they safely hid their paradise an hour away. Proclaimed a State Nature Preserve in 1931, the rocks of Czech Paradise were formed by the sedimentation of sandstone, marl, and slate on the bottom of the Mesozoic sea. High, narrow towers and pillars separated by deep, cramped gorges make for stellar climbing as well as a series of stunning views for those who prefer not to grapple. The 588 acres of the preserve are interwoven by a dense network of trails, with options for hikers of all ages and abilities. The ideal base for exploring the region is the "fairy-tale" town of Jičín, which itself warrants a visit.

## JIČÍN                                                        ☎(0)433

Once upon a time there was a small town in the northern Czech Republic named Jičín. It was full of friendly residents and fine cafes, but lived in the shadow of its big sister Prague. Only a lucky few knew that the best reason to come to Jičín was its proximity to some of the best hiking and mountain climbing sites in the country, known as the Czech Paradise. Then in the 17th-century, the great lord Albrecht Valdštejn (Wallenstein) began to build it up in his name, creating its magnificent square, stone tower, and St. James Church. Jičín attracted attention and came to be called "the Gateway to Czech Paradise." Today the secret is out and those dedicated travelers who do visit Jičín take home a piece of a town that lives happily ever after. The End.

**⊏ TRANSPORTATION. Buses** from Prague to Jičín (1½hr., 7 per day, 53Kč) are the best means of transportation to the town. The **train station** is at Dělnická 297. (☎503 11 11. Info office open daily 6am-5:30pm.) Trains run from **Prague** (2½hr., 8 per day, 66Kč), but usually require a stopover.

**▉▮ ORIENTATION AND PRACTICAL INFORMATION. Valdštejnovo náměstí** (Wallenstein Square) serves as the center of town. **Revoluční,** one of the main streets leading out of the square, contains a series of trees known as **Lípová alej** (Linden Alley). **Husova,** another main street, is filled with various shops, cafes, and restaurants. **Šafaříkova,** just off Husova, leads to the **bus station.** The **tourist office,** Information Centre, is at Valdštejnovo nám. 1. (☎/fax 53 43 90; mic@eurodata.cz. Open M-F 9am-6pm, Sa 9am-2pm, Su 9am-noon.) **GE Capital Bank,** Žižkovo nám. 4, **exchanges cash** for a 1% commission and **traveler's checks** for a 2% commission. (Open M-F 7:30am-noon and 1-4pm.) An **ATM** sits next to the tourist office in the square. There's a **pharmacy** at Tylova 812, just off Žižkovo nám. (Open M-F 8am-5pm, Sa 8am-noon.) The **police station** is at Balbínova 27. (☎58 43 01. Open M and W 8am-5pm; reception open daily 7:30am-3:30pm.) The only internet joint in town, **Internet Café Jičín,** Husova 1058, has some of the best rates in the country. (☎223 78. 66Kč per hr., students 56Kč. Open M-F 10am-10pm, Sa-Su 6pm-10pm.) The **post office** is at Šafaříkova 141. (☎58 54 32. Open M-F 8am-5:30pm, Sa 8-11:15am.) **Telephones** can be found outside the post office and in the main square. **Postal Code: 506 01.**

**▚▙ ACCOMMODATIONS AND FOOD.** The most inexpensive lodgings are at **Motel Rumcajs,** Koněva 331, where camping spaces and beds are always available. From the main square, take Nerudova to B. Němcové, turn right and head to Komenského nám., then bear left onto Kollárova, which becomes Koněva. (☎53 10 78. Singles 200Kč; doubles 300Kč; quads 600Kč; camping 35Kč per person plus 50-70Kč per tent.) The pricier **Hotel Start** is at Revoluční 863. To get there, walk to Žižkovo nám. and then take Havlíčkova until it becomes Revoluční. The hotel's clean rooms, with balconies, compensate for the bland exterior and old elevators. (☎52 38 10; fax 52 39 16; box@hotelstartjc.cz; www.hotelstartjc.cz. Singles with shower 650Kč.) In the center of town is **Hotel Paříž,** Žižkovo nám. 3, whose highlights include a disco that gets rowdy on weekends and a cheap buffet-style eatery. (Singles 450Kč; doubles 650Kč. Disco open W, F, and Sa 8am-4am.)

Jičín is full of restaurants, most of which serve decent food at affordable prices. **Restaurant Lucie,** Fügnerova 191, is trendy as hell. (☎211 92. Main dishes 60-120Kč. Open M-F 11am-10pm, Sa-Su noon-10pm.) For Czech specialities, head over to **U Matěje,** Nerudova 45, and relax in the beer garden. The chicken with peach and ham (125Kč) is very good. (☎226 41. Open daily 11am-10pm.) **Mini-marts** are all over the town; one of the best supermarkets is **Fa Market,** Komenského nám. 57. (☎53 17 08. Open M-F 6am-6pm, Sa 6am-noon, Su 7am-11am.)

**▣▟ SIGHTS AND ENTERTAINMENT.** The entrance to the main square is through the **Valdice Gate.** The **gate-tower** and its creaky stairs, built in 1568-78, are worth climbing for a view of the town. (Open daily May-Aug. 9am-5pm. 8Kč.) Next door is the **Church of St. James.** Constructed between 1627 and 1634 from a Greek-style layout, it boasts a mesmerizing painted dome. (Open daily 9am-5pm.) In the southeast corner of the square sits the Italian-designed **château,** home to the regional **museum,** which consists of eight rooms filled with artifacts and archaeological finds from the Jičín region. Also in the chateau is a **gallery** with various exhibits of 20th-century Czech art. (Museum and gallery open Tu-Su 9am-5pm.)

**▨ HIKING AND OUTDOORS.** Numerous **trails** criss-cross the **Český Ráj National Preserve.** Green signs on the trees and rocks mark the roundabout route, yellow signs guide hikers through the most challenging path, and red signs mark the ever-long **Golden Trail,** which connects Prachovské skály (Prachovské Rocks) to Hrubá skála (Rough Rock).

From Jičín, **buses** run to **Prachovské skály** (15min., every hr., 9Kč). You can also walk to the park along the relatively easy 8km yellow trail, beginning at the Rumcajs Motel in Jičín. From Valdštejnské nám., turn onto Palackého, and go left on Jiráskova, continuing through its name change to Kollárova. From the bus stop at Prachovské skály, take a right at the fork; a 10min. walk brings you to the **ticket office** at the base of the rocks. Prachovské skály are sandstone creations that offer some of the finest rock-climbing in the Czech Republic. The rocks boast 17 stunning vistas, the ruins of the 14th-century rock **castle** Pařez, and the rock pond Pelíšek. (Open Apr.-Oct. daily 8am-5pm. 25Kč, students 10Kč. Swimming in rock pond May 1-Sept. 1.)

To get to Hrubá Skála, take a **train** from Jičín to **Turnov** (1hr., 12 per day, 24Kč). Get off at Turnov-Město and follow the signs to the red trail. Hrubá skála is a rock town surrounding a hilltop castle-turned-hotel, where hikers enjoy the best view of the sandstone rocks. Trails resemble those in Prachovské skály, but tend to be more level after the initial climb. From the Hrubá Skála castle, the red trail leads up to the remains of **Valdštejnský hrad** (Wallenstein Castle), where composer Josef B. Foerster wrote some of his finest pieces.

# EAST BOHEMIA

Oft in the shadow of the better-known regions of the Czech Republic, East Bohemia has no less to show. From the fertile lowlands of the Elbe to the mountain ranges that create a natural border with Poland, East Bohemia has skiing, sightseeing, and swimming to spare. Under Habsburg rule, it was largely in the villages of East Bohemia that the Czech language was kept alive. Not surprisingly, many of the 19th-century Czech intellectuals and champions of national sovereignty came from here. Today, Hradec Králové, the region's administrative and cultural center, surprises with its marvelously preserved medieval buildings and lively pace. Litomyšl, birthplace of composer Bedřich Smetana, enchants with one of the most beautiful Renaissance chateaus north of Italy.

## HRADEC KRÁLOVÉ         ☎ (0) 49

At the confluence of the Elbe and the Orlice rivers, Hradec Králové (HRA-dets KRAh-loveh), literally "Queens' Castle," once served as a depository for Czech royal widows. A definite case for multiple personalities, Hradec lures visitors with an exceptional Staré Město (Old Town) and a fully loaded commercial district. The city's old-school feel is shaped by a number of well-preserved Gothic, Renaissance, and Baroque buildings, while great Czech architects Jan Kotera and Josef Gočar brought life to the town's second personality with ground-breaking modern structures. Great daytrips and a compact city center that feels like a miniature Prague—minus the hordes of tourists—merit the city's exploration.

### ■ ORIENTATION

Hradec Králové can be viewed as two separate towns separated by the Elbe (Labe in Czech) River. The west side contains the shop-infested Nové Město (New Town), while the east side is home to the church- and cafe-filled Staré Město (Old Town). The **train** and **bus stations** sit next to each other, on the edge of Nové Město away from the river. To get to the center, **Velké náměstí** (Great Square), from the stations, follow follow **Gočárova** all the way to the river, cross the bridge, and continue for one block. When you hit **Čs. armády**, take a left and a quick right onto **V kopečku**, which leads to Velké nám. Alternatively, buses #1-3 and 5-17 all go to the center from the train station.

# ◧ TRANSPORTATION

**Trains:** Riegrovo nám. 914 (☎502 22 29; info ☎502 51 71). Trains to **Prague** (2hr., every hr. 6am-8pm, 75Kč; round-trip 141Kč, indirect 98Kč). Open daily 3am-11:30pm; info center open M-F 5:15am-6:15pm, Sa 6:15am-3:45pm, Su 8:15am-5:45pm.

**Buses:** S.K. Neumanna 1138 (☎553 35 30), next to the train station. Consists only of numbered terminals and an information center. Buses to **Prague** (2hr. every hr., 70-80Kč) leave from in front of the train station. Open M-F 5:30am-6pm.

**Public transportation:** 7Kč per ride. Buy tickets at kiosks or the train station.

**Taxi: Sprint Taxis** (☎140 14), wait in front of the train station.

# ◪ PRACTICAL INFORMATION

**Tourist Office: Information center,** Gočárova třída 1225 (☎/fax 553 44 82). Helpful English-speaking staff. Open M-F 8am-6pm, Sa 10am-4pm; off-season closed Sa.

**Budget Travel: Čedok travel,** Gočárova 1228 (☎553 46 20), down the street from the tourist office. Offers discounted airline and bus tickets to travelers under 26. English spoken. Open M-F 8:30am-6pm, Sa 9am-noon.

**Currency Exchange: Komerční Banka,** Čelakovského 642 (☎581 55 50), at Masarykovo nám., charges 2% on all currency exchanges. **ATM** inside.

**Luggage storage:** At the train station. 5Kč per bag per day; lockers 5Kč per day. Open daily 5am-10pm.

**International Bookstore: Skippy Bookstore,** Gočarova 30 (☎337 79). Small English section on the 2nd floor. Open M-F 8am-6pm, Sa 8am-noon.

**Police:** Haškova, near the train station. Open 24hr.

**Pharmacy: Centrální lékárna,** Masarykovo nám 637 (☎551 16 14), across from Komerční Bank. Open M-F 7am-7pm, Sa 8am-1pm.

**Hospital:** Sokolska (☎583 11 11), just south of the old town.

**Internet access: Jowin Digital,** Gočárova 1261 (☎553 65 95), just across from the tourist office, 2nd floor. Fast, but not cheap. 1Kč per min. Open M-Sa 10am-6pm.

**Post Office:** Riegrovo nám. (☎553 37 15), next to the train station. Send large packages at window #8. Card **telephones** out front. Open M-F 7am-7pm, Sa 8am-noon.

**Postal Code:** 500-00.

# ◩◯ ACCOMMODATIONS AND FOOD

You won't find budget accommodations in the center of town. The best rooms for your buck are at **Hotel Dům,** Heyrovského 1177, a 15-minute walk from **Staré Město** (the Old Town). Rooms here all have fridges and desks. (☎551 11 75; fax 551 24 68. Reception 24hr. 150Kč per person.) Also outside the center, **Hotel Garni,** Na Kotli 1147, is one step up despite its bland exterior—all rooms have baths. (☎576 36 00. Reception 24hr. Singles 560Kč; doubles1460Kč. Breakfast included.) **Hotel Stadion,** Komenského 1214, is a more expensive option located directly in Staré Město. Fabulous rooms, a relaxing TV lounge, and next-door bar help redefine the word "convenience." (☎551 46 64; fax 551 46 67. Reception 24hr. Lone doubles 910Kč; doubles 960Kč; triples 1110Kč; quads 1260Kč.)

Most restaurants in Hradec Králové serve non-Czech food, so for authentic meals stick to the pubs. **Pivnice Gobi,** Karla IV 522, is an underground hangout with inexpensive meals. (☎551 10 03. Main dishes 39-84Kč. Open M-Th 2:30pm-1am, F 2:30pm-3am, Sa 5pm-3am, Su 5pm-1am.) The best lunch option is **Jídelna Praha,** Gočárova 1229, whose fully fledged buffet serves high quality at a low price. (☎61 87. Main dishes 33-50Kč. Open M-F 6:30am-4pm, Sa 9am-12:30pm.) The **supermarket** giant, **Tesco,** Nám. 28. Října 1610, has all the goodies plus some English **newspapers** and magazines. (☎507 21 11. Open M-F 7am-8pm, Sa 7am-6pm.)

## 👁 🎵 SIGHTS AND ENTERTAINMENT

Most sights in Hradec Králové are in **Velké nám.**, the center of Staré Město. Here, the 1307 **Church of the Holy Spirit** (Kostel Svatého Ducha) serves as testament to the town's historical significance, with priceless items such as a 1406 tin baptismal font (one of the oldest in Bohemia) and tower bells affectionately named Eagle (Orel) and Beggar (Žebrák) from 1496 and 1538, respectively. (Open M-Sa 10-11am and 2:30-3:30pm, Su 2-3:30pm.) The 1580 **White Tower** (Bílá věž), standing beside the church, originally served as a water tower. The landmark is a full 71m tall and contains Bohemia's second largest bell. (Open Tu-Su 9:30-11:30am. 10Kč.) In the middle of the square, the **Gallery of Modern Art** (Galerie moderního umění), at #139, showcases the works of Czech artists. Rotating exhibitions on the first level focus on a particular artist. (Open Tu-Su 9am-noon and 1-6pm. 20Kč, students 10Kč.) Walk across the square from the museum to the **Church of the Assumption of the Virgin Mary** (Kostel Nanebevzetí Panny Marie), constructed by Jesuits from 1654-1666. Prussian soldiers destroyed its interior in 1792, but 19th- and 20th-century renovations have revived its former beauty. Fish lovers can find peace at the **Ohří Aquarium**, Baarova 1663, where 130,000L of water hold vegetarian piranhas. To get there, cross the Elbe River, turn left onto Střelecká, then right onto V. Lipkách; Baarova will be on the left. The exhibit is small, but a walk through the simulated rainforest is pretty therapeutic. (☎553 45 55. Open Th-Su 9am-6pm. 55Kč.)

In late October, Hradec Králové's largest festival, **"Jazz Goes to Town,"** features jazz musicians from all over the world. The action takes place at the Aldis Center, Eliščino náb. 357 (☎60 01 11), but you can buy tickets at the tourist office. The **Theater Festival of European Regions** is usually held in the last two weeks of June. Classic and modern plays are performed daily all over town by professional groups from non-capital European cities. Tickets are available at the tourist office. If you're just looking for a relaxing pub, **Hogo Fogo Bar**, Eliščino náb., on the water, is where all the students flock when the sun goes down. (☎55 15 92. Beer 19Kč. Open M-F 11am-midnight, Sa-Su 2pm-midnight.)

## 🚌 DAYTRIPS FROM HRADEC KRÁLOVÉ

### THE ZOO AT DVŮR KRÁLOVÉ NAD LABEM ☎(0)437

*Štefánikova 1029. ☎82 95 15. Buses run from outside the train station in Hradec Králové (1hr., every hr., 34Kč). Turn right out of the bus station onto Listopadu, then walk 2 blocks and turn left onto Švehlova. Cross the town square diagonally and follow Palackého to Husova, then follow the zoo signs downhill to the park. Open daily 9am-6pm. 60Kč, parking 40Kč. Ticket price includes the park, gallery, safari bus, and toilets.*

So what do you do when your elephants and hippos start to multiply? Open up a zoo, like they did in Dvůr Králové nad Labem. Opened in 1946 with the help of volunteers, the zoo is the largest and most impressive animal park in the Czech Republic and houses all of your four-legged friends, plus monkeys and reptiles. In the summer (May 15-Sept. 30, weather permitting) follow the signs to the **safari bus** (15-20min., every 25min.), which embarks on a journey through the wild side of the park. While the 2km walk to the safari is the highlight with its rhinos and zebras, there is also a **mini-train** (5-10min.) that leaves from outside the restaurant "Rotunda." The **gallery** is to the left of the main entrance and contains colorful dinosaur portraits. (Open daily 10am-6pm.) The area between the gallery and summer exhibit is where you'll find the monkeys and birds.

For a great lunch, grab a tray at **"U Lemura"** at the zoo's entrance and fill up on its homestyle meals for 52-64Kč. (☎66 70 66. Open daily 9am-6pm.) The **ticket office** at the main entrance has free zoo **maps** and sells a handy English guidebook (55Kč).

### LITOMYŠL ☎(0)464

*Buses run from outside the train station in Hradec Králové (1hr., 2 per hr., 50Kč). Trains are infrequent; avoid them. Exit the bus station to the right and take the main street*

*Mařákova, down across the river. Turn left onto Tyršova and bear left at Braunerovo nám. to get to the square. Chateau open Tu-Su 9am-noon and 1-5pm. 50Kč, students 25Kč. English guide 50Kč. Last tour 1hr. before closing.*

Home to many famous Czech intellectuals, Litomyšl has made a big name for itself in the world of arts and politics. The town's sights consist of artists' homes and galleries, all of which lie minutes from the banana-shaped Staré Město (Old Town). Dating back to the 10th century, Litomyšl is the only small town that can lay claim to bringing seven Central European presidents together, which happened here in 1994. Litomyšl's magnificent **chateau** is just a 5-minute walk uphill from the square. Take J. Váchala from the square to the covered stairway, then go up the stairs and continue on straight. The chateau was built in a high Renaissance style from 1568-1581 by Vratislav of Perštejn, the supreme chancellor of the Czech kingdom. Perštejn had it built for his wife Marie Manrique de Lara of the Spanish Mendoza family, who missed the Renaissance architecture of her native country after moving to Bohemia. The exterior of the chateau is adorned with letter-shaped *sgrafitti*, each with a different design. The main attraction is the 1797 **theater** inside. The courtyard houses the **Smetana Opera Festival** (June 21-July 1; call ☎ 61 90 33 for tickets). Within the castle grounds lies the birthplace of composer **Bedřich Smetana.** The house seems as if it had been left unwatched for years and visitors can stroll through as they listen to some of his pieces. (Open May-Sept. Tu-Su 9am-noon and 1-5pm; off-season Sa-Su only or by appointment. 20Kč, students 10Kč.)

Outside the chateau walls in the city center is the **Portmoneum,** Terezy Novákové 75, a 1920s house whose walls are graced with the art of painter **Josef Váchal.** For further information about Litomyšl and its sights, go to the **tourist office, Informāní Centrum Litomyšl,** Smetanovo nám. 72, in the main square. (☎/fax 61 21 61; ic@litomysl.cz; www.litomysl.cz. Open M-F 9am-7pm, Sa 9am-4pm, Su 10am-3pm; off-season M-F 8:30am-5:30pm, Sa 9am-2pm.)

# MORAVIA

Wine-making Moravia makes up the easternmost third of the Czech Republic. Home of the country's finest folk-singing tradition and two leading universities, it's also the birthplace of a number of Central European notables: Tomáš G. Masaryk, founder and first president of Czechoslovakia, composer Leoš Janáček, and psychoanalyst Sigmund Freud. Johann Gregor Mendel founded modern genetics in his pea garden in a Brno monastery. Brno and Olomouc are the towns most worth visiting, but South Moravia also harbors the remarkable caves of the Moravský Kras and the architectural pearl Telč.

# BRNO
☎ (0)5

The Czech Republic's second-largest city, Brno (berh-NO; pop. 388,900) is a mecca of business and industry and the streets show it: scores of "erotic club" sirens call out to lonely men, while restaurant menus list prices with corporate expense accounts in mind. The city does have an upside: an extensive array of Gothic and Baroque churches, splendidly cheap opera, and amazing ice cream. While there are more exciting and beautiful places to visit in the Czech Republic, Brno lets travelers escape the tourist hordes and experience a living Czech city.

## ■ ORIENTATION

Brno's compact center makes everything in town accessible by foot. Several streets radiate from **Nám. Svobody** (Freedom Sq.), the main square. From the train station's main entrance, cross the three tram lines on **Nádražní** to **Masarykova,** which leads to Nám. Svobody. From the bus station, follow **Plotní** as it becomes **Dornych** and turn left at the train station onto **Nádražní;** Masarykova will be on the right.

CZECH REPUBLIC

## ⬚ TRANSPORTATION

**Trains:** ☎42 21 48 03. To: **Prague** (3hr., 16 per day, 164-224Kč); **Bratislava, SLK** (2hr., 9 per day, 115Kč); **Vienna, AUS** (2hr., 1 per day, 525Kč); and **Budapest, HUN** (4½hr., 2 per day, 872Kč). The international booking office in the train station handles Wasteels tickets. Open 24hr.

**Buses:** ☎43 21 77 33. On Zvonařka, go down Plotní from the trains. Follow it to Tesco and then under the train station. To **Prague** (3hr., many, 112-167Kč) and **Vienna, AUS** (2½hr., 3 per day, 250Kč).

**Public Transportation: Trams, trolleys,** and **buses** 11Kč; luggage 4Kč; 24hr. pass 44Kč. Buy tickets at a *tabák* or any kiosk. Ticket checks do happen. Fine for riding ticketless 600-1000Kč. Some tram routes run all night; the rest run 5am-8pm.

**Taxis: Radiotaxi,** ☎45 22 45 22.

## ▨ PRACTICAL INFORMATION

**Tourist Office: Kulturní a informační centrum města Brna,** Radnická 8 (☎42 21 10 90; fax 42 21 07 58). Turn left off Masarykova onto Květinářská just before Svobody. Follow Nám. Svobody to Zelný trh; the office is across the square. Multilingual staff books hotels, private rooms (from 400Kč), and hostels (200Kč), and sells city **maps** (6-69Kč). Open M-F 8am-6pm, Sa-Su 9am-5pm.

**Budget Travel: GTS International,** Vachova 4 (☎42 22 19 96; fax 42 22 10 01). English spoken. Open daily 9am-6pm.

**Currency Exchange: Komerční banka,** Kobližná 3 (☎212 71 11), at the corner of Nám. Svobody. Gives Visa **cash advances,** cashes **traveler's checks** for a 2% commission (minimum 50Kč), and has an AmEx/Cirrus/MC/Visa **ATM.** Open M-F 8am-5pm.

**American Express,** Starobměnská 20 (☎42 21 81 33). Open M-F 9am-noon and 1:30-5pm.

**Luggage storage:** At the train station. 10Kč per bag per day. Lockers 10Kč per day.

**Pharmacy:** Kobližná 7 (☎42 21 21 10). Open M-Sa 7am-7pm, Su 8am-1pm.

**Internet Access: @InternetCafe,** Lidická 17 (☎41 24 53 44). 2 levels of speedy PCs. 2Kč per min. Open M-F 10am-10pm, Sa-Su 2-10pm.

**Post Office:** Poštovská 3/5 (☎42 32 11 01). **Poste Restante** at #1 or 23. Open M-F 7am-7:30pm, Sa 8am-12:30pm.

**Postal code:** 601 00.

## ▰ ACCOMMODATIONS

Brno's hotel scene is geared toward business visitors, so it's no surprise that one of the budget hotels was replaced by the "Moulin Rouge Erotic Night Club disco." There are a few budget options around, and the tourist office can arrange **private rooms** in the center.

**Interservis (HI),** Lomená 48 (☎/fax 45 23 42 32). Take tram #9 or 12 from the train station to the end at Komárov. Continue along Hněvkovského and turn left onto the unmarked Pompova (the 2nd-to-last turn before the railroad overpass); the hostel is on the right. Friendly staff and great views of the city brighten up this otherwise lackluster hostel, which is far from the center. 260Kč per person, students 230Kč; with breakfast 310Kč, students 270Kč. MC/Visa.

**Hotel Astorka,** Novobranská 3 (☎42 51 03 70; fax 42 51 01 06; astorka@jamu.cz). From the train station, head up Masarykova and take the 1st right onto Josefská, which leads to Novobranská; Astorka is the light purple building on the right. Brand new and centrally located, with upstairs bar and restaurant. Doubles 420Kč per person, students 210Kč; triples 315Kč, 157.50Kč.

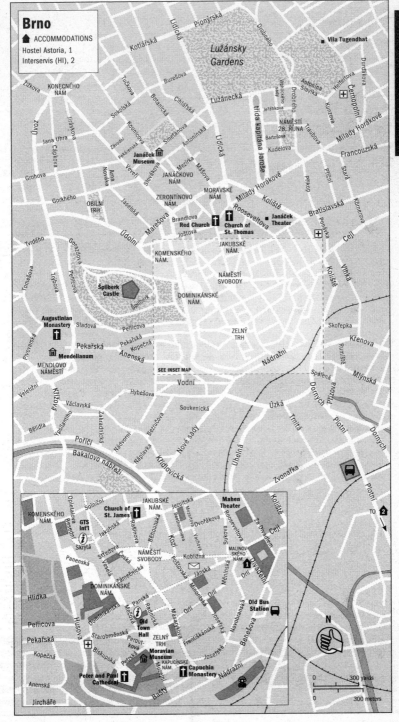

**Brno**

♦ ACCOMMODATIONS
Hostel Astoria, 1
Interservis (HI), 2

## FOOD

Street-side pizza joints far outnumber traditional *párek* peddlers. A fruit and vegetable **market** (open M-F 9am-6pm) thrives on Zelný trh, while a **Tesco** awaits your purchase behind the train station. (Open M-F 7am-8pm, Sa 7am-7pm, Su 8am-6pm.)

**Livingstone,** Starobrněnská 1 (☎/fax 42 21 46 45), across from Zelný trh. Cure-playing, angst-filled student pub. Daily menu 45Kč. Open M-F 10am-2pm, Sa-Su 5pm-2am.

**Aviatik Klub a Restaurace,** Jakubská 7 (☎ 42 21 45 55). From Nám. Svobody, walk up Česká past McDonald's and turn right on Jakubská. Hand-painted hot-air balloon murals lead to this bistro. Czech favorites 49-86Kč. Open M-Sa 11am-11pm.

**Fischer Cafe,** Masarykova 8/10 (☎ 42 22 18 80). This cafe does not quite pull off its intended New York chic, but it serves good salads at fairly steep rates (55-95Kč). Open M-Sa 8am-10pm, Su 10am-10pm.

**Bufet Vesmír,** Kobližná 8. From Nám. Svobody, head down Kobližná; it's on the right. Great for a quick, cheap, and filling meal (50Kč). Open M-F 7am-7pm.

## SIGHTS

**PETER AND PAUL CATHEDRAL.** (Biskupská katedrála sv. Petra a Pavla.) You may hear the bells strike noon at eleven o'clock. Allegedly Brno was saved from the Swedish siege one day in 1645 when the besieging general gave his army until noon to capture the town; after noon, he would withdraw. When the townsfolk learned of this, they rang the bells early and the Swedes slunk away. The bells have been striking noon at 11am ever since. *(On Petrov Hill. Cathedral open daily 8am-6pm, tower 10am-6pm, crypt 11am-6pm. Church free. Tower 20Kč, students 15Kč. Crypt 20Kč, students 15Kč.)*

**ŠPILBERK CASTLE.** (Hrad Špilberk.) Once home to Czech kings and later a mighty Habsburg fortress, Špilberk has a checkered past. After a brief period of serving as the city's main defense against the Swedes, it was used as a prison, first in the 1700s to hold Hungarian, Italian, Polish and Czech patriots and revolutionaries, then during World War II by the Nazis. A journey through its corridors is more intriguing than the rather weak collection of torture-related exhibits. The ground floor's exhibit "Prison of Nations" covers the history of the prison from the 18th to 20th centuries, while the first floor shows the history of Brno. The second floor displays art, from Renaissance to modern. *(From Nám. Svobody, take Zámečnická through Dominikánské nám. and turn right on Panenská to Husova, heading uphill. ☎ 42 21 41 45. Open May-Sept. Tu-Su 9am-6pm; Oct.-Apr. 10am-5pm. English cassettes 60Kč, students 30Kč. Call to reserve an English tour guide. All exhibitions 60Kč, students 30Kč. 1 exhibition 25Kč, 10Kč.)*

**CAPUCHIN MONASTERY CRYPT.** (Hrobka Kapucínského kláštera.) If you liked Kutná Hora (see p. 245), you'll love this morbid resting place. The monks at the Capuchin Monastery Crypt developed a revolutionary embalming technique involving extensive ventilation, preserving more than 100 18th-century monks and assorted worthies. The results are now on display to enlighten the living: the crypt begins with the Latin inscription, "Remember death," and ends with an uplifting slogan in a room full of dead monks, "What you are, we were. What we are, you will be." *(Just to the left of Masarykova from the station. ☎ 42 21 23 32. Open M-Sa 9am-noon and 2-4:30pm, Su 11am-noon and 2-4:30pm. 40Kč, students 20Kč.)*

**AROUND MENDL SQUARE.** (Mendlovo náměstí.) In the heart of Old Brno, the high Gothic **Basilica of the Assumption of the Virgin Mary** (Basilika Nanebevzetí Panny Marie) houses the 13th-century Black Madonna, the Czech Republic's oldest wooden icon, which purportedly held off the Swedes in 1645. *(From the castle, walk downhill on Pelicova and take the stairs to Sladová. Go left onto Úvoz to Mendlovo nám. Open M-Sa 5-7:15pm, Su 7am-12:15pm and 5-7:15pm.)* The Augustinian monastery next door was the home of **Johann Gregor Mendel,** the father of modern genetics. It took the scientific world 50 years to appreciate his work, but as his words, now carved in stone, predicted *"Má doba přijde!"* ("My time will come!"). The **Mendelianum,** Mendlovo nám. 1a, documents Mendel's life and work, explaining his remarkable experiments with peas and bees. The Lysenkoist Communists took down his statue—it's now back in the courtyard. *(Open daily July-Aug. 9am-6pm; Sept.-June 8am-5pm. English info book 85Kč. 8Kč, students 4Kč.)*

**OLD TOWN HALL.** (Stará radnice.) This building is the stuff of legends. The Old Town Hall's strangely crooked Gothic portal purportedly became that way after the carver working on it blew his commission on too much good Moravian wine. Another story has it that the dismayed stone face inside is the petrified head of a burgher who met his doom behind the wall after siding with the Hussites in 1424. The most famous tale involves the stuffed "dragon" hanging on the wall. The story goes that the medieval reptile was on the rampage. In an attempt to stop him, a valiant knight stuffed an ox carcass with quicklime and offered it to the beast. After devouring the bait, the dragon quenched his thirst in a nearby river; the lime began to slake, and the poor creature's belly exploded—thus the seam along his stomach today. The dragon is actually an Amazonian crocodile offered to the town by Archduke Matyáš to garner favor among the burghers. *(Radnická 8, just off Zelný trh. Open daily Apr.-Oct. 9am-5pm; last tour 4:30pm. 20Kč. Tower 20Kč.)*

**AROUND NÁMĚSTÍ SVOBODY.** The partially gold **Plague Column** (Morový sloup) in the center of the square has successfully warded off infections for the last 300 years (if you don't count the recent arrival of fast food chains). North of Nám. Svobody along Rašínova, the **Church of St. James** (Kostel sv. Jakuba), with its strangely thin tower pointing skyward, was built for Brno's medieval Flemish and German communities. The church has undergone more than 10 renovations since its construction. The French Huguenot Raduit de Souches, who helped save Brno from Swedish invasion in 1645, rests inside in a great stone monument. Returning to the square, go left along Kobližná and turn left on Rooseveltova for an exercise in comparative architecture. On the left is the grand **Mahlen Theater** (Mahlenovo divadlo), built by the Viennese duo Helmer and Fellner in the 19th century; on the right stands the 1960s **Janáček Theater** (Janáčkovo divadlo), home to Brno's Opera.

## 🎵🎭 ENTERTAINMENT AND NIGHTLIFE

The Old Town Hall hosts frequent concerts; buy tickets at the tourist office's **ticket agency,** Běhounská 16. (Open M-F 9am-5pm.) Get **theater and opera** tickets at Dvořákova 11. **Cinemas** abound, usually showing Hollywood flicks (50-200Kč). **Kapitol Kino,** Divadelní 3 (☎42 21 33 51), shows American blockbusters; **Lucerna,** Minská 19 (☎74 70 70), shows British and American indie films. Look for posters advertising **techno raves,** Brno's hottest summer entertainment. Surprisingly, it's easier to find a *pivnice* than a wine pub in the heart of wine-producing Moravia, but there is that occasional *vinárna* (wine cellar; bottles 80-120Kč).

   **Divadelní hospoda Veselá husa** (Merry Goose Theatrical Pub), Zelný trh 9 (☎42 21 16 30). At the back of the building. An eclectic crowd gathers for impromptu performances and improv comedy. *Pilsner* 22Kč. Open M-F noon-midnight, Sa-Su 3pm-midnight.

   **Pivnice Minipivovar Pegas,** Jakubská 4 (☎42 21 01 04). This newfangled microbrewery has a loyal following. Pints 18Kč. Open daily 9am-midnight.

   **Mersey,** Minská 14 (☎41 24 06 23). Take tram #3 or 11 from Česká to Tábor. Hosts visiting bands and DJs, sometimes from "overseas." Mostly rock, but some techno and jungle. Beer 14Kč. Open Tu-Sa 7pm-late.

   **H46,** Hybšova 46 (☎43 23 49 45). A 10min. walk left with your back to the train station, or a few stops on tram #1 or 2. Ring the bell if the door is locked. A mostly gay/partly lesbian/others welcome bar. *Pivo* 16Kč. Open nightly 4pm-4am.

## DAYTRIPS FROM BRNO

### MORAVSKÝ KRAS CAVES                                    ☎(0)506

*Get there early, as tours are likely to sell out. A train from Brno to Blansko at 6:50am (30min., 7 per day, 17Kč) will get you to the caves before 9am. From here, either hike the 8km on the green trail from Blansko to Skalní Mlýn or take the bus (15min., 5 per day, 6Kč) from the station up the road from the trains. Don't skip the trip if you can't get to the caves until later; just make reservations. At Skalní Mlýn, there's a ticket and info office (☎41 35 75) and a shuttle to the cave (round-trip 40Kč, students 30Kč). Or, walk the 1.5km along the yellow trail. The BVV travel agency in Brno, Starobrněnská 20, organizes afternoon tours (☎42 21 77 45; 640Kč per person, 4 person minimum).*

Inside the forested hills of Southern Moravia, a network of caves comprising Moravský Kras (MO-rahv-skee krahs) has been opened to visitors. The most popular is **Punkevní,** where tour groups pass magnificent stalactites and stalagmites, many with their own silly names (like *rokoková panenka*, "rococo doll") to emerge at **Stepmother Abyss** (Propast Macocha). The story goes that a wicked stepmother from a nearby town threw her stepson into the gaping hole. When villagers found the boy suspended from a branch by his trousers, they saved him and threw in the woman instead. Over the last 20 years, 50 people have committed suicide by jumping off the abyss's 140m ledge. During the summer, spelunkers row along the underground Punkva river. Bring a sweater; it gets very chilly. (Apr.-Sept. tours 8:20am-3:50pm; Jan.-Mar. and Oct.-Dec. tours 8:20am-2pm; closed Dec. 24-26. Buy tickets for the tour at Skalní Mlýn's bus stop or in the entrance. 70Kč, students 25Kč. Photos 10Kč; video 50Kč.) Those craving more can explore the other caves: **Balcarka** (45min. tour; open Apr.-Sept. M-F 7:30am-3:30pm, Sa-Su 8:30am-2:30pm; Oct. M-F 7:30am-1:30pm, Sa-Su 8:30am-2:30pm; Feb.-Mar. 9am, 11am, 1:30pm tours; 40Kč, students 20Kč), **Kateřinská** (30min. tour; open April-Sept. 8:20am-4pm; Oct. 8:20am-2pm; Feb.-Mar. 10am, noon, 2pm tours; 30Kč, students 15Kč), and **Sloupskošošůvské** (1hr. tour; open Apr.-Sept. 7:30am-3:30pm; Oct. 8am-1:30pm; Feb.-Mar. 10am, noon, 2pm tours; 40-60Kč, students 20-30Kč).

### TELČ                                                     ☎(0)66

*Buses from Brno to České Budějovice stop at Telč (2hr., 8 per day, 70-80Kč). The bus station lies 5min. from Nám. Zachariáše z Hradce. Follow the walkway and turn right on Tyršova, then left on Masarykovo. Pass under the archway on the right to enter the square.*

The Italian aura of Telč (TELCH) stems from a trip **Zachariáš of Hradec,** the town's ruler, took to Genoa, Italy, in 1546. He was so enamored of the new Renaissance style that he brought back a battalion of Italian artists and craftsmen to spruce up his humble Moravian castle and town. Stepping over the cobblestone footbridge into the main square makes it easy to see why UNESCO named the Gingerbread town of Telč a World Heritage Monument: the square is flanked by long arcades of peach-painted gables, lime-green Baroque bays, and time-worn terracotta roofs.

While it's easy to get caught up browsing the center's porticos and watching local children in traditional Moravian costume sing and dance, don't miss a tour of Telč's castle. There are two options—*trasa A* and *trasa B*, both 45min. Buy your ticket and wait in the courtyard; when there are enough people and a guide is ready, a tour will begin. *Trasa A* goes through the Renaissance hallways past tapestries, through the old chapel, and under extravagant ceilings; *trasa B* leads through the rooms decorated in the 18th and 19th centuries. Any of the guidebooks on sale around town (from 30Kč) provide useful commentary in English. (☎724 39 43. Open May-Aug. Tu-Su 9-noon and 1-5pm; Mar.-Apr. and Sept.-Oct. Tu-Su 9am-noon and 1-4pm. Final tour leaves 1hr. before the closing. English tour 90Kč, students 45Kč.) In the arcaded courtyard, a **museum** displays examples of Telč's folklore. (Last admission 30min. before closing. 20Kč, students 10Kč. English leaflets available.) The **gallery** off the walled garden is a memorial to artist **Jan Zrzavý** (1890-1977), who trained as a neo-Impressionist, dabbled in Cubism, and produced some religious paintings.

This collection of his wacky work is definitely worth a look (see **History,** p. 204). English guidebook at reception. (Same hours as museum. 20Kč, students 10Kč.)

You can also rent a **rowboat** from Půjčovna lodí, on the shore, to view the castle and town from the lake in the company of swans. (Open June 20-Aug. daily 10am-7pm. 20Kč per 30min.) Beside the castle grounds stands the town's **tower.** Climb to the top, if you can bear the winding stairs and unstable ledges, to enjoy a magnificent view of Telč. (Open Tu-Sa 10am-noon and 1-6pm, Su 1-6pm. 15Kč.) For further information, go to the **tourist office,** Nám. Zachariáše z Hradce 10 (☎724 31 45; fax 724 35 57) right in the town hall. It has plenty of accommodations info and can find *pensions* in the square for 250Kč per person (with bath). **Privat Nika,** in the corner of the square opposite the castle, which has great little rooms and an award-deserving breakfast. (☎724 31 04. Reservation necessary. 350Kč, 400Kč with breakfast.)

# OLOMOUC                                                   ☎(0)68

More chic than Brno but quainter than Prague, Olomouc (OH-lo-mohts; pop. 104,800), the historic capital of North Moravia, is a university city which embodies the best aspects of the Czech Republic. The masterfully rebuilt town center offers a charming network of cobblestone paths, triangular squares, and Baroque architecture with a dose of modern sleekness. Restaurants feature tofu platters and boutiques sell only the hippest Eurofashions. Surprisingly, Olomouc remains virtually undiscovered by umbrella-toting tourists, who are far outnumbered by local scholars of Comenius and Hus, lending the squares an eerie quiet in the evenings.

## ⚹ ORIENTATION

With a little imagination, Olomouc's Staré Město (Old Town) forms a triangle, in the center of which is the enormous **Horní náměstí** (Upper Square). **Dolní nám.** (Lower Square) is beside Horní nám. The main street, **Masarykova třída,** leads east to the train and bus stations. All trams from the **train station** head downtown (5 stops, 6Kč per ticket). The **bus station** lies one stop beyond the trains, heading away from the center on tram #5. Take the tram to Koruna and the gigantic cement block **Prior** department store, then follow 28. října 50m to Horní nám.

## ▐ TRANSPORTATION

**Trains:** Jeremenkova 60 (☎472 21 75). To **Brno** (1½hr., 7-8 per day, 66Kč) and **Prague** (3hr., 19 per day, 164Kč).

**Buses:** Sladkovského 37 (☎332 91). To **Brno** (1½hr., 10 per day, 82Kč) and **Prague** (4hr., 3 per day, 200Kč).

**Public Transportation:** The city's **trams** and **buses** all require 6Kč tickets, sold at kiosks marked with a big yellow arrow. Most run between the train station and Prior.

**Taxis: Ekotaxi** (☎44 95 41). On the street in front of the train station or at the intersection between Riegrova and Národních hrdinů.

## ▐ PRACTICAL INFORMATION

**Tourist Office:** Horní nám. (☎551 33 85; fax 522 08 43; inforcentrum@olomouc.cz.), in the *radnice* (town hall). Books hotels, hostels, and private rooms (from 200Kč per person). In summer, posts student-housing fliers. English spoken. Open daily Mar.-Nov. 9am-7pm; Dec.-Feb. 9am-5pm.

**Budget Travel: CKM,** Denišova 4 (☎522 21 48; fax 522 39 39). Sells ISIC cards (200Kč) and train tickets. Open M-F 9am-5:30pm.

**Currency Exchange: Komerční banka,** Svobody 14 (☎550 91 11) and Denišova 47 (☎550 91 69), cashes most **traveler's checks** and gives MC **cash advances** for a 2% commission. Denišova branch gives AmEx/MC cash advances. Open M-F 8am-5pm.

**ATMs:** All over Horní nám.

**Luggage storage:** At the train station. 10Kč per piece per day; 24hr. lockers 5Kč. At the bus station. Lockers 5Kč.

**Pharmacy:** At Ostružnická and Horní nám. Open M-F 8am-6pm, Sa 8am-noon.

**Internet Access: Internet Cafe,** Ostružnická 20 (☎523 22 09). 15Kč per 15min. 20% off after 1st hour. Open M-F 9am-8pm, Su 1-7pm.

**Post Office:** Horní nám. 27. Open M-F 7am-7pm, Sa 8am-noon.

**Postal code:** 771 00.

# ▌ ACCOMMODATIONS

The cheapest beds (200Kč) pop up in summer when **university dorms** open to tourists. Olomouc levies a 15Kč tax on all rooms, but it's usually included in the price.

▨ **Pension na Hradbách,** Hrnčířská 14 (☎/fax 523 32 43). From Horní nám., head down Školní, go straight along Purkrabská, and turn right onto Hrnčířská. A small, friendly *pension* in the quiet old streets of the town center. Like living at home, except no one bothers you. Not much space, so call ahead. Luxurious singles with private bath and TV a steal at 500Kč; doubles 600Kč; triples 900Kč.

**Hostel Betánie,** Wurmova 5 (☎523 38 60; fax 522 11 27). Take tram #2 or 4 for 3 stops to U Domu on 1. máje; Wurmova is on the left. Spacious bedrooms and baths make this place a bargain. 5min. from the center. No curfew. Reception 6am-10pm. Doubles 200Kč per person; lone double 320Kč.

**Hostel Plavecký stadion,** Legionářská 11 (☎41 31 81; fax 541 32 56), at the swimming stadium. Take any tram from the train station to Nám. Hrdinů. Go back through the bus park, head right under the airplane, and go around the pool buildings. The hostel is part of the pool complex—airy in the morning, but with a chlorinated tang by afternoon. Swimming 25Kč. Triples 400Kč; quads 500Kč.

# ◖ FOOD

For do-it-yourselfers, a **24hr. grocery** sits at Komenského 3. (☎522 50 32.) For I-can't-do-it-myselfers, Olomouc has some acceptable Czech fare.

**U červeného volka** (At the Red Bull), Dolní nám. 39 (☎522 60 69). Tofu pioneers. Delicious soy, meat, and pasta dishes 50-70Kč. Open M-Sa 10am-11pm, Su 11am-11pm.

**Cafe Caesar,** Horní nám. (☎522 92 87), in the town hall. Caesar was, they say, the founder of Olomouc. Garlicky pizzas (30 varieties; 25-130Kč) and cheap plates of pasta (45-95Kč). When it's packed, there's a bit of a wait. Open 9am-midnight.

**Restaurace U Huberta,** 1. máje 7 (☎522 40 17). Minutes from Nám. Republiky and the museum, Huberta serves nothing but traditional Czech food. Fresh meals (35-45Kč) are above average. Open M-Sa 10am-10pm.

# ◉ SIGHTS

The massive 1378 **town hall** *(radnice)* and its spired clock tower dominate the center. The tourist office arranges trips up the tower for 10Kč. (Daily at 11am, 12:30pm, 3pm, and 5pm.) A wonderful astronomical clock is set in the town hall's north side. In 1955, communist clockmakers replaced the mechanical saints with steelworkers, who strike the hour with their glorious hammers and sickles. The 35m black-and-gold **Trinity Column** (Sloup Nejsvětější Trojice) soars higher than any other Baroque sculptures in the Czech Republic. It will be under construction until late 2001. Farther along 28. října, next to the massive copper cube of the Prior department store, the blocky Gothic **Church of St. Maurice** (Kostel sv. Mořice) might well have been the minimalist eyesore of its day, but its rich interior more than makes up for it. One of Europe's largest Baroque organs bellows on Sunday in the church's resonant hall and stars in Olomouc's **International Organ Festival,** which occurs yearly during the first half of September. Buy tickets at the tourist office or before the show at the church.

From Horní nám., take Mahlerova to the **Jan Sarkander Chapel** (Kaple sv. Jana Sarkandra) on the right, which honors the Catholic priest tortured to death by Protestants in 1620 after he refused to divulge a confessee's secret. There's an exhibit on his "threefold torture" inside. Continue on Mahlerova, turn left onto Univerzitní, and then right onto Denisova. On the left, the **Museum of National History and Arts** (Vlastivědné muzeum), Nám. Republiky 5, presents the history of *homo olomouciensis* from mammoth to noble, as well as the pre-Communist history of the town hall's astrological clock. (☎ 522 27 41. Open Tu-Su 9am-6pm. 30Kč, students 15Kč.)

Leave Nám. Republiky on Mariánská to reach Biskupské nám., home of the Renaissance **Archbishop's Palace** (Arcibiskupský palác), a 17th-century palace and the site where Franz Josef ascended the Habsburg throne during the revolutionary turbulence of 1848. Turn right on Wurmova, cross 1. máje, and climb up Dómská to reach Václavské nám. Let the spires of the **Metropolitan Church of St. Wenceslas** (Metropolitní Kostel sv. Václava) lead the way. The church interior is in impeccable condition, having been reworked virtually every century since it caught fire in 1265. The crypt exhibits Christian paraphernalia, including the gold-encased skull of Olomouc's protectress, St. Pauline. (Sv. Pavlína. Open M, W, and F-Sa 9am-5pm, Th 9am-4pm, Su 11am-5pm.) The **Přemysl Palace** (Přemyslovský palác) next door is a Gothic cloister with fine 15th-century frescoes and the 13th-century **Chapel of John the Baptist** (Kaple sv. Jana Křtitele). Across the square sits the **former Capitular Deaconry** (bývalé Kapitulní děkanství), where an 11-year-old Mozart composed his Symphony in F major while his buddies were learning to tie their shoelaces.

## 🌑 NIGHTLIFE

It's no secret that the students of Olomouc provide the juice for night-time activities; when they are gone for the summer things turn down a notch. Popular among the young'uns, **Depo No. 8,** Nám. Republiky 1, pours *Staropramen* (Pilsner Urquell; 20Kč) in three underground rooms with metallic decor and comfy seats. In the wee hours, the basement becomes Olomouc's most happening student dance club. (☎ 522 12 73. Occasional cover 30Kč. Snacks served all night. Open daily 7pm-4am.) If it's nice out, dance the night away at **Exit Discoteque,** Holická 8, the Czech Republic's largest outdoor club. From Horní nám., walk to Dolní nám., then follow Kateřinská to 17. listopadu. Turn left, then right onto Wittgensteinova. Cross the bridge; the club is on the right (25min.). Listen to all kinds of music until you have to exit. (☎ 523 20 84. Cover 50-100Kč. Open June-Sept. F-Sa 9pm-5am.) Closer to town is **Barumba,** Mlýnská 4, a new techno-pumper with cheap beer. Follow Pavelčákova out of Horní nám. and turn left onto Mlýnská. (☎ 08 12 67. *Krušovice* 13Kč. Cover 30-60Kč, women free. Open M-Th 7pm-2am, F 9pm-6am, Sa 9pm-5am.)

# ESTONIA (EESTI)

**IF YOU'RE HERE FOR...**

**4-6 DAYS.** Spend a couple of days touring the museums of Tallinn and then hit the mud baths of Pärnu for some seaside relaxation.

**2 WEEKS.** Make a loop around the country: from Tallinn, head to Tartu to scope out the university and night scene. Then head to Pärnu, stopping by the castle ruins of Viljandi, on the way to hiking, biking, and driving around the cliffs of the Estonian Islands.

Happy to shuck its Soviet past, Estonia seems quick to revive its historical and cultural ties to its Nordic neighbors, as Finnish money (and tourists) revitalizes the nation. The fancy cars, cellular phones, designer shops, and ever more stylish youngsters that litter the capital indicate that Estonia is benefitting from its transition to democracy and capitalism. Material trappings, however, mask the declining living standards that lurk outside of big cities, as well as the chagrin of the ethnically Russian minority (35%) over Estonia's Finnish leanings. Still, having overcome successive centuries of domination by the Danes, Swedes, and Russians, Estonians are now proud to take their place as members of modern Europe.

## ESTONIA AT A GLANCE

**OFFICIAL NAME:** Republic of Estonia

**CAPITAL:** Tallinn (pop. 471,608)

**POPULATION:** 1,400,000 (65% Estonia, 28% Russian, 7% other)

**LANGUAGES:** Estonian (official), Russian, Ukrainian, English, Finnish

**CURRENCY:** 1 Estonian kroon (EEK) = 100 cents

**RELIGION:** Evangelical Lutheran, Russian Orthodox, Estonian Orthodox

**LAND AREA:** 45,226 km$^2$

**GEOGRAPHY:** Lowlands, marshes

**BORDERS:** Latvia, Russia

**ECONOMY:** 70% Services, 24% Industry, 6% Agriculture

**GDP:** $5500 per capita

**EMERGENCY PHONE NUMBERS:** Police, Ambulance, and Fire 112 (In Tallinn, add leading 0)

**COUNTRY CODE:** 372

**INTERNATIONAL DIALING PREFIX:** 800

# HISTORY

**VIKINGS AND GERMANS.** Estonia's new-found freedom stands against a history of foreign domination and repression. Ninth-century **Vikings** were the first to impose themselves on the Finno-Ugric people who had settled the area long before. In 1219, King Valdemar II of **Denmark** conquered northern Estonia. Shortly thereafter, Livonia, now southern Estonia and northern Latvia, fell to the crusading German knights of the **Teutonic Order,** who purchased the rest of Estonia in 1346.

**RUSSIANS, A SWEDISH INTERLUDE, THEN MORE RUSSIANS.** German domination continued until the emergence of Muscovite Tsar Ivan the Terrible, who, in 1558, crushed many of the tiny feudal states that had developed in the region. In an attempt to force Ivan out, the defeated states searched for foreign assistance: northern Estonia capitulated to Sweden, while Livonia yoked itself to the Polish-Lithuanian Commonwealth. By 1581, Russia had lost control of the country, and the rest of Estonia devolved to Sweden with the 1629 Truce of Altmark.

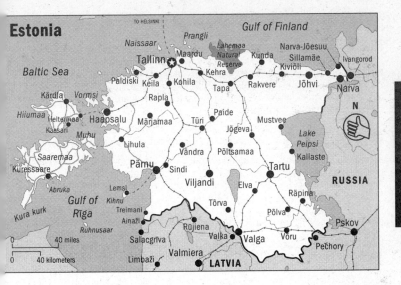

Estonia

TO HELSINKI
Gulf of Finland
Prangli
Naissaar
Lahemaa
Natural
Reserve
Narva-Jõesuu
Maardu
Kunda
Sillamäe
Kiviõli
Ivangorod
Tallinn
Kehra
Baltic Sea
Paldiski
Keila
Kohila
Tapa
Rakvere
Jõhvi
Narva
Kärdla
Vormsi
Rapla
Hiiumaa
Heltermaa
Haapsalu
Märjamaa
Türi
Paide
Jõgeva
Mustvee
Lake
Peipsi
Kassari
Muhu
Lihula
Vändra
Põltsamaa
Kallaste
N
Saaremaa
Pärnu
Sindi
Tartu
RUSSIA
Kuressaare
Viljandi
Elva
Abruka
Lemsi
Tõrva
Räpina
Gulf of
Kihnu
Põlva
Võru
Kura kurk
Rīga
Treimani
Ainaži
Rūjiena
Pskov
Ruhnusaar
Salacgrīva
Valka
Valga
Pechory
0       40 miles
0       40 kilometers
Limbaži
Valmiera
LATVIA

ESTONIA

The **Swedish Interlude** (1629-1710), a relative improvement for the Estonian peasantry, brought an end to the worst abuses of the feudal system. During this era,
Estonian-language schools and the **University of Tartu** were established. Tolerance
ended in 1721 when the **Peace of Nystad,** concluding the **Great Northern War,** handed
the Baltics to Peter the Great. Russian rule reinforced the power of the nobility and
serfs lost all rights until Estonian serfdom was finally abolished by **Tsar Alexander I**
in 1819, 45 years earlier than in Mother Russia herself. Even under Russian rule,
however, Estonia was a center of German culture. Benefitting from a wave of
Enlightenment reforms, Estonian peasants owned two-fifths of all private land by
the end of the 19th century, and the population was 97% literate. Following the coronation of reactionary **Tsar Alexander III** in 1881, however, Russia clamped down,
replacing the Baltic civil and criminal codes with Russian ones and making Russian
the language of instruction. This prompted an Estonian nationalistic backlash led
by **Konstantin Päts,** peaking in a failed bid for independence during the **Russian Revolution of 1905,** which was brutally repressed by the Tsarist authorities.

**WAR: WHAT IS IT GOOD FOR?** At the outbreak of **World War I,** Estonians were in a
difficult position; many were drafted into the Russian Army, but the Estonian-Ger-
man population sympathized with Prussia. The **Russian Revolution of 1917** intensified the Estonian struggle for independence. After occupation by Germany, Estonia
declared independence in 1918 but was subsequently taken by the Red Army. The
Estonians fought off the Soviets with British and Finnish help and embarked upon
self-rule. From 1919-33, a succession of some 20 coalition governments ruled.
Although the country prospered, the **Depression** allowed extreme right-wing parties,
led by veterans from the war for liberation, to gain public support, causing president **Konstantin Päts** to proclaim a state of emergency in 1934. Päts ruled as a benevolent dictator until calling and winning a referendum on his rule in 1938.

In 1940, as agreed to in the **Nazi-Soviet Non-Aggression Pact,** Estonia was occupied
by the Soviets. Päts and other Estonian leaders, as well as a significant portion of
the Estonian population, were arrested, deported, or killed. Soon after, **Hitler**
reneged on the pact and Germany re-took the country, remaining from 1941 to
1944. As the Red Army slowly pushed the Nazis out, thousands of Estonians fled to
Germany or Sweden; thousands more died at sea trying to escape.

The 1950s saw extreme repression and Russification under **Soviet rule,** when internal purges removed the few native Estonians in the ruling elite. *Glasnost* and *perestroika* eventually allowed enough breathing room for an Estonian political renaissance. In 1988, the **Popular Front** emerged in opposition to the Communist government, pushing a resolution on independence through the Estonian legislature. Nationalists won a legislative majority in the 1990 elections and successfully declared independence after the failed 1991 coup in the Soviet Union. In 1992 the newly-independent nation adopted a new constitution and held free elections, with **Lennart Meri** winning the presidency.

# POLITICS

Estonia today is a parliamentary democracy, with a much weaker presidency than most other post-Soviet states. The 1992 general election, the first following Estonia's declaration of independence, saw the rejection of the government of **Edgar Savisaar,** who had founded the Popular Front in the twilight of Soviet rule. Savisaar's regime was replaced by a coalition of parties committed to radical economic reform, a trend which has continued to the present day. The government has taken important steps to remove the obstacles to economic development left over from the Soviet planned economy, privatizing industry and lowering trade barriers. These measures, along with the constitutionally mandated balanced budget, have made Estonia the darling of many Western investors, but the hardships of transition to the free market led voters to install a new center-left coalition in 1995. The new regime was quickly toppled by charges of corruption, however, and replaced by a succession of similarly short-lived alliances. None of these fundamentally altered the economic course of the country. The most recent elections in 1999 brought yet another coalition government to power, this time composed of three center-right parties: **Pro Patria, the Reform Party,** and the **Moderates. Under President Lennart Meri** and **Prime Minister Mart Laar** the government has made **NATO** and **EU** accession its top priorities, with the former goal hoped for by 2002 and the latter by 2003.

Relations with **Russia** remain troubled, largely due to Estonia's treatment of its nearly 30% Russian minority. Following independence in 1991, the government imposed a number of policies designed to promote Estonian language and culture, denying citizenship to those unable to speak Estonian, including many Russians. Such discriminatory practice brought pressure on the Estonian government, both from Russia and from the European Union, and in 1998 citizenship was automatically extended to the children of Russian speakers born in Estonia.

President Meri will have to step down at the end of his second term in 2001, but his successor in the largely honorary post is not expected to make major policy changes—most of the president's power lies in influence over the appointment administrators such as the governor of the central bank.

| NATIONAL HOLIDAYS IN 2001 | |
| --- | --- |
| **JANUARY 1** New Year's | **JUNE 23** Victory Day |
| **FEBRUARY 24** Independence Day | **JUNE 24** Jaanipäev (St. John's Day, Mid-summer) |
| **APRIL 13** Good Friday | |
| **APRIL 15** Catholic Easter | **AUGUST 20** Restoration of Independence |
| **MAY 1** Spring Day | |
| **JUNE 3** Pentecost | **DECEMBER 25-6** Christmas |

# CULTURE
## LITERATURE

**EARLY LITERATURE.** The oldest surviving Estonian-language book is a Lutheran Catechism from 1535. Most of the literature published through the 18th century was religious. The most notable publication of this period was **Anton Thor Helle's** 1739 translation of the Bible, which created a common Estonian language based on the northern dialect. Helle's work heralded the **Estophile period** (1750-1840), which produced lyric poetry rooted in national folktales and Finnish epics. Folklore also provided the basis for **Friedrich Reinhold Kreutzwald's** *Kalevipoeg* (1857-61). Kreutzwald's 19,023-line epic described the conquests of *Kalevipoeg* (Kalev's son), mythical ruler of Estonia, ending with his death at the hands of invaders. This tale became the rallying point of Estonian national rebirth in the Romantic period.

**MY GENERATION.** Deepening class barriers throughout the 1800s shifted the intelligentsia's attention from national problems to social ones. Toward the end of the century, the Neo-Romantic nationalist **Noor-Eesti** (Young Estonia) movement appeared. Led by the poet **Gustav Suits** and the writer **Friedebert Tuglas**, the writers of the movement focused on literary form in creating works unmatched in emotional force. Suits devised the group's slogan: "More European culture! Be Estonians but remain Europeans!"

The interwar years saw the development of tragic poetry haunted by visions of human suffering and war. **Anton Tammsaare's** prose evolved from the Noor-Eesti approach toward Realism, and his *Truth and Justice* (*Tõde ja õigus*, 1926-33), which documents the development of the Estonian nation in the guise of a family chronicle, is essential to the Estonian canon. The resurgence of Realism, however, did not dampen the Estonian literati's interest in mysticism, as **Marie Under's** earthy love sonnets gained popularity in the 1930s. The strictures of **Socialist Realism** under Soviet rule sent many authors abroad or into temporary exile in Siberia, but creativity blossomed once more under Khrushchev's thaw in the early 1960s. This period saw the introduction of modernistic imagery to Estonian poetry by **Artur Alliksaar** and the grotesquerie of **Juhan Viiding**. Later, **Jaan Kross** managed to criticize the realities of Soviet life in *The Tsar's Madman* (1978). In the same year, **Aimée Beekman** addressed women's plight in *The Possibility of Choice*.

## VISUAL ARTS

Pagan sculptors produced animal figures; some art from the transition to Christianity incorporates both Christian and pagan symbols. During the Middle Ages much of the art was imported from France or Germany, but the Renaissance saw the emergence of Estonian artists. Among baroque artists woodcarvers **Elert Thiele** and **Christian Ackermann** are acknowledged masters, the former for the 1667 Tallinn Town Hall Frieze (see **Sights**, p. 288) and the latter for his ornate altars. Not until 1803 was the first art school in Estonia, the drawing school at Tartu University, founded.

The first nationally conscious Estonian art emerged at the close of the 19th century with painters **Johann Köler** and **Amandus Adamson** and sculptor **August Weizenberg**. Realism was initially dominant, but with the turn of the century artists began to turn to symbolism and mysticism. By the time of the *Noor-Eesti* movement **expressionism** and **symbolism** were dominant. The neo-impressionist paintings of **Konrad Mägi** and the landscapes of **Nikolai Triik** moved increasingly toward abstraction. The later painting of the 1920s and 1930s was heavily influenced by European trends including cubism and the principles of the German *Bauhaus*.

Visual art suffered in solidarity with its comrade literature under Soviet rule. Those artists lucky enough to escape abroad frequently expressed either extreme pessimism or painful longing for Estonia. With the **thaw** in the 1960s art emerged once more, albeit in fragmented form, with a variety of "isms" battling for aesthetic supremacy in a fight to the finish. The 1970s and 1980s saw several Estonians, including **Taevo Gans**, achieve recognition in the design of ceramics and jewelry.

ESTONIA

# RELIGION

The first Christian missionaries reached Estonia in the 11th century, but the population was not widely converted to the Roman Catholic faith until the early 13th century. With the reformation in the 1520s Catholicism declined and Estonian became the language of worship. With the annexation of Estonia by Russia following the Northern War of 1700-1721, though, Eastern Orthodoxy began to gain converts; eventually followers of the Orthodox church grew to 20% of the population. By the first half of the 20th century Lutheranism had become the dominant faith, claiming 80% of the population as adherents. Under later Soviet occupation religious practice was discouraged, but since independence the Lutheran faith has grown in strength. Small Catholic and Orthodox communities still practice, the former bolstered by the visit, in September 1993, of Pope John Paul II.

# FOOD AND DRINK

Estonia's cuisine used to be characterized by the same assortment of drab sausages and cold fried potatoes that plagues much of the former USSR. Things have since changed for the better. While schnitzel (a breaded and fried pork fillet) still figures prominently on nearly every menu, dishes like salads, pasta, pizza, curries and more innovative meat preparation can now be had. Estonian specialties include the typical Baltic *seljanka* meat stew and *pelmenid* dumplings, plus smoked salmon and trout. Pancakes with cheese curd and berries are a delicious and common dessert option. Bread is usually dark and dense. If you visit the islands, try picking up some *Hiumaa leib;* a loaf of this black bread easily weighs a kilo. Food tends to be fried and doused with sour cream. *Õlu* (beer) is the national drink in Estonia for good reason—not only is it inexpensive, but it's delicious and high-quality. The national brand *Saku* is excellent, as is the darker *Saku Tume.* Local brews, like *Saaremaa* in Kuressaare, can be volatile. The Estonian brand of carbonated mineral water, *Värska*, is particularly salty.

# CUSTOMS AND ETIQUETTE

Businesses take hour-long **breaks** at noon, 1pm, or 2pm, and most are closed on Sunday. No one **tips** in Estonia, although a service charge might be included in the bill. Estonian fashion is an interesting blend of cutting edge Scandinavian fashion and 1980s Soviet throwbacks. Sneaker-wearers be prepared: women dress to kill and almost exclusively wear heels. **Smoking** is common, except at transport stations, as is **spitting. Women** traveling alone are a rarity, so expect curious glances. **Homosexuality** is legal in Estonia, but public displays are not socially accepted, even in bigger cities. Much of the late-night entertainment in cities and resort towns caters to *mafiosi* and the like, although not as predominately as in the rest of the former USSR.

# LANGUAGE

Estonians speak the best **English** in the Baltic states; most young people know at least a few phrases. Many also know **Finnish** or **Swedish,** but **German** is more common among the older set and in resort towns like Pärnu, Saaremaa, and Tartu. **Russian** used to be mandatory, but Estonians in secluded areas are likely to have forgotten much of it since few, if any, Russians live there. Estonians are usually averse to using Russian. Always try English first, making it clear you're not Russian, and then switch to Russian if necessary. The clear exception to this is along the border in eastern Estonia, where many prefer it to **Estonian.** Estonian is a Finno-Ugric language, with 14 cases and all sorts of letters. You won't master it in a day, but basic words help: *bussijaam* (BUSS-ee-yahm; bus station); *raudteejaam* (ROWD-tee-yahm; train station); *avatud* (AH-vah-tuht; open); and *suletud* (SUH-leh-tuht; closed). Take offense if you're called a *pudru pää:* it means porridge head. For common words and phrases, see **Glossary,** p. 282 and **Phrasebook,** p. 283.

# ADDITIONAL READING

*Estonia and the Estonians*, by Toivo U. Raun, offers a comprehensive history of the country. Jaan Kross's *The Tsar's Madman*, a historical novel about a 19th-century Baltic nobleman, is arguably the best Estonian fiction available. See **Lithuania: Additional Reading** (p. 408) for a good survey of Baltic history.

# TRAVELING ESSENTIALS

Citizens of Australia, Ireland, New Zealand, and the US can visit Estonia visa-free for up to 90 days in a six month period, UK citizens for 180 days in a year. Canadians and South Africans must obtain a visa at the nearest Honorary Consulate. You may also use a Latvian or Lithuanian visa to enter the country. To apply for a visa include a passport, a photo, an invitation or letter from a contact in Estonia, proof of solvency (such as plane tickets or hotel reservations), and a health insurance policy valid in Estonia with a coverage of at least 160,000 EEK for the entire duration your stay. Single-entry visas (valid for 30 days) are US$13, multiple-entry (length of validity varies with consulate) US$61. Single-entry transit visas (72hr.) cost US$13, double-transit (72hr.) US$19. Single-entry urgent visas (issued within 48hr.) are US$25. Although Estonian visas are available at the border, it is cheaper and more convenient to arrange them beforehand; it is also possible to use a Latvian or Lithuanian visa to enter. To obtain a visa extension, contact the visa department of the Immigration Department, Lai 40. For further visa information consult the Estonian Ministry of Foreign Affairs website at www.vm.ee. Note that prices vary monthly with exchange rate. There is no fee for crossing an Estonian border. The easiest means of entering or exiting Estonia is to take a direct bus or train from Tallinn to Moscow, St. Petersburg, or Riga. Estonian customs officials are quite slow; expect several hours of delay when crossing the border.

# TRANSPORTATION

Entering Estonia is easiest by plane or boat. Either way will save you hassles with customs officials, and traveling by ferry from Finland or Sweden is extremely cheap (200-300EEK). On the islands, bike (100EEK per day) and car (350-900EEK per day) rentals are an excellent means of exploration.

**BY PLANE.** Several international airlines offer flights to Tallinn. For more information, see **Tallinn: Practical Information,** p. 285.

**BY BOAT.** It is easiest to enter by ferry from **Helsinki** or **Sweden,** as several ferry lines connect to Tallinn's harbor (☎631 85 50); for options, see **Tallinn: Practical Information,** p. 286. For contact details of ferry companies across the Baltic in Helsinki, see **Helsinki,** p. 810.

**BY TRAIN.** If you're coming from another Baltic state or **Russia,** trains may be even cheaper than ferries, but expect more red tape when crossing the border.

**BY BUS.** Domestically, buses are the best means of transport, as they are much cheaper and more efficient than trains. It's even possible to ride buses direct from the mainland to island towns (via ferry) for less than the price of the ferry ride. During the school year (Sept.-June 25), students receive half-price bus tickets.

**BY TAXI.** Taxis are a safe means of transportation. The average rate is 7EEK per km, compared to 0.4EEK per km for buses.

**BY THUMB.** *Let's Go* does not recommend hitchhiking. Those who choose to do so should stretch out an open hand. Or, call the agency **Vismutar** (☎8290 01 050) and leave your name, number, destination, and time of departure. The agency will match you with a driver going your way and contact you no less than 24hr. before you leave. Although drivers are not paid, they have incentive in the form of a 500EEK lottery at the end of each month.

# GLOSSARY

| ENGLISH | ESTONIAN | PRONOUNCE |
|---|---|---|
| one | üks | euwks |
| two | kaks | kahks |
| three | kolm | kõlm |
| four | neli | NEH-lee |
| five | viis | veese |
| six | kuus | koose |
| seven | seitse | SAYT-seh |
| eight | kaheksa | KAH-heks-ah |
| nine | üheksa | t'EUW-eks-ah |
| ten | kümme | KEUW-meh |
| twenty | kakskümmend | KAHKS-keuwm-mehnd |
| thirty | kolmkümmend | KÕLM-keuwm-mend |
| forty | nelikümmend | NEH-lee-keuwm-mend |
| fifty | viiskümmend | VEES-keuwm-mend |
| sixty | kuuskümmend | KOOS-keuwm-mend |
| seventy | seitsekümmend | SAYTS-seh-keuwm-mend |
| eighty | kaheksakümmend | KAH-hek-sah-keuwm-mend |
| ninety | üheksakümmend | EUW-hek-sah-keuwm-mend |
| one hundred | sada | SA-da |
| one thousand | tuhat | TU-hat |
| Monday | esmaspäev | EHS-mahs-pav |
| Tuesday | teisipäev | TAYS-ee-pav |
| Wednesday | kolmapäev | KOHL-mah-pav |
| Thursday | neljapäev | NEHL-yah-pav |
| Friday | reede | REE-eed |
| Saturday | laupäev | LAH-oo-pav |
| Sunday | pühapäev | PEUW-hah-pav |
| a day | üks päev | EUWKS pav |
| a few days | mõni päev | MEUH-nee pav |
| a week | üks nädal | euwks na-DAHL |
| morning | hommik | HÕM-meek |
| afternoon | õhtupool | EUH-too-põõl |
| evening | õhtu | EUH-too |
| today | täna | TA-nah |
| tomorrow | homme | HÕM-me |
| spring | kevad | keh-VAHD |
| summer | suvi | SOO-vee |
| fall | sügis | SEUW-gees |
| winter | talv | tahlv |
| hot | kuum | koom |
| cold | külm | keuwlm |
| single room | üheline | EUW-heh-LEE-neh |
| double room | kaheline | KAH-heh-LEE-ne |
| with shower | duššiga | DOOSH-ee-gah |
| pharmacy | apteek | ahp-TEEK |

| ENGLISH | ESTONIAN | PRONOUNCE |
|---|---|---|
| post office | post kontor | põst KÕN-tör |
| stamp | mark | mahrk |
| airmail | lennu post | LEHN-noo põst |
| departs | väljub | VAL-yoob |
| arrives | saabub | SAH-boob |
| one-way ticket | üheotsa piletit | EUW-heh-OHT-sah PEE-leh-teet |
| round-trip | edasi-tagasi piletit | Eh-dah-see-TAH-gah-see PEE-leh-teet |
| luggage | bagaaž | BAH-gahzh |
| train | rong | rõng |
| bus | buss | boos |
| airport | lennujaam | LEHN-noo-yahm |
| station | jaam | yahm |
| ticket | pilet | PEE-leht |
| grocery | toidupood | TÕY-doo-PÕÕD |
| breakfast | hommiku söök | HÕM-mee-koo seuhk |
| lunch | lõunasöök | LEUH-nah-seuhk |
| dinner | õhtusöök | EUH-too-seuhk |
| menu | menüü | MEH-neuh |
| bread | leib | LAY-eeb |
| vegetables | juurvili | YOOR-vee-lee |
| beef | loomaliha | LÕÕ-mah-lee-hah |
| chicken | kana | kah-nah |
| pork | sealiha | seh-ah-LEE-hah |
| fish | kala | kah-lah |
| coffee | kohv | kohv |
| milk | piim | peem |
| beer | õlu | elu |
| sugar | suhkur | SOOH-koor |
| eggs | munad | MOO-nahd |
| holiday | püha | PEUW-hah |
| open | avatud/lahti | AH-vah-tood/LAH-tee |
| closed | suletud/kinni | SOO-leh-tood/KEEN-nee |
| bank | pank | pahnk |
| police | politsei | POH-leet-say |
| exchange | valuutavahetus | vah-loo-TAH-vah-heh-toos |
| toilet | tualett | twa-LET |
| square | plats/väljak | plahts/val-yahk |
| castle | loss | lõs |
| church | kirik | kee-reek |

| ENGLISH | ESTONIAN | PRONOUNCE |
| --- | --- | --- |
| tower | torn | tõrn |
| market | turg | toorg |
| on the left | vasakul | VAH-sah-keul |

| ENGLISH | ESTONIAN | PRONOUNCE |
| --- | --- | --- |
| passport | pass | pahs |
| bakery | pagar | PAH-gahr |
| on the right | paremal | PAH-reh-mahl |

## PHRASEBOOK

| ENGLISH | ESTONIAN | PRONOUNCIATION |
| --- | --- | --- |
| Yes/no | Jaa/Ei | jah/ay |
| Please/You're welcome | Palun | PAH-loon |
| Thank you | Tänan | TA-nahn |
| Hello | Tere | TEH-reh |
| Good-bye | Head aega | heh-ahd EYE-gah |
| Good morning | Tere hommikust | TEH-re höm-mee-KOOST |
| Good evening | Head õhtut | heh-ahd EUW-toot |
| Good night | Head ööd | heh-ahd euwd |
| Sorry/Excuse me | Vabandage | vah-bahn-DAHG-eh |
| Help! | Appi! | AHP-pee |
| When? | Millal? | meel-LAL |
| Where is...? | Kus on...? | koos õn |
| I'd like to go to... | Soovin minna... | söö-veen MEEN-nah |
| How much does this cost? | Kui palju? | kwee PAHL-yoo |
| Do you have...? | Kas teil on...? | kahs tayl õn |
| Do you speak English? | Kas te räägite inglise keelt? | kahs teh raa-GEE-teh een-GLEE-seh kehlt |
| I don't understand. | Ma ei saa aru. | mah ay sah AH-roo |
| I don't speak Estonian | Ma ei räägi Eesti keelt. | mah ay RAA-gee ehs-tee kehlt |
| Please write it down. | Palun kirjutage maha. | PAH-loon KEER-yoo-TAH-geh MAH-hah |
| Speak a little slower, please. | Palun rääkige natuge aeglasemalt. | PAH-loon RAA-kee-geh nah-too-geh EYE-glah-seh-mahlt |
| I'd like to order... | Ma sooviksin... | mah SOO-veek-seen |
| I'd like to pay/We'd like to pay. | Ma sooviksin maksta | ma SOO-veek-seen MAHKS-tah |
| I think you made a mistake... | Arvan et eksisite... | AHR-vahn eht EHK-see-see-teh |
| I'd like to make a reservation. | Sooviksin broneerida tuba. | SÕÕ-veek-seen BRÕ-neh-ree-dah too-bah |
| Do you have a vacancy? | Kas teil on vaba tuba? | kahs TAYL õn vah-bah TOO-bah |
| I'd like a room. | Ma sooviksin tuba. | mah SOO-vik-sin TUH-bah |
| May I see the room? | Kas võiksin tuba näha? | kahs VEUWK-seen too-bah NA-hah |
| No, I don't like it. | Ei meeldi/Ei sobi. | ay mehl-dee/ay sõ-bee |
| Yes, I'll take it. | Jaa, võtan. | Yah, VEUW-tahn. |
| Will you tell me when to get off? | Palun öelge kus ma pean väljuma? | PAH-loon EULL-geh koos mah peh-ahn VAL-yoo-mah |
| Does this train/bus go to...? | Kas see rong/buss läheb...? | kahs seh rõng/boos LA-hehb |
| I want a ticket to... | Ma sooviksin ühte piletit... | mah SOO-veek-seen EWKH-teh PEE-leh-teet |
| How long is the trip? | Kui pikk on reis? | koo-wee peek õn rays |
| When is the first/next/last train to... | Millal lahkub esimine/järgmine/viimane et minna... | meel-lahl lah-koob EHS-ee-mee-neh/JARG-mee-neh/VEE-mah-neh eht meen-nah |
| Where is the bathroom/nearest telephone booth/center of town? | Kus on tualett/kõige lähedam telefon/kesklinn? | koos õn twa-LEHT/keuw-geh LA-heh-dahm teh-leh-fõn/kehs-kleen |
| I've lost my... | Olen kaotanud... | õ-lehn KAÕ-tah-nood |
| Would you like to dance? | Soovite tansida? | soo-vee-teh tahn-SEE-dah |
| Go away. | Minge ära. | MEEN-geh A-ra |

ESTONIA

# TOURIST SERVICES AND MONEY

| CURRENCY | | |
|---|---|---|
| US$1 = 17EEK (ESTONIAN KROONS) | 10EEK = US$0.57 | |
| CDN$1 = 12EEK | 10EEK = CDN$0.85 | |
| UK£1 = 25EEK | 10EEK = UK£0.39 | |
| IR£1 = 20EK | 10EEK = IR£0.50 | |
| AUS$1 = 10EEK | 10EEK = AUS$9.90 | |
| NZ$1 = 7.50EEK | 10EEK = NZ$1.30 | |
| SAR 1 = 2.50EEK | 10EEK = SAR 4.00 | |
| DM 1 = 8.00EEK | 10EEK = DM 1.25 | |

Unlike most of the former Soviet Union, Estonia is grasping the importance of tourist services; most small towns now offer city maps, while larger towns and cities may have well-equipped tourist offices with literature and English-speaking staff. Generally, such offices are quite knowledgeable about accommodations and the local scene, but less so about transportation. Booths marked with a green "i" sell maps and give away brochures.

The unit of currency is the **kroon** (EEK), divided into 100 **senti** and tied to the Deutschmark. **Inflation** is around 3%, so prices and exchange rates should be relatively stable. The biggest and most stable banks in the country, Hansapank and Eesti Ühispank, cash **traveler's checks.** Many restaurants and shops take credit cards, mostly **MasterCard** and **Visa. ATMs** are common in all towns covered in *Let's Go.* When purchasing items in a shop, cash is not usually passed between hands, but is instead put in a small tray on counter tops.

# HEALTH AND SAFETY

Public **toilets** (tasuline), marked by "N" or a triangle pointing up for women and "M" or a triangle pointing down for men, usually cost 3EEK and include a very limited supply of toilet paper. **Medical services** for foreigners are few and far between, and most often you'll have to pay cash. **Pharmacies** (look for the "Apteek" sign) are usually Scandinavian chains, and as a result, are well-equipped and modern. They only sell medicine; try grocery stores for toiletries. While Tallinn water is generally OK, it never hurts to drink **bottled water,** especially in the rest of the country. While the petty **crime** rate is low, **women** should avoid going to bars and clubs alone or walking alone at night, even during white nights. **Minorities** in Estonia are few; they receive stares but generally experience little discrimination. As always, for English-speaking help in an emergency, contact your embassy.

# ACCOMMODATIONS AND CAMPING

Each **tourist office** will have listings and prices of accommodations in its town and can often arrange a bed for visitors. There is little distinction between hotels, hostels, and guesthouses; some upscale hotels still have hall toilets and showers. The word *võõrastemaja* (guesthouse) in a place's name usually implies that it's less expensive, but not always. Many hotels provide **laundry** services for an extra charge. Some hostels are part of larger hotels, so be sure to ask for the cheaper hostel rooms. Rooms are almost always 200EEK per night, though the range is 80-450EEK. **Homestays** are common and cheap, but not as cheap as the cheapest hostels. For info on HI hostels around Estonia, contact the **Estonian Youth Hostel Association,** Tatari (☎646 14 57; fax 646 15 95; puhkemajad@online.ee).

# KEEPING IN TOUCH

**Telephone calls** are paid for with digital cards, available at any bank or newspaper kiosk. Cards come in denominations of 30, 50, and 100EEK. **International access numbers** include: **AT&T Direct** ☎80 08 00 10 01; **BT Direct** ☎800 800 10441; and **Canada**

**Direct** ☎ 800 800 1011. **International calls** can be made at post offices. Calls to the Baltic states cost 5EEK per min., to Russia 10EEK. Phoning the US is expensive: US$1-4 per min. When calling Estonia, preface the phone code with an 8.

**PHONE MAYHEM** The phone system in Estonia proves that, indeed, the universe tends toward chaos. To call Tallinn from outside Estonia on the digital system, first dial 372 (note that all calls within Estonia must be prefaced by the 8 which we list in parentheses in front of city codes.) No other cities require a special code to be dialed first. To call a cell phone anywhere in the country, first dial 37 25. Eesti Telefon's information number is ☎ 07. For help, call the English-speaking Ekspress Hotline at ☎ 0 11 88.

**Mail** can be received general delivery through **Poste Restante**. Address envelope as follows: Katie (First name) HEIKKINEN (LAST NAME), POSTE RESTANTE, Narva mnt. 1 (Post office address), Tallinn (City) 0001 (Postal code), ESTONIA. An airmail letter costs 5.50EEK to Europe and the CIS, and 7EEK to the rest of the world. Postcards are only 5.20EEK to Europe and the CIS or 6.70EEK everywhere else. **Internet access** is becoming more widespread, and averages 30-60EEK per hour. English-language **books** and **newspapers** are relatively easy to find in Estonia, especially in Tallinn. The English-language *City Paper—The Baltic States*, available at hotels, kiosks, and tourist info points (US$1.50), covers all three Baltic countries. The info-packed *Tallinn in Your Pocket* has detailed information and entertainment listings for Tallinn and Tartu.

# TALLINN ☎ (8)2

As one approaches Tallinn (pop. 430,000) by ferry, German spires, Danish towers, and Russian minarets loom alongside the industrial cranes in the process of restoring them. The hip new shops, bars, and cosmopolitan youth, as well as the modern glass structures downtown, complement the medieval serenity tourists have long come to see. Sadly, the ubiquitous mobile phones and BMWs of the pastel Old Town cannot efface Tallinn's drab outskirts, which remain as if frozen under Soviet rule. In places like Kopli and Kadrioru Park, capitalism has brought nothing but increased crime. Nevertheless, when the sun sets over the white beaches that curve around the bay and the thin church steeples that pierce the pink evening sky, any doubt of the beauty and dynamism of that first view of Tallinn fades.

## ■ ORIENTATION

Tallinn's **Vanalinn** (Old Town) is an egg-shaped maze ringed by five main streets, all running into one another: Rannamäe tee, Mere pst., Pärnu mnt., Kaarli pst., and Toompuiestee. The best entrance to Vanalinn is through the 15th-century **Viru ärarad**, the main gate in the city wall. **Hotel Viru** is Tallinn's central landmark. The old town has two sections: **All-linn**, or Lower Town, which is the larger, busier section, and **Toompea**, a rocky, fortified hill. **Raekoja plats** (Town Hall Square) is the scenic center of the Old Town.

## ■ INTERCITY TRANSPORTATION

**Flights: Tallinn Airport,** Lennujaama 2 (☎ 621 10 92; www.tallinn-airport.ee). Estonian Air, Finnair, Lufthansa, and SAS have flights to Tallinn. Bus #2 runs approx. every 20min. to Hotel Viru, Viru väljak 4.

**Trains:** Toompuiestee 35 (☎ 615 68 51). Trams #1 and 2 travel between the station and Hotel Viru. International trains are modern, with English announcements. Get international tickets on the 2nd floor and domestic tickets on the ground floor. English spoken at info desk but not in ticket booths. To: **Riga, LAT** (9hr., 155EEK); **St. Petersburg, RUS** (10hr., 1 per day, 155EEK); and **Warsaw, POL** (27hr., 1 per day, 519EEK).

**Buses:** Lastekodu 46 (☎601 03 86), just south of Tartu mnt. and 1.5km southeast of Vanalinn. Trams #2 and 4 and bus #22 connect the bus station to the city center. Catch trams at the Vero stop on the side of Hotel Vero; get off at Bussijaam. To: **Riga, LAT** (5-6hr., 4 per day, 180EEK); **St. Petersburg, RUS** (10hr., 4 per day, 200EEK); and **Vilnius, LIT** (10hr., 2 per day, 300EEK).

**Ferries:** (☎631 85 50.) At the end of Sadama, 15min. from the center. 4 different terminals, specific to each company. Boats, hydrofoils, and catamarans cross to **Helsinki.**

**Eckerö Line,** Terminal B (☎631 86 06; fax 631 86 61). 3½hr.; 1 per day; 205EEK, students 165EEK.

**Nordic Jet Line,** Terminal C (☎613 70 00; fax 613 72 22). 1½hr.; 6 per day; 430-510EEK.

**Silja Line,** Terminal D (☎611 66 61; fax 611 66 65). 1½hr.; 4 per day; 260-840EEK.

**Tallinn Express,** Terminal D (☎632 83 20, fax 631 83 25). 1½hr.; 3 per day; 225-775EEK.

# █ LOCAL TRANSPORTATION

**Public Transportation: Buses, trams,** and **trolley-buses** cover the entire metropolitan area; 6am-midnight. Tickets (talong; 10EEK) can be bought from kiosks around town. Validate them in the metal boxes on board. 460EEK fine for riding without ticket.

**Taxis:** ☎612 00 00, 655 60 00, 644 24 42, or 627 55 55. Check the cab for a meter and expect to pay 4-6EEK per km.

**Car Rental: Europcar,** Magdaleena 3 (☎650 25 59, airport office ☎638 80 31; fax 650 25 60), is cheaper than others. Reserve 2 days ahead. Open M-F 9am-5pm.

# ▮ PRACTICAL INFORMATION

## TOURIST AND FINANCIAL SERVICES

**Tourist Office: Tourist Information Center** (TIC), Raekoja pl. 10 (☎645 7777; fax 645 7778; turismiinfo@tallinnlv.ee; http://tourism.tallin.ee). Across from the town hall. Sells and gives out brochures and maps. *Tallinn In Your Pocket* 16EEK. Open M-F 9am-6pm, Sa-Su 10am-4pm. Branch on Sadama 25 (☎485 73 49; fax 485 56 72), at the harbor (Terminal A). Open daily 9am-6pm. A **Tallinn Card,** available at either location, entitles the holder to a city tour, unlimited public transport, and entry to most museums, but at a steep price: 1 day 195EEK, 2 days 270EEK, 3 days 325EEK.

**Tours: CDS Reisid,** Jaama 2 (☎611 43 59; fax 631 36 66). English walking tours of Vanalinn starting at Raekoja plats 17 (1½hr., daily May 15-Sept. 15 at 2pm, 75EEK). Office open M-F 10am-8pm, Sa 10am-6pm, Su 10am-2pm. **REISI Ekspert,** Roosikrantsi 17 (☎445 276; fax 442 258), gives tours daily at 9:30am, noon, and 2:30pm. Buy tickets (150EEK) at Hotel Viru.

**Embassies: Canada,** Toomkooli 13 (☎627 33 11; fax 627 33 12). Open M, W, and F 9am-noon. **Latvia,** Tõnismägi 10 (☎646 13 13; fax 631 13 66). Open M-F 10am-noon. **Russia,** Pikk 19 (☎646 41 69; fax 646 41 78). Open M-F 9am-noon. **UK,** Wismari 6, (☎667 47 00; fax 667 47 23). **US,** Kentmanni 20 (☎631 20 21; fax 631 20 25). Open M-F 9am-noon, 2-5pm.

**Currency Exchange: Eesti Ühispank,** in the same building as the main post office.

**ATMs:** Everywhere.

**American Express:** Suur-Karja 15, 10140. (☎626 62 62; fax 626 62 12; sales@estravel.ee). Books hotels and tours, sells airline, ferry, and rail tickets, and arranges visas to former Soviet republics and Russia. Open summer M-F 9am-6pm, Sa 10am-5pm; off-season M-F 9am-6pm.

## LOCAL AND EMERGENCY SERVICES

**Luggage Storage:** 4-12EEK per day at the bus station. Open daily 6:30-11am, 11:30am-7:30pm, and 8-10:30pm.

**International Bookstore:** Viruvärava Raamatu Kauplus (☎631 31 95), centrally located on Viru 23, has a small collection. Open M-F 10am-7pm, Sa 10am-6pm, Su

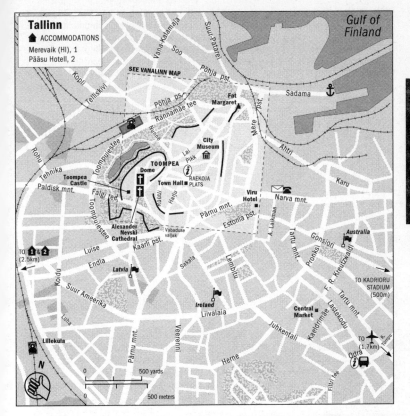

Tallinn

ACCOMMODATIONS
Merevaik (HI), 1
Pääsu Hotell, 2

11am-3pm. For a great selection, try **Allecto**, Juhkentali 32-5, a bit far from the center near the bus station. Open M-F 9am-6pm, Sa 11am-4pm.

**Laundromat: Sauberland,** Maakri 23 (☎646 65 81). Self-service 55EEK per load.

**Pharmacy: Tallinna Linnaapteek,** Pärnu mnt. 10 (☎644 22 62). Open M-F 8am-8pm, Sa 9am-4pm, Su 10am-3pm.

**Hospital: Tallinn Central Hospital,** Ravi 18 (info ☎620 70 10).

**Telephones:** Narva mnt. 1 (☎640 26 66). All over the city; buy a phone card (30, 50, or 100EEK) from any convenience store or kiosk. For instructions on how to place a phone call to and from Tallinn, see **Keeping in Touch,** p. 284.

**Internet Access: Cafe ENTER,** Gonsiori 4 (☎626 73 67), is behind Hotel Viru. A funky cellar bar that serves drinks to sip in the neon glow of 20 computer screens. 60EEK per hr. Open daily 10am-midnight. The **National Library of Estonia,** Tõnismägi 2, is more tranquil but has fewer computers. 40EEK per hr.

**Post Office:** Narva mnt. 1, 2nd Floor (☎625 73 00), across from Hotel Viru. Open M-F 7:30am-8pm, Sa 8am-6pm.

**Postal code:** 0001.

# ▐ ACCOMMODATIONS

Tallinn's hostels fill quickly in summer; it's wise to book in advance. If you're in a bind, inquire at the information desk in the **bus station** about beds there (doubles 170EEK per person). **Rasastra**, Mere 4 (☎641 22 91), finds rooms in private homes in Tallinn, throughout the Baltics and in St. Petersburg from 149EEK per person. **CDS Reisid** (see **Tours,** p. 286) also arranges private rooms. Call ahead.

■ **Hostel Vana Tom** (The Barn; formerly Hotell Küün), Väike-Karja 1, 2nd fl. (☎/fax 631 32 52), in Vanalinn. From the train station, take the pass under Toompuis and follow Nunne through the park to Vanalinn. From the steepled end of the town hall in Raekoja plats, head down Vanaturu Kael. Take a right onto Vana Turg and a left onto Suur Karja, bearing left. The hostel is through an arch on your left. Unbeatable cleanliness and location in the heart of Old Town. Strip club on 3rd floor but noise doesn't carry. Towel rental 10EEK and next-day laundry service 50-75EEK. Reception 24hr. Dorms 195EEK; doubles with shared bath 550EEK. 15EEK off with HI.

**Hotell Gasthaus Esdlitall,** Dunkri 4, 2nd floor (☎631 37 55; fax 631 32 10). Head down Dunkri around the Town Hall on the far side of the steeple. Prime location, with colorful and clean private rooms. Breakfast 36EEK. Singles 450EEK; doubles 585EEK.

**Pääsu Hotell,** Sõpruse pst. 182 (☎52 00 34; fax 654 20 13), in Mustamäe. Take trolley bus #4 from the railway station or trolley bus #2, 3, or 9 from the center of town to the "Linnu tee" stop. Backtrack a bit, turn left on Linnu tee, then left again on Nirgi and follow the white signs with the pale blue swallow icon. Big, comfortable rooms, complete with cable TV and refrigerator. 2 rooms share a bath. Sauna 150EEK per hr. Singles 360EEK; doubles 460EEK; triples 540EEK. Breakfast included.

# ◖ FOOD

Restaurants in Vanalinn are becoming increasingly expensive as the kroon sinks and tourism surges. For cheaper, more casual fare, try eating at pubs or cafes, found around Old Town Square. **Stockman's,** on the corner of Livonia and A. Lauteri between Old Town and the bus station, is a mammoth Finnish department store-cum-supermarket. (Open M-F 10am-10pm, Sa-Su 10am-9pm). **Open-air markets** set up most days near Lastekodu 10.

**Irish Dubliner,** on Suur Karja next to the hostel, is a cheap pub serving a mix from Italian pasta to Indian curries. (Open M-Sa 11am until the last guest leaves, Su noon-1am.)

**Merevaikus,** Rahukohtu 5, on Patkuli vaateplats in Toompea. This cafe/restaurant has some of the best views of medieval Tallinn and the Baltic in Toompea. An ideal place to woo your sweetie or just plain relax. Crepes, salads, soups, and herring with potatoes, all 30-50EEK. Main dishes 75-100EEK. Open daily 11am-11pm.

**Eeslitall** (Donkey Stable), Dunkri 4/6 (☎631 37 55). There's been a restaurant in these halls since 1362. This one serves American and Balto-Russian cuisine. Main dishes around 140EEK. Pint of *Tartu au Coq* 25EEK. Call ahead for dinner in summer. Open Su-Th 11am-11pm, F-Sa 11am-1am. MC/Visa.

# ◖ SIGHTS

## ALL-LINN

The summer brings fun times to the Town Hall Square (Raekoja plats), as local troupes perform folk songs and dances while beer flows throughout the outdoor cafes. The 14th-century **town hall** is the oldest in Europe. (☎644 08 19. Open daily 9am-5pm. Guided tours 30EEK; call ahead.) From the square, head north on Mündi and turn right on Pühavaimu, where the 14th-century **Church of the Holy Ghost** houses a 15th-century bell tower and an intricate 17th-century wooden clock. (☎644 14 87. Open M-Sa 10am-4:30pm. Free music recitals M at 6pm.) **St. Olev Church** (Oleviste kirik), is the tallest church in town. From the Church of the Holy Ghost, turn left on Pühavaimu and right on Pikk; St. Olev will be near the end of Pikk on the left. The murals inside the adjoining chapel illustrate the architect's death: he fell from the tower. (Open M-F 10am-2pm.)

The Viru City Gate (Viru ärarad) is to the east of the square. Just inside the gate along Müürivahe, which runs north-south, a large sweater market sets up in summer; in winter, it moves to the flower stalls that line Viru. Walking toward the center from the gate on Viru, turn right on Vene to reach the **Dominican Cloister** (Dominiiklaste Klooster), Vene 16. Founded in 1246 as a missionary base, it's com-

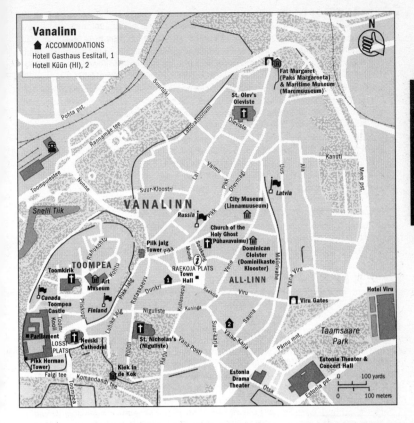

prised of a Gothic limestone courtyard, two Catholic churches, a windmill, stone carvings, and a granary. (☎515 54 89. Open daily 11am-7pm. 225EEK.)

To get to **St. Nicholas Church** (Niguliste kirik), at the south end of Vanalinn, take Dunkri from the southwest corner of the square, turn left on Rataskaevu and continue until you reach the church. With its mighty spire, St. Nicholas houses the ghoulish 1520 gravestone of Johannes Ballivi and anachronistically modern stained-glass windows. It also contains a museum of medieval art. (☎644 99 11. Open W-F 10am-6pm, Sa-Su 11:30-6pm. 15EEK.)

# TOOMPEA

The center of Toompea is **Castle Square** (Lossi pl.). From St. Nicholas Church, turn left onto Niguliste kirik, which turns into Lühike jalg. Uphill, Toompea leads to Castle Square. The **Alexander Nevsky Cathedral** in the center of the square was dominated by the Russian minarets of this cathedral, begun under Tsar Alexander III and finished just in time for the Bolshevik Revolution. A marble marker from 1910 recalls Peter the Great's 1710 victory over Sweden. (Open daily 8am-7pm. Services 9am and 6pm.) **Toompea Castle,** the present seat of the Estonian **Parliament** (riigikogu) stands on the square, but its doors are shut to prying eyes. Directly behind it, a fluttering Estonian flag tops **Tall Hermann** (Pikk Hermann), Tallinn's tallest tower and most impressive medieval fortification. To get to **Toomkirik,** head north from the square on Pilskopi. The 13th-century spires of this Lutheran Cathedral tower over Toompea. (Open T-Su 9am-6pm.) The three best views of the lower town from Toompea are at the end of Kohtu and at Patkuli vaate plats.

# 🏛 MUSEUMS

**City Museum** (Linnamuuseum), Vene 17 (☎644 18 29). The history of Tallinn, from its founding in 1219 until becoming the capital of the 1st republic, is condensed into the City Museum. Particular attention is paid to the brief period of independence from 1918-1940 (see **History**, p. 276). Open M and W-Su 10:30am-5:30pm. 5EEK.

**Maritime Museum** (Meremuuseum), Pikk 70 (☎641 41 12). At the northern end of Pikk. In the large, squat tower known as Fat Margaret (Paks Margareeta), this museum houses temporary exhibits on Tallinn's port history. Scale models of ships are set among nautical charts. Open W-Su 10am-6pm, final admission 5:30pm. 15EEK, students 7EEK.

**Theater and Music Museum** (Teatri-ja Muusikamuuseum; ☎644 21 32). On the 2nd street to the left from Viru Gate. Over 500 musical instruments, from rare pianos to the inventions of 19th-century farmboys. Open W-Su 10am-5:30pm. 10EEK.

**Peek in the Kitchen Tower** (Kiek in de Kök), Komandandi 2 (☎44 66 86). This 1475 tower presents a look at medieval Tallinn, complete with cannon-ball-embedded walls. Also miniature models of the old town wall and voyeuristic panoramas of 16th-century Tallinn homes. Open Tu-F 10:30am-5:30pm, Sa-Su 11am-4:30pm. 10EEK, students 5EEK.

**Art Museum** (Eesti Kunstimuuseum), Kiriku plats 1 (☎ 644 14 78). Displays Estonian art from the 19th century to the 1940s and shows how Estonia handled impressionism, realism, art deco, and other schools of art. Open W-Su 11am-6pm. 10EEK, students 5EEK.

# 🎵 ENTERTAINMENT

*Tallinn This Week*, free at the tourist office and hotels, lists performances. The premier theater in town, **Estonia Theater**, Estonia pst. 4, offers opera, ballet, musicals, and chamber music. (☎626 02 15; www.oopu.ee. Ticket office open daily noon-7pm.) **Eesti Kontsert**, Estonia pst. 4, has classical music nearly every night. (☎614 77 60; fax 614 77 69; www.concert.ee. Box office open M-F noon-7pm, Sa noon-5pm. Students 30EEK.) The **Church of the Holy Ghost** (see p. 288) holds performances by students of the Estonian Music Academy and Tallinn's conservatory. **St. Nicholas Church** (see p. 289) holds organ concerts and choir performances. (Recitals Sa-Su 4pm. Tickets available Tu 3-7:30pm, W 3-5:30pm, and Th 11:30am-5:30pm.) Check the athletic complex in Kadrioru Park for national **sports** events. Get tickets for international matches at the stadium gate (100-150EEK). On Sundays, Tallinn converges on the **beach** at Pirita (buses #1, 1a, 8 or 114) on the city's outskirts.

# 🎐 FESTIVALS

Tallinn loves music festivals. During the **Old Town Days,** usually the last week of May into the first week of June, the city hosts open-air concerts throughout Vanalinn, as well as fashion shows, singing, and skits at Raekoja pl. The first week of July provides just one more excuse (as if one were necessary) to loose the taps in Tallinn bars, as **Beersummer** celebrates all things hoppy. During the **Organ Festival** (Aug. 1-10), churches around town host recitals. Tickets are sold at St. Nicholas Church (see p. 289). The **National Song Festival**, which occurs once every four to five years (next in 2004), proved instrumental to Estonia's drive to independence in the "singing revolution" of 1990-91.

# 🎵 NIGHTLIFE

Bars have sprouted up on almost every street of Vanalinn; most have a loyal clientele, although all but the most popular empty by 11pm as the local scene moves to the nightclubs. While young mafiosos dominate some, expats and tourists are also carving out a niche. In an effort to keep their clientele suave and sophisticated, many establishments enforce an age minimum of 21-23, applied mostly to men. Barhopping with older friends should help admission.

**STONE-COLD** Estonian folklore, as recorded by Friedrich Reinhold Kreutzwald in the national epic *Kalevipoeg*, has an interesting take on the origins of Toompea. As the story goes, the eponymous young protagonist was out hunting with his brothers when a Finnish sorcerer, already jilted once by the lad's mother Linda, pounced on her and dragged her off to his northern fortress to make his solitude a little less solitary. Linda's cries for help went unheeded until the magician had lugged her nearly to the shores of the Baltic, when the forces of nature—never sympathetic in Estonia—intervened. In a twist of fate that can only leave feminists shaking their heads, a bolt of lightning stunned the villain but also turned his ill-gotten prize into the rocky mound where the Estonian Parliament now stands.

**Nimeta Baar** (The Pub with No Name), Suur-Karja 4 (☎ 64 11 515). This Scottish-owned pub draws a boisterous crowd on weekend nights, often ending in shot-drinking competitions. Open M-Sa 11am-2am, Su noon-1am. MC/Visa.

**Nimega Baar** (The Pub *with* a Name), Suur-Karja 13. This nearby bar has a classier crowd, sleeker interior, and ambient jazz perfect for chilling. Beer 32EEK. Open M-Th 11am-2am, F-Sa 11am-4am, Su noon-2am. MC/Visa.

**Flamingo,** Merivälja Str. 5 (☎630 01 23). Take bus #1, 1a, 8, 38, or 114 from Hotel Viru. On the beach at Pirita, it boasts a gorgeous view of the sea. Dancing upstairs. Attracts a cheery crowd of 20- and 30-somethings, locals, and tourists. Cover up to 100EEK. Open M-Tu and Su noon-midnight, W-Th noon-3am, F-Sa noon-6am.

**Club V.S.** (Voitlev Sona), Parnu mnt. 28 (☎627 26 27). This bar has a polished steel and purple neon decor and is a local favorite. Beer 30EEK. Open daily 11am-4am.

**Von Krahli Teater/Baar,** Rataskaevu 10 (☎626 90 96 and 626 90 90), on the west edge of lower Vanalinn. Lights up with elaborate multimedia spectacles, including blends of Gregorian chants and techno and performances by local bands. Theater active most nights 7-9pm. Theater and band tickets from 40EEK. Cover for dance shows 60-70EEK. 21+. Open Su-Th noon-1am, F-Sa noon-3am.

# 🔁 DAYTRIP FROM TALLINN

### ROCCA-AL-MARE
*From Tallinn's train station, take bus #21 or 21a. Museum at Vabaõhumuuseumi 12 (☎654 91 00). Chapel open daily May-Oct. 10am-8pm, Nov.-Apr. 10am-6pm. 25EEK, students 9EEK.*

Rocca-al-mare is a peninsula 10km west of central Tallinn. It contains the **Estonian Open Air Museum,** a park full of 18th- to 20th-century wooden mills and homesteads, collected from all over Estonia and rebuilt here. Visitors can duck into log cabins, climb rickety stairs, and explore stables and dirt paths leading to the sea. The 208-acre museum has 68 buildings, including the **Sutlepa Chapel** (kabel), where a choir sings in Estonian and Swedish during holidays. Intricately attired Estonian folk troupes perform regularly.

# COASTAL ESTONIA

Sun, sand, natural preserves...and mud. East of Tallinn, Lahemaa National Park shelters precious coastline, historic villages, and endangered species from the ravages of tourism. Hip Pärnu and quiet Haapsalu, on the other hand, welcome weary travelers with open—albeit muddy—arms. Both are famed for their spas and travelers to Haapsalu are only a ferry away from the unspoiled Estonian islands.

# LAHEMAA NATIONAL PARK     ☎(8)232

Founded in 1971, Lahemaa National Park was the USSR's first; today it is Estonia's largest. It covers nearly 500 sq. km, 75% of them woodland, and frames a jutting and rocky coastline. Four peninsulas stretch like stubby fingers from the mainland, sheltering quiet bays and beaches from the caprices of the Baltic Sea. Further inland, nature trails lead through forest clearings and bogs flecked with purple lupin and white tufts of grass. Lahemaa is home to 838 plant species and some striking fauna, including elk, storks, and lynx. The park serves as a cultural as well as an ecological reserve, sheltering fishing villages and 18th-century German-Baltic estates from modernity. All the same, the region has taken progressive steps to boost its tourist appeal, from renovated historical sights and improved museums to expanded lodging and dining opportunities.

**◪⑫ ORIENTATION AND PRACTICAL INFORMATION.** The most convenient city from which to explore the area is Palmse, where you will find the **Lahemaa National Park Visitor Center.** (☎341 96; ekal@estpak.ee. English spoken. Open daily May-Aug. 9am-7pm, Sept. 9am-5pm, Oct.-Apr. M-F 9am-2pm.) To get to the park, call ahead to the Visitor Center for the bus schedule from Viitna to Palmse Mõis. Then, take the **Rakvere** bus from Tallinn to **Viitna** (1hr., 9 per day, 13 per day return to Tallinn, 35EEK). From there, catch a bus to Palmse Mõis or walk the 7km down the road. Buses are infrequent and some run only on alternate days; biking and hiking are the only ways to get around if you don't want to wait. Luckily, most destinations lie within a two-hour walk of one another. For direct access to the coast, inquire at the Tallinn station about buses to **Võsu** (3 per week). These can also be used for direct transport to the Palmse Manor House. **Postal code:** 45202 (Viitna).

**⌖⌗ ACCOMMODATIONS AND FOOD.** The Palmse information center offers advice on the wide variety of accommodations in Lahemaa and can sometimes arrange for private-room owners to pick you up by car. Situated a scenic 8km hike from Võsu in the village of Käsmu, **Lainela Puhkemajaad,** toward the end of Neema, offers small, tidy rooms within 50m of the sea. Free access to a basketball court, two tennis courts, a sauna, and the nearby Kásmús Maritime Museum (see below) are all available. (☎381 33. Triples 140EEK. Tent space 100-120EEK.) For more luxurious, inland lodging, try the newly opened hotel/hostel at **Sagadi Mõis.** 8km from Palmse Mõis (9km from Võsu), the hostel has six rooms with a total of 17 beds. They also **rent bikes** to guests. The restaurant inside offers tasty meals, including a full vegetarian menu. (☎588 78. Bikes 20EEK per hr.; 150EEK per day. Main dishes 50-100EEK. Singles 180EEK; triples and up 100EEK per person.) The **campground** at Viitna is 400m past the bus stop and through the wooden arch on the right. The lakeside camping office can set you up with tent space or rooms in log cabins. It also **rents bikes.** (☎936 51. Bikes 19EEK per hr. Singles 100EEK; doubles 150EEK.)

In the wilds of Palmse Mõis, the **Park Hotell Restaurant** prepares fresh salads for 15-20EEK and the obligatory schnitzel for 60EEK. (☎236 26. Open daily noon-7pm.) The **tavern** in Viitna, located opposite the bus stop, dishes up hearty local food for 50-100EEK. (☎435 43. Open daily noon-midnight.)

**◉ SIGHTS. Palmse Manor** is among the best restored and most historically significant estates in Lahemaa. From 1677, members of the von Pahlen family resided among the manor's ostentatious gazebos and swan ponds until the government reclaimed all private land in 1923. Peter Ludwig was involved in the 1801 assassination of Russian Tsar Paul I and Alexander initiated the building of the Tallinn-St. Petersburg railroad in 1879. The estate includes eclectic furniture carted in from all over the country. (☎341 91. Open Apr.-Aug. M and W-Su 10am-7pm.)

Next to the Lainela Puhkemajaad, the **Kásmús Maritime Museum** introduces visitors to the history of the surrounding fishing village, which once served as a ship-building center and a school for sailors. Ask the proprietor, old salt Aarne Vaik, for a tour. (☎252 97 135. Open 24hr. Free.) On the far side of the Puhkemajaad Neemetee, a path through the woods opens to a rocky beach where the **stone hill** grants wishes to those who contribute new rocks to the mound. Ice Age glaciers carried boulders all the way from Finland; they remain here, 8m tall in the sand.

The extensive grounds of Sagadi Mõis (see above) attempt to recreate the days of the German aristocracy that once presided over Lahemaa. Inside the manor itself, ornate 18th- and 19th-century furniture and countless mirrors betray the vanity of the estate's former residents. The **Museum of Forestry**, the first white building on the left through the gates, features exhibits on the park's plant and tree life, its historical uses, and the sobering impact of humans on the ecosystem. (☎252 58 88. Museum and manor open May 15-Sept. 30 Tu-Su 11am-6pm. Joint ticket 30EEK, students 10EEK; separately 20EEK, 7EEK.)

During the 1950s, the Soviets closed much of the northern coast off with barbed wire and banned fishing; **Altja** is one of the few fishing villages remaining. The fishing huts on the cape are part of an open-air museum. (Open 24hr.) As you continue around the cape and cross the river, white stripes on the trees mark a short trail that runs through the coastal forest and loops back to town. The small island visible is **Vergi**, connected to the cape by a land bridge 2.5km farther along the road.

# PÄRNU ☎(8)44

The "summer capital" of Estonia, Pärnu (PAER-noo), long a Hanseatic center trade center, got its makeover as a resort in the early 19th century, and hasn't looked back since. Called the "Cinderella of the Baltic" by turn of the century poets, the town of 50,000 has certainly made a fairy-tale comeback. After toiling long under its wicked Soviet stepmother, Pärnu has gone from sooty to muddy once again, as crowds flock there to experience its famous mud baths and sandy beaches. A warm breezy climate and relaxed holiday groove make Pärnu *the* place to be in the summer. And, with cultural festivals adding to the excitement, Pärnu is ready to take the ball by storm.

## ◢◤ ORIENTATION

Pärnu is bisected by the River Pärnu and framed by water. The town center is on the seaside, stretching from the inlet **Vallikraav** to the **bus station** on Ringi. The main street is **Rüütli**. A short walk down Nikolai and Supeluse from the center leads to the mud baths and the beach. **Ranna pst.** runs along the beach.

## ▆ TRANSPORTATION

**Trains:** ☎226 67. 3km east of the center, by the corner of Riia and Raja; take bus #40 from the post office to Raeküla Rdtj. 5EEK. To **Tallinn** (3hr., 2 per day, 30EEK).

**Buses:** Ringi 3 (☎71 00 21; Eurolines ☎41 755). Best way to reach Pärnu. To: **Haapsalu** (3hr., 2 per day, 60EEK); **Kuressaare** (3hr., 2-3 per day, 110-125EEK); **Tallinn** (3hr., 36 per day, 70EEK); **Tartu** (5hr., 11 per day, 105EEK); **Rīga, LAT** (4hr., 5 per day, 105EEK); and **St. Petersburg, RUS** (10hr., 1 per day, 231EEK).

**Taxis:** ☎412 40 and 311 11. 6-7EEK per km.

**Bike Rental:** Rattapood, Riia 95 (☎324 40). 75EEK per day. Open M-F 10am-6pm, Sa 10am-3pm.

## ▐ PRACTICAL INFORMATION

**Tourist office:** Rüütli 16 (☎730 00; fax 730 01; info@parnu.tourism.ee; www.parnu.ee). Provides **maps**, *Pärnu In Your Pocket,* and help with lodging. Open M-F 9am-6pm, Sat 9am-4pm, Su 10am-3pm.

**Currency Exchange:** Eesti Ühispank, Rüütli 40a (☎771 11). Cashes **traveler's checks**, gives **cash advances**, and has a Cirrus/Plus **ATM**. Open M-F 9am-6pm, Sa 9am-2pm. In a pinch, Hotel Pärnu has bad rates but is open all hours except 1-2pm.

**Telephones:** Rüütli 5 (☎707 27). Around the corner from the post office to the right. Open M-F 8am-6pm, Sa 9am-4pm.

**Internet access: Museum of New Art,** Esplanaadi 10. 25EEK per hr. Open Tu-F 1-7pm, Sa 10am-3pm.

**Post office:** Akadeemia 7 (☎711 11). At the west end of Rüütli, 1km from bus station. Open M-F 8am-6pm and Sa 9am-3pm; packages M-F 8am-7pm and Sa-Su 9am-3pm.

**Postal code:** 80001.

## THE DIRTIEST BATH THIS SIDE OF THE BALTICS
Mud has never looked or felt better than at Pärnu's Neo-Classical **Mudaravila**, Ranna pst. 1. Since the health resort was founded in 1838, the privilege of rolling around in gooey mud has not been limited to pigs and small children. Workers at the mud bath (as well as many health professionals) insist that Pärnu's sea mud has a curative effect on disorders of the bones, joints, and peripheral nervous system—there's even a special ward for patients with myocardial infraction and cardiovascular diseases. After a brief consultation, patients can choose between General or Local Mud; the first involves being hosed with mud while lying on a table in the buff, while the latter consists of mud compresses (90-130EEK). No day at the mud bath is complete without a massage (220EEK), a "curative" bath or shower (60-75EEK), and a cup of restorative herb tea. (☎255 20; info@mudaravilla.ee. Open daily 8am-3pm.)

### ACCOMMODATIONS AND FOOD

Now that Pärnu is popular again, many hotels are renovating and raising their prices. Places fill fast, so reserve ahead. The tourist office can also book rooms. **Kalevi Pansionaat,** Ranna 2, is a beach-side hotel on the side of the Parnu stadium that seems to have been designed for Spartans: it has hard beds, hall bathrooms, and not much else. It is, however, right on the beach. (☎430 08. Breakfast 30EEK. Doubles and triples 200EEK.) **Linnakämping Green,** Suure-Jõe 50b, is 3km from the town center along a deserted, unlit, and unpaved street on the river. Take bus #9 or 40 from the bus station along Riia. Get off at the "Tammsaare" stop, back-track to turn right onto Kastani, and right again onto Suur-Jõe. This is Pärnu's cheapest and most basic accommodation. Facilities include gnome-sized cabins, a bar, a basketball court, and immaculate bathrooms. (☎437 76. Open June-Aug. Breakfast 30EEK. Tent site 60EEK; cabin bed 95EEK.)

A *turg* (market) is at the intersection of Sepa and Karja. (Open Tu-Su 7am-1pm. (☎/fax 445 67. Main dishes 30-80EEK. Open daily 10am-midnight.) **Georg,** on the corner of Rüütli and Hommiku, is a cafeteria-style joint that's dirt cheap and packed with locals. (Main dishes under 35EEK. Open M-F 7:30am-10pm, Sa-Su 9am-10pm. Visa.)

### SIGHTS AND ENTERTAINMENT

Adjacent to Hotell Pärnu at Rüütli 53, the **Pärnu Regional Museum** (Pärnu Rajoonide Vaheline Koduloomuuseum), displays everything from taxidermy to Stone Age tools. The final display case contains heart-wrenching letters from local children to their parents, who were deported to Siberia. (☎434 64. Open W-Su 10am-6pm. 10EEK, students 5EEK.) The **Lydia Koidula Museum,** Jannseni 37, across Pärnu river, commemorates the 19th-century poet who revived Estonian verse and drama. (See **Literature,** p. 279. ☎416 63. Open W-Su 11am-5pm. 5EEK, students 3EEK.) At the corner of Uus and Vee one block north of Rüütli, the Russian Orthodox **Catherine Church** (Ekateriina kirik) is a multi-spired, silver-and-green church built in the 1760s under the order of Catherine the Great. Rüütli ends at an **open-air theater,** where music and drama performances are given in summer, starting in July. Turn left off Rüüli before you reach the open-air theater to pass through the formidable **Tallinn Gate** (Tallinna värav), the only way into the city during Swedish rule and the only surviving Baltic town gate from the 17th century.

The broad, tree-lined street stretching south from Tallinna värav leads to a long pedestrian zone just behind the white-sand **beach.** The water is clean, if a bit shallow and cold before July. Women can bathe **nude** if they wander up the beach to the right. Swings, jungle-gyms, and trampolines are set up on the sand, and a whirly waterslide is open in summer. On summer evenings, drinking, partying, and sunset-watching center around the temporary bars that set up along the beach.

For a more grandiose setting, try **Tallinna Bar,** a ceilinged stone tavern, atop the grand Tallinn Gate. (☎450 73. Open daily noon-11pm. Main dishes 20-80EEK. *Saku* 20EEK.) Housed in a 1930s wooden dance hall on the beach, **La Pera Vida,** Mere 22, spins pop and techno for a Bohemian crowd, with occasional theme nights. (☎432 79. Open daily 10am-1am. Occasional 25EEK cover.) There's a **cinema** in the same building; films are usually in English (30EEK). In the first weekend of July, the **Pärnu Jazz Festival** attracts artists and listeners from around the world.

# HAAPSALU ☎(8)047

Seaside Haapsalu (HAAP-sa-loo) sprawls out from the ruins of the Bishop's Castle, the 13th-century seat of the Saare-Lööne bishopric that once ruled most of western Estonia. The town was almost destroyed during the Russo-Livonian War (1558-1583), before being conquered by Swedes in 1581 and Russians in 1710. In the 19th century it was famed throughout the Russian Empire for its curative mud baths, but during Soviet times the resort image crumbled like dry mud as the town became a military airbase. Today, with the rebuilding and renovation of the sanatoriums and the sailing harbor, Haapsalu is a rapidly Westernizing tourist attraction. The loudest noises, however, still come from nature, as the protected caves just off the main peninsula serve as a breeding ground for thousands of squawking ducks and swans.

**TRANSPORTATION.** The **bus station,** Raudtee 2, occupies a massive covered platform built by Nicholas II to ensure that none of his party would get wet while disembarking. (☎347 91. Ticket office open daily 5-8:30am, 9am-1pm, 2-4:30pm, and 5-7pm.) Buses go to: **Tallinn** (2 hr., 22 per day, 55EEK); **Pärnu** (2-3hr., 3 per day, 64EEK); and **Kärdla** (3 hr., 3 per day, 65EEK). **Taxis** (☎335 00) are 5EEK per km.

**ORIENTATION AND PRACTICAL INFORMATION.** To reach the center from the bus station, head straight down Jaama to **Posti,** the main street. Get your bearings at the **tourist information office** in the train station complex. The English-speaking staff sells **maps** for 15EEK. (☎33 248; fax 33 464; info@haapsalu.tourism.ee; www.haapsalu.ee. Open May 15-June 14 and Aug. 15-Sept. 14 M-Sa 10am-7pm; June 15-Aug. 14 M-Sa 10am-7pm, Su 10am-3pm; Sept. 15-Dec. 29 M-F 10am-5pm.) **Exchange money** or use a 24hr. **ATM** at **Hansapank,** Posti 41. (Open M-F 8:30am-5:30pm, Sa 9am-2pm.) The **telephone office** is at Tallinna mnt. 1. (☎332 24. Open M-F 9am-6pm, Sa 9am-3pm.) The library, Posti 3, has free **internet access.** (☎451 65. Open T-F 10am-6pm, Sa 11am-4pm.) The **post office** is at Nurme 2. (☎333 42. Open M-F 7:30am-6pm, Sa 8am-3pm.) **Postal code:** 90501.

**ACCOMMODATIONS AND FOOD.** The ■ **Jahtklubi** (Yacht Club), Holmi 5a, is a 20-minute walk to the end of the peninsula from the bus station. Follow Posti north as it merges with Karja, then turn left on Ehte. Follow the right edge of the lake, continue on to Kaluri, and Holmi is on your right. Enter via the stairs underneath the tower in the back. You can also take city bus #2. Jahtklubi sports spotless rooms with sinks, hall baths, a bar behind the front desk, and a small outdoor restaurant. (☎455 82; fax 455 36. Breakfast 35EEK. Restaurant open daily 11am-9pm. Main dishes 20-50EEK. Singles 170EEK; doubles 330EEK, up to 2 extra people for 50EEK each.) The **Paralepa Puhkemaja** is on a gorgeous beach 10 minutes from the bus and train station. Look for the low, unmarked wooden building that looks like a beach bar behind the Fra Mare Sanatorium. The rooms are spartan but clean. (☎25 10 67 35. Open in summer. Doubles, triples, and quads 140EEK per person.)

The **market** (turg) is one block from the bus station on the corner of Jürlöö and Jaama. (Open Tu-Su 7am-3pm.) There are several good **supermarkets,** including **Rema 1000,** Linula 3. (Open 9am-9pm. MC/Visa.) Locals at **Restaurant Central,** Karja 21, hang out in the cellar bar or dine in style upstairs, enjoying such dishes as chicken in white wine sauce for 64EEK. (☎44 673. Main dishes 25-75EEK. Open Su-Th noon-10pm, F-Sa noon-2am.)

**FULL-MOON CAPITALIST FEVER** Haapsalu's economic viability relies as much on the legend of the White Lady as it does on its famous curative mud. Monks at the castle were supposed to be chaste, and women were never to enter the cathedral's halls. Love found a way, though, and in 1280 a wayward monk snuck his mistress in dressed as a choirboy. The truth soon came out, and what could a responsible bishop do to teach his clergy a lesson? He threw the monk into prison to starve and walled the poor girl up with nothing but a cup of water and slice of bread. Her fate was sealed, but it didn't stop her nocturnal visits after death. According to legend, she makes an apparitional appearance in the cathedral window on the full moon of each August. The event is celebrated by a week-long festival, including dramatizations of the legend that draw people from all over the country. In order to avoid disappointment if she fails to emerge or on cloudy nights, budding Estonian capitalists set up projectors to generate an approximate image on the chapel windows; they keep the tourists flooding in, and allow the White Lady an occasional rest from her timeless woe.

**SIGHTS. Bishop's Castle** (Piiskopilinnus), where the Bishop of Saare-Lääne lived until moving to Saaremaa in 1358, is located about halfway up the peninsula. To get to the castle, follow Kalda or Posti from the bus station to the town center. There they converge onto Karja and flow into **Castle Square** (Lossiplats). From the square, one can enter **Castle Park;** the castle sits within. (Park open 7am-11pm.) The oldest parts of the castle were built in 1265, and it has been home to the powerful, tyrannical ruler-bishops of the Saare-Lääne bishopric in 1302. Left in ruins after a huge fire in 1688, the castle was briefly restored in the late 1800s only to fall into disrepair again under the Soviets. A large portion of the castle has since been repaired and now houses a **museum,** which exhibits period costumes, a scale model of the old castle, and informative plaques on the town's history. (Open Tu-Su 10am-6pm. 15EEK, students 5EEK.) Included in museum entry is the **Episcopal Church,** a dazzlingly renovated chapel dating from 1270. You can also climb the steep and ragged steps of the castle tower for a view of Haapsalu and the marshy seas that surround it (10EEK). The **Africa Beach** (Aafrikarand) promenade, northeast of the castle at the end of Rüütli, runs 2km to the yacht club. **Kaluri,** farther east, makes for beautiful walks amid weathered wooden houses, marsh grasses, and ducks. Quack.

# ESTONIAN ISLANDS

Estonia extends far out to sea, with over 1500 islands speckling the Baltic. The largest three, Saaremaa, Hiiumaa, and Muhu, are hot new vacation destinations, yet still preserve the flavor of pre-World War II Estonia. Worried about providing an easy escape route to the West, the Soviets prohibited foreigners and mainland Estonians from visiting the islands. As a result, the islands are a preserve of all that is distinctive about Estonia before the rest of the world got involved—from the outdoor museums of Saaremaa to the exotic flora and fauna on Hiiumaa, to the remarkable Gothic church on Muhu. The islands also offer such curiosities as a tragically ineffective lighthouse on Hiiumaa, deserted Soviet bases, and the annual cops-versus-hooligans soccer match in Kuressaare. History aside, the simple pleasure of a long bicycle ride in idyllic surroundings make the islands worth visiting.

## SAAREMAA ISLAND

The largest and most touristed of the Estonian islands, Saaremaa (SAA-reh-maa) is often reckoned to be more Estonian than mainland Estonia. Silent windmills lining hilltops survey a countryside of traditional farms and stone churches. From mysterious meteorite craters and bubbling springs to the rugged coast and astounding cliffs, natural beauty abounds. Come summer, young Estonians from the mainland arrive in increasing numbers to party beachside, adding a surge of energy and revelry to the otherwise subdued serenity of the island.

# Estonian Islands

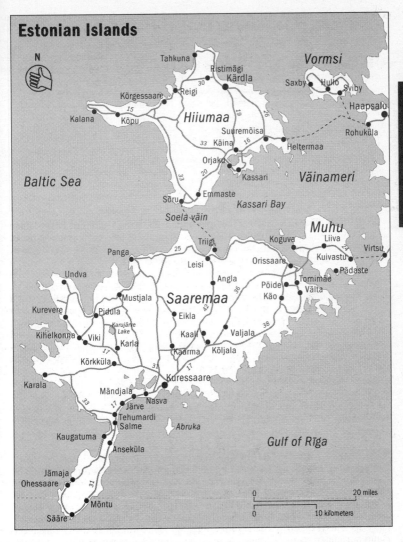

N

Tahkuna

Vormsi

Ristimägi
Kärdla

Saxby  Hullo  Sviby

Körgessaare  Reigi

Haapsalu

Kalana  Köpu  *Hiiumaa*

15

Suuremõisa

Rohuküla

33  Käina  16

*Baltic Sea*

Orjaku

Heltermaa

Kassari  *Väinameri*

20

Sõru  Emmaste

33

Kassari Bay

Soela väin

*Muhu*

Triigi  Koguva  Liiva

Panga  25  Virtsu

Leisi  Orissaare  Kuivastu

Undva  Angla  Pädaste

Pöide  Tornimäe

Mustjala  *Saaremaa*  Käo  Välta

Kurevere  Pidula  Eikla

Karujärve
Lake

Kihelkonna  Viki  Kaali  Valjala  38

Karla

Käarma  Kõljala

Körkküla  31

Kaugatuma  Anseküla

Karala  Mändjala  Nasva

Järve

Tehumardi  *Abruka*

Salme

Kaugatuma

*Gulf of Rīga*

Anseküla

Jämaja
Ohessaare

31

Möntu

Sääre

| 0 | 20 miles |
| 0 | 10 kilometers |

> Saaremaa is in the process of upgrading its telephone systems. As a result, numbers listed here might be incorrect. Check with the tourist office in Kuressaare for the most up-to-date telephone information.

## KURESSAARE

☎ (8)245

A major resort before Soviet occupation, Kuressaare (KOO-res-saa-re), on Saaremaa's south coast, is making a comeback. An abandoned 16th-century fortress attracts tourists, while new bars and hotels make the most of the returning crowds.

▸ **TRANSPORTATION.** Direct **buses**, which get priority on the ferries, are the fastest way to get to the mainland. Buses, Pihtla tee 2 (☎573 80), at the corner of Tallinna, head to **Pärnu** (3hr., 2 per day, 115EEK) and **Tallinn** (4hr., 7per day,

150EEK). A new **ferry** route island-hops between **Triigi** on Saaremaa and **Sõru** on Hiiumaa (65min., 2 per day M-Tu and Th-Su, 50EEK). **Taxis** run from behind town hall, the bus station, and Smuuli pst. (☎533 33. 4-5EEK per km.)

**⬛🔢 ORIENTATION AND PRACTICAL INFORMATION.** The town is centered around the narrow **Raekoja pl.** (Town Hall Square). **Raatapood,** Tallinna 26, near the bus station, rents **bikes.** (☎571 18. 120EEK per day.) **Polar Rent,** Tallinna 9, offers **car rentals.** (☎336 60. From 590EEK per day.) The **tourist office,** Tallinna 2, inside the *raekoda* (town hall), sells a useful **map** (15EEK) and answers questions on food, lodging, and special events. (☎/fax 331 20; info@oesel.tourism.ee; www.tourism.ee/oesel. Open May-Sept. 15 M-Sa 9am-7pm, Su 10am-3pm; Sept. 16-Apr. M-F 9am-5pm.) **Exchange currency,** cash **traveler's checks,** and get MC/Visa **cash advances** at **Eesti Ühispank,** Kohtu 1. (☎215 00. Open M-F 9am-4pm, Sa 9am-2pm.) The **post office,** Torni 1, is on the corner of Komandandi, a block north of Tallinna. (☎543 45. Open M-F 8am-6pm, Sa 8:30am-3pm.) **Postal code:** 93 813.

**📁🔢 ACCOMMODATIONS AND FOOD.** New hotels open all the time; check with the tourist office. **Saaremaa Uhisgumnaasium Uhiselamu,** Hariduse 13A, in the school on Hariduse, has comfortable rooms, an internet lab, and a sauna. From Hariduse, turn down Kingu, and enter at the second gate.(☎543 88; fax 572 26. Dorms 65EEK; triples 80EEK per person.) **Hotell Pärna,** Pärna 3, is a converted house in a relaxed part of town. The hotel has large, uniquely-shaped rooms and a kitchen. (☎/fax 575 21. Sauna 150EEK per hr. Doubles 400EEK, with bath 550EEK. Breakfast included.) **Mändjala Puhkeküla,** Kuressaare Vald, lies 11km outside town at the "Kämping" stop on the Kuressaare-Järve bus. It offers tent space and spacious cabins along a small beach. (☎441 93; fax 540 35. Open May-Sept. Dorms 155EEK, breakfast included. Campsites 40EEK.)

**Supermarket EDU,** Tallina 1, is well stocked. (Open daily 9am-10pm.) **Vanalinna,** Kauba 8, one of the best eateries in town, serves delicious fish for 60-80EEK and wild boar for 160EEK. (☎553 09. Open daily noon-midnight. MC/Visa.) The 100-year old **Restoran Veski,** Pärna 19, serves steak and seafood (40-99EEK) to four floors of eager eaters in an old windmill. (☎531 61. Open Su-Th noon-midnight, F-Sa noon-2am.) Like the adjoining hotel, **Kass Restaurant,** Vallimaa 5a, is run by hotel-school students and offers a cheap lunch. (Main dishes 40-50EEK. ☎246 50. Open daily 11:30am-3:30pm. MC/Visa.)

**⬛🔢 SIGHTS AND ENTERTAINMENT.** Seventeenth-century buildings line **Town Hall Square** (Raekoja pl). The most notable is the 1670 Nordic Baroque **Town Hall** (raekoda), built by Swedish landowner Marcus Gabriel de la Gardie. Past the square's south end a **statue** commemorating the 1918-20 struggle for independence is actually a 1990 replica of the original, erected in 1928 but destroyed by the Soviets. Heading south of Raekoja pl. along Lossi, through a sleepy park and across a moat, lies the ◼ **Bishopric Castle** (Piiskopilinnus). Built in 1260 after the Teutonic Order conquered the island, it was renovated in the 1300s for the Bishop of Saare-Lääne, who liked it so much that in 1358 he declared it the bishopric's administrative center. The **Saaremaa Regional Museum,** in the castle, is one of the more interesting museums in Estonia. It displays an eclectic collection from the island's history, including intricately carved coats-of-arms, carriages, and military and maritime objects. (☎563 07. Open daily May-Aug. 11am-7pm, last admission 6pm; Sept.-Apr. W-Su. 30EEK, students 15EEK.)

At night, a mellow crowd gathers at **Budweiser Pub,** Kauba 6, a popular Irish bar. (☎532 40. Open daily 10am-2am.) For a livelier time, head from Nimeta Pub across Raekoja pl. to **Punane Baar,** where twenty-somethings grind to American tunes under red lights. (Cover 30EEK and up. Open daily 10pm-4am.) On weekends in July, a bandstand occupies the park around the castle; on it's a brass band on Saturdays and a small orchestra on Sundays. The first weekend of August brings **Maritime Days,** which feature sailing competitions and musical performances.

**COPS AND ROBBERS** Mention hooliganism at soccer matches to most people, and visions of pub brawls between drunk, starved fans come to mind. The relation between ne'er-do-wells and the world's most popular sport, however, is a global phenomenon, as evinced by the annual match between the punks and the police in Kuressaare. Someone had the bright idea a few years back to put these mortal foes together on the pitch to let out their aggressions. Since then, every June, the cops in their blue shirts and badges and the punks with their rainbow mohawks have had at each other with a flurry of slide tackles and obscenities. The quality of the footballing is usually rather poor, a fact only compounded by the keg of beer on the punks' sideline. Nonetheless, the game is a town spectacle, with almost everyone there supporting the underdogs against the long foot of the law.

## WEST SAAREMAA

As distances are long and buses infrequent, you'll need to rent a car to see the entire island. Those traveling by bike or bus will have to pick and choose among accessible sights. Alternatively, take your bike on the bus for the price of a second ticket and tour via bike before taking another bus home. Whatever you choose, it is advisable to consult with the tourist office before beginning.

To get to **Karujärve Lake,** take the road to Saîa (just before Kaarema) about 15km to Kärla. At the main intersection in Kärla, turn right onto the paved road. After 5km, on the left you'll see the Karujärve **campground,** Kärla vald, which has campsites (30EEK) and small A-frame cabins for two (250EEK). There is swimming and horseback riding nearby. (☎421 81; fax 420 34. Open May 15-Sept. 15.) The main road heads toward **Kihelkonna,** passing the **Mihkli Farm Museum** (Mihkli Talumuuseum) in Viki along the way. Nineteenth-century farmhouses cluster around a garden. (☎766 13. Open daily 10am-6pm. 10EEK, students 4EEK.) Farther along the road, turn right down the hill to Kihelkonna, where the relief on the tower of the 13th-century **Kihelkonna Church** depicts archangel Michael fighting a dragon.

Continuing down the road to Silla, turn right on the unpaved road to **Pidula** to reach the bubbling **Odalästi Springs,** rumored to bring eternal youth to young ladies who splash the spring's water on their faces. Look closely for the churning earth where the water wells up from underground. Backtracking to the head of the road, you'll find the **Pidula fish farm.** Here they raise 'em, release 'em, catch 'em, and fry 'em. Ah, the circle of life. (100EEK per kg.) You can stay on the lake after your meal, in one of two available rooms. (☎465 13. Sauna 100EEK per hr.; boat rental 30EEK. Rooms 300-350EEK.) Follow the signs to **Käsitöösahver,** for sandwiches (from 5EEK) grilled on an open fire. (Open daily 11am-7pm.)

From Mustjala you have your choice of peninsulas—either the impressive shoreline of **Tagaranna** or the even more impressive 25m drop at **Panga,** depicted on the back of the 100EEK note. If you go to Tagaranna, skirt the tip of the peninsula to reach a former **Soviet training facility,** with trenches and barbed wire now overgrown with lupin. If you choose Panga, climb up the "lighthouse," a ladder enclosed by steel scaffolding. Use caution: the steps are steep and wind blustery.

## SOUTHWEST SAAREMAA

Renting a bike is one of the best ways to explore Southwest Saaremaa, which starts at Kuressaare and stretches down to the Sõrve peninsula. The first stop on the route south should be the quiet beaches of **Mändjala** and **Järve,** 8-12km west of Kuressaare. To reach Mändjala, take the first left after the "Mändjala 1" bus stop. For the beach in **Järve,** turn left after the "Ranna" bus stop. At **Tehumardi,** a giant concrete sword marks the location of a 1944 World War II battle, now honored by rows of memorials for the dead soldiers. Farther on, the town of **Salme,** 17km out of Kuressaare, makes a good lunch stop. The restaurant **Ago & Co.,** on the main road, serves the usual fare, including fried perch with cheese for 52EEK and *seljanka* for 14EEK. (☎715 34. Main dishes 50-80EEK. Open daily 11am-10pm.)

About 2km from Salme, a sign points along an unpaved road to **Iide,** cutting over to the west side of **Sõrve poolsaar** (the peninsula), where the choppy waters of the open Baltic meet rockier beaches. The "cliffs" at **Kaugatuma** are overrated, but you can sunbathe beside grazing cows on the fossil-strewn, pebbly beaches. Five kilometers farther down the road, the ruins of the **World War II defense line** are visible. At **Sõrve säär,** the very tip of Sõrve poolsaar, clear weather reveals a view of Latvia, 25km south across the Baltic. On the trip back, the road through **Mõntu** (in the opposite direction from Jämaja) passes through the **national park.** The ride may leave you with a sore keister, so bring cushioning, as well as bug repellent.

## EAST SAAREMAA

The East is the most rapidly developing part of Saaremaa and also features some of the island's more impressive religious sights. One of the island's most beautiful churches is in **Kaarma.** You can bicycle the 15km here by taking Tallinna mnt. north out of Kuressaare and turning left at the sign to Upa (after about 3km), then right to Kaarma. Across the road from the 13th-century **Kaarma Church** are the earthen remains of the 12th-century **Kaarma Stronghold** (Maalinn). To leave, take the dirt road back to the paved one. Turn left and then right toward Kaali, where you'll find several **meteorite craters,** the largest of which is big enough to necessitate steps down to the pond at its bottom. **Kalli Trahter,** across the road from the crater parking lot, serves tasty, reasonably priced dishes in a new building trying to look rustic. (☎911 82. Shrimp in cream sauce 84EEK. Open daily 10am-11pm.)

To reach the easternmost parts of the island, catch a bus from Kuressaare to **Orissaare.** The **Püharisti Hotel,** Ranna pst. 11, 200m off the main road, offers comfortable rooms in its two scenic cabins by the sea. (☎451 49. 240EEK per person. Breakfast included.) An inexpensive **24hr. restaurant** sits 100m away. South of Orissaare lies **Pöide** and its **church.** Built as a Catholic church in the 13th century, it later became Lutheran, Russian Orthodox, and then Lutheran again. It also doubled as a fortress for the Teutonic Knights. The stairs up the tower are unlit and shaky, but the top offers a fantastic panorama. Southwest of Orissaare in the small town of **Valjala** sits **Valjala Church,** the oldest stone church in Estonia.

# MUHU ISLAND

Between Saaremaa and the mainland, Muhu bears witness to centuries of Estonian religious history. The **Muhu Church,** in Liiva, is an edifice dating from at least 1276. With no steeple and a bright asymmetrical interior, it looks a bit avant-garde. Amazingly, portions of 13th-century murals still survive within the church walls. Portraits of saints and angels are covered in layers of whitewash, with which they were plastered during the Reformation. While the short, modest pulpit reflects the Lutheranism still practiced here, the trapezoidal tombstones in the churchyard recall the paganism that found a refuge on these islands when mainland Estonia was converted. Slightly east of Liiva and off the main highway, a dirt road veers right 8km to Muhu's south shore and the tall **Pädaste Manor** (Mõis), which dates from the 17th century and is currently under renovation. **Buses** run from **Kuressaare** to **Kuivastu** on Muhu (2hr., 11 per day, 30EEK). If you stay on Muhu, **Vanatoa Tunsmitalu,** Muhu vald in Koguva, has somewhat luxurious accommodations at very moderate prices. (☎488 84. 250EEK per person. Breakfast included.) **Mesimaja Trahler** offers decent meals for 70-120EEK. (☎488 00. Open daily noon-midnight.)

# HIIUMAA ISLAND

By restricting access to Hiiumaa (HEE-you-ma) for 50 years, the Soviets unwittingly preserved many of the island's rare plant and animal species, as well as its unhurried way of life. Native residents tell stories of ghosts, giants, trolls, and devils who inhabited Hiiumaa before them: visitors find unadorned churches, history-laden lighthouses, and the birthplace of legends. A woody wilderness unblemished by human habitation, Hiiumaa is a haven for all weary spirits.

More than two-thirds of all the plant species in Estonia exist only on Hiiumaa. Due to this biodiversity, much of the island now belongs to the West-Estonian Islands Biosphere Reserve. Hiking and camping are permitted and encouraged, but be sure to pick up info at the tourist office about off-limits regions. Motor vehicles are not allowed on the seashore and certain other areas. Because of dry conditions, campfires are prohibited. Apart from the reserve, the most interesting parts of the island lie on the coast. With distances so short and buses so infrequent, a bike is the best means of transportation. By bike, you can see all of the sights in two long daytrips from Kärdla: one to Kõpu and one to Kassari.

## KÄRDLA
☎(8)246

The Swedish settlers who first stumbled across this sleepy spot on Hiiumaa's north coast named it "Kärrdal," meaning "lovely valley." Hardly an urban center, Kärdla (pop. 4200) still contains as many creeks and trees as houses. This town is the gateway to Hiiumaa, with easy access to the beach and bike rentals.

**TRANSPORTATION.** To reach the mainland, it's best to catch a bus from Kärdla or Käina (ticket price includes the ferry). From the **bus station**, Sadama 13 (☎320 77; open daily 7am-7pm), north of Keskväljak, catch buses to: **Haapsalu** (3hr., 3 per day, 65EEK); **Tallinn** (4hr., 3 per day, 115EEK); and points around the island (0.40EEK per km). A **shuttle** from the station runs to **Heltermaa** (45min., 4 per day, 11EEK) and **Sõru** (1hr., 2 per day, 18EEK). **Ferries** go to **Heltermaa** from Rohuküla, south of Haapsalu (info ☎316 30 in Heltermaa, ☎24 73 36 66 in Rohuküla) and **Sõru** from Triigi (1hr., 2 per day, 20EEK per person, 150EEK per car). **Local buses** are infrequent. **Taxis** are in Keskväljak. (☎316 95. 5EEK per km.)

**PRACTICAL INFORMATION.** The island's only **tourist office**, Hiiu 1, in **Keskväljak,** the main square, provides info on accommodations and sells **maps** (10-85EEK) and guides to sights on Hiiumaa. (☎222 33; fax 222 34; info@hiiumaa.tourism.ee; www.hiiumaa.ee. Open May-Sept. M-F 9am-6pm, Sa-Su 10am-2pm; Oct.-Apr. M-F 9am-4pm.) At **Eesti Ühispank**, on Keskväljak, you can **exchange currency,** get Visa **cash advances,** and find an **ATM.** (Open in summer M-F 9am-4pm, Sa 9am-4pm; off-season M-F 9am-4pm.) Rent **bikes** (100EEK per day) and **cars** (500EEK) from **Kertu Sport,** Vabrikuväljak 1, just across the bridge from the bus station. (☎963 73. Open M-F 10am-6pm, Sa 10am-3pm.) **Telephones** are at Leigri väljak 9. (☎315 37.) There's **internet access** upstairs in the yellow cultural center, on the main square at Rookopli 18. (☎963 22. Open M-F 2-6pm; closed July to early Aug.) The island's main **post office** is at Posti 13, about 200m north of the bus station, opposite the church. (☎963 18. Open M-F 8:30am-5:30pm, Sa 9am-3pm.) **Postal code:** 92412.

**ACCOMMODATIONS AND FOOD.** ▧ **Nuutri Matkamaja,** Nuutri 4, seven minutes from the center, has 12 beds in three rooms, with a common room, shower, sauna, kitchen, fireplace, and TV. Follow Polla past the stadium, then cross the bridge and turn right on Nuutri. Bear right at the immediate fork, and there will be a small footbridge to your right. The hostel, a brown unmarked building, will be on your right. (☎964 68 and mobile 050 588 96; fax 046 311 78. 200EEK per person.) Farther away from town on the water is **Hausma Village,** a hostel with cabins and camping space. From the town square, take Uus past Ranna until it ends, then go right. Hausma is 2km along the unmarked Hausma Road near the ocean. Rooms in the house are large, while the cabins are a good deal. (☎319 29. Rooms 200EEK per person; cabins 150EEK per person. Breakfast included. Camping 20EEK per person.)

While you won't find great cuisine on Hiiumaa, a few good meals can be had. **Konsum,** in Keskväljak, is the central **supermarket.** (Open daily 9am-9pm. MC/Visa.) The big green building in the town square houses **Arteesia Kohvik,** Kärdla's most centrally located restaurant, which serves cheap and starchy eats. (☎918 43. Main dishes 40-80EEK. Open Su-Th 9am-10pm, F-Sa 9am-midnight.) **Rannapaargu,** by the beach at the end of Lubjaahju, is perfect for a drink by the sea. (☎965 09. Open M-Th, Su noon-8pm F-Sa noon-8pm and 10pm-4am.)

ESTONIA

🔲 **SIGHTS. Hiiumaa Museum**, in Vabriku Valjak, houses displays on the history of Kärdla and the island in general, including authentic period furniture. (10EEK, students 5EEK. Open daily 10am-5pm.) On a nice day, you might want to head to **Rannapark**, at the end of Lubjaahju, with a shallow beach, walking trails, and mini-golf.

🚲 **BIKING TO KÕPU.** Heading west out of Kärdla toward Kõrgessaare, you'll encounter the **Hill of Crosses** (Ristimägi), on your left after about 6km. The crosses were placed there to commemorate the Hiumaa Swedes who were deported to Ukraine by Catherine the Great in 1781. Farther down the road, a right turn leads to the **Tahkuna Lighthouse** (11km). Built in Paris in 1874, the lighthouse was consistently ineffective in warning ships about the coast's shallow waters. This didn't hurt the economy much, though, since salvaging loot and rescuing passengers from the ships was quite profitable. Not without irony, a memorial to those lost in the 1994 sinking of the ocean liner *Estonia* now stands here alongside Soviet-era gun emplacements and bunkers. Well past Luidja, the highway gives way to a dirt road as it approaches the most impressive sight in Western Hiiumaa, **Kõpu Lighthouse**. This pyramid-shaped tower on Hiiumaa's west peninsula was constructed in the early 1500s by the Hanseatic League. The stairwell was an afterthought, hacked out of solid rock to provide access to the top. The view from the top gives a panorama of the Baltic Sea, including all of Hiiumaa and, on a sunny day, the island of Saaremaa to the south. (10EEK.) The island's most renowned restaurant hides in the hamlet of **Kõrgessaare** (also called Viskoosa), 17km west of Kärdla. Take Kõrgessaare mnt., marked "Sadama," about 1km to get there. The large rose-granite building that **Viinaköök** (Vodka Kitchen) inhabits was originally a 19th-century silk factory and later a vodka distillery. (☎933 37. Main dishes 40-90EEK. Open Su-Th 11am-midnight, F-Sa 11am-2am.)

🚲 **BIKING TO SUUREMÕISA, KÄINA, AND KASSARI.** For the journey south from Kärdla to Kassari, you could take the direct route to Käina, but the road through **Suuremõisa** is more scenic. **Pühalepa Church**, in Suuremõisa, contains the graves of the Baltic-German Count Ungern-Sternberg's family. The Count, who came to the island in 1781, the year Catherine the Great deported Hiiumaa's Swedes, wanted to acquire the entire island, but his shipping and salvage business was cut short when he killed one of his ship captains during a dispute. From the church parking lot, take a right onto a gravel road. It leads about 150m to the **Contract Stones** (Põhilise leppe kivid), which were placed by human hands and whose purpose is a mystery. Backtrack from the stones to the highway; the left directly before the bridge that crosses the Suuremõisa River leads to **Suuremõisa Palace**, a beautiful example of northern Baroque architecture. The palace was built on the estate of the Swede Jakob de la Gardie, who purchased the entire island in 1624. He lost it in 1710, but his great-granddaughter reclaimed the land and built the manor house in 1755. The ill-fated Ungern-Sternberg was also an owner; it was in one of the manor's rooms that the murder occurred. Though it currently houses a school, the Manor is still open for tours in the summer. (Open June 22-Aug. 15 M-F 9am-4pm; Aug. 16-June 21 M-F 9am-4pm. 7EEK, students 3EEK.)

With a population of 200, **Käina**, southwest of Suuremõisa, remains Hiiumaa's second-largest town. The **Käina Church** had been the focus of the Käina settlement since 1422, but a German air attack in 1941 left it in ruins. **Lilia Restoran**, Hiiu mnt. 22, in Käina, serves fancy-pants food like chicken Kyiv and roast salmon with mushrooms at normal-pants prices. (☎361 46. Main dishes 32-140EEK. Open daily noon-11pm.) If you want to crash nearby, 🏠 **Puulaiu Matkamaja** (Campground Puulaid), is only a short distance from Käina. Ask the bus driver to let you off at Puulaid. It's among the nicer budget hotels in Estonia. It also rents boats for 16EEK per hr. (☎361 26. Breakfast 40EEK. Rooms and tents 20EEK per person.)

The tiny island of 🏠 **Kassari** (ka-SA-ree), south of Käina, is home to even thicker woods and wilder sights. The most beautiful of the island's sights is **Sääretirp**, a 1.3m wide peninsula jutting 3km into the sea, lined with wild strawberry and juniper bushes. Legend holds that this is what's left of a bridge built by the giant Leiger between Hiiumaa and Saaremaa so that his brother Suur Tõll could come for a visit. Today most visitors aren't there for work, but to sunbathe at one of the many beaches that line the peninsula. For a break from the sun, you might want to stop in at **Hiumaa Museum,** just off the main road in the middle of the island. Displaying the history and wildlife of Hiumaa, its highlight may be the historical display on the communist period. (☎971 81. Open daily 10am-5:30pm. 5EEK, students 3EEK.)

# INLAND ESTONIA

The roads that head inland from Tallinn lead to Tartu, the geographic, intellectual, and historic heart of the country. The juxtaposition of a student population with the oldest city in the Baltics makes for an appealing mix of history and youthful energy. Along another fork of the road, travelers can rekindle dragon-slaying fantasies of their youth while climbing what's left of the medieval fortress at Viljandi.

## TARTU                                                                      ☎(8)7

Tartu (pop. 100,000) may be one of the oldest city in the Baltics, but it is also a fountain of youth, having been razed and rebuilt five times since its founding in 1030. Today, that youthfulness persists at the University, long a wellspring of Estonian nationalism and the source of the youthful buzz that keeps the city hopping. Tartu may slow down a bit in summer when its budding intellectuals scamper to the coast, but there's still plenty of music, theater, and nightlife to keep the residents of Estonia's second largest city entertained.

### ■ ORIENTATION

The **bus** and **train stations** border the center of town on opposite sides. The main artery, **Riia mnt.,** runs into the center from the southwest and ends by the bus station. Perpendicular to it near the **Emajõgi River** is **Turu pst.,** which turns into **Vabaduse pst.** and runs from the bus station along the river toward the northeast. **Raekoja plats** (Town Hall Square), the city's geographical and social center, stretches west from the Emajõgi river toward the old castle hills. **Rüütli** heads north from the square; its end at Lai marks the boundary of the historic center. Behind the town hall, **Lossi** meanders uphill between the two peaks of **Toomemägi** (Cathedral Hill) and intersects **Vallikraavi,** a crooked, cobblestone road that follows the path of the old moat circling the hills and joins **Kuperjanovi,** leading to the train station.

### ■ TRANSPORTATION

**Trains:** Vaksali 6 (☎37 32 20). At the intersection of Kuperjanovi and Vaksali, 1½km from the city center. Info booth open daily 7am-noon and 1-7pm. To **Tallinn** (3½hr., 3 per day, 70EEK).

**Buses:** Turu 2 (☎47 72 27). On the corner of Riia and Turu, 300m southeast of Raekoja plats along Vabaduse. The best way to get to Tartu. To: **Tallinn** (2-5hr., 44 per day, 85-90EEK); **Pärnu** (4hr., 12 per day, 84-100EEK); **Rīga, LAT** (5hr., 1 per day, 150EEK); and **St. Petersburg, RUS** (10hr., 2 per day, 160EEK). Info booth open daily 8am-8pm.

**Public Transportation:** Bus tickets 6EEK from kiosks, 8EEK on board. Buses #5 and 6 go from the train station to Raekoja plats and the bus station. Bus #4 travels down Võru. Buses #3, 8, 2, 22 and 11 travel away from the river on Riia; #3, 6, 7, 8, 11, and 21 head towards it.

**Taxis:** Outside the bus and train stations (6EEK per km).

### ■ PRACTICAL INFORMATION

**Tourist Office:** Raekoja plats 12 (☎/fax 43 21 41; info@tartu.turism.ee; www.tartu.ee). Provides English info, orders guides and rental cars, and arranges lodging. **Maps** 10E-90EEK. Open M-F 10am-6pm, Sa 10am-3pm; in summer also Su 10am-2pm.

**Currency Exchange:** Best rates at banks. **Eesti Ühispank,** Ülikooli 1, gives **cash advances,** cashes AmEx **traveler's cheques,** and has an **ATM.** Open M-F 9am-6pm.

**Luggage Storage:** In the bus station. 4-12EEK per bag. Open M-Sa 6am-10pm, Su 7am-10pm, with a lunch break daily 3-3:30pm.

**24hr. Pharmacy: Raekoja Apteek** (☎43 35 28), on the north side of the Town Hall.

**Telephones:** Lai 27 (☎43 16 61; fax 43 39 93). At the corner of Rüütli. Card phones and **fax** machine. Open M-F 8am-6pm, Sa-Su 9am-4pm.

**Internet Access: Cafe Virtual,** Pikk 40 (☎40 25 09). A sleek cafe with several computers and TVs. 30EEK per hr. Open daily 11am-midnight.

**Post Office:** Vanemuise 7 (☎44 06 05). Open M-F 8am-7pm, Sa 9am-3pm.

**Postal code:** 51003.

# ACCOMMODATIONS

Tartu has a number of small, inexpensive bed and breakfasts that are often better than hostels. Contact the tourist office for information.

**Külalistemaja Salimo,** Kopli 1 (☎/fax 47 08 88), 3km southeast of the train station off Võru. Take bus #4 from the beginning of Riia opposite the Kaubamaja to "Alasi." Walk 25m to your left, cross Võru, and turn left onto Kolpi. Although a bit far from town, Salimo is brighter and cleaner than others more centrally located. 2 rooms share bath. Renovated doubles 320EEK per person; unrenovated triples 210EEK per person.

**Hostel Tartu (HI),** Soola 3 (☎43 20 91; fax 43 30 41), in the center of town directly across from bus station. Aging yellow building houses big rooms with big beds. A bargain only for HI members. Sauna 140EEK per hr. Check-out noon. Singles with toilet 200EEK, nonmembers 410EEK; doubles 720EEK, 990EEK. MC/Visa.

**Külalistemaja Tähtvere,** Laulupeo pst. 19, 2nd floor (☎42 17 08). From the bus station, follow Riia across Turu and turn right on Ülikodi. A block beyond the pink hall, turn left on Jakobi. Go uphill and turn right on Laulupeo. This 16-bed hotel in a sports hall has the town's cheapest rooms. No English spoken. Singles 100EEK; doubles 200EEK.

# FOOD

A large combination **supermarket** and department store, Tartu Kaubamaja, is at Riia 2 (☎47 62 31; open M-F 10am-8pm, Sa 10am-6pm, Su 11am-5pm; MC/Visa). The indoor *turg* (market) on the corner of Vabaduse and Vanemuise, opposite the bus station, is not only a great place to buy inexpensive meats and produce, but also provides a bustling glimpse of Estonian culture. (Open M-F 7:30am-5:30pm, Sa 7:30am-4pm, Su 7:30am-3pm.)

**Tavern,** Raekoja plats 20 (☎431 22 22). Yummy international meat dishes, several vegetarian dishes, and a wine list is as long as the menu. Main dishes 50-100EEK; beer 23EEK; 0.75L of wine 150EEK. Open Su-Th 11am-midnight, F-Sa 11am-1am.

**Pool Russ,** Rüütli 1 (☎256 220 372), just off Raekoja plats. Has a unique build-your-own menu (meat 39-79EEK, side dishes 5-16EEK). Also serves cheap pub grub (blood dumplings 30EEK). Happy hour 5:30-6:30pm; beer 15EEK. Open daily noon-4am. The Mexican **Arriba,** in the same building, serves Tex-Mex for 35-50EEK.

**Rotundi Kohvik,** the low wooden octagon in the park on Toomemägi near Angel's Bridge. Get your grub on with ample portions of Estonian favorites while surrounded by windows that provide a great view of the park. No English menu, so be sure to know your *schnitzel* and *pelmenid* beforehand. Main dishes 40-50EEK. Open daily 11am-8pm.

# SIGHTS

**TOWN HALL SQUARE.** (Raekoja plats.) The 1775 Town Hall Square is the social center of Tartu. The **town hall** was constructed in Dutch style. In front stands a fountain of a couple kissing in the rain, one of Tartu's trademarks. Near the bridge, Raekoja plats 18, now leans (much like the student population here) a little to the

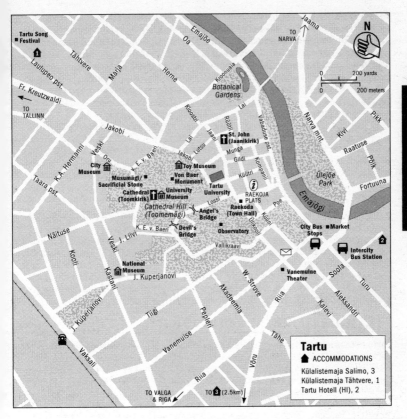

**ESTONIA**

**Tartu**
♦ ACCOMMODATIONS
Külalistemaja Salimo, 3
Külalistemaja Tähtvere, 1
Tartu Hotell (HI), 2

left. Inside is the **Tartu Art Museum** (Tartu Kunstimuuseum), which hosts temporary exhibits. (☎44 10 80. Open W-Su 11am-6pm. 5EEK, students 2EEK; F free.)

**TARTU UNIVERSITY.** (Tartu Ülikool.) Founded in 1908 to teach government officials and Protestant clergy, it was modeled after Uppsala University in Sweden. Inside the main building sits the **Museum of Classical Art,** which houses copies of Greek and Roman statues and a scary 4,000-year-old baby mummy. You can also see the assembly hall or the lock-up where naughty students were punished. The only university in the Russian empire with the right to have fraternities after the Great Northern War, Tartu used the privilege well: the **Estonian National Awakening** began here with the founding of the Estonian Student Association (Eesti Üliõpilaste Selts) in 1870. The nationalists who constituted the fraternity became so central to Estonia's struggle for independence that when the country won its freedom in 1919, the frat's colors (blue, black, and white) became those of the national flag. (Ülikooli 8. Follow Ülikooli from behind the town hall. ☎46 53 84. Open M-F 11am-4:30pm. Museum 7EEK, students 4EEK. Lock-up 5EEK, 2EEK. Assembly hall 10EEK, 4EEK.)

**OTHER SIGHTS ON ÜLIKOOLI.** Farther up Ülikooli (which becomes Jaani), **St. John's Church** (Jaani-kirik), completed in 1323, is unique among Gothic structures with its thousands of terracotta saints, martyrs, and other figures. Only a few hundred figures remain from the Russian recapture of Tartu in 1944. (Lutsu 16/24.) At the intersection of Lai and Toomemägi Hill, a path leads up to the **Tartu Toy Museum** (Mänguasja Muuseum), which entertains with a collection of antique dolls and toys from around the world. (Lai 1. ☎25 08 25 36. Open W-Su 11am-6am. 4EEK.)

**CATHEDRAL HILL.** (Toomemägi.) The hill's central site is the ruins of the once-majestic 15th-century **Cathedral of St. Peter and Paul.** An adjoining building houses the ▨ **Tartu University Museum** (Museum Historicum Universitatis Tartuensis), which features scientific instruments and history of the university. The faint-hearted should avoid the jarred human fetuses. (☎ 37 56 74. Open W-Su 11am-5pm. 10EEK, students 5EEK. English tours.) Near the church and two Swedish 17th-century cannons, **Kissing Hill** (Musumägi), once part of a prison tower, is now a makeout spot and the site of an ancient pagan sacrificial stone. Two bridges lead to the east hump of Toomemägi—the pink wooden **Angel's Bridge** (Inglisild) and the concrete **Devil's Bridge** (Kuradisild). An annual competition between the university choirs takes place on these bridges—women on the former, men on the latter. Cathedral Hill is also littered with **statues.** At the bottom of the hill stands Nikolai Pirogov, a 19th-century pioneer in the field of anaesthesia while on the hill itself stands Krist-jan Joak Peterson, national poet and the first Estonian to attend Tartu University. Embryologist Karl Ernst von Baer, who graces the 2EEK banknote, tops the hill, awaiting the annual spring ritual of biology students dousing him with champagne.

**OTHER MUSEUMS.** The **Estonian National Museum** (Eesti Rahva Muuseum) displays folk costumes, furniture, and model houses. (J. Kuperjanov 9. Follow Riia uphill from the bus station. Turn right on Pepleri and follow it around the bend to the left as it becomes Kuperjanovi. ☎ 42 13 11. Open W-Su 11am-6pm. 10EEK, students 8EEK. F free.) Tartu's **City Museum** (Linnamuuseum) houses the table on which the Peace Treaty of Tartu was signed between Russia and the nascent Estonian Republic on February 2, 1920, ending the Estonian War of Independence, but was closed for renovation at press time. (New location will be 23 Narva mnt.; call the tourist office for more info.)

## ▣ ▨ ENTERTAINMENT AND NIGHTLIFE

Tartu comes alive in the evenings with bar-hoppers roaming **Raekoja plats.** Bulletin boards in the lobby of the main university building (Ülikooli 20) advertise week-end happenings. Less frequent events include the end of May's "Rock Box" Festi-val, showcasing Estonian bands. The **Dionysia** arts festival, held from late March to early April, includes drama and dance performances, film screenings, and art exhi-bitions all over Tartu (for information, call the Vanemuine theater, below). The 1st Estonian-language theater, **Vanemuine,** Vanemuise 6, founded in 1870, stages operas and classical concerts; it is closed in the summer. (☎ 434 059. Box office open M-Sa 9am-7pm.) **Eesti Suve Teater** (Summer Theater) picks up the slack, with swashbuckling Estonian renditions of western classics on the riverside or in the medieval church on Cathedral Hill. (Performances run July-Aug. ☎ 427 471.)

- ▨ **Wilde Bar,** Vallikraavi 4 (☎ 30 97 64; fax 30 97 61). A bronze Oscar Wilde meets his Estonian counterpart Eduard on the bench outside this Wildely popular haunt. Irish and Estonian vittles served with national brews. 0.5L domestic beer 25EEK. Live music F and Sa nights. Open Su-Tu noon-midnight, W-Th noon-1am, F-Sa noon-2am.

- ▨ **Krooks,** Jakobi 34 (☎ 44 15 06), at the bottom of Toomemägi. Rock album covers and neon lights provide the backdrop for a relaxed crowd to chat and drink. 0.5L Guinness 28EEK. Open daily noon-4:30am.

- **Atlantis,** Narva mnt 2 (☎ 44 15 09), across the river. This super-disco looks like it dropped out of the sky onto the banks of the River Emajõgi. Patrons in the round glass restaurant look out over the river as others gamble or shoot stick in the casino and bil-liard hall below. Later, everyone converges on the groovy "underwater" dance floor. 21+. Dress code. Cover 35-85EEK. Disco open T-Th 10pm-3am, F-Sa 10pm-4am. Res-taurant open Su-Th noon-midnight, F-Sa noon-1am. Casino open 7pm-7am. MC/Visa.

## ▣ DAYTRIPS FROM TARTU

### OTEPÄÄ ☎ (8)276

Buses go between Tartu and Otepää (50-70min., approx. every hr., 18EEK). The tourist office, Lippuväljak 13, sells maps for 10EEK. (☎ 553 64; fax 612 46. otturinf@estpak.ee.

*www.tourism.ee/otepaais. Open M-F 9am-6pm, Sa-Su 10am-3pm.) Kassin Racing Center, Tartu mnt. 1a, across from the tourist office, rents bikes. (☎615 23 and mobile ☎250 37 152. Open M-F 10am-6pm; Sa-Su 10am-3pm. 200EEK per day.)*

Otepää is a small town only an hour away from Tartu by bus but ages away in atmosphere. Located in a scenic region of green fields and blue waterways, the village is quietly dominated by **Pühajärve** (Holy Lake). Pühajärve, so named after having been blessed by the Dalai Lama in October 1991, is surrounded by forests so lush they seem almost primeval—a day spent exploring the many inlets and islands of the lake by canoe makes a welcome reprieve from city life. To get to the lake, follow Pühajärve tee until you reach the parking lot. Take the small rocky path which hugs the shores of the lake, passing the amphitheater and onto the beach. On your way, be sure to stop by the **Dalai Lama monument,** behind the amphitheater. (Beach open daily 10am-7pm. 50-100EEK.) Continue up Pühajärve tee as it becomes Tartu mnt. Follow the signs for a wide right. To the right on Võru will be the 1890 **Lutheran Church.** (☎550 75. Open by appointment only.) Near the church gates is a path leading to **Otepää Linnamägi,** the hilltop remains of Otepää's 18th-century fortress. The smell of the wildflowers growing among the ruins is almost as intoxicating as the views of the surrounding countryside.

**Kesklinna Hostel,** Lipuväljak 11, diagonally across from the tourist office, is conveniently located and features clean bright, rooms. (☎255 77 414. Reception 24hr. 150EEK per person.) Grab a bite to eat at the pub **Edgari Trahter,** Lipuväljak 10. (☎546 34. Main dishes 15-55EEK. Open M-Sa 9am-10pm, Su 10am-10pm.)

# VILJANDI ☎ (8)43

*Buses, Ilmarise 1 (☎336 80), run to: Tartu (2hr., 14 per day, 35-45EEK); Pärnu (2hr., 9 per day, 50-65EEK); and Tallinn (2½-3hr., 20 per day, 70-85EEK). Cashier open daily 5:30am-11am and noon-5:30pm. Luggage 5:30am-8pm. The tourist office, at Tallinna 2b (☎/fax 337 55; info@viljandi.tourism.ee; www.tourism.ee/viljandi), has maps. Open daily May-Aug. 9am-6pm; Sept.-Aug. M-F 10am-5pm, Sa 10am-2pm.*

Viljandi, a small town littered with picturesque old buildings and footbridges, is a gratifying exception to the flatness of the rest of Estonia. Its imposing **Order's Castle** (Ordulinnuse varemed), now in ruins, was founded by the Knights of the Sword in the 13th century. One of the largest in the Baltics, the fortress once spanned three hilltops with high-flying bridges. Today, the ruins afford not only an impressive view of **Viljandi Lake** (järv), but also numerous opportunities for exploration, starting with the stone archway that leads to the last remaining wall of the **keep** and is now used as a backdrop for spooky summer productions. Around the back of the keep, the 1879 **suspension footbridge** (Rippsild) leading to town was sent to Viljandi in 1931 by a German count to stop his daughter from racing her horses over it. The easiest way to the castle from the bus station is to walk down Tallinna, the main street, towards the river as the road becomes Tasuja pst. At the end of Tasuja, the small path slightly to your left which leads to the castle. In the central castle park is the medieval **St. John's Church** (Jaani kirik. Open daily 10am-5pm.) Along the longer route on **Lossi,** the main street of the Old Town, you'll pass by **Viljandi Museum,** Laidoneri plats 10. It features some crazy taxidermy—check out the wild-eared prehistoric squirrel—and a model of the fortress in its glory days. (☎333 16. Open summer W-Su 11am-6pm; off-season 10am-5pm. 6EEK, students 3EEK.) When you're done, head down to the **lake** for a swim or a beer from the roving bars along the water.

In a run-down building by the lake, **Kalevi Viljandi Motel,** Ranna 6, is a hostel with twin rooms and quite possibly the cleanest bathrooms in Eastern Europe. From the bus station, turn off Tallinna onto Kauba and follow it down the stairs. Turn left at the statue of the hyperventilating runner; it's the first building on the left. (☎472 70. 80EEK per person.) **Tasuja Kohvik,** Vadabuse plats, has schnitzel for 60EEK. (☎331 42. Open M-F 9am-9pm, Sa 11am-10pm, Su 11am-9pm.) **Rema 1000,** Tallinna 24, is a huge **grocery store.** (Open daily 8am-10pm.)

# HUNGARY (MAGYARORSZÁG)

## IF YOU'RE THERE...

**3-5 DAYS.** Indulge yourself in **Budapest's** (p. 318) hedonistic Turkish baths, sinful restaurants, and opulent Opera House.

**1-2 WEEKS.** If you can bring yourself to leave **Budapest,** daytrip to **Esztergom** (p. 340) or **Szentendre** (p. 338). Then take one of the following trips: go east to **Eger** (p. 375), whose abundant wine cellars attract the region's most discriminating drunks; south to the cosmopolitan **Pécs** (p. 361), whose contemporary art museums and nightlife are the best outside of Budapest; or east to the charming **Győr** (p. 342) and culturally-enlightening **Archabbey of Pannonhalma** (p. 344).

Communism was a mere blip in Hungary's 1100-year history of repression and renewal. Today, the nation appears well at ease with its new-found capitalist identity. Budapest remains Hungary's social and economic keystone, although it by no means has a monopoly on cultural attractions, and intriguing provincial capitals lie within a three-hour train ride. Nonetheless, with luscious wine valleys nestled in the northern hills, a rough and tumble cowboy plain in the south, and a bikini-worthy beach resort in the east, the beauty of the countryside should not be forsaken for a whirlwind tour of the capital. Otherwise, you'll have seen the heart of Hungary, but missed its soul entirely.

## HUNGARY AT A GLANCE

**OFFICIAL NAME:** Republic of Hungary

**CAPITAL:** Budapest (pop. 1.9 million)

**POPULATION:** 10 million (90% Magyar, 4% Roma, 3% German, 2% Serb, 1% other)

**LANGUAGE:** Hungarian (Magyar)

**CURRENCY:** 1 forint (Ft) = 100 filler

**RELIGION:** 68% Roman Catholic, 20% Calvinist, 5% Lutheran, 7% other

**LAND AREA:** 92,340 km²

**CLIMATE:** Continental

**GEOGRAPHY:** Mostly plains; low mountains and hills on Slovakian border

**BORDERS:** Austria, Croatia, Romania, Slovakia, Slovenia, Ukraine, Yugoslavia

**ECONOMY:** 67% Services, 30% Industry, 3% Agriculture

**GDP:** US$4340 per capita

**EMERGENCY PHONE NUMBERS:** Ambulance 104, Fire 105, Police 107

**COUNTRY CODE:** 36

**INTERNATIONAL DIALING PREFIX:** 00

# HISTORY

**THE MIGHTY MAGYARS.** Modern Hungary was inhabited by hunters, gatherers, Neolithic farmers, and Scythians into the Late Stone Age, as evidenced by the Istálósk cave near Budapest (see **Szilvásvárad,** p. 379). In the third century BC, **Celtic tribes** forced their way onto the territory and were soon followed by the **Romans** (see **Aquincum,** p. 332), who founded the provinces of Pannonia and Dacia in the early post-Augustan period and maintained them through the 4th century AD.

The **Magyars,** mounted warrior tribes from Central Asia, arrived in AD 896. Led by **Prince Árpád,** it took them only a few years to conquer the middle basin of the Danube River. Árpád's descendant, **Stephen I,** was crowned King of Hungary with the benediction from Pope Sylvester II on Christmas Day, 1000. Canonized in 1083, Stephen is considered the founder of the modern Hungarian state.

Hungary

**THE GOLDEN YEARS.** A series of strong monarchs developed a system of imperial control over the next hundred years, generating a lot of revenue and uniting the country. The nobility grew restless with the blunders of Andrew II, however, and in 1222 he was forced to sign the **Golden Bull,** granting rights to the people and restricting the powers of the monarchy. The devastating Mongolian invasion came just under two decades later and in 1301 the Árpáds died out and were replaced by a variety of families from across Europe. As leadership changed hands in the 14th century, Hungary reached its **Golden Age,** so named for both its military stability and the gold mines controlled by its monarchs.

**ONLY THE GOOD DIE YOUNG.** Unfortunately, royal infighting gradually weakened the country and in the mid-15th century, Mátyás Hunyadi, known as **Matthias Corvinus** (1458-1490), was imprisoned in Prague by claimants to the throne after the death of his father **János Hunyadi.** Corvinus was freed and coronated by the nobility, and presided over Hungary's Renaissance, stressing the importance of art and science and cultivating an extensive library. Following Matthias' death, the bourgeoisie ensured that nearly all his reforms were undone. The peasants, horribly oppressed, staged an unsuccessful rebellion in 1514, leading to civil rights setbacks that took hundreds of years to repair. The army, in disarray, was easily defeated by the Turks at **Mohács** in 1526.

**THE RISE AND DEMISE OF THE AUSTRO-HUNGARIAN EMPIRE.** Conflict among the Protestant nobility, the Ottomans, and the Holy Roman Empire plagued Hungary for the next 150 years, until the Austrian Habsburgs took over in the early 17th century. A new war of independence began in 1848, led spiritually by the young poet Sándor Petőfi and politically by Lajos Kossuth. Together, they convinced the Diet (parliament) to pass a series of reforms that became known as the **April Laws.** Kossuth's state held out for one year, but in the summer of 1849 Habsburg Emperor Franz Josef I retook Budapest with the support of Tsar Nicholas I of Russia. Despite a period of repression, Hungary (under the leadership of Ferenc Deák) was granted its own government by the **Compromise of 1867,** resulting in the **Dual Monarchy** of the **Austro-Hungarian Empire.** Nationalist sentiment grew, leading to linguistic and institutional policies in the empire that favored the Magyars. Opposition movements emerged among Romanians, Serbs, Croats, and Slovaks in response. These divisions erupted during World War I, resulting in the permanent destruction of the Austro-Hungarian Empire. After the war, Hungary gave up two-thirds of its territory to several countries of the Allied Powers in the 1920 **Treaty of Trianon**.

**APOCALYPSE.** The Bourgeois Democratic Revolution that overthrew the monarchy in 1918 was followed by the 133-day Communist Hungarian Republic of Councils under the leadership of **Béla Kun.** Counter-revolutionary forces eventually took control, though, brutally punishing those involved with the Communist administration. **Admiral Miklós Horthy** then settled in for 24 years of control (1920-44), initially overseeing a democratic government run by István Bethlen, but always ultimately maintaining dictatorial control. The depressed interwar years were followed by a tentative alliance with Hitler in **World War II,** then by a year-long Nazi occupation and the near-total destruction of Budapest during the two-month Soviet siege of 1945. Two-thirds of Hungary's Jews, whose numbers had approached one million before the war, were murdered. Nearly all survivors fled the country.

**BACK IN THE USSR.** In 1949 Hungary became a People's Republic under **Mátyás Rákosi** and the Hungarian Workers' Party. Under his leadership, the country became tied to the USSR economically and politically, often serving as a "workshop" to fulfill Soviet industrial needs. Rákosi lost control in the **1956 Uprising,** a violent rebellion in Budapest in which **Imre Nagy** declared a neutral, non-Warsaw Pact government. Soviet troops crushed the revolt and executed Nagy and thousands of protesters.

**FIGHT FOR YOUR RIGHT (TO PARTY).** Over the next three decades Nagy's replacement, **Janos Kádár,** oversaw the partial opening of borders and a rise in the national standard of living. Inflation and stagnation halted progress in the 1980s, but democratic reformers in the Communist Party pushed Kádár aside in 1988, pressing for a market economy and increased political freedom. In autumn 1989 Hungary broke away from the Soviet orbit and the first free elections in 1990 transferred power to the Hungarian Democratic Forum. Slow progress, skyrocketing inflation, and unemployment, however, eroded its popularity. The renamed-and-revamped Socialists returned to power as prime minister **Gyula Horn** of the **Hungarian Socialist Party** won in the elections of 1994, promising a moderate course.

# POLITICS

The **president**, who serves a five-year term, is commander-in-chief of the armed forces but has authority over little else. The 386-member National Assembly has the real power, as it elects the **prime** and **cabinet ministers** that comprise the Council of Ministers in addition to electing the president. Members are elected to parliament every four years. Six parties participate regularly in parliament: the Hungarian Democratic Forum, the Alliance of Free Democrats, the Independent Smallholders' Party, the Christian Democratic People's Party, the Federation of Young Democrats, and the Socialist Party.

May 1998 elections favored the conservative **Hungarian Citizens' Party,** whose leader, 36-year-old **Victor Orbán,** is the youngest prime minister in Europe. On June 6, 2000, 69-year-old law professor **Ferenc Madl**, also conservative, was elected president. Although he ran uncontested and is supported by the majority parties in parliament, it took three rounds to elect him. He replaced outgoing president **Árpád Göncz** on August 4. Göncz, Hungary's most popular political figure, is a former political prisoner who served two terms as Hungary's first non-Communist president.

With increasing integration into the West, the only visible vestiges of the old regime are now benign: efficient public transportation, clean parks and streets, and a low incidence of violent crime. Hungary has lowered inflation, stemmed rising unemployment, and is experiencing consistent GDP growth. **EU** accession negotiations began in March 1998, although the EU is not expected to let in new members until 2003. Hungary accepted **NATO membership** in 1999, but change has not been easy, and Hungary's economic transition remains incomplete. Like most other budding capitalist countries, Hungary's hot political topics include wages and inflation.

The 1999 conflict in Yugoslavia had little effect on Hungary, despite bombings in the ethnically Hungarian Yugoslavia province of Vojvodina, 10km from Szeged.

**Neo-Nazism** is unfortunately on the rise, particularly in Budapest and Szombathely. In early 1999, neo-Nazis staged a pan-European conference in the capital. Whether the rise in Nazi-related graffiti adorning Hungarian buildings is directly related to the high-profile conference is unclear. What is clear, however, is that a veritable spray-paint war is being fought on Hungarian bricks. In general, neo-Nazism does not effect tourists and is more rhetoric than action.

# CULTURE

## NATIONAL HOLIDAYS IN 2001

| | |
|---|---|
| **January 1** New Year | **June 3-4** Pentecost |
| **March 15** National Day | **August 20** Constitution Day |
| **April 15-16** Easter | **October 23** Republic Day |
| **May 1** Labor Day | **December 25-26** Catholic Christmas |

## LITERATURE

The generation of writers that lived through the Revolution of 1848 played an important role in Hungary's history. Most notably, the Populist, anti-Romantic **Sándor Petőfi** (1823-1849) fueled the nationalistic rhetoric that drove the revolution. Hungarian literature matured with the founding of the *Nyugat* (West) literary journal in 1908, while the avant-garde poet and artist **Lajos Kassák,** unconnected with *Nyugat,* concerned himself with Hungarian working-class life. After World War II, Communism forced Magyar writers to adopt the doctrine of **Socialist Realism,** but eventually a new generation appeared that was able to develop individual styles more freely. **György Konrád,** one of the most important Hungarian authors of the century, wrote novels that were crucial in defining the dissident movements of Central Europe. Less concerned with social issues than with the Postmodern exploration of the meaning and use of words themselves, **Péter Esterházy** began a new movement, returning Magyar literature to the world cultural scene.

## MUSIC AND OTHER ARTS

Music is the element of Hungary's cultural tradition that has gained the most international acclaim. The greatest piano virtuoso of his time, **Franz Liszt** (1811-1886) was also the most prolific musician in Hungary's history. Liszt's contributions to music range from advancing the technique of piano composition to give the piano a fuller sound to inventing the **symphonic poem.** Even though he spoke German, not Hungarian, and is not commonly associated with Hungary, his heritage shines through in his Hungarian Rhapsodies. Nineteen in sum, they are are based on the spirit of Hungarian folk music. Liszt eventually wrote "Hungarian songs became the blood of my soul." Similarly, **Béla Bartók** (1881-1945) was influential for his use of folk material to create music that expressed a deep sense of nationalism. His most famous works include his string quartets and his *Concerto for Orchestra.*

**EGOLISZTICAL** The virtuoso Liszt was so vain that he initiated the practice of performing concerts in profile so the audience could admire the contour of his face. He also played the piano so violently that it shook at times, and he took to performing with 2 pianos on stage so he would have an extra in the event that he broke the strings on the first instrument...or sometimes the piano itself. Silliness aside, in spite of his reputation as a self-centered prima donna, Liszt actually did much to promote his colleagues' work—by transcribing symphonic and other works for piano, he made these pieces accessible to the public.

The 20th century also saw **Lajos Kassák** and **László Moholy-Nagy** as internationally significant avant-garde painters and **Miklós Jancscó** and **István Szabó** as pioneers in Hungarian film. One of the staples of Hungarian culture is **folk dancing. Csárdás** is the national dance that includes women's circle and men's bootslapping dances. All begin with a slow section (lassu) and end in a fast section (friss). Dancers don embroidered costumes and perform to lively music in duple time.

## FOOD AND DRINK

Hungarian food is more flavorful and varied than standard Eastern European fare. **Paprika,** Hungary's chief agricultural export, colors most dishes red. In Hungarian restaurants (*vendéglő* or *étterem*), begin with *halászlé,* a deliciously spicy fish stew. Alternately, try *gyümölesleves,* a cold fruit soup topped with whipped cream. The Hungarian national dish is *bográcsgulyás* (goulash), a stew of beef, onions, green pepper, tomatoes, potatoes, dumplings, and plenty of paprika. *Borjúpaprikás* is veal with paprika and potato-dumpling pasta. Vegetarians can find recourse in the tasty *rántott sajt* (fried cheese) and *gombapörkölt* (mushroom stew) on most menus. In general, Hungarian food is fried, and fresh vegetables other than peppers and cabbage are a rarity.

In a *cukrászda* (confectionery), you can satisfy your sweet tooth for dangerously few *forints. Túrós rétes* is a chewy pastry pocket filled with sweetened cottage cheese. *Somlói galuska* is a fantastically rich sponge cake of chocolate, nuts, and cream, all soaked in rum. The Austrians stole the recipe for *rétes* and called it "strudel," but this delicious concoction is as Hungarian as Zsa Zsa Gabor. *Kávé* is espresso, served in thimble-sized cups and so strong your veins will be popping before you finish the first sip.

Hungary produces a diverse array of fine wines (see **A Mini-Guide to Hungarian Wine,** p. 382). *Sör* (Hungarian beer) ranges from the first-rate to the merely acceptable. *Dreher Bak* is a rich, dark brew. Good light beers include *Dreher Pils, Szalon Sör,* and licensed versions of *Steffl, Gold Fassl, Gösser,* and *Amstel.* Hungary also produces different types of *pálinka,* a liquor that resembles brandy. Among the best tasting are *barackpálinka* (similar to apricot schnapps) and *szilvapálinka* (plum brandy). *Unicum,* advertised as the national drink of Hungary, is a very fine herbal liqueur that Habsburg kings used to cure digestive ailments.

## CUSTOMS AND ETIQUETTE

**Business hours** in Hungary are Monday to Friday 9am-5pm (grocery stores tend to open earlier and close later). Banks close around 1-3pm on Friday. **Museums** are usually open Tuesday to Sunday 10am-5pm, with Tuesdays an occasional free day. ISIC holders usually get discounts on admission. Rounding up the bill as a **tip** is standard for a job well done—especially in restaurants, but also for everyone from taxi-drivers to hairdressers. Remember in restaurants to hand the tip to the server when you pay, as it's rude to leave it on the table. Waiters usually expect foreigners to tip 15%, although locals never give more than 10%. Bathroom attendants get 30Ft.

The frequency and extent of public displays of affection among young and old alike may be startling, or at least distracting—every bus has a couple exchanging bodily fluids. Taste in **clothing,** especially for men, is casual and unpretentious; you may see men over 50 sweeping the streets in Speedos. Modesty is not a strong point of Hungarian women's fashions, but people in small towns dress more conservatively. Hungarians are serious about cigarettes; **smoking** seems to be a national pastime. Dogs are family members and tend to be far bigger than the European average—no poodles here, thank you—and are spoiled rotten.

Because **paprika** is one of Hungary's most important commodities, exporting it is illegal. If you attempt to take it duty-free, border patrol will accost you—on trains, they check under every seat.

# LANGUAGE

**Hungarian** is distantly related to Turkish and even more distantly to Estonian and Finnish. After Hungarian and **German**, **English** is Hungary's third language. *"Hello"* is often used as an informal greeting or farewell. *"Szia!"* (sounds like "see ya!") is another greeting—you'll often hear friends cry: "Hallo, see ya!"

A few starters for pronunciation: *"c"* is pronounced "ts" as in "pots"; *"cs"* is "ch" as in "which"; *"gy"* is "dy" as in *"adieu"*; *"ly"* is "y" as in "yak"; *"s"* is "sh" as in "shard"; *"sz"* is "s" as in "cell-phone"; *"zs"* is "zh" as in "fusion"; and *"a"* is "a" as in "paw." The first syllable is always stressed. For common words and phrases, see **Glossary**, p. 314 and **Phrasebook**, p. 315.

# ADDITIONAL READING

*A History of Modern Hungary 1867-1994*, by Jorg K. Hoensch, provides a brief contextualization of Hungarian history, while *A History of Hungary*, edited by Peter Sugar, Peter Hanak, and Tibor Frank, is more exhaustive in its treatment. Gyorgy Konrad's collection of essays, *The Melancholy of Rebirth*, covers more recent events. *The Bridge at Andau*, by James Michener, is a popular account of the 1956 Uprising and Janos Nyiri's *Battlefields and Playgrounds* is a highly acclaimed recent novel on the Holocaust in Budapest. For modern fiction, anything by Peter Esterházy is outstanding, most notably *The Glance of Countess Hahn-Hahn* and (if you're willing to be seen with it) *A Little Hungarian Pornography*.

# TRAVELING ESSENTIALS

Citizens of Canada, Ireland, South Africa, the UK, and the US can visit Hungary without visas for 90 days, provided their passport does not expire within six months of their journey's end. Australians, and New Zealanders must obtain 90-day tourist visas from a Hungarian embassy or consulate. (See **Embassies and Consulates**, p. 18.) For US residents, visas cost: single-entry US$40, double-entry US$75, multiple-entry US$180, and 48hr. transit US$38. Non-US residents pay US$65, US$100, US$200, and US$50. Visa processing takes a few days and requires, in addition to the visa application and form, proof of transportation (such as an airplane ticket), a valid passport, three photographs (5 for multiple-entry visas), a money order, and a self-addressed, stamped (certified mail) envelope. Hungarian visas are occasionally available at the border, but always priced exorbitantly; it is safer and cheaper to arrange a visa before visiting. Visa extensions are rare; apply at local police stations. There is no fee for crossing a Hungarian border. In general, Hungarian customs are efficient; a border crossing should add no more than 30 minutes to your journey. The easiest way to enter or exit Hungary is to take a direct bus or train to or from Budapest to a neighboring country's capital.

# TRANSPORTATION

**BY PLANE.** Hungary's national airline, **Malév,** has daily direct flights from New York to Budapest and from London (both Gatwick and Heathrow) to Budapest. It also offers flights to neighboring countries. Otherwise, several international airlines fly into Budapest.

**BY TRAIN.** Most trains *(vonat)* pass through Budapest. They are generally reliable and inexpensive, although theft is frequent on the Vienna-Budapest line. **Eurail** and **EastRail** are valid in Hungary. Students and travelers under 26 are sometimes eligible for a 30% discount on train fares; inquire ahead and be persistent. An **ISIC** commands discounts at IBUSZ, Express, and station ticket counters. Flash your card and repeat "student," in Hungarian, *"diák"* (DEE-ahk). Book international tickets in advance.

*Személyvonat* trains are excruciatingly slow; *gyorsvonat* (listed on schedules in red) cost the same and move at least twice as fast. Large provincial towns are accessible by the blue *expressz* lines. Air-conditioned *InterCity* trains are fastest.

# GLOSSARY

| ENGLISH | HUNGARIAN | PRONOUNCE |
|---|---|---|
| one | egy | edge |
| two | kettő | ket-tuuh |
| three | három | hah-rom |
| four | négy | naydj |
| five | öt | uh-t |
| six | hat | hut |
| seven | hét | hayte |
| eight | nyolc | nyoltz |
| nine | kilenc | kih-lentz |
| ten | tíz | tease |
| twenty | húsz | hoose |
| thirty | harminc | har-mintz |
| forty | negyven | nedj-ven |
| fifty | ötven | ut-ven |
| sixty | hatvan | hut-von |
| seventy | hetven | het-ven |
| eighty | nyolcvan | nyoltz-van |
| ninety | kilencven | kih-lentz-ven |
| hundred | száz | saaz |
| thousand | ezer | eh-zehr |
| Monday | hétfő | hayte-phuuh |
| Tuesday | kedd | ked |
| Wednesday | szerda | sayr-dah |
| Thursday | csütörtök | chew-ter-tek |
| Friday | péntek | paine-tek |
| Saturday | szombat | SAWM-baht |
| Sunday | vasárnap | VAHSH-ahr-nahp |
| evening | ôhtul | EHKH-tul |
| today | ma | mah |
| tomorrow | holnap | HAWL-nahp |
| spring | kevad | KE-vad |
| summer | suvi | SU-vi |
| fall | sügis | SEW-gis |
| winter | talv | talv |
| holiday | ünnepnap | ewn-nap-nop |
| single/double | ühelist/kahelist | EW-hel-ist/KA-hel-list |

| ENGLISH | HUNGARIAN | PRONOUNCE |
|---|---|---|
| post office | posta | pawsh-tuh |
| stamp | bélyeg | BAY-yeg |
| airmail | légipostán | LAY-ghee-pawsh-tahn |
| departure | indulás | IN-dool-ahsh |
| arrival | érkezés | ayr-keh-zaysh |
| one-way | csak oda | chok AW-do |
| round-trip | oda-vissza | AW-do-VEES-so |
| train | vonat | VAW-not |
| bus | buss | busss |
| airport | repülőtér | rep-ewlu-TAYR |
| station | pályaudvar | pa-yo-OOT-var |
| ticket | jegyet | YED-et |
| grocery | élelmiszerbolt | Ay-lel-meser-balt |
| breakfast | reggeli | REG-gell-ee |
| lunch | ebéd | EB-ayhd |
| dinner | vacsora | VOTCH-oh-rah |
| menu | étlap | ATE-lop |
| bread | kenyér | KEN-yair |
| vegetables | zöldségek | ZULD-segek |
| beef | marhahúst | MOR-ho-hoosht |
| pork | sertéshúst | SHER-taysh-hoosht |
| fish | hal | hull |
| water | víz | veez |
| juice | gyümölcslé | DYEW-murl-chlay |
| coffee | kávé | KAA-vay |
| milk | tej | tay |
| beer | sör | shurr |
| wine | bor | bawr |
| market | suur toidukau-plus | suuur TOI-du-KAUP-lus |
| bakery | leivapood | LEI-va-POOOD |
| pharmacy | apteek | AP-teeek |
| bank | bank | bonk |
| city center | linnakeskus | LIN-na-KES-kus |
| exchange | valutabeváltó | VO-loo-tob-be-vaal-taw |
| left | vasakul | VA-sa-kul |
| right | paremal | PA-re-mal |

A *potegy* (seat reservation) is required on trains labeled "R." While you can board an *InterCity* train without a reservation, the fine for doing so is 1000Ft in addition to the cost of the reservation; purchasing the reservation on board will double the price of the ticket. Some basic vocabulary will help you navigate the rail system: *érkezés* (arrival), *indulás* (departure), *vágány* (track), and *állomás* or *pályaudvar* (station, abbreviated *pu.*); see the **Hungarian Glossary,** below. The *peron* (platform) for arrivals and departures is rarely indicated until the train approaches the station, and then the announcement will be in Hungarian. Many train stations are

# PHRASEBOOK

| ENGLISH | HUNGARIAN | PRONOUNCIATION |
|---|---|---|
| Yes/no | Igen/nem | EE-ghen/nem |
| Please | Kérem | KAY-rem |
| Thank you | Köszönöm | KUH-suh-num |
| Hello | Szervusz | SAIR-voose |
| Good-bye | Viszontlátásra | Vi-sont-lah-tah-shraw |
| Good morning | Jó reggelt | YOH reh-gehlt |
| Good night | Jó éjszakát | YOH ay-sokat |
| Excuse me | Elnézést | EL-nay-zaysht |
| When? | Mikor? | MI-kor |
| Where is...? | Hol van...? | hawl von |
| How do you get to...? | Hogy jutok...? | hawdj YOO-tawk |
| How much does this cost? | Mennyibe kerül? | MEN-yee-beh KEH-rewl |
| Do you have...? | Van...? | von |
| Do you speak English? | Beszél angolul? | BESS-ayl ON-goal-ool |
| I don't understand. | Nem értem | nem AYR-tem |
| I don't speak Hungarian. | Nem tudok magyarul. | Nehm TOO-dawk MAH-dyah-rool |
| Please write it down? | Kérem, írja fel. | KAY-rem, EER-yuh fell. |
| Speak a little slower, please. | Kérem, beszéljen lassan | KAY-rem, BESS-ayl-yen LUSH-shun |
| I'd like to order... | ...kérek. | KAY-rek |
| Do you have a vacancy? | Volna valami? | VAWL-na VO-lom-mee |
| I'd like a room. | Ma sooviksin tuba. | ma SOO-vik-sin TU-ba |
| May I see the room? | Kas ma saaksin tuba näha? | kas ma SAAAK-sin TU-ba NÆ-ha |
| No. I don't like it. | Ei. See ei meeldi mulle. | ei. seee ei MEEEL-di muLL-le |
| That's fine. I'll take it. | See sobib. Ma võtan selle. | seee SO-bib. ma VEH-tan SEL-le |
| Is this the right train/bus to...? | Kas see rong läheb...? | kas seee rong LÆ-heb RIII-ga |
| I want a ticket to... | Ma sooviksin ühte piletit... | ma SOO-vik-sin ewkh-te PI-le-tit |
| Will you tell me when to get off? | Palun öelge kus ma pean väljuma? | PA-lun UH-EL-geh kus |
| When is the first/next/last train to...? | Millal läheb esimene/järgmine/viimane rong...? | MI-llal LÆ-heb E-si-mene/YÆRG-mine/VII-mane rong |
| Where is the *bathroom*/nearest *telephone booth*/(public phone)/*center of town*? | Kus on lähim (avalik telefon)? | kus on LÆ-him (A-va-lik TE-le-fon) |
| I've lost my... | Ma olen oma...ära kaotanud. | ma O-len O-ma...Æ-ra KAO-ta-nud |
| Go away. | Tävozzék. | TAH-vawz-zayk |
| My name is... | ...vagyok | vah-djawk |
| What is your name? | Hogy hívják | hawdj HEE-vyahk |
| Check, please. | A számlát, kérem. | uh SAHM-lot KAY-rem |
| with shower/bath? | zahanyzós/fürdoszobás? | ZOO-hon-y-aw-yawsh/FEWR-dur-saw-baash |
| I'm lost. | Ma olen ära eksinud. | ma O-len Æ-ra EK-si-nud |

not marked; ask the conductor what time the train is expected to arrive (just point at your watch and say the town's name) and watch for a stop at that time.

**BY BUS.** Use buses to travel between the outer provincial centers. The cheap, clean, and crowded bus system links many towns that have rail connections only to Budapest. The **Erzsébet tér** bus station in Budapest posts schedules and fares. *Inter-City* bus tickets are purchased on board (arrive early if you want a seat). In larger cities, tickets for local transportation must be bought in advance from a newsstand

and punched when you get on; there's a fine if you're caught without a ticket. In smaller cities, you pay when you board (usually 60Ft).

**BY BIKE.** IBUSZ and Tourinform can provide brochures about cycling in Hungary that include maps, suggested tours, sights, accommodations, bike rental locations, repair shops, and border-crossings. If you feel like you're moving in circles, remember that streets names change arbitrarily, and many in Budapest occur more than once. Always check the district as well as the kind of street: **út** is a major thoroughfare, **utca** (u.) a street, **körút** (krt.) a circular artery, and **tér** a square.

# TOURIST SERVICES AND MONEY

| CURRENCY | | |
|---|---|---|
| US$1 = 290 FORINTS (FT, OR HUF) | | 100FT = US$0.34 |
| CDN$1 = 200FT | | 100FT = CDN$0.51 |
| UK£1 = 430FT | | 100FT = UK£0.24 |
| IR£1 = 330FT | | 100FT = IR£0.30 |
| AUS$1 = 170FT | | 100FT = AUS$0.60 |
| NZ$1 = 120FT | | 100FT = NZ$0.80 |
| SAR 1 = 42FT | | 100FT = SAR 2.40 |
| DM 1 = 130FT | | 100FT = DM 0.75 |

**Tourinform** has branches in every county, and is generally the most useful tourist service in Hungary. They can't make reservations, but they'll check on vacancies, usually in university dorms and private *panzió.* Tourinform should be your first stop in any Hungarian town, as they always stock maps and tons of local info. **IBUSZ** offices throughout the country book private rooms, exchange money, sell train tickets, and charter tours, although they are generally better at helping with travel plans than at providing information about the actual town. Snare the pamphlet *Tourist Information: Hungary* and the monthly entertainment guides *Programme in Hungary* and *Budapest Panorama* (all free and in English). **Express,** the former national student travel bureau, handles hostels and changes money. The staff usually speaks German, and sometimes English. Regional agencies are most helpful in the outlying areas. **Tourist bureaus** are generally open in summer Monday through Saturday 8am-8pm.

The national currency is the **forint,** divided into 100 **fillérs,** which are quickly disappearing from circulation. The rates given above are those for September 2000; **inflation** is hovering around 10%, so expect prices to increase over the next year. Make sure to keep some US dollars or Deutschmarks for visas, international train tickets, and (less often) private accommodations. New Zealand and Australian dollars, as well as South African rand and Irish pounds, are not exchangeable. Rates are generally poor at exchange offices with extended hours. The maximum permissible commission for cash-to-cash exchange is 1%. Allow 30min. to exchange money, and never change money on the street. **American Express** offices in Budapest and IBUSZ offices around the country convert **traveler's checks** to cash for a steep 6% commission; go instead to **OTP Bank** and **Postabank** offices. **Cash advances** are available at most OTP branches, but with the already abundant and ever-increasing number of **ATMs,** many banks no longer give them. Currency exchange machines are popping up all over and have excellent rates, although they tend to be slow. Major **credit cards** are accepted at expensive hotels and in many shops.

# HEALTH AND SAFETY

Medical assistance is most easily obtained in Budapest, where embassies carry a list of Anglophone doctors; additionally, most hospitals in the capital staff English-speaking doctors. Outside Budapest, try to bring a Hungarian speaker with you. All medical services must be paid for in cash. Tap water is usually clean and drinkable (except in the town of Tokaj, where it bears an uncanny resemblance to the neighboring Tisza River). Bottled water is available at every food store. Public bathrooms vary tremendously in cleanliness: pack soap and a towel, and be prepared to pay the attendant 30Ft. Also carry a roll of toilet paper with you, as hostels rarely have it and the single square you get in a public restroom is less than useful. Gentlemen should look for *Férfi*, and ladies for *Női* signs. *Gyógyszertar* (pharmacies) are well-stocked with Western brands and always carry hefty supplies of tampons and condoms. In bigger towns, there are most always 24hr. pharmacies. Violent **crime** in Hungary is low, but in larger cities, especially Budapest, foreign tourists are favorite targets of petty thieves and pickpockets. **Homosexuality,** although legal, is still not fully accepted in Hungarian society; discretion is wise.

# ACCOMMODATIONS AND CAMPING

Many travelers stay in **private homes** booked through a tourist agency. Singles are scarce—it's worth finding a roommate, as solo travelers must often pay for a double room. Agencies may try to foist off their most expensive rooms on you. Outside Budapest, the best and cheapest offices are region-specific (e.g. EgerTourist in Eger). These agencies will often make advance reservations for your next stop. After staying a few nights, you can make arrangements directly with the owner, thus saving yourself the agencies' 20-30% commission. **Panzió,** run out of private homes, are the next most common option, although not necessarily the cheapest.

Hotels exist in some towns, but most have disappeared. As the industry develops and room prices rise, **hosteling** is becoming more attractive, although it is rare outside Budapest. Hostels are usually large enough to accommodate summer crowds, and **HI cards** are increasingly useful. Sheets are rarely required. Many hostels can be booked through Express, the student travel agency, or sometimes the regional tourist office. From June through August, university **dorms** become hostels. Locations change annually; inquire at Tourinform and always call ahead.

More than 300 **campgrounds** are sprinkled throughout Hungary; most sites stay open from May through September. If you rent a bungalow you must pay for unfilled spaces. Tourist offices offer the annual booklet *Camping Hungary* for free. For more info and maps, contact Tourinform in Budapest.

# KEEPING IN TOUCH

The Hungarian **mail** system is somewhat reliable; airmail *(légiposta)* takes 5-10 days to the US and the rest of Europe, and two weeks to South Africa, New Zealand, and Australia. **Mail** can be received general delivery through **Poste Restante.** Address envelope as follows: Jessica (First name) BERENBEIM (LAST NAME), POSTE RESTANTE, Varoshaz u. 18 (Post office address), Budapest (City) 1052 (Postal code), HUNGARY.

Almost all phone numbers have six digits. For intercity calls, wait for the tone and dial slowly; "06" goes before the phone code. **International calls** require red phones or new digital-display blue ones. Although the blue phones are more handsome than their red brethren, they tend to cut you off after 3-9 minutes. Phones increasingly require *telefonkártya* (phone cards), available at kiosks, train stations, and post offices in denominations of 800Ft and 1600Ft. Direct calls can also be made from Budapest's phone office. To call **collect,** dial 190 for the international operator. To reach international carriers, put in a 10Ft and a 20Ft coin (which you get back), dial 00, wait for the second tone, then dial the appropriate number: **AT&T Direct** (☎ 06 800 01111); **BT Direct** (☎ 06 (wait for dial tone) 800 04411); **Canada Direct** (☎ 06 800 01 211); **MCI WorldPhone** (☎ 00 800 01411); and **Sprint** (☎ 00 800 01 877).

**Internet** access is increasing throughout the country, and is ubiquitous in Budapest and major provincial centers. However, be prepared to go without access at Lake Balaton or in Szombathely and Kecskemét. The Hungarian keyboard differs significantly from English-language keyboards. When you first log on, go to the bottom right-hand corner of the screen and look for the "Hu" icon; click here to switch the keyboard setting to "Angol."

English-language press can be found in many Budapest kiosks and large hotels, but rarely in other cities. The weekly *Budapest Sun* (280Ft) mostly includes news and business information, but its Style section will help navigate the capital's cultural life. English-language radio and TV programming is found in *Budapest Week*, which also has excellent listings, survival tips, and articles about life in Hungary (published Thursday; 145Ft, free at AmEx offices and larger hotels). Also published weekly, the Magyar flyer *Pesti Est* lists movies, concerts, and performances in Budapest; pick up a free copy in restaurants, theaters, and clubs. Three radio stations have Anglophone programming: Juventus, Radio Bridge, and Danubius. The frequencies vary from region to region, but in the Budapest area they are 89.5, 102.1, and 103.3FM, respectively.

# BUDAPEST ☎ 1

Budapest (pop. 1.9 million) doesn't feel very Hungarian. While the rest of the country seems to linger in a slower, friendlier state, Budapest speeds along with a backdrop of crowded streets, hip nightclubs, towering apartment buildings, and neon-bedecked Western companies. Cosmopolitan and confident, Budapest is reassuming its place as a major European capital; even 40 years in a communist coma couldn't kill the spirit of this stronghold of Magyar nationalism. Originally two separate cities, Budapest was created in 1872 with the joining of Buda and Pest, and immediately went on to become the Habsburg Empire's number-two city. Endowed with an architectural majesty befitting royalty, the Hungarian capital is only enhanced by the now-tattered landscape. World War II punished Budapest, but the Hungarians rebuilt it from rubble with the same pride that fomented the ill-fated 1956 Uprising, weathered the Soviet invasion, and overcame decades of subjugation. No toyland Prague, Budapest is bigger, dirtier, and more vibrant—flashing lights and legions of tourists may have added tinsel to its streets, but beneath the kitsch, the indefatigable spirit of Budapest charges on.

## ✸ ORIENTATION

Originally Buda and Pest, two cities separated by the **Duna** (Danube) River, modern Budapest preserves the distinctive character of each. Elegant **Buda** inspires artists with its hilltop citadel, trees, and cobblestone Castle District. On the east side, bustling **Pest,** the city's commercial engine, is home to wide shopping boulevards, theaters, Parliament, and the Opera House.

Three central bridges tie Budapest together. **Széchenyi lánchíd** connects Roosevelt tér to the base of the cable car that scurries up **Várhegy** (Castle Hill). To the south, slender **Erzsébet híd** runs from near **Petőfi tér** and **Március 15 tér** to the St. Gellért monument at the base of **Gellért-hegy** (Gellért Hill). Farther along the Danube, the green **Szabadság híd** links **Fővám tér** to the south end of Gellért-hegy, topped by **Szabadság Szobor** (Liberation Monument). **Moszkva tér,** just down the north slope of Várhegy, is Budapest's bus and tram transportation hub. **Batthyány tér** lies opposite **Parliament** (Országház), one metro stop past the Danube in Buda. This is the starting point of the **HÉV commuter railway,** which heads north through **Óbuda** to **Szentendre** (40min.; every 15min. 5am-9pm; buy tickets past Békásmeyger, Milleniumtelep, or Ilonatelep on the train). Budapest's **Metro,** built in 1896, is the oldest in continental Europe and third oldest in the world after London and Boston. Its three lines (the yellow M1, the red M2, and the blue M3) converge at **Deák tér** in District V, beside the main international bus terminal at **Erzsébet tér.** Deák tér lies at the core of Pest's loosely concentric boulevards and spoke-like avenues. Two blocks west toward the river lies **Vörösmarty tér.** Facing the statue of Mihály Vörösmarty, the main pedestrian shopping zone, **Váci u.,** is to the right.

Addresses in Budapest begin with a Roman numeral representing one of the city's 23 **districts.** Central Buda is I; central Pest is V. As many streets have shed their Communist labels, an up-to-date **map** is essential. The **American Express** and **Tourinform** offices have good free tourist maps, as does *Belváros Idegenforgalmi Térképe*, available at any Metro stop (199Ft).

# ⊡ INTERCITY TRANSPORTATION

**Airplanes: Ferihegy Airport** (☎296 96 96; info ☎296 715, 296 70 00, and 296 80 00; reservations toll-free ☎(0680) 212 121 M-F 7:30am-6pm, Sa 7:30am-2pm). Malév (Hungarian airlines) international flights terminal 2A, all other airlines terminal 2B. The cheapest way to the center is to take the Ferihegy/red **bus #93**, followed by the M3 to Köbanya-Kispest (50min.). Or, **Centrum buses** go to Erzsébet tér (45min., every 30min. 5:30am-9pm). The **Airport Minibus** (☎296 85 55) serves the entire city 24hr.; call 1 day in advance for airport service. One-way 1500Ft; round-trip 2500Ft.

**Trains:** ☎461 54 00. *Pályaudvar,* often abbreviated "pu.," means train station. The 3 main stations—**Keleti pu., Nyugati pu.,** and **Déli pu.**—are also Metro stops. Railway stations are the favorite haunts of Budapest's infamous thieves and pickpockets, so be careful. Most international trains arrive at Keleti pu., but trains to and from a given location do not necessarily stop at the same station—trains from Prague may stop at Nyugati pu. or Keleti pu. Each station has schedules for the others. To: **Vienna, AUS** (3hr.; 17 per day; 7150Ft, 700Ft reservation fee); **Prague, CZR** (*EuroCity* 7hr., 5 per day, 13,564Ft; night train 9hr., 1 per day, 12,064Ft; 800Ft reservation fee); **Warsaw, POL** (11hr.; 2 per day; 12,857Ft, 2000Ft reservation fee); **Berlin, GER** (12hr., 1 per day, 20,400Ft; night train 15hr., 1 per day, 35,200Ft; 2500Ft reservation fee); and **Bucharest, ROM** (14hr., 7 per day, 12,000Ft). The daily **Orient Express** stops on its way from **Paris, FRA** to **Istanbul, TUR**. Prices listed are approximate—they vary wildly depending on where you purchase your ticket.

**Train Tickets:** For student discounts, show your ISIC and destination and tell the clerk "*diák*" (DEE-ak; student). **International Ticket Office,** Keleti pu. Open daily 7am-6pm. **IBUSZ** (see **Tourist Offices,** p. 322) offers generous discounts on international rail tickets; buy several days in advance. **MÁV Hungarian Railways,** VI, Andrássy út 35 (☎/fax 322 8405; www.mav.hu), with branch offices at all train stations, sells domestic and international tickets. 30-40% off international fares with ISIC. Open Apr.-Sept. M-F 9am-6pm, Oct.-Mar. 9am-5pm. **Carlson Wagonlit Travel,** V, Dorottya u. 3 (☎429 21 10; fax 266 25 85), just off Vörösmarty tér. 15-20% off international fares for those under 25 or over 65. Open M-F 9am-5pm. AmEx/MC/Visa.

**Buses:** ☎117 29 66. Most buses to Western Europe leave from **Volánbusz main station,** V, Erzsébet tér (international ticket office ☎317 25 62; fax 266 54 19). M1, 2, or 3: Deák tér. The international cashier upstairs will help you with Eurail passes and reservations. Open M-F 6am-6pm, Sa 6:30am-4pm. Buses to most of Eastern Europe depart from **Népstadion,** Hungária körút 48/52 (☎252 18 96). M2: Népstadion. To: **Vienna, AUS** (3½hr., 5 per week, 5190Ft); **Prague, CZR** (8½hr., 1-3 per week, 9900Ft); and **Berlin, GER** (14½hr., 2-5 per week, 16,110Ft). **Domestic buses** are cheaper but take longer than trains. Buses to the Danube Bend leave from outside the **Árpád híd Metro station.**

# ⊡ LOCAL TRANSPORTATION

**Public Transportation:** The subway, buses, and trams are inexpensive, convenient, and easy to navigate—by far the best way to get around town. Pick up free **route maps** from hostels, tourist offices, and train stations.

**Night Transportation:** The Metro stops around midnight but gates lock at 11:45pm. Buses and trams stop at 11pm. Buses whose numbers are marked with an "É" run along major routes midnight-5am. Bus #7É and 78É run along the same route as M2, and bus #14É runs along the same route as M3.

**Tickets:** All public transport uses the same blue tickets (95Ft; no transfers), sold in Metro stations, *Trafik* shops, and by some street vendors. Punch them in the orange boxes at the Metro gate and on buses and trams. **Passes** are worthwhile if you're going to be in town for more than a day. Day pass 740Ft; 3-day 1500Ft; 1-week 1850Ft; 2-week 2400Ft; 1-month 3600Ft.

**Fines:** The fine for riding ticketless is 1360Ft or 3000Ft if you can't pay on the spot. Inspectors will also fine you for failing to punch a new ticket when switching lines and for losing the cover sheet to the 10-ticket packet.

**Car Rental:** There are several reliable rental agencies in Budapest, which charge roughly US$38-49 per day for the cheapest cars. Few agencies rent to those under 21. **Vista** (see **Tourist Offices,** below) can help you find the most affordable option.

HUNGARY

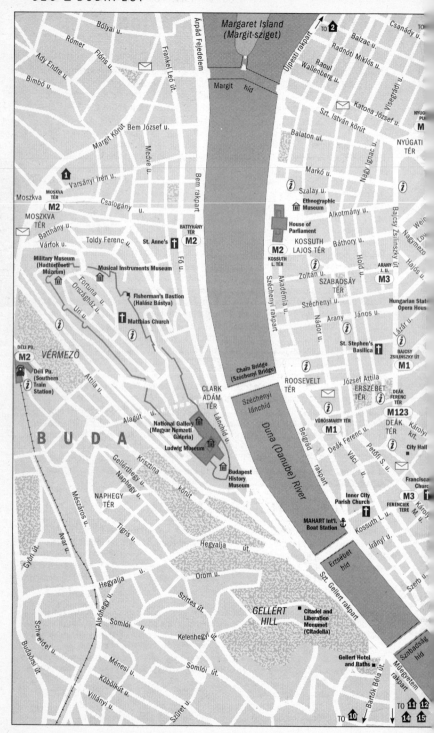

Margaret Island (Margit-sziget)

Margit híd

TO 2

Csanády u.
Balzac u.
Radnóti Miklós u.
Raoul Wallenberg u.

Újpesti rakpart

Katona József u.

NYÜGATI PU.
M

Szt. István körút

NYÜGATI TÉR

Bólyai u.
Römer
Flóris u.
Ady Endre u.
Bimbó u.
Árpád Fejedelem
Frankel Leó út.

Bölyai u.

Bem József u.
Margit Körút
Medve u.
Margit híd

Varsányi Irén u.

Moszkva
MOSZKVA TÉR
M2
MOSZKVA TÉR

Csalogány u.

Batthyány u.
Várfok u.
Toldy Ferenc u.
St. Anne's
BATTYHÁNY TÉR
M2

Military Museum (Hadtörténeti Múzeum)
Musical Instruments Museum
Fortuna u.
Országház u.
Fő u.

Fisherman's Bastion (Halász Bástya)

Úri u.

Matthias Church

VÉRMEZŐ

DÉLI PU.
M2

Déli Pu. (Southern Train Station)

Attila u.

Alagút u.

CLARK ADÁM TÉR

Lánchíd u.

BUDA

National Gallery (Magyar Nemzeti Galéria)

Ludwig Museum

Budapest History Museum

Krisztina
Gellérthegy u.
Naphegy u.
NAPHEGY TÉR

Mészáros u.
Avar u.
Tigris u.
Körút

Győri út.

Hegyalja
Hegyalja út.
Orom u.
Szirtes út.

Schweidel u.
Budaörsi út
Alsóhegy u.
Somlói u.
Mészáros u.

Ménesi u.
Kőbálkút u.
Villányi u.
Szüret u.
Somlói út.
Kelenhegy u.

GELLÉRT HILL

Citadel and Liberation Monumet (Citadella)

Gellert Hotel and Baths

Bartók Béla út

Bem rakpart

Balaton ul.
Markó u.
Szalay u.

Ethnographic Museum

House of Parliament

KOSSUTH LAJOS TÉR
M2
KOSSUTH L. TÉR

Akadémia u.
Széchenyi rakpart
Zoltán u.
Nádor u.
Arany János u.
Széchenyi u.

Alkotmány u.
Báthory u.
Hold u.

SZABADSÁY TÉR

Nagy Ignác u.

Vizsgrádi u.

Bajcsy Zsilinszky u.
Nagymezo
Hajós u.
Weine
Lon

ARANY J. U.
M3

Hungarian State Opera House

St. Stephen's Basilica

Lázár u.

BAJCSY ZSILINSZKY ÚT
M1

Chain Bridge (Széchenyi Bridge)

Széchenyi lánchíd

ROOSEVELT TÉR

József Attila u.
ERZSÉBET TÉR

DEÁK FERENC TÉR

VÖRÖSMARTY TÉR
M1

DEÁK TÉR
M123

City Hall

Duna (Danube) River

Belgrád rakpart
Deák Ferenc u.
Váci u.
Petőfi S. u.

Károlyi krt.

Inner City Parish Church

MAHART Int'l. Boat Station

Kossuth L. u.
Irányi u.

Franciscan Church

FERENCIEK TERE
M3

Károly M. u.

Erzsébet híd

Szt. Gellért rakpart

Szerb u.

Szabadság híd

Müegyetem rakpart

TO 10
TO 11 12
14 15

**Budapest**

SEE ALSO COLOR INSERT

🏠 ACCOMMODATIONS

Backpacker's Guesthouse, **11**
Bakfark Hostel, **1**
Caterina, **5**
Hostel Apáczai, **7**
Hostel Diáksport, **3**
Hostel Landler, **15**
Hostel Rózsa, **13**
Hostel Schönhutz, **10**
Martos, **14**
Museum Guesthouse, **8**
Nicholas's Budget Hostel, **12**
Station Guest House, **6**
Strawberry Y.H., **9**
Weisses Haus, **2**
Yellow Submarine Y. H., **4**

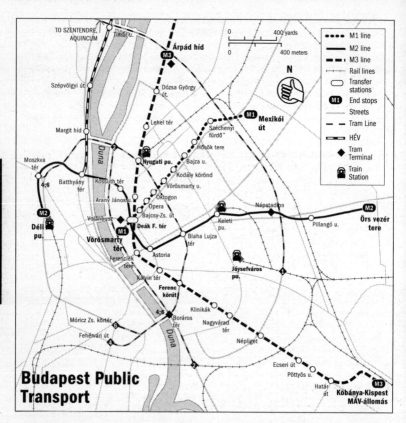

**Budapest Public Transport**

**Taxis:** One of Budapest's most spectacular rip-offs. Check that the meter is on and negotiate a price beforehand to make sure it hasn't been rigged against tourists. Prices should not exceed the following: 6am-10pm basic fee 200Ft, 200Ft per km or 50Ft per min. waiting; 10pm-6am basic fee 280Ft, 280Ft per km or 70Ft per min. waiting. Taxis ordered by phone are considerably cheaper than those hailed on the street. **Budataxi** (☎233 33 33) has the best rates, at 100Ft per km on the street and 90Ft by phone. **Főtaxi** (☎222 22 22), **City Taxi** (☎211 11 11), and **Rádió Taxi** (☎377 77 77) are also reliable companies with standardized rates.

# ⁊ PRACTICAL INFORMATION

## TOURIST AND FINANCIAL SERVICES

**Tourist Offices:** All tourist offices and metro stations sell the **Budapest Card** (Budapest Kártya), a worthwhile investment if you plan on seeing all the major sights and museums in one swoop. You get public transportation, entrance to all museums, reduced rates on car rental and the airport minibus, and discounts at many shops and restaurants. (2-day card 2800Ft; 3-day card 3400Ft.)

**Tourinform,** V, Sütő u. 2 (☎317 98 00; fax 317 95 78), off Deák tér behind McDonald's. M1, 2, 3: Deák tér. The best place for info about events, tours, and performances. Open daily 8am-8pm.

**Vista Travel Center: Visitor's Center,** Pauley Ede 7 (☎267 86 03), deals with city tourist info. **Travel Agency,** Andrássy út 1 (☎266 33 00), gives advice on travel outside Budapest. M1, 2, 3: Deák tér. Exit on Bajcsy-Zsilinszky út. Efficient, multilingual staff arranges accommodations, books transportation, and handles car rentals. Open M-F 9am-6:30pm, Sa 9am-2:30pm.

**IBUSZ,** V, Ferenciek tér 10 (☎485 27 00). M3: Ferenciek tér. Books discounted tickets and polyglot sightseeing tours (3hr. 5500Ft, with Budapest Card 3400Ft), finds accommodations, and **exchanges currency.** Open M-F 8:15am-6pm, Sa 9am-1pm for currency exchange only. AmEx/MC/Visa accepted for some services.

**Budget Travel: Express,** V, Zoltán út 10 (☎311 98 98). Offers same youth discounts on rail travel as the train station. 10-30% off flights. Open M-Th 8am-4:30pm, F 8:30am-3pm. **Malév Airlines,** V, Dorottya u. 2 (☎235 35 62). Entrance in Ápaczai út. M1: Vörösmarty tér. 10-30% off flights. Open in summer M-W and F 8am-5pm, Th 8am-6pm, Sa 8:30am-noon; off-season closed Sa. **IBUSZ** and **Vista Budget Travel** (see **Tourist Offices,** above) also sell discounted plane, train, and bus tickets.

**Embassies and Consulates: Australia,** XII, Királyhágó tér 8/9 (☎457 97 77). M2: Déli pu., then bus #21 to Királyhágó tér. Open M-Th 9am-5pm, F 9am-2pm, Sa-Su 9am-noon. **Canada,** XII, Budakeszi út 32 (☎275 12 00). Take bus #158 from Moszkva tér to the last stop. Open M-F 9am-noon. **South Africa,** VII, Rákóczi út 1/3 (☎266 21 48). **UK,** V, Harmincad u. 6 (☎266 28 88), near the intersection with Vörösmarty tér. M1: Vörösmarty tér. Open M-F 9:30am-noon and 2:30-4pm. **US,** V, Szabadság tér 12 (☎267 45 55; emergency ☎266 93 31). M2: Kossuth Lajos. Walk 2 blocks down Akademia and turn on Zoltán. Open M and W 8:30-11am, Tu and Th-F 8:30-10:30am. **New Zealand** and **Irish** nationals should contact the UK embassy.

**Currency Exchange: Magyar Külkereskedelmi Bank,** V, Szent István tér 11 (☎269 09 22). M1, 2, 3: Deák tér, at the basilica's entrance. One of the few banks that gives MC/Visa **cash advances** and cashes **traveler's checks** into US$ (2% commission, US$20 minimum). Outdoor Cirrus/MC/Visa **ATM.** Open M-Th 8am-4:30pm, F 8am-3pm. **Budapest Bank,** V, Váci u. 1/3 (☎328 31 55; fax 267 30 40). Offers credit card **cash advances, Western Union** services, cashes **traveler's checks** into US$ for a 3.5% commission, and has great exchange rates. Open M-F 8:30am-5pm, Sa 9am-2pm.

**American Express:** V, Deák Ferenc u. 10 (☎235 43 30; fax 267 20 28). M1: Vörösmarty tér. Next to Hotel Kempinski. Cardholders can receive mail. AmEx ATM. Open June-Sept. M-F 9am-6:30pm, Sa-Su 9am-5:30pm; Oct.-May M-F 9am-5:30pm, Sa 9am-2pm.

## LOCAL SERVICES

**Luggage storage:** At **Keleti pu.** large yellow lockers sit across from the international cashier (200Ft). Lockers are also available at Déli pu. and Nyugati pu. for 200Ft. Nyugati pu. has a 24hr. luggage desk in the waiting room next to the ticket windows. 140Ft per day, 280Ft for large bags. The **Volánbusz** main bus station has smaller lockers for 90Ft per day. Open M and F-Sa 6am-8pm, Tu-Th and Su 6am-7pm. **Vista Travel Center** (see **Tourist Offices,** above) has lockers big enough to hold a pack. 100Ft per hr.

**International Bookstores: Bestsellers KFT,** V, Október 6 u. 11 (☎/fax 312 12 95), near the intersection with Arany János u. M1, 2, 3: Deák tér; M1: Vörösmarty tér. Carries *The Phone Book,* a free business directory invaluable for long stays. Open M-F 9am-6:30pm, Sa 10am-5pm, Su 10am-4pm. **CEU Academic Bookshop,** V, Nador u. 9 (☎327 30 96), has a more erudite selection, particularly strong on all things Eastern European. Open daily Aug. 10am-4pm; Sept.-July 8am-6pm. AmEx/MC/Visa. **Rhythm 'N' Books,** V, Szerb utca 21-23 (☎266 98 33 and 266 22 26). Has 2nd-hand books "from pulp to philosophy." 1-for-1 book exchange. Open M-F noon-7pm.

**Gay Hotline: Gay Switchboard Budapest** (☎(0630) 932 33 34; fax 351 20 15). A volunteer organization that provides a comprehensive gay guide on the internet and a daily Info-Hotline service for gay tourists in Budapest. (See also **Gay Budapest,** p. 337.)

**Laundromats: Irisz Szalon,** V, Városház u. 3/5 (☎317 20 92). M3: Ferenciek tére. Wash 1100Ft per 7kg, 1400Ft per 10 kg; dry 450Ft per 15min. Request services and pay cashier before you start. Open M-F 7am-7pm, Sa 7am-1pm.

## EMERGENCY AND COMMUNICATIONS

**Tourist Police: Kulföldiket Elenörzö Osztály (KEO),** VI, Városligeti Fasor 46/48 (☎443 50 00, ask for "KAY-o"). M1: Hősök tér. Walk 3 blocks up Dósza György út and turn right on Városligeti Fasor. Staffs interpreters in summer to help deal with tourist crime and visa extensions, but don't expect them to be kind. Open Tu 8:30am-noon and 2-6pm, W 8:30am-1pm, Th 10am-6pm, F 8:30am-12:30pm.

**24hr. Pharmacies:** II, Frankel L. út 22 (☎212 44 06); III, Szentendrei út 2/A (☎388 65 28); IV, Pozsonyi u. 19 (☎389 40 79); VII, Rákóczi út 39 (☎314 36 95); IX, Boráras tér 3 (☎217 07 43); X, XII, Alkotás u. 1/B (☎355 46 91). At night, call the number on the door or ring the bell; you will be charged a small fee for the service. Medicine (including aspirin) is sold only at state pharmacies; little is displayed but all is dispensed from behind the counter. Look for a tan-and-white motif with *Gyógyszertár, Apotheke,* or *Pharmacie* in black letters in the window.

**Medical Assistance: Falck Személyi Olvosi Szolgálat (SOS) KFT,** II, Kapy út 49/B (☎200 01 00 and 275 15 35). English spoken. Ambulance service. First aid free for foreigners. Open 24hr. The US embassy has a list of English-speaking doctors.

**Telephones: Domestic operator** ☎191; **international operator** ☎190. Most phones use **phone cards,** available at newsstands, post offices, and Metro stations. 50-unit card 800Ft, 120-unit card 1800Ft. Use card phones for **international calls.** They will automatically cut you off after 20min., but that's more time than the coin phones will give you. Open M-F 8am-8pm, Sa 9am-3pm.

**Internet Access:** Cybercafes litter the city, but computers still need to be reserved well ahead of time; 3hr. lines are not uncommon. Avoid afternoon peak hours. Internet access is also available at many of Budapest's hostels.

**Telephone,** Petőfi Sandor u. 17. M1, 2, 3: Deák tér. Lots of computers, but expect to wait at least 1hr. 300Ft per 30min; 500 Ft per hr. Open M-F 9am-8pm, Sa 10am-3pm.

**Vista Travel Center,** Panlay Ede u. 7 (☎268 0888; see **Tourist Offices,** p. 322). Pricier, but lines are shorter. 11Ft per min. Open M-F 8am-11pm, Sa-Su 10am-11pm.

**Eckermann,** VI, Andrássy út 24 (☎374 40 76). M1: Opera. Free. Call 2-3 days ahead. Open M-Sa 8am-10pm, Su closed.

**Center for Culture and Communication (C3),** I, Orozágház u. 9 (☎214 68 56), inside the castle walls. Free. Reserve 2-3 days in advance. Open M-F 9am-9pm.

**Post Office:** V, Városház u. 18 (☎318 48 11). **Poste Restante** (Postán Mar). Open M-F 8am-8pm, Sa 8am-2pm. **Branches** at Nyugati pu. (☎312 12 00), VI, Teréz krt. 105/107 and Keleti pu. (☎322 14 96), VIII, Baross tér 11/C open M-F 8am-9pm, Sa 8am-2pm.

**Postal code:** 1052.

# ■ ACCOMMODATIONS

The city fills with tourists in July and August; save yourself some blisters by phoning first or stashing your pack while you seek out a bed for the night. Travelers arriving at Keleti pu. enter a feeding frenzy as hostel solicitors elbow their way to tourists in order to hawk rooms. Don't be drawn in by promises of free rides or special discounts; the hostel-hawkers have been known to stretch the truth. Be cautious, but keep an open mind—these hostels may be as good as anything else you'll find at the last minute, and best of all, they come to you.

## ACCOMMODATION AGENCIES

**Private rooms** are slightly more expensive than hostels (2000-5000Ft per person; prices decrease with longer stays), but usually offer what hostels can't: peace, quiet, and private showers. Accommodation agencies populate nearly every square in Budapest. Arrive when they open to secure the lower-priced rooms. Haggle stubbornly and bring cash.

**Budapest Tourist,** I, Deli Pálaudrar (☎212 46 25). Well-established. Singles in Central Pest 5000-7000Ft; doubles 6000-10000Ft; triples 6000-12000Ft. Off-season prices considerably lower. Also rents apartments for stays longer than 1 week. 3000-7000Ft per day, less for stays over 2 months. Open M-F 9am-5pm.

**IBUSZ,** V, Ferenciek tér (☎485 27 00). M3: Ferenciek tér. Rents rooms at a base price plus 1050Ft per day. Doubles 3500Ft; triples 4500Ft; quads 5000Ft. Also rents centrally located Pest apartments with kitchen and bath. 1-bedroom doubles from 5000Ft; 2-bedroom triples and quads from 6000Ft. Open M-F 8:15am-6pm.

**Non-Stop Hotel Service,** V, Apáczai Csere J. u. 1 (☎318 48 48; fax 317 90 99), M1: Vörösmarty tér. Tourist office and accommodation service for rooms in Pest. Singles 6000Ft; doubles from 7500Ft in summer, off-season 6000Ft; triples and quads from 8000Ft, 7000Ft. English spoken. Open 24hr.

# YEAR-ROUND HOSTELS

Budapest's hostels are generally social centers, each with its own quirks. Most don't have curfews and some hostel common rooms are as alluring as the city's expat bars and clubs. Many hostel accommodations, including university dorms, are now run under the aegis of the Hungarian Youth Hostel Association, which operates from a small office in Keleti pu. Their representatives wear Hostelling International t-shirts and will—along with legions of competitors—accost you as soon as you get off the train, if not before. Get your bearings before you accept any room and make sure that the hostel is easily accessible by public transportation, preferably the Metro. Although the hostels are generally legit, see the room before you hand over any cash. Theft is rampant in hostels. Unless otherwise noted, all have luggage storage, kitchens, and a TV in the common room.

## BUDA

▨ **Backpacker's Guesthouse,** XI, Takács Menyhért u. 33 (☎/fax 385 89 46; backpackguest@hotmail.com; www.backpackbudapest.hu), 12min. from central Pest. From Keleti pu. or anywhere along Rákóczi út, take bus #7 or 7A toward Buda. Get off at Tétenyi u., 5 stops past the river, walk back under the railway bridge, and make a sharp left turn. Take the 3rd right; it's on the left side of the street. Budapest's quirkiest hostel. Themed rooms, weekly spelunking trips (2100Ft), and Gen-X slacker-guests who never leave the kitchen. Bathrooms, though tidy, are packed—10am can be brutal. The key to a good stay: bring your own sheets; get a padlock for your locker; and exploit the superb CD and video collections, internet access (20ft per min.), satellite TV, and laundry service (1000Ft). Reception 24hr. Reserve 1-2 weeks in advance. 5- to 8-bed dorms 1600Ft; small dorm 1900Ft; "love shack" double 2400Ft per person.

## PEST

**Station Guest House (HI),** XIV, Mexikói út 36/B (☎221 88 64; station@mail.matav.hu). Near the train station. From Keleti pu., take bus #7 1 stop to Hungária Körút, walk under the railway pass, and take an immediate right onto Mexikói út; walk for 2 blocks. Look for the HI logo. Very eccentric—they provide paints for guests to graffiti the walls. It's set up for a party, with billiards, satellite TV, liquor at the reception, and live music twice a week. Ask for a kitchen-floor room if you plan to sleep. All rooms well-kept with private lockers. Breakfast 300Ft. Internet access 20Ft per min. Laundry 600Ft per 4kg. Reserve 1 day in advance or end up on a mattress in the attic. Attic 1400Ft, drops to 1200 by 3rd night; 6- to 8-bed dorms 2000Ft, 1400Ft by 4th night; 2- to 3-bed dorms 2800Ft, 2200Ft by 4th night. All prices 200Ft more for nonmembers.

**Ananda Youth Hostel,** IX, Alsoérdósor út. 12 (☎322 0502; anandyn@hotmail.com). Close to Keleti pu. Run by the same management as the popular Museum Guesthouse (see below), this relatively new hostel shares its older sibling's decorative scheme but has a larger kitchen—better suited for socializing. Internet, laundry facilities, and kitchen. Reception 24hr. 8-bed dorms 2000Ft; doubles 3500Ft.

**Yellow Submarine Youth Hostel,** VI, Teréz Körút 56, 3rd fl. (☎/fax 331 98 96). Across from Nyugati pu. Big bright rooms and friendly staff. Large kitchen. Laundry 500Ft wash, 500Ft dry. Check-out 9am, but full day luggage storage. 8-10-bed dorms 2200Ft; 4-bed dorms 3800Ft; double 7000Ft. 10% off with HI. Breakfast included. MC/Visa.

**Royal Youth Guesthouse,** VIII, Német út. 13. M2: Blaha Lujza tér. From the Metro, walk down Jószef Körú and take a left at the far end of Rájcócz tér; Német will be the 2nd right. Smaller (15 beds) and cozier than most. Beds vary in comfort, but low numbers mean low shower and kitchen traffic. Internet 400Ft per hr. after 6pm. Laundry 1000Ft. 4-6 bed dorms 1800Ft; doubles 2800Ft.

**Hostel Diáksport,** XIII, Dózsa György út 152 (☎340 85 85 and 329 86 44; fax 320 84 25; travellers@matavnet.hu). M3: Dózsa György. Enter on Angyalföldi, 50m from the river. Huge and social, with a 24hr. bar. Recently renovated and run by eager new management, this prefab hostel is fully loaded with all the amenities. Internet access 350Ft per 30min., billiards, laundry, cable TV, and breakfast—they'll even transport you from Keleti pu. (just try to stop them). Reserve by fax or email with credit card. 6- to 12- bed dorms 2400Ft; singles 3800Ft; doubles 3000-3600Ft, with shower 3800Ft; triples and quads 2900Ft. 10% off with HI.

# SUMMER HOSTELS

Many university dorms reinvent themselves as hostels in July and August. Conveniently accessible by tram, the majority are clustered around Móricz Zsigmond Körtér in district XI. Although they often provide in-room refrigerators and TV rooms on each floor, they can't quite make up for the fact that most rooms have bunk beds and linoleum floors. Surprisingly enough, these multi-leveled monsters are generally quieter than their year-round counterparts. Unless otherwise noted, all have kitchens, luggage storage, and TV in the common room.

## BUDA

**Hostel Bakfark,** I, Bakfark u. 1/3 (☎343 0748). M2: Moszkva tér. From the Metro, walk along Margit krt. with Burger King to the right. Take the 1st street after passing Mammut; the street isn't marked, but the hostel is. Some of the most comfortable hostel rooms in town, with lofts instead of bunks. The showers sparkle but are far from the rooms. Check-out 10am. Reservations recommended. Open June 15-Aug. 31. 4- to 6-bed dorms 2700Ft. 300Ft off with HI.

**Hostel Landler,** XI, Bartók Béla út 17 (☎463 36 21). Take bus #7 or 7A across the river and get off at Géllert. It's a short walk on Bartók Béla út away from the river. Lived-in college dorms, Madonna pin-ups and all. Bring flip-flops for the shower. Laundry available. Some English spoken. Check-out 9am. Open July 5-Sept. 5. Singles 4800Ft; doubles 3200Ft per person; triples and quads 2900Ft per person. 10% off with HI.

**Hostel Rózsa,** XI, Bercsényi u. 28/30 (☎463 42 50). M2: Blaha Lujzatér. Continue on tram #4 and get off 3 stops after the river. Although it lacks accessories, it's strong on the basics, with freshly painted walls and squeaky-clean (but curtainless) showers. Refrigerators in all rooms. Laundry (160Ft, wash only) requires your own detergent and the kitchen your own pots. Free transport from bus or train station. Open July-Sept. 5. Doubles 3200Ft per person. 10% off with HI.

**Hostel Schönhertz,** XI, Irinyi u. 42 (☎372 51 69). M2: Blaha Lujza tér. From the Metro, take tram #4 to the 2nd stop after crossing the Danube. Cross the street and walk on the left side facing away from the river; the hostel is the blue building behind the OTP. This massive hostel fills to capacity in summer, drawing people to its in-room showers and thumping basement disco. Unfortunately, the disco closes at 1am and the personal showers are only in triples and quads, leaving everyone else to brave the curtainless co-ed showers down the hall. Wash 250Ft, dry 250Ft. Open July-Aug. Doubles 3800Ft per person; triples and quads 3500Ft per person. 10% off with HI. Breakfast included.

**Martos,** XI, Stoczek u. 5/7 (☎463 37 76; ☎/fax 463 36 50; reception@hotel.martos.bme.hu). Near the Technical University. From Keleti pu., take red bus #7 to Móricz Zsigmond Körtér and trek back 300m toward the river on Bartók Béla út. Turn right onto Bertalan Lajos at the large square. Stoczek u. is the 3rd right; the hostel is near the corner. This independent, student-run hostel is one of Buda's best deals, with cheap, clean rooms. Free laundry and internet. Satellite TV. Check-out 9-10am. Singles 2500Ft; doubles, triples, and quads 1800Ft person.

## PEST

**Strawberry Youth Hostels,** IX, Ráday u. 43/45 (☎218 47 66), and Kinizsi u. 2/6 (☎217 30 33). M3: Kálvin tér. With Hotel Mercure on the right, walk down Vámház krt. Ráday is 1 block toward the river on the left. Big, sunny bunk-less rooms with fridge, drying rack, and a view of the building next door. There's a small pub downstairs; ask for a

3rd-floor room if you're not into heavy bass. Coin-operated laundry (400Ft wash). Free Keleti pu. pickup. Check-out 10am. Open June 29-Sept. 1. Doubles 3200Ft; triples and quads 2900Ft. 10% off with HI.

**Hostel Apáczai**, V, Papnövelde u. 4/6 (☎267 03 11), M3: Ferenciek tér. Follow Károlyi M. u. with the river to the right; Papnövelde u. is 3 blocks later on the right. The beds are back-breakers, but with the heart of Budapest nightlife at your doorstep, who needs a bed? Mr. Clean would approve of these convent-like accommodations; the bigger rooms resemble army barracks. Check-out 9am. Open July-Aug. Dorms 2700Ft; 6-bed dorms 2700Ft per person; quads 2900Ft person. 10% off with HI.

## GUEST HOUSES

Guest houses and rooms in private homes lend a personal touch for slightly more forints than an anonymous hostel bed. These should not be confused with *panzió*, which are larger and rarely charge less than 4000Ft per person. Although not always fluent in English, friendly owners will usually pick travelers up at the train station or the airport. Most allow guests to use their kitchens and are on hand to provide general advice or help. Visitors receive keys to their rooms and the house; while trying not to wake a sleeping household as you tiptoe down the hall might trigger high-school flashbacks, you'll be free to come and go as you please.

■ **Museum Guesthouse**, VIII, Mikszáth Kálmán tér 4, 1st fl. (☎318 95 08 and 318 21 95). M3: Kálvin tér. Take the left exit from the stop onto Baross u.; when it forks, take the left branch, Peviezky u. At the open square, go to the far right corner and ring the buzzer at gate #4. In the heart of a hopping bar scene and near the Metro. Laid-back atmosphere keeps them chatting for hours in the tiny kitchen. Run by young, hostel-style management ready to hook you up to the internet (1000Ft per hr.; free after 6pm), do your laundry (1000Ft wash and dry), and offer advice on Hungarian wines. Spacious lofts, bunks, and single beds hide its capacity, but the morning line for the single shower and electric kettle will soon remind you. 500Ft locker and key deposit. English spoken. Reception 24hr. Check-out 10am. Reserve the morning of your stay. 1800Ft per person.

**Caterina**, VI, Andrássy út 47, 3rd fl., apt. #18, ring bell 11. (☎291 95 38; mobile ☎(0620) 346 398; fax 352 61 47; caterina@mail.inext.hu). M1: Oktogon. Or, trams #4 or 6. Across from Burger King. In a century-old building on Andrássy near central Pest, you'll find the home of "Big" Caterina Birta and her daughter, "Little" Caterina. If you've ever wondered what staying with your doting (but stern) grandmother would be like, this is it: fresh linens, a kitchen floor you could eat off, and—though there's no curfew—quiet hours after 10pm. TV in all rooms. Internet access 550Ft per 30min. Laundry 700Ft per 5kg. Eger outings in the family minivan 2500Ft. English understood. Reception 24hr. Check-out 9am. Lockout 10am-2pm. Reserve by fax or email. Triple 2000Ft; 2-bed loft 2700Ft; dorm 2000Ft; 6-person room US$10 per person.

**Weisses Haus**, III, Erdőalja út 11 (☎/fax 387 82 36; mobile ☎(0620) 343 631). M3: Árpád híd. Continue on Béci ut.-bound tram #1 to Floriantér; from there, take bus #137 to the Iskola stop. A family-owned villa in a nice neighborhood 30min. from the center. More peaceful than a hostel. Breakfast lovingly prepared by family matriarch Mama Zsuzsa. Some English spoken. Laundry 1000Ft per 4kg. No curfew, but bus #137 stops at 11:30pm. 4 doubles with a great view of distant Pest US$10 per person.

## CAMPING

More suburban than rustic, Budapest's campgrounds allow travelers to escape the city's crowded streets and enjoy them at the same time. For a listing of all of Hungary's campsites, pick up *Camping Hungary*, availabe at tourist offices.

**Zugligeti "Niche" Camping**, XII, Zugligeti út 101 (☎/fax 200 83 46). Take bus #158 from "Moszkva tér" to the last stop. An easy commute to central Budapest, located right next to the János Negyi chairlift. A grassy campsite with shady walks and friendly people. The on-site restaurant provides cheap food, but the young clientele usually spends its evenings in the city. Communal showers and a safe. English spoken. 850Ft per person. Tents 500Ft, big tents 900Ft. Cars 700Ft. Electricity 500Ft. MC/Visa.

**Római Camping**, III, Szentendrei út 189 (☎368 62 60; fax 250 04 26). M2: Batthyány tér, then take the HÉV to "Római fürdő" and walk 100m toward the river. A huge 3-star site with tip-top security, a grocery store, and tons of restaurants. Enjoy the big swimming pool (300Ft), and the vast shady park and Roman ruins nearby. Communal showers and kitchen. Open mid-Apr. to mid-Oct. Tents 1950Ft; bungalows with cold water 1350-2000Ft. 10% off with HI. MC/Visa.

# ⚫ FOOD

Eating at family joints can be tastier and more fun than eating in regular restaurants. A 10% tip is generally expected; add another 10% if your meal is accompanied by live music. Explore the cafeterias beneath "Önkiszolgáló Étterem" signs for something greasy and cheap. (Meat dishes 300-500Ft.) Seek out the *kifőzés* or *vendéglő* in your neighborhood for a taste of Hungarian life. For kicks, the **world's largest Burger King** is on Oktogon, and for staples, **Non-Stop** stores and corner markets are the best options. The king of them all is **Grand Market Hall**, IX, Fővamtér 1/3, next to Szabadság híd (M3: Kálvin Tér). First built in 1897, the hall's 10,000 square meters of market stalls make it a tourist attraction in itself.

## BUDA

**Söröző a Szent Jupáthoz**, II, Retek u. 16 (☎212 29 23). M2: Moszkva tér. Huge wooden tables, huge menu, and huge portions. Main dishes 595-1709Ft. Open 24hr.

**Marcello's**, XI, Bartók Béla út 40 (☎466 62 31). Just before Móricz Zsigmond Körtér, on the river side. With imported "cigarette" bread-sticks, fresh flowers, classy high-heeled waitresses, and real tomato sauce (a rarity in Budapest), this place is pizza all grown up. Pizzas 480-650Ft. Reservations recommended. Open M-Sa noon-10pm.

**Paksi Halászcsárda**, II, Margit Körút 14 (☎212 55 99). Tram #4 or 6 to Margit Híd. Dimly lit, elegant restaurant where red wine and collared shirts rule the roost. Well-executed Hungarian standbys. Main dishes 760-2500Ft. Open daily noon-midnight.

**Remiz**, II, Budakeszi út 8 (☎275 13 96). Take bus #122 from Moszkva tér 3 stops to Szépilona. Known for its outdoor BBQ, where ribs and steak are prepared on lavastone. Main dishes 980-1780Ft. Open daily 9am-1am; BBQ May-Sept. AmEx/MC/Visa.

**Marxim**, II, Kisrókus u. 23 (☎316 02 31). M2: Moszkva tér. Walk along Margit krt. facing away from the castle-like building, then turn left down the industrial road. Communist-kitsch dishes served in barbed wire booths. Great pizzas 300-900Ft. Linger over your Cold War Cup ("ice-cream with frozen dreams and hopes," 300Ft) with a crowd of hip young people. Open M-F noon-1am, Sa noon-2am, Su 6pm-1am.

**Borpatika** (Wine Pharmacy), XI, Bertalan L. u. 26 (☎204 26 44). Take tram #47 or 49 from Deák tér to Bertalan Lajos. A bustling tavern with lively patrons, a boisterous happy hour, and a dearth of expats. If the drinking songs and friendly bartender can't cure your ills, the huge jugs of *Furmint* might. Cozy candlelit cellar dining room. Main dishes 350-2100Ft. Open 8am-midnight.

**Nagyi Palacsintázója**, I, Hattyú u. 16 (☎201 86 05). M2: Moszkva tér. For those late-night crepe cravings. A precarious ladder leads to a 2nd floor perch. *Palacsintá* (Hungarian crepes) from 50Ft, set menus 365-695Ft. English menu on request. Open 24hr.

## PEST

▨ **Fatâl Restaurant**, V, Váci út 67 (☎266 26 07). Packs them in for large and hearty Hungarian meals. Giant, carefully garnished main courses from 860Ft. Popular with tourists. Reservations only. Open daily 11:30am-2am.

▨ **Marquis de Salade**, VI, Hajós u. 43 (☎302 40 86). M3: Arany János. At the corner of Bajcsy-Zsilinszky út, 2 blocks from the Metro. Chic cuisine served by waiters clad head-to-toe in black. Elaborate opium-den decor. Dishes from Azerbaijan, France, India, Italy, Japan, and Hungary. Main dishes 700-2200Ft. Open daily noon-midnight.

**Falafel Faloda**, VI, Paulay Ede u. 53 (☎267 95 67). M1: Opera. From the opera, cross Andrássy, head straight on Hajós u., and turn left on Paulay Ede. Fast food at its best:

make-your-own-falafel with real tahini and fresh vegetables. Sandwich 360Ft; salad 350-420Ft. Open M-F 10am-8pm, Sa 10am-6pm.

**Gandhi,** V, Vigyázó Ferenc u. 4 (☎269 16 25). From the meditation guides at the door to the trickling waterfall inside, this cellar establishment takes its customers to a higher plane. A superior vegetarian restaurant, without the fat, meat, and fried cheese of traditional Hungarian food, but also without its generous portions. New menu every day (lunar and solar), herb teas, organic wines, and wheat beers sure to generate good karma. Main dishes 860-1080Ft. Open M-Sa noon-10:30pm. AmEx/MC/Visa.

**Dankó Vendéglő,** V, Hercegpámás u. 18 (☎269 0220). Generous portions of good Hungarian food at especially low prices. Main dishes 540-1200Ft.

**Korona Passage,** V, Kecskeméti u. 14 (☎317 41 11). M3: Kálvin tér. Across from the Mercure Korona Hotel. Watch as giant *palacsintá* are prepared to order. Sweet and savory crepes 460-650Ft. Open daily 11am-10pm.

**Iguana Bar and Grill,** V, Zoltán u. 16 (☎331 43 52). M2: Kossuth tér. 2 blocks down Akadémia u. Though the food is OK, the American-style service, Texan-sized portions, and a few macho menu items like the "whoop-ass beef" cheer lively crowds of homesick American travelers. Reservations recommended. Main dishes 1080-2580Ft. Brunch Sa-Su until 4:30pm. Happy hour M-F 4-6pm. Open daily 11:30am-2am. AmEx/MC/Visa.

# CAFES

Once the haunts of Budapest's literary, intellectual, and cultural elite as well as its political dissidents, head to a cafe to both experience a bit of history and enjoy cheap and absurdly rich pastries.

**Művész Kávéház,** VI, Andrássy út 29 (☎352 13 37). M1: Opera. Diagonally across from the Opera. The name means "artist cafe," and—unlike most remaining Golden Age coffeehouses—the title fits. A mix of cell-phoning Italians, Hungarian grandmothers, and starving artists congregate here. Enjoy a *Művész torta* (jam and hazelnut cake; 190Ft) and cappuccino (200Ft) on the terrace. Open daily 9am-midnight.

**Cafe New York,** VII, Erzsébet krt. 9-11 (☎322 38 49). M2: Blaha Lujza tér. Once the biggest swing club in Eastern Europe, this symbol of the city's *fin-de-siècle* Golden Age fell into disrepair under communism. The exterior still bears scars left by a Soviet tank, but the gorgeous interior, resplendent with exquisite velvet, gold and marble, has been restored as a tourist attraction. Ice cream and coffee delights priced accordingly (750-1150Ft). Pastries 300-550Ft. Open daily 10am-midnight. AmEx/MC/Visa.

**Ruszwurm,** I, Szentháromság u. 7 (☎375 52 84). Just off the square on Várhegy in the Castle District. This cafe has been confecting since 1827, and the sweets that once attracted the Habsburgs now cater to the castle's visitors rather than its residents. Homemade ice cream 60Ft; chocolate cake 220Ft. Open daily 10am-7pm.

**Litea Literatura & Tea,** I, Hess András tér 4 (☎375 69 87). In the Fortuna Passage. Choose from an immense selection of teas at this airy gardenhouse cafe inside a bookshop. Coffee 130Ft; cappuccino 150Ft. Open daily 10am-6pm. AmEx/MC/Visa.

**Faust Wine Cellar,** I, Hess András tér 1-3 (☎214 30 00). Enter the Hilton in the Castle District and descend into the 13th-century Dominican cloisters. Located deep under the hotel, this cellar serves nothing but wine and features an overwhelming array of excellent Hungarian vintages. 290-5000Ft per glass. Open daily 3-11pm.

# SIGHTS

In 1896, Hungary's 1000th birthday bash prompted the construction of what are today Budapest's most prominent sights. Among the works commissioned by the Habsburgs were **Heroes' Square** (Hősök tére), **Liberty Bridge** (Szbadság híd), **Vajdahunyad Castle** (Vajdahunyad vár), and continental Europe's first metro system. The domes of **Parliament** (Országház) and **St. Stephen's Basilica** (Szent István Bazilika) are both 96 meters high—vertical references to the historic date. Slightly grayer for wear, war, and communist occupation, these monuments still attest to the optimism of a capital on the verge of its Golden Age. See these sights, gain an orientatation of the city, and meet other travelers with **The Absolute Walking Tours.** Their basic tour is

2500Ft for 3½ hours and meets daily at 9:30am and 1:30pm at Déak tér and 10am and 2pm from the Heroes' Square. They also offer a range of specialized tours, from architectural to pub crawl. (Info ☎211 88 61. Tours 2½-5½hr.; 2500-5500Ft.)

# BUDA

## CASTLE HILL (VÁRHEGY)

Towering above the Danube, the castle district has been razed and rebuilt three times in its 800 years of existence, most recently in 1945 when the Red Army left Castle Hill nearly uninhabitable. With its winding, statue-filled streets, breathtaking views, and a magnificent hodge-podge of architectural styles, the UNESCO-protected district—the view itself is classified as a World Heritage site—now appears much as it did in Habsburg times, with the addition of tour buses and gift shops.

**THE CASTLE.** (Vár.) Budapest's castle was originally built in 1242, but was quickly leveled by a Mongol invasion. Centuries later, Good King Mátyás (see **History,** p. 308) made Buda the site of his Renaissance palace. The Turks, however, wouldn't have it and the castle suffered again in 1541. One hundred and forty-five years later, Habsburg forces razed the reconstruction in order to oust the Ottomans. Another reconstruction was completed just in time to be destroyed by the Germans in 1945. Determined Hungarians pasted the castle together once more, only to face the Soviet menace—bullet holes in the facade recall the 1956 Uprising. In the post-Soviet period, sorely needed resources have been channeled into the restoration of the castle, but nearly nothing from the good ol' days stands. Rather, the entire hill is largely a reproduction of what was once there. The World War II bombings revealed artifacts from the original 1242 version of the castle, which are now housed in the **Budapest History Museum** (Budapesti Történeti), in the Royal Palace (Budavári palota) at the southernmost end of the district. For a full description of Castle Hill museums, see **Museums,** p. 333. (*M1, 2, 3: Deák tér. From the Metro, take bus #16 across the Danube. Get off just after the river at the base of the Széchenyi Chain Bridge and take the funicular (sikló) up the hill. 300Ft up; 250Ft down. Runs daily 7:30am-10:30pm; closed 2nd and 4th Monday of the month. The upper lift station sits just inside the castle walls, only a few meters from the Hungarian National Gallery (Nemzeti Galéria). Or, take the Metro to M2: Moszkva tér, walk up to the hill on Várfok u., and enter the Castle at Vienna Gate (Becsi kapu).*)

**MATTHIAS CHURCH.** (Mátyás templom.) The Gothic Matthias Church is one of the most-photographed buildings in Budapest, largely due to its multi-colored roof. The church still bears the marks of Turkish rule: when Ottoman armies seized Buda on Sept. 2, 1541, it was converted into a mosque overnight. In 1688, the Habsburgs defeated the Turks, sacked the city, and re-converted the church. Descend the stairway to the right of the altar to enter the **crypt** and **treasury;** explanations are only in Hungarian. The stunning marble bust of Habsburg Queen Sissy sits guard at the entrance to the adjacent **St. Stephen's Chapel** (Szent István Kápelna). A second side chapel contains the **tomb of King Béla III,** the only sepulcher of the Árpád dynasty not looted by the Ottomans. (*M1, 2, 3: Deák tér. From the Metro, take bus #16 to the top of Castle Hill. High mass with full orchestra and choir Su 7, 8:30, 10am, noon, and 8:30pm; come early for a seat. Organ, orchestral, and choral concerts most W and F at 7:30pm. 1000Ft, occasionally free. Call Tourinform (see p. 322) for info. Treasury open daily 9:30am-5:30pm. 200Ft. English guide to church 500Ft.*)

**FISHERMAN'S BASTION.** (Halászbástya.) The grand equestrian monument of **King Stephen** bearing his trademark double cross sits in front of the Fisherman's Bastion. This arcaded stone wall supports a squat, fairy-tale **tower,** built as a romanticized reconstruction of the original. The amazing view is still the same, although you pay to see across the Danube. (*Behind Matthias Church. M free; Tu-Su 200Ft.*)

**CASTLE LABYRINTHS.** (Budvári Labirinths.) After seeing the sights above ground, it's worth exploring the ones below. The caverns beneath Buda Castle, formed by thermal springs and rich in stone formations, were created when Budapest's only residents were unicellular. There's no minotaur in the center, but children under 14, young mothers, and people with a heart condition are advised not to participate. (*Úri u. 9. ☎212 02 07. Open daily 9am-7:30pm. 900Ft, students 700Ft.* )

## ELSEWHERE IN BUDA

More disjointed than Pest, Buda tumbles down from Castle and Gellért Hills on the east bank of the Danube, sprawling out from their bases into Budapest's main residential areas. Buda is older and more conservative than Pest, but with the city's best parks, lush hills, and Danube islands, it's no less worth exploring.

**GELLÉRT HILL.** The Pope sent Bishop Gellért to the coronation of King Stephen, the first Christian Hungarian monarch, to assist in the conversion of the Magyars (see **History**, p. 308). Those unconvinced by his message hurled the good bishop to his death from atop the hill that now bears his name. Watching over the city from atop Gellért Hill (Gellért-hegy), **Liberation Monument** (Szabadság Szobor) was created to honor Soviet soldiers who died "liberating" Hungary; the Soviet star and the smaller military statues have only recently been removed. The adjoining **Citadel** was built as a symbol of Habsburg power after the failed 1848 Revolution. The view from the top of the hill is spectacular at night, when the Danube and its bridges shimmer in black and gold. Only a short walk down from the Citadel through the park, the **statue of St. Gellért**, complete with colonnaded backdrop and glistening waterfall, overlooks Erzsébet híd. At the base of the hill sits the **Gellért Hotel and Baths**, Budapest's most famous Turkish bath (see **Baths**, p. 335). The grounds are worth exploring even if you're not getting wet. *(Take tram #18 or 19 to Hotel Gellért. Follow Szabó Verjték u. to Jubileumi Park and continue on the marked paths to the summit. Alternatively, take bus #27 to the top; get off at Búsuló Juhász and walk another 5min. to the peak.)*

**MARGIT ISLAND.** (Margitsziget.) Off-limits to private cars but not to buses, Margit Island offers thermal baths, garden pathways, and numerous shaded terraces, but don't expect the unexpected: the island is fairly small and fairly crowded. It is named after King Béla IV's daughter; he vowed to rear young Margit as a nun if the nation survived the Mongol invasion of 1241. The Mongols left Hungary decimated, but not destroyed, and Margit was confined to the island convent. Visitors can come and go as they please. The outdoor **pool** is especially popular with Hungarian kids and their Speedo-clad dads. (550Ft. Open May-Aug. 8am-7pm, Sept.-Apr. 10am-6pm.) You can **rent bikes** or **bike-trolleys**, a Flintstone-esque way to pedal around the island. (750Ft per 30min., 1250Ft per hr.) Open-air clubs to the west entertain evening crowds. *(M3: Nyugati pu. Continue from the Metro on bus #26 or 26A; get off on Margit híd or on the island itself.)*

**PÁL-VÖLGYI CAVES.** These popular caves give first-time spelunkers a taste of the real thing, with tricky paths, challenging climbs, and stalactites close enough to bring out the claustrophobe in anyone. Be sure to wear warm clothing, even in the summer. *(Take bus #86 from Batthyány tér to Kolosyi tér, then bus #65 5 stops to the caves. Open Tu-Su 10am-4pm; last admission 3pm. Tours every hr. 280Ft, students 140Ft.)*

# PEST

Pest has become Budapest's animated commercial and administrative center. Although downtown Pest dates back to medieval times, its overall feel is decidedly modern. Her winding streets were constructed in the 19th century; today, they meander among European chain stores, Hungary's biggest corporations and banks, and myriad monuments. The old Inner City (Belváros) which centers around the pedestrian Váci u. and Vörösmarty tér, swarms with tourists, street vendors, the elegant, the trendy, and tacky-old-world architecture animated by 21st-century life.

**PARLIAMENT.** (Országház.) Filled with souvenir shops, Pest's riverbank sports a string of luxury hotels leading up to its magnificent Neo-Gothic Parliament. Built from 1885 to 1904, with 96 steps symbolizing the date of Hungary's millenium anniversary, the palatial parliament was modeled after Britain's, right down to the riverside location. The massive structure has always been too big for Hungary's government; today, the legislature uses only 12% of the building. *(M2: Kossuth Lajos tér. ☎ 268 49 04. English tours M-F 10am and 2pm, Sa-Su 10am only—come early. Purchase tickets at gate #10; enter at gate #12. Reservations recommended. 900Ft, students 500Ft.)*

HUNGARY

**ST. STEPHEN'S BASILICA.** (Sz. István Bazilika.) By far the city's largest church, St. Stephen's Basilica was decimated by Allied bombs in World War II. Its Neo-Renaissance facade is under reconstruction, but its ornate interior continues to attract both tourists and worshippers. The **Panorama Tower** remains Pest's highest vantage point, and its 360° balcony offers an amazing view. The church's highlight is St. Stephen's mummified right hand, one of Hungary's most revered religious relics. For the devout and the macabre, a 100Ft donation dropped in the box will light the hand up, allowing two minutes of closer inspection. *(M1, 2, 3: Deák tér. Open May-Oct. M-Sa 9am-5pm; Nov.-Apr. M-Sa 10am-4pm. Tower open daily June-Aug. 9:30am-6pm; Sept.-Oct. 10am-5:30pm; Apr.-May 10am-4:30pm. Tower 400Ft, students 300Ft.)*

**SYNAGOGUE.** (Zsinagóga.) Pest's other major religious sight is the largest synagogue in Europe and the second largest in the world, after the temple Emmanuel in New York City. The Moorish building was designed to hold 3000 worshippers. During World War II it housed a German telecommunications system. The synagogue has been under renovation since 1988, and much of the artwork is likely to be blocked from view. In the garden is a **Holocaust Memorial,** an enormous metal tree that sits above a mass grave for thousands of Jews killed near the end of the war. Each leaf bears the name of a family that perished. *(M2: Astoria. At the corner of Dohány u. and Wesselényi u. Open May-Oct. M-Th 10am-5pm, F 10am-3pm, and Su 10am-2pm; Nov.-Apr. M-F 10am-3pm, and Su 10am-1pm. 500Ft.)*

**ANDRÁSSY ÚT AND HEROES' SQUARE.** (Hősök tére.) Hungary's grandest boulevard, Andrássy út, extends from Erzsébet tér in downtown Pest to Heroes' Square. Built in 1872, the elegant balconies and gated gardens evoke Budapest's Golden Age. Perhaps the most vivid reminder of this era is the gorgeous Neo-Renaissance **Hungarian National Opera House** (Magyar Állami Operaház). If you can't actually see an opera, be sure to take a tour; the 24-karat gilt interior glows on performance nights. *(Andrássy út 22. M1: Opera. ☎332 81 97. English tours daily 3 and 4pm. 900Ft, students 450Ft. 20% off with Budapest card.)* Andrássy út's most majestic stretch lies near its end at Heroes' Square, where a view of the **Millennium Monument** (Millenniumi emlékmű) dominates the street. The structure, built in 1896 for the city's 1000-year anniversary, commemorates the nation's most prominent leaders. The seven horsemen at the base of the statue represent the seven Magyar tribes who settled the Carpathian Basin, while overhead the Archangel Gabriel towers, offering St. Stephen the crown of Hungary. *(Andrássy út stretches along M1 from Bajcsy-Zsilnszky út to Hősök tére.)*

**CITY PARK.** (Városliget.) The shady paths of City Park are perfect for an afternoon stroll. Inside, ice cream vendors, balloon men, and hot dog stands herald the presence of a permanent circus, a rather run-down amusement park, and a respectable zoo. Adding to this whimsical atmosphere, the nostalgic lakeside **Vajdahunyad Castle** sits in the park's center. Created for the millennium celebration of 1896, the facade is a collage of Romanesque, Gothic, Renaissance, and Baroque styles intended to chronicle the history of Hungarian architecture. Outside the castle broods the hooded statue of **Anonymous,** King Béla IV's scribe and the country's first historian, who recorded everything about medieval Hungary but his own name. Sit in his lap and get a picture taken or rent a **rowboat** on the lake next to the castle and explore the banks. From here you can also rent **ice skates** in the winter or **bike-trolleys** in the summer. *(M1: Széchenyi Fürdő. Boat and bike-trolley rental open June to mid-Sept. M-F 10am-8pm, Sa-Su 9am-8pm; boats 400Ft per 30min.; bike-trolleys 300Ft per 30min. Ice skates rented daily Nov.-Mar. 9am-1pm and 4-8pm; 300Ft per 30min.)*

**AQUINCUM.** In north Budapest, the ruins of the Roman garrison town Aquincum crumble in the outer regions of the third district. What look like a few fallen stones by the highway are actually the most impressive vestiges of a 400-year Roman occupation. The settlement's significance increased steadily over time; eventually, it attained the status of *colonia* and became the capital of Pannonia Inferior, a region covering most of Western Hungary. Marcus Aurelius and Constantine blessed the town with a visit. Unfortunately, the remains don't reflect the site's former grandeur. The **museum** on the grounds contains a model of the ancient city, so at least you know what you're looking at. *(Szentendrei út 139. From M2: Batthyány tér, take the HÉV to Aquincum; if you face the Danube, the site is about 100m to the right of the HÉV stop. ☎368 82 41. Open Apr. 15-30 and Oct. 9am-5pm, May -Sept. 9am-6pm.)*

# 🏛 MUSEUMS

The magnificent buildings that house Budapest's eclectic collection of museums often delight as much as their contents. Thoughtful visitors can find backroom gems and underlit masterpieces that a see-the-sights plan of attack will surely miss. Happily, most museums are small enough to invite the necessary wandering, and they're not mobbed—you'll have the space to enjoy a painting that in any other European city would require battling huge crowds.

**Buda Castle,** I, Szent György tér 2 (☎375 75 33). M1, 2, 3: Deák tér. From the Metro, take bus #16 across the Danube to the top of Castle Hill. Leveled by the Soviets and Nazis, the reconstructed palace now houses fine museums. 400Ft, students 200Ft; 1 ticket valid for all 3 wings.

　**Wing A** (☎375 91 75) contains the **Museum of Contemporary Art** (Kortárs Művészeti Múzeum) and the smaller **Ludwig Museum** upstairs, devoted to Warhol, Lichtenstein, and other household names in modern art. This unassuming museum is easy to miss, but rotating special exhibits feature the best in contemporary art (exhibit calendars are at most tourist offices). The real highlight, though, is the impressive collection of works by Eastern European artists, many of whom were suppressed under Soviet rule. Open Tu-Su 10am-6pm.

　**Wings B-D** hold the **Hungarian National Gallery** (Magyar Nemzeti Galéria; ☎375 75 33), a definitive collection of the best in Hungarian painting and sculpture. Its treasures include works by the Realist Mihály Munkácsy and Impressionist Pál Mersei, and Károly Markó's Classical landscapes. No, you won't recognize most of the names, but in this massive gallery you're bound to discover a new favorite. Open Tu-Su 10am-6pm. English tour by appointment.

　**Wing E** houses the **Budapest History Museum** (Budapesti Történéti Múzeum; ☎355 88 49). If you've seen all the monuments and are sick of brochure history blurbs, this museum (complete with English translations) will connect the dots. Open daily May 16-Sept. 15 10am-6pm; Sept. 16-Oct. and Mar.-May 15 M and W-Su 10am-6pm; Nov.-Feb. M and W-Su 10am-4pm.

**Museum of Fine Arts** (Szépművészeti Múzeum), XIV, Dózsa György út 41 (☎343 97 59). M1: Hősök tére. A simply spectacular collection of European art—from Raphael to Rembrandt, Gauguin to Goya, these are the paintings you've never seen in books, but should not miss. Highlights include an entire room devoted to El Greco, the Italian Renaissance galleries, and the range of the Impressionist collection. Open 10am-5:30pm. 500Ft, students 200Ft. Tours for up to 5 people 2000Ft.

**Museum of Applied Arts** (Iparművészeti Múzeum), IX, Üllői út 33-37 (☎217 52 22). M3: Ferenc körút. The eclectic collection of Tiffany glass, furniture, and various other *objets d'art* warrants diligent exploration and excellent temporary exhibits highlight specific crafts in more detail. The museum building itself serves as an excellent example of "applied arts." Built for the 1896 millennium celebration, the Eastern-influenced Hungarian Art Nouveau design is as much a part of the exhibit as the pieces inside. Open Mar. 15-Oct. Tu-Su 10am-6pm; Nov.-Mar. 10am-4pm. 300Ft, students 100Ft.

**Jewish Museum** (Zsidó Múzeum), VII, Dohány út 2 (☎342 89 49). M2: Astoria. Juxtaposes a celebration of Hungary's rich Jewish past with haunting photographs and documents from the Holocaust. Open M-F 10am-3pm, Su 10am-2pm. 500Ft, students 250Ft.

**Hungarian National Museum** (Magyar Nemzeti Múzeum), VIII, Múzeum krt. 14/16 (☎338 21 22). M3: Kálvin tér. Two permanent exhibitions chronicle the history of Hungary. The first extends from the founding of the state to the 20th century, including the Hungarian Crown Jewels, weathered after the wear of a war-torn millennium but intriguing nonetheless. The 2nd exhibition covers Hungary in the 20th century—a cheery Stalin reaches out to guide you to rooms devoted to Soviet propaganda. Captions have English translations; often Hungarians' presentation of their own history is more interesting than the history itself. Open Mar. 15-Oct. 15 Tu-Su 10am-6pm; Oct. 16-Mar. 14 Tu-Su 10am-5pm; last admission 30min. before closing. 400Ft, students 150Ft. English tour 500Ft per person; inquire about group rates.

**Museum of Ethnography** (Néprajzi múzeum), V, Kossuth tér 12 (☎ 312 48 78). M2: Kossuth tér. An exhibition of international folk culture from the late 18th century to World War I housed in a monumental gilt structure constructed for the Supreme Court. Open Mar.-Oct. Tu-Su 10am-6pm; Nov.-Feb. Tu-Su 10am-5pm. 300Ft, students 150Ft.

**Museum of Military History** (Hadtörténeti Múzeum), I, Tóth Árpád Sétány 40 (☎ 356 95 22), in the northwest corner of Várhegy. An intimidating collection of ancient and modern weapons, assembled to relate Hungary's historic moments of violence. Not a difficult task, considering the its legacy of wars, executions, martyrs, murders, sackings, and suicides. Includes a day-by-day chronicle of the 1956 Uprising. Open Apr.-Sept. Tu-Su 10am-6pm; Oct.-Mar. 10am-4pm; closed Dec. 16-Jan. 250Ft, students 80Ft.

**Statue Park Museum** (Szoborpark Múzeum; ☎ 227 74 46), XXII, on the corner of Balatoni út and Szabadkai út. Take tram #47 or 49 to its end at Kosztolányi tér, then take the yellow long-distance bus toward Érd (every 15min. from terminal #6; 20min.). An arresting outdoor collection of communist statuary removed from Budapest's parks and squares after the collapse of Soviet rule. Open daily Mar.-Nov. 10am-dusk, Dec.-Feb. weekends and holidays only. 200Ft, students 150Ft.

# 🎵 ENTERTAINMENT

Budapest's cultural life, somewhat deadened during communist rule, flourishes anew with a series of performance events throughout the year. **Óbudai Island** hosts the week-long **Sziget Festival,** Europe's biggest **open-air rock festival,** in mid-August. (☎ 372 06 50. Day ticket 2000Ft, 1500Ft if purchased in early summer; week 9000Ft.) The best of all worlds come together in the last two weeks of March for the **Budapest Spring Festival** (☎ 33 23 37 or inquire at Tourinform), a showcase of Hungary's premier musicians and actors. If you miss international pop culture, many of the world's biggest shows pass through Budapest. Prices are reasonable; check the **Music Mix 33 Ticket Service,** V, Váci út 33. (☎ 266 70 70. Open M-F 10am-6pm, Sa 10am-1pm.) *Programme in Hungary, Budapest Panorama,* the "Style" section of the *Budapest Sun,* and *Budapest in Your Pocket* (300Ft) are the best English-language guides to entertainment, listing everything from festivals to cinemas to art showings. All are available at most tourist offices and hotels. Although it may take some translating, *Pesti Est* (found at every pub, club, and McDonald's) is hands-down the best local entertainment guide. It features an English section on weekly cinema; films listed as *szinkronizált* or *magyarul beszélő* have been dubbed into Hungarian. (Tickets 500-600Ft.)

## THEATER AND CLASSICAL MUSIC

Like any large city, Budapest hosts a world of intimate theaters, smoky club performances, and showcases of local talent, many of which merit at least as much attention as the gilt stages of Budapest's grand cultural venues. The **Central Theater Booking Office,** VI, Andrássy út 15, next to the Opera House (☎ 312 00 00 and 267 12 67; open M-F 10am-6pm), and at Moszkva tér 3 (☎ 212 56 78; open M-F 10am-6pm), sells tickets to almost every performance in the city for no commission. In late summer, the Philharmonic and Opera take a break, but Budapest's theaters keep up the pace. Touring companies *à la* Andrew Lloyd Webber sometimes drop into town— watch out for *Cats* on roller skates. Buy tickets at the **Madách Theater Box Office,** VII, Madách tér 6. (☎ 322 20 15. Open M-Sa 2:30-7pm.)

**State Opera House** (Magyar Allami Operaház), VI, Andrássy út 22 (☎ 332 81 97). M1: Opera. One of Europe's leading performance centers. For less than US$5 you can enjoy an opera in the splendor of Budapest's Golden Age, provided you ditch the blue jeans. The box office (☎ 353 01 70), on the left side of the building, sells unclaimed tickets at even better prices 30min. before showtime. Open M-Sa 11am-5pm, Su 2-5pm.

**Philharmonic Orchestra,** V, Vörösmarty tér 1 (☎/fax 318 44 46). The ticket office is on the side of the square farthest from the river; look for the Jegyiroda sign. Equally grand music in a slightly more modest venue. Concerts almost every evening Sept.-June. Open daily 9am-3pm. 1200-1700Ft, less on the day of the show.

**Margitsziget Theater** (☎340 41 96), XIII, on Margitsziget. Tram #4 or 6 to Margitsziget. Opera and Hungarian folk concerts on an open-air stage. Summer only.

**Pesti Vigadó** (Pest Concert Hall), V, Vigadó tér 2 (☎318 99 03; fax 375 62 22). On the Danube near Vörösmarty tér. Flashy costumes and lots of vibrato. Hosts operettas every other night. Box office open M-Sa 9am-6pm.

**Buda Park Theater** (☎366 99 16), XI, Kosztolányi Dezső tér. Folk-dancers stomp across the stage of this small theater. Box office at V, Vörösmarty tér 1. Open M-F 11am-6pm. Tickets 90-350Ft.

# BATHS

To soak away weeks of city grime, crowded trains, and yammering camera-clickers, sink into a thermal bath, the essential Budapest experience. The baths were first built in 1565 by Arslan, a Turkish ruler of Buda who feared that a siege of the city would prevent the population from bathing. Thanks to his anxiety, nothing will keep you from bathing, either: the range of services—from mud baths to massage—are cheap enough to warrant indulgence without guilt. Some baths are meeting spots for Budapest's gay community.

▩ **Gellért**, XI, Kelenhegyi út 4/6 (☎466 61 66). Bus #7 or tram #47 or 49 to Hotel Gellért, at the base of Gellért-hegy. Venerable indoor thermal baths, segregated by sex. Accustomed to slightly bewildered tourists, this is the only spa with signs in English. Boasts a rooftop sundeck and an enormous outdoor wave pool. Offers a huge range of inexpensive à la carte options, including mudbaths, ultrasound, and the new "Thai massage," featuring "the world famous masseuses of the Bangkok wat po": women trained to use their feet, elbows, and knees in an exhausting 1½hr. massage of strategic pressure points (7500Ft, call for reservations). Open May-Sept. M-F 6am-6pm, Sa-Su 6am-4pm; Oct.-Apr. M-F 6am-6pm, Sa-Su 6am-1pm. Pools open daily May-Sept. 6am-6pm; Oct.-Apr. M-F 6am-6pm, Sa-Su 6am-4pm. Thermal bath 1000Ft, under 18 900Ft; with pool privileges 1600Ft. 15min. massage 1200Ft.

**Széchenyi Fűrdő**, XIV, Állatkerti u. 11/14 (☎321 03 10). M1: Hősök tére. Indoor baths attract the city's gentry while the large outdoor swimming pools delight their grandchildren. Great for relaxing and people-watching: old men play chess on floating chessboards in the warm outdoor pool. For a maximum amount of sun, there are sex-segregated nude sundecks on the roof. Open daily May-Sept. 6am-7pm; Oct.-Apr. M-F 6am-7pm, Sa-Su 6am-5pm. July-Aug. thermal steambaths are men only Tu, Th, and Sa; women only M, W, and F. 1000Ft deposit to enter with money returned if you leave in 5hr. Massage 1200Ft per 15min.

**BUCK-NAKED IN BUDAPEST** Treatment at a Budapest bath is royally indulgent, if somewhat intimidating for the virgin bather. When you first arrive, you'll be given what is essentially a dish-rag with strings: a bizarre apron no bigger and no less dingy. Modesty requires that you tie it around your waist. After depositing your belongings in a locked stall (the attendant keeps the the key), proceed to the baths. In general, women put the apron aside as a towel while men keep theirs on. Bring your bathing suit, because custom varies greatly by establishment, but either way, it's a good idea to do as the locals do—there's nothing more conspicuous (or embarrassing) than a Speedo-clad tourist among the naked natives. Once you've cycled through the sauna and thermal baths, repeat for good measure, and enter the massage area. If you're looking for a good scrubbing, go with the sanitary massage (vízi); if you're a traditionalist, stick to the medical massage (orvosi). In both cases, the masseuse will blithely ignore you, chattering away in Hungarian while pummeling your back. All of the baths provide a much-needed rest area once the whole process is complete. Refreshed, smiling, and somewhat sleepy, tip the attendant, lounge over mint tea, and savor your afternoon of guilt-free pampering and scrubbing.

HUNGARY

**Király,** I, Fő u. 84 (☎201 43 92). M2: Batthány tér. The basic bath experience, elevated by the splendor of Turkish cupolas and domes. The men's half has a reputation as a meat-market for gay men. Men-only M, W, and F 9am-9pm; women-only Tu and Th 6:30am-7pm, Sa 6:30am-1pm. 500Ft. Massage 750Ft per 15min.

**Rudas,** Döbrentei tér 9 (☎375 83 73). Take bus #7 to the 1st stop in Buda. Right on the river under a dome built by Turks 400 years ago, this is the gorgeous one you see in all the brochures. Unfortunately, women will have to make do with the photographs—centuries haven't altered the dome, the bathing chamber, or the "men-only" rule. This is more of an old-boys-club than a boys' club, though—Rudas has a reputation for being one of the straightest baths in Budapest. Steambaths open M-F 6am-8pm, Sa-Su 6am-1pm; baths M-F 6am-7pm, Sa 6am-1pm; pool M-F 6am-6pm, Sa-Su 6am-1pm. 1½hr. bath 1000Ft. Swimming pool open to women. 600Ft.

# ◪ NIGHTLIFE

On any given night out in Budapest, you can experience an amazing diversity of scenes, from the lively atmosphere of all-night outdoor parties to the decadent elegance of after-hours clubs. Global village alterna-teens wearing the usual labels and grinding to an electronic beat make the club scene in Budapest familiar to anyone who has ever partied in the West. Despite the throbbing crowds in the clubs and 4am chatter in the pubs, the streets themselves—often lit only by a single dim bulb—are surprisingly empty at night, echoing pre-capitalist times. To find out what's going on where and when, pick up a copy of *Budapest Week* (126Ft).

## BARS

**Old Man's Pub,** VII, Akácfa u. 13 (☎322 76 45). M2: Blaha Lujza tér. Although the name implies otherwise, this crowd is still in the larval phase of yuppie-dom. The lively atmosphere is more clean-cut hip than smoke-filled pub. For the horn-rimmed glasses set, this packed bar is pretty much the place to be on a Saturday night. Live blues and jazz every evening—check the schedule and arrive very early. Then relax in the restaurant (open until 4am) or grind in the "funky disco." Open M-Sa 3pm-4:30 or 5am.

**Fat Mo's Speakeasy,** V, Nyári Pal u. 11 (☎267 31 99). M3: Kálvin tér. "Spitting prohibited" in this Depression-era bar. Drinking, however, isn't. Fourteen varieties of draught beer (0.5L 350-750Ft) and live jazz (Su, M, and Th 9-11pm) to make the booze flow quicker. Gets crowded early with the loyal patronage of "permanent tourists:" wanderers who stopped in Budapest for a few days and wound up staying indefinitely. Once the they show up (around midnight or 1am), you can forget about such trivialities as moving or breathing. Th-Sa DJ from 11:30pm. Open M-F noon-2am, Sa-Su 6pm-4am.

---

**AN OFFER YOU CAN'T REFUSE** Communism may be dead in Hungary, but the mafia is alive and well in post-Soviet Budapest. Don't look for the usual Adidas-clad, gold chain-bedecked thugs; Budapest's agent extraordinaire might wear plenty of gold, but she also wears a miniskirt and high-heeled shoes. You'll meet her—an English-speaking, Hungarian hottie known as the "consumption girl"—at a swank bar or on the street around Váci út. Things will start off smoothly as she suggests a new venue. Of course you join her. She asks you to buy her a drink, and of course you do. When the bill comes, it is accompanied at last by the *beezneezmen* you'd expect from the post-Soviet mafia. US$1000 for a single Sloe Gin Fizz? It's no mistake, they assure you. And what do you give a 300lb. gorilla? Anything he wants. You *will* pay, because there is no recourse for the victimized. Ask to see the menu and there it is, written in black-and-white. Not enough cash in your wallet? Don't worry, the mafia has learned at least a few tricks from capitalism: they now accept major credit cards. The US Embassy has advised against patronizing a number of establishments in the Váci út area, including Fontana Cabaret, Mephisto Café, Muskátli Eszpresszó, and Tropical Bar.

**Petőlfi híd,** park on the Buda side (also known as "Green Park"). In the summer, this balmy outdoor party rocks all night every night; music varies widly (in genre and quality), but the drinks are always cheap and the view is always great.

**Morrison's Music Pub,** VI, Révay u. 25 (☎269 40 60). M1: Opera. Just left of the opera. With bar overflow onto the dance floor and dance floor overflow into the bar, this jostling nightspot pulls in a crowd ready to party in any language. British telephone booth inside actually works but moonlights as a shameless make-out spot. June-Aug. cover 500Ft; women free. Open M-Sa 8:30pm-4am.

**Crazy Cafe,** VI, Jokai u. 30 (☎302 40 03). M3: Nyugati pu. A great place to start a long evening on the town. With belly-baring waitresses serving up 40 kinds of whisky (shots 450-1190Ft), 13 kinds of tequila (350-550Ft), and 17 kinds of vodka (280-450Ft), the scene has been known to get more than a little rowdy. Live music nightly 9pm. Stick to the weekends—Su and M are karaoke nights. Open daily 11am-1am.

**Long Time Music Club and Restaurant,** VII, Dohány u. 22 (☎322 00 06). Billiards-and-darts bar, with live jazz, blues, soul, and funk every night at 9pm. Restaurant open 4-9pm, club 6pm-2am.

## CLUBS

**⚑ Undergrass,** VI, Liszt Ferenc tér 10 (☎322 08 30). M1: Oktogon. Or, tram #4 or 6. The hottest spot in Pest's trendiest area. The slick underground bar has only a few chairs, but most are happy to stand, kissing cheeks, waving across the room, and generally expressing the life-is-grand giddiness of the young and beautiful. A glass, soundproof door allows all this to go on while an equally-packed disco spins funk and pop. Open daily 8pm-5am; disco Tu-Su 10pm.

**Piaf,** VI, Nagymező u. 25 (☎312 38 23). A much-loved after-hours place and the final destination of any decent pub crawl in Budapest. Guests are admitted only after knocking on a rather inconspicuous—albeit intimidating—door and meeting the approval of the club's matron. Actresses relax in the red velvet lounge after the show. You'll feel like a cliché but you won't care. The beautiful staff is icy because they can be. 500Ft cover includes 1 drink. Open daily 10pm-6am, but don't come before 1am.

**Fél 10 Jazz Club,** VIII, Baross u. 30 (mobile ☎(0660) 31 84 67). M3: Kálvin tér. A short walk down Baross u. A sophisticated bar and disco, "Fel TEEZ" covers 2 floors with a convoluted layout *à la* M.C. Escher. No one seems to mind, though, since the live "jams" can be heard everywhere and the drinks—once you navigate the bottleneck at the bar—are potent. Cover 400Ft. Open M-F noon-dawn, Sa-Su 6pm-dawn.

**Club Seven,** Akácfa u. 7 (☎478 90 30). More upscale and less of a dive than the average Budapest club, but just as crowded. Music ranges from funk to soul to jazz to disco, depending on the night. M-F no cover; Sa-Su men 1000Ft, women free. Coffeehouse open 9pm-4am, restaurant 6pm-midnight, dance floor 10pm-5am.

**Franklin Trocadero Cafe,** V, Szent István körút 15 (☎311 46 91). The sign outside—flashing purple and green—typifies this self-consciously "Latin" dance club. DJ spins good salsa, occasionally mixed with pop Latin music, to an intermittent crowd ranging from devotees to novelty-seekers. Cover 400Ft. Open Tu 9pm-3am, W-Th and Su 9pm-4am, F 9pm-6am, Sa 9pm-5am.

## GAY BUDAPEST

For decades, gay life in Budapest was completely underground; it is only just beginning to make itself visible. The city still has its share of skinheads, so it's safer to be discreet. If there are problems of any sort, call the **gay hotline** (☎0630 932 33 34; fax 351 20 15). The establishments below are either gay-friendly or have gay clientele. Unfortunately, the gay scene in Budapest is exactly that: a *gay* scene. There are no venues other than Capella Cafe frequented by (or even welcoming to) lesbians. Ask around though—other clubs occasionally sponsor special nights or events.

**Capella Cafe,** V, Belgrád rakpart 23 (☎318 62 13). With glow-in-the-dark grafitti and an underground atmosphere, this popular spot draws a mixed crowd for a line-up that varies from transvestite lip-synchs to W night stripteases. Nightly shows at midnight. Women welcome. Cover 500Ft; 500Ft minimum. Open Tu-Su 9pm-5am.

**Angel Bar,** VII, Szövetség u. 33 (☎351 64 90). The 1st gay bar in Budapest. Until a few years ago, the club moved weekly; now this huge 3-level disco, cafe, and bar is packed for its weekend programs: F and Su nights bring drag shows, Sa is men only. Cover 500Ft, F 600Ft. Open Th-Su 10pm-dawn.

**Action Bar,** V, Magyar u. 42 (☎266 91 48). M3: Kálvin tér. As the name implies, this smoky basement pub is a pickup spot. Video-viewing room. Men only. 700Ft minimum. Open daily 9pm-4am.

# THE DANUBE BEND

North of Budapest, the Danube sweeps in a dramatic arc called the Danube Bend (Dunakanyar), deservedly one of the finest tourist attractions in Hungary. Ruins of first-century Roman settlements cover the countryside, Esztergom's cathedral and Visegrád's castle overlook the river as reminders of medieval glory, and an artists' colony thrives amid the museums and churches of Szentendre. All this is within two hours of Budapest by bus or a longer and more scenic ferry ride upriver.

## SZENTENDRE                                                    ☎(0)26

A short commute from Budapest, Szentendre (sen-TEN-dreh) appears at first to be a rural town. Upon closer inspection, though, the overwhelming abundance of credit-card signs lurking in shop windows, upscale art galleries, and overpriced restaurants in its cheery squares reveal its insidious modernity. After providing refuge for Serbian refugees fleeing the Turks in the 14th to 17th centuries, the cultural and religious center of Hungarian Serbs then became an artistic center for all of Hungary; it remains so today.

**▐ TRANSPORTATION. HÉV** travels from **Budapest's** Batthyány tér (45min., every 10-15min., 118Ft). **Buses** run from **Budapest's** Árpád híd Metro station (30min., every 20-40min., 172Ft); many continue to **Visegrád** (45min., 216Ft) and **Esztergom** (1½hr. from Szentendre, 432Ft). **MAHART boats** leave from a pier 10-15 minutes north of the town center; with the river on the right, walk along the water to the sign. May 17-Aug. boats run to: **Budapest** (3 per day, 650Ft); **Visegrád** (3 per day, 650Ft); and **Esztergom** (1 per day, 700Ft).

**◢▐ ORIENTATION AND PRACTICAL INFORMATION.** The **HÉV, train,** and **bus station** is a 10-minute walk from Fő tér; descend the stairs outside the station, go through the underpass, and head up Kossuth u. At the fork in the road, bear right onto Dumsta Jenő út, which leads to the **1763 Plague Cross** in the town center. **Tourinform,** Dumsta Jenő u. 22, between the center and the station, provides free **maps** and brochures. (☎31 79 65 and 31 79 66. Open in summer M-F 10am-1pm and 1:30-5pm, Sa 9:30am-6:30pm, Su 10am-2pm; off-season M-F 10am-1pm and 1-5pm.) **OTP Bank,** Dumsta Jenő u. 6, makes up for its sloth with great **exchange** rates, no commission on **traveler's checks,** and a Cirrus/MC/Visa/Plus 24hr. **ATM.** (☎31 02 11. Open M 7:45am-6pm, Tu-F 7:45am-5pm.)

**▐▛ ACCOMMODATIONS AND FOOD.** Although Szentendre can be visited in a day, there are a surprising number of (overpriced) lodging options. **IBUSZ,** Bogdányi u. 11, will hook you up with a private double for 3000Ft. (☎361 81; fax 31 35 97. Open M-F 9am-4pm, Sa-Su 10am-3pm.) **Ilona Panzió,** Rákóczi Ferenc u. 11, in the center of town, rents small but comfortable doubles with tiny personal showers. The friendly proprietors serve a generous breakfast on their terrace. (☎31 35 99. 3500Ft for 1 person; 4600Ft for 2. Breakfast included.) The sociable and beautiful **Pap-szigeti Camping** sits 1km north of the center on its very own island in the Danube. Walk along the water with the river to your right; the short bridge to the island will be obvious. (☎31 06 97; fax 31 37 77. Open May-Oct.15. Tent sites 2500Ft for 2; US$3.50 per extra person. 3-5 bed bungalows US$3-12 per person. Hostel singles, doubles, triples, and quads US$4-6. *Panzió* doubles with shower US$15.)

The constant flow of tourists has made restaurants in town expensive by Hungarian standards—budget travelers will do best to return to Budapest or continue to Visegrád for dinner. For one of the best deals in town, walk through a beaded curhead to **Kedvac Kifőzde**, Bükköspart 21. Perfect for a light lunch, this tiny corner restaurant serves up good soups and delicious menus for 300Ft. (☎31 91 86. Open M-F 11:30am-8pm.) Stop for a pastry and a "Nostalgia cappuccino" at the ▨ **Nostalgia Cafe,** Bogdángi u. 2. Photographs of the opera-singing owners adorn the cozy inside room—the couple sometimes holds concerts in the cafe's courtyard. (☎311 660. Pastries 250-450Ft, wine 800-5000Ft. Open Th-Su 10am-10pm.) There's also a **grocery store** near the rail station. (Open M-F 9am-7pm, Sa-Su 10am-5pm.)

▨▧ **SIGHTS AND ENTERTAINMENT.** Start your visit by climbing **Church Hill** (Templomdomb), above the town center in Fő tér, to visit the 13th-century Catholic church—one of the few medieval churches left in Hungary—which features the best view in town. Facing it, the **Czóbel Museum** exhibits the work of Béla Czóbel, Hungary's foremost Impressionist painter, including his "Venus of Szentendre," reclining in red bikini. (Open Mar. 15-Oct. W-Su 10am-4pm; Nov.-Mar. 14 F-Su 10am-4pm. 200Ft, students 100Ft.) Just across Alkotmány u., the museum at the red Baroque **Serbian Orthodox Church** (Szerb Ortodox Templom) displays the religious art of Szentendre's Serbian community. (Open Tu-Su 10am-8pm. 200Ft.) The church's ornate interior, an Orthodox take on Baroque, is also definitely worth a look. Szentendre's most frequented museum, **Margit Kovács Museum,** Vastagh György u. 1, exhibits miles of sentimental ceramic sculptures and tiles by the popular 20th-century Hungarian artist Margit Kovács. (Open daily Mar. 18-Oct. 10am-6pm; Nov.-Mar. 14 Th-Su 10am-4pm. 380Ft, students 150Ft.) **Szabó Marzipan Museum and Confectionary,** Dumtsa Jenő u. 7, tests the limits of its medium. It's like a summary of all the other museums in Hungary—folk art, treasuries, decorative arts, icons—but in candy. The huge marzipan Parliament is impressive, but the real thriller is the larger-than-life chocolate statue of Michael Jackson, made in Budapest in 1995. (☎31 19 31. Open daily 10am-6pm. 150Ft.) Hungary's ethnological **Open Air Village Museum** is a 10-minute bus ride from Szentendre; take the "Skazer" bus from terminal #7 (schedule varies; call ☎312 089 for info). The museum reconstructs traditional settlements and architecture from each separate region of Hungary. Craftsmen and artisans bring it to life each weekend with basket weaving, butter making, and other traditional skills. (☎502 500, 502 501, and 312 304. Open Apr.-Oct. Tu-Su 9am-5pm. 400Ft, students 200Ft.) The annual **Danube Carnival** celebrates folk art with performances by dance groups from along the river. (Mid-Mar. to late Apr. Call Tourinform (see **Practical Information,** above) for details. From mid-June to late August, **Szentendre Summer Festival** (Szentendrei Nyár Fesztivál) draws a procession of music and theater performances to the city.

# VISEGRÁD
☎(0)26

Now a sleepy rural town, Visegrád (VEE-sheh-grad) hosted the royal court in medieval times. The town's significance began to diminish after the 15th century, but was truly devastated when the Habsburgs destroyed its citadel in an early 18th-century struggle against freedom fighters. Since then, Visegrád has been rediscovered as an archaeological site. The town's slow pace and splendid views have also made it a popular holiday town, where people retreat to escape its successor, Budapest.

▣ **TRANSPORTATION.** There is no bus or train station in Visegrád. **Buses** from **Esztergom** (45min., hourly, 216Ft) and **Budapest's** Árpád híd Metro station (1½hr., 30 per day, 344Ft) pass through on route #11 along the Danube. The bus from Budapest will drop you off in front of a large parking lot. **MAHART boats** run to: **Szentendre** (1¼hr., 3 per day, 650Ft); **Esztergom** (2hr., 3 per day, 650Ft); and **Budapest** (2½-3hr., 5 per day, 700Ft).

■▪🔢 **ORIENTATION AND PRACTICAL INFORMATION.** To get to the center from the bus stop, cross the parking lot and turn right on Fő út, the road parallel to the river. About five minutes later you'll reach the Catholic Church at the town center, where Mátyás Király út and Fő út meet. **Visegrád Tours,** Rév u. 15, can help with info. Turn right at the church in the town center; the office is at the very end of the street. (☎39 81 60. Open daily Apr.-Oct. 9am-5pm; Nov.-Mar. M-F 10am-3:30pm.) They have a few **private rooms** nearby. (Doubles 20DM per person.)

▐▝▐ **ACCOMMODATIONS AND FOOD.** If you prefer to avoid the tourist agency, look for *Zimmer frei* signs along Fő út past the center. Also a few minutes past the center on Fő út, the brand new but traditional-style **Haus Honti,** Fő út 66, offers extremely clean, spacious doubles with TV, shower, and fans. (☎39 81 20. 4000-7500Ft. Breakfast included.) **Elte Guest House,** Fő út 117, is in a multi-level modern building five minutes down on the left. It has carpeted rooms with bath and—if you're lucky—a balcony. There's also a **restaurant** downstairs. (☎39 81 65. Night guard. Reception 24hr. 2990Ft per person.) **Gulás Csárda,** Nagy Lajos u. 4, prepares five excellent Hungarian dishes each day in a cozy family restaurant; you can smell the delicious garlic scent even in the outside garden. (☎39 83 29. Main dishes 350-1250Ft. Open daily 11:30am-10pm.) On a sunny day, the grassy banks of the Danube provide a perfect spot for a picnic. **ABC supermarket,** across from Visegrád Tours at the end of Rév u., sells necessities. (Open M-F 7am-7pm, Sa-Su 7am-3pm.)

▣▪🔒 **SIGHTS AND ENTERTAINMENT.** Visegrád's main attraction is the 13th-century **citadel,** visible for miles from its perch high above the Danube. Formerly a Roman outpost, the site commands a dramatic view of the river and surrounding hills. The local **bus** only shuttles back and forth from town twice a day (96Ft); if you haven't planned ahead and can afford it, save time with a minibus (☎39 73 72; 1800Ft) to the fortress; otherwise, make the arduous 30-minute hike up Kalvaria, lined with icons depicting the Stations of the Cross. The citadel also has a **wax museum** *(panoptikum)* devoted to medieval torture. (Open daily Apr.-Nov. 9:30am-6pm. 260Ft, students 200Ft.) King Matthias' **Royal Palace** (Királyi Palota), built in 1259 in the foothills above Fő út, was thought to be a myth until it was discovered by archaeologists in 1934. (☎39 80 26; fax 39 82 52. Open Apr.-Oct. Tu-Su 9am-5pm. 120Ft, students 60Ft.) During the second weekend of July, the grounds re-live their glory days for the **Viségrad Palace Games** (☎(01) 365 60 32 and (01) 209 34 59), with royal parades, jousting tournaments, concerts, medieval crafts, and cooking. Named for a king imprisoned here in the 13th century, the hexagonal Romanesque **Solomon's Tower** (Alsóvár Salamon Torony), at the end of Salamontorony u., provides a fine view of Hungary's one-time Camelot. The **King Matthias Museum** inside displays a large Lion Fountain and other artifacts from the palace ruins. (Open Apr.-Oct. Tu-Su 9am-5pm; last admission 4:30pm. 200Ft, students in a group 100Ft each, students alone free.)

# ESZTERGOM ☎(0)33

One thousand years of religious history revolve around a solemn hilltop cathedral that makes Esztergom (ESS-ter-gom), nicknamed "the Hungarian Rome," worthy of its religious pilgrims. The birthplace of King (and Saint) Stephen and the first Royal Court of Hungary, it is still the center of Hungarian Catholicism today.

▐ **TRANSPORTATION. Trains** go to **Budapest** (1½hr., 22 per day, 1286Ft). Catch **buses** three blocks away from Rákóczi tér on Simor János u. (the street lined with fruit and clothing stands). To **Visegrád** (45min., every hr., 216Ft) and **Szentendre** (1½hr., every hr., 432Ft). Buses from **Budapest** (2hr., 15 per day, 570Ft) leave from the M3 Árpád híd Metro station—follow the signs to the Volanbusz terminal. **MAHART boats** (☎41 35 31) depart from the pier at the end of Gőzhajó u. on Primas Sziget Island for **Budapest** (4hr., 3 per day, 440Ft) via **Visegrád** (1½hr., 600Ft) and **Szentendre** (2¾hr., 650Ft).

**⊞⊡ ORIENTATION AND PRACTICAL INFORMATION.** The train station is an easy 10-minute walk from town. Facing away from the station, turn left on the main street. Make a right onto Kiss János Altábornagy út, which becomes Kossuth Lajos u. as it proceeds toward the square. From the bus station in Esztergom, walk up Simor János u. toward the **street market,** which brings you directly to Rákóczi tér. **Grantours,** Széchenyi tér 25, at the edge of Rákóczi tér, provides **maps** (250Ft) and helps locate *panzió* doubles for 8000Ft or cheaper, less central **private rooms** for 2000Ft. (☎/fax 41 37 56. Open July-Aug. M-F 8am-6pm, Sa 9am-noon; Sept.-June M-F 8am-4pm, Sa 9am-noon.) **K&H Bank,** also on Rákóczi tér, has the best **exchange** rates in town and cashes **traveler's checks** for no commission. (Open M 8am-5pm, Tu-Th 8am-4pm, F 8am-3pm.) A **currency exchange machine** and an AmEx/Cirrus/MC/Plus/Visa **ATM** stand outside.

**⊡⊡ ACCOMMODATIONS AND FOOD.** Several pensions cluster around the square. **Platán Panzió,** Kis-Duna Sétány 11, in an old-fashioned yellow building between Rákóczi tér and Primas Sziget, rents small, plain, but very comfortable rooms with shared bath and a view of the courtyard rose garden. (☎41 13 55. Hot water. Reception 24hr. Singles 2500Ft; doubles 4000Ft.) **Gran Camping,** Nagy-Duna Sétány, in the middle of Primas Sziget, rents tent space in a lush park on the banks of the Danube, with its own restaurant and grocery store. Take a dip in the pool or at the small river beach and enjoy a great view of the Danube. (☎40 25 13; fax 41 19 53. Reception 24hr. 800Ft per person. Tents 750Ft.) Nearby, **Szalma Csárda,** at Primas Sziget near the pier at the end of Gőzhajó u., serves fish straight from the Danube in a beautiful restaurant with family-style tables. (☎31 10 52. Main dishes 800-1600Ft. Open daily noon-10pm.) **Csülök Csárda,** Battyány u. 9, serves up fine Hungarian dishes, adding over a dozen creative variations to the usual repertoire of roasts and stews. (☎31 24 20. Main dishes 620-1650Ft. Open daily noon-midnight.) There's also a **Julius Meinl** supermarket just off of Rákóczi tér. (Open M-F 6:30am-6:30pm, Sa 6:30am-1pm.)

**◼ SIGHTS.** A basilica was originally built here in 1010, but the present Neoclassical colossus—Hungary's biggest **church**—was consecrated in 1856. One of the finest collections of religious ornamentation in Hungary lies in the treasury, while the Basilica offers one of the finest views in the country. Climb to the top of the cathedral cupola (100Ft) for an incredible echo and the ◼ **best view** of the bend, extending all the way to the Low Tatras in Slovakia—you're on the edge of an enormous building with only a tiny guardrail between you and what feels like the entire country. Then descend into the solemn **crypt** to honor the remains of Hungary's archbishops. (Open daily 9am-4:45pm. 50Ft, pilgrims free.) The **Cathedral Treasury** (Kincstáv), whose entrance is to the right of the main altar, is Hungary's most extensive ecclesiastical collection, a treasure trove of ornate gold and silver relics and textiles spanning a millennium. The easy-to-miss jewel-studded cross, labeled #78, in the case facing the entrance to the main collection, is the 13th-century **Coronation Oath Cross** (Koronázási Eskűkereszt), on which Hungary's rulers pledged their oaths until 1916. (Open daily 9am-4:30pm. 200Ft. English guide 80Ft.) The red marble **Bakócz Chapel,** on the left side of the nave as you face the altar, is a masterwork of Tuscan Renaissance craftsmanship. It was dismantled during the Turkish occupation, then reassembled here from over 1000 separate pieces. (Open daily Mar.-Oct. 9am-4:30pm; Nov.-Dec. Tu-F 11am-3:30pm, Sa-Su 10am-3:30pm.) Beside the cathedral stands the restored 12th-century **Esztergom Palace.** Inside is the **Castle Museum** (Vár Múzeum), with pieces of St. István's original palace on display, as well as some interesting medieval fresco fragments. (☎31 59 86. Open in summer Tu-Su 9am-4pm; off-season 10am-3:30pm. 200Ft, students 100Ft.) At the foot of the cathedral hill, the **Christian Museum** (Keresztény Múzeum), Berenyi Zsigmond u. 2, houses a marvelous collection of Renaissance and medieval religious art. It exhibits Hungarian versions of Biblical scenes—such as a crucifixion painting in which the Romans wear Turkish dress—as well as some of the world's finest tryptychs. (☎413 880. Open Tu-Su 10am-5:30pm. 200Ft. Last admission 5pm.)

**HUNGARY**

# THE ŐRSÉG

In the far west corner of Hungary, low-flying storks guard the pastoral region known as the Őrség (EWR-shayg). During the Cold War, authorities discouraged visitors and Hungarians alike from entering the Őrség, as it was too close to the capitalist Austria and Tito-era Yugoslavia. Thus a region that had always been a little behind the times—electricity didn't arrive until 1950—became even more distanced from the pace of the modern world. Today the rural areas still feel wonderfully old-fashioned and unspoiled. The landscape is gentle, rather than dramatic, with rolling hills and farmland perfect for relaxing walks or bicycle rides. From the beautiful architecture of Sopron to the outstanding museums of Győr, tourists come to catch this slice of timelessness.

## GYŐR
☎(0)96

The cobbles streets of Győr's (DYUR) inner city wind peacefully around a wealth of religious monuments, superb museums, and prime examples of 17th- and 18th-century architecture. Horse-drawn carriages accompany rush-hour traffic and Győr's industrial outskirts leave the city just real enough to placate the traveler weary of too much storybook charm. The large and lively population makes the old town exciting as well as aesthetically pleasing. Add a packed riverside waterpark, an array of terrace restaurants, and throngs of young people on weekend evenings, and you have a living, breathing combination of history and recreation that begs visitors to stay just one more day.

### ✳ 🛈 ORIENTATION AND PRACTICAL INFORMATION

The **train station** lies only five minutes from the city center; the underpass that links the rail platforms leads back to the **bus station.** To reach the center, head out the front of the train station and go right until you come to the bridge. Turn left just before the underpass, then cross the big street to the pedestrian **Baross Gabor u.**

**Trains:** To **Budapest** (2½hr., 26 per day, 974Ft) and **Vienna, AUS** (2hr., 13 per day, 5116Ft).

**Buses:** To **Budapest** (2½hr., every hr., 1144Ft).

**Tourist Office: Tourinform kiosk,** Árpád u. 32 (☎31 17 71). At the corner with Baross Gabor u. Provides free **maps.** Open June-Aug. M-F 8am-8pm, Sa 9am-3pm, Su 9am-1pm; Sept.-May M-Sa 9am-4pm.

**Budget Travel: IBUSZ,** Kazinczy u. 3 (☎31 17 00). A few blocks farther up Baross Gabor u., turn left on Kazinczy u. Extensive accommodation info and assistance. 10% off on international train and bus tickets for those under 26. Open June-Aug. M-F 8am-6pm, Sa 8am-noon; Sept.-May M-F 8am-4pm. AmEx/MC/Visa.

**Currency Exchange: OTP Bank,** at the corner of Baross u. and Kisfaludy u. Good exchange rates. Open M 7:45am-4pm, Tu-F 7:45am-3pm. Cirrus/MC/Visa/Plus **ATM** outside. Cash **AmEx traveler's cheques** at the *Postabank* desk in the post office (see below) for no commission.

**Pharmacy:** Jedlik Á. u. 16 (☎32 88 81). Open M-F 7am-6pm, Sa 7am-2pm.

**Post office:** Bajcsy-Zsilinszky út 46 (☎31 43 24). Open M-F 8am-8pm. EMS parcel post open 8am-6pm.

**Postal code:** 9021.

### ▸ ACCOMMODATIONS

Accommodations in downtown Győr overflow in July and August, making reservations essential. Tourinform (see above) can help you find a *panzió* or hotel room, and will make reservations if you call ahead. IBUSZ (see above) offers a few **private rooms,** but expect to pay a 30% surcharge if you stay under four nights. (Singles from 2000Ft, doubles from 3000Ft.)

**Hotel Szárnyaskerék,** Vasut u. 5 (☎31 46 29). Right across the street from the train station. If you can stand the icy reception, it's a good value, although rooms are spartan. Beds are comfy, bathrooms decent. Doubles 4250Ft, with bath 6600Ft.

**Széchenyi Istvan Főiskola Kollégiuma,** Hédevári út 3, entrance K4 (☎50 34 00). Also across the Moscow-Dune River. Heading up Baross Gabor u. from the train station, turn right on Bajcsy-Zsilinszky u. and left onto Czuczor Gergely u., which becomes Jedlik Ányos. Cross the bridge and take a sharp left onto Kúlóczy tér, cross the parking lot, and look for the Bufé. Entrance K4 is on the left; after 9pm enter at K3. Standard dorms in modern buildings arranged around a courtyard. Weak showers and no toilet paper. Reception 24hr. Check-out 9am. Open July-Aug. Airy triples 2000Ft per person.

**Kiskút liget Camping** (☎31 89 86), on Kiskút liget. Catch local bus #8 in front of the train station, going toward the overpass; the stop is clearly marked. Year-round motel, bungalows, and campsite. Easily accessible from the city center and in a good area for cycling. Open Apr.-Oct. 15. 300Ft per person. Tents 300Ft. 2-person bungalows 3800Ft. Motel singles 3600F; doubles 4350Ft.

# FOOD

The sprawling **Kaiser's supermarket** sits at the corner of Alany János u. and Aradi vértanúk. (Open M 7:30am-7pm, Tu-F 6:30am-7pm, Sa 6:30am-2pm.)

**Matróz Restaurant,** Dunakapu tér 3 (☎32 49 55). Off Jedlik Ányos facing the river. With folksy tavern decor but a more upscale restaurant atmosphere, Matróz fries up succulent fish dishes. Cozy, brick dining room decorated with fishing nets and furnished with dwarf-sized wooden chairs. Main dishes 380-790Ft. Open daily 9am-10pm.

**Paradiso,** Kazinczy u. 20 (☎31 28 56). The upstairs bistro offers decent Hungarian fare for decent prices. Don't venture downstairs unless you're in the market for something a little more racy. Main dishes 450-1600Ft. Open daily 9am-1am.

**Stinger Pub,** Aradi u. 3 (☎32 46 65). A good place for a break from Hungarian food. Sidewalk cafe tables sit on a pleasant street near the top of the hill. Offers delectable pizza (490-790Ft) and pasta (440-590Ft) and an assortment of salads (160-350Ft).

# SIGHTS

Most sights in Győr lie within a small area near the center of town. Going east of the Rába River you will cross Bécsi kapu tér, Chapter Hill, and then Széchenyi tér.

**CHAPTER HILL.** (Káptalandomb.) Walking uphill on Baross Gabor u. will bring you to Chapter Hill, the oldest sector of Győr. The striking **Ark of the Covenant statue** (Frigylada szobov), built by King Charles III in 1731 with the proceeds of taxes levied on his mercenaries to keep them impoverished and in line, marks the way to Chapter Hill. The Episcopal **Cathedral** (Székesegyház), at the top of the hill, has suffered constant additions since 1030; its exterior is now a hybrid of Romanesque, Gothic, and Neoclassical styles. The Baroque splendor inside deserves more attention, with dozens of gilded cherubim perched above magnificent frescoes. A priest fleeing Oliver Cromwell in the 1650s brought the miraculous **Weeping Madonna of Győr** all the way from Ireland. Legend has it that on St. Patrick's Day in 1697 the image spontaneously wept blood and tears for three hours in sympathy for persecuted Irish Catholics. On the opposite side of the cathedral, the Hédeváry chapel holds the **Herm of King St. Ladislas,** a medieval bust of one of Hungary's first saint-kings. For a larger dose of religious art, the **Ecclesiastical Treasury** (Egyházmegyei Kincstáv) hides at the end of a small side alley, which leads off the square from the back right corner of the cathedral. It displays primarily 14th-century gold and silver religious artifacts, but be sure to see the 15th- and 16th-century illuminated manuscripts as well. It also includes some interesting recent pieces, such as a 19th-century gold reliquary with about 30 neatly-arranged saints' fingernails visible inside. *(Open Tu-Su 10am-4pm. 150Ft, students 75Ft. English captions.)*

**OTHER SIGHTS.** The **Imre Patkó Collection** (Patkó Imre Gyűjtemény), Széchenyi tér 4, whose entrance is on Stelczera is housed in the **Iron Log House** (Vastuskós ház), named for a stump into which traveling 17th-century craftsmen drove nails when they spent the night. The collection contains two floors of modern Hungarian art and an attic full of Asian and African works that Patkó amassed in his travels. *(Open Tu-Su 10am-6pm. 140Ft, students 70Ft.)* A short walk down Kenyér Köz from Széchenyi tér, the **Margit Kovács Museum** (Kovács Margit Gyűjtemény), Rózsa Ferenc u. 1, displays the artist's distinctive ceramic sculptures and tiles (kitschy or sweet, depending on your taste). *(Open Mar.-Oct. Tu-Su 10am-6pm; Nov.-Feb. Tu-Su 10am-5pm. 200Ft, students 100Ft. To get to Széchenyi tér from Chapel Hill, go left down Király u.)*

The **Carmelite Church** (Karmelita-templom) and the remains of a **medieval castle** built to defend the town from the Turks sit on Bécsi kapu tér. A branch of the **János Xanthus Museum** (Xantus János Múzeum), housing an underground lapidarium filled with fragments of Roman ruins, is built into the castle. *(From Széchenyi tér, following Király u. will bring you to Bcsi kapu tér. Open Apr.-Oct. Tu-Su 10am-6pm. 140Ft.)*

## 🎵🎶 ENTERTAINMENT AND NIGHTLIFE

In summer, do as the locals do—splash in the water and enjoy the sun. Across the river from the center of town, thermal springs serve as the basis for a large 🌊 **water park** (furdő). It feels as though the entire city is there, with three generations of Hungarians having the time of their lives in the pool or at one of the ice cream bars. (Cziráky tér 1. From Széchenyi tér, take Jedlik Ányos to the main bridge, take a left on the other side, and walk along the sidewalk until you come to a smaller footbridge on the left. Cross this; the park is to the left. Open daily 8am-7pm. 400Ft, students 300F; after 3pm 290Ft, 220Ft.) Győr frolics away June and July with **Győri Nyár,** a festival of daily concerts, drama, and the city's famous ballet. Buy tickets at the box office on Baross Gábor út or at the performance venue. Schedules are at Tourinform and IBUSZ (see p. 342).

Győr has an active nightlife, with music spilling from cellar bars onto streets full of teens in their Saturday-night best. Crowded at 5pm and still packed at midnight, the terrace of **Komédiás Biergarten,** in the courtyard at Czuczor Gergely u. 30, inspires loud conversation and general merrymaking. (☎31 90 50. Amstel 200Ft. Open M-Sa 11am-midnight.) If you're wistful for a Guinness, **Dublin Gate Irish Pub,** Bécsikapu tér 8, across from the yellow Carmelite Church, draws a lively young crowd (☎31 06 88. Guinness 290Ft. Open M-Sa noon-midnight, Su noon-11pm.) You're sure to incur a mean hangover after a visit to **Trófea Borozó,** Bajcsy-Zsilinszky 16, with a selection of wines cheap enough to bring out the snob in anyone. (Open M-F 6am-10pm, Sa 7am-10pm. Wine 225Ft, beer 145-195Ft.)

## 🚌 DAYTRIP FROM GYŐR

### ARCHABBEY OF PANNONHALMA                    ☎(0)96

*Pannonhalma is an easy daytrip from Győr on the bus from stand #11 (45min., 7 per day, 216Ft). Ask for Pannonhalma vár and look for the huge gates. Some of the buses only go as far as the town, 1km away.*

Visible at a distance from Győr, the hilltop Archabbey of Pannonhalma (Pannonhalmi Főapátság) has seen 10 centuries of destruction and rebuilding since it was established by the Benedictine order in 996. The working abbey now houses a 13th-century basilica, a staggering 360,000-volume library, a small art gallery, and one of the finest boys' schools in Hungary. Among the treasures to be found here are a 1055 deed founding a Benedictine Abbey, the oldest document bearing Hungarian words, and a charter from 1001 with St. Steven's classic medieval signature. Although the most recent renovation for the Pope's visit in 1996 left the abbey halls looking a bit spiffy for their age, Hungary's oldest graffiti is still visible in the wall: a soldier defending the hill against the Turks "was here" in 1578. Continual additions to the abbey illustrate the layers of influences on Hungarian religious art. Keep an eye out for eccentric stone carvings hiding in corners and on columns. Legend has it that if you fit into St. Steven's wooden throne in the Gothic-Romanesque crypt, the wish you make there will be granted. You can hear **Gregorian chants** every Sunday at the 10am mass. Classical music concerts also take place frequently in the halls of the abbey; inquire at **Pax Tourist** (☎57 01 91). To see the abbey, join an hourly tour group at the Pax Tourist office to the left of the entrance. English-speaking guides are available in summer only for the mandatory one-hour tour at 11am and 1pm. Some written information is also available in English. (Abbey open daily 8:30am-4pm. Hungarian tour with English text 400Ft, students 120Ft; English tour 800Ft, 400Ft. AmEx/MC/Visa.)

# TATA ☎(0)34

The quiet vacation town of Tata (TAW-TAW) stretches around lakes, canals, and a 14th-century castle, providing a restful training ground for the Hungarian Olympic team. If you'd rather go for the beach than the gold, the glassy lake is perfect for sunbathing, boating, and fishing. Visitors relax, enjoy the town's casual atmosphere and laid-back pace, and watch the sun set over the lake from the castle walls.

**HUNGARY**

**◤ TRANSPORTATION. Trains** from **Budapest's** Keleti Station (1¼hr., 16 per day, 450Ft) pass through—be sure *not* to get off at Tatabánya, one stop before Tata when coming from Budapest—but you can avoid the 1.5km hike into town by taking the **bus** from **Budapest's** Árpád híd station (1¼hr., 2 per day, 658Ft).

**◤◪ ORIENTATION AND PRACTICAL INFORMATION.** From the train station, exit on Gesztenye u., then take a left on Bacsó Béla u. After 10 minutes, turn right on Somogyi Béla u., which ends at Országgyűlés tér. Bear left to **Ady Endre u.,** Tata's main street, or take local bus #1 to Tata's main bus station (90Ft). From the bus station, walk down the road toward the lake and the castle, following the shore as it curves to the left. Bear right onto Alkotmány u. when Bartok B. u. splits. A moment later, you'll be on Ady Endre u. **Tourinform,** Ady Endre 9, **exchanges currency,** offers a **map** (170Ft), and helps with accommodations. (☎38 48 06. Open in summer M-F 8am-3:30pm, Sa 8am-11:30am.) The **OTP Bank** on Ady Endre, to the left coming out of Tourinform, cashes **traveler's checks** for no commission. (Open M 7:45am-5pm, Tu-F 7:45am-4pm.) There's a Cirrus/MC/Plus/Visa **ATM** outside. The central **post office** lies off Országgyűlés tér, to the right opposite a church. (Open M-F 8am-6:30pm, Sa 8am-noon.) **Postal code:** 2890.

**◤◪ ACCOMMODATIONS AND FOOD.** Tata is a popular summer vacation destination for foreigners and Hungarians alike, so rooms fill quickly—call ahead. **Hattyú Panzió,** Ady Endre u. 56, supplies tidy, well-furnished triples with shared bath. Reception is in the friendly tavern downstairs. (☎38 36 53. Breakfast 5600Ft. Tavern open daily noon-10pm. 4400Ft.) Several inexpensive options lie a bit farther out from the town center. Coming from the town center, turn right down Ady Endre from the Spar, then turn left on the main road (út Május I) that leads off the far end of Országgyűlés tér. Take a right onto Oroszlányi u. (across from the Profi Supermarket), which becomes Fényes fasor (30min.). Down Fényes fasor, *Zimmer frei* and *lovas iskola* (riding school) signs point left toward **Maestoso.** The spiffy, bright pension in a peaceful field offers outstanding rooms with beautiful private bathrooms. There's a sauna (900Ft per hr.), a pool table, ping-pong, bike rentals, a tanning salon, and **horseback riding.** (☎/fax 48 50 39. Horseback riding 2200Ft per hr.; 30min. lesson 1560Ft. Rooms 3850Ft. Breakfast included.) Ten minutes up Fényes fasor from Maestoso is **Fényes-Fürdö Camping,** which rents 4-person bungalows (4500Ft) and tents (550Ft plus 410Ft per person) in a country club with swimming pools, tennis courts, and a laundromat. (☎/fax 48 12 08. Open May-Sept.) To reach the campground from the bus station, follow the *Bad-Camping* (an inadvertent combination of English and German)/*Fényes Fürdö* signs.

At **Halaszcsárda,** Tópart u. 10, one of many lakefront restaurants, big families seated around big picnic tables enjoy fresh fish dishes and sunsets over the lake. (☎38 01 36. Main dishes 510-700Ft. Open Su-Th noon-10pm, F noon-midnight, Sa noon-1am.) A well-stocked **Supermarket Spar** sits across the street from Tourinform on Ady Endre. (Open M-F 6:30am-7pm, Sa 6:30am-2pm, Su 7am-noon.)

🔲🗄 **SIGHTS AND ENTERTAINMENT.** From the center, head down Alkotmány u. (the first left coming from Tourinform away from the Spar) to the lakeshore and Tata's two main draws. Follow the lake to the right to the grassy, ruin-filled grounds of the **Old Castle** (Öregvár). Inside is Tata's main tourist attraction, **Kuny Domokos Múzeum,** covering two millennia of regional history. Breeze through the two lower floors and head for the third, which contains the wood, metal, and porcelain work of 18th-century master craftsmen. (Open Tu-Su 10am-6pm. Su-F 250Ft, Sa 150Ft.) The real gem of the museum is not its collection, but its coffeehouse: the 🔲 **Múzeum Presszó** has a panoramic view of the lake from its rooftop terrace. The Baroque **Eszterházy mansion,** built in 1765 and now used as a hospital, sits a few meters farther down the shore. The family name came to be linked with the gentle yellow color of the house's exterior; many churches and monuments throughout the country are painted this "Eszterházy yellow." A converted and crumbling synagogue (the white building), across the street from the mansion, houses the eccentric **Greco-Roman Statuary Museum** (Görög-Római Szobormásolatok Múzeum), which has a collection of faux-ancient statues. (Open Tu-Su 10am-6pm. 80Ft, students 50Ft.) They once lined the paths of **Angol Park,** Hungary's first English-style park, right off Ady Endre u. Its wide paths, small waterfalls, and public swimming pool maintain the park's elegance and serenity. On warm weekends, live bands play outside on the south shore of the lake.

Locals party late at **Zsigmond borozó,** a hip bar located in underground caverns on the castle grounds. The entrance is a stairway that descends into the hill in front of the castle. (☎309 69 09 49. Open 2pm-midnight.)

# SOPRON ☎(0)99

With soaring spires and winding cobblestone streets, the well-preserved historical monuments of Sopron's (SHO-pron) medieval quarter feel decidedly Austrian. As any local will remind you, though, Sopron is considered "Hungary's most loyal town." In 1920, the Swabians of Ödenburg (as Sopron was then called) voted to remain part of Hungary instead of joining their linguistic brethren in Austria. Fidelity notwithstanding, Sopron is deluged daily by Austrians drawn by both cheap medical care and good sausage.

## ✴ ORIENTATION

Belváros (Inner Town), the historic center, is a 1km long horseshoe bounded by three main streets. **Ógabona tér** and **Várkerület** form an arc while **Széchenyi tér** connects the two longer roads near the train station. **Fő tér,** the site of many of the museums and notable buildings, sits within this region, at the end farthest from the train station. The **train station** is a five-minute walk from the city center on Mátyás Király út, which leads to Széchenyi tér and becomes Várkerület, curving around the Inner Town. The **bus station** is also five minutes from the center. Exit the station and make a right onto Lackner Kristóf út, then turn left at the Ciklámen Tourist office to reach Várkerület near Fő tér.

## 🔲🗄 TRANSPORTATION AND PRACTICAL INFORMATION

**Trains:** To: **Győr** (1½hr., 12 per day, 612Ft); **Budapest** (3-4hr., 6 per day, 1508Ft); and **Vienna, AUS** (1-2hr., 13 per day, 2410Ft).

**Buses:** To: **Győr** (2hr., 1 per hr., 654Ft) and **Budapest** (4hr., 5 per day, 1510Ft).

**Tourist Office: Tourinform,** Előkapu u. 11 (☎33 88 92). Follow the trail of info signs to the shiny new office right off Várkerület u. Gives free **maps,** advice, and accommodations info, and sells more detailed city **maps** of Sopron (400Ft). Also carries some travel information on Austria. Open M-F 9am-5pm, Sa 9am-noon.

**Currency Exchange:** Head to **Budapest Bank,** Színhaz u. 5, which also cashes **traveler's checks** for no commission. Open M-Th 8am-5pm, F 8am-3pm. There's an AmEx/Cirrus/MC/Plus/Visa **ATM** outside Julius Meinl (see **Food,** below), Várkerület 100/102.

**Internet Access:** At the public library in the Magyar Művelődes Háza (MMH; Hungarian Cultural House), on Liszt Ferenc ut. 1 just off Széchenyi tér. It also has a good selection of **English books.**

**Post Office:** Széchenyi tér 7/10 (☎31 31 00). Just outside of Belváros. Open M-F 8am-8pm, Sa 8am-noon.

**Postal code:** 9400.

# ◤ ACCOMMODATIONS

Tourinform (see above) can get you settled into a comfy **private room** near the center. (Singles 1800Ft; doubles 3600Ft.) **Ciklámen Tourist,** Ógabona tér 8, on the way to city center from the bus station, can also set you up with a convenient private room. (☎31 20 40. Doubles 3640Ft; with bath 5000Ft first night, 4000Ft thereafter. Open M-F 8am-4:30pm, Sa 8am-1pm.) If you'd prefer a *panzió,* **Locomotiv Turist,** Várkerület 90, locates the cheapest options. (☎31 11 11. Doubles with TV, shower, and fridge from 4500Ft. Open M-Sa 8:30am-4:30pm.)

**Ringhofer Panzió,** Balfi u. 52 (☎32 50 22; fax 32 60 81). From Széchenyi tér on Várkerület, take the 2nd right onto Torna u. Follow the street as it becomes Bem u. and turn left onto Balfi u. Breakfast 400Ft. Bicycle rental 1000Ft per day. Reception 24hr. Check-out 10am. Doubles with shower 4000Ft. Tourist tax 300Ft.

**Lővér Campground** (☎/fax 31 17 15). Take bus #12 from the city center (one pickup point is Erzsébet u. 2); the last stop is "Camping." Bus #12A also goes there—get off at its last stop on Köszegi u., follow the road curving left, and look for the fork with the "camping" sign to reach this friendly, relaxed campsite. Open Apr. 15-Oct. 15. 350Ft per person; 500Ft per tent. 2-3 person bungalows 2000-3800Ft; 2-person hut 2000Ft.

# ◖ FOOD

Of the many small grocery stores, the ubiquitous **Julius Meinl,** Várkerület 100/102, has perhaps the best collection. (Open M-F 6:30am-8pm, Sa 6:30am-3pm.)

**Várkerület Restaurant,** Várkerület 83 (☎31 92 86). Near Széchenyi tér. A traditional Hungarian menu, as well as some of its own specialties ("house-proud dishes"). Prompt service brings the meaty main courses (650-1700Ft) to warmly-lit tables in the dining room and a beer garden surrounded by trees. Open daily 11am-midnight.

**Pince Csárda,** Széchenyi tér 5 (☎34 92 76). Serves a tremendous array of chicken, venison, and veal dishes. Main dishes 590-1750Ft. Open M-Th 10am-11pm, F-Sa 10am-midnight, Su 10am-4pm.

**Perkovátz-HÁZ/John Bull English Pub,** Széchenyi tér 12 (☎31 68 39). Perfect for homesick Brits, with one exception—the food is actually good here. Chicken, fish, and veggie dishes with 3 types of genuine English beer on tap. Main dishes 400-2380Ft; Guinness 700Ft per pint. Open daily 10am-2am. MC/Visa.

# ◉ SIGHTS

**BENEDICTINE CHURCH.** (Bencés Templom.) Built in the 13th century by a happy herder whose goats stumbled upon a cache of gold, the Benedictine Church has been the site of the royal coronations for two queens and one king. The small monastery (kolostor), next door at Templom u. 1, also dates from the 13th century. Visitors can enter its Chapter Hall, a room full of textbook Gothic architecture decorated with 10 allegorical sculptures of human sin. Information sheets (available in several languages) explain their meaning, while taped Gregorian chants add atmosphere. *(On Fő tér. Open daily 10am-noon and 2-5pm.)*

**OLD AND NEW SYNAGOGUES.** Two of the few medieval synagogues left standing after World War II, both are now museums dedicated to the daily life of the local Jewish community expelled in 1526. **Old Synagogue** (Középkori Ó-Zsinagóga) was first built around 1300 and has been reconfigured to show the separate rooms for men and women, the stone Torah ark, the wooden *bima*, and the ritual bath well. *(Új u. 22. Open M and W-Su 9am-5pm. 100Ft, students 50Ft.)* **New Synagogue** (Új-Zsinagóga), only 50 years newer, is now being restored after centuries of neglect—its exterior is visible through the courtyard at Szent György u. 12, on the opposite side of the block. *(Új u. 11. Open M 1-5pm, W-Th 9am-3:30pm, F 9am-noon.)*

**FIRE-WATCH TOWER.** (Tűztorony.) The main symbol of Sopron, this tower consists of a 17th-century spire atop a 16th-century tower on a 12th-century base that straddles a Roman gate. Its clock is the source of the chimes heard throughout town. Squeeze up a spiral staircase to the balcony for a view of the surrounding hills. *(Opposite the front side of Tourinform. Open Tu-Su 10am-6pm. 150Ft, students 80Ft.)*

**FABRICIUS HOUSE.** Of the three exhibits in the house, the high-vaulted cellar contains the best one. Originally a Gothic chapel, and now the coolest place in town on a hot day, the **Roman Lapidarium** (Római Kőtár) houses tombs and statues dating to Sopron's origins as the Roman colony of Scarbantia. *(Fő tér 6. Open Tu-Su 10am-6pm. 100Ft for the 1st 2 exhibits, students 60Ft. Lapidarium 150Ft, students 80Ft.)*

**STORNO HOUSE.** (Storno-ház.) Storno House's exterior restorations are unimpressive. Its residents, Swiss-Italian restorers of monuments and cathedrals, however, had impeccable taste in interior design. They collected furniture and artwork from the Renaissance to the 19th century. *(Fő tér 8. Open Tu-Su 10am-6pm. Brief written information available in English. 80Ft, students 40Ft.)*

**BAKERY MUSEUM.** (Pékmúzeum.) Illustrating the history of professional baking from the 15th to 20th centuries in the restored shop of a successful 19th-century baker, the Bakery Museum denies patrons the full sensory experience—there are no goodies for sale. *(☎31 13 27. Bécsi út 5. From Várkerület, enter onto Ikva-Dorfmeister u. near the small branch of the post office. Take the 2nd left onto Jégverem Halász u. and follow it through Sas tér as it becomes Bécsi út. Open Tu-Su 10am-noon. 100Ft, students 50Ft.)*

## 🎵 ENTERTAINMENT

For information on cultural events in and around Sopron, visit Tourinform (see **Tourist Office,** above), and pick up a free copy of the monthly *Soproni Ünnepi Hetek* (Sopron Program), which lists local events. Watch out for regular appearances by the "Beatles," Hungary's popular take on the original mop-tops. During the **Sopron Festival Weeks** (late June to mid-July), the town hosts opera, ballet, and concerts. Some are set in the **Fertőrákos Quarry,** 10km away, served by hourly buses from the bus terminal. (Quarry 30Ft for students. Concerts 500-600Ft.) Buy tickets for all events from the **Festival Bureau,** on Széchenyi tér across from the post office. (Open M-F 9am-5pm, Sa 9am-noon; closed mid-July through mid-Aug.)

## 🍸 NIGHTLIFE

**Cézár borozó,** Hátsókapu 2 (☎31 13 37). Near Fő tér. The drink selection is so good, you'll never want to leave this 17th-century home. 1dL red wine 40Lt; 0.5L Gösser 250Ft; shots from 300Ft. Open M-Th 11am-10pm, F-Sa 11am-midnight, Su 11am-9pm.

**La Playa Cafe and Bar,** Várkerület 22 (☎34 03 34). So packed with Sopron youth that it's hard to appreciate the eclectic decor, complete with a sombrero, a sewing machine, and a *Gone With the Wind* poster. Scarlett might have believed that "tomorrow is another day," but she wasn't dealing with a hangover brought on by Corona (420Ft) or Rolling Rock (180Ft). Open F-Sa 6pm-2am, Su-M and W-Th 6pm-1am.

**The Ex-Rockline Freestyle Music Club,** Ágfalvi u. 2 (☎34 23 46). The best place for clubbing, if you're not too exhausted from the trek out here. Despite its inconvenience, the Freestyle is swamped nightly by a devoted crowd of regulars who came to dance and celebrate. Beer 150-230Ft; shots 200-380. Open W-Sa 9pm-4am.

## 🏛 DAYTRIP FROM SOPRON

### FERTŐD                                      ☎(0)99
*Buses leave for Fertőd from platform #11 in Sopron's station on Lackner Kristóf (45min., every hr., 265Ft). They continue on to Győr (2hr., 5 per day, 523Ft).*

27km east of Sopron, Fertőd (FER-tewd) is home to the magnificent Baroque ■ **Eszterházy Palace,** Joseph Haydn 2, nicknamed the "Hungarian Versailles." Miklós Eszterházy, known as Miklós the Sumptuous before he squandered his family's vast fortune, ordered the palace built in 1766 to host his extended bacchanal feasts, claiming boldly, "What the emperor can afford, I can afford as well." The mansion grounds were once home to an opera house, a Chinese pavilion, and a puppet theatre. The tour (1hr.) explains everything from the marble floors to the painted ceilings, including the cleverly concealed door in the prince's bedroom—it's only in Hungarian, but the English information sheet is fairly extensive and additional historical information is available at the register. Used as a stable and then a hospital during World War II, the mansion was restored with much-needed government funds directly after the 1957 revolution. Josef Haydn spent 30 years composing here; ■ **concerts** during the annual fall **Haydn Festival** recreate the premieres of his most famous works. (☎37 09 71. Palace open Apr. 16-Oct. 15 Tu-Su 9am-5pm; Oct. 16-Apr. 15 Tu-Su 9am-4pm. 600Ft, students 250Ft. Concerts 4500Ft and 7000Ft; check at Tourinform in Sopron for a schedule.)

There is a **hotel** inside the mansion; for reservations, particularly during the Haydn Festival in early September, book with Ciklámen Tourist in Sopron. Call the hotel directly at ☎37 09 71 or fax 37 01 20 for information.

# SZOMBATHELY                              ☎(0)94

The seat of Vas county and a major commercial crossroads between Transdanubia and Austria, Szombathely (SOM-ba-tay; "Saturday's Place") holds 2000-year-old ruins obscured by modern storefronts and scattered baroque facades. Though it lacks much in atmosphere, it still fills each weekend with tourists looking for a taste of the Hungarian lifestyle—or at least good lager—on the terrace of one of the city's many restaurants and cafes.

**🚆 TRANSPORTATION. Trains** (☎31 14 20) go to: **Győr** (2hr., 4 per day, 834Ft; *InterCity* 1¼hr., 4 per day, 834Ft plus 310Ft reservation fee); **Keszthely** (2½hr., 3 per day, 820Ft); and **Budapest** (3¾hr., 9 per day, 1624Ft; *InterCity* 2¾hr., 4 per day, 1624Ft plus 310Ft reservation fee). Tickets can be purchased at MÁV offices at the train station or at Király u. 8/a. (Open M-F 8am-5pm, Sa 8am-noon.) **Buses** (☎31 20 54) run to: **Győr** (2½hr., 8 per day, 964Ft); **Keszthely** (2½hr., 6 per day, 834Ft); and **Budapest** (3½hr., 6 per day, 2194Ft).

**🏛 ORIENTATION AND PRACTICAL INFORMATION.** It takes only 20 minutes to walk the inner city of Szombathely. The town focuses around several squares, the largest of which is **Fő tér,** one of Hungary's largest squares and home to the main tourist offices. To get there from the **train station,** take Széll Kálmán u. to Mártírok tére. Turn left onto Király u., which ends in **Savaria tér,** a smaller square that opens onto the wide Fő tér. The **bus station** sits on the opposite side of the inner city; turn left on the street parallel to the station and follow it as it curves to the left. Cross Kiskar u. and then head straight to the narrow pedestrian Belsikátor, which ends in Fő tér.

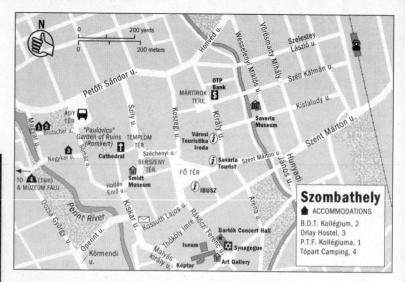

For English brochures and pamphlets go to **Városi Touristikai Iroda** (Town Tourist Office), Belsikátor 1, off Fő tér. (☎34 18 10. Open M-F 10am-5pm.) Tourinform-licensed **Savaria Tourist** provides info and **maps** (200Ft). Its three central locations are at Király u. 1 (☎32 58 31; fax 32 58 30), Mártírok tére 1 (☎51 14 35 and 51 14 36), and Berzsenyi tér 2 (☎/fax 34 00 86). All locations **exchange currency** and cash **traveler's checks** for no commission. (Open M-F 8:30am-4:30pm, Sa 8am-noon.) Exchange currency at **OTP Bank,** Fő tér 4. (Open M 7:45am-6pm, Th-F 7:45am-5pm.) There's also a currency exchange machine and a Cirrus/MC/Plus/Visa **ATM** outside. A **pharmacy** sits at both Fő tér 9 (☎31 24 66) and 31 (☎31 25 83; both open M-F 7:30am-6:45pm, Sa 8am-1pm.) A **doctor** is on call at Wesselényi Miklós u. 4 (☎31 11 00). The **post office** is at Kossuth Lajos u. 18. (☎31 15 84. Open M-F 8am-8pm, Sa 8am-2pm.) **Postal code:** 9700.

**⌐⌐ ACCOMMODATIONS AND FOOD.** To find one of the few **private rooms** available in Szombathely, go through either **Savaria Tourist** (see above; central doubles 3000-3800Ft) or **IBUSZ,** Fő tér 44 (☎31 41 41; open June-Aug. M-F 8am-5pm, Sa 9am-noon; Sept.-May M-F 8am-4pm; singles 3120Ft; doubles 3640Ft). **Orlay Hostel,** Nagykar u. 1/3, is next to the bus station. Cross the street parallel to the station and walk left to the statue in the pedestrian area; it's on the left across from the Xerox center. Pristine rooms are more spacious than most dorm accommodations, but showers are shared and lack curtains. (☎31 23 75. Open daily July-Aug.; Sept.-June Sa-Su only. Dorms 900Ft.) **Puskás Tivadar Fém és Villamosipari Szakközépiskole Kollégiuma,** Ady tér 2, is in the park opposite the bus lot. This hostel with a big name has small but clean rooms. (☎31 21 98. Ask for Dr. Őri Imréné (EW-ry EEM-ray-nay) to make a reservation. Open July-Aug. only. Dorms 850Ft.) To get to **Tópart Camping,** Kenderesi u. 14, take bus #7 from the station to the lake terminal and walk five minutes to the other side of the lake. This picture-perfect campsite, complete with swans, has peace and quiet. (☎50 90 38; fax 50 90 39. Open May-Sept. 700Ft per person, 300Ft per tent. Doubles 4100Ft; 2-person bungalows 6700Ft; 3- and 4- person 8800Ft; 5-person 9800Ft. Tourist tax 120Ft.)

Most of the town's restaurants line Fő tér's pedestrian walkway. **Julius Meinl** supermarkets sit at Fő tér 17 (open M-F 7am-8pm, Sa 7am-2pm) and behind the bus station (open M 6am-6pm, Tu-F 6am-7pm, Su 6am-noon). They may not be the best stocked, but both accept MC and Visa. ■ **Gődőr Étterem,** Hollán Ernő 10/12, dishes up huge portions of Hungarian specialties from a menu so descriptive it makes your mouth water ("fried; so it's not good for you, but it's so delicious you won't care;" ☎51 00 78; main dishes 750-1690Ft; open M-Th 11am-11pm, F-Sa 11am-midnight, Su 11am-3pm). **Belvárosi Vendéglo**, Savaria tér 1, is near the end of Fő tér. This no-nonsense eatery has a quick staff and heaping plates of meat (540-1480Ft). Enjoy a smoke, a beer (0.5L Heineken 380Ft), and a steak (1310Ft) at the counter or on the terrace with the rest of town. There are even some vegetarian dishes. (☎31 49 67. Open daily 8:30am-10pm.)

🏛🎭 **SIGHTS AND ENTERTAINMENT.** Szombathely's 1797 **cathedral**, built in Baroque and Neoclassical styles, is Hungary's third-largest. To its right stands the entrance to **"Paulovics" Garden of Ruins** (Paulovics Romkert), Templom tér 1, the center of the original first-century AD Roman colony, with town walls, a bathhouse, remains of a palace, and floor mosaics. From Fő tér, go left onto Széchenyi u., right onto Szily János u., and straight to Templom tér. (☎31 33 69. Open Apr.-Nov. Tu-Sa 9am-5pm. 100Ft, students 60Ft.) The **Smidt Museum**, Hollán Ernő u. 2, is a testament to Dr. Lajos Smidt's obsession with collecting just about anything he could get his retired hospital superintendent hands on. Like a garage sale gone berserk, each case is packed with weapons, watches, coins, clothing, tableware, Roman artifacts, and ancient maps. Check out Franz Liszt's pocket watch and a beer mug inscribed with the largely unheeded warning *Bier ist Gift!* ("Beer is Poison!"). From Fő tér, walk through the tiny Belsikátor u. to Hollán E. u., the main street; it's on the corner across the street. (☎31 10 38. Open Tu-Su noon-5pm. 120Ft, students 80Ft.) The **Savaria Museum**, Kisfaludy Sándor u. 9, unearths the roots of Vas county. Watch your step in the first exhibit—the floor has been modeled to reflect a topographical map of the region, complete with two-inch gradations between altitude lines. Take Király u. left from Savaria tér, at the end of Fő tér across from the McDonald's, then make the first right onto Kisfaludy Sándor. (☎31 25 54. Open Tu-F 9am-5pm, Sa-Su 10am-4pm. 120Ft, students 80Ft.) The **Village Museum** (Múzeum Falu), Árpád u. 30, on the outskirts of town, consists of 150- to 200-year-old farmhouses, whose rooms are furnished authentically, transplanted from throughout the region. Take bus #7 from the train station to the lake, make a left onto Árpád út, and walk along the lakeshore until you reach the parking lot. (☎31 10 04. English-speaking tour guide usually off on Sa. Open Apr.-Oct. 8 Tu-Su 10am-6pm. 150Ft, students 100Ft.)

🎭🎶 **ENTERTAINMENT AND NIGHTLIFE.** A series of **parks** nestles around the lake. Around summer solstice, the parks on the west side of town host the **Szentivánéji Festivities,** with bands, beer-drinking contests, and magic shows. Nightlife in Szombathely is centered around **Fő tér**. The square hosts summer performances, impromptu concerts, and ice cream stands that stay open late into the night. Enjoy a gooey pastry (100-240Ft) or an ice cream concoction (300-470Ft) at the charming and cozy **Claudia Cukrászda**, Savaria tér 1. (☎31 33 75. Open daily 9am-8pm.) Next to the synagogue, the **Szinfonia Café**, Rákóczi u. 3, is a regular meeting place for musicians who perform in Bartok Hall. It draws a pleasant, if somewhat subdued, crowd and the red plush seats and black-and-white bar give the impression that you're enjoying your coffee inside a piano. (☎32 26 89. Open 8am-about midnight.)

# LAKE BALATON

An idyllic land of beaches and wine, Lake Balaton has become one of the most coveted vacation spots in Central Europe. The freshwater lake is so warm and shallow that it feels more like a bath than a "Hungarian sea." Villas first sprouted along its shores under the Romans; when a railroad linked the lake to its surrounding towns in the 1860s, the area became a summer playground of the Central European elite. More recently, it has grown into a favorite spot for German university students, who spend their infamous seven-day weekend with liquor flowing liberally on the waterfront. The commercialized south shore now sports such flashy resorts as Siófok and Balatonföldvár, while the north—with its elegant Festetics Palace, historic Tihany abbey, and welcoming vineyards—has cultural attractions that surpass its beaches. For Hungarians, "Balaton" means "holiday;" it's a pure pleasure-ground of museums, hikes, wine-tastings, and discos.

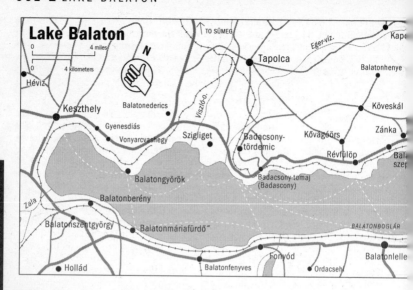

> ⚠ Storms roll in over Lake Balaton in less than 15min., raising dangerous white-caps on the usually placid lake. Amber lights on top of tall hotels and the Meteorological Research Center at Siófok's harbor give weather warnings; 1 revolution per 2sec. means stay within 500m of shore; 1 revolution per sec. means swimmers must be within 100m and boats must be tied on shore.

# SIÓFOK
☎ (0)84

More tourist offices per square kilometer congregate in Siófok than in any other Hungarian city, which says something about the number of surf-starved tourists who descend here annually. Siófok's street scene; filled with tacky t-shirt shops, pager-wielding teens, industrial strength discos, and low-riding convertibles with souped-up speakers, is the spitting image of a Florida vacation—minus the palm trees. Siófok has few sights to speak of (unless you count bronzed bodies), and the beach itself is not Balaton's best bathing spot, but the lake provides ample excuse for bikinis, beer, and the high hedonism that rules Hungary's summer capital.

## ORIENTATION AND PRACTICAL INFORMATION

Siófok's proximity to Budapest and excellent transportation services make it an ideal base from which to explore many of the lake's offerings. The **train** and **bus stations** lie next to each other, roughly in the center of town. The main **Fő u.** runs parallel to the tracks, directly in front of the station, on the other side of an impeccably maintained lawn. A **canal** runs perpendicular to the tracks, connecting the lake to the Danube and dividing the town. The **Arany-part** (Gold Coast) on the east side is home to the older, larger hotels, while the **Ezüst-part** (Silver Coast) on the west side hosts newer and slightly less expensive accommodations.

**Tourist Offices: Tourinform,** Fő u. 41 (☎315 355; fax 310 117; tourinf@mail.datanet.hu; www.siofok.com), in the base of the wooden water tower across from the train station. English-speaking staff finds cheap accommodations and carries free maps. Open July-Aug. M-Sa 8am-8pm, Su 10am-noon; Sept.-June M-F 9am-4pm. **IBUSZ,** Fő u. 61, 2nd floor (☎311 107; fax 311 481), a little farther down the street on the left. Exchanges money for no commission and books private rooms. Open M-F 8am-5pm.

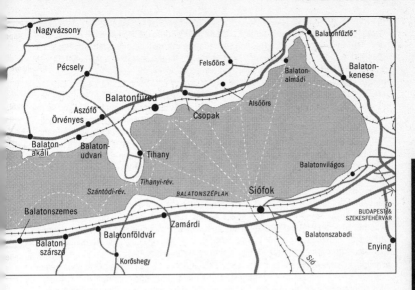

**HUNGARY**

**Currency Exchange: Postabank,** Fő u. 174-6 (☎310 400 and 310 833; fax 313 958). **Exchanges currency** for no commission and cashes AmEx **Traveler's Cheques** for a 1% commission. **ATM** and currency exchange machine outside. Open M-W 8am-3pm, Th 8am-6pm, F 8am-2pm, Sa 8am-noon.

**Police:** Sió u. 14 (☎310 700).

**Pharmacy:** Fő u. 202 (☎310 041). Stocks such Balaton necessities as suntan lotion and condoms. Open M-W 8am-6pm, Th 8am-7pm, F 8am-6pm, Sa 8am-2pm.

**Post Office:** Fő u. 186 (☎310 210). Open M-F 8am-7pm, Sa 8am-noon. **Telephones** stand outside.

**Postal code:** 8600.

# ▄ TRANSPORTATION

**Trains:** To **Budapest** (2½hr., every hr., 1040Ft). Siófok also sits on the Budapest line to: **Zagreb, CRO; Split, CRO; Ljubljana, SLN;** and **Venice, ITA.**

**Buses:** Express buses (gyorsjárat) leave for **Budapest** (1½hr., 7 per day, 1048Ft) and **Pécs** (3hr., 4 per day, 1240Ft).

**Ferries:** The quickest way to the north side of Balaton is by the hourly **MAHART ferry,** 10min. from the train station in the middle of the Strand. To **Tihany** (40min., one way 580Ft, round-trip 1100Ft).

# ▗ ACCOMMODATIONS

Due to the preponderance of affluent western tourists, weekend trips in Balaton are relatively expensive for everyone else. Myriad agencies offer **private rooms. Tourinform** (see above) sometimes charges a 300Ft commission per night and will mediate in the negotiation of rates. Doubles in the center of town average 3000-5000Ft per person in July and August; prices drop slightly in other months. **IBUSZ** (see above) offers doubles for 3000Ft in summer, but without a reservation you might end up paying more. There is a 30% surcharge for staying fewer than four nights. If you prefer to try your own luck: two residential streets close to the water—**Erkel Ferenc u.,** on the far side of the canal, and **Szent László u.,** to the left when leaving the train station—have rows of *Panzió* and *Zimmer frei* (room available) signs.

**Tuja Panzió,** Szent László u. 74 (☎314 996). Turn left as you leave the train station, and cross the tracks. Take an immediate right onto Ady Endre u., then turn left onto Tátra u. and right onto Szent László. The *panzió* will appear about 20min. later. Spacious doubles with a fridge for the pre-beach beer, a shower for the post-beach rinse, satellite TV, and black poodles. 3000Ft per person; off-season prices fall to 2000Ft.

**Hunguest Hotel Azúr,** Vitorlás u. 11 (☎312 033 and 312 259; fax 312 105), entrance on Erkel Ferenc u. With your back to the train station, go right onto Fő u. and right onto Mártirok u. just before the Fő u. bridge. Take the 1st left onto Indóház u. and cross the bridge on the far side of the tracks. Follow the street as it curves right to become Vitorlás u., then go left on Erkel Ferenc u. After 5min. the hotel's guard booth will appear on the right. Immense and immensely popular. Extensive resort-style complex complete with barber shop, tennis courts, and weight room. Reserve well in advance. Bright doubles with bathrooms June 17-July 8 8600Ft, July 9-Aug. 28 9600Ft, off-season 5000Ft.

**Hotel Viola,** Bethlen Gabor u. 1 (☎312 845, ☎/fax 310 157; violahot@matavnet.hu; www.siofok.com/viola). From the bus or train station, walk along Fő u. with the tracks on your right; cross at Bethlen G. u. and the hotel will appear on your left. Comfortable doubles in the big white block near the beach, but you'll face the nightly dilemma of whether to endure a stuffy room or the battalions of mosquitos outside your window. American guests still a novelty here. Friendly English-speaking staff. Reception 24hr. Doubles with bath and terrace 3100 including tax and breakfast.

**Aranypart Camping,** Szent László u. 183/185 (☎352 519). 5km out of the town center. Take bus #2 15min. to the camping sign. The most affordable option, if you don't mind the commute to the beach. No curfew, but relatively infrequent bus service stops at 9:30pm; luckily, the lively crowd brings the party back to camp with them and there are plenty of cafes and snack stands nearby. Open Apr.-Sept. Waterfront sites 5.6-6.6DM per person. 4-person bungalows 9.9DM. Tax 100Ft.

## ▐ FOOD

For beach provisions, a massive indoor fruit and vegetable **market** and **grocery** lies just across the canal off Fő u.; look for **Plus Discount**. (Open M-F 7am-7pm, Sa 7am-1pm, Su 8am-noon).

**Csárdás,** Fő u. 105 (☎310 642). Whips up tasty traditional Hungarian dishes to the tune of aggressive live folk music. Ask for a table on the warmly-lit terrace to avoid being immortalized in the "Family Trip to the Balaton" footage of the camcorder-wielding clientele. Main dishes 400-1490Ft. Open daily 11am-11pm. AmEx/MC/Visa.

**Restaurant-Café Kálmán,** Kálmán Imre sétány 1. In the shopping shantytown next to the train station. The usual fried fare in an unusually pleasant setting. Live music nightly 6pm. Main dishes 400-2400Ft. Open daily 10am-10pm.

## ▐ ENTERTAINMENT

Other attractions in Siófok pale in comparison with the **Strand,** which is a series of park-like lawns running to a sandless concrete shoreline. There are public and private sections, with private spots charging around 150Ft per person, depending on the location and whim of the owner. The most popular section is the town park, but swimming isn't allowed. The largest private part lies just to the right as you face the water. (Open M-F 8am-7pm.) Most sections rent an assortment of wacky water vehicles (100-200Ft per hr.); pedal-powered contraptions, along with the usual bikes and mopeds, are available all along the Strand. (Bikes 500-600Ft per hr.; mopeds 800-900Ft per hr.)

For a taste of culture beyond the *Elvis Goes to Hawaii* variety, check out one of the German operettas performed nightly in the **Kultúrcentrum,** Fő tér 2, near the water tower (get tickets at Tourinform). In the first week of July, the town hosts an annual, week-long **Golden Shell International Folklore Festival** (info ☎311 020 and 311 110; phsiofok@mail.datanet.hu), featuring folk music and dancing. Visit the **Kálmán Imre Múzeum,** Kálmán Imre sétány, next to the train station, for info on festival

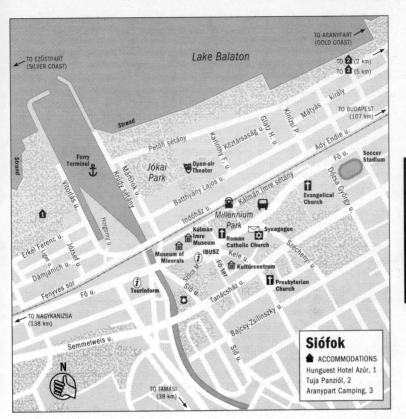

TO ARANYPART
(GOLD COAST)

TO EZÜSTPART
(SILVER COAST)

Lake Balaton

TO **2** (2 km)
TO **3** (5 km)

Strand

Kinisi P.

Mátyás király

TO BUDAPEST
(107 km)

Petőfi sétány

Kamilly F. u.

Köztársaság u.

Glatz H. u.

Ády Endre u.

Fő u.

Soccer
Stadium

Ferry
Terminal

Jókai
Park

Open-air
Theater

Dózsa György u.

Evangelical
Church

Mártírok u.

Krúdy sétány

Vitorlás u.

Horgony u.

Batthyány Lajos u.

Kálmán Imre sétány

Indóház u.

Millennium
Park

Kálmán
Imre
Museum

Synagogue

Roman
Catholic Church

Széchenyi u.

Erkel Ferenc u.

József u.

liget u.

Museum of
Minerals

IBUSZ

Kele u.

Fő tér

Damjanich u.

Szűcs M.

Fenyves sor

Fő u.

Kultúrcentrum

Presbyterian
Church

Tourinform

Tanácsház u.

TO NAGYKANIZSA
(138 km)

Sió u.

Bajcsy-Zsilinszky u.

Semmelweis u.

Sió u.

**Siófok**

▲ ACCOMMODATIONS
Hunguest Hotel Azúr, 1
Tuja Panzió!, 2
Aranypart Camping, 3

N

TO TAMÁSI
(38 km)

HUNGARY

schedules and tickets as well as some delightful exhibits of the hometown boy's "picture-book" illustrations. (Open Tu-Su 9am-5pm. 200Ft.) Slightly more sober, the church at Fő u. 57 holds biweekly evening organ concerts. (500Ft, students 400Ft.)

# ◪ NIGHTLIFE

Nightlife in Siófok wallows in decadence and hedonism, although of a somewhat self-conscious variety. **Nightclubs** of varying degrees of seediness line the lakefront. Many feature nude or semi-nude dancers; the ones with romance novel murals and sexy silhouettes may offer more skin than you would like to see. Amphibious lounge lizards frolic to ABBA and the Bee Gees aboard **disco boats** (☎310 050). Music ranges from disc jockeys to live pop. (Cover 800Ft. Departs nightly July 9-Aug. 21 7-9:30pm.)

▨ **Palace Disco,** Deák Ferenc Sétány 2 (☎350 698). Buses depart approx. every hour from the Tourinform water tower. A party complex—discos, bars, 2 restaurants, and open-air cocktail bar—all arranged around a brightly-lit courtyard. Men in silver shirts and women in practically nothing dance and drink in this Xanadu of Siófok, which at time can feel like an amusement park for 20-year-olds. Cocktails 980-1750Ft; cover 1000-3000Ft; disco open 10pm-5am. Camelot medieval restaurant open 5pm-midnight. Pizzeria open 11am-3am; decent pizza 700-990Ft.

▨ **Flört Disco,** Sió u. 4 (☎317 406). Just follow the spotlights scoping the sky, and do some scoping of your own at this 2-story Balaton institution (pronounced "flirt," with good reason). The top level is techno and the bottom 1980s standbys, with plenty of bass and bikinis in between. Beer 420-570Ft, shots 500-550Ft. Cover 1000-3000Ft. Open daily 10pm-6am.

**Sörbár,** Kálmán Imre Sétány. Just before the pedestrian overpass. A taste of home—if you're German. Boisterous beer garden with free-flowing *Tuborg* (220Ft) and *Weiselburger* (500Ft). Open daily 8pm-midnight.

# ⚡ DAYTRIPS FROM SIÓFOK

## SZÉKESFEHÉRVÁR

*Trains run along the lakeshore from Siófok (1hr., 28 per day, 286Ft). From the train station (☎312 293), on Béke tér, follow the "Centrum" sign in front of the station to Deák Ferenc u., the street that runs perpendicular to the tracks. After 15min., turn left onto the main Budai út, then right at the intersection with Várkörút. The inner city gates will appear on your left after 5min.; follow Koronázo tér straight from the gates to central Városház tér. Buses pass through wide fields of corn (1hr., 4 per day, 432Ft). From the bus station (☎311 057), on Piac tér, walk away from the McDonald's onto Liszt Ferenc u., which leads directly to Városház tér. Alternatively, pick up local bus #13, 34, or 35 from the train station and get off at the "Mozi" cinema stop on Varkörút (tickets from the train station paper shop 70Ft, from the driver 106Ft). Walk a few meters up Varkörút in the direction of the bus, and enter through the city gates on your left.*

Known as the place where Árpád—the nation's Magyar forefather—first set up camp, Székesfehérvár is technically Hungary's oldest town. Today, those traveling from Budapest to Balaton can visit this friendly, unpretentious city filled with historical significance en route, even if much of that history is still being excavated.

■ **BORY CASTLE.** (Bory-vár.) This whimsical castle could be the setting for the ultimate game of hide-and-seek. Over the course of 40 summers, architect and sculptor Jenő Bory built this iron, concrete, and brick mansion by hand in honor of his wife, his art, and his country's history. The rector of the Academy of Fine Arts from 1911-1945, Bory had been awarded the Knight's Cross for his abilities; he filled Bory-vár's towers, gardens, crooked paths, winding staircases, and stone chambers with dozens of his sculptures and studies. He decorated every inch of this fantastic and eccentric retreat, including colonnades lined with sculptures of Hungarian historical figures, and a chapel for his wife as the ultimate "monument to marital love." *(Take bus #32 from the train station to the intersection of Kassai u. and Vágújhelyi u. From here, backtrack along Kassai u. and turn right on Mária Völgyi u. to Bory tér. Tickets 70Ft at terminal, 106Ft on the bus. Castle at Bory tér on the city's outskirts. Open M-F 9am-5pm, Sa-Su 10am-noon and 3-5pm. 120Ft, students 60Ft.)*

**OTHER SIGHTS.** In the center of town, the **King St. Stephen Museum** (Szent István Király Múzeum) houses a permanent archaeology exhibit, including fantastic Roman artifacts that are more than just bits and pieces. *(Fő u. 6. ☎315 583. Open Tu-F 10am-4pm, Sa-Su 1-5pm. 100Ft, students 50Ft.)* The **Budenz House: Ybl Collection** (Budenz-ház: Ybl Gyűjtemény), is home to the collection of the Ybl family, including exquisite 18th- to 20th-century Hungarian art and furniture. *(Arany János u. 12, off Városház tér. ☎313 027. Open Tu-Su 10am-4pm. 100Ft, students 50Ft.)*

## TIHANY PENINSULA ☎(0)87

*MAHART ferries are the fastest way to reach Tihany from Siófok (40min., every hr., 580Ft, round-trip 1100Ft); overland transport can take up to 5hr. To reach the town from the ferry pier and neighboring Strand, walk toward the elevated road. Pass underneath and follow the "Apátság" signs up the steep hill to the abbey. Tihany's main drag, Kossuth Lajos u., sits just beyond the church at the top of the hill.*

With its scenic hikes, charming cottages and panoramic views, the Tihany (TEE-hahn) peninsula is known as the pearl of Balaton. Although every bit as touristy as the rest of the lake, Tihany retains a historical charm slightly more mature than its teeny-bopper beach-town brethren.

**BENEDICTINE ABBEY.** (Bencés Apátság.) The attraction that draws over a million visitors a year is the small but magnificent Benedictine abbey. Luminous frescoes and intricate Baroque altars make the interior distinctly photogenic; with so many blinding camera flashes going off at once, you might need to take a picture to see it properly. Below the abbey is the **András I crypt** (I. András kriptája), which contains the remains of King Andrew, one of Hungary's earliest kings and founder of the abbey. The **Tihany Museum** next door is the reincarnation of an 18th-century monastery, with the rather odd combination of contemporary psychedelic dreamscapes and large Roman artifacts displayed in a subterranean lapidarium. *(Abbey open daily 9am-6pm. To get to the crypt from the abbey, pass through the door next to the altar and descend below the church. Museum open Mar.-Oct. M-Sa 9am-5pm, Su 11am-5pm. Church and crypt 200Ft, students 100Ft, families 500Ft; Su free.)*

**☼HIKING.** Hiking across the Peninsula through hills, forests, farms, and marshes on one of the many well-marked trails takes only an hour or two and is well worth it. Another, shorter hike is also lovely: take the red-cross trail around Belső-tó; at the opposite side, turn right onto the red-line trail. The path will take you to the summit of Kis-erdő-hegy, from which you can see both of Tihany's interior lakes. If you're lucky you'll never see another person, save for the occasional vineyard tender. *(Get a map (300Ft) by the church before you start your hike, or pick one up at **Tourinform**, 8237 Kossuth Lajos ut. ☎438 016. tihany@tourinform.hu.)*

**OTHER SIGHTS.** Follow the "Strand" signs along the Promenade behind the church to descend to the **beach**. *(Beach open daily 9am-8pm. 180Ft.)* Continue a little longer along the panoramic walkway to reach **Echo Hill.** Named for its once "supercalifragilisticexpialidocious" echo, it is now just "super" due to landscape changes.

# KESZTHELY ☎(0)83

Sitting at the lake's west tip, Keszthely (KESS-tay) was once the toy-town of the powerful Festetics family, who left a legacy of 18th-century architecture, grand parks, and a "festetically" pleasing magnificent Baroque mansion. In the midst of all this class, the main promenade hosts an eclectic mix of pricey restaurants, small street cafes, and rogue tattoo parlors typical of a Balaton resort. Unlike the rest of the lake, this town does not depend solely on the summer tide of tourism; Keszthely's agricultural college, founded in 1797 by (who else) György Festetics, brings a large student population to pick up the slack after the tanned masses go home, and the nearby thermal spring attracts Austrians in any weather. Keszthely is a holiday town with a real-life feel (or, alternatively, a real town with a holiday feel).

## ◪ ORIENTATION AND PRACTICAL INFORMATION

The main **Kossuth Lajos u.** runs parallel to the shore, from **Festetics Palace** (Festetics Kastély) through the center at **Fő tér.** To reach the main square from the train station, walk straight up **Mártirok u.,** which ends in Kossuth Lajos u. Turn right; after 5min. you'll arrive in Fő tér. If you're coming from the ferry pier, walk toward the shore. Just after crossing the railroad tracks, turn left on **Kazinczy u.** This leads directly to the train and bus stations.

One of the best tourist offices on the Balaton, this **◪Tourinform,** Kossuth Lajos u. 28, sits on the palace side of Fő tér, with plenty of **maps** (350Ft) and info. (☎/fax 314 144. Open Apr.-June and Sept. M-F 8am-4pm, Sa 9am-1pm; July-Aug. M-F 9am-5pm, Sa-Su 9am-1pm; Oct.-Mar. M-F 8am-4pm, Sa 9am-1pm.) **IBUSZ,** Fő tér 6/8, exchanges currency and books **private rooms** in town for approximately 200Ft commission. (☎510 560. Open June-Aug. M-F 8am-6pm, Sa 9am-1pm; Sept.-May M-F 8am-4pm. MC/Visa.) **OTP Bank,** at the corner of Kossuth Lajos u. and Helikon u., exchanges currency and **traveler's checks**, both for no commission. There is an **ATM** outside. Open M-Tu and Th-F 7:45am-4pm, W 7:45am-5pm. **Park gyógyszertar** is a **pharmacy** at Kossuth Lajos u. 64. (☎313 149. Open M-F 7:45am-7pm, Sa 8am-noon.) There are card **telephones** outside of the **post office** at Kossuth Lajos u. 48. (☎515 960. Open M-F 8am-6pm, Sa 8am-noon.) **Postal code:** 8360.

## ⊏ TRANSPORTATION

The **train station** is about 250m from the water on Kazinczy u. *Intercity* **trains** run between Keszthely and **Budapest** (2½hr., 13 per day, 1392Ft), while slow trains (személyvonat) serve **Szombathely** (2hr., 2 per day, 854Ft). The **bus terminal** is adja-

HUNGARY

cent to the train station. **Buses** beat trains for local travel to **Balatonfüred** (2hr., 9 per day, 502Ft) and **Pécs** (3hr., 5 per day, 620Ft). Some buses leave from the terminal while others use stops in the center at either Fő tér or Georgikan u. Each departure is marked with an "F" or a "G" to indicate which stop it uses; check the schedules. In summer, **boats** run to **Badacsony** (1¾hr., May 28-June 30 1 per day, July-Sept. 3 per day, 660Ft) and leave from the ferry pier at the end of the main dock.

## ACCOMMODATIONS AND FOOD

**IBUSZ** (see above) books central, private doubles with shower (3000Ft) and apartments with kitchen (5000Ft) for longer stays. **Zalatour,** Kossuth Lajos u. 1, also rents rooms, complete with bath and breakfast. (☎312 560; fax 314 301. Singles 3500Ft; doubles 4000Ft. Open June-Aug. M-F 8am-6pm, Sa 8am-1pm; off-season M-F 8am-4pm, Sa 8am-1pm.) If you'd like to avoid finder's fees and the language barrier, the multi-lingual folks at **Tourinform** (see above) offer a few private rooms near the center, starting at 2500Ft. You can try your own luck—homes with *Zimmer frei* signs are plentiful, especially near the Strand, off Fő tér on Erzsébet Királyné u., and near Castrum Camping (see below) on Ady Endre u. Go up Kossuth Lajos and take a right on Szalasztó u. immediately before the palace entrance; Ady Endre will be on the right a few streets down. **Castrum Camping,** Móra Ferenc u. 48, has tent sites with all the amenities, including tennis, beach access, a restaurant, and night spots. (☎312 120. July-Aug. tents 520Ft, plus 780Ft per person; Sept.-June tents 520Ft, plus 650Ft per person. Tax 250Ft.)

The fruit-and-flower **market** on Piac tér has been sitting on the same site since medieval times. At the center of the market's chaos, **Jééé supermarket** (pronounced "yay") provides everything else. (Open M-F 6:30am-7pm, Sa 6:30am-4pm, Su 7:30am-1pm. MC/Visa.) Most of the restaurants around Fő tér are obscenely overpriced, but more reasonable options can be found farther from the center. The **Oázis-Reform Restaurant,** Rákóczi tér 3, is not a mirage, although some vegetarians may think they're dreaming when they see the huge buffet of fresh, homemade dishes with no meat in sight. (☎311 023. 145Ft per 100g. Open M-Sa 11am-4pm.) **Corso Restaurant,** Erzsébet Királyné u. 23, closer to the Strand in the Abbázia Club Hotel, draws on the rich fish stocks of Lake Balaton for its culinary delights. (Main dishes 600-1500Ft. Open M-Sa 11am-10pm.) **Donatello,** Balaton u. 1/A, serves pizza and pasta in a lovely fish-pond courtyard. It somehow manages to retain its class, despite the Teenage Mutant Ninja Turtle sign out front. (☎315 989. Main dishes 330-870Ft. Open daily noon-11pm.)

## SIGHTS AND ENTERTAINMENT

Keszthely's pride is the ▧ **Helikon Palace Museum** (Helikon Kastélymúzeum) in the **Festetics Palace** (Kastély). Follow Kossuth Lajos u. from Fő tér toward the Tourinform office until it becomes Keszthély u. You can't miss the palace—it's the only one on the block. Built by one of the most powerful Austro-Hungarian families of the period, the storybook Baroque palace boasts fanciful architecture and a fascinating history. Once the site of Hungarian literary events hosted by György Festetics, he called it "Helikon" for Helikon Hill, home of the nine muses. Of the 360 rooms (yes, 360), tourists may visit only the central wing, but its mirrored halls, parquet floors, and extravagantly furnished chambers are captivating enough. The somewhat outrageous price is actually worthwhile, as it includes admission to the 90,000-volume, wood-paneled Helikon Library, an exotic arms collection that spans 1000 years, and an exhibit of the Festetics's elaborate porcelain pieces. The well-kept **English park** around the museum provides a vast strolling ground with plenty of photo-worthy vistas. (Open Tu-Su 9am-5pm; ticket office closes at 4:30pm. 1300Ft, students 650Ft. English tour, for groups booked in advance only, 3000Ft.) Popular chamber music **concerts** are frequently held in the mirrored ballroom; inquire at Tourinform (see above) for tickets. (900Ft, students and children 400Ft; charity concerts free, but donations appreciated.)

During the day, families throng to the **Strand,** on the coast to the right as you exit the train station. From the center, walk down Erzsébet u. as it curves right into Vörösmarty u. Go through the park on the left after the train tracks to reach the beach beyond. With rocks instead of sand and swamp instead of waves, it's a wonder that it's still so popular. (220Ft, children 150Ft.) Around the dock to the left of the main beach entrance glides a healthy population of swans, with benches on the shore for relaxing. The 1896 pastel green tower of the **Church of Our Lady,** on Fő tér, conceals the main part of the structure, which dates from 1386 and remains one of the most important standing works of Gothic architecture in Hungary. There are no Baroque frescoes here, but some beautiful stained glass and 14th-century wall paintings adorn the dark sanctuary.

# DAYTRIPS FROM KESZTHELY

## SÜMEG ☎ (0)87

*Buses come from Keszthely (1hr., every hr., 260Ft). From the station at Flórián tér, cross Petőfi Sandor u. to Kossuth Lajos u., the town's central street.*

Only a short distance from the Balaton shore, Sümeg feels a world away. It has some of the lake region's gaiety, but is much calmer; it's almost as festive, but less frantic. Baroque buildings line its quiet streets and the medieval **castle** (vár) recalls a history beyond the memory of most Balaton resorts. Sümeg's castle, among Hungary's largest and best-preserved strongholds, is strategically perched atop a limestone outcrop 270m above the town. Built in the 13th century as a last defense against the invading Mongols, the castle also resisted the Turks, standing until the Habsburg army, in the name of civilization, burned it in 1713. The stony walls were diligently restored in the 1960s, and the atmosphere inside is accordingly trippy, with magic shows, pony rides, archery ranges, and costumed characters performing to mandolin music. (☎ 35 27 37. Open daily 8am-8pm. 500Ft, students 250Ft.) The free **museum** inside exhibits medieval armor and the requisite torture chamber, full of pointy metal objects that could be rendered red-hot when necessary. Remember to sample a glass of *Badacsony* wine (2dL 150Ft) from the small **cellar** on St. István tér (☎ 35 26 43), which enjoys a view of the castle. To get to the castle from the town center, walk up Vak Bottyán u. from the main Kossuth Lajos u., bear right at Szent István tér, and continue up the steep cobblestone street.

The castle's festivities may be the headliner in Sümeg, but it's the **Church of the Ascension,** at the corner of Deák Ferenc u. and Széchenyi György u., that quietly steals the spotlight. To get there, follow Deák Ferenc downhill from the intersection across from the OTP bank on Kossuth Lajos u. Its mundane exterior conceals a frescoed marvel known to locals as the Hungarian Sistine Chapel; the comparison is slightly hyperbolic, but one can't help but be impressed by Franz Anton Maulbertsch's 1757 Rococo masterpiece. It seems that Maulbertsch knew how magnificent his work was: he's the one mugging for you in the first fresco to the right as you enter the church (the cheese in his hand is supposedly a symbol of humility).

**Tourinform,** Kossuth Lajos u. 13, on the main drag, will give you a map and help you find an affordable private room, but ask for a *Zimmer frei*—they only speak German. (☎ 35 24 81. Open June-Aug. M-F 9am-5pm, Sa 9am-1pm; Sept.-May M-F 8am-4pm. Doubles 1500Ft, with bath 2000Ft.)

## HÉVÍZ ☎ (0)83

*Buses leave from Keszthely's Fő tér (30min., every 30min., 96Ft) to transport you (and groups of geriatric Germans) to Hévíz.*

Six kilometers out of the city, Hévíz is home to the world's largest ▧ **thermal lake,** covered in gigantic lilies most of the year. The slightly radioactive water is supposed to have miraculous healing powers—according to legend, it once cured the beautiful, crippled daughter of the lord of Tátika Castle. At a calm-inducing 26-33°C (77-91°F), you too can live happily ever after, soaking in the hot springs all year-round. The 11-acre lake is surprisingly large, but the spring that fills it pumps so fast that the water is entirely replaced every 28 hours. To take advantage of this amazing spot, head out to the *fin de siècle* **bathhouse.** It sits on stilts above the center of the lake; the entrance is at Dr. Schülhof Vilmos sétány 1, across from the bus station. (☎34 04 55; fax 34 04 64. Open daily 8:30am-5pm. 490Ft for 3hr.)

## BADACSONY

*Buses pass through town from Keszthely (1hr., 7 per day, 8 on Su, 260Ft).*

Nestled at the base of a basalt outcrop jutting over the northern shore of the lake, the Badacsony (BAD-uh-chone) region offers open wine cellars, relaxing hikes, and a welcoming beach-side marketplace. Technically, four resort towns lie at the foot of Balaton Hill (Badacsonyhégy), but **Badacsony-tomaj** (BAD-uh-chone TOE-my) is by far the most popular, and hence the one Hungarians refer to as Badacsony. The town's main draw is the small community of **wine cellars** clustered on the southern face of the hill, where you can sample a vintage or purchase it by the 5L plastic jug (500Ft and up). The 3km walk up to the vineyards is not exactly pleasant on a blazing Balaton day; cheat a little instead and pick up one of the jeeps parked in front of the post office for a rough-and-tumble ride up the rocky slope. (500Ft per person, 800Ft round-trip; jeeps leave whenever four customers arrive.) Get off at the **Kisfaludy Ház** restaurant and sip the region's finest wines in an idyllic but tourist-ridden setting. (3 1dL samples with Hungarian cold plate 15DM; open daily 10am-11pm). Otherwise, wander back down the road and turn left onto the cobblestone Hegyalya u. (part of the yellow-cross hiking trail) for the less-pricey smaller cellars. One of the best is the **Bormúzeum Pince** (Wine Cellar Museum), Hegyalya 6 (☎431 262). You can either sit in the cool and comfortable vaulted cellar or in the dining room with huge windows and lovely views while tasting the local white wines. Grey Monk, a demi-sweet, is the most famous; they also serve both sweeter and dryer wines, along with delicious Hungarian sausages. (3 1dL samples with Hungarian cold plate 970Ft. Open daily 10am-10pm.)

If you can still walk straight after a round of "samples," head farther uphill—about 100m past the spring next to Kisfaludy Ház—to try one of the Badacsony's shady **hikes.** Fill up before you embark, as the soda stands (if not the crowds) end here. A short trek on the red trail leads to **Rose Rock** (Rózsa-kő), where legend has it that a couple that sits facing away from the water will be married within a year. Local lore also has it that the Rock's daunting prophecy is the source of more break ups than hook ups, so proceed with caution. An hour's hike farther up rocky stairs will bring you to **Kisfaludy Tower** (Kisfaludy kiláto), where a predictably breathtaking vista rewards the journey. For those willing to make a day of it—or simply desperate to escape the tourist ranks—a **stone gate** (*kőkapu*) awaits still farther down the trail, a dramatic cliffside basalt formation resembling the gate to an airy underworld. badacsony's **beach** is rather small and swampy (open daily 8am-9pm; 200Ft, children 100Ft), but the carnival-esque **marketplace** around it captures the essence of a Balaton Strand, with blaring Britney Spears, low-rent bikini stalls, and cheap *palascinta*.

If the wine makes a return to Keszthely impossible, **Tourinform office Badacsony,** Park u. 6 (☎131 046). Walk away from the pier and turn right after the marketplace. Gives advice on private rooms and other budget accommodations, and also sells **maps.** (Maps 250Ft. Open daily 9am-7pm in high season, 9am-5pm in off-season.) **Postal code:** 8261. **Phone code:** 87.

# SOUTHERN TRANSDANUBIA

Framed by the Danube to the west, the Dráva River to the south, and Lake Balaton to the north, Southern Transdanubia is known for its rolling hills, sunflower fields, mild climate, and good wine. Once the southernmost portion of the Roman province of Pannonia, the region later suffered through the Turkish occupation, which ended in 1566 with the bloody battle of Szigetvár, halting the Ottoman advance toward Vienna. The Austro-Hungarian Empire subsequently rewarded its people with fine churches and elegant 18th century architecture.

# PÉCS

☎(0)62

Tucked at the southern base of the Mecsek mountains, Pécs's (PAYCH) warm climate, incomparable vistas, and captivating architecture slow the pace of any walk through the city. With a 2000-year history, Pécs's monuments reveal a rich legacy of Roman, Ottoman, and Habsburg influence, and the city's many fine collections of modern art pick up where the sights leave off. These features, along with a happening nightlife fueled by university students, make the city one of Hungary's most worthwhile weekend excursions.

## ◣◪ ORIENTATION AND PRACTICAL INFORMATION

Pécs rests on the knees of the Mecsek mountain range; conveniently, north and south correspond to up and down the hillside. Tourists bustle through the historic **belváros** (inner city), a rectangle bounded by the remnants of the city wall. The middle of the inner city is **Széchenyi tér,** where most tourist offices are located. Belváros is small enough for pack-toters to traverse on foot; it takes less than 20min. to cross it going downhill.

**Tourist Offices: Tourinform,** Széchenyi tér 9 (☎211 134; fax 213 315). Offers photocopied **maps** (free) and color maps (350Ft), sells phone cards and stamps, and **exchanges currency.** Also gives info on local entertainment and travel connections. Open June 16-Sept. 30 M-Sa 9am-5:30pm, Su 9am-2pm; Oct. M-Sa 8am-4pm; daily Nov. 1-Apr. 30 8am-4pm; May 1-June 15 Su-F 8am-4pm, Sa 9am-2pm. **Mecsek Tours,** Széchenyi tér 1 (☎513 370; fax 214 866). Arranges travel, sells phone cards, **exchanges currency,** and books rooms. English spoken. Also has an **ATM.** Open M-F 9am-5pm, Sa 9am-1pm.

**Currency Exchange: K & H Bank,** on the corner of Széchenyi tér and Jókai u (☎233 100). Cashes most traveler's checks and exchanges currency for no commission. Open M 8am-5pm, Tu-Th 8am-4pm, F 8am-3pm. Cirrus/Plus **24hr. ATM** inside. ATM also at **OTP Bank,** Rákóczi út 44 (☎211 288), which cashes traveler's checks and exchanges currency for no commission. Open M 7:45am-6pm, Tu-F 7:45am-5pm.

**Internet Access: Matáv Pont,** Rákóczi u. 17 (☎212 670). English-language keyboards. 300Ft per 30min., 500Ft per hr. Open M-F 8am-7pm, Sa 8am-2pm.

**Post Office:** Jókai Mór u. 10 (☎506 000). Two-floor monster offers so many services there's an info desk to guide you. Open M-F 8am-8pm, Sa 8am-2pm.

**Postal code:** 7621.

## ▐ TRANSPORTATION

**Trains:** The station is just beyond the bottom of the city's historic district. Take bus #30, 32, or 33 from the center of town or do the 20min. walk from Jókai u. to Széchenyi ter. From **Villány** (45min., 10 per day, 230Ft) and **Budapest** (3½hr., 3 per day, 1624Ft; InterCity 2½hr., 6 per day, 1964Ft). Four trains per day leave for various towns around Lake Balaton. Purchase all tickets at the **MÁV travel office** in the station (☎312 443) or at Rákóczi út 39c (☎212 734. Open M-F 9am-5pm).

**Buses:** ☎215 215 and 215 665. To **Budapest** (4½hr., 7 per day, 1750Ft).

**Local Transportation:** City bus tickets cost 85Ft at kiosks and 105Ft on the bus.

## ▐ ACCOMMODATIONS

For central accommodations, **private rooms** are the best budget option. Pécs's excellent bus system, however, makes cheap dorm rooms a little farther out almost as convenient.

**Szent Mór Kollégium,** 48-as tér 4 (☎311 199). Take bus #21 two stops from the main bus terminal to 48-as tér. It's a gorgeous old building in a shaded university quadrangle that houses spiffy triples. Hall bathrooms are cleaned daily, and toilet paper is never lacking. Laundry done by request. Common kitchen. 24hr. reception—ring the bell. Check-out 10am. Lockout midnight. Open June-Aug. 30. 1000Ft, students 700Ft.

**Hotel-Camping Mandulás,** Angyán János u. 2 (☎315 981). Take bus #34 from the train station right to the campground. This large camping complex—complete with its own post office and grocery store—offers accommodations in varying degrees of rusticity. It's within walking distance of both panoramic views and local restaurants. **Currency exchange** at 24hr. reception. Breakfast 300Ft. Call Mecsek Tours (see **Orientation and Practical Information,** above) to reserve, or just show up. Open Apr.-Oct. 500Ft per person; tents 500Ft.

**Szántó Kovács János u. 1** (☎/fax 501 000, ext. 6100). Not as central as other options. Take bus #21 from the main bus terminal to Nendtvich Andor út. The university that corresponds to these dorms is across the main road and to the left. Neat triples with floor bathrooms and lacy curtains. The lower floors stay cooler, but offer less protection from mosquitoes. No curfew, but bus service ends at 11pm. 800Ft, apartments 1400Ft.

**Janus Pannonius University** has several campuses around the city; dormitory rooms are nearly always available in July and August, but call ahead in September and June to see if there is space.

**Universitas u. 2** (☎311 966; fax 324 473). Take bus #21 from the main bus terminal to the wooded 48-as tér. Turn left and walk past the McDonald's; the dorm will be on your right, set back from the street. Slightly rough around the edges, but the rooms are spotless. ATMs outside. Reception 24hr. 3-bed dorms 1000Ft.

# 🍴 FOOD

The countless restaurants, cafes, and bars that line Pécs's touristy streets are one of the city's biggest attractions. Reservations are necessary on Friday and Saturday nights at the more popular places, but a walk down Király u., Apáca u., or Ferencsek u., each packed with terraced cafes, should yield a table and an excellent dinner. **Konzum,** the main supermarket on Kossuth tér, is good in times of low cashflow. (Open M-F 6:30am-7pm, Sa 6:30am-2pm.) When sweet tooth cravings hit, sink your teeth into Hungarian sweets at **Caflisch Cukrászda Café,** Király u. 32. Pastries from 79Ft. at the best—and trendiest—cafe in town. (☎310 391. Open daily 8am-10pm.)

**DÓM Vendéglő Restaurant,** Király u. 3 (☎210 088). Through the courtyard, it's the last door on the right. The interior is an impressive 2-level wooden reproduction of the Pécs Cathedral, complete with stained-glass windows. Serves various forms of roasted meat (200-1500Ft), pizza (500-650Ft), and salads (290-400Ft). Open daily 11am-11pm.

**Ferences Vendéglő,** Ferences ut. 24 (☎325 239). Serves delicious food to familes and regulars relaxing indoors or at sidewalk tables. Main dishes 800-1350Ft for 1 person, 2100Ft for 2-3 people. Vegetable dishes 440-670Ft, beer 260-360Ft.

**Liceum Söröző,** Király u. 35 (☎327 284). Opposite the Liceum church and through a courtyard; restaurant is downstairs. Low prices make this a favorite of the student community. Everything is fried, but with 0.5L of Gold Fassl at 230Ft, no one seems to mind. Main dishes 300-780Ft. Open M-Th noon-10pm, F 11am-11pm, Sa 6pm-11pm.

# 👁 SIGHTS

**GHASI KHASIM PASHA INNER CITY PARISH CHURCH.** (Ghasi Khasim Pase Belvarosi Templom.) Ornate Baroque buildings on Széchenyi tér circle the striking church. Nicknamed the "Mosque Church," the elegant green-domed building is a former Turkish mosque, which itself was built on the site of an earlier Christian church. Verses from the Koran remain as decorative wall designs in the church's interior, and a former absolution basin—where the Turks washed their feet before entering the mosque—now serves as a baptismal font. The largest structure from the Ottoman occupation still standing in Hungary, the church is an exciting fusion of Christian and Muslim traditions; as such, it has become an emblem of the city. (Open daily Apr. 16-Oct. 14 10am-4pm; Oct.15-Apr. 15 10am-noon.)

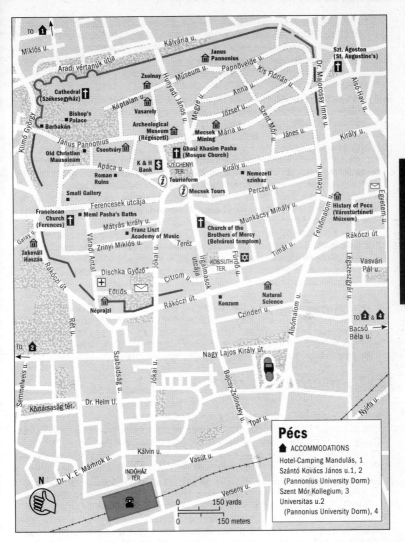

**Pécs**

⚓ ACCOMMODATIONS

Hotel-Camping Mandulás, 1
Szántó Kovács János u.1, 2
  (Pannonius University Dorm)
Szent Mór Kollegium, 3
Universitas u.2
  (Pannonius University Dorm), 4

**CATHEDRAL AND BISHOP'S PALACE.** The neo-Romanesque cathedral *(bazilika)*, with its extraordinarily ornate altarpiece and frescoed chapels, stands proudly as Pécs's centerpiece. Masons have been piling on additions to its fourth-century foundation since the first bricks were laid. Together with the Elegant Bishop's Palace and nearby shaded gardens, it makes the hilltop a peaceful refuge in the middle of the city. *(On Dóm tér. From Széchenyi tér, walk left on Janus Pannonius u., take the 1st right, and then go left on Káptalan to Dóm tér. Cathedral open M-Sa 9am-1pm and 2-5pm, Su 1-5pm. Palace not open to the public. 300Ft, students 150Ft.)*

**SYNAGOGUE.** The stunning 1869 synagogue is well worth a peek, with intricate paintings covering the ceiling and a fabulous Ark of the Covenant hiding in its sanctuary. Look up at the decorated ceiling, entrance, and delicately carved oak "Women's Gallery." The temple still holds services for the city's Jewish population, which today hovers at a mere 300. *(On Kossuth tér. Walk downhill from Széchenyi tér on Irgalmasok u.; the square on the left is Kossuth tér. Open M-F and Su 10am-11:30am and noon-4pm. 100Ft, students 50Ft.)*

**ROMAN RUINS.** Near the cathedral in the neighboring Szent István tér, 4th-century Roman ruins have been slowly decaying since Jupiter and Venus went out of business. Underneath lies the largest known burial site in Hungary, and a crypt with Roman Christian wall paintings. *(Cross Janus Pannonius from the cathedral or make the 5min. walk from Széchenyi tér; look for the sunken ruins on the left, in the park's corner. Open Tu-Su 10am-6pm.)*

**BARBAKÁN.** Surrounding Dom tér, the old city walls provide a popular walking spot. Follow along behind the cathedral to find the circular *barbakán*, a vestige of the great double-walled defense of the 15th century.

## 🏛 MUSEUMS

🖼 **Csontváry Museum,** Janus Pannonius u. 11 (☎310 544). Follow Janus Pannonius to the left from Széchenyi tér; the museum is on the left. This museum displays the works of Tivadar Csontváry Kosztka (1853-1919), a local artist who gained an international reputation despite less than 20 years of work. The well-assembled, well-lit exhibit emphasizes the master's thematic interests and luminous, expressionistic skies, making it clear why he is known as the Hungarian Van Gogh. Open Tu-Su 10am-6pm. 200Ft, students 150Ft.

**Zsolnay Museum,** Káptalan u. 2 (☎324 822). Walk up Szepessy I. u. from the back of the Mosque Church, then turn left onto Káptalan u. There's nothing mass-produced at the Zsolnay Museum, which exhibits the finest pieces of the world-famous Zsolnay porcelain. This porcelain is hand-crafted at the family workshop, which has been a Pécs mainstay since the mid-19th century. Open Tu-Su 10am-6pm. 350Ft, students 150Ft.

**Vasarely Museum,** Káptalan u. 3. The neighboring Vasarely Museum houses works of one of the most important 20th-century Hungarian artists, Pécs-born Viktor Vasarely, who founded the Op-Art movement that defined the look of the 1960s. The images will transport you to the era, and after 20min. of trippy 3D graphics, you'll probably have the headache to prove it. Open Apr.-Oct. Tu-Su 10am-6pm. 300Ft, students 140Ft.

## 🎵🎭 ENTERTAINMENT AND NIGHTLIFE

A good place to combine music and wine is at Pécs's ■**World Festival of Wine Songs** in late September. For information, contact Pécsi Férfikar Alapitvány, Színház tér 2 (☎/fax 211 606 or 994 6380). The flighty Pécs **nightlife** scene is one of the best in Hungary. It generally settles in the crowded, colorful bars near Széchenyi tér, especially on the first two blocks of Király u. For brain-busting beats and body piercings aplenty, the local alternative scene is unrivaled outside of Budapest.

🖼 **Dante Cafe,** Janus Pannonis u. 11 (☎21 06 61), in the same building as the Csontváry museum. Originally founded to finance the Pécs literary magazine *Szép Literaturari Ajándék*, the cafe is the center of literary, art, and theater scene—and a great place to chill. Open daily 10am-1am, later on weekends.

**Hard Rák Cafe,** Ipar u. 7 (☎50 25 57), at the corner of Bajcsy-Zsilinszky u. The name refers to the music, not the American chain. Cave paintings will inspire your primal urges, if the liquor hasn't already. Live rock, alternative, and hard-core performances in summer on Friday and Saturday nights. Cover Su-Th 200Ft., F-Sa 400Ft. Open M-Sa 7pm-6am.

**Rózsakert Söröző,** Janus Pannonius u. 8/10 (☎31 08 62). Locals come here to enjoy a sobering breeze, live Hungarian Gypsy music, and a lantern-adorned terrace. 0.5L *Gold Fassl* 180Ft. Open M-Sa 10am-2am, Su 10am-11pm.

## 📷 DAYTRIP FROM PÉCS

### SZIGETVÁR CASTLE

*Buses (☎31 26 58) run from Pécs (40min., 8 per day, 300 Ft), and stop at the town's south end. Walk straight up Rákóczi u. 15min. to the castle. Museum open Tu-Su May-Sept. 9am-6pm; Oct.-Apr. 9am-4pm. 150Ft, students 90Ft. The Turkish House, Bástya u. 3, is open May-Sept. Tu-Su 10am-3pm. 30Ft, students 15Ft.*

# Call the USA

"feel free to call"

1-800-COLLECT

1 8 0 0
COLLECT

**When in Ireland**
**Dial: 1-800-COLLECT (265 5328)**

**When in N. Ireland, UK & Europe**
**Dial: 00-800-COLLECT USA (265 5328 872)**

*Member of*
**Dublin Tourism**

| Australia | 0011 | 800 265 5328 872 |
| Finland | 990 | 800 265 5328 872 |
| Hong Kong | 001 | 800 265 5328 872 |
| Israel | 014 | 800 265 5328 872 |
| Japan | 0061 | 800 265 5328 872 |
| New Zealand | 0011 | 800 265 5328 872 |

In 1566, 50,000 Turks besieged the Croatian viceroy Miklós Zrínyi and his 2500 soldiers in **Szigetvár Castle**. After a month-long struggle, with their drinking water exhausted and the inner fortification in flames, Zrínyi's army decided to go out with a bang, opening the castle gates and launching a desperate suicidal attack against their aggressors. They were wiped out, but managed to take a quarter of the Turkish force with them, halting the Ottoman Empire's planned expansion into Vienna and ending Turkey's march on Europe. The castle ruins are remnants of a structure built well after the battle; the mostly red brick walls now house a pleasant park and the **Zrínyi Miklós Museum,** which chronicles the siege. The Szigetvár of the Turkish period is portrayed in the exhibits at the 16th-century **Turkish House.**

# THE GREAT PLAIN (NAGYALFÖLD)

Romanticized in tales of cowboys and bandits, Nagyalföld is an enormous grassland stretching southeast of Budapest over almost half of Hungary. Also called the *puszta*, meaning "plain," this tough region is certainly no longer empty, with arid Debrecen, fertile Szeged, and the vineyards of Kecskemét rising out of the flat soil like Nagyalföld's legendary mirages. Brimming with universities, fine art museums, and elegant architecture, these civilized spots offer an excellent opportunity to experience Hungarian high culture at its best.

## DEBRECEN ☎(0)52

Protected by the mythical Phoenix, Debrecen (DE-bre-tsen; pop. 210,000) has risen from the ashes of over 30 devastating fires, the fate of a land-locked city on the dry Great Plain. Happily, the last rebuilding left the city with refreshing parks and wide boulevards where 19th-century architecture mixes comfortably with its modern counterpart—a relaxed urban setting that offers big-city action without the grit of big-city life. The unofficial capital of eastern Hungary and Hungarian Protestantism, Debrecen is most famous as a university town. Its Reformed College is one of Hungary's oldest and largest, drawing students worldwide. This massive student population keeps the pace lively, whether lounging in Nagyerdei Park by day or pub-crawling through city streets until sunrise.

### ■ ORIENTATION

The town center is a 15-minute walk from the train station. Facing away from the station, walk down **Piac u.**, the main street to the left, which runs perpendicular to the station. Piac u. ends in **Kálvin tér,** where the huge yellow **Nagytemplom** (Great Church) sits watching the city's center. Debrecen's other main hub lies about 3km farther along Piac u., which becomes Péterfia u. at Kálvin tér, running north to **Nagyerdei Park** and **Kossuth Lajos Tudományegyetem** (KLTE; Kossuth Lajos Technical University). The **bus station** is 15 minutes from the center. Exit the station at Terminal 2 and turn left onto Arany János u., continue until the street ends, and then make a left onto Piac u., which leads directly to Kálvin tér.

### ■ TRANSPORTATION

**Trains:** ☎326 777. To: **Miskolc** (2½-3hr., 5 per day, 920Ft); **Budapest** (3hr., 13 per day, 1530Ft; *InterCity* 2½hr., 5 per day, 1850Ft); **Eger** (3hr., 3 per day, 786Ft) via **Fúzesabony;** **Szeged** (3½hr., 7 per day, 1750Ft) via **Cegléd;** and **Tirgu Mureş, ROM** via **Oradea, ROM** ( 3½hr. or more depending on border crossing, 1 per day, 1360Ft).

**Buses:** ☎413 999. At the intersection of Nyugari u. and Széchenyi u. To: **Miskolc** (2hr., every 30min.-1hr., 828Ft); **Tokaj** (2hr., 2 per day, 746Ft); **Eger** (2½hr., 4 per day, 1160Ft); **Szeged** (4-5½hr., 3 per day, 1990Ft); **Kecskemét** (5½hr., 2 per day, 1990Ft); and **Oradea, ROM** (3½hr., 1 per day, 704Ft).

HUNGARY

**Public Transportation:** Public transport is by far the most convenient way to navigate the city. Tram #1 (the one and only) runs from the train station at Petőfi tér through Kálvin tér and then loops around the park, past the university, and back to Kálvin tér. Ticket checks are frequent and menacing (fine 2000-5000Ft)—get tickets from the kiosk by the train station (80Ft) or pay the driver (100Ft). The price changes frequently, so check on the back of the driver's seat to confirm. Once you board the tram, validate your ticket in the black contraptions. Trams only stop on the way in; to return to the center of town you must ride the loop. The tram is the best route to the center from the train station; get off at the stop after McDonald's for tourist offices and most other necessities.
**Taxis:** ☎444 444 and 444 555.

## 2 PRACTICAL INFORMATION

**Tourist Office: Tourinform,** Piac u. 20 (☎412 250; fax 314 139), in the cream-colored building on the right as you come from the train station just before Kálvin tér. Friendly agents fluent in English will provide **maps** and info on events and dorm accommodations. Open daily May 15-Sept. 15 8am-8pm; Sept. 16-May 14 M-F 9am-5pm.

**Currency Exchange: OTP,** Hatvan u. 2/4 (☎506 500), has fairly good rates, gives MC **cash advances,** accepts most **traveler's checks,** and has a 24hr. Cirrus/MC/Plus/Visa **ATM.** Open M-Tu and Th-F 7:45am-4pm, W 7:45am-5pm.

**Pharmacy:** Hatvan u. 1 (☎415 115). Open M-F 8:30am-6pm, Sa 8:30-1pm.

**Medical Assistance: Medical emergency room** (☎414 333) is across the street from the bus station at the intersection of Erzsébet u. and Szoboszlój u.—look for the building with the blue and white *"Mentők, orro si ügyelet"* sign.

**Post office:** Hatvan u. 5/9 (☎315 206). Open M-F 7am-8pm, Sa 8am-2pm.

**Postal code:** 4001.

## ACCOMMODATIONS

**Hajdútourist,** Kálvin tér 2 (☎415 588; fax 319 616), arranges central **private rooms.** (Doubles 2500Ft. Tourist tax 120Ft. Open M-F 8am-5pm. AmEx/MC/Visa.) **IBUSZ** does the same on Széchenyi u. near Piac u. (Doubles 2600Ft; triples 3200Ft. Open M-F 8am-5:30pm, Sa 8am-noon. AmEx/MC/Visa.) In July and August, many of the **university dorms** rent rooms (1500-2000Ft per person)—ask at Tourinform (see above), but be warned: many of the dorms they list only rent rooms to groups, so let your fingers do the walking and call before trekking across the city. Be sure to book ahead around festivals, especially during the Flower Carnival (see below).

**Hotel Stop,** Batthyány u. 18 (☎420 301). From Kossuth tér, head down Piac u. and go left on Kossuth u.; Batthány u. will be on the right in a nice courtyard. Despite ongoing exterior construction, the rooms are clean and bright. Breakfast 600Ft. Reception 24hr. Check-out 11am. Doubles with shower 4900Ft; triples with shower and TV 5900Ft.

**Hotel Fönix,** Barna u. 17 (☎413 355; fax 413 054). Close to the train station, right off Piac u. Rooms are spotless, if occasionally stuffy. Breakfast 500Ft. Free luggage storage. Reception 24hr. Singles 2200Ft, with shower 4000Ft; doubles 3800Ft, 6000Ft; triples 4900Ft, 7200Ft. MC/Visa.

**Termál Camping,** Nagyerdei körút 102 (☎/fax 412 456), is hidden in Nagyerdei Park. From the train station take tram #1 or bus #10 or 14. Get off the tram once you're in the park—you should see Hotel Termál on the left—and follow the tracks for a few minutes until you strike Nagyerdei Körút. Turn right, away from the tracks; the campground is 5min. down the road. Reserve 1 month ahead. Open May-Oct. Tents for 2 1700Ft. Caravans 2000Ft per person. Quads 2400Ft, with shower 5400Ft. Tourist tax 200Ft.

## FOOD

The tiny **supermarket** at Hatvan u. 8 is open 24hr. The **University Dining Halls** offer lunch for 100-250Ft per item during the school year, with cheap leftovers until approximately 4pm for 50-100Ft. Directly behind the main university building on

Egytem tér, follow the center path straight through the park; bear right when you see the tennis courts—the "Menza" is on the second floor of the white building. (Open daily Sept.-June 11:30am-2:30pm.) **Csokonai Söröző,** Kossuth u. 21, is in a classy, candle-lit cellar. Waiters enthusiastically greet their customers and then allow them to roll dice for a free meal. The city's best menu includes English translations and photographs of its excellent meals. (☎410 802. Main dishes 395-1250Ft. Veggie soups and salads 295-475Ft. Open M-Su noon-11pm.) To get to **Sütöde,** walk down Kossuth u. from Piac u. Make a right down the small alley just before the Drogerie Markt—or simply follow the delicious aroma from several blocks away. Sütöde is a small, store-front bread stand where locals get breakfast and daily supply of sweet-smelling baked goods. (Breads 80Ft per kg. Open daily 7am-7pm.)

### 🔆 🎵 SIGHTS AND ENTERTAINMENT

Hungary's largest Protestant church and Debrecen's town symbol, the 1863 twin-spired **Great Church** (Nagytemplom), looms over Kossuth tér's northern end. The bell tower offers a great view of the town, but don't look down—the narrow wooden stairs become progressively more rickety as you near the top. Hear the huge organ in action every Friday at noon. (☎412 695. Open M-F 9am-4pm, Sa 9am-1pm, Su noon-4pm. 60Ft, students 30Ft. Concerts 1hr.; free.) The **Református Kollégium,** Kálvin tér 16, behind the church, was established in 1538 as a center for Protestant education. The present building housed the government of Hungary twice—in 1849, when Lajos Kossuth led the Parliament in the Oratory, and again in 1944. Today it houses Calvinist schools, as well as a collection of religious art and an exhibit on the history of Protestantism in Debrecen. The highlight, though, is the 650,000-volume **library** which also displays 16th-century Bibles. (☎414 744. Open Tu-Sa 9am-5pm, Su 9am-1pm. 120Ft. English information 200Ft.)

The **Déri Museum** displays a collection ranging from local history to Japanese lacquerware. Upstairs are awe-inspiring murals by Mihály Munkácsy of Christ's trial and crucifixion. Spot the artist's self-portrait in *Ecce Homo* as an old man in the crowd, next to the arch. Coming from Kossuth tér, walk to the left of the Great Church and take the first left onto Múzeum u.—it's on the right with the sculpture garden. (☎41 75 77. Open Nov.-Mar. Tu-Su 10am-4pm; Apr.-Oct. 10am-6pm. 200Ft, students 100Ft; special exhibits 100Ft. No cameras.)

Debrecen is famous for its young population, the largest in Hungary, chiefly found in **Nagyerdei Park.** The park also has bike lanes, paddle boats, bars, tattoo salons, and an overabundance of leering single men lounging in tank tops. Nagyerdei's highlight is the **municipal thermal bath,** where you can soak nude in steamy baths with other Debreceners. (☎346 000. Open M-F 8am-noon and 1-6:30pm. Thermal bath 500Ft; 30min. massage 350Ft.) Debrecen hosts a series of summer events, ranging from equestrian competitions to musical performances and air shows. Every spring the **Jazz Days** festival features well-known musicians and bands. In July of even years the **Béla Bartók Choir Festival** attracts choirs worldwide. (Info ☎319 311. See Tourinform for schedules and tickets (300-1000Ft).) The fête season culminates in the hugely popular **Flower Carnival** parade (info ☎319 311) on August 20.

At night head to the smoky **El Tornado,** Pallagi u. 2, in Nagyerdei Park. This saloon-style pub even cranks out country music every so often. (0.5L *Borsodi* 130Ft. ☎34 05 90. Open daily 5pm-4am.) The more mellow and mature **Yes Jazz Bár,** Kálvin tér 4, is usually filled with quiet conversation set in time to live jazz and blues. (☎418 522. Guinness 390Ft. Open daily 2pm-2am.) The **Apolló Cinema,** Miklós u. 1 (☎417 847), offers refuge from oppressive summer heat in its three movie theaters.

# SZEGED ☎(0)62

The easygoing charm of the Great Plain's cultural capital has prompted some to describe Szeged (SAY-ged) as a Mediterranean town on the Tisza. After an 1879 flood practically wiped out the city, streets were laid out in orderly curves punctuated by large, stately squares, giving the only planned city in Hungary a quiet cosmopolitan atmosphere closer to Europe's seaside cities than to anything else in landlocked Hungary. Instead of the usual Baroque facades, rows of colorful Art Nouveau buildings line the busy walkways, and the town's exciting and intellectual social life, largely dictated by its university population, complements the lively architectural mood.

## ORIENTATION AND PRACTICAL INFORMATION

Szeged is divided by the **Tisza river,** with the city center on the west bank and the parks and residences of **Újszeged** (New Szeged) to the east. The city center forms a semicircle against the river, bounded by **Tisza Lajos krt** and centered at **Széchenyi tér,** the main square. Across **Híd u.** (Bridge St.) from Széchenyi, shops and cafes cluster on the pedestrian **Klauzál tér.** Large multilingual **maps** litter the city's squares.

**Tourist Office: Tourinform,** Victor Hugo út 1 (☎425 966; fax 420 509). From the tram stop at Széchenyi tér and Vár u., walk 1 block back along the tracks to Híd u. Turn left and then right on Oskola u., which runs along the river. The first right is Victor Hugo út. Free **maps** and accommodations info. Open M-F 10am-6pm.

**Currency Exchange: OTP,** Klauzál tér 5 (☎480 380). Cashes **traveler's checks** for no commission and gives MC/Visa **cash advances.** Open M-W and F 7:45am-4pm, Th 7:45am-5pm. **Budapest Bank Ltd.,** Klauzál tér 4 (☎485 585), doubles as a **Western Union.** Open M-Th 8am-5pm, F 8am-3pm. **K&H Bank,** Kárász u. 2, has the best exchange rates and a Cirrus/Plus **24hr. ATM.**

**Luggage Storage:** At the train station. 60Ft per bag 4am-4pm, 120Ft 4-11pm. Open 4am-11pm.

**International Bookstore: Studium Könyvesbolt,** Victor Hugo út 4, is a university bookshop with a handful of English books. Open M-F 9am-6pm, Sa 9am-1pm.

**24hr. Pharmacy: Kígyó Richter Referenciapatika,** Klauzál tér 3 (☎420 131). Ring bell outside 8pm-7am.

**Medical Assistance:** Kossuth Lagos sgt. 15/17 (☎474 374). From the Town Hall, walk up the center of Széchenyi tér and turn left onto Vörösmarty u., then follow it as it becomes Kossuth Lagos sgt. The medical center is on the right at the intersection with Szilágyi u. Some English spoken. Open M-F 5:30pm-7:30am, Sa 7:30am-M 7:30am. Ring bell after hours.

**Internet Access: Cyber Cafe,** Dugonics tér 11 (☎426 216). 500Ft per hr. Open daily 9am-midnight.

**Post Office:** Széchenyi tér 1 (☎476 276). At the intersection with Híd u. Open M-F 8am-8pm, Sa 8am-2pm, Su 8am-noon.

**Postal Code:** 6720.

## TRANSPORTATION

**Trains: Szeged pu.** (☎421 821), on Indóház tér on the west bank of the Tisza. International cashier on 2nd floor. Open daily 6am-5:45pm. To: **Kecskemét** (1hr., 15 per day, 650Ft, *InterCity* 910Ft); **Budapest** (2½hr., 15 per day, *InterCity* 1420Ft); and **Debrecen** (3-4hr., 3 per day, 1709Ft) via **Cegléd.**

**Buses:** On Mars tér (☎421 478). From the station, cross the street at the traffic light and walk down Mikszáth Kálmán u. towards the Tisza, which intersects Széchenyi tér 10min. after becoming Károlyi u. To: **Kecskemét** (1¾hr., 10-14 per day, 820Ft); **Budapest** (3½hr., 7 per day, 1590Ft); **Pécs** (4½hr., 7 per day, 1705Ft); **Eger** (5hr., 2 per day, 2140Ft); **Debrecen** (5¼hr., 2-4 per day, 1910Ft); and **Győr** (6hr., 2 per day, 2350Ft).

**Public Transportation:** Tram #1 connects the train station with Széchenyi tér (4 stops). Otherwise it's a 20min. walk. To get to the bus station, continue 2 more stops to the corner of Pacsirta u. and Kossuth L. sugárút; facing the same direction as the tram, turn left on Pacsirta u. and walk 2 blocks to reach Mars tér. Tickets from kiosks 79Ft; from the driver 105Ft. The fine for riding ticketless is 1500Ft, and they *do* check.

**Taxis:** ☎470 470, 480 480, 488 488, and 490 490. 100Ft base fare; 80Ft per km if booked ahead by phone; 120Ft per km on the street.

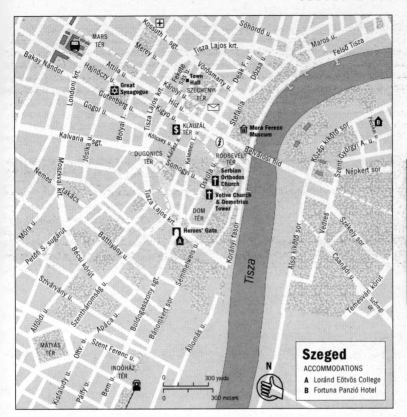

**Szeged**
ACCOMMODATIONS
A  Loránd Eötvös College
B  Fortuna Panzió Hotel

# ACCOMMODATIONS

**Tourinform** (see above) carries info on **private rooms** (central doubles with shower 2400-4500Ft) and other budget accommodations. University dorms are generally cheapest, especially for solo travelers, but are only available in July and August.

**Hotel Tisza,** Széchenyi tér 3 (☎/fax 478 278; tisza@zenon.eunet.hu; www.zenon.eunet.hu/home/tisza). This elegant 1886 hotel lies in the center and offers a few rooms at very reasonable prices. Béla Bartók performed in its concert hall and Hungarian literary figures once frequented its restaurant. English spoken. Reception 24hr. Check-out noon. Lone doubles with with sink 4200Ft, with shower and sink 5500Ft; for 2 people 6800, 8100Ft; for 3 people 9800, 10,900Ft. Breakfast included.

**Loránd Eötvös College,** Tisza Lajos krt 103 (☎544 124). The hostel is to the left of Hero's Gate; its entrance is hidden from the street, to the left of the restaurant. Cheap, central dorms with such perks as mosquito-proof screens and clean bathrooms. Well-lit and pleasant. Laundry service included. Doubles 1800Ft 1st night, 1500Ft thereafter.

**Fortuna Panzió,** Pécskai u. 8 (☎/fax 431 585 and 431 907). Worth the walk for that rare luxury in Hungary—A/C. The spacious rooms are peaceful and bright, although the neighborhood dogs may interrupt your solace. Doubles with bath 5400Ft. MC/Visa.

**Napfény,** Dorozsmai u. 4 (☎421 800; fax 467 579). Take tram #1 to the last stop, go up the overpass, then turn right. After 10min. you'll see Napfény on the left. Next to international route E75, this hotel and campground feels like a typical highway motel. An agreeable place to crash for the night with 2restaurants to boot. Reception 24hr. 6300Ft per person; tents 6300Ft. Motel doubles 2600Ft. Tourist tax 100Ft.

FOOD

Szeged is home to Hungary's finest lunchmeat—Pick salami—and the best place for *halászlé* (spicy soup made with fresh Tisza fish). The town's distinctive cuisine, combined with a hungry student population, makes dining out a favorite pastime. The **24-hour ABC market** on Mars tér, near the corner of Londoni krt. and Mikszáth Kálmán u., provides late-night munchies. You can buy pick salami in all its varieties at the **Szeged Pick Korzó Márkaáruház,** at the corner of Karasz u. and Kölcsey u. (Open M-F 6am-9pm, Sa-Su 7am-9pm). For the non-sausage fans, there is a **kosher** restaurant in the Jewish Community Building at Gutenberg u. 20 (☎423 849).

▨ **Roosevelt téri Halászcsárda (Sótartá Étterem),** Roosevelt tér 14 (☎424 111). Next to the river, across from the Móra Ferenc Museum. Sit on the peaceful shaded terrace or in the vaulted downstairs dining room; the famously spicy *szegedi halászlé* or any of the *hallé* (fish soup) dishes with fiery green paprika on the side will appease your taste-buds. Main dishes 350-1500Ft. Open daily 11am-11pm.

**At Aranykorona Étterem,** Victor Hugo u. 6 (☎425 704). Traditional Hungarian food in the pleasant garden, sidewalk cafe, or dining room. Main dishes 590-1750Ft, including vegetarian meals. Open M-F 11am-10pm, Sa 11:30am-midnight, Su 11:30am-5pm.

**Roxy Cafe and Pizzeria,** Deák Ferenc u. 24. Chic restaurant serves pizzas (400-650Ft) and a daily vegetarian platter (580Ft) to Szeged's hippest university students. The perfect post-party, pre-hangover stop. Open M-Th 10am-midnight, F 10am-2am, Sa noon-2am, Su noon-midnight.

**Bounty Pounty,** Stefánia 4 (☎432 233), across from Roosevelt tér. This kitschy, ship-like restaurant specializes in "lava rock grilling," a process in which gravy is steamed in with meat. More than 70 types of whiskey (250-3400Ft) for seafarers. Main dishes 790-1800Ft. Restaurant open daily 11am-midnight; bar open daily noon-3am.

◉ SIGHTS

▨ **SYNAGOGUE.** (Zsinagóga). Widely acknowledged as the most beautiful of its kind in Hungary, the 1903 synagogue is Szeged's absolute must-see. This temple is a goulash of styles; its Moorish altar and gardens, Romanesque columns, Gothic domes, and Baroque facades constitute an awe-inspiring display of craftsmanship. The cupola, decorated with symbols of infinity and faith, symbolizes the world and seems to grow more profound the longer you look up at it. Its 24 pillars stand for both the 24 hours in a day and the 24 books of the Old Testament. The vestibule walls are lined with the names of the 3100 members of the congregation killed in concentration camps. Today Szeged has an active Jewish community, and the Szegedi Zsinagóga is still a house of worship. (*Jósika u. 8. From Széchenyi tér, walk away from the river along Híd u. through Bartók tér; turn left onto Jósika. The synagogue is on the left. 150Ft, students 60Ft.*)

**MÓRA FERENC MUSEUM.** This riverside museum houses an eclectic collection of 18th- to 20th-century folk art in a gorgeous Neoclassical palace. On your way upstairs, linger to inspect panoramic paintings of Szeged during the devastating flood of 1879. The first floor details the life of the long-vanished Avar tribe with an impressive series of papier-maché mannequins, complete with yarn hair. (*Roosevelt tér 1/3. From Széchenyi tér, turn right on Vár u., which brings you to Roosevelt tér. ☎470 370. Open Apr.-Oct. Tu-Su 10am-5pm; Nov.-Mar. 10am-3pm. 100Ft, students 50Ft.*)

**VOTIVE CHURCH.** (Fogadalmi Templom). This neo-Romanesque, red-brick church pierces the skyline with its twin 91m towers. The cathedral was completed in 1930 after the great flood as a means of asking God's protection against future deluges. At least this monster is in no danger of washing away, with bulky towers sitting heavily on the square. Hungary's fourth-largest church houses a 9040-pipe organ that often exerts itself for afternoon or evening concerts. Alongside the church stands the 12th-century **Demetrius Tower** (Dömötör Torony), Szeged's oldest monument and all that remains of the church that originally stood on the site. On the walls surrounding the cathedral, the **National Pantheon** portrays the faces of 90 Hungarian political, literary, and artistic figures. *(From Széchenyi tér, turn left on Híd u., then right on Oskola u., which leads to Dom tér. Open Tu-Su 10am-6pm, Su 12:30-6pm.)*

**TOWN HALL.** (Városháza). The yellow town hall, reshingled with red and green ceramic tiles after the 1879 downpour, overlooks grassy Széchenyi tér at the town's center. The bridge connecting the bright building to the drab one next door (which once held the tax office) was built so Habsburg Emperor Franz Joseph wouldn't have to walk up and down the stairs. *(Széchenyi tér 10.)*

**SERBIAN ORTHODOX CHURCH.** (Palánki Szerb Templom). The 1778 Serbian Orthodox Church features impressive artwork. The iconostasis holds 80 gilt-framed paintings, and the ceiling fresco of God creating the Earth is covered with stars. *(Somogyi u. 3a. ☎ 325 278. Open by request. 100Ft.)*

**HERO'S GATE.** (Hősök Kapuja). Hero's Gate was erected in 1936 to honor Horthy's White Guards, who brutally cleansed the nation of "Reds." The propagandistic murals are now gone, but skeletal soldiers remain. *(Start at Dóm tér and head away from the center to reach the gate, in the adjacent Aradi Vértanuk tér.)*

## 🎵🎭 ENTERTAINMENT AND NIGHTLIFE

The **Szeged Open Air Festival,** held from July 10 to August 21, is Hungary's largest outdoor performance event. International troupes show off folk dances, operas, and musicals in an amphitheater, with the looming cathedral as a backdrop. Tickets (700-3000Ft) are sold at Tourinform (see **Orientation and Practical Information,** p. 368) and at Deák u. 28/30. (☎471 466; fax 471 322; szabadteri@mail.tiszanet.hu; www.tiszanet.hu/szabadteri. Open M-F 10am-5pm.) Swimming pools, baths, and people in lawn chairs line the **Partfürdo Strand;** from Szeged, cross the Belváros bridge and walk left along the river. Most of these establishments are open every day, and charge 200-400Ft admission. Pick up a communist-era bargain at one of Szeged's vintage clothing stores, such as **Cián Káli Underground Second Hand,** Deák Ferenc u. 26. (Open daily 10am-7pm.)

**Grand Cafe,** Deák Ferenc u. 18, 3rd fl. (☎420 578). Skip the strobe lights and save your voice at Sophisticate Central. Here you can watch a film in the art movie theater and sip red wine (140Ft) while mellow jazz glosses over the low conversation of young Hungarians. Open in summer 5-11pm, off-season 2-11pm.

**Gin-tonic Club,** 53 Széchenyi tér 3, in the Tisza Hotel building. Terrifically chic and well-decorated underground vault, where stylishly dressed people listen to funk, jazz, blues, or swing W-Sa. Beer 350-400Ft, wine 380Ft, shots 600-800Ft. No cover. Open M-W 7pm-1am, Th-Sa 7pm-4am, Su 7pm-1am.

**Sing-Sing,** on Mars tér. Disco ducks migrate here in colder weather. The DJ churns out popular beats for a ready-to-rave crowd. 0.5L *Amstel* 200Ft. Open daily 10pm-dawn.

**Jate Klub,** in the Toldy u. entrance to the central university building on Dugonies tér. During the school year, join *Szegedi* students on their own turf. With an area set aside for chatting with—or chatting up—co-eds, undergraduate pretention never had such a great soundtrack. 0.5L *Rolling Rock* 150Ft. Cover 300Ft. Open Th-Sa 9pm-4am.

**HBH Bajor Serfőzde** (Beer House), Deák Ferenc u. 4 (☎42 03 94). In the center of the city. Watch beer being made behind the bar and then disappearing down your throat. 150-254Ft per glass. Open M-Sa 11:30am-midnight, Su 11:30am-11pm.

# KECSKEMÉT ☎(0)76

Ensconced in vineyards, fruit groves, and the dusty *puszta* (plains), Kecskemét (KETCH-keh-MATE) lures tourists with its shady, park-like central square, its famous *barack pálinka* (apricot brandy), and the musical methods of native composer Zoltán Kodály (1882-1967). First described in 1368 as a market town, "the garden city" sprung up as the crossing point of trade routes between Istanbul and Hamburg. Today, Kecskemét is also famous for its exceptional and eclectic architecture, which culminates in its pink Art Nouveau town hall.

## ✦🛈 ORIENTATION AND PRACTICAL INFORMATION

The town sprawls around a loosely connected string of squares. The largest, **Szabadság tér** (Liberty Square), is orbited by three satellite squares, **Kossuth tér, Kálvin tér,** and **Széchenyi tér.** To get to Szabadság from the **train station,** turn left as you exit, take a quick right on Rákóczi út, follow it through the park, and walk straight for 10min. The **bus station** is around the corner on the right from the train station.

**Tourist Office: Tourinform,** Kossuth tér 1 (☎/fax 481 065). From the train station, walk through the park to the left and down Rákóczi út. Continue straight past McDonald's, then head toward the town hall (a huge pink building to your left); the office is in the corner of the building. Info on exploring the *puszta.* English spoken. Open July-Aug. M-F 8am-6pm, Sa 9am-1pm; Sept.-June M-F 8am-5pm, Sa 9am-1pm.

**IBUSZ,** Kossuth tér 3 (☎486 955; ☎/fax 480 557), in the Aranyhomok hotel, behind the fountain as you come from the station. The staff cheerfully assists with visas, pension rooms (see below), and international bus, train, and plane tickets. Discounts for travelers under 26. Open summer M-W and F 8am-4:45pm, Th 8am-3:45pm. MC/Visa.

**Currency Exchange: OTP,** at the intersection of Szabadság tér and Arany János u., has the best exchange rates in town and also cashes traveler's checks, both for no commission. Open M-W and F 7:45am-4pm, Th 7:45am-5pm. A 24hr. Cirrus/Plus **ATM** sits outside. The OTP **branch** next to the synagogue on Koháry I. krt. is open until 6pm.

**Luggage storage:** At the train station. 100Ft per day. Open daily 7am-7pm.

**Pharmacy: Mátyás Kírály Gyógyszertár,** Szabadság tér 1 (☎480 739). Open M-F 7:30am-8pm, Sa 8am-4pm, Su 8am-2pm.

**Post Office:** Kálvin tér 10/12 (☎486 586; fax 481 034). Open M-F 8am-8pm, Sa 8am-2pm.

**Postal code:** 6000.

## ▐ TRANSPORTATION

**Trains:** Kodály Zoltán tér (☎322 460), at the end of Rákóczi út. To: **Szeged** (1hr., 17 per day, 500Ft); **Budapest** (1½hr., 13 per day, 786Ft); and **Pécs** (5hr., 1153Ft) via **Kiskunfélegyháza**.

**Buses:** Kodály Zoltán tér (☎321 777). To: **Budapest** (1½hr., 26 per day, 790Ft); **Szeged** (1¾hr., 13 per day, 710Ft); **Eger** (2½hr., 3 per day, 1290Ft); **Debrecen** (5hr., 2 per day, 1507Ft); and **Pécs** (5hr., 3 per day, 1507Ft).

**Local Transportation: Volán buses.** The main local bus terminal is a block away from Kossuth tér; make a right from the terminal on Sík S. Timetables are posted at most stops—service winds down around 10pm. (75Ft from kiosks, 90Ft from the driver)

## ▐ ACCOMMODATIONS

Summer brings all sorts of bargains, but winter travelers have fewer options. While some are overpriced, the best deals are in pensions. Most tourist agencies (see above) will help in the quest for an affordable bed. **IBUSZ** (see **Orientation and Practical Information,** above) rents private, fully loaded 4-bed flats near the center (3500-5000Ft), and can set you up with an equally convenient pension (doubles and triples 3500Ft, with shower 4000Ft).

**Hotel Pálma,** Arany János u. 3 (☎/fax 321 045 and 322 094), in the heart of the city. From Tourinform, turn left past McDonald's; the hotel is in the sea-green building on the right. This ex-college dorm with beachy decor is calm despite the shops located on its ground floor. Recently renovated, with agreeable bathrooms. 3- and 4-bed dorms with private showers and phones. Beware of overheated top floor rooms. English spoken. Reception 24hr. Checkout 10am. Prices vary according to number of people in each room: 2985Ft for 1, 5100Ft for 2, 6050Ft for 3, 7400Ft for 4. Breakfast included.

**Tanitóképzo Kollégiuma** (Teacher's College), Piaristák tére 4 (☎489 777), 5min. from Kossuth tér. Coming from the train station, turn right on Koháry I. Krt., and follow to where it forks at Piaristák tére. The Kollégiuma is on the right, facing the large church.

Although somewhat run-down, the Kollégiuma is serviceable and extremely convenient. Friendly staff. Little English spoken. Laundry 150Ft. Reception 8am-2am. Doubles, triples, and quads 1700Ft per person.

**Autós Camping,** Csabay Gréza Krl. 5 (☎329 398). 15min. southwest of town on Volán bus #1 or 11. Get off at the swimming pool and follow the signs to this somewhat sandy site. Electricity 400Ft. Open mid-Apr. to mid-Oct. 600Ft per person; 500Ft per site; 2-person caravans 2000Ft; 4-bed bungalows 5000Ft. Tax 100Ft. Parking included.

# ◖ FOOD

Kecskemét is the home of apricots; not surprisingly, it is also the home of apricot brandy. Don't let the sweet name fool you: the stuff may taste great, but it will put hair on the chest of any greenhorn. **Alförd supermarket,** Deák tér 2, just off Kossuth tér, fulfills more practical culinary needs. (Open M-F 6:30am-1pm.)

■ **Liberté Kavéház,** Szabadság tér 2 (☎480 350), serves more than just coffee in leafy, terraced elegance. Hungarian specialties not seen elsewhere and an atmosphere perfect for lingering. Main dishes 750-1600Ft. Open daily 9am-11pm. Afterwards, grab dessert (100-450Ft) at the adjoining **Fodor Cukrászda.** Open in summer daily 9am-8:30pm, off-season 9am-6:30pm.

**Göröd Udvär Étterem,** Hornyik J. 1 (☎492 513). Sit on doric stools at mosaic tables or in the more peaceful garden. This Greek oasis serves terrific *suvlaky* (810Ft) and gyros (550Ft), plus a few traditional Hungarian meals. Main dishes 500-1500Ft. Open daily 10am-11pm.

**Őregház Vendéglő,** Hosszú u. 27 (☎496 973). From Széchenyi tér, follow Mária ut. for about 15min. until it intersects with Hosszú ut. Large portions of Hungarian-style meat 'n' potatoes in a spacious neighborhood restaurant. Main dishes 450-550Ft; 20% off Sa-Su. Open M-Th and Su 11am-10pm, F-Sa 11am-11pm; last seating 10:15pm.

# ◉ SIGHTS

The salmon-colored **town hall,** Kossuth tér 1, was built in 1897 during the height of the Hungarian Art Nouveau movement; its pink facade and painted Gala Hall serve as excellent examples of the style. It dominates Kecskemét's main square, and its bells chime the songs of Zoltán Kodály throughout the town of his birth. The **Zoltán Kodály Institute of Music Education** is nearby at Kéttemplom-Köz 1/3, set back from the street in what was once a Fransiscan monastery. Just around the corner is the **Hungarian Museum of Photography,** Katona József tér 12, the only one of its kind in the country. (☎483 221. www.c3.hu/~fotomuz. Open W-Su 10am-5pm. 150Ft, students 100Ft.) Another example of Kecskemét's "Hungarian Secessionist" architecture is the **Kecskemét Gallery** (Kecskeméti Képtár), Rákóczi út 1, across the square from the town hall. Once a boarding house with a casino and ballroom, the gallery now features an upstairs hall lined with colorful peacock reliefs. While it also displays the work of local artists, the gallery's whimsical building is the main attraction. (☎480 076. Open Tu-Sa 10am-5pm, Su 1:30-5pm. 200Ft, students 60Ft.) The same could be said for the cupola-topped synagogue, Rákóczi út 2, which is now the **House of Science and Technology** and has 15 fake Michelangelo sculptures. (☎487 611. Open M-F 8am-9:30pm. 40Ft, students 20Ft.) The 1806 Roman Catholic **Great Church** asserts itself with a gorgeous Neoclassical facade and an interior of elaborate frescoes. (Usually open Tu-F 9am-noon and 3-6pm.) You can brave its rickety wooden floors and wobbly stairs to find a broad view of town atop the Church's **tower.** (Open June-Aug. Sa-Su 10am-8pm. 200Ft, students 100Ft.)

# ▥ MUSEUMS

■ **Museum of Naive Artists** (Naív Művészek Múzeum), Gáspár András u. 11 (☎324 767). Follow Déak Ferenc tér away from the Great Church (see **Sights,** above) to visit this museum, which fills halls with the folksy, often intriguing work of local amateurs. At the second major intersection of Deák Ferenc, turn right on Dobó István Körút; the entrance is on the left behind the strip mall. Open Tu-Su 10am-5pm. 150Ft, students 100Ft.

**Toy Museum** (Szórakaténusz Játékmúzeum és Műhely), Gáspár András u. 11 (☎481 469). Houses a fun collection of antique miniature trains, castles, and dolls, and also has hands-on workshops for children. Toymaker's workshop open Mar. 15-Dec. 31 W and Sa 10am-noon and 2:30-5pm and Su 10am-noon. 200Ft, students 100Ft; Su free. Open Mar. 15-Dec. 31 Tu-Su 10am-12:30pm and 1-5pm.

**Museum of Hungarian Folk Art** (Magyar Népi Iparművészet Múzeuma), Serfőző u. 19 (☎327 203). From the Tourinform office, turn left on the main street and follow it as it becomes Petőfi Sandor and then Dózsa Gy. út. Take the first right after the Arpád Körút onto Lajita u., then the first left onto Serfőző; the museum is on the right (10min.). This museum's extensive collection of costumes, furniture, ceramics, horse whips, and easter eggs fosters appreciation for many of the visual themes in Hungarian folk art. You also can't go wrong with the room of immortalized high-concept gingerbread. Open Tu-Sa 10am-5pm. 200Ft.

## 🎵🎭 ENTERTAINMENT AND NIGHTLIFE

Shakespeare may lose something in translation, but the elegant stage at the **Katona József Theater** (*Színhaz*), Katona tér 5, would lend grace to any script. (☎483 283; www.kecskemet.hu/szinhaz. Tickets 1000Ft. Box office open Sept.-June M-F 10am-7pm.) At **Club Robinson**, Akadémia krt. 2, platform heels stomp to Abba. (☎485 844. 0.5L beer 150Ft. Open daily 7pm-3am.) For a more laid-back evening, try **Kilele Music Cafe**, Jokai 34. The sign outside may suggest a raging inferno, but the downstairs is more cool than hot, with live jazz on the weekends. (☎326 774. 400Ft cover. Beer 140-380Ft. Open M-F 5pm-2am, Sa 6pm-3:30am, Su 6pm-1am.)

Kecskemét has produced such greats as composer Zoltán Kodály (1882-1967) and author József Katona (1791-1830); its artistic tradition continues each March with the **Kecskemét Spring Festival**, featuring music, theater, and literary readings. Duing the last week of August and the first week of September live it up and gain a few pounds at the **Hírös Food Festival**, when the Hungarian food industry dishes out its best creations.

## 🏇 DAYTRIP FROM KECSKEMÉT

### BUGAC HORSE SHOW

*The horse show is 6km north of Bugac and not directly accessible by public transportation. The narrow-gauge **train** leaves from **Kecskemét K.K.** (not the main station), on Halasi u. ☎ 322 460. To get to the station, head down Batthyány u. from the Hungarian Museum of Photography (see above) and cross the overpass (40min. walk). Or, take local bus #2 from the central bus terminal behind the Aranyhomok Hotel (176Ft). The train stops at 4 places in the Bugac area; get off at the 2nd stop (Bugac town) for a private room, the 3rd stop (Bugac-Felső) to be near the riding school, or the 4th stop (Bugaci Karikás Csárda; see below) to buy horse show tickets. From the 4th stop, continue along the tracks until a sand path crosses them, turn right, and follow the path (10min.) to the Bugaci Karikás Csárda (see below), where the tickets are sold. 3 trains per day (1hr.). Tickets 176Ft; buy them on the train. **Buses** depart from the main **Kecskemét** station (45min., 5 per day, 344Ft). There is no stop for Csárda; bring a brochure to show the driver, and remind him when you see the beige sign for Bugac Csárda.*

Bugac (boo-GATS), a giant rural area 35km outside Kecskemét, is adjacent to Kiskunság National Park. Sand lizards and vipers share the park with gray cattle, twisted-horned sheep, and the Mangalica pig. It may look as thought it's been around forever, but the *pustza* is really just a huge garden—the landscape was created by irrigation, and was a swamp as recently as 150 years ago. Even the "traditional"-looking octagonal thatched houses are merely symbolic representations of the shepherds' tents. To make the most of your day, start with a visit to **Bugac Tours**, Szabadság tér 5/A, Kecskemét, which also arranges daytrips. (☎/fax 482 500;

bugac@mail.datanet.hu; www.datanet.hu/~bugac. Open daily Apr.-Oct. 8am-8pm).
The most popular destination for those with fast-shutter cameras is the 40min.
**horse show.** Cowboys, constantly on the move to avoid raids, taught their horses
such tricks as lying down to hide. When the Nonius steeds perform now, it's all for
show: tricks include horses sitting at the dinner table and shaking hands with their
masters. The performance culminates in the breathtaking "Koch five-in-hand," in
which a horseman drives a band of five horses at a staggering speed while he stands
with one foot on the rumps of the two back horses. (Shows May-Sept. 15 1:15 and
3:15pm, Apr. and Oct. with enough people. Carriage departs from bus stop 1hr.
before show. Admission and a carriage ride 2000Ft, students 1000Ft; without carriage ride 1000Ft, students 500Ft.)

The national park offers some lovely hikes and bike rides in the juniper forest.
**Táltos Panzió** (☎ 372 633; fax 372 580), next to Bugaci Karikás Csárda in Bugac-Felső,
or **Bugac Tours** in Kecskemét (see above), arrange horseback riding (1500-2200Ft
per hr.), carriage rides (800-1500Ft per hr.), bike rentals, and wintertime sledding.
At the bus stop where Beton út meets Főld út, a summer souvenir shop offers **tourist information** and directions. The national park **ticket office,** about 1km past the
souvenir shop and just before Bugac-Puszta, offers info, but the staff's English ability depends on who is working that day. If you get hungry out on the range, try
■ **Bugaci Csárda** (Bugac Tavern), whose interior is decorated with pictures of the
horse-mad British royal family it has served in the past. The delectable Hungarian
specialties (600-2500Ft) are more than a few steps above cowboy grub, but who
says that budget travelers need to rough it *all* the time? (☎ 372 688. Open daily daily
8am-10pm.) Another option is the more boisterous (and touristy) **Bugaci Karikás
Csárda** (Bugac Horsewhip Tavern), right near the Bugac Tours Outpost. (☎ 372 688.
Main dishes 400-1500Ft. Open daily 9am-5pm.)

# NORTHERN HUNGARY

Hungary's northern upland is dominated by a series of six low mountain ranges
running northeast from the Danube Bend along the Slovak border. Their soils yield
unique wines and their terrain provides endless opportunities for outdoor exploration. From the famous wines of Eger and Tokaj to the Lipizzaner ponies of Szilvásvárad, it seems every town has its own distinctive export. Meanwhile, the Bükk and
Aggtelek National Parks beckon hikers with scenic trails and complex caves.

# EGER ☎(0)36

The siege of Eger Castle and István Dobó's subsequent defeat of the overwhelming
Ottoman army figures prominently in Hungarian national lore. The key to victory:
the strengthening powers of local *Egri Bikavér* (Bull's Blood) wine. The legacy
remains alive today in the vibrant cellars of the Valley of the Beautiful Women and
the dozens of historical monuments scattered throughout the city. Eger seduces
visitors with infectious tipsiness and friendliness.

## ◤ ORIENTATION

The **train station** lies on the outskirts of town; take bus #11, 12, or 14 to get to the **bus
station** (95Ft). To get to the center, head straight from the station and take a right
onto Deák u. After about 10 minutes, take a right onto Kossuth Lajos u. and an
immediate left onto Széchenyi u., between the cathedral and the Lyceum. A final
right onto Érsek u. leads to **Dobó tér** (20min.), the main square. To get to the center
from the bus station, exit from terminal #10 , head right on **Barkoczy u.,** and turn
right on the first street, Brody u. Follow the stairs down to the end of the street and
turn right onto Széchenyi u; a left down Érsek u. leads to Dobó tér. Most sights are
within a 10-minute walk of the square.

## ◨ TRANSPORTATION

**Trains:** Vasút u. (☎314 264). Sends trains to: **Szilvásvárad** (1¼hr., 6 per day, 180Ft); **Budapest** (2hr., 12 per day, 498Ft) via **Füzesabony** (20min., 112Ft); **Budapest's** Keleti station (2hr., 5 direct per day, 1050Ft); and **Szeged** (4½hr., 1 per day, 812Ft). Budapest trains split in Hatvan—confirm with other passengers or the conductor that your car is going to Budapest.

**Buses:** Barkóczy u. (☎410 552). To: **Szilvásvárad** (45min., every 30min.-1hr., 246Ft); **Budapest** (2hr., 15-20 per day, 1080Ft); **Aggtelek** (3hr., 8:45am, 5pm return, 910Ft); and **Debrecen** (3hr., 5-6per day, 1080Ft).

## ◪ PRACTICAL INFORMATION

**Tourist Office: Tourinform,** Dobó tér 2 (☎/fax 32 18 07; tourinfo@agria.hu). The English-speaking staff gladly provides accommodations info and **maps** (280Ft). Open M-F 9am-6:30pm, Sa-Su 9:30am-1pm; off-season M-F 9am-5pm, Sa 9:30am-1:30pm.

**Bank: OTP,** Széchenyi u. 2 (☎31 08 66), gives AmEx/MC/Visa **cash advances** and cashes AmEx **traveler's cheques** for no commission. A Cirrus/MC/Plus/Visa **ATM** stands outside. Open M-Tu and Th-F 7:45am-5pm, W 7:45am-6pm; currency desk open M, Tu, and Th until 2:45pm, W until 4:30pm, F until noon.

**Pharmacy:** Dobó tér 2 (☎/fax 312 219), stocks American and Western European products. Open M-F 7:30am-6pm, Sa 8am-12:30pm.

**Telephones:** Inside the post office.

**Internet: PC Club,** Mecset u. 2 (☎310 506). Turn left just after crossing the bridge leaving Dobó tér; the office faces the parking lot. 480Ft per hr. Open daily 10am-10pm.

**Post Office:** Széchenyi u. 22 (☎313 232). Open M-F 8am-8pm, Sa 8am-1pm.

**Postal code:** 3300.

## ◤ ACCOMMODATIONS

The best and friendliest accommodations are **private rooms;** look for *Zimmer frei* signs outside the city center, particularly on Almagyar u. and Mekcsey u. near the castle. It's best to go knocking at lunchtime. (Around 2000Ft.) **Eger Tourist,** Bajcsy-Zsilinszky u. 9, arranges private rooms in the center. (☎41 17 24; fax 41 17 68. Open M-F 9am-5pm. Around 3000Ft. Breakfast included.)

**Eszterházi Károly Kollégiuma,** Leányka u. 2/6 (☎520 430), is cheap, but the way isn't well-marked. Facing away from the church at Dobo tér, exit the square to the right, walking over the river and past the outdoor cafes. Turn right again on Dobó u., walk through Dózsa Gry. tér, and turn left as if to enter the castle. Take the stairs to the right just before the castle gate (Var Köz). After the underpass, you'll emerge on Leanyka u.; the Kollégiuma is the multi-level cement building on the left. Open July-early Sept. Call ahead. Triples and quads 1200Ft plus 250Ft per person.

**Tourist Motel,** Mekcsey u. 2 (☎42 90 14). A favorite of tour groups. The curfew-breaking pre-teens can get loud, but the rooms are tidy and spacious. May be gone in 2001. Doubles 2800Ft, with bath 3600Ft; triples 3450Ft, 4350Ft; quads 4800Ft, 5600Ft.

**Autós Caravan Camping,** Rákóczi u. 79 (reserve through Eger Tourist), 20min. north of the center on bus #5, 11, or 12. Get off at the Shell station and look for signs to the campground. Open Apr. 15-Oct. 15. 320Ft per person; tents 250Ft.

## ◖ FOOD

There are plenty of food options along **Széchenyi u.,** but grocery stores are usually the cheapest and quickest way to eat. A giant **ABC supermarket** has its own little square directly off Széchenyi u. between Sandor u. and Szt. Janos u. (Open M-F 6am-6:30pm, Sa 6am-4pm.) A daily fruit and vegetable **market** sits off Széchenyi u.—

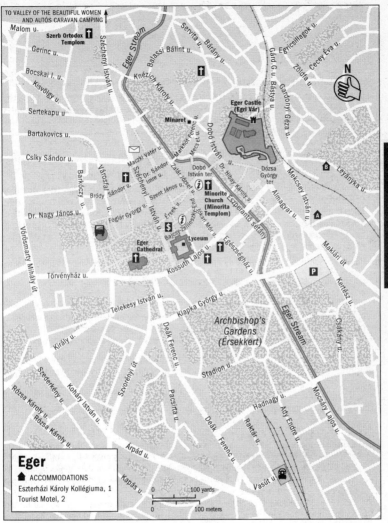

**Eger**

🔺 ACCOMMODATIONS
Eszterházi Károly Kollégiuma, 1
Tourist Motel, 2

turn right on Arva Köz; it's on the right. (Open in summer M-F 6am-6pm, Sa 6am-1pm, Su 6-10am; off-season M-F 6am-5pm, Sa 6am-1pm, Su 6-10am.)

**HBH Bajor Söház,** Bajcsy-Zsilinsky u. 19 (☎316 312), off Dobó tér across from the pharmacy. Beer house serving "Hungarian standards" such as cold brains, ham knuckles, and goose liver. Polyglot waiters and an English menu make the dining experience less intimidating, if less exotic. Main dishes 600-1500Ft. Open daily 10am-10pm.

**Kulacs Csárda Borozó** (☎/fax 311 375), in the Valley of the Beautiful Women, has the best location and makes the most of it. The vine-draped courtyard keeps the crowds coming with a menu featuring Hungarian specialties and some rare non-fried options. Meals 720-1100Ft. Open Tu-Su noon-10pm.

**Gyros Étterem Sérozc,** Széchenyi u. 10 (☎310 135), serves gyros (320-350Ft) and roasts (685-1400Ft) in a pleasant pub-like atmosphere.

**Dobos,** Szécheny u. 6. Proves why Hungarians don't diet with its decadent pastries and other desserts. Try a marzipan snail or rose (220-250Ft), a candy frog (90Ft), or one of their gorgeous and inventive pastries (95-155Ft). Open daily 9am-10pm.

## ENTERTAINMENT

**VALLEY OF THE BEAUTIFUL WOMEN (SZÉPASSZONYVÖLGY).** After a morning of exploring Eger's historical sights, spend the early evening in the wine-cellars of the Valley of the Beautiful Women. Following World War II, cheap land prices allowed hundreds of cellars to sprout on this volcanic hillside. Most of the 25 open cellars consist of little more than a 20m tunnel and a few tables and benches, but each has its own personality: some are subdued, while others are rowdy with Hungarian and Roma sing-alongs. Although locals pride themselves on white wines as well, Eger is Hungary's red wine capital; the most popular libations are the famous *Bikavér* and the sweeter *Medok* or *Medina*. The valley is for people serious about buying, but many spend hours lingering in the friendly, smoky cellars, or outside chatting, wine-filled tupperware in hand. Visitors push coins into the spongy fungus on cellar walls—supposedly if your coin sticks, you'll return. **Cellar #16** is usually still kicking when others have begun to close, probably because they serve the best *Medok* in the valley. Taste a glass of *Bikavér* at the less rowdy, but equally warm, **Cellar #17** next door. Although the budget gospel dictates otherwise, the smart (and kind) thing to do here is to enjoy all the samples you want, and then buy a bottle of your favorite—this way the cellars can continue to give free tastings. *(Start on Széchenyi u. with Eger Cathedral to the right. Turn right onto Kossuth Lajos u. and then left onto Deák u., although the signpost on Kossuth Lajos u. directs you otherwise. Continue on Deák u. and make the 1st right onto Telekessy u. Go straight past the intersection; after the cemetery, follow the fork to the left onto Szépasszony-völgy. 15min. Most cellars open 10am-6 or -7pm, some until 4am. Best to visit in the afternoon. 100mL 30-50Ft; 1L 300Ft, less if you bring your own container.)*

**EGER CASTLE.** (Egri Vár.) Egri Vár's innards include subterranean barracks, catacombs, a crypt, and a wine cellar. One ticket buys admission to the three museums in the castle: a **gallery** with Hungarian paintings from as early as the 15th century; the **Dobó István Vármúzeum,** which displays excavated artifacts, armor, and an impressive array of weapons; and the **dungeon exhibition,** a collection of torture equipment that will inspire sadists and masochists alike. The 400-year-old **wine cellars** are also open to the public for tastings. Be careful, though, because the bar is in the same room as the hands-on archery exhibit where 10-year olds are taught to shoot longbows with real arrows. *(☎312 744 ext. 111. Castle open daily 8am-8pm. Museums open Tu-Su 9am-5pm. Wine cellars open Tu-Su 10am-5pm. Underground passages open M only. Castle 120Ft, students 60Ft. All 3 museums Tu-Su 300Ft, 150Ft; M 250Ft, 120Ft. Wine cellars 60Ft. English tour 300Ft per person.)*

**LYCEUM.** The fresco in the library on the first floor of the Rococo Lyceum depicts an ant's-eye-view of the Council of Trent, out of which came the edicts of the Counter Reformation—hence the lightning bolt blasting a pile of heretical books. Upstairs, a small **astronomical museum** houses 18th-century telescopes and instruments from the building's old observatory. *(Open Th-Su 9:30am-3:30pm. 200Ft, students 100Ft. Museum 200Ft.)* A marble line in the floor represents the meridian; when the sun strikes the line through a pin-hole aperture in the south wall, it is astronomical

**RED BULL.** In 1552, Egri Vár was besieged by 100,000 Ottoman soldiers. To prepare for the attack, Dobó István and his 2000 men downed barrels of the region's wine, which stained their beards red. When the Hungarians didn't succumb to the overwhelming Turkish force, it was rumored among the Turks, who did not drink themselves because of Muslim law, that the fierce Hungarians were quaffing the blood of bulls for strength. The rumor gave the wine a name—*bikáver*, or Bull's Blood.

noon. Two floors up a *camera obscura* satisfies the Peeping Tom in everyone. The mechanism projects a live picture of the surrounding town onto a table, providing a god-like view of the world below in a tower room so hot you won't forget your mortality. *(At the corner of Kossuth Lajos u. and Eszterházy tér.)*

**EGER CATHEDRAL.** Built in 1837 by Joseph Hild to be the largest in Hungary, the only Neo-Classical building in Eger was quickly eclipsed by Hild's larger church in Esztergom. This is still the more beautiful one; pastel colors and soaring architecture make it feel less oppressive and decadent than the more typical Baroque interior. Exquisite organ and soprano **concerts** (30min.) are held here from May to mid-October. *(On Eszterházy tér just off Széchenyi u. Concerts M-Sa 11:30am, Su 12:45pm. 300Ft.)*

**OTHER SIGHTS.** The pink Baroque **Minorite Church** (Minorita Templom) in Dobó tér was built in 1758. It has an elaborate carved wooded interior, and the facade overlooks a statue of Captain Dobó and two Hungarian defenders, including a woman poised to hurl a rock at an unfortunate Turk. From Dobó tér, walk down Mescet u. on the right to reach the 40m, 17th-century **Minaret,** the Ottomans' northernmost phallic symbol. The steep spiral staircase is not much wider than the average 20th-century person—only the intrepid make it to the top. *(Open Apr.-Oct. 10am-6pm. 50Ft.)* The 18th-century **Serbian Orthodox Church** (Szerb Ortodox Templom), on Vitkovics u. at the center's northern end drips with gilt ornamentation. Follow Széchenyi u. from the center and enter at #15. *(Open Tu-Su 10am-4pm.)*

## ♫ ❀ ENTERTAINMENT AND FESTIVALS

In summer, the **open-air baths** (a.k.a. swimming pools) offer a desperately needed respite from the sweltering city as well as curative power for such ailments as bone disease and "weariness." To get there from Dobó tér, take Jókai u. to Kossuth Lajos u. and continue down Egészségház u.—the baths are across from the Archbishop's garden. (☎411 619. Open May-Sept. M-F 6am-7:30pm, Sa-Su 8am-7pm; daily Oct.-Apr. 9am-7pm. 320Ft, students and pensioners 170Ft.)

Eger revels in its heritage during the **Baroque Festival,** held over two weeks in late July and early August. Nightly performances of operas, operettas, and medieval and Renaissance court music are held on Dobó tér, at the Basilica, and around the city. Buy tickets at the venue. (500Ft, 750Ft, and 1000Ft; info ☎410 324, or ask at Tourinform.) The **Eger Bull's Blood Festival** is in the beginning of July. An international folk dance festival, **Eger Vintage Days,** is held in early September. Inquire at Tourinform (see p. 376) for schedules.

## ⛰ DAYTRIP FROM EGER

### BARADLA CAVES ☎(0)48

*The bus leaves Eger at 8:45am daily, whizzes through Szilvásvárad at 9:25am, and arrives in Aggtelek at 11:25am in front of Cseppkő Hotel (910Ft). The returning bus leaves from the same stop at 3pm; the bus to Miskolc is at 5pm. To get to the cave from the bus stop, walk out behind the hotel and, facing away from it, cut across the field toward the street. Once on the road, the national park is to the right. ☎/fax 350 006. Mandatory 1hr. Hungarian tours daily 10am, 1pm, 3pm; in the high-season also 5pm and whenever more than 10 people assemble. 600Ft, students 300Ft. More difficult, longer tours covering the entire main branch of the cave (5hr., 7km) can be arranged through Naturinform. ☎343 073; call ahead. 3200Ft, students 1600Ft.*

The spectacular Baradla Caves wind for over 25km, straddling the Hungarian-Slovak border. In each chamber, a forest of dripping stalactites, stalagmites, and fantastically shaped stone formations tower over the visitor. The entrance in Hungary is at **Aggtelek** (AWG-tel-eck). A large chamber inside the cave with perfect acoustics has been converted into an auditorium, and the tour takes a dramatic pause here for a low-tech **light show** set to apocalyptic music. Another hall contains an **Iron Age cemetery** where 13 people, thought to be recent crime victims when the cave was first discovered, are buried. The temperature is 10°C year-round, so bring a jacket.

HUNGARY

# SZILVÁSVÁRAD
☎ (0)36

Beloved for its carriages, Lipizzaner horses, and surrounding national parks, Szil-vásvárad (SEAL-vash-vah-rod) trots along at its own dignified clip. One of only four places in the world to breed the prize-winning Lipizzaners, Szilvásvárad takes pride in its modest claim to international prominence—locals will attempt to bridge all language barriers whenever the conversation turns equine.

**▐ TRANSPORTATION. Trains** run to **Eger** (1¼hr., 8 per day, 202Ft). Szilvásvárad has two stations; get off at the first, "Szilvásvárad-Szalajkavölgy." There is no bus station. **Buses** are generally the most convenient transport, running to **Eger** (45 min., every 30min.-1hr., 260Ft) and **Aggtelek** (1¾hr., 9:25am, 629Ft). Don't get off at the first bus stop in town, unless you want to investigate the *Zimmer frei* (rooms available) signs. The second stop is on Egri út, within sight of Szalajka u.

**▆▐ ORIENTATION AND PRACTICAL INFORMATION.** The town's main street, **Egri út,** extends straight from the Szilvásvárad-Szalajkavölgy train station and bends sharply at the race course's tollbooth-ticket office. The booth marks the entrance to **Szalajka u.,** which leads directly to the national park. Farther north, Egri út turns into **Miskolci út.** There's no tourist office in town, so get information and a basic map at the **Eger Tourinform** (see p. 376) before heading out. **Hiking maps** are available at the tollbooth-ticket office (150Ft) and are posted throughout the park along hiking trails. More detailed hiking maps of the surrounding mountains (200Ft) are available at the small **bank,** behind the second bus stop on Egri út. (☎355 453. Open M-F 8am-noon and 12:30-4pm.)

**▐▗▐ ACCOMMODATIONS AND FOOD.** Although Szilvásvárad seems scaled perfectly for a daytrip, it can be a very relaxing place to stay. **Private rooms** are the cheapest option (1500Ft without amenities), but their price rises during the Lipicai Festival (see below). **Hegy Camping,** Egri út 36a, offers great views of the valley from the groomed campground. (☎355 207. Open Apr. 15-Oct. 15. Tent for 2 people 1500Ft; each additional person 650Ft. Bungalow doubles with bath 3400Ft; triples 4200Ft; quads 5000Ft. Tourist tax 300Ft.)

**Csobogó,** Szalajka u. 1, on the road to the national park, stands out among the restaurants. In addition to traditional meals toned down for tourists, it offers a selection of "international" dishes, including vegetarian meals. (☎(30) 415 249. Main dishes 380-680Ft. Open daily 11am-8pm; summer also Sa-Su 11am-midnight.) For picnic supplies, the cheapest food in town is at the **Mini Coop Market,** Egri út 6. (Open M-F 7am-6pm, Sa 7am-1pm, Su 8am-noon.)

**▆▐ SIGHTS AND ENTERTAINMENT.** Although the town is only one street long, outdoor opportunities abound, from leisurely biking in the Szalajka Valley to hikes in the low Bükk mountains. The arena on Szalajka u., just to the right of the park entrance, hosts **horse shows** on weekends (800Ft per person), and a festival (see below) in late July. You can jump into the thick of things by learning how to drive a carriage, brandish a whip, or ride a steed. Many farms offer horse riding, especially in July and August. Friendly Péter Kovács, Egri út 62 (☎355 343), **rents horses** (1500Ft per hr.) and **two-horse carriages** (4500Ft per hr.). **Lipicai Stables,** the stud farm for Szilvásvárad's Lipizzaner breed, is where it all begins. Walking on Egri út away from the park entrance, make a left onto Enyves u. and follow signs to the farm. (☎35 51 55. Open daily 8:30am-noon and 2-4pm. 80Ft.) In late July, the extremely popular **Lipicai Festival** (call the stables for information) attracts carriage drivers from across the globe for a grand three-day competition.

Shaded walks through the **Bükk mountains** and the **Szalajka valley** are beautiful, but not always relaxing—in June the trails swarm with school groups, packs of 14-year-olds, and families with more children than you can eat. At the **Fátyol waterfall,** the lazy trailside stream transforms into the most dramatic—and most popular—of the park's attractions. It only takes 45 minutes to walk here along the green trail, or 15 minutes by the little open-air train, which departs just to the right of the stop sign at the park's entrance. (100Ft, students 60Ft.) A 30-minute hike along the green trail beyond the waterfalls leads to the **Istálósk Cave,** home to a bear cult during the Stone Age (see **History,** p. 308). After clearing the brook, the trail becomes extremely steep—either bring a walking stick or wear shoes with good traction. One way of avoiding crowds is to **rent a bike** at Szalajka u., just past the stop sign at the entrance to the park. Pick up one of their excellent free **cycling maps** and tourist guides, and hit the trails—the paths are just rough enough to make it interesting. The shop also arranges trips to the local plateaus for groups of 10 or more for the cost of a day's rental. (☎(60) 352 695. 500Ft 1st hr., 200Ft thereafter; 1500Ft per day. Open daily in summer 9am-dusk; off-season in good weather only.)

# TOKAJ ☎(0)47

King Louis XIV of France called Tokaj (toke-EYE) "the wine of kings and the king of wines," which lends a note of somewhat incongruous grandeur to this sleepy Hungarian village. Tokaj is just one of many small towns at the foot of the Kopasz Mountains (er, hills) that produce unique whites, yet it lends its name to the entire class of wine (Tokaji Féherbör). Even the scent hangs in the air above the wide, sunny streets by the banks of the Tisza river. If Tokaj gives the wine its name, the wine gives Tokaj its flavor, with days split between leisurely exploration of the famed local cellars and outdoor activity in the hills and waters.

**🖪 TRANSPORTATION. Trains,** Baross G. u. 18 (☎352 020), go to **Miskolc** (1hr., 12 per day, 348Ft); and **Debrecen** (2hr., 8 per day, 794Ft) via **Nyíregyháza** (30min., 13 per day, 218Ft). **Buses** leave from the train station, but only service local towns.

**🖪🔂 ORIENTATION AND PRACTICAL INFORMATION.** The trek from the train station to the town's center takes 15 minutes. Facing away from the entrance of the station, walk left along the railroad tracks to an underpass, then turn left on Bajcsy-Zsilinszky u. At the Hotel Tokaj fork, stay on the left road. It only takes 10 minutes to walk across Tokaj's center. The main **Bajcsy-Zsilinszky u.** becomes **Rákóczi u.** after the Tisza bridge, transforming again after **Kossuth tér** to become **Bethlen Gábor u.** Some brochures from pensions and wine cellars include simple street **maps. Tourinform,** Serház u. 1, on the right side of Rákóczi u. as you walk into town, arranges **private** and **hotel rooms** for no fee, and can set you up with a horse, canoe, or rafting tour. (☎/fax 352 259 and 352 539; tokaj@tourinfor.hu. Open Apr.-Oct. M-Sa 11am-7pm; off-season M-F 10am-4pm.) **Exchange currency,** cash **traveler's checks,** or get MC/Visa **cash advances** at **OTP,** Rákóczi u. 35. (☎35 25 21. Open M-Th 7:45am-3:15pm, F 7:45am-2:15pm.) A Cirrus/MC/Plus/Visa **ATM** sits outside. The **pharmacy** next to the Bacchus Etterem restaurant on Kossuth tér has regular hours; ring after hours for emergencies. (Open M-F 8am-5pm, Sa 8am-4pm, Su 8am-noon and 12:30-4:30pm.) **Telephones** are in the post office and in the center. The **post office** is at Rákóczi u. 24. (☎35 24 17. Open M-F 8am-5pm, Sa 8am-noon.) **Postal code:** 3910.

**🖪🔂 ACCOMMODATIONS AND FOOD.** See what **Tourinform** has to offer (see above), but *Zimmer frei* and *Szoba Kiadó* (rooms available) signs abound—your best bet is to walk along Rákóczi u. and venture down random streets to choose one you like. (Singles average 1500-2000Ft; doubles 3000-5000Ft.) Don't be afraid to bargain, but beware: your host may well talk you into sampling—and buying—her expensive homemade wine. *Zimmer frei* etiquette dictates that you not go ringing on doors after 8:30pm. **Grof Széchenyi István Students Hostel,** Bajcsy-Zsilinszki u. 15/17, the white building with the statue out front as you walk from the train station toward the center, is the best deal around, with fresh, recently renovated doubles (3800Ft per person with bath) and sparse but clean quads (3000Ft). It has a pleasant, rather than an institutional atmosphere, and is five minutes from the center of town. (☎35 23 55. Reception approx. 24hr. Open July-Aug.) The friendly and convenient **Makk Marci Panzió,** Liget Köz 1, in the center, is steps from some of the town's best wine cellars. (☎352 336; fax 353 088. Reception 24hr. Singles 3360Ft; doubles 5040Ft; triples 7280Ft; quads 8400Ft. Breakfast included.) There's also a **pizzeria**

# A MINI-GUIDE TO THE WINES OF TOKAJ

Wine connoisseurs have been aware of the merits of Hungarian wines for years, and budget travelers have long appreciated the low prices. The exotic names on the labels, however, might intimidate those used to *Chardonnay*. In order from driest to sweetest (and lightest to darkest in color), the main varieties are:

**Furmint,** a basic dry white that goes well with seafood, fish, and game dishes.

**Szamorodni,** which comes in dry (Száraz) and sweet (Édes) varieties, has a more complex flavor. While the dry can accompany most main meals, the sweet goes well with pâté, delicate cheeses, and ice-cream.

**Aszú,** *Furmint* sweetened with *aszú* grapes (grapes which ripen and dry out more quickly than others in the same bunch), is the most famous. According to local lore, *Aszú* wine was invented when Máté Szepsi Laczkó neglected his harvest in 1630—fearing Turkish invasion, he left his grapes to rot on the vine. The fruit produces an extremely sweet dessert wine that soon became popular among farmers. Sweetness is measured in 3, 4, 5, or 6 *puttonyos*, or the number of baskets of sweet *Aszú* grapes added. (*Szamorodni* contains a mix of both *Aszú* and regular grapes.)

**Aszú Eszenela,** the "imperial elixir," is too sweet to be described in terms of *puttonyos;* drink it alone or accompanied by "great Havana cigars."

1972, 1975, 1983, 1988, 1993, and 1999 are considered good vintages. Some vintners believe the overall quality of their wines increased after the privatization of the vineyards in 1991. To be an expert, or just look like one, sample wines in order from driest to sweetest. In the opposite order, dry wines will taste bitter or acidic.

downstairs. (Pizzas 390-550Ft. Open daily 10am-10pm.) **Lux Panzió,** Serház u. 14, provides sunny rooms suffused with pink. To get there, turn right onto Vároháza-köz from Rákóczi u., just after OTP. The *panzió* is the bright yellow building. Ask for the double with the shower in the room—it's the same price as those with a shower down the hall. (☎35 21 45. Doubles 3500Ft; triples with TV 5200Ft. Tourist tax 125Ft.) To camp out with the mosquitoes, take the Tisza bridge (5min. from the center). The mega-center **Camping Tisza,** on the right as you cross the river, rents out waterfront campsites and tiny bungalows to the traveling hordes, keeping them busy into the wee hours with a casino and a disco. (Check-in 2pm. Check-out 10am. Camping 600Ft per person. 2-bed bungalow 2500Ft; 4-bed 4400Ft.)

Soak up the regional wines at **Toldi Fogado,** Hajdú Köz, at Rákóczi u., which serves good Hungarian food in a pleasant dining room and garden. (☎353 403. English menu available. Main dishes 550-700Ft. Open daily 11am-10pm.) **Bacchus Etterem,** centrally located at Kossuth tér 17, is like a local diner. (☎35 20 54. Goulash 400Ft. Breakfast 250-300Ft. Open M-Sa 8am-10pm, Su 9am-10pm.) The **ABC-Coop supermarket** is at Kossuth tér. (Open M-F 6:30am-6:30pm, Sa 6:30am-1pm, Su 8-11am.)

**◉ ♫ SIGHTS AND ENTERTAINMENT.** *Bor Pince* signs herald **private wine cellars** whose owners are generally pleased to let visitors sample their wares (approx. 1000Ft for 5 or 6 1dL samples). Walk in or be bold and ring the bell if the cellar looks closed. The big flashy cellars on the main road are more touristy—explore the side streets for higher-quality wines. Serious commercial tasting takes place at the most respected and largest of the lot: **Rákóczi Pince,** Kossuth tér 15. This 1.5km system of tunnels served as the imperial wine cellar for two centuries until the end of World War I. In 1526, János Szapohjai was elected king of Hungary in the elegant and surprisingly large subterranean hall. Five-hundred years worth of dripping, spongy fungus chill in the 10°C cellar. Wine tastings and group tours of the cellar and hall usually occur on the hour, but can be pre-empted by tour groups. Individual tours can also be arranged at any time. English-speaking guides may be available July-August. (☎35 20 09; fax 35 21 41. Open daily 10am-8pm. 1350Ft for 30min. tour and 6-glass tasting; 2600Ft with *Aszú* tasting. MC/Visa.) The young ▓ **Tokaji Hímesudvar Cellars,** Bem u. 2, produce phenomenal Aszú wines—their 1993 *5-put-*

*tonyos* received several international awards. The friendly, English-speaking Várhelyi family will be glad to guide you through the history of the region and the subtleties of the Tokaj wines. To get to the royal hunting lodge where the cellar is located, take the road to the left of the church in Kossuth tér and follow the signs to the cellar. (Open daily 9am-9pm. Tastings 1000Ft for 5 wines, 1200Ft for 6.) The **Tóth family cellar** at Óvár út 40 produces five exceptional whites, including a 1988 *6-puttonyos* Aszú. Follow the street that begins at Rákóczi u. across from Tourinform. (5 glasses 300Ft, 1L of *5-puttonyos* 3100Ft, 1L of 6-*puttonyos* 3500Ft.)

**Outdoor** recreation in Tokaj is as popular as the wine that brings people here. **Vízisport Centrum,** at the campground to the left after crossing the bridge, rents bikes (500Ft per day) and canoes (100Ft per 30min., 1200Ft per day), will drive you to the beginning of the Tisza for a long canoe trip (100Ft per km), and arranges horseback-riding (600Ft per hr., 1000Ft with trainer). **Camping Tisza** also rents canoes. (4-seater 1500Ft per day.) **Veres Szekér Söröző,** Rákóczi u. 30/32, is a tavern that packs in students and young people for an after-dinner round. (0.5L beer 80-130Ft; 100mL wine 30-180Ft; pool 60Ft per game. Open daily 2pm-2am.)

HUNGARY

# LATVIA (LATVIJA)

**IF YOU'RE HERE FOR...**

**3 DAYS.** Spend a day in swanky **Rīga** (p. 390), see the spectacular **Rundāles Palace** (p. 398), and check out the beaches of **Jūrmala** (p. 399).

**1 WEEK.** Go on to the castle ruins and brewery of **Cēsis** (p. 401), **Turaida Castle** (p. 399), and the red tile roofs of **Kuldīga** (p. 402).

With the smallest majority of natives of the three Baltic States, Latvia remains the least affluent and developed. Attitudes toward the many Russians who still live in the country are softening, but evidence of national pride abounds, from patriotically renamed streets bleeding with crimson-and-white flags, to a rediscovery of native holidays predating even the Christian invasions. Rīga, Latvia's only large city, is a westernized capital luring more and more international companies. The rest of the country is mostly a provincial expanse of green hills dominated by tall birches and pines, dairy pastures, and quiet settlements.

## LATVIA AT A GLANCE

**OFFICIAL NAME:** Republic of Latvia

**CAPITAL:** Riga (pop. 874,000)

**POPULATION:** 2.4 million (56.5% Latvian, 30.4% Russian)

**LANGUAGE:** Lettish (official), Lithuanian, Russian

**CURRENCY:** 1 Latvian lat = 100 santims

**RELIGION:** Lutheran, Roman Catholic, Russian Orthodox

**LAND AREA:** 64,589 km²

**GEOGRAPHY:** Low plain

**BORDERS:** Belarus, Estonia, Lithuania, Russia

**ECONOMY:** 65% Services, 28% Industry, 7% Agriculture

**GDP:** $4100 per capita

**EMERGENCY PHONE NUMBERS:** Fire 01, Police 02, Emergency 03

**COUNTRY CODE:** 371

**INTERNATIONAL DIALING PREFIX:** 00

# HISTORY

Latvia stands at the Baltic crossing of two different historical and religious strains. Latgale, or southeastern Latvia, was historically tied to Catholic Lithuania and Poland. Northern Latvia, on the other hand, took the Estonian path, influenced mainly by Lutheran Scandinavian powers.

Latvia has consistently struggled under the yoke of foreign rule. The first invaders to subjugate the native Balts were the Germans, who arrived in the late 12th century eager to trade and convert the locals to Christianity. In 1237 the Germanic Brothers of the Sword, who had conquered all of present-day Latvia, merged with the Teutonic Knights and established the **Confederation of Livonia,** which ruled over the territory for nearly 300 years. The population lived poorly under the Germans; the native nobility was forced out, while the peasants labored under a heavy tax burden imposed by their conquerors. The confederation collapsed when Russian Tsar Ivan IV (the Terrible) invaded, beginning the 25-year **Livonian War** (1558-83) and a half-century of partition. The 1629 Truce of Altmark brought an extended period of relative stability and freedom known as the **Swedish interlude,** achieved by ceding control of eastern Livonia to the Poles and giving Rīga and the northern regions to Sweden. Sweden, however, was forced to cede the Livonian territories to Peter the Great under the Peace of Nystad in 1721, and with the second partition of Poland in 1795 the entire country fell under Russian control. The Latvian peasantry, which

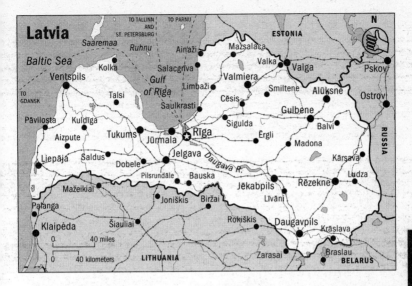

became increasingly prosperous after the abolition of serfdom in 1861, continued to struggle for freedom from the Russian empire throughout the 19th century. Nationalism flared with particular strength during the Russian Revolution of 1905, when the idea of a Latvian state was openly put forward.

Reacting to the Bolshevik coup of November 1917, the **Latvian People's Council** proclaimed independence on November 18, 1918, establishing a government in Rīga led by **Kārlis Ulmanis.** Over the next few years, the country was overrun by battling armies. Latvians, Germans, White Russians, British, French, Estonians, Lithuanians, and the Red Army all fought for supremacy. By 1920 the Latvians were in control. The constitution of 1922 provided for a republic governed by a president and a unicameral parliament, but the large number of political parties in the legislature, or Saeima, kept the political situation unstable. Ulmanis encountered increasing problems as German elements within Latvia became sympathetic to the Nazi party, and in 1934 he declared a state of emergency. Two years later he became President. Under the secret provisions of the **Nazi-Soviet Nonaggression Pact,** Latvia fell under the control of the USSR in 1938. Germany reneged on the Pact, however, and in 1941 occupied Latvia. In 1945 the Red Army drove them back out and the Soviets annexed their smaller neighbor.

Latvia entered the **Soviet Union** as one of its wealthiest and most industrialized regions. Under Soviet rule, though, it was torn by radical economic restructuring, political repression, and a thorough Russification of its national culture. Some 35,000 Latvians, including many members of the intelligentsia, were deported to Russia during the first year of the occupation. Encouraged by the Soviet government, immigrants from the rest of the USSR poured into the country. Few bothered to learn the local language or to identify with the indigenous population, and immigrants subsequently dominated local politics. Within four decades, ethnic Latvians accounted for only half the population.

Never reconciled to their incorporation into the Soviet Union, the Latvians were more than ready to take advantage of Gorbachev's willingness to reform the Soviet system. Under **glasnost** and **perestroika,** Latvians protested en masse against the communist regime and created the **Popular Front** of Latvia in 1988. The Communists were trounced in the 1990 elections. On May 4, 1990, the new legislature declared independence, but Soviet intervention sparked violent clashes in Rīga in 1991. Following the failed Moscow coup in August, the Latvian legislature reasserted **independence** and most of the world recognized Latvian sovereignty in September 1991.

> **WHEN LIFE GIVES YOU LEMONS...** Hey, having a disgruntled Russian population and a depressed economy isn't all bad, right? The former circumstance has given Latvia a fairly healthy vodka industry, while the latter has kept prices down and made distributors eager to get supply to a burgeoning international demand. Recently, smugglers took a page from the playbooks of collegiate binge drinkers, running their 300m pipeline down the throat of an Estonian border town en route from Rīga to Tallinn. The project was a smashing success (vodka costs 60% more in economically robust Estonia), until the international authorities busted the party and confiscated the hardware. What's next...a toga party?

## POLITICS

Internal politics remain turbulent, with numerous parties, including the **For Fatherland and Freedom Party,** the **People's Party,** and the **Latvian Way Party,** jockeying for position in the **Saeima** (Parliament). The office of Prime Minister has turned over rapidly as coalitions have come and gone—on April 12, 2000, Prime Minister Andris Skele resigned for the third time. The rapid political turnover, spurred in part by conflict over the pace of privatization of large government holdings in telecommunications and energy, has caused delays in economic reform. The current President, Vaira Vike-Freiberga, a psychology professor who spent most of her life in Canada, was elected in June 1999 after seven rounds of voting in the Saeima.

The **EU** was sufficiently satisfied with the progress of economic reform to add Latvia to its list of candidates for membership in December 1999, but if future reforms are slowed by domestic political woes the Latvian government could find itself at odds with both the EU and the IMF. Current Latvian timetables call for EU membership in 2003, but many observers expect that date to slip to 2004 or 2005.

Relations with **Russia** remain thorny. Tension flared especially over the Latvian State Language Law, which set stringent requirements for residents to gain proficiency in Latvian and for business to be conducted in Latvian. The law was seen by Moscow as undermining the rights of the large ethnic Russian population in Latvia, and the Russian Duma threatened, but did not enact, economic sanctions. Under pressure from both Russia and the EU, Latvia revised the bill.

## CULTURE

**NATIONAL HOLIDAYS**

| | |
|---|---|
| **January 1** New Year's | **June 23-4** Midsummer Celebrations |
| **April 13** Good Friday | **November 18** Independence Day |
| **April 15-16** Easter Sunday | **December 25** Christmas |
| **May 1** Labor Day | **December 31** New Year's Eve |

## LITERATURE

The legacy of the ancient Balts is powerful in Latvian literature. The **daina,** a folk song reflecting the pagan reverence of nature and a strong sense of ethics, has never left the Latvian memory. The first written literature, although late in coming, shows clear evidence of folk influence. The 17th-century poet **C. Fuereccerus** made use of the *daina*'s stylistic elements, while **G. Mancelius,** founder of Latvian prose, simultaneously fought good-naturedly against the influence of the pagan songs.

The mid-19th century brought a national awakening as the country asserted its literary independence. The *daina*'s spirit was reflected in *Lāčplēsis* (*Bearslayer*), **Andrējs Pumpurs's** 1888 national epic. Legend foretold that Pumpurs's hero would return to free Latvia, and believers say his 20th-century reappearance in the form of

**Māra Zālīte's** rock opera helped the cause. Realism and social protest became important with the arrival of the **New Movement** in the last years of the 19th century. **Jānis Rainis** used folk imagery to depict contemporary problems, while his wife, **Aspazija,** fought for women's rights.

New literary forms diversified Latvia's literature after the country achieved independence in 1918. **Jānis Akurāters's** romantic lyrics exhibit Nietzschean influence. Other poets, like **Kārlis Zariņš,** grappled with the aftermath of World War I. **Aleksandr Caks** used the ballad to caricature urban and suburban life, although his most outstanding work was *Marked by Eternity (Muzibas skartie),* a haunting cycle about the Latvian riflemen of World War I. Many Latvian writers turned to psychological detail in the 20th century: **Anslavs Eglitis** reveled in intensifying human traits to the point of absurdity.

Following World War II the Soviets imposed **Socialist Realism** on Latvian literature. Their censorship, however, failed to drown other trends. **Jānis Medenis,** exiled to a labor camp in Siberia, longed for a free Latvia in his poetry; **Imants Ziedonis** also managed to foster independent Latvian literature despite the authorities' tight censorship. **Martis Ziverts,** who wrote one-act plays, is generally regarded as the best 20th-century Latvian playwright.

# FOOD AND DRINK

Latvian food is heavy and starchy, but tasty. Big cities offer foreign cuisine, and Rīga is one of the easiest places to be a **vegetarian** in all the Baltics. Tasty national specialties include the holiday dish *zirņi* (gray peas with onions and smoked fat), *maizes zupa* (bread soup usually made from cornbread, and full of currants, cream, and other goodies), and the warming *Rīgas* (or *Melnais*) *balzams* (a black liquor great with ice cream, Coke, or coffee). Dark rye bread is a staple. Try *speķa rauši,* a warm pastry, or *biezpienmaize,* bread with sweet curds. Dark-colored *kaņepju sviests* (hemp butter) is good but too diluted for "medicinal" purposes. Latvian **beer,** primarily from the Aldaris brewery, is stellar, particularly *Porteris.*

# CUSTOMS AND ETIQUETTE

If a **tip** is expected where you're dining, it will most often be included in the bill. Expect to be bought a drink if you talk with someone a while; repay the favor in kind. If you're invited to a meal in someone's home, bring a **gift** for the hostess (an odd number of flowers is customary). **Shops** sometimes close for an hour or two between noon and 3pm. Rīga is the melting pot of the Baltics. Clubs catering to **gays and lesbians** advertise themselves as such freely, although attitudes are far less tolerant outside the city.

# LANGUAGE

Heavily influenced by German, Russian, Estonian, and Swedish, **Latvian** is one of two languages (the other is Lithuanian) in the Baltic language group. Life, however, proceeds bilingually. **Russian** is in disfavor in the countryside but universally spoken; it is much more acceptable and widespread in Riga. Many young Latvians study **English,** but don't rely on it. The older set know some **German.** *Alus* (beer) is a crucial word in any language. Key words include *autoosta* (bus station), *stacija* (train station), *lidosta* (airport), *viesnīca* (hotel), and *pasts* (post office). To find an English speaker ask, *"Vai jūs runāyat angliski?"* For common words and phrases, see **Glossary,** p. 388 and **Phrasebook,** p. 389.

# ADDITIONAL READING

See **Lithuania: Additional Reading** (p. 408) for a good survey of Baltic history. *The Testimony of Lives: Narrative and Memory in Post-Soviet Latvia* by Vieda Skultans eloquently examines the recent difficulties experienced by Latvians.

LATVIA

## GLOSSARY

| ENGLISH | LATVIAN | PRONOUNCE |
|---|---|---|
| one | viens | vee-yenz |
| two | divi | DIH-vih |
| three | trīs | treese |
| four | četri | CHEH-trih |
| five | pieci | PYET-sih |
| six | seši | SEH-shih |
| seven | septini | SEHP-tih-nyih |
| eight | astoņi | AHS-toh-nyih |
| nine | devini | DEH-vih-nyih |
| ten | desmit | DEZ-miht |
| twenty | divdesmit | DIHV-dehs-miht |
| fifty | piecdesmit | PEE-AHTS-dehs-miht |

| ENGLISH | LATVIAN | PRONOUNCE |
|---|---|---|
| one hundred | simts | sihmts |
| one thousand | tūkstots | TOOKS-twats |
| one-way | vienā virzienā | VEEA-nah VIR-zee-an-ah |
| round-trip | turp un atpakaļ | toorp oon AT-pakal |
| station | stacija | STAH-tsee-uh |
| grocery | pārtikas veikals | PAHR-tih-kas VEY-kalss |
| bread | maizi | MAI-zi |
| vegetables | dārzeņi | DAR-ze-nyih |
| coffee | kafija | KAH-fee-yah |
| beer | alus | AH-lus |
| left | pa kreisi | PAH kreh-ih-sih |
| right | pa labi | PAH lah-bih |

# TRAVELING ESSENTIALS

Irish, UK, and US citizens can visit Latvia for up to 90 days without a visa. Citizens of Australia, Canada, New Zealand, and South Africa require 90-day visas, obtainable at a Latvian consulate (see **Essentials: Embassies and Consulates,** p. 18). Travellers may obtain visas at the airport in Rīga, however these are valid for a maximum stay of 10 days. Single-entry visas cost US$15; multiple-entry cost US$30 to US$75; for 48-hr. processing the fee is doubled and for 24-hr. processing it is quadrupled. Allow ten days for standard processing. Send the application with your passport, one photograph, and payment by check or money order. Visas are not available at the border. For extensions, apply to the Department of Immigration and Citizenship (see **Rīga: Passport Office,** p. 393).

# TRANSPORTATION

**BY PLANE.** Flights to Latvia use **Rīga** airport. **Air Baltic, SAS, Finnair, Lufthansa,** and others make the hop to Rīga from their hubs.

**BY TRAIN.** Trains link Latvia to **Berlin, Moscow, St. Petersburg, Tallinn, Lviv, Odessa,** and **Vilnius.** Trains are cheap and efficient, but stations aren't well-marked, so get a map. The **suburban rail** system renders the entire country a suburb of Rīga. For daytrips from Rīga, you're best off taking the **electric train;** as a rule, a crowded train is more comfortable than a crowded bus.

**BY BUS.** Latvia's efficient long-distance bus network reaches Prague, Tallinn, Vilnius, and Warsaw. Buses, usually adorned with the driver's bizarre collection of Christian icons, stuffed animals, and stickers, are quicker than trains for travel within Latvia. Beware the standing-room-only long-distance jaunt.

**BY FERRY.** Ferries run to Rīga from Stockholm, Sweden and Kiel, Germany, but are slow and expensive.

**BY THUMB.** Hitchhiking is common, but hitchers may be expected to pay. *Let's Go* does not recommend hitchhiking.

## PHRASEBOOK

| ENGLISH | LATVIAN | PRONOUNCIATION |
| --- | --- | --- |
| Yes/no | Jā/nē | yah/ney |
| Please/You're welcome | Lūdzu | LOOD-zuh |
| Thank you | Paldies | PAHL-dee-yes |
| Hello | Labdien | LAHB-dyen |
| Good-bye | Uz redzēšanos | ooz RE-dzeh-shan-was |
| Good morning | Labrīt | LAHB-reet |
| Good night | Ar labu nakti | ar LA-boo NA-kti |
| Help! | Palīga! | PAH-lee-gah |
| When? | Kad? | KAHD |
| Where is...? | Kur ir...? | kuhr ihr |
| How do I get to...? | Kā es varu nokļūt uz...? | kah ess VA-roo NOkly-oot ooz |
| How much does this cost? | Cik maksā? | sikh MAHK-sah |
| Do you have...? | Vai jums ir...? | vai yoomss ir |
| Do you speak English? | Vai jūs runājat angliski? | vai yoos ROO-nah-yat AN-glee-ski |
| I don't understand. | Es nesaprotu. | ehs NEH-sah-proh-too |
| I'd like to order... | Es vēlos... | ess VE-lwass |
| I'd like to pay/We'd like to pay. | Lūdzu rēķinu. | LOOD-zu RAY-tyi-noo |
| Do you have a vacancy? | Vai jums ir brīvas istabas? | vai yums ir BREE-vas IS-tab-as |
| May I see the room? | Vai es varu redzēt istabu? | vay ehss VAH-roo REHD-zeht IHS-tah-boo |
| Will you tell me when to get off? | Lūdzu pasakiet, kad jāizkāpj? | LOOD-zoo pah-sah-kee-aht, kahd YAH-IHS-kah-pye |
| I want a ticket to... | Es vēlos biļeti uz... | ehss VAAL-wass BIHL-yet-ih ooz |

# TOURIST SERVICES AND MONEY

| CURRENCY | | |
| --- | --- | --- |
| US$1 = 0.61LS (LATS) | | 1LS = US$1.60 |
| CDN$1 = 0.41LS | | 1LS = CDN$2.40 |
| UK£1 = 0.89LS | | 1LS = UK£1.10 |
| IR£1 = 0.69LS | | 1LS = IR£1.40 |
| AUS$1 = 0.35LS | | 1LS = AUS$2.80 |
| NZ$1 = 0.26LS | | 1LS = NZ$3.80 |
| SAR1 = 0.09LS | | 1LS = SAR 11 |
| DM1 = 0.28LS | | 1LS = DM 3.60 |

Look for the green "i" marking some tourist offices, which are rather scarce. Private tourist offices such as **Patricia** are much more helpful.

The Latvian currency unit is the **Lat. Inflation** averages around 4%. There are many **ATMs** in Rīga linked to Cirrus, MC, and Visa, and at least one or two in larger towns. Larger businesses, restaurants and hotels accustomed to Westerners accept **MC** and **Visa. Traveler's checks** are harder to use; both AmEx and Thomas Cook can be converted in Rīga, but Thomas Cook is a safer bet outside the capital. It's often difficult to exchange currencies other than US dollars and Deutschmarks.

# HEALTH AND SAFETY

**Bathrooms** are marked with an upward-pointing triangle for women, downward for men. Latvians claim that Rīga **tap water** is drinkable, but boil it for 10 minutes to be safe. **Bottled water** is available at grocery stores and kiosks, although it is usually carbonated. **Pharmacies** are well-stocked with German brands of tampons, condoms, and band-aids. Most **restrooms** require you to bring your own toilet paper. If you feel threatened, *"Ej prom"* (EY prawm) means "go away"; *"Lasies prom"* (LAH-see-oos PRAWM) says it more offensively, and *"Lasies lapās"* (LAH-see-oos LAH-pahs; "go to the leaves"), poetic though it may be, is even ruder. You are more likely to find English-speaking help from your **consulate** than from the police.

## ACCOMMODATIONS

College dormitories, which open to travelers in the summer, are often the cheapest places to sleep. In Rīga, **Patricia** arranges homestays and apartment rentals for around US$15 per night (see **Rīga: Tourist Offices**, p. 392). Many towns have only one **hotel** (if any) in the budget range; expect to pay 3-15Ls per night.

## KEEPING IN TOUCH

Latvia is by far the most difficult of the Baltic states from which to call the US; there's no way to make a free call on a Latvian phone to an international operator. Most telephones take **cards** (available in 2, 3, 5, or 10Lt denominations) from post offices, telephone offices, and large state stores. Try to make **international** calls from a telephone office, although they may simply sell you a phonecard for a booth. Access numbers include **AT&T Direct,** ☎700 70 07 in Rīga, ☎827 00 70 07 otherwise, and **MCI,** ☎800 88 88. The gradual switch to digital phones has made making a connection comparable to cracking a safe—sometimes you must dial a 2 before a number, sometimes a 7, and sometimes an 8 from an analog phone. To call abroad from an analog phone, dial 1, then 00, then the country code. From a digital phone, simply dial 00, then the country code. Phone offices and *Rīga in Your Pocket* have the latest information on phone system changes.

Ask for *gaisa pastu* if you want to send something by **airmail.** The standard rate for a letter abroad is 0.40Ls; for a postcard 0.30Ls. **Mail** can be received general delivery through **Poste Restante.** Address envelope as follows: Jennifer (First name) O'BRIEN (LAST NAME), POSTE RESTANTE, Stacijas laukums 1 (Post office address), Riga (City) LV-1050 (Postal code), LATVIA. **Email** is only available in Rīga.

# RĪGA                                                      ☎(8)2

> Huge, restless, alluring and slippery, Riga remains a city without a handle, forever eluding the grasp of the terms and powers that have sought to contain it.
> —David Beecher

The self-proclaimed capital of the Baltics, sprawling Rīga (pop. 874,000) feels strangely out of proportion as the capital of small, struggling Latvia. More Westernized and cosmopolitan than the rest of the country, Rīga envisions itself as the "Paris of the East," a city of fascinating museums, architectural splendor, and diplomatic importance. True, the city is more urbane and cultured than either Tallinn or Vilnius, and the *Jugendstil* buildings are stunning, but it nonetheless feels more like Las Vegas than Paris, with 24-hour casinos on every street, showgirls parading through posh hotels and cabarets, and the tell-tale tinted windows of German luxury automobiles. In the last nine years, both Rīga and Latvia have been coping with rebuilding, new political and economic systems, and at long last testing out what it means to be Latvian. While the city has a long way to go to becoming a major European capital, it has established a new identity as the cultural and social center of the Baltics. Like the freedom monument in the center of the city, Rīga stands above her surging and seedy streets with allusive and optimistic majesty.

LATVIA

**800 BOTTLES OF BEER ON THE WALL.** If you've ever considered heading to the Baltics' flashy center of fast cars and faster women, 2001 is the year to go as Riga celebrates her 800th birthday in high style. The festival schedules for 2001 aren't yet set, but rest assured they will include music, gambling, and enormous amounts of beer. Check out the official web site at www.riga800.lv. Need another reason to party? 2001 also marks 10 years of Latvian independence from Soviet rule.

## ✈ TRANSPORTATION

**Flights: Lidosta Rīga** (Rīga Airport; ☎720 70 09, 8km southwest of Vecrīga (Old Riga). Take bus #22 from Gogol iela (0.20Ls). **Air Baltic** (☎720 74 01; airbaltic@mail.bkc.lv) flies to many European capitals. **Lufthansa** (☎721 71 83; fax 720 70 26) flies to **Frankfurt, Finnair** (☎720 70 10; fax 720 77 55) to **Helsinki.**

**Trains: Centrālā Stacija** (Central Station), Stacijas laukums (☎583 30 95), down the street from the bus station. Housed in 2 buildings; long-distance trains depart from the larger building, to the left as you face the station. Departures (atiešanas) on the board to the right as you enter. To reach **Berlin, GER** and **Warsaw, POL** on the Baltic Express, you must go via Vilnius. To: **Vilnius, LIT** (8hr., 1 per day, *coupé* 14Ls); **St. Petersburg, RUS** (13hr., 1 per day, *coupé* 26Ls); and **Moscow, RUS** (15½hr., 2 per day, *coupé* 32Ls). **Suburban trains,** running as far as the Estonian border at **Valka/Valga,** leave from the smaller building. The Lugaži line includes **Cēsis** and **Sigulda.** Buy same-day tickets in the halls and advance ones in the **booking office** (☎583 33 97) off the right side of the suburban hall. Open M-Sa 8am-7pm, Su 8am-6pm.

**Buses: Bus station** (Autoosta), Prāgas 1, (☎721 36 11). 200m from the train station in the direction of the Daugava River along Prāgas iela, across the canal from the central market. Open daily 5am-midnight. To: **Tallinn, EST** (5-6hr., 7 per day, 6-7Ls); **Vilnius, LIT** (6hr., 3 per day, 6Ls); **Kaunas, LIT** (7hr., 2 per day, 5-6Ls); and **Minsk, BLR** (10hr., 2 per day, 6.90Ls). Book buses to **Warsaw, POL** (14hr., 1 per day, 15Ls) and **Prague, CZR** (30hr., 1 per week, 38Ls) through **Eurolines** (☎721 40 80; fax 750 31 34), at the bus station right of the ticket windows. Open M-F 8am-7pm, Sa 9am-6pm.

**Public Transportation: Buses, trams,** and **trolleybuses** run 5:30am-12:30am. Buy tickets on board. 0.20Ls.

**Taxis:** Private taxis have a green light in the windshield. **Taxi Rīga** (☎800 10 10; taxi@parks.lv) charges 0.30Ls per km during the day, 0.40Ls per km at night.

**Car Rental: Europcar Interrent,** Basteja bul. 10 (☎721 26 52; fax 782 03 60), rents Opels for US$96 per day. Open daily 9am-11pm.

## ✷ ORIENTATION

The city is neatly divided in half by **Brīvības bulvāris,** which leads from the outskirts to the **Freedom Monument** in the center, continuing through **Vecrīga** (Old Riga) as **Kaļķu iela.** With the trains behind you, turn left onto Marijas iela and right onto one of the small streets beyond the canal to reach Vecrīga. *Rīga In Your Pocket* (0.60Ls), available at kiosks and travel agencies, provides a comprehensive list of the city's sites. The informative *The City Paper—The Baltic States,* available in the same places (US$1.50), covers current and cultural events in English.

## 🛈 PRACTICAL INFORMATION

### TOURIST AND FINANCIAL SERVICES

**Tourist Offices:** The good-humored, multilingual staff at **Patricia,** Elizabetes iela 22-26, 3rd Fl. (☎728 48 68, after hours ☎925 67 31; fax 728 66 50; tourism@parks.lv; www.rigalatvia.net), 2 blocks from the train station, arranges homestays in Vecrīga (US$15 per person; breakfast US$5), and rent apartments (US$45 per night; min. 3 night stay). They can also help with Russian visas (6 days US$80). Open M-F 9:15am-8pm, Sa-Su 10:15am-1pm.

**Passport Office:** For a visa extension, go to the **Department of Immigration and Citizenship,** Raiņa bulv. 5 (☎ 721 91 81; fax 782 01 56).

**Embassies: Belarus,** Jēzusbaznīcas 12 (☎ 732 25 50; fax 732 28 91). Open M-F 8:30am-5pm. **Canada,** Doma laukums 4, 3rd and 4th fl. (☎ 722 63 15; fax 783 01 40; canembr@bkc.lv). Open M-F 9am-3pm. **Estonia,** Skolas iela 13 (☎ 781 20 20; fax 781 20 29). Open M-Tu and Th-F 10am-1pm. **Lithuania,** Rūpniecības iela 24 (☎ 732 15 19; fax 732 15 89). Open M-F 9:30am-12:30pm. **Russia,** Antonijas iela 2 (☎ 721 25 79; fax 783 02 09), entrance on Kalpaka bulv. Open M-F 9am-5:30pm. **Ukraine,** Kalpaka bulv. 3 (☎ 724 30 82; fax 732 55 83). Open M-F 10:30am-12:30pm. **UK,** Alunāna iela 5 (☎ 733 81 26; fax 733 81 32). Open M-F 9am-1pm and 2-5pm. **US,** Raiņa bulv. 7 (☎ 721 00 05; fax 782 00 47). Open M-F 9am-noon and 2-4pm.

**Financial Services:** At any of the innumerable **Valutos Maiņa** kiosks or shops in the city. **Unibanka,** Kaļķu iela 13, gives MC/Visa **cash advances** for a 4% commission and cashes AmEx and Thomas Cook **traveler's checks** for a 3% commission. Open M-F 9am-9pm, Sa 9am-6pm. **24hr. exchange desks** are at branches at Basteja bulv. 14, Brīvības 30, and Merķeļa 10. Cirrus/Plus **ATMs** are popping up all over.

**American Express:** There is a representative at **Latvia Tours,** Kaļķu iela 8 (☎ 708 50 01; fax 782 00 20). Open M-F 9am-6pm.

## LOCAL SERVICES

**Luggage Storage:** In the **bus station,** on guarded racks near the Eurolines office (0.20Ls per 10kg for 2hr.). Open daily 6:30am-10:30pm. At the **train station** lockers (0.60Ls) are in the tunnel under the long-distance tracks. Open daily 5am-1am.

**Bookstore: Globuss,** Vaļņuiela 26 (☎ 722 69 57). Good selection of English novels and classics. Open M-F 9am-7pm, Sa 10am-6pm. MC/Visa. **Jāņa Rozes,** Kr. Baronas iela 5. Open M-F 10am-7pm, Sa 10am-5pm. MC/Visa. **Rastāmlietas Grāmatas Bērniem,** Elizabetes iela 85 (☎ 728 66 36), through a courtyard and on the right. English fiction on the 1st floor. Open M-F 10am-7pm, Sa 10am-5pm.

**Bi-Gay-Lesbian Services:** Puškina 1a (☎ 951 95 51; info@gay.lv). Open 9am-11pm; call before stopping by.

**Laundromat: Miele,** Elizabetes iela 85a (☎ 721 76 96), in the courtyard opposite the bookstore. Groaning machines take almost 2hr. to wash a load, so plan ahead. Wash 1.95Ls; dry 0.70Ls. Overnight full service 4.10Ls per load. Open 24hr. MC/Visa.

## EMERGENCY AND COMMUNICATIONS

**Pharmacies: Grindex,** Audēju 20 (☎ 721 33 40). Open M-F 8am-9pm, Sa 9am-5pm. MC/Visa. Late at night, try the **24hr. Mēness aptieka,** Brīvības 121 (☎ 737 78 89).

**Telephone Office:** Brīvības bulv. 19 (☎ 701 87 38). Smaller office at post office by the train station. Open 24hr. Cirrus/MC/Visa **ATM.**

 The phone code in Riga is 2 for all 6-digit numbers; there is no phone code for 7-digit numbers.

**Internet Access: Internet Club,** Kaļķu iela 10, 2nd fl. (☎ 750 35 95). This internet addict's dream is open 24hrs. 1.80Ls per hr. **Latnet,** Raiņa 29 (☎ 721 12 41). 0.22Ls per hr. Open M-Th 9am-6pm, F 9am-5pm. Other internet cafes are popping up all along Elizabetes iela, generally open noon-10pm for 1.80Ls per hr.

**Post Offices:** Stacijas laukums 1 (☎ 701 88 04), near the train station. **Poste Restante** service at window #2. Open M-F 8am-7pm, Sa-Su 8am-4pm.

**Postal code:** LV-1050.

## ACCOMMODATIONS

Rīga's prices for decent rooms are the highest in the Baltics. If you are interested in a private room, try **Patricia** (see **Tourist Offices,** p. 392).

**Arena,** Palasta iela 5 (☎ 722 85 83). The cheapest place in town, Arena hides in an unmarked building by Dome Cathedral. Hall shower and kitchen; some rooms have sinks. Beautiful views of Vecrīga. Open Apr.-Oct. (the rest of the year circus performers live here). 3- to 4-bed dorms 4Ls.

**Studentu Kopmītne** (Student Dormitories), Basteja bulv. 10 (☎721 62 21). From the bus station, cross under the railroad tracks and take the pedestrian tunnel under the highway. Bear right onto Aspazijei bul., which becomes Basteja bul. Enter through the Europcar Interrent office on the edge of Vecrīga. Run by the University of Latvia for guest lecturers. Make reservations early. Great location in Vecrīga. Midnight curfew. Call ahead. 4-5Ls per person; with private bath 8-9Ls.

**Saulite,** Merķela iela 12 (☎722 45 46), directly across from the train station. Spiral seafoam-green staircase branches off to clean rooms and communal toilets. Spartan 1930s-style rooms with TVs and minutes away from Vecrīga. English spoken. Singles 6Ls, with bath 16Ls; doubles 10Ls, 20Ls; triples 9Ls, 25Ls. Shared shower 0.40Ls. MC.

**Viktorija,** A. Čaka iela 55 (☎701 41 11; fax 701 41 40; reservations@hotel-viktorija.lv; www.hotel-viktorija.lv). 8 blocks from the trains on Marijas iela (which becomes Čaka iela), or 2 stops on trolleybus #11 or 18. Newly renovated rooms with private bath, TV, and fridge, as well as cheaper rooms with hallway toilets. Singles 8-9Ls, with bath 26Ls; doubles 10-12Ls, 38Ls. Breakfast included. MC/Visa.

# ◔ FOOD

Look for 24hr. food and liquor stores along Elizabetes, Marijas, and Gertrūdes iela. The 24hr. **Interpegro,** Raiņa bulv. 33 (☎722 90 44), stocks liquor, water, and produce. Occupying five immense zeppelin hangars behind the bus station, **Centrālais Tirgus** (Central Market) is one of the largest in Europe. It has the best selection at the cheapest prices, but remember to haggle. (Open M-Sa 8am-5pm, Su 8am-3pm.)

**Alus Arsenāls,** Pils Laukums 4 (☎732 38 96). Descend from the entrance on Arsenāla, marked by a bursting keg of *alus* over the door, down into an oak lodge-styled interior, or sit on the deck outside. Serves excellent, inexpensive Latvian cuisine. Service is faster inside. Main dishes 3-4.50Ls. Open daily 11am-midnight. MC.

**Nostalgia,** Kaļķu 22 (☎722 23 38), about 250m from the freedom monument. Dine in high bourgeois style surrounded by Soviet murals glorifying the revolution. That sound? Marx and Lenin spinning in their graves. Ample main dishes from 4Ls, but less expensive starters can be meals in themselves. Open 10am-2pm; disco Th-Sa 7pm-5am.

**Lido Bistro,** Elizabetes 65 (☎722 13 18). Cafeteria dining and a large, tiled interior somehow add up to one of the most popular fast-food places in Rīga. Come early or late to beat the crowds. Greasy but decent Latvian meals 2-3.50Ls. Open daily 8am-11pm.

**Kirbis** (Pumpkin), Doma laukums 1 (☎949 54 09), directly across from the Dome Cathedral. A treat for vegetarians, with outstanding eggplant and mushroom dishes, served cafeteria-style. Funky stone and wood surroundings—note the cave-paintings of hunters and the hunted. Main dishes 2-4Ls. Open M-F 9am-11pm, Sa-Su 10am-11pm.

**Tower,** Smilšu 7 (☎721 61 55). An elegant international menu with offerings from fettuccine alfredo to T-bone steak. Eat outdoors or dine in the medieval tower. Prices are moderate, but beware the hidden extras: 10% service charge and a whopping 0.60Ls for small glasses of water. Main dishes 5-10Ls. Open M-F 11am-1am, Sa-Su noon-1am.

**Rozamunde,** Maza Smilsu 8 (☎722 77 98), 1 block off Filharmonija laukums. Many foreigners dine at this small, elegant restaurant, which serves ample portions of Latvian cuisine. Sample the air of 1920s Rīga and recipes preserved from the 17th century. Live jazz nightly. Main dishes 8-16Ls. Open M-F 11am-11pm, Sa-Su noon-11pm.

# ◉ SIGHTS

Most of Rīga's sights lie densely clustered in Vecrīga, but even the "modern" parts of town generally date from the mid-19th century and offer architectural pearls of their own. An exploration of Vecrīga should begin with the towering Freedom Monument, then branch out slowly to the side streets and hidden sights.

**FREEDOM MONUMENT.** (Brivibas Piemineklis.) The beloved monument stands in the center of the city. "Milda," as she is affectionately known, stands upon her towering obelisk raising her arms skyward, as three gold stars seem to levitate above her fingertips. She was dedicated in 1935, during Latvia's brief tenure as an independent republic. To survive the subsequent Russian occupation, Milda masqueraded as a Soviet symbol; Intourist used to explain that the mighty figure represented Mother Russia supporting the three Baltic states. (It actually shows Liberty raising up the three main regions of Latvia—Vidzeme, Latgale, and Kurzeme.) Two steadfast honor guards protect Milda 9am-6pm; the changing of the guard occurs every hour on the hour. *(At the corner of Raiņa bul. and Brīvības iela.)*

**BASTEJKALNS.** The central park of the region inside the old city moat (Pilsētas kanāls), Bastejkalns houses ruins of the old city walls. Across and around the canal, five red stone slabs stand as **memorials** to the dead of January 20, 1991, when Soviet special forces stormed the Interior Ministry on Raiņa bul. The dead included a schoolboy and two cameramen recording the events. At the north end of Bastejkalns, on K. Valdemāra iela, two sculptured men bear the weight of the **National Theater** on their shoulders. It was here that Latvia first declared its independence on November 18, 1918. *(☎ 732 29 23. Open daily 10am-7pm.)*

**DOME SQUARE.** Vecrīga's cobblestoned central square may feel timelessly serene, but in fact it only dates from 1936; Latvian prime minister Kārlis Ulmanis (see **History,** p. 384) created the square by tearing down acoustically offensive buildings so his voice could be heard during a speech. On the far side of the square stands Rīga's centerpiece, **Dome Cathedral** (Doma baznīca), begun in 1226. The largest in the Baltics, the cathedral once boasted a collection of gorgeous stained-glass windows—only 12, however, survived the bombing of World War II. The immense pipe organ contains 6,768 pipes ranging from 7mm to 10 meters in height. *(Proceed down Kaļķu iela from the Freedom Monument, then turn right on Šķūņu iela. ☎ 721 32 13. Cathedral open Tu-F 1-5pm, Sa 10am-2pm. 0.50Ls. Camera 2Ls. Concerts (☎ 961 85 95) W at 7pm.)*

**ST. PETER'S CHURCH.** (Sv. Pētera baznīca). Towering above Rīga, St. Peter's dark spire is visible throughout the city. First built in 1209, the church as it is now dates from 1408. Its tower, for a long time the largest in Europe, hasn't been as lucky, catching fire several times throughout the centuries. Destroyed again by artillery fire during World War II, it was rebuilt, complete with an elevator, in the 70s. From the top of the 123m spire, you can see the entire city and the Baltic. *(Proceed down Kaļķu iela from the Freedom Monument, then turn left on Skāmu iela. Open Tu-Su 10am-7pm. Church free; tower 1.50Ls, students 1Ls; exhibitions 0.50Ls, students 0.30Ls.)*

**ST. JOHN'S CHURCH.** (Sv. Jāņa baznīca). This small 1297 church was built by Dominicans but taken over by Lutherans after the Reformation in 1582. It also served a stint as an armory. Through an alleyway on the left, **St. John's Courtyard** (Jāņa sēta) is the oldest populated site in Rīga; part of the old city wall is preserved here. *(Skāmu iela on the corner with Jāņa iela. ☎ 722 40 28. Open 11am-6pm.)*

**THE THREE CEMETERIES.** On the south end of **Mežaparks** lie the three main cemeteries of Rīga, powerful symbols of the struggle for Latvian nationhood. **Brothers' Cemetery** (Brāļu Kapi) is dedicated to soldiers who fell during the World Wars and the 1918-20 struggle for independence. The poet Jānis Rainis rests in the smaller **Rainis Cemetery** (Rainis Kapi), along with other nationalists, literary figures, and important Communists of the last 50 years. **Forest Cemetery** (Meža Kapi) is a peaceful area. *(Take tram #11 to Braļu Kapi, 11 stops from the starting point at the train station.)*

---

## THE BOY WHO CRIED "NAPOLEON!" In 1812,

Rīga was devastated by a single herd of cattle. Traveling happily through the countryside, the nefarious bovines raised a cloud of dust that was clearly visible to the city's residents. Believing the herd to be Napoleon's army, the people set fire to the city, razing 740 buildings and hundreds of acres of farmland. The citizens later realized that the fearsome marauders were really only looking for grass and a good human to milk them. Meanwhile, Napoleon entered via a different route, wreaking his own havoc.

LATVIA

**SOVIET SIGHTS.** Outside the Occupation Museum stands the **Latvian Rifleman Monument,** three granite soldiers guarding the square. Dedicated during Soviet times, the figures honor the crack team of Latvian riflemen who served as Lenin's bodyguards after the revolution. The statue was one of the few Soviet monuments not torn down, since the Rifleman gained fame in the fight for Latvia in World War I, but some still would like to see the statue go. More insulting to the eyes, if not Latvian national pride, is the orange tiered tower of the **Academy of Sciences.** Nicknames for the building range from "the Kremlin" to "Stalin's birthday cake."

# 🏛 MUSEUMS

Some of the best museums of 20th-century Baltic history are in Rīga, ensuring that the horror of war and occupation does not fade too quickly from memory.

🏛 **Occupation Museum** (Okupācijas muzejs), Strēlnieku laukums 1 (☎721 27 15), in the appropriately black-walled building behind the Latvian Rifleman statue. The finest museum in the Baltics. Top-notch exhibits with multilingual explanations in excruciating detail—allow several hours to see it all. The initial Soviet occupation is depicted so vividly that you can almost hear the Red Army marching. Walk through the reconstructed gulag barrack. Open daily 11am-5pm. Free.

🏛 **Latvian Museum of War** (Latvijas kara muzejs), Smilšu iela 20 (☎722 81 47). From the freedom monument, walk into Vecrīga, turning right on Valņu iela. Located inside Powder Tower, with nine cannonballs still lodged in its 14th-century walls; it's not clear why they're on the side facing the city. Rīga's most interesting military site, this huge museum jams the history of war, from the Middle Ages to the present, into 8 floors. Open Tu-Su 10am-6pm. 0.50Ls, students 0.25Ls. English tours 3Ls. Camera 2Ls.

**Motor Museum** (Rīgas Motormuzejs), Eizenšteina 6. Take bus #21 from the even-numbered side of Brīvības iela to the suburbs and get out at the Pansionāts stop in the Mežciems region. Walk right and follow the street which bears left (Eizenšteina). This highly-touted museum has a wacky collection of cars and related objects old and new, including Stalin's 7-ton armored Chaika limousine and Brezhnev's crashed Rolls Royce Silver Shadow, complete with wax test-dummies of the former dictators. (Note the look on Brezhnev's face as he collides with a truck.) Allow at least 1 hr. Open Apr.-Oct. M 10am-3pm, Tu-Su 10am-6pm. 1Ls.

**Open-Air Ethnographic Museum** (Etnogrāfiskais brīvdabas muzejs) Brīvības g. 440 (☎799 41 06), on the shores of Juglas Ezers (Juglas Lake). Take tram #6 from Aspazijas iela in front of the freedom monument to the end of the line. Walk across the bridge and turn right onto Brīvības iela. The collection includes nearly 100 18th- and 19th-century buildings from all over Latvia, and features artists and craftsmen churning out their traditional wares. Open daily May-Oct. 10am-5pm. 2Ls, students 1Ls.

# 🎵 ENTERTAINMENT

For centuries Rīga has prided itself as one of the cultural hotspots of Eastern Europe. Today it still offers the best and widest array of musical and performance art in the Baltics—except in the off-season, mid-June through August. Check out the Opera House or Dome Cathedral for summer special events. The **Latvian National Opera** performs in the **Opera House,** Aspazijas bulv. 3 (☎722 58 03; fax 722 82 40), where Richard Wagner once presided as director. The **Latvian Symphony Orchestra** (☎722 48 50) has frequent concerts in the Great and Small Guilds off Filharmonija laukums. Smaller ensembles perform throughout the summer in **Wagner Hall** (Vāgnera zāle; Vāgnera iela 4; ☎721 08 14). At the Dome Cathedral, popular organ concerts (ērģeļmūzikas koncerts) employ the world's 3rd-largest organ. Buy tickets at Doma laukums 1, opposite the main entrace at *koncertzales kase.* (☎721 34 98. Open daily noon-3pm and 4-7pm.) The **Rīga Ballet** carries on the proud dancing tradition of native star Mikhail Baryshnikov.

The **ticket offices** at Teātra 10/12 (☎722 57 47; open daily 10am-7pm) and Amatu iela 6 (☎721 37 98 and 722 36 18), on the 1st floor of the Great Guild, cover nearly all concerts in Rīga.

Rīga has several **cinemas,** including the magnificent **Kino "Rīga,"** Elizabetes iela 61, which shows American films with Latvian and Russian subtitles. (☎728 11 05. Tickets 1.90Ls; Tu 1Ls). Check the paper *Diena* for local listings.

#  NIGHTLIFE

The rebellious socialite of the Baltics, Rīga thrives to jive every day of the week, scoffing at your need for sleep and the summer sun—dawn at 3am marks the mid-point of Rīga's nightlife. Waste hours and money at the ever-multiplying 24hr. casi-nos or dance the night away at the *diskotekas*. The social scene is centered in **Vecrīga.** Be careful, as some of the big and bad of Rīga hang out in some of the shad-iest, and most popular, areas of town. Be prepared to take a taxi.

## PUBS AND BARS

**Paddy Whelan's,** Grēcineku iela 4 (☎721 02 49). Rīga's first Irish pub. Fast-flowing beer sates a noisy crowd of local students, backpackers and expats. The party spills into the streets during the Euro League Football season—every match is shown on the wide-screen TV. Guinness 1.50Ls. Open Su-Th 10am-midnight, F-Sa 10am-2am. MC/Visa.

**Ala** (Cave), Audēju iela 11 (☎722 39 57). Go through a glass door and walk through the building to the steps on the right. Subscribes to the "ant colony" school of bar design—tunnels and stairways connect little rooms of pool tables (2Ls per hr.), bars, slot machines, and young cave-dwellers. *Aldaris* 0.80Ls. Open daily 1pm-2am. MC/Visa.

**Pulkuedim Neviens Neraksta** (Nobody Speaks to the Colonel), Peldu 26/28 (☎721 38 86). A recently renovated refuge from the world of Russian and American techno. At night, trendy youth pack the backlit steel bridge, and a few even dance to the "alterna-tive" (mainstream American rock) sounds. After 9pm, 1Ls cover Sa, 2Ls F. Open Su-Th noon-3am, F-Sa noon-5am.

## CLUBS AND DISCOS

**Vernisāža,** Tērbatas 2 (☎709 24 00). Rīga's favorite club is set to carry its nightlife to infinity...and beyond. Descend the glass stairway into a smokey inferno complete with space-age lights and lasers, a moving stainless steel dance floor, and a rising central pedestal that takes dancers higher. Cover 5Ls. Open W-Su 11pm-6am.

**Hamlet Club,** Jāņa Sēta 5 (☎722 99 38), in the heart of Vecrīga. Hosts the excellent Latvian Raubiško jazz ensemble M and Su nights at 9pm. Call ahead to reserve a table. The club hosts a musical cabaret by Kārlis Streips every other Th, as well as the occa-sional open-mike night. Open daily 7pm-5am.

**Groks Stacija,** Kaļķu iela 22, near the Freedom Monument (☎721 63 81). The disco downstairs is meant to evoke a Metro stop, complete with fluorescent graffiti. Instead of elevator music, techno pulses throughout the club to the delight of tireless hipsters. *Aldaris* 0.70Ls. Open daily noon-6am.

**Underground,** Slokas 1 (☎761 54 56). One of the more popular clubs in Rīga, but the trek across the river from Vecrīga should not be made alone. Cover 3Ls. M, W-Th, and Sa 20+; F students only. Open M-F 9pm-6am, Sa 9pm-8am.

## BI-GAY-LESBIAN NIGHTLIFE

**Purvs,** Matīsa 60/62. No signs, so just walk down the hall and inside. Neon-and-techno madness, with the air of being the cool place to be. Cover 0.50-1.50Ls. Open M and W-Sa 8pm-6am.

**Teritorija,** A. Kalniņa 8. Go into the drive and turn left. The fabulous lights and fun tunes make up for the somewhat sketchy decor. Mainly a male locale. Cover 2Ls. Open daily 6pm-5am.

LATVIA

# ▐ DAYTRIPS FROM RĪGA

## ▨ SALASPILS MEMORIAL

*Green electric trains run to Dārziņi (20-30min., 14 per day, 0.30Ls). Make sure the train will be stopping at Dārziņi before leaving Rīga. Do not take the train to "Salaspils."*

The Salaspils Memorial marks the remains of the Kurtenhof concentration camp, which claimed 100,000 victims during World War II. The inscription over the entrance reads, "Beyond this gate the earth moans." Four clusters of massive sculptures—Motherhood, Solidarity, The Humiliated and The Unbroken—watch over the Way of the Suffering, the circular path connecting barrack foundations in which flowers now grow. A black box emits a low ticking, like the pulse of a beating heart.

## ▨ PILSRUNDĀLE ☎ (8)239

*Take the bus to Bauska, (1¾hr., express 1¼hr.; 22 per day, last bus 8:20pm; 1.20Ls); then change to the bus to Jelgava and ask the driver to drop you off at "Pilsrundāle" (25min., 8-10 per day, 0.30Ls). From there, go left at the big Pilsrundāle sign and walk 1.5km. The palace is around a hedge to the left. Before leaving Bauska, ask for the times of returning buses. Ticket office ☎ 622 74. Open May-Oct. W-Su 10am-6pm, Nov.-Apr. 10am-5pm. 2Ls, students 1Ls, camera 3Ls. English guidebook 1.20Ls. 1½-2hr. info-packed tours 3Ls for a group; call ☎ 621 97 to arrange in advance.*

Located in the heart of the Latvian countryside, the magnificent **Rundāles Palace** (Rundāles pils) long served as a summer retreat for Baltic, Russian, and German nobility. In the late 18th century, **Ernst Johann von Bühren** employed 15,000 laborers and artisans to build his stately pleasure dome, a maze of 138 gilded ballrooms and cavernous halls. Bartolomeo Rastrelli, the Italian master who also planned St. Petersburg's Winter Palace (see p. 649), designed the palace in 1736; it wasn't until 1768 that the interior wall decorations were completed by Johann Michael Graff under the patronage of Catherine the Great.

The motto under the eagle guarding the East Wing, "Faithfulness and Jealousy," captures the story of its construction. Empress-to-be Anna married Frederick, Duke of Courland, who was bringing her to his estate in Jelgeva when he died en route. Abandoned among peasants, Anna was taken in by Von Bühren (Bīrons in Latvian), a local noble who became her adviser and lover. When she became Empress in 1727, Von Bühren suddenly found himself a rather wealthy count with the means to build an architectural symbol of his power.

At the top of the grand staircase is the **Gold Room** (Zelta Zāle), the marble and gold-leaf home to the throne, with dramatic murals and soldiers' graffiti from 1812. The **White Room** (Baltā Zāle) was the ballroom; cherubs represent the four seasons and the four elements. It'll cost you more, but the exhibit of art recovered from churches brutalized by the Soviets is worthwhile.

## SAULKRASTI

*Take the commuter train (1hr., 1-2 per hr., 0.54Ls) to the Saulkrasti train station (☎ 95 13 37), a large, pale yellow building, which also serves as the bus station (☎ 95 15 51). The station borders a paved road, Alfrēda Kalniņa iela (it becomes Raiņa iela), which leads to the center of Pētrupe; follow it left out of the station, past the cemetery. For the beach, follow Raiņa past Unibanka into the woods.*

Saulkrasti, formed by the confluence of the Neibāde, Pēterupe, and Katrinbāde villages, is a quiet seaside town of about 5000. Tranquil waves roll across dark, thick sand, creating a quieter and more secluded shoreline than in crowded Jūrmala. More and more beachgoers discover Saulkrasti every year, but it's still ideal for relaxing by the Gulf of Rīga. A seaside picnic is the way to go for lunch; stock up at **grocery store "Giva,"** where Raiņa iela meets Ainažu iela at Ainažu 8. (☎ 95 12 76. Open 24hr. MC.) For prepared food, the **LN Saulkrasti Kafejnīca** at the corner of Rīgas iela (Ainažu becomes Rīgas) and Murjāņu iela serves chicken filet for 1.80Ls and salad for 0.70Ls along with *Aldaris* for 0.50Ls. (☎ 514 88. Open noon-2am. MC.)

## JŪRMALA REGION ☎(8)7

*The commuter rail runs 1 train every 30min. in both directions from 5am-11:30pm. Trips to Majori take 30 min. and cost 0.40Ls. Public buses (18 santīmi) and microbuses (0.20-0.30Ls) string together Jūrmala's towns.*

Sun-bleached, powder-fine sand, warm waters and festive boardwalks have drawn crowds since the late 19th century to this narrow spit of sand 20km from the capital between the Gulf of Rīga and the Lielupe River. Towns dot the coast; from Rīga, beachless Priedaine is the first train stop in Jūrmala; the tracks then pass over the Lielupe river and quickly run through Lielupe, Bulduri, Dzintari, Majori, Dubulti, Jaundubulti, Pumpuri, Melluži, Asari, and Vaivari before heading back inland to Sloka, Kudra, and Ķemeri. In 1959, 14 of the towns were incorporated into the giant city-resort Jūrmala (YOUR-ma-la; pop. 60,000). It became a popular summer resort with the Soviet elite and as a result Latvian independence dealt quite a blow to the local economy. Nonetheless, Jūrmala is swiftly recovering as crowds of tourists rediscover its beaches and shops.

Any of the towns between **Bulduri** and **Dubulti** are popular for sunning and swimming, but if you're looking for Jūrmala's social center, go to **Majori**. Trainloads of people file to the beach or wander along **Jomas iela**, lined with cafes, restaurants, and shops. From the train station, cross the road, walk through the cluster of trees in the small park and turn right. The **tourist office**, Jomas iela 42, has **maps**, brochures and bustling, English-speaking employees willing to help with anything. (☎642 76 and 644 93; fax 646 72; jurmalainfo@mail.bkc.lv; www.jurmala.lv. Open M-F 9am-5pm.) Dining and drinking options abound along **Jomas iela**.

The crowds that frolic in Majori taper off at either end of the beaches of Jūrmala. **Lielupe**, the town with beach access closest to Rīga, offers dramatic sand dunes. At the other end of Jūrmala, **Ķemeri** was once the prime health resort of the Russian Empire. Therapeutic mud baths, sulfur water, and other cures have operated here since the mid-18th century. The impressive white 1936 **Sanatorium**, built vaguely in the style of an Art Deco ocean liner, is an aging palace: it is in such major need of renovation as to make its future uncertain. It could always become a disco-bar.

# NEAR RĪGA

## SIGULDA ☎(8)29

The hills around Sigulda, 50km east of Rīga, boast legendary caves and the ruins of two castles, all connected by a string of nature trails in a picturesque stretch of the Gaujas Valley. Part of the Gaujas National Park, a bobsled run, bungee jumping, and hot-air ballooning make it a popular daytrip from the capital.

**▐ TRANSPORTATION. Trains** run from **Rīga** on the Rīga-Lugaži commuter rail line (1hr., 15 per day, 0.98Ls). **Buses** travel from **Rīga** (1½hr., 15-20 per day, 0.80Ls) and drop passengers off at a station on the edge of Sigulda, at the corner of Gātes and Vizdemes. Walking back toward Rīga, take the first right onto Gātes and walk across the train tracks to reach the *autoosta*. (Open daily 6am-8pm.)

**▐ PRACTICAL INFORMATION.** From the **bus** and **train stations**, walk up Raiņa iela to reach the center. Continue as it turns into Gaujas iela, which, after the Gaujas Bridge, becomes the steep Turaidas iela and passes **Turaida Castle**. Bus #12 runs from the station to **Hotel Senleja** (0.20Ls), then to **Turaida Castle**; **maps** (0.50Ls) are sold here. The **Sigulda Tourist Information Center**, Pils 4a, in a hut behind the bus station, also sells maps (0.80Ls; ☎/fax 721 07; open daily 9am-7pm). Just before Gaujas iela reaches the Gaujas Bridge, take a left on Peldu iela and follow it 650m to get to **Makara Turisma Birojs**, Peldu iela 1 (☎737 24; fax 24 49 48). They **rent bikes** (5Ls per day) and **canoes** (1 day with return transportation 24Ls). The staff also organizes bike adventures and supplies ski instruction (Dec.-Mar.). **Exchange money** and get MC/Visa **cash advances** at **Latvijas**

**Unibanka,** Rīgas iela 1. (☎ 711 99. Open M-F 9am-5pm.) The **post office** sits at Pils iela 2. (Open M-F 8am-noon and 1-5pm, Sa 8am-2pm.) **Telephones** are inside. (Open daily 7am-9pm.) **Postal code:** LV-2150.

**▐▌▐▌ ACCOMMODATIONS AND FOOD. Hotel Senleja,** Turaidas iela 4, lies below Turaida castle and near Gūtmaņ ala. Rooms come with TV and bath. (☎ 721 62; fax 701 02. Singles 15Ls; doubles 22Ls. Tent space 4Ls.) To reach **Hotel Vējupe,** Televizijas 19 (☎ 731 21), turn right onto Ausekla iela from the train station and follow it as it becomes Dárza iela and finally Televīzijas iela; the hotel is in a field. It rents spacious rooms with baths and has a fallout shelter in the basement. Enjoy the sauna and bar. (Sauna 5Ls per hour. Singles 10Ls; doubles 16-20Ls.)

Located inside the newest castle, the 19th-century **Sigulda Dome** (see p. 400), Pilsmuiža, Pils 15, is one of the best restaurants in the region. (☎ 713 95. Main dishes 2.50-5Ls. Open daily noon-2am.) **Kafejnīca/Bistro,** Raiņa iela 1, across the street from the train station, sells salads, pork chops, chicken kebabs, and rice by weight. (Main dishes 1.50Ls. Open daily 7am-10pm. MC/Visa.) There's a **grocery store** next to the Kafejnīca. (Open M-Tu and Th-Su 8am-11pm, W 8am-10pm. MC/Visa.)

**▣▐▌ SIGHTS AND ENTERTAINMENT.** "The wheel of history with its many wars, damage, and suffering has rolled over our little land," proclaims a caption outside ▨ **Turaida Castle** (Turaidas Pils). The restored brick fortifications are visible throughout the Gauja valley and surrounding hilltops. Work on the castle began in 1214, initiated by German crusaders seeking to convert the Liivs. Ascend the steep staircase of the main tower (restored in 1958) for views of the region. An adjacent building houses the **History Museum** (Siguldas novadpētniecības muzeja), Turaidas iela 10. It contains impressive displays on the history of the Liiv people, from their immigration to Latvia in the 3rd century to their near-elimination in the 12th-century crusades, complete with English descriptions and *faux* ancient music. (Open daily 10am-6pm. Castle, tower, and museum 1Ls, students 0.40Ls.)

Walk 10-15min. back down the hill along Turaidas iela to reach the legendary **caves** of Sigulda. The chiseled mouth of **Gutman's Cave** (Gūtmaņa ala), inscribed with coats of arms and mottos from generations of Latvians and other visitors since the 16th century, continues to erode. Climb the wooden stairway behind the cave for a walk along the high ridge above the valley. After steep rises and falls, you'll arrive at the ruins of the 13th-century **Krimulda Castle** (Krimuldas pilsdrupas). There's barely anything left, as the bulk of it fell in the 1601 Polish-Swedish war, but hints of magnificence make for a pleasant walk. Perched on a ridge to the right of Gauja iela, on the near side of the gorge, is the **Sigulda Dome,** the "new" castle-palace where the Russian Prince Kropotkin once lived. Behind, the immense ruins of **Siguldas Castle** (Siguldas pilsdrupas) are a mere glimmer of their former glory. Constructed by the German order of the Knights of the Sword between 1207 and 1226, the fortress was destroyed in the Great Northern War (1700-1721).

**▟ OUTDOOR ACTIVITIES.** An excellent 2km walk follows the Gauja River to the steep **Piķenes Slopes,** where two caves, the deep **Devil's Cave** (Velna ala) and **Devil's Little Cave** (Mazā velnala), merit mention. The nearby spring is purportedly a **Fount of Wisdom** where ambitious mothers bathe their babes. Another good hike goes from Siguldas Castle down to the Gauja and heads upstream to cross Vējupite creek. Another 100m upstream, stairs rise to **Paradise Hill** (Paradīzes kalns), where 19th-century Latvian painter Jānis Rozentāls made the valley view famous. The **Gauja National Park Center,** Baznicas iela 3, has 2-hour guided English tours. (☎ 713 45. Open daily 9am-5pm. Minimum 10Ls per guide, not including cable car and museum prices.) Call two days in advance to arrange tours.

Visible from the commuter rail, the Olympic-sized **bobsled and luge run** plummets from Sveices iela 13. From October to March, you can take the plunge—in summer do it on wheels. (☎ 739 44; fax 790 16 67. Open Sa-Su 10am-8pm. 3Ls.) From the Gaujas Bridge, a thin rope supports a tiny red **cable car.** This is the local **bungee**

**jumping** base; call ☎762 51 for reservations. To go one-on-one with gravity, climb the wooden stairs, sign a release, and jump. (Open on weekends; 15Ls.)

Try **Dukšte Gunars** (☎761 16 14; mobile ☎934 03 20) for **hot-air balloon** rides (70Ls per person per hr.); just don't float into Belarus. The **International Ballooning Festival** floats out of town in late May. Next to the Turaidas Museum, Turaidas 10, **horses** are available for hire. (☎745 84. Open Tu-F noon-6pm, Sa-Su noon-7pm. 7Ls per hr.)

# CĒSIS                                                                    ☎(8)412

Entrancing medieval streets, majestic castle ruins, and the nearby hills and streams draw foreigners and Latvians alike to Cēsis (TSEH-siss; pop. 19,471). The conquering knights of the Livonian Order once made this their headquarters, raising a magnificent castle. The town also has a bloody history with Russia—in 1703, Peter the Great invaded and in 1919, it was the site of a crucial battle in a rebellion against Russia. Today it's a quiet cluster of beautiful old buildings and spectacular ruins.

**7 TRANSPORTATION AND PRACTICAL INFORMATION.** From Rīga, Cēsis is easily reached via suburban **trains** (1½-2hr., 12 per day, 1.50Ls) and **buses** (2hr., 1-2 per hr. 6am-9pm, 1.30Ls). Ask the cashier at the **bus** and **train station** (☎227 62; open daily 8am-2pm and 3-7pm) to **store luggage. Local transportation** consists of two buses (0.20Ls): bus #9 runs west to the Gauja River while bus #11 runs east from the bus station along Poruka iela and down Lapsu iela. **Raunas iela** runs to the town center from the station and empties into the main square, **Vienības laukums. Rīgas iela** and **Valnu iela,** heading downhill at the square's south end, meet at **Līvu laukums,** the original 13th-century heart of the city. **Lenču iela,** which runs away from Vienī bas laukums, travels to **Cēsu pils** (Cēsis Castle). Free **maps** are available at the **Cēsis Hotel,** Vienības laukums 1 (☎201 22). The **tourist office,** Pils 9 (☎/fax 12 18 15; martins@cesutic.appollo.lv), in the building on the left as you enter the castle grounds from Lenču iela, functions more as a travel agency. (Open M-F 10am-4pm, Sa 11am-2pm.) **Exchange currency** upstairs at **Unibanka,** Raunas iela 8, which cashes MC/Thomas Cook/Visa **traveler's checks** and gives MC/Visa cash advances. (☎220 31. Open M-F 9am-5pm, Sa-Su 9am-2pm.) The **post office,** Raunas iela 13, sits at the corner of Vienības laukums in a new red brick building. (☎227 88. Open M-F 8am-6pm, Sa 8am-4pm.) The **telephone office** is in the yellow building across the street. You can send a **fax** (234 81) for 1Ls. (☎078. Open daily 9am-7pm.) **Postal code:** LV-4100.

**⬛⬛ ACCOMMODATIONS AND FOOD. Putniχkrogs,** Saules iela 23, isn't bad as far as Soviet-style accommodations go, and you can't beat the price. Follow the train tracks and the unmarked road to your right through the low bushes until it becomes paved. The hotel is the 2nd brick building on the right after the dirt bike track; enter around the back. (☎202 90. Singles 4Ls; doubles 8Ls. Showers 1Ls.) The **Cēsis Hotel,** Vienības Lakums 1, is pure luxury, from the sumptuous lobby to the huge bed and sparkling private baths. (☎201 22; fax 201 21. Singles 30Ls; doubles 42Ls. Breakfast included. 25% discount F-Su. English spoken.)

There's a **market** on Uzvaras Bulvaris between Vienības laukums and the tourist office. (Open 8am-4pm.) The Hotel Cēsis has its own **Cafe Popular,** a bistro until 5pm and a full restaurant thereafter. Housed in the basement, it sports loud music and fresh meals. (Main dishes 2-3Ls. Open M-Th 10am-11pm, F-Sa 10am-midnight, Su noon-10pm. MC/Visa.) The more elaborate **Restoran Alexis,** Vienības laukums 1, upstairs in the hotel serves a wide array of Latvian, international and vegetarian dishes. (☎223 92. Full meals 4-8Ls. Open daily noon-11pm.) **Kafejnīca Raunis,** where Rauna iela meets the square, serves plentiful if somewhat bland meals. The location is well-suited for people-watching, should anyone actually stroll through the square. (☎238 30. Main dishes 1-2Ls. Open daily 8am-10pm.)

**⬛⬛ SIGHTS AND ENTERTAINMENT.** Begun in 1206 by the Germans, the town's **castle** (☎226 15), with 4m thick walls, was completed in the 1280s. By the late 16th century, the Livonian Order's power lapsed, but when Russia's

> **OUT, OUT DAMNED SPOT!** In an effort to win back Cēsis from the Livonian Order that had taken the town in 1209, the Letgal tribe—ancestors of modern-day Latvians—went to battle against the knights in 1272. Legend has it that during the battle, the Letgal chief fell slain on a white sheet, staining it a deep crimson on two sides but leaving the middle section white. Some grief-stricken warrior flew the sheet and the tribe rallied around it. Today, that red-and-white pattern still adorns the Latvian flag, making it the 2nd-oldest national banner in Europe.

**Ivan IV** (the Terrible) laid siege to the fortress in 1577, the men chose to fill the cellars with gunpowder and blow themselves up rather than surrender. It was later rebuilt, but when Russians invaded again in 1703 under **Peter the Great**, the castle was bombarded and left in its ruined state. Ask an attendant to point out the **Lenin statue,** now resting under a giant wood crate resembling a coffin. **Cēsis History Museum** (Cēsis vēstures muzejs), Pils iela 9, in the newer of the two castles (the one with a roof and all four walls), exhibits coins and jewelry. After viewing the displays, climb to the roof for a view of the other castle's ruins. (☎226 15. Open Tu-Su 10am-5pm. 0.50Ls, students 0.30Ls. Cameras 2Ls. Tour 3Ls, in English 10Ls.)

 **Cēsis Brewery** (Cēsu alus daritava), Lenču iela 9/11, the oldest brewery in Latvia, has been producing fine beverages since the 1870s. The shop parts with its wares for 0.23-0.26Ls a bottle. Tours are possible if you contact the director in advance (☎235 29. Open M-F 8am-7pm, Sa 8am-5pm, Su 8am-1pm.) To access the older section of town, take Torņa iela from the parking lot by the castle. The Gaujas River flows along the east side of town, and a number of good **hiking** trails lead along the many cliffs lining the river. Bus #9 from the hotel on Vienības laukums leads 3km along Gaujas iela to the base of the trails. The best cliffs are to the south.

## KULDĪGA ☎(8)33

Legend has it that Kuldīga's (kool-DEE-ga; pop 13,920) Rumba, the town's waterfall, formed after a rooster's call frightened the Devil, making him drop a sack of rocks into the river. After Satan was through, the politicians moved in as Kuldīga rose to prominence as the seat of the Duchy of Courland. The city later fell to Russia in the Great Northern War and was consigned to provincial status. Anonymity has had its perks—left relatively unscathed by Soviet rule, Kuldiga's Baltic red-tile-roofed architecture and Venta River make it one of the prettiest stops in the region.

 **◪ ORIENTATION AND PRACTICAL INFORMATION.** Kuldīga's town center can be traversed in just 10min. The main street, **Liepājas iela,** intersects Baznīcas iela, which heads downhill to the castle park and the Venta river. **Buses** arrive from **Rīga** (3-4hr., 6 per day, 2.40Ls) at the **bus station,** Stacijas iela 2. (Open daily 4:30am-9pm.) To get to the center, turn right out of the station and walk to the black and brown barn. Take a left on Jelgavas iela and follow it until it turns into Mucenieku iela, then take a right on Putnu iela to reach Liepājas iela. (15min.) The **Tourist Information Office,** Pilsētas lankums 5, is located off Liepājas iela in the small kiosk and building in the town square. (☎222 59, mobile ☎926 25 83; fax 222 38. Open M-F 9am-5pm.) **Exchange money** at **Zemes Banka,** Liepājas iela 15, which cashes AmEx traveler's cheques and gives MC cash advances. (Open M-F 10am-4pm.) The **post office** is at Liepājas iela 34. (Open M-F 8am-6pm, Sa 8am-4pm.) **Postal code:** LV-3301.

 **▮▮ ACCOMMODATIONS AND FOOD.** The Soviet **Viesnīca Kuršu,** Pilsētas laukums 6, stands tall, wide, and gray over the town square. Old but clean singles with cold-water showers cost 6Ls. Doubles 9Ls, with hot water and TV 16Ls. (☎224 30; mobile ☎ (8) 29 35 73 98.) The new **Jāņa Nams Hotel,** Liepājas iela 36, offers doubles with private bath for 22Ls. (☎234 56.)

Jāņa Nams Hotel has a **cafe** in front whose dishes (2-3.50Ls) make up in taste what they lack in size. (Open daily 7am-11pm.) Crowded **Staburadze Kafejnica,** Liepājas iela 8, a little closer to the river, provides some of the cheapest meals in town. Pork *carbonade* (fried in egg) with greasy fries costs 1.66Ls. (☎ 235 99. Open M-Sa 11am-midnight, Su 11am-6pm.) **Rumba Cafe,** on Pils iela at the top of the castle park, provides drinks and snacks but no full meals. (*Aldaris* 0.50Ls. Open daily 11am-1am.) For **groceries,** hit the **Tirdzniecības Centrs,** in the town square next to Viesnīca Kuršu. (Open daily 7am-10pm.)

**▣ SIGHTS.** The most famous church in Kuldīga, **St. Katrina's** (Sv. Katrīnas baznīca), is a large white building on Baznīcas iela. Built in 1655 and rebuilt during the 19th and 20th centuries, it was used as a museum by the Soviets. (Services Su 10am-noon.) An 1807 **water mill** stands down the hill across the rickety wooden bridge. Turn left onto the high bridge or bear right uphill for an impressive view of the river and its **waterfall.** Outside, the **Regional Museum** (Kuldīgas Novada Muzejs), Pils iela 5, a single-vaulted room of the castle whose top is covered by earth and glass, forms part of a **sculpture garden.** (☎ 223 64. Open Tu-Su 11am-5pm. 2Ls.) The **Lutheran Church of St. Anne,** Dzirnavu iela 12, is a brick giant with green-coned tops. The stained glass near the pipe organ shows an absurd Soviet scene of bounty and family virtue. (Open daily 10am-5pm.)

# LITHUANIA (LIETUVA)

**IF YOU'RE HERE FOR...**

**3 DAYS.** Check out beautiful, charming **Vilnius** (p. 411).

**1 WEEK.** Get your dose of culture in **Kaunas** (p. 420), the "most Lithuanian city in Lithuania," and unwind in the spa town of **Druskininkai** (p. 425).

**2 WEEKS.** Go on to the beautiful **Baltic Coast** (p. 426).

Once part of the largest country in Europe, stretching into modern-day Ukraine, Belarus, and Poland, Lithuania has since faced oppression from tsarist Russia, Nazi Germany, and Soviet Russia. The first Baltic nation to declare its independence from the USSR in 1990, Lithuania has become more Western with every passing year. Its spectacular capital city of Vilnius welcomes hordes of tourists into the largest old town in Europe, recently covered in a bright new coat of paint from city-wide renovations. In the other corner of the country, the mighty Baltic Sea washes up against Palanga and the called Curonian Spit.

## LITHUANIA AT A GLANCE

**OFFICIAL NAME:** Republic of Lithuania

**CAPITAL:** Vilnius (pop. 590,000)

**POPULATION:** 3.6 million (80.6 % Lithuanian, 8.7% Russian, 7% Polish)

**LANGUAGE:** Lithuanian, Polish, Russian

**CURRENCY:** 1 Lithuanian litas = 100 centas

**RELIGION:** Primarily Roman Catholic, Lutherans largest minority

**LAND AREA:** 65,200 km²

**CLIMATE:** Maritime and continental

**GEOGRAPHY:** Lowlands with numerous lakes

**BORDERS:** Belarus, Latvia, Poland, Russia

**ECONOMY:** 55% Services, 32% Industry, 13% Agriculture

**GDP:** $4900 per capita

**EMERGENCY PHONE NUMBERS:** Fire 01, Police 02, Emergency 03

**COUNTRY CODE:** 370

**INTERNATIONAL DIALING PREFIX:** 810

# HISTORY

**PAGAN AND PROUD.** Although the date of migrations of Baltic peoples to the region is a point of contention among scholars, it is clear that the people were well established by the beginning of the Christian era. From there on, a litany of would-be conquerors tested the resilience of the settlers, beginning with the Teutonic Order at the dawn of the Middle Ages. The Lithuanian tribes rose to the challenge, uniting under **Mindaugus,** who accepted **Christianity** in 1251 and was named the country's first Grand Duke by Pope Innocent IV in 1253. Mindaugas reverted to paganism, however, and was assassinated, along with two of his sons, in 1263.

Lithuanian territory soon swelled to imperial proportions, swallowing modern Belarus and northern Ukraine, as **Grand Duke Gediminas** consolidated power in the 14th century. Under Gediminas the capital of the Lithuanian state was at Vilnius and the ruling caste was Lithuanian, however intermarriage with the subject East Slav tribes was common and many Lithuanians accepted **Eastern Orthodoxy.** After the death of Gediminas, disputes weakened the state.

LITHUANIA

Lithuania

**COME TOGETHER. Jogaila,** Gedminas's grandson, married the 12-year-old Polish Princess Jadwiga and became Władisław II Jagiełło, King of Poland, in 1385. With this union, Jogaila introduced **Roman Catholicism** to Lithuania, converting the nobility. Turning his attention to Poland, Jogaila delegated control of Lithuania to **Vytautus Didysis** (the Great). Together, they expanded their empire until Vytautus' death in 1430, at which point Lithuanian territory stretched from the Baltics to the Black Sea, from Vilnius to a mere 160km away from Moscow.

Lithuania solidified its ties to Poland with the 1569 **Union of Lublin,** which created the **Commonwealth of Two Peoples** (or Polish-Lithuanian Commonwealth), heralding a period of prosperity and cultural development. Under the Union each state retained its own laws and administration under a joint sovereign and parliament, but the Lithuanian nobility became almost entirely Polonized, while the peasantry retained the old language and culture.

**DECLINE AND FALL.** In the mid-17th century, unrest among Ukrainian Cossacks and wars against Sweden over Livonia left the commonwealth vulnerable. In the 18th century the growing power of Russia and Prussia led to the three **Partitions of Poland** (see **Poland: History,** p. 456), which erased the Commonwealth from the European map. By 1815, Russia controlled all of Lithuania.

Nationalist uprisings in Poland in 1830-31 and 1863 provoked intensified campaigns of Russification in Lithuania; the tsars closed the 250-year-old University of Vilnius and banned the use of Lithuanian in public places. As Russia's empire began to crumble, Lithuania was subjected to the geopolitical whims of its mighty neighbors. German troops returned to Lithuania in 1915, 500 years after the defeat of the

Teutonic knights, only to leave at the end of 1918, when the Soviets tried and failed to regain hold of the country. The Lithuanians expelled the Red Army in 1919, but during the confusion Poland took Vilnius—the population of the city, though the historical capital of the Lithuanian state, was predominantly Polish—and refused to give it up. A dispute also arose with Germany over the port of Klaipėda, a predominantly German city that represented the Lithuanian state's only hope for a viable harbor on the Baltic. Under intense pressure, Lithuania ceded the port to Germany.

**THAT OLD FAMILIAR FEELING.** Deprived of its capital and primary port, Lithuania's independence was short-lived. A parliamentary democracy collapsed in 1926 in a coup, as dictator **Antanas Smetona** banned opposition parties. Whatever autonomy remained disappeared with the 1939 **Nazi-Soviet Nonaggression Pact** and subsequent treaties, which invited the Soviets to invade. In June 1941, the Soviets began pulling Lithuanians from their homes; **deportations** to desert regions of the USSR displaced some 35,000 people. The Nazi occupation only caused greater hardship, as Lithuania lost another 250,000 citizens, including most of its Jewish population.

The Soviets returned in 1944, although they were opposed by Lithuanian guerrilla fighters—at their height 40,000 strong—into the early 1950s. It was not until the 1960s that **Antanas Sniečkus** managed to solidify Soviet rule. Resistance to the regime persisted through the stagnation of the 1970s and 1980s, as the republic generated more *samizdat* ("self-made" dissident publications) per capita than any other in the Soviet Union. **Mikhail Gorbachev's** reforms fell on dangerously fertile ground, and on March 1, 1990, Lithuania shocked the world when it declared **independence.** Moscow immediately retaliated, attempting futilely to disconnect the region's oil and gas resources. In a public relations disaster for Gorbachev, the Soviets launched an assault on Vilnius's radio and TV center, leaving 14 dead. Only in the wake of the failed Soviet *putsch* of August 1991 did Lithuania achieve any meaningful independence. Despite internal divisions, the country rejoiced on August 31, 1993, when the last Russian soldiers left Lithuania.

# POLITICS

Lithuania got off to an early start on economic reforms, and has been labeled by investors as one of Eastern Europe's economic "tigers." Recently, however, many of its reforms have run aground. Approximately 80% of the population is officially poor, and disenchantment with government institutions has grown, due as much to corruption as the decline in GDP. An associate member of the **EU** since 1995, the country nonetheless remains heavily dependent on Russia for fuel and has therefore suffered from Russia's financial woes. Lithuania ranks first among the Baltic states in meeting EU membership requirements regarding the treatment of minorities, however it currently lags behind both of its northern neighbors in economic categories. Russia remains opposed to the **NATO** membership Lithuania seeks. Still, of the Baltic states Lithuania maintains the most cordial relations with its former ruler, due largely to the smaller Russian population on its soil. Among the Baltic states, its chances for NATO membership are thought to be the greatest, both because of its good relations with Russia and its ties to NATO-member Poland.

Prime Minister **Roland Paksas** resigned in 1999 to protest a deal to sell state oil concern **Mazeiku** to US energy giant Williams Corp and was succeeded by the respected but relatively unpopular **Andrius Kublius.** The ruling right-center coalition, composed of the **Homeland Union-Lithuanian Conservatives** (TS-LK) and the conservative **Christian Democrats,** has attempted to catch up by implementing IMF austerity measures, but the resulting short-term decline in living standards has hurt the ruling coalition. The system of representation used in Lithuania's parliament has generally made it less fragmented than those of Latvia and Estonia, contributing to a lower rate of turnover in coalitions. The Lithuanian **presidency,** as in the other Baltic states, is a relatively weak one; the President's primary power is in shaping foreign policy. **Valdas Adamkus,** elected in January 1998, currently holds the office.

# CULTURE

**NATIONAL HOLIDAYS IN 2001**

| | |
|---|---|
| **January 1** New Year's | **June 23** Midsummer Night |
| **February 16** Independence Day | **July 6** Day of Statehood |
| **March 11** Restoration of Independence | **November 1** All Saints' Day |
| **April 15-16** Easter | **December 25-26** Christmas |

## LITERATURE AND ARTS

The earliest Lithuanian writings were the Chronicles of the Grand Duchy of Lithuania, written in an East Slavic dialect. During the Middle Ages and the Renaissance, Polish and Latin were the primary languages of Lithuanian literature. The first book in Lithuanian, a Lutheran catechism, was printed in 1547. The year 1706 saw the appearance of secular literature alongside sacred with the publication of *Aesop's Fables*. A Lithuanian translation of the **New Testament** was published in 1701 and a Lithuanian Bible in 1727. The first Lithuanian dictionary was the 1629 *Dictionarium trium linguarum* by **K. Sirvydas.**

After 1864, many writers violated the Tsarist ban on publishing Lithuanian works in Latin letters (as opposed to Cyrillic), seeking to overthrow Russian political and Polish cultural control. The first modern Lithuanian periodical was founded in 1883 by **Jonas Basanavicius;** *Dawn (Ausra)* lent its name to the next literary generation. Known for both dramatic and lyric poetry, "the poet-prophet of the Lithuanian renaissance" was **Jonas Mačiulis,** whose 1895 *Voices of Spring (Pavasario balsai)* launched modern Lithuanian poetry. After independence, ex-priest **Vincas Mykolaitis-Putinas** pioneered the modern Lithuanian novel with *In the Altar's Shadow (Altorių šešėly)*. Soviet rule again gagged and shackled Lithuanian writers, but new expressive modes were attempted in the philosophical poetry of **Alfonsas Nyka-Niliunas,** and the novels of **Marius Katiliskis.** *Pre-Dawn Highways*, by **Bronius Radzevicius,** which depicts an intellectual alienated from his national culture, is considered the strongest work of the late Soviet period.

Both Lithuanian **music** and **painting** have been heavily influenced by the folk culture from which they emerged. Much of the visual arts' development has centered around the **Vilnius Drawing School,** founded in 1866, and much is also owed to the work of composer/painter **Mikolojus Ciurlionis,** who died in 1911. **Jonas Mekas,** born in Lithuania, was a prominent filmmaker of the last half-century.

## RELIGION

Lithuania was Europe's last pagan stronghold, with the bulk of the population converting to Christianity only in the late 14th century. While German Lutheranism and Soviet atheism have strongly influenced the cultures of Estonia and Latvia to the North, Lithuania remains predominantly **Catholic.** Its Russian **Orthodox** minority, too, is small in comparison to the other Baltic republics.

## FOOD AND DRINK

Lithuanian cuisine is heavy and more often than not very greasy. Keeping a **vegetarian** or **kosher** diet will prove difficult, if not impossible. Restaurants serve various types of *blynai* (pancakes) with *mėsa* (meat) or *varške* (cheese). *Cepelinai* are heavy, potato-dough missiles of meat, cheese, and mushrooms, launched from street stands throughout Western Lithuania. *Šaltibarščiai* is a beet and cucumber soup prevalent in the east. *Karbonadas* is breaded pork fillet, and *koldunai* are meat dumplings. Lithuanian beer is very good. *Kalnapis* is popular in Vilnius and most of Lithuania, *Baltijos* reigns supreme around Klaipėda, and the award-winning *Utenos* is widely available. Lithuanian **vodka** *(degtinė)* is also very popular.

LITHUANIA

## GLOSSARY

| ENGLISH | LITHUANIAN | PRONOUNCE |
|---------|------------|-----------|
| one | vienas | VYEH-nahss |
| two | du | doo |
| three | trys | treese |
| four | keturi | keh-TUH-rih |
| five | penki | PEHN-kih |
| six | šeši | SHEH-shih |
| seven | septyni | sehp-TEE-nih |
| eight | aštuoni | ahsh-too-OH-ni |
| nine | devyni | deh-VEE-nih |
| ten | dešimt | deh-SHIMT |
| one hundred | šimtas | SHIM-tahs |
| one thousand | tukstantis | TOOK-stan-tis |
| today | šiandien | SHYEHN-dih-ehn |
| tomorrow | rytoj | ree-TOY |

| ENGLISH | LITHUANIAN | PRONOUNCE |
|---------|------------|-----------|
| departure | išvyksta | ish-VEEK-stah |
| arrival | atvyksta | at-VEEK-stah |
| one-way | i vieną galą | ee VIE-naa GAH-laa |
| round-trip | grįžtamasio bilieto | GREEZH-tah-mah-sio BI-lieto |
| train | traukinys | trow-kih-NEES |
| bus | autobusas | ow-TOH-boo-suhs |
| station | stotis | stow-TISS |
| grocery | maisto prekės | MYE-stoh PREH-kays |
| bread | duona | DWOH-na |
| vegetables | daržovė | dar-ZHO-ve |
| coffee | kava | KAH-vah |
| beer | alus | AH-lus |
| left | kairę | KAH-ihr-aa |
| right | dešinę | DEHSH-ihn-aa |

# CUSTOMS AND ETIQUETTE

Reserve informal greetings for those you know personally. A *"laba diena"* (good day) whenever you enter a shop ensures good feelings, and you can never say *"prašau"* too many times (both "please" and "you're welcome"). Handshakes are the norm for men; women get handshakes and perhaps a peck on the cheek. **Tipping** is not expected, but some Lithuanians leave 10% for excellent service. When eating in someone's home or, oddly enough, going to the doctor, bring a gift of flowers or chocolates. Feel free to **smoke** anywhere. **Homosexuality** is legal but not always tolerated. Lithuania has the most nightclubs, hotlines, and services for gays and lesbians in the Baltics. Contact Vladimiras or Eduardas of the **Lithuanian Gay League** (☎/fax (2) 63 30 31; lgl@gay.lt; www.gay.lt), P.O. Box 2862, Vilnius 2000. **SAPHO**, P.O. Box 2204, Vilnius 2049, is a prominent lesbian organization.

# LANGUAGE

**Lithuanian** is one of only two Baltic languages (Latvian is the other). All "r"s are trilled. **Polish** is helpful in the south, **German** on the coast, and **Russian** most places, although it is not as prominent as in Latvia. You may need the words *atidarytas* (ah-tee-DAR-ee-tass; open), *uždarytas* (oozh-DAR-ee-tass; closed), *viešbutis* (vee-esh-BOO-tees; hotel), and *turgus* (tuhr-GUHSS; market). If someone seems to sneeze at you, they're just saying *ačiu* (aa-choo; thank you). For commonly used words and phrases, see **Glossary,** above and **Phrasebook,** p. 409.

# ADDITIONAL READING

*The Baltic Revolution: Estonia, Latvia, Lithuania and the Path to Independence,* by Anatol Lieven, contrasts the Baltic states' respective histories. Masha Greenbaum's *The Jews of Lithuania* is a must for anyone interested in Jewish history. On a different track, *There is no Ithaca: Idylls of Semeniskiai & Reminiscences,* by Jonas Mekas, is a series of historical reflections from a Lithuanian who left the country to become an underground New York filmmaker.

## PHRASEBOOK

| ENGLISH | LITHUANIAN | PRONOUNCIATION |
|---|---|---|
| Yes/no | Taip/ne | TAYE-p/NEH |
| Please/You're welcome | Prašau | prah-SHAU |
| Thank you | Ačiū | AH-chyoo |
| Hello | Labas | LAH-bahss |
| Good-bye | Viso gero | VEE-soh GEh-roh |
| Good morning | Labas rytas | LAH-bahss REE-tahss |
| Good night | Labanaktis | lah-BAH-nahk-tiss |
| Sorry/Excuse me | Atsiprašau | aHT-sih-prh-SHAU |
| Help! | Gelbėkite! | GYEL-behk-ite |
| When? | Kada? | KAH-da |
| Where is...? | Kur yra...? | Koor ee-RAH |
| How do I get to...? | Kaip nueti į...? | KYE-p nuh-EH-tih ee |
| How much does this cost? | Kiek kainuoja? | KEE-yek KYE-new-oh-yah |
| Do you have...? | Ar turite..? | ahr TU-ryite |
| Do you speak English? | Ar kalbate angliškai? | AHR KULL-buh-teh AHN-gleesh-kye |
| I don't understand. | Aš nesuprantu | AHSH neh-soo-PRAHN-too |
| I'd like to order... | Norėčiau... | nor-RAY-chyow |
| I'd like to pay/We'd like to pay. | Sąskaitą, prašau | SAHS-kai-ta, prah-SHAU |
| Do you have a vacancy? | Ar turite laisvų kambarių? | ahr TU-ryite lai-SVOO KAHM-bah-ryoo |
| May I see the room? | Ar galiu pamatyti kambarį? | ahr gah-LEE-OO pah-mah-TEE-tih KAHM-bah-ree |
| I want a ticket to... | Aš norėčiau bilieto į... | ahsh nohr-YEH-chee-ah-oo BYEE-lee-eh-toh ee... |

# TRAVELING ESSENTIALS

Citizens of Australia, Canada, Ireland, New Zealand, the UK, and the US do not need a visa for visits up to 90 days. Citizens of South Africa who have visas from Estonia or Latvia can use those to enter Lithuania; otherwise, regular 90-day visas are required. Send a completed application, one recent 33x44mm photo, your passport, the application fee (by check or money order), and a stamped, self-addressed envelope to the nearest Lithuanian embassy or consulate (see **Embassies and Consulates,** p. 18). No invitation is required for citizens of South Africa. Single-entry visas cost US$20; multiple-entry visas US$50; transit visas (good for 48hr.) US$5; double-transit visas US$15. Regular service takes two weeks; rush service costs US$20 extra for 24hr. or US$15 extra for 72hr. service. There is no fee for crossing a Lithuanian border. Visas are not available at the border, but Estonian and Latvian visas can double as a Lithuanian transit visa. Avoid crossing through Belarus to enter or exit Lithuania; not only do you need a transit visa for Belarus (US$20-30 at the border) but border guards will also demand an unofficial border crossing "surcharge." Land travel in Lithuania often involves lengthy waits at customs, especially at the Polish border. Obtaining a visa extension may be a wild goose chase, but start at the Immigration Service in Vilnius, Virkių g. 3 #6 (☎75 64 53) or at the Immigration Department, Saltoniškių 19 (☎72 58 64).

# TRANSPORTATION

**BY PLANE.** Planes land in Vilnius from **Berlin, Moscow, Stockholm,** and **Warsaw.**

**BY TRAIN.** Two major lines cross Lithuania: one runs north-south from **Latvia** through **Šiauliai** and **Kaunas** to **Poland,** and the other runs east-west from **Belarus** through **Vilnius** and Kaunas to **Kaliningrad,** or on a branch line from Vilnius through Šiauliai to **Klaipėda.**

**BY BUS.** Domestically, buses are faster, more common, and only a bit more expensive than the often-crowded trains. Vilnius, Kaunas, and Klaipėda are easily reached by train or bus from **Belarus, Estonia, Latvia, Poland,** and **Russia.**

**BY FERRY.** Ferries connect Klaipėda with **Kiel, GER** and **Muhkran, GER.**

# TOURIST SERVICES AND MONEY

| CURRENCY | | |
|---|---|---|
| US$1 = 4.00LT (LITAI) | 1LT = US$0.25 |
| CDN$1 = 2.70LT | 1LT = CDN$0.37 |
| UK£1 = 5.90LT | 1LT = UK£0.17 |
| IR£1 = 4.60LT | 1LT = IR£0.22 |
| AUS$1 = 2.30LT | 1LT = AUS$0.43 |
| NZ$1 = 1.70LT | 1LT = NZ$0.58 |
| SAR1 = 0.58LT | 1LT = SAR1.70 |
| DM1 = 1.80LT | 1LT = DM0.54 |

**Litinterp** is generally the most helpful tourist office; they will reserve accommodations, usually without a surcharge. Vilnius, Kaunas, and Klaipėda each have an edition of the *In Your Pocket* series, available at newsstands and some hotels.

The unit of **currency** is the **Litas** (1Lt=100 centų), plural Litai. Since March 1994, it has been fixed to the US dollar at US$1 = 4Lt. Prices are stable, with inflation hovering at just under 1%. Except in Vilnius, exchange bureaus near the train station usually have poorer rates than banks; it's often difficult to exchange currencies other than US dollars and Deutschmarks. Most banks cash **traveler's checks** for a 2-3% commission. Cash advances on **Visa** cards can usually be obtained with minimum hassle. **Vilniaus Bankas,** with outlets in major cities, accepts major credit cards and traveler's checks for a small commission. If you're planning on traveling off the touristed path, be aware that most places catering to locals don't take credit cards. **ATMs,** especially Cirrus, are readily available in most cities.

# HEALTH AND SAFETY

A triangle pointing downward indicates men's **bathrooms;** an upward-facing triangle indicates women's bathrooms. Many restrooms are nothing but a hole in the ground. Well-stocked **pharmacies** are everywhere. Drink bottled mineral water, and **boil tap water** for 10 minutes first if you must drink it.

# ACCOMMODATIONS AND CAMPING

Lithuania has several **youth hostels**. HI membership is nominally required, but an LJNN guest card (US$3 at any of the hostels) will suffice. The head office is in Vilnius (see **Vilnius: Practical Information,** p. 412). Their *Hostel Guide* is a handy booklet with info on bike and car rentals, reservations, and maps. Vilnius has a number of good budget accommodations, but elsewhere you'll be lucky to find more than two cheap places. In that case, have **Litinterp** hunt something down.

# KEEPING IN TOUCH

There are two kinds of public phones: rectangular ones accept magnetic strip cards and rounded ones accept chip cards. Both are sold at phone offices and many kiosks in denominations of 3.54Lt, 7.08Lt, and 28.32Lt. Calls to **Estonia** and **Latvia** cost 1.65Lt per minute; **Europe** 5.80Lt; and the **US** 7.32Lt. Most countries can be dialed directly. Dial 8, wait for the second tone, dial 10, then enter the country code and number. **International direct dialing** numbers include: **AT&T Direct,** ☎ (8) 80 09 28 00; **BT Direct,** ☎ (8) 80 09 00 44; **Canada,** ☎ (8) 80 09 10 04; and **Sprint Express,** ☎ (8) 80 09 10 04. For countries to which direct dialing is unavailable, dial 8, wait for the second tone, and dial 194 or 195 for English-speaking operators.

**Airmail** *(oro pastu)* **letters** abroad cost 1.70Lt, postcards 1.20Lt, and usually take about one week to reach the US. **Mail** can be received general delivery through Poste Restante. Address envelope as follows: Matthew (First name) GIBSON (LAST NAME), POSTE RESTANTE, Laisves al. 102 (Post office address), Kaunas (City) LT-3000 (Postal code), LITHUANIA. **EMS** international mail takes three to five days. The internet has yet to become a major force in Lithuania, so checking email outside major cities can be difficult. Most major cities have **internet access.**

# VILNIUS ☎(8)22

Deluged by new businesses and foreign investment, Vilnius (pop. 579,000) races forward with her Baltic sisters. Once the political and cultural heart of Eastern Europe, the city remains self-conscious, proud, and staunchly Lithuanian. While the narrow, cobblestoned streets wind past examples of German- and Russian-influenced architecture, Vilnius absorbs them into its own slightly schizophrenic, but distinctly national personality. Founded in 1321 after a prophetic dream by Grand Duke Gediminas, within 60 years Vilnius was among the chief cities of the Polish-Lithuanian Commonwealth, the largest empire in Europe. After World War II, the city fell into the grip of the USSR. While it suffered at the hands of the Soviets, Vilnius managed to resist the mass Sovietization of other provincial capitals. Today it's the most beautiful city in the Baltics.

## ▟ ORIENTATION

The **train** and **bus stations** are directly across from each other. With your back to the train station, walk right on **Geležinkelio g.** and turn left at its end. This is the beginning of **Aušros Vartų g.**, which leads downhill through the **Aušros Vartai** (Gates of Dawn) and into **Senamiestis** (Old Town). Aušros Vartų g. changes its name first to **Didžioji g.** and then **Pilies g.**, before reaching the base of Gediminas Hill. Here, the **Gediminas Tower** of the Higer Castle presides over **Arkikatedros aikštė** (Cathedral Sq.) and the banks of the river **Neris. Gedimino pr.**, the commercial artery, leads west from the square in front of the cathedral's doors.

## ▣ INTERCITY TRANSPORTATION

**Flights:** The **airport** *(oro uostas)*, Rodūnės Kelias 2 (info ☎30 66 66; advance booking ☎75 26 00), lies 5km south of town. Take bus #1 from the train station, or bus #2 from the Sparta stop of trolley bus #16 on Kauno g. (15-20min.). **LOT** (☎73 90 20; fax 73 90 19) flies to **Warsaw, POL; SAS** (☎39 55 00; fax 39 55 01) to **Copenhagen, DEN; Estonian Air** (☎73 90 22; fax 26 03 95) to **Tallinn, EST; Lithuanian Airlines** (☎75 25 88; fax 72 48 52) to most European capitals.

**Trains:** Geležinkelio Stotis, Geležinkelio g. 16 (☎33 00 86, 33 00 87, and 33 00 88). Tickets for all trains are sold in the yellow addition left of the main station; windows #3 and 4 are specifically for trains to western Europe. Tickets for trains originating outside of Lithuania can be bought no earlier than 3hr. before departure. The **reservation bureau** (☎62 69 47) is in the main station hall on the right. Open M-F 6-11am, noon-6pm. All international trains (except those heading north) pass through Belarus; you'll need a Belarussian visa to complete the trip (see **Belarus: Essentials**, p. 77). To: **Minsk, BLR** (5hr., 2 per day, *coupé* 57Lt); **Kaliningrad, RUS** (7½hr., 5 per day, *coupé* 70Lt); **Rīga, LAT** (7½hr., 2 per day, *coupé* 72Lt); **Warsaw, POL** (11hr., 1 per day, *coupé* 115Lt); **Moscow, RUS** (17hr., 3 per day, *coupé* 128Lt); **St. Petersburg, RUS** (18hr., 3 per day, *coupé* 110Lt); and **Berlin, GER** (22hr., 1 per day, 317Lt).

**Buses:** Autobusų Stotis, Sodų g. 22 (☎26 24 82 and 26 24 83; reservations ☎26 29 77; international ☎33 52 77), opposite the train station. Purchase tickets from the driver for short trips. **Tarpmiestinė Salė** covers long-distance buses; windows #13-15 serve destinations outside the former Soviet Union. Open daily 7am-8pm. To: **Kaliningrad, RUS** (10hr., 2 per day, 38-47Lt); **Minsk, BLR** (5hr., 9 per day, 19Lt); **Rīga, LAT** (6½hr., 5 per day, 30-40Lt); **Warsaw, POL** (9½hr., 4 per day, 60-80Lt); and **Tallinn, EST** (10hr., 2 per day, 81Lt).

LITHUANIA

# ▐▀ LOCAL TRANSPORTATION

**Public Transportation: Buses** and **trolleys** run throughout the city, linking downtown with the train and bus stations and the suburbs. All lines run daily 6am-midnight. Buy tickets at any kiosk (0.60Lt) or from the driver (0.75Lt); punch them on board to avoid the hefty fine. Those staying in the city for a few days and planning to hop a trolley often will find buying a monthly pass a better bargain with various levels of discounts (students 5Lt, an 80% discount).

**Taxis: State Taxis** (☎ 22 88 88). 1.30Lt per km. **Private taxis** show a green light in the windshield; arrange the fare before getting in.

**Car Rental: Hertz,** Kalvarijų 14 (☎ 72 69 40; fax 72 69 70; hertz@auste.elnet.lt). Open M-F 8am-6pm, Sa-Su 9am-4pm.

# ▐▛ PRACTICAL INFORMATION

## TOURIST AND FINANCIAL SERVICES

**Tourist Offices: Tourist Information Centre,** Pilies str. 42 (☎/fax 62 07 62; turizm.info@vilnius.sav.lt; www.vilnius.lt), provides information about travel and events throughout Lithuania, organizes tours, and sells *Vilnius in Your Pocket* (4Lt). Also posts current train and bus schedules. English and Russian spoken. Open M-F 9am-6pm, Sa noon-6pm. **Lithuanian Youth Hostels Head Office,** Filaretų g. 17 (☎/fax 25 46 27; filaretai@post.omnitel.net), at the Filaretai Hostel (see below). Arranges travel and hostel reservations. Open daily 8am-5pm.

**Budget Travel: Lithuanian Student and Youth Travel,** V. Basanavičiaus g. 30, #13 (☎ 22 13 73). Great deals for travelers under 27. Sells student tickets for buses, trains, and planes. Open M-F 8:30am-6pm, Sa 10am-2pm.

**Passport Office: Imigracijos Taryba,** Verkių 3, #3 (☎ 75 64 53), 2km north of Senamiestis. Extends visas for those who demonstrate proof of need to stay in Lithuania (61Lt). Open M-F 9am-4:30pm.

**Embassies and Consulates: Australia,** Gaona 6 (☎/fax 22 33 69; aust.con.vilnius@post.omnitel.net). Open M, W, and F 11am-2pm. **Belarus,** Mindaugo 13 (☎ 25 16 66; fax 25 16 62), visas at Muitinės g. 41 (☎ 33 06 26). Open M-Tu and Th-F 8:15am-3:30pm. **Canada,** Gedimino pr. 64 (☎ 22 08 98; fax 22 08 84). Open M and W 9am-noon. **Estonia,** Mickevičiaus g. 4a (☎ 75 79 70; fax 22 04 61), visas Tu-Th 10am-noon, 2:30-3:30pm. **Latvia,** M. K. Čiurlionio g. 76 (☎ 23 12 60; fax 23 11 30; lietuva@latvia.balt.net), visas Tu and F 9am-noon. **Russia,** Latvių g. 53/54 (☎ 72 17 63, visa ☎ 72 38 93; fax 72 38 77, visa fax 72 33 75). Open M-F 8:30am-12:30pm, 2:30-5pm. **Ukraine,** Teatro 4 (☎ 22 15 36; fax 22 04 75), visas at Justiniškių g. 64 (☎ 70 51 15), M-Tu and Th-F 9am-noon. **UK,** Antakalnio g. 2 (☎ 22 20 70; fax 72 75 79; bevilnius@post.omnitel.net). Open M-F 9-11am. **US,** Akmenų g. 6 (☎ 22 30 31; fax 31 28 19). Open M-Th 8:30am-5:30pm.

**Currency Exchange:** Geležinkelio 6 (☎ 33 07 63), to the right as you face the train station, has the best rates. Open 24hr. **Vilniaus Bankas,** Gedimino pr. 12 (☎ 68 28 12; fax 22 62 88). Gives MC/Visa cash advances for no commission. Also cashes AmEx and Thomas Cooke traveler's checks. Open M-Th 8am-3:30pm, F 8am-3pm. **Bankas Snoras (Zzzz...),** A. Vivulskio g. 7 (☎ 26 27 71; fax 65 23 95). Cashes all traveler's checks and gives Visa cash advances for a 2% commission at circular blue and white kiosks throughout the city. Open daily 8am-8pm.

**ATMs:** Cirrus machines are at **Vilniaus Bankas,** the airport, and **Lithuanian Savings Banks,** Vilniaus 16 and Piles 9.

## LOCAL SERVICES

**Luggage Storage:** At the bus station. 1.50Lt per bag. Open daily 7am-10pm. Also in the tunnels under the train station. 1.50Lt per small bag, 2.50Lt for large bags and backpacks; 2Lt each additional day. Open 24hr.

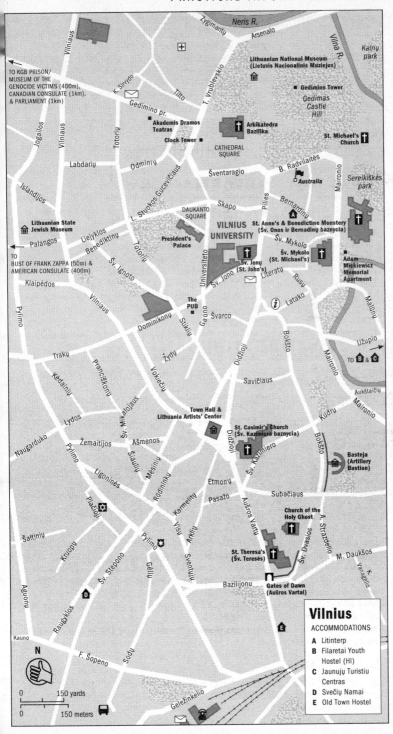

Neris R.

Žygimantų
Arsenalo

Vilniaus

K. Sirvydo

Tilto

Gedimino pr.

Lithuanian National Museum
(Lietuvis Nacionalinis Muziejus)

Kalnų
park

Vilna R.

Gedimino Tower

Gedimas
Castle
Hill

St. Michael's
Church

TO KGB PRISON/
MUSEUM OF THE
GENOCIDE VICTIMS (400m),
CANADIAN CONSULATE (1km),
& PARLIAMENT (1km)

Akademis Dramos
Teatras

Clock Tower

Arkikatedra
Bazilika

CATHEDRAL
SQUARE

Totorių

Jogailos

Vilniaus

Labdarių

Odminių

Šventaragio

B. Radvilaitės

Australia

Maironio

Sereikiškės
park

Islandijos

Palangos

Lithuanian State
Jewish Museum

L. Stuokos-Gucevičiaus

Lieyklos

Benediktinų

Totorių

DAUKANTO
SQUARE

Skapo

President's
Palace

VILNIUS
UNIVERSITY

Šv. Mykolo

St. Anne's & Benedictine Monstery
(Šv. Onos ir Bernadinų baznycia)

Bernardinų

Šv. Mykolo
(St. Michael's)

Adam
Mickiewicz
Memorial
Apartment

TO
BUST OF FRANK ZAPPA (50m) &
AMERICAN CONSULATE (400m)

Klaipėdos

Šv. Ignoto

Vilniaus

Pylimo

The
PUB

Universiteto

Šv. Jono

Šv. Jonų
(St. John's)

Literatų

Rusų

Latako

Trakų

Dominikonų

Stiklių

Gaono

Švarco

Didžioji

Bokšto

Maironio

Malūnų

Užupio

TO B & C

Kėdainų

Pranciškonų

Žydų

Vokiečių

Savičiaus

Aukštaičių

Maironio

Lydos

Šv. Mikalojaus

Ašmenos

Rodūninkų

Town Hall &
Lithuania Artists' Center

Kūdrų

Bokšto

Naugarduko

Pylimo

Žemaitijos

Šiaulių

Mėsinių

St. Casimir's Church
(Šv. Kazimiero baznycia)

Šv. Kazimiero

Didžioji

Basteja
(Artillery
Bastion)

Ligoninės

Placioji

Etmonų

Pasažo

Subačiaus

A. Strazdelio

Karmelitų

Aušros Vartų

Church of the
Holy Ghost

Šaltinių

Pylimo

Visų

Arklių

Kruopų

Gėlių

Šventurų

St. Theresa's
(Šv. Teresės)

Šv. Dvasios

M. Daukšos

K. Vanagelio

Bazilijonų

Gates of Dawn
(Aušros Vartai)

Aguonų

Šv. Stepono

Raugyklos

Kauno

N

0    150 yards
0    150 meters

F. Šopeno

Sodų

Geležinkelio

LITHUANIA

**English Bookstores: Penki Kontinentai** (Five Continents), K. Stulginskio g. 5 (☎22 14 81), off Gedimino pr. Open M-F 9am-6pm, Sa 9am-1:30pm. **Neta-Foreign Books,** Trakų 5 (☎61 04 16). Wide selection. Orders books. Open M-F 9am-6pm, Sa 10am-3pm.

**Bi-Gay-Lesbian Services: Gay Information Line,** (☎33 30 31; www.gay.lt). Info about organizations, events, and accommodations for gay men. The **Lithuanian Gay and Lesbian Homepage** (www.gayline.lt) lists gay and lesbian establishments in Lithuania. **The Gay Club** (☎ 8 299 85 009; vgc@takas.lt) keeps listings and locations in Lithuania.

**Laundromat: Slayana,** Latvių g. 31 (☎75 31 12), in Žvėrynas, 5min. west of Senamiestis across the Neris. Take tram #7 from the train station or tram #3 from Senamiestis. Self-service wash and dry 12Lt; full service 20Lt. Detergent 3Lt. Open M-F 8am-3pm.

## EMERGENCY AND COMMUNICATIONS

**24-Hour Pharmacy: Gedimino Vaistinė,** Gedimino pr. 27 (☎61 06 08 and 62 49 30).

**Medical Assistance: Baltic-American Medical & Surgical Clinic,** Antakalnio g. 124 (☎34 20 20; fax 76 79 42), at Vilnius University Hospital. Open 24hr.

**Telephones:** In the main post office (☎62 55 11). Phones take cards (from 8Lt) and allow direct dialing abroad.

**Internet Access: V002,** Ašmenos 8 (☎79 18 66). 8Lt per hr. Open 8am-midnight. **Interneto Kavine,** Gedimino pr. 4 (☎22 14 81). Open 8am-8pm. 8Lt/hr. Both offer speedy connections. **Martynyas Mavydas National Library,** Gedimino pr. 51 (☎61 70 28). Library card (7Lt) required. Open M-F 8am-8pm, Sa 10am-5pm.

**Post Office: Centrinis Paštas,** Gedimino pr. 7 (☎61 67 59), west of Arkikatedros aikštė. Letter to the US 1.35Lt. **Poste Restante** at the window that says *"iki pareikalavimo";* 0.50Lt to pick up mail. Open M-F 7am-7pm, Sa 9am-4pm.

**Postal code:** LT-2000.

# ▐ ACCOMMODATIONS

▨ **Old Town Hostel (HI),** Aušros vartų g. 20-15a (☎62 53 57; fax 22 01 49; livijus@pub.osf.lt), 100m from the "Gates of Dawn" in the Old Town. The outgoing proprietor offers coffee or tea upon arrival, free email access, large communal fridge, a washing machine, and deals at restaurants and bars around town. The hostel is currently undergoing renovations, tripling the size of the dorm-style oasis, adding more showers and toilets, and even a sauna. Hosts such fetes as "Pin the Mole on the Babushka." Dorms 32Lt, non-members 34Lt; singles and doubles 40-60Lt.

**Filaretai Youth Hostel (HI),** Filaretų g. 17 (☎25 46 27; fax 22 01 49; filareta@post.omnitel.lt). Take bus #34 from the right of the station (across from McDonald's), 10min. to the 7th stop (10min.). Clean kitchen, satellite TV and local info, but without the Old Town's personal touch. Breakfast 6Lt. Washer/dryer 10Lt per load. Reception 7am-midnight. Curfew in summer 1am, off-season midnight. Reservations recommended June-Sept. and weekends. Cozy, comfortable 2- to 8-bed dorms 29-37Lt 1st night, 8Lt off afterward, non-members 5Lt off. MC/Visa.

**Litinterp,** Bernardinų 7, #2 (☎22 38 50; fax 22 35 59; litinterp@post.omnitel.net; www2.omnitel.net/litinterp). Quieter than the Old Town. Sparkling rooms. Shared bath. Reception M-F 8:30am-5:30pm, Sa. 8:30am-3:30pm. Reservations recommended. Singles 70-100Lt; doubles 120-140Lt. Breakfast included. Apartment with kitchen and bath from 200Lt per night. 5% off rooms and car rentals with ISIC.

**Jaunujų Turistiu Centras,** Polocko 7 (☎61 35 76 and 61 15 47; fax 62 77 42). Take bus #34, which leaves from the right of the station (across from McDonald's) to the 7th stop (10min.). Offset slightly from the road, you'll find quaint rooms and an obliging staff. Marvel at their spotless single-sex showers and bathrooms—they surpass even the highest of standards. Little English spoken. 3- to 4-bed dorms 20Lt.

**Svečių Namai,** Šv. Stepono 11 (☎26 02 54). With you back to the train station, head straight down Stoties and turn left on F. Šopeno, then right on Šv. Stepono. Hidden away in a residential area of town, with more privacy then other hostels. Rooms with bath, TV and fold-out beds. No English spoken. 3- to 4-bed dorms 40Lt.

# ◌ FOOD

**Iki supermarkets,** which stock foreign brands, are all over Vilnius. A new Iki, the most convenient, recently opened next to the bus station. (Open 8am-10pm.)

## RESTAURANTS

Trendy, inexpensive restaurants are popping up everywhere. A full meal can be as cheap as US$4-6, but quality and price are closely related.

▨ **Ritos Smuklė** (Rita's Tavern), Žirmūnų g. 68 (☎77 07 86). Too far to walk; take trolley-bus #12, 13, or 17. Rita aims to capture the "spirit of Lithuania's past as it really was," from Lithuanian dishes to traditional music and costumes. Fun and folksy atmosphere, amusing English menu. Be sure to sample the acorn coffee (3Lt) and try something from the outside grill. Main dishes 15-30Lt. Live folk music W-Th from 7pm, F-Sa from 8pm. Open M-F 5pm-midnight, Sa-Su noon-midnight.

**Ritos Slėptuvė** (Rita's Hideaway), A. Goštauto g. 8 (☎62 61 17; fax 31 65 15). Along the Neris, a giant wooden plate and spoon are the only markers of Rita's. Why the secrecy? It was designed as a bomb shelter in case of a US attack on the USSR. Funky American decor and food with an Lithuanian twist. "No sweat suits allowed"—seemingly a subtle ban on the local mafia. Eat well for under 10Lt. Come before 4pm, after which the menu shrinks as the place becomes a **bar.** Live music Sunday nights. Open M-Th 7am-2am, F 7am-6am, Sa 8am-6am, Su 8pm-2am.

**Stikliai Aludė** (Beer Bar), Gaono g. 7 (☎62 45 01). A cozy, folksy, subterranean haunt. The specialty of the house is its array of local brew: *Biržai Grafas* 4.50Lt, *Kalnapilis* 3Lt. Main dishes 16-28Lt. Open daily noon-midnight.

**Cabare,** Mėsinių 5/2 (☎62 49 70). Don't expect a live floor show—but do expect a quick and mouth-watering Lithuanian meal. In pleasant weather dining outside is an option, otherwise sit by the polished bar or antique decor. Try *troskinla jautiena*, potato pancakes with beef and sauce (12 Lt). Main dishes 12-16Lt. Open M-Su 10am-11pm.

## ◧ CAFES

**Cafe Filharmonija,** Aušros vartų g. 5 (☎22 13 83). Next to the National Philharmonic, with the style to match. Of the cafes lining Aušros Vartų, this is the pick of the litter, with its scrumptious treats and perfect location for people-watching. Marked by a golden *"Kavinė"* sign over the door and a relaxed crowd outside. Main dishes 7-12Lt. Excellent ice cream 5-8Lt. Open daily 9am-11pm.

**Cafe Afrika,** Pilies g. 28 (☎61 71 90), smack in the center of it all. If the vibrant yellow decor and the purple-and-yellow striped Zebra sign don't grab your attention, the fun-loving clientele filling the tables will. Soup, salad, and gourmet coffee for less than 12Lt. Open daily 10am-11pm.

**Užupio Kavinė,** Užupio g. 2 (☎22 21 38), between Senamiestis and the Filaretai hostel. On a warm and breezy day, come take advantage of the tree-shaded deck seating overlooking the bubbly Vilnia River. A meal with your intellectual pretensions? Don't forget to eat between games of chess. Rowdier by night. 0.5L of *Dvaro* beer 6Lt. Open daily 9am-11pm.

## ◉ SIGHTS

**GATES OF DAWN AND BEYOND.** (Aušros Vartai.) The Gates of Dawn, the only surviving portal of the old city walls, have guarded **Senamiestis** (Old Town) since the 16th Century. In 1671 a **Chapel** (Koplyčia) was built inside the portal as a shrine for a gilded portrait, said to have been either an icon of the Virgin Mary captured in Ukraine by Grand Duke Vytautas or a portrait of a 16th-century princess. *(Through the gates, enter the 1st door on the right. Open 9am-6pm.)* At the building's end stands **St. Theresa's Church** (Šv. Teresės bažnyčia), known for its Baroque sculptures, multi-colored arches, frescoed ceiling, and stained glass. A few steps farther down, a gateway leads to the shockingly bright 17th-century **Orthodox Church of the Holy Spirit**

(Šv. Dvasios bažnyčia), seat of Lithuania's Russian Orthodox Archbishop. A functioning monastery, the church is the final resting place of Saints Antonius, Ivan, and Eustachius, martyred in 1371. Their bodies, usually clad in red in a glass case under the altar, wear white for Christmas and black for Lent. *(Aušros Vartų 10. ☎62 64 59.)*

**ST. CASIMIR'S CHURCH.** (Šv. Kazimiero bažnyčia.) Named after the country's patron saint, St. Casimir's is Vilnius's oldest Baroque church, built by the Jesuits in 1604. In 1832, it gained a Russian Orthodox dome; during World War II, the Germans made it Lutheran. After "liberating" Vilnius, the Soviets turned the temple into a shrine to atheism, but it's been back in the Catholic fold since 1989. *(Didžioji g. 34. Beyond the gates, Aušros Vartų g. turns into Didžioji g., leading to the church. ☎22 17 15. Open M-Sa 4-6:30pm, Su 8am-1:30pm.)*

**TOWN HALL SQUARE.** (Rotušės aikštė.) Located on Didžioji g., Town Hall Square is an ancient marketplace dominated by the columns of the 18th-century **town hall,** now home to the **Lithuanian Artists' Center** (Lietuvos Menininkv Rumai). Just north of the square on Didžioji g. lies **St. Nicholas's Church** (Šv. Mikalojaus bažnyčia). Lithuania's oldest church, St. Nicholas' was built in 1320 for the city's Hanseatic merchants. *(Šv. Mikalojaus g. 4. ☎62 30 69.)*

**VILNIUS UNIVERSITY.** (Vilniaus Universitetas.) Founded in 1579, the Jesuit university was a major player in the Counter-Reformation. On the east side of the main courtyard, the 1387 **St. John's Church** (Šv. Jonų bažnyčia), served as a science museum under the Soviets. *(Šv. Jono g. 12.)* Go through the arches opposite St. John's to the 17th-century **Astronomical Observatory,** once rivaled in importance only by Greenwich and the Sorbonne. The university **library,** with more than five million volumes, remains one of Europe's largest. *(Universiteto g.)* The nearby **Church of the Holy Spirit** (Šventosios Dvasios bažnyčia), a gold and marble Baroque masterpiece last rebuilt in 1770, was the first Gothic church in Vilnius. *(Dominikonų g. 8, near the corner of Pilies g. and Šv. Jono g. Open daily 7am-10am and 5-7pm.)*

**ST. ANNE'S CHURCH AND BERNARDINE MONASTERY.** (Šv. Onos ir Bernardinų bažnyčia.) A red-brick structure built at the height of the Gothic style, St. Anne's Church and Bernadine Monastery is so beautiful that Napoleon supposedly wanted to carry it back to France. The Bernardine monastery in back, part of the city walls in 1520, houses the Art Academy and Design School of the University of Vilnius. *(Maironio g. 8. From Cathedral Square at the base of the castle hill, follow B. Raduvilaites along the park and turn right on Maironio g.)*

**CATHEDRAL SQUARE.** (Arkikatedros aikštė.) A church has stood here since 1387, when Grand Duke Jogaila converted his country to Catholicism to win the Polish throne (see History, p. 404)—prior to that it was the site of the principal temple to Perkūnas, Lithuanian god of thunder. Today's 18th-century **Cathedral** (Arkikatedra Bazilika) resembles a Greek temple, perhaps a nod to the pagan past. Inside, to the right of the altar, peek into the early Baroque **Chapel of St. Casimir** (Šv. Kazimiero koplyčia), home to a royal mausoleum. Out in the square, the freestanding octagonal 1522 **bell tower** contains county bells from throughout the country. *(In the square, down Pilies g. or Universiteto g. Open M-Sa 7am-1pm and 2:30-8pm, Su 7am-2pm.)*

**HIGHER CASTLE MUSEUM AND GEDIMINAS TOWER.** The tower, proudly sporting the Lithuanian flag, dominates the hill behind the Cathedral. Follow the winding path to the top of the hill, which has been crowned by a castle since 200-100 BC. The Higher Castle Museum (Aukštutinės Pilies Muziejus) offers an exhibit on the history of the castle and city and a collection of medieval weapons, but the main attraction is the magnificent view of Senamiestis and Gedimino pr. *(Castle Hill, Arsenalo 5. ☎61 74 53. Open Tu-Su 11am-5pm. English captions. 4Lt, cameras 10Lt.)*

**PARLIAMENT.** In January 1991, the world watched as Lithuanians raised barricades to protect their parliament from the Soviet army. A section of the **barricade** remains as a memorial; more sections are housed at the Lithuanian National Museum (**see Museums,** p. 417). President Ladsbergis later said that all of the deputies expected to become martyrs on the night of January 13, but the main attack came instead at the TV tower. *(Gedimino 53, just before the Neris.)*

**HILL OF THREE CROSSES.** (Trjių Kržių kalnas). The Hill of Three Crosses is visible throughout Vilnius. White crosses were originally set here in the 18th century to commemorate seven 13th-century Franciscans crucified on the hill by pagan tribes. During Lithuania's first period of independence, 1919-1939, a white stone memorial of three crosses appeared on the hilltop. Torn down by the Soviets in the 50s, the present monument is a 1989 copy; legend dictates that two of the crosses can be seen from anywhere in the city, while a third remains hidden.

**ST. PETER AND PAUL CHURCH.** (Sv. Apaštalv Petro ir Povilo bažnyčia). Built in 1688, St. Peter and Paul Church features an baroque interior decorated with over 2000 figures—note the chandelier styled like a sailing ship. The church's humble founder is buried next door; his tombstone reads *Hic jacet peccator*—"Here lies a sinner." *(Antakalnio g. 1. Take trolleybus #2, 3, or 4 from Senamiestis. ☎ 34 02 29.)*

**TV TOWER.** (Televizijos Bokštas). Fourteen unarmed civilians were killed at the TV tower as the Red Army forced the station off the air. Crosses and memorials surround the spot today, and streets in the neighborhood have been renamed in honor of the 14 martyrs. The huge tower, with its revolving top, is visible from the city center. *(Sausio 13-Osios 10. Take trolleybus #11 going from Skalvija on Žaliasis bridge's south end toward Pašilaičai (14 stops). ☎ 45 88 77. Open daily 9am-9pm. 15Lt.)*

**FRANK ZAPPA MONUMENT.** Yes, you read right. Perhaps the most random monument in Eastern Europe after Slovakia's Andy Warhol Museum (see p. 732), this bust of Frank was installed in 1995 after the **Museum of Theater, Music, and Cinema** turned it away. *(Shoots skyward off Pylimo between Kalinausko 1 and 3.)*

**JEWISH CULTURAL CENTRE.** A Jewish community has called Vilnius home since 1325; later the city gained fame as "The New Jerusalem," an international center of Jewish learning and culture. Vilnius was once a center of Jewish life comparable only to Warsaw and New York, with a Jewish population of 100,000 (in a city of 230,000) at the outbreak of World War II. Only 6,000 survivors remained by the time the Red Army retook the city in 1944. The Centre provides information on locating ancestors or on the Jewish Quarter in general. *(Šaltinių g. 12. ☎ 41 88 09.)*

**PANERIAI GENOCIDE MEMORIAL.** (Panerių Memorialas.) The Paneriai Genocide Memorial sits on the site of the former Paneriai concentration camp. Between 1941 and 1944, 100,000 people, including 70,000 Jews, were shot, burned, and buried here. Paved paths connect the pits that served as mass graves and execution sites. A small museum holds artifacts and documents the excavation of the sites. *(Agrastų g. 15. A 10-15min. train ride from Vilnius in Paneriai (1.30Lt). Facing away from the tracks, head right and follow Agrastų g. straight to the memorial. Return by bus; cross the pedestrian bridge over the railroad tracks and catch bus #8 from the stop to the right of the bridge. ☎ 64 18 47. Open M and W-Sa 11am-6pm. Captions in English.)*

**SYNAGOGUE.** (Sinagoga.) Built in 1903, this synagogue was the only one of Vilnius's 105 to survive WWII. The Nazis used it to store medical supplies; it's now undergoing its first exhaustive restoration. Services are now held regularly on Saturday mornings. *(Pylimo g. 39. ☎ 61 25 23.)*

# 🏛 MUSEUMS

▨ **Museum of Genocide Victims** (Genocido Aukų Muziejus), Gedimino pr. 40, (☎ 62 24 49). Enter around the corner at Aukv g. 4. Housed in the old KGB prison. One of the staff, G. Radžius, was a prisoner here; find someone to translate what he says. The stately building was originally constructed in 1899 by Tsar Nicholas II to serve as a court, but it was captured by the Nazis during WWII and turned into a Gestapo headquarters. It later became Vilnius' KGB headquarters. The prison is as the Soviets left it, outfitted with torture and execution chambers; notice the dark, damp rooms in which prisoners were tortured and beaten, and then left to stand in solitude for as long as a week. Tours in Lithuanian and Russian, captions in English. Open May 15-Sept. 15 Tu-Su 10am-6pm, Sept. 16-May 14 Tu-Su 10am-4pm.

**Lithuanian National Museum** (Lietuvis Nacionalinis Muziejus), Arsenalo g. 1. (☎62 94 26). Behind the Gedimino Tower. Founded in 1855, the museum chronicles the history of the Lithuanian people through 1940. Don't miss the exhibit on the 1918-40 Lithuanian republic. Also check out the newest exhibit on the struggle for independence in the early 1990s—the last glass case contains pieces of the barricades where Lithuanians denounced their Soviet possessions, nailing their internal passports into the wall. Some English captions. Open W-Su 10am-5pm. 4Lt, students 2Lt, free with ISIC.

**Applied Art Museum** (Taikomosios Dalies Muziejus), Arsenalo 3a (☎22 18 13). Next to the National Museum. Home of the recently unveiled exhibit *Christianity in Lithuania's Art*, the Applied Art Museum exhibits a collection of over 270 pieces of gold, silver, and jeweled religious objects hidden in 1655 on the eve of the Russian invasion and rediscovered in the walls of the cathedral in 1985. They were concealed from the Soviets and finally revealed to the public in 1998. Open Tu-Su 11am-6pm. 4 Lt.

**Artillery Bastion** (Basteja), Bokšto g. 20/18 (☎61 21 49). Cannons, armor, and rusty swords fill the Artillery Bastion, a restored section of the city's 17th-century defenses against the Russians and Swedes. In a stroke of irony, restoration of the ruins began in 1960 under the Russians. Open W-Su 10am-5pm. Free.

**Adam Mickiewicz Memorial Apartment** (A. Mickevičiaus Memorialinis Butas), Bernardinv g. 11 (☎61 88 36). The yellow door with the lion's head, next to Litinterp, marks the apartment. The famous Lithuanian-Polish poet (see **Poland: Literature and Arts**, p. 458) lived here in 1822 and it still contains his possessions and work. Although Mickiewicz wrote in Polish, he is beloved by Lithuanians for penning the national epic, *Pan Tadeusz*. English captions. Open Tu-F 10am-5pm, Sa-Su 10am-2pm. Free.

**Museum of Architecture**, Šv. Mykolo g. 9 (☎61 64 09). Housed in the Renaissance **St. Michael's Church** (Šv. Mykolo), which was built in 1625 to house a family mausoleum. English captions. Open M 10am-5pm, W 11am-6pm. 1Lt.

**The Green House**, Pamenkalnio g. 12 (☎62 07 30). Set back from the street. Chronicles the destruction of Vilnius's Jewish community. It also documents where 90% of Lithuania's 240,000 Jews were exterminated during the war. Ben-Zvi (1884-1963) and Š.Z. Šazaras (1889-1974), Israel's second and third presidents, respectively, were both originally from Vilnius; their pictures now hang in the museum as testimony to the enduring vigor of the city's Jewish community. Printed tours in English. Open M-Th 9am-5pm, F 9am-4pm. Donations requested.

**Lithuanian State Jewish Museum**, housed in 2 buildings at Pylimo g. 4 (☎61 79 17). An **exhibition on Jewish life** houses rotating exhibits and a permanent collection of items salvaged from the rubble of synagogues. The **Gallery of the Righteous** (Teisuoliu Gallerija; ☎62 45 90 and 74 24 88) honors the Lithuanians who sheltered Jews during the war. The museum also arranges guided tours of Jewish Vilnius in English, Yiddish, Russian, and Lithuanian. Open M-Th 9am-5pm, F 9am-4pm. Donations requested.

# ▣ ENTERTAINMENT

In summer, festivals and pop concerts come to town; check *Vilnius in Your Pocket* or the Lithuanian morning paper *Lietuvos Rytas* for performances. Consult the tourist office at Pilies g. 42 (☎62 64 70; fax 62 07 62) for info on obtaining tickets. See English-language movies at **Lietuva Cinema**, Pylimo g. 17 (☎62 34 22), and **The Vilnius**, Gedimino pr. 5a (☎61 26 76). **Kino Centras Skalvija**, Goštauto g. 2 (☎61 14 03), shows the best non-Hollywood films in the city. Consult *Lietuvos Rytas* or www.kinas.lt for locations and show times.

**National Philharmonic Orchestra** (Lietuvos Naciolinė Filharmonija), Aušros Vartų 5 (☎22 22 90; fax 62 28 59; info@filharmonija.lt). Internationally renowned. Box office open M-F 10am-6pm, Sa 11am-6pm, Su 11am-1pm; Tickets 10-150Lt. Performances begin at 7pm. Also organizes the **Vilniaus Festivalis** (www.filharmonija.lt/vilnaiusfestivalis), a month of concerts starting in late May. MC/Visa.

**Opera and Ballet Theater** (Operos ir Baleto Teatras), Vienuolio 1 (☎62 06 36; tickets ☎62 07 27). Open M-F noon-2:30pm and 3:30pm-6pm, Sa 1-5pm, Su 10am-2:30pm and 3:30-6pm. Performances begin at 6 or 7pm.

**Academic Drama Theater** (Akademinis Dramos Teatras), Gedimino pr. 4 (☎62 97 71). Look for the 3 muses carved into black stone wearing golden masks. From Tennessee Williams to Federico García Lorca. Box office open Tu-Su 10am-6pm.

# ◪ NIGHTLIFE

New discos, bars, and clubs are springing up daily to entertain the influx of foreigners and the city's younger crowd. Check out posters in the Old Town or wander down Gedimino pr. toward the thumping music. Lithuanian hipsters Eduardas and Vladimiras organize a **gay disco** every Saturday night at a different venue. Call them (☎8 287 25 879) for more information (Cover 15Lt. Usually open F-Sa 10pm-6am.)

## PUBS AND BARS

**The PUB (Prie Universiteto Baras),** Dominikonų g. 9 (☎61 83 93), in the heart of Senamiestis, and near the university. Traditional English pub with wooden interior and a cozy, 19th-century dungeon. Usually packed with foreigners and local students. W night jazz, Su night disco. Cover 8Lt. Open daily 11am-2am. Visa/MC.

**Savas Kampas** (Your Corner), Vokiečių g. 4 (☎22 32 03). A laid-back option for a more mature set who like to hear 60s, 70s, and 80s tunes. Look for the saxophone sign on the corner or the giant outdoor complex on the green. Local Lithuanian bands play live F-Sa nights. Great mix of jazz, blues, and rock. Open daily midnight-3am. Visa/MC.

**Amatininskv Užeiga,** Didžiogi g. 19, #2 (☎61 79 68). A wooden carving of a man swinging his mug of *alus* hangs over the door. Mingle with the locals at the bar or descend into the recently discovered medieval basement for a more intimate atmosphere. Open M-F 8am-5am, Sa-Su 11am-5am.

## CLUBS

**Naktinis Vilkas** (Night Wolf), Lukiškių g. 3 (☎22 47 51). Groove or grab a booth with local students. Full of communist kitsch, the Night Wolf is reputed to have the best singles scene in town. 21+. Cover M-Sa 5-10Lt. Open daily 10pm-6am.

**Ministerija,** Gedimino pr. 46 (☎62 16 06). Local studs practice American dance crazes—from 6 years ago. A "no techno" rule is mercifully enforced. Th Ladies' Night. 20+. Cover 5-15Lt. Open M-Th 6pm-3am, F-Sa 6pm-5am.

**Ultra,** Goštauto g. 12 (☎62 00 29). Frequented by a trendy younger crowd that gladly dances to anything with a beat. Cover 5-10Lt. Open Th-Sa 9pm-5am.

# ◪ DAYTRIP FROM VILNIUS

## TRAKAI CASTLE

*Trakai, 28km east of Vilnius, is an easy daytrip by bus (under 45min., over 25 per day, 2.90Lt; buy tickets on the bus). The last bus for Vilnius departs nightly at 9:07pm, but it occasionally leaves early. Bus station open daily 5am-11:30pm. The easiest way to navigate Trakai is by boat; boat owners usually line the lake shore by the footbridge to the castle. The going rate is 5-7Lt per hr. Alternatively, board a yacht in front of the castle for a 45-minute guided tour (10Lt). Museum open daily 10am-7pm. 7Lt, students 3.5Lt. 1hr. tours 40Lt, students 15Lt; foreign-language tours 50Lt; students 25Lt. Cameras 4Lt.*

Trakai's fairy-tale castle has inspired legends since its construction at the beginning of the 15th century. With the summer of 1410 and the defeat of the Teutonic Order at the Battle of Grunwald, Trakai became the home of Grand Duke Gediminas and the capital of Lithuania. By this time the original castle of Gediminas was looking a little the worse for wear, and Vytautas upgraded to a nicer one. Vytautas's new digs were short-lived, however, for in 1665 the Russians accomplished what the Germans could not, plundering the town and razing the castle. Trakai has been relegated to provincial status ever since, but the castle itself has been revived. Thanks to a lengthy process of restoration from 1952 to 1980, five stories of red bricks now tower over some of the most beauti-

**GETTING HEAD** Legend has it the gorgeous and serene rippling waters surrounding the castle are more sinister than they seem. Lake Galvė derives its name from the Lithuanian word for "head;" it seems the zealous Grand Duke Vytautas got a little carried away in his victory dance after defeating the Germanic crusaders of the Teutonic Order and spiked the head of a decapitated crusader into the lake's sparkling waters. The lake fell head over heels for this mortal morsel and now will not freeze before it takes its "head," usually a drowned drunkard or a lost tourist.

ful lakes and woods in Lithuania. A combined admission ticket is valid for both the **Insular Castle's** 30m brick watchtower and the **City and Castle History Museum** (☎55 294). The rooms in the tower chronicle the history of Lithuania after it came under the rule of tsarist Russia in 1795, as well as the history of the independent Lithuanian republic that existed between the wars. Across from the tower, the museum features Lithuanian period furniture from the 18th to 20th centuries, the clock collection of Bronius Kasperavicus, handmade marble postal stampers, and an immense collection of tobacco and opium pipes. Facing away from the footbridge leading to the Insular Castle, walk left and explore the ruins of the Gediminas's **Peninsular Castle** and Dominican monastery.

# INLAND LITHUANIA

The geographic heart of Lithuania also contains the figurative heart of its people. While flashier Vilnius attracts foreigners' attention and investment, inland Lithuania has always been where the country turned when times went bad. Kaunas has rebuilt itself countless times to bear the standard of Lithuanian culture, and Šiauliai is home to the Hill of Crosses, a symbol of resistance to communist rule.

## KAUNAS                                                        ☎(8)827

Would-be dictators beware: staunchly nationalist Kaunas (KOW-nas; pop. 415,800) has always boded ill for foreign invaders. Napoleon planned his star-crossed campaign against imperial Russia in 1812 while encamped here. During World War II Hitler converted the city's Ninth Fort into a concentration camp, from which 64 prisoners and resistance fighters escaped in 1943—the only successful mass escape from the Nazi death camps. Stalin didn't have much luck either—Kaunas resisted Sovietization to the point where Russian "colonists" planted in the city started to speak Lithuanian and adopt local customs. (The always-cuddly "Uncle Joe" responded by sending the settlers to Siberia.) Through it all, Kaunas, has been called the "most Lithuanian" city in Lithuania and the "cradle of Lithuanian culture." A contemplative, serene city, Kaunas keeps its unhurried pace despite the growing number of bars, restaurants, and shops.

### ✳ ORIENTATION

At the confluence of the **Nemunas** and **Neris** rivers, Kaunas is on a peninsula pointing west, with **Senamiestis** (Old Town) at the western tip and the bus and train stations at the southeast point. **Naujamiestis** (New Town) fills the middle, bisected by **Laisvės al.** At the fork with **Šv. Gertrūdos g.**, Laisvės al. merges with **Vilniaus g.** at the entrance to Senamiestis and runs to **Rotušės aikštė**. The **train station** lies at the end of **Vytauto pr.** where it intersects with M. K. Čiurlionio; the **bus station** is about 300m from the train station on Vytauto pr. Continue along Vytauto pr. and Kęstučio g. and Laisvės al. are to the left. **Bus #7** runs parallel to Laisvės al., never more than a block distant. *Kaunas in Your Pocket*, an excellent yearly guidebook with detailed listings on the city (4Lt), is available at **Lintinterp** or the **Tourist Office** (see below).

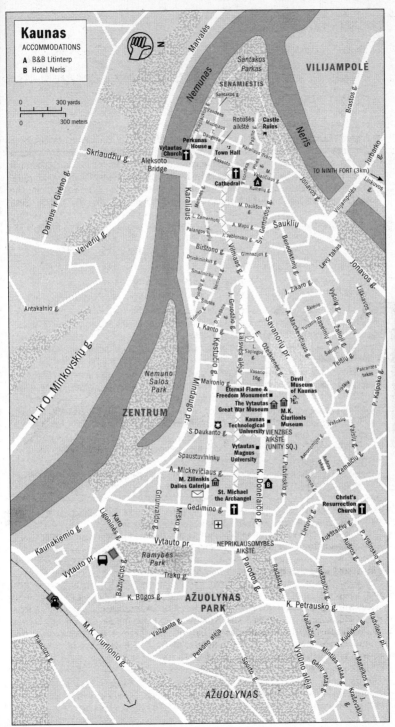

# Kaunas

ACCOMMODATIONS

**A** B&B Litinterp
**B** Hotel Neris

N

0        300 yards
0        300 meters

VILIJAMPOLĖ

Nemunas

Marvalės

Santakos
Parkas

SENAMIESTIS

Santakos g.

Prieplaukos

Vandens

Muziejaus

Daugirdo

Rotušės
aikštė

Castle
Ruins

Perkūnas
House

Vytautas
Church

Town Hall

Karaliaus gtvd.

Aleksoto

Pilies g.

Skrlaudžiu g.

Aleksoto
Bridge

Cathedral

M.
Valančiaus g.

Kumeliu g.

Neris

TO NINTH FORT (3km)

Jonavos g.

Vilijampolės

Linkuvos

Jurbarko

Brastos g.

Danaus ir Girėno g.

Veiverių g.

Karaliaus

Muiuneas

Bonų

M. Daukšos
g.

L. Zamenhofo

A. Mapu g.

J. Jablonskio g.

Palangos

Birštono g.

Druskininkų g.

Smalininkų

Vilniaus g.

Sv. Gertrūdos

Šaulių

Benediktinų g.

Gimnazijos g.

A. Mackevičiaus g.

Levų takas

Jonavos g.

Liškiavos g.

Antakalnio g.

H. ir O. Minkovskių g.

Nemuno
Salos
Park

ZENTRUM

Poldia g.

Silutes

Trento g.

Podba

J. Gruodžio g.

Kęstučio g.

I. Kanto g.

Laisvės alėja

J. Zikaro g.

E. Ožeškienės g.

Savanorių pr.

Vyšnių g.

Turžėnu

Raseinių g.

Skleno

Šarūpos g.

Žaliojų g.

Orbulių

Telšių g.

Pakrantės
takas

Mindaugo pr.

Maironio g.

L.
Sapiegos g.

Vasario
16g.

Eternal Flame &
Freedom Monument

The Vytautas
Great War Museum

Kaunas
Technological
University

S Daukanto g.

Devil
Museum
of Kaunas

M.K.
Čiurlionis
Museum

VIENYBĖS
AIKŠTĖ
(UNITY SQ.)

Brokių g.

P. Kalpoko g.

Vašokilu

LITHUANIA

Vaisių g.

Spaustuvininkų

Vytautas
Magnus
University

A. Mickevičiaus g.

M. Žilinskis
Dalies Galerija

St. Michael
the Archangel

Gedimino g.

Gruvaldo g.

Miško g.

K. Donelaičio g.

V. Putinskio g.

Katonomijos g.

Dinca g.

Aušros
takas

Žemaičių g.

Christ's
Resurrection
Church

Vytauto pr.

Kaunakiemio g.

Karo
Ligoninės g.

Bažnyčios g.

Ramybės
Park

Vytauto pr.

Trakų g.

K. Bugos g.

NEPRIKLAUSOMYBĖS
AIKŠTĖ

AŽUOLYNAS
PARK

Parodos g.

Radastų g.

Lietuvių g.

Aukštaičių g.

Aušros g.

P. Višinsko g.

Aukštaičių g.

P.
Valaičio g.

K. Petrausko g.

Pranciskų g.

M. K. Čiurlionio g.

Valžganto g.

Valganto g.

Pertono alėja

Sporto g.

Vydūno alėja

Mintes alėja

Gėlių ratas

V. Kudirkos g.

Radvilėnų pl.

Matelkos g.

J.
Kraševskio

AŽUOLYNAS

# ▐▀ TRANSPORTATION

**Trains:** M. K. Čiurlionio g. 16 (☎29 22 60), at the end of Vytauto pr. To: **Vilnius** (2hr., 15 per day, 7.30-8.70Lt) and **Rīga, LAT** (6hr., 1 per day, 39Lt, *coupé* 61Lt). Schedule varies for other connections, including **Kaliningrad, RUS, Tallinn, EST** and **Warsaw, POL.**

**Buses:** Vytauto pr. 24/26 (☎22 79 42; international reservations ☎20 19 63; info ☎20 19 55). To: **Vilnius** (2hr., 25 per day, 12.40Lt); **Klaipėda** (4hr., 8 per day, 31Lt); and **Palanga** (4hr., 7 per day, 33Lt).

**Hydrofoils:** Raudondvario pl. 107 (☎26 13 48), in the town of Vilijampolė, across the Neris. Take trolleybus #7 from the train and bus stations, or #10 or 11 from the stop at the west end of Laisvės al.; get off at Kedainiu, the 3rd stop across the river. In summer, *Raketa* hydrofoils splash to **Nida** via **Nemunas** (4hr., 1 per day, 59Lt).

**Local Transportation:** Tickets for buses and trolleybuses are available from kiosks (0.60Lt) or the driver (0.70Lt). The best way to get around the city, however, is by the **maršrutinis taksis** vans that speed along bus routes in large numbers. To stop one, stick out an arm. Tell the driver where you want to get off (1Lt).

**Taxis: State Taxi Co.,** ☎23 66 66. 1Lt per km. **Private Taxi,** ☎23 98 80, rates vary so be sure to bargain.

# ▐ PRACTICAL INFORMATION

**Tourist Office: Regional Tourist Information Center,** A. Mickevičiaus 36/40 (☎32 34 36; fax 20 36 78; turizma@takas.lt). Helpful staff sells maps and can arrange tours. Open Apr.-Sept. M-F 9am-7pm, Sa 9am-3pm; Oct.-Mar. M-F 9am-6pm.

**Currency Exchange:** Look for Valiutos Keitykla signs on Laisvės al. and Vilniaus g. **Lietuvos Taupomasis Bankas,** Laisvės al. 82 (☎20 66 36), gives MC **cash advances,** cashes AmEx/MC/Thomas Cook **traveler's checks,** and has a Cirrus 24hr. **ATM.** Open M-F 8am-4pm.

**Luggage Storage:** In a tunnel under the train station. 1Lt per bag. Open daily 8:30am-2:15pm, 3-8pm, and 8:30pm-8am. At the bus station, store luggage outside the main building, to the left. 1Lt per bag. Open daily 7am-9pm.

**English Bookstore: Centrinis Knygyas,** Laisvės al. 81 (☎22 95 72), stocks classics, best-sellers, and books on Lithuania and Kaunas. Open M-F 10am-7pm, Sa 10am-5pm.

**Bi-Gay-Lesbian Services: Gay Information Line** (☎(8) 22 33 30 31; www.gay.lt) provides general information. **The Gay Club,** out of Vilnius, (see p. 414; ☎(8) 299 85 009; vgc@takas.lt) keeps listings and locations in Lithuania.

**Telephones:** To the left as you enter the post office; card phones in the main lobby. Open daily 8am-10pm. Europe 5.80Lt per min., North America 10.50Lt per min.

> Lithuanian Telecom has been changing many of the phone numbers in Kaunas. In an attempt to smooth the transition, they have set up an info line at (8-800) 22 22 22. For directory assistance dial 09. The tourist office also keeps track of changes.

**Internet Access: Kavinė Internetas,** Daukšos 12 (☎22 53 64). Open 10am-10pm.

**Pharmacies: Aesculaturas,** Gedimino 36 (☎20 48 02). English spoken. Open M-F 8am-6pm, Sa 9am-4pm. **24hr. pharmacy** at Savanoriu 66 (☎20 57 96).

**Post Office:** Laisvės al. 102 (☎32 42 86; fax 32 43 41). **Poste Restante** window #11; 0.50Lt per package. Open M-F 7:30am-6:30pm, Sa 7:30am-4:30pm.

**Postal Code:** LT-3000.

# ▐▞ ACCOMMODATIONS AND FOOD

Only one cheap option survives: **Litinterp,** Kumeliu 15, #4 (☎/fax 22 87 18; litinterp@kaunas.omnitel.net), in Senamiestis, which finds excellent private rooms in the Old Town. Buy any of the Lithuanian *In Your Pocket Guides* here. (Open M-F

9am-6pm, Sa 9am-4pm. Singles 60-80Lt; doubles 100-120Lt; triples 150-180Lt.) The restaurant situation is thankfully much better.

**Astra,** Laisvės al. 76 (☎22 14 04). Eat well to live jazz among splatter-painted canvases. You can also enjoy comfy outdoor seating on the city's main walkway. International main dishes 20-35Lt. English menu available. Live music M-Th 8pm, F-Sa 10:30pm. Open M-Th 8am-midnight, F-Sa 8am-1am, Su 11am-midnight.

**Miesto Sodas,** Laisvės al. 93 (☎22 55 76). Rub shoulders with the elite for an affordable price. The lighter menu options are a refreshing alternative to Baltic fare. Eat well for under 30Lt. Open daily 11am to midnight. MC/Visa.

**Tête-à-Tête,** Vytautos 56 (☎22 04 62; fax 22 61 31). Considered by many the best restaurant in Lithuania. A few (but not many) main dishes come in under 25Lt. The desserts are divine and easier on the wallet. Open M-Tu noon-midnight, W-Su noon-2am.

**Pas Pranciška,** Zamenhofo 11 (☎20 38 75). Offers simple, mid-range elegance with maritime decor. Main dishes 20-25Lt. Open daily 9:30am-9pm. MC/Visa.

**Arbatinė,** Laisvės 100 (☎32 37 32). The veggie-lover's dream. Decorated as a nature cabin—complete with a white picket fence—Arbatinė offers a **vegan** menu, with main dishes under 25Lt. Open M-Sa 8:30am-7:30pm.

# 🔎 SIGHTS

Sights in Kaunas cluster around two regions. St. Michael's Church and Unity Square lie toward the end of Laisvės al, the city's main pedestrian boulevard; at the boulevard's other end you'll find Senamiestis and its cathedral, town hall, and smaller attractions. Pažaislis Monastery and Church and the Ninth Fort are outside the city.

**ST. MICHAEL THE ARCHANGEL CHURCH.** The church was built for the Russian garrison that came to man the nine forts around Kaunas in the 1890s. The sumptuous, symmetric neo-Byzantine exterior and silver-blue domes are a feast for the eyes. (*Nepriklausomybės Sq, at the end of Laisvės al. opposite Senamiestis.* ☎22 66 76. *Open M-F 8am-4pm, Sa-Su 8:30am-2pm. Services M-F noon, Sa 10am, Su 10am and noon.*)

**UNITY SQUARE.** (Vienybės aikštė.) On the south side, **Vyatauto Didžiojo University** and the older **Kaunas Technological University** draw in a student population of more than 16,000. Across the street, in an outdoor shrine to Lithuanian statehood, busts of famous Lithuanians flank a corridor leading from the **Freedom Monument** (Laisves paminklas) to an eternal flame commemorating those who died for freedom in 1918-20. These symbols of nationhood disappeared during the Soviet occupation, but emerged in St. Michael's in 1989. On a hill behind the Čiurlionis Museum (see p. 424), **Christ's Resurrection Church,** a famous Modernist creation, waits to be finished. Started in 1932, construction stopped in 1940 on account of Stalin's meddling. While in the area, check out the nearby **Devil Museum** and the **Vytautas the Great War Museum** (see p. 424). (*Two blocks down Laisvės al. from St. Michael's and right on Daukanto g.*)

**KAUNAS CATHEDRAL.** (Kauno Arkikatedra Bažnyčia.) One of Lithuania's largest churches, the Kaunas Cathedral is thought to have been built during the 1408-13 Christianization of Low Lithuania. Its breathtaking interior, which dates from 1800, is cut in sharp Gothic lines. A pillar at the back of the church holds the **tomb of Maironis,** the beloved priest from Kaunas whose poetry played a central role in Lithuania's 19th-century National Awakening. (*Vilniaus 26. Where Laisvės al. ends, Senamiestis begins; follow Vilniaus g. through an underpass and inside the medieval city walls, and then 3 blocks farther to the cathedral.* ☎22 75 46. *Open 7am-4pm.*)

**OLD TOWN SQUARE.** (Rotušės aikštė.) Just past the cathedral, the **town hall,** a confused stylistic concoction constructed in stages from 1542 to 1771, presides over Old Town Square in the city center. Behind and to the left of the town hall stands a **statue of Maironis.** His hand hides his clerical collar, a ploy that duped the atheist Soviets into allowing the city to erect a statue of a priest. Up Karaliaus dvaro, which leads off the square to the right of Maironis's statue, the Neris and Nemunas rivers meet at **Santakos Parkas.** The remains of the 13th-century **Kauno castle** (pilis) stand here. Next to it is the decaying late-Baroque **St. Francis Church and Jesuit Monastery.**

Follow Aleksoto g. toward the river from the corner of Rotušės aikštė opposite Karaliaus d. to get to the quirky 15th-century **Perkūnas House** (Perkūnas namas), a late-Gothic edifice built for Hanseatic merchants on the site of a temple to Perkū nas, god of thunder. At the end of the street is the Gothic **Vytautas Church** (Vytauto bažnyčia), also built in the early 1400s.

**PAŽAISLIS MONASTERY AND CHURCH.** This vibrant Baroque ensemble, with rich frescoes, sits on the right bank of the Nemunas 10km east of central Kaunas. The church was designed by three Florentine masters in the 17th century. Used as a KGB-run "psychiatric hospital" and then as a resort, the monastery was returned to the Catholic Church in 1990. Classical music concerts are held here, as is the much-touted Pažaislis Music Festival from late May through August. *(Kauno jūros 31. Take trolleybus #5 or 9 from the train station to the end of the line; the church is 1km down the road past a small beach. ☎ 75 64 85. Hours vary, so call ahead. Free tour after 11am mass.)*

■ **NINTH FORT.** (IX Fortas.) Across the Neris from the castle lies the town of **Vili-jampolė,** which gained infamy during World War II as the Jewish Ghetto of Kaunas, vividly immortalized in Avraham Tory's *Kovno Ghetto Diary*. The Ninth Fort, a few kilometers north of the ghetto, was one of the nine forts constructed in the 1880s around Kaunas as the first line of defense against the German Empire. During World War II it was used as a Soviet deportation center until it became a Nazi concentration camp; still later, it served as the site of KGB atrocities. The museum focuses on the Nazis, but also includes newer exhibits on the mass deportations of Lithuanians in the 1940s and 50s. Part of the museum is housed in the fort's prison cells, where 30,000 Jews were murdered. Outside looms the monument unveiled in 1994 as a memorial to the dead, with contorted figures etched into the twisting stone. The surrounding fields are mass graves for over 50,000 people. *(Žemaičių pl. 73. Catch microbus #46 and ask to stop at IX Fortas (2-5 per hr. 2am-9pm). ☎ 23 76 68 and 23 74 47. Open W-Su 10am-6pm. Each part of the museum 2Lt, students 1Lt. Tunnel connecting the prison with the barracks can be explored with a guide for 10Lt. Cameras 20Lt.)*

# 🏛 MUSEUMS

Museums abound in Kaunas; with a few notable exceptions, the most interesting ones lie around Unity Square (Vienybės aikštė), off Laisvės al.

■ **Devil Museum** (Velnių muziejus, formally the A. Žmuidzinavičiaus Art Collection), V. Putvinskio g. 64 (☎ 20 84 72), near Unity Square. Lithuanian artist and collector Anta-nas Žmuidzinavičiaus collected more than 260 devils (or 20 devil dozens); the museum now boasts over 2000 devils from Lithuania, Africa, Siberia, the Urals and South Amer-ica. Most notable is "The Division of Lithuania," featuring Devil Hitler and Devil Stalin chasing each other across bone-covered Lithuania. Open Tu-Su 11am-5pm; closed last Tu of the month. 4Lt, students 2Lt.

■ **Museum of Exiles and Political Prisoners** (Tremties ir rezistencijos muziejus), Vytauto pr. 46 (☎ 22 75 26 and 20 64 88), near Ramybės Park and a short walk from St. Michael's. Small collection of photographs and artifacts of the resistance to Soviet rule, as well as evidence of the life of exiles in Siberia. One of the women there was an exile herself—get someone to translate her tour from Lithuanian, German, or Russian. Bro-chure in English. Open W-Su 10am-4pm. Donation requested.

**M. K. Čiurlionis Museum,** Putvinskio 55 (☎ 20 44 46; guided tours 22 97 38), in Unity Sq. behind the War Museum. Displays works by the revered artist and composer who sought to combine music and image to depict ideas in their pre-verbal state. Čiurlionis has been described as "a cross between Monet on acid and Dalí on valium." High-qual-ity 20th-century Lithuanian works fill the other halls. Open Tu-Su 11am-5pm; closed last Tu of every month. 5Lt, students 2.50Lt.

**Vytautas the Great War Museum** (Vytauto Didžiojo Karo Muziejus), Donelaičio g. 64 (☎ 22 26 06), in Unity Sq. behind 2 soccer-playing lions. Houses all sorts of weapons and the aircraft *Lituanica*, in which 2 Lithuanian-Americans, Darius and Girėnas, tried to fly from New York to Kaunas non-stop in 1933; they crashed in Germany. Another exhibit follows Napoleon's journey through the Baltics en route to his ill-fated Russian campaign. Open W-Su 11am-6pm. 2Lt, students 1Lt.

**Mykolo Žilinsko Dailės Galerija,** Nepriklausomybės 12 (☎20 13 81), just south of St. Michael's. Hosts rotating exhibits of Modernist art and a collection of mummies, porcelain, and 19th-century paintings. Cézanne, Renoir, and Manet await on the upper levels. Open Tu-Su noon-6pm; closed last Tu of each month. 5Lt, students 2.50Lt.

## 🎵🎭 ENTERTAINMENT AND NIGHTLIFE

**Muzikinis Teatras** (The Musical Theater), Laisvės al. 91 (☎20 09 33), performs operettas. The **Kaunas Philharmonic,** Sapiegos g. 5 (☎20 04 78), is known for its classical concerts (9-15Lt). Some of Kaunas's outdoor bars offer live music in the evenings.

**Siena** (The Wall), Laisvės al. 93 (☎22 55 76), beneath Miesto sodas. Spacious dance floor that tends to fill quickly as local bands play and the house DJs drop mad-phat beat. Live jazz Su. Open W-Th and Su 9pm-2am, F-Sa 9pm-4am. MC/Visa.

**Amerika Pirtyje,** Vytauto 71 (☎29 32 44), at the Hotel Baltija. Rough wood, coiled rope, and picnic tables make this disco feel like a converted barn. Concerts every Saturday at 9pm. Open M-W and Su noon-2am, Th noon-3am, F-Sa noon-4am.

**Skliautai,** Rotušės aikštė 26 (☎20 68 43). In the courtyard, more peaceful than the night clubs along Laisvės al. Older sophisticates mellow out and sip the beer. 0.50L *Kalnapilis* 5Lt. Open daily 10am-midnight. MC.

## ⌘ DAYTRIPS FROM KAUNAS

### ŠIAULIAI
*Take the train from Kaunas (2hr., 5 per day, 6Lt). Buses now run directly to Šiauliai as well. Do not take a bus to Kryžkalnis; it's 30km south of Šiauliai. From the bus stop, a marked road leads down for about 2km. To get back, take any bus heading toward Kaunas. The last train leaves at 5:45pm, and the last bus at 6pm.*

On a sunny morning in 1236, the German Knights of the Sword, returning from a campaign to Christianize Lithuania, were ambushed and massacred. The town founded on the site, Šiauliai (SEE-ow-oo-lee-eye; pop. 146,500), took its name from the shining sun *(saulė)* of that bloody day. To commemorate the bloodshed, people began the **Hill of Crosses** (Kryžių Kalnas), 14km northwest of the city. After the Lithuanian uprisings of 1831 and 1863, people from across the country brought crosses to remember the dead and the deported, and the collection grew. During Soviet occupation the hill became a veritable mound of anti-Russian sentiment and despite three bouts with a bulldozer, the memorial survived. Independence has brought a new eruption of crosses, as emigré Lithuanians and relatives of the exiled have returned to add their own monuments. In 1993, Pope John Paul II added a crucifix of his own to the pile, which now rattles audibly in the breeze.

# DRUSKININKAI                                    ☎(8)370

Cradled by the Nemunas River and sprinkled by a host of lakes and mineral springs, Druskininkai (pop. 20,000) has been calming the nerves and healing the sick of Europe since 1794, when it was declared a center for treatment by the Grand Duke of Lithuania. It also happens to be the birthplace of revered Lithuanian artist Mikolojus Konstantinas Čiurlionis (see **Literature and Arts,** p. 407). Druskininkai houses eight sanatoria and boasts of curative mineral springs. Poles once flocked to Druskininkai to put mud on their faces and bathe in its natural spring waters; after World War II, the town became a favorite vacation resort among Russians. These days, the Russians are gone, while the Poles are returning in droves.

**⌐ TRANSPORTATION.** The **train station,** Gardino g. 3, sends trains to **Vilnius** via **Pariečė, BLR** (☎534 43; you need a visa to get off; 4hr., 3 per day, 13Lt) and **Hrodna, BLR** (1½hr., 2 per day Sa-Su, 6Lt). Get to Hrodna on weekdays by boarding an early train headed for Vilnius and switching to a Hrodna-bound train in Parieče (1½hr., 6.50Lt). **Buses** remain the more convenient choice, heading from the station, Gardino g. 1 (☎513 33), to: **Vilnius** (2hr., 5 per day, 13.90Lt); **Kaunas** (3hr., 10 per day, 14.50Lt); **Hrodna, BLR** (1¾hr., 3 per day, 6Lt); and **Warsaw, POL** (7-7½hr., 1 per day, 52Lt). To get to town, go left after exiting either station and walk down Gardino g., which soon becomes V. Kudirkos g., and leads directly to the main artery, M. K. Čiurlionio g. (5min.). For maps and info, go to the **Tourist Information Center,** Gardino 1, upstairs from the bus station. (☎/fax 517 77; druskininkutib@post.omnitel.net; www.druskonis.lt/info. Open M-F 8:30am-12:30pm, 1:15-5:15pm.) The bus station has **luggage storage** (0.50Lt). **Postal code:** LT-4690. Phone code: 370.

**⛏️◌ ACCOMMODATIONS AND FOOD. Druskininkai Hotel,** V. Kudirkos g. 43, on the corner of Taikos g., directly across the street from the Roman Catholic church, is visible while following V. Kurdirkos g. into town. The spartan yet clean rooms are as cheap as they come in Druskininkai. (☎525 66; fax 522 17. Singles with bath and balcony 50Lt; doubles 66-80Lt; triples 75-96Lt. MC/Visa.) The **French Bakery,** M. K. Čiurlioni g. 63, sells pastries fresh out of the oven for a pittance. (Croissant 1Lt. Open 8am-9:30pm; MC/Visa.) **Sicilija,** Taikos g. 9, serves up delicious pizza (5-13Lt) and makes a worthwhile stop for those hankering for a menu with English translations or a vegetarian option. (☎518 65. Open M-Su 11am-11pm. MC/Visa.)

**◙⬛ SIGHTS AND ENTERTAINMENT.** "You hear the murmur of the pines, so solemn, as if they were trying to tell you something," avant-garde artist, composer, and mystic M.K. Čiurlionis wrote in 1905. Čiurlionis was born and spent many of his days in Druskininkai, although, to the locals' regret, he died and was buried in Poland. The artist's unique works are kept alive at **M.K. Čiurlionis Memorialinis Muziejus,** M.K. Čiurlionio g. 35, which tells the artist's story in four buildings, including the house in which he worked. The museum has mostly prints and focuses on the artist's life and times. (☎511 31. Open Tu-Su 11am-5pm; closed last Tu of the month; 1Lt, students 0.50Lt.) **Piano concerts** on Sunday evenings in the summer feature Čiurlionis's own compositions, as well as those of Bach, Debussy, and Beethoven. (1hr. performances at 5pm. 8Lt.) To take advantage of Druskinkai's therapeutic offerings, follow one of the **cleansing paths** marked in the map from the Tourist Office or explore a **sanatorium** with foot massages (1Lt) and other delights.

# COASTAL LITHUANIA

The chilly Baltic Sea dominates the secluded, thickly forested world of coastal Lithuania. The carnival resort town of Palanga offers fun-filled summer days and nights, while the bustling port of Klaipėda continues to enjoy economic prominence and political importance. Klaipėda also guards the gateway to Lithuania's share of the Curonian Spit (Neringa). Down the Spit, Juodkrantė showcases delightful, devilish Lithuanian art and farther yet, near the border with Kaliningrad, Nida nestles among towering sand dunes.

## PALANGA                                    ☎(8)236

Palanga (pop. 18,000) is the hottest summer spot in Lithuania—at least that's what the national government and president apparently think, having chosen Palanga as their summer residence. About 82,000 other summer settlers agree, drawn by magnificent beaches, charming streets lined with cafes and shops, and rollicking nightlife. Don't get turned off by the crowds; with the largest park in the country and over 20km of shoreline, there's room on the beach for all.

**⬛ TRANSPORTATION.** The **bus station,** Kretinjos 1 (☎533 33), sends buses to: **Kaunas** (3hr., 16 per day, 30Lt); **Vilnius** (4-5hr., 9 per day, 41Lt); and **Druskininkai** (5hr., 1 per day, 40Lt). **Microbuses** leave for **Klaipėda** from the bus station (20min., every 30min., 2.50Lt; buy tickets from the driver).

■▪**🄵** **ORIENTATION AND PRACTICAL INFORMATION.** Palanga's main streets are **Vytauto gatrė,** which runs parallel to the beach past the bus station, and **J. Basan-avičiaus,** which runs perpendicular to Vytauto g. and finishes in a boardwalk. The pedestrian **Meilės alėja** runs south of the pier alongside the beach, becoming **Birutės alėja** in the Palanga Park and Botanical Garden.

English **tourist information** is available from the center to the right of the bus station entrance. (Open M-F 9am-1pm, 2-6pm.) **Lietuvos Taupomasis Bankas,** Juratės g. 15/2, **exchanges currency,** cashes AmEx/MC/Thomas Cook **traveler's checks,** and processes MC **cash advances. Western Union** services are available inside and a 24hr. **ATM** stands outside. (☎512 09. Open M-F 7:30am-6:30pm, Sa 8am-2pm.) The **post office,** Vytauto g. 53 (☎531 47), also exchanges currency. (Open M-F 9am-6:30pm, Sa 9am-2pm.) The **telephone office** is in the same building. (☎/fax 482 25. Open M-F 8am-10pm, Sa 8am-2pm.) **Postal code:** LT-5720.

▛▞▟ **ACCOMMODATIONS AND FOOD.** Finding inexpensive rooms can be tricky. **Litinterp** in Klaipėda (see **Practical Information,** p. 429) arranges **private rooms** in Palanga for slightly higher rates. **"Palangos Žuvėdra" Viešbutis,** Birutės alėja 52, offers rooms in a multi-building complex near the shore, complete with the sound of crashing waves. From the bus station, head left on Vytauto g. for several blocks, turn right onto Kestučio, and then left onto Birutės. Call ahead, as tour groups often book the entire place. Clean but bare doubles with shared bath for 60Lt. (Info ☎538 52; registration ☎532 53. Breakfast, lunch, and dinner 16.52Lt.) **Vyturio Korpusas,** Dariaus ir Girėno g. 20, is popular with both backpackers and older travelers. From the bus station, go left on Vytauto g. to Danaus ir Gireno g. and right opposite the soccer fields. This complex includes a sauna and pool. (☎491 47; fax 491 98. Breakfast 8Lt; lunch 11Lt; dinner 8Lt. Singles 74Lt; doubles 116Lt; triples 159Lt. MC/Visa.)

The Palangan pedestrian will have no trouble finding food. **Vytauto g.** and **J. Basan-avičiaus g.** are lined with cafes blaring music. Innumerable street vendors sell soft-serve ice cream (1Lt), *čeburekai* (meat-filled dough pastries; 2Lt), and waffles-dipped-in-chocolate-on-a-stick (3-4Lt). **Senoji Dorė,** J. Basanavičiaus g. 5, at the end of the major pedestrian street, offers Lithuanian cuisine amid nautical decorations. (☎53 455. Main dishes 16-28Lt. 5% service charge. Open 10am-midnight.) For an alternative to Palanga's many "themed" restaurants, try **Monika,** J. Basanavičiaus g. 12, which serves Lithuanian and Italian dishes. (☎525 60. Veggie pizza 9Lt; other dishes 17-26Lt. Open M-F 11am-midnight, Sa-Su 10am-midnight. MC/Visa.) Serious carnivores may enjoy **Elnio Ragas,** J. Basanavičiaus g. 25. This smoky hunting lodge—complete with fireplace and trophy boar's head—uses up lots of tongue in its dishes. If those or boiled pigs' ears (12Lt) aren't to your taste, there are always chicken fingers (7Lt; ☎535 05; open 11am until the last guest leaves; MC/Visa).

🄶 **SIGHTS.** Palanga's pride and joy, the **Amber Museum** (Gintaro muziejus), resides in the mansion built in 1897 by Count Tiškevičius, at the heart of the Botanical Gardens. It displays a large portion of its 15,000 inclusions—amber with primeval flora and fauna trapped inside (check out the rare reptile inclusion in Case 13). (☎513 19. English captions. Open June-Aug. Tu-Su 10am-8pm, Sept.-May Tu-Su 11am-7pm; ticket office closes 1 hour early. 5Lt, students 2.50Lt. "Common ticket," including the Clock Museum and the Picture Gallery of Klaipėda, 4.50Lt.) The **Palanga Botanical Gardens** include landscaped flower gardens, wooded paths, and a pond that hosts a family of trumpet swans. Through the main entrance to the gardens, on the corner of Vytauto g. and S. Dariaus ir S. Girėno g., stands **Eglė,** Queen of the Serpents, one of the most famous statues in Lithuania. Follow the path past the manor to the right to reach the **beach.** The pine-covered hill to the left before the boardwalk is **Birutė Hill,** once the site of a pagan shrine to Praurimė, named for the vestal virgin of the shrine who was kidnapped and made a Grand Duchess (look for her grave nearby). A 19th-century octagonal **chapel** with brilliant stained glass windows now invades Praurimė's turf. Leaving the Botanical Garden through the main gate, walk left down Vytauto to the **Dr. Jonas Šliūpas Memorial Gardens and House,** Vytauto g. 23a, where the famous "cultural worker and public man" lived from 1930-

44. Dr. Šliūpas was a Lithuanian patriot who founded newspapers, participated in the brief Lithuanian government between the world wars, and worked as a doctor, teacher, and even brewmaster in Palanga before being forced into exile; he died in the US. (☎545 59. Open W-Su 11am-5pm. Free.)

🎭 **ENTERTAINMENT.** Street vendors rent **bikes** (5-10Lt per hr.), **in-line skates** (7Lt per hr.), and a host of other wheeled vehicles. Alternatively, go nuts with **minigolf** (15Lt) next to Ritos Virtuvė on J. Basanavičiaus g. **Bumper boats** (5Lt for 3min.) are set up in front of the **Summer Theatre** (Vasaraos Estrada) at Vytauto g. 43. The hall hosts **concerts** by the Lithuanian National Philharmonic and Klaipėda Philharmonic, as well as visiting performers. (☎522 10. Box office open daily 11am-noon and 1-8pm.) Many of the cafes lining Basanavičiaus g. and Vytauto g. feature live bands and dancing at night. **Kinoteatras Naglis,** Vytauto g. 82, shows Hollywood's latest vehicles of cultural imperialism with Lithuanian subtitles (8Lt).

Stick around for **sunset** to take part in Palanga's most famous tradition. Join locals and visitors-in-the-know in strolling out onto the pier to bid farewell to the sun as it vanishes over the vast Baltic Sea—a serene and spectacular moment before Palanga's swinging nightlife kicks in.

# KLAIPĖDA                                          ☎(8)26

Guarding the Curonian Lagoon with its fortress at the tip of the Neringa peninsula, Klaipėda (klai-PAY-da; pop. 202,484), Lithuania's third-largest city, is a little too strategically located for its own good. Known as Memel until 1923, the city passed from Lithuanian to Polish, Swedish, Russian, and Prussian hands over the course of a few centuries. In 1807 it became the temporary capital of Prussia while Napoleon roamed the continent; the city remained German until it went to France in the 1919 Treaty of Versailles. Lithuania reclaimed it as Klaipėda in 1923 and all was well until Hitler personally stormed its shores in 1939. (He left when the Soviets moved in.) The legacy of conquest lives on in Klaipėda's architectural hodgepodge and the city's location still makes it an ideal base for tourist invasions of the dramatic coast.

## ✳ ORIENTATION

The **Danė River** divides the city into south **Senamiestis** (Old Town) and north **Naujam-iestis** (New Town). Kuršių marios (Curonian Lagoon) to the west cuts off **Smiltynė**, Klaipėda's Kuršių Nerija (Curonian Spit) quarter. **H. Manto g.,** the main artery, becomes Tiltų g. as it crosses the river into Senamiestis, and finally Taikos g. as it enters the more modern (read: Soviet) part of the city. Pick up *Klaipėda in Your Pocket*, with **maps** and info on Palanga, Juodkrantė, and Nida (4Lt), at **Litinterp** (see below). All of mainland Klaipėda lies close to the **bus** and **train stations,** which are separated by Priestoties g. Facing away from the bus station, turn left onto Priesto-ties g. and left again onto S. Nėries g. Follow S. Nėries g. away from the train station to its end, then take a right on S. Daukanto g. to reach the heart of the city.

## 🚌 TRANSPORTATION

**Trains: Geležinkelio stotis,** Priestoties 1 (☎31 36 76; reservations ☎29 62 91). To: **Vilnius** (5hr., 3 per day, 40Lt) and **Kaunas** (6½hr., 1 per day, 26Lt). Station open daily 3:30am-10:30pm.

**Buses: Autobusų stotis,** Butkų Juzės 9 (☎41 15 47; international ☎41 15 02; reserva-tions ☎21 14 34). To: **Palanga** (20min., every 30min., 2.50Lt); **Kaunas** (2-4hr., 13 per day, 20-25Lt); and **Vilnius** (4-7hr., 10 per day, 30-37Lt).

**Ferries: Old Castle Port,** Žveju 8 (☎31 42 57; info ☎31 11 57), sends ferries to **Smiltynė** (10min., 1-2 per hr. 5:30am-2am, round-trip 1.40Lt, students 0.70Lt). Ticket window open 5:15am-11:30pm. Microbuses on the other side complete the connection to **Juodkrantė** (20min., 5Lt) and **Nida** (1hr., 7Lt). **Private boats** advertised across from Old Castle are more expensive and wait until the boat is filled.

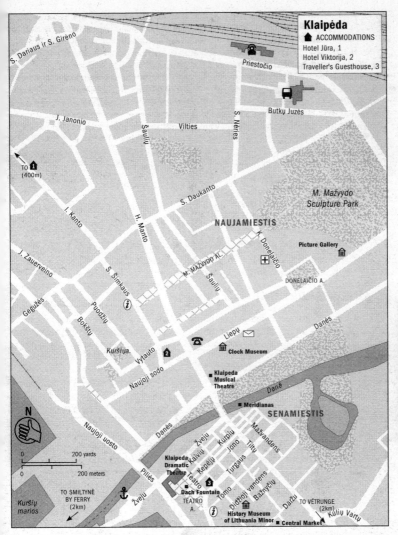

**Klaipėda**

🏠 ACCOMMODATIONS
Hotel Jūra, 1
Hotel Viktorija, 2
Traveller's Guesthouse, 3

S. Dariaus ir S. Girėno

Priestočio

Butkų Juzės

J. Janonio

Šaulių

Vilties

S. Nėries

TO 🏠
(400m)

I. Kanto

H. Manto

S. Daukanto

M. Mažvydo
Sculpture Park

NAUJAMIESTIS

K. Donelaičio

Picture Gallery 🏛

J. Zauerveino

M. MAŽVYDO AL.

Šaulių

DONELAIČIO A.

Geguzės

S. Šimkaus

Puodžių

Bokštų

Kuršių.

Vytauto

Liepų ✉

🏛 Clock Museum

Danės

Danės

📞

Naujoji sodo

■ Klaipėda
Musical
Theatre

Danė

■ Meridianas

SENAMIESTIS

N

Naujoji uosto

Danės

Žvejų

Kalvių

Kurpių

Jono

Mažvandens

Tiltų

0        200 yards

0        200 meters

Kuršių
marios

TO SMILTYNĖ
BY FERRY
(2km)

Pilies

Žvejų

Klaipėda
Dramatic
Theatre

Teatro

Kepėjų

Turgaus

Didžioji vandens

Bažnyčių

Tomo

TEATRO
A.

🏛 Dach Fountain

ℹ

🏛 History Museum
of Lithuania Minor

Darių

TO VĖTRUNGE
(2km)

Kūlių Vartų

■ Central Market

LITHUANIA

**Public Transportation: City buses** (0.60Lt per ride) and the wonderfully convenient **maršrutinis taksis** (route taxis) run all over town. The latter pick up and deposit passengers anywhere along the way. Stick out an arm to hail one (1Lt 6am-11pm; 2Lt 11pm-6am). #8 travels from the train station down H. Manto g. through Taikos g.

**Taxis: State company** (☎006). 1.20Lt per km is the standard fare. Several **private companies** roam the streets for 0.90-1.20Lt per km.

## 🛈 PRACTICAL INFORMATION

**Tourist Offices: Tourism Information Centre,** Tomo g. 2 (☎41 21 86 and 41 21 81; fax 41 21 85; kltic@takas.lt). Sells maps, provides brochures, and arranges tours. Staff speaks fluent English. Open M-F 8:30am-5pm, in summer also Sa 9am-3pm. **Litinterp,** S. Šimkaus g. 21/8 (☎31 14 90 and 41 18 14; fax 41 18 15;

litinterp@klaipeda.omnitel.net; www1.omnitel.net/litinterp-klaipeda). Arranges private rooms in: **Klaipėda** (singles 70Lt; doubles 120Lt; apartments 160-180Lt); **Palanga** (singles 100-120Lt; doubles 140Lt); and **Nida** (see p. 432). They also **rent bikes** (20Lt per day, US$100 deposit), sell **maps,** and answer questions. English spoken. Open M-F 8:30am-5:30pm, Sa 10am-3pm.

**Currency Exchange:** At kiosks around the bus and train stations, or at the many banks. **Lietuvos Taupomasis Bankas** at Taikos g. 22 (☎48 46 28) cashes AmEx/Thomas Cook/Citibank traveler's checks for a 0.25% commission. **Western Union** services. **Branch** at H. Manto g. 4 (☎21 72 13). Open M-F 9am-5pm, Sa 9am-3pm. Other branches advertise these services but won't actually perform them.

**ATM:** There's a Visa ATM in the post office (see below).

**Luggage Storage:** Lockers at far end of the train station (0.50Lt for a small locker) or racks at the bus station (1.50Lt per bag). Both open daily 5:30am-11:30pm.

**Telephones: Central Telephone Office,** H. Manto g. 2 (☎41 10 33). Pay the attendant or use card phones. Open daily 8am-10pm.

**Internet Access:** 2nd floor of the **library,** Tilžes 9 (☎25 89 02). 7 terminals at 3Lt per hr. Open M-F 11am-7pm, Sa 10am-3pm. Also at the telephone office. 10Lt per hr.

**Post Office: Central Post Office,** Liepų g. 16 (☎31 50 22; fax 31 50 45), in a neo-Gothic building. Houses a 48-bell carillon (the largest musical instrument in the country), which rings Sa-Su at noon. Visa ATM inside. Open M-F 8am-7pm, Sa 8am-4pm.

**Postal code:** LT-5800.

# ▐ ACCOMMODATIONS

The ever-obliging folks at **Litinterp** (see **Tourist Offices,** above) arrange **private rooms** with local families or can set you up in their own **guest house** near the M. Mažvydo pedestrian street. (Singles 70Lt; doubles 120Lt. MC/Visa.) Klaipėda's reasonably priced rooms provide a convenient base for coastal explorations, and can be easier on your wallet than rooms in the resort towns.

**Hotel Viktorija,** S. Šimkaus g. 2 (☎40 00 55 and 41 12 44; fax 41 21 47). Heading down H. Manto g. from the bus and train stations, turn right onto Vytauto g., the next street after the pedestrian walkway M. Mažvydo al. The hotel is on the corner at the end of the block. The best location in town for the best price. Old rooms are clean and hall showers have been recently renovated, but the shared toilets leave something to be desired (e.g. seats and toilet paper). Cheerful staff. Hall shower 3.50Lt. Reception 24hr. Singles 40Lt, with TV 45Lt; doubles 60Lt, 65Lt, private baths 120Lt.

**Klaipėda Traveller's Guesthouse (HI),** Turgaus 3/4 (☎21 49 35; oldtown@takas.lt), in the Old Town. Walk left from the train station (right from the bus station) down Trilapio and turn right on Liepu, then left H. Manto g., which crosses the river. Turgaus is the 2nd left after the bridge. The place to go to meet other backpackers or find local advice. Free beer and bike rental for reserving by email. Dorms 32Lt, non-members 34Lt.

**Hotel Jūra,** Malūnininkų 3 (☎39 98 57; fax 39 32 67), in the northwest part of town. From the bus station, turn left onto Priestoties g. and follow it across the bridge as it changes names. Turn right onto Sportinikų and left onto Malūninkų. The lobby and 2nd floor of this hotel have been beautifully renovated; new rooms come with Western furniture, phone, TV, and private baths. Older rooms transport you to the 1970s, complete with old-school decor and rotary phones. Sauna 50Lt per hr. Singles 90Lt, renovated 150Lt; doubles 100Lt, 250Lt. Breakfast included. MC/Visa.

# ◖ FOOD

The **central market** is on Turgas aikštė; follow Tiltų g. through Senamiestis and take a hard right at the first rotary. (Open daily about 8am-6pm.) The **IKI supermarket,** M. Mažvyado 7, has everything you could want in air-conditioned comfort within walking distance of the Old Town. (Open daily 9am-10pm.)

■ **Skandalas,** I. Kanto 44 (☎21 28 85). The only thing scandalous here is the Hollywood kitsch decor, which includes a pinstriped swing band nightly after 8pm. Tasty American cuisine—especially steaks—with rivers of beer to wash it all down. Main dishes 15-44Lt. 30% off on meals before 6pm. Open daily noon-3am. MC/Visa.

■ **BonTon,** Turgaus 4/2 (☎21 24 88). Excellent Senamiestis location, with the entrance tucked into an alleyway. Try to sit in the beautiful courtyard, which includes a garden and a stone waterfall. Good, fast, and insanely cheap local dishes (2-8Lt); ask for the English menu. Open M-F 8am-8pm, Sa-Su 10am-7pm.

**Luiza Kavine,** Puodžių 4 (☎21 98 82), opposite the gargantuan Hotel Klaipėda. Outside bar by the fountain and a slightly fancier cellar. Specializes in divine less-standard local fare. English menu. Squid stuffed with rice and vegetables 22Lt, stewed veal 15.40Lt, *Baltijos* 4.50Lt. Open daily 11am-midnight.

#  SIGHTS

## MAINLAND KLAIPĖDA

One would never guess that the lush, cheery **M. Mažvydo Sculpture Park** (M. Mažvydo Skulptūrų Parkas), between Liepų g. and S. Daukanto g., once served as the town's central burial ground. More sculptures by Lithuanian artists await at the **Picture Gallery** (Paveikslų galerija), Liepų 33, along with an extensive collection of striking 20th-century paintings—perhaps the finest art exhibit in Lithuania. (☎41 04 12. Open Tu-Sa noon-6pm, Su noon-5pm. 3Lt, students 1.50Lt. "Common ticket," including the Clock Museum and Palanga's Amber Museum, 4Lt.) Exiting the gallery, continue right down Liepų g. to the **Clock Museum** (Laikrodžių Muziejus), Liepų g. 12, next to the post office. Home to every conceivable time-keeping device, from Egyptian sundials to Chinese candle clocks to a modern quartz watch-pen, this bizarre little museum is a worthwhile stop. (☎41 04 13. Open Tu-Su 9am-5:30pm. 4Lt, students 2Lt. English tour 40Lt.)

The **Klaipėda Drama Theater** (Klaipėdos Dramos Teatras; tickets ☎31 44 53), Teatro aikštė, on the other side of H. Manto g., dominates the center of the Old Town. Built in 1857, the theater is famous as one of Wagner's favorite haunts, and infamous as the site where Hitler personally proclaimed the reincorporation of the town into the *Reich* in 1939. In front, the **Simon Dach Fountain** spouts water over the symbol of Klaipėda, a statue of Ännchen von Tharau. The original statue disappeared in World War II; some say it was taken by the Nazis, who didn't want her back to Hitler during his speech. The copy standing today was erected by German expatriates in 1989. Clothing, maps, rusty swords, coins, and buttons from the Iron Age to the present fill the **History Museum of Lithuania Minor** (Mažosios Lietuvos Istorijos Muziejus), Didžioji vandens g. 6. The extensive photographic exhibit on Klaipėda in World War II and after is worth a close look. (☎41 05 24. Open W-Su 11am-7pm. 2Lt, students 1Lt.) **Aukštoji g.,** near the history museum, is one of the best preserved areas of Senamiestis, lined with several examples of exposed-timber *Fachwerk* buildings for which pre-war Klaipėda was well-known.

## SMILTYNĖ

The ■ **Maritime Museum, Aquarium, and Dolphinarium** (Lietuvos Jūrų Muziejus), Smiltynė 3, is housed in an 1860s fortress that once guarded Klaipėda's bustling port. Now Baltic seals and sea lions frolic in the inner moat, while the fort's inner sanctum houses the aquarium. (☎39 11 19 and 39 11 33. Open June-Aug. Tu-Su 11am-7pm; May and Sept. W-Su 11am-7pm; Oct-Apr. Sa-Su 11am-6pm. 5Lt, students 3Lt. Camera 2Lt.) Don't miss the highly amusing **sea lion show,** featuring two North Sea sea lions and their trainer, budding comedians all. (11am, 1pm, and 3pm. 3Lt.) Dolphins leap, paint, and dance at the museum's **Dolphinarium.** (Noon, 2pm, and 4pm; 10Lt, students 5Lt.) Follow the road to the right as you step off the ferry. Museums dot the 1.5km stroll to the pier at the head of the Spit. The **Nature Museum** (Kuršių nerijos nacionalinio parko gamtos muziejus), Smiltynė 9-12, exhibits the region's natural and human history, including dioramas of villages now buried by the shifting sand dunes. (☎39 11 79. Open June-Aug. Tu-Su 11am-6pm, May and Sept. W-Su 11am-6pm. 2Lt., students 1Lt.) The **Fishermen's Village** (Ethnografinė Pajūrio Žvejo Sodyba) is a reconstruction of a 17th-century settlement. (Open 24hr. 2Lt.) Just down the road, four ships sit on pillars in the **Garden of Veteran Fishing Boats** (Žvejybos Laivai-veteranai). Forest paths lead west about 500m to the **beaches**. If you walk north before crossing over you can get a patch of sand to yourself. Signs mark gender-restricted areas for **nude bathing**—women to the right, men to the left, and the **public beach** in between.

## 🎵🎭 ENTERTAINMENT AND NIGHTLIFE

Nights in Klaipėda are generally spent mellowing in a beer garden with friends, listening to live bands perform Lithuanian hits and American classics. The best bar-hopping lies along H. Manto g., although most places close around midnight. Those searching for a more cultured experience will find it at the **Klaipėda Musical Theater** (Muzikinis teatras), Danės g. 19, which hosts operas and other musical events. (☎41 05 56. Ticket office open Tu-Su 11am-2pm and 4-7pm.) If you hit town in early June, a **Jazz Festival** will be in full swing.

  🏅**Meridianas,** Dauės Krautinė (river bank; ☎21 68 51), next to the bridge. The decks of this permanently moored schooner slope toward the bar. Old salts and sea pups alike imbibe while a skeleton (likely the only sober mate aboard) mans the wheel. Disco down below from 10pm. Cover 20-30Lt. Open daily 3pm-5am.

  **Paradox,** Minijos 2 (☎31 41 05). From the rotary at the end of Tiltų g., turn right onto Gallnio Pylimo g., which after another rotary becomes Minijos. The paradox? You'll figure it out after 5 or 6 beers. Work your way up or down 3 floors, from the pulsing disco to the mellow pool room to the relaxed bar as the night progresses. Open W noon-3am, Th-Su noon-6am. MC/Visa.

  **Kalifornija,** Laukininkų 17 (☎22 97 35), on the edge of town but still the most popular place around. Follow Taikos through Senamiestis away from the river. Take a left on Smiltelės and a right on Vingio. A taxi ride costs around 12Lt. Book a table well in advance, or just crowd the undersized dance floor. No cover. 20+. Open 8pm-6pm.

## 🔲 DAYTRIP FROM KLAIPĖDA

### WITCH'S HILL
*Nearly all of the microbuses running between Klaipėda and Nida stop at Juodkrantė—ask the driver to be sure (30min., 5Lt).*

Goblins, devils and, amused mortals frolic on Witch's Hill (Raganų Kalnas) in Juodkrantė. Set aside an hour to wander the worn trail (when in doubt, veer right, the path loops back to the beginning) through the dense magical wood lined with over 100 fantastic and mythical wooden sculptures in high Lithuanian folk-art style. Knights slay dragons, fishermen sail to sea, imps throw a party, and even Satan himself joins in on the fun. Don't miss the chance to cut in on a game of cards between the devil and a witch—they've left two seats free for you. Follow the "Sveikatingumo takas" path to the left or just head towards the sound of crashing water to find the **beach** on the Baltic side of the Spit. While Juodkrantė has been a site of mirth and ritual since the Stone Age, modern legend claims Witch's Hill is the place to be on Midsummer's Eve and St. John's Day.

# CURONIAN SPIT (NERINGA)

Majestic dunes, trails through lush forests, and swimming in the Baltic await on what is essentially a giant sandbar. The **Kuršių Nerija National Park** works to preserve this pristine natural wonder; you'll have to pay a 3Lt "environmental tax" when entering the Spit by microbus or hydrofoil.

# NIDA ☎ (8)259

The magical rise of wind-swept, white-sand dunes has long drawn summer vacationers to Nida (pop. 2000), only 3km north of the Russian Kaliningrad region on the Curonian Spit. From the remains of the immense sundial—the highest point on the Spit—you can look down on the glorious vista of the dunes, the Curonian Lagoon, the Baltic, and nearby Russia.

**☰ TRANSPORTATION.** The **bus station**, Naglių 20 (☎523 34), is basically a schedule and a few chairs encased by four walls. **Microbuses** run to **Smiltynė** (1hr., 7.50Lt); buy tickets on board. The last one (10pm) should get you there in time to catch the 11:15pm **ferry** back to **Klaipėda** (1hr., 7Lt). A **hydrofoil**, Naglių 16, goes to **Kaunas**. (4hr., Tu-Su 1 per day, 49Lt. ☎523 33. *Kasa* open daily 12:30-3:30pm and 6-9pm).

**⚐ PRACTICAL INFORMATION.** From the hydrofoil port, **Taikos g.** runs west inland. Perpendicular to Taikos g., **Naglių g.**, eventually becomes **Pamario g.** The **Tourist Information Center**, Taikos g. 4, opposite the bus station, offers the standard Neringa **map**, arranges private rooms for a 5Lt fee, and has good accommodation and transport info. (☎523 45; fax 523 44. Open June-Aug. M-Sa 10am-8pm, Su 10am-3pm; Sept.-May M-F 9am-noon and 1-7pm.) **Lietuvos Taupomasis Bankas**, Taikos g. 5, **exchanges currency**, cashes AmEx and Thomas Cook **traveler's checks** for a 0.5% commission, and gives MC/Visa **cash advances**. (☎522 41. Open M-F 8:30am-12:30pm and 1:30-5:30pm, Sa 9am-1pm and 2-7pm, Su 10am-4pm.) The **post office**, Taikos g. 13, lies up the road. (☎526 47. Open daily 8am-5pm.) The adjacent **telephone office** has card phones. (☎520 07. Open daily 8am-11pm.) **Postal code:** LT-5870.

**▟▟ ACCOMMODATIONS AND FOOD.** The **tourist office** (see above) arranges **private rooms** (30-50Lt per person). **Urbo Kalnas**, Taikos g. 32, on a pine-covered hill above town, rents large rooms with clean hot showers, TVs, and fridges. Walk uphill along Taikos g. from the center. (☎524 28. Singles 150Lt; doubles 210Lt; triples 275Lt. Breakfast included.) The budget traveler's dream awaits just past the Thomas Mann house at **Nidos Pušynas**, Purvynės 3—if that dream is a conveniently-located one-room shack with bathrooms across the street. (☎522 21. 12-20Lt.) **Litinterp** hikes its prices for private rooms in Nida. (☎(26) 31 14 90), in Klaipėda (see p. 429). Singles 100-120Lt; doubles 140-150Lt.)

The local specialty is *rūkyta žuvis* (smoked fish), which is best eaten with beer; selection varies from nondescript "fish" to eel and perch. **Seklyčia**, at the end of Lotmiško g., serves outstanding Lithuanian dishes. *Shashliks* and *blyni* are the cheapest meals. (☎529 45. Main dishes 22-35Lt. Open daily 9am-midnight.) **Ešerinė**, Naglių 2, is a wacky collection of thatched-roofed, glass-walled huts with wonderful views of the dunes. (☎527 57. Main dishes 20-27Lt. Open daily 10am-midnight.) Nida's largest **grocery store** is **Kuršis**, Naglių 29. (Open 9am-9pm.)

**◪ SIGHTS.** The ▨ **Drifting Dunes of Parnidis** rise south of town, across the bay from the shore-side restaurants at the end of Naglių and Lotmiško. Walk along the beach or through forest paths to reach steep stairs that lead to the peak of the tallest sand dune, marked by the remains of an immense sundial with ancient Baltic carvings—it was smashed by a huge storm in 1999. After enjoying the wonderful views of the lagoon and Baltic Sea, roam the surreal mountains and gorges of white sand carved by the wind. The nature preserve farther south is off-limits, which is just as well since going there you'd run the risk of straying into Russia.

All of the **wooden houses** clustered along Lotmiškio g. are classified as historic monuments; another two whole villages of them are buried somewhere under the sand. From the center of town, walk along the promenade by the water and bear right onto Skruzdynės g. to reach the renovated **Thomas Mann House** (Thomo Manno Namelis) at #17. Mann built the cottage in 1930 and wrote *Joseph and His Brothers* here, but had to give it up when Hitler invaded. The house now contains photos of Mann and his family and newspaper articles on the writer. (☎522 60. Open Tu-Su 10am-6pm, 1Lt.) The **Thomas Mann Cultural Center** puts on classical concerts in the living room for the **Thomas Mann Festival** in July.

# MACEDONIA (МАКЕДОНИЈА)

Although years of UN- and Greek-enforced trade embargoes damaged its economy, Macedonia is slowly regaining its place among southern European resorts. Its greater problem now may be the escalating unrest between the country's different ethnic groups—especially its large, underprivileged Albanian minority. Current problems notwithstanding, Macedonia's historical and geographical treasures remain intact, accessible, and welcoming, particularly the spectacular mountain basin that is home to Lake Ohrid, making Macedonia a necessary and memorable addition to any Balkan itinerary.

## MACEDONIA AT A GLANCE

**OFFICIAL NAME:** The Former Yugoslav Republic of Macedonia (FYROM)

**CAPITAL:** Skopje (pop. 450,000)

**POPULATION:** 2 million

**LANGUAGES:** Macedonian, Albanian

**CURRENCY:** 1 Macedonian denar (MKD) = 100 deni

**RELIGION:** Eastern Orthodox 67%, Muslim 30%

**LAND AREA:** 25,333 km²

**GEOGRAPHY:** Mountainous

**CLIMATE:** Warm, dry summers and relatively cold winters with heavy snowfall

**BORDERS:** Albania, Bulgaria, Greece, Serbia and Montenegro

**ECONOMY:** 20% Agriculture, 39% Industry, 41% Services

**GDP PER CAPITA:** US$1,050

**EMERGENCY PHONE NUMBERS:** Ambulance 94, Fire 93, Police 92

**COUNTRY CODE:** 389

**INTERNATIONAL DIALING PREFIX:** 99

**WHAT'S IN A NAME?** For brevity's sake, *Let's Go* uses the name "Macedonia" to refer to the Former Yugoslav Republic of Macedonia. *Let's Go* does not endorse any perceived claims of the former Yugoslav Republic to the Greek territory of the same name.

# HISTORY

**ALEXANDER THE GREAT.** Archaeological evidence shows a flourishing civilization in Macedonia between 7000 and 3500 BC. In the first millennium BC, a mixed population of Thracians, Illyrians, and Celts wandered into the Balkan Peninsula. The Greek culture to the south seeped into the fringes of the area, then known as **Paeonia,** and **King Philip II** of Macedonia (then situated just to the south of the modern Republic of Macedonia) joined Paeonia with his kingdom in 358 BC. Under his son **Alexander the Great,** their kingdom would stretch from Albania to India.

Following the death of Alexander the Great and the many years of shifting territories that followed, Macedonia allied with Carthage and Egypt and was finally defeated Rome in the First and Second **Macedonian Wars.** Through five centuries of Roman rule, Paeonia saw the construction of cities that still exist today, notably Heraclea Lyncestis (present-day Bitola) and Skupi (present-day Skopje).

**A MELTING POT.** Change came in the 3rd century, when Balkan Slavs tore through the area; they continued to do so for the next 300 years. When the Roman Empire split in the 4th century, these ancestors of Macedonia's modern inhabitants fell

F.Y.R. Macedonia

N

YUGOSLAVIA

Djakovica
Uroshevac
Prizren

St. Nikita
Matejcha
Kumanovo

Kriva
Palanka
Osogovo

Kyustendil

BULGARIA

Pschaca

Skopje

Tetovo
Matka
Andrija
Gostivar
St. Pantelejmon
Mustafa
Pashina
Markov

Lesnovo

Kochani

Sveti
Nikole

Berovo

Titov
Veles

Shtip

Peshkopi

Mavrovo

Vardar R.

Kavadarci

Strumica

Kichevo

Zerqan

Krushevo

Prilep

St. Bogorodista
and St. Atanasie
Struga

Ohrid

Gevgelija

Lake
Ohrid

Yeni and
Isak Jamiya

Bitola

Kilkis

St.
Naum

Lake
Prespa

GREECE

Pogradec

ALBANIA

Árnissa
Edessa

Giannitsá

Florina

0     20 miles
0     20 kilometers

MACEDONIA

under the Byzantine thumb. The **Byzantines** and **Bulgarians** periodically warred over the territory from the 7th to 14th centuries. Serbian control, which began in 1331, ended with the 1389 **Battle of Kosovo,** and over the next 70 years the territory was wholly absorbed into the **Ottoman Empire.** The diverse heritage of Greek, Turkish, and Slavic origins has laid the foundation for contemporary conflict in Macedonia. The Christian culture brought by the Greek-speaking Byzantines competed with the traditions of the Serbs and later the religion of the Ottoman Turks, who ruled the region from the end of the 14th century to 1913.

In the 19th century, South Slavs began agitating for independence. Russia managed to force the Ottoman Empire to reinstate Bulgaria (then including Macedonia) in 1878, but Austria-Hungary, Britain, France, and Prussia, interested in the territories of the faltering empire, restored the lands to Turkey. One domestic reaction to these international pressures was the 1893 creation of the **International Macedonian Revolutionary Organization** (IMRO), whose slogan was "Macedonia for the Macedonians." Twelve years later, every power in the Balkans fought over Macedonia in the **First Balkan War.** The Ottomans were quickly defeated, but the victors could not agree on how to divide the spoils. Bulgarian troops turned on their Serbian and Greek allies, causing the **Second Balkan War.** The Bulgarians were defeated, and most of what would eventually become the Republic of Macedonia fell to Serbia. In 1941, Macedonia was partitioned again, this time among the **Axis powers.**

**MACEDONIA, TAKE TWO.** After **World War II,** Macedonia was incorporated into **Yugoslavia** as one of its constituent republics. Under Yugoslav leader **Tito,** Macedonian language, literature, and culture experienced a revival. In 1958, the Archbishopric of Ohrid was restored, signifying a break with the Serbian Church. Macedonia was the least successful of the Yugoslav republics economically. Eventually, popular support for sovereignty could not be denied, and on December 19, 1991, Macedonia declared its independence from Yugoslavia.

# POLITICS

Macedonia has a unicameral parliament elected for a 4-year term. President **Kiro Gligorov**, elected in 1996 for another 5-year term, continues to lead the country since 1991 after surviving an assassination attempt by car bomb in October 1995. **Ljubico Georgievski**, Prime Minister since 1998, heads an interesting coalition government, which is a mix of right- and left-wing parties.

There are half a million more sheep in Macedonia than there are people, but the people often don't get along as well as the sheep. Ethnic tensions remain high in this nation, with its mix of Slavic Macedonians, Albanians, Serbs, Bulgars, and Turks. Once weakened by U.N.-enforced embargoes from the north and Greek trade blockades from the south, Macedonia is now making a comeback. In October 1995, Greece, which originally contended that the new nation's name, currency, flag, and constitution all implied pretensions to the Greek province of the same name, lifted its embargoes. Recently, Macedonia's economy further suffered by the influx of Albanian refugees from Kosovo, whom it was unable to accommodate. The country aspires to membership in the EU and NATO, but its position as a neighbor of the ever-unstable Serbia continues to be a curse.

# CULTURE

## NATIONAL HOLIDAYS

| | |
|---|---|
| **January 1** New Year | **May 1** May Day |
| **January 6-7** Orthodox Christmas | **May 24** Sts. Cyril and Methodius Day |
| **April 15** Easter | **August 2** Ilinden Day |
| **March 8** International Women's Day | **September 8** Independence Day |

# LITERATURE

Tracing the roots of Macedonian-Slav literature is as problematic as giving the fledgling country a politically acceptable name. Occupied by foreign powers for so long, Macedonian was not even officially recognized as a literary language until 1946, when the country became a constituent republic of Yugoslavia.

Little was written in Macedonian during the period of Ottoman rule until the 19th century, when **Konstantin Miladinov** began to produce lyric poems, laying the foundation for a modern Macedonian literature. Further efforts came with **Kosta Misirkov**. Post-Yugoslavia literary development was stunted by various economic and political problems. With the 1995 lifting of the Greek trade embargo, however, a wonderful wealth of works poured forth. **Ante Popovski's** collection *Prividenija (Providence)*, which intertwines history and theosophy, won the Braca Miladinović Award at the Struga Poetry Festival, while **Sande Stojcevski's** *A Gate in the Cloud*, featuring over 50 of the poet's best lyrics, was published in an elegant English translation by David Bowen et al. The short stories of **Petre Andreevski**, collected in *Site lica na smrtta (All the Faces of Death)*, combine folk wisdom with modernity, and are read as metaphors for Macedonian life today.

*Before the Rain*, a critically acclaimed film by Milcho Manchevski, which earned nomination for the Academy Award in 1995, has been by far the most successful product of Macedonian culture in the international scene.

**MACEDONIA**

# FOOD AND DRINK

Food is not cheap in Macedonia. Macedonian food shows strong Serbian and Greek influences. Sesame seeds are the name of the game. Kiosks sell **grilled meats** (скара; skara), especially small hamburgers (плескавица; pleskavitsa; 50dn) and **burek** (бурек; warm, filo-dough pastry stuffed with veggies, feta cheese, or meat; 30-35dn). Macedonian *chebubs* (чебаб) and hamburgers may not be what you expect: they are often made of a mix of meat from various animals that even the most die-hard carnivores may find challenging. You can buy fruits and vegetables at an out-door market, or *pazar* (пазар). *Letnitsa*, a type of trout found only in Lake Ohrid, is expensive. *Eyeyar* and *rindzur* are tomato-based pasta dishes. *Chorba* (чорба; a thick soup) is a popular mid-morning snack. Wash it all down with delicious Macedonian *vino* (вино; wine) or *rakiya*, a grape or plum brandy. The water is drinkable, and public fountains abound, although they are often filthy.

# CUSTOMS AND ETIQUETTE

**Tipping** is appropriate in small amounts. A tip of 10% will be perceived as generous. When restaurants are crowded, share a table with the locals and practice your Macedonian. People are generally unwilling to wait in lines to purchase tickets or board a bus and push their way to the front. Local **gypsies** are treated as stray dogs; **minority** travelers will be stared at. In summer Macedonian **women** are dressed in small skimpy clothes that show as much skin as possible. In churches, sleeveless T-shirts and short skirts are theoretically not allowed. **Homosexuality** is illegal in Macedonia, and there is a general lack of tolerance toward lesbians and gay men. Life here will be easier if you do not express views or preferences openly.

# LANGUAGE

**Macedonian** is a south Slav language that uses the **Cyrillic** alphabet. It is closely related to Serbian and Bulgarian. **Russian** is widely understood, as are **Serbian** and **Croatian**. **English** is quickly becoming the 2nd language of choice in Macedonia. Older Macedonians may reverse the Western style of **head movements** for "yes" and "no;" confirm everything with words. Helpful words include *bilet* (билет; ticket), *voz* (воз; train), *zheleznitsa* (железница; railway), *avtobus* (автобус; bus), *stanitsa* (станица; station), *povraten bilet* (повратен билет; return ticket), *liniya* (линија; track), *peron* (перон; platform), *informatsiya* (информација; information), *trugvanye* (тругвање; departures), *pristignuvanye* (пристигнување; arrivals), *kola za spienye* (кола за спиење; sleeping car), and *avtobuska/tramvajska stanica* (автобуска/трамвајска станица; bus/tram stop).

# TRAVELING ESSENTIALS

Irish, New Zealand, and UK citizens need only a valid passport to enter Macedonia. Citizens of Australia, Canada, and the US can obtain single-entry visas at the border or at the nearest Macedonian embassy or consulate. Processing at embassies and consulates is generally completed in one day; only a valid passport and a passport-size photo are required. Fees vary from consulate to consulate and at the border, but are generally free for US citizens and under $5 for others. Upon entry, you will be issued a card which will be required when leaving the country. Business and multiple-entry visas are issued only at Macedonian embassies and consulates. No additional documents are required for multiple-entry visas; however, for business visas a cover letter is required. Macedonia has no diplomatic representation in South Africa; South Africans traveling to Macedonia may obtain 90-day single-entry visas at the border for US$15.

MACEDONIA

# TRANSPORTATION

As the country lurches out of its communist past, some street names have changed but some old street signs remain. When asking for directions, use both the new and the old names; locals may be unaware of the change. Get a copy of a new map in English as soon as you arrive. Additionally, **addresses often lack a street number and instead list bb—**_bez broj;_ "no number."

**BY PLANE.** Both Skopje and Ohrid have airports. While Skopje's airport closes in winter, Ohrid's stays open all year. There are flights from Ohrid to **Greece.**

**BY TRAIN OR BUS.** Buses and trains travel around the country with comparable speed and comfort, but buses are usually more frequent. Domestic tickets may be purchased in _denars_, Deutschmarks, or US dollars. Nearly all international travel must be done through Skopje. Due to political tensions, there are no bus or train connections from Ohrid to Greece—to cross, you will have to walk across the border or backtrack to Skopje. Be warned: border crossings can take a long time, as there are often traffic backups for miles.

**BY TAXI.** Taxis are often the only way to get to a particular destination (e.g., distant sights or the Greek border if you plan to cross it by foot). Rates are generally fair, but settle the price before the ride.

# TOURIST SERVICES AND MONEY

| CURRENCY | | |
|---|---|---|
| US$1 = 60DN (DENARS) | 10DN = US$0.17 | |
| CDN$1 = 41DN | 10DN = CDN$0.24 | |
| UK£1 = 64DN | 10DN = UK£0.16 | |
| IR£1 = 67DN | 10DN = IR£0.15 | |
| AUS$1 = 35DN | 10DN = AUS$0.29 | |
| NZ$1 = 26DN | 10DN = NZ$0.38 | |
| SAR1 = 8.60DN | 10DN = SAR1.16 | |
| DM1 = 27DN | 10DN = DM0.37 | |

There are **tourist offices,** mostly private, in Skopje and Ohrid; getting information in English elsewhere ranges from problematic to impossible. Offices give out maps, rent private rooms, and sell train and airline tickets. Look for the **"i"** signs. **Shops** are generally open Monday through Friday 8am to 8pm; weekend hours vary. Some **banks,** especially in tourist areas, are open daily. Expect an hour break anytime between noon and 2pm at most offices and shops.

The monetary unit is the **denar,** which comes in notes of 10, 50, 100, 500, 1000, and the rare 5000dn, and in coins of 1, 2, and 5dn. The exchange rates given above are those for summer 2000; Macedonian **inflation** is a remarkably low 3%, so rates and prices should be stable. The best exchange rates are available at **change bureaus,** the worst at hotels. **Traveler's checks** can only be cashed at banks. Most currency prices in Macedonia are given in Deutschmarks (DM), but most banks will readily accept US dollars or British pounds and cash **AmEx** traveler's checks. Few places accept **credit cards,** and some major hotels accept only cash. All **ATMs** accept MC and Cirrus; they offer the best exchange rates available but are scarce.

Throughout Macedonia, the US dollar will be accepted for goods and services. When paying with US dollars, however, be careful not to receive change in another currency. Not only is exchanging on the street illegal and punishable by heavy fines, you'll also get ripped off.

# HEALTH AND SAFETY

Recent political events have made it inadvisable to enter Albania or Kosovo in Yugoslavia; even traveling near the border may be dangerous, due as much to bandits as to soldiers and occasional **landmines**.

Pack a **soap** and some **toilet paper**. The concept of **deodorants** has not yet reached Macedonia; bring your own. Basic **medicines** are widely available in Macedonian **pharmacies** (аптека; apteka). *Analgin cafetin* is aspirin, and *arbid* is cold medicine. Bandages are *Flexogal*. Other useful expressions include: *alergija* (алергија; allergy), *treska* (треска; fever), *glavobolka* (главоболка; headache), and *stomakot* (стомакот; stomachache). **Feminine hygiene products** are widely available. If you are seriously ill, the Faculty of Medicine at the University in Skopje and the Military Hospital are the best options. A list of **medical specialists** can be obtained from the US Embassy in Skopje. Credit cards are accepted at hospitals.

# ACCOMMODATIONS AND CAMPING

A hotel or hostel will take your passport at check-in: all businesses offering accommodations are required by law to **register** passports with the police. You'll get the passport back at the end of your stay; try to get it back earlier if you are expecting **Poste Restante** or if you plan to cash traveler's checks. If you are staying with friends, they are required to do this as well, although this law is often ignored.

In areas other than Lake Ohrid, **private rooms** are expensive (900dn) and difficult to find; check with the nearest tourist office. In the resorts, you'll be met by room-renting locals at the bus and train stations—prices improve with haggling ($10-15). All accommodations provide bedding, but some lack towels. **Hotels** are exorbitantly expensive (4000-5000dn per person in summer). **Youth hostels** are rare. Many **campgrounds** are in a state of disarray; call ahead. Freelance **camping** is popular, but you risk a fine and it's not safe. Camping in reserve areas is prohibited.

# KEEPING IN TOUCH

To make an international call with a calling card use one of the following direct access numbers: **AT&T Direct** ☎99 800 42 88; **BT Direct** ☎99 800 00 44; **Canada Direct** ☎99 800 42 77; **MCI WorldPhone** ☎99 800 42 66. International calls from card-operated phones are ridiculously expensive; use phones at the post office instead. To get an international line, dial ☎99. Calls to the US average US$3-4 per minute. To make local calls from public phones, you must buy a microchip **phone card** (100 or 200dn) at a post office or kiosk. **Internet** is by far the most convenient way of communicating with the outside world—cyber hangouts are everywhere. **Mail** can be received general delivery through **Poste Restante**. Address envelope as follows: Jonathan (First name) DAWID (LAST NAME), POSTE RESTANTE, Skopje (City) 91101 (Postal code), MACEDONIA.

**Faxes** can be sent at most phone centers for prices comparable to phone calls. **Photocopy** centers abound; look for the sign "фотокопир." Prices range from two to 10dn per copy. Large hotels televise **CNN** in their lobbies, kiosks sell *Newsweek* and *Time*, some radio stations occasionally switch to **Voice of America** and **BBC** broadcasts, and local TV features subtitled American movies.

# SKOPJE (СКОПЈЕ) ☎(0)91

The rolling hills, tilled fields, and orange-roofed suburbs that surround Skopje (SKO-pye; pop. 600,000) lend the city a sense of rural serenity—an impression quickly corrected upon the first choking attempt to breathe the smog-filled air in the nation's bustling capital. Miraculously, the disastrous earthquake that destroyed 90% of Skopje in 1963 spared the town's Old Bazaar, and ancient mosques and churches still rise above the otherwise concrete landscape. Due to its proximity to Kosovo, Skopje has been filled with humanitarian organizations in the last two years—if humanitarian work is not your *raison d'être*, head south to Lake Ohrid for more pleasant surroundings.

>  There are landmines in Skopje's immediate vicinity, particularly to the north at the border with Yugoslavia; stay on paved roads.

## ✦ ORIENTATION

Most of Skopje's points of interest lie along a small stretch of the **Vardar River** (Вардар) and **Samoilova** (Самоилова), the street on the western edge of the **Stara Charshiya** (Стара Чаршија; Old Bazaar). Several bridges, most notably the pedestrian **Kamen most** (Камен мост; Stone Bridge), connect the old and new sections of the city. The **trgovski tsentar** (трговски центар; central shopping center) is on the river next to **Ploshtad Makedoniya** (Плоштад Македонија; Macedonia Square). **Maps** of Skopje are sold at bookstores and kiosks for 150 to 200dn. While some street signs are in Latin script, most are printed in Cyrillic. To add to the confusion, city leaders have changed "red" names (but not signs) to democratic ones.

## ✦ TRANSPORTATION

**Flights: Skopje Airport/Aerodrome Petrovec** (☎711 024 and 235 156), 23km away in Petrovec. A taxi costs 600-1200dn.

**Trains:** Be sure to ask for the *new* **train station** (Нова Железница Станица; Nova zheleznitsa stanitsa), bul. Jane Sandanski (Јане Сандански). Purchase tickets through **Feroturist** (Феротурист; ☎163 248), in the station. Open M-F 7am-8pm, Sa 7am-2pm). To **Thessaloniki, GRE** (6 hr., 1 per day, 669dn). To get to Budapest or other destinations in the west, it's necessary to change trains in **Belgrade, YUG** (8hr., 3 per day, 1166dn), where a visa is required. *Let's Go* does not recommend traveling through Yugoslavia. There are no direct trains to **Istanbul, TUR**—go through **Thessaloniki, GRE**.

**Buses:** At the entrance to the Old Town (info ☎236 254). From the train station walk 3 blocks to the river, keeping the mountains on the left, and cross the stone bridge. Buses run to **Ohrid** (3½hr., 11 per day, 310dn). Purchase international tickets at **Tourist Agency Proleter** (Пролетер; ☎237 532), in the bus station. To **Sofia, BUL** (8hr., 3 per day, 590dn) and **Istanbul, TUR** (18hr., 1 per day, 1850dn).

**Public Transportation:** Buy **bus tickets** from kiosks and travel agencies (20dn) or from the driver (30dn); stamp them on board. **Private buses** run the same routes (10-15dn, pay on the bus).

**Taxis: Radiotaxi Vodno** (☎91 91), **Radiotaxi Vardar** (☎91 95), or **Radiotaxi Tatto** (☎91 98). 50dn for the 1st 2.5km, then 15dn per km. No ride in Skopje should cost 100dn. Haggle with the driver before you get in or ask him to turn on the meter.

**PLAYING WITH FIRE** Skopje's streets are often dotted with men playing "matchbox games," a betting game where a marble is hidden under one of three matchboxes, the boxes are rotated, and passersby challenge the "spinner" as to under which box the marble hides when it stops—only to have the boxes switched in the microsecond they spend glancing into their wallets to offer the challenge. While the solution seems easy—hold the proper box down with your foot while reaching for your money—resist the temptation. Beating the spinner at his own game will bring taunts and accusations of mafia affiliations from the small crowds on hand.

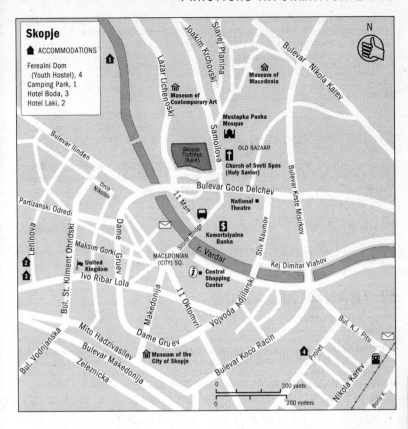

**Skopje**

🏠 ACCOMMODATIONS

Ferealni Dom
  (Youth Hostel), 4
Camping Park, 1
Hotel Boda, 3
Hotel Laki, 2

# ⚡ PRACTICAL INFORMATION

**Tourist Office:** 🛈 **Skopje Tourist Information** (Скопје Туристичка Информација; ☎ 116 854), around the corner from the bus station, across from the Turkish baths in the shopping center **Most** (Мост). Cheery English speakers provide **maps** and answer any and all questions. Open July-Aug. M-F 8am-7pm, Sa 9am-4pm; off-season M-F 9am-6pm, Sa 9am-4pm. **Kompas Holidays** (☎ 222 441; fax 110 089), in the central shopping center, sells **maps** of the city (150dn), **exchanges currency,** rents cars, and sells international plane, train, and bus tickets. Open M-Sa 8am-8pm.

**Embassies: UK,** Velyko Vlahovik 26, 4th floor (Ве ко Влаховик; ☎ 116 772; fax 117 005). **US,** Bulevar Ilinden bb (Булевар Илинден; ☎ 116 180; fax 117 103). Both open M-F 9am-5pm; registration services M-F 9am-noon. Citizens of **Australia, Canada,** and **New Zealand** should contact the UK office.

**Currency Exchange: Komertsiyalna Banka** (Комерцијална Банка; ☎ 112 077; fax 113 494), in the gigantic white office building across from the bus station. Exchanges currency and cashes AmEx **traveler's cheques** at good rates. Open M-F 7:30am-8:30pm, Sa 7:30am-1:30pm. Also on the ground floor of the *trgovski tsentar.* Open M-F 7am-7pm, Sa 7am-1pm.

**ATM:** In the *trgovski tsentar.*

**Luggage Storage: Garderoba** (Гардероба). At the domestic bus station. 40dn per piece. Open daily 6am-9:30pm. At the train station; 22dn per piece. Open 24hr.

**International Bookstore: Svet** (Свет), Bul. Vasil Glavinov 3 (Васил Главинов; ☎129 124), across from St. Klement Ohridski Church, has an abundant supply of English and American periodicals and books. Publishes a monthly English-language magazine *Svet*.

**Pharmacy: Apteka** (Аптека), on the ground floor of the central shopping center (☎130 333). Open daily 7am-midnight.

**Medical Assistance: Medical Faculty Hospital,** Vodnanska (Воднанска; ☎147 147). The **US Embassy** (see above) provides a list of medical specialists (info ☎116 180).

**Telephones:** In the 2 post offices (see below). Open 24hr. at Varder, during office hours at the train station. Phonecards can also be purchased at post offices and kiosks and used throughout the country, even for international calls (180dn for 100 impulses, 300dn for 200 impulses).

**Internet Access: Cyberia Club,** Dimitrie Cupovski bb (☎298 0600). 80dn per hr. Open daily 10am-4am. **Internet Contact** (☎296 365), on the top floor of the central shopping center. 100dn per hr. Open M-Sa noon-8pm, Su 2-8pm.

**Post Office:** Cross Kamen bridge from the bus station, take a right along the Vardar, and follow the yellow "ПТТ" signs to the circular, 1960s-style cement fortress. **Poste Restante** (6dn) at window #24. Open M-F 7am-8pm, Sa-Su 7am-2pm. **Postal code:** 91101. Branch at the train station on Nikola Karev, under the "ПТТ" sign. **Poste Restante** (6dn) at window #18 or 19. Open M-Sa 7am-8pm.

**Postal code:** 91000.

# ▌ ACCOMMODATIONS

Affordable accommodations abound, but so do their patrons. Due to the large number of humanitarian organizations, cheap hotels (1000-3000dn) are usually booked. If you're unable to confirm a reservation beforehand, go with one of the locals offering **private rooms** at the bus station (800-1000dn).

■ **"Fereaini Dom" Youth Hostel Skopje (HI),** Prolet 25 (Пролет; ☎11 48 49; fax 23 50 29). From the train station, walk toward the river along Kuzman Yosifovski and take the 2nd left onto Prolet; it's the 3-story building on the right. Recently renovated, with sparkling clean rooms and private baths. Dorms with ISIC/HI 935dn, others 1280dn; singles 1280dn, 1590dn. Breakfast (7-9am) in the adjacent restaurant included.

**Hotel Boda** (Хотел Бода), Ivo Ribar Lola 22 (☎221 023), on the corner of Leninova. Homey atmosphere. Rooms with skylights and TV. Shared bath. Reception open daily until midnight. Singles 30DM; doubles 50DM.

**Hotel Laki** (Хотел Лаки), Leninova 79 (Ленинова; ☎128 120, 116 827, and 116 836). Head west on Ivo Ribar Lola, then right on Leninova; it's the 2nd building on the right. Rooms with private showers, TV, and phones. 35-50DM per person. Breakfast included.

**Camping Park,** in the park behind the stadium. Cozy 4-person cabins 475dn per person; tents 190dn per night.

# ◘ FOOD

You'll find some of Skopje's best dishes toasting over hot coals in the streets of the **Old Bazaar.** *Chorba* (чорба; a thick, meat-based soup) is a popular dish, as are the more substantial *shish kebab*, grilled peppers, and *tavche gravche* (тавче гравче; greasy beans topped with *shish kebab* bits). Kiosks specialize in inexpensive and generous stuffed pastries (20-50dn). The Old Bazaar's north end hosts a huge **vegetable market** and the adjacent **Bitpazar** (Битпазар; flea market) has everything else. A new craze has recently erupted in Skopje: *skara na kilo* (скала на кило; grill by the kilo) restaurants let you pick raw meat of your choice and wait while it's grilled freshly for you. **Vegetarians** will have to settle for eggs and beans. Request *"neshto bez meso"* (something without meat).

▨ **Pivnitsa An** (Пивница Ан; ☎221 817), down the steps and through the wooden gates in Stara Charshiya's fountain square. In the courtyard of a restored old house. Enjoy *filet mignon* (филе миюон; 330dn), less substantial grills (120-160dn), or stuffed grape leaves (сарма от винова лоза; sarma ot vinova loza; 200dn), a Balkan specialty. Baklava and other desserts 100dn. English menu, nice staff. Open daily 9am-midnight.

**Dal Metu Fu** (Дал Мету Фу), pl. Makedoniya (☎112 486). Imaginative pizzas (170dn), as well as pasta and assorted meat dishes (150-800dn) in a huge, bright joint. English menu. Open M-Th 8:30am-midnight, F-Sa 8:30am-1am, Su 10:30am-midnight.

**Idadiya III** (Идадија III), Rade Konchar bb (Раде Кончар; ☎110 522). Go west on Ilinden, take the 6th left, and walk 1 block to the intersection with Orce Nikolov. Classic Macedonian cuisine. The *svinsko file* (pork tenderloin filled with cheese and wrapped with bacon; 120dn) is delicious. Open Su-Th 8am-midnight, F-Sa 8am-1am.

# ◑ SIGHTS

Skopje takes anything that could potentially look appealing and promptly defaces it—the entire city is filled with trash and graffiti and impatiently awaits better days. Most historical sights are an easy walk from the bus station. To reach Samoilova (Самоилова), go to the left side of the Most shopping center and climb the stairs. Below, the **Old Bazaar** section of the city preserves a taste of traditional Macedonian, Albanian, and Muslim culture. It is connected to the modern part of the city by a 6th-century **Stone Bridge** (Камен мост; Kamen Most), one of the lucky structures that survived the 1963 earthquake but which has not withstood an invasion of cheap T-shirt and fake-Marlboro peddlers. The the 15th-century **Turkish Bathouse** (Даут-Пашин Амам; Daut-Pashin Amam) is a well-preserved building with typical star-spotted dome ceilings, sitting at the edge of the Old Bazaar up the street past the bus station. It now serves as an art gallery with rotating exhibitions. (☎133 102. Open Tu-Su 10am-1pm and 5-9pm. 50dn, students 20dn.) Perfect acoustics make the Bathouse a desirable venue for classical concerts during the **Skopje Summer** festival (Скопско Лето; Skopsko Leto), which takes place annually from mid-June to mid-July. **Sveti Spas** (Свети Спас; Saint Spas), with a masterful walnut iconostasis that took three artisans seven years to carve, also sits at Samoilova. Much of the interior is below ground level—Christian churches were once prohibited from being taller than mosques. In the courtyard, there's a sarcophagus holding revolutionary Gotse Delchev, who died in 1903, and an exhibit on his life and death. (☎233 812. Open Tu-F 9am-5pm, Sa-Su 9am-3pm. 60dn, students 30dn.) Farther up the street, **Mustafa Pashina Mosque** (Мустафа Пашина џамија; Mustafa Pasha Jamiya) marks its 506th year. Its key-holder will let you in any time he's around, usually between 5am and 10pm. Every Friday at 1pm, hundreds gather to listen to the preaching of the Hodzha, or Imam. The mosque with the amazingly tall minaret belonged to Mustafa Pasha's brother, **Jaja Pasha,** who decided to match the height of Mustafa's temple despite the inferior valley site. Perched on a hill overlooking the city is the crumbling **Turkish Fortress** (Кале; Kale); its less-crumbling parts provide a great spot for a picnic.

The elegant **Turkish Inn** (Куршумли Хан; Kurshumli Han) in the Old Bazaar, is part of the **Museum of Macedonia** (Музеј на Македонија; Muzey na Makedoniya). Its three permanent exhibits—archaeological, ethnographic, and historical—present a nationalistic picture of the country's past. (☎116 044. Open M-F 8am-4pm, Sa 9am-3pm. 50dn, students 20dn. English tour included.) Farther up Samoilova, the **Museum of Modern Art** (Музеј на Современата Уметност; Muzey na Sovremenata Umetnost) occupies the highest point in central Skopje. (Open Tu-Sa 10am-5pm, Su 9am-1pm. 30dn, students 10dn.)

There is a fair amount of turnover in the hot spots of Skopje's nightlife. New clubs are always popping up in the park near the stadium and in the shopping center on bul. Makedonija. A classic disco scene thrives at the **Coloseum,** off Dimitrie Cupovski, near Dame Gruev. (Open nightly 9am-3am.)

**MACEDONIA**

# 🖪 DAYTRIP FROM SKOPJE

## MATKA

> *Bus #60 from Skopje, which runs frequently on weekends but less often during the week, goes to Matka village (30min., 30dn). A taxi costs 200-250dn (15min.).*

The village, canyon, and lake that share the name Matka lie on the Treska River, 15km southwest of Skopje. The canyon's natural beauty provides a blessed relief from Skopje's smoggy summer heat. Several short day hikes lead to churches and monasteries in the vicinity, while the lake offers excellent swimming and cliff-jumping. Just a minute from Matka village, up the road behind Restaurant Monastery Peshtera Matka (see below), sits **Sveta Bogoraditsa.** Built by one woman in the 14th century out of stone, sand, and egg whites, it has survived seven earthquakes and is amazingly well preserved. (Open daily 7am-8pm.) From the village, follow the river upstream until you reach the hydroelectric dam. The bridge crossing the river at the bottom of the dam leads to the **Sveti Nikola** trail, marked by faded red and white bull's eye trail markings. The 30-minute hike is well worth the effort; the view of the canyon from the steep cliffs is breathtaking. To reach the lake, follow the paved path to the right of the dam (5min.). Just past the arches labeled "Matka," you'll find **Sveti Andreja.** Built in 1389, the monastery is an excellent example of traditional Byzantine architecture and preserves many vibrant frescoes. (Open daily 10am-10pm.) Next door to Sveti Andreja, the **Matka Restaurant** (☎352 655) sells picnic food and sporadically ferries people across the lake (before 10pm). Past the restaurant, a large map board outlines many **hiking** and **spelunking** routes, including the rugged, occasionally treacherous hike along the river's edge. For tips on safe hiking, see **Camping and the Outdoors,** p. 37. The best dining in the area is at **Restaurant Monastirska Peshtera Matka,** across from the outgoing bus stop in the village. Built inside a cave, it serves the region's specialties. (☎352 512. Main dishes 250-1000dn. Open daily 10am-midnight.)

# LAKE OHRID

Rocky Lake Ohrid is perhaps Macedonia's greatest natural treasure. Its clean water (visibility 22-25 meters) has been flowing from the southeastern springs for four million years. Surrounded by mountains on all sides, its shores are dotted with hundreds of small churches and monasteries, interspersed with grassy and sandy beaches. Tourists aren't the only ones attracted to the warm water; eels and trout thrive in Lake Ohrid and are culinary specialties throughout the area.

## OHRID (ОХРИД)                    ☎(0)96

Ohrid is Macedonia's premier summer resort and possibly its most beautiful town. Before the war in Bosnia, 300,000 foreign tourists visited Ohrid annually. That number has dropped dramatically, but those who make it here won't be disappointed. The town's lake shore is lined with cafes facing the Albanian coast and small shops and churches dot the sloping cobblestone streets of the Old Town. Ohrid has been Roman, Slavic, Ottoman, and was even the capital of Bulgaria in the late 10th and 11th centuries. Thanks to UNESCO's designation of Ohrid as a protected town, the architectural legacy of Yugoslav socialism is scarcely visible.

🖪 **TRANSPORTATION.** Buses go to **Bitola** (2hr., 9 per day, 150dn) and **Skopje** (3½hr., 11 per day, 310dn). Due to strained relations with Greece, there are no international buses out of Ohrid. Unless you plan to walk or hitchhike across the Greek border, the best options for transportation into Bulgaria or Greece are from Skopje. *Let's Go* does not recommend hitchhiking across the Greek border or elsewhere.

**⚠️🏠 ORIENTATION AND PRACTICAL INFORMATION.** To get to the center from the bus station, exit on the post-office side, make a right onto Partizanska (Партизанска), and turn left on bul. Makedonski Prosvetiteli (Македонски Просветители) until you reach the lake. The collection of orange-roofed white houses on the hill is the Old Town. At the foot of the hill, **Sveti Kliment Ohridski** (Климент Охридски) serves as Ohrid's pedestrian main street. The **tourist office AD Galeb-Bilyana** (АД Галеб-Билјана; ☎ 224 94; fax 241 14), Partizanska 3, in the bus station building, finds **private rooms** (500-700dn per person) and sells **maps** (150dn). Large maps are posted on boards in the center. **Ohridska Banka** (Охридска Банка), on the corner of Makedonski Prosvetiteli and Turistichka bul. (Туристичка), **exchanges currency** and cashes AmEx **traveler's cheques** for 0.55% commission. (☎ 314 00. Open daily 8am-5pm. Branch offices keep longer hours—try the one on Sv. Kliment Ohridski.) There are **no ATMs** in Ohrid. There's **luggage storage** at the bus station (50dn). **Cyber City,** on the corner of Makedonski Prosvetiteli and Partizanska, has **internet access.** (60dn per hr. Open 24hr.) The **post office** sits on Makedonski Prosvetiteli. (☎ 26 01 11. Open M-Sa 7am-8pm.) **Telephones** and **faxes** (fax 322 15) are in the post office. (Open M-Sa 7am-9pm.) **Postal code:** 96000.

**📷📍 ACCOMMODATIONS AND FOOD.** If you don't book a room through an agency (see above), people at the bus station offer rooms in their homes. The rates for **private rooms** are good (500-700dn), but may not include the daily 20dn tax. Find out the location of the room and exactly what the price includes, then bargain away. **Hotel Park,** 2km south of Ohrid, has singles with bath for DM30 and **campsites** for DM9. (☎ 261 521 and 263 671; fax 260 061. Reception 24hr.)

Vendors in the **town market** (градско пазариште; gradsko pazarishte) hawk fruits and vegetables daily 8am-8pm between Gotse Delchev and Turistichka. **Fast food** restaurants along Kliment Ohridski add some cholesterol to your system with burgers (70dn) and chicken filets (пилет филет; pilet filet; 100dn), served with french fries and lots of ketchup and mayo unless you request otherwise. The ⬛ **Ohrid Fish Restaurant** (Охридска пастрмка рибен ресторан; Ohridska pastrmka riben restoran), in the center behind the rose gardens, serves the best of the lake's specialties. (☎ 263 827. Main dishes 300-600dn. Open daily 7am-2am.) **Restoran Dalga,** Kosta Abrash 7, cooks up classic Macedonian cuisine on the lake shore. (☎ 319 48. Meat dishes 250-500dn. Salads 50-80dn. Open daily 10am-midnight.)

**📷📍 SIGHTS AND BEACHES.** You could spend the better part of a week visiting Ohrid's churches and monasteries. Almost every monastery provides an English guidebook. To get to **Sveta Sofia** (Света Софија), take Kliment Ohridski toward the lake and turn right on Tsar Samoil (Цар Самоил); the church is 300m up on the left. Ohrid's oldest church, it was built in the 9th century on the foundations of an even earlier church. The 11th-century frescoes, in surprisingly good shape, depict scenes from the Old and New Testaments. Under the Ottoman yoke the church served as a mosque. (Open Tu-Su 9am-10pm. 50dn, students 20dn.) Sveta Sofia also hosts performances for **Ohridsko Leto** (Охридско лето; Ohrid Summer), an annual festival of classical music. (Info ☎ 26 23 04; www.ohridsummer.com.mk.) Go uphill on Ilindenska (Илинденска) and turn right before the stone arches to reach **Sveti Kliment** (Свети Климент). The frescoes of this church, home to the Ohrid archbishopric during Ottoman rule, depict saints, the Virgin, and the Last Supper. (Open daily June-Sept. 9am-7pm; off-season shorter hours. 100dn, students 50dn.) Across from the church, the **Icon Gallery** displays works spanning seven centuries. (Open Tu-Su 9-10:30am, 11am-1pm, and 4-8pm. 100dn, students 50dn.) The 13th-century **Sveti Jovan** (Свети Јован) perches on the lip of a cliff overlooking the lake. Go left on Kočo Ratsin (Кочо Рацин) and follow the cliff path to the church to see great view of Ohrid as the sun sets in technicolor over the lizard-covered rocks. (Church open daily 9am-1pm and 5-7pm. 100dn, students 20dn.)

Ohrid's best **beaches** are on the lake's eastern side, starting at Hotel Park (Хотел Парк), 5km from town. They get even better farther away, around Lagadin

(Лагадин), where paunchy privateers erect their villas. **Water-taxis** wait on the shores of the town center to transport sun-bathers to the better beaches. (40dn if you wait for the boat to fill up; otherwise, hire the whole boat for 300dn round-trip to the 1st beach, 400dn to the 2nd, 500dn to the 3rd.)

■ **NIGHTLIFE.** Ohrid is filled with crowded bars and cafes blaring Eurocheese into the wee hours, but a mellower scene can be had at the **Jazz Inn,** Kosta Abrash 74. Here you can nod your head with the hepcats at Macedonia's first jazz club. (Open daily 10pm-sunrise.) If you're brimming with energy, **Scorpion,** on Kliment Ohridski, is worth a visit, with Ohridians of all ages dancing to Eurobeats and "La Bamba." (Cover 50dn. Open daily in summer 1pm-5am, off-season F-Sa only.)

# NEAR OHRID

## SVETI NAUM (СВ. НАУМ)

*A boat leaves Ohrid daily 10am and returns 5pm (1½hr., 100dn). Buses run alongside the shore (1hr., 7 per day, 80dn). To get to the monastery from the bus, follow the beach.*

Twenty-eight kilometers south of Ohrid, on the Albanian border, sits Sveti Naum, a monastery that was built in the 9th century, destroyed in the 15th, and built again over the next two centuries. Today, its inner chapel is regarded as one of Macedonia's most precious treasures, housing two original pillars and frescoes more than 200 years old. St. Naum is buried in the right chamber of the church—believers say they can still hear his heartbeat by pressing their right hand and ear on his tomb. (Open daily 7am-8pm. 100dn, students 30dn.) Next to the church are the spring of St. Naum, part of the Galicia National Park (Галициа), and the source of the river Drim. Cross the bridge to the only **restaurant** for an unbeatable dining setting at the springs' edge. (Main dishes 300-900dn. Open daily 9am-midnight.). Past the restaurant, rowboats depart for hour-long trips through the clear waters and past many unusual birds (80dn). Near the springs, the shores of Lake Ohrid are lined with picnickers and vacationers relaxing on the beach.

## BITOLA (БИТОЛА)

*Buses run from Ohrid (2hr., 7 per day, 150dn) and Skopje (6hr., 10 per day, 310dn). Trains also come from Skopje (7hr., 4 per day, 280dn). To reach the Roman ruins, turn left on Ribar Lola from the bus, heading away from the center, bear right at the fork, then turn right to reach the gate. Tickets at the cafe up the hill. 100dn, students 50dn.*

During Ottoman rule Bitola was second only to Istanbul and Thessaloniki in importance and served as a center for diplomacy with Europe. Founded by Philip of Macedon (Alexander the Great's father) in the 4th century BC, Bitola can no longer rely on its once-strategic location for prosperity and now depends solely on **Heraclea Lyncestis** (Хераклеја Линкестис), a complex of ruins, to attract tourists. At the turn of the millennium, it was an Episcopal seat; two basilicas and the Bishop's palace have survived; their floor mosaics are completely intact. The amphitheater is being rebuilt to accommodate the **Heraclean Nights** (Хераклејски Вечери; Herakleyski Vecheri), an eight-week music, poetry, and drama festival held every summer. Contact the Bitola Cultural Center (*Dom na Kultura;* ☎ 300 50 and 339 67) for info or check the schedule posted at the cafe inside the gate. Many of Heraclea's most precious finds sit in the **Institute, Museum and Gallery** (Завод, Музеј, і Галерија; Zavod, Muzey, i Galeriya), an elegant building looming over a lawn at the north edge of the park, near the start of Marshal Tito. Built in 1848, the museum was once a high school—Kemal Atatürk studied here—and later an army barracks. It houses archaeological exhibits, as well as artifacts from Atatürk's life. (☎ 353 87. Open M-F 7am-8pm, Sa-Su 10am-1pm and 5-8pm. 50dn, students 20dn.) The opposite end of town is dominated by two mosques. **Yeni Jamiya** (Јени Үамија) sits at the end of Marshal Tito near the clock tower. Built in 1558 on the foundation of a Christian church, St. George, the interior preserves 18th-century frescoes and now serves as

Bitola's **Gallery of Modern Art.** (Уметника Галерија; Umetnika Galeriya. ☎221 915. Open June-Aug. Tu-Su 9am-1pm and 7-10pm; off-season Tu-Su 9am-1pm and 6-9pm. Free.) Just across the river is **Isak Jamiya** (Исак Уамија), built in 1580 and still operating as a mosque. Bitola is also home to the impressive 1830 Orthodox church, **Sveti Dmitri** (Свети Дмитри). To get there, turn left before the park with the clock tower at the end of Marshal Tito, then take another left; the church is 20m down on the right. It has the sunken floor common to many Ottoman-era Orthodox churches and features an iconostasis, in front of which is stored the head of a Christian decapitated by the Turks before the church was built. (Open daily 7am-6pm. Free.) Bitola's **Stara Charshiya** (Стара Чаршија; Old Bazaar) sits just east of Isak Jamiya. With a multitude of shops and cafes, it's chock full of atmosphere.

---

**UNDERGROUND IN THE BALKANS** After spelunking through your 10th church in the caves of Macedonia, you might wonder, "What were these crazy Christians thinking?" The answer lies not in monkish asceticism, but rather in 5 centuries of Ottoman domination. The regime imprisoned or tortured Christian teachers and decreed that all churches remain physically, as well as symbolically, lower than mosques. To avoid persecution, congregations moved to secret grottoes in the outskirts, but, as the three Struga monks who got walled into their own temple found out, the empire had ears everywhere. Most churches from the Ottoman era still operate in cellars. Hermit churches throughout the Macedonian countryside were fortunate enough to escape the humiliation bestowed on their big-city cousins like Sveta Sofia in Ohrid, which had to wear a minaret until 1912.

---

# MOLDOVA

A long-time part of Moldavia, one of the three historical provinces of Romania, this region languished under Soviet rule for 45 years. While 70% of Moldova's land and people live on the west bank of the Dniester (called the Nistru by Romanians), a high concentration of Russians and Ukrainians hold out on the other side, many clamoring for greater independence. Not many tourists stumble over Moldova on their travels—if you do, look for the country's glamour in its scenic countryside rather than its cities. Perhaps the most fascinating aspect of the country is its multilingual locals, who will switch from Russian to Romanian and back without blinking an eye. Despite having one of the slowest developing economies in Europe, the country is rebuilding and will hopefully build itself all the way to the EU.

## MOLDOVA AT A GLANCE

**CAPITAL:** Chişinău (pop. 676,700)
**POPULATION:** 4,460,000
**LANGUAGE:** Moldovan (Romanian), Russian, Gagauz (Turkish dialect)
**CURRENCY:** 1 leu (plural lei) = 100 bani
**RELIGION:** 98.5% Eastern Orthodox

**BORDERS:** Romania, Ukraine
**EMERGENCY PHONE NUMBERS:** Fire 901, Police 902, Ambulance 903, Information 909
**COUNTRY CODE:** 373
**INTERNATIONAL DIALING PREFIX:** 810

## POLITICS AND CULTURE

Moldova today is a mixture of political and economic mayhem and a westward vision for the future. On May 8, 1997, Moldovan President **Petru Lucinschi** (elected in December 1996) and Transdniestr leader **Igor Smirnov** signed a **Memorandum of Understanding,** affirming a united Moldovan state with substantial autonomy for the Transdniester region. Nonetheless, the Transdniestr remains firmly Soviet and refuses to acknowledge any Moldovan hand in its business. Russian troops, stationed in the region on an arms reduction mission, have only heightened tensions.

Despite a few differences, **"Moldovan"** and **Romanian** are fundamentally the same. To learn some useful phrases, see the section on **Language** in our Romania chapter (p. 556). Everybody also speaks **Russian** (less so in the countryside), so check out the **Language** section of Russia, p. 597. **Cuisine** doesn't differ from Romanian fare and most Moldovan customs derive from those of Romania and Russia. While most Moldovans are very courteous, **anti-homosexual** and **anti-Semitic** attitudes abound.

## TRAVELING ESSENTIALS

**VISAS.** Citizens of Australia, Ireland, New Zealand, South Africa, and the UK need visas and invitations to enter Moldova; citizens of the US and Canada need visas, but not invitations. For US citizens, single-entry visas cost US$50 (valid one month), multiple-entry visas run US$50-80 (depending upon length of stay), and transit visas are US$35 for single-entry, US$50 for double-entry. For other nationalities, single-entry visas are US$60 (valid one month), double-entry US$70 (valid one month), multiple-entry US$90-220, single-transit US$40, and double-transit $60. Regular service takes seven business days; two-day rush service costs an additional US$20. Together with a visa application and invitation (if applicable), you must submit your passport, photograph, and fee by money order or company check to the nearest Moldovan embassy or consulate (see **Essentials: Embassies and Consulates,** p. 18). US citizens can also get visas at the airport in Chişinău, although getting one ahead before your trip will save your time and sanity. Invitations can be obtained from acquaintances in Moldova, or from **Moldovatur** (see **Practical Information,** p. 452) after booking a hotel room in Chişinău.

Moldova

TRANSPORTATION. **Trains** are inefficient; **buses** are crowded and old but provide a much cheaper and more comfortable way of getting in, out, and around Moldova. The Iaşi-Chişinău train trip takes about 6 hours, of which only two are spent in motion; border controls and wheel-changing take up the rest. There are direct train and bus connections from Chişinău to Bucharest, Kyiv, or Odessa. If possible, **avoid traveling through Tiraşpol or Dubăsari,** both of which are in Moldova's politically unstable breakaway Transdniester Republic. You will be given a sheet on which to **document the money you are changing.** Be sure not to lose it—it might be demanded by customs when you leave the country. Internally, trains from Chişinău go to Băltsi, Tiraşpol, and Ungleni, but the railroad network—built when Moldova and Ukraine were one country—crisscrosses their border in several places. The two classes are regular *platzkart* and the more comfortable and secluded *coupé.*

**TOURIST SERVICES AND MONEY. Moldovatur** is the main tourist office. Its employees usually speak English and are a good source of all types of information. Do not confuse the Moldovan *leu* with the Romanian currency of the same name. The currency rates below are those for September 2000. **Bringing cash is necessary** since few places outside Chişinău take traveler's checks or give cash advances. There are only a few **ATMs** in the capital, and even fewer elsewhere in the country.

| CURRENCY | | |
|---|---|---|
| US$1 = 12 LEI | 10 LEI = US$0.81 |
| CDN$1 = 8.30LEI | 10 LEI = CDN$1.20 |
| UK£1 = 18 LEI | 10 LEI = UK£0.56 |
| IR£1 = 14 LEI | 10 LEI = IR£0.71 |
| AUS$1 = 7.00 LEI | 10 LEI = AUS$1.40 |
| NZ$1 = 5.30 LEI | 10 LEI = NZ$1.90 |
| SAR1 = 1.81 LEI | 10 LEI = SAR 5.50 |
| DM1 = 5.60 LEI | 10 LEI = DM 1.80 |

**HEALTH AND SAFETY.** In Chişinău, streets are poorly lit at night, and it is **unwise to stay out late.** Pharmacies in Moldova are generally well-equipped with western products; a chain called Farmacia Felicia is open 24hr. In hospitals, pay with cash or a credit card. Carrying toilet paper and insect repellent is always a good idea.

**ACCOMMODATIONS.** Hostels are nonexistent, and the cheapest options for the budget traveler are private rooms (14-40 lei).

**KEEPING IN TOUCH.** AT&T Direct and similar **phone** services are not yet available; collect calls also remain impossible. Most local phones use Moldtelecom cards (from 12 lei), available at the post office or in kiosks. When calling Moldova from Ukraine and other former Soviet republics, you need only to dial the city code, not the country code. **Mail** can be received general delivery through *Poste Restante;* service in the post office in Chişinău is slow but dependable to most countries. Address envelope as follows: Anne (First name) CHISHOLM (LAST NAME), *Poste Restante,* bd. Ştefan cel Mare 134 (Post office address), Chişinau (City) 2012 (Postal code), MACEDONIA. **Email** is cheap and widely available in Chişinău. Expensive and efficient, **DHL** has landed in both Chişinău and Tiraşpol.

# CHIŞINĂU (КИШИНЭУ)   ☎(8)2

Once famous for excellent wine, Chişinău (KEE-shee-nao; Russian kee-shee-NYOF; pop. 657,775) has lost its energy, and is only uneasily playing the role as its country's capital. Built on a rectangular grid, its sparseness is punctuated only by concrete monsters on a Stalinist scale. The city has tried, however, to shed its provincial feel and bring Moldova into the 21st century, undertaking new construction and renovating old buildings. Indicators of the city's political, social, and economic future are as fascinatingly mixed as its architecture—traditional marketplaces are complemented by stores packed with western imports and the cell phone has begun to infiltrate the city's transit system, but the streets still fall eerily quiet come night.

**▪ ORIENTATION.** Thanks to its grid layout, Chişinău is very easy to navigate. **Bd. Ştefan cel Mare şi Sfint** (Stefan the Great and Saint) spans the city center from southeast to northwest; most sights are clustered around it. It intersects **str. Tighina** about 10min. up from the **train station;** turn right to find the marketplace and the **bus station.** From the bus, a 10-min. walk along bd. Ştefan cel Mare leads to the central **Piaţa Naţională. Trolleys** #1, 4, and 8 run from the train station to the center, while #1, 5, 8, and 22 run along bd. Ştefan Cel Mare. **City maps** are available for 15lei from Moldova Tur or most bookstores.

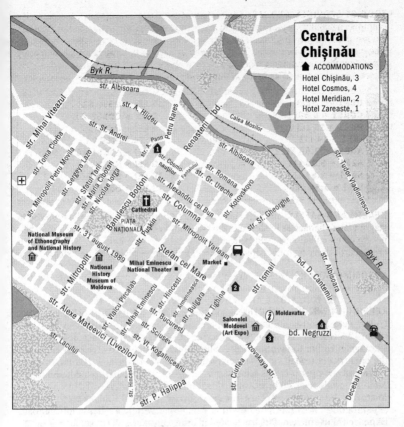

**Central Chişinău**

♠ ACCOMMODATIONS
Hotel Chişinău, 3
Hotel Cosmos, 4
Hotel Meridian, 2
Hotel Zareaste, 1

■ **TRANSPORTATION.** The **airport** (☎ 52 54 12) is 12km from downtown; take bus #65 from the corner of Izmail and Ştefan Cel Mare. **Voiaj Travel,** bd. Negruzzi 10, near Hotel Naţional, arranges flights to **Frankfurt, Moscow, Athens, Istanbul,** and just about anywhere in the world. (☎ 54 64 64. Open M-Sa 8am-7pm, Su 9am-5pm. MC/Visa.) The **train station** (☎ 25 27 35) is in the southwest corner of town. Buy tickets on the 2nd floor or get them for 10 lei extra from the English-speaking **Moldovatur** (see below). To: **Odessa, UKR** (4½hr., 2 per day, 24 lei); **Bucharest, ROM** (12½hr., 1 per day, 178 lei); **Kyiv, UKR** (18hr., 2 per day, 180 lei); **Simferopol, UKR** (19hr., 1 per day M, W, and F, 150 lei); **Varna, BUL** (21hr., 1 per day M, W, and F, 425 lei); **Minsk, BLR** (26hr., 1 per day M and F, 200 lei) and **Moscow, RUS** (27hr., 2 per day, 205 lei). The following trains pass through Chişinau: Varna, ROM to Minsk, BLR; Sofia, BUL to Saratov; and Ivano-Frankivsk-Odessa, UKR. **Buses,** Str. Mitropolit Varlaam 58 (☎ 21 20 84), leave for: **Iaşi** (5hr., 4 per day, 30 lei); **Odessa, UKR** (5hr., 1 per hr., 33 lei); **Kamyanets-Podilsky, UKR** (9hr., 2 per day, 62 lei); **Bucharest, ROM** (10hr., 2 per day, 92 lei); **Simferopol, UKR** (1 per 2 days, 130 lei); and **Kyiv, UKR** (1 per day, 200 lei). Ticket booth open daily 9:30am-6:30pm. **Kavasoglu lines** (☎ 54 98 22) and **Ozguleu lines** (☎ 26 37 48) each run buses to **Istanbul, TUR** from the train station (400 lei).

Chişinău has an extensive local **trolley and bus** system. (0.75 lei per ride, 1 lei on new buses. Pay on board.) *Marshrutki* (converted minivans) follow the same routes (numbers and destinations are on the windshield, along with an "A" (bus) or "T" (trolley) to indicate which route they follow) and are a quick alternative (1 lei). Hold out your hand to hail one if you're not at a stop. If possible, avoid overpriced **taxis** (☎ 907 or 908).

**MOLDOVA**

**◪ PRACTICAL INFORMATION.** The **tourist office, Moldovatur,** bd. Ştefan cel Mare 4, in the left corner of the 1st floor of Hotel Naţional, arranges hotel reservations and tours. It also provides city **maps** for 15 lei. (☎54 03 01 or 54 04 94. jur@dnt.md; www.ipm.md/mtur. Open M-F 8:30am-5pm.) There's a **US Embassy** on str. Alexe Mateevici 103. (☎23 37 72; fax 23 30 44. Open M-F 9am-6pm, citizens' services W 2-4pm.) Citizens of other countries should contact their embassies in Romania (see **Bucharest: Embassies,** p. 564). **Currency exchange** business is booming; look for the "schimb valutar" or "обмен валют" signs. The best rates are at **Eximbank,** bd. Ştefan cel Mare 3. (Open 9am-2pm and 3-8pm.) **Victoriabank,** bd. Ştefan cel Mare 77, exchanges traveler's checks for a 1.5% commission and gives MC/Visa cash advances for a 2-3% commission. A Plus/Visa **ATM** stands outside. (☎22 59 24. Open M-F 9am-5pm, Sat 9am-2pm.) **Western Union** is everywhere—look for the black and yellow signs. A **24hr. pharmacy, Felicia Farmacia,** has several locations; one is at bd. Ştefan cel Mare 128 (☎22 37 25). The **hospitals** on Str. Puşkin 51 (☎22 32 66 or 21 22 91) and on Toma Ciorba 1 treat foreigners. **Oxford University Press,** Str. Mihai Eminescu 63, offers a wide selection of English books. (Open M-F 10am-6pm, Sa 10am-3pm.) **24hr. telephones** are at the corner of str. Tighina and bd. Ştefan cel Mare. **Internetclub Mobile Arena,** Renasterii 8, boasts fast connections (7 lei per hour). There's a **post office** (oficiul poştal) at bd. Ştefan cel Mare 134, right across from city hall and the Mihai Eminescu Theater. (Open M-Sa 8am-7pm, Su 8am-6pm. Fax services daily 9am-2pm.) **Postal code:** 2012.

**▛▜ ACCOMMODATIONS AND FOOD. Coopertiva Adresa,** bd. Negruzzi 1, across from Hotel Cosmos, rents **private rooms** (☎54 43 92. All with TV, bath, A/C. English spoken. Open M-F 9am-9pm, Sa-Su 9am-6pm. 10-60 lei.) All hotels levy a 9 lei tourist tax. **Hotel Meridian,** str. Tighina 42, is friendly and conveniently next to the bus station. (☎27 06 20. Barest rooms 30 lei per person; singles with toilet and sink 100 lei; doubles 120 lei, with bath 225 lei.) **Hotel Zareaste,** Anton Pann 4, has bare rooms with TV, shared bath, and hot water. From the center, go right down bd. Bodoni and left on Alexandru cel Bun. Pann is the 1st right; the hotel is on the right. (☎22 76 25. Doubles 48.60 lei per person; triples 45.60 lei per person.) At the **marketplace Piaţa Centrala,** off Ştefan cel Mare on str. Tighina, you can find vendors selling fresh fruit and vegetables, *buterbrod* (open-faced sandwiches with meat and veggies; 1-2 lei), and pastries. (Open in summer Tu-Su 6:30am-6pm; off-season 7am-4pm.) Also look for **Alimentari** (food stores). The one on the corner of Ştefan cel Mare and Str. Tighina is open 24 hours. **▨ Restaurant Indian Tandoori,** bul. Renasteri 6, will fill you with Indian and Persian classics. They have so many vegetarian dishes, you might just forget you're in Moldova. (☎24 50 23. Main dishes 15-80 lei. Open M-F noon-midnight, Sa-Su 3pm-midnight. MC/Visa.) For the best traditional fare, try **Barracuda,** Puşkin 35. (☎20 21 02. Main dishes from 25-100 lei. Open daily noon-11pm.)

**◨▞ SIGHTS AND ENTERTAINMENT.** Up bd. Ştefan cel Mare, at the intersection with str. Puşkin, is **Piaţa Naţională,** Moldova's main square. The 1841 **Triumphal Arch** stands in front of a park that houses the **Catedrala Naşterea Domnului Clopotniţa,** a temple-like cathedral and bell-tower. On the square's upper left corner stands the statue of the legendary **Stephen the Great** (Ştefan cel Mare şi Sfînt), wielding sword and cross. The **▨ National History Museum of Moldova** (Muzeul Naţional de Istorie a Moldovei), Str. 31 August 1989, is so spectacular it might even make you believe that Moldova is the center of universe. (☎24 43 25. Open in summer Tu-Su 10am-6pm; off-season 9am-5pm. Closed last F of the month. 2 lei, students 1 lei.) For the Moldovan take on Russian Pushkin-mania, visit the **A. S. Pushkin House and Museum** (Casa-Muzeu A.S. Pushkin) at Str. Anton

MOLDOVA

Pann 19. Pushkin lived in Chişinău from 1820 to 1823 while working on *Eugene Onegin*. (☎29 26 86 or 29 41 38. Open Tu-Su 10am-5pm. 2 lei.) For a bastion of serenity, walk about five blocks up str. Puşkin from the center to stroll around the **city park,** and rent a boat from its small **beach** (12 lei per hr.) Tire yourself during the day, as nightlife is lacking (most likely because it isn't safe to go out alone after dark). The cafes near the opera house are popular with the young.

**▶ DAYTRIP FROM CHIŞINĂU: VADUL LUI VODĂ.** About 12km northeast of Chişinău, this relaxing riverside resort is a summertime haven for Moldovans. On a hot summer day the **beach** is packed with Chişinău residents. *(Bus #31 runs directly from the market in Chişinău (4 per day, 21 lei). Behind the bus station, on Str. Bulgara, Marshrutki taxis marked "31A Vadul lui Voda" depart as they fill up. 3 lei.)*

MOLDOVA

# POLAND
# (POLSKA)

## IF YOU'RE HERE FOR...

**5 DAYS.** Wander the streets and kick back in cellar jazz joints in historical **Kraków** (p. 481), the cultural heart of Poland.

**2 WEEKS.** See reconstructed **Warsaw** (p. 465).

**1 MONTH.** Experience the cosmopolitan flair of the **Tri-city area** (p. 531), the serenity of the village of **Hel** (p. 544), and the grunting bison of **Wolin National Park** (p. 530).

Poland has always been caught at the threshold of East and West, and its moments of freedom have been brief. It is easy to forget that between 1795 to 1918, Poland simply did not exist on any map of Europe, and that its short spell of independence thereafter—like so many before it—was brutally dissolved. Ravaged by World War II and viciously suppressed by Stalin and the USSR, Poland has at long last been given room to breathe, and its residents are not letting the opportunity slip by. The most prosperous of the "Baltic tigers," Poland now has a rapidly expanding GDP, a new membership in NATO, and a likely future membership in the E.U. With their new wealth, the legendarily hospitable Poles have been returning to their cultural roots and repairing buildings destroyed in the wars, a trend popular with the growing legions of tourists that visit each year. Capitalism brought with it Western problems, like rising crime and unemployment, issues politicians have begun to recognize as serious. But there are few Poles complaining about the events of the past ten years. Political and economic freedoms have helped this rich culture to occupy its own skin once again, even if it's now wearing a pair of Levi's.

## POLAND AT A GLANCE

**OFFICIAL NAME:** Republic of Poland

**CAPITAL:** Warsaw (pop. 1,640,000)

**POPULATION:** 39 million

**LANGUAGE:** Polish

**CURRENCY:** 1 zloty (zł) = 100 groszy

**RELIGION:** 95% Roman Catholic (about 75% practicing)

**LAND AREA:** 312,683 km²

**CLIMATE:** Temperate

**GEOGRAPHY:** Plains, southern mountains

**BORDERS:** Belarus, Czech Republic, Germany, Lithuania, Russia, Slovakia, Ukraine

**ECONOMY:** 68.3% Services, 26.6% Industry, 5.1% Agriculture

**GDP:** $6,800 per capita

**EMERGENCY PHONE NUMBERS:** Police 997, Fire 998; Emergency 999

**COUNTRY CODE:** 48

**INTERNATIONAL DIALING PREFIX:** 00

# HISTORY

**BEGINNINGS.** Between AD 800 and 960, a number of the West Slavic tribes occupying modern Poland joined to form small states. When **Prince Mieszko I** of the Piast dynasty converted to Catholicism in 966, he united many of the tribes. His son, **Bolesław Chrobry** (the Brave), was crowned Poland's first king in 1025 (see **Gniezno**, p. 518). Poland was devastated by the Mongols in 1241, but the 14th century—particularly under **King Kazimierz III Wielki** (Casimir III the Great)—developed into a time of

prosperity and unprecedented religious and political tolerance. Poland also became a refuge for Jews expelled from Western Europe, guaranteeing their freedom and prohibiting forcible baptism. A **university** was founded at Kraków, the cultural and political capital of Poland, in 1364.

**YOU KNOW WHAT THEY SAY ABOUT LITHUANIAN MEN.** In 1368 the Polish nobles, eager to bring Christianity to Lithuania and to expand trade, married Kazimierz's only child Princess Jadwiga to Jagiełło, Grand Duke of Lithuania. Jagiełło was crowned King Wladyslaw II Jagiełło of Poland and the Polish nobles gained a powerful ally against the aggressive **Teutonic Knights.** The decision proved fortuitous. After the death of Casimir III in 1370, Poland experienced increasing difficulties with the knights, who took East Prussia and cut off access to the Baltic. Troubles with the knights continued until 1410, when Polish and Lithuanian forces dealt them a crushing defeat at the **Battle of Grunwald,** establishing Poland as a European power. In 1447 Casimir IV assumed power. Continuing the war against the Teutonic Knights, he succeeded in reopening the road to the Baltic.

**LET'S GET TOGETHER.** Poland and Lithuania drew closer with the 1569 **Union of Lublin,** which established the **Polish-Lithuanian Commonwealth** under an elected king and a common legislature and customs union, but with separate territories, laws and armies. The Renaissance reached Poland in the 16th century under **King Zygmunt I Stary** (Sigmund the Old). Shortly thereafter, Mikołaj Kopernik, an astronomer from Toruń better known by his Latin name, **Copernicus,** developed the heliocentric model of the solar system (see **Toruń,** p. 519). Though the Reformation made some progress in Poland, its gains were largely eliminated by the Catholic Counter Reformation, led by the Jesuit Order.

POLAND

In the early 17th century, the Swedish **Zygmunt III Waza** moved the capital to Warsaw. Zygmunt also embroiled the state in conflicts with Turkey and Muscovy and though he was often victorious in battle, his campaigns weakened the state. His successor, **Wladyslaw IV,** angered the Cossacks, formerly allies of the Polish state, by subjugating Orthodoxy to Catholicism, creating the **Uniate church.** The Cossacks, under **Bohdan Khmelnitsky,** subsequently rebelled, and after lengthy conflict with Poland finally allied themselves with Muscovy. The Poles succeeded in putting down the Cossacks, but then, from 1648-67, faced a wave of **Swedish invasions.**

Under pressure from Russian troops, Prince Janusz Radziwill submitted to Sweden and Poland proper capitulated in 1655. The brutal Swedish occupation soon provoked resistance, however, and with the aid of the Habsburgs, Denmark, and Prussia the occupation was lifted in 1660. Polish nobles used the wars as leverage to extract power from the monarch. In 1652 the *Sejm*, the Polish parliament, adopted the principle of *liberum veto*, under which one dissenting vote could block a proposed measure. With separate Polish and Lithuanian administrations and a weakened monarch, the Polish state had become infirm. The next few decades witnessed a string of ineffective monarchs, increasingly dominated by Russia. During the same period, though, Enlightenment ideas penetrated Poland, leading to the establishment of the Knights' School, the first secular college in Poland.

**THE RUSSIANS ARE COMING.** In 1768 nationalist Poles, opposed to Russian influence in domestic affairs and desirous of maintaining the primacy of the Catholic faith, formed the **Confederation of Bar.** This formation precipitated a civil war which threw the nation into anarchy until 1772. France and Turkey aided the confederates, while Russia backed the monarchy. Fearful of losing its influence in Poland, the Russian government began to hearken to Prussian ruler Frederick the Great's schemes to partition Poland.

Russia, Prussia, and Austria each took sizable chunks of the Polish-Lithuanian Commonwealth in 1772. Paradoxically, Polish culture flourished in the period after partition despite the presence of Russian troops. Following the dissolution of the Jesuit order the educational system was reformed; the economy boomed and literature blossomed. Russia remained fearful of a strong Polish state, however, and a legal reform attempted by Stanislaw II was blocked by Moscow.

**DÈJA VU.** In 1788 Polish noblemen convened a special meeting of the *Sejm* to draft a state constitution. This "Great Sejm" took four years of debate, during which the American Revolution was frequently invoked, to produce a constitution calling for a parliamentary monarchy. Signed on May 3, 1791, the new constitution was the second of its kind in the world; it established Catholicism as the national religion, set up a plan for the election of political leaders, provided for a standing army and abolished the liberum veto. The prospect of a renascent state, however, made both Russia and Prussia nervous, leading to…

**DÈJA VU ALL OVER AGAIN.** In response to these attempts at independence, Russia and Prussia divided Poland again in 1793. The Polish government was forced to capitulate and many patriots fled abroad. The following year, **Tadeusz Kościuszko,** a hero of the American Revolution, led an uprising against Russian rule. He ended up in prison, and Poland was divided one last time in 1795 (see **Racławice Panorama,** p. 510). The three **Partitions of Poland** removed the country from the map of Europe for the next 123 years, during which time Russia attempted to crush the nationalist spirit expressed in the rebellions of 1806, 1830, 1846, 1848, 1863, and 1905.

Poland didn't win back its independence until 1918, after **Marshal Józef Piłsudski** pushed back a new invasion by the Red Army. A Polish delegation led by **Roman Dmowski** worked Polish statehood into the Treaty of Versailles. From the 1920s until 1935, Piłsudski ruled with only formal preservation of parliamentary authority.

**WORLD WAR II.** The signing of the **Nazi-Soviet Nonaggression Pact** in August 1939 rendered Poland's defense treaties worthless. In September, Nazi and Soviet forces attacked Poland simultaneously from west and east. Germany occupied the western two-thirds of the country, while the Soviet Union got the rest. More than six million Poles were killed, including three million Jews. Five years later, as the Nazis lost control of the country to the invading Red Army, freedom fighters loyal to the government in exile in London initiated the **Warsaw Uprising** of 1944 to take back their city before the Soviets "liberated" it. The Germans retaliated ruthlessly, however, while the Soviets waited in the suburbs. When Red tanks finally rolled in, they took Warsaw with little opposition and inaugurated 45 years of **communist** rule. The first few years brought mass migrations, political crackdown, and social unrest that contributed to the 1946 Jewish **pogrom**. Even after the country grudgingly submitted, **strikes** broke out in 1956, 1968, and 1970; all were violently quashed.

**THE RISE OF SOLIDARITY.** In 1978, **Karol Wojtyła** became the first Polish pope, taking the name John Paul II. His visit to Poland during the following year helped to unite the Catholic Poles and was an impetus for the birth of **Solidarność** (Solidarity), the first independent workers' union in Eastern Europe, in 1980. Led by the charismatic **Lech Wałęsa,** an electrician at the Gdańsk shipyards, Solidarity activities resulted in the declaration of **martial law** in 1981 by head of Polish government **General Wojciech Jaruzelski.** Wałęsa was jailed and released only after Solidarność was officially disbanded and outlawed by the government in 1982.

In 1989, Poland spearheaded the fall of Soviet authority in Eastern Europe. Solidarity members swept into all but one of the contested seats in the June elections, and **Tadeusz Mazowiecki** was sworn in as Eastern Europe's first non-Communist premier in 40 years. In December 1990, Wałęsa became the first elected president of post-Communist Poland. The government opted to swallow the bitter pill of capitalism all in one gulp by quickly eliminating subsidies, freezing wages, and devaluing the currency. This threw the antiquated economy into recession and produced the first true unemployment in 45 years. Following this short period of rising crime and painful reform, Poland has rebounded toward economic and political stability.

# POLITICS

In Poland's tightly contested November 1995 presidential election, **Lech Wałęsa**—former leader of the Solidarity movement—lost to **Aleksander Kwaśniewski.** A 1980s Communist and head of the ex-Communist Democratic Left Alliance, Kwaśniewski was elected on a platform of moderately paced privatization and stronger ties with the West. Following Kwaśniewski's election, however, the **Solidarity Electoral Action (AWS)** party saw success in local elections, marked by the ascendance of **Jerzy Buzek** to the post of prime minister in October 1997. Solidarity's stock has since plummeted, particularly following the collapse of the Solidarity-Freedom Union coalition government in June 2000. Wałęsa, meanwhile, has become a political outcast both within the party he founded and on a national level.

# CULTURE

| NATIONAL HOLIDAYS IN 2001 | |
|---|---|
| **Jan 1** New Year's Day | **August 15** Assumption Day |
| **April 15-16** Easter | **November 1** All Saints Day |
| **May 1** Labor Day | **November 11** Independence Day |
| **May 3** Constitution Day | **December 25** Christmas |
| **June 14** Corpus Christi | **December 26** 2nd day of Christmas |

POLAND

# LITERATURE

Like its social and political history, the course of Polish literature changed forever when the nation chose to follow Roman—not Byzantine—Christianity. Accordingly, Poland's medieval texts, mostly religious works and chronicles, were written in Latin. With the onset of the European Renaissance, Poland's Western alphabet and religion helped it become an immediate participant, and generated a literary culture that flourishes to this day. Self-taught 16th century author **Mikolaj Rej,** the first to write consistently in Polish, combined medieval and renaissance styles in his work and is regarded as the father of Polish literature. His contemporary **Jan Kochanowski,** who remains one of the most important Slavic poets, shed the archaic elements present in Rej's work; His *Treny (Laments)*, a cycle of poems about the death of his young daughter, brought the Polish literary language to full maturity.

Loss of statehood in 1795 paved the way for **Romanticism,** which held nationalism as a primary ideal. The most prominent writers of this great period—**Adam Mickiewicz, Juliusz Słowacki,** and **Zygmunt Krasiński,** exiles all—depict Poland as a noble, suffering martyr. The Lithuanian-born Mickiewicz is widely regarded as Poland's national poet and his *Pan Tadeusz* is still considered the country's primary epic.

Another failed uprising in 1863 brought the Romantic period to an end. Characterized by naturalistic and historic novels, late 19th-century **Positivism** advocated simple work and participation in one's community. Nobel Prize-winner **Henryk Sienkiewicz's** 1896 novel *Quo Vadis?*—a tale of early Christianity amid Roman decadence under Nero—argues that society rests on individual morality.

The daily grind provided inspiration only until the turn of the century; the early 20th-century neo-romantic **Młoda Polska** (Young Poland) movement was laden with pessimism and apathy. In his mystery-filled *Wesele* (The Wedding), one of the finest pieces of the period, playwright **Stanisław Wyspiański** addressed many of the problems that defined Poland in his era.

Later, the "thaw" following Soviet attempts to enforce **Socialist Realism** brought about an explosion of new work addressing life under communism's thumb. **Zbigniew Herbert** developed the character *Pan Cogito*, while **Tadeusz Różewicz** concentrated on very short, poignant lyric poems and plays. Later, the **Generation of '68** ushered in a new wave of authors whose poems and essays tackle the dilemmas of living at a historical crossroads. Recent Polish authors include Nobel Prize-winner **Czesław Miłosz,** whose controversial *The Captive Mind (Zniewolony umysł)* remains an essential commentary on communist control of individual thought. In 1996, **Wisława Szymborska,** a prominent female poet, became the second Polish writer in 16 years to receive the Nobel Prize.

# MUSIC

Polish music has long been rooted in folk culture and sacred music developed during the renaissance. The first Polish opera, Jan Stefani and Wojciech Boguslawski's *The Pretended Miracle; or, The Krakovians and the Highlanders (Cud mniemany czyli Karakowiacy i Górale)* appeared in 1794. Polish music is best defined by the 19th-century work of **Frédéric Chopin** (in Polish, Fryderyk Szopen), a master composer and the first of many internationally acclaimed Polish instrumentalists (among them pianist **Artur Rubinstein**). Popular contemporary composers include Witold Lutoslawski and Krzysztof Penderecki. Poland is also a jazz hotbed.

# VISUAL ARTS AND FILM

Fine examples of both Romanesque and Gothic **architecture** still stand in Poland. The wooden altar of **Wit Stwosz,** in St. Mary's Church in Kraków (see p. 486), is a masterpiece, as is the red-brick castle of **Malbork** (see p. 538), formerly the headquarters of the Teutonic Knights. The town hall of **Poznań** (see p. 517) is a fine example of the Polish take on Renaissance style, while the town of **Zamość** (see p. 495) has been preserved in 16th century form. Several palaces, including the **Wawel Castle** (see p. 487) in Kraków, present fine specimens of Classical architecture.

Polish **films** have consistently drawn international acclaim. Filmmaker **Andrzej Wajda** is known for explorations of his country's internal conflicts in such films as *Pokolenie (A Generation)* and *Czlowiek z marmuru (Man of Marble)*. He received an honorary Oscar in 2000. Polish directors **Roman Polański** and **Krzysztof**

Kieślowski have achieved international recognition, the latter primarily for his trilogy *Three Colors: Red, White and Blue*. Polański's first film, *Knife in the Water* (1962), made while he was a student at the acclaimed Łodz film school, was nominated for an Academy Award for best foreign language film.

# RELIGION

Poland is one of the most uniformly **Catholic** countries in the world and the Catholic church enjoys both immense respect and tremendous political power. Polish Catholicism has been bolstered since 1978 by the election of the Polish Pope John Paul II, the first non-Italian pope since the 16th century. **Protestant** groups are generally confined to small geographic areas bordering Germany. A few communities of Polish **Jews** remain, but these represent a tiny percentage of the population.

# FOOD AND DRINK

Monks, merchants, invaders, and dynastic unions have all flavored Polish cuisine—a blend of dishes from the French, Italian, and Slavic traditions. Polish food favors meat, potatoes, cabbage, and butter.

A Polish meal always starts with **soup,** usually *barszcz* (clear broth), *chłodnik* (a cold beet soup with buttermilk and hard-boiled eggs), *kapuśniak* (cabbage soup), or *żurek* (barley-flour soup loaded with eggs and sausage). Filling **main courses** include *gołąbki* (cabbage rolls stuffed with meat and rice), *kotlet schabowy* (pork cutlet), *naleśniki* (cream-topped crepes filled with cottage cheese or jam), and *pierogi* (dumplings with various fillings—meat, potato, cheese, blueberry).

Poland bathes in **beer, vodka,** and **spiced liquor.** *Żywiec* is the most popular strong (12%) beer; *EB* is its excellent, gentler brother. *EB* also makes *EB Czerwone*, a darker, heavier, stronger variety. Other available beers include *Okocim* and *Piast*. *Wódka* (vodka) ranges from wheat to potato. *Wyborowa, Żytnia,* and *Polonez* usually decorate private bars, while *Belweder* is Poland's proudest alcoholic export. "Kosher" vodka is rumored to be top-notch, although what makes it kosher remains a mystery. The herbal *Żubrówka* vodka comes with a blade of grass from the region where the bison roam. It is sometimes mixed with apple juice (*z sokem jabłkowym*). *Miód* and *krupnik*—two kinds of mead—are beloved by the gentry, and many grandmas make *nalewka na porzeczce* (black currant vodka).

# CUSTOMS AND ETIQUETTE

**Business hours** tend to be Monday to Friday 10am to 6pm and Saturday 9am to 2pm. Saturday hours vary, as some shops in Poland distinguish "working" (*pracująca*) Saturdays, when they work longer hours, from "free" (*wolna*) ones, when hours are shorter. Unfortunately, each store decides for itself which Saturdays are which, so it may be difficult to prepare a shopping plan for any given weekend. Very few stores or businesses are open on Sunday. **Museums** are generally open Tuesday to Sunday, 10am to 4pm. They are ordinarily closed on holidays or the day after a holiday. In restaurants, tell the server how much change you want back, leaving the rest as a 10% **tip.** If you're paying with a credit card, give the tip in cash. When arriving as a **guest,** bring a female host an odd number of flowers. When addressing a man, use the formal *"Pan"*; with a woman, use *"Pani."* It is not uncommon for **restaurants** to be mostly empty, especially in the evening. **Drinking** is common on the street, but **smoking** is often prohibited indoors. **Homosexuality** is legal and a frequent topic of media debate, although its practice remains fairly underground.

# SPORTS

**Football** (soccer) is very popular in Poland, where Legia Warszawa, Polonia Warszawa, Ruch Chorzów and Wisla Kraków are the top teams. The national team, once relatively strong, has failed to qualify for the past three World Cups. (Their die-hard fans, however, continue to invoke the 3rd place in the 1974 World Cup in a tone approaching religious reverence.) **Volleyball,** once very popular, has declined in popularity while basketball has drawn an increasingly large following.

# LANGUAGE

**Polish** varies little across the country. The two exceptions are the region of Kaszuby, whose distinctive, Germanized dialect is classified by some as a separate language, and Karpaty, where the highlanders' accent is extraordinarily thick. In western Poland and Mazury, **German** is the most commonly known foreign language, although many Poles in big cities, especially students, will speak **English.** Elsewhere, try English and German before **Russian,** which many Poles understand but show an open aversion to speaking. Most Poles can understand **Czech** or **Slovak** if they're spoken slowly. Students may also know **French.**

The fully phonetic spelling is complicated by some letters not in the Latin alphabet: "*ł*" sounds like a "w"; "*ą*" is a nasal "on"; "*ę*" is a nasal "en." "*Ó*" and "*u*" are both equivalent to an "oo." "*Ż*" and "*rz*" are both like the "s" in "pleasure"; "*w*" sounds like "v." A few consonantal clusters are easier to spit out than they seem: "*sz*" is "sh," "*cz*" is "ch," and "*ch*" and "*h*" are equivalent, and sound like the English "h." "*C*" sounds like an English "ts," "*dż*" is "dg" as in "fridge," "*dź*" is "j" as in "jeep," "*ć*" or "*ci*" is "chyi," and "*zi*" or "*ź*" is "zhy." For commonly used words and phrases, see **Glossary,** p. 462 and **Phrasebook,** p. 463.

# ADDITIONAL READING

Both *Heart of Europe: A Short History of Poland*, by Norman Davies, and *The Polish Way: A Thousand Year History*, by Adam Zamoyski, provide a good sense of Polish history, with all its quirks and intricacies. James Michener's *Poland* provides an outstanding fictional account of three Polish families over eight centuries. *Pan Tadeusz*, by Adam Mickiewicz, and *Teutonic Knights*, by Henryk Sienkiewicz, are both classics that include some interesting history, and *The History of Polish Literature* by the Czesław Miłosz covers the genre in fascinating style.

# TRAVELING ESSENTIALS

Citizens of Ireland and the US can travel to Poland without a visa for up to 90 days and UK citizens for up to 180 days. Australians, Canadians, New Zealanders, and South Africans all need visas. Single-entry visas (valid for 180 days) cost US$60 (children and students under 26 pay US$45); multiple-entry visas cost US$100 (students US$75); 48hr. transit visas cost US$20 (students US$15). A visa application requires a valid passport, two photographs, and payment by money order, certified check, or cash; a visa with work permit also requires a work permit issued by the Labor Office or a certificate of employment. Regular service takes four days; 24hr. rush service costs an additional US$35. See **Essentials: Embassies and Consulates,** p. 18, for a list of Polish embassies. No visas are available at the border. To extend your stay, apply at the local province office (urząd wojewódzki); or in Warsaw to the Ministry of Internal Affairs at ul. Kruzca 5/11 (☎ (022) 625 59 04).

# INTERNATIONAL TRANSPORTATION

**BY PLANE.** LOT, British Airways, and Delta fly into Warsaw's **Okęcie Airport** from **London, New York, Chicago,** and **Toronto** (among other cities).

**BY TRAIN AND BUS.** Trains and buses connect to all neighboring countries, but Eurail passes are not valid in Poland. **Almatur** offers ISIC holders a discount of 192zł. Wasteels tickets and Eurotrain passes, sold at Almatur, Orbis, and major train stations, get those under 26 40% off international train fares. Thefts have been known to occur on international overnight trains; try not to fall asleep, or sleep in shifts with a friend (for more on train safety, see **Safety and Security,** p. 25).

**BY FERRY.** Ferries run from **Sweden** and **Denmark** to Świnoujście, Gdańsk, and Gdynia. In summer a ferry runs from Gdynia to **Kaliningrad,** Russia.

# DOMESTIC TRANSPORTATION

**BY TRAIN.** For all but daytrips, trains are preferable to and, for long hauls, usually cheaper than buses. Train stations have boards that list towns alphabetically, and posters that list trains chronologically. *Odjazdy* (departures) are in yellow; *przyjazdy* (arrivals) are in white. *InterCity* and *Ekspresowy* (express) trains are listed in red with an "IC" or "Ex" in front of the train number. *Pośpieszny* (direct; also in red) are almost as fast. *Osobowy* (in black) are the slowest but are 35% cheaper than *pośpieszny*. All *InterCity, ekspresowy,* and some *pośpieszny* trains require seat reservations; if you see a boxed R on the schedule, ask the clerk for a *miejscówka* (myehy-TSOOF-kah; reservation). Buy surcharged tickets on board from the *konduktor* before he or she finds (and fines) you. Most people purchase *normalny* tickets, while students and seniors buy *ulgowy* (half-price) tickets. **Beware:** foreign travelers are not eligible for discounts on domestic buses and trains. You risk a hefty fine by traveling with an *ulgowy* ticket without Polish ID. On Sundays, tickets cost 20% less. Train tickets are good only for the day they're issued. Allot time for long, slow lines or buy your ticket in advance at the station or an Orbis office. Stations are not announced and are sometimes poorly marked. Foreign students are eligible for *ulgowy* bus and tram tickets in some cities.

**BY BUS.** PKS buses are cheapest and fastest for short trips. Like trains, there are *pośpieszny* (direct; marked in red) and *osobowy* (slow; in black). Purchase advance tickets at the bus station, and expect long lines. However, many tickets can only be bought from the driver. In the countryside, PKS markers (steering wheels that look like upside-down, yellow Mercedes-Benz symbols) indicate bus stops, but drivers will often stop if you flag them down. Traveling with a backpack can be a problem if the bus is full, since there are no storage compartments.

**BY TAXI.** Taxi drivers generally try to rip off foreigners; either arrange the price before getting in or be sure the driver turns on the meter. The going rate is 1.50-2zł per km. Cabs arranged by phone are more reliable than those hailed on the street.

**BY THUMB.** Though legal, **hitchhiking** is rare and more dangerous for foreigners. Hand-waving is the accepted sign. *Let's Go* does not recommend hitchhiking.

# TOURIST SERVICES AND MONEY

| CURRENCY | |
|---|---|
| US$1 = 4.40ZŁ (ZŁOTY, OR PLZ) | 1ZŁ = US$0.23 |
| CDN$1 = 3.00ZŁ | 1ZŁ = CDN$0.34 |
| UK£1 = 6.40ZŁ | 1ZŁ = UK£0.16 |
| IR£1 = 5.00ZŁ | 1ZŁ = IR£0.20 |
| AUS$1 = 2.50ZŁ | 1ZŁ = AUS$0.40 |
| NZ$1 = 1.90ZŁ | 1ZŁ = NZ$0.53 |
| SAR 1 = 0.63ZŁ | 1ZŁ = SAR 1.59 |
| DM 1 = 2.00ZŁ | 1ZŁ = DM 0.50 |

POLAND

City-specific offices are generally more helpful than the bigger chains. You can count on all offices to provide free info in English and to be of some help with accommodations for a nominal fee. Most provide good free maps and sell more detailed ones. **Orbis,** the state-sponsored travel bureau staffed by English speakers, operates luxury hotels in most cities and sells transportation tickets about the same price as station offices. **Almatur,** the Polish student travel organization, sells ISICs, helps find dorm rooms in summer, and sells student transportation tickets. Both provide maps and brochures, as do **PTTK** and **IT** (Informacji Turystycznej) bureaus. The *Polish Pages,* a free annual information and services guide available at larger hotels and tourist agencies, is also helpful.

## GLOSSARY

| ENGLISH | POLISH | PRONOUNCE |
|---|---|---|
| one | jeden | YEH-den |
| two | dwa | dvah |
| three | trzy | tshih |
| four | cztery | ch-TEH-rih |
| five | pięć | pyench |
| six | sześć | sheshch |
| seven | siedem | SHEH-dem |
| eight | osiem | OH-shem |
| nine | dziewięć | JYEH-vyench |
| ten | dziesięć | JYEH-shench |
| twenty | dwadzieścia | dva-JESH-cha |
| thirty | trzydzieści | tshi-JESH-chee |
| forty | czterdzieści | chter-JESH-chee |
| fifty | pięćdziesiąt | pyench-JESH-ont |
| sixty | sześćdziesiąt | sheshch-JESH-ont |
| seventy | siedemdziesiąt | shed-em-JESH-ont |
| eighty | osiemdziesiąt | ohsh-em-JESH-nt |
| ninety | dziewięćdziesiąt | JYEH-vyench-JESH-ont |
| one hundred | sto | stoh |
| one thousand | tysiąc | TIH-shonts |
| Monday | poniedziałek | poh-nyeh-JAH-wehk |
| Tuesday | wtorek | FTOH-rehk |
| Wednesday | środa | SHROH-dah |
| Thursday | czwartek | CHVAHR-tehk |
| Friday | piątek | PYAWN-tehk |
| Saturday | sobota | soh-BOH-tah |
| Sunday | niedziela | nyeh-JEH-lah |
| a day | dzien | j-EHN |
| a week | tydzien | TI-jehn |
| morning | rano | RAH-no |
| afternoon | popołudnie | poh-poh-WOOD-nyeh |
| evening | wieczor | v-YEH-chohr |
| today | dzisiaj | JEESH-eye |
| tomorrow | jutro | YOO-troh |
| spring | wiosna | v-YOH-snah |
| summer | lato | LAH-toh |
| fall | jesień | YEH-shen |
| winter | zima | ZHEE-mah |
| single room | pokój jednoos-bowy | POH-kooy yehd-noh-oh-soh-BOH-vih |

| ENGLISH | POLISH | PRONOUNCE |
|---|---|---|
| post office | poczta | POH-chtah |
| stamp | znaczki | ZNATCH-kee |
| airmail | lotniczą | loht-NYEE-chawng |
| departure | odjazd | OHD-yazd |
| arrival | przyjazd | PSHEE-yazd |
| one-way | w jedną stronę | VYEHD-nong STROH-neh |
| round-trip | tam i z powrotem | tahm ee spoh-VROH-tehm |
| luggage | bagaż | BAH-gahsh |
| seat reservation | miejscówka | myeh-TSOOF-ka |
| train | pociąg | POH-chawnk |
| bus | autobus | ow-TOH-booss |
| airport | lotnisko | laht-NEE-skoh |
| station | dworzec | DVOH-zhets |
| ticket | bilet | BEE-leht |
| grocery store | sklep spożywczy | sklehp spoh-ZHIV-chih |
| breakfast | śniadanie | sh-nyah-DAHN-yeh |
| lunch | obiad | OH-byaht |
| dinner | kolacja | koh-LAH-tsyah |
| menu | menu | MEH-noo |
| bread | chleb | khlehp |
| vegetables | vegetables | jarzyny |
| beef | beef | wołowina |
| chicken | kurczak | KOOR-chak |
| pork | wieprzowina | vye-psho-VEE-nah |
| fish | ryba | RIH-bah |
| coffee | kawa | KAH-vah |
| milk | mleko | MLEH-koh |
| beer | piwo | PEE-voh |
| sugar | cukier | TSOOK-yehr |
| eggs | jajka | y-EYE-kah |
| open | otwarty | ot-FAR-tih |
| closed | zamknięty | zahmk-NYENT-ih |
| bank | bank | bahnk |
| police | policja | poh-LEETS-yah |
| pharmacy | apteka | ahp-TEH-ka |
| left | lewo | LEH-voh |
| right | prawo | PRAH-vo |
| church | kościół | kosh-CHOOW |
| market | rynek | RIH-nehk |

# PHRASEBOOK

| ENGLISH | POLISH | PRONOUNCIATION |
|---|---|---|
| Yes/no | Tak/nie | tahk/nyeh |
| Please/You're welcome | Proszę | PROH-sheh |
| Thank you | Dziękuję | jen-KOO-yeh |
| Hi! | Cześć | cheshch |
| Good-bye | Do widzenia | doh veedz-EN-yah |
| Sorry/Excuse me | Przepraszam | psheh-PRAH-shahm |
| Help! | Na pomoc! | nah POH-mots |
| When? | Kiedy? | KYEH-dih |
| Where is...? | Gdzie jest? | g-JEH yest |
| How do I get to...? | Którędy do...? | ktoo-REN-dih doh |
| How much does this cost? | Ile to kosztuje? | EE-leh toh kohsh-TOO-yeh |
| Do you have...? | Czy są...? | chih sawn |
| Do you (male/female) speak English? | Czy pan(i) mówi po angielsku? | chih PAHN(-ee) MOO-vee poh ahn-GYEL-skoo |
| I don't understand. | Nie rozumiem. | nyeh roh-ZOOM-yem |
| I don't speak Polish | Nie mowię po polsku | nyeh MOO-vyeh poh POHL-skoo |
| Please write it down. | Proszę napisać. | PROH-sheh nah-PEE-sahch |
| I'd like to order... | chciałbym zamówić... | kh-CHOW-bihm za-MOOV-eech |
| I'd like to pay. | chciałbym zapłacić | kh-CHOW-bihm zap-WACH-eech |
| I think there is a mistake in the bill. | Myślę, ze jest błęd w rachunku | MIHSH-leh zheh yest bwend v ra-KHOON-koo |
| Do you have a vacancy? | Czy są jakieś wolne pokoje? | chih sawn YAH-kyesh VOHL-neh poh-KOY-eh |
| I (male/female) would like a room. | Chciał(a)bym pokój. | kh-CHOW-(ah)-bihm POH-kooy |
| May I see the room? | Czy mogę zobaczyć pokój? | chi MOH-geh zoh-BAH-chihch POH-kooy |
| No, I don't like it. | Nie, nie podoba mi się. | nyeh, nyeh poh-DOH-bah mee shyeh. |
| Yes, I'll take it. | Tak, go wezmę. | tahk, goh VEH-zmeh. |
| Will you tell me when to get off? | Proszę mi powiedzieć kiedy wysiąść? | PROH-sheh mee pohv-YEDGE-ehch KYEH-dih VIH-shonshch? |
| Is this the right train/bus to...? | Czy to pociąg/autobus do...? | chih toh yehst POH-chawng/ow-TOH-booss doh |
| I want a ticket to... | Poproszę bilet do... | poh-PROH-sheh BEE-leht do... |
| How long does the trip take? | Jak długo trwa podróż? | yahk DWOO-goh tr-fah POHD-roosh |
| When is the first/next/last train to... | Kiedy jest pierwszy/następny/ostatni pociąg do...? | KYEH-dih yehst PYEHR-fshih/nah-STEH-pnih/oh-STAHT-nyee POHT-shawng do... |
| Where is the bathroom/nearest telephone booth/center of town? | Gdzie jest łazienka/najbliziej budka telefoniczna/centrum miasta? | g-JYEH yest wahzh-YEHN-ka/neye-BLEEZH-ay BOOT-kah teh-leh-foh-NEE-chnah/TSEHN-troom MYAH-stah |
| I've lost my... | Zgubiłem... | zgoo-BEE-wehm |
| Get away! | Spadaj! | SPAHD-eye! |

The Polish **złoty**—plural *złote*—is fully convertible (1 *złoty* = 100 *grosze*). The rates given are those for September 2000; Polish inflation is around 6% so rates should be reasonably stable. For cash, private **kantor** offices (except for those at the airport and train stations) offer better exchange rates than banks. **Bank PKO S.A.** also has fairly good exchange rates; they cash **traveler's checks** and give MC/Visa **cash advances. ATMs** (Bankomat) are everywhere except the smallest of villages. **MC** and **Visa** are the most widely accepted ATM networks. Budget accommodations rarely, if ever, accept **credit cards,** although some restaurants and pricier shops will.

In January 1995, the National Bank cut four zeroes off all prices and introduced new bills and coins. The old currency has been invalid since January 1, 1997. Learn the difference between old and new (posters at the airport and train stations depict the currencies), and never accept old currency. When changing money, it helps to ask for small bank notes (10zł or 20zł), since businesses and hostels may not be able to give change for the larger notes (50zł or higher).

# HEALTH AND SAFETY

**Public restrooms** are marked with an upward-pointing triangle for men and a circle for women. They range from pristine to nasty and can cost up to 0.70zł, even if they're gross. Soap, towels, and toilet paper all cost extra. **Pharmacies** are well-stocked, and at least one in each city will be open 24hr. There are usually clinics in major cities with private, Anglophone doctors. Expect to plunk down 30-70zł per visit. Avoid the state hospitals if you can help it. **Tap water** is theoretically drinkable, but **bottled mineral water,** available carbonated (gazowana) or flat (nie gazowana), will spare you from some unpleasant metals and chemicals. **Criminals** feed off naive Western tourists, and as unemployment grows, so do the ranks of con artists. Always be on your guard at big train stations. Be on the lookout for pickpockets, especially when aboard crowded public buses and trams.

# ACCOMMODATIONS AND CAMPING

Grandmotherly **private room** owners drum up business at the train station or outside the tourist office. Private rooms are usually safe, clean, and convenient, but can be far from city centers. Expect to pay about US$10 per person. **Youth hostels** (schroniska młodzieżowe) abound and average 9-25zł per night. They are often booked solid, however, by school or tour groups; call at least a week in advance. **PTSM** is the national hostel organization. **University dorms** transform into spartan budget housing in July and August; these are an especially good option in Kraków. The Warsaw office of **Almatur** can arrange stays in all major cities. **PTTK** runs a number of hotels called **Dom Turysty,** which have multi-bed rooms as well as budget singles and doubles. Hotels generally cost 30-50zł per night. Many towns have a **Biuro Zakwaterowań,** which arranges stays in private homes. Rooms come in three categories based on location and availability of hot water (one is the best).

**Campsites** average US$2 per person; with a car, US$4. **Bungalows** are often available; a bed costs about US$5. *Polska Mapa Campingów* lists all campsites. Almatur runs a number of sites in summer; ask for a list at one of their offices.

# KEEPING IN TOUCH

**Mail** is becoming increasingly efficient, although there are still incidents of theft. Airmail *(lotnicza)* usually takes a week to reach the US. Mail can be received general delivery through **Poste Restante.** Address envelope as follows: Katharine (First name) HOLT (LAST NAME), POSTE RESTANTE, ul. Długa 22/25 (Post office address), Gdańsk (City) 80-800 (Postal code), POLAND. Letters abroad cost 1.60zł (air mail 1.80-2.20zł) for up to 20g. When picking up **Poste Restante,** you may have to pay a small fee (0.70-1zł) or show your passport. Most mid-sized towns and cities have at least one **internet club/cafe.**

**POLSKI PHONE HOME?** After making a call from one of Warsaw's spiffy new magnetic card telephones, you may find yourself accosted by any number of locals—from young girls to elderly gentlemen—staring at your card longingly and bargaining at you in Polish like a used-car salesman. Before you write these poor souls off as free-loaders who couldn't bother to buy their own phone card, know that the opposite is more likely true: they probably have plenty of cards and are looking to add yours to their collection. If you need confirmation of this bizarre factoid, most collectors will whip out their collection with great pride if asked. The cards with pictures on the back are the most coveted; if you find you're holding the Honus Wagner of phone cards—a 1999 Pope John Paul II—you'll have to fend off an ugly mob to escape.

**Card telephones** have become the public phone standard. Cards, which come in several denominations, are sold at post offices, Telekomunikacja Polska offices, and most kiosks. In some cities Telekomunikacja Polska offices also offer **internet access.** Long-distance access numbers are: **AT&T Direct, ☎** 00 80 01 11 11 11; **BT Direct,** ☎ 00 80 04 41 11 44; **Canada Direct,** ☎ 00 80 01 11 41 18; **MCI WorldPhone,** ☎ 00 80 01 11 21 22; and **Sprint,** ☎ 00 80 01 11 31 15. To make a **collect call,** write the name of the city or country and the number plus "*Rozmowa 'R'*" on a slip of paper, hand it to a post office clerk, and be patient.

# WARSAW (WARSZAWA)  ☎(0)22

Warsaw's motto, *contemnire procellas* (to defy the storms), has been put to the test in the city's long history. According to legend, Warsaw (pop. 1,640,000) was created when the fisherman Wars netted a mermaid (Polish *syrena,* now the city's emblem). She begged him to release her and told him that if he and his wife established a city on the spot, she would protect it forever. The mermaid has been busy for the past 1000 years as invaders from the north, east, and west have all taken a shot at this bastion of Polish pride. Most recently, World War II saw two-thirds of the population killed and 83% of the city destroyed. Even that devastation was seen by the Varsovians as an opportunity to rebuild and revitalize.

Once again the world's largest Polish city (a title long held by Chicago), Warsaw is quickly throwing off its Soviet legacy to emerge as an important international business center. A crop of new skyscrapers has emerged in the city center, while tourists come to take in the museums, listen to the concerts, and feast in the many restaurants. The university infuses Warsaw with young blood, which keeps the energy high and the night lively. All things considered, the *syrena* appears to have kept her promise, though it is unlikely that she, or any other Varsovian, will soon forget the storms that the city has weathered. For now, at least, all of its dynamism remains hand in hand with its history; in Warsaw there is no escape from the comparison between what is and what was.

## ✦ ORIENTATION

The busy city center, **Śródmieście,** is on the west riverbank of the **Wisła** (Vistula) **River,** which bisects the city. In the middle of it all, **Warszawa Centralna,** the main train station, lies on **al. Jerozolimskie,** between **al. Jana Pawła II** and **ul. Emilii Plater.** Nearby, the gargantuan **Pałac Kultury i Nauki** (Palace of Culture and Science) hovers above **pl. Defilad** (Parade Square) and its vast marketplace. **Ul. Marszałkowska** and **al. Ujazdowskie** are the city's main north-south avenues. Marszałkowska leads north to **Ogród Saski** (Saxon Gardens); the intersection serves as a major stop for most bus and tram lines. Al. Jerozolimskie continues east to intersect the other main north-south avenue, **al. Ujazdowskie,** at **rondo Charles de Gaulle.** A left here runs north up **ul. Nowy Świat,** which becomes **ul. Krakówskie Przedmieście,** and leads directly to **Stare Miasto** (Old Town) and the Royal Palace. A right at rondo Charles de Gaulle leads to **al. Ujazdowskie,** which finds the **Łazienki Palace** by way of embassy row.

POLAND

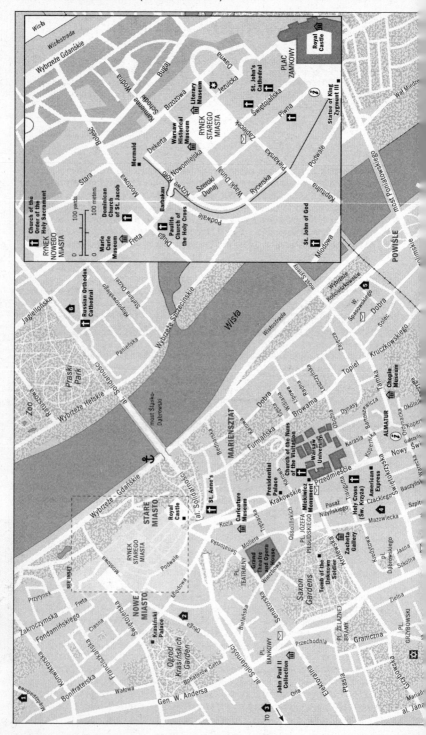

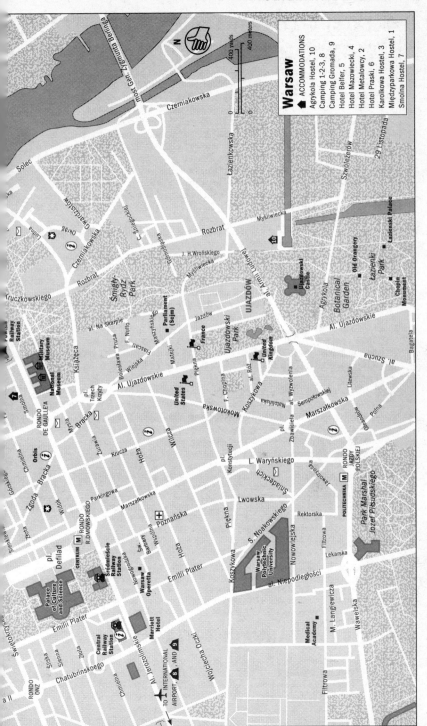

## Warsaw

**ACCOMMODATIONS**
Agrykola Hostel, 10
Camping 1-2-3, 8
Camping Gromada, 9
Hotel Belfer, 5
Hotel Mazowiecki, 4
Hotel Metalowcy, 2
Hotel Praski, 6
Karolkowa Hostel, 3
Międzyparkowa Hostel, 1
Smolna Hostel, 7

# ■ INTERCITY TRANSPORTATION

**Flights: Port Lotniczy Warszawa-Okięcie,** ul. Żwirki i Wigury (airport information desk ☎650 41 00), referred to as "Terminal 1." Take bus #175 to the center (after 11pm, bus #611); buy tickets at the Ruch kiosk in the departure hall or at the *kantor* outside. 2.40zł, students 1.20zł. Extra ticket required for a large suitcase or backpack. Open M-F 7:30am-8pm. There are also hotel minibuses that run to the city center. Tickets, available on board, are more expensive than for the bus, but the ride is faster.

**Airline Offices: Aeroflot,** al. Jerozolimskie 29 (☎628 17 10). Open M-F 8am-4pm. **Air France,** ul. Krucza 21 (☎628 12 81; fax 621 89 50) and at the airport (☎650 45 09; fax 650 45 06). **British Airways,** ul. Krucza 49 (☎628 94 31; airport office ☎650 45 03 and 650 45 20), off al. Jerozolimskie. Open M-F 9am-5pm. **Delta,** ul. Królewska 11 (☎827 84 61). Open M-F 9am-5pm. **KLM,** (☎622 80 00), at the aiport. Open M-F 9am-5pm. **LOT,** al. Jerozolimskie 65/79 (☎952 and 953), in the Hotel Marriott. LOT flies directly to New York (9 per week) and Chicago (9 per week). Open M-F 8am-8pm, Sa 8am-3pm. **Lufthansa,** ul. Nowy Swiat 19 (☎828 8505; fax 826 3970; warszawa@lufthansa.pl). Open M-Th 9am-5pm, F 9am-4:30pm.

**Trains:** There are 4 railway stations in Warsaw; the most convenient is **Warszawa Centralna,** al. Jerozolimskie 54 (☎825 50 00, international info ☎620 45 12, domestic info ☎620 03 61). Lines can be long, and most employees speak only Polish. Write down where and when you want to go, then ask them to write down which *peron* (platform) number to head for ("*Który peron?*" means "Which platform?"). Yellow signs list departures, white signs arrivals. To: **Berlin, GER** (7-8hr., 3 per day, 110zł); **Bratislava, SLK** (8hr., 2 per day, 136zł); **Budapest, HUN** (10hr., 2 per day, 190zł); **Minsk, BLR** (12hr., 1 per day, 105zł); **Vilnius, LIT** (12hr., 1 per day, 136zł); **Prague, CZR** (12-14hr., 3 per day, 153zł); **Kiev, UKR** (22-24hr., 2 per day, 147zł); **St. Petersburg, RUS** (26hr., 1 per day, 160zł); **Moscow, RUS** (27-30hr., 3 per day, 250zł); and almost every corner of Poland, including **Kraków** (2½hr., 14-18 per day, 33-63zł), **Poznań** (3hr., 14-18 per day, 33-63zl); and **Gdańsk** (3½-4½hr., 5-16 per day, 35-65zł).

> **Warning:** Theft is rising on international overnight trains to and from Berlin and Prague, as well as in train stations. Travelers should be mindful of their safety and protect their property (see **Accommodations and Transportation,** p. 27).

**Buses:** Warsaw sends buses from three separate stations:

**PKS Warszawa Zachodnia,** al. Jerozolimskie 144 (☎822 48 11, domestic info and reservations ☎94 33; international info ☎823 55 70) shares a building, address, and bus stop with the Warszawa Zachodnia train station. It can be reached by taking bus #127, 130, or 517 (or #601 at night) from the center to Zachodnia. For information about international bus tickets, check with the ticket booking office, **Centrum Podróży AURA,** at the Zachodnia station (☎823 68 58; open daily 6am-9:30pm) or at al. Jerozolimskie 63, in the Marriott Hotel (☎628 62 53). Buses depart to such foreign cities as **London, BRI** (450zł), **Paris, FRA** (399zł), **Prague, CZR** (94zł), **Minsk, BLR** (84zł), **Copenhagen, DEN** (330zł), and **Venice, ITA** (340zł).

**PKS Warszawa Stadion** on Zielaniecka, on the other side of the river. Take bus #101, #509, or tram #12 from the center of town. Buses head from here to the east and south.

**Polski Express,** al. Jana Pawła II (☎630 03 20), in a kiosk near Warszawa Centralna (see above), is a private company that offers faster and more comfortable bus service from Warsaw to such cities as **Gdańsk** (6hr., 2 per day, 37zł); **Kraków** (6hr., 2 per day, 33zł); **Łódź** (2½hr., 7 per day, 17zł); and **Lublin** (3hr., 7 per day, 17zł); and **Szczecin** (9½hr., 2 per day, 33zł). Discounts for students under 26. Open M and Sa 6am-8:30pm, T-Th 6:30am-8:30pm, F and Su 6:30am-9:30pm.

# ▐ LOCAL TRANSPORTATION

**Public Transportation: Bus** and **tram** lines are marked on some maps. Day trams and buses (including express lines) 2.40zł, with ISIC 1.20zł; night buses 7.20zł. Large baggage 1 ticket per piece. Day pass 7.20zł, with ISIC 3.60zł. Weekly pass 26zł, with ISIC 13zł. Buy tickets at most kiosks, or from the driver at night. Punch the ticket (on the end marked by the arrow and *tu kasować*) in the machines on board or face a 140zł fine,

POLAND

plus another 48zł for your pack. Bus #175 goes from the airport to Stare Miasto (Old Town) by way of the central train station, the center of town, and ul. Nowy Świat; watch out for pickpockets. Bus #130 connects Zachodnia Station, Centralna Station, and Wilanów in the south. Warsaw's **Metro** has only a single line, which connects the southern border of town with the center. Bus, tram, and subway share the same tickets and prices. Urban transport runs from 5am-11pm.

**Taxis: MPT Radio Taxi** (☎919) or **Sawa Taxi** (☎644 44 44). Overcharging is still a problem; if possible, call these companies to arrange pickup. State-run cabs with a mermaid sign are generally safer. Fares start at 4zł plus 1.60zł per km; the legal maximum is 2zł per km during the day, 2.40zł per km at night. MPT accepts MC/Visa.

**Car Rental: Avis,** at the Marriott Hotel (☎/fax 630 73 16). Open daily 8am-6pm. Airport office (☎650 48 72) open daily 7am-10pm. Prices start at 119DM per day. **Budget** (☎630 72 80), also at the Marriott. Open daily 8am-8pm. At the airport (☎650 40 62). Prices from 168DM per day.

# 🛈 PRACTICAL INFORMATION

## TOURIST AND FINANCIAL SERVICES

**Tourist Offices: Informacji Turystyczna (IT),** al. Jerozolimskie 54 (☎/fax 524 51 84 and 654 24 47, info ☎94 31), inside the central train station. English-speaking staff provides maps (some free, some 6zł), guidebooks, currency exchange, and hotel reservations. Open M-F 8am-8pm, Sa-Su 9am-7pm. **Branch** at Rynek Starego Miasta 28, inside the Historical Museum. Open daily May-Sept. 8am-8pm, Oct.-Apr. 9am-6pm. English publications, including the indispensable *Warsaw Insider* (6zł) are on sale in kiosks just outside the office. Smaller offices at Zachodnia Station and the airport. The **tourist office** in the back of the main train station sells a map of the whole city, including the public transportation lines (6zł).

**Budget Travel: Almatur,** ul. Kopernika 23 (☎826 35 12 and 826 26 39; fax 826 45 92), off ul. Nowy Świat. Sells international bus, ferry and plane tickets at student discounts. ISIC cards 35zł. Often has vouchers for hotels in major Polish cities. Open M-F 9am-7pm, Sa 10am-2pm. **Orbis,** ul. Bracka 16 (☎827 07 30 and 827 01 72; fax 827 76 05), with the entrance on al. Jerozolimskie near ul. Nowy Świat, sells train, ferry, and bus tickets. Open M-F 8am-7pm, Sa 9am-3pm.

**Embassies:** Most near ul. Ujazdowskie. **Australia,** ul. Nowogrodska 11 (☎617 60 81). Open M-F 9am-1pm and 2-4pm. **Belarus,** ul. Ateńska 67 (☎617 32 12, visas 617 39 54). Open M-F 8am-4pm. **Canada,** al. Jerozolimskie 123, 5th floor (☎629 80 51). Open M-F 8am-4:30pm. **Russia,** ul. Belwederska 49, bldg. C (☎621 34 53). Open W and F 8am-1pm. **South Africa,** ul. Koszykowa 54 (☎625 62 28). Open M-F 9am-noon. **Ukraine,** al. Ujazdowskie 13 (☎625 01 27). Open M-F 10am-4pm. **UK,** al. Róż 1 (☎628 10 01). Open M-F 9am-noon and 2-4pm. **US,** al. Ujazdowskie 29/31 (☎628 30 41). Open M-F 8:30am-5pm.

**Currency Exchange:** At hotels, banks, tourist offices, and private *kantori* (which have the best rates) throughout the city. **24hr. currency exchange** is available at Warszawa Centralna and the international airport departures area. **Bank PKO S.A.,** on pl. Bankowy 2 (☎637 10 61), in the blue skyscraper; ul. Mazowiecka 14 (☎661 25 59); or ul. Grójecka 1/3 (☎658 82 17), in Hotel Sobieski, cashes AmEx/Visa **traveler's checks** for a 1-2% commission. MC/Visa **cash advances.** Most branches have a Cirrus **24hr. ATM.** All branches open M-F 8am-6pm, Sa 10am-2pm. 24hr. Euronet ATMs, which accept most major credit cards, are popping up everywhere. 24hr. AmEx ATMs at American Express and the airport. **Western Union,** ul. Krakówskie Przedmieście 55 (☎636 56 88), in Prosper Bank S.A. Open M-F 8am-6pm, Sa 9am-1pm. Other **branches** in Powszechny Bank Kredylowy, ul. Nowy Świat 6/12 (☎661 77 18), and al. Jerozolimskie 91 (☎629 27 58), in Bank Zachodni.

**American Express:** ul. Krakówskie Przedmieście 11 (☎551 51 52; fax 828 75 56). Open M-F 9am-6pm. Services also available at the **Marriott Hotel.** Open M-F 8am-8pm, Sa-Su 10am-6pm.

## LOCAL SERVICES

**Luggage Storage:** At Warszawa Centralna train station, below the main hall. Lockers come in 3 sizes: "A," 6zł per day, "B," 8zł per day, and "C," 14zł per day. Open 24hr. Storage also available in Zachodnia Station; 4zł for a large pack. Open 7am-7pm.

**English Bookstores: American Bookstore,** ul. Koszykowa 55 (☎660 56 37). Good but pricey selection of fiction, reference books, and periodicals. Open M-F 10am-7pm, Sa 11am-6pm. Also inside **Księgarnia Leksykan,** ul. Nowy Świat 41. Open M-F 11am-7pm, Sa 11am-3pm. **Empik Megastore,** ul. Nowy Świat 15/17, on the corner of al. Jerozolimskie and ul. Nowy Świat (☎627 06 50), stocks a wide array of international newspapers. Open M-Sa 9am-10pm, Su 11am-7pm. AmEx/MC/Visa.

**Bi-Gay-Lesbian Services: The Lambda Center Hotline** (☎628 52 22) is available in English and Polish. They'll tell you what's up and where. Open Tu-W 6-9pm, F 4-10pm. Located at Czerniakowska 178 (#16). Call ahead before visiting. The **Ola Archive** (☎060 465 64 44; olga@kki.net.pl) is working on collecting lesbian resources, such as books, films, and journals. Open M and Th 5-8pm.

**Laundromat:** ul. Karmelicka 17 (☎831 73 17). Take bus #180 north from ul. Marszałkowska toward Żoliborz, and get off at ul. Anielewicza; backtrack 1 block to ul. Karmelicka. Detergent 3zł. Wash and dry 23.10zł. Open M-F 9am-5pm, Sa 9am-1pm. Call ahead to make a reservation. Some English spoken.

## EMERGENCY AND COMMUNICATIONS

**24hr. Pharmacy: Apteka Grabowskiego** (☎825 13 72), at Warszawa Centralna.

**Medical Assistance: American Medical Center,** ul. Wilcza 23 m. 29 (☎622 04 89; 24hr. emergency ☎0 602 24 30 24; fax 622 04 97). Provides English-language medical and dental referrals, as well as guidance through the byzantine Polish medical system. Call in an emergency and they will meet you at the hospital. General practice clinic open M-Sa 8am-6pm. **24hr. service and ambulance: Central Emergency Station,** ul. Hoża 56 (☎999).

**Telephones:** At the post office. Tokens and phone cards available at the post office and in many kiosks. **Directory assistance:** ☎913.

**Internet Access:**

**Planeta 8C8,** ul. Królewska 2 (☎828 91 07), just of Krakowskie Przedmieście. English spoken. 8zł per hr., 5zł per 30min. Open M-F 10am-midnight, Su noon-8pm.

**Casablanca,** ul. Krakówskie Przedmieście 4/6 (☎828 14 47). Next to Burger King. English spoken. 12zł per hr. Open M-Th 9:30am-1am, F 9:30am-2am, Sa 10am-2am, Su 10am-midnight.

**Empik Zaprasza,** ul. Marszałkowska 104, on the 3rd floor of the store in Galleria Centrum. 8zł per hr. Open M-Sa 9am-10pm, Su 11am-7pm. English spoken.

**Piękna Internet Pub,** ul. Piękna 68A (☎622 33 77). Coffee, tea, and alcohol (draft beer 5zł). 4zł per 15 min., 7zł per 30 min., 10zł per hour. Open M-Th 10am-11pm, F 10am-midnight, Sa noon-11pm, Su noon-11pm.

**Post Office:** ul. Świętokrzyska 31/33 (☎827 00 52, info ☎826 75 11). The computer at the entrance doles out tickets; take a number and wait your turn. For stamps and letters, push "D." For packages, push "F." For **Poste Restante,** go in the room to the left and push "C" at the computer there. Pick up at window #12. Open 24hr. **Photocopy** and **fax** bureau (fax 30 00 21), open 7am-10pm. *Kantor* open 7am-10pm. **Postal code:** 00-001.

# ▛ ACCOMMODATIONS

Rooms become scarce and prices rise in the summer. Hostel vacancies are the first to go, so reserve at least a week in advance. Differences in hotel prices often do not reflect a difference in quality; some hotels just aim for the business traveler and charge more. For help finding **private rooms,** check with **Syrena,** ul. Krucza 17 (☎628 75 40; fax 628 56 98), off al. Jerozolimskie. The staff speaks English. (Open M-Sa 9am-7pm, Su 2-7pm. Singles from 72zł per night, 61zł per night for 3 or more nights;

doubles at 96zł per night, 84zł per night for 3 or more nights.) **Almatur** (see **Budget Travel, p.** 469) can arrange for travellers to stay in **university dorms** in July and August. The city tourist offices maintain a list of all accommodations in the city and can help with reservations. Hotels, and especially hostels, have many cancellations and no-shows; keep checking back even if they claim to be booked.

# HOSTELS

**Schronisko Młodzieżowe (HI),** ul. Karolkowa 53a (☎632 88 29; fax 632 97 46). Take tram #22 or 24 west from al. Jerozolimskie or the train station to "Okopowa." Cross at the corner near Pizza Hut and continue down al. Solidarności. The hostel will be to your right; follow the green IYH signs. Cafe, kitchen, free storage facility, and spotless bathrooms with gorgeous showers. Doubles and triples include TV and fridge. 140 beds total. English spoken. Sheets 3.50zł. Reception 6-10am and 5-11pm. Lockout 10am-5pm. Curfew 11pm. 7- to 14-bed dorms 22.50zł, nonmembers 30zł; singles 50zł, with bath 120zł, with kitchen 140zł; doubles 100zł; triples and quads 40zł per person.

**Schronisko Młodzieżowe (HI),** ul. Smolna 30, top floor (☎827 89 52), across from the National Museum. Close to the train station; take any tram east 3 stops to "Muzeum Narodowe." Great location, but bathrooms are crowded and not sufficient for 120 people. English spoken. Kitchen and storage available. Sheets 4zł. 3-day max. stay. Reception 6-10am and 5-11pm. Lockout 10am-4pm. Curfew 11pm. Call 2 weeks in advance. Dorms 21zł, nonmembers 28zł; singles 45zł; doubles and triples 38zł per person.

**Schronisko Młodzieżowe "Agrykola,"** ul. Myśliwiecka 9 (☎622 91 10 and 622 91 11; fax 622 91 05). Near Łazienki Park. From Marszałkowska, take bus #107, 404 or 520 to "Rozbrat." Continue on Rozbrat as it turns into Myśliwiecka. Built only 2 years ago. The paint's barely dry, the bedspreads haven't frayed, and the bathrooms still sparkle. Cable TV. English spoken. Curfew midnight. Singles 200zł; doubles 250zł; triples and quads 60zł per person. Breakfast included. MC/Visa.

**Schronisko Młodzieżowe (HI),** ul. Międzyparkowa 4/6 (☎831 17 66), between 2 parks near the river. Take tram #2, 6, or 18 north from ul. Marszałkowska to "K.K.S. Polonia." It's on the left as you continue down the road. The least formal hostel in town, located in an old sports complex. Caters to school groups and attracts few foreigners. Sheets 5zł. Lockout 10am-5pm. Curfew 11pm. Supposedly open Apr. 15-Oct. 15 but may operate only in July and August. Call ahead. 6- to 8-bed dorms 12zł; nonmembers 30zł.

# HOTELS

**Hotel Metalowcy,** ul. Długa 29 (☎831 40 21, ext. 29; fax 635 31 38). Take bus #175 from the train station to "pl. Krasińskich," backtrack to ul. Długa and turn right. Affordable and centrally located. Clean rooms (if you don't mind the occasional odd smell) and decent communal bathrooms. Singles 56zł; doubles 88zł; quads with bath 155zł.

**Hotel Mazowiecki,** ul. Mazowiecka 10 (☎687 91 17, ☎/fax 827 23 65). Little more than a block from ul. Krakówskie Przedmieście off ul. Świętokrzyska. One of the toniest budget hotels in the downtown area, with hardwood floors. Mildew-free bathrooms. Check-in 4pm. Check-out 2pm. Singles 125zł; doubles 170zł; triples 210zł.

**Hotel Praski,** al. Solidarności 61 (☎/fax 818 49 89; www.polhotels.com/warsz/Praski). Just across the river from Stare Miasto. Take tram #4 from Marszałkowska to "Park Praski." A new, well maintained hotel. Weekdays: singles 133zł; doubles 184zł, with bath 248zł; triples 222zł, with bath 321zł. Weekends: singles 121zł; doubles 168zł, with bath 201zł; triples 201zł, with bath 291zł. AmEx/MC/Visa.

**Hotel Belfer,** ul. Wybrzeże Kościuszkowskie 31/33 (☎625 55 62; ☎/fax 625 51 85). From the train station, take any tram east to "Most Poniatowskiego," then go down the stairs and cross the overpass. Walk along ul. Wybreże Kościuszkowskie for 2 blocks. A little rough around the edges (including the ones in the bathrooms), but bright and roomy, with some very good views from the higher floors (though it's hard to avoid spying the Stalinist Palace of Culture). English spoken. Singles 122zł, with bath 165zł; doubles 165zł, with bath 188zł. Breakfast included. AmEx/MC/Visa.

## CAMPING

**Camping "123,"** ul. Bitwy Warszawskiej 1920r. 15/17 (☎822 91 21; ☎/fax. 823 37 48), by the main bus station. Take bus #127, 130, or 517 to "Zachodnia" and cross the street at the traffic circle. Bitwy Warszawskiej is to the left. Close to the city center, well-shaded by trees, and near a popular swimming pool, this expansive complex includes a small hotel and bungalows. Guarded 24hr. English spoken. 10zł per person. Small tent space 8zł, large 10zł. Electricity 10zł. Bungalows: double 69zł, with bath 99zł; triple 90zł, with bath 135zł. Hotel: double 99zł; triple 128zł; quad 143zł.

**Camping Gromada,** ul. Żwirki i Wigury 32 (☎825 43 91). Take bus #175 in the direction of "Port Lotniczy" to "Akademia Medyczna." Cross the street, turn left, and follow the cheerful signs to the slightly more hard-core campsite. Fenced in. English spoken. Reception 8am-4pm. Check-in 2pm. Check-out noon. Open Apr.-Sept. 10zł per person. 1-2 person tent space 6-7zł, 3-4 person space 9zł.

# 🗒 FOOD

Countless food stands dot the square beneath the Pałac Kultury, and many more lie under the train station. For a decent meal, **milk bars** *(bar mleczny)* or **cafeterias** *(stołowki)* offer good bang for your buck. There's a **24hr. grocery store** at the central train station, as well as several **24hr. delikatesy,** including those at ul. Nowy Świat 53 (☎826 03 22; open 7am-5am) and al. Solidarności 82a. Some restaurants in Warsaw sell fish, poultry, and meat by weight. Ask in advance how much the average weight is to avoid a nasty surprise when the check arrives. There are any number of very good restaurants dotting both the Old and New Town Squares, but these areas are heavily touristed and the prices are correspondingly high.

**▨ Pod Samsonem,** ul. Freta 3/5 (☎831 17 88). Between Stare Miasto and Nowe Miasto. Hearty Polish-Jewish cuisine is supposed to make you big and strong like Samson. Interior is decorated with photos of Jewish life in pre-war Warsaw. Meals 15-30zł. Open daily 10am-10pm. AmEx/MC/Visa.

**▨ Mata Hari,** ul. Nowy Świat 52 (☎828 64 28). Budget-conscious omnivores rejoice! Incredibly cheap, mostly Indian vegetarian dishes, including a variety of soups and samosas. Full meals under 10zł. Open M-F 11am-7pm, Sa 11am-5pm.

**Bong Sen,** ul. Poznańska 12 (☎621 27 13), just south of the train station (Poznańska runs parallel to al. Marszałkowska.) The decidedly Polish waitstaff won't created any illusion that you're in the Far East, but the food might fool you. Main dishes 19-30zł. Open daily 11am-10pm. AmEx/MC/Visa.

**Gospoda Pod Kogutem,** ul. Freta 48 (☎635 82 82). A shining star in the Old Town for unmistakably local food. No tourist hordes here, just crowds of hungry Poles. Main dishes 15-22zł, draft beer 5zł. Open daily 11am-midnight. MC/Visa.

**Bar Mleczny Familijny,** ul. Nowy Świat 39. A giant version of a Polish grandmother's kitchen. Soups 1zł; main dishes 2-6zł. Open M-F 7am-8pm, Sa-Su 9am-5pm.

**Bar Uniwersytecki,** ul. Krakówskie Przedmieście 16/18. As Polish and as fattening as it gets. Menu available in English at the cashier. Salad 1-2zł, soups 1zł, main dishes 2-4zł. Open M-F 7am-8pm, Sa-Su 9am-5pm.

**Dong Nam,** ul. Marszałkowska 45 (☎621 32 34), on the 2nd floor. An excellent (and ever so elaborately, if not tastefully, decorated) source for Vietnamese and Chinese food. Main dishes 15-40zł; all you can eat buffet 39zł (call ahead to check). Open daily 11am-11pm. MC/Visa.

**Restauracja Ekologiczna "Nowe Miasto,"** Rynek Nowego Miasta 13/15 (☎831 43 79). Warsaw's 1st natural foods restaurant. Organically grown vegetarian main dishes 20-40zł, fish 45-60zł. Whole grain desserts, healthy soups, crepes, and an ensemble cast of salads (19-21zł). Breakfast 8-15zł. Polish beer (0.5L Żywiec 9zł) and many wines. Live music nightly 7-10pm. Open daily 10am-midnight. AmEx/MC/Visa.

**Zapiecek,** ul. Piwna 34/36 (☎831 56 93), at the corner of ul. Piwna and ul. Zapiecek in Stare Miasto. For the Deutsch and Deutschland-loving crowd, Zapiecek offers Germantinged Polish cuisine by candlelight. Main dishes 7-18zł, side orders 1-4zł. Outdoor dining. Open daily noon-11pm. AmEx/MC/Visa.

**Restauracja-Kawiarnia "Chmielna,"** (☎827 14 84), at the corner of ul. Chmielna and ul. Zgoda. Walk down al. Jerozolimskie from the city center toward the river, then turn left on ul. Krucza. The cafe, full of fake street lamps and brimming with plants, dishes out a better deal than the restaurant, but both offer lively dining on a pedestrian street. Vegetarian lasagna 12.90zł, salads 4-11zł, main dishes 7-24zł. Cafe open M-Sa 11am-11pm; restaurant open M-Sa noon-11pm. AmEx/MC/Visa.

**Lody,** Nowomiejska 9. The most popular ice cream shop in Stare Miasto. 1.50zł per scoop, with flavors like "smurf" and tiramisu. Open daily 10am-7pm.

# ▐ CAFES

▧ **Pożegnanie z Afryka,** ul. Freta 4/6. The name means "Out of Africa," although most of the myriad coffees (7-8zł) are actually South American; regardless, it's the best cafe in town. Worth the wait for 1 of the 6 tables. Open daily 11am-9pm.

**Antykwariat Cafe,** ul. Żurawia 45 (☎629 99 29) 2 blocks south of Rondo de Gaulle'a. Take bus #116 or 122 south along Nowy Świat to "Pl. Trzech Krzyży." Book-lined, comfortable, and delicious. Popular with students. Coffee 6-8zł. Open M-F 10am-10pm, Sa-Su noon-10pm.

**Kawiarnia Bazyliszek,** Rynek Starego Miasta 9/11/13 (☎831 32 35). A fancy cafe with relaxed outdoor seating. Great views of the restored splendor of Stare Miasto and the tourists here to see it. Tortes 7-10zł. Coffee 6-8zł. Open daily 11am-11pm.

**Casablanca,** ul. Krakówskie Przedmieście 4/6 (☎828 14 47). To the right of Burger King. Bogey will watch over you (from the posters on the walls) as you surf the Net until late into the night. (see **Internet Access,** p. 470). English spoken. Coffee (7zł) and alcohol. Open M-Th 9:30am-1am, F 9:30am-2am, Sa 10am-2am, Su 10am-midnight.

# ▣ SIGHTS

Razed to something resembling the surface of the moon, Warsaw had to be almost entirely rebuilt after World War II. Thanks to the wonders of Soviet upkeep, though, most of the buildings look much older than their 50 years. Sights are very spread out, and exploring the city in full takes several days.

## STARE AND NOWE MIASTO

*Warsaw's postwar reconstruction shows its finest face in the narrow, cobblestoned streets and colorful facades of Stare Miasto (Old Town), at the very end of ul. Krakówskie Przedmieście in pl. Zamkowy. To get here, take bus #175 or E3 from the center to "Miodowa."*

**ROYAL CASTLE.** (Zamek Królewski.) In the Middle Ages, it was home to the Dukes of Mazovia. In the late 16th century it replaced Kraków's Wawel as the official royal residence; still later it became the presidential palace. Burned down in September 1939 and plundered by the Nazis, the castle was elevated to martyrdom by Polish freedom fighters. Many Varsovians risked their lives hiding its priceless works in the hope that one day they could be returned. After Poland gained independence in 1945, the castle's plans and some of the treasures were retrieved and for 30 years, thousands of Poles, Polish expats, and dignitaries worldwide sent contributions in hopes of restoring this symbol of national pride. Work began in 1971 and was completed in 1984. The kingly abode is an impressive example of restoration; visitors will marvel that anything so regal was built in the 1970s (see **Museums,** p. 477). *(At the right side of the entrance to Stare Miasto.)*

**STATUE OF ZYGMUNT III WAZY.** Constructed in 1644 to honor the king who transferred the capital from Kraków to Warsaw, the statue stood for 300 years before being destroyed in World War II. The king's figure, now rebuilt, has watched over pl. Zamkowy for centuries; his vigil continues today, albeit over youngsters drinking beer on the steps below. *(Stands proudly above the square in front of the castle.)*

**ST. JOHN'S CATHEDRAL.** (Archi-Katedra św. Jana.) Decimated in the 1944 Uprising, Warsaw's oldest church was rebuilt after the war in the Vistulan Gothic style. The documents from the 1339 case against the Order of Teutonic Knights, who had broken a pact made with Duke of Mazovia Konrad Mazowiecki, are hidden within its walls. In its depths, **crypts** hold the dukes of Mazovia and such famous Poles as Nobel Laureate Henryk Sienkiewicz and Gabriel Narutowicz, the first president of independent Poland. A side altar contains the tomb of Stefan Cardinal Wyszyński, primate of Poland from 1948-1981. *(Just up ul. Świętojańska from pl. Zamkowy. Open daily dawn-dusk, except during services. Crypts 2zl, students 1zl.)*

**OLD TOWN SQUARE.** (Rynek Starego Miasta.) A stone plaque at the entrance commemorates the reconstruction of the Renaissance and Baroque square, finished in 1953-54. On the *rynek's* southeast side at #3/9, **Dom Pod Bazyliszkiem** immortalizes the Stare Miasto Basilisk, a legendary reptile with a fatal breath whose stare brought instant death to all who crossed its path. Apparently, the monster's breath was no match for the modern firepower of World War II. The houses around the *rynek* were all but demolished during the 1944 Uprising, though large fragments of the ruins were used in reconstruction. *(On ul. Świętojańska.)*

**BARBAKAN.** A rare example of 16th-century Polish fortification, the Barbakan is also a popular spot for locals and tourists to duck out of the traffic for a rest. The **Little Insurgent Monument,** to the left near ul. Kilińskiego, is less a miniscule memorial than a marker of the heroism of little people; it honors the youngest soldiers of the 1944 Uprising. Around the Barbakan are the remains of the walls that used to enclose Stare Miasto; they are marked by the **Mermaid** (Warszawska Syrenka), the symbol of the city. *(Follow Ul. Krzywe Koło (Crooked Wheel) from Old Town Square.)*

**OTHER SIGHTS.** The Barbakan opens onto ul. Freta, the edge of Nowe Miasto. The district is only relatively new; only the Old Town existed earlier. Also destroyed during World War II, its 18th- and 19th-century buildings have enjoyed an expensive face lift. The great physicist and chemist **Maria Skłodowska-Curie,** winner of two Nobel prizes, was born at ul. Freta 16 in 1867 (see **Museums,** p. 477). Ul. Freta leads to **New Town Square** (Rynek Nowego Miasta), the site of the **Church of the Holy Sacrament** (Kościół Sakramentka), founded in 1688 to commemorate King Jan III Sobieski's 1683 victory over the Turks (see **History** p. 454). Its interior is only a ghost of its past glory, but the Baroque dome still inspires awe. *(Open daily dawn-dusk.)*

# TRAKT KRÓLEWSKI

*The 4km Trakt Królewski (Royal Way) begins on pl. Zamkowy at the entrance to Stare Miasto and continues along ul. Krakówskie Przedmieście. From ul. Krakówskie Przedmieście, Trakt Królewski continues as ul. Nowy Świat (New World Street).*

The Royal Way, so named because it leads south in the general direction of Kraków, Poland's former capital, is lined with palaces, churches, and convents built when the royal family moved to Warsaw. The name of the street dates to the mid-17th century, when a new settlement was started here, composed mainly of working-class people. It was not until the 18th century that the aristocracy started moving in, embellishing it with ornate manors and residences. Today, there's nothing working-class about it; it's the most fashionable street in town and the best urban route for a walk. Traffic and crowds of tourists now detract from its once regal splendor, but a stroll down this Polish memory lane is really a must.

**AROUND PL. ZAMKOWY.** On the left as you leave pl. Zamkowy, St. Anne's Church (Kościół św. Anny), with a large figure of Christ above the entrance and striking gilded altar, dates from the 15th century but was rebuilt in the Baroque style. *(Open daily dawn-dusk.)* Farther down the street, a monument to Adam Mickiewicz, Poland's national poet (see **Literature and Arts,** p. 458), gazes toward pl. Piłsudskiego and Saxon Garden (Ogród Saski), which contains the **Tomb of the Unknown Soldier** (Grób Nieznanego Żołnierza). Urns hold earth from battlefields marked by Polish blood and from the graves of Polish officers murdered by the Soviets in Katyń. The **changing of the guard** takes place on Sundays and national holidays at noon.

**CHOPIN LEGACY.** The next stretch of the Trakt is a requisite pilgrimage sight for Frédéric Chopin (in Polish, Fryderyk Szopen) fans (see **Literature and Arts,** p. 458). Chopin spent his childhood in the neighborhood near ul. Krakówskie Przedmieście, and gave his first public concert in **Pałac Radziwiłłów** (a.k.a. **Pałac Namiestnikowski**) 46/48, the building guarded by four stone lions. Today it's the Polish presidential mansion and a guard stands watch alongside his feline counterparts. A block down the road, the **Church of the Visitation Nuns** (Kościół Wizytek) once resounded with the romantic ivory pounding of the mop-topped composer. *(Open daily dawn-dusk.)* **Pałac Czapskich,** Chopin's last home before he left for France in 1830, provided the setting for many of his best-known compositions. Now the palace houses the **Academy of Fine Arts** and **Chopin's Drawing Room** (Salonik Chopinów; ☎ 826 62 51, ext. 267). Enter through the gate at ul. Krakówskie Przedmieście 5; the entrance is on the left. *(Open M-F 10am-2pm, closed holidays. 3zł, students 2zł.)* Chopin died abroad at the age of 39 and was buried in Paris, but his heart belongs to Poland; it now rests in an urn in the left nave of **Holy Cross Church** (Kościół św. Krzyża).

**UNIVERSITY OF WARSAW.** (Uniwersytet Warszawski.) In front of Kościól św. Krzyża and behind the swarms of students, a complex of rebuilt palaces on the left belongs to the University of Warsaw, founded in 1816. **Pałac Kazimierzowski,** at the end of the alley leading from the main entrance to the university, now houses the rector's offices, but was once the seat of the School of Knighthood. Its alumni include General Tadeusz Kościuszko, who fought in the American Revolutionary War and later fought unsuccessfully against the partition of the country. The **Copernicus Monument** (Pomnik Mikołaja Kopernika) and **Pałac Staszica,** home of the Polish Academy of Sciences, mark the end of ul. Krakówskie Przedmieście.

# ŁAZIENKI PARK

*South of Stare Miasto, Łazienki Park sprawls along al. Ujazdowskie and Trakt Królewski. Take bus #116 or 195 from ul. Nowy Świat or #119 from the city center south to Bagatela. The park is just across the street. Open daily dawn-dusk.*

The park and the palaces within were built in the late 18th century for Stanislaw August Poniatowski, the last king of Poland, but peacocks and swans rule the roost today. The real draw of the park isn't any one building, but rather the grounds, which attract Varsovians eager for a weekend retreat. Near the entrance is the **Chopin Monument** (Pomnik Chopina), site of free concerts (Spring-Autumn Su noon and 4pm) and the new statue of Henryk Sienkiewicz.

**PAŁAC ŁAZIENKOWSKI.** Farther into the park is the striking Neoclassical Pałac Łazienkowski, also called the **Palace on Water** (Pałac na Wodzie) or **Palace on the Isle** (Pałac na Wyspie). This, like most palaces in the park, is the creation of benefactor King Stanisław August and his beloved architect Dominik Merlini. Galleries of 17th- and 18th-century art await inside. *(Open Tu-Su 9:30am-4pm, barring rain. Kasa closes at 3:15pm. 11zł, students 8zł. Guided tour in English 55zł.)*

**THE OLD ORANGERY.** (Stara Pomarańczarnia.) Nearby, the orangery houses both the 1788 **Stanisławowski Theater** and the **Gallery of Polish Sculpture** (Galeria Rzeźby Polskiej), which exhibits sculptures from the 16th century through 1939. *(Orangery open Tu-Su 9:30am-3:30pm. 6zł, students 4zł. Guided tour in Polish 35zł, in English 66zł.)*

**OTHER SIGHTS.** Near the orangery stands the 1774 **White House,** which remarkably survived the war unscathed *(Open Tu-Th 9am-4pm, F-Su 9:30am-5pm. 5zł, students 3zł).* Just north of Łazienki along al. Ujazdowskie are the soul-soothing **Botanical Gardens.** *(Open June-Aug. M-Th 9am-8pm; F-Su 10am-8pm; Sept. daily 10am-6pm; Oct. daily 10am-4pm. Kasa closes 1hr. before the gardens. 4zł, students 2zł.)* Continuing north along al. Ujazdowskie, turn right on ul. Matejki and you will reach the **Sejm** (Parliament) and Senate building, built in 1925 and rebuilt after World War II. *(Closed to the public.)*

# THE FORMER WARSAW GHETTO

*The Jewish Visitor's Center can provide more information about Jewish sites. ☎ 652 21 50. The buildings surrounding the Nozyk Synagogue also house Our Roots, ul. Twarda 6 (☎/fax 620 05 56), a Jewish travel agency that arranges English tours of Jewish Warsaw, Auschwitz, Treblinka, and Majdanek. Open M-F 9:30am-1:30pm. Tours US$25-70.*

POLAND

Still referred to as the Ghetto, the modern Muranów neighborhood (literally, "walled"), north of the city center, holds few vestiges of the nearly 400,000 Jews who comprised one-third of the city's prewar population.

**MONUMENTS.** The **Umschlagplatz,** at the corner of ul. Dzika and ul. Stawki was the railway platform where the Nazis gathered 300,000 of the Jews for transport to the death camps. A large monument, with writing in Polish, Hebrew, and Yiddish, now stands in its place. *(Take tram #35 from ul. Marszalkowska to "Dzika.")* With the monument to the left, continue down Stawki and turn right on ul. DuBois, which becomes ul. Zamenhofa. You will pass a mound of earth with a monument on top marking the location of the underground command bunker of the **1943 ghetto uprising** (see **History,** p. 454). Further on, in a large park to your right stands the large **Monument of the Ghetto Heroes** (Pomnik Bohaterów). Nearby, a marker commemorates the **Relief Council for Jews,** an organization sponsored by the government in exile that worked to rescue the Jews from the Holocaust. Signs near the Monument indicate the future location of the **Museum of the History of Polish Jews.** *(Ul. Jelinka 48. ☎ 833 00 21.)*

**JEWISH CEMETERY.** (Cmentarz Żydowski.) Thickly wooded and stretching for kilometers, the cemetery is the final resting place of 200,000 of Warsaw's Jews. Sadly, many of the tombstones are shrouded in undergrowth and thousands have long since disappeared. *(In the western corner of Muranów. From Dzielna, follow al. Jana Pawła II to Anielwicza and take a left. Alternatively, take tram #22 from the city center to "Cm. Żydowski." ☎ 838 26 22. Open M-Th 9am-3pm, F 9am-1pm. 3zł.)*

**NOZYK SYNAGOGUE.** This beautifully restored building is a living remnant of Warsaw's Jewish life. The only synagogue to survive the war, it was spared for use as a stable by the Wehrmacht. Today it serves as the spiritual home for the few hundred observant Jews who remain in Warsaw. *(Ul. Twarda 6. From the city center, take any tram north along ul. Jana Pawła II to "Rondo ONZ." Turn right on Twarda and left at the Jewish Theater (Teatr Żydowski). ☎ 620 43 24. Open M-F 10am-3pm, Su 11am-3pm. Morning and evening services daily; contact the synagogue for a schedule. 5zł.)*

**GHETTO WALL.** Early in the occupation of Warsaw, the Nazis confined Jews to the Ghetto, building a wall around the entire neighborhood. A small section of the original ghetto wall still stands between two apartment buildings on ul. Sienna and ul. Złota, just west of al. Jana Pawła II and near Warszawa Centralna station. Enter the courtyard at ul. Sienna 55; the wall is on the left.

## COMMERCIAL DISTRICT

**PALACE OF CULTURE AND SCIENCE.** (Pałac Kultury i Nauki.) The center of Warsaw's commercial district, southwest of Stare Miasto and adjacent to the train station, is dominated by the 70-story Stalinist Gothic Palace of Culture and Science. Originally christened the Joseph Stalin Palace, the building has since been dubbed "The Wedding Cake" because of its tiered architecture. Locals claim "the cake" offers the best view in Warsaw. Why? It's the only place from which you can't see the building. This palatial eyesore houses over 3000 offices, exhibition and conference facilities, three theaters, several cinemas, a shopping center, a cafe, and two museums. Below, **pl. Defilad** (Parade Sq.), Europe's largest square (yes, even bigger than Moscow's Red Square) swarms with bazaar capitalists. *(On ul. Marszałkowska.)*

## WILANÓW

*Take bus #180, 410, or 414 from ul. Marszałkowska, or bus #130 or 519 from the train station south to "Wilanów." Cross the street; the road to the palace is on the right. ☎ 842 81 01. Open June 15-Sept. 15 M and W-Sa 9:30am-2:30pm, Su 9:30am-4:30pm; Sept. 16-June 14 9:30am-2:30pm. 15zł, students 8zł. Th free. Admission and English tour for fewer than 5 people 100zł; for 6-35 people, 20zł per person. The cost of admission is for a spot in a slow-moving Polish-language tour, but it is better to break off and explore on your own. English captions. Gardens open M and W-F 9:30am-dusk. 3zł, students 2zł.*

POLAND

In 1677 King Jan III Sobieski bought the sleepy village of Milanowo, had its existing mansion rebuilt as a Baroque palace, and named the residence Villa Nova (in Polish *Wilanów*). Over the years, a long line of Polish aristocrats have called the palace home. One of the bluebloods, Duke Stanisław Kostka Potocki, thought it might be nice to share it with his subjects. In 1805 he opened it to visitors, founding one of the first public museums in Poland. Since then, **Pałac Wilanowski** has functioned both as a museum and as a residence for the highest-ranking guests of the state. Inside are lovely frescoed rooms, countless 17th- to 19th-century portraits, and extravagant royal apartments. The surrounding **gardens** form strict, formal patterns and feature an army of bottle-shaped topiary creations. The greenery becomes less sculpted near the meandering river as the gardens merge with neighboring parks, where many people take refuge from the urban sprawl of central Warsaw.

## PRAGA

*Take tram #4 from ul. Marszałkowska to "Park Praski."*

The **Praga** neighborhood, connected to Stare Miasto by the Śląsko-Dąbrowski bridge, offers a Victorian contrast to the contemporary architecture of the city center. To one side is the massive **Cathedral of St. Michael and St. Florian,** completed in 1902 and rebuilt after World War II. (Open daily dawn-dusk. Free.) On the other side of al. Solidarności is the lush **Park Praski,** which leads to the **Warsaw Zoo.** *(Open daily 9am-7pm. Kasa closes 6pm. 8zł, students 4zł.)* Head here to see polar bears and penguins in their not-so-natural habitat. A short walk farther along al. Solidarności ("Dw. Wileński" stop) leads to the **Russian Orthodox Church** (Katedra Kościóła Prawosławnego), a five-domed structure with a Byzantine layout and Renaissance facade. The traditional gold interior, including the elaborate iconostasis, is magnificent. *(Open dawn-dusk. Sunday liturgy at 7:30am, 8:30am, and 10am.)*

## 🏛 MUSEUMS

- 🖼 **Royal Castle** (Zamek Królewski), pl. Zamkowy 4 (☎657 21 78). The palace recreates the world of Poland's kings with paintings and artifacts dating from several periods. The Royal Apartments are stunning. Tickets and guides at the *kasa* inside the castle courtyard. There are 2 routes for viewing—Route 1 snakes through the parliament chambers and apartments, while route 2 hits the more arresting apartments of the King. Route 1 open M 11am-4pm, Tu-Sa 10am-4pm. 8zł; students 3zł. Route 2 open M 11am-4pm, Tu-Sa 10am-6pm, Su 11am-6pm. 12zł, students 6zł. *Kasa* closes 1hr. before the museum. Admission to the "highlights" free on Sundays. English tour M-Sa 50zł.

- 🖼 **Center of Contemporary Art** (Centrum Sztuki Współczesnej), al. Ujazdowskie 6 (☎628 12 71), inside the Ujazdowski Castle near the botanical gardens. Very "cutting edge" and often wonderfully bizarre, featuring post-anti-retro-neo-formalism-structuralism at its finest. If you have to ask, you'll never get it. English info at the *kasa*. Open Sa-Th 11am-5pm, F 11am-9pm. 8zł, students 4zł.

- **National Museum** (Muzeum Narodowe), al. Jerozolimskie 3 (☎629 30 93). Founded in 1862 as a museum of fine arts and converted into a national museum in 1915, this is Poland's largest museum. Gives an impressive illustration of the evolution of Polish art. Also houses a Gallery of Medieval Art and a Gallery of European Art, which include 14th- to 18th-century Italian works, 15th- to 16th-century German art, and 17th-century Dutch and Flemish paintings. Open Tu-W and F 10am-4pm, Th noon-5pm, Sa-Su 10am-5pm. Closed the day after public holidays. 13zł, students 7zł, Sa free.

**OUT OF LINE** If you're in any reasonably touristed spot you'll likely encounter "Kwierunek Zwiedzania" arrows that point out the proper sightseeing route. Note that these aren't mere suggestions; should you decide to peruse the paintings/costumes/ice fishing equipment in your own order, you'll be accosted by flustered museum employees. Be an individual—stick to the road more travelled by.

**POLAND**

**Museum of Pawiak Prison** (Muzeum Więzienia Pawiaka), ul. Dzielna 24/26 (☎831 13 17). Built in the 1830s as a model prison for common criminals, Pawiak later served as Gestapo headquarters under the Nazis. From 1939-1944, over 100,000 Poles were imprisoned and tortured here; 37,000 were executed and another 60,000 were transferred to concentration camps. The Nazis dynamited the prison during the 1944 Warsaw Uprising and it has never been fully rebuilt. Housed in a small, reconstructed section of the prison, the museum exhibits photographs and artifacts, including the artwork and poetry of many former prisoners. English captions. Open W 9am-5pm, Th and Sa 9am-4pm, F 10am-5pm, Su 10am-4pm. Donation requested.

**Frédéric Chopin Museum** (Muzeum Fryderyka Chopina), ul. Okólnik 1 (☎827 54 71 and 827 54 72), enter from ul. Tamka. A small but fascinating collection of original letters, scores, paintings, and keepsakes, including the composer's last piano and his first published piece—the Polonaise in G Minor, penned when Fryderyk was but a precocious tyke of 7. English captions. Open May-Sept. M, W, and F 10am-5pm, Th noon-6pm, Sa-Su 10am-2pm; closed holidays. 8zł, students 4zł. Audio guides in 5 languages 4zł.

**John Paul II Collection**, pl. Bankowy 3/5 (☎620 21 81), in the old Stock Exchange and Bank of Poland building. Over 400 impressive paintings from a single private collection. Artists include Dalí, Titian, Rembrandt, Van Gogh, Goya, Renoir and others. One of the most significant pieces is a massive mural of the Crucifixion by the Polish painter Gerson. The museum tends to be strangely deserted; it's usually possible to encounter these masterpieces 1-on-1. Open Tu-Su 10am-5pm. *Kasa* closes at 4pm. 5zł, students 3zł. Polish tour 1zł per person.

**Zachęta Gallery**, Plac Małachowskiego 3 (☎827 69 13). Having just celebrated its 100th birthday with a renovation of its exhibition rooms, the gallery, though not very large, is magnificent. Dynamic contemporary art; don't be surprised to find some of the sculptures alive. Open Tu-W and F-Su 10am-6pm, Th 10am-8pm. 10zł; students 7zł. Guided tour in Polish 40zł, in English 60zł. Schedule tours 2 days in advance.

**Polish Military Museum** (Muzeum Wojska Polskiego), al. Jerozolimskie 3 (☎629 52 71 and 629 52 72). Could equip its own army with its collection of Polish weaponry and uniforms through the ages. Documents the nation's fight for freedom during World War II. Open May 15-Sept. 30 W-Su 11am-5pm, Oct. 1-May 14 W-Su 11am-4pm. 5zł, students 3zł, F free. Guided tours in English 20zł.

**Adam Mickiewicz Literary Museum** (Muzeum Literatury im. Adama Mickiewicza), Rynek Starego Miasta 20 (☎831 40 61). The main exhibition is a shrine to Poland's national poet, but the 1st floor focuses on the 20th-century literary world. Most information in Polish. Open M-Tu and F 10am-3pm, W-Th 11am-6pm, Su 11am-5pm. 4zł, students 3zł.

**Warsaw Historical Museum** (Muzeum Historyczne Miasta Warszawy), Rynek Starego Miasta 42 (☎635 16 25). Chronicles the evolution of style in the city's architecture and clothing from the 13th century to the present. Top floors illustrate the inescapable topic of how destructive World War II was. Some English captions. Open Tu and Th 11am-6pm, W and F 10am-3:30pm, Sa-Su 10:30am-4:30pm. 5zł, students 2.50zł, Su free.

**Maria Skłodowska-Curie Museum** (Muzeum Marii Skłodowskiej-Curie), ul. Freta 16 (☎831 80 92), in the Skłodowskis' former house. Founded in 1967, on the 100th anniversary of Maria's birth, the exhibit chronicles her life in Poland, emigration to France, and marriage to scientist Pierre Curie, with whom she discovered radium, polonium, and marital bliss. Open Tu-Sa 10am-4pm, Su 10am-2pm. 5zł, students 2zł.

**Poster Museum** (Muzeum Plakatu; ☎842 48 48; ☎/fax 842 26 06), next to Pałac Wilanowski. Displays over 450 of its collection of 50,000 posters from the last century, from Soviet propaganda to old movie posters. Open Tu-F 10am-4pm, Sa-Su 10am-5pm. 7zł, students 5zł; W free.

# 🎵 ENTERTAINMENT

It's hard to take a step in Warsaw without seeing a notice about a performance. To get the latest schedule of events, call the tourist info number (☎94 31).

Like any other major European capital, Warsaw is brimming with culture—classical music aficionados, particularly, will have a field day. Tickets aren't only for the upper crust; it's possible to get standby tickets for major performances for under 10zł. Inquire about concerts at the **Warsaw Music Society** (Warszawskie Towarzystwo Muzyczne), ul. Morskie Oko 2 (☎849 68 56). Take tram #4, 18, 19, 35, or 36 to "Morskie Oko" from ul. Marszałkowska. The society is to your left as you pass the Japanese Ambassador's residence on the right; it hosts concerts frequently, though not in the summer months. The **Warsaw Chamber Opera** (Warszawska Opera Kameralna), al. Solidarności 76B (☎831 22 40), hosts a Mozart festival each year during early summer, with performances throughout the city. The **Chopin Monument** (Pomnik Chopina), nearby in Łazienki Park, hosts free Sunday performances by classical artists. (May-Oct. noon and 4pm.) **Teatr Wielki,** pl. Teatralny 1 (☎692 07 58; www.teatrwielki.pl), Warsaw's main opera and ballet hall, offers performances almost daily. The **National Philharmonic** (Filharmonia Narodowa), ul. Jasna 5 (☎826 72 81), gives regular concerts, but is closed in summer.

Jazz, rock, and blues fans have quite a few options, especially in summer, when Stare Miasto is alive with street music. Usually the best bets are bars (see below). **Sala Kongresowa** (☎620 49 80), in the Pałac Kultury on the train station side with the casino, hosts serious jazz and rock concerts with famous international bands. Enter from ul. Emilii Plater. Keep your eyes peeled in June for the annual **Warsaw Summer Jazz Days** it hosts. For tickets to rock concerts, call **Empik Megastore** (☎625 12 19).

# ◼ NIGHTLIFE

Warsaw has a lot to offer in the way of evening revelry. A wide variety of pubs attract big crowds and often have live music, and cafes (*kawiarnie*) around Stare Miasto and ul. Nowy Świat serve coffee and beer late into the night. In the summer, large beer gardens complement the pub scene.

## BARS

Warsaw's pubs—despite their relatively high prices—are popular with both trendy locals and visitors looking for a comfortable nook.

▨ **Morgan's,** ul. Okólnik 1 (☎826 81 38), enter on ul. Tamka under the Chopin Museum. Ollie Morgan runs this comfortable, friendly Irish haunt for expats and visitors. Ollie says he pours the best Guinness in Poland, and he's probably right (0.5L, 15zł). If you're hungry, try the shepherd's pie (20zł). Occasional live music, but usually not in the summer. Draws an older crowd. Open daily 2pm-midnight.

**Empik Pub,** ul. Nowy Świat 15/17 (☎625 10 86). In the basement and outside of the Empik Megastore; enter from al. Jerozolimskie. Hosts local bands of varied ilk, many of which are quite good. The place for blues in Warsaw. Live music M-Sa 9pm, Su 8pm. No cover. Open 9am until the last guest leaves.

**Drink Bar,** ul. Wspólna 52/54 (☎629 26 25) near ul. Marszałkowska south of the train station. Looking for a darker place? Maybe one where people have more piercings? Where the furniture doesn't match quite so well? Here's your place. It's all of the above, in a good way. Draught beer 7zł. Open daily noon-midnight, Su 5pm-midnight.

**Club Giovanni,** ul. Krakówskie Przedmieście 24 (☎826 92 39), on the premises of Uniwersytet Warszawski. Enter from the street via the narrow stairway next to the main gate. A hangout for a low-key student set, complete with faux-graffiti on the walls. Live music Th nights. Plenty of beer on tap (8-10zł). Cheap food, too; vegetarian pizza 15zł. Open M-Th 10am-1am, F 10am-3am, Sa 1pm-3am, Su 1pm-1am. AmEx/MC/Visa.

**Harenda Pub,** ul. Krakówskie Przedmieście 4/6 (☎826 29 00), at Hotel Harenda, just off the street. Enter from ul. Karasia. Dimly lit, with pictures of the owners in bow ties doing chummy things like taking road trips and going on brewery tours. Outdoor beer garden especially popular after work with the professional crowd. Beer 0.50zł. Live jazz sessions, usually Tu and W. Open daily 8am-3am.

## NIGHTCLUBS

As in any city, nightclubs in Warsaw tend to be hit-or-miss. Posters around town have the latest info on special club and disco nights.

POLAND

**Piekarnia,** ul. Młocinska 11 (☎636 49 79), downstairs from Rondo Babka, out al. Jana Pawła. So hip it hurts. Packed dance floor, little clothing and good music, often from top DJs. Cover F-Sa 25zł. Open F-Sa 10am-4am.

**Ground Zero,** ul. Wspólna 62 (☎625 43 80 and 625 39 76), just south of the central railway station. Deep in an old fall-out shelter, Warsaw's first big dance club is still kicking after 6 years. With a capacity of 800 people, you'll find all sorts of groovers in the black light. Not exactly cutting-edge, but definitely good for dancing. W student techno, Th 70s, 80s, and karaoke, F ladies' night, Sa dance party. Cover W 18zł, students 10zł; Th 18 zł; F 28zł, women 5zł 9-11pm; Sa 28 zł. Open W-Su 9pm-4am.

**Underground Music Cafe,** ul. Marzałkowska 126/134 (☎826 70 48; fax 826 70 47). Across from the Pałac Kultury; walk down the steps in front of McDonald's. Top floor has a bar with ample seating, downstairs is an expansive dance floor. Just make your way past the chain-link fence to the steps. Beer 7-8zł. Check the schedule outside the door. Usually M, Tu, and Sa house, W-Th funky, F dance, Su mellow. No cover Su-Tu, W-Sa 8-20zł. Open M-Sa 1pm-last guest leaves, Su 4pm-last guest leaves. Usually discounts for women before 10 or 11pm.

## BI-GAY-LESBIAN NIGHTLIFE

Unless visitors have come to Warsaw for a black eye, they do not advertise their homosexuality. Warsaw is largely a community of conservative businesspeople, and those gay clubs that do exist are rare and ephemeral. Establishments are often secluded and always discreet (on the outside, anyway). For the latest info, call the gay and lesbian **hotline** (see **Bi-Gay-Lesbian Services,** p. 470). Kiosks sell *Inaczej* and *Filo*—magazines listing gay entertainment throughout the country.

**Między Nami,** ("Our Place") ul. Bracka 20. A left off al. Jerozolimskie when coming from the Pałac Kultury; turn right on Bracka; it's the unmarked restaurant on your left. Mixed 20- to 30-something crowd during the day, sizable gay crowd in the evening. Classy "industrial" interior. 0.5L Żywiec 5.50zł. Salads 11.5zł. main dishes 15zł. Open M-Th 9am-11pm, F-Sa 9am-midnight, Su 4-10pm.

**Mykonos,** al. Jana Pawła II 73 (☎838 04 77), next to the Hotel Maria near Rando Babka. "Greek" murals look out on weekly drag and cabaret shows (F and Sa nights; 20 zł). One of the best places in Warsaw for lesbians. Open daily 4pm-2am.

**Paradise,** at the corner of ul. Wawelska and ul. Żwirki i Wigury, (☎(0)604 25 6682) on the grounds of the "Skra" sports complex, next to the tennis courts. Take bus #175 (or night bus #611) to "Pomnik Lotnika." A bit farther out, with a large dance floor and a patio. During the day it's a gay pub with bright colors and mood lighting. Younger crowd (of both men and women) than at the 2 other clubs. Beer 6zł. Disco F-Sa nights. Cover F 20 zł after 11pm, Sa 20 zł after 10pm. Open M-Th noon-midnight, F-Sa noon-5am.

## ⚡ DAYTRIP FROM WARSAW

### ŻELAZOWA WOLA

*Two buses daily pass through Żelazowa Wola (53km west of Warsaw), but none of the signs in Warsaw mention it. Take the bus headed to Wyszogrod. Żelazowa Wola is a regular stop on the route (6.70zł), but tell the driver where you want to get off ahead of time. Only the 9:45am bus arrives (11am) in time to take it all in; the other one arrives after the museum closes. There are no direct buses back after 4:30pm. Or, take a commuter train from Warszawa Śródmieście to the small town of Sochaczew (1 hr., 25 per day, 7.80zł). A Sochaczew city bus runs to "Żelazowa Wola" every hr. M-F, and every other hr. Sa-Su.*

The birthplace of Fryderyk Chopin, Żelazowa Wola is a must-see on any Chopin fan's itinerary. In the early 19th century, the town was the site of a manor that belonged to Count Skarbek, for whom the composer's father, a Frenchman named Nicolas Chopin, worked as a French tutor. There he met and married Justyna Krzyżanowska, a distant cousin of the count. They had 4 children—3 daughters and Fryderyk, who was born February 22, 1810. The Chopin family didn't remain at Żelazowa Wola for very long; just months after the genius-to-be was born, they headed for the city, settling in Warsaw in October 1810. The sight consists of the Chopins' cottage and the surrounding gardens. The museum in the house (☎/fax (46) 863 33 00) features rooms devoted to each of Chopin's parents. It lacks the family's original furniture, but the cottage does display a few tokens of Chopin's life and genius; his birth certificate, a page of an 1821 *polonaise* and the cover page of his first published piece (dreamt up when he was seven) all hang from the walls.

Although the gardens are beautiful and the collection in the cottage is authentic, the best reason to make the trip is to catch a **concert** of Chopin's works. From May to September, music fans gather here on Sundays to listen to Polish musicians deliver Frydryk's goods. (Concerts 11am and 3pm.) The schedule of music and performers, posted throughout Warsaw, is available at the Chopin museum (see **Museums,** p. 478); both change weekly. Concerts are free if you're content to listen from the park benches just outside the music parlor. The performers will come out to acknowledge the crowd afterwards. Seats in the parlor itself cost 30zł and are available at the *kasa* at the entrance to the grounds. Chopin's house and park 10zł, students 5zł. Park only 4zł, students 2zł. English audio tour 20zł.

# LESSER POLAND (MAŁOPOLSKA)

The Małopolska uplands lie in Poland's southeast corner, stretching from the Kraków-Częstochowa Uplands in the west, strewn with medieval castle ruins, to Lublin in the east. Kraków, which suffered only minimal damage during World War II, remains Poland's cultural and social center, drawing flocks of travelers. Daytrips from the city run the gamut of human accomplishment and suffering, from the artistry of the salt caves at Wieliczka to the unspeakable horror of Auschwitz-Birkenau and of Tarnów, a *Roma* town until the Nazi invasion. To the northeast stands Lublin, with another concentration camp, Majdanek, on its outskirts. Zamość to the east was inspired by the artistry of Padua, Italy. Finally, near the Ukrainian border, Łańcut stands out for its opulent castle.

# KRAKÓW ☎(0)12

Although Kraków (KRAH-koof; pop 745,500) only recently emerged as a trendy, international city, it has long held a distinguished place in the heart and history of Poland. This ancient capital sheltered centuries of Central European kings and garnered astounding architectural achievements in the process, many of which still stand in the maze of the multi-colored Old Town. Its narrow streets offer all sorts of treasures, including the country's oldest—and best—university. Unlike those in other major Polish cities, Kraków's original structures remain intact; the city survived even World War II unscathed.

The city has always confronted destruction: the notorious Nowa Huta steelworks in the eastern suburbs are a grim reminder of the Stalinist era and the Auschwitz-Birkenau death camp from the Nazi occupation lies only 70km to the west. It is this combination of vitality and darkness that lends the city its dynamism, as well as the protection and advocacy of all those who visit it. In the face of destructive pollution from the steelworks, UNESCO named Kraków to its original list of World Heritage Sites; today, UNESCO considers the city one of the 12 most important cultural monuments in the world. The flocks of tourists seem to agree, descending on the city to experience its relaxed atmosphere and underground network of hip pubs, clubs, and galleries. By no means undiscovered, Kraków remains the highlight of Poland.

POLAND

# ■ ORIENTATION

For both tourists and locals, the true heart of the city remains the huge **Rynek Główny** (Main Marketplace), in the center of **Stare Miasto** (Old Town). Ringing Stare Miasto are the **Planty** gardens and, a bit farther out, a ring of roads that includes Basztowa, Dunajewskiego, Podwale, and Westerplatte. Just south of the Rynek Główny looms the gigantic **Wawel Castle**. The **Wisła** (Vistula) river snakes past the castle and borders the old Jewish village of **Kazimierz,** which is accessible from the Rynek by ul. Starowiślna. The **bus** and **train** stations are located just to the northeast of the Planty ring. To reach the Rynek from either, follow the signs that read *do centrum;* they'll take you left out of the train station and right out of the bus station to the underpass. When you ascend from the depths, you'll be in Planty garden. There are a number of paths and streets that cut from here into the Rynek (10min.).

## ✈ INTERCITY TRANSPORTATION

**Airplanes: Balice airport** (☎411 19 55 and 285 50 70), 15km west of the center. Connected to the main train station by northbound **bus** #152 or 208 (40min.) or **express bus** 502 (30min.). Major international carriers include Swissair, British Airways, Austrian Airlines, KLM, Delta, SAS, and LOT. Open daily 4am-midnight. **INT Express Travel Agency,** ul. św. Marka 25 (☎423 04 97; fax 421 79 06), books tickets on most airlines. Open M-Sa 8am-8pm.

**Trains: Kraków Główny,** pl. Kolejowy 1 (☎624 54 39). To: **Warsaw** (3hr., 30 per day, 50.69zł); **Zakopane** (5½hr., 15 per day, 37.44zł); **Gdańsk** (6½hr., 12 per day, 60.86zł); **Poznan** (8hr., 7 per day, 60zł); **Bratislava, SLK** (8hr., 1 per day, 112zł); **Berlin, GER** (8½hr., 2 per day, 110zł); **Prague, CZR** (8½hr., 1 per day, 145zł); **Vienna, AUS** (9hr., 2 per day, 149zł); **Lviv, UKR** (10½hr., 1 per day, 85zł); **Budapest, HUN** (11hr., 1 per day, 145zł); and **Kyiv, UKR** (22hr., 1 per day, 180zł). Tickets sold both at the station and at many travel offices. Some trains to southeast Poland leave from **Kraków Płaszów,** pl. Dudzinskich 1 (☎933). Take the train from Kraków Główny or tram #3 or 13 from the center south to ul. Wielicka.

**Buses:** ☎936. On ul. Worcella, directly across from Kraków Główny. **Sindbad** sells international tickets in the main hall (☎266 19 21). Open M-F 9am-4:30pm. To: **Zakopane** (2hr., 26 per day, 10zł); **Warsaw** (5hr., 4per day, 40zł); **Vienna, AUS** (9hr., 7 per week, 100zł); **Lviv, UKR** (10hr., 1 per day, 50zł); **Budapest, HUN** (11hr., 2 per week, 116zł); **Prague, CZR** (11hr., 3 per week, 139zł); and **Berlin, GER** (12hr., 3 per week, 142zł).

## ⊏ LOCAL TRANSPORTATION

**Public Transportation:** Buy tickets at kiosks near **bus** and **tram** stops (2zł) or on board (2.50zł); punch them on board. Large backpacks need their own tickets. Night buses 4zł. Buy tickets in advance, as many kiosks are not open late. Day pass 8zł; weekly 20zł. 60zł fine if you're caught ticketless, 40zł if your bag is. Foreigners are fined frequently, so be sure your ticket is in order. Student fares are for Polish students only.

**Taxis: Express Taxi** (☎644 41 11); **Hellou** (☎644 42 22); and **Major** (☎636 33 33). Cabs that display a call sign and phone number are the most reasonably priced.

## 🛈 PRACTICAL INFORMATION

### TOURIST AND FINANCIAL SERVICES

**Tourist Offices: IT,** ul. Pawia 10 (☎422 60 91; ☎/fax 422 04 71), between the bus station and the train station. A great place to start. Information in English about budget accommodations, tours, and transportation. Also sells the incredibly handy *Kraków in Your Pocket* (5zł) and assorted maps (Kraków 5zł). Open May-Oct. M-F 8am-6pm, Sa 9am-1pm; Nov.-Apr. M-F 8am-4pm. **MCI** (Małopolskie Centrum Informacji), Rynek Główny 1/3 (☎421 77 06; fax 421 30 36). English-speaking staff offers maps and organizes tours. Open May-Sept. M-F 9am-8pm, Sa 9am-3pm; Oct.-Apr. M-F 9am-6pm.

**Budget Travel: Orbis,** Rynek Główny 41 (☎422 40 35; fax 422 28 85). Sells international tickets and arranges trips to the Wieliczka salt mines and Auschwitz. **Currency exchange.** English spoken. Open Apr.-Oct. M-F 9:30am-6pm, Sa 9am-2pm, Su 10am-

**Kraków: Stare Miasto**

SEE ALSO COLOR INSERT

▲ ACCOMMODATIONS

Camping Krak, 3
Dom Studentcki Zaczek, 4
Dom Wycieczkowy Pod Sokotem, 6
Hotel Mistia, 7
Hotel Poloni, 8
Hotel Studencki Piast, 2
Schronisko Młodzieżowe, 5
Strawberry Youth Hostel, 1

2pm; Nov.-Mar. M-F 9am-6pm, Sa 9am-1pm. **Almatur,** ul. Grodzka 2 (☎422 67 08; fax 422 61 40). Open M-F 9am-6pm, Sa 10am-4pm.

**Consulates: UK,** sw. Anny 9 (☎421 70 30), 4th floor. Open M-F 9am-4pm. **US,** ul. Stolarska 9 (☎429 66 55; emergency ☎429 66 58). Open M-F 8:30am-4:30pm.

**Currency Exchange:** *Kantory,* except those around the train station, have the best rates. **Bank PKO S.A.,** Rynek Główny 31 (☎422 60 22), cashes traveler's checks for a 1-2% commission (10zł min.), gives MC/Visa cash advances. Open M-F 8am-6pm, Sa 8am-2:30pm. For a better rate, exchange your traveler's checks for US$ here and take the cash to a *kantor*. Most are open only during business hours, but the **Forum Hotel,** ul. M. Konopnickiej 28 (☎261 92 12), has a 24hr. currency exchange. **ATMs** are plentiful.

**American Express:** Rynek Główny 41 (☎422 91 80), in the Orbis office (see above). Open Apr.-Oct. M-F 8:30am-6pm, Sa 9am-2pm, Su 10am-2pm; Nov.-Mar. M-F 9am-6pm, Sa 9am-1pm.

**Luggage Storage:** At Kraków Główny. 1% of value plus 3.90zł per day. Open 24hr.

**English Bookstore: Znak,** Sławkowska 1. Open M-F 10am-6pm, Sa 8am-2pm. MC/Visa. **Szawal,** ul. Długa 1 (☎421 53 61) and ul. Gołębia 8/1 (☎430 24 29). Open M-F 10am-6pm, Sa 10am-2pm.

**Laundromat:** Ul. Piastowska 47, on the ground floor of Hotel Piast (see **Accommodations,** below). 3hr. drop-off. Wash 8zł; dry 8zł. Open July-Aug. M-Sa 8am-8pm; Sept.-June 10am-7pm. **Betty Clean,** ul. Duga 17 (☎632 67 87), past the end of ul. Florionska. More of a dry cleaner than a landromat, but they'll clean all sorts of garments. Priced by item (shirt 7zł, sweater 9zł, nun's habit 20zł). Express service (3hr.) and super-express service (1½hr.) available. Open M-F 8am-7:30pm, Sa 8am-2pm.

## EMERGENCY AND COMMUNICATIONS

**Pharmacies: Apteka Pod Złotym Tygrysem** (Under the Golden Tiger), Szczepańska 1 (☎422 92 93), just off Rynek Główny. Posts a weekly list of 24hr. pharmacies in its window. Open M-F and Su 8am-8pm, Sa 8am-2pm.

**Medical Assistance: Medicover,** ul. Krótka 1 (☎422 76 33; after hours emergency ☎430 00 34). English speaking staff can help you navigate the Polish medical system. Ambulance services. Open M-F 8am-8pm, Sa 9am-2pm. **Profimed,** Rynek Główny 6 (☎421 79 97) and ul. Grodzka 26 (☎422 64 53). Open M-F 8am-8pm, Sa 9am-1pm.

**Telephones:** At the post office and opposite the train station, ul. Lubicz 4. Both open 24hr. **Telekomunikacja Polska,** Rynek Główny 18 (☎429 17 11; fax 423 00 19). Open daily 8am-10pm.

**Internet Access:** Available at **Club U Louisa** (see **Entertainment,** p. 489) for 5zł per hr. Open daily 11am-11pm. **Internet Cafe Looz,** Mikołajska 11 (☎422 37 97). 2zł per 15min., 6zł per hr. Open daily 10am-midnight. **Point Internet Club,** ul. Grodzka 2. 1zł per 15min., 6zł per hr. Open daily 10am-10pm. **Centrum Internetowe,** Rynek Główny 9 (☎431 32 84). 2zł per 15min., 5zł per hr. Open 24hr.

**Post Office:** Ul. Westerplatte 20 (☎422 51 63 and 422 86 48; fax 422 36 06). Take a number from the computer and wait your turn unless you are waiting for Poste Restante, to send packages, or to buy stamps. **Poste Restante** at counters #1 and 3. Open M-F 7:30am-8:30pm, Sa 9am-2pm, Su 9-11am.

**Postal code:** 31-045.

# ▐ ACCOMMODATIONS

Reservations are a good idea year-round, but necessary in summer. Call at least a few days ahead. **Waweltur,** ul. Pawia 8 (☎422 16 40; fax 422 19 21), arranges **private rooms.** (Open M-F 8am-8pm, Sa 8am-2pm. Singles 75zł; doubles 128zł, 117zł outside of the center. Stays over 1 week singles 64zł; doubles 96zł.) Locals also rent private rooms; watch for signs or solicitors in the train station.

### HOSTELS

▨ **Dom Wycieczkowy Pod Sokołem** (Vacation Home Under the Falcon), ul Sokolska 17 (☎292 01 99; ☎/fax 292 01 98), across the river from Kazimierz. Take tram #8 or 10 from the train station towards "Kagiewniki" and get off at the 1st stop after the bridge. Head down the stairs; it will be just ahead. Great new hostel (without a curfew!) features 12 extraordinarily clean rooms. Kitchen facilities. Dorms 30zł per person.

**Schronisko Młodzieżowe (HI),** ul. Oleandry 4 (☎633 88 22). Take tram #15 from the train station and get off when the main drag turns into ul. 3-go Maja. Take the first right up 3-go Maja onto Oleandry. 350 cheap but dingy beds, with bathrooms on each floor that don't keep up with the traffic. Decent showers; good location. 15min. by foot from the center. Kitchen facilities. English spoken. Flexible lockout 10am-5pm. Curfew midnight. 2- to 4-bed dorms 26zł; 5- to 8-bed dorms 22zł; 16-bed dorms 18zł.

**Dom Studencki Żaczek,** ul. 3-go Maja 5 (☎633 54 77). Across from Hotel Cracovia. Accessible by tram #15; get off just after the National Museum. Excellent location, but the communal bathrooms could smell better, and the nearby disco may keep you up. Check-out 10am. Singles 60zł, with bath 70zł; doubles 70zł, 110zł; triples 84zł, 135zł.

**Strawberry Youth Hostel,** ul. Radawicka 9 (☎636 15 00). Take tram #4, 8, or 13 from the train station to Urzędnicza. Walk in the direction of the tram, then take a right on Nowomiejska. After a block, it turns into Radawicka. Check-out 10am. Open July-Aug. Doubles, triples, and quads 40zł per person.

### HOTELS AND CAMPING

**Hotel Studencki Piast,** ul. Piastowska 47 (☎637 49 33). Take tram #4 or 12 from the train station to "Wawel." Walk in the direction of the tram to the 1st intersection and turn left. Go straight for a few blocks and Piast will be on the left. The location is a bit remote, but the tidy rooms make this a great option otherwise, as the many English speakers staying in the summer months attest. Laundromat in basement and cafe on ground floor. Check-out 10am. Singles 50zł (only in July and Aug.), with bath 85zł (year-round); doubles 74zł, 110zł; triples with bath 120zł.

**Hotel Mistia,** ul. Szlak 73a (☎/fax 633 29 26 and 634 16 70), on the corner of ul. Warszawska. Ah, the feeling of clean wall-to-wall carpeting and the sight of perfectly folded bedspreads! Marvelously maintained and close to the train station. 10min. by foot to the center. Check-in 2pm. Check-out 10am. Singles 90zł, with bath 130zł; doubles 110zł, 150zł; triples 170zł. Breakfast included. MC/Visa.

**Hotel Bydgoska 19,** ul. Bydgoska 19 (☎636 80 00; ☎/fax 638 77 88). Take tram #4 or 8 from the train station toward "Os. Bronowice Nowe" and get off at "Biprostal." Take the 1st left on al. Kijowska, walk 2 blocks, then take a right on Misjonarska, which quickly intersects Bydgoska. Sits in the middle of a park, with light and airy rooms. Comfortable, but certainly not a masterpiece of modernity. Grocery store, cafe, and post office downstairs. Check-in 2pm. Check-out 10am. Open July-Sept.; there are only a few rooms available year-round. 4- to 7-bed dorms 22zł; singles 45zł, with bath 90zł; doubles 58zł, 112zł; triples 78zł, 132zł.

**Hotel Polonia,** ul. Basztowa 25 (☎422 12 33; fax 422 16 21). Across from the train station. Convenient if you arrive too early or late to check into more affordable accommodations. Breakfast 16zł. Check-in 2pm. Check-out noon. Singles 153zł, with bath 250zł; doubles 187zł, 297zł; triples 330zł, 435zł. AmEx/MC/Visa.

**Camping Krak,** ul. Radzikowskiego 99 (☎637 21 22 and 637 29 57; fax 637 25 32). Take tram #4, 8, or 13 from the train station to Balicka Wiaduct. If it stops at Wesele, take bus #313 the last 2 stops. Walk down to ul. Armu Krajowej, the street under the tram line, and turn left up the hill for 10min. On the grounds of a complex of hotels, near a McDonald's. Open May 15-Sept. 15. Tents 18zł per person; cars 14zł.

# ◘ FOOD

The restaurants and cafes on and around Rynek satisfy Kraków's huge tourist population. Grocery stores surround the bus and train stations, with more in the city center. Street vendors sell *obwarzanki*, Polish soft pretzels (round and "soft" only about half the time) with sesame seeds, poppy seeds, or salt, for less than a złoty. Any *bar mleczny* (milk bar) provides a hearty, inexpensive dose of Polish fare. A traditional one sits at ul. Piłsudskiego 1. (Open M-F 8am-6pm, Sa 8am-4pm.)

▩ **Chimera,** ul. św. Anny 3 (☎423 21 78), in the cellar and ivy garden. The oldest and most famous salad joint in town, Chimera remains popular, especially with students. Huge sampler of 6 of their 20 cruciferous creations costs 10zł; slightly smaller plate 7zł. Meat dishes 15-30zł. Live music nightly 8pm. Open M-Sa 9am-11pm, Su 9am-10pm.

▩ **Cafe Zakątek,** Grodzka 2 (☎429 57 25). Fresh sandwiches (4-6zł), salads, and a stack of old albums. Frank Sinatra will croon in the corner while you munch your *kanapka* (sandwich). Breakfast 6zł. Open in summer M-Sa 8:30am-10pm; off-season 9am-7pm.

**Jadłodajnia u Stasi,** ul. Mikołajska 16. A one-person operation named after the owner's mom, Pani Stasia. Definitely budget. Famous for its traditional Polish food, including both meat- and fruit-filled *pierogi*. Come early afternoon for the best selection, but be prepared to wait in line. Open M-F 12:30pm until the food runs out—usually 4-5pm.

**Vega Bar Restaurant,** ul. św. Gertrudy 7 (☎422 34 94). Elegant vegetarian eatery with dried chiles over the counter and lace-draped pianos. Salads, soups, and creative manipulations of traditionally meat-based Polish cuisine (2-5zł). Open daily 9am-10pm.

**Piwnica Pod Ogródkiem,** ul. Jagiellońska 6 (☎421 60 29). "French" crepes and galettes packed full of meats, sweets, or vegetables 10-12zł. Good-sized portions. Offers a break from *naleśniki*, if Polish pancakes have tired you out. Open daily 1pm-midnight.

**Różowy Słoń (Pink Elephant),** ul. Straszewskiego 24 (☎423 07 57). Batman speaks Polish! Or at least he does in the comic book murals on the walls of this popular fast food restaurant. Polish dishes under 5zł. Open M-Sa 9am-9pm, Su 10am-9pm. Other locations at ul. Sienna 1 and ul. Straszewskiego 24 (near the train station).

**Balaton,** ul. Grodzka 37 (☎422 04 69). If you hit this popular Hungarian joint when it's hopping, you'll probably rave. Catch it at an off moment, however, and you might wonder where the appeal is in the higher-priced main dishes and the overly thematic red and green decor. Main dishes 10-40zł. Open daily 9am-10pm.

**Restauracja Ariel,** ul. Szeroka 18 (☎/fax 421 79 20), in the old Jewish district of Kazimierz, a 15min. walk south of Rynek. Outdoor cafe tables and elegant, antique interior with a creative, non-kosher mix of Polish and Jewish cuisine (10-36zł). Lots of tour groups. Jewish music nightly 8pm (cover 20zł). Open daily 9am-midnight.

# ⌗ CAFES

**Camelot,** ul. św. Tomasza 17 (☎421 01 23). Popular with students, artists, and foreigners alike. Adorned with handcrafted wooden dolls and original paintings. Salad 18-20zł. Breakfast, including muesli with yogurt and fresh fruit, 8zł. Music or cabaret W and F 8pm. Open daily 9am-midnight.

**Szuflada** (The Drawer), ul. Wiślna 5 (☎423 13 34). Doubles as a restaurant (main dishes 9-27zł) and as a shaken-up gallery. Fragments of art under the glass tabletops; walls with distorted angles and patterns that, on their best days, don't quite match. If you feel drunk upon entering, don't be surprised. Live music. Open daily noon-1am.

**Cafe Botanica,** ul. Bracka 9 (☎422 89 80). As the name suggests, plant life takes center stage. Packed full of greenery, but there's space to sip coffee or tea (3-6zł) or devour dessert. Open M-Sa 9am-10pm, Su 10am-10pm.

**Pożegnania z Afryka** (Out of Africa), ul. Św. Tomasza 21. Every good-sized Polish city has one, with good reason. Extensive selection (70 varieties) of rich, high-class coffee 6-8zł. Dark wood tables and thick aroma. No smoking. Open daily 10am-10pm.

**Kawiarnia Jama Michalika,** ul. Floriańska 45 (☎422 15 61). More than a century old, this is one of Kraków's most famous, and best decorated, cafes. Former haunt of the Polish intelligentsia. Evening cabaret. Open daily 9am-10pm.

# ◉ SIGHTS

Unlike many Polish cities, Kraków was spared from destruction in World War II. It was not, however, lucky enough to escape the effects of Soviet-style industrialization; for years the fumes emitted by the Nowa Huta Steelworks eroded the city's monuments. Kraków has scraped off the grime, however, revealing the extensive beauty and character that make it one of Eastern Europe's most treasured cities.

## STARE MIASTO

At the center of the Stare Miasto spreads **Rynek Główny,** replete with seas of cafes and bars. It's a convenient central point for exploring the nearby sights.

**ST. MARY'S CHURCH.** (Kościół Mariacki.) The two towers of St. Mary's were built by two brothers with different working styles: one hurried, the other deliberate. Eventually the hasty brother realized that the work of his careful sibling would put his own to shame, and killed him in a fit of jealousy. The murder weapon is on display in the Cloth Hall (see below). The deep blues and golds of the church's Baroque interior encase a 500-year-old wooden altarpiece carved by Wit Stwosz. Dismantled by the Nazis, the altar was rediscovered by Allied forces at the war's end. Now reassembled, its narration of the joy and suffering of St. Mary, complete with life-sized figures, is unveiled at noon each day. A trumpet call blares from the towers once in each direction every hour. Its abrupt ending recalls the destruction of Kraków in 1241, when the invading Tatars are said to have shot down the trumpeter in the middle of his song. *(At the corner of Rynek closest to the train station. Open daily noon-6pm. Altar 2.50zł, students 1.50zł. No photography. Video camera 5zł.)*

**CLOTH HALL.** (Sukiennice.) In the middle of Rynek, the yellow Italianate Cloth Hall remains as mercantile now as when cloth merchants actually used it: the ground floor is lined with wooden stalls hawking souvenirs. Upstairs, the **Cloth Hall Gallery,** part of the National Museum (see below), houses a gallery of 18th- and 19th-century Polish sculptures and paintings. Particularly striking are Józef Chełmoń-

POLAND

ski's *4 in Hand* and Henryk Siemiradzki's enormous *Nero's Torches*. (☎ *422 11 66. Open Tu-W and F-Su 10am-3:30pm, Th 10am-6pm. Last admission 30min. before closing. 5zł, students 2.50zł, Su Free.*) During the academic year, students cruise the area and wait for their friends under the **statue of Adam Mickiewicz,** Poland's most celebrated Romantic poet, between Cloth Hall and St. Mary's.

**UL. FLORIAŃSKA.** Ul. Floriańska runs from the corner of Rynek closest to the train station to the **Barbakan,** the only remnant of the city's medieval fortifications. Ul. Floriańska was once part of the Royal Way—the road leading to the castle—and many of the houses date from the 14th century. At the top of the street, **Floriańska Gate,** the old entrance to the city, is the centerpiece of the only surviving remnant of the city wall. In the 19th century, a local painter convinced city officials that the wall blocked the destructive north wind, thereby rescuing it from demolition.

**CZARTORYSKICH MUSEUM.** Among other masterpieces, this branch of the National Museum displays Leonardo da Vinci's *Lady with an Ermine* and Rembrandt's *Landscape with a Merciful Samaritan.* It also exhibits objects of historical significance, including full sets of armor bedecked with feathers and pelts. (*Ul. św. Jana 19. Ul. św. Jana runs parallel to ul. Floriańska. From Rynek, head to the end of the street; it will be on the right. ☎ 422 55 66. Open Tu-Th and Sa-Su 10am-3:30pm, F 10am-6pm. Last admission 30min. before closing. 5zł, students 2.50zł, Su free. Cameras without flash 15zł.*)

**JAGIELLONIAN UNIVERSITY.** (Uniwersytet Jagielloński.) More than 600 years old, Kraków's Jagiellonian University ranks as the second oldest university in Eastern Europe (after Prague's Charles University). Astronomer Mikołaj Kopernik (Copernicus) and painter Jan Matejko are among its noted alumni. (*Ul. Jagiellonska 15. Walk down sw. Anny in the corner of Rynek near the Town Hall and turn left onto Jagiellonska. ☎ 422 05 49. Open M-F 11am-2:20pm, Sa 11am-1:20pm. University Museum 5zł, students 3zł.*)

**UL. KANONICZA.** Ul. Kanonicza runs parallel to ul. Grodzka, which extends from the corner of Rynek closest to the small **St. Wojciech's Church** (Kościół św. Wojciecha). This street, like Floriańska, was once part of the Royal Way. Several galleries line the path to Wawel, including **Cricot 2,** a funky museum exhibiting the works of an avant-garde group once led by the late Tadeusz Kantor. (*Kanonicza 5. ☎ 422 83 32. Open M-F 10am-2pm. 5zł, students 2zł.*)

**OTHER SIGHTS.** The permanent exhibitions of the **National Museum** include one on 20th-century Polish art. (*Not in Rynek proper, the imposing central building sits just off Józefa Piłsudskiego. Open Tu and Th-Su 10am-3:30pm, W 10am-6pm. 6zł, students 4zł.*) The **History Museum of Kraków** displays original ceiling frescoes and a variety of centuries-old documents from Kraków. Regular rotation of temporary exhibits. (*Rynek Główny 35. ☎ 422 99 22. Open Tu-W and F 9am-3:30pm, Th 11am-6pm. 4zł, students 2.50zł.*)

# WAWEL CASTLE

☎ *422 51 55; fax 422 16 97. Castle open Tu and F 9:30am-4:30pm, W-Th and Sa 9:30am-3pm, Su 10am-3pm. Cathedral open May-Sept. M-F 9am-5:15pm, Su 12:15-5:15pm; daily Oct.-Apr. 9am-3:15pm. Cathedral museum open Tu-Su 10am-3pm. Cave open daily 10am-5pm. Oriental collection open only by appointment. Royal chambers 12zł, students 7zł; treasury and armory 10zł, 6zł; cathedral tombs and Sigismund's bell 6zł, 3zł; cave 2zł. W free. English tours available; price varies with number of sights and size of the group. Call ahead.*

Wawel Castle (Zamek Wawelski) is one of the finest pieces of architecture in Poland. Begun in the 10th century but remodeled during the 1500s, the castle contains 71 chambers and a magnificent sequence of 16th-century tapestries commissioned by the royal family, among many other treasures. A visit to Wawel can last anywhere from half an hour to three hours, depending on the size of the crowds and one's interest. The **Crown Treasury** features the swords carried at many Polish coronations. The **Oriental Collection** has an amazing display of 17th- and 18th-century porcelain from China and Japan, all intricately painted. Poland's monarchs were crowned and buried in the **Wawel Cathedral** (Katedra Wawelska), next to the castle. Karol Wojtyła, who grew up in Kraków, was archbishop here before becoming Pope John Paul II. The cathedral houses the ornate tombs of kings and others—

poets Juliusz Słowacki and Adam Mickiewicz (see **Literature and Arts,** p. 458), and Polish military leader General Józef Piłsudski. The sarcophagus of King Kazimierz Jagiełłończyk was crafted by Wit Stwosz, who also designed the altar in Kościół Mariacki. St. Maurice's spear, presented by German Emperor Otto III in 1000 to the Polish prince Bolesław Chrobry (who became the country's first king in 1024), commemorates a spell of Polish-German friendship. Steep wooden stairs lead from the church up to **Sigismund's Bell** (Dwon Zygmunta). The climb affords a great view of Kraków—and the gargantuan ringer. Outside, the **statue of Tadeusz Kościuszko** glorifies the Polish patriot who fought in the American Revolution and organized the 1794 revolt against Russia (see **History,** p. 455). The entrance to **Dragon's Cave** (Smocza Jama), residence of Kraków's erstwhile menace, is in the southwest corner of the complex. It comes out onto the banks of the Wisła, so don't descend unless you're ready to leave or to hike back up on the other side of the hill.

## KAZIMIERZ: THE OLD JEWISH QUARTER

*Take tram #13 east from pl. Dominikańska, 1 block south of Rynek, and get off by the post office, at the intersection of ul. Miodowa and Starowiślna. Ul. Szeroka runs parallel to Starowiślna, on the right if you're looking in the same direction as the tram. By foot, the 15min. walk from Rynek leads down ul. Sienna past St. Mary's Church, and opposite the statue of Adam Mickiewicz. Eventually, ul. Sienna turns into Starowiślna. After 1km, turn right on Miodowa, then take the 1st left onto Szeroka.*

South of the Stare Miasto lies Kazimierz, Kraków's 600-year-old Jewish quarter. Founded in 1335, Kazimierz was originally a separate town. In 1495 King Jan Olbrecht moved Kraków's Jews there in order to get them out of the city proper. On the eve of World War II, 64,000 Jews lived in the Kraków area, many of them in Kazimierz, but Nazi policies forced most of them out. The 15,000 remaining were resettled in the overcrowded Podgórze ghetto in 1941. All were deported by March 1943, many to the nearby Płaszów and Auschwitz-Birkenau concentration camps. Despite the fact that only about 100 practicing Jews now live there, Kazmierz today is a focal point for the 5000 Jews still living in Poland and serves as a starting point for those seeking their heritage. The **Jarden Bookstore** organizes tours, including a two-hour tour of Kazimierz and the Płaszów concentration camp tracing the sites shown in the film *Schindler's List*. Płaszów is located in the south of Kraków and was completely destroyed by the Nazis on their retreat. Today, nothing remains apart from a long, overgrown field. *(Szeroka 2. ☎ 421 71 66. Open M-F 9am-6pm, Sa-Su 10am-6pm. Kazimierz tour 25zł per person, with ghetto 30zł; Schindler's List sights 45zł; Auschwitz 90zł, private tour 120zł. Discounts for students and groups larger than 8. Tours in English.)*

**REMUH SYNAGOGUE AND CEMETERY.** The tiny Remuh Synagogue is surrounded by Remuh's Cemetery, one of Poland's oldest Jewish cemeteries. Beautiful but overrun, the cemetery holds graves dating back to the plague of 1551-52. On the eastern side, there's a 20m wall composed of tombstones recovered in 1959 after being scattered and shattered during the Nazi occupation. *(Szeroka 40. Open M-F 9am-4pm. 5zł, students 2zł. Services F at sundown and Sa morning.)*

**CENTER FOR JEWISH CULTURE.** The center is housed in the former Bene Emenu prayer house, just off Plac. Nowy. It opened in November 1993 to organize cultural events and arrange heritage tours. *(Rabina Meiselsa 17. ☎ 430 64 49; fax 430 64 97.)*

**OLD SYNAGOGUE.** (Stara Synagoga.) Poland's oldest synagogue, and the one most emblematic of Jewish architecture, the Old Synagogue houses a museum depicting the history, traditions, and art of Kraków's Jews. *(Szeroka 24. ☎ 622 09 62. Open Mar.-Oct. W-Th and Sa-Su 9am-3pm, F 11am-6pm; Nov.-Feb. W-Th 9am-3pm, F 11am-5pm, Sa-Su 9am-4pm. Closed the 1st Sa-Su and open the 1st M of every month. 6zł, students 4zł, W free.)*

## 🎵 ENTERTAINMENT

**MCI** (see **Practical Information,** p. 482) offers monthly brochures on cultural activities. The **Cultural Information Center,** ul. św. Jana 2 (☎ 421 77 87; fax 421 77 31), sells the monthly guide *Karnet* (2zł) and tickets for upcoming events. (Open M-F 10am-7pm, Sa 11am-7pm.) Festivals abound in Kraków, particularly in summer. Notable among them are the **International Short Film Festival** (late May), the **Festival of Jewish Culture** (early July), the **Street Theater Festival** (early July), and the **Jazz Festival** (Oct.-Nov.). The city jumps with music, particularly jazz. Good sessions go on at **Indigo**, ul. Floriańska 26 (☎/fax 429 17 43), **U Muniaka**, ul. Floriańska 3 (☎432 12 05), and **Piec Art**, ul. Szewska 12 (☎429 64 25). Classical music buffs will appreciate the performances at **Sala Filharmonia** (Philharmonic Hall), ul. Zwierzyniecka 1. (☎429 13 45 and 422 94 77. Box office open M-Th 2-7pm, F 2-7:30pm, Sa-Su 1hr. before performance.) The **opera** performs at the **J. Słowacki Theater**, Plac Św. Ducha 1. (☎422 43 22. Box office open M-Sa 11am-2pm and 3-7pm, Su 2hr. before performance).

As a rule, films in Poland are shown in their original language with Polish subtitles. **Kino Pod Baranami**, Rynek Główny 27 (☎423 07 68), and **Kino Mikro**, ul. Lea 5 (☎634 28 97), are two of Kraków's more adventurous independent cinemas.

# ◪ NIGHTLIFE

After a day of sightseeing in and around Rynek, stick around for the best clubbing opportunities in the city, frequented by both local students and tourists. *Kraków in Your Pocket* will usually have good up-to-date information. For information on **gay nightlife**, see http://gayeuro.com/krakow/.

**Kredens,** Rynek Główny 20 (☎429 20 07). Convenient, laid-back, and packed with partygoers who aren't too chic to sing along. Couches and a moderately big dance floor. Żywiec 5.50zł. Cover 5zł. 21+. Open Th-Sa 4pm-4am.

**U Louisa,** Rynek Główny 13 (☎421 80 92). Draws a diverse crowd with good, loud jazz and blues on weekends and a cybercafe (see **Internet Access,** p. 484). Beer 4-7.50zł. Cover for shows 5-10zł. Open daily 11am until the last guest leaves.

**Klub Kulturalny,** ul. Szewska 25 (☎429 67 39), unmarked and hidden below ground. The kulture down below is dark and wonderfully dank, with a rotating stone sculpture on the ceiling. Slightly older crowd. Beer 5zł. Open M-F noon-2am.

**Piec Art,** ul. Szewska 12 (☎429 16 02). Reasonably priced food, a wide range of beers (5zł), and good live jazz (cover 5zł) every W at 8pm. Mellow, but usually crowded. Who could ask more from a pub? Open daily 3pm until the last guest leaves.

**Free Pub,** ul. Sławkowska 4 (☎222 24 06). Unmarked and easy to miss. Head under the archway, then down the stairs through the door on the right. Mostly mellow 20- and 30-somethings. Beer 5zł. Open daily 4pm until the last guest leaves.

**Pod Jaszczurami** (Under the Lizards), Rynek Główny 8 (☎222 22 19). A laid-back student hangout. Hosts a loud, smoky disco on F-Sa and occasional bands during the week. Cover for disco 8zł. Żywiec 5zł. Open daily 10am until 3 or 4am.

**Hali Gali,** ul. Karmelicka 10 (☎0048 603 51 01 72). Through the archway. A quiet bar where gay men can chat over a beer or coffee. Beer 5zł. Open Tu-Su 4pm-4am.

**Jazz Club "U Muniaka,"** ul. Floriańska 3 (☎422 26 53). Cafe run by well-known Polish jazz musician, Janusz Muniak, who hosts jam sessions with his friends. Concerts Th-Sa 9:30pm. 20zł at the door. EB 5zł. Open daily 5pm-midnight, 1am for concerts.

# ◪ DAYTRIPS FROM KRAKÓW

## AUSCHWITZ-BIRKENAU

*Buses run to Oświęcim from the central bus station. (1½hr., 10 per day, 7zł; get off at "Muzeum Oświęcim.") The bus back to Kraków leaves from a different stop across the parking lot. Trains leave from Kraków Główny (1¾hr., 3 per day, 8.70zł); times are inconvenient and trains may not be direct. More trains run from Kraków Plaszów. Tourist offices in Kraków offer tours that include transportation and knowledgeable guides. From outside the Oświęcim train station, buses #2, 3, 4, and 5 drop visitors off at the "Muzeum Oświęcim" stop. By foot, turn right as you exit the station, go 1 block, and turn left onto ul. Więźniów Oświęcimia; the road stretches 1.6km to Auschwitz, which will be on the right.*

POLAND

**KEEPING FAITH** It's difficult to visit the camps at Auschwitz and Birkenau without hearing the name of Maksymilian Kolbe, a priest who sacrificed his own life while a prisoner in Auschwitz. When another man was sentenced to death by starvation, Kolbe willingly took the man's place, submitting himself to even more ghastly torture than he was already enduring. After two weeks without food, Kolbe's strength had still not faded and he had not succumbed to death. At that time, frustrated by the length of time it was taking to kill him, the Nazis decided to accelerate the process of execution and shot him. For his tremendous bravery, Kolbe was later canonized, becoming a particularly strong symbol within the Catholic Church of the evidence of faith in the face of persecution. The man whom Kolbe replaced survived, living to see not only the liberation of the camp, but also old age. He died four years ago.

An estimated 1.5 million people, mostly Jews, were murdered, and thousands more suffered unthinkable horrors, in the Nazi concentration camps at **Auschwitz** (Oświęcim) and **Birkenau** (Brzezinka). The largest and most brutally efficient of the death camps, their names are synonymous with the Nazi death machine.

**MUSEUM.** Tours begin at the museum. As you walk through the barracks, with nothing but a plate of glass between you and the remnants of thousands of lives—suitcases, shoes, glasses, and more than 100,000lbs. of women's hair—the sheer enormity of the evil committed here comes into focus. Other rooms, such as the 2nd floor of Barrack 5, shock with minute detail, like the single pacifier atop a pile of children's clothing. There's an English-language showing at 11am and 1pm of a **film** shot by the Soviet Army, which liberated the camp on January 27, 1945. Children under 14 are strongly advised not to visit the museum. *(Open daily June-Aug. 8am-7pm; May and Sept. 8am-6pm; Apr. and Oct. 8am-5pm; Mar. and Nov.-Dec. 15 8am-4pm; Dec. 16-Feb. 8am-3pm. Free. Guided tour in English daily at 11:30am, 3½ hr. 20zł, film included. An English-language guidebook with maps and detailed information is sold at the entrance for 3zł.)*

**AUSCHWITZ I.** Prisoners were actually held at the this smaller camp, which lies within the limits of the town of Oświęcim. The grass that has grown among the eerily tidy red brick buildings seems almost collegiate, until the bitter irony of the inscription on the camp's gate—*Arbeit Macht Frei* (Work Makes You Free)—fully sinks in. Those prisoners who suffered the horrifying conditions at Auschwitz I escaped the immediate death waiting for those herded into Konzentrationslager Auschwitz II-Birkenau—the extermination camp created when the main Auschwitz crematorium was beyond its capacity.

**AUSCHWITZ II-BIRKENAU.** Do not leave Oświęcim without visiting this starker and larger camp, in the countryside 3km from the original camp, a 30min. walk along a well-marked route. Shuttles run here from the parking lot of the Auschwitz museum. *(Apr. 15-Oct. 31, 1 per hr. 11:30am-5:30pm, 1zł.)* Birkenau was constructed later in the war when massive numbers of Jews, Roma, Slavs, homosexuals, disabled people, and other "inferiors" were being brought to Auschwitz and a more "efficient" means of killing needed to be devised. Begin with the central watchtower, where you can view the immensity of the camp—endless rows of barracks, watchtowers, chimneys, gas chambers, and crematoria. Amazingly, this is only a small section of the original camp; the rest was destroyed by Nazis trying to conceal the genocide. The chimneys mark the spots where barracks stood until just after the war. The train tracks, which were reconstructed after the liberation, lead to the ruins of the crematoria and gas chambers, where an international memorial pays tribute to all those who died in the Auschwitz system. Near the monument lies a pond, still gray from the ashes deposited there a half century ago; fragments of bone can still be found in the area near the crematoria.

# ■ WIELICZKA

*Ul. Daniłowicza 10. Many companies, including Orbis, organize trips to the mine. The cheapest way to go is to take one of the minibuses that leave from the road between the train and bus stations (every 15min., 2zł). In Wieliczka, follow the old path of the tracks and then the "do kopalni" signs. ☎278 73 02. Open daily Apr. 16-Oct. 15 M-Sa 9am-8pm, Su 9:30am-4pm; Oct. 16-Apr. 15 M-Sa 9am-6pm. Tours 30zl, students 20zl. English guide available 3 times per day in June, 5 times per day July-Aug.*

The 1000-year-old **salt mine,** in the tiny town of Wieliczka, is 13km southeast of Kraków. Pious Poles carved a 20-chapel complex 100m underground entirely out of salt; in 1978, UNESCO declared the mine one of the 12 most priceless monuments in the world. Today, you can venture down and lick almost everything in sight—except the guide. The mandatory two-hour tour covers over 20 salt sculptures, a cafe, and a souvenir shop. Favorite Poles like Copernicus and Pope John Paul II, each of whom visited the museum in his respective time, are immortalized, but the most spectacular sight is the 60m-by-11m **St. Kinga's Chapel,** complete with salt chandeliers, an altar, and relief works. Take the lift 130m back to the surface or go on to the **underground museum,** which gives a history of the mines.

# TARNÓW ☎(0)14

*Ul. Krakówska 10. Tarnów lies 82km east of Kraków, connected by trains (1½hr., 43 per day, 8-11zł) and buses (2hr., 24 per day, 15zł), both of which arrive at pl. Dworcowy, 15min. from the center. From the main bus station, turn right on ul. Krakówska. The museum is a 10min. walk, en route to Rynek. ☎220 625. Open Tu and Th 10am-5pm, W and F 9am-3pm, Sa-Su 10am-2pm. 3zł, students 1.50zł. Camera 5zł.*

A Roma (gypsy) town before World War II, Tarnów still manages to preserve its legacy. Dedicated to "all travelers, past, present and, I hope, future," the **Ethnographic Museum** traces the history of the Polish Roma since 1401, when they first arrived here, displaying an exhibit on their culture and how it has developed through the years. Dolls, dresses, and, in the summer, vibrantly painted carriages attest to the vitality of the people's artistic tradition, as do the occasional performances organized by the museum. Of course, the Roma story is not entirely a happy one. They have been plagued, since their arrival in Europe, by persecution. World War II saw the liquidation of half the European Roma population; today, only 25,000 Polish gypsies remain. They have found strength as the museum notes, in the World Congress, an international association that enjoys observer status at the United Nations. When it first met in 1971, the Congress chose a national anthem and a flag. Its red wheel, set against a blue and green background, symbolizes the nomadic lifestyle that has always defined the Roma people.

# LUBLIN ☎(0)81

Lublin (LOO-bleen) can fool visitors with the slow pace of its surroundings, but its residents know their city is anything but provincial. Long an incubator of social and religious movements, Małopolska's former capital served as the center of the Polish Reformation and Counter-Reformation in the 16th and 17th centuries, and later housed the only independent institution of higher learning in the communist era, the Polish Catholic University. Today a bohemian presence flourishes around the city's two universities and in the historical depths of the Old Town.

## ✴️🛈 ORIENTATION AND PRACTICAL INFORMATION

The city's main drag, **ul. Krakówskie Przedmieście,** connects **Stare Miasto** (Old Town) in east Lublin to the **Katolicki Uniwersytet Lubelski** (Catholic University of Lublin KUL) and **Uniwersytet Marii Curie-Skłodowskiej** (Maria Curie-Sklodowska University) in the west, becoming **al. Racławickie** along the way and passing the urban oasis of the **Ogród Saski** (Saxon Garden). Take bus #5, 10, or 13 to town from the bus station. On foot, head toward the castle and climb **ul. Zamkowa,** which runs up to Stare Miasto. Changing names several times, Zamkowa emerges through **Brama Krakówska** (Kraków Gate) and intersects **ul. Krakówskie Przedmieście.** From the train station, take trolley #150 or bus #13 to the city center.

POLAND

**Tourist Office: IT,** ul. Narutowicza 54 (☎532 44 12), next to the Hotel Victoria. Walk or take bus #8, 9, or 11 south on Narutowicza from the city center. Carries maps (4zł) and brochures, and can help find accommodations. Open M-F 9am-5pm, Sa 10am-2pm.

**Budget Travel: Orbis,** ul. Narutowicza 31/33 (☎532 22 56; fax 532 15 30), handles international and domestic plane, train, and bus tickets, and is always excited to book rooms at their own hotels. Open M-F 9am-6pm, Sa 9am-2pm. Some English spoken.

**Currency Exchange:** *Kantor* has the best rates. **Bank PKO S.A.,** ul. Królewska 1 (☎532 10 16), accepts all types of traveler's checks (1.5% commission) and offers MC/Visa cash advances. Open M-F 7:30am-6pm, Sa 10am-2pm. **ATMs** are all over town.

**Pharmacy: Apteka Prowadzi,** ul. Bramowa 2/8 (☎535 32 31). Open daily 8am-8pm. Second location outside the Kraków Gate and down the hill at ul. Lubartowska 15 (☎532 27 30). Open M-Sa 8am-3pm.

**Telephones:** Inside and outside the post office, most take only Polish phone cards.

**Internet Access: Intercafe,** ul. Graniczna 13 (☎532 72 09; www.intercafe.com.pl), in a basement. 6zł per hr. **WWW.Cafe,** Rynek 8 (☎442 35 79; www-cafe.lublin.pl), on the fourth floor in the old square. 5zł per hr. Open 10am-10pm.

**Post Office:** ul. Krakówskie Przedmieście 50 (☎743 67 61/fax 532 50 61). **Fax** service available. Xerox at window #3, **Poste Restante** at #2. Open M-F 7am-9pm, Sa 8am-9pm, Su 9am-4pm. **Postal code:** 20-930.

# ⌐ TRANSPORTATION

**Trains:** pl. Dworcowy 1 (☎ 532 02 19; info ☎933). To **Kraków** (4hr., 2 per day, 36zł) and **Warsaw Central Station** (2½hr., 9 per day, 27zł).

**Buses:** ul. Tysiąclecia 4 (☎776 649; info ☎934). To **Warsaw** (3hr., 2 per day, 12zł). **Polski Express** (☎022 620 03 30) runs at odd hours and is worth the money for long rides. To **Warsaw** (2hr., 8 per day, 25zł) and **Kraków** (2 per day, 37zł).

**Local Transportation:** Buy tickets for buses and trolleys at kiosks. 10min. ride 1.70zł; 30min. 1.90zł.

# ▐ ACCOMMODATIONS

Room prices in Lublin are rising, but are still reasonable. There are no good hostels or inexpensive hotels available in or directly around Stare Miasto. Luckily, Lublin is not so large that the trek from budget accommodations is formidable; all those listed are a short ride away from the central part of town.

**Szkolne Schronisko Młodzieżowe,** ul. Długosza 6 (☎/fax 533 06 28), west of the center near the KUL. From the Ogród Saski bus stop, walk to the end of the park and take a right on ul. Długosza. Follow the blue hostel signs into the driveway on the left. With 22 beds in one of the dorm rooms and a kitchen open to all, this hostel is communal to the core. Isolated, but clean and quiet. Linen 4.50zł. Lockout 10am-5pm. Curfew 10pm. Dorms 18.29zł; triples 21.90zł per person.

**ZNP Dom Nauczyciela,** ul. Akademicka 4 (☎533 82 85; fax 533 37 45), near the KUL. From the Ogród Saski bus stop, cross the street and follow ul. Łopacińskiego until it turns into ul. Akademicka. Primarily for visiting teachers, but anyone can stay in one of its minimalist rooms. A good choice if you want to stay out late. Reception 24hr. 6-bed dorms 28zł (no shower); singles 65zł; doubles 134zł (with bath).

**Dom Noclegowy "Piast,"** ul. Pocztowa 2 (☎532 25 16), virtually on top of the train station. The first two floors of the building house a snack bar, but the top three have budget living written all over them. Reception 24hr. Singles 42zł; doubles 60zł.

# ◔ FOOD

Lublin's eateries cluster around ul. Krakówskie Przedmieście. A dozen **beer gardens** are situated immediately outside the gate to Stare Miasto, and several more can be found inside. To create your own culinary masterpiece, duck into one of the many

**Lublin**

ACCOMMODATIONS
A Schronisko Młodzieżowe (HI)
B ZNP Dom Nauczyciela
C Hotel Victoria

STARE MIASTO
(OLD TOWN)

Holy Trinity Church
Park Podzamcze
Lublin Castle/Museum
Dworzec PKS (Bus Terminal)
Al. Tysiąclecia
Nowy Plac Targowy
PL. ZAMKOWY
Grodzka Gate
Dominican Church
Old Town Hall
RYNEK
Cathedral
Krakow Gate
Bernardine Church
Church of St. John
PL. ŁOKIETKA
PL. OFIAR GETTA
Lubartowska

Ruska
Ruska
Nowy Plac Targowy
Browarna
Szewska
St. Staszica
St. Staszica
Karmelicka
Świętoduska
Zielona
Radziwiłłowska
Niecała
Dolna 3 Maja
3 Maja
Cicha
1 Armii W.P.
Chmielna
Ogrodowa
Czechowska
Gawarechich
Gawareckich
Czubachich
Czechowska
Spokojna
Lubomelska
Czugały
Party zancka
Czysta
Wieniawska
Krótka
Jasna
Ewangelicka
Krakowskie Przedmieście

Kapucyńska
Kościuszki
Peowiaków
Hempla
Kołłątaja
Narutowicza
Górna
Graniczna
Gminna
Środkowa
Wschodnia
Dolna Panny Marii

Orbis Office

Okopowa
Solna
Orla
Chopina
Hipoteczna
Sądowa
Chmielar czyka
Solna
Chopina
Krucza
Stajna
Lipowa

Al. Tysiąclecia

Ogród Saski

Lublin Catholic University

Leszczyńskiego
Al. Długosza
Popławska
Orzechówka
Snopkowska
al. Racławickie
Radziszewskiego
Łopacinskiego
Grottgera
Zbwizki i Wigury
Marii Skłodowskiej-Curie
Uniwersytecka
Obrotów Pokoju
Raabego
Akademicka

Wyszyńskiego
Misjonarska
Miedziana
Bernardyńska
Farbiarska

Al. Unii Lubelskiej

TO LUBLIN GŁÓWNY TRAIN STATION
TO MAJDANEK

Frumanska
Kowalska
Rybna
Olejna
Szambelanska
Jezuicka
Królewska
Grodzka
Archidiakońska
Dominikańska
Podwale
Złota
Zamkowa
Przechodnia
Wróblew skiego
Świętoduska
POLAND

200 yards
200 meters
0

N

well-stocked delicatessens, some of which stay open around the clock. **Delikatesy Nocne,** ul. Lubartowska 3 (☎534 42 46), just down the street from the Kraków Gate, is particularly popular with the late-night crowd.

**Café Szeroka 28,** ul Grodzka 21 (☎534 61 09), steps from the Grodzka Gate. Not just an eatery, but also an artistic project, with different rooms paying homage to a pre-war Polish street, Lublin Art Nouveau patterns, and a Jewish dressmaker's room. Terrace with a great view of the Stare Miasto and castle. Regional and international cuisine. Main dishes 5-10zł. Open Su-Th 11am-11pm, F-Sa 11am-midnight. Visa/MC.

**Pani Pizza,** ul. Kósciuszki 3 (☎532 61 59), behind the post office. With red-checked tablecloths and a variety of pizzas, it's almost a little bit of Italy. Almost—the house topping is ketchup. Main dishes 5-12zł. Open M-Sa 10am-9:30pm, Su 11am-9:30pm.

**Pod Basztą,** ul. Królewska 6. A spotless, brightly lit milk bar. Serves up a good selection of traditional Polish dishes and deserts. Main dishes 4-6zł. Open daily 10am-10pm.

**Old Pub Restauracja,** ul. Grodzka 8 (☎743 71 27). Popular, shockingly enough, with an older crowd. Enjoy a sandwich or an entree (28-38zł) in the garden or on an antique table inside. Open daily 11am-10pm. Visa/MC/AmEx.

**Bar Turystyczny Mleczny,** ul. Krakówskie Przedmieście 29. Great deals and authentic Polish dining. Spartan decor and total silence keep diners focused on the task at hand: ingestion. Soups 2zł, Main dishes 4-7zł. Open M-Sa 7am-6pm, Su 8am-5pm.

# 👁 SIGHTS

The 19th-century ochre facades of **ul. Krakowskie Przedmieście** lead into medieval Stare Miasto, home of Lublin's historical sights. Pl. Litewski showcases an **obelisk** commemorating the 1569 union of Poland and Lithuania and a **Tomb of the Unknown Soldier.** Pl. Lokietka, east of pl. Litewski, is home to the 1827 **New Town Hall** (Nowy Ratusz), seat of Lublin's government. To the right begins ul. Królewska, which runs down around the corner to the grand **Cathedral of St. John the Baptist and St. John the Evangelist** (Katedra Sw. Jana Chrzciciela i Jana Ewangelisty; 1586-1596). The cathedral's frescoes, gilded altar, and barrel vault make it worth a visit.

Ul. Krakówskie Przedmieście travels through pl. Łokietka to the fortified **Kraków Gate** (Krakowska Brama), which houses the **Historical Division of the Lublin Museum** (Oddział Historyczny Muzeum Lubelskiego), pl. Łokietka 3. Its four floors highlight the town's role in World War II and trace the changes in its appearance from 1585 to the present, with some info in English. (☎532 60 01. Open W-Sa 9am-4pm, Su 9am-5pm. 2zł.) The top of the spiral staircase offers a great view of Lublin. Across the gate, ul. Bramowa leads to Rynek, lined with early Renaissance houses. In Rynek's center stands the 18th-century Neoclassical **Old Town Hall** (Stary Ratusz). A walk along ul. Grodzka leads through the 15th-century **Grodzka Gate** (Brama Grodzka) to ul. Zamkowa, which runs to the massive **Lublin Castle** (Zamek Lubelski). Most of the structure was built in the 14th-century by King Kazimierz Wielki (see **History,** p. 454), but was restored in the 19th-century with a neo-Gothic exterior. During the Nazi occupation, the castle functioned as a Gestapo jail; the prisoners were shot en masse when the Nazis had to make a hasty retreat.

Inside the castle, the **Lublin Museum** (☎532 50 01, ext. 35) features historical paintings, armaments, and ornamental art. While its collection is interesting, the Russo-Byzantine frescoes in the attached **Holy Trinity Chapel** are truly stunning. The remarkably well maintained panels were completed in 1418 and depict various biblical scenes. (Open W-Sa 9am-4pm, Su 9am-5pm. 8zł for entry to both.)

# 📷 NIGHTLIFE

Thanks to its large student crowd, Lublin has an impressive number of cafes and pubs and an active music scene. The Stare Miasto is the definite center of nightlife.

**Colosseum Club,** Radziszewskiego 8 (☎534 43 00), near the University. This bootyshakin' university favorite features a great bar and disco. Mostly techno, although one or two polka-inspired Polish tunes slip into the mix. Cover fluctuates with the size of the crowd. On the

POLAND

weekend, expect to pay 10zł if you're male, half that if you're not. EB 4.50zł, bottled beers 4.50-10zł. The party starts at 8pm and rages until 1-4am.

**Zolo Ferari**, ul. Grodzka 1 (☎743 72 59). Subterranean, with graffiti on the stone walls. Advertises "4 shots for 14zł." Beer on tap 4.5zł. Open 4pm until the last guest leaves.

**Caffe Kardy**, ul. Królewska 4 (☎534 03 18), under the archway and down the stairs. Another stone-cold dungeon turned hip. Not much decoration, but the cheap beer tends to create its own atmosphere. EB, Herrelius 4zł. Open M-F noon-midnight, Sa-Su until the last guest passes out.

**Caffe Bilard**, ul. M.S. Skłodowskiej 26 (☎534 52 39). A few blocks from both KUL and UMCS, and so popular with students. Two pool tables (10zł per hr.) and a full bar. Open M-F 3pm-midnight, Sa-Su 5pm-midnight.

**Jazz Pizza**, ul. Krakówskie Przedmieście 55 (☎743 61 49). Portraits of Dizzy Gillespie preside over a full bar and the sounds of classic jazz records. Guinness 8zł, EB 4.50zł, pizza 8-10zł. Open M-Sa 2pm-midnight, Su 3-10pm.

**Café NATO**, ul. Kósciuszki 8. Celebrate Poland's acceptance into the Western military alliance at this dimly lit basement bar. Folding metal chairs add to the military ambiance. Tea 1.50zł, rum 9.50zł. Open M-F 10am-11pm, Sa-Su noon-11pm.

# ▐▞ DAYTRIP FROM LUBLIN

## MAJDANEK

*From Lublin, eastbound bus #28 from the train station, trollies #153 and 158 from al. Racławickie, and southbound trolly #156 from ul. Królewska all stop at the huge granite monument marking the entrance at Droga Męczenników Majdanka 67. Or, you can walk the 4km down the road from Lublin to Zamość, fittingly called Road of the Martyrs of Majdanek (Droga Męczenników Majdanka; 30 min.). ☎744 26 47 or 744 19 55; fax 744 05 26. Museum open May-Sept. Tu-Su 8am-6pm; Mar.-Apr. and Oct.-Nov. Tu-Su 8am-3pm. Call to arrange Dec.-Feb. visits. Free; children under 14 not permitted. Tours in Polish 60zł, in English 100zł. Call ahead for tours; the guides are busy and may not be available.*

During the Second World War, Majdanek was the largest concentration camp after Auschwitz. Approximately 235,000 people died here, including Jews, Poles, Soviets, and others from all over Europe. **Majdanek State Museum** (Panstwowe Muzeum na Majdanku) was founded in 1944 after the liberation of Lublin. The Nazis didn't have time to destroy the camp, so the original structures stand in their entirety, including the gas chambers, the crematorium, the third field prisoners' barracks, the watchtowers, the guardhouses, and the electrified barbed-wire perimeter.

A visit to Majdanek begins with the information building, whose staff supplies free information in several languages and shows a 25-minute documentary that includes the first footage taken after the camp's liberation. (Available in English, last showing 3pm. 2zł per person; minimum 10zł per show.) Walking through the entire camp takes 1½-2hr. The route begins with the gas chambers; signs in Polish, English, French, Russian, and German explain Nazi methods of extermination and experimentation. Guardhouses #43-45 contain historical exhibitions, including statistical displays, prisoners' clothes, instruments of torture, and a sample of the 730kg of human hair exported from Majdanek to a fabric factory in Germany. Perhaps the most overpowering single exhibit is piled up in guardhouse #52; 800,000 pairs of shoes the Nazis took from victims of Majdanek and neighboring camps fill the building. At the end of the main path through the camp, the intact crematorium ovens sit next to the concrete dome of the mausoleum, which stands as a massive mound of ash and human bone. Black crows still patrol the area.

# ZAMOŚĆ      ☎(0)84

After studying in Padua, young aristocrat Jan Zamojski wanted to recreate its beauty in his homeland. Venetian designer Bernardo Morando helped him realize his dream, and Zamość, with its immense *rynek*, opulent houses, and towering town hall, was born in 1580. Zamość withstood sieges by the Cossacks in 1648 and

POLAND

the Swedes in 1656, but diminished in importance after the partitions of Poland. After extensive restorations, this "Padua of the North" has emerged as a tourist favorite and has been added to UNESCO's list of World Cultural Heritage Cities. The colorful *rynek* is now a lovely place to relax with the locals.

**TRANSPORTATION. Trains** run from the station, ul. Szczebrzeska 11 (☎638 69 44), to: **Lublin** (3hr., 2 per day, 13.50zł); **Warsaw** (5hr., 1 per day, 34zł); and **Kraków** (6hr., 1 per day, 34zł). **Buses** run from the station, ul. Sadowa 6 (☎639 50 81), to **Lublin** (2hr., 30 per day, 16zł) and **Warsaw** (5hr., 5 per day, 34zł). For a **taxi**, call ☎96 22.

**ORIENTATION AND PRACTICAL INFORMATION.** To get to the *rynek* from the train station, turn right and walk toward the spires of Stare Miasto on ul. Szczebrzeska. After five minutes the road curves to the left and becomes Akademicka, which runs to the cathedral. A right up Staszica leads to the *rynek*. To reach the *rynek* from the bus station, turn right up Sadowa, which turns into ul. Goninna. After five minutes, turn right onto ul. Partyzantów. From here, take any city bus (1zł) one stop to the edge of the old town. Alternatively, walk right onto Lukasińskiego at the end of Partyzantów and take a left onto Staszica, going past the Franciscan church into the *rynek*. The **ZOIT tourist office,** Rynek Wielki 13 (☎639 22 92; fax 627 08 13), in the town hall, sells **maps. Bank PKO,** ul. Grodzka 2, cashes **traveler's checks,** gives MC/Visa **cash advances,** and has a Cirrus/MC/Visa **ATM** outside. (☎639 20 40. Open M-F 8am-6pm, Sa 10am-2pm.) **Apteka Rektorska** sits at Rynek 2. (☎639 23 86. Open M-Sa 8am-3pm). The **post office** and **telephones** are at ul. Kościuszki 9. (☎38 51 23. Open M-F 7am-9pm, Sa 7am-3pm.) **Postal code:** 22-400.

**ACCOMMODATIONS AND FOOD.** Hotels and hostels fill up fast in summer. Call at least a few days in advance to reserve a place. **Dom Turysty "Marta,"** ul. Zamenhofa 11, is in the center of town. Follow the directions to the *rynek* (see above), then walk up ul. Solna, passing the town hall on your left. Take the second right onto Zamenhofa. The friendly staff of this tourist hotel rents basic rooms with communal bathrooms, featuring clean showers. (☎639 26 39. 7-bed dorms 20zł; doubles 60zł.) **Hotel Garmizomowy,** ul. Lubelska 36, is farther away, but its decent and affordable rooms are a good option when more central accommodations are booked up. To get here, take ul. Solna out of the *rynek* to the rondo and go straight on ul Piłsudskiego for 10-15 minutes. Turn right onto ul. Koszary at the large airplane and then take the first left onto ul. Lubelska. The hotel is in the second house on the right, marked with a "Miejsca Noclegowe" sign. (☎638 48 42. Singles 35zł, with bath 40zł; doubles 60zł, 70zł; triples 80zł, 100zł; quads 100zł, 120zł.) To reach **Ośrodek Sportui Rekreacji,** Królowej Jadwigi 8, follow the directions to the *rynek*, then take ul. Staszica to the cathedral and turn right down Akademicka. Turn left on Królowej Jadwigi and walk for five minutes; the hotel is near a stadium and features clean rooms, all with bath. Reserve 3-4 days in advance or sports teams will beat you to the beds. (☎638 60 11. Singles 72zł; doubles 90zł; triples 105zł; quads 121zł.) **Camping Duet,** Królowej Jadwigi 14, is in a wooded area down the street. (☎39 24 99. Campsites 3.50zł per person. Tents 6zł. 4-bed bungalows with bath and fridge 60zł for 1 person; 70zł for 2; 90zł for 3; 110zł for 4.)

Culinary options in Zamość center on the pleasant outdoor cafes around the rynek. **Cafe-Restaurant Muzealna,** ul. Ormiańska 30, next to the town hall, features many tasty options. (☎638 64 94, ext. 4013. English menu. Main dishes 7-15zł. Open daily noon-midnight.) **Ratuszowa,** Rynek 13, in the town hall, serves traditional Polish fare in a relaxed cafe setting. (☎627 15 57. Main dishes under 17zł. Open daily 9am-11pm.) A **grocery** stands a few blocks up from the *rynek* on the corner of ul. Piłsudskiego and ul. Peowiaków. (M-F 6am-10pm, Sa-Su 8am-10pm.)

**SIGHTS.** Zamość is essentially one giant sight, and historical monuments fill the city center. A map from the tourist office (see above) will be helpful as you wander about through the **Zamojski Palace,** the old town gates, the churches, and the two remaining bastions. The splendidly preserved **Armenian burgher houses,** ul. Ormiańska 22, 24, 26, 28, and 30, in the northeast corner of the *rynek*, are especially worthwhile. These houses, complete with intricate woodwork and bright interiors, are what remains from Zamość's economic heyday. House #26 is the headquarters of the **Muzeum Okręgowe,** which displays religious art. (☎638 64 94. Open Tu-Su 9am-4pm. 3zł, students 1zł.) Master Carlo Dolci's *Annunciation* is inside the **cathedral,** ul. Kolegiacka; follow ul. Staszica from the *rynek* to get there. The region's religious riches—chalices, sculptures, and saints' relics—pack the adjoining **museum.** (Open May-Sept. M and Th-Sa 10am-4pm, Su 10am-1pm. 1zł.) If you're lucky, the cathedral's **bell tower** will be open. (2zł.)

**▮▮ ENTERTAINMENT AND FESTIVALS.** Pool tables abound in the bars and many residents and tourists head to the *rynek* for an evening *piwo* (beer); unfortunately, the good times wind down before midnight. **Jazz Club Kosz,** ul. Zamenhofa 3, hosts live jazz year-round; enter from the back of the building. (☎638 60 41. Open M-Sa noon-midnight, Su 4pm-midnight.) At the end of May, jazz musicians from Poland, Ukraine, and Belarus jam at the **Jazz na Kresach Festival** (Jazz in the Borderlands). In late September jazz singers gather for the **Międzynarodowe Spotkania Wokalistów Jazzowych** (International Festival of Jazz Vocalists.) For info, contact **Wojewódzki Dom Kultury (WDK),** ul. Partyzantów 13 (☎/fax 639 20 21).

# ŁAŃCUT ☎(0)17225

**▮ Łańcut Castle** (Zamek w Łańcucie) grants visitors a glimpse into the lavish lifestyle of Polish nobility. Dominating the town, the palace has a more intriguing history—and a better art collection—than many small European cities. Founded by King Kazimierz III Wielki in the mid-14th century, the palace survived Swedish and Turkish attacks in the 17th century, but was later transformed to fit the tastes of duchess Elźbieta Lubomirska z Czartoryskich. Although it was spared damage during World War II, the palace lost its soul when the last Lord of Łańcut fled Poland in 1944, taking 11 railway cars full of booty with him. The new government turned the complex into a **museum** showcasing what was left of the furniture and art.

The **ticket office** is just inside the palace park gate. The required tour includes the **Orangery** (Oranźeria), adjacent to the Palace, and the **Powozownia,** the largest display of carriages in Europe. If you don't speak Polish, you'll be allowed to wander without a group, so be sure to find the Powozovnia by heading left of the palace, outside the gate, and across ul. 3-ego Maja. (☎20 08. Open Apr.-Sept. Tu-Sa 9am-4pm, Su and holidays 9am-3pm; Feb.-Mar. and Oct.-Nov. Tu-Su 9am-3pm. Tours 12zł, students 7zł.) The grounds surrounding the palace provide a shady setting for walking or reading. The palace hosts an international **Music Festival** in mid-May.

To get to the palace from the **train station,** ul. Kolejowa (☎23 17), call a **taxi** (☎20 00), or head along ul. Żeromskiego and take the first right onto ul. Grunwaldzka (30min.). To reach the *rynek*, turn right where ul Grunwaldzka meets ul. Kościuszki, which leads to the palace gates. **Trains** run to: **Przemyśl** (1hr., 23 per day, 9.20zł); **Kraków** (2½hr., 9 per day, 14.50zł); and **Warsaw** (7hr., 2 per day, 46zł). The bus station, on ul. Sikorskiego (☎21 21), is across the street from the gates to the palace park. To reach the castle and hotel, cross the street and go right. To reach the *rynek*, turn right and walk 10 minutes along ul. Kościuszki. **Buses** roll to **Rzeszów** (30min., 7 per day, 3.20zł). The **Trans-Euro-Tours tourist office,** ul Kościuszki 2, provides accommodations info. (☎/fax 30 16. Open M-F 9am-5pm, Sa 9am-1pm.) A 24hr. **ATM** is across the street. **Postal code:** 37-100.

The **Hotel Zamkowy,** ul. Zamkowa 1, is attached to the palace, and fills up fast. The rooms are clean and well priced. (☎26 71. Check-out noon. Doubles 50-75zł, with bath 75-150zł; triples 85-150zł.) **Dom Wycieczowy PTTK,** ul. Dominikańska 1, off the *rynek*, occupies the old Dominican monastery. The rooms have been renovated recently and the bathrooms are passable. Call ahead for reservations. (☎45 12. 10-bed dorms 14zł; doubles 20-23zł per person.) The *rynek* houses restaurants. Among them, **Café Antico** offers Greek (6-15zł) and Polish (3-7zł) dishes, as well as pizza (6-15zł), in an elegant setting. (Open M 10am-10pm, Tu-Su 10am-2am.) **Delikatesy Asia** sits, sparkling new, on ul. Składowa 2. (Open M-Sa 7:30am-10pm, Su 8:30am-10pm.)

POLAND

# THE CARPATHIANS (KARPATY)

The Polish Carpathians lure millions of Poles and foreigners every year to their superb hiking and skiing. Zakopane sits within walking distance of the skyscraping Tatry, while Bielsko-Biała inspires with its old town and pleasant scenery.

> **TATRAN MAPS**  For a map of the Polish and Slovak Tatras, see p. 654-655 in the **Slovakia** chapter.

## ZAKOPANE ☎ (0)18

Set in a valley surrounded by jagged Tatran peaks and alpine meadows, Zakopane (zah-ko-PAH-neh; pop. 33,000), Poland's premier year-round resort, swells with hikers and skiers to a population of over 100,000 in the high seasons (mid-June to Sept. and Jan. to Feb.). Compared to the untouchable prices of the Swiss and Austrian Alps, meals and lodging here are still reasonable. As an added bonus, the native highlander culture—which has inspired Polish writers, musicians, and artists—continues to thrive today in architecture, folk costumes, and the local dialect.

### ✦ ORIENTATION

The **bus station** is on the corner of ul. Kościuszki and ul. Jagiellońska. The **train station** lies across ul. Jagiellońska. The center is a 10-15min. walk away along the tree-lined **ul. Kościuszki.,** which intersects **Ul. Krupówki,** the dining and shopping hub. The Tatras lie to the south, and Mt. Gievont is visible from nearly every part of the town.

### ▐ TRANSPORTATION

**Trains:** Ul. Chramcówki 35 (☎201 45 04). To: **Bielsko-Biała** (3½hr., 5 per day, 23.04zł); **Kraków** (3½hr., 8 per day, 24zł); and **Warsaw** (8hr., 3per day, 52zł).

**Buses:** Ul. Kościuszki 25 (☎201 46 03). To: **Kraków** (2hr., 22 per day, 12zł); **Warsaw** (9hr., 1 per day, 48zł); and **Poprad, SLK** (2½hr., 2 per day, 15zł). A **private express line** runs between Zakopane and Kraków (2hr., 14 per day, 9zł); buses leave from a stop on ul. Kościuszki, 50m toward the center from the bus station. Look for the "express" sign. Orbis (see **Budget Travel,** above) sells tickets. Buses are a much better option than trains.

**Taxis: Radiotaxi,** ☎919, 201 20 87, and 201 42 32.

**Bike Rental: Sukces,** ul. Sienkiewicza 39 (☎201 48 44), up the street from **IT** (see **Tourist Offices,** below). Mountain bikes 25zł per 5 hr., 35zł per day. Open high season M-Sa 9am-5pm, off-season M-Sa 10am-5pm. **Marek Malczewski Sport,** ul. Bronisława Czecha (☎201 20 05), near the "Pod Krokwią" campground. Turn right, take the 1st left, and walk 100m from the campground; the shop is a hut on your right. Mountain bikes 5zł per hr., 30zł per day. In-line skates 5zł per hr. Open Tu-Su 10am-6pm.

### ▐ PRACTICAL INFORMATION

**Tourist Offices:** ▧ **Tourist Agency Redykołka,** ul. Kościeliska 1 (☎/fax 201 32 53; king@zakopane.top.pl). Provides information on impeccable private rooms (25-35zł) and runs excellent English-language tours. Email in advance for priority service. Open May-Oct. M-Sa 9am-5pm, Su 10am-5pm; Nov.-Apr. M-Sa 9am-5pm, Su 10am-1pm. **IT,** ul. Kościuszki 17 (☎20 122 11; fax 20 660 51), at the intersection with ul. Sienkiewicza. Walk right from the bus station up ul. Kościuszki, and look for a light alpine hut. English spoken. Sells **maps** (4-5zł) and arranges private accommodations (25-30zł per person). Open daily 8am-8pm.

**Budget Travel: Orbis,** ul. Krupówki 22 (☎201 46 09; fax 201 22 38; orbis.zakopane@pbp.com.pl). Sells plane, bus, and train tickets, and arranges daytrips.

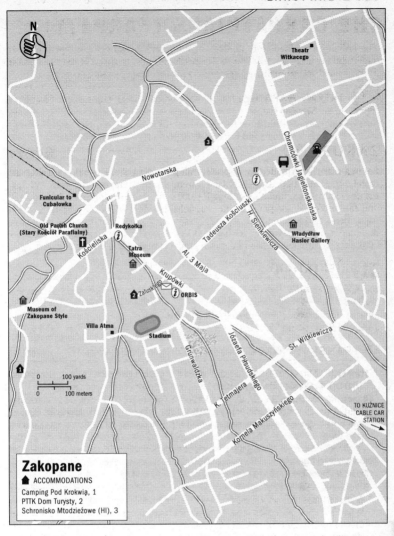

**Zakopane**

♠ ACCOMMODATIONS

Camping Pod Krokwią, 1
PTTK Dom Turysty, 2
Schronisko Mtodzieżowe (HI), 3

Open June 15-Sept. 30 and Dec. 1-Mar. 30 M-F 9am-7pm, Sa 9am-5pm; Oct.-Nov. and Apr.-June 15 M-F 9am-3pm.

**Currency Exchange: Bank PKO S.A.,** ul. Krupówki 71 (☎20 140 48). Cashes **traveler's checks** for a 0.5% commission and gives MC/Visa **cash advances.** Open M-F 7:45am-7pm, Sa 7:45am-2pm.

**ATMs:** AmEx/Cirrus/Plus in front of the bus station and along ul. Krupówki.

**Luggage Storage:** 3.95zł per day at the train station. Open 24hr. 2zł per day at the bus station. Open daily 8am-7pm.

**Pharmacy:** Ul. Krupówki 39 (☎206 33 31). Open M-F 8am-8pm, Sa 8am-3pm. List in the window posts names of other pharmacies.

**Mountain Rescue Service:** Ul. Piłsudskiego 63a (☎206 34 44).

**Telephones:** Ul. Zaruskiego 1 (☎/fax 201 44 21), in the post office building. Entrance under "Telekomunikacja Polska" sign. Phone cards and tokens sold, faxes sent, operator-assisted calls received. Open M-F 7am-9pm, Sa-Su 8am-9pm.

POLAND

**Internet Access: Internet Cafe,** Ul. Krupówki 2. 2zł per 15min. Open M-F noon-8pm, Sa-Su 10am-8pm.

**Post Office:** Ul. Krupówki 20 (☎206 38 58). Open M-F 7am-8pm, Sa 8am-3pm, Su 9am-noon.

**Postal code:** 34-500.

# ACCOMMODATIONS

During peak periods (mid-June to September, Christmas, February, and Easter), Zakopane is quite crowded and prices rise 50-100%. **IT** (see **Tourist Offices,** above) is a popular source for **private rooms** and pensions. To find your own private room, look for *pokój, noclegi,* or *Zimmer* signs. (25-30zł.) Hikers often stay in *schroniska* (mountain huts), but call at least three days in advance to avoid being stranded.

**"U Cukierow" (The Cukier Family),** ul. Za Strugiem 10. From the bus station, go right up ul. Kościuszki toward the center, turn right onto ul. Krupówki, then left onto Kościeliska. Ul. Za Strugiem is 10min. up the road on the left. Friendly highlander family provides clean rooms with original woodwork and embroidered curtains. Near hiking trails and a meadow with a view of Giewont. Curfew midnight. Reserve 3 days in advance with Mrs. Stanisława Cukier (☎206 66 29) or Mrs. Anna Puciło (☎206 29 20). Singles high season 40zł per person, off-season 30zł; doubles and triples 30zł, 25zł.

**PTTK Dom Turysty,** ul. M. Zaruskiego 5 (☎206 32 07; fax 206 32 07). A large chalet in the center of town. Walk down ul. Kościuszki from the bus station; it turns into ul. Zaruskiego. Decent-sized rooms and hot water. Check-out 10am. 4-bed dorms 19-45zł; 6- to 8-bed dorms 17-32zł; larger dorms 15-28zł.

**Schronisko Morskie Oko** (☎207 76 09), by the Morskie Oko lake, 9km from Zakopane (carriages make the trip from the bus drop-off; see **Hiking,** below). Take the bus from the station to Łysa Polana, or a direct minibus from opposite the bus station (40min.). A gorgeous, popular hostel overlooking a mountain lake and in an ideal hiking location. Check-out 10am. 3- to 6-bed dorms 35zł; 28zł in the old part of the hostel. Reception 8:30am-9:30pm. Call 1 week in advance.

**Schronisko Młodzieżowe (HI),** ul. Nowotarska 45 (☎206 62 03). From the bus station, walk down ul. Kościuszki toward the center, then take the 2nd right onto ul. Sienkiewicza and walk 2 blocks. Doubles and triples in a renovated building next door. Showers 5-10pm. Sheets 4zł. HI card required. Reception 24hr. Check-out 10am. 8- to 10-bed dorms 23zł. Doubles and triples 50zł per person. Breakfast included.

**Camping Pod Krokwią,** ul. Żeromskiego (☎201 2256; camp@regle.zakopane.pl), across the street from the base of the ski jump. From the train station, head left on ul. Jagiellońska; stay straight as Jagiellońska turns into Chałubińskiego at a 4-way intersection. Follow ul. Czecha from the roundabout and turn right on ul. Żeromskiego. Tents 9zł per person, students 7zł; bungalows 30zł per person.

# FOOD

Highlanders sell *oscypek* (goat cheese; 0.70zł), the local specialty, on the street. Watch out for anything that might spoil. Most restaurants cater to tourists and the food is priced accordingly. To escape, try the **Delikatesy grocery store,** on ul. Krupówki 41. (☎201 25 83. Open M-Sa 7am-10pm, Su 8am-10pm.)

**Bąkowo-Zohylina,** ul. Piłsudskiego 28a (☎201 20 45), has a genuine mountain lodge atmosphere, complete with animal pelts and an open hearth. Tables with an exceptional view of the Krokiew mountain and ski jump are scattered in the wild garden outside. Main dishes 7.50-22zł. Open daily 1pm-midnight.

**U Wandy,** ul. Sienkiewicza 10. Heading toward the train station from town on ul. Kościuszki, turn right on ul. Sienkiewicza. The restaurant is on the right in a private home. 3 large tables in a family dining room with books and pictures. Home-cooked meals so immense guests need help getting up. Main dishes 5-10zł. Open daily 2-6pm.

**Pizzeria Restauracja "Adamo,"** ul. Nowatarska 10 (☎201 52 90). Large portions, a great selection of Polish dishes, and 21 kinds of pizza. Friendly service and no waiters in regional costumes. Local clientele. Main dishes 7-30zł. Open daily 11am-midnight.

**Karczma Sopa,** ul. Kościeliska 52 (☎201 22 16). Walk 20min. west along historic ul. Kościeliska. Look for a barrel sign "Sopa" on the right. Live Carpathian music daily at 7pm. Highland fare 8-22zł. Open daily 4pm-midnight.

# ◣ HIKING

For outdoor fun, Poland's magnificent **Tatra National Park** (Tatrzański Park Narodowy) is not to be missed. Entrances to the park lie at the head of each trail. (2zł, students 1zł. Keep your ticket.) The best place to begin any number of forays into the mountains is **Kuźnice.** It's also possible to walk from the train station along ul. Jagiellońska, which becomes ul. Chałubińskiego. Then follow ul. Przewodników Tatrzańskich to the trailheads. The 1987m Kasprowy Wierch **cable car,** which runs to Zakopane, also starts in Kuźnice. (Open July-Aug. 7:30am-6:30pm; June and Sept. 7:30am-4pm; Oct. 7:30am-3pm. Round-trip 23zł, students 15zł.) The other popular cable car ascends **Gubałówka** (1120m) in the northern part of the city. To go up, walk north on ul. Krupówki to its end and then past the market. (Open daily 6:45am-8:50pm. 6zł.) There are breathtaking views of Zakopane from the top, and highlander huts and sheep populate the mountain slopes. You can walk down (30min.) or take a leisurely stroll west on the blue, black, or red trail to **Butorowy Wierch** (30min.) and descend on a chairlift. (Open daily May-Sept. 9am-6pm; Mar.-Apr. and Oct. 9am-5pm; Jan.-Feb. and Nov. 9am-4pm; Dec. 9am-3pm.) Before hiking, buy the map *Tatrzański Park Narodowy: Mapa turystyczna* at a kiosk or bookstore. For an overview of the Tatras and safety information, see p. 721; for more hiking info, see **Camping and the Outdoors,** p. 37.

**Valley of the Five Polish Tarns** (Dolina Pięciu Stawów Polskich; full day). One of the most beautiful hikes in the area. It departs from Kuźnice and leads along the blue trail to Hala Gąsienicowa. Refuel here at the mountain hut Schronisko Murowaniec, then continue to Czarny Staw (Black Tarn). On the incline to Zawrat Peak, you'll get to climb hand-over-hand up the chains. In the valley on the other side of Zawrat, another *schronisko* waits at Przedni Staw (Front Tarn) to shelter those exhausted by the hike or overwhelmed by the scenery. The blue trail ends 3km north, after several steep climbs and descents, at Morskie Oko, where you can eat, drink, or spend the night (see **Accommodations,** above). From the lake, a road travels 9km more down to Łysa Polana, which is connected to Zakopane by bus (an intense and long hike, for summer only). A shorter version of the hike (7-8hr.) begins at Łysa Polana. Head in the direction of Morskie Oko (see above). A green path takes off to the right about 1hr. into the hike, after the Mickiewicza Waterfall. This heads to Dolina Pięciu Stawów Polskich. Once you reach Wielki Staw (Great Tarn), head east toward Przedni Staw and follow the trail to Morskie Oko.

**Sea Eye** (Morskie Oko; 1406m; 7-8 hr.). The mountain lake Morskie Oko dazzles herds of tourists every summer. Take a bus from Zakopane's bus station (45min., 11 per day, 3.30zł), or a private minibus (6-10zł) from opposite the station to Łysa Polana. The 9km hike leads up a road that can also be covered by horse and carriage (high season 40zł up, 20zł down; off-season 20zł, 10zł). The trail is wildly popular and quite crowded, but all is forgiven when you reach the lake and the mountains surround you.

**Giewont** (1895m; 6hr.). Giewont's silhouette looks like a man lying down—hence the mountain's starring role in so many legends. The moderately difficult blue trail (7km) leads to the peak. Begin at the lower cable car station in Kuźnice and follow signs to the peak. Chains anchored into the rock help with the final ascent up some steep rocks. The top affords a great view north over Zakopane, as well as Slovakia and the highest Tatran peaks to the south and east.

**Dolina Kościeliska** (full day). An easy and lovely hike crossing the valley of Kościeliski. A bus shuttles from Zakopane to Kiry (every 30min., 2zł). From Kiry, a small road heads south toward Schronisko Ornak along a river; mountains hover on both sides and in front. It's about 1½hr. to the end of the road, and many trails lead off to various peaks and caves along the way. The valley is a popular day hike and bike route.

**Mulch Valley** (Dolina Chochołowska; full day). Take the westbound green trail from the entrance to Dolina Kościeliska at Kiry, which turns south onto a road after 3.5km. Head to the end of the road (1¼hr.) and go through a forested valley along the river. From there, a red trail takes off to Trzydniowiański Wierch (1765m), in the shadow of the Tatras, for a view of the valley. It's a longer hike than Kościeliska with fewer people.

**Red Peaks** (Czerwone Wierchy; 2122m; full day). The red trail leads west from the top of the cable car at Kasprowy Wierch (see above) along the ridge separating Poland and Slovakia. The ridge is part of the "West Tatras," a rounder, less rocky range running east of Kasprowy Wierch. Four of the 7 peaks along the way have paths that allow tired hikers to return to Zakopane. From the last peak, Ciemniak, the trail descends to Kiry.

**Rysy** (2499m; 8hr. from Morskie Oko, 12hr. from Zakopane). To claim you've climbed Poland's highest peak, follow the red trail from Schronisko Morskie Oko (see **Accommodations,** above) along the east lakeshore and up to Czarny Staw pod Rysami (Black Tarn). The arduous climb to Rysy begins in the tarn's southeast corner. Only for the fittest in good weather after mid-July. You can also tackle Rysy from Slovakia (see **Štrbské Pleso: Hiking,** p. 724) July-Sept., when the peak becomes an official border crossing.

## SIGHTS AND ENTERTAINMENT

There are seven houses along **ul. Kościeliska** built by architect and artist **Stanisław Witkiewicz** (1851-1915). Having lived here for much of his life, he invented the Zakopane style of building, characterized by tremendous ornamentation and design on the inside and outside of every building. Hugely popular, this became the Polish national style for over two decades at the beginning of the 20th century.

■ **Bandit's Hut** (Chata Zbójnicka), on ul. Jagiellońska, is by far the best place for raucous and intoxicating mountain nights. From the center, walk up Kościuszki to the bus station. Turn right onto ul. Jagiellońska and after 5min., head left up the gravel path with the big "Zbójnicka" sign. Mountain culture abounds here; enjoy an excellent shepherd's band and waitstaff who jitter to folk dances with willing partners. Some nights can get quite boisterous, as evidenced by the collection of cut-off ties and bras dangling from the ceiling. If the door is closed, beat on it. (☎201 42 17; fax 206 39 87. Open daily 5pm-midnight.) For a quieter evening, check out the cafes on ul. Krupówki. At **Piano-Cafe,** ul. Krupówki 63, burrow in a corner couch or sit at the glass-topped bar. (0.5L *Żywiec* 4zł. Open daily 3pm-midnight.)

**Air-Sport,** ul. Strążyska 13, arranges **paragliding** over the Tatras. If you've never jumped before, try a tandem jump off Nosal Mountain. (Mobile ☎(0) 60 180 03 85. 10-20min. flying time 100zł.) Natural hot springs (1600m below ground) have been turned into the swimming pool complex **Basen Antalowka,** ul. Jagiellońska 18. (☎206 39 34. Open daily July-Sept. 6am-9pm. Day pass 12zł.) During the last week of August, Zakopane resounds with the **Festival of Highlander Folklore** (Misąrynardowy Festival ziem Gòrskich), a week during which highland groups from all over the world participate in dancing and music on ul. Krupówki.

# BIELSKO-BIAŁA                     ☎(0)33

A composite of two towns that once belonged to different duchies, Bielsko-Biała (BYEL-skoh BYAH-wah; pop. 185,000) is one of the only places in Poland where two religions—Catholicism and Lutheranism—thrive side-by-side. Thanks to its religious tolerance, but also to its textile and car manufacturing industries, Bielsko-Biała continues to do well for itself. Known as "Little Vienna" for the architectural flavor left by over one hundred years of Austria-Hungarian rule, it is a diverse and dynamic community, and, with the Carpathians as a backdrop, a beautiful one, too.

POLAND

## ✴🛈 ORIENTATION AND PRACTICAL INFORMATION

Bielsko-Biała has two centers: Bielsko's castle and *rynek* (main square) in the west, and the Biała's *rynek* in the east. The latter is more commercial and is home to more cafes and shops, while the former remains a quieter and greener area that supports pubs and venues for live music. A 5min. walk along the city's main pedestrian artery, **ul. 11-go Listopada,** connects the two. To get to the Biała center from the train station, turn left out of the station down ul. 3-go Maja. After 15min., head down the stairs just past Hotel Prezydent to reach ul. 11-go Listopada. To reach Bielska's *rynek*, go a little farther on ul. 3-go Maja and turn right up Wzgórze.

**Tourist Office: Miejskie Centrum Informacji I Promocji Turystyki,** ul. Ks. Stojałowskiego 19 (☎819 00 50; fax 819 00 61; mci_bielsko@glowka.pol.pl; www.mcibielsko.pl). Follow directions to 11-go Listopada. Turn right onto Cechowa and left onto Ks. Stojałowskiego. Tourist office is over the river on the right. Sells maps, books rooms and provides general info. Open M-F 8am-6pm, Sa 8am-4pm.

**Budget Travel: Orbis,** ul. 3-go Maja 9a (☎812 40 00; fax 822 07 84). Arranges international rail and bus tickets. Open M-F 9am-5pm, Sa 10am-2pm.

**Currency Exchange: Bank PKO S.A.,** ul. 11-go Listopada 15 (☎816 52 31). Exchanges currencies at stiff rates, cashes AmEx/Visa traveler's checks for a 1.5% commission (5zł minimum), and offers MC/Visa cash advances. Open M-F 8am-6pm, Sa 9am-1pm. *Kantory* (exchange offices) congregate along ul. 11-go Listopada.

**ATMs:** Outside grocery stores.

**Pharmacy:** Apteka Pod Korona, ul. Cechowa 4 (☎812 48 93), at the intersection with ul. 11-go Listopada. Open M-F 8am-10pm, Sa 8am-4pm.

**Medical Assistance:** ☎999. Or, Emilii Plater 14, ☎812 3412.

**Telephones:** Near the post office.

**Internet Access: Cyber Czad,** ul. 11 Listopada 7 (☎822 94 14). 11 fast machines means little waiting. 30min. 4zł, 1hr. 6zł, 2hr. 10zł, every subsequent hr. 5zł. Open M-Sa 10am-10pm, Su 3pm-8pm.

**Post Office:** ul. 1-go Maja 2 (☎15 10 01; fax 81 26 900). Open M-F 9am-6pm. **Poste Restante** at window #9. **Postal code:** 43-300.

## ▐ TRANSPORTATION

**Trains:** Ul. Warszawska 2 (☎812 80 40; info ☎933). To: **Katowice** (1½hr., 27 per day, 7.80zł); **Kraków** (3hr., 26 per day, 11.40zł); **Warsaw** (6hr., 4 per day, 70.18zł); **Zakopane** (4hr., 3 per day, 23.05zł); and **Bratislava, SLK** (5½hr., 1 per day, 97.73zł).

**Buses:** Ul. Warszawska 7 (☎812 28 25). An overpass connects the bus station to the train station. To: **Oświęcim/Auschwitz** (1hr., 9 per day, 6.60zł) and **Kraków** (2¼hr., 30 per day, 15zł).

## ▌ ACCOMMODATIONS

**PTTK Dom Wycieczkowy,** ul. Krasińskiego 38 (☎812 30 19), 5min. from the bus and train stations. Turn left onto ul. 3-go Maja from the train station and right on ul. Piastowska. Krasińskiego is about 250m up on the left. Clean, spacious rooms with large windows in a quiet part of the city. Curfew 10pm-6am. Lockout 10am-2pm. Doubles 52zł, with bath 72zł; triples 75zł, 108zł; quads and quints 20zł per person.

**Youth Hostel "Bolka i Lolka,"** ul. Komorowicka 25 (☎816 74 66). From the train station, go up to the overpass and left over all the rail lines. Walk straight down the street at the end to intersection with Michata Grażyńskiego. Turn here and head left onto Zmożka, which goes across the river to Komorowicka. Named after 2 cartoon heroes, this hostel attracts schoolchildren. Some of the dorms (up to 8 beds) have TV. Sheets 3zł. Check-out 10am. Lockout 10am-5pm. Curfew 10pm. 16zł per person.

**Pod Pocztą** ("Under the Post Office"), ul. 1-go Maja 4a (☎815 16 92; fax 815 10 32). Turn left down ul. 3-go Maja from train station and walk 15min. to the post office. Upstairs from a restaurant and disco that will keep light sleepers awake on weekends. All rooms decent-sized with TV. Singles 70zł; doubles 80zł, 130zł. Breakfast included.

## ◔ FOOD

Bars and grocery stores are plentiful on and near the central ul. 11-go Listopada, but restaurants are tough to find. If you're in a hurry, stop at one of the many bars or buffet stands for a filling meal. **Savia**, ul. 11-go Listopada 38 (☎822 33 44), is one of the larger groceries. (Open M-F 6:30am-9pm, Sa 6:30am-8pm, Su 8am-4pm.)

**Restauracja Starówka**, pl. Smołki 5 (☎812 24 24), off ul. Wzgórze. Delicious Polish, French, and Chinese cuisine. The fountain at the entrance just inside the door is an indication of upscale prices. Main dishes 14-30zł. Open daily 10am-midnight.

**Pizzeria Margerita** (☎812 51 61), on ul. Cechowa. Serves 31 different specialty pizzas (7-26zł). Salads 8-11zł. Open M-Sa 11am until the last customer leaves, Su from noon.

**Kawiarnia Murzynek**, Listopada 21 (☎812 21 71), has many outdoor tables and serves pizza (11-18zł), as well as many varieties of coffee (3-3.50zł). Its central location makes it a great place to people-watch. Open daily 8am-midnight.

## ▦ SIGHTS

Bielsko's modest 14th-century **castle** stands above pl. Chrobrego. From the main tourist office, turn right up Ks. S. Stojałowskiego. Cross ul. 3-go Maja into pl. Chrobrego and turn left onto Wzgórze. The entrance is located up the hill on the square's south end at ul. Wzgórze 16. Its museum houses a collection of European paintings and artifacts from the castle's past. (☎812 53 53. Open Tu-W and F 10am-3pm, Th 10am-6pm, Sa 9am-3pm, Su 9am-2pm. 5zł, students 3zł.) The steeple of the early 20th-century **St. Nicholas's Cathedral** (Katedra św. Mikołaja), pl. Mikołaja 19 (☎812 45 06), can be seen from half the city. Follow directions to the castle and continue up Wzgórze to Rynek, then turn left down Kościelna. The church was bumped up from provincial status only a few years ago, when the Pope made the parish a bishopric. The grounds of the **Lutheran Church** (Kościół Ewangelicko-Augsburski), pl. Lutra 8 (☎812 74 71), feature Poland's only **statue of Martin Luther.** Follow directions to the castle but go straight through pl. Chrobrego up Nad Niprem. The tall towers of **Providence Church** (Kościół Opatrzności Bożej), decorate ul. Ks. Stojałowskiego 64 (☎814 45 07); turn right from the tourist office and head down Ks. Stojałowskiego. Peek in at its Baroque interior and don't miss the small gold pulpit depicting Jonah's escape from the whale.

Just a few kilometers south of Bielsko-Biała lies the sleepy town of **Żywiec** (ZHIH-vyets), home to Poland's best-known, hardest-hitting **brew** of the same name. **Trains** connect Bielsko-Biała and Żywiec daily (40min., 22 per day, 4.80zł). **Buses** also go there (40min., 10 per day, 4.30zł). Once you've arrived, the fastest and safest way to the factory of bottled miracles, the **Żywiec Brewery**, is to take bus #1 or 5 from the train station (1.60zł) to the "Browarna" stop; buy tickets at the kiosk next to the train station. **Trans-Trade Żywiec**, ul. Browarna 90, is unmistakable—a modern complex of buildings with trucks and trains pouring in and out. The brewery conducts tours only by special arrangement; call in advance. **Żywiecka Pub**, Browarna 88 (☎861 96 17), just next door, is a *piwarnia* (beer garden) that sells the freshest, cheapest beer in Poland; Żywiec products are sold at manufacturer's cost (0.5L 3zł) in a traditional setting. (Open Su-Th 11am-11pm, Fr-Sa 11am-midnight.)

## ♫ ENTERTAINMENT

**Bazyliszek Pub and Gallery**, ul. Wygórze 8, overlooks over the city from just past the castle. Original artwork adorns the walls, and the artists themselves might just be around to tell you about their work. A rattan bar serves *Okocim* (0.5L 4zł), and a back room with occasional live music and low-key patrons make the place a relaxing hangout. (Open M-Th noon-midnight, F-Sa noon-2am, Su 4pm-midnight.) Across from Banialuka (see above) sits **Café Dziupla**, ul. Mickiewicza 15, where a young crowd mixes in a pub atmosphere, complete with music, low lights, and a pool table. Moderately priced drinks (0.3L *Żywiec* 3.50zł) and live piano music on Tu at

7pm. The bar is non-smoking and the radio is tuned to folk music. (Open M-F 11am-11pm, Sa-Su 4-11pm.) Within a few days of **Corpus Christi** in late June, catch the annual **Garbus Volkswagon Rally and Show,** when enthusiastic owners celebrate by parking their beloved and specialized VW's outside the town hall on Pl. Ratuszowy.

# SILESIA (ŚLĄSK)

West of Kraków, Silesia became Poland's industrial heartland when uncontrolled Five-Year Plans guzzled the land's resources and filled the gaps with pollutants. Farther west, Dolny (Lower) Śląsk managed to staunch the bleeding, protecting its castles and Sudeten mountain spas. The regions' respective capitals, Katowice and Wrocław, reflect the varying impact of industrialization, and serve as bases for Catholic pilgrims to Częstochowa. Hikers eager to escape the industrial grime flock to Jelenia Góra, Karpacz and Sklarska Poręba, near Karkonosze National Park.

## KATOWICE                              ☎(0)32

An industrial core and business magnet, Katowice (ka-toe-VEE-tseh; pop. 367,000) is not likely to be anyone's final destination, but most travelers in Poland find themselves in this major transportation hub at some point.

**▐▀ TRANSPORTATION.** The **train station** has direct links to: **Kraków** (1½-2hr., 30 per day, 15.40zł); **Warsaw** (4½hr., 30 per day, 33.79zł); **Bratislava, SLK** (5hr., 4 per day, 112-135zł); **Vienna, AUS** (6hr., 2 per day, 142-167zł); **Prague, CZR** (7hr., 5 per day, 134.70-160zł); **Budapest, HUN** (8hr., 2 per day, 170-225zł); **Berlin, GER** (9hr., 2 per day, 106-138zł); **Lviv, UKR** (12hr., 1 per day, 115zł); and **Kyiv, UKR** (24hr., 1 per day, 200zł). The **bus station** is three blocks away on ul. Piotra Skargi (☎59 95 73). **PKS** buses run to **Kraków** (1½hr., 22 per day, 14zł) and **Warsaw** (4½hr., 1 per day, 36zł). Buses also run to many western European countries, including Austria, France, Germany, Italy, Norway, and the UK. **Biuro Podróży Daniel** offers information about international travel; other *kasy* don't. (Open M-F 9am-5pm, Sa 9am-2pm.)

**▐▌ PRACTICAL INFORMATION.** Exit the **train station** via the overpass to reach the pedestrian strip, **ul. Stawowa,** full of fast food and slightly overpriced but decent restaurants. Following Stawowa to its end at the Empik Megastore brings you within steps of the central **bus station,** which is just to Empik's left, on Piotra Skargi. There is **baggage storage** in the lower level of the train station. (1.70zł plus 0.45zł for every 50zł declared value. Open 24hr.) **Bank PKO,** ul. Chopina 1, between the bus and train stations, gives MC/Visa **cash advances** and cashes **traveler's checks.** (☎210 69 75 21 and 11 53 92 21. Open M-F 8am-6pm and Sa 9am-1pm.) To escape Katowice via computer, speed to **Supernet Internet Caffe,** ul. Mickiewicza 49, just around the corner from the bank. (☎781 58 80. 5zł per hour. Open M-Sa 9am-8pm, Su 11am-7pm.) If you're here for the night, **Hotel Centralny,** ul. Dworcowa 9, is directly behind the train station. The smoky, red-and-black decor might make you nervous, but the rooms are clean and all come with TVs and bottled water. (☎253 90 41. Singles 100zł, with bath 120zł; doubles 150zł, 180zł.) **La Strada,** ul. Warszawska 3, offers a variety of pizzas and pastas (12.50-21.50zł). From the train station, take a right and continue one block past the *rynek*. (☎253 05 30 and 206 96 36. Open M-F 11am-11pm, Sa-Su 2-11pm.) A **24hr. grocery** store is in the train station.

## CZĘSTOCHOWA                              ☎(0)34

In 1382, a haggard traveler arrived in Częstochova (chen-sto-HO-va) weary from her trials and tribulations and scarred from a scuffle with Hussite thieves. The visitor, a Byzantine icon in the prime of her life at only 800 years old, soon found refuge from the world and settled claim atop the hill of Jasna Góra, entrusting herself to the care of the monks living there. Since she moved in, the city's been defined by little other than her presence. As the most sacred of Polish icons, she draws millions of Catholic pilgrims to her bosom every year. They, and other visitors, descend upon the city to catch a glimpse of her, the famous *Black Madonna*.

## ✳ ORIENTATION

Częstochowa lies about 100km northwest of Kraków. The main **train** and **bus stations,** connected at the south end of the train station's platform #4, are near the town center. **Al. Najświętszej Marii Panny** (NMP; Avenue of Our Lady) links the stations to **Jasna Góra.** From the train station, go right onto al. Wolności to get to al. NMP. Take a left to reach Jasna Góra.

## ⁊ PRACTICAL INFORMATION

**Trains: Częstochowa Główna,** ul. Piłsudskiego 38 (☎324 13 37). To: **Katowice** (1-2hr., 32 per day, 16.80zł); **Kraków** (2hr., 6 per day, 23.04zł); **Wrocław** (3hr., 5per day, 26.88zł); and **Warsaw** (3½-4hr., 10 per day, 30.46zł). **Częstochova Stradom** sends trains to **Poznań** (5hr., 4 per day, 33.79zł).

**Buses:** Ul. Wolności 45/49 (☎24 66 16). Turn left onto ul. Wolności from the train station. To: **Katowice** (1½hr., 27 per day, 12zł); **Kraków** (3hr., 5 per day, 12-28zł); **Wrocław** (4hr., 5 per day, 18zł); **Warsaw** (4½hr., 4 per day, 28zł). **Polski Express** sends buses to: **Katowice** (1½hr., 3 per day, 17zł); **Kraków** (3hr., 3 per day, 28zł); and **Warsaw** (5hr., 2 per day, 28zł).

**Tourist Offices: WCIT,** al. NMP 65 (☎368 22 50; fax 368 22 60). Fanatically organized; provides maps and detailed info on hotels. Open M-F 9am-5pm, Sa-Su 9am-2pm. **Jasnogórskie Centrum Informacji (IT),** ul. Kordeckiego 2 (☎365 38 88; fax 365 43 43; information@jasnagora.pl), inside the monastery near the cathedral. English-speaking staff sells **maps** and English guidebooks (3-25zł), arranges monastery tours in English (100-150zł, depending on group size; it's possible to join a previously scheduled tour), and makes reservations for Dom Pielgrzyma (see below). Has a Cirrus/MC/Visa ATM. Open daily June 1-Oct. 15 7am-8pm; Oct. 16-Apr. 30 8am-5pm.

**Currency Exchange:** *Kantory* are throughout the city. **Bank PKO S.A.,** ul. Kopernika 17/ 19 (☎365 50 60), straight ahead from the train station, just off ul. Nowowiejskiego. Cashes traveler's checks for a 1% commission and gives MC/Visa **cash advances.** A Plus/Visa **24hr. ATM** stands outside. Open M-F 8am-6pm, Sa 10am-2pm.

**Luggage Storage:** At the train station. 8zł per day. Open 24hr. Also at the monastery, for a donation. Open daily June-Oct. 6am-6pm; Nov.-May 7am-5pm.

**Pharmacy: Apteka Nobia,** al. NMP 53 (☎324 68 52). Open M-Sa 8am-9pm.

**Internet Access: Centrum Internetowe,** al. NMP 12D (☎366 48 13), on the top floor of the Sklep shopping complex. 5zł per hr. Open M-Sa 9am-10pm, Su noon-10pm.

**Post Office:** Ul. Orzechowskiego 7 (☎24 44 43), between the bus and train stations. Open M-F 7am-9pm, Sa 7am-2pm. **Telephones** inside.

**Postal code:** 42-200.

## ▐ ACCOMMODATIONS

Reservations are strongly recommended year-round, but are a must for early May and mid- to late August, when pilgrims descend en masse.

**Dom Pielgrzyma im. Jana Pawla** (The Pilgrim's House), ul. Wyszyńskiego 1/31 (☎24 70 11; fax 65 18 70), outside the west gate of the monastery. A large operation run by nuns and cigarette-smoking priests. Immaculately conceived, with a crucifix in every room. Just pray for a vacancy. All rooms with bath. Check-in 3pm. Check-out 9am. Curfew 10pm. Dorms with communal bath 18zł; singles 55zł; doubles 70zł; triples 105zł.

**Dom Pielgrzyma—Hale Noclegowe,** ul. Klasztorna 1 (☎365 66 88, ext. 224), just southeast of Jasna Góra's west gate. For the ascetic pilgrim. Single-sex bedrooms and communal bathrooms. No hot water. Open May-Oct. 3- to 10-bed dorms 15zł.

**Schronisko Młodzieżowe,** ul. Jasnogórska 84/90 (☎24 31 21), 15min. from the train station and 10min. from Jasna Góra. From al. NMP, go right onto ul. Dąbrowskiego, then left onto ul. Jasnogórska. Take a right at the hostel sign and follow the alley to its end. The beds in this old school don't inspire thanks to the gods of cleanliness (or, for that matter, good maintenance), but they cushion the weary pilgrim for a decent price. Sheets 4zł. Reception daily 5-9pm. Curfew 10pm. Open July-Aug. 20zł per person.

**Hotel Ha-Ga,** ul. Katedralna 9 (☎24 61 73). A 5min. walk from the train station. Go left onto Piłsudskiego, then right onto Katedralna for 1 block. The hotel is on the right, through the gate after the Ha-Ga bar. Reasonably clean, if nothing to go ha-ga over. Check-in 2pm. Check-out noon. Singles 50zł, with bath and TV 70zł; doubles 60zł, 90zł; triples 70zł, 100zł; quads 80zł, 110zł.

**Camping Oleńka,** ul. Oleńki 10/30 (☎324 74 95), across the parking lot from the west gate of the monastery, near Dom Pielgrzyma. A sprawling complex with surprisingly clean and comfortable rooms; parties go late into the night. Kitchen facilities. Tent space 10zł per person. Triples 75zł; quads 100zł; quints 125zł, all with bath.

## ◖ FOOD

If you are supplementing your pilgrimage with a fast, Częstochowa's restaurants won't move you to temptation. Kiosks serve cheap snacks and there are endless gastronomic possibilities in the enormous **Supermarket Billa**, in the red building across from the bus station. (Open M-F 8am-9pm, Sa 8am-8pm, Su 9am-4pm.)

**Pod Gruszką** (Under the Pear), al. NMP 37 (☎365 44 90), next to Almatur in a court-yard. Popular student hangout with a small selection of salads (18zł per kg). *Żywiec* 4.50zł, *Naleśniki* 3-4zł. More of a cafe/bar at night. Open daily 10am-10pm.

**Restauracja Sphinx,** ul. Kościuszki 1 (☎366 41 85), just on the other side of NMP from al. Wolności. Nothing particularly pious about this outlet of the popular Polish chain, but it serves great pizza and sandwiches. Main dishes 6-30zł. Open daily 11am-11pm.

**Bar Pierożek,** ul. Kościuszki 7 (☎324 62 76). Cheap, basic spot serving typical Polish fare. *Pierogi* in five movements 4-5zł. Open M-F 11am-4pm, Sa noon-3pm.

**Art Caffe,** ul. Focha 16 (☎0605 523 116), near the Billa Supermarket (see above). Better for a snack than a meal. Coffee, tea, alcohol, and pizza (8-10zł). Open M-Th noon-midnight, F-Su noon until the last guest leaves.

**A. Blikle,** al. NMP 49. A dainty, deep green cafe serving coffee (2.50-4zł) and tortes (7-11zł). Open M-Th 9am-7pm, F-Sa 9am-8pm, Su 10am-8pm.

**Stacherczak,** ul. Racławicka 3 (☎24 62 35), just off NMP by the Pizza Hut. A classy Chinese establishment. Don't be put off if you have to ring to get in. Main dishes 10-25zł, including vegetarian dishes. Open daily 11am-11pm.

## ◖ SIGHTS

**Paulite Monastery** (Klasztor Paulinów), on top of **Jasna Góra** (Bright Mountain), is *the* sight in town. The monastery, which resembles a Baroque fortress, was founded in 1382 by Duke Władysław Opolczyk, who also donated the *Blessed Mother and Child* painting in 1384. The masses of pilgrims, however, are here to see the reportedly miraculous **Black Madonna** (Czarna Madonna; see "Black Madonna," below). The ornate 15th-century **Basilica** houses the icon inside the small **Chapel of Our Lady** (Kaplica Matki Bożej). Countless crutches, medallions, and rosaries strung up on the chapel walls attest to the faith of the pilgrims in the painting's otherworldly powers. (Chapel open daily 5am-9:30pm; icon revealed M-F 6am-noon and 1:30-9:30pm, Sa-Su 6am-1pm and 2-9:30pm. Free, but donations encouraged.)

The monastery also houses several small museums, all of which are free to the public (donations are requested). The **treasury** contains priceless art donated by pilgrims, including chalices, candelabra, liturgical vestments, and jewelry. The **Arsenal** exhibits weapons, military insignia, medals, and orders, including many from World War II. Wander through the **Museum of the 600th Anniversary** (Muzeum Sześćsetlecia), which commemorates the 1982 anniversary of the arrival of the icon at Jasna

**POLAND**

> **BLACK MADONNA** Jasna Góra's pilgrimage tradition dates to the monastery's founding in 1382. That year, Prince Władysław II of Opole invited Paulite monks to Poland, giving them the Jasna Góra hill and the picture that has come to be known by its 20th-century appellation, the Black Madonna. According to legend, the picture was painted by St. Luke on a plank of the table at which the Holy Family prayed and dined in Nazareth, though historians have surmised it is actually a 6th- or 7th-century Byzantine icon. She bears two scars on her right cheek—acquired, the story goes, in the hands of thieves (said to be followers of the Czech reformer Jan Hus, but more likely political opponents of the monastery's patron, King Władysław). The thieves, attempting to transport her away from her home, became frustrated with the weight of the picture and slashed her face, immediately drawing a torrent of blood. Her legend grew further following the Swedish invasions of 1655 and 1705, when the monastery remained unconquered while the surrounding countryside was overrun. Five million pilgrims come to Częstochowa each year to get a glimpse of the icon.

Góra. It also contains the Nobel Prize of Lech Wałesa and a huge collection of musical instruments. After the current renovation of the monastery is complete, it will again be possible to ascend it for excellent views of the region.

The largest pilgrimages and crowds converge on the monastery during the **Marian feasts and festivals.** These include: May 3 (Feast of Our Lady Queen of Poland), July 16 (Feast of Our Lady of Scapulars), August 15 (Feast of the Assumption), August 26 (Feast of Our Lady of Częstochowa), September 8 (Feast of the Birth of Our Lady), and September 12 (Feast of the Name Mary).

# NEAR CZĘSTOCHOWA

## TRAIL OF EAGLES' NESTS

Just when you've had it with crowded buses, churches, and regional history museums, a trip to the Trail of Eagles' Nests reminds you why you liked travel in the first place. Along the narrow 100km strip of land known as the **Kraków-Częstochowa Uplands,** numerous crags of Jurassic limestone erupt from rolling green hills. These outcroppings were often incorporated into the fortification of 12th-century **castles** built in the area, whose perches high on the rocky crags earned them the name "eagles' nests." As artillery grew more powerful, the effectiveness of the defensive walls diminished, and the fortifications proved no match for the invading Swedes. By the end of the 17th-century wars with the northern enemy, the fortresses had seriously deteriorated. Today, only a few remain whole, including **Wawel Castle,** in Kraków, and **Pieskowa Skała** just northwest of Kraków. The ruins of the rest still lie along the uplands, waiting to be discovered by trail or bus.

A **hiking trail** that runs along the entire 100km takes about seven days to trek. **PTTK** in Kraków or Częstochowa can provide **maps.** The trail is marked by red blazes, and maps are regularly posted along the way. The route leads through many small towns where hikers can find tourist info, provisions, and accommodations. The two biggest attractions on the trail, the Olsztyn Castle and the Pieskowa Skała Castle, are easy half-day trips from Częstochowa and Kraków, respectively.

Originally constructed in the 12th and 13th centuries, the ruins of Olsztyn Castle consist of upper and lower parts later flanked by two outer castles. The Swedish army ransacked the complex in 1655. In the 18th century, locals appropriated bricks from the partially destroyed castle to rebuild the local church, further reducing its glory. The sole preserved sections are in the **upper castle,** including two **towers.** Ghosts are rumored to haunt the castle; the two most famous apparitions are Maciek Borkowic, imprisoned here for his rebellion against King Casimir the Great, and a young bride lost in the dungeon. If they don't appear, there's always the spectacular view and the cows. Moo. (Take bus #58 (30min., every 2hr., 1.50zł) from ul. Piłsudskiego, across from the Częstochowa train station.)

# WROCŁAW ☎(0)71

Wrocław (VROTS-wahv), the capital of Dolny Śląsk (Lower Silesia), straddles the Oder River. Ever since the city's elaborate post-war reconstruction, only photos remind the viewer that 94% of it was destroyed by the Allies during World War II, when it became Festung Breslau under the Nazis, one of the last battlegrounds en route to Berlin. The city is developing rapidly, with construction tape and uprooted rocks strewn everywhere. Beneath the hubbub, Wrocław still charms visitors with the grace of its many bridges, parks, and refurbished 19th-century buildings.

## ◼ ORIENTATION

The political and social heart of Wrocław is the *rynek*. The **train** and **bus stations** lie 15min. southeast of the *rynek*, while accommodations cluster near the train station. With your back to the train station, turn left onto ul. Piłsudskiego, take the 3rd right onto ul. Świdnicka, go past **Kosciuszki pl.** (flanked by McDonald's and TGI Friday's) over the **Podwale river**, and into the *rynek*. The bus station is behind the trains. Alternatively, catch any tram in front of the Hotel Piast, on ul. Piłsudskiego, going toward **pl. Dominikanski**. Once at the square, head down Oławska away from ul. Janickiego for two minutes to reach the *rynek*.

## ◰ TRANSPORTATION

**Trains: Wrocław Głowny,** ul. Piłsudskiego 105 (☎368 83 33). A traveler's center with a 24hr. **exchange booth, pharmacy,** and eateries. Counters #17 and 18 handle international ticketing. To: **Poznań** (1hr., 21 per day, 26.88zł); **Kraków** (4hr., 11 per day, 32.13zł); **Warsaw** (5hr., 9 per day, 37.12zł); **Dresden, GER** (4½hr., 4 per day, 98.15zł); **Berlin, GER** (5½hr., 3 per day, 96.93zł); **Prague, CZR** (6½hr., 3 per day, 95.18zł); and **Budapest, HUN** (12hr., 1 per day, 177.02zł).

**Buses:** Ul. Sucha 1 (☎61 22 99 and 61 81 22), behind the trains. Open daily 5am-11pm. To: **Poznán** (3hr., 2 per day, 26zł); **Kraków** (destination "Krosno;" 7hr., 1 per day, 30zł); and **Warsaw** (8hr., 3 per day, 31zł).

**Public Transportation:** Tickets for **trams** and **buses** cost 1.80zł (students 1zł) per person and per backpack. 10-day pass 20zł. Express buses (designated by letters) 2.40zł. Night buses 2.80zł. Purchase tickets at kiosks; on the weekend pay on board.

**Taxis: HALLO Taxi,** ☎72 55 55 or 96 21. The trip from the train station to the *rynek* should cost approx. 12zł.

## ▰ PRACTICAL INFORMATION

**Tourist Office: IT,** Rynek 14 (☎344 31 11 and 344 11 09; fax 44 29 62). Stocked with useful **maps** (4-6.50zł) and brochures. Open M-F 9am-6pm, Sa 9am-4pm; off-season M-F 9am-5pm, Sa 10am-2pm.

**Budget Travel: Almatur,** ul. Kościuszki 34 (☎344 72 56; fax 78 18 45), in the student center "Pałacyk." Sells youth bus tickets and gives the skinny on student hostels. English spoken. Open M-F 9am-6pm, Sa 10am-2pm.

**Currency Exchange:** At *kantory* around the city and in the train station. **Bank PKO,** ul. Oławska 2 (☎344 44 54), cashes **traveler's checks** for a 1% commission (10zł minimum) and gives MC/Visa **cash advances.** Open M-F 8am-6pm, Sa 10am-2pm.

**24hr. ATMs:** Throughout the city, including one at pl. Solny 17 (Plus/Visa).

**Luggage Storage:** At the **train station.** 10zł per day for up to 400zł of declared value, 14zl for up to 500 zł of declared value, plus 2zł for every additional 100zł of declared value. Open 24hr. Also at the **bus station.** 4zł per day plus 1zł for every 50zł of declared value. Open 6am-10pm.

**Emergency:** ☎344 30 32.

**Pharmacy: Cefarm,** ul. Kościuszki 53 (☎344 82 31). Open M-F 8am-9pm, Sa 8am-3pm.

**Telephones:** Located inside and outside the post office.

**Internet Access: Cyberkawiarnia,** ul. Kuźnicza 29a (☎372 35 71; fax 372 30 58). Entrance around the corner on Nożownicza. 6zl per hr. Open M-Sa 10am-10pm, Su 4-10pm.

**Post Office:** ul. Małachowskiego 1 (☎344 17 17), to the right when exiting the train station. **Poste Restante** at window #22. Open M-F 7am-8pm, Sa-Su 7am-3pm.

**Postal code:** 50-900.

# ACCOMMODATIONS

Check with the tourist office for info about **private rooms** and **student dorms.**

**Youth Hostel (HI),** ul. Kołłątaja 20 (☎343 88 56), directly opposite the train station on the road perpendicular to ul. Piłsudskiego. Clean, secure, and spacious. Lockout 10am-5pm. Curfew 10pm. Call ahead. Dorms (and a few doubles) 20zł per person.

**Hotel Podróżnik,** ul. Sucha 1 (☎373 28 45), upstairs from the bus station. Great deal for the money, especially for groups. Rooms with TV and fan. Singles 88zł; doubles 130zł; triples 162zł; quads 196zł. Breakfast included.

**Dom Nauczyciela,** ul. Nauczycielska 2 (☎22 92 68; fax 21 95 02). Take tram #4 from the Hotel Piast stop toward Biskupin. Go left off pl. Grunwaldzki, then turn left again at the gas station. Singles 56zł; doubles 96zł; triples 99zł; quads 115zł; quints 134zł.

# FOOD

**Delikatesy grocery store,** pl. Solny 8/9, is near the *rynek.* (☎343 56 85. Open 24hr.)

**Bar Vega,** Rynek 27a (☎344 39 34). Two modern floors of veggie bliss. The menus differ by floor—the upstairs has an international flair. Imaginatively named menu comes with a joke phrasebook for translation. Full meals under 8zł. Downstairs open M-F 8am-7pm, Sa-Su 9am-5pm; upstairs M-F noon-6pm, Sa noon-5pm.

**Bar Miś,** ul. Kuźniczna 48 (☎342 49 63). The polar bear on the sign (and the crowds) outside point the way to this popular bargain cafeteria. Full meals 10-16zł. Open M-F 7am-6pm, Sa 8am-5pm.

**Spiż,** Rynek 9 (☎344 68 56; fax 344 52 67). Restaurant and microbrewery. Beer lovers lounge in this cool shelter on summer evenings. Stick to the pub grub, which runs 5-12.50zł per dish. Open daily 9pm-midnight.

**Tutti-Frutti,** pl. Kościuszki 1/4 (☎344 30 57). Endless ice cream desserts (4-12zł) and tortes (3-7zł). Bakery open M-Sa 9am-8pm, Su 9am-6pm; restaurant open daily 10am-10pm. Also at Rynek 22 (☎342 80 03). Open M-Th 10am-11pm, F-Su 10am-midnight.

# SIGHTS

■ **RACŁAWICE PANORAMA AND NATIONAL MUSEUM.** The 120m-by-15m **Panorama** depicts the 18th-century peasant insurrection led by Tadeusz Kosciuszko against the Russian occupation (see **History,** p. 454). Damaged by a bomb in 1944, the painting was moved from Lviv, UKR (then Lwów, POL) to Wrocław and put into storage. Officially, there were no specialists to restore it. In actuality, it was considered politically imprudent to permit the Poles to glorify independence from Russia. With the rise of Solidarity in 1980, the painting was restored and made available for 30-minute showings. Tickets are also valid for the **National Museum** (Muzeum Narodowe), in the brick building across the street. Check out the medieval Silesian paintings and sculptures, 16th- to 19th-century graphic art, and paintings by Canaletto and Grottger. *(Facing away from the town hall, bear left onto Kuźnicza for 2 blocks and then right onto Kotlarska, which becomes ul. Purkyniego. The Panorama is several blocks down on the right; the museum is at the end of the street on the left.* ☎ *344 23 44. Panorama and museum open Tu-Su 9am-4pm. English-language audio tour available. Joint admission 15zł; students 10zł.)*

**CATHEDRAL SQUARE.** (Pl. Katredralny.) The stately **Cathedral of St. John the Baptist** (Katedra św. Jana Chrzciciela) gives Cathedral Square its dignified character. Inside, a nun shows off the marble **Chapel of St. Elizabeth** (Kaplica św. Elżbiety; donation requested). Climb up the **tower** for an excellent view of the surrounding

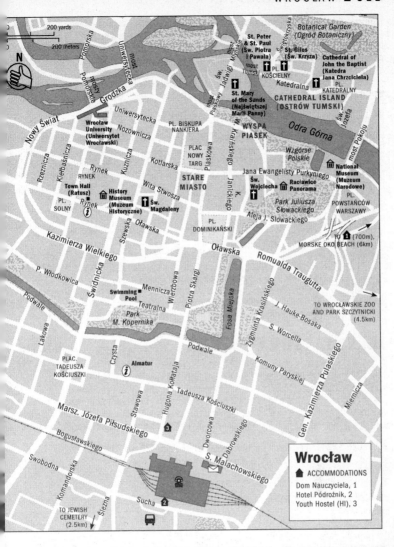

**Wrocław**

🏠 ACCOMMODATIONS

Dom Nauczyciela, 1
Hotel Pódroźnik, 2
Youth Hostel (HI), 3

churches. *(From the National Museum, turn left over Most Pokuju, then left again onto Kard B. Kominka. Open daily 10am-3pm. 4zł, students 3zł.)*

**WROCŁAW UNIVERSITY.** (Uniwersytet Wrocławski.) This center of Wrocław's cultural life houses many architectural gems. **Aula Leopoldina**, an 18th-century lecture hall with magnificent frescoes, is the most impressive. *(Pl. Uniwersytecki 1. Go down Nankiera through its name change to Uniwersytecki. On the 2nd floor of the main university building. ☎ 340 22 45. Open M, Tu, and Th-Su 10am-3:30pm. 2.50zł, students 1zł.)*

**AROUND THE RYNEK.** The Renaissance and Gothic **Town Hall** *(ratusz)*, and the **History Museum** (Muzeum Historyczne) comprise the heart of the city. One exhibit focuses entirely on ul. Świdnicka, a central street so beautiful that the Germans tried to have its stones moved. Take time to look at the collections of armor and old silver, including an amazing scepter. *(☎ 344 14 34. Open W-F 10am-4pm, Sa 11am-5pm, Su 10am-6pm. Last admission 30min. prior to closing. 4zł, students 2zł.)*

**JEWISH CEMETERY.** (Cmentarz Żydowski). Recently opened to the public, the **Jewish Cemetery** contains the remains of Ferdinand Lasalle and the family of Thomas Mann's wife, as well as fragments of Jewish tombstones dating from the 12th and 13th centuries found around Wrocław. *(Ul. Ślężna 37/39. Take tram #9 from the train station heading away from the center. Get off at the corner of Ślężna and Kamienna; go down Ślężna and the cemetery will be on your right. Gates open daily Apr.-Oct. 8am-6pm, but officially only on Su for a noon tour. 5zł, students 3zł.)*

## ENTERTAINMENT AND NIGHTLIFE

For event info, pick up *Co jest grane* (What's Playing), free at tourist offices. Wrocław is famous for its student and experimental theater; check out the **Grotowski Center,** Rynek 27 (☎44 53 20). May brings the international **Jazz nad Odrą Festival** (Jazz by the Oder) to Wrocław. Student clubs are the place to go for live music.

**Kalogródek,** ul. Kuźnicza 29B. In the center of the university district. Student crowd. Cheap beer (0.5L *Piast* 4zł; 0.5L *Strong* 4.50zł). Open daily 10am-midnight.

**Rura Jazz Club,** Lazienna 4 (☎344 33 20). Smooth jazz and an even smoother crowd have made this club well-known for years. Live music usually Tu-Su 9pm-midnight, but call ahead. No cover. Open daily 6pm-1am.

**Millenium,** ul. Szewska 6/7 (☎344 87 60), entrance around the corner. Twenty-somethings gather in this chic underground joint to hear DJs spin acid, jazz, soul, funk, R&B, and house. Open M-Th and Su noon-3am, F-Sa noon-4am.

**Kawiarnia "Pod Kalamburem,"** ul. Kuźnicza 29a (☎372 35 71), in the university quarter theater. A decadent, Art Nouveau artists' corner. Large cups of viscous caffeine 4zł. Open M-Sa 10am-midnight, Su noon-midnight. Piano concerts F and Sa at 9pm.

# JELENIA GÓRA ☎(0)75

In Poland's southwest corner, the land buckles along the Czech border to form the infamous Sudetenland. The crisp air and mineral springs in the Jelenia Góra valley have provided a welcome respite for centuries of city dwellers, including Goethe, Marysieńka Sobieska, and Henryk Sienkiewicz (see **Literature and Arts,** p. 457). At the foot of the Karkonosze range (part of the Sudety), Jelenia Góra makes a perfect starting point for treks to loftier hiking and skiing in Karpacz and Szklarska Poręba.

**TRANSPORTATION.** The **train station,** ul. 1-go Maja 77 (☎752 39 36), 15min. east of town, sends trains to **Wrocław** (3hr., 13 per day, 14.40zł; express 2¾hr., 23.04zł) and **Warsaw** (8hr.; 3 per day, off-season 2 per day; 40zł). To get to the center of town from the train station, turn right onto ul. 1-go Maja. Bear slightly right at the first large intersection and follow ul. 1-go Maja directly to Stare Miasto. The main **bus station,** ul. Obrońców Pokoju 1B (☎764 69 36), 10 minutes northwest of town, sends buses to **Wrocław** (3hr., 8 per day). From the bus station, make a left onto **Pokoju,** a right at the light, and a left onto **Jasna,** which brings you to the center. Most **buses** stop at (and many leave from) the train station.

**ORIENTATION AND PRACTICAL INFORMATION. Stare Miasto** (Old Town) is ringed by **ul. Podwale** in the north and west and **ul. Bankowa** in the south. The **IT tourist office,** Pl. Ratuszowy 2, is in the main square. The friendly staff provides brochures, **maps** (4-6zł), and advice. (☎767 69 25; ☎/fax 767 69 35; itratusz@box43.gnet.pl. Open M-F 8am-6pm, Sa 9am-1pm.) **Luggage storage** (5zł) is available at the train station. **Bank Zachodni,** ul. J. Kochanowskiego 8, the 2nd left after the train station, gives Visa **cash advances** and cashes **traveler's checks** for a 0.5% commission. **Western Union** services are also available. (☎764 62 25. Open M-F 8am-5pm, Sa 8am-1pm, Su 8am-noon.) There are AmEx/Cirrus/Plus **ATMs** outside Smok Restaurant on the *rynek* and in the train station. There is a **pharmacy, Apteka Karkonoska,** at ul. 1-go Maja 70. (☎/fax 752 33 47. Open M-F 8am-7pm, Sa 8am-3pm.) The **Internet Cafe** (at ADAX land), ul. Szkolna 3, is just off the square. (☎767 64 01. 5zł per hr. Open M-F 10am-6pm, Sa 10am-2pm.) **Telephones** stand outside the main

**post office,** ul. Pocztowa 9/10, which lies two minutes south of ul. 1-go Maja. (☎752 43 90. Open M-F 7am-9pm, Sa 8am-3pm, Su 9-11am.) **Postal code:** 58-500.

If you're visiting both Karpacz and Jelenia Góra, consider staying in Karpacz, where hotels are cheaper. Your best bet in Jelenia Góra is the cramped **Youth Hostel Bartek,** ul. Bartka Zwycięzcy 10, off ul. Kochanowskiego south of the train station. From ul. 1-go Maja, go left on ul. Kochanowskiego and turn right onto Bartka Zwyciezcy. (☎752 57 46. Reception 24hr. Lockout 10am-5pm. Knock on window if returning late. Bare-bones dorms from 20zł.) **Karczma Staropolska,** ul. 1-go Maja 33, serves tavern chow. (☎752 23 50. Main dishes 4-12.50zł. Open daily 7am-10pm.)

# KARPACZ                                                                    ☎(0)75

Going to Western Poland and skipping over Karpacz is like eating herring without vodka; both are simply unacceptable. Like nearby Szklarska Poręba, the town is an important gateway to Karkonosze National Park. Surrounding mountains throw long shadows over thickly forested valleys, and the raw beauty of the landscape—even from within Karpacz itself—is stunning.

**⌷ TRANSPORTATION.** Although there's no main station, **buses** stop along ul. 3-go Maja on the hill (see below). **Buses** head to **Jelenia Góra** (30min., 28 per day, 4.60zł).

**▉⁊ ORIENTATION AND PRACTICAL INFORMATION.** Karpacz's streets are poorly marked and follow the contours of the mountain, meandering uphill from the train station along **ul. 3-go Maja.** This main road is concealed from the station by trees—walk up the stairs from the bus station and follow the path to the left. Get off incoming buses at Karpacz Bachus and either go uphill to the Karpacz tourist office or downhill to **IT.** The **tourist office,** ul. 3-go Maja 52, **exchanges currency,** arranges private rooms (30zł), and makes reservations at hotels. (☎/fax 761 95 47. Open M-F 9am-5pm, Sa 9am-2pm.) **IT,** ul. 3-go Maja 25a, is less helpful but has indispensable English **maps** (10zł) and arranges private rooms for 20-30zł per person. (☎/fax 761 97 16. Open M-F 9am-5pm, Sa-Su 9am-2pm.) Ask at either tourist office about **bike, ski,** and **rock-climbing rentals, horseback riding,** and camping. **Bank Zachodni,** ul. 3-go Maja 43, cashes **traveler's checks** for a US$1.50 commission. (☎/fax 753 81 20. Open M-F 9am-5pm.) It also has a Plus/Visa **ATM** and **Western Union** services. There's a **pharmacy, "K-Med,"** at ul. 3-go Maja 82. (☎761 93 12. Open M-F daily 9am-8pm, Sa 9am-3pm, Su 9am-1pm.) The **post office** is at ul. 3-go Maja 21. (☎761 92 20; fax 761 95 85. Open M-F 8am-6pm, Sa 9:30am-2:30pm, Su 9-11am.) **Postal code:** 58-540.

**▛⌂ ACCOMMODATIONS AND FOOD. Private rooms** and **pensions** proliferate, especially on **Kościelna** street; the latter run 15-30zł. Unfortunately, some are open only part of the year—inquire at the Karpacz tourist office or at IT (see above) for current info. **Pension Celina,** in the center of town at ul. Kościelna 9, has all the comforts of Grandma's house. (☎761 94 55. Private baths. Breakfast 5zł. 30zł per person.) **D.W. Szczyt,** ul. Na Śnieżkę 6, is at the uphill end of town next to Świątynia Wang. Take the bus to Karpacz Wang—it's 1½ hours away. At 860m, the views from these comfortable rooms are incomparable. Make reservations at the Karpacz tourist office (see above; ☎761 93 60; 25zł). **FWP Piast,** ul. 3-go Maja 22, is downhill across the street from IT. Its spacious rooms are drab but the ping pong is free. (☎11 92 44. Meals 26zł. Doubles, triples, and quads 26zł per person.)

**Astra,** ul. Obrońców Pokoju 1, just uphill from IT, serves large, slightly pricey meals. Potato dumplings with meat and salad (8zł), salmon with fries and salad (20zł), and spaghetti (7zł) are all good choices. (☎761 93 14. Open daily 10am-10pm.) The grocery store **Delikatesy,** ul. 3-go Maja 29, stocks everything necessary for a picnic in the mountains. (☎761 92 59. Open M-Sa 8:30am-9pm, Su 10am-8pm.)

**▚⌇ SIGHTS AND HIKING.** The uphill hike to **Wang Chapel** (Świątynia Wang), ul. Śnieżki 8, at the upper end of town, takes 1½ hours but is worth it. This Viking church was built in southern Norway at the turn of the 12th century. In the early 1800s it sorely needed a restoration no one could afford, so Kaiser Friedrich Wilhelm III of Prussia had it transported to Karpacz for the Lutheran community to enjoy. Gaping dragons' mouths, stylized lions, and intricate plant carvings adorn the temple. (☎761 82 74. Open daily 9am-4pm. 3zł, students 2zł.)

**Hikers** of all ages aim for the crown of **Śnieżka** (Mt. Snow; 1602m), the highest peak in the Czech Republic. The border runs across the summit. Śnieżka and most of the trails lie within **Karkonosze National Park** (Karkonoski Park Narodowy; 1zł, students 0.50zł; 3-day pass 2zł, 1zł). To get to the summit as quickly (3-4hr.) and painlessly as possible, take the **Kopa chair lift** from ul. Strażacka just south of ul. Karkonoska, or follow the black trail from Hotel Biały Jar until you see the lift on the left. (Lift runs daily 8am-6pm; off-season 8am-4pm, weather permitting. 16zł, students 14zł; round-trip 20zł, 18zł.) From the top of the lift, the hike to the summit takes about an hour. A longer and less crowded trek starts at Świątynia Wang. Follow the blue route up to **Polana** (1080m; 1hr.), and then hike up to the scenic **Mały Staw** lake (1hr.). From here, it's 35 minutes to **Spalona Strażnica,** then an easy 30 minutes to the **Pod Śnieżką** pass (1394m); you can then ascend the peak (40min.).

Alternatively, you can take the red path up from behind Hotel Biały Jar's parking lot. Once you emerge above the tree line, it's difficult to ascend but still very manageable. The trek to Pod Śnieżką takes 2½ hours, and the summit rises another 30 minutes away. Endurance hikers follow the blue trail from Świątynia Wang to Polana (1hr.), then the yellow path to the **Pilgrims** (Pielgrzymy) stone formations (1204m; 25min.). Continue along the yellow route to another petrified protrusion at **Sunflower** (Słonecznik; 35min.). Turning left here, the red trail travels to Spalona Strażnica and Pod Śnieżką (1hr.), one mound from Śnieżka. There are two routes from Pod Śnieżką to the very top. The red **Zygzag** shoots straight up the north side; look for the cobblestone path (20-30min.). The blue trail, **Jubilee Way,** winds around the peak (1hr.). Once there, there's a fee to climb to the **observatory.** (Open daily 9am-5pm; off-season 9am-3pm. 2zł, students 1zł.)

# GREATER POLAND (WIELKOPOLSKA)

A train ride through the *Wielkopolski* lowlands reveals green fields and rolling hills, as well as a few dense woodlands. Except for a trio of urban centers—multifaceted Poznań; Toruń, home of Copernicus; and oft-neglected Łódź—Wielkopolska is as serene as it is culturally rich.

## POZNAŃ
☎(0)61

Parts of Poznań (POZ-nan; pop. 590,000) are frighteningly well-maintained and the town square has been reconstructed all too well, but the city surges with life nonetheless. It's hard to take a step without seeing a splash of color, be it on a wall plastered with graffiti or in the coats of paint on the buildings in the Rynek. It takes a little more work to discover the cultural opportunities in Poznań, though a rich music, art, and theater scene awaits, if you seek it out.

### ✦ ORIENTATION

Almost everything in town can be found in the central **Stare Miasto** (Old Town). The train station, **Poznań Główny,** sits on **ul. Dworcowa** in Stare Miasto's southwest corner; the **bus station** is 500m down ul. Towarowa. On foot, exit the main hall of the train station onto ul. Dworcowa and follow it until it ends, then go right onto **ul. Św. Marcin.** Continue to al. Marcinkowskiego. To get to **Stary Rynek** (Old Market), the heart of Stare Miasto, go left and take the second right, ul. Paderewskiego (20min.). Alternatively, catch any **tram** heading down Św. Marcin (to the right) from the end of ul. Dworcowa. Get off at the corner of Św. Marcin and Marcinkowskiego.

POLAND

## ☐ TRANSPORTATION

**Trains:** ul. Dworcowa 1 (☎866 12 12 and 869 38 11). To: **Szczecin** (2½hr., 15 per day, 29.63zł); **Warsaw** (3hr., 19 per day, 50.69zł); **Gdańsk** (4hr., 16 per day, 33.79zł); **Kraków** (6hr., 10 per day, 37.70zł); and **Berlin, GER** (3½hr., 8 per day, 122zł).

**Buses:** Ul. Towarowa 17/19 (☎833 16 55; international ☎833 83 43). No regular buses to major Polish cities. To: **Berlin, GER** (6½hr., 2 per week, 90zł) and **Paris, FRA** (18hr., 8 per week, 379zł). International office open M-F 9am-6pm, Sa 9am-1pm.

**Public Transportation: Tram** and **bus** tickets are sold in blocks of time rather than per ride: 10min. 0.90zł; 30min. 1.80zł; 1hr. 2.80zł. Prices double 11pm-4am. Tickets can be purchased at the Glob-Tour office in the train station or at the ubiquitous Ruch kiosks. 50zł fine for riding ticketless.

**Taxis: Radio Taxi** (☎919, 951, and 96 66).

## ▨ PRACTICAL INFORMATION

**Tourist Offices: Glob-Tour,** ul. Dworcowa (☎/fax 866 06 67), in the main lobby of the train station. Tourist info in English, maps (6zł), and **currency exchange.** Open 24hr. **Centrum Informacji Turystycznej (CIT),** Stary Rynek 59 (☎852 61 56), sells maps (6zł) and provides English accommodations info. Open M-F 9am-5pm, Sa 10am-2pm.

**Currency Exchange: Bank PKO S.A.,** ul. Św. Marcin 52/56 (☎855 85 58), has excellent rates and cashes traveler's checks for a 1% commission. Cirrus/Plus **ATM** inside. Open M-F 8am-6pm, Sa 10am-2pm. There are numerous *kantory* and banks in the city, especially on ul. Św. Marcin.

**Luggage Storage:** At the train station, opposite Glob-Tour. 2zł plus 0.15% of every 10zł of declared value. Open 24hr. with breaks from 7:45-8:15am and 7:45-8:15pm. Also in lockers at the train station. 8zł for a large bin, 4zł for a small one.

**International Bookstores: Omnibus Bookstore,** ul. Św. Marcin 39 (☎853 61 82). Open M-F 10am-7pm, Sa 10am-4pm. AmEx/MC/Visa. **Księgarnia Powszechna,** Stary Rynek 67 (☎851 82 07). Open M-Sa 11am-10pm, Su noon-9pm.

**24hr. Pharmacy: Apteka Centralna,** ul. 23 Lutego 18 (☎852 26 25).

**Medical Assistance:** Hospital at ul. Szkolna 8/12 (☎999 and 852 72 11).

**Internet Access: Internet Club,** ul. Garncarska 10 (☎853 78 18), to the right off Św. Marcin just past Hotel Royal. 5zł per 30min., 7zł per hr. Open M-Sa 10am-10pm. **Internet Club,** Plac Wolności 8 (☎852 79 33), across from Empik on the 2nd floor. 6zł per hr. Open daily 10am-10pm.

**Post Office:** ul. Kościuszki 77 (☎53 67 43). Open M-F 7am-9pm, Sa 8am-7pm, Su 9am-5pm. The branch next to the train station is open 24hr.

**Postal code:** 61-890.

## ▐ ACCOMMODATIONS

During its fairs (Mar., June, Oct.), the city fills quickly with tourists and businessmen, and prices rise 10%. During these times, getting a decently priced room without calling ahead is virtually impossible. For **private rooms** contact **Przemysław,** ul. Głogowska 16. (☎866 35 60; fax 866 51 63. Singles 37zł, during fairs 68zł; doubles 58zł, 96zł. Open M-F 8am-6pm, Sa 10am-2pm; closed some Sa in July and Aug.)

**Schronisko Młodzieżowe (HI),** ul. Berwińskiego 2/3 (☎866 40 40). Exit the train station through the tunnel toward McDonald's and turn left onto ul. Głogowska; ul. Berwińskiego is the 2nd street on the right. 52 beds in an old school. Sheets 4zł. Reception 5-9:30pm. Lockout 10am-5pm. Curfew 10pm. Dorms 18zł; doubles 22zł.

**Hotel Dom Turysty,** Stary Rynek 91 (☎/fax 852 88 93). Entrance on ul. Wroniecka. Exploit the cheap dorms of this upscale inn right on Stary Rynek. English spoken. Check-in noon; check-out 10am. Dorms without showers 50zł; singles with bath 150zł; doubles 160zł, with bath 240zł. Breakfast included. MC/Visa.

# 🍴 FOOD

There are several **24hr. grocery stores.** Try **Prospero,** ul. Wielka 18, for "just one more" bottle of *Lech Premium* (2.60zł). In summer, enjoy the fruits of local farms at the **outdoor market,** in the courtyard where ul. 23 Lutego meets Stary Rynek.

**Restauracja Sphinx,** ul. Św. Marcin 66/72 (☎852 07 02). Huge portions of middle-eastern main dishes and not-so-middle-eastern pizza. Only the sphinx can explain the forest decor. Main dishes 8-47zł, pizzas 8-15zł, salads 7-9zł. Open daily 10:30am-midnight; the attached **Sphinx burger** is open 24hr. 2nd branch at Stary Rynek 77.

**Bar Mleczny Pod Kuchcikiem,** ul. Św. Marcin 75. Traditional Polish food at unbeatable prices. Main dishes 1-3zł. Open M-F 8am-7pm, Sa 8am-4pm, Su 10am-4pm.

**Ali Baba,** on the corner of ul. 3 Maja and pl. Cyryla Ratajskiego. This middle-eastern joint is particularly popular late at night. Newly renovated interior and tasty kebabs. Main dishes 3.50-13zł; salads 4zł per 150g. Open 24hr.

# 👁 SIGHTS

Opulent 15th-century merchant homes, notable for their rainbow paint-jobs, line **Stary Rynek.** The houses surround the **town hall** (*ratusz*), a multicolored gem widely deemed the finest secular Renaissance structure north of the Alps. In front of town hall stands the **1535 whipping post,** whose construction was funded with fines levied on maids for their *risqué* garb. Nearby is the city's most interesting museum, the **Museum of Musical Instruments** (Muzeum Instrumentów Muzycznych), Stary Rynek 45/47. The collection's star, Chopin's piano, is backed by a chorus of instruments from Polynesia and Africa and an orchestra of antique instruments. (☎52 08 57. Open Tu 10am-5pm, W-Sa 9am-5pm, Su 11am-4pm. 5.50zł, students 3.50zł.)

In **Ostrów Tumski,** the oldest part of town, stands the first Polish cathedral, **Cathedral of St. Peter and St. Paul** (Katedra Piotra i Pawła), encircled by 15 chapels. The original church was built in 968, soon after the first Polish bishopric was established in Poznań. Lost to fire in 1945, it was rebuilt after the war in a neo-Gothic style. The tombs of two famous Piasts are in the **Golden Chapel** (Kaplica Złota): Prince Mieszko I (d. 992) and his oldest son, Bolesław Chrobry (the Brave; d. 1025), the first king of Poland. (Open to tourists daily 9am-4pm, except during mass. Entrance to crypt 2zł, students 1zł.) One of the most visible sights on ul. Św. Marcin hearkens from more recent history. The **park** on pl. Mickiewicz commemorates a 1956 clash over food prices between workers and government troops; 76 people died in the conflict. Two stark crosses knotted together with steel cable are emblazoned with the dates of workers' uprisings throughout Poland. An electronic recording tells the story from a console in front of the monument. (Free and in the language of your choice.) In the hot summer months, escape to **Malta Lake** (Jezioro Maltańskie). From the train station, take tram #6 eastbound to Rondo Środka.

# 🎭 ENTERTAINMENT

Poznań's music and theater scene is lively but mercurial. The monthly *Poznański Informator Kulturalny, Sportowy i Turystyczny (IKST)* contains many useful phone numbers and a supplement in English on all cultural events. (3.90zł; sold at bookstores and some kiosks.) The **Towarzystwo Muzyczne im. Henryka Wieniawskiego** (Music Society), ul. Świętosławska 7, provides concert info. (☎852 26 42; fax 852 89 91. Open M-F 9am-7pm.) It hosts the huge **International Theater Festival** at Malta Lake in late June and early July. **Centrum Informacji Miejskiej,** ul. Ratajczka 44, next to the Empik Megastore, provides info about cultural events and sells tickets. (☎94 31 or 851 96 45. Open M-F 10am-7pm, Sa-Su 10am-5pm.)

POLAND

## ☒ NIGHTLIFE

**The Dubliner,** ul. Św. Marcin 80/82 (☎853 60 81, ext. 147). Enter on al. Niepodłe-głości. A large, friendly pub with a devoted following. Irish food 8-20zł. Guinness 12zł, *Lech 8zł.* Live music in summer, Th-Sa 10pm. Open M-F noon-midnight or last guest, Sa-Su 4pm-midnight or last guest.

**Dziedziniec Zamkowy** (☎985 360 81 ext. 166), in the courtyard of the Zamek, just past The Dubliner. A backyard party without the house to trash. Tap the keg for 4zł per glass. Occasional rock shows (prices vary). Open daily 1pm until the last guest leaves.

**Stajenka Pegaza** (☎851 64 18), corner of ul. Fredry and ul. Wieniawskiego. The mix of fun-loving locals, tourists, and numerous draft beers more than make up for the remote location. Bring your favorite tape; they'll play it for you. *Żywiec 4.50zł.* Open M-F from 11am until last customer leaves, Sa noon, Su 3pm.

**Blue Note Poznań Jazz Club,** (☎/fax 851 04 08), entrance on ul. Kościuszki. 2 floors, 2 bars, large dance floor, and New Orleans eats. Live music: Su-W blues, rock, hip-hop, or flamenco; Th acid jazz, soul, or funk; F-Sa jazz concerts (cover 10-25zł). Open M-Sa from 5pm, Su from 7pm.

## ▐▌ DAYTRIP FROM POZNAŃ

### GNIEZNO

*Trains arrive from Poznań (50min., 35min. express; 21 per day; 7.80zł, 18.50zł express) and Toruń (1hr., 7 per day, 10.40zł). Buses arrive from Poznań (30min.-2hr., depending on the number of stops, 37 per day, 7.70zł) and Toruń (1hr., 1 per day, 15zł). To reach the rynek and the cathedral, head out of the train station onto ul. Lecha. Turn left onto ul. Chrobrego and follow the signs (10min.).*

Legend has it that Gniezno (g-NYEZ-no; "nest") was built as a perch by Lech, the mythical founder of Poland. With the refurbishments completed for the Pope's visit in June 1997, Gniezno is more charming than ever. Tourists (Papal and otherwise) continue to come to see the massive **Gniezno Cathedral** (Katedra Gnieźnieńska), at the end of ul. Chrobrego, past the *rynek* and a short walk up ul. Tumska. The first Polish king, **Bolesław Chrobry** (the Brave), was crowned here in 1025, 25 years after Gniezno had become the seat of Polish archbishops (see **History,** p. 454). The town was Poland's capital until it was razed by Czechs in 1038; the cathedral continued to host coronations into the 14th century. A forbidding statue of Bolesław (you'll recognize him from the 20zł note) guards the cathedral on the west side. Above the altar, in the archway, a 1430 crucifix hovers over parishioners. The true highlight, however, is not so easily spotted. Buy a ticket to see the 12th-century **bronze doors,** whose 18 bas-reliefs depict the life and martyrdom of St. Aldabert (Św. Wojciech), whose remains rest here. Light coming in at odd angles illuminates the side altars but leaves the main altar, with its ornate spiraling columns, dark and somber. (1.20zł, students 0.90zł. It costs an extra 8zł for a mandatory tour of the doors, but since the guides do not speak English, it's worth negotiating this point. Open M-Sa 10am-5pm, Su 1:30-5:30pm. English displays at the back 2zł.) Gniezno's other main attraction is the **Museum of the Origins of the Polish State** (Muzeum Początków Państwa Polskiego), ul. Kostrzewskiego 1, on the opposite end of Lake Jelonek from the cathedral. To get there, follow Bolesław's gaze down the hill from the cathedral to the lake and walk around it in either direction. Housed in a hideous Soviet building, the main exhibit hall features a display with ancient artifacts, weapons, books, and scale models of buildings and cities. (☎/fax 426 46 41. English captions. Open May-June Tu-Su 9am-6pm, otherwise Tu-Su 10am-5pm. 4zł, students 2.50zł; Su free.) The best way to return to the *rynek* and the stations is to backtrack along the lake; following the signs outside the front of the museum will lead you along a far less scenic (and much longer) stretch of highway.

# TORUŃ ☎ (0)56

Toruń (pop. 210,000) extols itself as the birthplace and childhood home of Mikołaj Kopernik, a.k.a. Copernicus, the man who "stopped the sun and moved the Earth" (see **History**, p. 454). After strolling the medieval cobblestoned streets, visiting the museum, and resting on the promenade along the river, you'll wonder why he ever left. In the city center, parishioners pray in 500-year-old churches and children play in the ruins of a Teutonic castle. All the while, life moves on in a place that has successfully matured into a modern city without losing its medieval charm.

## ◆ ORIENTATION

The main **train station**, Toruń Główny, lies across the Wisła (Vistula) River from most of the city. **Buses** #22 and 27 cross the river to the center; as you exit the main hall of the station, take the tunnel just outside and to your left. To find the **tourist offices**, get off at pl. Rapackiego, the first stop across the river. Head away from the bus and through the little park; **PTTK** will be on the left, while **IT**, in the town hall in the center of the square, is farther down on ul. Różana. On foot, take ul. Kujawska left from the train station, turn right onto al. Jana Pawła II, and hike over the Wisła. Pl. Rapackiego is on the right, after ul. Kopernika. To reach the center from the **bus station**, walk through the park to ul. Uniwersytecka. Take a left onto Uniwersytecka and follow it until it intersects with Wały Gen. Sikorskiego. Head right onto Sikorskiego until pl. Teatralny. At pl. Teatralny, turn left onto ul. Chełmińska, which leads to **Rynek Staromiejski** (Old Town Square). Most of the town's sights are here or in **Rynek Nowomiejski** (New Town Square). From Rynek Staromiejski, take ul. Szeroka and veer left onto ul. Krolowej Jadwigi to reach Rynek Nowomiejski.

## ▭ TRANSPORTATION

**Trains: Toruń Główny,** ul. Kujawska 1 (☎94 36). To: **Poznań** (2½hr., 4 per day, 15.60zł); **Gdańsk** (3hr., 6 per day, 29.63zł); **Warsaw** (3½hr., 5 per day, 30.46zł); **Szczecin** (5hr., 1per day, 35.46zł); and **Kraków** (7hr., 3 per day, 37.70zł). International *kasa* sells Wasteels and Interrail. Open M-F 7am-5pm, Sa-Su 7am-2pm.

**Buses: Dworzec PKS,** ul. Dąbrowskiego 26, (☎655 53 33). To: **Poznań** (3hr., 1 per day, 21zł); **Gdańsk** (3½hr., 2 per day, 28zł); **Warsaw** (4hr., 5 per day, 32zł); and **Szczecin**

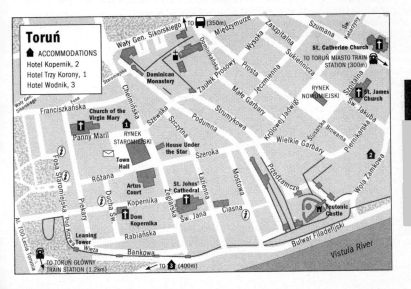

Toruń

**ACCOMMODATIONS**
Hotel Kopernik, 2
Hotel Trzy Korony, 1
Hotel Wodnik, 3

(5½hr., 1 per day, 42zł). **Polski Express** buses run from pl. Teatralny to: **Warsaw** (3½hr., 14 per day, 30-37zł) and **Szczecin** (5½hr., 2 per day, 36zł). Tickets at the Kolporter kiosk or at **Orbis** (see below). Students and seniors 30% off Tu-Th.

**Public Transportation:** Buy tickets at Ruch kiosks. Punch them at both ends when you board; students punch one end. (1.30zł; large luggage requires its own ticket.)

**Taxis: Radio Taxi,** ☎91 91 through 91 99; 91 96 for wheelchair-accessible transport. 4zł plus 1.60zł per km.

# ▋ PRACTICAL INFORMATION

**Tourist Offices: IT,** Rynek Staromiejski 1 (☎621 09 31; fax 621 09 30; www.it.torun.pl), in the Old Town Hall. English-speaking staff dispenses info and arranges accommodations. Sells maps (5.50zł). Open M and Sa 9am-4pm, Tu-F 9am-6pm, Su 9am-3pm; Sept.-Apr. closed Su. **PTTK,** pl. Rapackiego 2 (☎622 49 26; fax 622 82 28). Maps and brochures 3-6zł. 2hr. English city tour 110zł. Open M-F 8am-5pm, Sa 9am-1pm.

**Budget Travel: Kompas,** ul. Kopernika 5 (☎621 05 87; fax 621 00 16). Buy your train tickets here to avoid long lines. Also sells international bus and plane tickets. English spoken. Open M-F 9am-5pm, Sa 10am-1pm. **Orbis,** ul. Mostowa 7 (☎655 48 63; fax 654 91 44). Plane, rail, and bus tickets. Open M-F 9am-5pm, Sa 10am-2pm.

**Currency Exchange: Bank PKO,** ul. Kopernika 38 (☎621 09 15), cashes AmEx/Visa **traveler's checks** for a 1.5% commission (5zł minimum). AmEx/MC/Visa **cash advances.** Open M-F 8am-6pm, Sa 9am-1pm. Private kantory exchange cash.

**ATMs:** Machines abound along ul. Szeroka.

**International Bookstore: Księgarnia Lingwista,** ul. Szeroka 41 (☎621 01 08). Mostly reference books, but some fiction. Open M-F 10am-6pm, Sa 10am-2pm.

**International Press: Empik Megastore,** ul. Wielkie Garbary 18, sells English periodicals. Open M-F 10am-7pm, Sa 10am-4pm, Su 11am-5pm.

**Pharmacy: Apteka Panaceum,** ul. Odrodzenia 1 (☎622 41 59). Open M-F 8am-10pm, Sa 8am-2pm.

**Medical Assistance: Szpital Bielany,** ul. Św. Józefa 53/59 (☎610 11 00). Private doctors at ul. Szeroka 30 (☎652 12 32). Enter around the corner on ul. Szcytna. 50zł per visit. Open M-F 9am-9pm, Sa 9am-3pm.

**Internet Access: Internet Club Jeremi,** Rynek Staromiejski 33 (☎663 51 00). 5zł per hr. Open 24hr. **Hacker Pub,** ul. Podmurna 28 (☎663 56 21; www.hacker.komp.pl). 5zł per hr. Open M-Sa 10am-3am, Su 10am-midnight.

**Post Office:** Rynek Staromiejski 15 (☎621 91 00). **Telephones** inside. Open M-F 8am-8pm, Sa 8am-3pm. **Branch** at train station open 24hr.

**Postal code:** 87-100.

# ▌ ACCOMMODATIONS

There are still a number of reasonably priced accommodations right in the old town, but vacancies fill fast, so call ahead. **IT** (see above) can help arrange rooms.

▨ **Hotel Kopernik,** ul. Wola Zamkowa 16 (☎/fax 652 25 73). Right by Rynek Nowomiejski, one of the best values in town. Pleasant, newly-renovated rooms. Check-in 2pm, check-out noon. Singles 66zł, with toilet 81zł, with bath 106zł; doubles 71zł, 91zł, 131zł.

**PTTK Dom Wycieczkowy,** ul. Legionów 24 (☎/fax 622 38 55). From Rynek Staromiejski, follow ul. Chełmińska past Pl. Teatralny to the 2nd right after the park (ul. Grudziądzka), then take a left on Legionów. Or, take bus #10 from Pl. Rapackiego to "Dekerta." Close to the bus station. Caters to adults. Basic rooms and great prices. No curfew. Check-in 2pm; check-out noon. 4-bed dorms 28zł; singles 60zł; doubles 70zł; triples 90zł.

**Hotel Trzy Koruna,** Rynek Staromiejski 21 (☎/fax 622 60 31). You can't ask for a better location. Named for "3 crowns" of Polish royals who slept here. They probably didn't sleep on futons, but then they probably didn't have TVs either. Breakfast 10zł. Singles 80zł; doubles 90zł, with bath 190zł; triples 110zł, 230zł. AmEx/MC/Visa.

**Hotel Wodnik,** Bulwar Filadelfijski 12 (☎ 622 60 49; fax 622 51 14), near the river, just left of the bridge from the train station. Bigger rooms than Trzy Koruna, with satellite TV. Huge swimming pool in summer. Wheelchair accessible. Some English spoken. Singles 88zł, with bath 125zł; doubles with bath 170zł; triples with bath 190zł. AmEx/MC/Visa.

**Schronisko Młodzieżowe (HI),** ul. Św. Józefa 22/24 (☎ 654 41 07, ext. 33). From the train station, take bus #11 for 5 stops to "Św. Józefa." Basic rooms and a self-service kitchenette. Far from the center. 100 beds in summer, 30 off-season. Sheets 3zł. Lock-out 10am-5pm. Curfew 9pm. Reception 7am-10am and 5-9pm. Dorms 14zł, non-members 16zł; 2- to 4-person rooms 20zł, 22zł; singles (summer only) 32zł, 36zł.

# FOOD

Toruń still offers its centuries-old treat: **gingerbread** *(pierniki)*. Originally sold by Copernicus' father to put his son through school, it is now hawked in various forms, including chocolate-coated and Copernicus-shaped. Ingest the genius for under 3zł. There is a **24hr. grocery store** at ul. Chełmińska 22. The large market **Targowisko Miejskie** sits behind the "Supersam," one block north of Stare Miasto on ul. Chełminska, sells everything from plastic flowers to fish. (Open daily 8am-4pm.)

**Pizzeria Browarna,** ul. Mostowa 17 (☎ 622 66 74). Huge selection and huge portions. Pizza (8-21zł) and salads (8-14zł). Open daily 11am-midnight.

**Bar Mleczny,** ul. Różana 1. The modern milk bar incarnate. Serves mostly vegetarian Polish dishes, as well as a smattering of meat dishes. *Naleśniki,* the house-specialty pastries come with berries and cream *(z jagodami i śmietaną)* or with cheese *(z serem;* 3.90zł). Open M-F 9am-7pm, Sa 9am-4pm.

**Kebab Alladyn,** ul. Żeglarska 27 (☎ 663 57 00), behind the music store. Apparently, Alladyn asked the genie to bestow Middle Eastern eats upon the gingerbread-saturated residents of Toruń. Whether he requested the aquarium is another story. Main dishes, including falafel, kebabs, and salads 4-12zł. Open daily 9am-11pm.

**Stołówka Urząd Marszałkowskiego,** pl. Teatralny 2 (☎ 621 84 49). With your back to the theater, it's to the left, just across the street. Follow the "Stołówka" sign down through the underground passageway. A frugal diner's heaven: soup, main dish, and side dish for 8zł. Open daily 8am-8pm.

**Lotos,** ul. Strumykowa 16 (☎ 621 04 97). Far Eastern specialties in a Far Eastern setting, with the requisite bamboo and a tropical fish tank. Main dishes 7-34zł; vegetarian dishes 7-10zł. Open daily 11am-10pm. MC/Visa.

**Kopernik Factory Store,** ul. Żeglarska 25 (☎ 622 37 12), and Rynek Staromiejskie 6 (☎ 622 88 32). Stock up on Toruń's delicious *pierniki* in almost every imaginable form. Gets very crowded, so be patient while visions of gingerbread dance in your head. Prices range from 0.70zł for a small taste to 26zł for the top-of-the-line historical figures. Available by the kg or in pre-packaged form. Open M-F 10am-6pm, Sa-Su 10am-2pm.

# SIGHTS

An astounding number of attractions are packed into Toruń's medieval ramparts, particularly in **Stare Miasto** (Old Town), built by the Teutonic Knights in the 13th century. Nothing in Stare Miasto is more than a few minutes walk away.

**COPERNICUS' HOUSE.** (Dom Kopernika.) The birthplace of renowned astronomer Mikołaj Kopernik (February 19, 1473) has been meticulously restored and visitors can get a peek not only into the life of Copernicus, but also of 16th-century Toruń, with a miniature model of the city circa 1550. A "traditional" 16th-century sound and light show plays in Polish every 30 minutes; you might have to wait longer for a version in another language. *(Ul. Kopernika 15/17. ☎ 622 67 48. Open Tu-Su 10am-4pm. 5zł, students 3zł. Model of Toruń 7zł, students 5zł.)*

**TOWN HALL.** (Ratusz.) One of the finest examples of monumental burgher architecture in Europe, the building dominates the old town square. The original Gothic building's four wings were built in the late 14th century, and the turrets and other elements were added later. The town hall now contains the **Regional Museum** (Muzeum Okręgowe). Exhibits include a famous 16th-century portrait of Kopernik, an outstanding collection of Polish art from the 18th to mid-20th centuries, and a large figure in an ivy diaper riding a barrel. *(Rynek Staromiejski 1. ☎ 622 70 38. Open Tu-Su 10am-4pm. 3zł, students 2zł; Su free. Medieval tower 2zł, students 1zł. No English info.)*

**TEUTONIC STRUCTURES. The Teutonic Knights' Castle** continues to fascinate visitors. The 14th-century **toilet tower** served as its indoor plumbing and as a scatological defense—back in those days, one did more than just fart in the enemy's general direction. The 13th-century castle has been in ruins since 1454, when it was burned down by burghers of Toruń revolting against the Teutonic Order. *(Ul. Przedzamcze. Open daily 10am-6pm. 0.50zł.)* To the right as you face the river, the unique **Leaning Tower** manages to hold itself up, though the 15m structure deviates 1.5m from center at its top. The defect likely arose because the original architect was distracted—it was built in 1271 by a knight of the Order as punishment for falling in love with a peasant girl. The tower doesn't lean enough to scare away entrepreneurs, who have opened up a bar and souvenir shop inside. *(Ul. Krzywa Wieza 17.)*

**CHURCHES.** The **Cathedral of St. John the Baptist and St. John the Evangelist** (Bazylika Katedralna pw. Św. Janów) is the most impressive of the many Gothic churches in the region. Built in the 13th to 15th centuries, it mixes Gothic, Baroque, and Rococo elements, giving a disjointed but rich look at the architectural development of Toruń. Its great claim to fame does not concern its design, but rather its parishioners: the chapel witnessed baby Kopernik's baptism way back in 1473. *(At the corner of ul. Zeglarska and Św. Jana. Open M-F 9am-2pm, Sa 9am-1pm, Su for masses only.)* The **Church of the Virgin Mary** (Kościół Św. Marii), with its beautiful stained glass, has a less ornate feel than many Polish churches. The chancel holds the mausoleum of the Swedish queen Anna Wazówna. The information machine (in English, 2zł) details the transition of the church from one set of holy hands to another, chronicling its life with Bernardines, Franciscans, and Protestants. *(On ul. Panny Marii. Facing the front of the town hall, it's off the rynek to the left.)*

## 🎵 🎇 ENTERTAINMENT AND FESTIVALS

**Miś,** Św. Ducha 6 (☎622 30 49), downstairs. An artistic pub that bustles and boogies. Żywiec 4zł. Live music nightly, with DJs F and Sa. Open daily 6pm until late.

**Pub Czarna Oberża** (Black Inn), ul. Rabiańska 9 (☎621 09 63). Local students favor this billiards and beer hangout. Impressive selection of imported beer. Also serves Vietnamese dishes (20-25zł). Open M-Th 1pm-midnight, F-Sa 1pm-1am, Su 2pm-midnight.

**Kawiarnia Flisacza** (☎622 57 51), on ul. Flisacza, overlooking the Wisła. Don't be scared away by the spikes and barbed wire; you're welcome to come in, nosh on cafe treats, and enjoy the dark ambience. Beer 3.50-4.50zł. Open daily 4pm-midnight.

**Stara Fabryka,** ul. Św. Jakub 13 (☎652 17 75). Rock and roll in this old bread factory. Young crowd packs 2 floors and grooves to techno F and Sa. Open M-Th and Su 3pm-midnight, F-Sa 3pm-2am.

Toruń hosts a number of festivals, starting in May when **Probaltica,** the Baltic celebration of chamber music and arts, comes to town, followed later that month by an **International Theater Festival.** In June and July, during the **Music and Architecture Festival,** classical concerts are held in different historical buildings each weekend. The **Song of Songs** festival hits town in early July. The fun moves outside with **Summer Street Theater** in July and August and the season ends in November with the **National Blues Music Festival.** For information on events, head to **IT** (see **Tourist Offices,** p. 520), which publishes a schedule for each month.

It's still possible to achieve the festival high by jumping out of the sky with the **Aeroklub Pomorski** (ul. Bielańska 66; ☎622 24 74), which offers **skydiving** and **paragliding** from 50zł per hour. If you prefer to stay rooted, gaze up at the stars with the locals who gather in cafes around Rynek Staromiejska and along the Wisła.

# ŁÓDŹ

☎(0)42

Łódź (WOODGE; pop. 825,600), Poland's second-largest city, is often overlooked for international Warsaw to the northeast or picturesque Toruń to the north. This former textile town doesn't have a single attraction that could be placed on a post-card, but after strolling down the pedestrian ul. Piotrkawska, bustling by day and raucous by night, you'll wonder how Łódź could be ignored. Site of the largest ghetto in Europe during World War II, Łódź has also, more happily, been home for years to the famous Łódź film school, responsible for such luminaries as Andrzej Wajda and Krzysztof Kieślowski. This 15th-century city has many surprises in store, but they won't come with the fanfare found in more touristed Polish cities.

## █ TRANSPORTATION

**Trains: Łódź Fabryczna PKP** (☎935) sends trains to: **Warsaw** (2hr., 11 per day, 23.04zł) and **Kraków** (3hr., 2 per day, 33.12zł). **Łódź Kaliska** (☎934) send trains to: **Toruń** (2½hr., 6 per day, 26.88zł); **Kraków** (3hr., 2 per day, 33.12zł); and **Poznań** (4hr., 4per day, 31.30zł).

**Buses: Łódź Fabryczna PKS** (☎631 97 06) is attached to the Fabryczna train station. To: **Warsaw** (2½hr., 7 per day, 24zł); **Torun** (3½hr., 4 per day, 23zł); **Wrocław** (4-5hr., 3 per day, 31zł); **Poznań** (4½hr., 3 per day, 33zł); and **Kraków** (5hr., 6 per day, 30zł). Comfortable **Polski Express** buses to **Warsaw** (2½hr., 7 per day, 21-24zł) and **Kraków** (5hr., 3per day, 33zł).

**Local Transportation:** Trams and buses cost 1.80zł (students 0.90zł) for a ride of up to 30min., 2.70zł up to 1hr. (1.35zł), 3.60zł for 2hr. (1.80zł), and 7.40zł for a full-day pass (3.60zł). Prices double at night. Buy tickets at kiosks around town.

## █ ORIENTATION AND PRACTICAL INFORMATION

Restaurants and shops line **ul. Piotrkowska,** which runs north-south through the center of town and is closed to cars from **al. Pomorska** in the north to **al. Marsz. Józefa Piłsudskiego** in the south. The city center is within walking distance of both train stations. From **Łódź Fabryczna,** the main train station, cross under **ul. Jana Kilińskiego,** the wide street with multiple tram lines, and head toward Dom Kultury, the tall white building just across the way. Continue on Traugutta past Dom Kultury for two blocks to get to ul. Piotrkowska. From the **Łódź Kaliska** station, with your back to the entrance turn right on the highway (al. Włókniarzy), turn left onto **al. Adama Mickiewicza,** which becomes al. Marsz. Józefa Piłsudskiego, and continue about 15 minutes to the intersection with ul. Piotrkowska.

**Tourist Office: IT,** ul. Traugutta 18 (☎/fax 633 71 69), in Dom Kultury, across al. Jana Kilińskiego from Łódź Fabryczna (see above). Enter in back. Free maps and info on accommodations. English spoken. Open M-F 8:30am-4:30pm, Sa 10am-2pm.

**Budget Travel: Orbis,** ul. Piotrkowska 68 (flight info ☎636 35 33, bus info ☎633 21 14). Travel bookings and accommodations, especially helpful if you're Polish and planning a trip to Florida. Open M-F 9am-6pm, Sa 10am-3pm. **Almatur,** ul. Piotrkowska 59 (☎/fax 637 11 22). Open M-F 10am-5pm.

**Currency Exchange:** *Kantori* around ul. Piotrkowska. **PKO,** al. Piłsudskiego 12 (☎636 62 44), cashes **traveler's checks** for a 1-2% commission and gives MC/Visa **cash advances.** Also at al. Kościuszki 47. Both open M-F 8am-6pm, Su 10am-2pm.

**Luggage Storage:** There is a locked storage room at Łódź Fabryczna. 4zł for a large pack; go to *kasa* #9. Open daily 6:30am-5:45pm and 7-11pm. Storage is also available at the Kaliska station.

**English Bookstore: Empik,** ul. Piotrkowska 81 (☎632 83 55). Open M-F 10am-9pm, Sa 10am-5pm. Su 11am-5pm. MC/Visa. **OxPol,** ul. Piotrkowska 63 (☎630 20 13). Open M-F 10am-6pm, Sa 10am-3pm.

**24hr. Pharmacy: Apteka Hepatica,** ul. Piotrkowska 35 (☎630 35 39).

**Telephones:** At the post office. Open 24hr.

POLAND

**Internet Access: Cybergrota Internet Cafe,** ul. Więckowskiego 20 (☎ 632 81 00). Go through the courtyard, then down to the basement. 2zł per 15min., 3zł per 30min., 5zł per 1hr. Open M-F 10am-7pm, Sa 11am-7pm. **Internet Caffe,** ul. Piotrowska 122, 2nd floor, under the archway. 3zł per 30min., 5zł per 1hr. Open daily 8am-10pm. **Kawiarnia@Internetowa,** ul. Piotrowska 101, 2nd floor. 5zł per 1hr. Open daily 10am-10pm.

**Post Office:** ul. Tuwima 38 (info ☎ 633 54 40). Open 24hr. **Poste Restante** at window #19. Open M-F 7am-9pm, Sa 8:30am-3:30pm. Fax service (632 82 08).

**Postal code:** 90-001.

# ACCOMMODATIONS AND FOOD

A number of budget options are centrally located around ul. Piotrkowska. To reach the **Youth Hostel (HI),** ul. Legionów 27 (☎ 630 66 80; fax 630 66 83), walk north (as the street numbers descend) along ul. Piotrkowska to the end and turn left on ul. Legionów. This classy establishment on the north end of town will make you feel like you're in a fancy hotel. Almost. It provides 4- to 6-bed dorms (18zł, non-members 24zł), humongous, newly renovated singles with baths (45zł), and doubles and triples (30zł per person; linen 5zł; lockout 10am-5pm; flexible curfew 10pm). The not-so-modern subsidiary across town on ul. Zamenhofa 13 (☎ 636 65 99) sparkles less, but will keep you near the action. It offers dorm beds (20zł), doubles (25zł per person), and triples (22zł per person.) To reach this branch from the main station, walk to a left on Piotrkowska, following it (as the numbers ascend) to a right on Zamenhofa. (Linen 5zł. Lockout 10am-5pm. Curfew 10pm. Not always open on weekdays, so call ahead.) A little farther down Legionów from the youth hostel, the **Hotel Garnizonowy,** ul. Legionów 81 (☎ 633 80 23), offers spic, span, and comfortable rooms. Recently renovated, it's not quite a budget establishment, but a single bed in a double (85zł) or in a triple (68zł) is actually a very good value, especially since breakfast is included. (Singles 139zł; doubles 170zł; triples 204zł. MC/Visa.) If a curfew doesn't appeal to you, but you're not willing to jump into the upscale pool, there's always **Hotel Raff,** ul. Milionowa 25 (☎/fax 684 75 10). It's straight down from the central station on tram #1, 4, 5, or 16 down Jana Klińskiego (left with your back to the station). The rooms are a little cramped and very antiquated, but it's not far from Piotrkowska and certainly won't drain your wallet. (2- to 6-bed dorms 25zł; singles 37zł; doubles 70zł. Check in 2pm. Check-out 11am.)

Ul. Piotrkowska abounds with pizzerias that dish out huge portions for under 10zł. **Presto Pizza,** ul. Piotrkowska 67 (☎ 666 31 84) goes gourmet with some of its menu including the "San Francisco," topped with peaches and bananas. (Small pizzas 7.50-14zł, large 8.50-16zł. Open M-F noon-11pm, Sa noon-midnight.) At **In-Centro Pizza,** ul. Piotrkowska 153 (☎ 636 99 92), prices are similar but tables are scarce. (Open M-Sa noon-10pm, Su 1-10pm.) **Steakhouse Ramzes,** ul. Piotrkowska 40 (☎ 633 57 11), is a celebration of meat, with portions fit for a pharaoh. The steak is quite good, for Poland. (Main dishes 7-16zł. Open daily 11am-11pm. MC/Visa.) There is a **24-hour grocery** at al. Piłsudskiego 12. For a hot beverage to wash down the pizza pies, there's Poźegnane z Afryka (Out of Africa) at ul. Piotrkowska 88. (Open daily 10am-10pm). This chain doesn't feel like one, with dark wood tables and a world of coffees (6-8zł). **Teahouses** beckon at ul. Piotrkowska 67 (open M-Sa 10am-10pm, Su 10am-10pm) and ul. Piotrkowska 123 (open M-Sa 10am-8pm).

# SIGHTS

**JEWISH CEMETERY AND SYNAGOGUES.** The most affecting and beautiful sight in Łódź, the sprawling Jewish cemetery (Cmentarz Żydowski), is the largest in Europe. There are more than 200,000 graves and 180,000 tombstones, some quite elaborately engraved; especially noteworthy is the colossal Poznański family crypt. Near the entrance to the cemetery is a memorial to the Jews killed in the Łódź Ghetto. Signs lead the way to the **Ghetto Fields** (Pole Ghettowe), where Jews who died in the ghetto are buried in small but marked graves, something the local Nazi administration insisted upon. *(Take tram #1 from ul. Kilinskiego, #15 from ul. Legionyw, or*

ALPS          ASPEN

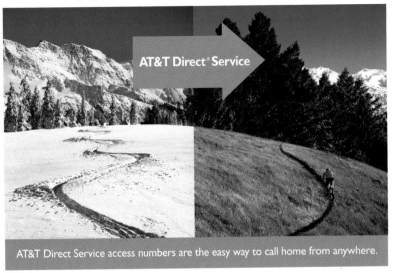

AT&T Direct® Service

AT&T Direct Service access numbers are the easy way to call home from anywhere.

Global
connection
with the AT&T
Network

**AT&T**
direct
service

www.att.com/traveler

---

# AT&T Direct® Service

The easy way to call
home from anywhere.

### AT&T Access Numbers

| | |
|---|---|
| Austria ● ......0800-200-288 | France ........0800-99-00-11 |
| Belarus × ........8♦800-101 | Gambia ● ...............00111 |
| Belgium ● ....0-800-100-10 | Germany ....0800-2255-288 |
| Bosnia ▲ ......00-800-0010 | Ghana ....................0191 |
| Bulgaria ▲ ......00-800-0010 | Gibraltar ..................8800 |
| Cyprus ● ........080-900-10 | Greece ● .....00-800-1311 |
| Czech Rep. ▲00-42-000-101 | Hungary ● ....06-800-01111 |
| Denmark ........ 8001-0010 | Iceland ● ..........800-9001 |
| Egypt ●(Cairo)‡....510-0200 | Ireland ✓.....1-800-550-000 |
| Finland ● ......0800-110-015 | Israel ......1-800-94-94-949 |

# AT&T Direct® Service

The easy way to call
home from anywhere.

### AT&T Access Numbers

| | |
|---|---|
| Austria ● ......0800-200-288 | France ........0800-99-00-11 |
| Belarus × ........8♦800-101 | Gambia ● ...............00111 |
| Belgium ● ....0-800-100-10 | Germany ....0800-2255-288 |
| Bosnia ▲ ......00-800-0010 | Ghana ....................0191 |
| Bulgaria ▲ ......00-800-0010 | Gibraltar ..................8800 |
| Cyprus ● ........080-900-10 | Greece ● .....00-800-1311 |
| Czech Rep. ▲00-42-000-101 | Hungary ● ....06-800-01111 |
| Denmark ........ 8001-0010 | Iceland ● ..........800-9001 |
| Egypt ●(Cairo)‡....510-0200 | Ireland ✓.....1-800-550-000 |
| Finland ● ......0800-110-015 | Israel ......1-800-94-94-949 |

The best way to keep in touch when you're traveling overseas is with **AT&T Direct® Service**. It's the easy way to call your loved ones back home from just about anywhere in the world. Just cut out the wallet guide below and use it wherever your travels take you.

For a list of AT&T Access Numbers, tear out the attached wallet guide.

AT&T

---

| | |
|---|---|
| Italy ● .............172-1011 | Russia (Moscow) ▶▲●755-5042 |
| Luxembourg✦ ..800-2-0111 | (St. Petersbg.)▶▲● ..325-5042 |
| Macedonia● ..99-800-4288 | Slovakia▲ ..00-42-100-101 |
| Malta .......... 0800-890-110 | South Africa ..0800-99-0123 |
| Monaco● ........800-90-288 | Spain ..........900-99-00-11 |
| Morocco ........002-11-0011 | Sweden ........020-799-111 |
| Netherlands ●...0800-022-9111 | Switzerland● 0800-89-0011 |
| Norway ..........800-190-11 | Turkey● ......00-800-12277 |
| Poland▲● ..00-800-111-1111 | Ukraine▲ ..........8✦100-11 |
| Portugal▲ ....800-800-128 | U.A. Emirates● ......800-121 |
| Romania●.......01-800-4288 | U.K..............0800-89-0011 |

**FOR EASY CALLING WORLDWIDE**
*1.* Just dial the AT&T Access Number for the country you are calling from.
*2.* Dial the phone number you're calling.　*3.* Dial your card number.

For access numbers not listed ask any operator for **AT&T Direct®** Service.
In the U.S. call 1-800-331-1140 for a wallet guide listing all worldwide AT&T Access Numbers.
Visit our Web site at: **www.att.com/traveler**
Bold-faced countries permit country-to-country calling outside the U.S.
● Public phones require coin or card deposit to place call.
▲ May not be available from every phone/payphone.
✦ Public phones and select hotels.
◆ Await second dial tone.
▶ Additional charges apply when calling from outside the city.
† Outside of Cairo, dial "02" first.
✗ Not available from public phones or all areas.
✔ Use U.K. access number in N. Ireland.

When placing an international call *from* the U.S., dial 1 800 CALL ATT.

EMEA　　　　　　　　　　　　　© 8/00 AT&T

---

| | |
|---|---|
| Italy ● .............172-1011 | Russia (Moscow) ▶▲●755-5042 |
| Luxembourg✦ ..800-2-0111 | (St. Petersbg.)▶▲● ..325-5042 |
| Macedonia● ..99-800-4288 | Slovakia▲ ..00-42-100-101 |
| Malta .......... 0800-890-110 | South Africa ..0800-99-0123 |
| Monaco● ........800-90-288 | Spain ..........900-99-00-11 |
| Morocco ........002-11-0011 | Sweden ........020-799-111 |
| Netherlands ●...0800-022-9111 | Switzerland● 0800-89-0011 |
| Norway ..........800-190-11 | Turkey● ......00-800-12277 |
| Poland▲● ..00-800-111-1111 | Ukraine▲ ..........8✦100-11 |
| Portugal▲ ....800-800-128 | U.A. Emirates● ......800-121 |
| Romania●.......01-800-4288 | U.K..............0800-89-0011 |

**FOR EASY CALLING WORLDWIDE**
*1.* Just dial the AT&T Access Number for the country you are calling from.
*2.* Dial the phone number you're calling.　*3.* Dial your card number.

For access numbers not listed ask any operator for **AT&T Direct®** Service.
In the U.S. call 1-800-331-1140 for a wallet guide listing all worldwide AT&T Access Numbers.
Visit our Web site at: **www.att.com/traveler**
Bold-faced countries permit country-to-country calling outside the U.S.
● Public phones require coin or card deposit to place call.
▲ May not be available from every phone/payphone.
✦ Public phones and select hotels.
◆ Await second dial tone.
▶ Additional charges apply when calling from outside the city.
† Outside of Cairo, dial "02" first.
✗ Not available from public phones or all areas.
✔ Use U.K. access number in N. Ireland.

When placing an international call *from* the U.S., dial 1 800 CALL ATT.

EMEA　　　　　　　　　　　　　© 8/00 AT&T

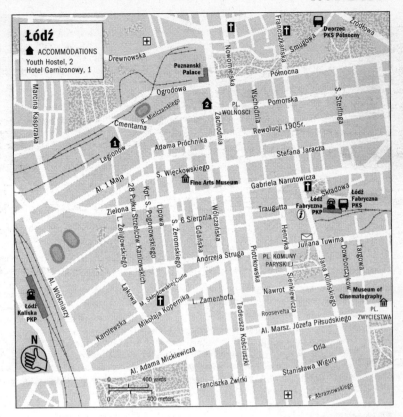

**Łódź**

**▲ ACCOMMODATIONS**
Youth Hostel, 2
Hotel Garnizonowy, 1

#19 from ul. Zachnodnia, north to Inflancka at the end of the line (30min.). Continue up the street to the first corner and make a sharp left turn onto the cobblestone ul. Zmienna before the car lot, and continue until the small gate in the wall. It is better to try this entrance than the main gate on ul. Bracka, which is usually locked for security purposes. Open May-Sept. M-F and Su 9am-5pm; Oct.-April M-F and Su 10am-3pm. Closed on Jewish Holidays. 4zł admission goes toward maintenance; free for those visiting the graves of relatives.) Back in the center of town, the **Jewish Community Center** (Gmina Wyznaniowa Żydowska) has more info. Walk through the gates and it's the second building on the right. (Ul. Pomorska 18. ☎ 633 51 56. Open M-F 10am-2pm. Services daily. English spoken.) The **old synagogue**—the only one to survive the war—is generally kept closed, but visits can be arranged through the Jewish Community Center. (Ul. Rewolucji-1905 28.)

**MUSEUM OF CINEMATOGRAPHY.** (Muzeum Kinomatografii.) International film giants Andrzej Wajda, Krzysztof Kieślowski, and Roman Polański (see **Literature and Arts,** p. 457) all got their start at Łódź's famous film school. They are now immortalized in the Museum of Cinematography, which is housed in a mid-19th-century mansion on al. Piłsudskiego. Rotating exhibits on Polish filmmaking are also featured, and local troupes occasionally put on productions here. (Pl. Zwycięstwa 1. Take tram #25 from al. Kosciuszki and get off when you see a park on your right. Tel. 674 09 56. Open Tu-F 10am-2:30pm, Sa-Su 11am-2:30pm. Closed last Su of the month. 3zł.)

**POZNAŃSKI PALACE.** A block northwest of the monument at **pl. Wolności,** which crowns the northern end of ul. Piotrkowska, stands the grandiose Poznański Palace, named for a family of wealthy Jewish industrialists who lived there in the late 19th and early 20th centuries. The ornate gray building houses the **Łódź Historical Museum** (Muzeum Historii Miasta Łódzi), which begins in the vast and beautiful pal-

**THE LUCKY FEW**   Established in 1940 as the largest Jewish ghetto in Łódź's ghetto was remarkably lucky (as far as ghettoes go) during World War II. For the early part of the war, the ghetto doubled as a giant Nazi textile factory, supplying winter uniforms for German soldiers in Russia. As Nazi-controlled ghettoes throughout Europe were being liquidated in 1942, only the elderly, the infirm, and the young children of Łódź were deported to concentration camps; the ghetto had become too valuable as a source of labor for the Nazis to destroy. By 1944, it was the last remaining ghetto in Poland. As the Red Army loomed only 150km away in August 1944, though, the Nazis decided it was time to liquidate the Łódź ghetto; its 70,000 residents were deported to Auschwitz, Birkenau, and Majdanek. 800 "lucky" Jews remained as a cleaning crew, but as the Russians were about to capture Łódź, the Nazis decided to execute the remaining few and built a mass grave in anticipation. Fortunately, the swift advance of the Russians interrupted the execution, and the 800 ghetto residents were saved. Of those deported to concentration camps, some 20,000 survived—the highest number of survivors of any European ghetto. Their fortune was due to their late deportation; by the end of the war, the death camps were quickly declining in murderous "efficiency." Those interested in exploring the ghetto (many of whose buildings are still standing) or in seeking the graves of relatives buried in the Ghetto's Jewish Cemetery should contact the Jewish community center.

ace dining room and has exhibits on Łódź's famous sons and daughters, including pianist Artur Rubenstein. (see **Literature and Arts,** p. 458) *(Ul. Ogrodowa 15. Tel. 654 03 23; fax 654 02 02. Open Tu and Th-Su 10am-2pm, W 2-6pm. 4zł, students 2zł. Su free.)*

**ŁÓDŹ FINE ARTS MUSEUM.** (Muzeum Sztuki w Łódźi.) The premier art collection in Łódź, the museum is home to 20th-century works by artists like Stanisław Wiłkiewicz, Henryk Stażewski, and Władysaw Strzeminski, as well as foreigners like Piet Mondrian and Max Ernst. *(Ul. Więckowskiego 36. Four blocks west of ul. Piotrkowska along ul. Więckowskiego. ☎ 674 96 98; fax 674 99 82. Open Tu 10am-5pm, W and F 11am-5pm, Th noon-7pm, Sa-Su 10am-4pm. 5zł, students 3zł; Tu-Th free.)*

 **NIGHTLIFE**

Łódź knows how to party. Piotrkowska, by day a pedestrian pizza and shopping drag, turns into publand a little after nine o'clock and there are plenty of places to throw back a drink or get your rump-shakin' groove on. At ■**Łódź Kaliska,** ul. Piotrkowska 102 (☎ 630 69 55), the packed crowd screams "hip" in unison. It sports two floors, two bars, more than your average number of pairs of capri pants, and bathrooms with tinted glass walls that let you keep one eye on the barstools and the other on the business at hand. (Draught beer 6zł.) For a little more of a low-key, younger crowd, head underground to the **Tunel Pub,** ul. Piotrkowska 80 (☎ (0)602 45 58 45). Students sit under a black light, sipping, smoking, or catching part of the game. Later in the night, the Tunel's neighbor, **Klub Fabryka,** also at ul. Piotrkowska 80 (☎ 630 16 44) starts kicking. The factory theme plays itself out with enormous metal doors and a warehouse atmosphere. Don't expect assembly lines; you'll get only pumping music and grinding dancers (open daily from 5pm).

# POMORZE

Pomorze, literally "along the sea," encompasses the murky swamps and windswept dunes of the Baltic Coast. In the face of shifting sands and treacherous bogs, fishermen built villages here millennia ago. A few hamlets grew into large ports—Szczecin on the lower Odra River is the largest, while others like Świnoujście are building themselves up around their shoreline assets. Meanwhile, Woliński National Park shelters hiking trails and bison from the ills of tourism and industry.

# SZCZECIN

☎ (0)91

Strategically situated on the Oder River, the port of Szczecin (SHCHEH-chin; pop. 420,000) has been the site of centuries of power plays, controlled by Sweden, Prussia, and finally Poland. Primarily an industrial and business center, the city serves as a major transport hub, and its railways and waterways now sprawl kilometers from the center. Think twice, though, before you leave Szczecin to the businessmen and economists. Rows of historic buildings and dense woods just out of town beautify this bustling boomtown, while the friendly attitude of the residents and the availability of budget accommodations encourage backpackers to visit.

**☐ TRANSPORTATION.** The train station, **Szczecin Główny**, sits at the end of ul. 3-go Maja. The the center of town is within walking distance, but for a quick ride into the city, take tram #3 toward "Las Arkoński." Trains run to: **Świnoujście** (2hr., 15 per day, 21.12zł); **Poznań** (3hr., 12 per day, 29.63zł); **Gdynia** (5hr., 5 per day, 35.46zł); **Toruń** (5hr., 1 per day, 35.46zł); **Warsaw** (5hr., 6 per day, 65.27zł); **Gdańsk** (5½hr., 5 per day, 37.12zł); and **Berlin, GER** (2hr., 4 per day, 82.81zł, under 26 72.67zł). The bus station sits on pl. Tobrucki, 2min. by foot from the train station. Exit left out of the main hall and take the 1st left up the hill. Purchase tickets at the station, through Orbis (see below), or on the buses from drivers. Buses run to: **Świnoujście** (2½-3½hr., 3 per day, 14.40zł) and **Toruń** (6½hr., 1 per day, 42zł). **Polski Express** buses to **Warsaw** and international destinations like **Berlin, GER**, and **London, BRI** leave from the train station. Tickets are available in **Euro ster**, the international coach lines office, in the main hall (☎/fax 88 41 37; open M-F 9am-5pm) or from **Orbis** (see below). The city's numerous **tram** and **bus** lines run along major roads. Tickets are sold in blocks of time rather than per ride (1zł per 10min., 1.50zł per 20min., 1.80zł per 40min., and 3.60zł per 2hr.; 5.10zł for all rides after 11pm). Schedules and tickets are available at kiosks around town. For a cab, try **Teletaxi Fullserwis** (☎ 9629).

**▨ ▨ ORIENTATION AND PRACTICAL INFORMATION.** Szczecin sits at the mouth of the **Oder River**. You'll need a map, so visit a tourist office; get off the train at the **Szczecin Główny** train station (the bus stop is a block away) and walk out the front of the station, which faces the river. Go left and the street turns into **ul. Dworcowa**. The main **tourist office** is just up the hill on the right. **Al. Niepodległości** stretches past the office to the right and heads to **pl. Brama Portowa**, the center of Szczecin and the best starting point for a tour of its sights. The English-speaking staff at **Centrum Informacji Turystycznej (CIT)**, al. Niepodległości 1, sells maps (7zł) and makes hotel reservations. (☎ 434 04 40; fax 433 84 20. Open M-F 9:30am-5pm, Sa 10am-2pm.) **Centrum Informacji Kulturalnej i Turystycznej (CIKiT)**, ul. Korsarzy 34, in the castle, provides English info about accommodations and events. (☎ 489 16 30, fax 434 02 86; cikit@zamek.szczecin.pl. Open daily 10am-6pm.) **Orbis**, pl. Zwycięstwa 1, sells bus, plane, and train tickets and exchanges currency. (☎ 434 44 25. Open M-F 10am-6pm, Sa 10am-2pm.) **Bank PKO**, pl. Żołnierza Polskiego 16, cashes all major **traveler's checks** for a 1-2% commission and gives AmEx/MC/Visa **cash advances**. (☎ 440 06 23. Open M-F 8am-6pm, Sa 10am-2pm.) *Kantory* have similar rates. **ATMs** are all over town. **Store luggage** downstairs by the exit to the platforms at the train station. (2zł, plus 0.50zł for every 50zł of declared value. Open 6am-10pm.) There's a **24hr. pharmacy** at ul. Więckowskiego 1/2. (☎ 434 26 27. Ring the bell 7pm-8am. 1.50zł surcharge for after-hours service.) The Post Office, ul. Bogurodzicy 1, has **telephones**. (☎ 440 13 02. Open M-F 7am-8pm, Sa 9am-2pm.) **Postal code:** 70-405.

**▨ ▨ ACCOMMODATIONS AND FOOD.** For a complete list of Szczecin's spartan summer youth hostels, contact either of the tourist offices (see above). ▨ **Schronisko Młodzieżowe (HI)**, ul. Monte Cassino 19a, features comfortable new bunk beds and light rooms. Take tram #1 from the center toward either "Głębokie" or "Zajezdnia Pogodno" and get off at "Piotra Skargi." Blue signs point the way from there; if you don't see them, backtrack to the 1st left onto Królowej Korony Polskiej and then take the first right onto Monte Cassino. (☎ 422 47 61; fax 423 56 96. Sheets 6zł. No lockout. Kitchen available for a 5zł deposit. 6-bed dorms 16zł, students 12zł; 8-

bed dorms 14.80zł, 10.80zł; 9- to 12-bed dorms 13.40zł, 9.40zł; singles 40zł, 32zł; doubles 40zł, 32zł; quads 70zł, 54zł.) For adequate rooms close to the center, try **Schronisko Młodzieżowe,** ul. Grodska 23. From the train station, follow the directions to the central tourist office, continue past it to the 1st right, then take a left on Grodska. (☎433 29 24. Reception 7-10am and 5-8pm. Lockout 10am-5pm. Curfew 10am. Call ahead. Open July-Aug. only. Dorms 14.80zł, students 10.80zł; singles 20zł, 16zł.)

A large supermarket, **Extra,** sits at ul. Niepodległości 27. (Open M-Sa 7am-8pm, Su 11am-7pm. MC/Visa.) Remember your old lunch lady at **Bar Turysta,** ul. Obrońców Stalingradu 6 (☎434 22 01. Full meals under 5zł. Open M-F 7am-7pm, Sa 8am-4pm, 1st and 3rd Su of the month 8am-3pm.) **Piramida,** al. Niepodległości 3, has great middle-eastern food and pizza. (☎488 16 63. Main dishes 8-15zł. Open daily 11am-11pm.) **Lucynka i Paulinka,** ul. Wojska Polskiego 18, treats customers to luxury food items downstairs and sinful desserts, coffee, and stiffer libations upstairs. Desserts and coffee start at 3zł. (☎434 69 22. Open daily 9am-10pm. MC/Visa.)

**🔲 SIGHTS.** The **Port Gate** (Brama Portowa) lends a Prussian flavor to the downtown area, with an inscription commemorating Emperor Friedrich Wilhelm I and a panorama of 18th-century Szczecin. The gate also features a likeness of Viadus, god of the Oder, leaning against a jug from which the river's waters flow. Originally called the Brandenburg and later the Berlin Gate, it was built in 1725 and spared during the removal of the city's fortifications in 1875 because of its architectural value. Close to the river on ul. Wyszynskiego, the **Cathedral of St. John the Evangelist** (Katedra Św. Jana Ewangelisty) rests on its 13th-century foundation, waiting to be restored in full. After the stained-glass windows are installed, the church will finally shine again with all the Gothic splendor lost in World War II. (Open daily 7am until the end of the last service, around 8pm.) The **town hall** *(ratusz)* stands one block from the cathedral on ul. Wyszynskiego. Built in 1450, it houses one of the three branches of the **National Museum** (Muzeum Narodowe). Check out the giant 19th-century music box masquerading as a mirror and, on the top floor, the bottle of vodka from 1615. Another branch—a chronicle of Pomeranian art—is in the Baroque palace of the **Pomeranian Parliament,** at ul. Stromlynska 27/28, just off Pl. Żolnierza Polskiego. (Both branches open Tu, Th and Sa-Su 10am-5pm, W and F 9am-3:30pm. 4zł, students 2zł; Th free.) Between the two museums, on ul. Korsarzy, the enormous, newly restored **Castle of Pomeranian Dukes** (Zamek Książąt Pomerań skich) overlooks the city from the site of Szczecin's oldest settlement. The seat of Pomeranian princes until 1630, it later belonged to Swedes and Prussians. Now it's occupied by an opera, a cinema, and a **museum** housing the dukes' exquisitely decorated sarcophagi. (Castle ☎434 73 91. Museum ☎489 16 30. Open daily 10am-6pm; temporary exhibits closed M. 3zł, students 2zł; temporary exhibits 5zł, 4zł.)

# ŚWINOUJŚCIE
☎(0)97

Visitors flock to Świnoujście's (shvi-noh-OOSH-che) main attractions: the shady parks and the Baltic shoreline, with its grassy dunes and relaxed beachcombing. The town's seafaring side becomes obvious from the ferry in. Colorful tugboats sit at the port, while sailors walk the streets; the **beach** and the **promenade** along ul. Żeromskiego are sights in themselves. Rent a bike from the office next to IT to peddle past the dunes or through the greenery. (3zł per hr., 15zł per day. Open daily 8am-6pm.) In the old town hall, the **Fishing Museum** (Muzeum Rybołówstwa) chronicles Świnoujście's maritime past. (Open Tu-F 9am-4pm; Sa-Su 11am-4pm. 3zł, students 2zł.) At ul. Matejka 35, the amphitheater hosts a number of productions, including circus acts and concerts. Check the schedules posted outside the entrance and around town. The century-old **lighthouse,** to the right as you face the ocean, is one of the city's most enduring symbols.

Świnoujście occupies of two islands, **Wolin** and **Uznam,** linked by a ferry across the **Świna River.** The **train** and **bus stations** and the international **ferry terminal** are all on the Świna's east bank, near the port on Wolin Island. **Trains** travel to: **Szczecin** (2hr., 14 per day, 21.80zł); **Katowice** (9hr., 3 per day, 41.73zł); **Warsaw** (9hr., 1 per day, 40.58zł); and **Kraków** (10hr., 2 per day, 43.17zł). **Buses** head to: **Międzydroje** (20min., 48 per day, 3.20, express 6zł); **Szczecin** (3hr., 2 per day, 15.50zł); **Gdynia** (8hr., 2 per day, 45zł); and **Gdańsk** (8½hr., 1 per day, 45zł). On Wolin, **Polferries**, ul. Dworcowa 1 (☎322 43 96; www.polferries.com.pl), sends ferries to: **Rönne, SWE** (6hr., 1 per week on Sa, 160zł, students and interail ticket holders 130zł); **Malmö, SWE** (6½hr., 1 per day, June-Aug. 510zł, 420zł; Sept.-May 440zł, 370zł); **Ystad, SWE** (7hr., 1 per day, June-Aug. 460zł, 370zł; Sept.-May 390zł, 320zł); and **Copenhagen, DEN** (10½hr., 5 per week, 340zł, 280zł). *Kasa* open daily 7am-11:30pm.

To get to the main part of town, on the west side of the river in Uznam, take the free **car ferry** (every 20min. 5am-11pm, every hr. midnight-5am) across the street from the train and bus stations. On the other side of the river, take a left on ul. Władsysław and then veer right on ul. Armii Krajowej at the small park. From here, a right on ul. Piłudskiego leads to the beach, while a left on ul. Grunwaldzka carries you to the outlying part of town, including the youth hostel (see below). A 25-minute walk down 2nd right off Grunwaldzka, ul. Komstytucji 3 Maja, leads to the German border. **Centrum Informacji Turystycznej (CIT)**, pl. Słowiański 15, issues free maps and brochures and helps find accommodations. (☎/fax 322 49 99; cit@for-net.com.pl. Open daily 9am-5pm.) **Bank PKO**, ul. Piłsudskiego 4, **exchanges money,** cashes **traveler's checks,** and handles **cash advances.** (☎321 57 33. Open M-F 8am-6pm, Sa 10am-2pm.) The **pharmacy** on ul. Piłsudskiego 23 provides a wide variety of drugs and displays a list of other *aptekas* in town in the window. (☎321 25 15. Open M-F 8am-6pm, Sa 10am-3pm, Su 10am-1pm. MC/Visa.) An **internet cafe** transports customers into cyberspace at Pl. Słowiański 10. (3zł per hr. Open M-F 11am-8pm, Sa 10am-2pm.) The **post office** is at ul. Piłsudskiego 1 (☎321 20 15; open M-F 8am-8pm, Sa 8am-6pm). **Postal code:** 72-600.

Rooms are plentiful from September to June, but in July and August it's a good idea to call ahead. **Private rooms** (25-30zł), arranged through CIT (see above), are a good option. The best deals close to the beach are in "tourist houses;" look for "Dom Wczasowy" signs. **DW Fala,** ul. Sienkiewicza 15 (☎321 20 87), offers beds for 35zł per person in July and August, 20zł at other times. To get there, take a left off of ul. Piłsudskiego, just after the park on the left ends. For a lot of character, stop by the **Pensjonat Wodnik,** ul. Matejki 20, and fight your way past the birdcages to negotiate a deal with the owners. There are no set prices in this very eccentric (but very clean) complex—the price depends on whether they have baths, how long they will be occupied, and other factors. (☎/fax 327 95 78. Singles June-Aug. 50-70zł; Sept.-May. 30-40zł.) **Camping Relax,** ul. Słowackiego 1, is near the beach. It doesn't offer much relaxation, as the crowds pack in and party on. (☎321 47 00; fax 321 39 12. 8zł, students 6zł, seniors 5zł. 2-person tents 4zł, 3- to 6-person 5zł, 6-person 8zł. 3-person bungalows 90-165zł, 4-person 120-205zł.) Farther from both center and beach, **Schronisko Młodzieżowe (HI)**, ul. Gdyńska 26, has free luggage storage and spotless bathrooms. Walk down ul. Grunwaldzka (10-15min.) then turn right onto ul. Grodzka. (☎327 06 13. Reception 6-10am and 5-10pm. Doubles and triples students 12.10zł, non-students 15.40zł, non-members 24.20zł; quads 9.90zł, 13.20zł, 20.90zł.)

Food stands by the dozen line ul. Żeromskiego. Try the inexpensive and delicious *gofry* (hot Belgian waffles with whipped cream and strawberries), or corn-on-the-cob for just 3.50zł. More substantial appetites can find a grilled *kiełbasa* and *piwo* for only 4zł. If you don't like eating while promenading, head to the end of Żeromskiego (to the right facing the beach) to **Pizzeria Muszla,** which serves a variety of good pies (9.50-18zł) in a slightly more civilized setting. (Open daily 11am-11pm.) Across from the post office at **Bar "Neptun,"** ul. Bema 1, you can feast on inexpensive Polish dishes (10-30zł) and homemade carrot juice. (☎321 26 43. Open M-Sa 8am-10pm, Su 9am-10pm.) **Grocery Kama,** ul. Chopina 2, has fresh bread, cheese, and meat. (☎327 04 73. Open M-Sa 7am-10pm, Su 10am-9pm.)

As the sun goes down, the food stands along ul. Żeromskiego transform into places for good times and cheap beer. Crowds of young fun-seekers also frequent the **nightclubs,** which are within easy walking distance. For a real culture shock, check out **Manhattan,** ul. Żeromskiego 1 (☎060 680 94 17), with its Big Apple decor and techno. (Beer 5zł. Cover Sa 10zł. Open daily 9pm-6am.) The coolest bar in town, ■**Jazz Club Teatralna,** upstairs at Pl. Słowiański 15, pleases students with its cheap beer (4zł) and frequent live music. (☎321 03 77. Open daily 6:30pm-4am.)

**POLAND**

# WOLIŃ NATIONAL PARK (WOLIŃSKI PARK NARODOWY)

☎(0)91

Amid quickly developing coastal resorts, Woliński National Park protects a pristine tract of Wolin Island containing glacial lakes, a bison preserve, and breathtaking views of the Baltic Sea. Pine-scented breezes stir its trails, while the dense woodland dampens the nearby road noise, leaving only silence and the cries of distant eagles. For those wary of the unfiltered Polish wilderness, fear not: the comforts of tiny Międzyzdroje, the best base for a trip into the park, are nearby.

**▣ TRANSPORTATION. Trains** run to Międzyzdroje (MYEN-dzi-ZDROY-eh) from **Świnoujście** (30min.; 14 per day; 3.80zł, express 5.12zł) and **Szczecin** (2hr.; 14 per day; 13.20zł, express 21.12zł). The easiest way to travel to and from **Świnoujście**, however, is by **bus** (20min.; 48 per day; 3.20zł, express 6zł). Buses also frequently travel to and from points along the hiking trails, including the towns of **Wisełka** and **Kołczewo,** both of which sit near astounding glacial lakes (20-30min., 6zł).

**◪ PRACTICAL INFORMATION.** Go right out of the train station and follow ul. Kolejowa down the hill to the center. There's a large map of town posted outside the train station. Maps of the park are posted at periodic intervals, so buying a one isn't essential. In the center of town at **PTTK,** ul. Kolejowa 2, you can obtain **maps** (3-6zł) and get info about the park and accommodations. The PTTK city/park map (4.50zł) is useful for hiking deeper into the woods. (☎328 04 62; fax 328 00 86. Some English spoken. Open M-F 7am-5pm, Sa 9am-1pm.) Maps also available from reception in the attached hotel. (Open 24hr.) There is a MC/Plus/Visa **ATM** at ul. Zwycięstwa 1. A **pharmacy** sits at ul. Zwycięstwa 9. (☎328 01 54. Open daily 8am-10pm.) Hop on the **internet** at ul. Krótka 4e, in the courtyard across from PTTK. (3zł per 30min., 5zł per hr. Open daily 11am-10pm.) The **post office** is at ul. Gryfa Pomorskiego 7. (Open M-F 8am-8pm, Sa 8am-7pm.) **Postal code:** 72-500.

**▐▝◪ ACCOMMODATIONS AND FOOD.** Keep an eye out for *"wolne pokoje"* (available rooms) signs, particularly along ul. Gryfa Pomorskiego, for a good deal on a **private room.** Alternatively, talk to **PTTK** (see above), which arranges stays in the summer (singles 32zł; doubles 40zł; triples 96zł) and runs the well-kept **PTTK Hotel,** in the same building as the office. (☎328 03 82. July-Aug. dorms 35zł; singles and doubles with sinks 45zł per person; Sept.-June 20zł, 35zł.) They also run a second hotel in summer at ul. Dąbrówski 11. The rooms are more expensive, but all have baths. (☎32 80 929; fax 32 80 086. July-Aug. singles 77zł, doubles and triples 132zł, quads 176zł; Sept.-June singles 40zł, doubles 70zł, triples 66zł, quads 88zł.) **Camping Gromada,** ul. Bohaterów Warszawy 1, has cabins (14-28zł per person) and tent sites (9-12zł) near the beach. (☎/fax 328 07 79 and 328 05 84. Reception open daily 8am-10pm.) Continue down Kolejowa as it becomes Gryfa Pomorskiego and later Dąbrówski; Gromada is at the end of the street on the right. Look for inexpensive **food** at the stands and restaurants along ul. Gryfa Pomorskiego and the beach.

**◪ HIKING.** Although Międzyzdroje is increasingly drawing crowds as a prime beach resort, the true accolades still belong to **Woliński.** The park is immaculately kept, with three main **hiking trails** (red, green, and blue—marked on trees and stones every 30m); stick to them or risk an encounter with park officials. All three are accesible from Międzyzdroje—the red at the northeast end of **ul. Bohaterów Warszawy,** the green at the end of **ul. Leśna** (follow the signs to the bison preserve), and the blue just off **ul. Ustronie Leśne.** The hikes are not especially strenuous. Check in the PTTK office (see above) for notices about where you can rent a bike.

The **red trail** alone makes the trip worthwhile. Part of a longer trek around Wolin Island, the trail's primary leg is a 15km stretch along the Baltic coast. Only a short climb from the trailhead, **Kawcza Góra** is the first of many scenic outlooks on the Baltic Sea. Look closely and you just might glimpse one of the park's famed eagles (*bieliki*). Snaking along the cliffs, the trail never strays far from the shoreline, with sea breezes keeping hikers refreshed. Just after Kawcza Góra, the trail hits a dead-end drop-off and a closed military area; backtrack a few steps and follow the trail right and down the hill to the road. Just up ahead, to the left, the red trail resumes. If you've just got to see a bison, instead of heading left on the road, cross it and head back into the park at the green trail.

It's worth renting a bike to check out the **green trail,** which has an extensive set of **bike paths** and which, by foot, has long stretches of less rewarding territory between the highlights. The 15km route heads into the heavily-forested heart of the park, rewarding the persistent hiker with serenity along glacial lakes. Just 1.2km from the trailhead is the small but popular **bison preserve** (*rezerwat żubrów;* open Tu-Su 10am-6pm; 3zł, students 2zł), home to deer, wild boar, eagles, and, of course, bison. After another 7km you'll come upon the lakes, at which point the trail, though still well marked, becomes slightly more confusing and heads in several directions as it snakes around the different lakes. Maps posted throughout the park help, but since all signs are in Polish, it's particularly important to gauge your own progress. After Lake Czajcze, head right along the road. Here, you can either continue on to Wisełka (3km) on the road past Lake Wisełka or head back onto the green trail to Kołczewo (7km), past Lake Kołczewa. Frequent buses run between the towns and from both towns to Międzydroje. The end of the green trail is 3km past Kołczewo, where it intersects the red trail.

The **blue trail** wanders south, covering more than 20km as it winds to Wolin, the island's southernmost point. Then it heads into the park right off ul. Ustronie Lesne by the train station; go under the bridge and take a right. Less traveled than the other two trails, it's a great escape from the mobs of tourists in town.

# TRI-CITY AREA (TRÓJMIASTO)

The Tri-city area (pop. 465,000) on Poland's Baltic coast is rapidly developing into a major tourist destination. The three cities of Gdańsk, Sopot, and Gdynia complement each other perfectly, forming a metropolis that is urban and cosmopolitan yet replete with beautiful beaches and stellar hiking. Efficient public transport makes it possible for travelers to find a bed in one city and explore the other two, as well as to venture farther afield on daytrips. The fishing village of Hel, the former concentration camp at Stutthof, the Teutonic castle of Malbork, the cathedral of Frombork, and the Curonian resort Krynica Morska all lie within two hours of the cities.

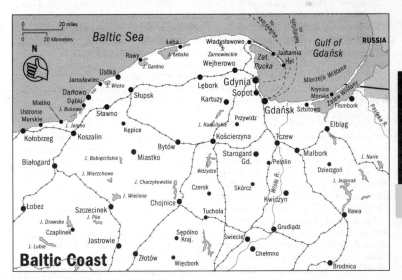

Baltic Coast

# GDAŃSK ☎(0)58

Gdańsk's (gh-DA-insk) strategic location, at the mouth of the Wisła (Vistula) on the Baltic Coast, has helped it flourish as a center of art and commerce for more than a millennium. Once the free city of Danzig, it was the site of the first deaths of World War II. After the war the city quietly began to restore its shattered center, but soon found itself in the spotlight again as the birthplace of Lech Wałęsa's Solidarity movement. Today Gdańsk offers visitors a staggering array of tastes, sights, and sounds. From the beaches of Brzeźno to the parks of Oliwa, the city and its environs have weathered the centuries with their charm intact.

## ✦ ORIENTATION

While Gdańsk technically sits on the Baltic Coast, its center lies 5km inland. From the **Gdańsk Główny** train station, the city center lies just a few blocks southeast, bordered on the west by **Wały Jagiellońskie** and on the east by the **Motława River.** Take the underpass in front of the train station, go right, exit the shopping center, then turn left on ul. Heweliusza. Turn right on ul. Rajska and follow the signs to **Główne Miasto** (Main Town), turning left on **ul. Długa.** Długa becomes **Długi Targ** as it widens near **Motława,** one of the most beautiful parts of town and home to the majority of sights and accommodations.

Gdańsk has several suburbs, all north of Główne Miasto. **Gdańsk-Brzeźno,** the center of the city's **beaches,** is accessible by tram #13 from the train station. **Gdańsk-Oliwa,** famous for its cathedral, can be reached by commuter rail or by tram #6 or 12 from the train station. **Westerplatte,** site of the opening shots of World War II, lies northeast of the center and can be accessed by bus #106 or 158, which head south and then loop up to the battleground. Also on trams #6 and 12 but closer to the center, bustling **Gdańsk-Wrzeszcz** contains a number of budget accommodations. Just north, on tram lines #2 and 8, **Gdańsk-Zaspa** is the site of a major hospital.

## ▉ TRANSPORTATION

**Trains: Gdańsk Główny,** ul. Podwale Grodzkie 1 (☎301 11 12). To: **Toruń** (3hr., 5 per day, 28.56zł); **Poznań** (4hr., 8 per day, 33.90zł); **Warsaw** (4½hr., 18 per day, 60.18zł); **Wrocław** (5½hr., 6 per day, 38.20zł); **Szczecin** (6hr., 6 per day, 37.02zł); **Katowice** (6½hr., 9 per day, 39.50zł); **Kraków** (6½hr., 9 per day, 41.10zł); **Berlin, GER** (8hr., 1 per day, 124.50zł); **Kaliningrad, RUS** (8hr., 1 per day, 30.50zł); **Prague, CZR** (14hr., June-Aug. 1 per day, 166zł); and **Odessa, UKR** (32hr., 1 per 2 days, 250zł). **City Fast Trains (SKM)** run to **Sopot** (20min., 2.50zł, students 1.25zł) and **Gdynia** (35min., 3.50zł, students 1.75zł) every 10min. during the day and less frequently at night. Punch your ticket at one of the big yellow *kasownik* machines before boarding.

**Buses:** ul. 3-go Maja 12 (☎302 15 32), behind the train station, connected by an underground passageway. To: **Krynica Morska** (2hr., 16 per day, 9.20zł); **Warsaw** (4½hr., 5 per day, 38zł); **Berlin, GER** (8½hr., 2 per week, 153zł; tickets available from Orbis or Almatur); and **Kaliningrad, RUS** (8½hr., 2 per day, 28zł).

**Ferries:** Passenger ferries run May-Sept. To: **Westerplatte** (50min.; every hr. 10am-6pm; 31zł, students 17zł); **Gdynia** (1½hr.; 3 per day; round-trip 50zł, 34zł); **Sopot** (1½hr.; 4 per day; 42zł, 30zł); and **Hel** (3hr.; 3 per day; 54zł, 37zł). **Polferries,** ul. Przemysłowa 1 (☎343 18 87 and 343 69 78; fax 343 65 74; www.polferries.com.pl), in Gdańsk-Brzeźno, sends ferries to **Nynäshamn, SWE** (19hr.; June-Sept. 1 per day, Oct.-May 1 per day Tu, Th, and Su, departs 6pm; 385zł, students 225zł).

**Local Transportation:** Gdańsk has an extensive bus and tram system. 10min. 1zł; 30min. 2zł; 45min. 2.50zł; 1hr. 3zł; day pass 5zł. Night buses: 30min. 3zł; night pass 5zł. Large pieces of luggage need their own tickets. Hefty fines for riding ticketless or without a ticket for baggage.

**Taxis:** It's a bird, it's a plane, it's...**Super Hallo Taxi,** ☎301 91 91. Not to be confused with the mild-mannered **Hallo Taxi,** ☎91 97. Both 1.80zł per km.

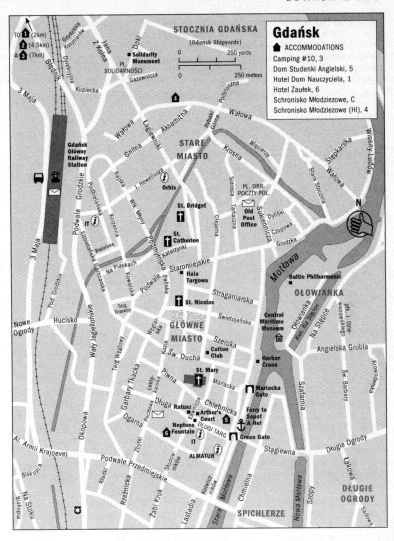

## Gdańsk

**ACCOMMODATIONS**

Camping #10, 3
Dom Studenki Angielski, 5
Hotel Dom Nauczyciela, 1
Hotel Zaułek, 6
Schronisko Młodziezowe, C
Schronisko Młodziezowe (HI), 4

## PRACTICAL INFORMATION

**Tourist Offices: IT Gdańsk,** ul. Długa 45 (☎/fax 301 91 51), in Główne Miasto. Open daily June-Aug. 8am-8pm, Sept.-May 8am-6pm. There's also a small office on the top floor of the train station. Open daily 10am-6pm.

**Budget Travel: Orbis,** ul. Podwale Staromiejskie 96/97 (☎/fax 301 84 12; orbis.gdanskpod@pop.com.pl). International and domestic ferry, train, and plane tickets. English tours of the city. Open M-F 9am-5pm, Sa 10am-2pm. **Branch** at ul. Heweliusza 22 (☎301 21 32; fax 301 31 10). **Almatur,** ul. Długi Targ 11, 2nd fl. (☎301 29 31; fax 301 78 18; almatur@combidata.com.pl), in Główne Miasto. ISICs (35zł), info about youth and student hostels, international ferry tickets, and Avis car rentals. Open M-F 8:30am-5:30pm, Sa 10am-2pm.

**Currency Exchange:** At hotels, banks, *kantory*, and certain post offices. The train station has a 24hr. *kantor* with decent rates. **Bank Gdański,** Wały Jagiellońskie 14/16 (☎307 92 12), cashes **traveler's checks** for a 1% commission and provides AmEx/MC/Visa **cash advances** for no commission. Open M-F 9am-6pm. **Orbis** (see above) exchanges AmEx traveler's cheques for no commission.

**24hr. ATMs:** On every street corner.

**Luggage Storage:** Downstairs at the train station. 3.95zł plus 0.45zł for every 50zł of declared value. Open 24hr.

**International Bookstore: English Books Unlimited,** ul. Podmłyńska 10 (☎301 33 73, ext. 114). Open M-F 10am-6pm, Sa 10am-3pm. **Empik Megastore,** at the end of the underpass in front of the train station, also sells **maps** and *Gdańsk in Your Pocket* (6zł). Small **internet cafe** inside. 5zł per hr. Open M-Sa 9am-9pm, Su 11am-7pm.

**24hr. Pharmacy:** At the train station (☎346 25 40). Ring the bell 8pm-7:30am.

**Medical Assistance: Private doctors,** ul. Podbielańska 17 (☎301 51 68). A big blue sign on the building says "Lekarne Specjaliśći." Internal medicine visit 35zł. For **emergency assistance** go to **Szpital Wojewodzki,** ul. Nowe Ogrody 5 (☎302 30 31), the hospital closest to the Old Town. From the train station, take a right out of the building and then the 1st right at the big traffic circle. The hospital is 1 block up on the left.

**Telephones:** At the post office (see below).

**Internet Access: Rudy Kot Internet Music Cafe,** ul. Garncarska 18/20 (☎301 86 49). Off Podwale Staromiejskie. 2.50zł per 30min., Open daily 10am-midnight. **Telokomunikacja Polska,** next to the post office at ul. Długa 22/28, lets customers check email for free. Spaces fill up; put your name on a list and come back later. Open M-F 10am-6pm.

**Post Office:** ul. Długa 22/28 (☎301 88 53). Take a number and wait your turn. **Fax** service. Open M-F 8am-8pm, Sa 9am-3pm.

**Postal code:** 80-801.

# ▐ ACCOMMODATIONS

With Gdańsk's limited tourist infrastructure and increasing popularity, it's best to reserve well ahead, especially in summer. If you're traveling in July or August, you can stay in a **university dorm.** Consult **IT, Almatur,** or *Gdańsk in Your Pocket* (6zł, available at some kiosks and at Empik) for info. Otherwise, private rooms are usually available and can be arranged through **Gdańsk-Tourist** (Biuro zakwaterowania), ul. Podwale Grodzkie 8, downstairs in the City Forum shopping complex, which is connected by the underground passage to the train station. (☎301 26 34; fax 301 63 01. Singles in the center 48zł, in the suburbs 39zł; doubles 80zł, 67zł. Open daily July-Aug. 8am-7:30pm; Sept.-June M-Sa 9am-5pm.) If you don't have any luck inside, try the posse of elderly women milling around outside the train station.

**Schronisko Młodzieżowe (HI),** ul. Wałowa 21 (☎301 23 13). Cross the street in front of the train station, head up ul. Heweliusza, turn left at ul. Łagiewniki, and right after the church onto Wałowa. Convenient location. Kitchen available. Old building with decent rooms. Reception on the 2nd floor. English spoken. Luggage storage 1zł. Sheets 3.21zł. Lockout 10am-5pm, but for 5zł you can stay during the day. Curfew midnight. Dorms 14.40zł, nonmembers 16zł; singles and doubles 27zł per person, 30zł.

**Dom Studencki Angielski,** ul. Chlebnicka 13/16 (☎301 28 16), 1 block off Długi Targ. Amazing location and unbeatable prices, with mattresses on the floor, no toilet paper in the bathrooms, and peeling paint. Funky murals (yes, that's Bob Marley on the 2nd floor) and garishly colored rooms, thanks to the art students who live here during the year. Sheets 3zł. No curfew. Open July-Aug. 22zł per person.

**Schronisko Młodzieżowe,** ul. Grunwaldzka 244 (☎341 41 08). From the train station, take tram #6 or 12 north (to the left facing away from the station) and get off 14 stops later at "Abrahama" (unmarked); you'll see several tram garages on the left (20-25min.). Turn right on ul. Abrahama, then right again on the highway-like Grunwaldzka; the hostel is just ahead. Immaculate rooms and bathrooms, but the location is less than ideal. Kitchen available. Luggage storage 1zł. Sheets 3zł. Reception 5-9pm. Lockout 10am-5pm. Curfew 10pm. Dorms 21.40zł; doubles 33.16zł, with bath 43.90zł.

**Hotel Zaułek,** ul. Ograna 107/108 (☎301 41 69). Ograna runs parallel to Długi Targ, 1 block farther when coming from the train station. Amazingly priced for its location, but you risk the occasional strange smell or tattered mattress. Fans of shower curtains will be sorely disappointed. Check-in and check-out noon. Singles 55zł; doubles 70zł; triples 90zł; quads 105zł; quints 120zł; 6-bed rooms 130zł.

**Hotel Dom Nauczyciela,** ul. Uphagena 28 (☎/fax 341 49 17 and 341 91 16), in Gdańsk-Wrzeszcz. Take tram # 6 or 12 north from the train station 7 stops to "Miszewskiego." Turn right on ul. Miszewskiego and take the next right onto Uphagena; the hotel will be ahead on the left, across from the tennis courts. Simple but clean rooms in an old building. Check-in 2pm. Check-out noon. Singles 48zł, with sink 68zł, with bath 123zł; doubles 70zł, 86zł, 176zł; triples 96zł, with sink 105zł.

**Camping #10,** al. Gen. J. Hallera 234 (☎343 55 31), in Gdańsk-Brzeźno. From the train station, take tram #13 north (to the left) toward "Breśno." Stay on the tram past the last stop; after it turns around (and starts heading back on a different street), get off at the 1st stop, when the Nightclub Balladynan is on the right (25min. total). The entrance to the campground is next door. Owned by Gdańsk-Tourist (see above), this large campground is a bit far from the center but right near the beach. English spoken. Reception 24hr. Check-in 2pm. Check-out noon. 10zł per person, students 8.15zł. Tents 8-15.50zł. Bungalows 24zł per person. Electricity and parking 8zł each.

# ▌ FOOD

For fresh produce, try **Hala Targowa** on ul. Pańska, in the shadows of Kościół św. Katarzyny just off Podwale Staromiejskie. (Open M-F 9am-6pm, first and last Sa of the month 9am-3pm.) If outdoor markets aren't your bag, baby, head to the **Super-Sam Supermarket,** Targ Węglowy 6, for groceries. (Open M-F 8am-9pm, Sa 8am-8pm, Su 10am-6pm.) The cafes, restaurants, and beer gardens that flank **Długa** and **Długi Targ** all provide prime people-watching and many dish out *pierogi* late into the night. **Herbiciarnia Cztery Pory Roku,** ul. Ogarna 73/74, off the end of Długi Targ, offers succulent teas for 4-6zł in a cozy setting. (☎301 19 94. Open Tu-Su noon-8pm.)

▨ **"La BoMbe" Cape of Good Taste,** ul. Rybackie Pebrzeże 5/7 (☎346 25 05), on the Motława. Tiny creperie-cum-gallery with hand-painted mugs and tables. Delectable crepes for lunch, dinner, or dessert (4-10zł). Open daily 9am-11pm.

▨ **Green Way Vegetarian Bar,** ul Garncarska 4/6 (☎301 41 21), serves vegetarian creations hearty enough for any carnivore. Stellar soups, samosas, stuffed pitas, and fruit juices. Main dishes 4-9zł. Open daily 10am-10pm.

**Tan Viet,** ul. Podmłyńska 1/5 (☎301 33 35). The Vietnamese cuisine is pricey, but worth it. Main dishes 15-40zł. Open daily noon until late. AmEx/MC/Visa.

**La Pasta,** ul. Szeroka 32 (☎301 51 91). No table service, but good food done cheap amid tasteful decor. Tasty (and very light) pizza 9-14zł; slightly less impressive pastas and lasagna in the same price range. Open daily 11am-10pm.

**Bar Mleczny Neptun,** ul. Długa 33/34 (☎301 49 88). Homestyle meat and veggie dishes in a traditional cafeteria. Full meal 5-10zł. Open M-F 7am-6pm, Sa-Su 9am-5pm.

**Bar Pod Ryba** (Under the Fish), ul. Długi Targ 35/38/1 (☎305 13 07), serves baked potatoes with all sorts of fillings, as well as good fish and chips. Most of the toppings, as the name suggests, are fish-based. Main dishes 6-15zł. AmEx/MC/Visa.

# ▌ SIGHTS

## GŁÓWNE MIASTO

The handsome main square, **Długi Targ,** forms the physical and social center of painstakingly restored Główne Miasto.

**ARTHUR'S COURT AND THE GDAŃSK HISTORY MUSEUM.** The original 16th-century facade of Arthur's Court (Dwór Artusa) faces out onto **Neptune's Fountain** (Fontanna Neptuna). The court, where medieval burghers held meetings, was fully restored in 1997 and now houses one branch of the **Gdańsk History Museum**

**POLAND**

(Muzeum Historii Gdańska). The highlight of the museum is the Renaissance architecture of the building itself, but the furnishings don't disappoint. Next to the fountain, where ul. Długa and Długi Targ meet, the 14th-century **Town Hall** (ratusz) houses another branch of the History Museum. Baroque paintings adorn the ceiling of the fantastic Red Chamber, while a magnificently gaudy Fabergé egg graces the Little Court Room. Another, more sobering exhibit shows the state of Gdańsk right after World War II—including some of the actual rubble. *(Both open Tu and Th 11am-6pm, W 10am-4pm, F-Sa 10am-5pm, Su 11am-5pm. Each branch 5zł, students 2.50zł. W free.)*

**CHURCH OF THE BLESSED VIRGIN MARY.** (Kościół Najświętszej Marii Panny.) The church was badly damaged during World War II, but has been almost completely rebuilt. Not all of the stained glass windows are in place and a few of the frescoes remain shadows of their former glory, but the intricate 1464 astronomical clock and the 1517 Dürer-inspired altarpiece still astound visitors. For 3zł you can climb the 405 steps to the top of the steeple for a phenomenal view of the city. In the foreground of the view on ul. Wielkie Młyny you'll find the 15th-century **St. Nicholas's Church** (Kościół św. Mikołaja) and behind it the 14th-century **St. Catherine's Church** (Kościół św. Katarzyny). Gdańsk's churches were often visited by Polish monarchs: King Władysław III Łokietek supervised 14th-century court trials in St. Catherine's, while King Zygmunt III received his electoral diploma in St. Nicholas's. Behind the Church of the Blessed Virgin Mary, the cobblestone **ul. Mariacka**, lined by galleries and "medieval" street musicians, ambles down to the river.

**NAUTICAL SIGHTS.** The huge medieval **Harbor Crane**, which once loaded cargo ships, towers over the riverside Długie Pobrzeże. This and the ship *Sołdek* are part of the **Central Maritime Museum** (Centralne Muzeum Morskie). The permanent exhibition in the crane focuses on the boats of non-European peoples (4zl, students 2.50zl), while the *Sołdek* houses exhibits on its construction and the Baltic shipyards (4zl, students 2.50zl). To reach the *Sołdek*, either take the boat that shuttles visitors across (3zł round-trip, students 1.50zl) or walk from the end of ul. Chlebnicka across the bridge at the end of Długi Targ. *(☎ 301 84 53. Museum open daily 10am-6pm. Ticket including all museums and ferry 10zł, students 6zł.)* The flags of Lech Wałęsa's trade union *Solidarność* (see **History,** p. 457) fly high once again at **Gdańsk Shipyard** (Stocznia Gdańska) and at the **Solidarity Monument,** on pl. Solidarności, just north of the center at the end of ul. Wały Piastowskie.

**MEMORIAL TO THE DEFENDERS OF THE POST OFFICE SQUARE.** On Sept. 1, 1939, the employees of the post office put up a desperate defense against the German army, fighting until the building was engulfed in flames. Those who survived the blaze were summarily shot. A museum inside the reconstructed, still-functioning post office commemorates the event. *(From Podwale Staromiejskie, go north on Olejarna and turn right at the sign for Gdańsk Post Office #1 (Urzad Poctowy Gdańsk 1). Open M-F 10am-4pm, Sa-Su 10:30am-2pm. 2.50zł, students 1.50zł.)*

## GDAŃSK-OLIWA

*Commuter trains run from the center (15min., 2.50zł, students 1.25zł). Trams #6 and 12 go more slowly (30-35min.). From the Oliwa train station, go up ul. Poczty Gdańskiej, turn right on ul. Grundwaldzka, then turn left at the signs for the cathedral on ul. Rybińskiego.*

**PARK OLIWSKI.** The most beautiful of Gdańsk's many suburbs, Oliwa provides a brief respite from the big city. To the right you'll find the lush green shade and ponds of the park. The oldest church in the Gdańsk area, the 13th-century **Oliwska Cathedral** (Katedra) is within the park's gates. A series of chapels surrounds the cathedral, whose main attraction is its magnificent 18th-century **organ**. The organ's pipes reverberate several times daily for tourists and during the summer, twice a week for the full-scale concerts of the **International Organ Music Festival.** *(Tickets 15zł, students 5zł. A few concerts take place in other venues; consult the Tourist Office for a complete schedule. Park open daily May-Sept. 5am-11pm; Mar.-Apr. and Oct. 5am-8pm.)*

**OLIWA ZOO.** The Oliwa Zoo, nestled in a forest right outside Oliwa proper, houses such exotic animals as Andean condors and Bactrian camels from the Gobi Desert. To get there, exit the park and walk farther along ul. Rybińskiego (with the park on the right) to the stop for bus #122. "Oliwa Zoo" is the last stop, 2½km away. *(Open daily May-Sept. 9am-7pm; Apr. 9am-6pm; Oct.-Mar. 9am-3pm. 6zł, students 3zł.)*

**TRI-CITY LANDSCAPE PARK.** (Trójmiejski park krajobrazowy.) A massive, thickly wooded wilderness set in gently rolling hills to the west of the three cities, the park offers excellent hiking on its numerous well-maintained trails. To plan your route, pick up the **map** "Nadleśnictwo Gdańsk" (7-9zł; available at some kiosks and the Empik Megastore). The park is most easily reached from Oliwa. Follow the directions for the zoo (see above) and look out for a blue-and-white-marked path across from the entrance to the zoo. You can also join the trail 10 minutes farther up ul. Rybińskiego. From there, a short and pleasant hike along the blue trail leads to the Sopot-Kamienny Potoh train station, where the commuter train runs back to Gdańsk. The trail begins with a rigorous climb to the top of a small hill; immediate gratification awaits with a stunning view of the city and sea in the distance. From here on, it's all trees; follow the markings carefully, as unmarked trails branch off from the main one. At the small road just past the high-tension power lines, turn left; the trail re-enters the woods about 5m down; the deceptive right arrow is for hikers coming in the opposite direction. The entire route is 10km and takes 2-3hr. The markings disappear at Sopot. As you descend past the small church, veer to the left onto ul. Małopolska and continue until you reach the train station; tickets are usually available at the nearby kiosks, but if you're coming through on a weekend after the buses have stopped running, bring tickets with you. *(2.50zł, students 1.25zł.)*

## OTHER SUBURBS

**WESTERPLATTE.** When Germany attacked on September 1, 1939, the little island fort guarding the entrance to Gdańsk's harbor gained the unfortunate distinction of being the target of the first shots of World War II. Its defenders held out for a week, until a lack of food and munitions forced them out. **Guardhouse #1** has been converted into a museum with an exhibit on the fateful week. *(Open May-Sept. 9am-dusk. 1.50zł, students 1zł. English info 6zł.)* The path beyond the exhibit passes the ruins of a command building and, farther up, the massive **Memorial to the Heroes of the Coast** (Pomnik Obrońców Wybrzeża). Follow the spiralling path up past the rose bushes for a closer look at the monument's giant granite figures and a glimpse of the shipyard and the sea. On a clear day, you can see across the Baltic all the way to the Hel Peninsula. *(From the train station, take bus #106 or 158 south to the last stop (20min.). The bus stop is just to the left of the station exit. A ferry (50min., every hr. 10am-6pm, round-trip 31zł, students 17zł) also runs to Westerplatte from the end of Długi Targ.)*

**BRZEŹNO.** For some fun at the beach, Brzeźno—though it may not be as trendy as Sopot—is perfect. What it does have over Sopot is **Park Brzeźnieński**, a wondrous escape full of tall pine trees. A few hundred meters to the left of the path the **pier**, the center of beach activity, juts out into the sea. The beach continues beyond Sopot. *(Take tram #13 north (to the left, facing away from the train station) to the last stop, "Brzeźno." Follow the footpath in the wooded area ahead to reach the beach.)*

## ♫ ENTERTAINMENT

Of the three cities that line this little stretch of the Baltic, Gdańsk draws the oldest and largest crowds to its incredible variety of activities. Street performances, often quite elaborate and captivating, liven up Długi Targ. The **Baltic Philharmonic** (Philharmonia Bałtycha), ul. Ołowianka 1 (☎305 20 40), performs free outdoor concerts during the summer; the audience listens from the other side of the Motława, near the end of Podwale Staromiejskie. Opera lovers can check out the **Baltic Opera** (Opera Bałtycha), al. Zwycięstwa 15 (☎341 01 34). Consult the tourist office (see **Tourist Offices**, p. 533) for more information on these and other venues.

POLAND

For those looking for more lowbrow fun, **U7**, pl. Dominikański 7, near the intersection of ul. Podwale Staromiejskie and ul. Podmłyńska, can't be beat. Housed in an old air-raid shelter, this complex is named for its seven attractions: bowling (7-14zł), billiards (15zł per hour), sauna (10zł), shooting range (12-20zł), fitness center (10zł), massage parlor (16-30zł), and bar. (☎305 55 77. Open daily 9am-midnight.)

The summer brings special events to the city, including a **Street Theater Festival** (early July), a **Shakespeare Festival** (early August), and the **International Organ Music Festival** at Oliwa (July-Aug.; see **Sights** above). The first two weeks in August also see the arrival of the gigantic **Dominican Fair,** a centuries-old trading party.

#  NIGHTLIFE

When the sun goes down, the crowds party on in Długi Targ, where bars and beer gardens abound. There are more pubbers than clubbers roaming the streets, but there's still plenty of dancing—especially on weekends—for those looking to shake their złoty-makers. 17th-century brewmaster and astronomer Jan Heweliusza, whose name and likeness grace Gdańsk's brew, would approve.

**Latający Holender Pub,** ul. Waly Jagielloński 2/4 (☎305 12 09), downstairs near the end of ul. Długa; look for the pub's namesake (skeletal) flying Dutchman outside. Doubles as a kind of a coffeehouse with guests lingering long in this popular space. Beer 6zł; coffee 4zł. Open daily noon-midnight.

**Jazz Club,** ul. Długi Targ 39/40 (☎301 54 09). Centrally located and extremely popular. A great spot for live music (F-Sa after 9pm) or a beer. Crowd is mostly over 30 but still kicking. 0.5L Żywiec 6zł. 5zł cover for concerts. Open June-Aug. 10am until the last guest leaves, Sept.-May from noon.

**Bar Apertif "Vinifera,"** ul Wodopój 7 (☎301 69 99), on the canal close to ul. Heweliusza and the Orbis hotel. This little cottage, whose interior looks like a diner with class, crowds in an older set for splendid glasses of wine (6zł and up) and all sorts of beer (Żywiec 5 zł). It was the model for the doll's house in *The Call of the Toad* by Nobel-prize winner Günter Grass. Open daily June-Aug. 3pm-midnight, Sept.-May 4pm-10pm.

**Cotton Club,** ul. Złotników 25/29 (☎301 88 13). A great place to play pool (10zł), catch live music on the weekends, or unwind at the end of the night. Draft beer 6zł. Open daily 4pm until the last guest leaves.

# DAYTRIPS FROM GDAŃSK

## MALBORK ☎(0)55

*Both trains (40-60min., 25 per day, 7.20zł, express 15.60zł) and buses (1hr., 8 per day, 7.20zł) run from Gdańsk to Malbork. Facing away from the station, walk right on ul. Dworcowa, then go left at the fork (sign points to Elbląg). Go up around the corner to the roundabout and cross to the street straight across the way, ul. Kościuszki, which runs between the apteka and the pizzeria. Follow it until you can veer right on ul. Piasłowska, where signs for the castle appear. Office ☎ 272 33 64; reservation ☎ 272 26 77. Courtyards, terraces, and moats open daily May-Sept. 9am-6pm, Oct.-Apr. 9am-4pm. Castle rooms open May-Sept. Tu-Su 9am-5pm, Oct.-April 9am-3pm. Sound and light show nightly May 15-Oct. 15. 18zł, students 10zł. Mandatory 3hr. tour in Polish included in the ticket price. To make it intelligible, buy the red English booklet sold in the kiosks for 6zł or get an English guide for 99zł. There's usually no problem securing one, but call ahead to be sure.*

One of the castles built by the Teutonic Knights, Malbork became the headquarters of the Teutonic Order in the 1300s. The Teutons first came to the region in 1230 at the request of Polish Duke Konrad Mazowiecki to assist the nation in its struggle against the heathen Prussians. The Teutons double-crossed the Poles, however, establishing their own state on conquered Prussian soil in 1309, with Malbork as its capital. The great period of Teutonic castle-building lasted until the Order was defeated at the Battle of Grunwald in 1410. Malbork withstood several sieges, but the Poles finally defeated their arch-enemies in 1457 under the leadership of King Kazimierz Jagiellończyk. For the next 300 years, Malbork served as a major arsenal and stronghold for the Kingdom of Poland. After the first partition of Poland in 1772, Malbork was incorporated into Prussia. Heavily damaged during World War II, the fortress was used by the Germans as a POW camp (Stalag XXB). After the war, Poland regained control of the largest brick castle in the world.

Malbork is a complex of three huge castles. Construction began in the mid-1270s with the monastery that became the **High Castle.** The rooms of the High Castle now exhibit a collection of 19th-century stained glass, Gothic sculptures, and the museum's most valuable possession, a tripartite altar from Tenkitten, Sambia. Between 1335 and 1341, a **tower** and a **bridge** over the Nogat River were incorporated. The most splendid additions were those of the Grand Master Winrich von Kniprode, for whom Rhenish architect Nikolaus Fellenstein designed the impressive **Master's Residence** in the **Middle Castle.** The guest lodgings are also in this part of the castle, along with the **Grand Refectory,** where feasts were held. Today, a marvellous **amber collection,** complete with several fossilized bugs, shines in the lower level of the east wing. Above it, the **weapons collection** exhibits the violent toys of the Polish hussars. Finally, the 14th and 15th centuries saw the development of the **Low Castle,** which included an armory, a chapel, and storerooms. The best point from which to see the entire castle is across the river, on the other side of the complex from the train and bus stations. Should you want to brave the waters, there's a **boat tour** (35min., every hr. 9am-10pm, 11zł, students 7zł). For advice, consult the English-speaking staff at the Maltur **tourist office,** ul. Sienkiewicza 15, near the traffic circle. (☎/fax 272 26 14 and 272 55 99. Open M-F 10am-4:30pm, Sa 10am-2pm.)

# FROMBORK ☎ (0)55

*Take a bus from Gdańsk (2hr., 5 per day, 10.90zł). Taking the train entails changing in Elbląg, which may take up to 4hr. The train station and the bus stop in Frombork are along ul. Dworcowa, with the docks right behind them. Return bus tickets must be purchased from the driver. Ferries run to Krynica Morska (30min., daily May-Sept. 15, 24zł, students 17zł; round-trip 33zł, 24zł) and Kaliningrad, RUS (2hr., daily May-Sept. 15, 70zł).*

Little Frombork is closely associated with the name and work of astronomer **Mikołaj Kopernik** (Copernicus), who lived here from 1510 until his death in 1543. It was in this town that Kopernik conducted most of his research and composed his (literally) revolutionary book, *De Revolutionibus Orbium Coelestium*. The tiny waterfront village surrounds a truly breathtaking and well-maintained **cathedral** complex perched majestically atop a hill. Follow the signs from the train and bus stops up the path straight ahead to get to the cathedral. The *kasa* on the left, just inside the complex's entrance, sells tickets to **Muzeum Kopernika,** the **cathedral,** the **tower** (wieża), and the less interesting **Tower of Copernicus** (Wieża Kopernika). The museum, on the right in the palace *(pałac)*, displays copies of *De Revolutionibus* and a number of Kopernik's documents, including a scrap of paper that served as his doctoral degree, circa 1503. (☎243 73 96. Open May-Sept. Tu-Su 9am-4:30pm; Oct.-Apr. Tu-Su 9am-3:30pm. 2zł, students 1zł.) Next door, in the cathedral itself, the 17th-century **organ** has a seven-second reverberation and impeccable sound quality. (Open May-Sept. M-Sa 9:30am-5pm; Oct.-Apr. M-Sa 9am-3:30pm. 3zł, students 2zł. Organ concerts M-Sa at noon and 3pm; July-Aug. Su 2pm.) Climb the tower for a phenomenal view of the cathedral, the town, and the lagoon. The gigantic Foucault pendulum inside continuously proves that the earth rotates. (Open daily May-Sept. 9:30am-5pm, Oct.-Apr. 9am-3:30pm. 3zł, students 2zł.)

**IT** (☎243 75 00) shares the tourist office with **Globus,** ul. Elbląska 2 (☎/fax 243 73 54); they are in the *rynek* at the end of the path from the stations. (Open daily May-Sept. 7am-7pm, Oct.-Apr. M-F 7am-3pm.) Should you need to stay the night, they can supply information about accommodations, including the youth hostel **Copernicus (HI),** ul. Elbląska 11. (☎243 74 53. Curfew 10pm. Lockout 10am-5pm. Dorms 11.98zł, nonmembers 14.98zł; triples and quads 17.12zł per person.)

# SOPOT
☎(0)58

As soon as you arrive in Sopot, you will realize that everything in this town exists to get you to and let you enjoy Sopot's incredible beaches. Let's re-emphasize this: beach beach beach. Beach. On the way there (to the beach, that is) you'll find wonderful shops, restaurants, bars, discos, street musicians, and more than a few rotisserie chicken stands, all of which make Sopot a fun place to be…but as soon you hit the famed 512m pier, look to either side and remember why you're here.

## ☞ TRANSPORTATION

**Trains:** The **commuter rail (SKM)** connects Sopot to **Gdynia** (15min., 2.50zł, students 1.25zł) and **Gdańsk** (20min., 2.50zł, 1.25zł). Trains depart from platform #1 every 10min. during the day and less frequently at night. Plainer **PKP trains** run to: **Toruń** (3hr., 6 per day, 30.46zł); **Warsaw** (4hr., 18 per day, 70.18zł); **Poznań** (4½hr., 8 per day, 70.18zł); and **Kraków** (6½hr., 15 per day, 77.86zł).

**Ferries:** ☎551 12 93. At the end of the pier. To: **Gdynia** (35min., 4 per day, round-trip 30zł, students 21zł); **Westerplatte** (35min., 2 per day, round-trip 30zł, 21zł); **Gdańsk** (1hr., 2per day, round-trip 42zł, 30zł); and **Hel** (1½hr., 4 per day, round-trip 44zł, 32zł).

## ✸❷ ORIENTATION AND PRACTICAL INFORMATION

**Ul. Dworcowa** begins at the train station and leads to the pedestrian **ul. Monte Cassino,** which runs along the sea to the **molo** (pier).

**Tourist Office: IT,** ul. Dworcowa 4 (☎550 37 83). In a wooden house next to the train station. English speakers behind the desk help secure accommodations, sell **maps** of Sopot and its sister cities (3-6zł), and provide info on the cultural scene. Open M-F 8am-7pm, Sa-Su 9am-7pm. In the same office, the **private accommodations bureau** (☎551 26 17) works its magic. Open M-F 8:30am-5pm, Sa-Su 9am-2pm.

**Budget Travel: Orbis,** ul. Hafferna 7 (☎/fax 551 41 42). Sells tickets for buses, ferries, and concerts around town. Open M-F 10am-5pm, Sa 10am-2pm.

**Currency Exchange: Bank Gdański,** pl. Konstytucji 3-go Maja 1 (☎551 32 32). Just down the hill from the train station. Gives AmEx/MC/Visa **cash advances,** cashes **traveler's checks,** and has a MC/Visa **ATM.** Open M-F 9am-6pm, working Sa 9am-2pm.

**International Press: Empik,** ul. Monte Cassino 55/57. Open M-F 10am-7pm, Sa 10am-3pm.

**24hr. Pharmacy: Apteka Pod Orłem,** ul. Monte Cassino 35 (☎551 10 18). Ring the bell 8pm-8am.

**Post Office:** ul. Kościuszki 2 (☎551 59 51). The 1st street on the right heading down ul. Monte Cassino. **Telephones** inside. Open M-F 8am-8pm, Sa 9am-3pm.

**Postal code:** 81-701.

## ☞ ACCOMMODATIONS

Sopot is one of Poland's most popular and expensive resorts, so reservations are a must in the summer. Consider renting a **private room;** visit the bureau in IT (see above) for help. (Nicest rooms: singles 46zł; doubles 78zł. One step down: singles 39zł; doubles 68zł; triples 90zł; quads 110zł.) If none of the following pan out, consider staying in Gdańsk, lest your *złotys* flutter away like a flock of seagulls.

**Hotel Wojskowy Dom Wypoczynkowy (WDW),** ul. Kilińskiego 12 (☎551 06 85; fax 626 11 33), is a 10min. walk from the pier. Facing the sea, turn right on ul. Grunwaldzka; ul. Kilińskiego is the 1st left after ul. 3-go Maja. This complex offers TV-equipped rooms and well-kept bathrooms. Check-in 2pm. Check-out noon. Singles 72zł, with bath 90zł; doubles 144zł, 180zł; triples 216zł, 270zł; quads with bath 304zł. Breakfast included.

**Hotel Chemik,** ul. Bitwy od Płowcami 61 (☎/fax 551 12 09 and 551 63 14). Facing the water, take a right on ul. Grunwaldzka from the pier, bear right at the fork, and then take a quick left. The hideous Chemik structure is on the left (10min.). The rooms are far more modern and comfortable than the exterior suggests. Check-in 12:30pm. Check-out 11am. Singles with bath 78zł; doubles 92zł, with bath 138zł; triples 138zł, 207zł.

**Hotel Miramar,** ul. Zamkowa Góra 25 (☎551 80 11; fax 551 51 64). Take the commuter rail (3min., every 10-20min., 1.25zł). From the Sopot-Kamienny Potok station, go down the right-hand stairs and turn left. Cross the street and pass the gas station. Miramar is behind an aquamarine monstrosity. Good-sized rooms, many with balconies. Check-in 2pm. Check-out noon. Singles 70zł, with bath 100zł; doubles 90zł, 160zł; triples 150zł, 180zł; quads 260zł. Breakfast included. AmEx/MC/Visa.

**Camping Nr. 19** (☎550 04 45), at the same address and phone number as Hotel Miramar. Separate reception desk and entrance on ul. Niepodłegłości, 300m from the end of the path from the Sopot-Kamienny Potok train station (go left). Outfitted with showers and a billiard hall. Check-in and check-out noon. 11zł per person; tents 6-11zł; 4 person cabins 75-80zł, with bath 85zł; doubles with bath 90zł.

# ⚫ FOOD

Ul. Monte Cassino is riddled with cafes and inexpensive food stands, many of which stay open into the wee hours. A small **24hr. grocery,** ul. Monte Cassino 60 (☎551 57 62), is but a step from the pier and the discos.

**▨ Happy Meals Vegetarian Kitchen,** among the kiosks at ul. Monte Cassino 67, sells huge portions of great samosas and cutlets topped with salads, as well as pitas bursting at the seams. Posters on the bright yellow walls apprise New Agers of goings on. Main dishes 4-9zł. Open Su-Th 11am-11pm, F-Sa 11am-midnight.

**Bar Rybny Pod Strzechą,** ul. Monte Cassino 42 (☎551 24 76). Serves simple but good fish dishes at unbeatable prices. Main dishes 4.50-12zł. Open daily 11am-11pm.

**Tivoli,** ul. Monte Cassino 16 (☎555 04 10). Cooks up Italian fare, including pizza and lasagna. Main dishes 10-25zł. Open daily noon until the last guest leaves.

**Saigon Restaurant,** ul. Grunwaldzka 8 (☎551 33 74). One block south of the pier. Vietnamese meals hover around 14-22zł, but a few creep into the 30-40zł range. Open daily noon-10pm. MC/Visa.

**Cukiernia Wiedeńska,** ul. Monte Cassino 11. Great for coffee, tea, and pastries. Everything under 4zł. Open M-F 7:30am-7pm, Sa 9:30am-5:30pm, Su 10:30am-4:30pm.

# 🎵 ENTERTAINMENT

As you may have gathered, Sopot's prominence is due largely to its **beach:** white, sandy, big, and adorned with all manner of recreational facilities, from waterslides to an outdoor theater. The most popular and extensive sands lie at the end of ul. Monte Cassino, where the longest **molo** *(pier)* on the Baltic begins. (M-F 2.10zł, Sa-Su 2.80zł) The town is just beginning to realize that the fun doesn't have to end when the tides come in, as evidenced by the growing number of street-side **cafes, pubs,** and **discos** along ul. Monte Cassino. **Kawiaret,** at 57/59, transforms from a mellow coffee-sipper's haven into a partier's playground when daylight fades. (☎551 53 31. Open daily 10am until the last guest leaves.) **Pub FM,** ul. Monte Cassino 36, offers traditional Polish fare (11-20zł) and American-wanna-be steaks (39-47zł) to a younger crowd, but most come here for the beer (0.5L Guinness 12zł) and cider. (☎551 33 59. Open daily 1pm-midnight. MC/Visa/AmEx.) Pierside discos and nightclubs are the latest rage; both **Non-Stop** (☎551 46 54; cover 10zł; open daily 10pm-late), and its neighbor **Fantom** (☎551 25 47; cover 10zł; open daily 10pm-late), haunted by an older crowd, are popular. Posters spread the word about special guest DJs at the clubs just out of town, accessible by commuter rail. **Opera Leśna,** an open-air theater, is a good place to get in on the local scene. Its open-air **rock and pop music festival** (☎551 18 12) dominates the area in mid-August. For tickets or information about other festivals, call the theater or contact **Orbis** (see above). If you can't bear to leave the beach, then look out for performers at **Teatr Atelier,** ul. Franciszka Mamuszki 2 (info ☎550 10 01), which stages shows on the sands; IT (see **Budget Travel,** p. 540) can give you a schedule.

# GDYNIA
☎(0)58

Young Gdynia (gh-DIN-ya; pop. 253,500), mostly built only after World War I, is in no hurry to grow up. Gdańsk might have the history and Sopot the glitz, but this town has the business—its residents are the wealthiest of any city in Poland, as some of the swankier shops suggest. If the city has become prosperous, though, it hasn't traded in its simple maritime life for too flashy a model. Evening strolls along the waterfront reveal a little slice of nautical heaven, recalling the time not long ago when the Gdynian life was not one of cyberspace, but of the sea.

## ▐▀ TRANSPORTATION

**Trains:** The Gdynia Główna train station welcomes a large volume of bus and train traffic. SKM commuter trains *(krolejka)* are the cheapest and easiest way to get to **Sopot** (15min., 2.50zł, students 1.25zł) and **Gdańsk** (35min., 3.50zł, 1.75zł). They depart every 10 minutes from *peron* (platform) #1. Punch your ticket in a yellow *kasownik* box before boarding. Trains to: **Hel** (2hr., 17 per day, 9.60zł); **Toruń** (3½hr., 5 per day, 30.46zł); **Warsaw** (4hr., 19per day, 63.18zł); **Poznań** (4½hr., 8 per day, 35.46zł); **Szczecin** (5hr., 6 per day, 35.46zł); **Katowice** (7hr., 10 per day, 40zł); **Kraków** (7hr., 10 per day, 41.15zł); **Wrocław** (7hr., 6 per day, 38.85zł); **Berlin, GER** (8½hr., 1 per day, 124.40zł); and **Prague, CZR** (15hr., July-Aug. 1 per day, 135.10zł).

**Buses:** Connections to **Hel** (2hr., 28 per day, 9.20zł) and **Świnoujście** (8hr., 2 per day, 43zł). **Polski Express** heads to **Warsaw** (4hr., 2 per day, 38zł, students 26.60zł). Tickets available at the PKS *kasa* or through Orbis (see below).

**Ferries:** leave from al. Zjednoczenia 2 (☎620 26 42; www.zegluga.gda.pl), on Skwer Kościuszki. To: **Sopot** (30min., 4 per day, 18zł, students 11zł); **Hel** (1hr., 10 per day, round-trip 42zł, 30zł); and **Gdańsk** (1½hr., 3 per day, 39zł, 28zł). July-Sept., from the same dock, a ferry runs to **Kaliningrad, RUS** (3hr., 2 per week, 110zł) via **Hel. Stena Line,** ul. Kwiatkowskiego 60 (☎660 92 00; fax 660 92 09) sends 1 ferry per day to **Karlskrona, SWE** (8½-10½hr., 300-385zł; duration and price depend on day of travel).

**Public Transportation:** Rides cost 1.60zł, students 0.80zł. If kiosks are closed, buy a book of 5 tickets (8zł, students 4zł) from the driver.

## ▄✳ ORIENTATION

Any of the roads running away and to the right from the train station will take you toward the beach and the pier; **ul. 10-go Lutego** is the most direct. If you end up on ul. Jana Kolna, ul. Wójta Radtkiego, or ul. Starowiejska, take a right at the end of the street and walk until you can take a left on ul. 10-go Lutego, where it hits the fountain-filled **Skwer Kościuszki.** For shopping, explore **ul. Swiętojańska,** which is perpendicular to 10-go Lutego. Explore ul. Swiętojańska, which is intersects ul. 10-go Lutego and where Skwer Kościuszki starts. The **beach** is to the right of the pier.

## ▐ PRACTICAL INFORMATION

**Tourist Office:** ul. 3 maja 27 (☎/fax 621 75 24), just off ul. 10-go Lutego near the train station, has free booklets on the Tri-city area, sells maps (6zł), and helps with finding accommodations. Open M-F 9am-5pm; Sa 9:30am-1pm.

**Budget Travel:** Orbis, ul. 10-go Lutego 2 (☎620 48 44; fax 620 89 50) meets most travel needs. Open M-F 8:30am-5:30pm; Sa 10am-2pm.

**Currency Exchange: Bank Gdański S.A.,** Skwer Kościuszki 14 (☎620 41 25), gives AmEx/MC/Visa **cash advances** and cashes AmEx/Visa/CitiCorps **traveler's checks.** Open M-F 8:30am-5pm, Sa 8:30am-2pm. The *kantor* to the right of the ticket counters in the train station is always open, but use it only if you're desperate; the rates are high.

**Luggage storage:** In the main hall of the bus/train station. 1.60zł plus 0.50zł for every 50zł declared value.

**24hr. Pharmacy: Apteka Pod Gryfem** (☎620 19 82), ul. Starowiejska 34.

**International Bookstore: Księgarnia Językowa,** ul. Świętojańska 14 (☎61 25 61), stocks English-language literature. Open M-F 10am-6pm, Sa 10am-3pm.

**Telephones:** In Telekomunikacja Polska, in the same building as the post office, but with a separate entrance. Open M-F 7am-9pm, Sa 9am-4pm, Su 11am-4pm.

**Internet Access: Com Net,** ul Świętojańska 18. 4zł per hr. Open daily 9am-8pm.

**Post Office:** ul. 10-go Lutego 10 (☎621 87 11), is between the train station and Skwer Kościuszki. Open M-F 7am-8pm, Sa 9am-3pm.

**Postal code:** 81-301.

# ACCOMMODATIONS

Cheap rooms are hard to come by in the city center; look for **private rooms. Turus,** ul. Starowiejska 47, opposite the train station, will help you find one. (☎621 82 65; fax 620 92 87. Singles 43.08zł; doubles 75.72zł. Open M-F 8am-6pm, Sa 10am-6pm.)

**Schronisko Młodzieżowe (HI),** ul. Morska 108c (☎627 00 05). Exit the train station through the tunnels under the platforms toward ul. Morska, then take bus #22, 25, 30, 105, 109, or 125 along ul. Morska for 4 stops. The entrance is in the back of building 108b. Rooms are basic but clean and the showers work well. Full kitchen. Sheets 3.21zł. Reception daily 8-10am and 5-10pm. Dorms 18.90zł, nonmembers 21zł.

**Dom Studencki Marynarza,** ul. Beniowskiego 24 (☎620 01 31), between the center and the hostel. A decent deal, particularly if you're staying for several nights. Follow the directions to Schronisko Młodzieżowe, but get off at the 2nd stop instead of the 4th. Backtrack and head up the hill on ul. Grabowo. Beniowskiego is the 2nd left. Check-out 9am. 55zł per person 1st night; 45zł 2nd-4th nights; 40zł thereafter.

**Hotel Lark,** ul. Starowiejska 1 (☎621 80 46), at the end of the road to the right of the train station. A short walk from the sights and the beach. Check-in 2pm; check-out noon. Singles 81.40zł; doubles 115.70zł; triples 132zł. AmEx/MC/Visa.

# FOOD

One of the most extensive markets in the Tri-city area, **Hala Targowa** stretches between ul. Jana Kolna and ul. Wójta Radtkiego. For a full sensory experience, check out the pungent **Hala Rybna** (Hall of Fish; open M-F 9am-6pm, Sa 8am-3pm.) Food stands, where a full meal can be had for less than 6zł, line the waterfront.

**Kawiarnia Artystyczna Cyganeria,** ul. 3 Maja 27, just off ul. 10-go Lutego. Offers excellent coffee (3-5zł) and an even better atmosphere, with velvet-covered couches, black-and-white photographs, and smoking students. Salads and chili 6-10zł. Open M-Th 10am-midnight, F-Sa 10am-1am, Su 4pm-midnight.

**Bistro Kwadrans,** Skwer Kościuszki 20 (☎620 15 92). Packs in the people with cheap pizza, Polish fare (6-13zł), and a set of breakfast menus for 6zł. Open M-F 9am-10pm, Sa 10am-10pm, Su noon-10pm.

**Restauracja Sphinx,** ul. 10-go Lutego 11 (☎661 87 95). Good pizza and hearty Middle Eastern sandwiches. Main dishes 7-25zł. Open M-F noon-11pm, Sa-Su noon-midnight.

**China Town,** ul. Dworcowa 11a (☎20 81 07), a stone's throw from the train station. Main dishes 11-30zł. Open daily noon-10:30pm.

# SIGHTS AND ENTERTAINMENT

Those looking to get nautical or naughty will not be disappointed by the city's pier off Skwer Kościuzki, where military history, marine biology, drinking, and dancing are all given their due. The only remaining Polish ship built before World War II, the destroyer **Błyskawica,** spends her days moored here. On board, an exhibition covers Polish naval history, including the ship's role in combat. (Open Tu-Su 10am-1pm and 2-5pm. 3zł, students 1.50zł. Free English info at the *kasa*.) The 1909 sailboat **Dar Pomorza** served as a school at sea for the Polish navy between 1930 and 1981, and won races in its competing days. (☎621 74 50. Open daily June-Aug. 10am-6pm, Sept.-May 10am-4pm. 5zł, students 3zł.)

POLAND

Crowds hang around well after meals to relax by the sea. **Bul. Nadmorski im F. Nowowiejskiego,** which heads to the right when facing the water, provides particularly good views along the beach. Follow it a few minutes to the outdoor **Cafe Bulwar** (☎ (0)50 109 93 51), a popular meeting point any time of the day or night. (Open 24hr. Disco nightly at 9pm.) **Gdynia Musical Theater** (Teatr Muzyczny w Gdyni; ☎621 60 24 and 621 78 16) puts on productions at pl. Grunwaldzki 1 and hosts concerts during the **Gdynia Summer Jazz Days** festival in early July. Call for a schedule or consult the tourist office (see p. 542). For a less formal show, head over to disco **Tornado**, below the restaurant Róża Wiatrów. (☎620 23 05. Open F-Sa 9pm-4am.)

# HEL
☎(0)58

Go to Hel—really. For almost a millennium, the sleepy village of Hel has lived off the fish of the Baltic Sea and booty from boats stranded on the Hel Peninsula (Mierzeja Helska). Recently, the town has awakened to the sound of tourists walking its clean, wide, gorgeous beaches. Hel opens the gates to a day of relaxation, serving up outstanding fish and a heavenly change of pace from crowded resorts.

**⌸ TRANSPORTATION.** Hel on earth exists on the tip of a peninsula jutting out into the Baltic, northeast of the Tri-city area. **Trains** (2hr., 17 per day, 9.60zł) and **buses** (2hr., 28 per day, 9.20zł) connect Hel to **Gdynia.** Hel can also be reached via **ferry** (☎301 63 35; www.zegluga.gda.pl) from: **Gdynia** (1hr., 10 per day, round-trip 42zł, students 30zł); **Sopot** (2hr., 4 per day, round-trip 44zł, 32zł); and **Gdańsk** (3hr., 3 per day, round-trip 42zł, 30zł). From July to September, a ferry also makes the short trip from to **Kaliningrad, RUS** (3hr., 2 per week, 110zł). It departs from Hel's dock on **Bulwar Nadmorski,** just down the hill from ul. Wiejska. When Hel freezes over (Nov.-Mar.), the ferry to Kaliningrad doesn't run. Tickets are sold in the white kiosk by the ferry landing. (☎675 04 37. Open daily 9am-6pm.)

**◪⋔ ORIENTATION AND PRACTICAL INFORMATION.** The **train station,** as well as the first of the town's two bus stops, is a short walk from **ul. Wiejska,** the main street. Facing away from the station, take **ul. Dworcowa** to the right as it follows a small park to intersect ul. Wiejska, then turn left to head into town. The **post office,** ul. Wiejska 55 (☎675 05 50) also **exchanges currency.** (Open M-F 8am-6pm, Sa 9am-1pm; *kantor* open M-F 8-11am and 3-6pm.) A Cirrus/Visa **ATM** sits across the street from the post office. **Postal code:** 84-150.

**⌂ ACCOMMODATIONS.** The cheapest accommodations in Hel are **private rooms.** Look for the *wolne pokoje* (available rooms) signs along the road from the train station through town. It's harder to find a single than a double or triple; if you're in limbo, call **Barbara Ptak-Formela** (☎/fax 67 50 996; hel@hel.com.pl; www.hel.com.pl; it's best to call after 2pm), who runs a fledgling tourist agency. She can arrange a room (single 30zł; doubles 50-80zł, with bath 100-160zł) or a stay in a *pensjonat* (80zł). Her office is at ul. Obroncow Helu 7, apt. #3. For a cheaper place to rest your bones, head to **Camping Helska Bryza,** ul. Bałtycka 5, near the lighthouse. Bear left at the end of ul. Wiejska to reach it. (☎675 08 93. Guarded 24hr. English spoken. Check-in noon. Check-out 11am. 10zł per person; tents 6zł; bungalows 30zł per person, with 3 meals 50zł.) If that plan gets shot to Hel, get in touch with the director of the Fishing Museum (see below), **Hanna Bulinska,** who may be able to put you up in her **pensjonat,** ul. Plażowa 5, a large, white stucco house a few hundred meters west of the museum. (☎675 08 48. 30zł per person.) **Tawerna "Helska,"** ul. Wiejska 82, has several newly renovated rooms, many with views of the sea. (☎675 06 40. Check-in 2pm. Check-out noon. 70zł per person. Breakfast included. AmEx/MC/Visa.) **Pensjonat Gwiazda Marza,** ul. Lesna 9b, on the way to the beach, has beautiful rooms with bath and TV. (☎675 08 59. 70zł per person.)

**⌷ FOOD.** It'll be a cold day in Hel before anyone starves; the town feeds its guests well. Most restaurants flank ul. Wiejska. The central **supermarket "Marina,"** ul. Wiejska 70, stocks groceries. (Open M-Sa 6am-10pm, Su 10am-4pm.) Near the ferry landing, **Izdebka,** ul. Wiejska 39, a white-and-brown fisherman's hut built in 1844, sells a variety of fresh fish for 3-10zł per 100g. (Open daily 10am-10pm.) The cafe in front of **Taverna "Helska"** sells great salads (3-5zł per 100g) and sandwiches (5-10zł; open daily 11am-10pm). If you're in the mood for dessert, stop for coffee (5zł) and sweets (6-10zł) at **Maszoperia,** ul. Wiejska 110, a 200-year-old hut with a traditional half-door. (☎675 02 97. Open daily 10am-midnight.)

🏛 **SIGHTS.** If, like Odysseus, you arrive in Hel by boat, the first thing you'll see after the harbor is its oldest building. Hel's bells top the red-brick **Church of St. Peter and Paul** (Kościół św. Piotr i Pawla; 1417-32), on Bulwar Nadmorski, which now houses the **Fishing Museum** (Muzeum Rybołówstwa). The museum displays nets, canoes, boats, and fishing and boat-building techniques of the last thousand years. Check out the fishermen's ice skates, the net-mending needles, and the giant eel-catching combs. (☎675 05 52. Open daily 9:30am-6pm. 4zł, students 2.50zł.) Facing the water, head right to see one Hel of a seal. "Balbin" has lived in the pool of the town **Fokarium** (☎675 05 52) since 1992. He and his six female playmates never fail to draw crowds with their frisky tricks. (Open daily 8am-10pm. 1zł.)

One of the Baltic Coast's best-kept secrets is the **beach** at the end of ul. Leśna. Take a left off ul. Wiejska onto ul. Leśna, from which a footpath continues through a park to the other side of the peninsula (15-20min.). **Ul. Wiejska,** the main artery, has retained much of its old character, thanks in part to the **19th-century fishermen's houses** at #29, 33, 39 and 110. These low-set huts are made of pine and bricks, and are also notable for facing the street sideways. Following ul. Wiejska as it turns into ul. Kuracyjna eventually leads to a military area closed to visitors. There, on the tip of the peninsula, sits the **Headland Battery,** site of the Polish defense at the beginning of World War II. If you bear left at the end of ul. Wiejska, you can reach the octagonal red lighthouse, which juts up of ul. Bałtycka. Follow the signs to "Latarni Marska." (2zł, students 1.50zł. Open daily 10am-2pm and 3-7pm.)

# KRYNICA MORSKA ☎(0)55

A small, popular seaside resort, Krynica Morska lies on the Curonian Spit (Mierzeja Wiślana), an outsized sandbar that stretches nearly 60km across the Baltic Sea. On one side of town lies the magnificent Baltic Sea and a gorgeous beach, on the other the serene Wiślany lagoon. Between the two, a pine forest provides serenity and good hiking. The **beaches** are the town's main draw. All lie on the Baltic and are quite nice: well-kept and wide with views of pine forests to either side. Right off the beach, numerous **trails** traverse the forest. Most of those near the center of town are only short routes, but there are longer ones in **Park Krajobrazowy,** which is on the beach side of the spit, off ul. Gdańska on the other side of town from the bus stop. The **lighthouse,** to the right (east) of the bus stop, provides stellar views. (Open 10am-1pm and 3-6pm. 1.50zł, students 1zł.) To get there, take a right on ul. Gdańska and a left up the hill on ul. H. Sienkiewicza. (15min. from the bus stop.)

Krynica Morska is 70km east of Gdańsk and less than 20km from the Russian border, which divides the Curonian Spit. The main **bus stop** is the third and final one within the town. It lies on the eastern edge of **ul. Gdańska,** the main thoroughfare. Looking back in the direction the bus came from, the lagoon lies to the left; ferries leave from the pier at the water's edge. **Buses** travel to: **Elbląg** (1½hr., 20 per day, 8.60zł), which has large train and bus stations; **Gdańsk** (2hr., 16 per day, 9.20zł); and **Warsaw** (5½ or 7hr., 2 per day, 47 or 43zł). **Polski Express** sends its comfortable coaches to Warsaw (5½hr., 2 per day, 45zł, students 31.50zł). There is also **ferry** service (☎247 60 23) to **Frombork** (90min., 6 per day, round-trip 33zł, students 24zł) and **Kaliningrad, RUS** (2hr. with customs clearance, daily May 1-Sept. 15, 70zł).

There's a map along the path from the bus stop to the lagoon pier. Ul. Bosmańska is on the lagoon side of ul. Gdańska, one block from the bus stop in the direction from which the buses come. Ul. Gdańska continues ahead through town. To the right, ul. Partowa runs over the hill. From its end, paths lead to the beach, about 10 minutes from the bus stop. The English speaking staff at **IT,** Bosmańska 1, gives out free maps and helps secure accommodations. (☎/fax 247 64 44; cit@mierzja.pl; www.mierzeja.pl. Open daily 10am-8pm.) There's a **pharmacy** at ul. Górników 15; coming from ul. Gdańska, take the first right off ul. Partowa and follow the signs. (☎247 66 11. Open M-F 8am-4pm, Sa 9am-1pm.) The **post office** is at ul. Gdańska 63. (Open M-F 8am-6pm, Sa-Su 9am-3pm.) **Telephones** are outside. **Postal code:** 82-120.

The best budget accommodations are **private rooms.** Look for the *Wolne Pokoje* and *Zimmer frei* signs along ul. Gdańska in the western part of town. Failing that, check along the unpaved ul. Rybacka, which runs parallel to ul. Gdańksa along the lagoon. From the bus stop, head into town and turn left on ul. Bosmańska; Rybacka is the first right. IT (see above) can also arrange rooms but charges slightly higher rates (singles 40zł, with bath 50zł). *Pensjonats* offer inexpensive quarters, but they fill up during the summer. **Pensjonat Riwera,** ul. Rybacka 37 (☎247 65 71), is family-run and offers 2- to 4-bed dorms with private bath, TV, and lagoon views for 30-35zł per person. **Dom Wypoczynkowy Morszczyn,** ul. Krynica 4, also has 2- to 4-bed dorms. Ul. Krynica is a 10min. walk from the bus station, heading west (left) on ul. Gdań ska. Check in the flower store (kwiaciarnia) if no one is in the reception area. (☎247 60 55. 25-30zł per person, with bath 35-40zł.) Finally, there are **campsites** on either side of the Spit. Swans wander the site at **Pensionat Dulka,** ul. Szałwiowa 8, which borders the lagoon. Off ul. Gdańska, it's a 20-minute walk from the bus station through town. (☎247 61 33. 9zł per person. Tents 4-9.5zł. Electricity 8zł.)

Krynica Morska is awash with eateries serving cheap tasty fish, *pierogi,* and other favorites for less than 10zł. A number of fruit and vegetable stands dot ul. Gdańska. Pick up an enormous sunflower head (słonecznik) full of seeds for 2.50zł. **Bar Kawiarnia Mariola,** ul. Gdańska 100, promises to feed you just like mama does. If you come from schnitzel- and potato-loving stock, then you're all set. (Main dishes 4-7zł; full lunch menu 10-14zł. Open daily 9am-8:30pm.)

During the summer, *Lunapark* arrives to supplement the natural entertainment, offering games and rides. The park lies across from the lagoon near the bus stop. At night many restaurants transform into **discos** and put up posters around town; look for signs advertising "Dancing," followed by one to five exclamation points. There's usually no cover, but when there is (5-10zł), beer is included.

# MAZURY

East of Pomorze, forested Mazury lives up to its nickname, "land of a thousand lakes." The region is actually home to about 4000 lakes; the largest, Śniardwy and Mamry, each cover an area of more than 100 sq. km. The myriad canals, rivers, and streams are ideal for kayaking and sailing. Mrągowo is the last outpost of civilization for tourists venturing out into the wild, beautiful waters.

## MRĄGOWO ☎(0)89

Tiny, orange-roofed houses speckle the endless lakes and rivers (once part of a Scandinavian glacier) where tourists come to boat, fish, swim, and water-ski. Known as Sensburg before 1947, Mrągowo (mrawn-GOH-voh) was named for Celesty Mrongowiusz, a patriot who fought the Germans so his countrymen could continue speaking Polish. The town center crowds the visiting population into its cafes and ice cream shops, but doesn't do much else; it depends on the adjacent lake and the surrounding hills to provide the entertainment—and the mosquitoes.

**⊏ TRANSPORTATION.** The **train station** (☎538 58 11), on ul. Kolejowa, receives trains from other towns in Mazury, such as **Olsztyn** (1½hr., 5 per day, 7.40zł), which has a large train station with many connections. It is far easier to travel to and from Mrągowo by bus, however, as buses run far more frequently and to more destinations. The **bus station** (☎741 32 11) at the end of ul. Skłodowskiej, sends buses to **Olsztyn** (1½hr., 21 per day, 7.70zł), **Białystok** (4hr., 2 per day, 26zł), **Warsaw** (4½ or 5hr., 6 per day, 31 or 30zł), and **Gdańsk** (5hr., 1 per day, 31zł).

**⚡🛈 ORIENTATION AND PRACTICAL INFORMATION.** To reach town from the train station, turn left on ul. Kolejawa, which runs in front of the station, then right on ul. Skłodowskiej, which runs down the hill. The bus station separates **ul. Warszawska,** a leg of Mrągowo's main thoroughfare, from **ul. Wojska Polskiego,** which leads out of town. Facing away from the station, bear right on ul. Warszawska to head into town (5min.). A right on **ul. Traugutta** drops down to **Jezioro Czos,** the biggest of the five surrounding lakes. Continue on ul. Warszawska to reach **ul. Ratuszowa** and then **ul. Królewiecka.** At ul. Ratuszowa 5, the large wooden doors lead to **Mrągowoska Agencja Turystyczna,** which sells maps for 5zł. (☎ 741 81 51 and 741 83 31. Open June-July M-F 9am-5pm, Sa 10am-2pm; Aug.-May M-F 9am-4pm, Sa 10am-1pm.) The tourist agency, **Mazur Travel,** at ul. Królewiecka 45, **rents bikes.** (English spoken. Open M-F 9am-5pm, Sa 9am-2pm.) For **currency exchange,** try one of the many *kantory* or **Bank PKO,** pl. Kajki 1, in the main square in the center of town. It cashes AmEx/Thomas Cook/Visa **traveler's checks** for a 1.5% commission (10zł minimum) and has a 24hr. Cirrus/MC/Visa **ATM.** (☎ 741 32 72. Open M-F 8am-6pm, Sa 10am-2pm.) There's a 24hr. ATM outside the **pharmacy** at ul. Królewiecka 23. (☎ 741 34 47. Open M-F and working Sa 8am-7pm, other Sa 9am-3pm.) The **post office,** ul. Królewiecka 39 (☎ 741 29 84; open M-F 7am-8pm, Sa 9am-2pm), has **telephones** outside. **Postal code:** 11-700.

**📷📂 ACCOMMODATIONS AND FOOD.** The best deal in town is the central, comfortable **Hotel Garnizonowy,** ul. Kopernika 1. From the bus station, turn left onto ul. Wojska Polskiego; Kopernika is the first left. (☎ 741 22 11. Singles 40zł, with toilet 50zł; doubles with toilet 70zł, with bath 100zł.) The summer-only **Schronisko Młodzieżowe (HI),** ul. Wojska Polskiego 2, right across from the bus station, is usually empty. Old but pleasant 1- to 4-bed dorms feature faded paintings and thriving plants. The showers in the basement are a little rustic. (☎ 741 27 12; fax 741 24 61. Sheets 6zł. Reception 6-10am and 5-10pm. Lockout 10am-5pm. Curfew 10pm. 9zł per person, nonmembers 12zł.) The rest of the hotels, most of which are more expensive, lie across the lake near the amphitheater, as does **camping** at **Centrum Sportowo Wypoczynkowo Szkoleniowe Troszczykowo,** ul. Troszczykowo. Take a left from ul. Traugułła and follow it around the lake (45-50min., 3½km). There is no direct bus, but you can take a taxi close to the entrance. (☎/fax 741 29 03. 10zł per person. Tents 7zł per person. 3-bed bungalows 75zł; 4-bed 100zł.)

Bars, snack shops, and ice cream joints pepper the town's main thoroughfare. **MaxDuet** supermarket, ul. Wojska Polskiego 22, advertises its one-stop shopping all over town. (Open M-F 6:30am-10pm, Sa 8am-10pm, Su 9am-8pm.) 🛑 **Restauracja Fregata,** just left off ul. Ratuszowa near ul. Dolny Zaułek, serves divine international and local cuisine from inside its communist-era shell. For a taste of the region, try the saucy *schab po mazursku* (Mazurian pork) for 13zł. (☎ 741 22 44. Main dishes 6-19zł. Open daily 11am-10pm.) Follow the delicious smells to the perpetually full 🛑 **Pizzeria "Margarita,"** ul. Królewiecka 5, and dig in. (☎ 741 48 88. Small pizza 7-11.50zł; large 10-14zł. Other dishes 5-12zł. Open M-F 10am-11pm.)

**📷📂 SIGHTS AND ENTERTAINMENT.** Don't go to Mrągowo expecting crazy or cosmopolitan living; you won't find any sign of it. Instead you'll find a taste of summer camp, at least along the lake. The **path** that snakes around the water left from ul. Traugułła is excellent for biking (see Mazur Travel, above, for rentals), running, or walking. The paved portion only lasts until it hits the **beaches**—at Plaża Miejska, 3-4km from town, there's guarded swimming and paddle boats and canoes for rent. The coolest late-night draw in town is **Bar Lasagne,** ul. Warszawska 7a (☎ 741 21 15), where locals gather until the wee hours to eat spaghetti or *kiełbasa,* washing it all down with Polish beer for 4zł. (Main dishes 4-9zł. Open daily 11am-1am.) When the **Lastar Saloon,** pl. Piłsudskiego, hosts live bands, the sound echoes throughout town. (Main dishes 5-15zł. Beer 5zł. Open daily 11am until the last guest leaves.) Proprietors of burgeoning discos try to lure patrons off the street while local hipsters gather at **Cocktail Bar Milano,** ul.

Królewiecka 53, a disco that plays pop and—yes—*Polish* hip-hop. (☎741 20 41. Cover 5zł. *Żywiec* 4zł. Open daily 10am until the last guest leaves.) Country music comes over Mrągowo's radio waves more frequently than elsewhere in Poland and to celebrate banjos and bandanas, the town holds the annual **Country Picnic Festival** during the last week in July.

# PODLASIE

Poland extends maximum environmental protection to this small, northeastern region, often called "the green lungs of Poland." Just a two-hour train ride from Warsaw, Podlasie is decidedly rural. Poland's few Russian Orthodox villages dot wide-open fields, shot through by the meandering Bug and Narew rivers. Białowieża Forest (Puszcza Białowieska), once the favorite hunting ground of Polish kings, is now a national park and the domain of the increasingly scarce European bison. Białystok, northwest of the preserve, is the region's student capital.

# BIAŁYSTOK ☎(0)85

Only 60km from the Belarussian border, Białystok (pop. 276,000) is a magnet for hawkers from Poland, Belarus, Lithuania, and Russia, who come to stock up on Polish goods at one of the largest markets in Eastern Europe. A healthy influx of students adds a cosmopolitan flair to this multilingual regional capital. Purported to be the birthplace of the famous *biały* roll, Białystok is the natural base for excursions to Białystok National Park (Białowieski Park Narodowy).

## ORIENTATION

The city center is organized along **ul. Lipowa,** which leads from the **bus** and **train stations** east to **Rynek Kościuszki,** the main square, and on to **pl. Branickich.** From the train station, cross the tracks via the overpass to reach the bus station. Facing away from the bus station, go left on ul. Bohaterów Monte Cassino (with the McDonald's on the right) and take the first right onto ul. Świętego Rocha. This leads directly to ul. Lipowa and, farther on, to Rynek Kościuszki (15min.). Ul. Sienkiewicza heads northeast (left, coming from the train station) from Rynek Kościuszki to several restaurants and budget accommodations and south (right) to the university. **Al. Piłsudskiego** runs parallel to ul. Lipowa, one block farther away from the stations.

## TRANSPORTATION

**Trains:** Ul. Kolejowa 1 (☎910). To: **Warsaw** (2½hr., 8 per day, 28zł); **Kraków** (8hr., 1 per day, 40zł); **Gdynia** (8hr., 2 per day, 38.27zł); **Hrodna, BLR** (4½hr., 4 per day, 17zł); **Vilnius, LIT** (8hr., 2 per day, 80zł); **Minsk, BLR** (10½hr., 1 per day, 130zł); **St. Petersburg, RUS** (15hr., 1 per day, 180zł); and **Moscow, RUS** (24hr., 1 per day, 250zł).

**Buses:** Ul. Bohaterów Monte Cassino 8 (☎936). To: **Białowieża** (2½hr., 2 per day, 12zł); **Warsaw** (3½-4½hr., 3 per day, 18.40-24zł); **Mrągowo** (4hr., 2 per day, 26zł); **Hrodna, BLR** (4½hr., 4 per day, 17zł); **Minsk, BLR** (9hr., 1 per day, 40zł); and **Vilnius, LIT** (9hr., 1 per day, 40zł). **Polski Express** buses also cruise to **Warsaw** (3½hr., 3 per day, F and Su 4 per day, 21-26zł).

**Local Transportation:** Buy bus tickets at kiosks throughout the city. 1.60zł per ride, students 0.80zł. Baggage requires its own ticket. 75zł fine for riding ticketless.

## PRACTICAL INFORMATION

**Tourist Offices: IT,** on Rynek in the Holiday Travel office, ul. Sienkiewicza 3 (☎653 79 50). English speakers field Białystok queries and find accommodations in the city and in Białowieski Park (see p. 551). Open M-F 9am-6pm, Sa 10am-2pm.

POLAND

**Budget Travel: Orbis,** ul. Rynek Kościuszki 13 (☎742 16 27 and 742 16 27). Provides **Western Union** services, MC/Visa **cash advances,** and **currency exchange.** Sells international train and bus tickets. Open M-F 8am-6pm, Sa 9am-3pm. **Almatur,** ul. Zwierzyniecka 12 (☎742 82 09). Follow ul. Legionowa from Rynek Kościuszki to a left on ul. Żwierzyniecka (15min.). Sells ISICs (35zł) and supplies information about university dorms that open up in the summer. Open M-F 9am-5pm, Sa 10am-2pm.

**Consulates: Belarus,** (☎744 55 01, fax 744 66 61). Visa department at ul. Bohaterów Monte Cassino 5 (☎744 45 62). Open M-F 10am-5pm.

**Currency Exchange:** *Kantory* flank ul. Lipowa. **Bank PKO,** ul. Sienkiewicza 40 (☎743 61 00), cashes all major brands of **traveler's checks** for a 1% commission. Open M-F 8am-6pm, Sa 10am-2pm.

**ATM:** There's a 24hr. Visa ATM at Rynek Kościuszki 16 and a MC ATM across the street.

**Luggage Storage:** At the train station, next to the restrooms. 4zł. Open 24hr. Don't be afraid to bang on the door at night.

**International Bookstore: Empik,** Rynek Kościuszki 6. International press downstairs; maps (4-6zł) and a small but adequate collection of fiction and non-fiction upstairs. Open M-F 9:30am-6:30pm, Sa 9:30am-3pm. **Księgarnia Językowa,** ul. Piłsudskiego 38 (☎743 65 55). Open M-F 10am-5pm, Sa 10am-2pm.

**24hr. Pharmacy:** Ul. Suraska 2 (☎742 04 53), just off Rynek Kościuszki to the right, coming from the stations.

**Telephones:** At the post office and throughout town.

**Internet Access: Internet Bar Jaff,** ul. Lipowa 37, has a bar inside that serves Mexican food. 5zł per hr. Open daily 8am-10pm. Less depressing, but less convenient, **Netcraft,** ul. Legionowa 9/1, packs in the gamers. Enter around back. Ul. Legionowa runs out of Rynek Kościuszki; follow it 10min. The complex is on the left.

**Post Office:** Ul. Warszawska 10. Open M-F 8am-8pm, Sa 8am-2:30pm. Smaller but more convenient **branch** at Rynek Kościuszki 13 (☎742 42 30 and 742 28 12). Open M-F 8am-8pm, Sa 10am-4:30pm.

**Postal code:** 15-900.

# ACCOMMODATIONS

Almatur (see above) can help find a **university dorm** room to sleep in during July and August, while IT (see above) can arrange a **private room** in Białowieski Park.

**Schronisko Młodzieżowe (HI),** al. Piłsudskiego 7b, a 15min. walk from the bus station. Take a left on ul. Bohaterów Monte Cassino and then the 1st right on Św. Rocha. In the square, go past the 1st right on ul. Lipowa and take the 2nd one; it's on the left behind the gray apartment buildings. Sheets 6zł. Friendly little cabin with a full-service kitchen and clean showers. Check-out 10am. No lockout. Flexible 10pm curfew. 6- to 14-bed dorms. Under 26 9.80zł, nonmembers 12zł; over 26 18zł, nonmembers 20.50zł.

**Dom Turysty Rubin,** ul. Warszawska 7 (☎777 23 35), in a stately old building. From ul. Lipowa, turn left on ul. Skłodowskiej and then right after the big intersection onto ul. Warszawska; the hotel is 3 blocks up, just past the park. Or, take bus #2 or 21 from the train station and get off at the 1st stop on ul. Warszawska (15min.). Big rooms with high ceilings, electric kettles, and TVs. Check-in 2pm. Check-out noon. Doubles 60zł, with bath 120zł; triples 75zł, 150zł; 2-person apartment 140zł; 3-person 200zł.

**Internat Nauczycielski,** ul. Sienkiewicza 86 (☎732 36 64). A 15min. walk from ul. Lipowa, on the right past the turn for Hotel Rubin and just before ul Złota. Enter through the courtyard in back. The simple rooms sparkle, but the place tends to fill up F-Sa, when pedagogical students come to town to study for exams. Negotiable 10pm curfew. 2- to 3-bed dorms 20zł; 5- to 6-bed dorms 18zł.

# FOOD

The city's best restaurants are on **ul. Lipowa** and around **Rynek Kościuszki. Supersam** sits at ul. Skłodowskiej 16. (☎742 06 41. Open M-Sa 6am-10pm, Su 10am-6pm. MC/Visa.) There's a **24hr. grocery** at Lipowa 12.

POLAND

■ **Bar El'Jot,** ul. Starobojarska 25 (☎ 732 63 16). A 10min. walk up ul. Sienkiewicza, on the right side. Small neighborhood haunt with a quiet terrace. The pizza, cutlets, and pepper steaks are only a half-step up from fast food, but they're tasty and cheap, and the grease factor is minimal. Main dishes 4.50-8zł. Great carrot juice 1.50zł; side of broccoli or cauliflower 2.50zł. Open daily 11am-midnight.

■ **Ananda Bar Wegetariański,** ul. Warszawska 30 (☎741 33 36). Two blocks past Hotel Rubin, Ananda is a much-needed respite for veggie lovers. If the Polish-only menu leaves you befuddled, rest assured that it's 100% vegetarian. The soups are particularly good. Main dishes 6-10zł. Open M-F 11am-10pm, Sa-Su noon-10pm. MC/Visa.

**Savona Pizza Club,** ul. Rynek Kościuszki 10 (☎743 51 35). Candlelit at night, but less romantic during the day, this basic parlor dishes out delectable pizzas. Medium (plenty for one, 9.80-12.50zł) and large (7.90-13.90zł) only. Open M-Th and Su 11am-midnight, F-Sa 11am-1am. MC/Visa. **Branch** at ul. Legionow 9/1, in the same building as Netcraft (see **Internet Access,** above).

**New York Bagels,** ul. Lipowa 12 (☎744 66 66). Excellent bagels 1.50zł, sandwiches 3.50-7zł, other main dishes 5-10zł. Open M-Sa 10am-10pm, Su 11am-10pm.

# 👁 SIGHTS

By far the most impressive building in Białystok is the 18th-century **Branickich Palace** (Pałac). Built by pretender Jan Klemens Branicki, it has been dubbed the "Versailles of Podlasie." It faces little competition for the title, since Baroque palaces are far and few between in this eastern wilderness, but that doesn't make it any less enchanting. The interior is closed to the public because the building now serves as a medical school, but the **park** and **gardens** offer sanctuary and occasional concerts. The entrance to the grounds is just past Rynek Kościuszki, across from pl. Jana Pawła II. (Open daily May-Sept. 6am-10pm, Oct.-Apr. 6am-6pm.)

An architectural and historical curiosity stands a few paces down ul. Lipowa at the end of Rynek Kościuszki—a small **parish church** connected to a giant **cathedral.** Under the tsars the Poles were forbidden to build any new Catholic churches. Their solution: attach a cathedral to the old church, even if the structures clashed. A short walk closer to ul. Lipowa (and the bus station), Białystok's **town hall** *(ratusz)* originally served as a trade center. It was demolished in 1940 by the Russians, who planned to put a monument to Stalin in its place. The statue never materialized and the site remained vacant until the present building was constructed in 1958.

# 🎵 ENTERTAINMENT

Pubs cluster around Rynek Kościuszki, hiding in basements and second floors as well as on the main drag. Just up ul. Lipowa, **Black Velvet Pub,** ul. Waryńskiego 4, lets customers collapse on its couch with a beer. (☎744 63 27. Beer 5zł. Open daily 4pm until the last guest leaves.) The hippest place in town is **Jazz Club Odeon,** ul. Akademicka 10/1. Enjoy the nightly concert from the balcony over the stage or take in the evening air out on the terrace. From Rynek Kościuszki, go right on ul. Sienkiewicza, right when it ends, and then left onto ul. Akademicka. Odeon is hidden across from the palace garden. (☎742 49 88. Beer 4.50zł, whiskey and Coke 7zł. Jazz concerts daily 8-11pm. Open Su-Th noon-1am, F-Sa noon-2am.) If you feel like grinding to techno, visit **Klub Muzyczny Metro,** ul. Białówny 9A, off ul. Malmeda. (☎732 41 54. Beer 4zł. Open daily noon-4am.) There are four **cinemas** in town and each plasters its posters on every available surface. Catch English-language films with Polish subtitles at **Kino Ton,** ul. Rynek Kościuszki 2 (☎/fax 743 53 82), **Kino Pokaj,** ul. Lipowa 14 (☎742 23 70), and **Kino Syrena,** ul. Św. Rocha 23 (☎744 58 96).

# ⌐ DAYTRIPS FROM BIAŁYSTOK

## BIAŁOWIESKI PARK NARODOWY

*Buses go to Białowieża from Białystok at 6:30am and 3pm, returning at 6am and 5pm (2½-3hr., 11.70-12zł). There are also only 2 straight back. Alternatively, take one of the frequent buses to Hajnówka (2hr., 25 per day, 8.30zł) and change there for Białowieża (45min., 9 per day, 4.70zł). Leave very early, as there may be a wait between buses. The main bus stop is not the final one. Once the bus reaches Białowieża, get off as you pass the post office and park gate on the left.*

**Białowieża Primeval Forest** (Puszcza Białowieska), a natural treasure of towering trees and European bison, sprawls out over oceans of flatland. Most travelers begin in the sleepy town of **Białowieża**, where there are plenty of inexpensive places in which to stay or camp. Bordering Białowieża is the park's main attraction, a large **bison preserve.** Only **guided tours** (see below) can enter this section of the park, where about 250 bison still lumber about. There would be far more, but many were wiped out by hungry soldiers in World War II. If you don't want to pay the price of a tour of the large preserve, there are two much smaller ones where bison and other animals are kept in tighter quarters. The closer of the two is 2½km away from town and accessible by the yellow trail, which leads from the PTTK office (see below) into the woods. (Preserve open Tu-Su 10am-5pm. 3zł, students 2zł.) The yellow, red, green, and blue trails all provide great biking (or walking) through flat, but beautiful and serene, wooded areas. They are all well-marked, and signs along the way post distances to the larger towns in the region.

In the gateway of the park entrance, the **IT** office awaits tourists. (☎681 29 01. Open daily 10am-5pm. English spoken.) They can point the way to accommodations (including the youth hostel) and can dispense info on such activities as horseback riding. **PTTK,** ul. Kolejowa 17, through the entrance to the park over the bridge to the left, rents **bikes** (2.50zł per hr., mountain bikes 3.50zł per hr.) and arranges **tours** of the park. (☎681 22 95. English-speaking guide for 1-25 people 120zł. Horse-drawn carriage tour for 1-4 people 100zł, plus 8zł for park carriage fee. All tours 3hr. 4zł per person park admission not included. Office open M-Sa 8am-4pm, Su 8am-3pm. AmEx/MC/Visa.) **Gulliwer Tourist Office,** ul. Kolejowa 3, down the street and to the left from PTTK, also arranges tours by carriage or foot. Their prices are the same as those of PTTK. (☎/fax 681 23 66. Open M-Sa 8:30am-3pm, Su by appointment.) To rent a bike, head to **Zimordek,** ul. Waszkiewicza 2, right across from the bus stop. When the door is closed, head around the corner to the youth hostel to find the owner. (☎/fax (85) 681 25 15. 2.50zł per hour, 22.50zł per day.)

# ROMANIA (ROMÂNIA)

**IF YOU'RE HERE FOR...**

**4-6 DAYS.** Stay in **Bucharest** (p. 561) long enough to take in Parliamentary Palace and hit a few clubs; then head to **Transylvania** (p. 570) for some hiking or skiing in the mountains and a history lesson on Dracula.

**1 WEEK.** Follow **Bucharest** (p. 561) and **Transylvania** (p. 570) with the secluded **Bukovina monasteries** (p. 585), whose beauty would make a believer out of anybody.

Romania, devastated by the lengthy reign of Communist dictator Nicolae Ceauşescu, now suffers under a government incapable of bridging its gaps with the West. The resulting state of flux has left the country disheartened, as the tourist industry flounders and offers sights packaged far less attractively than those of its more westernized neighbors. Bucharest, the center of the country's political and cultural existence, has been swallowed by concrete apartment blocks and sterile Communist squares. However, visitors who manage to avoid the beaten "Dracula" path and talk to common villagers will discover that Romania runs far deeper than Ceauşescu's effects. Here the joy of travel comes in peeling the layers from the nation's recent history to find what lies underneath. Romanians go out of their way to make visitors feel at home, and travelers daring enough to explore will find a dynamic people eager to grow and hopeful in spite of their past.

## ROMANIA AT A GLANCE

**OFFICIAL NAME:** Romania

**CAPITAL:** Bucharest (pop. 2.1 million)

**POPULATION:** 22,350,000

**LANGUAGES:** Romanian (official), Hungarian, German

**CURRENCY:** 1 leu (L) = 100 bani

**RELIGION:** 70% Romanian Orthodox, 6% Roman Catholic, 6% Protestant

**LAND AREA:** 230,340 sq. km

**CLIMATE:** Temperate and continental

**GEOGRAPHY:** Mountains and plains

**BORDERS:** Bulgaria, Hungary, Moldova, Ukraine, Yugoslavia

**ECONOMY:** 41% Industry, 40% Services, 19% Agriculture

**GDP:** US$4,050 per capita

**EMERGENCY PHONE NUMBERS:** Ambulance 961, Fire 981, Police 955

**COUNTRY CODE:** 40

**INTERNATIONAL DIALING PREFIX:** 00

# HISTORY

**ROOTS.** The Romanian ethnographic tree has its roots in the **Thracian** tribes that settled in the region as early as 2000 BC. Contact with **Greeks** and then **Romans** followed; the latter considered the flourishing Thracian (Dacian to the Romans) civilization threatening enough to warrant invasion. Romans are responsible for both the name "Romania" and the Latin from which the Romanian tongue descends. Another branch of Romania's tree came from the **Slavs,** who invaded in the 8th century. From the 8th to 10th centuries, **Bulgarians** provided the final crucial element, Orthodox Christianity, which better integrated Romanians with their neighbors.

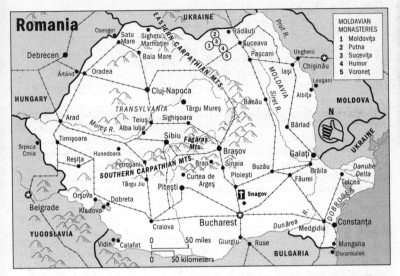

**Romania**

MOLDAVIAN
MONASTERIES
1 Moldoviţa
2 Putna
3 Sucevita
4 Humor
5 Voroneţ

**GROWING PAINS.** With the ethnic melange more or less complete, the Romanian people began carving a space for themselves; the first Romanian state, **Wallachia**, was established in the early 1300s. The second, **Moldavia**, was founded east of the Carpathians in 1349. The fledgling states had it rough, though, constantly defending against invasion by the **Ottoman Turks.** Moldavia's **Ştefan cel Mare** (Stephen the Great; 1457-1504) was most successful in warding off their attacks. During his 47-year rule, he built 42 monasteries and churches, one for each of his victories (see **Bukovina Monasteries,** p. 585). Alas, successful resistance died with Ştefan and Moldavia and Wallachia became Turkish vassals.

**HELP YOURSELF.** For the next four centuries, Austria-Hungary, Russia, Turkey and the Polish-Lithuanian Commonwealth fought for control of the region. Internally, many rulers enjoyed fleeting success at creating a unified Romania. **Mihai Viteazul** (Michael the Brave) tried in 1599 when he invaded Moldavia and Transylvania, but Polish, Hungarian, and Ottoman attacks left Mihai dead and the country in tatters. Moldavia and Wallachia united in 1859 by electing **Alexandru Cuza** prince and, this time, the union outlasted its ruler. **King Carol I** trounced corruption, built the first railroads, and strengthened the army that, in 1877, finally won independence from Turkey. On the heels of Austria-Hungary's defeat in **World War I,** Romania doubled its territory, gaining Transylvania, Bukovina, and Bessarabia (modern-day Moldova, which declared itself independent from the USSR in 1991). While the population doubled, expansion brought new minority groups and ethnic tensions.

The **1941 Nazi-Soviet Non-Aggression Pact** subjected Romania to a fate of its neighbors to the northwest, as it lost its new territory to the Axis powers. Hoping the Nazis would preserve an independent Romania, its dictator, **General Antonescu.,** chose to support Germany in World War II. In 1944, **King Mihai** orchestrated a coup and attempted to surrender to the Allies. The Big Three, however, had already decided Romania's fate and the Soviets moved in and proclaimed the **Romanian People's Republic** on December 30, 1947.

**TYRANNY AND DEATH.** Opposition was violently suppressed in the postwar era. More than 200,000 Romanians died in the purges of the 1950s, and farms were forcibly collectivized. In 1965 **Nicolae Ceauşescu** ascended to the top of the Communist Party. Although his attempts to distance Romania from Moscow's influence won praise from the West, his ruthless domestic policies were hardly laudable. His industrialization and trade programs often left the average Romanian without food, heat, and electricity. By the late 1980s Ceauşescu had whipped Romania into a police state, but rebellion seethed. In 1989 a **revolution** as ruthless as the dictator it would overthrow erupted. What began as a minor event in Timişoara, when the dreaded **Securitate** (Secret Police) arrested a popular Hungarian priest, soon ripped through the country. In December clashes with security forces in Bucharest brought thousands of protesters to the streets. Ceauşescu and his wife were arrested, tried, and executed—which was broadcast on TV—all on Christmas Day.

**OH, THE IRONY.** The enthusiasm that followed these December days didn't last, as **Ion Iliescu's National Salvation Front,** largely composed of former communists, seized power. Iliescu was himself a high-ranking communist official whom Ceauşescu pushed into minor positions because of his pro-Russian leanings. Despite his past, Iliescu won the 1990 presidential elections with 70% of the vote and began moderate reforms. In June 1990, Iliescu provoked international condemnation after calling on miners to repress student demonstrations in Bucharest. The miners terrorized the city for three days, beating anyone resembling a protester. Revolution, it seemed, had changed little.

# POLITICS

The constitution of 1991 provides for an elected **president** who serves a four-year term and nominates the **prime minister,** who with his cabinet, is responsible for implementing policy. **Members of Parliament** are elected to four-year terms.

In November 1996, **Emil Constantinescu** succeeded Ion Illiescu in the country's first democratic transfer of power. Constantinescu's **Romanian Democratic Coalition** (RDC) promised reforms, but spent most of its time settling disputes among its member parties. At press time, President Constantinescu had declared he would not run for reelection in November 2001, while both Prime Minister **Mugur Isarescu,** who champions entrance to the EU, and Illiescu had declared they would. The main objective of Romania's foreign policy is to join the EU; to this end the country has signed a treaty normalizing relations with Moldova.

# CULTURE

| NATIONAL HOLIDAYS IN 2001 | |
|---|---|
| **January 1-2** New Year | **May 1** Labor Day |
| **January 6** Epiphany | **December 1** National Day |
| **April 15-16** Easter | **December 25-26** Christmas |

# LITERATURE AND ARTS

The first sign of literary activity in Romania came with the Roman poet **Ovid,** who wrote his last works while exiled near what is now Constanţa. The Romanian national literary tradition is rooted in 15th-century translations of Slavonic religious texts, which culminated in the first Romanian translation of the **Bible** in 1688. The literary resurgence after the end of Ottoman oppression in the late 1700s is largely credited to the **Văcărescu family**: grandfather **Ienachita** wrote the first Romanian grammar, father **Alecu** wrote love poetry, and son **Iancu's** verse was so splendid that he, not his dad, is considered the father of Romanian poetry.

The early 19th century saw the cultivation of new genres; **Grigore Alexandrescu's** French-inspired fables and satires stand out. The next generation of writers—clustering around the literary magazine *Junimea*—penned the great classics of Romanian literature. Emulating German culture, their works combined cosmopolitan awareness and a preoccupation with national identity. For instance, **Ion Creangă's** (see **Iaşi,** p. 583) most important work, *Aminitiri din copilarie* (Memories of My

Boyhood), depicts life in his native village. **Mihai Eminescu** (see **Iaşi**, p. 583), considered the father of modern Romanian poetry, embodied **Romanticism** at its peak.

The end of World War II brought Nicolae Ceauşescu's communist regime and the strictures of **Socialist Realism. Geo Bogza** and **Mihail Beniuc** were among the prominent adherents, composing works glorifying the worker's state. Some native-born artists and scholars sought freedom in other lands and languages—absurdist dramatist **Eugène Ionesco** and religious scholar **Mircea Eliade** are the most prominent.

The most notable traditional crafts include **painting on glass** and elaborate **Easter egg** decoration. More contemporary artists include folk music composer **Georges Enesco** (1881-1955), painter **Nicolae Grigorescu** (1838-1907), who combined techniques he learned in France with his experience as an icon painter to immortalize the Romanian countryside, and sculptor **Constantin Brâncuşi** (1876-1957), who remains one of the greatest modernist sculptors of the 20th century and the preeminent Romanian artistic export.

# RELIGION

Unlike other communist regimes, the Romanian state placed few restrictions on religion. Though the government required all churches to register with the state, religious life still thrived. Today, the Roman Orthodox church is the largest, the Uniate church is prevalent in Transylvania, and Catholicism and Protestantism are favored by ethnic Hungarians.

# FOOD AND DRINK

Romanian food is fairly typical of Central Europe, with a bit of Balkan and French influence thrown in. Bucharest is the only place to find non-Romanian cuisine. Otherwise, lunch usually starts with a soup, called *supă* or *ciorbă* (the former has noodles or dumplings, the latter is saltier and usually has vegetables), followed by a main dish (typically grilled meat) and dessert. Soups can be very tasty; try *ciorbă de perişoare* (with vegetables and ground meatballs) or *supă cu găluşte* (with fluffy dumplings). Pork comes in several varieties, of which *muşchi* and *cotlet* are the best quality. For dessert, *clătite* (crepes), *papanaşi* (doughnuts with jam and sour cream), and *tort* (creamy cakes) can all be fantastic if they're fresh. Some restaurants charge by weight (usually 100g) rather than by portion. It's difficult to predict how many grams you will actually receive. *Garnituri*, the extras that come standard with a meal, are usually charged separately, down to that dollop of mustard. As a rule, you're paying for everything the waiters put in front of you.

In the mountains or resorts, peasants sell fruit and cheese. *Lapte* (milk) is fatty and often not homogenized; powdered milk is available in many shops. On the street, you can find cheap *mititei* (a.k.a. *mici;* barbecued ground meat) or Turkish-style kebabs, best when warm. "Fast food" in Romania means pre-cooked and microwaved. *Înghețată* (ice cream) is cheap and good, while the delicious *mere în aluat* (doughnuts with apples) and the sugary *gogoşi* (fried doughnuts) are delectable. Be sure to check the expiration dates on everything you buy.

# CUSTOMS AND ETIQUETTE

It is customary to give inexact change for purchases, generally rounding up to the nearest L500. Similarly, restaurants usually round up to the nearest L500 or give you candy instead of L100's. **Tipping** is not necessary but not unheard of. "Non-stop" cafes and kiosks can be found in all cities, but their names can be misleading; shops close arbitrarily when attendants run errands or go home early. **Posted hours** are not definite, and many banks and businesses may be closed on Friday afternoons. **Churches** services are lengthy (2½hr.), but people quietly come and go at all times.

Romanians take pride in their hospitality. Most will be eager to help, offering to show you around town or inviting you into their homes. When you're visiting, bring your hostess an odd number of flowers; even-numbered bouquets are only brought to graves. Romanians, especially the women, dress well, especially in cities, and shorts are a rarity for either sex on even the hottest days. **Men** are usually fairly respectful of women. **Women** traveling alone shouldn't go out alone after dark and should be prepared with a story about traveling with a male companion.

The Roma are the **minority** that experience the most discrimination; Hungarians who fit in well and other minorities are very rare. **Homosexuality** has been legal in Romania since 1996, but homosexual public displays of affection remain illegal. Outside major cities, many Romanians hold conservative attitudes toward sexuality, which may translate into harassment of gay, lesbian, and bisexual travelers. Homosexuals in Romania are well hidden, and gay hangouts are ephemeral when they exist at all. Nonetheless, women sometimes walk arm-in-arm without anyone batting an eye. **Child homelessness** continues to be a major problem in Romania.

# LANGUAGE

**Romanian** is a Romance language; those familiar with French, Italian, Spanish, or Portuguese should be able to decipher public signs. Romanian differs from other Romance tongues, however, in its Slavic-influenced vocabulary. Spoken mainly in Romania and Moldova, Romanian consists of four dialects that are very distinct; Daco-Romanian is the basis for the standard language. **German** and **Hungarian** are widely spoken in Transylvania. Throughout the country, **German** and **French** are a common second languages for the older generation, **English** for the younger. English-Romanian dictionaries are sold at book-vending kiosks everywhere. Spoken Romanian is a lot like Italian, but with three additional vowels: "*ă*" (pronounced like "e" in "pet") and the phonetically interchangeable "*â*" and "*î*" (like the "i" in "pill"). The other two characters peculiar to the Romanian alphabet are "*ş*" ("sh" in "shiver") and "*ţ*" ("ts" in "tsar"). At the end of a word, "*i*" is dropped. "*Ci*" sounds like the "chea" in "cheat," and "*ce*" sounds like the "che" in "chess." "*Chi*" is pronounced like "kee" in "keen," and "*che*" like "ke" in "kept." "G" before "e" or "i" sounds like "j" as in judge and "gh" before those vowels is like "g" in girl. For commonly used Romanian words and phrases, see **Glossary,** p. 558 and **Phrasebook,** p. 559.

# ADDITIONAL READING

The verbosely-titled *Taste of Romania: Its Cookery and Glimpses of its History, Folklore, Art and Poetry* is the most easily digested primer on Romanian culture. Acclimate yourself to the local proclivity for larded pork and sample the illustrations, folklore, and poetry interspersed throughout. For a more substantial and intriguing approach to poetry, pick up *When the Tunnels Meet*, an anthology of recent Romanian verse translated by Irish poets, including Northern Irishman and Nobel laureate Seamus Heaney. For art lovers, *Constantin Brâncuşi: 1876-1957* is one of the best books on the sculptor and has lots of pretty pictures to boot. Finally, in keeping with *Let's Go's* mission to debunk cultural myths, we recommend *Dracula, Prince of Many Faces: His Life and Times* by Radu R. Florescu, for the real story of Vlad Ţepeş.

# TRAVELING ESSENTIALS

US citizens do not need visas for stays of up to 30 days. Citizens of Australia, Canada, Ireland, New Zealand, South Africa, and the UK all need visas to enter Romania. Single-entry visas (US$35) are good for 30 days within three months of the date of issue, multiple-entry visas (US$70) for 180 days, and transit visas (US$35) for three days. Obtain a visa at a Romanian embassy (see **Essentials: Embassies and Consulates,** p. 18). To apply, submit a passport with expiration at least three months after your return from Romania, payment by money order, a letter stating the purpose of your visit and your approximate dates of departure and arrival, and a self-addressed, stamped envelope. At press time Romanian visas could be obtained at the border for the standard visa price. There were plans, however, to stop doing so after January 1, 2001. Also bear in mind that if you fly into Romania your airline may require that you have a visa before boarding. You can obtain a visa extension at a police station. There is no additional fee for crossing a Romanian border. The best way to cross the border is to take a direct train from Bucharest to the capital city of the neighboring country. The next best options are planes and buses.

# TRANSPORTATION

**BY PLANE.** Numerous airlines fly into Bucharest. **TAROM** (Romanian Airlines) is in the process of updating its aging fleet; it flies directly from Bucharest to **New York, Chicago,** and major European cities. Bucharest's Otopeni International Airport has improved its notoriously bad ground services, but the airport is still far from ideal.

**BY TRAIN.** Trains, a better choice of transport than buses, head daily to Western Europe via Budapest. There are also direct trains to and from Belgrade, Chişinău, Moscow, Prague, Sofia, Vienna, and Warsaw. To buy international tickets in Romania, go to the CFR (Che-Fe-Re) office in larger towns. Budapest-bound trains leave Romania through either Arad or Oradea; when you buy your ticket, you'll need to specify where you want to exit, and they'll want to see your papers. An ISIC might get you a 50% discount, but technically student discounts are for Romanians only.

**BY BUS.** Buses connect major cities in Romania to **Athens, Istanbul, Prague,** and various cities in Western Europe. Since plane and train tickets to Romania are often expensive, buses are a good—if slow—option. It is generally cheapest to take a domestic train to a city near the border and catch an international bus from there. Inquire at tourist agencies about timetables and tickets, but buying tickets straight from the carrier saves you from paying commission.

**BY LOCAL TRANSPORTATION.** CFR sells domestic **train** tickets one day before the train's departure. After that, only train stations sell tickets, which are only available one hour in advance. The timetable *Mersul Trenurilor* is useful in forming a plan of attack (L12,000; in English). Schedule info is available at ☎221 in most cities. **Interrail** is accepted; **Eurail** is not. There are four types of trains: *InterCity* (indicated by an "IC" on timetables and at train stations), *rapid* (in green), *accelerat* (red), and *personal* (black). International trains (often blue) are usually indicated by "i" on timetables. *InterCity* trains stop only at major cities such as Bucharest, Cluj-Napoca, Iaşi, and Timişoara, and have three-digit numbers. *Rapid* trains (also 3 digits) are the next fastest; *accelerat* trains have four digits starting with "1" and are slower and dirtier. The sluggish and decrepit *personal* have four digits and stop at every station. It's wise to take the fastest train you can, most often *accelerat*. There's not a big difference between **first class** (*clasa una;* wagons marked with a "1" on the side; 6 people per compartment) and **second class** (*clasa dova;* 8 people), except for on *personal* trains, where first class is markedly better. If you take an **overnight train,** shell out for first class in a *vagon de dormit* (sleeping carriage).

Use the local **bus** system only when trains are not available. Buses are more expensive, but still as packed and poorly ventilated. Look for signs for the *autogară* (bus station) in each town. Another good option for short distances are **minibuses,** which can be cheaper, faster, and cleaner than the alternatives. Look for signs posted on the bus and rates posted inside and pay the driver.

**BY THUMB.** *Let's Go* does not recommend hitchiking. If you do go, know that drivers generally expect a payment similar to the price of a train or bus ticket for the distance traveled, although some kind souls will take you for free or accept whatever you can afford. Hitchhikers stand on the side of the road and put out their palm, as if waving. Never hitchhike at night.

ROMANIA

## GLOSSARY

| ENGLISH | ROMANIAN | PRONOUNCE | ENGLISH | ROMANIAN | PRONOUNCE |
|---------|----------|-----------|---------|----------|-----------|
| one | unu | OO-noo | post office | poşta | POH-shta |
| two | doi | doy | stamps | timbru | TEEM-broo |
| three | trei | tray | airmail | avion | ahv-ee-OHN |
| four | patru | PAH-tru | departures | plecări | play-CUHR |
| five | cinci | CHEEN-ch | arrivals | soşiri | so-SHEER |
| six | şase | SHAH-seh | one-way | dus | doos |
| seven | şase | SHAHP-teh | round-trip | dus-întors | doos-in-TORS |
| eight | opt | ohpt | luggage | bagajul | bah-GAHZH-ool |
| nine | nouă | NO-uh | reservation | rezervarea | re-zer-VAR-eh-a |
| ten | zece | ZEH-cheh | train | trenul | TRAY-null |
| twenty | douăzeci | doh-wah-ZECH | bus | autobuz | AHU-toh-booz |
| thirty | treizeci | tray-ZECH | airport | aeroportul | air-oh-POR-tull |
| forty | patruzeci | pa-TROO-zech | station | gară | GAH-ruh |
| fifty | cincizeci | chin-ZECH | ticket | bilet | bee-LET |
| sixty | şaizeci | shay-ZECH | grocery | o alimentară | a-lee-men-TA-ra |
| seventy | şaptezeci | shap-teh-ZECH | breakfast | micul dejun | MIK-ul DAY-zhun |
| eighty | optzeci | ohpt-ZECH | lunch | prînz | preunz |
| ninety | nouăzeci | noah-ZECH | dinner | cină | CHEE-nuh |
| one hundred | o sută | o SOO-tuh | bread | pîine | PUH-yih-nay |
| one thousand | o mie | oh MIH-ay | beef | carne de vacă | CAR-ne de VA-cuh |
| Monday | luni | loon | pork | carne de porc | CAR-neh deh pork |
| Tuesday | marţi | marts | fish | peşte | PESH-teh |
| Wednesday | miercuri | MEER-kur | chicken | pui | poo-EE |
| Thursday | joi | zhoy | vegetables | legume | LEH-goom-eh |
| Friday | vineri | VEE-ner | salad | salate | sah-LAH-teh |
| Saturday | sîmbătă | SIM-buh-tuh | salt | sare | SAH-ray |
| Sunday | duminică | duh-MIH-ni-kuh | milk | lapte | LAHP-tay |
| today | azi | az | beer | bere | BE-reh |
| tomorrow | mîine | MUH-yih-neh | open | deschis | DESS-kees |
| spring | primăvară | PREE-mehr-vahr-ehr | closed | închis | un-KEES |
| summer | vară | VAH-rehr | bank | bancă | BAN-cuh |
| fall | toamnă | TWAM-nehr | exchange | un birou de de schimb | oon bee-RO deh skeemb |
| winter | iarnă | YAHR-nehr | toilets | toaleta | toh-AHL-eh-tah |
| hot | cald | kahld | passport | paşaportul | pah-shah-POHR-tool |
| cold | rece | REH-cheh | bakery | o brutărie | o bru-ter-REE-e |
| single room | cu un pat | koo oon paht | left | stinga | STUHN-guh |
| with shower | cu duş | koo doosh | right | dreapta | draap-TUH |

# TOURIST SERVICES AND MONEY

**ONT** (National Tourist Office) used to be one of the most corrupt government agencies in Romania. Times have changed, but while you won't have to bribe anyone, the information you get will not necessarily be correct. ONT also moonlights as a **private tourist agency,** providing travel packages for a commission, but big hotels are more reliable sources of information. Hotels and restaurants open and close all the time, and prices change with dizzying speed; double-check all important data. Get friendly locals to help you.

# PHRASEBOOK

| ENGLISH | ROMANIAN | PRONOUNCIATION |
|---------|----------|----------------|
| Yes/no | Da/nu | dah/noo |
| Please/You're welcome | Vă rog/Cu plăcere | vuh rohg/coo pluh-CHEH-reh |
| Thank you | Mulţumesc | mool-tsoo-MESK |
| Hello | Bună ziua | BOO-nuh zee wah |
| Good-bye | La revedere | lah reh-veh-DEH-reh |
| Good morning | Bună dimineaţa | BOO-nuh dee-mee-NYAH-tsa |
| Good night | Noapte bună | NWAP-teh BOO-ner |
| Sorry/Excuse me | Îmi pare rău/Scuzaţi-mă | im PA-reh rau/skoo-ZAH-tz muh |
| Help! | Ajutor! | AH-zhoot-or |
| I'm lost. | M-am rătăcit. | mahm rehr-tehr-CHEET |
| When? | Cind? | kihnd |
| Where is...? | Unde? | OON-deh |
| How do I get to...? | Cum se ajunge la...? | koom seh-ZHOON-jeh-la |
| How much does this cost? | Cît costă? | kiht KOH-stuh |
| Do you have...? | Aveţi...? | a-VETS |
| Do you speak English? | Vorbiţi englezeşte? | vor-BEETS ehng-leh-ZESH-te |
| I don't understand. | Nu înţeleg. | noo-ihn-TZEH-lehg |
| Please write it down. | Vă rog scrieţi aceasta. | vuh rog SCREE-ets a-CHAS-ta |
| A little slower, please. | Vorbiţi mai vă rog. | vor-BEETS my vuh rohg |
| I'd like to order... | Aş vrea nişte... | ash vreh-A NEESH-teh |
| Check, please. | Plata, vă rog. | PLAH-tah, VUH rohg |
| Do you have a vacancy? | Aveţi camere libere? | a-VETS KUH-mer-eh LEE-ber-e |
| I'd like a room. | Aş vreao cameră. | ash vreh-UH KUH-mehr-ahr |
| With private shower? | cu duş? | koo doosh |
| May I see the room? | Pot să văd camera, vă rog? | poht sehr vehrd KUH-mehr-uh vehr rohg |
| No, I don't like it. | Nu-mi place. | noomy PLAH-cheh |
| It's fine, I'll take it. | E bine, o iau. | yeh BEE-neh oh yah-oo |
| Will you tell me when to get off? | Puteţi să-mi spuneţi cînd să cobor? | poo-TEHT-sy sermy SPOO-nehtsy kihnd sehr koh-BOHR |
| I want a ticket to... | Vreau un bilet pentru... | vrah-oo oon bee-LEHT PEHN-troo |
| When is the first/next/last train to...? | La ce ora pleacă primul/urma-torul/ultimul tren spre...? | lah cheh OH-rehr pleh-UH-kehr PREE-mool/oor-mehr-TOH-rool/OOL-tee-mool trehn spreh... |
| Where is the bathroom/nearest public phone/center of town? | Unde este cameră de baie/un telefon prin apropiere/centrul oraşului? | OON-deh YEHS-teh KUH-mehr-ahr deh BAH-yeh/oon teh-leh-FOHN preen ah-proh-PYEH-reh |
| My name is... | Mă cheamă... | muh-KYAH-muh |
| What is your name? | Cum vă numiţi? | koom vuh noo-MEETS |

The Romanian unit of currency is the *leu*, plural *lei* (abbreviated L). The banknotes are L500, L1000, L5000, L10,000, L50,000, and L100,000. While many establishments accept US$ or DM, you should pay for everything in *lei* to avoid being ripped off and to save your hard currency for bribes and emergencies. The exchange rates given above are those for September, 2000; with Romanian **inflation** running at around 25% per year, expect rates and prices quoted in *lei* to change significantly over the net year. **ATMs,** which generally accept Cirrus, MC, Plus, and sometimes Visa and give *lei* at reasonable rates, are the best way to get money.

**ROMANIA**

| CURRENCY | | |
|---|---|---|
| US$1 = L23,000 (ROMANIAN LEI) | L10,000 = US$0.43 |
| CDN$1 = L16,000 | L10,000 = CDN$0.64 |
| UK£1 = L34,000 | L10,000 = UK£0.30 |
| IR£1 = L26,000 | L10,000 = IR£0.38 |
| AUS$1 = L13,000 | L10,000 = AUS$0.75 |
| NZ$1 = L10,000 | L10,000 = NZ$1.00 |
| SAR 1 = L3300 | L10,000 = SAR 3.00 |
| DM 1 = L11,000 | L10,000 = DM 0.94 |

ATMs are found everywhere except the smallest towns, are usually 24hr., and occasionally run out of cash. Because many Romanians stave off the inflation demons by carrying dollars or Deutchmarks, **private exchange bureaus,** which are better than banks for exchanging currency, litter the country; unfortunately, not many take **credit cards** or **traveler's checks.** Most banks will cash traveler's checks in dollars or Deutchmarks, then exchange them for *lei*, accumulating high fees in the process. Take the 20 minutes to walk around and see the going rates before plunking down your money. Dollars and Deutchmarks are preferred, although other Western currencies can usually be exchanged somewhere.

# HEALTH AND SAFETY

Most **public restrooms** lack soap, towels, and toilet paper, and those on trains and in stations smell rank. Attendants charge L1000-1500 for a single square of toilet paper. Pick up a roll at a newsstand or drug store and carry it with you everywhere. You can find relief at most restaurants, even if you're not a patron.

Beware the manic **drivers** in congested Bucharest. Roads are currently undergoing a government-sponsored repair, but they still have potholes. In the country, watch out for unlit carriages and carts, as well as sheep and cows.

*Farmacies* (drugstores) are a crapshoot and may not have what you need. *Antinevralgic* is for headaches, *aspirină* or *piramidon* for colds and the flu, and *saprosan* for diarrhea. *Prezervatives* (condoms) are available at all drugstores and at many kiosks. **Feminine hygiene** products are sold in cities, but it's a good idea to bring your own. Also bring insect repellant and contact solution. There are some American medical clinics in Bucharest that have some English-speaking doctors.

# ACCOMMODATIONS AND CAMPING

While some **hotels** charge foreigners 50-100% more than locals, lodging is still relatively inexpensive ($6-20). As a general rule, one-star hotels are on par with mediocre European youth hostels, so don't let the bed bugs bite—literally. Two-star places are decent, and those with three are good but expensive. In some places, going to ONT (in resorts, the *Dispecerat de Cazare*) and asking for a room may get you a price at least 50% lower than that quoted by the hotel. Reservations are a good idea in July and August.

**Private accommodations** are also a good option, but hosts rarely speak English; be aware that renting a room "together" means sharing a bed. Rooms run US$5-15 per person or $15+ in big cities, sometimes with breakfast and other amenities. See the room and fix a price before accepting. Many towns allow foreign students to stay in **university dorms** at remarkably low prices, although they may be hard to locate when you don't speak Romanian. **Campgrounds** are crowded and often have frightening bathrooms. Relatively cheap **bungalows** are often full in summer.

# KEEPING IN TOUCH

Almost all public phones are orange and accept **phone cards,** although a few archaic blue phones take L500 coins. Buy L50,000 and L100,000 phone cards at telephone offices, major Bucharest Metro stops, and some post offices and

ROMANIA

kiosks. Never buy cards not sealed in plastic wrap. Rates run L10,000 per minute to neighboring countries, L14,000 per minute to most of Europe, and L18,000 per minute to the US. International access numbers include: **AT&T Direct,** ☎ 01 800 4288; **BT Direct,** ☎ 01 800 4444; **Canada Direct,** ☎ 01 800 5000; and **Sprint,** ☎ 01 800 0877. Your best bet for using these numbers is to make calls in major cities from orange telephones; which will operate in English if you press "i." **Local calls** cost L595 per minute and can be made from any phone. Dial several times before giving up; a busy signal may just indicate a connection problem. It may be necessary to make a phone call *prin commandă* (with the help of the operator) at the telephone office, which takes longer and costs more. At the phone office, write down the destination, duration, and phone number for your call. Pay up front, and always ask for the rate per minute. At the post office, request *par avion* for **airmail,** which takes 2-3 weeks for delivery. **Mail** can be received general delivery through *Poste Restante.* Address envelope as follows: Katherine (First name) HODGE (LAST NAME), POSTE RESTANTE, Str. Nicolae Iorga 1 (Post office address), Braşov (City) 2200 (Postal code), ROMANIA.

# BUCHAREST (BUCUREŞTI)  ☎ (0)1

Once a fabled beauty on the Orient Express, Bucharest (pop. 2,040,000) is fabled today only for its infamous communist makeover under Romanian dictator Nicolae Ceauşescu. During his 25 years in power, Ceauşescu managed to entirely undo the city's splendor; Neoclassical architecture, grand boulevards, and Ottoman remnants were replaced with concrete blocks, wide highways, and communist monuments. Many parts of the city not standing in bitter memorial to the nefarious dictator are monuments to Romania's many post-Ceauşescu revolutions. Luckily, the country's current government is slowly beginning to pull itself together and to give Bucharest a desperately needed facelift. Newly restored parks and reconstructed historic buildings dot the cityscape while emerging museums provide indoor diversions from communist monoliths. Romanians have been trying to forget the past 50 years, but it's proving impossible when the entire city stands as a crumbling historical testament.

Be aware of your surroundings when traveling around Bucharest, as thieves will target inattentive tourists. Do not change money on the street; beware of anyone who asks to see your passport (especially those claiming to be police); try to take buses with few passengers; and be alert for pickpockets. Thieves are normally only after your money and personal safety is generally not an issue.

# ✈ ORIENTATION

One way to think about the city center is on a north-south and east-west axis. The main street, which changes from **Catargiu** to **Mugheru** to **Brătianu,** runs through all major north-south *piaţas* (squares), including **Piaţa Unirii, Piaţa Universităţii,** and **Piaţa Revolutiei.** The **main train station,** Gara de Nord, lies along the M3 Metro line just west of the Centru. Take a train headed toward Dristor II one stop to Piaţa Victoriei, then change to the M2 line headed toward Depoul. Take this train one stop to Piaţa Romana, two stops to Piaţa Universităţii, or three stops to Piaţa Unirii; all three stops are directly in the center of Bucharest and are a 15-minute walk apart. It's also possible to take trolley #79 or #133. **Maps,** scarce elsewhere in Romania, are sold throughout Bucharest, especially by street vendors in Piata Universitatii. You can pick up an extremely helpful copy of *In Your Pocket* (L20,000; covers Bucharest and Transylvania), at many museums, bookstores, and hotels.

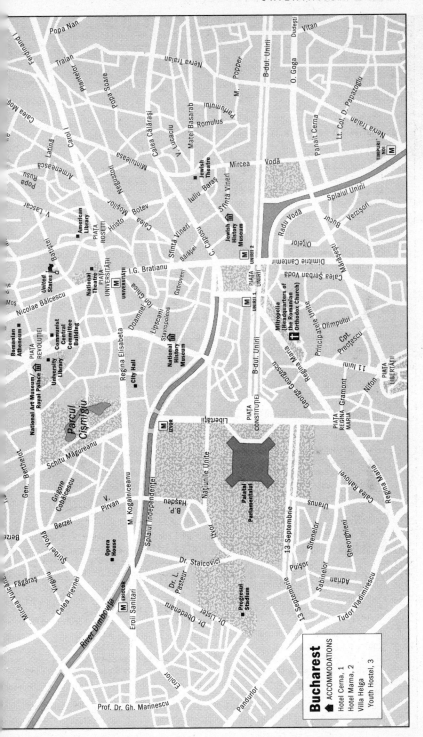

**Bucharest**

▲ ACCOMMODATIONS

Hotel Cerna, 1
Hotel Marna, 2
Villa Helga
Youth Hostel, 3

## ✈ INTERCITY TRANSPORTATION

**Flights: Otopeni Airport** (☎230 00 22), 18km outside the city. Buses leave every 15min. (30min. on weekends) from the airport for the Centru stop near Hotel Intercontinental Piaţa Universităţii (M2: Piaţa Universităţii; 40min.) Bus #783 to Otopeni leaves from Piaţa Unirii every 20min. **Băneasa Airport** (☎93 71), connected with Piaţa Romană by bus #131 and Gara de Nord by bus #205, handles domestic flights. Buy domestic plane tickets at **TAROM**, str. Brezoianu 10 (☎313 42 95 and 312 27 47.) Open 8am-7:30pm, Sa 8am-noon.

**Trains: Gara de Nord** (☎228 08 80) is the principal station. M3: Gara de Nord. L4000 fee to enter the station for nonpassengers. To: **Sofia, BUL** (10-12hr., 3 per day, L431,000); **Chişinău, MOL** (11hr., 1 per day, 276,000); **Budapest, HUN** (14-17hr., 6 per day, L606,000); **Istanbul, TUR** (20-24hr., 1 per day, L498,000); and **Kyiv, UKR** (30hr., 1 per day, L772,000). Domestic train tickets available at the **CFR**, str. Domniţa Anastasia nr. 10-14. (☎313 26 43 and 313 32 22.) From Piaţa Universiţii, with the National Theater on the left, turn right onto B-dul Regina Elisabeta. Turn left after McDonald's and left again at the next corner. Open 7:30am-7:30pm, Sa 8am-noon.

**Buses: Filaret**, Cuţitul de Argint 2 (☎335 11 40). M2: Tineretului. South of the Centru. Buses are the best way to reach **Istanbul, TUR** and **Athens, GRE**. To Athens, your best bet is **Fotopoulos Express** (☎335 82 49). To Istanbul, catch a **Toros** or a **Murat** bus from outside Gara de Nord. **Double T** (☎313 36 42), affiliated with Eurail, or **Eurolines Touring**, str. Ankara 6 (☎230 03 70; fax 315 01 66) can get you to Western Europe. All international bus companies are near Piaţa Dorobanţilor.

## ⊏ LOCAL TRANSPORTATION

**Public Transportation: Buses, trolleys,** and **trams** cost L2500 for one trip. Buy tickets from a kiosk; you can't always get them on board. Validate them to avoid a L100,000 fine; police may try to get more from foreign tourists. All **express buses** except #783 take only magnetic cards (L12,000 round-trip). Pickpocketing is a problem during peak hours. The **Metro** offers less crowded, reliable service. Runs 5am-11:30pm. Magnetic strip cards L7000 for 2 trips, L30,000 for 10 trips, or L9000 for a day pass.

**Taxis: Getax**, ☎95 31, **Cobălcescu**, ☎94 51, and **Cristaxi**, ☎94 61 are the most honest. Look for taxis with company logos and information displayed in the car; avoid those with simple "taxi" signs. Drivers have long been overcharging foreigners; they can now do it legally by setting the meter on *"Tarif #2."* Expect to pay at least L2000 per km. Arrange the price (preţul) beforehand; L30,000-60,000 is probably the best you'll get. Never pay more than US$12-15. Be especially careful traveling from the train station. Learn the phrase *"prea mult"* (too much) and bargain like a badass.

**Car Rental: Avis** (☎315 12 12). M2: Piaţa Universităţii. In Hotel Hilton, across the street from the Art Museum on Calea Victoriei. From US$33 per day for 1-3 days; US$28 for 4-6 days; US$24 for longer. US$0.33 per km. Insurance US$17 per day. AmEx/MC.

## ⚑ PRACTICAL INFORMATION

### TOURIST AND FINANCIAL SERVICES

**Tourist Office: ONT**, Caparti, Bd. Magheru 7 (☎314 19 22, fax 312 09 15). M2: Piaţa Romană. Not very helpful but has a **currency exchange** office open M and Su. Tourist services M-F 9am-7pm, Sa 9am-2pm. A number of private tourist offices are at Gara de Nord. Info can also be found at major hotels.

**Embassies: Australia**, Blvd. Unirii 74, Et. 5 (☎320 98 02; fax 320 98 02). M2: Piaţa Unirii. Open M-Th 9:30am-12:30pm. **Canada,** Str. Nicolae Iorga 36 (☎222 98 45; fax 312 03 66). M2: Piaţa Romană. Open M-F 8:30am-noon. **Irish Consulate,** Str. V. Lascăr 42-44 (☎211 39 67; fax 211 43 84). M2: Praţa Romana. Open M-F 10am-noon and 2-9pm. **UK,** Str. Jules Michelet 24 (☎312 03 03). M2: Piaţa Romană. Open M-Th 9am-noon, F 9-11am. **US,** Str. Tudor Arghezi 7/9 (☎210 40 42; after hours ☎210 01

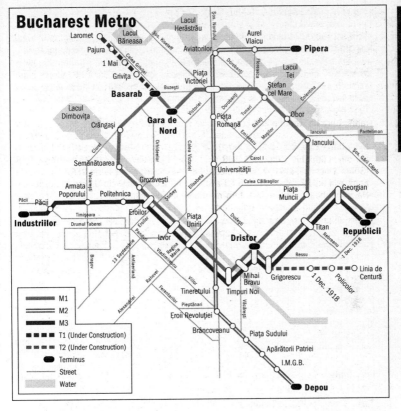

Bucharest Metro

49; fax 210 03 95). **M2:** Piaţa Universităţii. A block behind Hotel Intercontinental. Consular services at Str. Nicolae Filipescu 26 (☎210 40 42, ext. 629; fax 211 33 60). Open M-Th 8am-5pm. Citizens of **New Zealand** should contact the UK embassy. Citizens of **South Africa** should contact their embassy in Budapest (see p. 323).

**Currency Exchange:** Exchange houses are everywhere, with rates posted out front. Many refuse to give hard currency for *lei*. Banks usually charge a hefty commission (3-4% for traveler's checks). **ATMs** always give the best rate, and are located at most major banks, including **Banca Comerciala Romana**, near Piaţa Victoriei and Universităţii. Don't change money on the street—it's almost always a scam.

**American Express: Marshall Tourism,** Bd. Magheru 43, 1st floor, #1 (☎223 12 04). **M2:** Piaţa Romană. Doesn't cash traveler's cheques. Open M-F 9am-5:30pm, Sa 10am-1pm.

## LOCAL AND EMERGENCY SERVICES

**Luggage Storage:** At Gara de Nord. L7,100 or 14,200; passport necessary. Open 24hr.

**Bi-Gay-Lesbian Organization: Accept Bucharest,** Str. Lirei 10 (☎252 16 37; accept@fx.ro; http://accept.org.ro).

**24hr. Pharmacy: Farmadex,** Calea Moşilor 280 (☎211 95 60).

**Medical Assistance: Spitalul de Urgenţă** (Emergency Clinic Hospital), Calea Floreasca 8 (☎230 01 06). **M3:** Ştefan cel Mare. Open 24hr.

**Telephones:** Orange phone cards (L20,000, L50,000, or L100,000) are good for domestic and limited international calls from throughout the city. Order collect calls at the **telephone office,** Calea Victoriei 37 (☎400 21 65). Follow the small signs around to the obstructed entrance. Open M-F 8am-8pm, Sa 8am-2pm.

ROMANIA

**Internet Access: Internet Cafe,** Bd. Carol I 25, (☎313 10 48). M2: Piaţa Universităţii. Head east on Bd. Carol I past Piaţa Rosetti. 10:30am-9pm L15,000 per 30min.; 9pm-10:30am L10,000 per 30min. Open 24hr.

**Post Office:** Str. Matei Millo 10 (☎315 90 30). M2: Piaţa Universităţii. From the Metro, walk down Bd. Regina Elisabeta, turn right onto Calea Victoriei and left onto Str. Mille Constantin. Then take a right onto Str. Otetelesanu Ion; at the end of the street, continue left onto Matei Millo. Open M-F 7:30am-7:30pm, Sa 7:30am-2pm. **Poste Restante** is 3 doors down, next to Hotel Carpati.

**Postal code:** 70154.

# ▌ ACCOMMODATIONS

It's difficult to find good rooms for less than L300,000-400,000 per person. The ONT office (see **Tourist Offices**, p. 564) can arrange **private rooms** or **hotel** accommodations, which are a steep US$25. Tourist offices in the train station may be cheaper.

▨ **Villa Helga Youth Hostel,** Str. Salcâmilor 2 (☎610 22 14). M2: Piaţa Romană; bus #86, 79, or 133 2 stops from Piaţa Romană or 6 stops from Gara de Nord to Piaţa Gemeni (east along Bd. Dacia). From Bd. Dacia, continue across the square and trolley tracks 1 block and take a right; the hostel will be on the left-hand side after a block. Don't trust the supposed "staffers" at Gara de Nord; they're scam artists. The real staff, however, is friendly, funny, and provides 2-, 4-, and 8-bed dorms, free laundry service, and strong Romanian cigarettes. Reservations recommended during summer. US$12 per day; US$72 per week; US$196 per month. Breakfast and kitchen access included.

**Hotel Marna,** Str. Buzeşti 3 (☎659 67 33 and 650 68 20; fax 312 94 55). M3: Gara de Nord. Facing away from Gara de Nord, walk left along Calea Griviţei until you reach Str. Buzeşti. It's the 2nd building on your left. One-star hotel with decent rooms. Close to the train station and central Bucharest. Parking can be arranged. Singles L250,000; doubles L420,000, with TV L470,000, with shower L690,000. Breakfast included.

**Hotel Cerna,** Str. Golescu 29 (☎311 05 35). M3: Gara de Nord. One-star hotel right next to the train station. Comfortable rooms. Check-out noon. Singles L225,000, with bath L415,000; doubles L310,000, L640,000; triples L875,000.

# ◖ FOOD

**Open-air markets** that offer veggies, fruits, meat, and cheese abound in Bucharest—a good one is at **Piaţa Gemeni.** Facing away from Piaţa Universitaţii, at the intersection of B-dul Dacia and Str. Lasrăr, it's a 10-minute walk along B-dul Dacia. Markets are open daily but tend to be slower on Sundays. For excellent bread and pastries, try **Ana,** Str. Radu Beller 6 (☎230 67 00), or Calea Dorobanţilor 134 (☎230 57 32), both near Piaţa Dorobanţilor. (M2: Aviatorilor or M3: Ştefan cel Mare. Open M-Sa 7am-8pm, Su 9:30am-noon.)

▨ **Nicoreşti,** Str. Maria Rosetti 40 (☎211 24 80). M2: Piaţa Romană, or take trolley #79, 86, or 226. Head east on Bd. Dacia to Piaţa Gemeni, then walk 2 more blocks and take a right onto Toamnei; it's after an intersection on the right. Excellent cheap Romanian food. Open M-Sa 9am-11pm, Su 1-11pm.

**Caru' co Bere** (The Cart O'Beer), Str. Stavropoleos 3/5 (☎313 75 60). M2: Piaţa Universităţii. Big tourist stop. Live folk performances Tu-Su 8:30pm. Main dishes L30,000-60,000. Open daily 10am-midnight. AmEx/MC/Visa.

**Mes Amis,** Str. Lipscani 82 (☎312 29 10). M2: Piaţa Unirii or Piaţa Universităţii. In an alley between Lipscani and Gabroveni. Enjoy food and drink with artsy locals. Main dishes L25,000-35,000. Open M-Sa noon-2am, Su 5pm-2am; food until 12:30am.

**Paradis 2,** Str. Hristo Botev 10. M2: Piaţa Universităţii. Leave the square with Hotel Intercontinental on your left and take the 2nd right. Middle Eastern dishes come with fresh vegetables (L20,000-40,000). Open daily 9am-10:30pm.

# ◉ SIGHTS

Downtown Bucharest is a sprawl of concrete highrises, congested streets, once-grand buildings, and fledgling businesses. The memorials and sights worth seeing are not beautiful squares or opulent palaces; rather, Bucharest is worth exploring for the alluring feeling of a place in transition.

## ▨ CIVIC CENTER

In 1984, Ceauşescu fulfilled a long-standing plan and remodeled Bucharest after Pyongyang, North Korea's socialist capital. In order to create his perfect socialist capital, Ceauşescu destroyed 5 sq. km of Bucharest's historic center, demolishing over 9000 19th-century houses and displacing more than 40,000 Romanians. The result is today's Civic Center (Centru Civic), conveniently completed in 1989, just in time for his overthrow. It lies at the end of the 6km Bd. Unirii, intentionally built slightly larger than the Champs-Elysées (after which it was modeled).

**PARLIAMENTARY PALACE.** (Palatul Parlamentului.) With 12 stories, four underground levels, and 1100 rooms, the Parliamentary Palace is the world's second-largest building (after the Pentagon in Washington, D.C.), and the incomprehensibly huge centerpiece of the Civic Center. Begun in 1984, it took just four years, 70,000 slave laborers, and 700 architects to complete. Ceauşescu even ordered the construction of the world's largest one-piece rug, woven within the room because it would be too big to bring in whole. Today, the white monolith houses Romania's Senate and Parliament and the stark contrast of marble and wood opulence against the poverty of much of Romania is cause for both national frustration and pride. *(M1, 3: Izvor. For 45min. tours, enter at the entrance toward the left of the building. Open daily 10am-4pm. Tours L40,000; with ISIC L25,000. Cameras L30,000. Closed during special events.)*

**OTHER SIGHTS.** Amidst the madness, Ceauşescu inexplicably spared **Dealul Mitropoliei,** the hill on the area's southwest side. Atop the hill sits the headquarters of the **Romanian Orthodox Church,** located in one of the largest cathedrals in Romania. The cathedral also flanks the former **Communist Parliament Building.** This impressive Baroque construction now belongs to the church and periodically hosts free religious concerts. *(M2: Piaţa Unirii. Up Aleea Dealul Mitropoliei. Open M-Su 8am-7pm.)*

## SIGHTS OF THE REVOLUTION

Bucharest is slowly putting the tribulations of the fall of communism behind it, though crosses and plaques throughout the city commemorate the *eroilor revoluţiei Române,* heroes of the 1989 Revolution. The first shots of the Revolution were fired at **Piaţa Revoluţiei** on December 21, 1989. The square is surrounded by the newly-refurbished **University Library** (Bibliotecă) and the **Senate** (formerly the Communist Party headquarters). Ceauşescu delivered his final speech on the balcony now marked by a white marble triangle with the inscription "Glorie martirilor nostri" (Glory to our martyrs) commemorating the rioters. Just down the street on Bd. Nicolae Bălcescu, a black cross marks the spot where the first victim of the Revolution died. *(M2: Piaţa Universităţii. With Hotel Intercontinental on your left, turn right onto B-dul Regina Elisabeta and a right onto Calea Victoriei.)* **Piaţa Universităţii** houses memorials to victims of both the 1989 and 1990 Revolutions. Demonstrators perished while fighting Ceauşescu's forces here on December 21, 1989, the day before his fall. Crosses commemorating the martyrs line the center of the square and defiant anti-Iliescu graffiti decorates university walls and the **Architecture Institute,** across from Hotel Intercontinental. Piaţa 22 Decembrie 1989 was also the sight of the June 1990 riots: students had been protesting the ex-Communist government since April, and in June Iliescu bussed in over 10,000 Romanian miners to violently shut down the protestors. The rampage killed 21 students. *(M2: Piaţa Universităţii, behind the fountain.)*

# PARKS

**HERĂSTRĂU PARK.** This immense park directly north of downtown has diversions ranging from rowboat rentals to rollercoasters. At the southern end of the park on şos. Kiseleff stands the **Arcul de Triumf,** built to celebrate Romania's independence from Turkey in 1877. *(M2: Aviatorilor; bus #301, 331, or 131 from Piaţa Lahovari. The Metro station sits at the southern tip of the park, which sprawls along şos. Kiseleff. Open daily until sundown. Boat rentals L20,000 per hr.; L20,000 deposit.)*

**CIŞMIGIU GARDENS.** One of Bucharest's oldest parks, the Cişmigiu Gardens are filled with elegant paths and a small lake where you can rent paddle boats. The well-groomed park is, along with Herăstrău Park, the focal point of much of the city's social life during the summer. *(M2: Piaţa Universităţii. With Hotel Intercontinental on the left, make a right onto B-dul Regina Elisabeta and walk until you hit the park. Open daily 8am-8pm. Paddle boats L25,000 per hr.; photo ID as deposit.)*

**BOTANICAL GARDENS.** One of downtown Bucharest's prime grassy knolls served as a main demonstration sight during the 1848 revolution. *(M1: Politehnica; M3: Grozăveşti, Semănătoarea. Buses #62, 71,93,61, 306, and 336 stop at entrance. Şos. Cotroceni 32. Across from Cotroceni Palace. Open in summer M-Sa 8am-8pm, Su 9am-1pm; off-season 9:30am-3:30pm; last entrance 30min. before closing. Museum and greenhouses open Tu, Th, and Su 9am-1pm. L1,500, with student ID L1000. Camera L50,000. )*

## OTHER SIGHTS

The side streets just off Piaţa Victoriei and Calea Dorobanţilor, with names like Paris, Washington, and Londra, brim with villas typical of the beautiful Bucharest that once was.

**OBOR METRO.** If you're in the mood for something truly Romanian, visit the huge **market** at the Obor Metro stop, which often includes eggs, raw wool, rusty nails, Bulgarian cigarettes, Turkish Levis, shower heads, fly paper, ceramic plates, and ducks. Some vendors are well established in air-conditioned stores at the adjacent mall, while others stand in the crowd calling out their price for smuggled goods, ready to look innocent when the police arrive. *(M3: Obor. Immediately north of Obor Metro entrance. Hours generally 9am-5pm. Protect your valuables.)*

**FREE PRESS HOUSE.** (Casa Presei Libere.) In the good old days, a statue of Lenin stood on the steps of the ironically named Free Press House, a Stalinist monstrosity that housed the state propaganda machine. The building, constructed in the 1950s, still houses Romania's national press. *(M2: Aviatorilor. Follow Bd. Prezan from the Metro to şos. Kiseleff. Turn right after the Arcul de Triumf and walk along Herăstrău Park for quite some time; the communist relic will rise unmistakably before you.)*

# 🏛 MUSEUMS

Bucharest's museums can provide a nice break from the hectic pace on the city streets. The new **Circului Park** is a delightfully bizarre outdoor museum of painted sculptures carved into tree trunks. (M3: Ştefan cel Mare. Just off Str. Ştefan cel Mare, after the circus at the end of Aleea Circului.)

🏚 **Museum of the Romanian Peasant** (Muzeul Ţăranului Român), şos. Kiseleff 3 (☎650 53 60). M2 or 3: Piaţa Victoriei. Named best museum in Europe 1996-97. Though the written guides are in Romanian, the spectacularly beautiful presentation of the various aspects of peasant life—including clothing, religion, architecture, and education—will make you yearn for a lifestyle you never led. Open Tu-Su 10am-6pm; last admission 5pm. L20,000; cameras L100,000.

**Cotroceni Palace and National Museum** (Muzeul Naţional Cotroceni), B-dul Geniuluil (☎222 12 00). M1: Politehnica. With the train tracks on your right, head straight down B-dul Iuliu Maniu and continue on şos. Cotroceni; the entrance is on the right. Surrounded by the ruins of a monastery that Ceauşescu demolished, Cotroceni palace was built for Queen Maria from 1891-93. Check out the lovely Rococo flower room, the table where Mihai I signed his abdication in 1947, or, from a distance, the current home of Romania's president. Far from the center. Make an appointment to visit a day in advance. L50,000, students L25,000.

**Jewish History Museum of Romania** (Muzeul de Istorie a Comunitaţilor Evreieşti din România), Str. Mămulari 3 (☎315 08 37). M2: Piaţa Unirii. From the Metro entrance at Piaţa Unirii 2, turn right on Blvd. Coposu and take the 1st right across a parking lot. At the end of it, turn left onto Str. Mămulari; the museum is on the right in the synagogue. The central sculpture mourns the 350,000 Romanian Jews deported and murdered by the Nazis. English spoken. Open W and Su 9:30am-1pm. L5000.

# 🎵 ENTERTAINMENT

Bucharest hosts some of the biggest rock festivals this side of Berlin; guests include rising indie groups as well as falling stars like Michael Jackson (who responded to screaming fans with "Hello, Budapest!"). Inquire at the tourist office for upcoming performances. Cinemas show a variety of foreign films (L10,000-25,000), most from America and all with Romanian subtitles. For listings, check *Sapte Seri*, available at most hotels and restaurants. **Theater** and **opera** are inexpensive diversions in Bucharest. (Cheapest tickets L6,000-55,000.) As in other European cities, performances are on hiatus from June to September. Tickets are sold at box offices at the theater and go on sale the Saturday before the performance. Seats tend to go quickly, but whatever is left is available at half-price one hour before showtime. If a performance is sold out, ask to speak to the manager; he or she may be able to provide you with house seats.

**Atheneul Român,** Str. Franklin I, Piaţa Revoluţiei (☎315 68 75). M2: Piaţa Universitatii. Holds excellent classical music concerts in a gorgeous domed structure.

**Opera Românb,** Bd. M.L. Kogblniceanu 70 (☎313 18 57). M1, 3: Eroilor. Stages top-notch opera for ridiculously inexpensive prices.

**Teatrul Evreles,** Str. Iuliu Barasch 15 (☎323 45 30). M2: Piata Unirii. Europe's only state-run Jewish theater. The shows are in Yiddish and the translations in Romanian, but even if you can't understand what's going on it's one-of-a-kind. Performances throughout summer.

# 🏙 NIGHTLIFE

Pack a map and cab fare—streets are poorly lit and public transportation stops at 11:30pm. Bars and nightclubs around the center crawl with the *nouveau riche* and foreign businesspeople, while those near the M3: Semănătoarea and Grozăveşti are filled with students. Bucharest also suffers from the summer disease: clubs and popular hangouts slow down or close while everyone goes away for vacation.

**Maxxx.** M3: Semănătoarea or Grozăveşti. Take the last Metro (11:30pm) to Semănă toarea and let the noisy crowd lead you through the maze of dorms. The most popular disco in town Oct.-late June. Varied program and inevitable late-night jam sessions add to the great atmosphere. Beer L10,000 or less. Men L15,000 M-Th, F L25,000, women free M-F; Sa L20,000 until 11:30pm, L40,000 after.

**Underground,** Calea Victoria 26 (☎315 33 99). A trendy new bar with a red decorative theme that plays "underground" music. Borrowing the logo of the British subway, their motto tells you to "be different, feel different." Open midnight-3am.

**Club A,** Str. Blănari 14 (☎315 68 53). M2: Piaţa Universităţii. Walk down Bd. Brătianu and take the 3rd right; it's the unmarked place on the right. This club draws an international crowd and gets crowded by 11pm. Jazz Tu, blues W, alternative Th, disco F-Sa, oldies Su. Tu-Th men L25,000, women free; F-Sa L30,000. Open M-Th 11pm-5am, F 11pm-7am, Sa 9pm-7am, Su 9pm-5am.

**Swing House,** Str. Gabroveni 20 (☎092 58 90 58). M2: Piaţa Unirii. Hyper dance club pulls in an enthusiastic crowd. Live music nightly from 9:30pm, with weekly swing performances. L30,000 drink minimum. Open daily 3pm-6am.

# TRANSYLVANIA

Though the name evokes images of a dark, evil land of black magic and vampires, *Ardeal* (Transylvania) is actually a region of green hills and mountains descending gently from the Carpathians to the Hungarian Plain. This is Romania's most Westernized region, due to geographical location and the influence of both Austrian rule and ethnic minorities. Cities are cleaner, services are better, and the speech is slower and more musical, with a few regional expressions such as *"fain"* (good or cool) and the Austrian *"Servus!"* (hello). The intractable wilderness of some areas has remained largely untamed, making for good hiking from Sinaia into the Făgăraş Mountains. The vampire legends, however, do have root in remarkable architecture: Transylvanian buildings are tilted, jagged, and more sternly Gothic than anywhere else in Eastern Europe, as a visit to ancient Sighişoara will illustrate.

## SIGHIŞOARA ☎ (0)65

Sighişoara (see-ghee-SHWAH-rah) is perhaps the most pristine and enchanting medieval town in Transylvania. Crowning a green hill surrounded by mountains, its gilded steeples, old clocktower, and irregularly tiled roofs have survived centuries of attacks, fires, and dozens of floods. Today, the old city blends in beautifully with its colorful, tranquil surroundings.

**TRANSPORTATION.** Trains run to **Bucharest** (5hr., 10 per day, *accelerat* L70,000) and **Cluj-Napoca** (3½hr., 4 per day, L40,000). Store luggage at the train station. (L10,300 or 20,600 per item per day. Open 24hr.)

**ORIENTATION AND PRACTICAL INFORMATION.** To reach the center from the train station, take a right onto Str. Libertăţii, then take the first left onto Str. Gării. Veer left at the Russian cemetery, which commemorates victory over fascism. From there, turn right and cross the footbridge over the river Târnava Mare, then walk down Str. Morii, the street behind Sigma. A right at the fork leads to **Str. O. Goga** and the **Citadel**; a left leads to the main **Str. 1 Decembrie 1918** after a block. If all else fails, aim for the clock tower. The **tourist office, OJT Agenţie de Turism**, Str. 1 Decembrie 1918 10, helps find rooms in hotels, has an exchange office, and sells maps for L10,000. (☎77 10 72. Open M-F 9am-5pm, Sa 9am-1pm; exchange bureau open M-Sa 9am-5pm.) **IDM exchange office**, Str. Hermann Oberth 15, accepts AmEx/MC/Visa, and most traveler's checks. (☎77 49 49. Open M-F 8am-8:30pm, Sa 9am-1pm.) There is a **Western Union** (open M-F 8:30am-3pm) and an **ATM** at Banca Romana next to the telephone office (see below). Log onto cyberspace at **Kopling Internet Cafe**, Chendi 3. (Open M-F 10am-8pm, Sa 10am-4pm. L10,000 per hr.) Farther down, as Str. 1 Decembrie 1918 becomes Piaţa H. Oberth, lies the **post** and **telephone office**. (Open M-F 7am-8pm; telephones daily 7am-8pm.) **Postal code:** 3050.

**ACCOMMODATIONS AND FOOD.** At ■ **Bobby's Hostel**, Str. Tache Ionescu 18, you can enjoy the company of young travelers. The rooms are clean and plain. Look for a middle-aged man bearing a sign at the train station or take the scenic 30-minute walk. (☎77 22 32. Hot water 2hr. per day. Washing machines and cable TV. Open July 15-Aug. 30, but also try in the off-season. Dorms US$5; doubles US$6.) **Hotel Non-Stop,** directly across from the train station, offers spacious doubles. (Communal shower and toilet. Doubles L160,000, with TV L180,000.) In the Citadel, try **Restaurant Berarie**, Piaţa Cositorarilor 5, under the big metal dragon sign. The traditional meals and medieval decor are truly worth the extra *lei*. (☎77 15 96. Main dishes L20,000-50,000. Open daily 10am-midnight.) **Joker Restaurant,** across the street from Bobby's Hostel, serves Romanian food German-style. (Main dishes L25,000-30,000. Vegetarian options. Open M-Sa noon-11pm, Su 2-11pm.) The **grocery stores** along Str. 1 Decembrie 1918 will satisfy any remaining pangs of hunger.

**SIGHTS AND ENTERTAINMENT.** The **Citadel** (Cetate), built by Saxons in 1191, is now a tiny medieval city-within-a-city that houses three museums. Enter through the **Clock Tower** (Turnul cu Ceas), off Str. O. Goga. The **history museum** inside this old tower displays everything from Roman furniture to Apollo-program rocket science. (☎77 11 08. Signs in English. Open M 10am-3:30pm, Tu-F 9am-6pm, Sa-Su 9am-4pm. L10,000, students L5000.) Climb to the top to see the clock's mechanism and an expansive view of the area. To the left as you leave the tower, the **Museum of Medieval Armory** offers a small exhibit on Vlad Ţepeş (Dracula) and arms from all over the world. (Open Tu-F 9am-6pm, M and Sa-Su 9am-4pm. L6000, students L3000.) Underneath the clock tower, the **Torture Museum** displays racks, Spanish boots, and explicit descriptions in English. (Open M 10am-3:30pm, Tu-F 9am-6pm, Sa-Su 9am-4pm. L3000.) A three-museum pass for foreigners costs L25,000, which is curiously more expensive than a separate pass for each museum. For a walking tour of the Citadel, follow the white and red arrows that start next to Restaurant Berarie. Alternatively, from the clock tower, walk straight past Berarie and take a left onto Str. Şcolii. The 170-step covered wooden staircase that leads to the **School on a Hill** was built to make the climb easier for lazy 17th-century students.

# BRAŞOV ☎(0)68

Established as the center of Carpathian defense, Braşov (BRA-shohv) later became an international crossroads and is now an ideal starting point for excursions into the mountains. While the fortresses that surround the city testify to its past, the museums, restaurants, and churches of the pleasant city center demonstrate that Braşov is as suited to tourism as it has been to its more sinister roles.

**TRANSPORTATION.** Trains go to **Bucharest** (3-4hr., up to 25 per day, *accelerat* L31,000) and **Cluj-Napoca** (5-6hr., 6 per day, L70,000). Train info is posted at **CFR** on Str. Republicii. (Open M-F 8am-7pm, Sa 9am-4pm.) Buy bus tickets at the booths on the elevated sidewalk. (Open M-Sa 5:30am-8pm, Su 7am-7pm.) The **bus station** is at Autogară 2, sometimes called Gara Bartolomeu, on the western edge of the city. To get there take bus #10, or, facing away from the train station, head right three stops.

**ORIENTATION AND PRACTICAL INFORMATION.** To get to town from the **bus station,** take bus #4 toward Piaţa Unirii (L4700 for two rides; exact change) to the main square, **Piaţa Sfatului** (10min.); get off in front of Biserica Neagră, a large Gothic church. If you walk, cross the street in front of the train station and head straight down Bd. Victoriei, then follow Str. Mihail Kogălniceanu around the civic center until it ends. At the fork, take the soft right onto Bd. 15 Noiembrie (it becomes Bd. Eroilor) and turn left on Str. Republicii or Str. Mureşenilor (2km). To get to Piaţa Sfatului from the bus stop, walk up Bd. Eroilor, turn right onto Str. Mureşenilor, and then left at the plaza.

The best **maps** are at the kiosks on Str. Republicii for under US$1. Alternatively, Bd. Eroilor 9 has free maps. **St. O. Iosif,** Str. Muresenilor 14, sells maps and *In Your Pocket* guides. (☎14 41 00. Open M-F 8am-9pm, Sa 10am-2:30pm, Su 9am-1pm.) **Odeon "D" Travel,** Str. Mureşenilor 28, offers domestic and international transportation info. (☎47 08 16. Open M-F 9am-5pm.) **IDM,** in the circular building at the intersection of Bd. Eroilor and Str. Republicii, or on the left side of Str. Republicii as you head to the Piaţa, cashes AmEx **traveler's cheques** and gives MC/Visa **cash advances** for no commission. (☎41 02 19. Open M-F 7:30am-8:30pm, Sa 9am-6pm, Su 9am-5pm.) **ATMs** line the streets. A pharmacy, **Aurofarm,** is at Str. Republicii 27, near the Bayer sign. (☎41 12 48. Open daily 7:30am-midnight. MC/Visa.) Email away at **Internet Club,** Republicii 40 (☎47 64 02; L15,000 per hr; open daily 8am-10pm), or at many of the other stores around the piaţa. (Be careful of your possessions—slack-jawed typists have been known to get scammed.) The **post office,** Str. Nicolae Iorga 1, is on the street that parallels Bd. Eroiler across the long Parul Central. (☎41 51 64. Open M-F 7am-6pm, Sa 8am-1pm.) The **telephone office,** B-dul Eroilor 23, is between Str. Republicii and Str. Mureşenilor. (☎41 33 11. Open 7am-1:30pm and 2-7pm.) **Postal code:** 2200.

**▶☐ ACCOMMODATIONS AND FOOD.** The market for **private rooms** in Braşov is dominated by the legendary Maria Bolea, a short, zealous woman with dark hair and blue eyes who accosts backpackers at the train station. Alternatively, call ahead to Diana and Gigi Borcea (☎41 62 43) for a cozy double in an immaculate apartment right next to the station. Expect to pay US$10-15 for private rooms. To avoid negotiations at the station, go to **EXO,** Str. Postăvarului 6 (the unmarked door on the right), to get private room referrals. Check out rooms before renting. (US$7 per night. Open 11am-6pm, Su 11am-2pm.) If you prefer hostels to private rooms, try **Hotel Aro Sport,** at Sfantul Ioan 4, which has an ideal location and resonable prices. From Str. Mureşenilor, make a left on Sfantul Ioan and take Piaţa Sfantului to Sfantul Ioan 4. (☎14 28 40. Reception 24hr. Singles L224,000; doubles L280,000. )

A daily **market** on Str. Nicolae Bălescu, two blocks from the intersection with Bd. Eroilor, provides a cheap array of fresh and packaged foods. (Open M-F 7am-7pm, Sa 7am-2pm.) For a hearty meal and unusually splendid service, try ▧ **Bella Musica,** Str. G. Baritu nr. 2. Make your way through the music store and down the stairs on the right into a wine cellar transformed by candlelight. You can't beat the free shots of *palinka* or full menu of Romanian and Mexican food. (☎47 69 46. Open daily 1pm-midnight. *Ciorba* L22,000. Main dishes L50,000-70,000.)

**☐ SIGHTS.** Piaţa Sfatului and Strada Republicii are perfect for a stroll. Beyond the square along Str. Gh. Bariţiu looms the **Lutheran Black Church** (Biserica Neagră), Romania's most celebrated Gothic church, named as such after being charred by fire in 1689. (Open M-Sa 10am-5pm. L8000, students L4000. No photos. Organ concerts Tu, Th, and Sa 6pm in summer; L12,000.) The **History Museum** on the square used to be the city hall and courthouse; legend holds that the condemned had to jump from the tower to their deaths. Descriptions of artifacts are in Romanian, but it's doubtful you'll miss much—the armor is labeled "armor." (Open Tu-Su 10am-6pm. L4000.) From the main square, follow Str. Apollonia Hirschner and turn right onto Str. Poarta Schei to reach the city gate, **Poarta Schei,** built in 1828 to separate the old German citadel from the *schei* (the section allotted to the Romanian population). Behind the gate, a five-minute walk down Str. Prundului leads to Piaţa Unirii. Here stand 1495 **St. Nicholas Church** (Biserică Sfântu Nicolae) and **Romania's First School** (Prima Şcoala Românească; open 9am-6pm; L10,000, students L5000). You can take a *telecabina* (cable car) up Muntele Tâmpa from Aleea T. Brediceanu to get a view of the mountains. (Runs M noon-6pm, Tu 9:30am-noon, W-F 9:30am-7pm, Sa-Su 9:30am-8pm; every 15min.; L15,000, round-trip L20,000.) Take the stone steps or marked trails to go to the top. Alternatively, try the less-crowded trails on Aleea T. Brediceanu, which lead to the **Weaver's Bastion** and other medieval ruins.

**▶☐ ENTERTAINMENT AND FESTIVALS. Operas** tend to be low on production but high on vocal talent. (Tickets ☎14 41 38; open daily noon-4pm. L15,250, students L10,500.) Braşov also hosts an annual **International Chamber Music Festival** every July. (Tickets ☎47 18 89; info ☎14 31 13 and 14 73 78. Open 10am-6pm.) In late summer, Piaţa Sfatului holds the **Golden Stag** (Cerbul de Aur) **Festival,** which in past years has starred Ray Charles and MC Hammer. Students shake their booties at **discos;** ask around for the current hot spot. Unfortunately (or fortunately) most of the permanent entertainment options are strip clubs. One non-fleshy option is **Euro Billiard,** at Str. Grădinarilor 13. (☎47 28 46. Large table L30,000 per hr., small L25,000.)

# NEAR BRAŞOV

## BRAN CASTLE ☎(0)68

*From Braşov, take a taxi or one of the many trolleybuses to "Autogara 2" (a.k.a. "Gara Bartolomeu"); pay on board (45min., 1 per hr., L8000). Get off at the main bus stop by the sign that says "Cabana Bran Castle—500m." Take the main road back toward Braşov and take the 1st right. The tourist office, Compania Bran, is 2-3km back toward Braşov on the main road. (☎23 66 42 and 23 68 84. Tourist info ☎23 68 84. Open daily 8am-6pm.)*

**DRACULA, UNCENSORED** While Bran castle may be underwhelming, the gruesome exploits of its temporary tenant make the hack horror novel pale in comparison. Born in Sighişoara in 1431, Vlad Ţepeş' father (also Vlad) was a member of the Order of the Dragon, a society charged with defending Catholicism from infidels. Hence the name by which he ruled: Vlad Dracul ("Dragon"), and his son's moniker Dracula, "son of the dragon," which was corrupted to "son of the devil" as word of his atrocities spread. In 1444, Vlad's father shipped his two sons off to a Turkish prison to placate an Ottoman ruler. There Vlad learned the tortures for which he would become infamous. Of these, his personal favorite was impalement: a victim was pulled down a stake driven up his anus by two horses tied to his spread legs. When the Turks invaded Walachia in 1462, they were met by some 20,000 of their kinsmen impaled in this manner outside Dracula's territory. Horrified, the Turks retreated. Dracula also practiced such terror tactics on his own people. In order to combat poverty in his realm, for example, the benevolent ruler invited the destitute and disabled to his palace for a banquet...and then had them burned to death. By the height of his rule, his subjects were so terrified into obedience that Dracula placed a gold cup in Tirgovişte Square, which remained undisturbed for the length of his reign.

It's a dark and stormy night in the 19th century. As rain crashes down on the roofs of Bran and lightning illuminates its looming castle, an unfamiliar chariot navigates the Bran Pass—the tight road between the old principalities of Transylvania and Wallachia. This chariot was long thought to have belonged to Bram Stoker, who was said to have been so impressed by the scene that he wrote *Dracula*, a book which became the seed of the vampire myth and its zillions of re-interpretations. This myth, however, is no more true than the vampire story itself—Stoker never visited Romania. Sadly, the book also established Romania as a backward and superstitious country in the Western imagination. In reality, **Vlad Ţepeş Dracula** (literally "Vlad the Impaler, son of Dracul"), had little to do with either this overly-restored edifice or with vampires. As Prince of Wallachia during the 15th century, he was charged with protecting the Bran Pass, which played a crucial role during the Middle Ages in the development of Romanian trade. Today, Bran is a small town with a big castle of mythic importance, although it's not as beautiful or impressive as many other fortresses scattered across Romania.

The **castle,** which overlooks the pass, may have been the physical model for Stoker's, but Ţepeş actually resided in a castle near Curtea de Argeş. Despite its lack of blood-sucking significance, it contains a number of interesting exhibits, including an ethnographic village (with some English translations) and a small museum on Bran's economic importance. (Open Tu-Su 9am-5pm. L50,000, students L35,000.) Groups can take a thorough tour of the castle that includes all the details (real and fictional) of Ţepeş' life. **Hiking maps** are available near the entrance to the castle complex (L20,000-25,000). Follow the yellow triangle, red cross, or red stripe trails on Str. Valeriu Lucian Bologa to Omu peak (6-7hr.; see **Sinaia,** p. 574).

## POIANA BRAŞOV  ☎(0)68

*Buses run from the station on Bd. Eroiler in Braşov (2-3 per hr., L8000). Poiana Braşov's tourist office offers great 1-day excursions (US$5.50-46; discounts for large groups; ☎26 23 89; open M-F 8am-4pm). To get there from the bus station, turn away from the mountain and take the street veering to the right from the bus parking lot. Postal code: 2209.*

About 13km from Braşov, Poiana Braşov is a mountain niche that has long been vying with Sinaia for the title of Romania's best alpine resort. The beautiful green valley is perfect for hiking or skiing. Trails here are accessible to the average hiker, and the view atop **Mt. Postăvarul** (1802m) is glorious. **Centrul de Echitatie** (☎26 21 61), off the parking lot to the right when coming from Braşov, offers ponies, carriage rides, and horses. (Open daily 9am-7:30pm. Horse rides L100,000 per hr., in the woods L150,000 per hr; carriage rides L500,000 per hr.) In summer, swimming, tennis, and track facilities draw visitors to the town. In winter, Poiana Braşov offers downhill and cross-country **skiing** (with 10 downhill runs) and **ice skating**. Ski schools and rentals abound behind Hotel Teleferic at *telecabina* (cable-car) Poiana-Kanzel, and behind Hotel Sportul at *telecabina* Capra Neagra. (Open daily in summer 9am-9pm; off-season 8:30am-4pm. L20,000 round-trip.) **Hikers** have a choice of four main trails from Poiana Brașov. The blue stripe trail leads to Rîsnou, while the yellow stripe winds its way back to Brașov. You can take either the red cross or the blue cross to Cabina Potavarala; the former is less steep.

# SINAIA  ☎(0)44

Wedged into the Prahova valley and flanked by the Bucegi mountains on both sides, Romania's most celebrated year-round alpine resort made its mark as a favorite getaway of Romania's first royal family in the late 1800s. With its elegant villas and park, Sinaia is a resort town that still retains an aristocratic aura. Its cobblestone streets, magnificent hiking trails, and picturesque peaks draw throngs of sightseers, skiers, and trekkers to the best of alpine Romania.

**▓▓ TRANSPORTATION AND PRACTICAL INFORMATION. Trains** run to **Brașov** (1hr., every hr., L31,000) and **Bucharest** (2hr., every hr., *accelerat* L40,000). From the station, cross the street, climb two flights of stairs, and take a left onto a cobblestone ramp at the first landing. Climb the first steps and take two left turns onto **Bd. Carol I**, the main street. Large hotels, including the **Complex Economat** (see **Accommodations,** below), provide info and maps of Sinaia and bad maps of the trails (L4000). **Commercial Bank,** Bd. Carol I 49, does it all; it exchanges traveler's checks, gives credit card advances, sells international money orders, and charges steep commissions. It also has a Cirrus/EC/Plus **ATM.** (Open M-F 8am-noon, Sa 8:30am-12:30pm. Exchange office M-F 8am-5:30pm, Sa 8:30am-12:30pm.) Send an electronic yodel from the **internet cafe** located to the left, behind the park and across the street, as you emerge onto Bd. Carol I from the train station. Heading farther left down Carol I, you'll find a **post office** with a **telephone office** and train ticket information booth. (Post office open M-F 7am-8pm, Sa 8am-noon. Telephone office open M-F 8am-8pm, Sa-Su 10am-6pm.) **Postal code:** 2180.

**▓▓ ACCOMMODATIONS AND FOOD.** It's hard to go wrong in Sinaia, but in general, it's best to avoid the big hotels and do as the Romanians do: stay in private villas. Though they vary in quality, most provide comfortable and scenic rooms at very affordable prices. **Vila Retezatu,** Str. Kogalniceanu 64, is a homey place that offers decent doubles with communal baths and excellent views. With your back to the train station, head left on Bd. Carol I. When you reach the large digital clock, bear left. Make another left at the small bridge and follow Str. Mihail Kogalniceanu as it twists. (☎31 47 47. L200,000.) For more comfortable rooms and an equally central location, try **Vila Camelia,** Str. Spatar 2. At the clock, bear right; Vila Camelia will be on your left. (☎31 45 55. Doubles with bath L300,000.) A bit of a hike from the center, **Vila C** in **Complex Economat,** Str. Pelesului 2, has cozy, clean rooms with communal baths, an enchanting courtyard, and quick access to the major sights. Go straight up at the clock, bear right, continue up, and follow the right-most road, which slopes downward from Hotel Furnica. (☎31 11 51. Singles L150,000; doubles L300,000. MC/Visa.) If you're hungry from all that hiking, head back down the street to **Cabana Furnica,** Str. Furnica 50, for savory Romanian food in an old-world atmosphere. (☎31 18 51. Open 9:30am-9:30pm. Main dishes L20,000-L50,000. MC/Visa.)

**▓▓ SIGHTS AND ENTERTAINMENT.** When not in Budapest, the Romanian royal family lived in Sinaia. The family began the construction of ■ **Peleș Castle** (Castelul Peleș) in 1873 under the watchful eyes of Carol Hollenzollern-Sigmaringen, who finished it 10 years later as King Carol I of a newly-independent Romania (see **History,** p. 552). The enormous fortress features ornate rooms with woodwork from all over Europe, Venetian mirrors, 15th-century Spanish armor, and a number of Rembrandt duplicates. (Open W noon-5pm, Th-Su 9:15am-5pm; last entry

4:15pm. L75,000, students L45,000.) Electricity and German design are the only similarities between Carol I's Peleş and the equally striking ▧ **Pelişor Castle,** built nearby in the early 20th century as a summer residence for King Ferdinand, but designed and decorated by his wife, Queen Maria. An aspiring painter and writer, Maria wanted Pelişor to house artists and intellectuals. She designed it to fit contemporary tastes; witness the French Art Nouveau interior featuring bright, open spaces with simple wooden furniture. Vases and colored stones cover the bookcases and tabletops, while Maria's own paintings and stained glass decorate the walls. (Open W noon-5pm, Th-Su 9:15am-5pm. L60,000, students L30,000.) If you visit one of the houses, be sure to see the other as well; the stylistic changes wrought by 30 years are truly astounding. Both feature well-informed, multilingual tour guides. While you're in the neighborhood, wind your way down to the 17th-century **Sinaia Monastery,** Str. Mănăstirii, named for Mt. Sinai, where you can mingle with the monks and examine the ornate Neo-Byzantine murals. (☎31 49 17. Open dawn to dusk. Free.) After dark, dance the night away at the **Blue Angel,** across from Hotel Montana. (☎31 26 17. Cover M-F and Su L20,000, Sa L30,000. Open M-F and Su 9am-3am, Sa midnight-4am.)

**⚡ HIKING.** The *telecabina* to Cota 1400 (L20,000, round-trip L35,000) leads to alpine hikes and summer hang-gliding. **Ski slopes** descend from Cota 2000, which can be accessed by *telecabina* (cable car; L30,000, round-trip L50,000) or, in winter, *teleschi* (ski lifts). Along the Bucegi mountain range, the yellow stripe trail leads obsessive hikers on a strenuous 4-hour climb from Cota 2000, past **Babele** (2200m; accessible by cable car—see Buşteni below), whose rocks are said to represent two *babe* (women) and a sphinx, to **Omu** (2505m), the highest peak of the Bucegi. If you're feeling adventurous, it is possible to spend the night there at **Cabana Omu.** (L15,000. Open May-Dec.) While simple bedding is provided, bring a sleeping bag, since even the summer nights can be chilly. Meals are also available 7am-9pm (L10,000-30,000), but bringing your own provisions is a good idea. For the serious hiker, it's possible to hike the yellow trail all the way to **Bran Castle,** which takes about 6 hours.

# SIBIU ☎(0)69

One of Romania's oldest cities, Sibiu (SEE-bee-oo; pop. 170,000) was founded by German colonists in the 12th century and remains a town of medieval monuments and colorfully ornate houses. Culturally, Sibiu is marked by German and Hungarian influences, and socially by a lethargic pace of life. Now a popular vacation spot for Romanian yuppies, Sibiu's old town is an ideal location to store up energy before skiing or hiking, or to simply knock back a few beers.

**▢ TRANSPORTATION.** The only way to get to Sibiu is by train to **Bucharest** via **Braşov** (5-8hr., 5 per day, *accelerat* L35,600). **CFR,** Str. N. Bălcescu 6, near Hotel Împaratul Romanilor, sells tickets. (Open M-F 7:30am-7:30pm.)

**▦✠ ORIENTATION AND PRACTICAL INFORMATION.** To reach the center from the train station, walk 10 minutes up **Str. Generalu Magheru** (continue left at the fork) to **Piaţa Mare,** marked by a statue of Gheorghe Lazăr, founder of Romania's school system. The 18th-century **Roman Catholic Church** separates Piaţa Mare from **Piaţa Mică.** From Piaţa Mare, continue straight up **Str. Nicolae Bălcescu** to **Piaţa Unirii.** This *piaţa* is only a few minutes from the train station by **trolley** #T1 or T2 (L4700 for 2 trips); get off at the 3rd stop, when you see the Dumbrava department store or Hotel Bulevard. Go up the hill to Hotel Bulevard, then turn right onto the pedestrian Str. Nicolae Bblcescu.

**Prima Ardeleanu,** Piaţa Unirii 1, gives out free tourist **maps.** (☎21 17 88. Open M-F 10am-7pm, Sa 10am-2pm.) **EDF Asro,** Str. N. Bblcescu 41, **exchanges currency** and cashes **traveler's checks** for no commission. Enter the alleyway, go up the first stairway on the left, and take a left at the landing. (☎21 50 57. Open M-F 9am-6pm.) Cirrus/MC/Visa **ATMs** are at three locations: on Str. N. Blacesu at Banca Comerciala Română, on Calea Dumărăvii by the Brukentnal Art Museum, and by Hotel Bulevard. There are English-language books at **Thausiă**, Piata Mică 2. (☎21 57 74. Open M-F 9am-5pm.) **Telephones** are at the beginning of Str. N. Bălcescu. (Open M-Sa 7am-7pm.) To get to the **Efes Pilsner Internet Cafe,** from P. Mare, make a right off Str. Balesco after passing Hotel Împaratul Romanilor. (7am-midnight L15,000 per hr.; midnight-7am L40,000 per hr. Open 24hr.) The **post office** is on the corner of Str. Metropoliei and Str. Poștei. (Open M-F 7am-8pm, Sa 8am-1pm.) **Postal code:** 2400.

**▐▐▐ ACCOMMODATIONS AND FOOD.** Look for locals offering **private rooms** (L100,000) at the train station. **Hotel Bulevard,** Piața Unirii 2/4, has an ideal location, a majestic exterior, friendly staff, and modern rooms with small beds, TVs, fridges, private baths, and nonstop hot water. (☎21 60 60; fax 21 01 58. Singles L400,000; doubles L740,000. Breakfast included.) **Hotel Bar Pensione Leu,** Str. Mos Ion Roata 6, is clean and comfortable, with homey rooms. From Str. Magheru, cross Piața Mare heading right, past the Brokentnal Museum. Go down the stairs and make a left; Pensione Leu will be on your first left. (☎21 83 92. Communal bath. Reception 24hr. Call ahead for reservations. Singles L100,000; doubles L200,000; triples L300,000; quads L400,000. Breakfast included.)

To reach an **outdoor market,** take a right onto Bd. Corneliu Coposcu from Dumbrava (across Piața Unirii from Hotel Bulevard), then another right at the bus stop lined with street vendors. (Open 7am-8pm.) Munch around the clock at **Juventus Non-Stop,** Str. N. Bălcescu 40. ▧ **Crama Sibiul Vechi** (Wine Cellar of Old Sibiu), Str. Papiu Ilarian 3, features carved wooden chairs with fur cushions, waiters in folk costumes, and enough booze to intoxicate an elephant. Take the first real left heading down Bălescu away from P. Mare; it's below street level. (☎21 04 61. Filling main dishes L70,000. Open daily noon-midnight.) **Hotel Împaratul Romanilor,** Str. N. Bălcescu 4, is swank; formal attire for dinner is a must. A live band sometimes plays an evening tango, but the dance floor is under-used. (☎21 65 00. Meat dishes L20,000-50,000. Open daily 7am-midnight. MC/Visa.)

# HIKING AROUND SIBIU

## PĂLTINIȘ                                                                                  ☎(0)69

*A bus connects Sibiu's train station to Păltiniş (1¼hr.; 3 per day; L20,000, pay driver). Buses are 50m in front of the bus station (autogară), which is next to the train station. Sibiu's Agenția de Turism-Păltiniş, Str. Tribumei 5, off Piața Unirii, has schedules. (☎21 83 19. Open M-F 8am-6pm.)*

In the Cibin Mountains (Munții Cibinului), 32km from Sibiu, Păltiniş (pall-tee-NEESH) is Romania's oldest (1894), highest (1450m), and possibly smallest mountain resort. Its beautiful location, fresh air, and numerous hiking opportunities have made it a favorite of everyone from modern Romanian philosophers to German tourists. Between Mount Cindrel and the South Carpathians, Păltiniş becomes a major ski center in winter. In summer, most visitors are either daytrippers or destined for loftier locales along the hiking trails (trasee turistice). Trails are open in summer only. The **red dot trail** leads northwest toward **Cibinului Gorge** (Cheie Cibinului; 5km). Ride the bus to the ski lift (open in winter 9am-4:30pm) and follow the signs to start hiking the **red triangle** or **red cross trails.** To get to the **red dot trail,** follow the ski lift to the main street and turn right. The red cross trail/red stripe (4½hr. round-trip) follows an unpaved road for part of the way to **Old Woman's Peak** (Vf. Bătrâna; 1911m). Staying on the red stripe trail for 25km (7hr.) to **Cindrel Peak** (2244m) is more difficult, but more visually rewarding.

On the main street of Păltiniş, the **kiosk** to the left of Gasthaus zum Hans sells **hiking maps** for L25,000. (Open Tu-Su 10am-6pm.) Stock up on food in Sibiu before coming; there's no grocery store and only the **restaurant,** at the Cabana, opens for dinner. (Main dishes L10,000-40,000. Open daily 8am-10pm.)

# FĂGĂRAŞ MOUNTAINS

The Făgăraş mountain range extends more than 60km from the Olt Valley to the Piatra Craiului mountains; the tallest peaks, Moldoveanu and Negoiu, are both 2500m. Wildflower-strewn meadows, shrouded summits, and superb views of Wallachian plains and Transylvanian hills cure all fatigue. **Custura Sărăţii** (1hr. east of the Puha Saddle) is the ridge trail's most spectacular and difficult portion; for two hours you'll cling to rocks on a path sometimes less than a foot wide, with drop-offs on either side (an alternate path avoids this route). Many end their hike with a descent into the **Simbăta Valley** (red triangle trail); the ridge ends at Cabana Plaiul Foii near the Piatra Craiului mountains, about 30km from Braşov. To get down to the valley you may have to backtrack to find a suitable descent trail.

Those without a car should take a train to Ulcea and catch a bus to the mountains. From there, countless itineraries are possible; most start in the Olt Valley on the railway from Sibiu to the south. Most hikers enter the ridge at Lacul Avrig, a glacial lake reachable by the red stripe and blue dot trails, or the Puha Saddle (Şaua Puha) by the blue cross trail. You can reach both from the sleepy town of **Avrig** (1hr., 9 per day from Sibiu, personal L7100); plan a day's hike to reach the trails. Look for rudimentary **maps** in Păltiniş or Sibiu, pick up *Drumeţi În Carpaţi* in Bucharest or Braşov (L50,000), or look for maps and tips at www.geocities.com/Yosemite/2017. The hiking season lasts from July to mid-September, but the mountains are never crowded. Always be prepared for cold, snowy summits. The range can be traversed in about seven days; the usual route is from west to east, starting in Transylvania. It's possible to sleep in a cabana, but be prepared to camp if necessary. Some cabanas offer sleeping sacks (L30-50,000 per person) while others offer doubles with bath (L125-300,000); call **Cabana Salişte** in Sibiu (☎21 17 03) to make reservations for the latter. *Nobody* should hike alone in the Făgăraş. See **Essentials: Camping and the Outdoors**, p. 37, for more tips.

# CLUJ-NAPOCA ☎(0)64

The population of Cluj-Napoca (CLOOZH na-PO-ka, pop. 330,000), Transylvania's unofficial capital and student center, is not fully Romanian—a vocal Hungarian minority forms a third of the population. In an attempt to keep the town as Romanian as possible, Mayor Funar has ensured that the decorative street bulbs, bus and trolley tickets, and benches in the center are all blue, yellow, and red, the colors of the Romanian flag. The city's name reflects its rich heritage—Napoca from the city's Roman name, Cluj (derived from Klausenburg) from medieval German domination and life under the Habsburgs. A more upbeat city than Bucharest most of the year, Cluj-Napoca loses much of its vitality with the student exodus in June.

**▐ TRANSPORTATION. CFR trains** leave from Piaţa Mihai Viteazul. (☎19 24 75; info ☎952. Open M-F 7am-7pm.) To: **Alba Iulia** (2hr., 1 per day, *accelerat* L36,200); **Sibiu** (4hr., 1 per day, *accelerat* L50,000); **Braşov** (5hr., 8 per day, *accelerat* L80,000); **Timişoara** (5hr., 8 per day, *accelerat* L80,000); **Bucharest** (7hr., 7 per day, *accelerat* L45,600); **Iaşi** (9hr., 4 per day, *accelerat* L90,000) via **Suceava**; and **Budapest, HUN** (9-12hr., 4 per day, round-trip L400,000). **Buses** run from Str. Giordano Bruno 3 (☎43 52 78), near the train station, to **Sibiu** (3-4hr., 1 per day, L80,000) and **Budapest, HUN** (9hr., M-Tu and Th-F 7am, L180,000). **Local buses** and **trams** run from 5am to midnight; purchase tickets (round-trip L5000) at **RATUC** kiosks. Rows of **taxis** wait at the train and bus stations; look for one with a company sign listing a phone number and the price per km. (☎942, 946, and 948. Approx. US$0.25 per km.)

**▐▌ ORIENTATION AND PRACTICAL INFORMATION.** From the **train station**, walk to the right and turn right across a bridge to reach the **bus station**. Buses #3 and 4, to the left across the street from the train station, run to **Piaţa Mihai Viteazul** (round-trip L5000). Continue along the road away from the river and past McDonald's in the center of town, then turn right on Bd. 21 Decembrie 1989 to

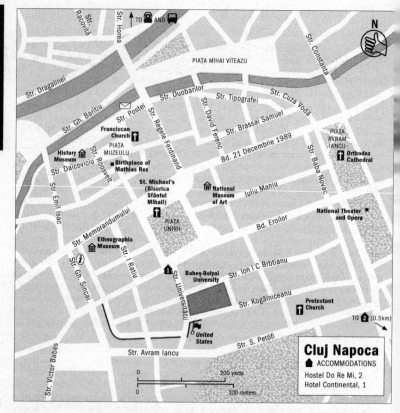

Cluj Napoca
▲ ACCOMMODATIONS
Hostel Do Re Mi, 2
Hotel Continental, 1

reach the center. On foot, cross the street and head down Str. Horea, which changes to **B-dul Regele Ferdinand** (formerly Str. Gh. Doja) after crossing the river. The main square, **Piaţa Unirii** (1km), spreads at the end of B-dul Regele Ferdinand.

**Ave Tour,** Str. Motilor nr. 1, three blocks from Unirii, sells **maps** (L20,000) and can get hotel rooms at cheaper prices. (US$9-20. ☎ 19 62 57. Open M-F 8am-8pm, Sa-Su 9am-12:30pm.) An information office of the **US Embassy** is at Str. Universităţii 7/9. (☎ 19 38 15. Open M and W 1-4pm and F 10am-noon.) **Bancă Transilvania,** Bd. Eroilor 36, off Piaţa Avram Iancu, cashes **traveler's checks** for no commission. (L5000 minimum. ☎ 19 45 67. Open M-F 8am-6pm, Sa 9:30am-12:30pm.) **Banca Româneasca,** on the corner of B-dul Ferdinand and Str. E Zola, offers **Western Union** services. (Open M-F 8:30am-2:30pm.) Cirrus/MC/Plus/Visa **ATMs** line B-dul Ferdinand leading to Piaţa Unirii and surround P. Unirii. The **telephone office** is behind the post office. (☎ 12 48 24. Open daily 7am-10pm; fax M-F 7am-8:30pm.) **Kiro Internet Cafe** is at B-dul Ferdinand 6, 3rd fl. (L7000 per hr. Open 24hr.) The **post office** sits at B-dul Ferdinand 33. (Open M-F 7am-8pm, Sa 7am-1pm.) **Poste Restante** is available at Str. Aurel Vlairu 3. (☎ 13 45 16. Open M, W, and F 8am-1pm.) **Postal Code:** 3400.

**📷🛏 ACCOMMODATIONS AND FOOD. Hotel Continental,** Str. Napoca nr. 1, on Piaţa Unirii, is an ornate, centrally located hotel with spotless communal bathrooms. (☎ 19 14 41. Reception 24hr. Singles and doubles with sinks US$9 per person. Breakfast included.) **Hostel Do Re Mi,** Str. Braşov nr. 2/4, is a good place to stop while passing through. Take bus #3 four stops, backtrack up Str. Mureşanu and take a right at Il Café; it's at the end of the street. (☎/fax 18 66 16. Reception 24hr. Open July-Aug. US$6 per person. 10% off with HI.)

When dining in Cluj, be sure to try *Doboş Cluj*, a local cake that has of layers of light, pudding-like chocolate. **Sora** grocery store, Bd. 21 Decembrie, across and farther down from Hotel Melody, is open 24hr. **Restaurant Privighetoarea** (Nightingale), B-dul Regele Ferdinand 16, is a classy joint. Savor delicious mushroom specialties and meat dishes for L20-45,000. (☎ 19 34 80. Open daily 10am-midnight. MC/Visa.)

■ **SIGHTS.** Most strolls begin at **Piaţa Unirii,** where the 80m Gothic steeple of the Catholic **Church of St. Michael** (Biserica Sf. Mihail) pierces the skyline. **Bánffy Palace,** Piaţa Unirii 30, is home to the **National Museum of Art** (Muzeul Naţional de Artă), which focuses on Romanian work. (☎ 19 69 52. Open W-Su 10am-5pm. L16,000.) The 1933 Byzantine-Romanian **Orthodox Cathedral** (Catedrala Arhiepiscopală) stands in **Piaţa Avram Iancu.** (Open Tu-F and Su 6:15am-8pm and M and Sa 6:30am-1pm and 5-8pm.) The Franciscan **church** (Biserica Franciscanilor) has a Baroque interior but was founded on a Roman temple site. Across the way, the **History Museum** (Muzeul de Istorie), Str. Constantin Daicoviciu 2, exhibits a flying machine built by a local professor in 1896. (Open Tu-Su 10am-4pm. L5000.) The **National Theater and Opera** (Teatrul Naţional şi Opera Română) in the square imitates Paris's Garnier Opera House. (Theater ☎ 19 53 63. Opera ☎ 19 34 68. Season Oct.-June.)

The University District lies south of the square on Str. Universiţatii. In front of the 15th-century **Protestant Church** stands a replica of St. George slaying a dragon (the original is in Prague). Many of the townsfolk took refuge here when the city was attacked; a cannonball is around and embedded in the left wall of the church, above the escape door at Kogălniceanu 21. One block behind the church is **Tailor's Bastion** (Bastionul Croitorilor), a remnant of the defense wall. In front is a statue of **Baba Novac,** whose Houdini-esque escape from a Turkish prison is legendary.

Cross the bridge from B-dul Regele Ferdinand and head left to the stairs to **Cetă-ţuie Hill;** a dazzling view awaits. Downhill and across the river is **Parcul Central.** (Open Apr.-Oct. M-F 9am-9pm, Sa-Su 9am-10pm. Boats L10,000 per 30min.) The **Botanical Garden** (Grădină Botanica), which includes a Japanese garden and greenhouses with orchids and palm trees, is one of the most relaxing and beautiful in Romania. (Open daily 9am-6pm. Map L3000. L5000; discount with student ID.)

■ **NIGHTLIFE.** For the latest on the night scene, pick up the free *Cap de Afiş* from the lobby of big hotels. The **Music Pub,** Str. Horea 5, is the place to be October to June. Kick back with students while you listen to the big names in rock, jazz, and ethnopop. (☎43 25 17. Open M-Sa 9am-3am, Su noon-3am.) **Terasa Muzeu,** in the courtyard of the National Museum of Art, is an outdoor cafe offering classic American movies to violin concerts to jazz. (Open June-Oct. 9am-11pm; entertainment from 9:30pm.) **Disco OK** is on the first floor of the complex in the middle of Piaţa Viteazul. (☎ 13 25 52. Disco F and Sa 10pm-4am; billiards Tu-Su 10pm-4am.)

# WESTERN CARPATHIANS

The Carpathians roll westward into the marshland traditionally known as the Banat and toward the Hungarian Great Plain. Indeed, the entire region is a means to a westward end: Timişoara is Romania's most Western-spirited city while Oradea is the main transportation link to Hungary. Like the even land that defines the terrain, the peaceful mixture of nationalities invites the traveler to unwind.

# TIMIŞOARA                                                    ☎(0)56

In 1989, 105 years after becoming the first European city illuminated by electric street lamps, Timişoara (Tee-mee-SHWAH-rah; pop. 334,000) ignited a revolution that left communism in cinders. Romania's westernmost city, it has always been on the forefront of its nation's cultural and economic change, heady with the ideals of the revolution. In addition, today's Timişoara is also a lively student center and transportation hub.

**TRANSPORTATION.** By train, get off at **Timişoara Nord** rather than Timişoara Est. **CFR** is at Piaţa Victoriei 2, 2nd floor. (☎ 19 18 89. Sells tickets a week in advance. Open M-F 8am-8pm.) It sends **trains** to **Bucharest** (8hr., 8 per day, *rapid* L170,000) and **Budapest, HUN** (5hr., 2 per day, round-trip L450,000).

**ORIENTATION AND PRACTICAL INFORMATION.** Timişoara lies 75km from the Hungarian border. Trolleys #11 and 14 run from the station to the center (2 trips L4700); get off when you see **Piaţa Victoriei** with its multicolored cathedral. Trolley #1 runs by the opera; get off when the tram turns left and backtrack a bit. Alternatively, turn left from the station and follow **Bd. Republicii** to the opera. To the left and up a bit, **Str. Alba Iulia** leads to **Piaţa Libertăţii**; to the right is **Piaţa Victoriei.**

**Colibri Travel and Tourism,** Bd. C. D. Loga 2, near Cinema Capitol, offers old but helpful **maps** for free. (☎/fax 19 40 74. Open M-F 9am-5pm.) Across from Bd. Republicii, **Exchange Trésor,** Str. Craiului 1, charges no commission. (Open M-F 8am-7pm, Sa 8am-4pm.) The **bank** next to Hotel Central exchanges **traveler's checks.** (Open M-F 9am-5pm, Sa-Su 9:30am-1:30pm.) There's a Cirrus/MC/Plus/Visa **ATM** ahead and to the right facing away from the opera. **Librăria Loi,** Str. Hector 2/4, offers a good selection of English books. Facing away from the opera, make a right from Piaţa Libertăţii onto Str. Proclamaţia de la Timişoara, then turn left onto Str. Hector. (☎ 22 09 49. Open M-F 10am-6pm, Sa 10am-2pm.) The **telephone office** is at Str. Mihail Eminesco 1. A machine out front sells L50,000 phone cards. (Open M-F 8am-2pm and 2:30-8pm, Sa 8am-1pm.) **Club 30,** Piaţa Victoriei 7, in the same building as Cinema Tiniş, has **internet access.** (☎ 22 99 05. L5600 per hr. Open 9am-3am.) The **post office,** Str. Piatra Craiului 1, is off Bd. Republicii and Piaţa Victoriei. (Open M-F 8am-7pm.) **Postal code:** 1900.

**ACCOMMODATIONS AND FOOD.** Old hotels in Timişoara are cheap and decent, with the best bathrooms in the country. Private rooms are hard to find, but you might get lucky in the dorms on Bd. Dr. Victor Babeş in **Complexul Studenţ esc.** Cross the bridge following Str. R. Ferdinand, continue down Str. Mihai Viteazul, and take a left onto Bd. Dr. Victor Babeş. (Open July-Aug. US$1-2.) **Casa Tineretului** (Home of Use), Str. Aries 16, attracts students. From the train station, take tram #8 10-15 minutes to Staţia Cluj. Walk toward the hospital in the direction the bus was going. The building is the large gray one on the left and also houses a theater, computer center, exchange office, and bar. The rooms are comfortable if basic. (☎ 16 24 19. Reception 24hr. Call 2-3 weeks in advance. Doubles L92,000; triples L66,120.)

Grocery stores and 24hr. snack shops saturate the Piaţa Victoriei area. An **outdoor market,** Piaţa 700, is on the corner of Str. C. Brediceanu and Str. Paris. (Open daily 7am-9pm.) Don't miss the *kandia* chocolates, available at almost any kiosk. **Restaurant N&Z,** Str. Alba Iulia 1, just before Piaţa Libertăţii on the left, is a young, modern restaurant with sleek metal chairs and cable TV. (☎ 19 39 77. Meaty main dishes L40,000. Open daily 9am-midnight.) At **Braseria Opera,** Piaţa Viabriei 1, waitresses in short red skirts balance opera-themed dishes to the latest Eurobeat hits. (☎ 19 07 90. Thick-crust pizza L20,000-40,000. Open daily 9am-11:30pm.)

**SIGHTS AND ENTERTAINMENT.** The National Theater (Teatrul Naţional) and Opera House (Opera Timişoara) are on one side of **Piaţa Victoriei** and the Metropolitan Cathedral is on the other. The square was a gathering place for protesters during the uprising against Ceauşescu. The metallic *troika* in the shape of a cross across the street and plaques at the entrance record the sacrifices made by the young revolutionaries of December 1989. Off the square but near the opera, the old **Huniazilor Castle** houses the **Banat Museum** (Muzeul Banatului), which traces Timişoara's history from pre-history to 1989. (Open Tu-Su 10am-4:30pm. L6000, students L3000. L2000 per photo.) **Metropolitan Cathedral,** off the square, was built between 1936 and 1946 in Moldavian folk style, with a rainbow-tiled roof and 8000kg bells. (Open 6:30am-8pm. Services M-F 6pm, Su 10am and 6pm.) An impressive **museum** downstairs displays religious artifacts. (Open W-Su 10am-1pm. L3000.) The **Park of Roses** (Parcul Rozelor), to the south, has cozy white benches surrounded by roses. It often hosts free concerts at night, as well as the annual **Interna-**

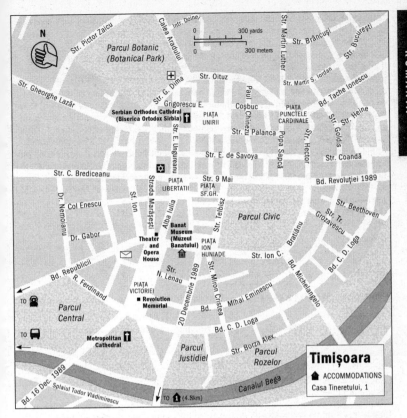

tional Folk Music Festival in June. Farther north is **Piața Unirii,** whose central fountain spouts water said to remedy stomach ailments. The 1754 **Catholic Cathedral** (Domul Romano-Catolic) has survived many a battle and the 1748 **Serbian Orthodox Church** (Biserica Ortodoxă Sârbă), Str. Ungureanu 12, has a mustard-colored facade. (Open M-Sa 8-9am and 5-6pm, Su 10am-noon.)

The **Opera House** box office is just up from the opera itself, on Str. Mărăşeşti. (Open daily 10am-1pm and 5-7pm. Closed in summer. Tickets L20,000-80,000, students half-price.) On the corner by the Serbian Church, **Cafe Colt,** Str. Ungureanu 10, has background music, smoke, and a friendly young crowd. (☎22 93 85. Open 24hr.) The **disco** operating out of what used to be the university cafeteria is a skin show once it starts up at midnight. Facing away from the opera, make a left past the National Cathedral over the bridge, and look for the crowds of students in the parking lot to the left. (Open daily 10pm until the last guest leaves. L25,000.)

# ORADEA
☎(0)59

Only 20km from Romania's northwest border, Oradea (oh-RA-day-ah; pop. 225,000) is a popular way to get to or from Hungary. The multi-colored, charming old city is a wonderful place to stroll through parks or gaze at the river before moving on.

**⌁ TRANSPORTATION. CFR** is on the corner of Str. Republicii before the river. (Open M-F 7am-7pm.) **Trains** go to: **Timişoara** (3-4hr., 2 per day, *accelerat* L50,000); **Bucharest** (11hr., 1 per day, *accelerat* L100,000); and **Budapest, HUN** (3hr., 4 per day, L40,000 round-trip).

**🛂 PRACTICAL INFORMATION.** To reach the center, take the **tram** that departs across the street from the station three stops to Str. Republicii (L5000). Alternatively, facing away from the train station, cross the street and head left. Take the first right, cut across the park, and take a right toward McDonald's. Bear right and follow the street on the left-hand side, crossing to the left onto Str. Republicii. **Luggage storage** is available at Bagaje de Mână in the train station. (L10,600. Open 24hr.) **Banca Naţională a României,** Parcul Traian 8, can do some last-minute *forint-lei* converting. There's an **ATM** at Banca Comerciala Româna on Str. Republicii. Stay in touch at **Liberty Internet Cafe,** Str. Republicii 35. (L10,000 per hr. Open 24hr.) If staying overnight, crash at the luxurious **Hotel Parc,** Str. Republicii 5. (☎41 16 99. Reception 24hr. Singles L200,000; doubles L300,000, with bath, TV, and minibar L400,000; triples L405,000, L510,000.) At **Restaurant Oradea,** Str. Iosof Vulcan 1, across from the CFR travel agency, muzak drones on as sonic wallpaper. (☎13 43 39. Main dishes L30,000-60,000. Open daily 8am-1am.) **Postal code:** 3700 .

# MARAMUREŞ

Nestled up against Ukraine and Hungary, the Maramureş region of northern Romania is known for its stunning woodcarving and reverence for sacred traditions. Many residents wear folk costumes, especially to church and during feasts and holidays. These days, few visitors find reason to venture into the area's rolling hills, but those who do are rewarded with the peaceful, seldom-seen traditions of village life.

## SIGHETU-MARMAŢIEI                                             ☎(0)62

In the northern town of Sighetu-Marmaţiei (see-GHEH-too mar-MAH-tsee-ay, or just Sighet), cars dodge horses running wild in the streets while farmers in modernized versions of traditional costume mingle with youths in clubwear. Sighet's dirty streets are unlikely to be called charming, but they do offer access to the unique surrounding countryside and a fascinating living study of Romanian history.

The **Memorial to the Victims of Communism and the Resistance** (Memorialul Victimelor Comunismului şi al Rezistenţei), on Corneliu Coposu Bvd., has earned worldwide acclaim and UNESCO patronage. The silent walls of this jailhouse-turned-museum witnessed the death of the Romanian elite, as the Communist Party imprisoned countless professors, doctors, ministers, and other intellectuals opposed to the Red wave. A partial list of those murdered between 1952 and 1955 hangs on the facade of the sobering building. Take the first right off the main street at the map board. (Open W-Su 10am-5pm. L4,000.) The decaying Soviet-era **Holocaust Memorial,** down Str. A. Muresan off Pţa. Libertăţii, commemorates the 38,000 Maramureş Jews killed by the Nazis. The **Outdoor Folk Architecture Museum** (Muzeul de Arhitectura şi Artă Populară), Str. Bicazului, on the Dobăieş Hill, can be reached from the center by bus (every hr., L5000). Get off when you see a sign for "Muzeul Statulai." Alternatively, walk down Ştefan cel Mare away from the yellow church and follow signs to the left at the roadwork (30min.). Near the old tracks, turn left up Str. Muzeului as the sign indicates. The museum is an idealized village and the most beautiful peasant houses in Maramureş have been transplanted here; ask the English-speaking guide to open them. The interiors reveal rooms embellished with handmade carpets and covers. (Open Tu-Su 10am-6pm. L5000, students L2000.)

The scenic **train** ride from **Cluj-Napoca** (7hr., 1 per day, L45,000) is worth every *leu*. Trains run to **Timişoara** (12hr., 1 per day, L65,000) and **Bucharest** (13½hr., 1 per day, L100,000). To reach the center, walk four long blocks down Str. Iuliu Maniu away from the train tracks to the yellow church; the center is to the left. The best **map** of town is posted on a large board several blocks to the left, at the other end of the center. **Banca Comercială,** Str. Iuliu Maniu 32, gives Visa **cash advances** and cashes **traveler's checks** for a 4.5% commission. (Open M-F 8am-2:30pm, Sa 8:30am-12:30pm.) An **ATM** stands out front here and at Hotel Tisa (see below). Access the **internet** at Zifer SRL, Iuliu Maniu nr. 20. (☎31 86 12. L10,000 per hr. Open M-F 8am-5pm, Sa 8am-2pm.) The **post office** is at Str. Bogdan Vodă. (Open M-F 7am-8pm, Sa

8am-noon.) Continue down the street, then turn left after the street with the small garden and statue to reach the **telephone office,** Str. Dragoş Vodă 2. (Open daily 7am-9pm.) **Postal code:** 4925.

**Mini-Hotel Măgură,** Str. Iuliu Maniu 44, 300m up the road from the train station, is your best bet for budget sleeps. Bring flip flops for the communal bathroom, which has hot water upon request. (Reception noon-midnight. Singles L75,000-100,000.) **Hotel Tisa,** Piaţa Libertăţii 8, offers clean rooms with color TV and hot baths. (☎31 26 45. Singles L315,000; doubles L300,000. Breakfast included.) In the center, tons of little markets offer variety at low prices. The **restaurant** in Hotel Tisa serves hot Romanian food. (Main dishes L10,000-30,000. Open 7am-10:30pm.)

# MOLDAVIA AND BUKOVINA

Eastern Romania, which once included neighboring Moldova, extends from the Carpathians to the Prut River. Moldavia saw its greatest glory in the late 15th century under the rule of Ştefan cel Mare (1457-1504; see **History,** p. 552). Starker than Transylvania but more developed than Maramureş, Moldavia, from the richness of cosmopolitan Iaşi to the distinctive religious ornaments of the Bukovina monasteries farther north, is an experience not soon forgotten.

## IAŞI                                                                      ☎(0)32

During the second half of the 19th century Iaşi (yee-ASH; pop. 340,000) was one of Romania's administrative and cultural centers. Its spiritual life revolved around the Junimea Society, founded by the country's top writers, nobles, and intellectuals, who filled Iaşi with Neoclassical homes and palaces. These buildings, remarkably well preserved after 45 grinding years of Soviet communism, draw tourists to the city's lovely modern streets, some of the cleanest in Romania.

**■ TRANSPORTATION. Trains,** Str. Silvestru, connect to: **Bucharest** (6hr., 10 per day, *accelerat* L100,000); **Timişoara** (16hr., 2 per day, *accelerat* L120,000) via **Cluj-Napoca;** and **Chişinău, MOL** (7hr., 1 per day, L100,000). **CFR,** Piaţa Unirii 9/11, sells tickets. (☎14 76 73. Open M-F 8am-8pm.) **Buses,** Str. Arcu (☎14 65 87), connect to: **Ungheni** (2hr., 2 per day, L30,000); **Braşov** (7hr., 1 per day, L110,000); and **Chişinău, MOL** (4hr., 4 per day, L90,000).

**■▐ ORIENTATION AND PRACTICAL INFORMATION.** To reach Iaşi's center, walk up the slope leading away from the train and bus stations, take a right on **Str. Arcu** (which becomes **Str. Cuza Vodă** at Piaţa Unirii), and follow the tram tracks. After a curve you'll hit **Piaţa Unirii.** The center is also accessible via tram #1 or 3 (L5000 round-trip) from directly in front of the train station and across the street from **Vama Veche** (Old Customs Tower). **Libraria Junimea,** Piaţa Unirii 4, offers helpful **maps** (L10,000) and info. (☎16 39 89. Open M-F 9am-7pm, Sa 9am-2pm.) **Banco Turco-Română,** on Str. Ştefan cel Mare, cashes AmEx **traveler's cheques** for a 1% commission. **ATMs** line Str. Ştefan cel Mare. **Luggage storage** is at the train station (L7100 per day for small bags, L14,200 for large) and at the bus station (L8000). For **telephones,** walk up Piaţa Unirii away from Str. Ştefan cel Mare, turn left and left again at the Romtelecom office; the office is down a bit on the right. Access the internet at **N@vigator,** B-dul Independentei nr. 11/13. (☎21 58 60. L12,000 per hr. Open 24hr.) The **post office** is at Str. Cuza Voda 3. (☎11 59 85. Open M-F 7am-8pm, Sa 8am-noon.) **Postal code:** 6600.

**▐▐ ACCOMMODATIONS AND FOOD. Hotel Continental,** Str. Cuza Vodă 4, has a good location and decent rooms with TV and phone. (☎21 18 46. Singles with bath L260,000; doubles L350,000, with bath L470,000; triples L480,000.) The central **Hotel Traian,** Piaţa Unirii 1, has rooms with pastel, silk-covered furniture except on the dingier third floor. (☎14 33 30. Singles L350,000; doubles L550,000-600,000. L45,000 breakfast credit included. Visa.)

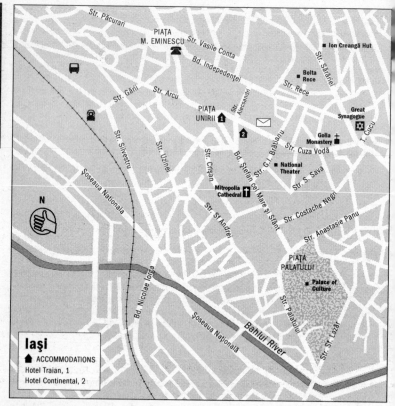

**Iaşi**

▲ ACCOMMODATIONS
Hotel Traian, 1
Hotel Continental, 2

For **groceries,** try **Rodex,** Str. Arcu 3/5, in the basement under the TAROM office. (Open 24hr.) The **market** is at Piaţa Mihai Eminescu near the intersection of Str. Copou and Bd. Independenţei. The 1786 ■ **Bolta Rece** (Cold Vault), Str. Rece 10, gets props for atmosphere. Walk down Str. Cuza Vodă past Hotel Continental and turn left onto Str. Brătianu. At Bd. Independenţei, continue straight across the street onto what becomes M. Eminescu, then turn left onto Str. Rece.

🎭 **SIGHTS.** The massive, neo-Gothic **Palace of Culture** (Palatul Culturii), marked by a clocktower that plays the anthem of the 1859 union of Moldovia and Walachia, contains historical, ethnographic, polytechnic, and art museums. (Open Tu-Su 10am-5pm. Each museum L10,000, students L5000.) The exterior walls of the gorgeous **Trei Ierarhi church,** on the right-hand side of Ştefan cel Mare as you walk to the Palace of Culture, display Moldavian, Romanian, and Turkish patterns in raised reliefs dating back to 1637. Gold covered the exterior until invading Tatars melted it down in 1653; the interior retains its original gold sheen. In 1821, the flag of the Eteria, a secret society for the liberation of Greece from Turkey, was sanctified here. (Church open daily 9am-noon and 3-5pm. L3000, students L1500; free for worshippers during service.) The **monastery,** home to the country's first printing press, displays valuable manuscripts, books, icons, and tapestries. (Monastery open 9am-noon and 3-5pm. L3000, students L1500. No cameras.) Writer Ion Creangă, "Romania's Mark Twain" (see **Literature and Arts,** p. 554) spent his last years in Iaşi in what is now known as the **Ion Creangă Hut,** Str. Simion Bărutiu 4. At the intersection of Golia and Bd. Independentei, go up Str. Sărăriei, 20 minutes past street #120, and follow the signs to "Bojdeuca." On March 1, large cultural celebrations honor Creangă's birthday. (☎ 11 55 15. Open Tu-Su 10am-5pm. L5000.) To get to **Copou Park,** Bd. Copou, take bus #35 from Piaţa Unirii. Inside the park created by Prince Mihail Sturza in 1836 is the famous **Mihai Eminescu linden,** the tree that shaded Romania's great poet as he composed (see **Literature and Arts,** p. 554). Statues of other artists line a nearby promenade. The adjacent **Eminescu Museum** exhibits pictures of the poet and some of his documents. (Open Tu-Su 10am-5pm. L2000 per person.)

# BUKOVINA MONASTERIES

Hidden among green hills and rustic farming villages, Bukovina's painted monasteries have witnessed many attacks over the centuries. Most recently, they endured early Soviet-era policies that forcibly ended the monks' lifestyle in favor of "reintegration." Built 500 years ago by Ştefan cel Mare and his successors, the exquisite structures mix Moldavian and Byzantine architecture, Romanian soul, and Christian dogma. Most of the monasteries are small, with stone walls and wooden roofs, surrounded by living quarters for monks or nuns and heavy stone walls that never quite deterred looters. Wear long sleeves and a long skirt or pants, or else borrow a skirt to wear over your shorts. Chew gum at your own risk. Smoking and taking pictures of the cloisters is prohibited, but taking pictures of the exteriors is allowed. Getting to monasteries other than Voroneţ and Humor by public transport unfortunately can be a trial of faith; instead, try one of the tours organized by Dispecerat de Cazare in Gura Humorului. A map is helpful for getting around. Young people often hitch, especially during summer, though *Let's Go* does not recommend hitchhiking.

## GURA HUMORULUI                                                ☎(0)33

Within walking distance of Humor and Voroneţ, and on the way to other monasteries, the small town of Gura Humorului is an ideal place to slumber while exploring the area. Though the town center itself could use a touch of the appeal of its divine surroundings, its peaceful side streets provide ample pleasure.

**▐ TRANSPORTATION.** Trains go to: **Suceava** (1hr., 5 per day, L25,000); **Iasi** (3hr., 4 per day, L74,000); **Cluj-Napoca** (6hr., 5 per day, L82,900); **Bucharest** (8hr., 1 per day, L131,1000); and **Timişoara** (12½hr., 2 per day, L165,800).

**▐ PRACTICAL INFORMATION.** To reach the town center, make a right on **Ştefan cel Mare** in front of the train station and continue over the bridge. The **bus station** is to the right as you emerge from the train station. Get info at ■ **Dispecerat de Cazare,** Str. Câmpului nr. 30, which offers car tours of the monasteries and a nearby underground salt mine that oddly features two chapels and a tennis court. From the train station, turn left onto Str. Ştefan cel Mare and left again on Str. Câmpului. (☎ 23 88 63; fax 23 23 87. Open 24hr. Tours US$20-30 per car.) Send your epiphanies at **Internet Cafe,** B-dul Bucovinii. (☎ 23 15 22. L15,000 per hr. Open daily 9am-11pm.)

Gura Humorului is a portal to scores of family-run, supremely comfortable villas in the sacred hills of Bukovina. If you arrange a room through **Dispecerat de Cazare** (see above) a guide will show you to your villa of choice. (July-Aug. 2-star double US$8-10; off-season 20-30% less, excluding holidays.) The staff can also arrange stays and meals at the actual monasteries; call in advance. Skip the mediocre restaurants and load up on groceries. Try the markets lining Str. Ştefan cel Mare or the 24hr. **Supermagazin** across the street from the Internet Cafe (see above).

## MONASTERIES

### VORONEŢ

*Take a bus from Gura Humorului (10min., M-F 3 per day, L10,000). On foot, turn left from the train station and again onto Cartierul Voroneţ; the monastery is at the end of a scenic 5km. Open daily 8am-8pm. L10,000; students L5,000. Cameras L20,000.*

Voroneţ Blue (Albastru de Voroneţ) is a phrase that haunts Romanian imaginations, from schoolchildren to art conservationists searching for a modern equivalent of this 15th-century paint. The blue that brought the monastery the name of "The Sistene Chapel of the East" is also the cause of its postponed restoration, since most work has to be put off until the paint is reproduced. The west wall depicts the Last Judgment in five levels. While the damned wear the faces of Moldavia's enemies, the Turks and Tatars, the blessed look ethnically Moldavian. Angels sport regional musical instruments and roll up the Zodiac around God, a demonstration of the passing of earthly time. Jesse's Tree, on the south wall, displays the genealogy of Jesus and ancient philosophers (look for Aristotle and Plato) while the north wall depicts scenes from Genesis and Adam's pact with the Devil. The church was built in 1488 by Ştefan cel Mare, supposedly on the advice of St. Daniel. If you listen carefully, you can still hear the bells tolling his name: "Ştefan-vodă."

## HUMOR

*Near the park in central Gura Humorului, follow Str. M. Humorulu and continue 6km to the monastery. Open daily 8am-8pm. L10,000, students 5000. Cameras L20,000.*

Dating from 1530, this convent was originally a monastery; its annexation to the Habsburg Empire in 1785 reinvented it as a parish church and then a storehouse. Humor has the oldest frescoes in Bukovina and is known for both its special red color and the south wall's depiction of the Virgin Mary's life. The mural, based on a poem by the patriarch of Constantinople, shows her saving Constantinople from a Persian attack in 626. With an eye toward current events, the artist substituted Turks for Persians and added weapons typical of the 16th century; he also painted huimself as a cavalier running a Turk through with his spear. The siege is part of a larger Hymn and Prayer to the Saints. The Last Judgment is on the porch, innovative for the time because of its open design.

## MOLDOVIŢA

*Buses run to Vatra Dornei from Gura Humorului (45min., 3 per day, L30,000). Open daily 7am-8pm. L5000. Cameras L20,000.*

Moldoviţa is the largest of the painted monasteries and its frescoes are among the best-preserved. Built in 1532 and painted in 1537, it portrays the Last Judgment, Jesse's Tree, and the monumental Siege of Constantinople. The siege of 626, painted on the exterior wall to the right of the entrance, depicts the ancient fortress in an uncanny 16th-century light. The monastery was closed from 1785 until 1945 and the north wall is badly weathered. Elaborately carved grapevine columns painted with gold jut out from the iconostasis. As in most of the monasteries, the founder is painted "al fresco" inside the nave, presenting the church to Jesus. The museum houses the wooden throne of Prince Petru Rareş, founder of numerous monasteries. Opposite the throne in the main room is the *Pomme d'Or* prize awarded to Bukovina in 1975 in recognition of its artistic importance. Be sure not to miss the giant religious tome donated by Catherine the Great.

## SUCEVIŢA

*Suceviţa lies 29km north of Moldoviţa (see above). The Moldoviţa-Rădăuţi bus between the Suceviţa and Moldoviţa monasteries features incredible scenery, including a large hand welcoming visitors to Bukovina (1hr., 1 per day, L15,000). Open daily 8am-8pm. L9000, students L5000. Cameras L20,000.*

Suceviţa, the newest of the monasteries at 405 years young, is set in fortified hills. Its frescoed south wall presents a Genealogy of Jesus and a procession of philosophers, including Pythagoras, Socrates, Plato, Aristotle, and Solon. The shade of green is unique to Suceviţa. Unlike the north faces of the other monasteries, Suceviţa's is well-preserved; souls climb a heavenly ladder of 30 rungs, each representing a virtue and a sin. The west wall remains unpainted—the artist fell from the scaffolding and his ghost supposedly prevents completion. The black stone head under the arch represents a woman who hauled stone for the construction with her oxen for 30 years to atone for her sins. Inside, the pro-nave depicts the deaths of 420 Orthodox saints, while the chamber contains an iconostasis carved from tisa wood. The altar, painted with scenes from the Old Testament, houses the tombs of the Movila dynasty. A door on the left leads to an emergency hiding place for relics and precious icons. The museum in one of the towers displays intricate tapestries, religious icons, and books, including an epitaph with 10,000 pearls.

## PUTNA

*For the scenic ride to Putna, catch direct trains from Suceava, 75km southeast (2½hr., 5 per day, L15,000). The last train leaves Putna around 9pm. The monastery lies 1km from the train station. Exiting the platform, turn right and then left at the 1st intersection and keep walking. Monastery open daily 8am-8pm. Free. Cameras L10,000. Museum open daily 9am-5pm. L5000, students L1500. Church open daily 9am-5pm. Free. No cameras.*

Immaculately white, Putna Monastery appears deceptively newer than its counterparts. Only one tower has survived the ravages of history, which have included fires, earthquakes, and attacks; not even the frescoes remain. The complex encompasses the marble-canopied tomb of Ştefan cel Mare (see **History,** p. 552), and a museum of religious artifacts and icons. In the church, Ştefan decays down on the right; his sons occupy the nearer tombs. Built between 1466 and 1469, Putna was the first of 38 monasteries founded by Ştefan, who built one church for each battle he won. He left Putna's location up to God: climbing a nearby hill to the left of the monastery (marked by a cross), he shot an arrow into the air. A piece of the oak it struck is on display at the museum, along with a number of manuscripts and religious garb. Midway to the railway station along the main road, stop by the 14th-century wooden church **Dragoş Vodă** (Biserica de lemn Dragoş Vodă), one of the oldest religious monuments in Bukovina. There are good hiking trails, but no maps. Tourists flood Putna on July 2, St. Ştefan's Day.

# RUSSIA (РОССИЯ)

## IF YOU'RE HERE FOR...

**1 WEEK.** Bust western-imperialist dance moves that would have brought a blush to Lenin's cheeks in the wild and woolly clubs of **Moscow** (p. 605).

**2 WEEKS.** Take the train to **St. Petersburg** (p. 637), which began as one man's pipe dream and remains one of the cultural centers of Europe.

**1 MONTH.** Ride the **Trans-Siberian Railroad** (p. 677) across Asia for a ridiculously low price while taking in some of the most dramatic scenery on Earth.

Ten years after the fall of communism, vast Russia stumbles forward without clear direction. Vaguely repentant former communists run the state under the standard of the market, while impoverished, outspoken pensioners long for a rosy-tinted Soviet past. Heedless of the failing provinces, cosmopolitan Moscow indiscriminately gobbles down hyper-capitalism, while St. Petersburg struggles not to resemble a ghost capital. Conservative monarchists, believers in the fundamental Orthodoxy of the Russian soul, rub elbows, albeit uneasily, with conservative nationalists, believers in Russian greatness through military strength. Neither have much affection for the West, by whom most Russians feel profoundly betrayed.

Russia is in many ways the ideal destination for a budget traveler—inexpensive and well-served by public transportation, with hundreds of neglected monasteries, kremlins, and churches. It can be a bureaucratic nightmare, but it can also offer a mixture of opulent tsarist palaces, fossilized Soviet edifices, and newfound symbols of ostentation—from GUM's designer shops to the mobile phones now ubiquitous among wealthy Russians—found nowhere else on Earth.

## RUSSIA AT A GLANCE

**OFFICIAL NAME:** Russian Federation

**CAPITAL:** Moscow (pop. 8.4 million)

**POPULATION:** 146 million (Russian 81.5%, Tatar 3.8%, Ukrainian 3%, Chuvash 1.2%, Bashkir 0.9%)

**LANGUAGE:** Russian

**CURRENCY:** 1 ruble (R) = 100 kopeks

**RELIGION:** 74% nonreligious, 16% Russian Orthodox, 10% Muslim

**LAND AREA:** 17,075,200km²

**CLIMATE:** Temperate to subarctic

**GEOGRAPHY:** Western plains, Ural Mountains, Siberian plateau

**BORDERS:** Belarus, Estonia, Latvia, Lithuania, Poland, Ukraine, Others

**ECONOMY:** 54% Services, 39% Industry, 7% Agriculture

**GDP:** $4000 per capita

**EMERGENCY PHONE NUMBERS:** Fire 01, Police 02, Emergency 03

**COUNTRY CODE:** 7

**INTERNATIONAL DIALING PREFIX:** 810

# HISTORY

Standing alone in the world, we have given nothing to the world, we have learnt nothing from the world...Today we form a gap in the intellectual order.
    —Pyotr Yakovlevich Chaadaev

**Western Russia**

**EARLY SETTLERS.** The earliest recorded settlers of European Russia were the **Varangians,** or Rus, though the area is believed to have been inhabited since the 2nd millennium BC. These Scandinavian tribesmen, exploring the area in search of furs and timber, followed river trade routes such as the Volga to the south, eventually reaching Baghdad and Constantinople in the mid-9th century. They gradually settled farther to the south, mingling with the East Slavic tribes they encountered. Consolidating their power in the early tenth century, these **Volga Rus** raided throughout the Caucasus and Central Asia.

Over the course of the tenth century one Varangian clan, led by **Prince Svyatoslav,** gained power over the others, establishing a new center of power in **Kyiv.** It was Svyatoslav's son **Volodymyr the Great,** however, who laid the foundations of **Kyivan Rus** by converting to **Orthodox Christianity** in AD 988. Volodymyr's decision established the Russian tradition of looking to Constantinople for political and cultural inspiration, which was to endure until the reign of Peter the Great (1682-1725). Following the death of Volodymyr in 1015, the Kyivan state was increasingly strained by wars between the clans and the declining importance of the Baltic-Black Sea trade route. Kyivan Rus disintegrated into numerous small principalities and city-states, chief among which were **Novgorod** and **Vladimir-Suzdal.**

**TARTAR CONTROL.** The lands of European Russia were in no position to resist the march of the Mongol **Golden Horde,** which arrived in 1223. Despite numerous myths to the contrary, the Mongol conquest was not particularly violent and most of the subjected city-states were able to carry on as before, albeit paying taxes to the Khans. Mongol influence on the culture of the Varangian and East Slavic tribes was minimal, but this period saw the emergence of **Muscovy** (today Moscow) as a commercial center and increasing contact with Western and Central Europe. Eventually the Mongol Khanate, like Kyivan Rus before it, fell victim to wars between competing local rulers, permitting Muscovy, **Lithuania, Novgorod** and the **Volga Bulgar Region** (later Kazan) to develop into powerful states.

**IVAN THE TERRIBLE.** Later **Ivan III**, Prince of Moscow, filled the void left by the departure of the Mongols and began a drive to unify all East Slavic lands—comprised of parts of present-day Belarus, Russia, and Ukraine—under his rule. Through a mixture of wily diplomacy and bashing in the heads of his competitors with a club, Ivan was able to subjugate many surrounding principalities while maintaining good relations with such neighbors as Kazan. Ivan also took the first steps toward the enserfment of the peasantry, limiting to St. Yuri's Day the period during which peasants might renounce tenancy of their land and move elsewhere. His son Vasily continued the expansion Ivan had begun, dying in 1533. He was succeeded by **Ivan IV (the Terrible),** the first ruler to take the title "tsar." He conquered neighboring Kazan and expanded westward, but alienated his generals and killed his oldest son and heir with his bare hands. Ivan's second son, **Fyodor I,** proved too weak to rule alone; his brother-in-law **Boris Godunov** secretly ruled in his stead. When Fyodor died childless in 1598, Boris became tsar. Conspiring against Godunov, the Russian **boyars** (nobles) brought forward a pretender named Dmitry who claimed Fyodor I had been his father. After Godunov's mysterious death, the *boyars* crowned this **"False Dmitry"** tsar. A decade of unprecedented instability and chaos followed, with the *boyars* striving for ever greater control over a succession of weak tsars. Finally, in 1613, **Mikhail Romanov** ascended to the throne, ushering in the dynasty that ruled until the Bolshevik Revolution of 1917.

**PETER THE GREAT (WELL, IT'S A MATTER OF OPINION).** Mikhail's grandson **Peter the Great,** whose reign began in 1682, dragged a reluctant Russia westward, producing the East-West schizophrenia that has plagued its national identity ever since. Peter created his own Westernized elite—he forced the Russian nobles to shave off their cherished beards—and built European-style St. Petersburg, his "window to the West," in the middle of a Finnish swamp. He killed innumerable workers in the process, hung the opposition, traipsed around Europe causing even more damage than the average *Let's Go* traveler, and left Russia with a severe statue and monument surplus when he died in 1725. With no male heir to the throne, the nobles took the opportunity to install a string of rulers firmly under their collective thumb, until the reign of **Catherine the Great,** 1762-96. The meek, homely daughter of an impoverished Prussian aristocrat, Catherine came to Russia to marry heir to the throne **Peter III,** whom she promptly overthrew after he came to power. Catherine extended the empire and partook of certain modish Enlightenment trends, but also increased landowners' power over their serfs, provoking the **Pugachov rebellion** in 1773. Claiming to be the deposed Tsar Peter III, Pugachov, a Don Cossack and an army veteran, led a peasant uprising that began east of the Volga and eventually engulfed much of European Russia. His army murdered numerous landlords before being put down by Catherine's troops. Following Catherine's death in 1796, her son **Paul I** set about undoing many of her reforms, endearing him to the populace but enraging the nobility. The nobles, with the tacit consent of Paul's son Alexander—his complicity was to haunt him for the rest of his life—assassinated the tsar in his bed in 1801. The reign of **Alexander I**, like so many Russian regimes, began with a flurry of reforms. Unfortunately for Russia, though, **Napoleon** began his rise to power in France at the same time.

Napoleon's invasion in 1812 foundered as the Russians burnt their crops and villages in retreat, leaving the French to face the harsh winter *sans* supplies. Victory over the little Corsican brought prestige and new contact with the rest of Europe, but led to internal strife. Russian officers returning from the West attempted a coup on December 14, 1825. Some **Decembrists** were hanged, most were exiled to Siberia, and for the next 30 years, **Tsar Nicholas I** made sure to stifle all dissent.

The 1840s saw a marked split in the intelligentsia between **Westernizers,** who considered Russia a backward, despotic country in need of reform, and the **Slavophiles,** who insisted that serfdom and autocracy were just bends along Russia's "special path" to saving Christianity and the world. The Westernizers bred a radical wing that would later take to Marxism and, more recently, consumer capitalism; Slavophilism, more amenable to the tsars, remains to this day the banner of extreme nationalism. Russia's loss to the West in the **Crimean War** (1853-1856) spurred reforms that included the **emancipation of the serfs** in 1861. Alexander II soon slowed the pace of reform, however, which prompted the radicals to move against him; he was assassinated shortly thereafter.

**WAR AND PEACE... AND WAR AGAIN.** The famine, peasant unrest, terrorism, and strikes of the late 1800s culminated in the failed **1905 Revolution.** Coupled with the humiliating loss of the Russo-Japanese War, the uprising forced **Tsar Nicholas II** to establish a legislative body, the **Duma,** and make vague attempts to address the demands of his people. **World War I,** stalemate with the Duma, and fermenting revolution led him to abdicate in March 1917. Vladimir Ilich Ulyanov, a.k.a. **Lenin,** leader of the Bolsheviks, steered the coup of October 1917: a few well-placed words to **Aleksandr Kerensky,** leader of the provisional government, and a menacing ring around the Winter Palace turned the nation Red. A **Civil War** followed the October Revolution, but Lenin died soon after the Red Army triumphed, and infighting began as Ioseb Dzhugashvili, a.k.a. **Joseph Stalin,** eliminated his rivals.

Stalin forced collectivization of Soviet farms and filled Siberian labor camps with "political" prisoners based on regional quotas. Priority was given to national defense and heavy industry, which led to shortages of consumer goods. His numerous purges of political opponents killed millions. Among world leaders, Stalin was able to find only one ally—**Hitler,** with whom he concluded the **Nazi-Soviet Non-Aggression Pact** in August 1939. Later that year the USSR helped Germany in its attack on Poland, and Red Army subsequently occupied Latvia, Lithuania and Estonia. After having purged most of his top generals, Stalin brought the USSR into **World War II** unprepared when the Nazi-Soviet relationship soured. Fortunately, a long winter, combined with the tactics of military commander **Georgy Zhukov,** helped the USSR fend off Hitler's treachery. The **Battle of Stalingrad** (today **Volgograd**), in which 1.1 million Russian troops are thought to have been killed, broke the German advance and turned the tide of the war on the Russian front. In 1945, the Soviets pushed through to Berlin and gained status as a postwar superpower. Stalin then reneged on the agreements made with the allies at Yalta, refusing to permit free elections in the nations of Eastern Europe. The USSR left its victorious Red Army in Eastern Europe and the **Iron Curtain** descended on the continent.

**I WANT MY KGB.** In 1949, the Soviet Union formed the Council for Mutual Economic Assistance, or **COMECON,** which incorporated all the Eastern European countries, reducing them to satellites of the Party's headquarters in Moscow. After Stalin's death in 1953, **Nikita Khrushchev** emerged as the new leader of the Soviet Union. In his 1956 "secret speech," he denounced the terrors of the Stalinist period. Krushchev also inaugurated the space race with the United States, putting the 184-pound **Sputnik** into orbit in 1957. A brief political and cultural **"thaw"** followed, lasting until 1964, when Khrushchev was ousted by **Leonid Brezhnev.** The Brezhnev regime remained in power until 1983, overseeing a period of political repression that witnessed the internal exile of writers such as **Alexsandr Solzhenitsyn** and **Joseph Brodsky.** Internal dissent was quashed as well, as in the case of exiled physicist **Andrei Sakharov,** the reluctant father of the Soviet H-Bomb, who had become a staunch advocate of disarmament. The brutal regimes of **Yuri Andropov** and **Konstantin Chernenko** followed Brezhnev in fortunately quick succession. As the decline of the aging elite consumed political circles, the army became frustrated with its losses in the war against the anti-communist Muslim guerillas in Afghanistan. The geriatric government finally gave way to 56-year-old firebrand **Mikhail Gorbachev** in 1985. Gorbachev's political and economic reforms were aimed at helping the country regain the status of a superpower. Reform began slowly, with **glasnost** (openness) and **perestroika** (rebuilding). The state gradually turned into a bewildering hodge-podge of near-anarchy, economic crisis, and cynicism. Gorbachev became the architect of his own demise; despite popularity abroad (and the 1990 Nobel Peace Prize), discontent with his reforms and a failed right-wing coup in August 1991 led to his resignation and the dissolution of the Union on Christmas Day, 1991.

**THE PARTY IS OVER.** With the collapse of the USSR **Boris Yeltsin,** President of the Russian Republic since June of 1991, assumed power. Most of the former Soviet republics nominally banded together in the **Commonwealth of Independent States (CIS),** but the confederation has become increasingly meaningless in all but the economic sense as the republics have drifted further along their own trajectories.

The constitution ratified in December 1993 gave the presidency sweeping powers, a provision whose shortcomings former Yeltsin's tenure exposed. Largely ineffective during his second term, Yeltsin was least lethargic when dealing with his cabinet, firing a succession of Prime Ministers. Those economic policies he did attempt came crashing down in August 1998, when the pyramid schemes Russia had played with its natural resources and bond sales were halted abruptly. The ruble was devalued in an attempt to lessen the country's foreign debt. As a result, **inflation** skyrocketed, hitting 84% by the end of 1998. Those with money in the bank languished in financial limbo, unable to withdraw their savings. Those with rubles in hand frantically bought up available resources through the nation's feeble distribution network and many Russians resorted to bartering for basic goods.

# POLITICS

Inadequate as he frequently was, Yeltsin did have the good sense to resign on December 31, 1999, installing ex-KGB official **Vladimir Putin** as Acting President. Yeltsin's peaceful departure marked the first-ever voluntary transfer of power by a Russian leader—Soviet leaders had maintained the tsarist tradition of either being forced from office or leaving in a casket. Like his predecessor, Putin has combined the ideas of a democrat with the methods of an autocrat, admittedly with greater sobriety and broader political support than Yeltsin ever displayed. While outwardly pledging support for democracy, Putin has alarmed Western observers with his often-brutal prosecution of the war in **Chechnya,** which has caused his domestic approval ratings to skyrocket. He was able to ride the wave of support for the war to victory in presidential elections the following March. Since his inauguration, Putin has displayed unquestionable political strength, persuading the Duma to ratify the START II disarmament treaty and to confirm his reform-minded Prime Minister, **Mikhail Kasyanov,** by an overwhelming majority. While Putin's charm and reformist pledges have earned him the adulation of the Western media, many in Russia and abroad are wary of his authoritarian leanings. Putin has taken steps to reduce the power of the Federation Council, the upper house of the Russian legislature, and ordered raids on television stations critical of his policy in Chechnya.

# CULTURE

RUSSIA

| NATIONAL HOLIDAYS IN 2001 | |
|---|---|
| **January 1-2** New Year's | **May 1-2** Labor Day |
| **January 7** Orthodox Christmas | **May 9** Victory Day |
| **February 23** Defenders of the Motherland Day | **June 12** Independence Day |
| **March 8** International Women's Day | **November 7** Day of Accord and Reconciliation |
| **April 15** Easter | **December 12** Constitution Day |

# LITERATURE

**THE GOLDEN AGE OF LITERATURE.** Ever since Catherine the Great exiled **Alexander Radishchev,** whose *Journey from St. Petersburg to Moscow* had documented the dehumanizing nature of serfdom, to Siberia, art and politics in Russia have been inextricably bound together. The country's most beloved literary figure, **Aleksandr Pushkin,** was sympathetic to the Decembrist revolution but ultimately chose aesthetics over politics. His novel in verse, *Eugene Onegin,* was a biting take on the poet's own earlier Romanticism. Pushkin could not escape the intrigues of the royal court, however, and died in a duel with a French officer. With his eulogy to Pushkin, **Mikhail Lermontov** accepted the poet's legacy, which included his own stint in exile and death in a duel.

The 1840s saw a turn, under the goading of Westernizer critic **Vissarion Belinsky,** to the realism and social awareness that would produce the masterpieces of Russian literature. While the absurdist works of **Nikolai Gogol** were hardly realist, they were read at the time as masterful social comments. His great comedy *The Government Inspector* exposed the corruption of Russian society, as did his great novel *Dead Souls.* **Ivan Turgenev's** *Fathers and Sons* was less ambiguously social, sadly recording the severance of the intellectual generations of the 1840s and 1860s. **Fyodor Dostoyevsky's** works, including *Crime and Punishment* and *The Brothers Karamazov,* have long outlasted various revolutionary and religious quests to save Russia. The same can be said for **Leo (Lev) Tolstoy,** whose psychological epics like *Anna Karenina* and *War and Peace* preceded the religious polemics of his old age. The 1890s saw the rise of **Maxim Gorky,** whose "tramp period" fictions explored the dregs of Russian society and foreshadowed his part in the Bolshevik Revolution. Realism's last great voice belonged to **Anton Chekhov,** whose short stories distilled the power of his verbose predecessors and whose plays are still part of repertoires worldwide.

**THE SILVER AGE AND THE REVOLUTION.** With the turn of the century literature entered its **Silver Age,** with many poets emulating French symbolism. **Aleksandr Blok,** whose talents may have exceeded those of the beloved Pushkin, tinted his verse with mystic and apocalyptic hues. For Blok and others, the Bolshevik revolution of 1917 seemed only to heighten the excitement in the air.

## CRIME AND PUNISHMENT

Fyodor Dostoyevsky earned his literary credentials the hard way—his involvement with the utopian-socialist Petrashevsky circle led to his arrest in 1849 and he was subsequently sentenced to death. After eight months of imprisonment, Dostoyevsky and his co-conspirators were brought into the courtyard of the Peter and Paul Fortress in St. Petersburg. A priest performed last rites and the firing squad marched into the courtyard. Just as hoods were placed over the heads of the condemned men, a messenger from Tsar Nicholas I thundered in on horseback, bringing a pardon; the execution had been staged in order to scare the prisoners straight. Thanks to the tsar's "mercy," Dostoyevsky spent ten years at hard labor in a Siberian prison and later wrote *The House of the Dead* about his experiences.

**LIFE SUCKS AND THEN YOU DIE** The life of a poet in Soviet Russia was not an easy one. **Sergei Yesenin**, a poet of peasant origin who initially welcomed the revolution, but later became disillusioned with the increasing mechanization and industrialization of Soviet society. Feeling alienated from the Bolsheviks and from the village of his youth, now permeated by communist slogans, Yesenin took to drinking and cocaine, trashing more hotels in America and Europe than Guns n' Roses and Aerosmith combined. In 1925 he hung himself in a Leningrad hotel room, after writing his final poem in his own blood. His fellow poet **Vladimir Mayakovsky** condemned Yesenin's suicide as an act of cowardice, masking his own deep reservations about the role of a poet in emerging Soviet society. Five years later Mayakovsky shot himself in his Moscow apartment, leaving behind a bitterly ironic suicide note: "love's boat has smashed against daily life."

Symbolism was soon challenged, however, by the **Acmeist** movement, which prized elegance and clarity over the metaphysical vagueness of the Symbolists. Among the members of the Acmeist moment, **Anna Akhmatova** became known for her haunting, sometimes melancholic love verses, and later for *Requiem*, her memorial to the victims of Stalin's purges. Competing with the Acmeists, the **Futurists** embraced industrialization and technology in their verse, with such poets as **Vladimir Mayakovsky** urging that Pushkin be "thrown from the steamship of modernity" as an superfluous relic of the past.

With the rise of Stalin in the late 20s, the state soon mandated **Socialist Realism,** a coerced glorification of international socialism. The regime turned its purges on the *literarati:* Akhmatova lost her husband to a firing squad and was subject to internal exile, as was **Boris Pasternak** for his Civil War epic *Doctor Zhivago*. Acmeist poet **Osip Mandelstam**, perhaps the greatest Russian poet of the 20th century, composed and memorized many of his greatest works in exile before dying in a Siberian gulag; they were later recorded by his wife. A few fortunate artists such as **Vladimir Nabokov** were able to emigrate.

Literature also pushed on at home, as **Mikhail Bulgakov** (for Bulgakov's house, see **Ukraine: Sights,** p. 776) slipped the leash of Socialist Realism with *The Master and Margarita* (it wasn't published for some thirty years, until 1966, and then appeared only in the West). The early sixties brought a "thaw" that allowed **Joseph Brodsky's** verse and **Alexander Solzhenitsyn's** shocking *One Day in the Life of Ivan Denisovich*, detailing life in a labor camp, to emerge. The accession of Leonid Brezhnev, however, plunged the arts into an ice age from which they have yet to fully recover. Post-modernists like **Dmitry Prigov** and **Lev Rubenstein** can publish freely, but the fabric of their world has hardly changed. **Lyudmilla Petrushevskaya,** for one, writes of people as unhappy as they were before.

# MUSIC

**Mikhail Glinka** began the modern Russian musical tradition, fusing folk melodies with the European harmonic system. His ballets *A Life for the Tsar* (1836) and the Pushkin-inspired *Ruslan and Lyudmila* (1842) remain in the repertoire of opera companies today. Glinka's successors were polarized into Westernizer and Slavophile camps. **Pyotr Tchaikovsky,** closest to Belinsky's Western-minded school,

**MY WIFE WON'T LEAVE ME ALONE** Life was a high-stress affair for Tchaikovsky, who suffered several breakdowns in his 53 years. The worst of these came in 1878, when he consented to marry one of his students, Antonina Milyukova (she had threatened suicide if he refused). She was shocked on the wedding night by the discovery that Tchaikovsky was homosexual, he by the discovery that she was a nymphomaniac. Tchaikovsky was so repulsed by his bride that he attempted suicide and later had to bribe her to keep his homosexuality a secret.

**SAY MY NAME** Shostakovich is known for his obsessive development of tiny thematic ideas, many of which occur in multiple works. Perhaps most curious is his repeated use of the sequence D-Eflat-C-B. What's that spell? Well, in the system of notation used in Russia, Eflat=S and B=h. "D-Eflat-C-B" spells "D. Sch," for Dmitri Schostakovich, the German spelling of the composer's name.

tempered native melodies with European restraint. His *Piano Concerto No. 1 in B Flat Minor* (1874-5) and *Symphony No. 6 "Pathetique"* (1893) are highly regarded and widely performed, as are his ballets, including *The Nutcracker* (1892). The work of **Nikolai Rimsky-Korsakov**, best known for the symphonic suite *Scheherazade* (1888), in contrast, was bombastically Slavophilic. **Modest Mussorgsky**, best known for his opera *Boris Godunov*, was of similar musical inclination.

The early 20th century brought revolutionary ferment and artistic experimentation. Virtuoso pianist and composer **Sergei Rachmaninov** fused the traditional romanticism of the Westernizer school with a unique lyricism, producing such lasting works as his four piano concerti and *Rhapsody on a Theme of Paganini*. This period also saw the fruitful collaboration between composer **Igor Stravinsky** and **Sergei Diaghilev**, impresario of the Paris-based **Ballets Russes**. It was for Diaghilev's company that Stravinsky wrote his three greatest ballets: *The Firebird* (1910), *Petrushka* (1911), and *The Rite of Spring* (1913). All three are now considered masterpieces, but *The Rite of Spring* represented such a departure—it is frequently used to mark the birth of the modern era due to its radical, unresolved dissonances—that it caused a riot in the theater following its Paris premiere.

The revolution of 1917 imposed ideological restrictions on such great composers as **Dmitri Shostakovich**. Despite repeated falls from official favor—the first of which was precipitated by Stalin's personal displeasure at the composer's opera *Lady Macbeth of the Mtsensk District*—Shostakovich maintained his stylistic integrity, often satirizing the unwitting Soviet authorities in his famous symphonies. His prolific contemporary **Sergei Prokofiev** enjoyed more consistent official favor, composing a variety of excellent pieces from the symphonic children's piece *Peter and the Wolf* to symphonies, concertos and films scores for Eisenstein's films *Alexander Nevsky*, *Ivan the Terrible* and *Battleship Potemkin*.

# VISUAL ARTS AND FILM

The young Soviet Union quickly produced **Sergei Eisenstein**, considered by some the greatest filmmaker to ever live. Eisenstein, who began his career as a theatrical costume and set designer, revolutionized film theory by juxtaposing symbolic images to increase the psychological effect of his films. His *Battleship Potemkin* (1925) was voted the greatest film ever made by an international poll of critics in 1958.

The period following the revolution saw the visual arts gain some of the prominence Russian music and literature had long enjoyed, with artists **Wassily Kandinsky, Marc Chagall** and **Natalya Goncharova** gaining international acclaim. Kandinsky, of Russian and Mongolian ancestry, is acknowledged as one of the pioneers of **Abstraction**; he was convinced as a child that each color had its own "internal life." Both Chagall and Goncharova left Russia a few years after the revolution, and both later worked designing sets for Diaghilev's Ballets Russes. Many later artists, confined by the strictures of Socialist Realism, were limited to painting canvases with such bland titles as, "The Tractor Drivers' Supper."

# RELIGION

The atheist programme of the Communist Party discouraged the open expression of religious faith, but with the demise of the Soviet Union Russian Orthodoxy, headed by **Patriarch Aleksei II**, has emerged from hiding and is now winning increasing numbers of converts. Numerous lands and buildings have been returned to the church, and Moscow's Cathedral of Christ the Savior (see p. 620), destroyed by the Soviets in 1931, has been rebuilt on its original site. The new Russian state has favored the Orthodox Church by making it difficult for other religious groups, such as Roman Catholics, to own property, distribute literature or worship in public.

Adherents to Orthodoxy are predominantly Slavic, although several Turkic peoples, such as the Chuvash, have converted. Most Turkic groups in Russia are Muslim and the few Mongolian-speaking groups, such as the Buryat, are Buddhist.

# FOOD AND DRINK

Russian cuisine is a medley of dishes both delectable and disgusting; tasty borscht can come in the same meal as *salo* (pig fat). Food is generally better in the south. If you're stuck in the culinary wasteland of the upper latitudes, look for a Georgian or Azerbaijani restaurant for some respite. The largest meal of the day, *obed* (обед; lunch), is eaten at midday and includes: *salat* (салат; salad), usually cucumbers and tomatoes or beets and potatoes with mayonnaise or sour cream; *sup* (суп; soup), either meat or cabbage; and *kuritsa* (курица; chicken) or *myaso* (мясо; meat), often called *kotlyety* (котлеты; cutlets) or *beefshteaks* (бифштекс; beefsteaks). Ordering a number of *zakuski* (закуски; small appetizers) instead of a main dish can save money. Dessert includes *morozhenoye* (мороженое; ice cream) or *tort* (торт; cake) with *cofe* (кофе; coffee) or *chai* (чай; tea), which Russians will drink at the slightest provocation. A cafe (кафе) or *stolovaya* (столовая; cafeteria) is cheaper than a restaurant, but the latter may be unsanitary.

**Dietas** (диета) sell goods for people on special diets (such as diabetics); **produkty** (продукты) and **gastronoms** (гастроном) offer a variety of meats, cheeses, breads, and packaged goods. The larger **universam** (универсам) simulates a supermarket with its wide variety. The **market** (рынок; rynok) sells abundant fruits and vegetables, meat, fresh milk, butter, honey, and cheese. Wash and dry everything before you eat it—Russian farmers use pesticides as if they were going out of style. Milk may not be pasteurized. A **bulochnaya** (булочная; bakery) usually sells fresh bread daily and sometimes sweet rolls, cakes, and cookies.

The **kiosks** found in every town act as mini-convenience stores, selling soda, juice, candy bars, and cookies; point to what you want. On the streets, you'll see a lot of *shashlyki* (шашлыки; barbecued meat on a stick) and *kvas* (квас), an alcoholic dark-brown drink (see **"Just for the Taste,"** p. 762). Kiosks often carry alcohol; imported cans of beer are safe (though warm), but be wary of Russian labels—you have no way of knowing what's really in the bottle. *Zolotoye koltso, Russkaya,* and *Zubrovka* are the best vodkas; the much-touted *Stolichnaya* is mostly made for export. Among local beers, *Baltika* (Балтика; numbered 1 through 7) is the most popular and arguably the best. *Baltika* 1 is the weakest (10.5%), *Baltika* 7 the strongest (14%). *Baltikas* 4 and 6 are dark; the rest are lagers. Numbers 3 and 4 are the most popular; 7 is extreme.

Vendors do not provide **bags** for merchandise. You can usually buy plastic bags in stores or at markets but bring your own to be safe. In stores, especially the older ones, decide what you want, then go to a *kassa* in the department you're buying from and tell the person working there the item and the price. The person will take your money and give you a receipt. You then take the receipt back to the counter. Give it to the person working there, and they will give you what you want.

# CUSTOMS AND ETIQUETTE

Decades of collective lifestyle forced people very close together; as a result, the notion of personal space is almost nonexistent in Russia. People pack tightly in lines and on buses, tolerating the discomfort with stoic patience. When boarding a bus, tram, or Metro car, forceful shoving is required. On public transportation, it's polite for women to give their seats to elderly or pregnant women and women with children. For men, it's gallant to yield a seat to all women. It's okay for everybody (especially *babushki*) to push and shove if polite requests don't get you anywhere.

On trains, even the hottest summer day, you may find the windows closed "for the winter" (no, there is no air-conditioning). If you luck out with a single window that does open, Russians will close it anyway—there's a national fear of drafts.

In St. Petersburg and Moscow (but nowhere else) a 5-10% **tip** is becoming customary. Most establishments, even train ticket offices, close for a **lunch break** sometime between noon and 3pm. Places tend to close at least 30 minutes earlier than they should, if they choose to open at all. "24hr." stores often take a lunch or "technical" break and one day off each week.

When visiting friends, bring flowers, cookies, or candy. Russians tend to dress up to go visiting, even if it's just across the street. Visiting a museum in shorts and sandals is regarded as disrespectful (they will give you a very hard time at the Hermitage). Many locals say that criminals spot foreigners by their sloppy appearances, so dress up and don't smile when stared at. Women in Russia generally wear skirts or dresses rather than pants. Never wear jeans to a performance, as Russians dress up for the theater and consider arriving for a performance in everyday clothes an insult to their culture. For polite requests, use first names and patronymics, which are middle names derived from one's father's first name (i.e. 'Mikhailovich' from Mikhail for men, or 'Mikhailovna' for women).

The concept of **sexual harassment** hasn't reached Russia yet. Local men will try to pick up women and will get away with offensive language and actions. The routine starts with an innocent-sounding *"Devushka..."* (young lady); just say *"Nyet"* (No) or simply walk away. Locations and intensity of pursuit vary, with intentions ranging from playfulness to physical abuse. And no, they don't wear deodorant—it's considered fine for Russian men to smell.

The laws outlawing **homosexuality** were taken off the books about seven years ago, but gay, lesbian and bisexual travelers should not expect tolerance of public displays of affection outside of the gay clubs that have sprung up in Moscow and St. Petersburg. Travelers of non-European descent will often receive rude treatment in stores or restaurants, as Russians **discriminate** against even their own non-Slavic citizens in the south. The authorities on the Metro will frequently stop and question dark-skinned individuals, particularly anyone who looks Chechen or Dagestani.

It is unwise, though not illegal, to take pictures of anything military or to do anything that might attract the attention of a man in uniform—doing something suspicious provides an excuse to detain you or possibly extort money.

# SPORTS

The Soviet Union consistently fared well at both the Summer and Winter Olympic Games and Russia has continued that tradition, making strong showings in ice hockey, figure skating, basketball, track and field, boxing and wrestling. Russian players such as **Sergei Fedorov** and **Pavel Bure** have been very successful in the NHL, while young tennis star **Anna Kournikova,** currently number fifteen on the WTP tour, has drawn huge crowds. Russia has also remained strong in figure skating, boasting stars such as **Maria Butyrskaya,** 1999 world champion, **Irina Slutskaya,** 2000 European champion, and **Alexei Yagudin,** world champion for the past three years.

Hockey and soccer are the most popular sports, but cross-country skiing and ice skating are also favorite pastimes among ordinary Russians. Chess is very popular; Russia has produced most of the world's great players since the introduction of an international championship in the late 19th century.

# LANGUAGE

Take some time to familiarize yourself with the **Cyrillic** alphabet. It's not as difficult as it looks and will make getting around and getting by immeasurably easier. Once you get the hang of the alphabet, you can pronounce just about any Russian word, though you will probably sound like an idiot. For more info on Cyrillic, see p. 15. Although more and more people are speaking **English** in Russia, come equipped with at least a few helpful Russian words and phrases (see **Glossary,** p. 598 and **Phrasebook,** p. 599).

# GLOSSARY

RUSSIA

| ENGLISH | RUSSIAN | PRONOUNCE |
|---|---|---|
| one | один | ah-DEEN |
| two | два | d-VAH |
| three | три | tree |
| four | четыре | chi-TIH-rih |
| five | пять | p-YAHT' |
| six | шесть | SHAY-st' |
| seven | семь | s-YEM' |
| eight | восемь | VOH-sem' |
| nine | девять | DYEV-it' |
| ten | десять | DYES-it' |
| twenty | двадцать | DVAH-dtsat' |
| thirty | тридцать | TREE-dtsat' |
| forty | сорок | SOR-ok |
| fifty | пятьдесят | pya-de-SYAHT |
| sixty | шестьдесят | shays-de-SYAHT |
| seventy | семьдесят | SYEM-de-sit |
| eighty | восемьдесят | VO-sim-de-sit |
| ninety | девяносто | de-vi-NO-sta |
| one hundred | сто | stoh |
| one thousand | тысяча | TIS-si-cha |
| Monday | понедельник | pa-ne-DYEL-nik |
| Tuesday | вторник | FTOR-neek |
| Wednesday | среда | sreh-DAH |
| Thursday | четверг | chet-VERK |
| Friday | пятница | PYAHT-nit-sah |
| Saturday | суббота | soo-BOT-tah |
| Sunday | воскресенье | vahsk-rees-SYEH-nyeh |
| a day | день | dyen |
| a few days | немногие дней | nee-m-NOG-iye dnei |
| a week | неделя | nee-DYEL-ya |
| morning | утром | OO-trum |
| afternoon | днём | d-NYOM |
| evening | вечером | VEI-cher-um |
| today | сегодня | see-VOHD-nya |
| tomorrow | завтра | ZAHV-trah |
| spring | весна | vehs-NAH |
| summer | лето | LYEH-ta |
| fall | осень | OHS-syen' |
| winter | зима | zee-MAH |
| hot | жаркий | ZHAR-ki |
| cold | холодный | khol-OD-nui |
| single room | на одного | nah AHD-nah-voh |
| double room | двойная комната | dvai-NA-ya KOM-na-ta |
| reservation | предварительный заказ | pred-va-RIT'-el-niy za-KAZ |
| with shower | с душом | s DOO-shom |
| pharmacy | аптека | ahp-TYE-kah |

| ENGLISH | RUSSIAN | PRONOUNCE |
|---|---|---|
| post office | почта | POCH-ta |
| stamp | марка | MAR-ka |
| airmail | авиа | AH-via |
| departure | отъезд | at-YEZD |
| arrival | приезд | pree-YEZD |
| one-way | в один конец | v ah-DEEN kah-NYETS |
| round-trip | туда и обратно | too-DAH ee ah-BRAHT-nah |
| luggage | багаж | ba-GAZH |
| reservation | предварительный заказ | pred-va-RI-tyel-nui za-KAZ |
| train | поезд | PO-yezd |
| bus | автобус | av-toh-BOOS |
| airport | аэропорт | ayro-PORT |
| station | вокзал | VOK-zal |
| ticket | билет | beel-YET |
| grocery | гастроном | gah-stra-NOM |
| breakfast | завтрак | ZAV-trak |
| lunch | обед | ob-YED |
| dinner | ужин | OO-zhin |
| menu | меню | men-YOO |
| bread | хлеб | khlyeb |
| vegetables | овощи | OH-va-shi |
| beef | говядина | ga-VYAH-dee-na |
| chicken | курица | KOO-ree-tsa |
| pork | свинина | svi-NEE-na |
| fish | рыба | REE-ba |
| coffee | кофе | KO-feh |
| milk | молоко | mah-lah-KOH |
| beer | пиво | PEE-vah |
| sugar | сахар | SA-khar |
| eggs | яйца | yai-TSAH |
| holiday | день отдыха | dyen OT-dui-kha |
| open | открыт | ot-KRIHT |
| closed | закрыт | za-KRIHT |
| bank | банк | bahnk |
| police | милиция | mee-LEE-tsi-ya |
| exchange | обмен валюты | ob-MEN val-YU-tui |
| toilet | туалет | too-a-LYET |
| square | площадь | PLO-shad' |
| castle | замок | ZAH-mak |
| church | церковь | TSER-kov |
| tower | башня | BASH-nya |
| market | рынок | RIHN-nak |
| passport | паспорт | PAS-pohrt |
| bakery | булочная | BOO-lahch-nai-yah |
| left | налево | nah-LEH-va |
| right | направо | nah-PRAH-va |

# PHRASEBOOK

| ENGLISH | RUSSIAN | PRONOUNCIATION |
|---|---|---|
| Yes/no | Да/нет | Dah/N-yet |
| Please/You're welcome | Пожалуйста | pa-ZHAL-u-sta |
| Thank you | Спасибо | spa-SEE-bah |
| Hello | Добрый день | DOH-brui DEN |
| Good-bye | До свидания | das-vee-DAHN-ya |
| Good morning | Доброе утро | DOH-braye OO-tra |
| Good evening | Добрый вечер | DOH-brui VEH-cher |
| Good night | Спокойной ночи | spa-KOI-nai NOCH-ee |
| Sorry/Excuse me | Извините | iz-vi-NEET-yeh |
| Help! | Помогите! | pah-mah-GHEE-te |
| When? | Когда? | kahg-DAH |
| Where is...? | Где? | g-dyeh |
| How do I get to...? | Как пройти...? | kak prai-TEE |
| How much does this cost? | Сколько стоит? | SKOHL'-ka stoit |
| Do you have...? | У вас есть...? | oo vas YEST' |
| Do you speak English? | Вы говорите по-английски? | vy ga-va-REE-tye po an-GLEE-ski |
| I don't understand. | Я не понимаю | ya nee pa-nee-MAH-yoo |
| I don't speak Russian | Я не говорю по-русски. | yah nyeh gah-vah-RYOO pah ROO-skee |
| Please write it down. | Напишите пожалуйста | nah-pee-SHEET'-yeh, pah-ZHAL-u-stah |
| Speak a little slower, please. | Медленее, пожалуйста | MYED-li-nyay-eh, pah-ZHAL-u-stah |
| I'd like to order... | Я хотел(а) бы | ya khah-TYEL(a) bui |
| I'd like to pay/We'd like to pay. | Счёт, пожалуйста | shchyot, pah-ZHAL-u-stah |
| I think you made a mistake in the bill. | Вы не ошиблись? | vih nee ah-SHIH-blis |
| Do you have a vacancy? | У вас есть свободный номер? | oo vahss yehst' svah-BOD-niy NO-mehr |
| I'd like a room. | Я бы хотел(а) номер. | yah bui khah-TYEHL(ah) NO-mehr |
| May I see the room? | Можно посмотреть номер? | MOZH-nah pah-smah-TREHT' NO-mehr |
| No, I don't like it. | Нет, мне не нравится. | nyeht, mnyeh nee NRAH-vit-sah |
| Yes, I'll take it. | Да, это подойдёт. | dah, EH-tah pah-dai-DYOHT |
| Will you tell me when to get off? | Вы мне скажете, когда надо выходить? | vui mnyeh skah-ZHIH-tyeh, kahg-DAH NAH-dah vui-hah-DEET |
| Is this the right train/bus to...? | Это поезд на...? | EH-tah PO-yezd nah |
| I want a ticket to... | Один билет до...., поиалуйста. | ah-DEEN bee-LYET dah...., pah-ZHAHLY-stah |
| How long does the trip take? | Долго ли надо ехать? | DOHL-gah lee NAH-dah YEH-khaht' |
| When is the first/next/last train to... | Когда первый/следующий/последний поезд на...? | kahg-DAH PYEHR-vui/pah-sly-ehd-nii PO-yezd nah |
| Where is the bathroom/nearest teleiphone booth/center of town? | Где находится туалет/ближайший телефон-автомат/центр города? | gdyeh nah-KHOHD-di-tsah TOO-ah-lyet/blee-ZHAI-shii te-le-FOHN-av-tah-MAHT/TSEN-ter GOR-rah-dah |
| I've lost my... | Я терял(а)... | ya teer-YAL-(a) |
| Would you like to dance? | Вы хотите танцевать? | vui kha-TEE-tye tan-tse-VAT' |
| Go away. | Уходите. | oo-khah-DEE-tye |

Note that улица (ulitsa; abbreviated ul./ул.) means "street," проспект (prospekt; pr./пр.) means "avenue," площадь (ploshchad; pl./пл.) means "square," and бульвар (bulvar; bul./бул.) is "boulevard." Кремль (kreml; fortress); рынок (rynok; market square); гостиница (gostinitsa; hotel); собор (sobor; cathedral); and церков (tserkov; church) are also good words to know.

## ADDITIONAL READING

James Billington's *The Icon and the Axe* is the classic study of Russian culture. Orlando Figes's *A People's Tragedy* is an amazing panorama of the Russian revolution. The most profound Western book on 19th-century Russian thought is probably Isaiah Berlin's *Russian Thinkers*, while Vladimir Nabokov's *Lectures on Russian Literature* are the best introduction 19th-century Russian literature could hope to have. Richard Pipes's *The Russian Revolution* remains the seminal history of the revolutionary period, while among accounts of Stalinism, nothing can match the moral force of Solzhenitsyn's *The Gulag Archipelago*. In the past several years, a number of "I-went-to-Russia-and-boy-was-it-crazy" books have popped up; these should be avoided, and don't even think of writing one yourself. David Remnick's fine study of the fall of the Soviet Union in *Lenin's Tomb* and his chronicle of post-Soviet life in *Resurrection* are both worthwhile exceptions. Hendrick Smith's *The New Russians* is also a well-executed portrait of Soviet life.

# TRAVELING ESSENTIALS

Citizens of Australia, Canada, Ireland, New Zealand, South Africa, the UK, and the US all require a visa to enter Russia. Several types of visas are available; the standard tourist visa is valid for 30 days of travel in Russia. Visas for longer stays require a lengthier application and cost more. All types of Russian visas require an invitation stating the traveler's itinerary and dates of travel. They are inherently difficult to get without a Russian connection. Travel agencies that advertise discounted tickets to Russia often are also able to provide visas. **Info Travel,** 387 Harvard St., Brookline, MA 02146 (☎(617) 566-2197; fax 734-8802; email info-study@aol.com) and **Academic Travel,** 1302 Commonwealth Ave., Boston, MA 02134 (☎(617) 566-5272; fax 566-3534; email actravel@myway.com), both provide invitations and visas to Russia starting at US$150, more with less than two weeks notice.

Low-cost visa assistance is also available on-line at www.visatorussia.com. This site provides the necessary supporting documents for several types of Russian visas, starting at $30 for the invitation necessary to secure a tourist visa. Invitations for longer stays or faster processing will cost extra. They provide similar services for visas to other CIS countries, including Ukraine, and can provide other services, such as hotel bookings. Contact them in the **US** at 4651 Roswell Road, Suite 301-D, Atlanta, GA 30342 (☎888-263-0023 and (404) 497-9190; fax (404) 497-9193; email info@gotorussia.net) or in **Russia** at 29 Leninsky pr., Suite 401-408, Moscow, 117912, RUSSIA (☎(095) 955 41 04, (095) 955 41 90, and (095) 955 42 98; fax (095) 954 42 78; email info@intelservice.ru).

A larger but significantly more expensive operation is **Russia House.** In the US, they are at 1800 Connecticut Ave. NW, Washington, D.C. 20009 (☎(202) 986-6010; fax 667-4244; email lozansky@aol.com). In Russia, contact them at 44 Bolshaya Nikitskaya, Moscow 125040 (☎(095) 290 34 59; fax 250 25 03; email aum@glasnet.ru). Invitations and visas are available to Russia, Belarus, and Ukraine starting at US$225.

The following organizations can also supply invitations and/or visas for individual tourists, but generally require that you book accommodations for your stay in Russia with them. Prices vary dramatically, so shop around.

**Host Families Association (HOFA),** 5-25 Tavricheskaya, 193015 St. Petersburg, Russia (☎/fax (812) 275 19 92; email hofa@usa.net or alexei@hofak.hop.stu.neva.ru). Arranges homestays in more than 20 cities of the former Soviet Union. Visa invitations (US$30) available for HOFA guests to Russia, Ukraine, and Belarus. Singles start at

US$25, doubles at US$40. Discount of US$5 per day for non-central locations and after the first week of a stay with the same family; US$10 after the second week with the same family (for non-central locations only). For an additional fee HOFA can also arrange for Russian tutors, theater tickets, meals, and transport to and from the airport.

**Red Bear Tours/Russian Passport,** Suite 11, 401 St. Kilda Rd., Melbourne 3004, **Australia** (☎ (03) 98 67 38 88; fax 98 67 10 55; email passport@travelcentre.com.au; www.travelcentre.com.au). Provides invitations to Russia and the Central Asian Republics, provided that you book accommodations with them. Also sells rail tickets for the Trans-Siberian, Trans-Manchurian, Trans-Mongolian and Silk routes and arranges tours.

**Traveler's Guest House,** Bolshaya Pereyaslavskaya 50, 10th Fl., Moscow, Russia 129401 (☎ (095) 971 40 59; fax 280 76 86; email tgh@startravel.ru). Arranges visa invitations, makes reservations, gets train tickets, and registers you upon arrival. For more, see **Moscow: Accommodations,** p. 612.

If you have an invitation from an authorized travel agency, apply for the **visa** in person or by mail at a Russian embassy or consulate (see **Essentials: Embassies and Consulates,** p. 18). Bring an original of your invitation; your passport; a completed application (available from an embassy or consulate or online at www.russianembassy.org); three passport-sized photographs; a cover letter stating your name, dates of arrival and departure, cities you plan to visit in Russia, date of birth, and passport number; and a money order or certified check for the amount of the visa fee made out to the embassy or the nearest consulate. (Single-entry, 60-day visas US$70 for 2-week processing, US$80 for 1-week service, US$150 for 3 business days, US$300 for same-day; double-entry visas add $50; prices change constantly, so check with the embassy.) If you have even tentative plans to visit a city, have it put on your visa. Many hotels will **register your visa** for you on arrival, as should the organizations listed above, however they can only do so if you fly into a city where they are represented. Some travel agencies in Moscow and St. Petersburg (see **Tourist and Financial Services,** p. 610 and p. 644) will also register your visa for approximately US$30. As a last resort, or if you enter the country somewhere other than the two major cities, you'll have to climb into the seventh circle of bureaucratic hell known is the central OVIR (ОВИР) office (in Moscow called UVIR—УВИР) to register. Many travelers skip this purgatory, but it is the law and taking care of it will leave one less thing over which bribe-seeking authorities can hassle you. OVIR is also where you should attempt to extend your visa, but it's far better to get a visa for longer than you plan on staying than to hang yourself with red tape.

# INTERNATIONAL TRANSPORTATION

In a perfect world, everyone would fly into St. Petersburg or Moscow, skipping customs officials who tear packs apart and demand bribes, and avoiding Belarus entirely. But it's not a perfect world, and you'll likely find yourself on a westbound **train.** If that train is passing through **Belarus** you will need a US$20-30 transit visa. If you wait until you reach the border, you'll likely pay more and risk missing your train. Travel between Finland and St. Petersburg is cheaper by bus than by train.

Upon your entrance to the country, you'll be given a **Customs Declaration Form** to declare all your valuables and foreign currency; don't lose it. Everything listed on the customs form must be on you when you leave the country. Anything that might be regarded by the customs officials as a work of art or any "old" books—that is, those published before 1975—must be assessed by the Ministry of Culture (located at 17 Malaya Morskaya in St. Petersburg and at Neglinnaya 8/10, office 29 in Moscow). These kind folks will look over your purchases and usually assess a 100% tax; be sure to have your receipt to establish the value of your item. You will not be permitted to take these items out of the country without a receipt proving you have paid the tax. Keep receipts for any expensive or antique-looking souvenirs. You cannot legally bring rubles into or out of the country: however, customs officials usually will not search your wallet and usually permit you to export small amounts of currency if they are declared on the customs form.

# DOMESTIC TRANSPORTATION

**BEFORE YOU GO** See **Essentials: Before You Go,** p. 28, for info on how to find the latest travel advisories. In August 1999, the US State Department issued a travel advisory regarding bringing Global Positioning Systems (G.P.S.), cellular phones, and other radio transmission devices into Russia. Failure to register such devices can (and does) result in search, seizure, and arrest.

**BY TRAIN.** Trains are generally the best way to move about the country. Weekend or holiday trains between Petersburg and Moscow sometimes sell out a week in advance; buy your ticket well ahead of time if you have an important connection to make or your visa is about to expire. If you plan far enough ahead, you'll have your choice of four **classes.** The best is *lyuks* (люкс), or *2-myagky* (2-person soft; мягкий)—a place in a two-bunk cabin in the same car as second-class *kupeyny* (купейний), which has four bunks. Both classes have the same type of beds: almost comfortable, with a roll-up mattress and pillow. On hot summer nights, air conditioned *lyuks*, which are only available on major lines, may be worth the added cost. The next class down is *platskartny* (плацкартный), an open car with 52 shorter, harder bunks. Aim for places 1-33. Places 34-37 are next to the unnaturally foul bathroom, while places 38-52 are on the side of the car and get horribly hot during the summer. Women traveling alone can try to buy out a *lyuks* compartment for security, or can travel *platskartny* with the regular folk and depend on the crowds to shame would-be harassers into silence. *Platskartny* is also a good idea on the theft-ridden St. Petersburg-Moscow line, as you are less likely to be targeted there. This logic can only be taken so far; the *obshchy* class may be devoid of crooks, but you'll be traveling alongside livestock. All first and second class cars are equipped with samovars that dispense scalding water for soups, hot cocoa, and coffee. In the upper classes, the car monitor will provide **sheets** for free or for around US$1; in *platskartny*, the grumpier monitors won't even let you use the mattress unless you've paid for sheets. *Elektrichka* (commuter rail; marked on signs as пригородные поезда; *prigorodnye poezda*) has its own platforms at each station; buy tickets at the *kassa*. These trains are often packed on weekends.

**BY BUS.** Buses, slightly less expensive than trains, are your best bet for shorter distances. They are often crowded and overbooked, however; don't be shy about ejecting people who try to sit in your seat. On the Hungarian **Ikarus** buses, you'll get seated in a fairly comfy reclining chair, and should be able to store luggage for free.

**BY THUMB OR TAXI.** Hailing a **taxi** is indistinguishable from **hitchhiking,** and should be treated with equal caution. Most drivers who stop will be private citizens trying to make a little extra cash (despite the recent restriction on this technically illegal activity). Those seeking a ride should stand off the curb and hold out a hand into the street, palm down; when a car stops, riders tell the driver the destination before getting in; he will either refuse the destination altogether or ask *Skolko?* (How much?), leading to protracted negotiations. Non-Russian speakers will get ripped off unless they manage a firm agreement on the price—if the driver agrees without asking for a price, you must ask *skolko?* yourself (sign language works too). Never get into a car that has more than one person in it.

# TOURIST SERVICES AND MONEY

There are two types of Russian tourist office—those that only arrange tours and those that offer general travel services. Offices of the former type are often unhelpful or even rude, but those of the latter are often eager to assist, particularly with visa registration. Big hotels are often a better bet for maps and other information. For **trekking** and **adventure travel,** consult Wild Russia (see **Tourist and Financial Services: Adventure Travel**, p. 645), which plans guided excursions to wilderness destinations throughout the country.

| CURRENCY | | |
|---|---|
| US$1 = 28R (RUSSIAN RUBLES) | 10R = US$0.36 |
| CDN$1 = 19R | 10R = CDN$0.53 |
| UK£1 = 41R | 10R = UK£0.25 |
| IR£1 = 32R | 10R = IR£0.32 |
| AUS$1 = 16R | 10R = AUS$0.62 |
| NZ$1 = 12R | 10R = NZ$0.84 |
| SAR1 = 4.0R | 10R = SAR2.5 |
| DM1 = 13R | 10R = DM0.78 |

RUSSIA

The **ruble** was redenominated in 1998, losing three zeros, and the old currency is gradually being fazed out. Government regulations require that you show your passport when you exchange money. Find an *Obmen Valyuty* (Обмен Валюты; currency exchange), hand over your currency—most will exchange US dollars and Deutschmarks, and some also accept British pounds—and receive your rubles. With **inflation** running at around 25%, expect prices quoted in rubles and **exchange rates** to undergo frequent, significant changes. **Do not exchange money on the street.** Banks offer the best combination of good rates and security. You'll have no problem changing rubles back at the end of your trip (just keep exchange receipts), but it's best not to exchange large sums at once, as the rate is unstable. 500R bills may attract unwanted attention and some establishments may be unwilling to make change for them.

**ATMs** (*bankomat;* банкомат) linked to all major networks and credit cards can be found all over most cities. Banks, large restaurants, ATMs and currency exchanges often accept major **credit cards,** especially **Visa.** Main branches of banks will usually accept **traveler's checks** and give cash advances on credit cards, most often Visa. Although you'll have to pay in rubles, it's wise to keep a small amount, US$20 or less, of dollars on hand. Be aware that most establishments do not accept crumpled, torn, or written-on bills of any denomination. Russians are also wary of the old US$100 bills; bring the new Benjamins if you bring any at all.

 **PAYING IN RUSSIA** Due to the fluctuating value of the Russian ruble, some establishments list their prices in US dollars. For this reason, some prices in this book may also appear in US$, but be prepared to pay in rubles.

# HEALTH AND SAFETY

Russian bottled water is often mineral water; you may prefer to boil or filter your own, or buy imported **bottled water** at a supermarket. Water in much of Russia is drinkable in small doses, but not in Moscow and St. Petersburg; boil it to be safe. An immunoglobulin shot will lower your risk of hepatitis A (see **Health,** p. 28). Check the expiration date before buying a packaged snack. Men's **toilets** are marked with an "M," women's with a "Ж." The 0.5-5R charge for public toilets generally gets you a hole in the ground and a measured piece of toilet paper; get into the habit of carrying your own. **Pharmacies** are among the few places where the positive effects of capitalism are apparent, with a range of Western medicine and hygiene products. For **medical emergencies,** either leave the country or go to the American Medical Centers at St. Petersburg or Moscow; these clinics have American-born and trained doctors and speak English. Traveler's health insurance is a must (ISIC provides some coverage; see **Essentials,** p. 18); it will cover the aforementioned clinics or evacuation.

Reports of **crime** against foreigners are on the rise, particularly in Moscow and St. Petersburg. Although it is hard to look Russian (especially with a huge pack on your back), try not to flaunt your true nationality. Your trip will be that much more pleasant if you never have to file a crime report with the local *militsia,* who will not speak English and will probably not help you. Reports of mafia warfare are scaring off tourists, but unless you bring a shop for them to blow up, you are unlikely to be a target. After the recent eruption of violence in the Northern Caucasus, the Dagestan and Chechnya regions of Russia are to be avoided.

# ACCOMMODATIONS

The only **hostels** in Russia are in St. Petersburg and Moscow, and even those average US$18 per night. Reserve well in advance, especially in summer. **Hotels** offer several classes of rooms. "Lux," usually two-room doubles with TV, phone, fridge, and bath, are the most expensive. "Polu-lux" rooms are singles or doubles with TV, phone, and bath. Rooms with bath and no TV, when they exist, are cheaper. The lowest priced rooms are *bez udobstv* (без удобств), which means one room with a sink. Expect to pay 300-450R for a single in a budget hotel. As a rule, and in small cities in particular, only cash is accepted as payment. In many hotels, **hot water**—sometimes all water—is often turned on only a few hours per day. Reservations are not necessary in smaller towns, but they may help you get on the good side of management, which is often inexplicably suspicious of backpackers.

**University dorms** offer cheap rooms; some accept foreign students for about US$5-10 per night. The rooms are liveable, but don't expect sparkling bathrooms or reliable hot water. Make arrangements with an institute from home. **Homestays**, often arranged through a tourist office, are often the cheapest (50-100R per night) and best option in the countryside.

# KEEPING IN TOUCH

Old local **telephones** in Moscow take special tokens, sold at Metro *kassy;* in St. Petersburg, they take Metro tokens. These old public phones are gradually becoming obsolete; the new ones take phonecards, are good for both local and intercity calls, and often have instructions in English. Phonecards are sold at central telephone offices, Metro stations and newspaper kiosks. When you are purchasing phonecards from a telephone office or Metro station, the attendant will often ask, "На улицу?" (Na ulitsu; On the street?) to find out whether you want a card for the phones in the station/office or for outdoor public phones. For 5-digit numbers, insert a "2" between the dialing code and the phone number. You can make **intercity** calls from private homes, telephone offices, your hotel room, or *mezhdugorodnye* (междугородные) phone booths. It will take awhile, but you can usually get through. Dial 8, wait for the tone, then dial the city code.

Direct **international** calls can be made from telephone offices and hotel rooms: dial 8, wait for the tone, then dial 10 and the country code. Calls to Europe run US$1-1.50 per min.; to the US and Australia about US$1.50-2.00. You cannot call collect, unless using AT&T service (same access number as listed below), which will cost your party dearly (US$8 first min.; US$2.78 each additional min. to the US). Prices for calls to the US range from 9R-25R per minute, depending on where you're calling from. To make calls from a telephone office, you can buy tokens or phone cards, or simply prepay your calls (depending on the city) and use the *mezhdugorodnye* telephones; be sure to press the ответ (reply; *otvet*) button when your party answers. If there are no automatic phones, pay for your call at the counter and have it dialed for you by the operator. Several hotels in Moscow now have direct-dial booths operated by a special card or credit card. The cost is astronomical (at least US$6 per min. to the US). Access numbers include: **AT&T Direct,** ☎755 50 42 in Moscow, ☎325 50 42 in St. Petersburg; **Australia Direct,** ☎810; **BT Direct,** ☎8 10 800 110 10 44; **Canada Direct,** ☎755 50 45 in Moscow, ☎747 33 25 in St. Petersburg, from other cities ☎8 10 800 110 1012; **MCI WorldPhone,** ☎747 33 22 in Moscow, ☎960 22 22 in St. Petersburg; **Sprint,** ☎747 33 24 in Moscow, ☎8 10 800 110 2011 in St. Petersburg. When calling from another city, dial 8-095 or 8-812 before these codes; you pay for the call to Moscow or St. Petersburg in addition to the international connection. Calling into the country is much less frustrating. Most countries have direct dial to Moscow and St. Petersburg; for other cities, go through the international operator. **Telegrams** to the US about 8.32R per word. **Faxes** cost 18-98R per page within Russia, 87.60R to Europe, 119R to the US, and 169R to Australia.

**Mail service** is more reliable leaving the country than coming in. Letters to the US will arrive as soon as a week after mailing; letters to other destinations take 2-3 weeks. Domestic mail will usually reach its destination; from abroad, send letters to Russian recipients via friends who are traveling there. Airmail is *avia* (авиа). Send your mail "заказное" (certified; 16R) to reduce the chance of it being lost. If you're sending anything other than paper goods into the abyss that is the Russian mail system, you must complete a customs form at the post office. Regular letters to the US cost 7R; postcards cost 5R. **Poste Restante** is "Писмо До Востребования" (Pismo Do Vostrebovania). **DHL** is in most large cities. Central post offices offer **fax service.** With a mail system mired in communist inefficiency and a phone stem with very capitalist rates, **email** is your best bet for keeping in touch.

# MOSCOW (MOCKBA) ☎(8)095

Like few other cities on Earth, Moscow (pop. 8,400,000) has an audacity about it, a sense of itself as a focal point of world history. Given the current shaky political, economic, and social climate, that audacity often translates into a feeling like having a wild party on the edge of a cliff. Muscovites, particularly the younger ones, don't seem to mind too much; after all, they are more accustomed than most to facing apocalyptic (or at least very trying) moments in history with a determination bordering on insanity. Under the leadership of the adorably chubby, horse-trading Mayor Yuri Luzhkov, Moscow is recreating itself as a beautiful capital, using the same resourcefulness that burned the city rather than leave it to Napoleon and that helped it engineer (and then survive) the greatest social experiment in history. Post-apocalyptic, post-capitalist, post-whatever-the-hell-you-want, Moscow at the millennium is in your face, down and dirty, and very, very Russian.

## ✈ ORIENTATION

A series of concentric rings radiates from the **Kremlin** (Кремль; Kreml) and **Red Square** (Красная площадь; Krasnaya ploshchad). The outermost street, **Moskovskoe Koltso** (Московское Кольцо; Moscow Ring), marks the city limits, but most sights lie within **Sadovoe Koltso** (Садовое Кольцо; Garden Ring). To the east of Red Square and the Kremlin is the 9th-century **Kitai-Gorod** (Китай-Город; Chinatown) neighborhood, packed with towering churches and bustling commercial thoroughfares. **Bely Gorod** (Белый Город; White Town), Moscow's nicest residential district and home to most of the city's cultural life, forms a semi-circle north of the Kremlin and Kitai-Gorod. **Ul. Tverskaya** (Тверская), one of Moscow's main shopping streets, begins in Bely Gorod and continues north along the green line of the Metro. **Zemlyanoi Gorod** (Земляной Город), the next concentric circle out from Bely Gorod, is the dividing line between the bourgeois center and the outskirts of the city. Zemlyanoi Gorod has the highest concentration of literary homes (see **Houses of the Literary and Famous**, p. 625) as well as the **Arbat** (Арбат) and **Novy Arbat** (Новый Арбат), Moscow's poshest and most commercialized streets, respectively. The old working-class neighborhood, **Krasnaya Presnya** (Красная Пресня), lies just to the southwest of Zemlyanoi Gorod and is notable primarily as the home to Russia's **Bely Dom** (Белый Дом; White House) and the highest proportion of New Russians. **Zamoskvareche** (Замоскварече) and **Krimskiy Val** (Крымский Вал), the neighborhoods directly south of the Kremlin and Red Square are home to myriad pubs, mansions, and monasteries, as well as **Gorky Park** (Парк Горкого; Park Gorkovo). The suburbs to the north and south are a concrete wasteland of apartment blocks.

If you familiarize yourself with the Cyrillic alphabet and orient yourself by the Metro, it's difficult to get lost. An extensive city **map** in English (30R) is available at at **Angliyskaya Kniga** (see p. 611) and Cyrillic maps are at kiosks all over the city. See this book's color insert for English and Cyrillic maps of the Metro and the city.

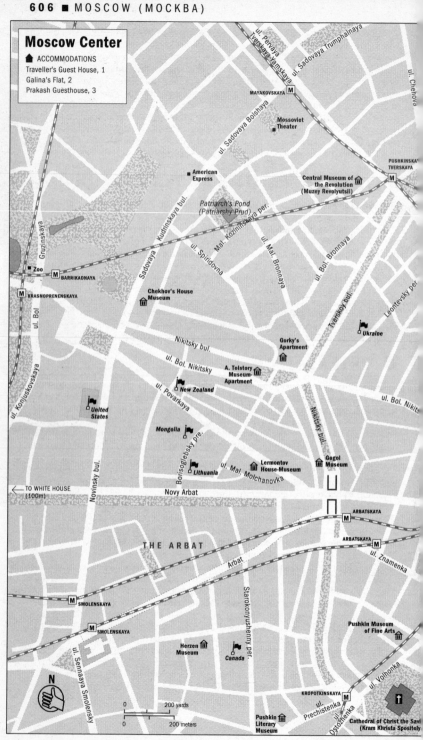

**Moscow Center**

⌂ ACCOMMODATIONS

Traveller's Guest House, 1
Galina's Flat, 2
Prakash Guesthouse, 3

ul. Pervaja Tverskaja Yamskaya
ul. Sadovaya Trumphalnaya
ul. Chehova

MAYAKOVSKAYA Ⓜ

Mossoviet Theater

PUSHKINSKA°
TVERSKAYA

American Express

Central Museum of the Revolution (Muzey Revolyutsii) Ⓜ

Patriarch's Pond (Patriarshy Prud)

ul. Sadovaya Bolshaya

Sadovaya Kudrinskaya bul.

Mal. Kozinihskaya per.

ul. Mal. Bronnaya

ul. Bol. Bronnaya

ul. Spindovna

Gruzinskaya

■ Zoo
Ⓜ BARRIKADNAYA

Ⓜ KRASNOPRENENSKAYA

ul. Bol

ul. Konjuskovskaya

Chekhov's House Museum

Nikitsky bul.

ul. Bol. Nikitsky

Gorky's Apartment

Tverskoy bul.

Leontevsky per.

⚑ Ukraine

A. Tolstory Museum-Apartment

⚑ New Zealand

ul. Povarkaya

ul. Bol. Nikits

United States

Mongolia

Borisoglebsky pre.

⚑ Lithuania

ul. Mal. Molchanovka

Lermontov House-Museum

Novinsky bul.

Gogol Museum

Nikitsky bul.

← TO WHITE HOUSE (100m)

Novy Arbat

ARBATSKAYA Ⓜ

ARBATSKAYA Ⓜ

ul. Znamenka

THE ARBAT

Arbat

Starokonyushenny per.

Ⓜ SMOLENSKAYA

Ⓜ SMOLENSKAYA

Pushkin Museum of Fine Arts

Herzen Museum

⚑ Canada

ul. Sennaya Smolensky

N

0    200 yards
0    200 meters

KROPOTKINSKAYA Ⓜ

ul. Volhonka

ul. Prechistenka

ul. Ostozhenka

Pushkin Literary Museum

Cathedral of Christ the Savi (Kram Khrista Spositely

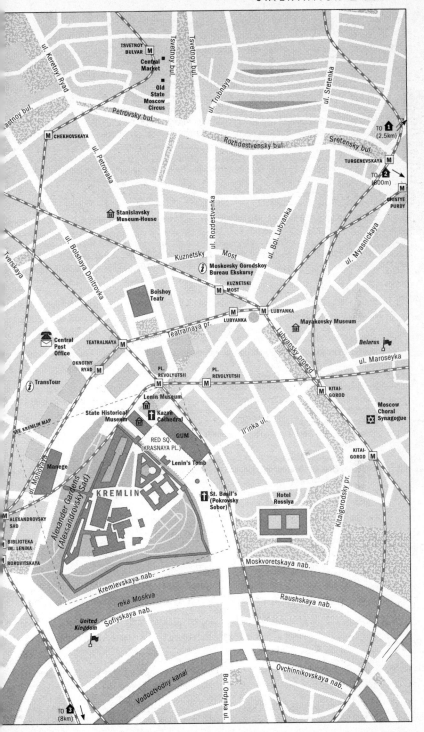

# ✈ INTERCITY TRANSPORTATION

**Flights:** International flights arrive at **Sheremetyevo-2** (Шереметьево-2; ☎956 46 66 and 578 91 01). Take the **van** under the "автолайн" sign in front of the station to M2: Rechnoy Vokzal (Речной Вокзал; 20min., every 10min. 7am-10pm, 10R). Or, take **bus** #851 or 551 to M2: Rechnoy Vokzal or bus #517 to M8: Planyornaya (Планёрная; 10R). Buses run 24hr. Most domestic flights and many flights within the former USSR originate at **Vnukovo** (Внуково; ☎234 86 56), **Bikovo** (Быково; ☎558 47 38), **Domod-edovo** (Домодедово; ☎234 86 55), or **Sheremetyevo-1** (☎578 23 72). Buy tickets at the *kassa* (касса) at the **Tsentralny Aerovokzal** (Центральный Аэровокзал; Central Airport Station), Leningradsky pr. 37a (☎155 09 22), 2 stops on tram #23 or trolley #12 or 70 from M2: Aeroport (sign on front of bus should say Центральный Аэровокзал). **Taxis** to the center charge more up to US$60—make sure to bargain (in June 2000 you could get it down to US$25). Agree on a price before getting into the cab.

**Airlines: Air France,** ul. Korovy Val 7 (Коровый Вал; ☎937 38 39; fax 937 38 38). Open M-F 9am-5:30pm. Also at Sheremetyevo-2, 6th floor (☎578 31 56). Open M-Sa 5:30am-11pm, Su 1-6pm. **British Airways,** Krasnopresnenskaya nab. 12, 19th floor, #1905 (Краснопресненская; ☎258 24 92; fax 258 22 72). Open M-F 10am-7pm, Sa 10am-2pm. **Delta,** 11 Gogolevsky Blv., 2nd floor (Гоголевский; ☎937 90 90; fax 937 90 91). Open M-F 9am-5:30pm, Sa 9am-1pm. **Finnair,** ul. Kuznetsky Most 3 (Кузнецкий мост; ☎292 17 62; fax 292 49 49). M7: Kuznetsky Most. Open M-F 9am-5pm. Also at Sheremetyevo-2 (☎/fax 956 46 36). **Lufthansa,** in Hotel Olympic Penta, Olimpiysky pr. 18/1 (Олимпийский; ☎737 64 00; fax 737 64 01; lhmowcust@glas-net.ru). M5, 6: Prospekt Mira. Open M-F 9am-5:30pm.

**Trains:** Moscow has 9 train stations arranged around the M5 metro line, known as koltsy-vaya linia (кольцывая линия; circle line) of the Metro. At all train stations, platform numbers are announced as the trains are arriving.

**Leningradsky Vokzal** (Ленинградский), Komsomolskaya pl. 3 (☎262 91 43). M1, 5: Komsomol-skaya. To: **St. Petersburg** (9hr. 15 per day, 84R); **Tallinn, EST** (14hr., 1 per day, 1297R); and **Helsinki, FIN** (15hr., 1 per day, 2800R).

**Kazansky Vokzal** (Казанский), Komsomolskaya pl. 2 (☎264 65 56 and 264 66 56). Opposite Leningradsky Vokzal. To the east and southeast, including **Kazan** (12hr., 1 per day, 145R); **Ros-tov-na-Donu** (20hr., 1 per day, 134R); and **Volgograd** (20hr., 1-2 per day, 191R).

**Yaroslavsky Vokzal** (Ярославский), Komsomolskaya pl. 5 (☎921 08 17 and 921 59 14). To: **Sibe-ria** and the **Far East**. The starting point for the legendary **Trans-Siberian Railroad** (see p. 677). To: **Novosibirsk** (48hr., 1 per 2 days, 385R).

**Paveletsky Vokzal** (Павлецкий), Pavletskaya pl. 1 (☎235 68 07 and 235 05 22). Trains to **Crimea, Eastern Ukraine, Georgia, Azerbaijan,** and **Armenia**. To: **Volgograd** (24hr., 1 per day, 191R) and **Astrakhan** (30hr., 1 per day, 162R).

**Kursky Vokzal** (Курский), ul. Zemlyanoi Val 29/1 (☎917 31 52 and 916 20 03). To: **Sevastopol, UKR** (30hr., 1 per day, 573R) and the **Caucasus**.

**Rizhsky Vokzal** (Рижский), Rizhkaya pl. 79/3 (☎971 15 88). Trains to **Latvia** and **Estonia**. To: **Riga, LAT** (16hr., 2 per day, 947R).

**Belorussky Vokzal** (Белорусский), pl. Tverskoi Zastavy 7 (☎251 60 93 and 973 81 91). To: **Minsk, BLR** (10hr., 6 per day, 377R); **Brest, BLR** (15hr., 3 per day, 493R); **Vilnius, LIT** (15hr., 1-2 per day, 1021R); **Warsaw, POL** (20hr., 3 per day, 2520R); **Kaliningrad** (22hr., 1-2 per day, 482R); **Berlin, GER** (27hr., 1 per day, 3780R); and **Prague, CZR** (33hr., 1 per day, 3360R).

**Kievsky Vokzal** (Киевский), pl. Kievskovo Vokzala (☎240 11 15 and 240 04 15). Trains to **Bul-garia, Romania, Slovakia,** and **Ukraine**. To: **Kyiv, UKR** (15hr., 4 per day, 374R); **Lviv, UKR** (17hr., 1 per day, 572R); and **Odessa, UKR** (26hr., 3 per day, 489R).

**Train Tickets:** Buying a train ticket in Russia can be enormously frustrating. If you don't speak Russian you may want to buy through **Intourist** or your hotel: you'll pay more, but you'll be spared the hassle of the *vokzal* (вокзал; station) experience, where lines can be long. Buy tickets for the *elektrichka* (local train) at the *prigorodnaya kassa* (пригородная касса; local ticket booths) in each station. Tickets for longer distances can be bought at the *Tsentralnoe Zheleznodorozhnoe Agenstvo* (Центральное Железнодорожное Агенство; Central Train Agency), to the right of Yaroslavsky Vokzal (see above). Buy tickets for Russian and CIS destinations at windows #10 and 11 and for international destinations at windows #5, 6, and 7. Your ticket will have your name and seat on it and tells you at which *vokzal* to catch your train. A complete schedule of stations, trains, destinations, and departure times is posted on both sides of the hall. *Kassa* open daily 8am-1:30pm and 2:30-7pm. 24hr. service is available at the stations themselves. Tickets to Helsinki are sold on the 2nd floor of Leningradsky Vokzal, at windows #27 and 28. Open daily 8am-10:30pm. If you plan to take the **Trans-Siberian Railroad,** you're probably better off with G&R Hostel Asia or Traveler's Guest House (see **Russia Essentials,** p. 601). They'll explain how the TSR works and can arrange a special ticket that allows you to get on and off the train at all major cities along the way. For slightly shorter lines in a more obscure location, try the other Tsentralnoe Zheleznodorozhnoe Agenstvo at Maly Kharitonevsky per. 6 (Малый Харитоневский; ☎262 06 04). M5: Turgenevskaya. Take a right off ul. Myasnitskaya (Мясницкая) and walk to the building on the right. Open daily 8am-1pm and 2-7pm.

# ▐ LOCAL TRANSPORTATION

**Public Transportation:** The **Metro** (Метро) is large, fast, and efficient—a masterpiece of urban planning. Its 10 lines stop within a 15min. walk of any place in town and serve as a continual reminder that 8.5 million people do live in Moscow—and all of them ride the Metro. Passages to different lines or stations are marked with a blue and white sign of a man walking up stairs; individual exit signs indicate nearby street names. A station serving more than one line may have more than one name. Trains run daily 6am-1am, but catch one by 12:30am to be safe. **Rush hours** 9-10am and 5-6pm. Buy token cards (4R) from the *kassy* inside stations. **Bus** and **trolley** tickets are available at kiosks labeled "проездные билеты" *(proyezdnye bilety)* and from the driver (4R). Punch your ticket when you get on, especially during the last week of the month when ticket cops need to fill their quotas—the fine for not doing so is 10R. **Monthly passes** (единые билеты; edinye bilety) let you take any form of transportation (240R). Buy them after the 20th of the preceding month. **Monthly Metro passes** (120R) are more cost-effective. Purchase either from the *kassa.* **Metro maps** are on the wall inside the entrance to every station and (in both Cyrillic and English) at the front and back of this book.

**Taxis:** If you don't speak Russian, it's tough to get a fair rate. Most drivers charge by destination—agree on a price by haggling before you set off. Taxi stands are indicated by a round sign with a green T. Consult the *Moscow Business Telephone Guide* (available at posh hotels) to order one over the phone. Meters tend to be purely ornamental, although a new law decrees that they must be used. Make sure the driver turns it on. Avoid taxis unless you know Moscow, as it is easy to get ripped off. It is fairly common—and generally cheaper than a taxi—to get a ride with ordinary motorists (see p. 602).

**Car Rental: Avis,** ul. Goncharnaya 24 (Гончарная; ☎/fax 915 13 89; avismosc@online.ru). US$55 per day. **Hertz,** ul. Chernyakhovskovo 4 (Черняховского; ☎937 32 74; fax 956 16 21; hertz.mos@co.ru). US$49 per day. 23+. Open M-F 9am-8pm, Sa-Su 9am-5pm. **Budget,** Volgogradsky pr. 43, bldg. 1 (Волгоградский; ☎737 04 07; fax 737 04 06). US$58-64 per day. 25+. Open M-F 9am-7pm.

---

**WE BRAKE FOR NO ONE.** Moscow drivers are notorious: unbelievably fast and blissfully ignorant of the gentle art of yielding to pedestrians. Should you dare venture from your curbside security onto the blacktop, they will honk, yell, and gesticulate obscenely, but they will not touch their brakes. One day of such confrontations will suffice to convince you that the underpass beneath nearly every intersection—called a *perekhod* (переход; crossing)—is there out of dire necessity. The only time that a car *might* stop for you is if you're female, alone, and out at night—and that's only because the driver thinks you're a prostitute. Perhaps more disturbing is the Muscovite fondness for driving, often in reverse, on the sidewalks, which they use for parking lots, driveways, and passing lanes. On the roads of Moscow, there are pedestrians and there are drivers. And pedestrians are most decidedly not wanted.

---

# ⚂ PRACTICAL INFORMATION

## TOURIST AND FINANCIAL SERVICES

**Tourist Offices: TransTours Voyages,** Nikitsky per. 4a (Никитский; ☎203 32 24 and 203 19 54; fax 203 31 59) M1: Okhotny Ryad (Охотны Ряд). Visa registration.

**Tours: Moskovskoye Gorodskoye Excursionnoye Byuro** (Московское Городское Екскурсионное Бюро; City of Moscow Bureau of Excursions; ul. Rozhdestvenka 5 (Рождественка; ☎924 94 46; fax 921 50 19). Excellent 1½hr. bus tours of the main sights. Tours leave from Krasnaya pl., between the Lenin Museum and GUM; look for the person with the microphone. Russian only. Daily 9am-8pm. 100R. **Intourist,** ul. Mokhovaya 16 (Моховая; ☎292 52 30 and 203 69 62). General information. Branch at Stoleshnikov per. 11 (Столешников; ☎923 57 63; fax 928 48 13). Museum tours and translation services.

**Budget Travel: Student Travel Agency Russia (STAR),** ul. Baltiyskaya 9, 3rd floor (Балтийская; ☎797 95 55). M2: Sokol. Discount plane tickets, ISICs, and worldwide hostel booking. Open M-F 10am-6pm, Sa 11am-4pm. **Moskovsky Sputnik** (Московский Спутник), Maly Ivanovsky per. 6, kor. 2 (Малый Ивановский; ☎925 92 78; fax 230 27 87). M6, 7: Kitai-Gorod. Student travel, ISICs, and tickets. Open M-Th 9am-6pm, F 9am-5pm. For visas, call ☎923 2092.

**Passport Office: UVIR** (УВИР), ul. Pokrova 42 (Покрова). M1: Krasnye Vorota. From the Metro, turn right onto Sadovaya Chernogryazskaya, continue down until ul. Pokrova, and turn right (10min.). UVIR is possibly the 7th circle of Russian bureaucratic hell—to avoid an unpleasant encounter, secure a visa invitation and stamp from your 1st night's accommodation whenever possible. Most hotels register you automatically and give you a card to prove you're staying there. Open M-F 10am-1pm and 3-6pm, Sa 10am-1pm. W is designated for foreigners; Sa for urgent questions.

**Embassies and Consulates:**

**Australia,** Kropotkinsky per. 13 (Кропоткинский; ☎956 60 70; fax 956 61 70). M3: Smolenskaya (Смоленская). Open M-F 9am-12:30pm and 1:30-5pm.

**Belarus,** ul. Maroseyka 17/6 (Мароseйка; ☎924 70 31; fax 928 64 03; visa ☎924 7095; visa fax 928 6403).

**Canada,** Starokonyushenny per. 23 (Староконюшенный; ☎956 66 66 and 956 61 58; fax 232 99 48). M1: Kropotkinskaya. Open M-F 8:30am-1pm and 2-5pm.

**China,** ul. Druzhby 6 (Дружбы; ☎147 42 83, 143 19 51, and 956 11 68; fax 938 21 32; visa ☎143 15 40; visa fax 956 11 69).

**Estonia,** Maly Kislovsky per. 5 (Кисловский; ☎290 50 13; fax 202 3830). Consular services at Kalashny per. 8 (Калашний; ☎290 31 78; fax 291 10 73). M3: Arbatskaya. Open M-Th 10am-noon.

**Ireland,** Grokholsky per. 5 (Грохольский; ☎742 09 07; fax 975 20 66; visa ☎742 09 01; visa fax 742 09 20). M5, 6: Prospekt Mira. Open M-F 9:30am-1pm and 2:30-5:30pm.

**Lithuania,** Borisoglebsky per. 10 (Борисоглебский; ☎291 26 43 and 291 16 98; fax 202 3516; visa ☎291 15 01; visa fax 291 75 86). M3: Arbatskaya. Open M-F 9-11:30am.

**Mongolia** consular section, Spasopeskovsky per. 7/1 (Спасопесковский; ☎241 15 48, 244 78 67; fax 291 61 71).

**New Zealand,** ul. Povarskaya 44 (Поварская; ☎956 35 79; fax 956 35 83; visa ☎/fax 956 26 42). M5, 7: Krasnopresnenskaya. Open M-F 9am-5:30pm.

**South Africa,** Bolshoy Strochenovsky per. 22/25 (Большой Строченовский; ☎230 6869; fax 230 6865). Open M-F 8:30am-5pm.

**UK,** Sofiyskaya nab. 14 (Софийская; ☎956 7200; fax 956 7420). M1, 3, 9: Borovitskaya. Open M-F 9am-5pm.

**Ukraine,** Leontyevsky per. 18 (Леонтьевский; ☎229 10 79; visa ☎229 69 22), off ul. Tverskaya. M3: Tverskaya. Open M-F 9:15am-12:30pm.

**US,** Novinsky 19/23 (Новинский; ☎252 24 51 through 58; fax 956 42 61). Consular section (☎956 42 42 and 255 95 55; fax 956 42 61) only helps with major passport/visa problems. M7: Krasnopresnenskaya. Flash a US passport and cut the long lines. Open M-F 9am-6pm.

**Currency Exchange:** Banks are on almost every corner; check ads in English-language newspapers. The *Moscow Express Directory*, updated biweekly and free in most luxury hotels, lists the addresses and phone numbers of many banks, as well as places to buy and cash **traveler's checks.** Few besides main branches of large banks change traveler's checks or issue **cash advances;** a posted sign is no guarantee.

**ATMs:** Nearly every bank and hotel has an ATM. A particularly reliable one stands in the lobby of the **Gostinitsa Intourist Hotel** (Cirrus/MC/Plus/Visa). There is an **AmEx** ATM in the lobby of the AmEx office (see below). It allows withdrawals in either US$ or rubles. US$5-10 service charge per transaction; 4% if making greater than a US$250 withdrawal. Beware of ATMs protruding from the sides of buildings on the Arbat; not only do they work irregularly, but standing out in the middle of a busy street getting money invites muggers. **Rossiyski Credit** (Российски Кредит), Usacheva 35 (Усачева; ☎119 8250), offers **Western Union** services. Left entrance. M1: Sportivnaya. Exit to the right; it's on the right, next to the Global USA Shop. Open M-F 9am-7pm, Sa 9am-3pm.

**American Express:** ul. Sadovaya-Kudrinskaya 21a, Moscow 103 001 (Садовая-Кудринская; ☎755 90 00; fax 755 90 04). M2: Mayakovskaya (Маяковская). Exit the Metro, cross through the street/parking lot directly ahead and turn left onto ul. Bolshaya Sadovaya (Большая Садовая), which becomes ul. Sadovaya-Kudrinskaya. One of the only places in Moscow that cashes **traveler's cheques.** Open M-F 9am-5pm, Sa 10am-2pm.

## LOCAL SERVICES

**International Bookstores: Angliyskaya Kniga** (Английская Книга), ul. Kuznetsky most 18 (☎928 20 21). M7: Kuznetsky most. Large selection. Open M-F 10am-2pm and 3-7pm, Sa 10am-2pm and 3-6pm. MC/Visa. **Shakespeare and Co.,** 1 Novokuznetsky per. 5/7 (1-й Новокузнецкий; ☎951 93 60). M2: Pavletskaya. New and used books. Open M-Sa 11am-7pm, Su noon-6pm. **Anglia British Bookshop,** Khlebny per. 2/3 (Хлебный; ☎203 58 02; fax 203 06 73). M3: Arbatskaya. Large selection. Open M-F 10am-7pm, Sa 10am-6pm. AmEx/MC/Visa.

**International Press:** Two free English-language newspapers are easy to find in hotels and restaurants. *The Moscow Times* (more widely read and distributed) and *The Moscow Tribune* have foreign and national articles, sports, etc. for news-starved travelers. Both also have weekend sections (on Fridays) that list exhibitions, theatrical events, English-language movies, and housing and job opportunities. The Moscow Times web site (www.themoscowtimes.com) has a special section for travelers. An "alternative" paper, The *eXile*, is one of the funniest, most irreverent and offensive papers on Earth. Its nightlife section is brutally and indispensably candid. The *Moscow Business Telephone Guide* and *What and Where in Moscow*, both free, are excellent info resources.

**Cultural Centers:** The Western powers have all ganged up and put their cultural centers in the **Foreign Library,** ul. Nikoloyamskaya 1, 3rd floor (Николоямская). M5, 8: Taganskaya (Таганская). The **American Cultural Center** (☎777 65 30) has a library full of reference materials. Open M-F 10:30am-8:30pm, Sa 10am-6pm. The **British Council Resource Centre** (☎234 02 01) is next door. Open M-F noon-7pm.

**Laundromat: Traveler's Guest House** (see **Accommodations,** p. 613) does your laundry for 80R per load. **California Cleaners,** Pokhodny 24 (Походный, ☎493 5311), has 20 locations around Moscow. Free pickup and delivery. Wash and dry 90R per kg, slightly more with ironing. Open daily 9am-9pm.

## EMERGENCY AND COMMUNICATIONS

**Emergencies:** To report **offenses by the police:** ☎299 11 80. **Lost children:** ☎401 99 82. **Lost credit cards:** ☎254 45 05 for AmEx, ☎284 41 51 or 284 47 13 for all others. **Lost property:** Metro ☎222 20 85; other transport ☎923 87 53. **Lost documents:** ☎200 99 57.

**24hr. Pharmacies:** Look for "круглосуточно" (kruglosutochno; always open) signs. Leningradsky pr. 74 (Ленинградский; ☎151 45 70). M2: Sokol. Ul. Tverskaya 25/9 (Тверская; ☎299 24 59 and 299 79 69). M2: Tverskaya. Ul. Zemlyanoi Val 25 (Земляной Вал; ☎917 12 85). M5: Kurskaya.

**Medical Assistance: American Medical Center,** Grokholsky per. 1 (Грохольский; ☎ 933 77 00; fax 933 77 01). M5: Prospekt Mira. Walk-in medical care for hard currency. US$175 per visit. Membership US$55 per month, students $40; US$375 per year, students US$250. Open M-F 8am-8pm, Sa 9am-5pm; 24hr. for **emergencies,** although you will pay more. **Mediclub Moscow,** Michurinsky pr. 56 (Мичуринский; ☎931 5018 and 931 5318). M1: Prospekt Vernadskovo. Private Canadian clinic offering full-scale emergency service. Medical consultations 515R. Payment in rubles or by credit card only (MC/Visa). Open M-F 9am-8pm.

**Telephones: Moscow Central Telegraph** (see **Post Offices,** below). To **call abroad,** go to the 2nd hall with telephones. Collect and calling card calls not available. Prepay at the counter for the amount of time you expect to talk. You will then be given the number of a stall from which to dial directly. Use the *mezhdunarodnye telefony* (международные телефоны; international telephones). To get a refund if you do not reach your party, you must stand in line again at the same counter. Open 24hr. International calls can also be placed from private homes (dial 8-10-country code-phone number); private homes are also often the only way to use a calling card. For calling card access numbers, see **Russia Essentials: Communication,** p. 604. **Local calls** require new phone cards, available at some Metro stops and kiosks.

**Internet Access: Image.ru** (Имидж.ру), ul. Novoslobodskaya 16 (Новослободская; ☎737 37 00, ext. 146). M9: Mendeleevskaya. 40R per hr. **Partiya Internet Cafe** (Партия), Volgogradsky pr. 1. M7: Proletarskaya. US$3 per hr. Open daily 10am-8pm. **VDNKh** (ВДНХ) **Metro Exhibition Hall.** From the Metro, take the ВВЦ exit and head left through the main gates to the exhibition hall. At the back of the hall on the ground floor is a computer store with an internet salon. 1R per min. M-F 10am-6:30pm. Also at **Traveler's Guest House** for 3R per min. and **G&R Hostel Asia** for US$1 per 15min.

**Post Offices: Moscow Central Telegraph,** ul. Tverskaya 7, a few blocks uphill from the Kremlin. M1: Okhotny Ryad. Look for the globe and the digital clock in front. **International mail** service at window #32. **Faxes** at #11-12. **Telegram** service. Open M-F 8am-2pm and 3-9pm, Sa 8am-2pm and 3-7pm, Su 9am-2pm and 3-7pm. For **Poste Restante,** address mail: "Москва 103 009, До востребования (POSTE RESTANTE), ARTHUR, Taryn." Pick it up at windows #38 and 39, although they might send you to Myasnitskaya 26 (Мясницкая) if they don't have it. **Poste Restante** also at the **Gostinitsa Intourist Hotel post office,** ul. Tverskaya 3/5, just past reception and to the right. Address mail "BULGAKOV, Mikhail, До востребования, К-600, Гостиница Интурист, ул. Тверская 3/5, Москва." To mail **packages** (paper-made contents only: books, manuscripts, etc.), bring them unwrapped; they will be wrapped and mailed while you wait. Intourist post office open M-F 9am-noon and 1-8pm.

**Postal code:** 103 009.

# ACCOMMODATIONS

The lack of backpacking culture in Moscow results in slim pickings and overpriced rooms. Call at least a week ahead in summer, although the city's two hostels generally have room for drop-ins. Women standing outside major rail stations rent **private rooms** or **apartments** (as low as 200-250R per night; don't forget to haggle); just look for the signs advertising rooms (сдаю комнату; sdayu komnatu) or apartments (сдаю квартиру; sdayu kvartiru). If you're interested in a **homestay,** book it in advance (see **Russia Essentials,** p. 588). The **Moscow Bed and Breakfast** is a US-based organization that rents out apartments in the city center; contact them before you arrive in Moscow. (US ☎603 585 3347; fax 603 585 6534; jkates@top.monad.net. Singles US$35; doubles US$52.) The places below are as cheap as it gets.

■ **G&R Hostel Asia,** ul. Zelenodolskaya 3/2 (Зеленодольская; ☎378 00 01; fax 378 28 66; hostel-asia@mtu-net.ru; www.hostels.ru). M7: Ryazansky Prospekt (Рязанский Проспект). On the 14th floor of the tall gray building with "Гостиница" in large letters on top, visible from either Metro exit. Clean rooms, helpful staff and low prices. TV and fridge in each room. Far from the center, but close to the Metro. Transport to and from the airport US$20. Visa invitations US$25. Reception open 9am-9pm. Dorms US$13; singles US$18, with bath US$22; doubles US$15, with bath US$21.50. 10% off with HI, RYHA, or ISIC. MC/Visa.

**Traveler's Guest House (TGH)**, ul. Bolshaya Pereyaslavskaya 50, 10th floor (Большая Переяславская; ☎971 40 59; fax 280 7686; tgh@glas.apc.org). M5, 6: Prospekt Mira (Проспект Мира). From the Metro, walk north along pr. Mira (10min.) and take the 3rd right on Banny per. (Банный). Turn left at the end of the street. TGH is the white, 12-story building across the street. Its greatest virtue is its clientele: almost every budget traveler in town stays here and the bulletin board serves as a forum for travel advice. Clean rooms and kitchen facilities. Staff's fluency in English compensates somewhat for their brusqueness. Airport pickup and drop-off US$40. Visa invitations US$40. Phone cards for calls abroad from 140R. Laundry service US$2 for 3-5kg. Check-out 11am. Dorms US$18; singles US$36; doubles US$48, with bath US$54. MC/Visa.

**Galina's Flat**, ul. Chaplygina 8, #35 (Чаплыгина; ☎921 60 38; galinas.flat@mtu-net.ru), in a beautiful old neighborhood. M1: Chistye Prudy (Чистые Пруды). From the Metro, head down bul. Chistoprudny (Чистопрудный) past the statue of Griboedov. Take the 1st left onto Kharitonevsky per. (Харитоньевский) just after the blue Kazakh Embassy and then the 2nd right on Chaplygina. Go through the courtyard (under the blue sign), turn right, and enter the building with the "Уникум" sign next to the doorway; the flat is on the 5th floor, on the right. Galina and her sidekick Sergei welcome you to their homey Russian apartment. Easygoing atmosphere. Hot showers. Kitchen facilities. Only 8 beds, so call ahead. 5-bed dorm US$8; comfortable double US$10 per person, US$15 as a single. If an 8th person arrives, an extra cot will appear.

**Gostinitsa Kievskaya** (Гостиница Киевская), ul. Kievskaya 2 (☎240 14 44 and 240 53 78). M3, 5: Kievskaya. Just outside the train station. Spacious old rooms and soft beds in a great location. Singles with bath 345R; doubles with bath 455R.

**Prakash Guesthouse**, ul. Profsoyuznaya 83, kor. 1 (2nd entrance), 3rd floor, (Профсоюзная; ☎334 82 01 and 335 08 76; fax 334 25 98; prakash@misa.ru). M6: Belyaevo (Беляево). From the Metro, take the exit nearest the last car of the train and follow the *perekhod* to the end; exit from the last stairway on the left side. The guest house is in the 4th building on your right, at the 1st intersection. Go through the gate around to the back and go into the last entrance, 2 doors to the right of the main entrance. Office is on the 2nd floor, room 201. Call ahead and they'll meet you at the Metro. Friendly but remote lodge caters (but not exclusively) to Indian guests. Shower, toilet, and telephone for local calls in each room. Free email. Breakfast US$6; dinner US$12. Reception 7am-11pm; call ahead if you're arriving earlier or later. Dorms US$40; singles US$30; doubles US$40.

# 🍴 FOOD

> Many restaurants list prices in US dollars to avoid having to change their menus to keep up with inflation, but payment is always in rubles.

Eating out in Moscow ranges from expensive to insanely expensive. The ubiquitous and varied kiosk fare offers a cheap alternative, with *sloiki* (3-5R), *bliny* (15-20R), and a multitude of pre-packaged offerings. Restaurants can, however, be affordable if you look for local cuisine and many of the higher priced establishments have begun to offer business lunch (бизнес ланч) specials, which are typically available noon-4pm and cost US$4-6. Russians tend to eat late in the evening, so you can avoid the crowds by eating earlier. Prices for full meals include soup (суп) or salad (салат), an appetizer, and a main dish.

## RESTAURANTS AND CAFES

### RUSSIAN

🖼 **Vremya Est** (Время Есть; Time to Eat), ul. Lesnaya 1/2 (Лесная; ☎251 68 73). M5: Belorusskaya. In the complex across the street from Belorussky Vokzal. Tavern-like restaurant serving Russian food with a creative, European twist. Friendly service and one of Moscow's largest selections of beer, from *Baltica* (25R) to *Murphy's Irish Red* (65R). Main dishes 145-195R. Happy hour M-F 3-7pm. Open daily noon-5am.

RUSSIA

**A HANDY BLINY REFERENCE** After you've gone through all the trouble of dressing like a Russian, speaking no English in public and hiding your camera in your bag, there's nothing more embarrassing than having to whip out your dictionary in front of a sidewalk stand to figure out what's inside a *bliny* or *pirozhok*. The fillings on the menu are printed following the word "c," meaning "with," pronounced like a hissing sound before the main word. Relative to most Russian eateries, *bliny* and *pirozhok* stands offer a number of vegetarian options: with cheese (с сыром; ss-SEER-um), with cabbage (с капустой; ss-ka-POOST-ay), with potatoes (с картофелем; ss-kar-TOF-felyem), with mushrooms (с грибами; ss-GREEB-am-ee), and with sour cream (с сметаной; ss-smet-AN-ay). Carnivores can opt for: with liver (с печеней; ss-PYE-che-ney) or with meat (с мясом; ss-MYA-sum). Travelers with a sweet tooth have many delicious alternatives, including: with chocolate (с шоколадом; ss-shaka-LAD-am), with apples (с яблоками; ss-YAB-lak-a-mee), and with jam (с вареньем; ss-var-EN-yem). *Pryatnovo appetita* (прятного аппетита; bon appetit)!

**Cafe-Bar Rioni** (Риони), Arbat 43 (☎241 78 46). M3: Smolenskaya. Dim interior and (artificial) plants make this cafe a hideaway from the bustle of the Arbat. If you don't need to hide, sit out on the patio and enjoy fabulous people-watching and even more fabulous borscht (55R). Full meals 250R. Open daily 11am-11pm.

**Praga** (Прада), Arbat 2 (☎290 31 37), near the corner of Novy Arbat. M3: Arbatskaya. Home of the famous "Praga" torte sold all over Moscow. The restaurant itself is astronomically expensive, but the bakery around back sells delectable pastries and mini-cakes for 8R per piece. Open daily 10am-9pm.

**Zaidi i poprobuy** ("Drop In and Try"; Зайди и попробуй), pr. Mira 124 (Мира; ☎/fax 286 81 65). M6: Alekseevskaya, then walk right for 7min. Entrance on Malaya Moskovskaya ul. (Малая Московская). Good, cheap Russian cuisine in a simple but elegant dining room. Full meals 150-200R. Open daily noon-midnight.

**Evropeyskoe Bistro** (Европейское Бистро), Arbat 16 (☎291 71 61), with an orange-and-blue awning. Serves cafeteria-style "Eurofood"—basically Russian cuisine with a snazzy name. Patio seating facilitates people-watching. Salads 50-60R, main dishes 70-85R. Open daily 8am-midnight.

**Cafe Margarita** (Кафе Маргарита), ul. Malaya Bronnaya 28 (☎299 65 34), at the corner of Maly Kozikhinsky per. (Малый Козихинский). M2: Mayakovskaya. Exiting the Metro, take a left onto Bolshaya Sadovaya, then left onto Malaya Bronnaya. A small cafe serving Russian and Georgian food, opposite the Patriarch's Ponds, where Bulgakov's *The Master and Margarita* begins. Enjoy the house specialty—tomatoes stuffed with garlic and cheese (130R)—or sip a cup of tea and enjoy the dark, cozy atmosphere. Attracts expats and tourists, with consequently high prices. Full meals 400-500R. Live piano music after 7pm (cover 30R). Open daily 1pm-midnight.

**Flamingo,** pr. Mira 48. M4: Prospekt Mira. Look for the large pink flamingo on the door. This is the place for larger-than-average portions of better-than-average Russian food. The chintzy exterior hides a moderately classy interior and the service is impeccable. Eat, drink, and be merry for 250-300R. Open daily noon-1:30am.

## ETHNIC

■ **Moscow Bombay** (Москва Бомбей), Glinishchevsky per. 3 (Глинищевский; ☎292 97 31; fax 292 93 75). M7: Pushkinskaya. Exiting the Metro, walk 5min. downhill on Tverskaya and turn left onto Glinishchevsky. Dark carved wood, soothing Indian music, and gracious service make for a relaxing atmosphere in which to enjoy the Indian specialties. English menu, including a full page of vegetarian options. Appetizers 110-220R, *naan* 150R, main dishes 100-375R. 10% student discount. Reservations recommended, especially on weekends. Open daily noon-midnight. MC/Visa.

**Mama Zoya's,** Sechenovsky per. 18 (Сеченовский; ☎201 77 43). M1: Kropotkinskaya. From the Metro, walk 4 blocks down ul. Ostozhenka (Остоженка) and take a right on

Sechenovsky. Turn right at the Mama Zoya's sign and head to the basement in the back of the building. Mama cooks up inexpensive, family-style Georgian feasts. Main dishes 50-80R. Live Georgian music. Open daily noon-midnight.

**Guria's,** Komsomolsky pr. 7/3 (Комсомольский; ☎246 03 78), on the corner of ul. Frunze, opposite St. Nicholas of the Weavers and behind Dom Modeley (Дом Моделей). M1, 5: Park Kultury. Tasty Georgian fare for some of the city's lowest prices. Cabbage leaves stuffed with rice and meat (60R) are a must. Most main dishes 40-90R. Open daily 11am-10pm.

**Patio Pizza,** ul. Tverskaya 3 (☎292 08 91). M1: Okhotny Ryad. Also at ul. Volkhonka 13a (Волхонка; ☎298 25 30). M1: Kropotkinskaya. Four additional locations around the city. This place rocks, and everyone in Moscow knows it—the delicious thin-crust pizzas have the crowds lining up after 7pm. One of the only restaurants in Moscow whose concept of salad actually includes vegetables. Pizzas US$2.50-12.50. All-you-can-eat salad bar US$6. Open daily noon-midnight. AmEx/MC/Visa.

**Kishmish** (Кишмиш), ul. Novy Arbat 28 (Новый Арбат; ☎291 20 10). M3: Arbatskaya. Also at ul. Barrikadnaya 8/9 (☎202 10 83). M7: Barrikadnaya. Popular restaurant serving Central Asian cuisine. Lamb and chicken *shashliks* (45-55R), *plov* (105R), and a great salad bar (105R). English menu. Arbat location open 11am-3am; Barrikadnaya location open 11am-midnight.

**Starlight Diner,** ul. Bolshaya Sadovaya 16 (Большая Садовая; ☎290 9638). M2: Mayakovskaya. Turn left out of the Metro; it's in the courtyard on the other side of the Tchaikovsky Conservatory. Another location at ul. Korovy Val 9 (☎959 89 19). M5: Oktyabrskaya. Neon and chrome on the outside, Americana on the walls inside. This place is authentic—they flew the decorations in from Florida. Large selection of American favorites to comfort homesick expats. The delicious milkshakes are well worth US$5. Burgers US$7-9, main dishes US$8-10. Drink menu extensive but expensive (US$6-7). Open 24hr. AmEx/MC/Visa.

**Krizis Zhanra,** per. Prechistensky 22/4 (Пречистенский; ☎241 29 40). M1: Kropotkinskaya. From the Metro, walk down ul. Prechistenka (Пречистенка) away from the Church of Christ the Savior. Take the 3rd right onto Prechistensky. Walk through the gate across from the Danish embassy into a courtyard and turn left; the entrance is the 1st large door on the left. Caters to pensive, artsy types—bring your *Crime and Punishment*. Snacks and beers 200-250R. Open Tu-Su 11am-11pm.

## THE CHAINS (OR, HOW UNCLE SAM WON THE COLD WAR)

**McDonald's** (Макдоналдс—not that you need the Cyrillic, ye seeker of the Golden Arches). Ronald now has 21 outlets in Moscow, included here because *Let's Go* endorses the steady homogenization of world culture. The lines are horrendous and they charge for ketchup (3.50R). Everywhere you look, but Bolshaya Bronnaya 29 (Большая Бронная), M7: Pushkinskaya, and ul. Arbat 50/52 (Арбат), M3: Smolenskaya, are the biggest. Big Mac 29R. Large fries (большая порция картофеля-фри; bolshaya portsiya kartofelya-fri) 26R. Hours vary by location.

**Russkoe Bistro** (Русское Бистро). Moscow's stellar, cheaper answer to McDonald's, with locations all over town (particularly near the Pushkinskaya Metro, where you can see 3 of them at once). Just like the kiosks, only indoors. Traditional food, fast. Premade salads 13-15R, filled pies 12-30R. Open daily 9am-11pm.

**Rostik's** (Ростик'с). Moscow's answer to Kentucky Fried Chicken. The largest of these popular eateries is located diagonally across from M2: Mayakovskaya; another inside the GUM shopping center (see p. 619). Look for the deranged, grinning rooster holding a knife and fork. 3 pieces of "Rostik's original" chicken 60R, salads and soups 10-40R. Combo meals 60-85R. Open daily 10am-11pm.

**Baskin Robbins,** all over the place; there's a big one on the Arbat, near Arbat 20. M3: Arbatskaya (Арбатская). In spite of the Russian national obsession with chocolate ice cream, the 31 flavors incline toward the fruit-based. Small scoop 20R. Arbat location open daily 10am-10pm, elsewhere hours vary.

## SUPERMARKETS

The number of supermarkets is increasing just as the need for them is decreasing—many goods can be found more cheaply in kiosks and in smaller, neighborhood markets selling Russian and foreign food. If nothing else, the convenience of knowing you can find everything you need without being trampled is tempting. Listed below are a few of the largest.

**Eliseevsky Gastronom** (Елисеевский), ul. Tverskaya 14 (☎209 07 60). M2: Tverskaya. With stained glass, high Baroque ceilings, and high-flying chandeliers, Moscow's most famous grocery is as much a visual spectacle as it is a place to buy food. Stocked with foreign goods. Higher prices than most other groceries (if you dare demean it by calling it a grocery). Open M-F 8am-9pm, Sa 10am-7pm.

**Gastronom Tsentralny, a.k.a. Sedmoi Kontinent** (Седмой Континент), ul. Bolshaya Lubyanka 1½ (Большая Любянка), behind Lubyanka Prison. M1, 8: Lubyanka. This 24hr. supermarket stocks everything. AmEx/MC/Visa.

**Dorogomilovo** (Дорогомилого), ul. Bolshaya Dorogomilovskaya 8 (Большая Дорогомиловская). M5: Kievskaya. Left of McDonald's, across the park from Kievsky Vokzal. A wide array of Western foods and other products at reasonable prices. Open M-Sa 9am-9pm, Su 9am-7pm.

## MARKETS

Vendors bring everything from a handful of cherries to an entire produce section to Moscow's many markets. A visit is worthwhile just for the sights: sides of beef, tomatoes, peaches, grapes, and pots of flowers crowd together in a visual bouquet. Wash everything with bottled water before eating. The bigger markets include the **central market** (центральный рынок; tsentralny rynok), Tsvetnoi bul. 15 (Цветной бул.), M9: Tsvetnoi Bulvar, next to the Old Circus, the **Rizhsky Market** (Рижский), Prospekt Mira 94-96; M6: Rizhskaya and **Veshchevoy Market** (Вещевой), M3, 5: Kievskaya. Impromptu markets also spring up around Metro stations; some of the best are at Turgenevskaya, Kuznetsky Most, Aeroport, Baumanskaya, and between Novoslobodskaya and Mendeleevskaya. Vendors arrive around 10am and leave by 8pm, though stragglers stick around until 10pm. Produce, sold by the kilogram, is far cheaper than in grocery stores; bags are rarely provided, so bring your own.

## ◉ SIGHTS

Moscow's sights reflect the city's strange history: one can choose from 16th-century churches or Soviet-era museums, but there's little in between. The city suffers from the 200 years when St. Petersburg was the Tsar's seat—there are no grand palaces—but the city's art museums contain the very best of Russian art. Tourists will notice that the political upheaval of the last decade has taken its toll on the museums dedicated to Lenin, Marx, and Engels, which are closed indefinitely while their political significance is reassessed. Yet the "political reconstruction" of the capital has also led to physical renovation, and the city seems to be constantly under construction, with new buildings going up practically overnight. Despite the fact that 80% of Moscow's pre-revolutionary splendor was torn down by the Soviet regime, the capital still packs enough sights to occupy you for over a week. For information on guided tours of the city's sights, see **Tours**, p. 610.

## RED SQUARE

Red Square (Красная площадь; Krasnaya ploshchad), a 700m long lesson in history and culture, has been the site of everything from a giant farmer's market to public hangings, from political demonstrations to a renegade Cessna landing. There's nothing red about it; *krasnaya* meant "beautiful" long before the Communists co-opted it. On one side, the **Kremlin** stands as both the historical and religious heart of Russia and the seat of the Communist Party for 70-odd years; on the other, **GUM**, once a market, then the world's largest purveyor of Soviet "consumer goods," is now an upscale shopping mall. At one end, **St. Basil's Cathedral** (Покровский

Собор; Pokrovsky Sobor), the square's second oldest building, rises high with its crazy-quilt onion domes; at the other end sit the **History** and **Lenin Museums.** Lenin's historical legacy has come into question, but his mausoleum still stands in front of the **Kremlin,** patrolled by several scowling guards. Moscow's mayor had a church built to block the largest entrance to the square, ensuring that Communist parades will never again march through; it's now the domain of tourists.

## KREMLIN

*Open M-W and F-Su 10am-5pm. Buy tickets at the kassa in Alexander Gardens, on the west side of the Kremlin, and enter through Borovitskaya gate tower in the southwest corner if you're going to the Armory; enter between the kassy if you're skipping it. Entrance to all cathedrals 200R, students 110R; after 4pm 90R, students 45R. Camera 30R. English-speaking guides offer tours at outrageous prices; haggle away. Local hotels also offer tours.*

Like a spider in its web, the Kremlin (Кремль; Kreml) sits geographically and historically in the center of Moscow. Here, Ivan the Terrible reigned with his iron fist and Stalin ruled the lands behind the Iron Curtain. Napoleon simmered here while Moscow burned, and the Congress of People's Deputies dissolved itself here in 1991, ending the USSR. Although this one-time fortress has been the scene of tremendous political history, its magnificent churches remain the real attraction. Much of the Kremlin is still government offices; the watchful police will blow whistles if you stray into a forbidden zone.

**ARMORY MUSEUM AND DIAMOND FUND.** (Оружейная и Выставка Алмазного; Oruzheynaya i Vystavka Almaznovo Fonda.) The Armory Museum lies just to the left as you enter. All the riches of the Russian Church and many of those of the state can be found in these nine rooms. Room 2, on the second floor, holds the legendary **Fabergé Eggs** and the royal silver. Room 6 holds pieces of the royal wardrobe (Empress Elizabeth is said to have had 15,000 gowns, only one of which is on display). The horses' dress harnesses, only slightly less elaborate than their human counterparts' attire, are on display in Room 8. Room 9 contains royal coaches and sleds—Elizabeth (not one for understatement) had her sled pulled by 23 horses. The display is a must-see to comprehend the opulence of the Russian court. The **Diamond Fund,** in an annex of the Armory, has still more glitter, including a 190-carat diamond given to Catherine the Great by Gregory Orlov, a "special friend." *(Armory and Diamond Fund open M-W and F-Su 10-11:30am, noon-1:30pm, 2:30-4pm, 4:30-6pm. Armory 290R, students 145R. Diamond Fund 250R. Large bags and cameras must be checked before entering the Diamond Fund.)*

**CATHEDRAL SQUARE.** (Соборная Площадь; Sobornaya Ploshchad.) From the Armory, follow the eager masses to Cathedral Square, home of the most famous gold domes in Russia. The first church to the left, **Annunciation Cathedral** (Благовещеиский Собор; Blagoveshchensky Sobor), guards the loveliest iconostasis in Russia, with luminous icons by Andrei Rublyov and Theophanes the Greek. Originally only three-domed, the cathedral was enlarged and gilded by Ivan the Terrible. The second, southeast entrance is also his work; Ivan's four marriages made him ineligible to enter the church so he was forced to stand in the porch during services as penance. Across the way, the square **Archangel Cathedral** (Архангельский Собор; Arkhangelsky Sobor), gleaming with vivid icons and frescoes, is the final resting place of many tsars prior to Peter the Great. Ivans III (the Great) and IV (the Terrible) are behind the south end of the iconostasis; Mikhail Romanov is in front.

**ASSUMPTION CATHEDRAL.** (Успенский Собор; Uspensky Sobor.) The center of Cathedral Square is Assumption Cathedral, the oldest cathedral in the Russian state. The icons on the west wall date from the 15th century; the others are from the 1640s. Ivan the Terrible's throne still stands in the armory. Napoleon, eager to improve his already-stellar rapport with the Russians, used this place as a stable in 1812. To the right of Uspensky Sobor stands **Ivan the Great Belltower** (Колокольня Нвана Велнкого; Kolokolnya Ivana Velikovo). It's visible from more than 30km away, thanks to Boris Godunov, who raised the tower to 81m.

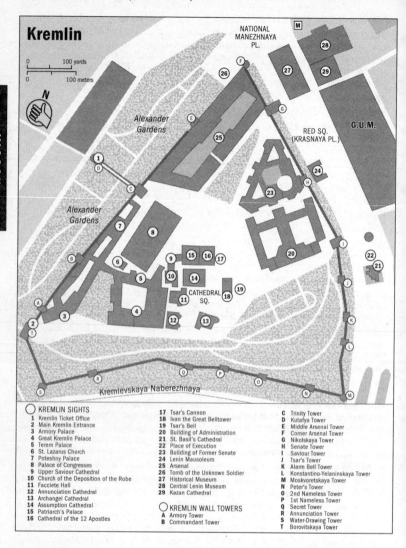

# Kremlin

NATIONAL MANEZHNAYA PL.

Alexander Gardens

RED SQ. (KRASNAYA PL.)

G.U.M.

Alexander Gardens

CATHEDRAL SQ.

Kremlevskaya Naberezhnaya

**○ KREMLIN SIGHTS**
1 Kremlin Ticket Office
2 Main Kremlin Entrance
3 Armory Palace
4 Great Kremlin Palace
5 Terem Palace
6 St. Lazarus Church
7 Poteshny Palace
8 Palace of Congresses
9 Upper Saviour Cathedral
10 Church of the Deposition of the Robe
11 Facciete Hall
12 Annunciation Cathedral
13 Archangel Cathedral
14 Assumption Cathedral
15 Patriarch's Palace
16 Cathedral of the 12 Apostles

17 Tsar's Cannon
18 Ivan the Great Belltower
19 Tsar's Bell
20 Building of Administration
21 St. Basil's Cathedral
22 Place of Execution
23 Building of Former Senate
24 Lenin Mausoleum
25 Arsenal
26 Tomb of the Unknown Soldier
27 Historical Museum
28 Central Lenin Museum
29 Kazan Cathedral

**○ KREMLIN WALL TOWERS**
A Armory Tower
B Commandant Tower

C Trinity Tower
D Kutafya Tower
E Middle Arsenal Tower
F Corner Arsenal Tower
G Nikolskaya Tower
H Senate Tower
I Saviour Tower
J Tsar's Tower
K Alarm Bell Tower
L Konstantino-Yelaninskaya Tower
M Moskvoretskaya Tower
N Peter's Tower
O 2nd Nameless Tower
P 1st Nameless Tower
Q Secret Tower
R Annunciation Tower
S Water-Drawing Tower
T Borovitskaya Tower

**OTHER KREMLIN SIGHTS.** Directly behind the belltower is the **Tsar Bell** (Царь-колокол; Tsar-kolokol). The world's largest, this bell has never rung and probably never will (unless Mayor Luzhkov undertakes another one of his reconstruction projects): an 11.5-ton piece broke off after a 1737 fire. Behind the Assumption Cathedral stands the **Patriarch's Palace** (Патриарший Дворец; Patriarshiy Dvorets), site of the **Museum of 17th-Century Russian Applied Art and Life** and the **Church of the Twelve Apostles** (Собор Двенадцати Апостолов; Sobor Dvenadtsati Apostolov), built by Patriarch Nikon in the 17th century. The only other place inside the Kremlin you can actually enter is the **Kremlin Palace of Congresses,** a square white monster built by Khrushchev in 1961 for Communist Party Congresses. It's also a theater, open in summer for concerts and ballets.

## OTHER SIGHTS IN RED SQUARE

**STATE DEPARTMENT STORE GUM.** (Государственный Универсальный Магазин; ГУМ; Gosudarstvenny Universalny Magazin.) Built in the 19th century, GUM was designed to hold 1000 stores. Its arched wrought-iron and glass roofs resemble a Victorian train station. During Soviet rule, going to GUM was a depressing experience; the sight of 1000 empty stores is pretty grim. These days, it's depressing only to those who can't afford it (almost everyone). The complex has been completely renovated and is now a mall of which any American metropolis would be proud. Some stores quote prices in US dollars or Deutschmarks; pay in rubles. *(M3: Ploshchad Revolutsii (Площадь Революции). From the Metro, turn left, then left again at the gate to Red Square.* ☎ *929 33 81. Open M-Sa 9am-9pm, Su 11am-8pm.)*

**ST. BASIL'S CATHEDRAL.** (Собор Василия Блаженного; Pokrovsky Sobor or Sobor Vasiliya Blazhennovo.) There is perhaps no more familiar symbol of Moscow than St. Basil's Cathedral. Completed in 1561, it was commissioned by Ivan the Terrible to celebrate his 1552 victory over the Tatars in Kazan. The nine main chapels are named after the saints' days on which Ivan won his battles, but the cathedral itself bears the moniker of a holy fool, Vasily—Basil in English—who correctly predicted that Ivan would murder his own son. Before the Kazan victory, Vasily died and was buried in the church that once stood on this ground. The grand cathedral that replaced it has seen the addition of a few minor domes since Ivan's time, as well as the colorful patterns for which the domes are known. *(M3: Ploshchad Revolutsii (Площадь Революции). Open W-M 11am-6pm; kassa closes at 5:30pm. Buy tickets from the kassa to the left of the entrance, then proceed upstairs. 90R, students 45R.)*

**LENIN MAUSOLEUM.** (Мавзолей В.И. Ленина; Mavzoley V.I. Lenina.) You've seen his likeness in bronze all over the city, now see him in the eerily-luminescent flesh. In the glory days, this squat red structure in front of the Kremlin was guarded by fierce goose-stepping guards, and the line to get in was three hours long. The line is still long, and the guards are still stone-faced, but on the whole amused curiosity pervades the atmosphere. No photos are allowed of Vlad's embalmed remains, and bags must be checked at the cloakroom in Aleksandrovsky Sad. Pulling out a camera in the tomb might get you escorted out to the gates of Red Square. Entrance to the mausoleum also gives access to the **Kremlin wall,** where Stalin, Brezhnev, Andropov, Gagarin, and John Reed (author of *Ten Days that Shook the World*) are buried. As you admire the mausoleum on your stroll around Red Square, note the balcony on top, where Russia's leaders stood during May 1 and November 7 parades. Rumor has it that the plushest bathroom in Moscow is hidden in the back. Unfortunately it's not open to the public. *(Open Tu-Th and Sa-Su 10am-1pm.)*

**KAZAN CATHEDRAL.** (Казанский Собор; Kazansky Sobor.) The pink and white Kazan Cathedral has been reopened for services after being demolished in 1936 to make way for May 1 parades. The interior of the faithful 1990s reconstruction is plainer than that of most Russian churches, and the iconostasis is free of golden Baroque madness. *(M3: Ploshchad Revolutsii (Площадь Революции). Stands on the opposite end of Red Square from St. Basil's, just to the left of the main entrance. Open daily 8am-7pm. Services M-F 8am and 5pm, Su 7am, 10am, and 5pm.)*

**ALEXANDER GARDENS.** (Александровский Сад; Aleksandrovsky Sad.) More than just the place to buy Kremlin tickets, the Alexander Gardens are a green respite from the carbon monoxide fumes of central Moscow. At the north end of the gardens at the **Tomb of the Unknown Soldier** (Могила Неизвестного Солдата; Mogila Neizvestnovo Soldata), an eternal flame burns in memory of the catastrophic losses suffered in World War II, known in Russia as the Great Patriotic War. Twelve urns containing soil from the Soviet Union's "Hero Cities," which withstood especially heavy casualties, stand there as well. It used to be the trendy (and macabre) spot to have a picture taken on your wedding day—that and Lenin's mausoleum. *(M3: Ploshchad Revolutsii, to the left of the exit.)*

# RELIGIOUS SIGHTS

If the grime and bedlam get to you, escape to one of Moscow's hidden houses of worship. Before the Revolution, the city had more than 1000 operational churches; today, there are fewer than 100. Shorts are not permitted in Orthodox monasteries and women should cover their heads.

**CATHEDRAL OF CHRIST THE SAVIOR.** (Храм Христа Спасителя; Khram Khrista Spasitelya.) No one should leave Moscow without visiting the city's most controversial landmark, the enormous, gold-domed Cathedral of Christ the Savior, visible from just about anywhere in west Moscow. Believe it or not, the city government of Moscow, led by Mayor Yuri Luzhkov, constructed the cathedral that stands here today in a mere two years, on the site of the former Moscow swimming pool. Nicholas I had originally placed a cathedral on this spot to commemorate Russia's victory over Napoleon, but in 1934 Stalin had it dynamited, claiming it interfered with the city's biannual military parades. The minute the church was leveled, however, the truth came out: Stalin intended to erect a "Palace of the Soviets," which he wanted to be the tallest building in the world, on the spot. The so-called "Palace" was to be topped with a 100m statue of Lenin (the world's tallest statue). The ground on which the edifice was to stand ultimately proved too soft to hold a building of such weight, and after Stalin's death Khrushchev abandoned the project and instead turned the site into the Moscow outdoor swimming pool. Although 20,000 people per day used the pool, in the early 90s it was discovered that vapor from the heated water damaged paintings at the nearby Pushkin Museum, so the pool was closed. In 1994-95 a controversy erupted over what was to become of the site; the Orthodox Church and Moscow's mayor finally won out and raised funds to build the US$250 million cathedral that stands here today. As for where they got the money—well, let's just say it was a miracle. *(M1: Kropotkinskaya. Between ul. Volkhonka (Волхонка) and the Moscow River. ☎ 201 28 47. Museum open daily 10am-6pm. Closed last M of the month. Service schedule varies. Free but donations welcome.)*

**NOVODEVICHY MONASTERY AND CEMETERY.** (Новодевичий Монастырь.) The high brick walls of one of Moscow's most famous monasteries are crumbling slightly and its golden domes are undergoing some much-needed repair, but they're still worth seeing. A few well-known 16th-century Russians are buried within the monastery's walls, but all the truly famous folks are entombed at the cemetery next door (see below). **Smolensk Cathedral** (Смоленский Собор; Smolensky Sobor), in the center of the convent, shows off Russian icons and frescoes. English/Cyrillic keys decode the elaborate maze of scenes depicted on the walls. Other buildings of interest include **Assumption Church** (Успенская Церковь; Uspenskaya Tserkov), to the right of Smolensky, and a small three-room **exhibit hall** at the far end of the grounds. *(M1: Sportivnaya. Take the exit out of the Metro that does not go to the stadium. Turn right and the monastery is several blocks down on the left. ☎ 246 85 26. Open M and W-Su 10am-5:30pm; cathedrals close at 4:45pm. Closed 1st M of each month. Avoid Sunday, when tour buses hog the place. Entrance to the grounds 30R, students 15R; Smolensk Cathedral 68R, students 38R; special exhibits 68R, students 38R. English tour 300R; call to arrange.)*

Exiting the monastery gates, turn right and follow the exterior wall back around to the **cemetery** (кладбище; kladbishche), a massive pilgrimage site that cradles the graves of famous artists, politicians, and military men. Many tombstones are decorated with stylized representations of the deceased. Gogol, Chekhov, Stanislavsky, Bulgakov, Shostakovich, and Mayakovsky lie to the right of the path, while Eisenstein, Gromyko, Prokofiev, and Scriabin lie to the left. Once closed to prevent crowds from flocking to Khrushchev's tomb (straight through the entrance at the back of the cemetery), it's now open to the public. The writers are conveniently clustered near each other. *(Open daily in summer 9am-7pm; off-season 9am-6pm. 20R; buy tickets at the small kiosk across the street from the entrance. Cyrillic maps of cemetery 5R.)*

**MOSCOW CHORAL SYNAGOGUE.** First constructed in the 1870s, the Moscow Choral Synagogue is a much-needed break from the city's ubiquitous onion domes. Although it functioned during Soviet rule, KGB agents stationed across the street were instructed to take pictures of anyone entering, preventing all but the boldest of Moscow's Jews from participating in services. Today more than 200,000 Jews officially live in Moscow, and services are increasingly well attended, especially on holidays. The synagogue has two prayer rooms; the main room is marked by 10 chandeliers and a patterned ceiling that protects the upper level, where women must sit. The graffiti occasionally sprayed on the building serves as a sad reminder that anti-Semitism in Russia is not dead. Regular services are held every morning and evening. A **restaurant** on the premises serves kosher food. *(Bolshoy Spasoglinish-chevsky per. 10 (Большой Спасоглинищевский). M6, 7 Kitai-Gorod. Go north on Solyansky Proezd (Солянский Проезд) and take the first left.* ☎ *923 96 97. Open daily 9:30am-8pm; Sabbath services Sa 9am. Restaurant open Su-M 9am-6pm.)*

**CHURCH OF ST. NICHOLAS OF THE WEAVERS.** (Церковь Николы в Хамовниках; Tserkov Nikoly v Khamovnikakh.) One of Moscow's better-known churches, St. Nicholas's reddish-brown and green trim gives it the appearance of a giant Christmas ornament or something designed by the witch from Hansel and Gretel. Enter off ul. Lva Tolstovo for the best view of the low ceilings and equally vivid interior. *(M1, 5: Park Kultury. At the corner of Komsomolsky pr. and ul. Lva Tolstovo. Open daily 6am-8pm. Services M-F 6am and 5pm, Sa-Su 6:30am and 5pm.)*

**DANILOVSKY MONASTERY.** (Даниловский.) This monastery is home to the Patriarch, head of the Russian Orthodox Church—hence the men in uniform overrunning the place. The well-preserved and recently restored pastel exterior is complemented by stunning grounds and long-robed monks; unfortunately, visitors can see no more than these exterior views. The Patriarch's office is hard to miss, marked by an enormous mosaic of a stern-looking man watching over the visitors to his domain. *(M9: Tulskaya. Turn right from the Metro and then take another right onto Danilovsky vul. The monastery is 3-4 blocks down on the right. Open daily 6am-8pm. Services M-F 7am and 5pm, Sa-Su 6:30am, 9am, and 5pm.)*

**SPASO-ANDRONIKOV MONASTERY.** (Спасо-Андроников.) Dating from the 1360s, Spaso-Andronikov is famed for its preservation of life-sized 16th-century icons and a biblical text from the 14th century. Master of iconography Andrei Rublyov was a monk here from the beginning of the 15th century until his death in 1430; he is buried inside the walls. The tiny **Museum of Andrei Rublyov** (Музей им. Андрея Рублёва; Muzey Andreya Rublyova), on the grounds of the monastery, showcases several beautiful icons but, unfortunately, nothing by Rublyov. *(Andronik-ovskaya pl. (Андрониковская). M8: Ploshchad Ilicha. Exit the Metro and go right on ul. Sergiya Radonezhskovo (Сергия Радонежского). Stop across the street from a blue and silver church; the monastery is across the street and through the trees to the right.* ☎ *278 14 67. Open M-Tu and Th-Su 11am-6pm. Closed last F of the month. Kassa closes 5:30pm. 35R, students 10R.)*

# AREAS FOR WALKING

**MOSCOW METRO.** (Московское Метро.) The Metro, one of the most beautiful in the world, is worth a tour of its own. All of the stations are unique, and those inside the Circle Line are elaborate, with mosaics, sculptures, stained glass, and crazy chandeliers. It's only 4R and you can stay as long you as like. Stations **Kievskaya, Mayakovskaya,** and **Ploshchad Revolutsii** are particularly noteworthy, as are **Komso-molskaya, Novoslobodskaya, Rimskaya,** and **Mendeleevskaya.** Note the molecular-model light fixtures in the Mendeleevskaya station. *(Open daily 6am-1am.)*

**ARBAT.** (Арбат.) A pedestrian shopping arcade, the Arbat was once a showpiece of *glasnost* and a haven for political radicals, Hare Krishnas, street poets, and *met-allisty* (heavy metal rockers). Today, the flavor of political rebellion has been replaced by the more universal taste of capitalism, including McDonald's and Benetton. Popular with native Muscovites, the Arbat is nonetheless peppered with kiosks tempting tourists with everything from *matryoshka* dolls to Soviet military caps. Still, some of the flavor of the old Arbat remains, particularly in the large numbers of street performers and guitar-playing youths. The many outdoor cafes provide the ideal venue for people-watching. Intersecting, but nearly parallel to, the Arbat runs **Novy Arbat**, a thoroughfare lined with foreign businesses (such as the Arbat Irish House), and massive Russian stores. *(M3: Arbatskaya.)*

**PUSHKINSKAYA PL.** (Пушкинская пл.) This square in central Moscow has inherited the Arbat's mantle of political fervor. Missionary groups evangelize while amateur politicians gather to hand out petitions. All the major Russian news organizations are located in this region and the square is the center of free speech. Everything here is large—from the golden arches to the **Kinoteatr Rossiya**, Moscow's largest movie theater, which brought *Terminator* to the masses. Follow ul. Bolshaya Bronnaya, next to McD's, down to the bottom of the hill, turn right, and follow ul. Malaya Bronnaya to **Patriarch's Pond** (Patriarshy Prud; Патриарший Пруд), where Mikhail Bulgakov's *The Master and Margarita* begins. This area, known as the Margarita, is popular with artsy students and old men who play dominoes by the shaded pond. *(M7: Pushkinskaya. Halfway up ul. Tverskaya from Krasnaya pl.)*

**VICTORY PARK.** (Парк Победы; Park Pobedy.) The recently opened Victory Park, is a popular gathering point. The entire park and its museum (see **Historical Museums**, p. 625) were built as a lasting monument to World War II, in which 27 million Russians perished. The main square showcases stones, each inscribed with a year that the Soviet troops fought in the war (1941-45). The gold-domed **Church of St. George the Victorious** (Храм Георгия Победоносного; Khram Georgiya Pobedanosnova) commemorates those who died in battle. *(M3: Kutuzovskaya.)*

# PARKS

**GORKY PARK.** (Парк Горкого; Park Gorkovo.) In summer, out-of-towners and young Muscovites promenade, relax, and ride the roller coaster at Moscow's **amusement park**. In winter, the paths are flooded to create a park-wide **ice rink**. Those seeking an American-style amusement park will be disappointed—attractions are far outnumbered by ice cream kiosks and the rides are on their last legs. Nevertheless, it's a fun place to mingle with delighted children, teenage couples, and a menagerie of "pet" animals, including monkeys and alligators. Night may be the best time to go—the rides are illuminated and the children are home sleeping. *(M1, 5: Park Kultury or M5, 6: Oktyabrskaya. From the Park Kultury stop, cross Krimskiy most. From Oktyabrskaya, walk downhill on Krimskiy val. and enter through the main flag-flanked gate. Park open daily 10am-midnight. General admission M-F 20R, Sa-Su 25R. Most rides 25-75R.)*

**KRASNAYA PRESNYA AND ZOOPARK.** One of the largest of the city's serene green areas, **Krasnaya Presnya** (Красная Пресня) attracts small children and readers with its scattered wooden playgrounds and quiet benches. *(M6: Ulitsa 1905 goda (Улица 1905 года). Exit to and then cross ul. Krasnaya Presnya; the park stretches alongside ul. 1905 goda.)* The action is livelier two blocks down ul. Krasnaya Presnya at the **Zoopark** (Зоопарк). Going to the zoo used to be a bit like watching calves raised for veal, until Mayor Luzhkov directed his energy and fundraising talents toward improving the animals' quality of life. Now the zoo is a good place to keep the kids (and yourself) amused for a couple of hours. *(On both sides of ul. Bolshaya Gruzinskaya (Большая Грузинская). ☎ 255 53 75. Open Tu-Su 10am-8pm; kassa closes at 7pm. 30R.)*

**KOLOMENSKOE SUMMER RESIDENCE.** The tsars' summer residence sits on a wooded rise above the Moskva River. Stroll through the grounds to the main gate, overlooking the river. Red-coated guards with handy axes and fur-lined hats patrol the entrance, an authentic if kitschy blast from the past. Directly in front stands the 16th-century **Assumption Cathedral** (Успенский Собор; Uspensky Sobor), the first example of a brick church built like a traditional wooden building (St. Basil's is the more famous example). Inside the main gate you can buy tickets to the museums on the grounds. Most notable is Peter the Great's 1702 **log cabin**. *(M2: Kolomenskaya. Follow the exit signs to "к музею Коломенское." Exiting the Metro, turn right and walk about 400m down the shaded, merchant-lined path to the main entrance gate. Grounds open daily 7am-10pm. Free. Museums open Tu-Su 11am-6pm. 60-70R, students 30-35R.)*

**IZMAYLOVSKY PARK.** (Измайловский Парк.) Your grandfather wants a *matry-oshka* doll, your little brother wants Communist propaganda posters, and Uncle Bob wants "one of them Russkie fur hats." Your one-stop-shop for all of your souvenir needs is Izmaylovsky Park, whose colossal weekend market, **Vernisazh** (Вернисаж), unfortunately overshadows its lush greenery. Arrive late Sunday afternoon, when people want to go home and are willing to make a deal. Compare prices—the first painted box you see will not be the last, guaranteed. *(M3: Izmaylovsky Park. Go left and follow the hordes. Open daily 9am-6pm. 10R entrance fee on weekends.)*

**TSARITSYNO.** (Царицыно.) This Tsar's park is most famous for its unhappy history. Conceived for Catherine the Great, the project was headed by Vasily Bazhenov, a Paris-educated serf, and included several pavilions, a system of palaces, arches, and bridges. Bazhenov had barely set up some pavilions and started the palaces when the capricious Catherine changed her mind and canceled the project. Bazhenov was devastated, but the blueprints survived. The Soviet authorities began restorations of the palaces many a time, but always ran out of funds. Three years ago some of the palaces were completed, along with the arches and bridges. Now, the red and white buildings, fragile and exotic, stand out against the gray Moscow sky. Many believe the place was cursed some 250 years ago and its bad luck still looms over the ancient trees. *(M2: Orekhovo (Орехого). Exit to "Царицыно" from the front of the train platform and go left out of the tunnel. Walk right down the sidewalk for 10min. Turn left at the end; after a few minutes you'll see the bridge that leads to the palace.)*

**VDNKh.** The **Exhibition of Soviet Economic Achievements** (Выставка Достижений Народного Хозяйства—ВДНХ; Vystavka Dostizheny Narodnovo Khozyaystva—VDNKh) has changed a great deal since its original conception. Now that the world knows that there were no Soviet economic achievements, this World's Fair-esque park filled with pavilions has ironically become a giant shopping mecca. *(M6: VDNKh. Exiting the Metro to "ВВЦ," go left down the kiosk-flanked sidewalk. Enter through the large main gate. Shops open 10am until dark.)* Outside the gates of the main complex, almost buried in the hoard of kiosks by the Metro, an ugly monument to Soviet space achievements stands atop the **Cosmonaut Museum** (Музей Космонавтики; Muzey Kosmonavtiki), equally garish in its Star Trek-esque displays of life in space and aboard Sputnik, complete with cosmonaut food: freeze-dried borscht. *(pr. Mira 111. ☎ 283 79 14. Open Tu-Su 10am-7pm; closed last F of the month. 45R, students 20R.)*

# 🏛 MUSEUMS

## ART GALLERIES AND MUSEUMS

🖼 **Tretyakov Gallery** (Третьяковская Галерея), Lavrushinsky per. 10 (Лаврушинский; ☎230 77 88, 951 13 62, and 238 13 78; www.tretyakov.ru). M8: Tretyakovskaya. Exiting the Metro, turn left and then left again, followed by an immediate right onto Tolmachevsky per. (Толмачевский пер.) Walk 2 blocks and turn right onto Lavrushensky per. Founded through Tretyakov's 1892 donation of his private collection, this gallery is a veritable treasure chest of Russian national art. 18th- and 19th-century portraits and 19th-century landscapes comprise most of the collection, although it contains works by turn-of-the-20th-century artists. The gallery also plays host to a magnificent collection of icons, including works by Andrei Rublyov and Theophanes the Greek. Allow several hours to see it all. Open Tu-Su 10am-8:30pm. 210R, students 120R. Camera 30R; video 60R. Call in advance for an English tour (390R; ☎953 52 23) or rent one on tape (100R for each of the 2 parts of the musuem).

🖼 **State Tretyakov Gallery** (Государственная Третьяковская Галерея; Gosudarstvennaya Tretyakovskaya Galereya), ul. Krymsky Val 10 (Крымский Вал; ☎238 13 78). M1, 5: Park Kultury. Directly opposite the Gorky Park entrance on the right side. Built to house newer works and exhibitions of Russian art, it shares a building with the Central House of Artists; the State Tretyakov is the building at the back, with an entrance to the right side. Picks up chronologically where the Tretyakov leaves off. The collection starts on the 3rd floor with early 20th-century art and moves through the neo-primitivist and futurist schools, culminating in a room of Malevich. His famous *Black Square* hangs in the corner like an icon. The 2nd floor holds temporary exhibits that often draw huge crowds; it's best to go weekday mornings. Behind the gallery to the right lies a **graveyard for fallen statues.** Once the main dumping ground for decapitated Lenins and Stalins, it now contains plaques and neat pathways to ease your journey among sculptures of Gandhi, Einstein, and Niels Bohr. A controversial statue of Soviet secret police founder Dzerzhinsky was nearly returned to its original location before the Duma passed legislation to keep it in the graveyard. Open Tu-Su 10am-7:30pm; *kassa* closes 6:30pm. 210R, students 120R. Call to arrange an English tour (390R).

**Pushkin Museum of Fine Arts** (Музей Изобразительных Искусств им. А.С. Пушкина; Muzey Izobrazitelnykh Iskusstv im. A.S. Pushkina), ul. Volkhonka 12 (☎203 95 78). M1: Kropotkinskaya. Across from the Cathedral of Christ the Savior. The museum houses a large collection of European Renaissance, Egyptian, and Classical art. The Pushkin was founded in 1912 by poet Marina Tsvetaeva's father, who wanted his art students to have the opportunity to see original specimens of Classical art. Today—no doubt to his chagrin—those originals hang alongside several mere reproductions, and plaster copies of Greek statues dominate most of the floor space. The Egyptian art and the French Impressionists (including some great Monets) are the most noteworthy collections. Open Tu-Su 10am-7pm; *kassa* closes at 6pm. 210R, students 120R. Call ahead to arrange an English tour (☎203 74 12), or rent a taped one (100R plus 200R deposit).

**Museum of Private Collections,** housed in the aquamarine building to the left of the Pushkin. Exhibits famous foreign and Russian art from the 19th and 20th centuries. The museum began when Ilya Siberstein donated his collection to the state and asked that it be placed in the old Prince Yard Hotel, frequented by Ilya Repin and Maxim Gorky. Open W-Su noon-7pm; *kassa* closes at 6pm. 40R, students 20R.

**Central House of Artists** (Центральный Дом Художника; Tsentralny Dom Khudozhnika), ul. Krymsky Val 10 (☎238 96 34). M1, 5: Park Kultury. In the same building as the State Tretyakov Gallery (see above). One part art museum, one part gallery, and one part upscale gift shop (if you need to ask, you can't afford it). Dilettantes and serious collectors alike come to look at the cutting edge exhibits. Consult *The Moscow Times* for info. Open Tu-Su 11am-8pm. *Kassa* closes at 7pm. 15R.

**Manezh** (Манеж), 1 Manezhnaya pl. (Манежная; ☎202 89 76). M1: Okhotny Ryad. A big yellow building with white columns, across from the main entrance to the Alexander Gardens. Enter from the north end, on the square. A one-time riding school for the military is now the Central Exhibition Hall and often features interesting modern Russian exhibits. Open Tu-Sa 11am-8pm.

**All-Russia Museum of Decorative and Applied Folk Art** (Все-российский Музей Декоративно-прикладного; Vsye-rossiysky Muzey Dekorativno-Prikladnovo), Delegatskaya ul. 3 (Делегатская; ☎923 17 41 and 921 01 39). M9: Tsvetnoi Bulvar. Turn left out of the Metro, cross Sadovaya-Sukharevskaya, turn left and walk 10min. This is what the junk they sell on the Arbat is supposed to look like. The first building, where you buy your tickets, displays painted and lacquered wood, 17th- and 18th-century textiles, and samovars. The 2nd building at ul. Delegatskaya 5 is more interesting—the 1st room juxtaposes 19th-century Russian peasant costumes with what the St. Petersburg glitterati were wearing at the time. Open Tu-Sa 10am-6pm, Su 10am-5pm; last entrance 30min. before closing. Closed last Th of the month. 15R, students 10R.

**MARS Gallery,** ul. Malaya Filevskaya 32 (Малая Филевская; ☎146 84 26; fax 146 63 31). M3: Pionerskaya. Widely known for contemporary and avant-garde art. Open Tu-Sa noon-8pm, Su noon-6pm.

**Bakhrushin Theater Museum,** ul. Bakhrushina 31 (Бахрушина; ☎953 44 70). M2, 5: Paveletskaya. Across the street from the station. One of the numerous theater museums in Moscow, it boasts a chronologically arranged permanent exhibit of costumes, dressers, programs, and photos. English pamphlet. Open M noon-6pm, Tu-Su noon-7pm. Closed last M of the month. 10R, students 5R.

**Exhibition Hall of the Russian Academy of Art,** ul. Prechistenka 21/12 (Пречистенка; ☎201 58 40). M1: Kropotkinskaya. Near the Pushkin Literary Museum, 2 blocks down on the left. Displays the work of trendy artists. Exhibits change periodically. Open W-F noon-8pm, Sa-Su 10am-6pm; last entrance 1hr. before closing. 5R.

# HISTORICAL MUSEUMS

**Museum of Contemporary Russian History** (Центральный Музей Современной Истории России; Tsentralny Muzei Sovremennoi Istorii Rossii), ul. Tverskaya 21 (☎ 299 67 24). M7: Pushkinskaya. Exiting the Metro, walk 1 block uphill on Tverskaya and walk the gates on the left. Housed in the former mansion of the Moscow English club, the museum covers Russian history from the Revolution of 1905 to the present in exhausting detail. Complements its Cold War propaganda posters with newly displayed statistics on the ill effects of socialism. The bullet-ridden door has a recent story to tell; it was damaged in the Oct. 1993 attack on the White House. Museum open Tu-Sa 10am-6pm, Su 10am-5pm. 10R. Photos 75R, video 150R. Call ahead for English tour.

**Central Museum of the Armed Forces of the USSR** (Tsentralny Muzey Vooruzhennykh Sil SSSR; Центральный Музей Вооруженных Сил СССР), ul. Sovetskoy Armii 2 (Советской Армии; ☎ 281 48 77). M5: Novoslobodskaya. Walk down ul. Seleznevskaya (Селезневская) for 10min. to the square/rotary. Pass a huge theater on the left and bear right at the fork. The museum is 1 block down on the right. Uniforms, weapons, and artwork from the time of Peter the Great through to Chechnya. Displays the milepost 41 marker from the Moscow-Leningrad highway, the closest the Nazis ever got to Moscow. Open W-Su 10am-5pm. Closed 2nd Tu and the last week of the month. 15R, students 10R. Camera 15R, video 50R. Call ahead for English tour.

**State Historical Museum,** Krasnaya pl. 1 (☎ 292 37 31). M1: Okhotny Ryad. Just to the right of the entrance to Red Square. Traces Russian history from the Neanderthals to Kyivan Rus to modern Russia. Excellent exhibition on the Tsars. Open M and W-Su 11am-7pm; last entrance 6pm. Closed the 1st M of the month. 150R, students 75R.

**Borodino** (Бородино), Kutuzovsky pr. 38 (☎ 148 19 67). M3: Kutuzovskaya, then 10min. to the right down Kutuzovsky pr. A giant statue of General Kutuzov stands in front of the large circular building that houses the Borodino panorama, which commemorates the bloody battle against Napoleon in August 1812 (see **History, p. 591**). The 360° painting and accompanying exhibitions usually draw long lines, but even *War and Peace* fans may find the mandatory Russian tour tedious. Open M-Th and Sa-Su 10am-4:45pm. Closed last Th of the month. 20R, students 10R. Camera 20R, video 50R.

**Museum of the Great Patriotic War** (Музей Отечественной Войны; Muzey Otechestvennoy Voyny), pl. Pobedy (Победы; ☎ 449 80 44). M3: Kutuzovsky. Devoted to the soldiers and heroes of the Great Patriotic War (World War II). This was one of Mayor Luzhkov's most ambitious building projects, and the glitz of the building itself often undermines the solemnity of its subject matter. In the park behind the museum is the **Museum of War Technology** (Музей Военной Техники; Muzey Voyennoy Tekhniki), an outdoor display of several WWII fighter planes and helicopters. Open Tu-Su 10am-6pm. Closed last Th of the month. Most exhibits free; access to the rest 80R, students 40R. Camera 10R, video 15R. Some signs in English.

# HOUSES OF THE LITERARY AND FAMOUS

Russians take immense pride in their formidable literary history, preserving authors' houses in their original state, down to half-empty teacups on the mantelpiece. Each is guarded by a team of fiercely loyal *babushki*. Plaques on buildings throughout the city mark where writers, poets, artists, and philosophers lived and worked. Most take 45-60 minutes to visit thoroughly.

▨ **Leo Tolstoy Estate,** ul. Lva Tolstovo 21 (Льва Толстого; ☎ 246 94 44). M1, 5: Park Kultury. Exiting the Metro, walk down Komsomolsky pr. toward the colorful Church of St. Nicholas of the Weavers; turn right at the corner on ul. Lva Tolstovo. The estate is 3 blocks up on the left. The author lived here during the winters of 1882-1901. Exhibits on both the glamorous aspects of Tolstoy's life—such as the room where he entertained Rachmaninoff, Chekhov, and other famous friends—and the mundane, including what he ate and drank for breakfast. English captions. The *kassa* is to the right of the entrance gate or, if that is closed, in a small building down a path to the left, inside the entrance. Open in summer Tu-Su 10am-6pm; off-season 10am-3:30pm. Last entrance 1hr. before closing. Closed last F of the month. 100R, students 50R.

**Mayakovsky Museum** (Музей им. В. В. Маяковского; Muzey im B.B. Mayakovskovo), Lubyansky pr. 3/6 (Лубянский; ☎928 25 69). M1, 8: Lubyanka. Look for the bust of Mayakovsky surrounded by huge crimson metal shards; the museum hides in the building behind it. More of a walkthrough work of futurist art than a museum, with the poet and artist's papers and art arranged in a 4-story assemblage of bizarrely oriented chairs, spilled paint, and chicken wire. Mayakovsky lived here in a communal apartment from 1919 until he shot himself in 1930. His room, at the top of the building, chronicles his initial love affair with the Revolution and his travels abroad. Open M-Tu and F-Su 10am-6pm, Th 1-9pm. 50R. Call ahead for an English tour (600R; ☎921 93 87).

**Pushkin Literary Museum** (Литературный Музей Пушкина; Literaturny Muzey Pushkina), ul. Prechisterka 12 (Пречистерка), at the corner with Khrushchevsky per. (Хрущевский). M1: Kropotkinskaya. If you haven't seen Pushkin-worship first-hand, this gigantic museum will either convert or frighten you. Open Tu-Su 11am-7pm; *kassa* closes 6pm. Closed last F of the month. 15R, students 8R.

**Tolstoy Museum** (Музей Толстого; Muzey Tolstovo), ul. Prechistenka 11 (Пречистенка). M1: Kropotkinskaya. From the Metro, walk 3 blocks down Prechistenka in the opposite direction from the Cathedral of Christ the Savior; the museum is on the left. This yellow and white building in the neighborhood of Tolstoy's first Moscow residence displays original texts, paintings and letters related to Tolstoy's masterpieces. Another room is dedicated to the religious philosophy that almost got him excommunicated. English captions. Open Tu-W 11am-5pm; *kassa* closes at 4:30pm. Closed last F of the month. 50R, students 30R. Camera 30R.

**Gorky Museum-House** (Музей-дом Горкого; Muzey-dom Gorkovo), ul. Malaya Nikitskaya 6/2 (Малая Никитская; ☎290 51 30). M3: Arbatskaya. From the Metro, cross Novy Arbat and turn right onto Merzlyakovsky per. (Мерзляковский пер.) Cross the small park and to the apartment. The entrance is on the street just to the left and through the small courtyard. A pilgrimage site more for its architectural interest than for its collection of Maxim Gorky's possessions. Designed by Shekhtel in 1900, this is one of the best examples of Art Nouveau. The main staircase is modeled to project the feeling and movement of waves on the sea. English captions. Open W and F noon-7pm, Th and Sa-Su 10am-5pm. Closed last Th of the month. Free; 5-10R donations requested.

**Stanislavsky Museum-House** (Музей-дом Станиславского; Muzey-dom Stanislavskovo), Leontevsky per. 6 (Леонтьевский; ☎229 24 42 and 229 28 85). M7: Pushkinskaya. Walk down ul. Tverskaya and take a right onto ul. Leontevsky. The respected theater director held lessons and performances in his home. Ask the *babushka* at the *kassa* if you can see the collections of costumes in the basement used for famous productions of Gogol's *The Government Inspector* and Shakespeare's *Othello*. Open Th and Sa-Su 11am-6pm, W and F 2-8pm. Closed last Th of the month. Concerts in June and July (info ☎488 88 92). Museum 70R; students 20R. Camera 10R.

**Gogol Museum** (Музей Гоголя; Muzey Gogolya), Nikitsky bul. 7 (☎291 12 40). M3: Arbatskaya. Cross Novy Arbat and take the 1st right onto Nikitsky bul. through the large courtyard on the left; the entrance is on the right. Gogol worked on the 2nd volume of *Dead Souls* while living here in the house of his friend A.P. Tolstoy (a distant cousin of Leo). The furniture in the bedroom/study where Gogol worked standing up and slept sitting up was reconstructed from descriptions by Turgenev. On the other side of the foyer is the library where Gogol first read *The Inspector General* and where he died at age 42. Open M and W-F noon-7pm, Sa-Su noon-5pm. Closed last day of the month. Free.

**Chekhov Museum-House** (Музей-дом Чехова; Muzey-dom Chekhova), ul. Sadovaya-Kudrinskaya 6 (Садовая-Кудринская; ☎291 61 54). M7: Barrikadnaya. Exiting the Metro, turn left onto ul. Barrikadnaya, then left again onto Sadovaya-Kudrinskaya; the house is on the right. Chekhov lived here with a baffling number of relatives from 1886 until 1890, writing, receiving patients, and thinking deep thoughts. English captions. Open Tu, Th, and Sa-Su 11am-5pm, W and F 2-6pm; last entrance 1hr. before closing. Closed last day of the month. 10R, students 8R.

**Lermontov House-Museum** (Дом-музей Лермонтова; Dom-muzey Lermontova), ul. Malaya Molchanovka 2 (Малая Молчановка; ☎291 52 98). M3: Arbatskaya. Off Novy Arbat, in the pink house behind the Sport Bar (Спорт Бар). A display devoted to the life and works of Pushkin's poetic heir. Open Th and Sa-Su 11am-4pm, W and F 2-8pm. Closed last F of the month. 5R.

# 🎵 ENTERTAINMENT

Moscow is a fast-paced metropolis, with the recreational options to prove it. Renowned theater, opera, and ballet companies provide a healthy injection of culture to go with the sights and shopping. Fortunately for moviegoers, many new cinemas offer imports in English. Of these, the **American House of Theater**, Radisson-Slavyanskaya Hotel, Berezhovskaya nab. 2, 2nd floor is the largest. (☎ 941 87 47. M4: Kievskaya. 200R.) **Dom Khanzhonkova** (Дом Ханжонкова), Triumphalnaya pl. 1, to the left of the Mayakovskaya Metro stop, is the only cinema in Moscow that consistently shows new Russian films, even when they're awful. (☎ 251 58 60. Tickets 25-100R.) **Muzey Kino** (Музей Кино), Drushinikovskaya ul. 15, on the left side of the Cinema Center building, shows classics, some with subtitles. (M6: Krasnopresnenskaya.) Check the Friday *Moscow Times* for all movie listings.

## THEATER, BALLET, AND OPERA

Summer is the wrong season for theater in Moscow. Russian companies not on vacation are on tour and the only folks playing in Moscow are touring productions from other cities, which, with the exception of those from St. Petersburg, tend to be of lesser quality. Starting in September and running well through June, however, Moscow boasts some of the world's best theater, ballet, and opera, as well as excellent orchestras. If you buy tickets far enough in advance and don't demand front row center, you can attend very cheaply (US$2-5). Tickets can usually be purchased from the *kassa* located inside the theater. (Usually open noon until curtain.) Tickets to most events are also sold at the "Театры" kiosks around the city.

Scalpers and Intourist (see **Tours, p. 610**) often snatch up tickets to performances at the Bolshoy and the Tchaikovsky Concert Hall, so if you have no luck at the box office, hang outside the theater. Scalpers look around a lot and ask if tickets are needed with the not-so-subtle *"Bilety nada?"* or *"Bilety nuzhny?"* ("Need tickets?"). Haggle over what you think is a fair price. Always check back at the *kassa* to be sure you're not getting hosed. At the *kassa*, ask for the cheapest tickets (самый дешёвый; samy deshovy), which usually go for 30-250R at the Bolshoy Theater and 30-100R at the Tchaikovsky Concert Hall.

**Bolshoy Teatr,** Teatralnaya pl. 1 (Большой Театр; ☎ 292 00 50; fax 292 90 32). M2: Teatralnaya. Literally, "The Big Theater." Home to both the opera and the world-renowned ballet companies, Bolshoy performances are consistently excellent. Champagne and caviar served at intermission under crystal chandeliers. *Kassa* open noon-7pm. Daily performances Sept.-June at noon and 7pm. Tickets 30-1000R.

**Maly Teatr,** Teatralnaya pl. 1/6 (Малый Театр; ☎ 923 26 21). M2: Teatralnaya. Just right of the Bolshoy. Literally, "The Small Theater." Affiliate at Bolshaya Ordynka 69 (☎ 237 31 81 and 237 44 72). Shows a different production every night, mostly Russian classics of the 19th and 20th centuries. All performances in Russian. *Kassa* open Tu-Su noon-3pm and 4-6:30pm. Daily performances at 7pm. Tickets start at 20-35R.

**Musical Operetta Theater,** ul. Bolshaya Dmitrovka 6 (☎ 292 04 05), to the left of the Bolshoy. Completes the M2: Teatralnaya theater triumvirate. Famous operettas staged year-round. Performances M-Th 11am or noon and 7pm, F-Su 6pm. Tickets 25-250R.

**Tchaikovsky Conservatory's Big and Small Halls,** Triumfalnaya pl. 4/31 (☎ 299 36 81 and 299 39 57). M2: Mayakovskaya. During intermission, locals sneak into the Bolshoi Zal (Большой Зал; Grand Hall) to admire its pipe organ and chandeliers. Scalpers may lie and say no tickets are available when the *kassa* will sell them more cheaply. Concerts almost daily at 7pm plus Su 2pm. *Kassa* in big hall open daily noon-7pm. 100 to several thousand rubles, depending on the program. Back-row tickets for the Maly Zal (Малый Зал; Small Hall) 5R. Closed in summer.

**Taganka Theater** (Театр Таганкой), Zemlyanoi Val 76 (Земляной Вал; ☎ 915 12 17). M5, 7: Taganskaya. Directly across the street from the ring line exit. This avant-garde theater is the only reason to come to this oppressive square on the loud and dusty Garden Ring. *Kassa* open daily noon-3pm and 4-8pm. Performances at 7pm.

**Stanislavsky Theater,** ul. Tverskaya 23 (Тверская; ☎ 299 72 24). M2: Tverskaya. Avant-garde productions. *Kassa* open daily Sept.-June 30 noon-3pm and 4-7pm. From 30R.

## CIRCUS

**Old Moscow State Circus,** Tsvetnoi Bulvar 13 (☎200 06 68). M9: Tsvetnoi Bulvar. Turn right and walk half a block; it's on the right, recently renovated. Animal acts in the 1st half and a glittery acrobatic performance in the 2nd. Great for non-Russophones. Don't miss the motorcycle acrobat act of Oleshchenko and Shavro or Piotr Prostetsov's trained dogs. New lions and tigers act. Plan on buying your ticket to the popular show 2-3 days in advance, or shop around among the eager scalpers outside. Performances M and W-F 7pm, Sa-Su 3pm and 7pm. *Kassa* open daily 11am-7pm. Tickets 100-150R.

## BANYAS

If weeks of traveling on sweltering, crowded trains and living out of a backpack have you feeling not-so-fresh, a trip to a Russian *banya* (bath) is in order. Similar in theory to a Turkish bath, the *banya* experience is a cyclical whirlwind of hot and cold extremes that rejuvenate via shock therapy. The men's and women's sections of each *banya* are divided into four rooms. First stop is the dressing room, staffed by attendants who rent linen, assign places, and sell drinks and snacks. Next comes the shower room, the self-explanatory step. The *paulka* (steam room) is the 3rd and most lavishly praised room of the *banya*. With temperatures upwards of 110°F and the air thick with the fragrance of scented oils, the steam's magic will draw out your tensions, along with a lot of sweat. Before you pass out, escape to the cooling relief of the dipping pool, designed to quickly lower the body temperature. The final stage is a return to the *paulka*, this time engaging in the quasi-masochistic tradition of the birch branches. While showering, soften a bundle of birch branches with hot water, then beat yourself vigorously to exfoliate dead skin, improve circulation, or simply blend in with the locals. *Banya* sessions typically last two hours; prices are listed for the standard experience, but myriad other services, including massages and manicures, can be enjoyed at an additional cost. Save a few rubles by bringing a towel, sheet, soap and shampoo.

**Sandunovskie Bani** (Сандуновские Бани), ul. Neglinnaya 14 (Неглиння; ☎925 46 31). M1: Kuznetsky Most. Moscow's oldest and most luxurious *banya* features high ceilings, cavernous rooms, and classical statues. 2hr. sessions 200-500R, depending on luxury. Extra services available, with massages starting at 200R. Open daily 8am-8pm.

**Bani Na Presnye** (Бани На Пресне), Stolyarny per. 7 (Столярный; ☎255 53 06). M7: Ulitsa 1905 goda. Large and sparsely decorated, this modern *banya* is crowded on weekends. Ice-cold dipping pool and refreshing lemon-infused chai tea (pot 25R). 2hr. sessions 200R, weekends 250R. Open M and W-Su 8am-10pm, Tu 2-10pm.

## ◨ NIGHTLIFE

Moscow's nightlife boasts the most kickin' action this side of the Volga and is certainly the most varied, expensive, and dangerous in Eastern Europe. Unfortunately, many of the more interesting clubs enjoy flaunting their high cover charges and strict face-control policies. Restaurants often transform into dance clubs after dark, while myriad casinos stay open all hours of the night. Check the weekend editions of *The Moscow Times* or *The Moscow Tribune* for club reviews and music festival listings, including the annual jazz festival. *The Moscow Times'* Friday pull-out section, *The Beat*, provides an excellent synopsis of each week's events, as well as up-to-date restaurant, bar, and club reviews. Cheaper and more popular bars on isolated streets may be a better time than the dark, *faux*-elegant, expensive "bars" close to the center, which cater to New Russians or to no one at all.

## DANCE AND LIVE MUSIC

▨ **Propaganda** (Пропаганда), Bolshoy Zlatoustinsky per. 7 (Большой Златоустинский; ☎924 57 32). M6, 7: Kitai-Gorod. Exiting the Metro, walk down ul. Maroseika and take a left on Bolshoy Zlatoustinsky per.; the club is on the right. Once voted 1 of the best clubs in Europe, Propaganda is the best place in Moscow to dance without feeling like you're in a meat market. Hip, unpretentious student crowd with a hefty percentage of backpackers. DJs drop ill beat. Hopping, even on Su. Beer 50-65R. Cover F-Sa 70R. Open M-W and Su noon-12:30am, Th noon-3am, F 10pm-6am, Sa 3pm-6am.

**Hungry Duck,** Pushechnaya ul. 9 (Пушечная; ☎923 61 58). M1: Kuznetsky Most. Just left of the Metro station. Enter the courtyard and follow the red neon arrows in. There's no sign, which is just as well since no one can agree whether it's called "Fiesta" or "Hungry Duck." (see **Hungry for More,** above). Lively crowd dances on the table, the bar, and everywhere in between (until they fall over drunk, that is). Tu Ladies' Night: women drink free while watching male strippers. W Oktoberfest: all-you-can-drink beer for 200R. Th Latin Night: 2-for-1 Corona and an erotic dance by a 250lb. woman. Beer 60-90R. Cover for men 100-200R, women free-50R. Open daily 8pm-6am.

**TaxMan,** Krymsky Val. 10 (Крымский Вал; ☎238 08 64). M6: Oktyabrskaya. Exiting the Metro, walk downhill on Krymsky val. TaxMan is on the right side of the Central House of Artists, opposite the entrance to Gorky Park. Inexpensive drinks and musical variety attract a mixed but low-key crowd. Bar and dancing downstairs, bar and billiards upstairs. Beer 40R. Cover (after 7pm) varies, usually 70-90R. Open daily noon-6am.

**Krizis Zhanra,** Prechistensky per. 22/4 (Пречистенский; ☎241 19 28). M1: Kropotkin-skaya. From the Metro, walk down ul. Prechistenka (Пречистенка) away from Church of Christ the Savior. Take the 3rd right onto Prechistensky per. Enter the courtyard on the right at #18 and turn left; club is on the left. One of the best places in Moscow to grab a beer. Extremely popular with local and foreign students alike. Czech beers 50R. Live concerts pack 'em in daily 8:30-11pm—arrive early. Open daily 11am-11pm.

**Trety Put** (Третий Путь; 3rd Way), ul. Pyatnitskaya 4 (Пятницкая; ☎951 87 34). M2: Novokuznetskaya. Turn right out of the Metro onto ul. Pyatnitskaya. The club is on the left side, on the 2nd floor. A sign informs visitors that the club's name refers to an ideal state of communion of souls without language. Whether or not it reaches that state, this funky apartment welcomes guests to a number of little rooms to watch videos, play chess, or dance to psychedelic music. Cover 50-100R. Open F-Sa 10pm-6am.

**Respublika Beefeater,** ul. Nikolskaya 17 (☎928 46 92). M2, 3: Pl. Revolutsii. Follow the signs to ul. Nikolskaya and walk away from Red Square; the bar is on the left. Great dance music and a student crowd. Beer 60R. Occasional live music, Th jazz. Cover F-Sa men 100R, women 50R; variable when there's a concert. Open daily 11am-6am.

**Master** (Мастер), ul. Pavlovskaya 6 (Парловская; ☎237 37 91). M9: Serpukhovskaya. Turn right onto Stremyanny per., then take the 1st right on bul. Serpukhovskaya. Follow it for 10 min.; the club is on the right, just after the giant intersection. Mostly main-stream techno. 2 dance floors, 4 bars. Beer 35-50R. Female strippers F and Sa. Cover 50-70R before 1am, 100R after. Open W 7pm-11:30pm, Th-Su 7pm-6am.

**HUNGRY FOR MORE** Almost as much of a Moscow landmark as the Kremlin, the Hungry Duck was known internationally for its debauched parties and Sodom-and-Gomorrah-esque Ladies' Nights. Women were cattle-called into the bar hours before men to consume mass quantities of alcohol and participate in strip shows and bar-dancing. By the time the women were too drunk to protest, hordes of desperate men—backpackers, mafiosos, and Russian businessmen alike—were let loose, and the floodgates of testosterone were opened. If the live sex shows weren't enough, bathrooms, bars, and not-so-dark corners all became impromptu bordellos as the masses got busy to the sonic sex pulsing over the sound system. By the end of a Ladies' Night, over 200 people would get laid, at least three plastered women would have to be carried out of the bar, and more than a few fights broke out. The Hungry Duck closed without explanation in 1999. Since then, the true heir to the Hungry Duck's legacy has been a subject of dispute. The club in the original location, after a brief period under the name Fiesta, has reverted to the old and infamous name with a lot of the old and infamous action. Some claim, however, that the true spirit of "the Duck" now resides at the Boar's Head Cafe, or that it fled to TaxMan, near the State Tretyakov Gallery.

**Bednye Lyudi** (Бедные Люди; Poor Folk), ul. Bolshaya Ordynka 11/6 (Большая Ордынка; ☎951 33 42). M8: Tretyakovskaya. Follow the signs to ul. Bolshaya Ordynka out of the Metro, and walk toward Red Square. The club is on a side street to the right. Converted basement has live rock/alternative nightly. Separate rooms for dancing, chatting, and billiards make it a favorite haunt for young Russians. Beer 20-55R. Cover Su-Th 60R; F-Sa 100R. Open daily 5pm-5am.

## EXPAT HANGOUTS

**Doug and Marty's Boar House,** Zemlyanoi val 26 (☎917 01 50). M3: Kurskaya, opposite the train station. Formerly known as the Chesterfield Cafe (the giant papier-mache boar's head over the bar serves as a reminder of the change). About as American as you can get in Moscow, prices included. Packed on weekends. Happy hour 3-6pm. 50% discount on food 5am-9pm. Beer 50-110R. Cover for men 100R, women 60R. Open 24hr. AmEx/MC/Visa.

**Moosehead Canadian Bar,** ul. Bolshaya Polyanka 54 (Большая Полянка; ☎230 73 33). M5: Dobryninskaya. Take a left through the *perekhod,* then another left onto Bolshaya Polyanka. Moosehead is in a little enclave on the left. Nondescript Western bar could be in any North American city, from Winnipeg to Williamstown. Popular with Russians as well as expats. Good food, cheap drinks. Buffalo wings (Tu 3 for US$1). Beer US$2-3. Happy Hour M-F 6-8pm. Open Su-W noon-2am, Th-Sa noon-5am.

**Sports Bar,** Novy Arbat 10 (☎290 43 11). M3: Arbatskaya. A true paradise for Eurosport fans: 8 TVs and a large screen display the game from every angle. The 2 floors fill up fast for big games; at other times, head upstairs to shoot pool, throw darts, and watch New Russians compare their New Cellular Phones. The disco is a late-night hotspot. Higher drink prices than your neighborhood sports bar—think 100R per beer. Live music nightly 8-11pm. Happy Hour 5-8pm featuring 2-for-1 beer. Bar open daily noon-6am; disco 11pm-6am. AmEx/MC/Visa.

**John Bull Pub,** ul. Krasnaya Presnya 25 (Красная Пресня; ☎252 55 40). M7: Ulitsa 1905 Goda. 2 blocks down from McDonald's. Also at Smolenskaya Pl. 4 (☎241 06 44). M3: Smolenskaya. An English pub with US$5 draft beers. Live pop bands, karaoke, and blues nights. Open Su-Th noon-midnight, F-Sa noon-2am. AmEx/MC/Visa.

**Rosie O'Grady's,** ul. Znamenko 9/12 (Знаменко; ☎203 90 87). M9: Borovitskaya. Go right out of the Metro, then right on ul. Znamenko. Pub is on the left, at ul. Marxa i Engelsa. Typical Irish pub. Guinness 135R. Open daily noon until the last guest leaves.

## BI-GAY-LESBIAN NIGHTLIFE

**Shans** (Шанс; Chance), ul. Volochayevskaya 11/5 (Волочаевская; ☎956 71 02; www.gay.ru/chance), in Dom Kultury Serp i Molot (Дом Культуры Серп и Молот). M8: Ploshchad Ilicha. Walk down ul. Sergia Radonezhskovo all the way through the 3rd open driveway on your right. When you see tram tracks on the road, turn and walk up the stairs. It's on top of the hill, straight ahead. The oldest gay club in Moscow, with 3 bars, a restaurant, nightly strip shows, and aquariums—some with naked men in them. The club is popular with everyone and the crowd is a mixture of ravers, punks, students, and New Russians; it's more "gay-friendly" than strictly gay. Downstairs dance music; upstairs Russian pop. Plush sofas ensure you get to know even those too timid to dance. Very Euro—black attire is *de rigeur*. Beers 40-60R. Cover up to 200R depending on time, day, and gender. Open daily 11pm-6am.

# 🔃 DAYTRIP FROM MOSCOW

## SERGIEV POSAD (СЕРГИЕВ ПОСАД)

Elektrichki *(commuter trains)* run to Sergiev Posad from Yaroslavsky Vokzal *(1½hr., every 30-40min., 32R round-trip). Departure times are listed immediately outside the prigorod-naya kassa (suburban cashier; пригородная касса). Any train with the destination "Sergiev Posad" or "Aleksandrov" (Александров) will get you there. The announcement boards in front of the trains often don't work, but tiny strips on the sides of the trains show their destinations. Alternatively, purchase a one-way train ticket (16R) and return via the*

*"Москва-ВВЦ" bus outside the Sergiev Posad station (10R, every 15min.). To get to the monastery from the station, turn right and follow the road that goes past the right side of the rynok (рынок; market) until you see the domes. Open 8am-6pm. English tours 240R. Museums open 10am-5:30pm; kassa closes 4:45pm. Free, but fees for the ramparts, the sacristy, the art museum, and the historical museum. Cameras 100R.*

Possibly Russia's most famous pilgrimage point, Sergiev Posad attracts wandering Orthodox believers with a mass of churches huddled at its main sight—**St. Sergius's Trinity Monastery** (Троицко-Сергиева Лавра; Troitsko-Sergieva Lavra). During Soviet times Sergiev Posad was called Zagorsk and many locals still use the name. After decades of state-propagated atheism, the stunning monastery, founded in the 1340s, has again become a religious center and monks pace the paths among the colorful churches and gardens. The patriarch of the Russian Orthodox Church, also known as the Metropolitan, resided here until 1988, when he moved to the Danilovsky Monastery in Moscow (see **Religious Sights**, p. 620).

Each church is exquisite, but Russian Orthodoxy's opulent colors come out in the **Trinity Cathedral** (Троицкий Собор; Troitsky Sobor), filled with gilded Andrei Rublyov icons. The **Refectory** (Трапезная; Trapeznaya), with its vine-clad columns, delights with a magnificently frescoed ceiling. The **Chapel-at-the-Well** (Надкладезная Часовия; Nadkladeznaya Chasoviya) has an appropriately superstitious history—one day, a spring with magical healing powers allegedly appeared inside a tiny chapel in the monastery. *Babushki* still come here with empty bottles to carry the holy water home. Next door, **Assumption Cathedral** (Успенский Собор; Uspensky Sobor), was modeled after the eponymous cathedral in Moscow's Kremlin and proves its equal in splendor. Outside the door on the left is the grave of Boris Godunov, who, among other things, has the distinction of being the only Russian tsar not buried in Moscow's Kremlin or St. Petersburg's St. Peter and Paul Cathedral. As in any active Orthodox monastery, women should cover their heads.

# GOLDEN RING (ЗОЛОТОЕ КОЛЬЦО)

To the north and west of Moscow lies a series of towns known as the Golden Ring (Zolotoye Koltso), home to ancient churches and kremlins (fortresses) widely considered the most beautiful in Russia. Many reached their zenith in the 12th century, as power shifted north with the weakening of Kyiv, and have spent the subsequent years trying to maintain their importance in a constantly changing nation. Vladimir and Suzdal were once Russian capitals and still maintain kremlins of extraordinary elegance; Yaroslavl was the capital of its own principality in the 13th century and is today one of the most attractive cities in Russia. An array of architectural monuments and slow pace of life make the Golden Ring a truly unique part of Russia.

## YAROSLAVL (ЯРОСЛАВЛЬ)  ☎(8)852

Yaroslavl (yi-ra-SLAH-vl) acquired its wealth and prosperity from 16th-century trade with the Middle East and the West, and has fought hard to have things its own way. Case in point: when Prince Yaroslav the Wise considered settling here, the townspeople chased him out of town with a wild bear. This century, the citizens of Yaroslavl have fought just as fiercely to ward off Soviet architectural monstrosities. With its wide, green boulevards, romantic river walks, numerous parks, and proximity to Moscow, Yaroslavl offers the best of two worlds—provincial charm with capital-city comforts.

### ◼ ORIENTATION

Yaroslavl lies at the confluence of the **Volga** and **Kotorosl** (Которосль) **Rivers,** 280km northeast of Moscow. Locals call the corner where the Kotorosl meets the Volga *strelka* (стрелка; promontory). From Glavny Vokzal (Главный Вокзал; Main Station), ul. Svobody (Свободьи) leads to the center at **pl. Volkova,** the origin of most bus lines. Ul. Kirova (Кирова) runs north out of this square toward the Volga. **Ul. Komsomolskaya** (Комсомольская) and **ul. Pervomayskaya** (Первомайская) are the center's main west-east thoroughfares; at the southern end the streets converge on **pl. Bogoyavlenskaya** (Богоявленская). Here, the six-lane Moskovsky pr. (Московский пр.) runs east across the Kotorsol to **Moskovsky Vokzal,** the secondary train and primary bus station. From Moskovsky Vokzal, cross Moskovsky pr. and take trolley #9 three stops to pl. Volkova. From Glavny Vokzal, trolley #1 reaches pl. Volkova in six stops. In an attempt to avoid confusion, street signs often list a whole genealogy of names, resulting in posts bearing up to four different plates. Cyrillic **maps** of the center are sold at the House of War Books (Дом Военной Книги) at Pervomayskaya 39 (Первомайская) for 20R. It's best to avoid Yaroslavl around June 20th, graduation day for the town's two military academies.

## ▐ TRANSPORTATION

**Trains: Glavny Vokzal** (☎ 79 21 12 and 79 21 11), connected to pl. Volkova by trolley #1. Trains run to: **Vologda** (4hr., 2-3 per day, 40-43R); **Moscow** (4½hr., 13 per day, 44-48R); and **St. Petersburg** (13hr., 2 per day, 80-113R). From **Moskovsky Vokzal,** on trolley lines #5 and 9 from Bogoyavlenskaya pl., trains leave for **Nizhny Novgorod** (8½hr., 1 per day, 67R). *Kassa* #4 open 24hr.

**Buses: Avtovokzal,** in the same building as Moskovsky Vokzal. Buses to: **Vologda** (4½hr., 1 per day, 77R) and **Vladimir** (5½hr., 1 per day, 80R).

**Local Transportation:** Yaroslavl's local transportation system is excellent, even by Russian standards; trolleys and buses stop every 2min. Trolley #9 runs up and down Moskovsky pr. through pl. Volkova to Leninsky pr. (Ленинский). Trolley #1 travels from Glavny Vokzal to the center. Buy tickets (2R) at the light-blue kiosks next to main stops labeled "яргортранс продажа проездных документов;" once aboard, hand your ticket to the person with the black waist pouch. 8R fine for getting caught ticketless.

## ▐ PRACTICAL INFORMATION

**Tourist Office: Intourist,** Kotoroslnaya nab. 11a (Которосльная; ☎ 72 65 65; fax 30 54 13), on the 1st floor of Gostinitsa Yubileynaya (see below). English-speaking staff leads tours, sells pamphlets, and books hotel rooms for less than most places, but for a commission. Open M-F 9am-5pm.

**Currency Exchange:** One of the best options is **Sberbank,** ul. Kirova 16, which also cashes AmEx and Thomas Cook **traveler's checks** for a 3% commission. Open M-Sa 8:30am-1pm and 2-6:30pm, Su 9am-1pm and 2-4pm.

**ATM:** There is a Cirrus/Plus ATM in the post office (see below).

**Luggage Storage:** Available at Glavny Vokzal for 8.50R per day. Open 24hr.

**Telephone Office:** In the same building as the post office. Prepay at the counter to get a booth. 3 tones mean the call has yet to go through. Press the "ответ" button when someone answers. Buy tokens for local and intercity calls (1.43R and 4.72R) at the same booth; for the latter, use phones labeled "междугородный автомат" (intercity automatic; mezhdugorodny avtomat), which malfunction frequently. Open 24hr.

**Post Office:** 22/28 Bogoyavlenskaya pl. (Богоявленская; ☎ 22 37 28), opposite the monastery and down ul. Komsomolskaya from pl. Volkova. Open M-Sa 8am-8pm, Su 8am-6pm.

**Postal code:** 150 000.

## ▐ ACCOMMODATIONS

Yaroslavl has always been popular among both Russians and foreigners, and its hotel prices are consequently high. Foreigners are often charged more than Russians. With some luck and some sacrifice of convenience, it is possible to get by on a tight budget. Rooms are scarce come summer. Ask what kind of room you're getting; if they have no vacancies in the kind you're requesting, they may upgrade you to a more expensive room without telling you until they hand you the bill.

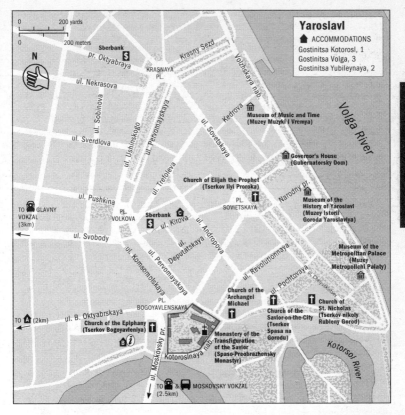

**Yaroslavl**

🏠 ACCOMMODATIONS
Gostinitsa Kotorosl, 1
Gostinitsa Volga, 3
Gostinitsa Yubileynaya, 2

RUSSIA

**Gostinitsa Kotorosl** (Которосль), ul. B. Oktyabrskaya 87 (Б. Октябрьская; ☎21 15 81; fax 21 64 68). 2 stops on tram #3 from Glavny Vokzal. This pink palace offers brand-new rooms at reasonable rates. All rooms with TV and telephone. Singles with private bath 310R; doubles with bath 560R.

**Gostinitsa Volga** (Волга), ul. Kirova 10 (☎30 81 31; fax 72 82 76). From pl. Volkova, walk south toward pl. Bogoyavlenskaya and take a left on ul. Kirova. Excellent location and spacious rooms, but watch out for the mosquitoes. Check-out noon. Singles with bath 830R; doubles 240R, with bath 1160R; triples 270R. 25% added to first night if you reserve in advance.

**Gostinitsa Yubileynaya** (Юбилейная), Kotoroslnaya nab. 11a (Которосльная; ☎30 92 59; call Intourist (see above) for English info. From pl. Volkova, walk down Komsomol-skaya ul. to pl. Bogoyavlenskaya (Богоявленская). Pass the church on your left and turn right at the river. This 7-floor hotel is comfortable. In the summer, ask for a room on the back side if you're not paying the extra charge for A/C; front ones have a nice view but get incredibly hot. Singles US$30; doubles US$50.

**Gostinitsa Yuta** (Юта), ul. Respublikanskaya 79 (Республиканская; ☎21 87 93). Old but spacious rooms. Eager, helpful staff. TV, phone, and private bath in every room. Singles 380R; doubles 450R.

## 🍴 FOOD

Sidewalk cafes hawking beer, ice cream, and sweet rolls reign supreme in Yaroslavl, where restaurants seem outnumbered by cathedrals. Stock up on produce at the **tsentralny rynok** (центральный рынок; central market), ul. Deputatskaya 15 (Депутатская; open M-Sa 8am-6pm, Su 8am-4pm). The central and crowded **grocery** at Kirova 13 sells just about everything else. (Open daily 8am-10pm.)

**Cafe Aktyor** (Актёр; actor), ul. Kirova 5 (☎ 72 75 43). Follow the cartoons up the stairs to this little Russian cafe. A stage, velvet curtains, and theater posters. The chocolate-banana *bliny* (30R) are heavenly. Full meals with beer 125R. Open daily 8am-11pm.

**Restaurant Rus** (Ресторан Русь), ul. Kirova 10 (Кирова; ☎ 72 94 08). Typical Russian cuisine, but with more veggies than most. Fortunately, the prices aren't as high as the green velvet draperies suggest. Full meals 200-250R. Open daily noon-midnight.

**Cafe Lira** (Лира), Volzhskaya nab. 43 (☎ 22 21 38), 1 block south of the river station. The food is unexciting, but for romance this cafe's location by the Volga can't be beat. Full meals 150R. Open daily noon-11pm.

## ◉ SIGHTS

**MONASTERY OF THE TRANSFIGURATION OF THE SAVIOR.** (Спасо-Преображенский Монастырь; Spaso-Preobrazhensky Monastyr.) The fortified monastery, pl. Bogoyavlenskaya 25, has been guarding the banks of the Kotorosl since the 12th century. The high white walls surround a number of buildings and exhibitions, which, frustratingly, all have separate entrance fees. Enter the grounds through the **Holy Gate** (Святые Ворота; Svyatye Vorota), on the side facing the Kotorosl. Climb to the top of the popular **bell tower** (звонница; zvonnitsa) just inside, for a spectacular view of the city. *(Open daily 10am-5:30pm. 20R, students 7R.)* To the right behind the bell tower sits a cluster of museum exhibits. The best of these is the **Old Russian Art exhibit** (Древнерусское и Народно-Прикладное Искусство; Drevnerusskoye i Narodno-Prikladnoe Iskusstvo), containing icons, embroidery, enamel work, and wood sculpture. *(12R, students 4R.)* On the other side of the complex is the **exhibit** on the **Song of Igor's Campaign** (Экспозиция Слово о Полку Игореве; Ekspozitsiya Slovo o Polku Igoreve), dedicated to the discovery and publication of one of the first literary creations of Old Russia, dating from the 12th century and found on the monastery grounds in the late 18th century. *(12R, students 4R.)* The exhibits are often difficult to understand, as foreign-language guides are not available, and only the art museum has scattered English signs. *(Monastery open daily 8am-7pm. Exhibitions open Tu-Su 10am-5:30pm; kassa closes at 4:30. Monastery 12R, students 4R. Entrance free with purchase of tickets to museum.)*

**CHURCH OF THE ELIJAH THE PROPHET.** (Tserkov Ilyi Proroka; Церковь Ильи Пророка.) Perhaps Yaroslavl's most beautiful church, the Church of Elijah the Prophet lies on Sovetskaya pl. (Советская) at the end of ul. Kirova. Built in the 17th century in traditional Yaroslavl style, its elaborate and lovingly-restored iconostasis and frescoes flood the interior with color. *(Open M-Tu and Th-Su 10am-1pm and 2-6pm. 20R, students 7R. Camera 20R, video 50R.)*

**ART MUSEUM.** (Художественный Музей; Khudozhestvenny Muzey.) The Art Museum has two branches. The first, **Museum of the Metropolitan Palace** (Музей Митрополичьи Палаты; Muzey Metropolichi Palaty), displays the best of Yaroslavl's icons—the intricate ones in the 3rd room are especially beautiful. *(Volzhskaya nab. 1. ☎ 72 92 84 and 30 86 65. Open Sa-Th 10am-5pm; kassa closes 4:30pm. 60R, students 30R.)* The modern branch, in the former **Governor's house,** displays 18th- to 20th-century Russian paintings and sculpture, mostly by local artists, with a few famous names thrown in. *(Volzhskaya nab. 23. ☎ 30 35 04. Open Tu-Su 10am-6pm; kassa closes 5pm. 60R. Camera 20R, video 50R.)*

**CHURCH OF THE EPIPHANY.** (Церковь Богоявления; Tserkov Bogoyavleniya.) Across from the monastery and farther from the Volga, the red-brick Church of the Epiphany shows off fragments of frescoes recovered from destroyed Yaroslavl churches. The main room has an ornately carved Baroque iconostasis and several beautiful frescoes in dire need of restoration. *(Pl. Bogoyavlenskaya. Open W-M 10am-1pm and 2-5pm. Knock on the door if the church seems closed. 12R, students 4R. Camera 10R.)*

**CHURCH OF THE ARCHANGEL MICHAEL.** (Церковь Архангела Михаила; Tserkov Arkhangela Mikhaila.) Across from the corner of the monastery nearest the *strelka*, the Church of the Archangel Michael thrusts a similar set of red brick and green domes skyward, and also shelters frescoes by local artists. *(Open daily 9am-8pm. Services F-Su 5pm, liturgy Sa-Su 9am.)*

# VLADIMIR (ВЛАДИМИР)  ☎ (8)922

RUSSIA

Once the capital of Russia and headquarters of the Russian Orthodox Church, Vladimir (vlad-IH-mir) suffered at the hands of the Tatars and eventually fell to Moscow in the early 14th century. Until that time, it had rivaled Kyiv in size and splendor. Now marked by 12th-century white stone monuments and splendid cathedrals, this city of 360,000 has old-world charm to spare. Avoid straying too far outside the older parts of the city, however; the sheer ugliness of the Soviet industrial buildings serves as a sad reminder of the "progress" that has occurred since the construction of the treasures of Vladimir.

## ▐ TRANSPORTATION

**Trains:** The station is on Vokzalnaya ul. (Вокзальная). To: Moscow's **Kursky Vokzal** (3hr., 8-10 per day, 40-55R) and **Nizhny Novgorod** (4hr., 6 per day, 65-80R). Trips to Moscow can be made on a regular train, or more cheaply and conveniently on a *prigorogny* (пригорогный; suburban) *elektrichka* train.

**Buses:** Across from the train station. To: **Moscow** (3½hr., 12-15 per day, 57-63R); **Yaroslavl** (5hr., 1 per day, 67-80R); and **Nizhny Novgorod** (5½hr., 6 per day, 65-77R).

## ▌▐ ORIENTATION AND PRACTICAL INFORMATION

The old city stretches the length of a small ridge, along whose crest runs **ul. Bolshaya Moskovskaya** (Большая Московская), sometimes called by its former name, **ul. III-ego Internatsionala** (III-его интернационала), a 5min. walk uphill from the train station. Nearly everything of interest to tourists is on or near this street.

**Tourist Office: Excursionny Otdel** (Экскурсионный Отдел), ul. B. Moskovskaya 43 (☎ 34 42 63), arranges English-language tours of Vladimir and Suzdal. Open 9am-6pm.

**Currency Exchange: Sberbank,** ul. B. Moskovskaya 31, offers the most financial services, giving MC/Visa **cash advances** and cashing **traveler's checks** (AmEx, Visa, Thomas Cook, and Citicorp) for a 3% commission. It also has an **ATM** inside. Open M-F 9:20am-12:30pm and 1:30-5pm.

**Telephones:** The train station houses a 24hr. **telephone office** that serves only Russian cities. A 25R **telephone card** is required to use these phones (good for about 4min. to Moscow). For **international calls**, head to Peregovorny Punkt (Переговорный Пункт), Gorkovo 60 (Горького). Take trolley #2 or 8 down ul. Gagarina between the Cathedrals and the Golden Gate off ul. B. Moskovskaya to pl. Lenina.

**Internet Access:** Slow but functional internet connections are available on the 3rd floor of ul. Gagarina 2. Walk southwest on B. Moskovskaya from Gostinitsa Vladimir (see below), then take a right on ul. Gagarina (Гагарина) at the 1st traffic signal after Cathedral Square. Open M-Th 8:30am-6pm, F 8:30am-4:45pm. 0.75R per min.

**Post Office:** Ul. Podbelskovo 2; head down ul. Muzeynaya near the Excursionny Otdel, then turn left on Podbelskova. Open M-F 8am-8pm, Sa-Su 8am-6pm.

**Postal code:** 600 000

## ▐☼ ACCOMMODATIONS AND FOOD

Heading uphill on the far left path from the train station leads to **Gostinitsa Vladimir** (Гостиница Владимир), ul. B. Moskovskaya 74. Blissfully untroubled by competition, it rents clean and pleasant rooms with sinks. (☎ 32 72 39; fax 32 72 01. Singles 180R, with bath 400R; doubles with bath 600R.) Fax ahead to reserve, and expect a 25% first-night surcharge if they can save you a spot. The **grocery** next door is well-stocked and has non-carbonated mineral water at 6.70R for 1.5L. (Open M-F 9am-8pm, Sa 9am-7pm, Su 9am-5pm.) For cheap and greasy fare, the **Pirozhki Bar** at ul. B. Moskovskaya 22 (*pirozhki* 3-5R, main dishes 15-18R; open M-Sa 8am-8pm) and the **Pizzeria** (Кафе Пицца), ul. B. Moskovskaya 14 (pizza 30-40R; open daily 11am-3pm and 4-11pm) are excellent. For a bit more money and a lot less grease, **U Zolotykh Vorot** (У Золотых Ворот; By the Golden Gates), ul. B. Moskovskaya 15, will turn out a tasty Russian meal for around 200R. (☎32 31 16. Open daily noon-midnight.)

## ◉ SIGHTS

Walking left on B. Moskovskaya from Gostinitsa Vladimir, a fenced wooded park appears on the left. Go though the park to the drive behind it, then left to the 12th-century **St. Dmitry's Cathedral** (Дмитриевский Собор; Dmitrievsky Sobor), the only surviving building of Prince Vsevelod III's palace. Lavishly carved in stone, the cathedral's outer walls display the stories of Hercules, King David, and Alexander the Great. At press time, locked doors prevented visitors from viewing the Byzantine frescoes inside, as a major restoration project was underway. Farther down the hill, the brick **Museum of the History of the Vladimir Region** (Музей Истории Владимирского Края; Muzey Istorii Vladimirskovo Kraya), ul. B. Moskovskaya 64, has a satisfying—if predictable—collection of artifacts from the Stone Age through 1917, including mammoth tusks, suits of armor, and a model of the city as it looked in the 12th century. (☎34 22 84. Open Tu and F-Su 10am-4:30pm, W-Th 10am-3:30pm. Closed last Th of each month. 15R.) Directly in front of the drive behind the park is the yellow and white **Vladimir-Suzdal Historical, Archaeological, and Artistic Museum,** ul. B. Moskovskaya 58. As the name implies, there are a slew of exhibits, each with a separate entrance fee. The most worthwhile are: the Walk Through the Old City (Прогулка по старому городу; Progulka po staromu gorodu), whose period-costumed *babushki* delight children; the Picture Gallery (Картинная Галерея; Kartinnaya Galereya), which displays paintings from the 18th-20th centuries; and the exhibit on the lifestyle of the nobility (Минувших Оней Очарованье; Minuvshikh Onei Ocharovanye; ☎22 24 29; open Tu-W 10am-4pm and Th-Su 10am-5pm; closed last Th of the month; each exhibit 15R.) Up the hill, to the right of the museum, stands **Assumption Cathedral** (Успенский Собор; Uspensky Sobor). It once guarded one of the most famous icons in Russia, until it was taken by Moscow's Tretyakov Gallery. Fortunately, the Tretyakov couldn't take the frescoes by renowned artists Andrei Rublyov and Daniil Chiorny. The cathedral was begun in 1158, and in 1189 received four more domes and two more aisles—try to ignore the 19th-century bell tower. (Open Tu-Su 1:30-5pm. 15R. Respectful attire required.) In front of Assumption Cathedral lies **Cathedral Square** (Соборная Площадь; Sobornaya Ploshchad), a pleasant place to sit and watch the world go by.

Farther down ul. B. Moskovskaya, the 12th-century **Golden Gate** (Золотые Ворота; Zolotye Vorota; ☎22 25 59) stands triumphantly marking the end of the old city, unaware of all the traffic problems it causes by occupying the middle of the street. Just before you reach it, a path off to the left leads to the **Exhibit of Old Vladimir** (Выставка Старого Владимира; Vystavka Starovo Vladimira), in an old water tower. It displays assorted items from life in 19th-century Vladimir and offers a panoramic view of the old city. (☎254 51. Open Tu and F-Su 10am-5pm, W-Th 10am-4pm. Closed last F of the month. 15R.) Climb to the top of the Golden Gate itself for a brief military history of the city. Get the *babushki* to play the English version of the melodramatic soundtrack to the diorama of the 1238 battle against the Mongols. (Open M and Th 10am-4pm; and W and F-Su 10am-5pm. Closed last Th of the month. 15R.) Just beyond the gate, the early-20th-century **Trinity Church** houses an exhibit of **crystal** and **lacquer crafts.** (☎32 48 72. Open M and W 10am-4pm, Th-Su 10am-5pm. Closed last F of the month. 15R.)

# THE NORTHWEST

The Northwest provides a glimpse of the diverse types of beauty that vast Russia has to offer. The man-made glory of the Orthodox church and the tsars is the most famous—the kremlins and monasteries of Novgorod and Pskov, along with St. Petersburg and its nearby palaces, remind tourists of Russian opulence both sacred and secular. A subtler and yet equally appealing natural beauty lies in the lush greenery and lakes that dominate the landscape on the island of Schlisselburg. Finally, the pastoral charm of the countryside, where horse-drawn carts and *babushki* on bicycles traffic the landscape, confronts the traveler with the Russia that has puzzled intellectuals and politicians since the time of Peter the Great.

# ST. PETERSBURG ☎(8)812
# (САНКТ-ПЕТЕРБУРГ)

Remember, St. Petersburg is Russian...but it is not Russia.
—Tsar Nicholas II

Fed up with the backwardness of Moscow, Peter the Great set out to turn a Finnish swamp into his new capital—a "window on the West" that would architecturally and intellectually resemble the rest of Europe. Replete with grand palaces and graceful canals, Petersburg formed an ideal seat of government from which to write legislation aimed at dragging the rest of Russia toward the "enlightened" West.

Peter certainly did not intend for his beautiful capital to become the center of the revolutionary movement that would eventually oust his descendants from power and rename his city for their own leader, V.I. Lenin. Soviet authorities, however, particularly Stalin, remained suspicious of Leningrad's continued intellectualism and they turned away from the northern city in favor of proletarian Moscow. Even the damage caused by Soviet neglect paled in comparison to the fate that Leningrad suffered at the hands of the Nazis, during perhaps the worst 900 days of *any* city's history. The Germans besieged the city; many of those who survived the bombardments starved to death during the winter.

Reluctant as the Soviets were to embrace the city, they did shell out the funds for its reconstruction after the Nazi devastation, and today St. Petersburg stands once more as a modern "window on the West," with Italian fashion and American fast food storming the streets. The cultured intellectualism that has always defined the city continues to flourish; the multitude of world-class concert halls and theaters regularly fill up with attentive audiences. Many of the natives themselves, however, opt to pass the day in one of the city's many parks, where time drifts by almost unnoticed. Indeed, the passage of time means very little in this city, where the glory and suffering of the past seem as close to the surface as if they had occurred a decade ago, rather than a lifetime. Moscow may be the embodiment of Mother Russia's bold, post-apocalyptic youth, but St. Petersburg remains the majestic and mysterious symbol of Peter's great Russian dream.

## ◤ ORIENTATION

St. Petersburg sits at the mouth of the **Neva river** (Нева) on the **Gulf of Finland** (Finsky Zaliv; Финский Залив), occupying 44 islands interspersed among 50 canals. The city center lies on mainland St. Petersburg between the south bank of the Neva and the north bank of the **Fontanka River. Nevsky Prospekt** (Невский Проспект) is the cultural heart of the city. Most of St. Petersburg's major sights—including the Winter and Summer Palaces, the Hermitage, and the city's three main cathedrals—are on Nevsky pr. South and east of the Fontanka on the mainland are the **Liteyny, Smolny,** and **Vladimirskaya** districts. These are central St. Petersburg's newest neighborhoods, developed primarily in the late 19th century, and house the Smolny Insti-

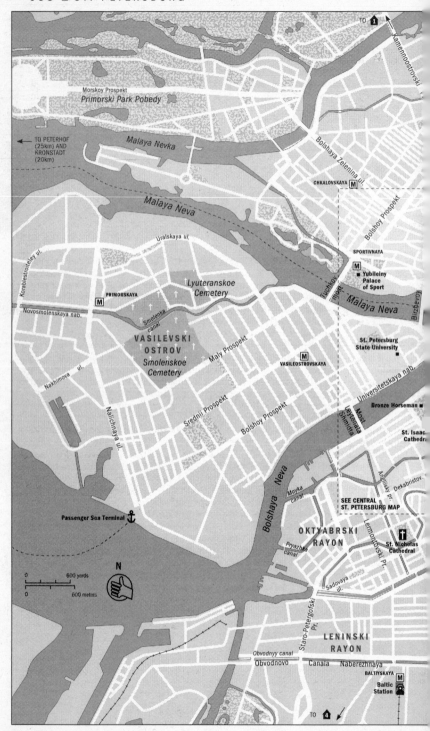

TO ■1

Morskoy Prospekt
*Primorski Park Pobedy*

TO PETERHOF
(25km) AND
KRONSTADT
(20km)

*Malaya Nevka*

Bolshaya Zelenina ul.

CHKALOVSKAYA Ⓜ

*Malaya Neva*

Bolshoy Prospekt

Uralskaya ul.

SPORTIVNAYA

Ⓜ **Yubileiny
Palace
of Sport**

Korablestroiteley ul.

*Malaya Neva*

PRIMORSKAYA Ⓜ

*Lyuteranskoe
Cemetery*

Tuchkov

Birzhevoy

Novosmolenskaya nab.

Smolenka
canal

**St. Petersburg
State University** ■

**VASILEVSKI
OSTROV**

Maly Prospekt

*Smolenskoe
Cemetery*

Nakhimova ul.

Ⓜ
VASILEOSTROVSKAYA

Universitetskaya nab.

Nalichnaya ul.

Srednii Prospekt

**Bronze Horseman** ■

Bolshoy Prospekt

Most
Leytenanta
Shmidta

**St. Isaac
Cathedra.**

Moyka
canal

Angliysky pr.

Dekabristov.

**SEE CENTRAL
ST. PETERSBURG MAP**

**Passenger Sea Terminal** ⚓

*Bolshaya Neva*

**OKTYABRSKI
RAYON**

ⓘ **St. Nicholas
Cathedral**

Pryazhka
canal

Lermontovski Pr.

N

0 ──── 600 yards
0 ──── 600 meters

Sadovaya ul.

**LENINSKI
RAYON**

Staro-Petergofski Pr.

Obvodnyy canal

Obvodnovo    Canala    Naberezhnaya

BALTIYSKAYA
Ⓜ

**Baltic
Station** 🚉

TO ■4 ↙

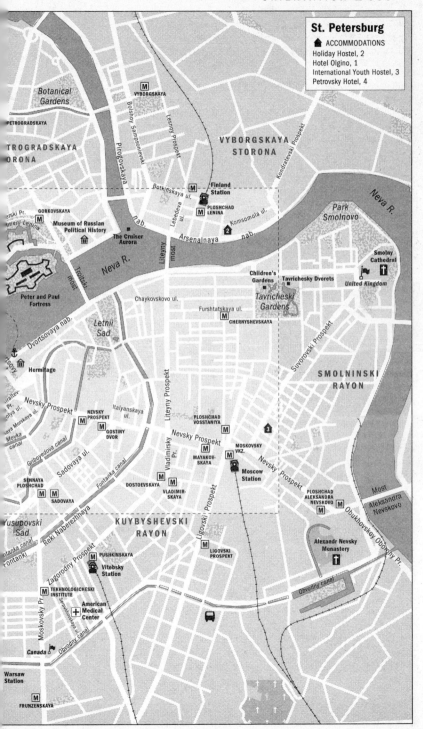

St. Petersburg

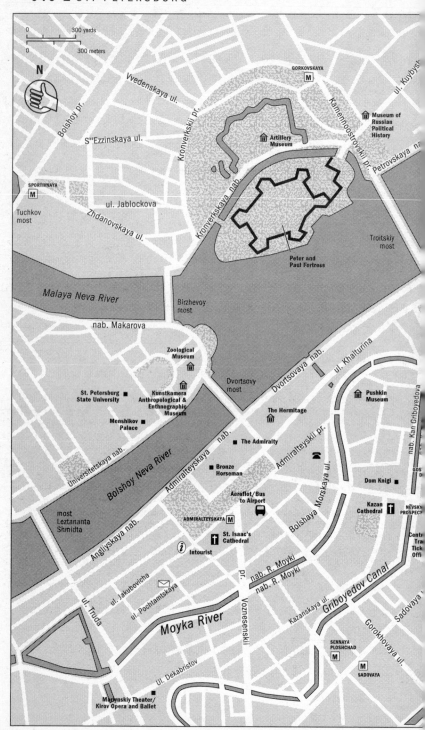

0      300 yards

0      300 meters

**N**

Bolshoy pr.

Vvedenskaya ul.

GORKOVSKAYA
M

ul. Kuybysh

S"Ezzinskaya ul.

Kronverkskii pr.

Kamennoostrojskii pr.

Museum of
Russian
Political
History

Artillery
Museum

Petrovskaya na

SPORTIVNAYA
M

ul. Jablockova

Kronverkskaya nab.

Zhdanovskaya ul.

Tuchkov
most

Troitskiy
most

Peter and
Paul Fortress

Malaya Neva River

Birzhevoy
most

nab. Makarova

Zoological
Museum

Dvortsovaya nab.

ul. Khalturina

Dvortsovy
most

Pushkin
Museum

St. Petersburg
State University

Kunstkamera
Anthropological &
Enthnographic
Museum

The Hermitage

nab. Kan Griboyedova

Menshikov
Palace

Admiralteyskaya nab.

The Admiralty

Admiralteyskii pr.

GOS
D

Universitetskaya nab.

Bronze
Horseman

Dom Knigi

Bolshoy Neva River

Aeroflot/Bus
to Airport

Bolshaya Morskaya ul.

Kazan
Cathedral

NEVSKY
PROSPECT

Angliyskaya nab.

ADMIRALTEYSKAYA
M

Centr
Tra
Tick
Offi

most
Leztananta
Shmidta

St. Isaac's
Cathedral

Intourist

ul. Jakubovicha

nab. R. Moyki

nab. R. Moyki

pr. Voznesenski

Griboyedov Canal

ul. Pochtamtskaya

Kazanskaya ul.

Sadovaya

ul. Truda

ul. Pochtamtskaya

Moyka River

Gorokhovaya ul.

SENNAYA
PLOSHCHAD
M

ul. Dekabristov

SADOVAYA
M

Mariynskiy Theater/
Kirov Opera and Ballet

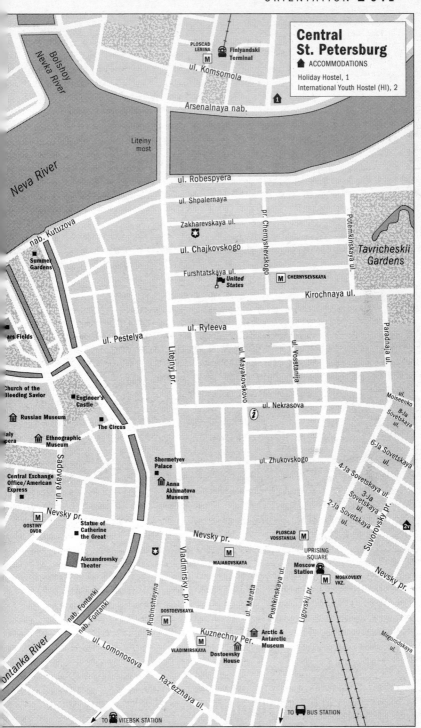

**Central St. Petersburg**

♠ ACCOMMODATIONS

Holiday Hostel, 1
International Youth Hostel (HI), 2

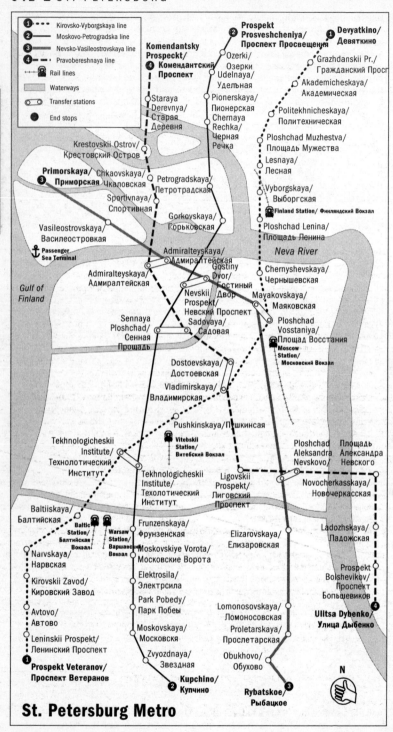

**Legend:**
- ① ‑‑‑‑‑ Kirovsko-Vyborgskaya line
- ② Moskovo-Petrogradska line
- ③ Nevsko-Vasileostrovskaya line
- ④ ‑‑‑ Pravobereshnaya line
- Rail lines
- Waterways
- Transfer stations
- End stops

Komendantsky Prospeckt/
④ Комендантский Проспект

Prospekt Prosveshcheniya/
② Проспект Просвещения

Devyatkino/
① Девяткино

Ozerki/
Озерки

Grazhdanskii Pr./
Гражданский Прос

Udelnaya/
Удельная

Akademicheskaya/
Академическая

Staraya Derevnya/
Старая Деревня

Pionerskaya/
Пионерская

Politekhnicheskaya/
Политехническая

Chernaya Rechka/
Черная Речка

Ploshchad Muzhestva/
Площадь Мужества

Krestovskii Ostrov/
Крестовский Остров

Lesnaya/
Лесная

Primorskaya/
③ Приморская

Chkaovskaya/
Чкаловская

Petrogradskaya/
Петроградская

Vyborgskaya/
Выборгская

Sportivnaya/
Спортивная

Finland Station/ Финляндский Вокзал

Vasileostrovskaya/
Василеостровкая

Gorkovskaya/
Горьковская

Ploshchad Lenina/
Площадь Ленина

Passenger Sea Terminal

Neva River

Admiralteyskaya/
Адмиралтейская

Admiralteyskaya/
Адмиралтейская

Gostiny Dvor/
Гостиный Двор

Chernyshevskaya/
Чернышевская

Nevskii Prospekt/
Невский Проспект

Mayakovskaya/
Маяковская

Gulf of Finland

Sennaya Ploshchad/
Сенная Прощадь

Sadovaya/
Садовая

Ploshchad Vosstaniya/
Площад Восстания

Moscow Station/
Московский Вокзал

Dostoevskaya/
Достоевская

Vladimirskaya/
Владимирская

Pushkinskaya/Пушкинсая

Tekhnologicheskii Institute/
Технолотический Институт

Vitebskii Station/
Витебский Вокзал

Ploshchad Aleksandra Nevskovo

Площадь Александра Невского

Tekhnologicheskii Institute/
Техолотический Институт

Ligovskii Prospekt/
Лиговский Проспект

Novocherkasskaya/
Новочеркасская

Baltiiskaya/
Балтийская

Baltic Station/
Балтийская Вокзал

Warsaw Station/
Варшавский Вокзал

Frunzenskaya/
Фрунзенская

Elizarovskaya/
Елизаровская

Ladozhskaya/
Ладожская

Narvskaya/
Нарвская

Moskovskiye Vorota/
Московские Ворота

Kirovskii Zavod/
Кировский Завод

Elektrosila/
Электросила

Prospekt Bolshevikov/
Проспект Большевиков

Avtovo/
Автово

Park Pobedy/
Парк Побеы

Lomonosovskaya/
Ломоносовская

Ulitsa Dybenko/
④ Улица Дыбенко

Leninskii Prospekt/
Ленинский Проспект

Moskovskaya/
Московскя

Proletarskaya/
Прослетарская

Prospekt Veteranov/
① Проспект Ветеранов

Zvyozdnaya/
Звёздная

Obukhovo/
Обухово

Kupchino/
② Купчино

Rybatskoe/
③ Рыбацкое

N

# St. Petersburg Metro

tute and the Aleksandr Nevsky Monastery. **Moskovsky Vokzal** (Moscow Train Station; Московский Вокзал), the city's main train station, is in the middle of this district, located near the midway point of Nevsky pr.; **Vitebsky Vokzal** (Витебский Вокзал) is at the southern edge of this district on Litiyny pr. (Литейний пр.).

East of the city center and across the Neva sprawls **Vasilevsky Island,** the city's largest island and the original, intended site of Peter's dream city. Most sights on the island are among St. Petersburg's oldest and are on its eastern edge in the **Strelka** neighborhood. The western portion of the island is a sprawl of grid-patterned streets and apartment complexes; the city's **Sea Terminal,** the ferry port, is at the island's far western tip on the Gulf coast.

On the north side of the Neva and across from the Winter Palace is a small archipelago housing the Peter and Paul Fortress, the **Petrograd Side** residential neighborhood, and the wealthy **Kirov Island** trio; this is the historic heart of St. Petersburg. North and south of the city center on the mainland are the southern suburbs and the **Vyborg Side** neighborhoods; both are vast expanses of tenements and factories and are of little interest to most tourists aside from the train stations they house, including **Finlyandsky Vokzal** (Finland Train Station; Финляндский) in the north and **Varshavsky Vokzal** (Warsaw Train Station; Варшавский) in the south. The city makes promenading a pleasure, and fortunately most major sights are close together.

---

The pipes and drainage system in St. Petersburg have not changed since the city was founded. There is no effective water purification system, making exposure to giardia very likely. Always boil tap water at least 10 minutes, dry your washed veggies, and drink bottled water. Also see Essentials: Health, p. 28.

---

# ✈ INTERCITY TRANSPORTATION

**Flights:** The main airport, **Pulkovo** (Пулково), has 2 terminals: Pulkovo-1 for domestic and Pulkovo-2 for international flights. M2: Moskovskaya. From the Metro, take bus #39 for Pulkovo-1 (30-40min.) or bus #13 for Pulkovo-2 (25-30min.). Hostels can often arrange a taxi (usually US$30-40). **Air France,** Bolshaya Morskaya 35 (Большая морская; ☎325 82 52). Open M-F 9am-5pm. **British Airways,** ul. Malaya Konyushennaya 1/3 (Малая конюшенная; ☎329 25 65). Open M-F 9am-5:30pm. **Delta Airlines,** Bolshaya Morskaya 36 (☎311 58 19 and 311 58 20; fax 325 62 28). Open M-F 9am-5:30pm. **Finnair,** ul. Kazanskaya 44 (Казанская; ☎326 18 70). Open M-F 9am-5pm. **Lufthansa,** Voznesensky pr. 7 (Вознесенский; ☎314 49 79). Open M-F 9am-5:30pm. **SAS/SwissAir,** Nevsky pr. 57 (Невский; ☎325 32 50). Open M-F 9am-5pm.

**Trains: Tsentralnye Zheleznodorozhnye Kassy** (Центральные Железнодорожные Кассы; Central Ticket Offices), Canal Griboedova 24 (Грибоедого). Open M-Sa 8am-8pm, Su 8am-6pm. Foreigners must purchase **domestic tickets** at **Intourist** windows #100-104 and **international tickets** at windows #2-4 on the 2nd floor. Expect long lines and few English-speaking tellers. For prices, go to the information booths (4R per question). Prices vary slightly depending on the train running (see **Local Transportation,** p. 602), and fluctuate widely over time. There are also Intourist offices at each of St. Petersburg's 4 train stations; go there to purchase tickets on the day of departure. For schedule and fare info in Russian, dial 055 from your hotel; you'll be billed later at 6-8R per call. Check your ticket to see from which station your train leaves.

**Varshavsky Vokzal** (Варшавский Вокзал; Warsaw Station; ☎168 26 90). M1: Baltiskaya (Балтийская). To: **Riga, LAT** (12hr., 1 per day, 825-1400R); **Tallinn, EST** (8hr., 1 per day, 325-560R); **Vilnius, LIT** (13hr., 1 per day, 640-980R); and **Warsaw, POL** (27hr., 1 per day, 1090-1340R).

**Vitebsky Vokzal** (Витебский Вокзал; Vitebsk Station; ☎168 58 07). M1: Pushkinskaya (Пушкинская). To: **Kiev, UKR** (28hr., 2 per day, 506-803R) and **Odessa, UKR** (36hr., 1 per day, 650-1100R).

**Moskovsky Vokzal** (Московский Вокзал; Moscow Station; ☎168 45 97). M1: Pl. Vosstaniya (Восстания). To: **Novgorod** (4½hr., 1 per day, 306R); **Moscow** (6-9hr., 15 per day, 170-400R); and **Sevastopol, UKR** (36hr., 1 per day, 770-1200R). Anna Karenina threw herself under a train here.

**Finlyandsky Vokzal** (Финляндский Вокзал; Finland Station; ☎168 76 87). M1: Pl. Lenina (Ленина). To **Helsinki, FIN** (6hr., 2 per day, 1330-2300R).

**Buses:** nab. Obvodnovo Kanala 36 (Обводного Канала; ☎166 57 77). M4: Ligovsky pr. Take tram #19, 25, 44, or 49, or trolley #42, from the M1 stop across the canal. Facing the canal, turn right and walk 2 long blocks. The station is on your right; enter through the back. Cheaper and more comfortable than trains during the day, but queue up early for the over-booked short-distance jaunts. Buy tickets several hours before departure to avoid a 5R surcharge. One-way tickets only. Open daily 8am-8pm. For destinations in the Baltic States, consult the **Eurolines Agency** (Agenstvo Evrolains; Агенство Евролайнс), ul. Shkapina 10 (Шкапина; ☎168 27 40). M1: Baltiiskaya. Deals with buses to **Tallinn, EST, Riga, LAT,** and **Vilnius, LIT.**

# ⌷ LOCAL TRANSPORTATION

**Local Transportation:** The **Metro** (Метро) is a comprehensible, efficient, and safe method of exploring the city. Runs daily 5:30am-12:30am. Always packed, but avoid the peak hours from 8-9am and 5-6pm. Four lines lead from the outskirts of the city through the center. A Metro **token** (zheton; жетон) costs 3R; stock up, as lines are often long and cutting is common. **Buses, trams,** and **trolleys** run fairly frequently, depending on the time of day. Read the destination of each numbered line off the signs at the bus stop, or read the list of stops posted on the outside of the bus. Trolleys #1, 5, and 22 go from pl. Vosstaniya to the bottom of Nevsky pr., near the Hermitage. Buses are often packed and brutally hot in the summer. Bus, tram, and trolleys run 6am-midnight; tickets (2R) should be purchased from the driver. A **monthly transportation card** (175R) is good for unlimited public transportation; purchase one at any Metro station starting on the 25th of the month and running throughout the following month. Half-month passes 85R.

**Taxis:** Both marked and private cabs operate in St. Petersburg. Marked cabs operate off a metered rate of 5R per km; add 20R if you call ahead. Unofficial cabs involve haggling over a flat fare based on your destination. They are safe for the most part, but never get into a car with more than one person already in it.

# ⚐ PRACTICAL INFORMATION

## TOURIST AND FINANCIAL SERVICES

**Tourist Office: Ost-West Contact Service,** ul. Mayakovskovo 7 (Маяковского; ☎327 34 16; fax 327 34 17; sales@ostwest.com; www.ostwest.com). Resourceful staff provides maps of the city and free info on anything from clubs to pharmacies. It also arranges homestays (US$20 in center, US$15 elsewhere), hotel bookings, boat and bus tours, and theater tickets. Provides visa invitations and registration. English spoken. Open M-F 10am-6pm, Sa noon-6pm.

**Budget Travel: Sindbad Travel (FIYTO),** ul. 3-ya Sovetskaya 28 (3-я Советская; ☎327 83 84; fax 329 80 19; sindbad@sindbad.ru; www.sindbad.ru). In the International Hostel. Geared toward students and budget travelers. Arranges plane, bus, ferry, and train tickets, as well as package tours and adventure trips. 10-80% discounts on airplane tickets. English spoken. Open M-F 9:30am-8pm, Sa-Su 10am-5pm. Also at Universitetskaya nab. 11 (Университетская наб.; ☎/fax 324 0880). Open M-F 10am-6pm.

---

**NOT IN IVAN'S BACKYARD** With so many sights clustered at the end of Nevsky Prospekt and just across the Neva, you may find yourself nursing blisters and wondering if the 20-minute walk from the Hermitage to the nearest Metro station is just Soviet planning in all its glory or Stalin's legacy of torment for Western tourists. It's actually neither—a station, Admiralteystvo (Адмалтейство), does exist in the area and some maps even show it. The problem? After construction was completed, area residents refused to allow the authorities to build an entrance or exit connecting the station to the surface. Wave at the empty station as the train flies by.

**Adventure Travel: ☒ Wild Russia,** ul. Mokhovaya 28-10 (Моховая; ☎273 6514; fax 279 2856; yegor@wildrussia.spb.ru or RRi9521029@aol.com; www.wildrussia.spb.ru). In addition to arranging expensive and exotic expeditions to the outermost regions of Russia, Wild Russia also provides guides, gear, and accommodations for outdoor excursions near St. Petersburg. One weekend US$40-100.

**Consulates: Canada,** Malodetskoselsky pr. 32 (Малодетскосельский; ☎325 84 48; fax 325 83 93). M1: Tekhnologichesky Institut (Технологический Институт). Open M-F 9:30am-1pm and 2-5pm. **UK,** pl. Proletarskoi Diktatury 5 (Пролетарской Диктатуры; ☎320 32 00; fax 320 32 11). M1: Chernyshevskaya. Open M-F 9:30am-1pm and 2-5:30pm. **US,** ul. Furshtatskaya 15 (Фурштатская; ☎275 17 01; 24hr. emergency ☎274 86 92; fax 110 70 22; acs_stpete@state.gov). M1: Chernyshevskaya. Open M-F 9:30am-5:30pm, services for US citizens 9:30am-1:30pm. Citizens of **Australia** and **New Zealand** should contact their embassies in Moscow but can use the UK consulate in an emergency.

**Currency Exchange:** Look for "Обмен валюты" (obmen valyuty) signs everywhere. The black market is less prevalent than a few years ago, but should be avoided in any case; many of the bills are counterfeit. **Central Exchange Office,** ul. Mikhailovskaya 4 (Михайловская; ☎110 55 48). Off Nevsky pr. across from Grand Hotel Europe. M3: Gostiny Dvor. All major credit cards and traveler's checks accepted for a 3% commission. Open M-Sa 9:30am-1:30pm and 2:30-8pm, Su 9:30am-1:30pm and 2:30-7pm. Keep your exchange receipts if you plan to change rubles back into hard currency, but they still might not be accepted.

**ATMs:** *Bankomat* (Банкомат) are multiplying rapidly. All upscale hotels and most large banks now have them; on Nevsky pr., there's one every 100m. There's a particularly safe and reliable one at Nevsky 40. Most take Cirrus/Plus/Visa/MC.

**English-Language Bookstore: Anglia British Bookshop** (Англия), nab. Reki Fontanki 40 (Реки Фонтанки; ☎279 8284). Petersburg's only English bookstore stocks a wide variety of titles, including sizeable literature and recent fiction sections. Open M-F 10am-7pm, Sa-Su 11am-6pm.

**Laundry Service:** ☎560 29 92. Pick-up, next-day laundry service. 60R for 4.5kg. Pick-up 10R, delivery 60R.

## EMERGENCY AND COMMUNICATIONS

**Emergency and Police:** Police and ambulance drivers generally do not speak English. There is now a multilingual police office which deals specifically with crimes against foreigners at ul. Zakharevskaya 19 (Захаревская; ☎278 30 14). Completely user-unfriendly; you'll probably want to enlist the aid of your consulate to report a crime.

**Pharmacy:** Nevsky pr. 22. Stocks Western medicines and toiletries. Open M-F 8am-10pm, Sa 9am-9pm, Su 11am-7pm.

**Medical Assistance: American Medical Center,** ul. Serpukhovskaya 10 (Серпуховская; ☎326 17 30; fax 326 17 31). M1: Tekhnologichesky Institut. Staffs Western doctors. **Hospital #20,** Gastello ul. 21 (Гастелло; ☎108 4821), treats foreigners.

**Internet Access: Tetris Internet Cafe** (Тетрис), Chernyakhovskovo 33 (Черняховского; ☎164 48 77). M4: Ligovsky Prospekt. Exit the Metro, turn left onto Ligovsky pr., and walk straight for 5min. Turn left at the sign and follow that street to the end, then turn left on Chernyakhovskovo. 5 min. down on the right. 70R per hr. **Cityline Internet,** Nevsky pr. 88. 15R per 10min., 70R per hr. Only four terminals. Both **Hostel Holiday** and **International Youth Hostel (HI)** (see **Accommodations,** p. 646) let you send and receive email free at the hostel's web address only.

**Telephones: Central Telephone and Telegraph,** Bolshaya Morskaya ul. 3/5 (Большая Морская). Facing the Admiralty, it's right off Nevsky pr. near Dvortsovaya pl. For intercity calls, use one of the *mezhdugorodny* (междугородный) phone booths; they take special grooved *zhetony* (tokens; жетоны) sold across from the booths (5R). Pre-pay your phone call in the *kassa* in the 2nd (for intercity) or 3rd (for international) hall, and get change for unspent time. English instructions available. When making long-distance calls, dial 8 and wait for the tone before proceeding. When your party answers, push the round button bearing an arrow for a few seconds. Open 24hr. **Intercity calls** can also

RUSSIA

be made from any public phone on the street that takes phone cards (25 units 60R, 400 units 331R; 1 unit per min. for local calls; 48 per min. to US). Cards, good for both local and intercity calls, can be purchased at the Central Telephone Office, Metro stations, or news kiosks. Certain phones also take Metro tokens for local calls. For **AT&T Direct,** call ☎ 325 50 42; you can also use this service to call collect from most international phones, except credit card phones.

**Post Office:** ul. Pochtamtskaya 9 (Почтамтская). From Nevsky pr., go west on ul. Malaya Morskaya, which becomes ul. Pochtamtskaya. It's about 2 blocks past Isaakievsky Sobor on the right, before an overhanging arch. Change money or make intercity or international calls. Regular mailing services are unreliable for international letters and parcels—the extra 8-10R for certified mail may help the post office to not lose it. International airmail letters 7R; postcards 5R. International mail is sent from window #24. For **Poste Restante,** address mail: "DOGG, Snoop Doggy, До Востребования, 190 000 Санкт-Петербург, Главпочтамт, Russia." Held up to 1 month at windows #1 and 2. Open M-Sa 9am-8pm, Su 10am-6pm.

**Postal Code:** 190 000.

# ▐ ACCOMMODATIONS

Nowhere is Russia's politico-economic flux more apparent than in the accommodations industry. Where once travelers were assigned a hotel by Intourist, now they can choose among deluxe new joint ventures, old Intourist dinosaurs, **hostels,** and **private apartments.** *The St. Petersburg Times* lists apartments for rent, both long-and short-term; pick up a free copy in the Grand Hotel Europe or at one of the hostels. The International Youth Hostel's *Traveler's Yellow Pages* has current listings of accommodations options.

That said, budget accommodations are rare and not very "budget." Russian speakers may want to consider a **homestay,** which can be arranged by the **Host Families Association (HOFA;** ☎/fax 275 19 92; alexei@hofak.hop.stu.neva.ru), based at the St. Petersburg Technical University. They provide bed and breakfast in apartments within 5km of the city center. The most economical B&B package includes only room and breakfast: if your host meets you at the station or treats you to a home-made dinner, expect to be charged extra. Also available are deluxe B&B (includes dinner) and full service (all meals and a car) packages. Rates are cheaper if you go hunting on your own.

The national **Russian Youth Hostels Association (HI)** in St. Petersburg accepts reservations by phone, provides assistance with visas, books train tickets, and provides rides to the airport. They also sell maps and bottled water.

▦ **International Youth Hostel (HI),** 3-ya Sovetskaya ul. 28 (3-я Советская; ☎ 329 80 18; fax 329 80 19; ryh@ryh.ru; www.ryh.ru). M1: Pl. Vosstaniya. Walk along Suvorovsky pr. (Суворовский) for 3 blocks, then turn right on 3-ya Sovetskaya ul. Floral curtains, helpful staff, superb security, and a wide range of services lend this cheery hostel a home-away-from-home feel. Minimal kitchen. TV and small library in common room. English films nightly 8pm. Internet after 8pm. Offers city tours from US$8. Communal showers 8-11am and 4-11:30pm. Laundry service (US$4 for 4kg). Reception 9am-midnight. Check-out 11am. Curfew 1am. Member of the International Booking Network (IBN). 2- to 5-bed dorms $19, $2 off with HI, $1 with ISIC. Breakfast included. Visa/MC.

**Hostel "Holiday" (HI),** nab. Arsenalnaya 9 (Арсенальная; ☎ 327 10 70; fax 542 73 64; info@hostel.spb.ru; www.hostel.spb.ru). M1: Pl. Lenina. Exit at Finlyandsky Vokzal, turn left on ul. Komsomola (Комсомола), then right on ul. Mikhailova (Михаилова). At the end of the street turn left on nab. Arsenalnaya. The hostel is on the left. Large rooms overlooking the Neva river. Internet access and visa support (single-entry US$30). Beds range from rock-hard to low-slung. Hall baths and toilets. Check-out noon. Call ahead. 3- to 5-bed dorms US$14; doubles US$38 per person. US$1 off with HI or ISIC; US$2 after 5 days. Breakfast included. MC/Visa.

**Petrovsky Hostel,** ul. Baltiiskaya 26 (Балтийская; ☎ 252 75 63; fax 252 40 19). M1: Narvskaya. From the Metro, turn left on pr. Stachek (Стачек). Don't cross the street into the park; instead turn left on ul. Baltiskaya. The hostel is a few blocks ahead on your left in the Petrovsky College building, where students study, among other things, tourism. Though a little ways from the center, the clean, comfortable rooms and low prices attract many guests. Kitchen, common room with TV. A few private *luks* (luxury) rooms with bath, TV, and phone. Check-in noon-midnight. Check-out noon. Call 2-3 months ahead for summer housing. 2- to 3-bed dorms 150-170R; *luks* room 300-500R.

**Hotel Olgino** (Отель Ольгино), Primorskoe Shosse 18 (Приморское Шоссе; ☎238 36 71; fax 238 34 63). M4: Staraya Derevnya (Старая Деревня). From the Metro, take bus #110 or 210 (20-25min.). The bus will make a U-turn and stop in front of the hotel immediately afterward. The grungy exterior conceals recently renovated and comfortable rooms. Located outside the city, the hotel offers quiet and the opportunity to camp, but makes sightseeing a long commute. Horseback riding (200-300R per hr.), bowling (270-600R per hr.), billiards (70R per hr.), and tennis (50R per hr.) available. Showers and kitchen on-site. Sauna (200-300R per hr.). Check-in 24hr. Check-out noon. Call a few days ahead, a full week in summer. Camping US$7 per person; parking US$2. Singles US$28; *luks* room US$45; doubles US$31. Some English spoken.

# ☐ FOOD

St. Petersburg's menus vary little, but many restaurants harbor top-secret methods of preparing old Russian favorites worth tasting. The few great restaurants fill up fast, and getting there often requires a hefty walk. Unfortunately, even in highly touristed regions, menus are often exclusively in Cyrillic.

Fast food venues are springing up all over and many are open 24 hours. More than a few serve hamburgers and french fries, though several chains have fairly good Russian food. For those craving good old American fare, **Pizza Hut, KFC,** and **Baskin-Robbins** are all over town. Or, bask in the glow (and cultural hegemony) of the Golden Arches at **McDonald's;** the one at 11 Bolshaya Morskaya, two blocks from St. Isaac's Cathedral, is open 24 hours.

Markets stock fresh produce, meat, cheese, bread, pastries, honey, and the occasional greasy prepared dish, but are more expensive than state-owned stores. They are a truly Russian experience and require energy on the part of all involved. Sellers easily spot foreigners and try to cheat them; watch out for fingers on the scales and count your change. If you are not satisfied, simply walk away; a simple *nyet* will do wonders to bring the price down. Bargaining is what these places are all about. Don't forget to bring bags and jars, although some vendors provide them for a couple of rubles. The **covered market,** Kuznechny per. 3 (Кузнечный), just around the corner from M1: Vladimirskaya, and the **Maltsevsky Rynok** (Мальцевский Рынок), ul. Nekrasova 52 (Некрасова), at the top of Ligovsky pr. (Лиговский; M1: Pl. Vosstaniya), are the biggest and most exciting.

## RUSSIAN RESTAURANTS

▨ **The Idiot** (Идиотъ), nab. Moyki 82 (Мойки; ☎315 16 75). M4: Sadovaya. 5min. down the Moyka from Isaakievskaya pl. Named for a Dostoyevsky novel, this spacious but homey cafe captures the feel of a Silver Age salon. Menu in English and Russian showcases a true rarity—predominantly vegetarian Russian cuisine. A few seafood dishes. Homemade meals 75-120R. Happy hour 6:30-7:30pm offers 2-for-1 beer or wine. Open daily noon-11pm.

**Kafe Khutorok** (Хуторок), 3-ya Sovetskaya ul. 24. M1: Pl. Vosstaniya. Right next to the International Youth Hostel. Don't be fooled by the Polynesian decor; this basement cafe whips up amazing Russian food, while English- and Spanish-language pop add to the incongruous international flavor. The menu revolves around seafood and a list of alcoholic drinks (8-90R) ad nauseam; vegetarians might find it a better place for a sweet snack than a full meal. Main dishes 75-125R. Open daily 10am-11pm.

**Kafe Bistro** (Кафе Бистро), ul. Malaya Morskaya 14. A rare non-smoking cafe, on the way to St. Isaac's from Nevsky pr. The traditional array of Russian food in an eye-pleasing display that works as well as a menu. *Bliny* 8-10R. Open M-Sa 10am-9pm, Su 11am-8pm.

**Kolobok** (Колобок), ul. Tchaikovskovo 40 (Чайковского). M1: Chernyshevskaya. Turn right on pr. Chernyshevskovo for 1 block until ul. Chaikovskovo. Cheap, greasy, and fast. Sweet and savory rolls 4-10R; main dishes 25-50R; 15% discount with ISIC. Open daily 7:30am-9pm.

**Green Crest** (Грин Крест), Vladimirsky pr. 7 (Владимирский). M1: Vladimirskaya or M4: Dostoevskaya. 12 varieties of picturesquely displayed fresh salads sold by weight (50g salad 7.35R). One of the very few non-smoking eateries in St. Petersburg, so breathe deep. Open daily 9am-11:30pm.

## ETHNIC RESTAURANTS

☑ **Tbilisi** (Тбилиси), ul. Sytninskaya 10 (Сытнинская; ☎ 232 93 91). M2: Gorkovskaya. Follow the wrought-iron fence that wraps around Park Lenina away from the fortress until the Sytny (Сытный) market; Tbilisi is just behind it. Georgian restaurants offer some of the best food in Russia, and Tbilisi has low-lit ambiance thrown in at no extra charge. Main dishes 50-75R. Open daily noon-11pm.

**Tandoor** (Тандур), Voznesensky pr. 2 (☎ 312 38 86). M2: Nevsky Prospekt. On the corner of Admiralteysky pr. (Адмиралтейский), 2 blocks to the left after the end of Nevsky pr. Between the Indian decor and the English conversations of expats, Tandoor makes it easy to forget that Russia is just outside the door. The quality Indian cuisine is well worth the relatively high price. Many vegetarian dishes. Some English spoken. Dinner 420-700R. Lunch special daily noon-4pm (280R). Open daily noon-11pm.

**La Cucaracha,** nab. Fontanki Reki 39 (Фонтанки Реки; ☎ 110 40 06). M3: Gostiny Dvor. Hold back your cockroach jokes, cynical wanderer; any bugs here were scared off by the over-the-top Tex-Mex decor and live music on Tu, F, and Sa evenings. The quesadillas (160R) are a shot of adrenaline to the over-borschted palate. Main dishes 150-250R. Happy hour 6-8pm (drinks 60R). Open M-Th and Su noon-1am, F-Sa noon-5am.

**Koreysky Domik** (Korean House; Корейский Домик), Izmailovsky pr. 2 (Измайловский; ☎ 259 93 33). M1, 2: Tekhnologichesky Institut. Savory South Korean cuisine served against a background of paper fans and wooden screens. Full meals with soup, salad, and main dish for around 250R. Vegetarians beware; even the vegetable soup (50R) and the "noodles with vegetables" (85R) have meat in them. Open daily 1-11pm.

## FAST FOOD

**Koshkin Dom** (Кошкин Дом; Cat's House), Liteyny pr. 23 (Литейный) and ul. Vosstaniya 2. M1: Pl. Vosstaniya. English menu available. Carnivores can tear into Russian entrees and soups for 30-75R. Both locations open 24hr.

**Skazka** (Сказка; Fairy Tale), 1-ya Sovetskaya 12. M1: Pl. Vosstaniya. *Bliny* stuffed with your choice of savory or sweet fillers, ranging from the proletarian cabbage (10R) to the intensely bourgeois caviar (40R). Fast service and unbeatable prices. Open 24hr.

**Minutka** (Минутка), Nevsky pr. 20. M2: Nevsky Prospekt. Large sandwiches, small prices. Meat, seafood, and vegetarian 12-inch sandwiches 55-75R, 6-inch 25-40R. Prepared salads (mostly meat) 35-40R. Open daily 10am-10pm.

## SUPERMARKETS

**Magazin #11** (Магазин), Nevsky pr. 105. M1, 3: Pl. Vosstaniya. The usual elevated supermarket prices but a bigger selection than most. Probably the only place in town that stocks herbs and spices. Open daily 10am-10pm.

**Eliseevsky** (Елисеевский), Nevsky pr. 56. M2: Nevsky Prospekt. Across from pl. Ostrovskovo. A gastronomical and decorative delight. Fancy stained glass and elaborate chandeliers elegantly frame Russian delicacies. Open daily 9am-1pm and 2-9pm.

**Produkty** (Продукты), ul. Komsomola (Комсомола). M1: Pl. Lenina. 5min. from Hostel Holiday. The only reasonably priced supermarket in St. Petersburg. Open 24hr.

# 📷 SIGHTS

St. Petersburg is a city that doesn't let you forget its past. Citizens speak of the time "before the Revolution" as though it had occurred only a few years ago, and of dear old Peter and Catherine as if they were first cousins. Signs such as the one at Nevsky pr. 14 recall the harder times of WWII: "Citizens! During artillery bombardments this side of the street is more dangerous." Even if you don't go inside any of St. Petersburg's major sights, take the time to stroll through the city to experience the grace of its architecture.

## ■THE HERMITAGE

*Dvortsovaya nab. 34 (Дворцовая; ☎ 110 96 25; www.hermitage.ru/html_En/index.html). M2: Nevsky Prospekt. Exiting the Metro, turn left and walk down Nevsky pr. to its end at the Admiralty. Head right, onto and across Palace Square. Kassa located on the river side of the building. Lines can be long, so come early or on a weekday. Allow at least 3-4hr. to see the museum, although an entire day is better. It's easy to latch onto a tour group, especially if you speak Russian. Open Tu-Su 10:30am-6pm, Su 10:30am-5pm; cashier and upper floors close 1hr. earlier. 250R, students free. Cameras 75R; video 200R.*

Originally a collection of 225 paintings bought by **Catherine the Great** in 1764, the State Hermitage Museum (Эрмитаж), the world's largest art collection, rivals both the Louvre and the Prado in architectural, historical, and artistic significance. After commissioning its construction in 1769 and filling it with works of art, Catherine II (the Great) wrote of the treasures: "The only ones to admire all this are the mice and me." This, to the public's great fortune, is no longer true; the collection was made public in 1852.

Today, the museum takes up five buildings. Ask for an indispensable English floor guide at the information desk near the *kassa;* otherwise, consult those found on each level. The rooms are numbered, and the museum is organized chronologically by floor, starting with **Egyptian, Greek,** and **Roman** art on the ground floor of the Small and Great Hermitages, and **prehistoric artifacts** in the Winter Palace. On the second floors of the Hermitages are collections of 17th- and 18th-century French, Italian, and Dutch art. It is impossible to absorb the whole museum in a day or even a week—indeed, only 5% of the three-million-piece collection is on display at any one time. Rather than attempting a survey of the world's artistic achievements, pick a building or time period to focus on. If you're running late, visit the upper floors first—the museum closes from the top down.

**THE WINTER PALACE.** Commissioned in 1762, the Winter Palace (Зимний Дворец; Zimny Dvorets), reflects the extravagant tastes of Empress Elizabeth, Peter the Great's daughter, and the architect Rastrelli. On the third floor **Impressionist, Post-Impressionist,** and **20th-century** European and American art is on display.

**THE SUMMER PALACE.** The paintings and sculptures on display in the Summer Palace (Летний Дворец; Letny Dvorets) are often outshone by the rooms that contain them. Room 189 on the second floor, the famous **Malachite Hall,** contains six tons of malachite columns, boxes, and urns, each painstakingly constructed of thousands of matched stones to give the illusion of having been carved from one massive rock. If you wondered why the revolution occurred, decadence like this might clear up your confusion. The Provisional Government of Russia was arrested in the adjacent dining room in October 1917. In rooms 226-27 an exact copy of **Raphael's Loggia,** commissioned by Catherine the Great, covers the walls just as in the Vatican.

**OTHER BUILDINGS.** By the end of the 1760s, the collection amassed by the empress had become too large for the Summer Palace, and Catherine appointed Vallin de la Mothe to build the **Small Hermitage** (Малый Эрмитаж; Maly Hermitage), where she could retreat by herself or with one of her lovers. The **Great Hermitage** (Великий Эрмитаж; Veliky Hermitage) and the **Hermitage Theater** (Эрмитажный Театр; Hermitazhny Teatr) were completed in the 1780s. Stasov, a famous imperial Russian architect, built the fifth building, the **New Hermitage** (Новый Эрмитаж; Novy Hermitage), in 1851. The tsars lived with their collection in the Zimny Dvorets and Hermitage complex until 1917, after which the museum complex was nationalized.

**PALACE SQUARE.** The huge windswept expanse in front of the Winter Palace, Palace Square (Дворцовая Площадь; Dvortsovaya Ploshchad) has witnessed many turning points in Russia's history. Here, Catherine took the crown after overthrowing her husband, Tsar Peter III. Later, Nicholas II's guards fired into a crowd of peaceful demonstrators on "Bloody Sunday," which precipitated the 1905 revolution. Still later, Lenin's Bolsheviks seized power from Kerensky's provisional government during the storming of the Winter Palace in October 1917. Today, vendors peddle ice cream and souvenirs while the angel at the top of the **Aleksander Column** (Александрийская Колонна; Aleksandryskaya Colonna) waits for another riot. The column commemorates Russia's defeat of Napoleon in 1812. The inscription on the Hermitage side reads, "To Aleksandr I from grateful Russia"; the angel's face is said to resemble the Tsar's. The column itself weighs 700 tons, took two years to cut from a cliff in Karelia, and required another year to bring to St. Petersburg. With the help of 2000 war veterans and a complex pulley system, it was raised in just 40 minutes and is held in place by its massive weight alone.

## ST. ISAAC'S CATHEDRAL

*At the corner of Admiralteysky and Voznesensky pr. M2: Nevsky Prospekt. Exiting the Metro, turn left and walk to the end of Nevsky pr. Turn left onto Admiralteysky pr. ☎ 315 97 32. Cathedral open Tu-Su 11am-6pm. Museum open M-Tu and Th-Su 11am-5pm. The kassa is to the right of the cathedral, but foreigners buy tickets inside the church. Cathedral 200R, students 100R; colonnade 80R, students 40R. Museum 15R.*

Glittering, intricately carved masterpieces of iconography await beneath the dome of **St. Isaac's Cathedral** (Исаакиевский Собор; Isaakievsky Sobor), a massive example of 19th-century architecture. On a sunny day, the 100kg of pure gold that coats the dome shines for miles. The cost of this opulent cathedral was well over five times that of the Winter Palace and 60 laborers died from inhaling mercury fumes during the gilding process. Construction took 40 years, due in part to architect Auguste de Montferrand's lack of experience and also to a superstition that the Romanov dynasty would fall with the cathedral's completion. The cathedral was completed in 1858, but alas, the Romanovs endured until 1917. While the exterior is chipped as a result of German artillery fire during the siege of the city and perpetually covered in scaffolding, the interior remains overwhelming; after one gets used to the grandeur of the place, its details merit a look. Some of Russia's greatest artists have worked on the murals and mosaics inside, which are thankfully titled in both English and Russian. Although officially designated a museum in 1931, the cathedral still holds religious services. Both the 260-step climb and the 360-degree view of St. Petersburg atop the **colonnade** are breathtaking.

## FORTRESS OF PETER AND PAUL

*M2: Gorkovskaya. Exiting the Metro, turn right on Kamennoostrovsky pr. (Каменноостровский), the street in front of you (there is no sign). Follow it to the river and cross the wooden bridge to the island fortress. ☎ 232 94 54. Open M and Th-Su 11am-6pm, Tu 11am-5pm; closed last Tuesday of the month. Bastion and cathedral US$3, students US$1.50; additional sights 10-40R. Purchase a single ticket for most sights at the kassa located in the "boathouse" in the middle of the island or in the smaller kassa to the right just inside the main entrance. English tours approx. 40R.*

Across the river from the Hermitage, the walls and golden spire of the **Fortress of Peter and Paul** (Петропавловская Крепость; Petropavlovskaya Krepost) beckon. In summer, locals try to sunbathe on the rocky embankment; in winter, walruses and masochists in Speedos swim in holes cut through the ice. Construction of the fortress began on May 27, 1703, a date now considered the birthday of St. Petersburg. Originally intended as a defense against the Swedes, it never saw battle; Peter I defeated the northern invaders before the bulwarks were finished. With the Swedish threat gone, Peter turned the fortress into a prison for political dissidents. Sardonic etchings by inmates now cover the citadel's stone walls. The **Military History Museum** (see **Museums**, p. 655) can be found in the old arsenal. The fortress also houses a gold-spired cathedral that gives the complex its name (see below).

**PETER AND PAUL CATHEDRAL.** (Петропавловский Собор; Petropavlovsky Sobor.) The main attraction within the fortress, the cathedral glows with walls of rose and aquamarine marble and a breathtaking Baroque iconostasis. From the ceiling, cherubs keep watch over the ornate sarcophagi of Peter the Great and most of his successors. Before the main vault sits the recently restored **Chapel of St. Catherine the Martyr.** The bodies of the Romanovs—Nicholas II, his family, and their faithful servants—were entombed here on July 17, 1998, the 80th anniversary of their murder at the hands of the Bolsheviks. Just outside the church, Mikhail Shemyakin's controversial bronze statue of Peter the Great at once fascinates and offends Russian visitors with its scrawny head and elongated body.

**NEVSKY GATE.** (Nevskoe Vorota; Невское Ворота.) The site of numerous executions, the gate stands beyond the statue, to the right. The condemned awaited their common fate at the **Trubetskoi Bastion** (Трубецкой Бастион), in the fortress's southwest corner, also the site where Peter the Great held and tortured his first son, Aleksei. Dostoyevsky, Gorky, Trotsky, and Lenin's older brother spent time here as well. Plaques in Russian next to each cell identify other notable inmates.

**PETER'S CABIN.** (Домик Петра Первого; Domik Petra Pervovo.) The first building constructed in St. Petersburg, the Cabin served as home to Peter the Great while he supervised the construction of the city. Now it's a shrine, with exhibits on the founding of the city and the Tsar's victory over Sweden; don't be surprised if the furniture is more exciting. *(In a small brick house in the park on the Petrograd Side of the fortress. Open M and W-Su 10am-5:30pm; closed last Monday of the month. 25R, students 15R.)*

**CRUISER AURORA.** (Аврора; Avrora.) Initially deployed in the Russo-Japanese war, the ship later played a critical role in the 1917 Revolution when it fired a blank by the Winter Palace, scaring the pants off Kerensky and his Provisional Government. Inside there are exhibits on revolutionary and military history. *(Farther down the river past Peter's Cabin. Open Tu-Th and Sa-Su 10:30am-4pm.)*

# ALEXSANDER NEVSKY MONASTERY

*M3, 4: Pl. Aleksandra Nevska. The 18th-Century Necropolis, officially called the Lazarus Cemetery, lies to the left of the entrance, while the Artists' Necropolis, officially the Tihkin Cemetery, lies to the right. Cemeteries open M-W and F-Su 10am-5pm. Cathedral services daily 6:45, 10am, and 5pm. Admission to both cemeteries 30R, students 15R. Cameras 20R; video 50R. Free admission to cathedral, but donations requested. No shorts allowed in the monastery. Women are supposed to wear skirts and cover their heads, but the rule is often overlooked when no services are going on.*

A major pilgrimage spot and a peaceful place to stroll, Alexsander Nevsky Monastery (Александро-невская Лавра; Aleksandro-Nevskaya Lavra) derives its name and fame from Prince Aleksandr of Novgorod, whose body was moved here by Peter the Great in 1724. In 1797, it received the highest monastic title of *lavra*, bestowed on only four Orthodox monasteries. Placement of the dead has always been a concern of Russian Orthodoxy; cemeteries are of major importance, and gravestones are carefully sculpted. Many of the tombs in Aleksandro-Nevskaya Lavra's two cemeteries are extremely elaborate. A cobblestone path lined with souvenir-sellers and beggars connects the cathedral and the two cemeteries. Maps of the grounds indicate the graves of famous people and small black signs mark the individual graves.

**18TH-CENTURY NECROPOLIS.** The 1716 18th-Century Necropolis, also known as the Lazarus Cemetery (Лазаревское Кладбище; Lazarevskoye Kladbishche), is the city's oldest burial ground. Going around the edge of the cemetery to the left leads to the plain black tomb of **Natalya Goncharova,** the wife of Aleksandr Pushkin. The tomb is marked N. N. Lanskaya (Н. Н. Ланская) on the maps. Smack in the tiny cemetery's middle lie the graves of two famous St. Petersburg architects: **Andrei Voronikhin,** who designed the Kazan Cathedral (see p. 653), and **Adrian Zakharov,** architect of the Admiralty (see p. 653).

**ARTISTS' NECROPOLIS.** The Artists' Necropolis (Некраполь Мастеров Искусств; Nekropol Masterov Uskusstv), also known as the Tikhvin Cemetery (Тихвинское Кладбище; Tikhvinskoye Kladbishche), next to Lazarus Cemetery, is newer and larger, and is the permanent home of a still more distinguished group. **Fyodor Dostoyevsky** could only afford to be buried here thanks to the Russian Orthodox Church; his grave is around to the right, fairly near the entrance and always strewn with flowers. Continuing along the cemetery's right edge, you arrive at the cluster of famous musicians: **Mikhail Glinka,** composer of the first Russian opera and a contemporary of Pushkin's, and **Mikhail Balakirev,** to the left of Glinka, who taught **Nikolai Rimsky-Korsakov.** Rimsky-Korsakov's grave is recognizable by its unfriendly angels and white marble Orthodox cross. Many are drawn to **Aleksandr Borodin's** grave by the gold mosaic of a composition sheet from his famous String Quartet #1. **Modest Mussorgsky, Anton Rubinstein,** and **Pyotr Tchaikovsky** are in magnificent tombs next to Borodin. Once Tchaikovsky's homosexuality was discovered and publicized, the Conservatory deemed it more appropriate that the musician commit suicide than disgrace its hallowed halls. Whether the composer truly complied or died of natural causes is, like most of Russian history, still unclear, but black angels watch over his magnificent tombstone.

**OTHER SIGHTS.** The **Church of the Annunciation** (Благовещенская Церковь; Blagoveshchenskaya Tserkov), farther along the central stone path on the left, was the original burial place of the Romanovs, who were moved to Peter and Paul Cathedral in 1998 (see p. 650). The church now houses military heroes and minor members of the royal family. The **Holy Trinity Cathedral** (Svyato-Troitsky Sobor; Свято-Троицкий Собор), at the end of the path, is a functioning church, teeming with priests in black robes and *babushki* devoutly crossing themselves and kissing icons. The large interior contains many altars and icons.

## SMOLNY INSTITUTE AND CATHEDRAL

*Take bus #46, 134, or 136 from the stop across the street from M1: Chernyshevskaya to the Smolny (Смольный) complex. Or, just head north 20min. on Suvorovsky pr. (Суворовский) from Nevsky pr.* ☎ *271 91 82. Open M-W and F-Su 11am-6pm; kassa closes 5:30pm. Exhibition 100R; tower 100R.*

Once a prestigious school for aristocratic girls, the **Smolny Institute** (Смольный Институт) earned its place in history when Trotsky and Lenin set up the headquarters of the **Bolshevik Central Committee** here in 1917 and planned the Revolution from behind its yellow walls. Today it serves as the municipal office of St. Petersburg. The gate to the buildings at the end of the drive reads, from left to right, "First Soviet of the dictatorship of the proletariat" and "Proletariats of all nations, unite!" Farther down, again from left to right, are busts of Engels and Marx. Next door the blue-and-white **Smolny Cathedral** (Смольный Собор; Smolny Sobor) rises, notable for combining Baroque and Orthodox Russian architectural styles. The church now functions as an exhibition and concert hall. Climb to the top of a 68m high bell tower and survey Lenin's—er, Peter's—city.

## SUMMER GARDENS AND PALACE

*M2: Nevsky Prospekt. Turn right on nab. Kanala Griboedova, cross the Moyka, and turn right onto ul. Pestelya (Пестеля). The palace and gardens are on your left, behind the Russian Museum and directly across the river from Petropavlovskaya Krepost.* ☎ *314 04 56. Garden open daily summer 10am-11:30pm; off-season 11am-7pm. 5R, students 3R, children 2R. Palace open May-Nov. M and W-Su 11am-6pm; closed last M of the month. 50R, students 25R. Palace signs in English.*

The Summer Gardens and Palace (Летний Сад и Дворец; Letny Sad i Dvorets) are lovely places to rest and cool off. Two entrances at the north and south lead to long, shady paths lined with replicas of Classical Roman sculptures and busts. In the northeast corner of the Garden sits Peter's **Summer Palace.** The decor reflects Peter's European tastes, with everything from Spanish and Portuguese chairs to Dutch tile and German clocks. Peter lived downstairs, while his wife Catherine and children lived above; upon his death in 1725 she became Russia's first female ruler. The **Coffee House** (Кофейный Домик; Kofeyny Domik), also in the Garden, houses a small exhibit, while the nearby **Tea House** (Чайный Домик; Chayny Domik) holds a gift shop and cafe.

**Mars Field** (Марсово Поле; Marsovo Pole), so named because of military parades held here in the 19th century, extends next to the Summer Gardens. The broad, open park is now a memorial to the victims of the Revolution and the Civil War (1917-19). There is a monument in the center with an eternal flame. Don't walk on the grass; you'd be treading on a massive common grave.

## ALONG NEVSKY PROSPEKT

The easternmost boulevard of central St. Petersburg, Nevsky pr. is the city's equivalent of Paris's Champs-Elysées. Like nearly everything else in the city, Nevsky pr. was constructed under Peter the Great. In accordance with his vision for St. Petersburg, the avenue is of epic scale, running 4.5km from the Neva in the west to the Alexander Nevsky Monastery in the east; the golden dome of the Admiralty is visible all the way from pl. Vosstaniya, two-thirds of the way down the avenue. In addition to housing many of St. Petersburg's most monumental sights, Nevsky pr. is also notable for its variety of architectural styles and vibrant street life.

**ADMIRALTY.** (Адмиралтейство; Admiralteystvo.) The Prospekt begins at the Admiralty, whose golden spire towers over the Admiralty gardens and Dvortsovaya pl. The spire was painted black during WWII to disguise it from German artillery bombers. The **tower**—one of the first buildings in St. Petersburg—supposedly allowed Peter to supervise the continued construction of his city. He also directed Russia's new shipyard and navy from its offices. The **gardens,** initially designed to allow for a wider firing range when defending the shipyard, now hold statues of important Russian literary figures. *(M2: Nevsky Prospekt. Exit the Metro, turn left and walk to the end of Nevsky pr.)*

**BRONZE HORSEMAN.** This hulking statue of Peter the Great astride a rearing horse terrorized the protagonists of works by Pushkin and Bely by coming to life and chasing them through the streets of St. Petersburg. In real life, the statue hasn't moved from the site on which Catherine the Great had it set in 1782. The menacing effect of sculptor Etienne Falconet's bronze piece is undermined by nearby ice cream vendors and a playground, yet the likeness of the city's founder remains a powerful symbol of St. Petersburg. Set on a rock from the site where he first surveyed the city, Peter gazes across the Neva while crushing a snake beneath his horse's hooves. *(M2: Nevsky Prospekt. To the left of the Admiralty as you face it.)*

**KAZAN CATHEDRAL.** (Казанский Собор; Kazansky Sobor.) This colossal edifice across the street from Dom Knigi was modeled after St. Peter's in Rome but designed and built by Russian architects (and left to decay by the Soviets). Completed in 1811, the cathedral was originally created to house Our Lady of Kazan, a now-lost sacred icon of the Romanovs. Kazan Cathedral is far less touristed then many of the other cathedrals—incense hangs heavily in the air and the icons are illuminated by candles lit by the faithful. *(M2: Nevsky Prospekt. ☎ 219 45 28. Services M-Sa 10am and 6pm, Su 7:30am and 10am. Tours daily noon-6pm. Cathedral free; tour 25R.)*

**CHURCH OF THE BLEEDING SAVIOR.** (Спас На Крови; Spas Na Krovi). The colorful Church of the Bleeding Savior, also known as the Savior on the Blood, sits on the site of Tsar Aleksandr II's 1881 assassination. Reopened after 20 years of Soviet condemnation, the church has been beautifully renovated. The walls are covered with 7000 square feet of mosaics, restored to correspond with the designs of the original Russian artists. The adjacent chapel houses an exhibit paying homage to the life and death of the reformer Aleksandr II. *(M2: Nevsky Prospekt. 3 blocks off Nevsky pr. up Canal Griboedova from the House of Books. ☎ 315 16 36. Open Su-Tu and Th-Sa 11am-7pm; kassa closes at 6pm. Church 250R for foreigners, foreign students with ID 100R, Russians 15R, Russian students with ID 7R, children under 12 free; foreigners not always charged the higher rate. Aleksandr II exhibit 20R, students with ID 10R.)*

**OSTROVSKOVO SQUARE.** (пл. Островского; Pl. Ostrovskovo.) Ostrovskovo Square is home to a monument to Catherine the Great surrounded by the principal political and cultural figures of her reign: Potemkin (her favorite), Marshall Suvorov, Princess Dashkova, poet Derzhavin, and others. To the right is St. Petersburg's main public library, decorated with sculptures and reliefs of ancient philosophers. The oldest Russian theater, **Aleksandrovsky** (Александровский), built by the architect Rossi in 1828, is behind Catherine's monument. The first production of Gogol's *The Inspector General* was staged here in 1836. On ul. Zodchego Rossi, behind the theater, is the **Vaganova School of Choreography,** which graduated such greats as Vaslav Nizhinsky, Anna Pavlova, Rudolf Nureyev, and Mikhail Baryshnikov. *(M3: Gostiny Dvor. Exit the Metro and head right on Nevsky pr. The square is on the right.)*

**SHEREMETYEV PALACE.** (Дворец Шереметьевых; Dvorets Sheremetevykh.) Constructed in the early 1700s as a residence for Peter the Great's marshal, Boris Sheremetyev, and recently restored to its original grandeur after decades of Soviet neglect, the palace doubles as a music museum and a stunning example of imperial decadence. Non-Russian speakers may find the monolingual signs and eager-to-help guides awkward, but music lovers may not resist the collection of antique instruments and the pianos of Rubenstein, Glinka and Shostakovich. The palace's mirrored hall hosts concerts on weekends. *(Nab. Fontanki 34. M3: Gostiny Dvor. ☎ 272 38 98. Open W-Su noon-4pm; closed last Wednesday of the month. 50R, students 25R. Concerts October-May, F 6:30pm, Sa-Su 4pm. 5R.)*

**UPRISING SQUARE.** (пл. Восстания; Pl. Vosstaniya). Some of the bloodiest confrontations of the February Revolution took place in Uprising Square, highlighted by the moment the Cossacks turned on police during a demonstration. The obelisk in the center, erected in 1985, replaced a statue of Tsar Aleksandr III that was removed in 1937. Across from the train station, the green Oktyabrskaya Hotel bears the words "Город-герой Ленинград" (Leningrad, the Hero-City), in remembrance of the crippling losses suffered during the German siege. *(M1: ploshchad Vosstaniya. The halfway point of Nevsky pr., near Moskovsky Vokzal.)*

# OCTOBER REGION

St. Petersburg's most romantic quarter, the October Region (Октябрьский Район; Oktyabrsky Rayon) sees Canal Griboedova meander through quiet neighborhoods with leafy parks.

**ST. NICHOLAS CATHEDRAL.** (Никольский Собор; Nikolsky Sobor). A magnificent blue-and-gold structure, St. Nicholas Cathedral was constructed in striking 18th-century Baroque style. The bells atop the spectacular tower supposedly possess special mystic powers. Inside, candles lit by the faithful illuminate gold-plated icons. *(M4: Sadovaya. Turn right off ul. Sadovaya (Садовая) and cross the canal onto ul. Rimskovo-Korsakovo (Римского-Корсакого), near the Mariinsky Theater and Conservatory. Enter through the gate on the right side. Services daily at 10am and 6pm.)*

**YUSUPOVSKY GARDENS.** (Юсуповский Сад; Yuspuovsky Sad.) On the outer borders of the October Region, the large Yusupovsky Gardens—named after the prince who succeeded in killing Rasputin only after poisoning, shooting, and ultimately drowning him—provide a patch of green in the middle of the urban expanse. Locals come here to relax, make out, and knit (not usually at once) along the edges of the large pond that occupies much of the park. *(M4: Sadovaya. At the intersection of ul. Sadovaya and ul. Rimskovo-Korsakovo.)*

**LARGE CHORAL SYNAGOGUE OF ST. PETERSBURG.** St. Petersburg's only functioning synagogue is also Europe's second-largest. The synagogue celebrated its 100th anniversary in 1993 and has only around 100 regular members, down from 5000 in 1893. The synagogue is currently undergoing massive renovation, scheduled for completion by Rosh Hashanah of 2003, the year of St. Petersburg's 300th anniversary. In the meantime, services are held in the small synagogue in back. *(Lermontovsky pr. 2. M4: Sadovaya. Turn right off ul. Sadovaya and cross the canal onto ul. Rimskovo-Korsakovo, continuing to Lermontovsky pr. and turning right. ☎ 114 11 53. Open daily 9am-9pm. Morning services daily at 9am.)*

## OTHER SIGHTS

**MENSHIKOV PALACE.** (Васильевский Остров; Vasilevsky Ostrov.) In the middle of the Strelka district on Vasilevsky Island, Menshikov Palace is an unassuming yellow building with a small courtyard. Aleksandr Menshikov was a good friend of Peter I and governor of St. Petersburg. Peter entertained guests here before he built the Summer Palace, and then gave it to the Menshikovs, who employed Catherine I as a serving-girl before she became Peter's second wife. The museum displays a "Russian Culture of Peter's Time" exhibition, with fragments of original 18th-century interiors and Dutch tiles. Call ahead for the English tour, without which the museum is lovely but rather incomprehensible. *(Universitetskaya nab. 15 (Университетская). M3: Vasileostrovskaya. It's better, however, to cross the bridge north of the Admiralteystvo and walk left. ☎ 323 11 12. Open Tu-Su 10:30am-4:30pm. 125R, students with ID free. English tour 125R.)*

**PISKARYOV MEMORIAL CEMETERY.** (Пискарёвское Мемориальное Кладбище; Piskaryovskoye Memorialnoye Kladbishche.) To understand St. Petersburg's obsession with WWII, come to the remote and hauntingly tranquil Piskaryov Memorial Cemetery. Close to a million people died during the 900 days that the German army laid siege to the city; this cemetery is their grave. An eternal flame and grassy mounds bearing the year are all that mark the dead. The place is nearly empty, yet the emotion is palpable—this is the grave of a Hero City (Город-Герой). The monument reads: "No one is forgotten; nothing is forgotten." *(M2: Ozerki (Озерки). Exit the Metro and go right out of the exit to catch bus #123. Ride about 16 stops (30min.) until you reach a large flower shop on the right and the cemetery on the left, marked by a low granite wall and two square stone gate buildings, each with four columns.)*

## 🏛 MUSEUMS

There are three kinds of museums in St. Petersburg: the giant, famous ones, fast-disappearing Soviet shrines, and recreated homes of cultural figures. The first are a must, despite high foreigner prices and yammering tour groups. The second appeal largely to lovers of the absurd and/or military history. The third are pilgrimage sites for those seeking such relics as a famous author's pen and toothbrush, but are less revealing for those who don't read Russian.

---

**A MUSEUM-GOER IN A STRANGE LAND** Like many in Eastern Europe, museums in Russia charge foreigners much higher rates. In desperation, some travelers don a fluffy fur hat, snarl a little, push the exact number of rubles for a Russian ticket toward the *babushka* at the *kassa*, and remain stoically mute. Go ahead and try; it might work. Once inside, don't worry about forgetting to see anything—the *babushki* in each room will make sure of that. Many museums, with floors made of precious inlaid wood, will ask visitors to don *tapochki*, giant slippers that go over your shoes and transform the polished gallery floor into a veritable ice rink. There are no guard rails—only irreplaceable imperial china—to slow your stride. Try to keep your figure skating fantasies in check, or after navigating dozens of slippery wooden exhibition rooms you might meet an unfortunate end on the marble stairs.

## ART AND LITERATURE

■ **Russian Museum** (Русский Музей; Russky Muzey; ☎219 16 08; fax 314 41 53). M3: Gostiny Dvor. In the yellow 1825 Michael Palace (Mikhailovsky Dvorets; Михаиловский Дворец), behind the Pushkin monument. Go down ul. Mikhailovsky past the Grand Hotel Europe. Enter through the basement in the right corner of the courtyard; go downstairs and turn left. Or, enter through the Benois Wing on Canal Griboedova. Boasts the 2nd-largest collection of Russian art after Moscow's Tretyakov Gallery, and the title of 1st public museum of Russian art (1898). 12th- to 17th-century icons, 18th- and 19th-century paintings and sculpture, and Russian folk art arranged chronologically. Benois Wing with avant-garde art of the early 20th century, including internationally famous artists like Kandinsky and Chagall alongside lesser-known but similarly great artists like Malevich and Filonov. Signs in English. Open M 10am-5pm, W-Su 10am-6pm; *kassa* closes M 4pm, W-Su 5pm. 240R, students 120R.

**Theater and Music Museum** (Музей Театрального и Музыкального Искусства; Muzey Teatralnovo i Muzykalnovo Iskusstva), pl. Ostrovskovo 6, 3rd fl. (☎311 21 95). M3: Gostiny Dvor. Showcases memorabilia from Imperial- and Soviet-era performances, including a model of a set design by famous artist Liubov Popova. The room devoted to ballet honors famous dancers and displays costumes such as those from the 1895 premiere of Tchaikovsky's *Sleeping Beauty*. Open M and Th-Su 11am-6pm, W 1-7pm; closed last F of the month. 50R, students 2R. Concerts and lectures 5-25R.

**Dostoyevsky House** (Дом Достоевского; Dom Dostoevskovo), Kuznechny per. 5/2 (Кузнечный; ☎164 69 50). M1: Vladimirskaya, around the corner to the right, just past the market. Dostoyevsky wrote *The Brothers Karamazov* here, surrounded—unlike most of his dysfunctional characters—by a supportive wife and loving children. The area resembles Dostoyevsky's St. Petersburg, though *Crime and Punishment* junkies should check out Sennaya pl. (Сенная), the setting of the book's grisly murder. Open Tu-Su 11am-6pm; *kassa* closes 5:30pm; closed last W of each month. 60R, students 30R. Film versions of Dostoyevsky's novels Su at noon; 10R, students 5R. Expensive (250R) neighborhood tours available.

**Pushkin Museum** (Музей Пушкина; Muzey Pushkina), nab. Reki Moyki 12 (Реки Мойки; ☎311 38 01). M2: Nevsky Prospekt. Walk right on Nevsky from the Metro, then turn right onto nab. Reki Moyki and follow the canal; it's the yellow building on the right. Enter through the courtyard; the *kassa* is on the left. The former residence of Russia's adored poet displays his personal effects, while the adjacent literary exposition exhibits his drafts and sketches—Pushkin apparently loved to draw funny-looking people in his margins. In the library where Pushkin died, the furniture is original, and the clock is stopped at the time of his death. Interesting to literary buffs, but not many others. Open M and W-Su 10:30am-5pm; closed last F of the month. Residence 25R, students 10R; English-language residence tour 60R. Literary exposition 30R, students 10R.

**Anna Akhmatova Museum** (Музей Анны Ахматовой; Muzey Anny Akhmatovoi), Liteiny pr. 53 (Литейный; ☎272 18 11). In the Sheremetev Palace. Enter through an archway; keep left and follow the signs. Personal possessions of the poet whose courageous Soviet-era writings made her a national hero. Akhmatova lived here at intervals from 1927-52. English films on Akhmatova and Joseph Brodsky. Open Tu-Su 10:30am-5pm; closed last W of month. Museum 60R, students 40R. Recorded tour in English 60R.

## HISTORICAL AND SCIENTIFIC

**Ethnographic Museum** (Музей Этнографии; Muzey Etnografii), Inzhenernaya ul. 4, bldg. 1 (Инженерная; ☎210 43 20). Next to the Russian Museum. Established at the end of the 19th century, the museum exhibits the arts, traditions, and cultures of the 159 peoples of the former Russian empire. All signs in Russian; English speakers can admire the exquisite costumes and crafts of one of the most diverse regions of the world. Open Tu-Su 11am-6pm; *kassa* closes at 5pm. 40R, students 20R.

**Kunstkamera Anthropological and Ethnographic Museum** (Музей Антропологии и Этнографии—Кунсткамера; Muzey Antropology i Etnografy—Kunstkamera), Universitetskaya nab. 3 (☎328 14 12). The museum faces the Admiralty from across the river; enter on the left. A natural history museum with a morbid twist. "Lives and habits" of the world's indigenous peoples join Peter's anatomical collection, featuring severed heads and deformed fetuses bathed in formaldehyde. Don't miss the two-headed calf. Open Tu-Su 11am-6pm; *kassa* closes at 4:45pm. Closed last Tu of the month. 100R, students 20R. English tour 520R; call ahead.

**Museum of Russian Political History** (Музей Политической Истории России; Muzey Politicheskoi Istorii Rossii), ul. Kuibysheva 4 (Куйбышева; ☎233 70 52). M2: Gorkovskaya. Go down Kamennoostrosky toward the mosque and turn left on Kuybysheva. Housed in the former mansion of Matilda Kshesinskaya, prima ballerina of the Mariinsky Theater and a lover of Nicholas II. Contains an exhibit about her and a memorial to Lenin, whose Bolsheviks briefly occupied the mansion after the revolution. The east wing displays a range of Soviet propaganda, focusing on the 1905 and 1917 revolutions, as well as artifacts from WWII, known in Russia as the Great Patriotic War. Several photos of a tipsy-looking Boris Yeltsin on the 2nd floor. Open M-W and F-Su 10am-6pm. 60R, students 30R.

**Zoological Museum** (Зоологический Музей; Zoologichesky Muzey), Universitetskaya nab. 1 (☎318 01 12). Next door to the Anthropological and Ethnographic Museum. While the stuffed Siamese cat is a bit odd, the Zoological Museum does contain 40,000 other animals, fish, insects, and specimens, including the enormous skeleton of a blue whale. Open M-Th and Sa-Su 11am-6pm; *kassa* closes at 4:50pm. 15R, students 8R. Live insect zoo 15R.

**Military History Museum** (Военно-Исторический Музей; Voenno Istorichesky Muzey), Aleksandrovsky Park 7 (Александровский Парк; ☎238 47 04). M2: Gorkovskaya. One of the oldest museums in the city. Opened in 1756, it moved to its present site—in the old arsenal of the fortress of Peter and Paul—in 1868. Showcases military hardware from 15th-century armor to the 20th-century tanks in the courtyard. Exhibits on all of the (many) major Russian wars of the 19th and 20th centuries. The section on the war of 1812 features General Kutuzov, glorified in Tolstoy's *War and Peace*. Open W-Su 11am-6pm. Closed last Th of the month. 100R, students 50R.

**Arctic and Antarctic Museum** (Музей Арктики и Антарктики; Muzey Arktiki i Antarktiki; ☎113 19 98 and 311 25 49). M3: Mayakovskaya. On the corner of Kuznechny per. and ul. Marata (Марата). The best place in town to learn about penguin taxidermy, the museum chronicles Russian forays into the polar regions, exhibiting model ships, nautical instruments, and other cold-weather accoutrements. Make sure the guides show you the Northern Lights exhibit. Open W-Su 10am-6pm; *kassa* closes 5pm. Closed last Sa of each month. 75R, students 25R. 45min. tour 100R, 90min. 200R.

# 🎭 ENTERTAINMENT

St. Petersburg's famed White Nights lend the night sky a pale glow from mid-June to early July. In summer, couples stroll under the illuminated heavens and watch the bridges over the Neva go up at 1:30am. Remember to walk on the side of the river where your hotel lies—the bridges don't go back down until 4-5am, though some close briefly from 3 to 3:20am.

The city of Tchaikovsky, Prokofiev, and Stravinsky continues to live up to its reputation for classical performing arts. It is fairly easy to get tickets to world-class performances for as little as 20-30R, although many renowned theaters are known to grossly overcharge foreigners. Buying Russian tickets from scalpers will save you money; be *very* sure that they aren't for last night's show. If you do get Russian tickets, dress up and speak no English, or the ushers may ask to see your passport. The **Mariinsky Ballet,** one of the world's best companies and the place where Russian ballet won its fame, often has cheap tickets. In the third week of June, when the evening sun barely touches the horizon, the city holds a series of outdoor evening concerts as part of the **White Nights Festival,** which lasts throughout the month of June. Check kiosks, posters, and the monthly *Pulse* (free at most upscale hotels) for more info. The theater season ends around the time of the festival and begins again in early

September, but check for summer performances at ticket offices at Nevsky pr. 42, across from Gostiny Dvor, or at kiosks and tables near Isaakievsky Sobor and along Nevsky pr. It may be more productive to try the *kassa* of the theater where the performances are held.

In general, theaters start selling tickets 20 days in advance, and only cheap ones are still available by the day of the performance. *Yarus* (ярус) are the cheapest seats, and, close to the start of a performance, some viewers manage to sneak into this section for free. Performances often start a few minutes late. Russians dress up for the theater and consider foreigners who arrive for a performance in everyday clothes an insult to their culture.

For the most part, Russian performers are at their best when doing Russian pieces. While the Maly Opera's rendition of *La Traviata* may be the worst Italian opera you've seen, Tchaikovsky's *Queen of Spades* (Пиковая Дама; Picovaya Dama) will easily make up for it; likewise, choose Prokofiev over Strauss at any orchestral performance. As with opera and orchestral music, Russian plays in Russian are generally better than Shakespeare in Russian. The Russian circus, while justly famous, is not for animal lovers. In fact, even those who come garbed in fur coats and hats may want to run home and throw red paint on themselves after seeing a bear whipped into walking a tightrope. Nonetheless, the circus can be amusing and, of course, you don't need to speak Russian to enjoy it.

## BALLET AND OPERA

**Mariinsky Teatr** (Мариийнский), a.k.a. the "Kirov," Teatralnaya pl. 1 (Театральная; ☎ 114 43 44). M4: Sadovaya. Walk 10min. along Canal Griboedova, then turn right onto the square. This imposing aqua building, where Tchaikovsky's *Nutcracker* and *Sleeping Beauty* both premiered, is one of the most famous ballet halls in the world. Pavlova, Nureyev, Nizhinsky, and Baryshnikov all started here. For 4 weeks in June, the theater hosts the **White Nights Festival,** for which tickets are relatively easy to get. Evening performances 7pm; matinees Sept.-June 11:30am. *Kassa* open W-Su 11am-3pm and 4-7pm. Tickets (20R and up, as much as 300R for foreigners) go on sale 10 days in advance.

**Maly Teatr** (Small Theater; Малый Театр), a.k.a. "Mussorgsky," pl. Iskusstv 1 (Искусств; ☎ 219 19 49 and 219 19 78), near the Russky Muzey. Open July-Aug., when the Mariinsky is closed. Similarly impressive concert hall hosting excellent performances of Russian ballet and opera. Bring your passport; documents are checked at the door. Evening performances 7pm; matinees at noon. *Kassa* open daily 11am-3pm and 4-7:15pm. Tickets for foreigners up to 200R, Russians 5-30R.

**Conservatoriya** (Консерватория), Teatralnaya pl. 3 (☎ 312 25 19), across from Mariinsky Teatr. M4: Sadovaya. Excellent student ballets and operas often performed here. Evening performances M-F 6:30pm, Sa-Su 6pm; matinees at noon. *Kassa* open daily noon-6pm. Tickets from 15R.

## CLASSICAL MUSIC

**Shostakovich Philharmonic Hall,** Mikhailovskaya ul. 2 (☎ 110 42 57), opposite the Grand Hotel Europe. M3: Gostiny Dvor. Large concert hall with both classical and modern concerts. Acoustics are flawed due to its original use for Boyar Council meetings, which had no need for sonic subtlety. One of the few arenas offering cheap tickets to foreigners. The Philharmonic is on tour for most of the summer. Other groups perform 4 and 7pm daily. *Kassa* open daily 11am-3pm and 4-7:30pm. Tickets from 20R, depending on the concert and day.

**Akademicheskaya Kapella** (Академическая Капелла), nab. Reki Moyki 20 (☎ 314 10 58). M2: Nevsky Prospekt. Small hall for choirs, solos, and small orchestras. Concerts at 7pm. *Kassa* open daily noon-3pm and 4-7pm. Prices from 20R.

**Glinka Maly Zal,** Nevsky pr. 30 (☎ 312 45 85). Part of the Shostakovich Philharmonic Hall, but has better acoustics than the main hall. Concerts 7pm. *Kassa* open daily 11am-3pm and 4-8pm. Tickets from 20R, depending on the concert and day.

## THEATER

**Aleksandrinsky Teatr** (Александринский Театр), pl. Ostrovskovo 2 (☎ 110 41 03). M3: Gostiny Dvor. Turn right on Nevsky pr., then right at the park with Catherine's statue and head straight back. Ballet and theater—mostly Western classics like *Hamlet* and *Cyrano de Bergerac*. Attracts some of Russia's most famous actors and companies; locals wait in line for hours to see some Moscow troupes. Summer ballet season starts July 25. Performances throughout the summer M-F 7pm, Sa-Su 8pm. *Kassa* open M-F 11am-3pm and 4-7:15pm, Sa-Su 11am-3pm and 4-6:15pm. Tickets (10-80R) available 20 days in advance.

**Bolshoy Dramatichesky Teatr** (Большой Драматический Театр), nab. Reki Fontanki 65 (Реки Фонтанки; ☎ 310 92 42). M3: Gostiny Dvor. Conservative productions of Russian classics. Season ends mid-June. Performances 11:30am and 7pm. *Kassa* open daily 11am-3pm and 4-6pm. Tickets 5-50R.

## CIRCUS

**Tsirk** (Цирк; Circus), nab. Fontanki 3 (☎ 314 84 78). M3: Gostiny Dvor, near the Russky Muzey. Russia's oldest traditional circus, made more interesting by a non-traditional live orchestra. Closed mid-June to Sept. Matinees 11:30am, afternoon shows 3pm, evening shows 7pm. *Kassa* open daily 11am-7pm. Tickets from 20R.

# ◩ NIGHTLIFE

During the pre-Gorbachev era, St. Petersburg was the heart of the Russian underground music scene; today, the city still hosts a large number of interesting clubs. There are plenty of expensive dance clubs for Russian *biznessmeni*, too, but better evening fare is hidden away in former bomb shelters off the main drag. Be careful going home late at night, especially if you've been drinking—loud, drunk foreigners might as well be carrying neon signs saying, "Rob me!" Taking taxis home is common and fairly safe, but check to see when your bridge rises or you may be stuck on the wrong side of the river. Clubs last no longer than most high school relationships; the hip scene tends to get infatuated and then grow quickly bored. HI hostels can often recommend the newest places. Check the Friday issue of the *St. Petersburg Times* and *Pulse* for current events and special promotions. For info on jazz clubs around St. Petersburg, call Jazz-inform (☎ 327 38 65).

▨ **Mama,** ul. Malaya Monetnaya 3b (Малая Монетная; ☎ 232 31 37). M2: Gorkovskaya. Walk left on Kamenoostrovsky, take the 2nd right (Divenskaya; Дивенская), then the 1st right (Mal. Monetnaya). Look for the mob outside the apparently abandoned building. Game rooms and bar downstairs, dance floor and 2 bars upstairs. Very hip, very young, very techno, and raging very late. Drinks 15-30R. Cover 60R-100R. Open F-Sa 11:50pm-6am.

**Griboyedov,** ul. Voronezhskaya 2A (Воронежная; ☎ 164 43 55). M4: Ligovsky Prospekt. Exit the Metro and go down through the *perekhod* (Переход; crossing). Cross under the street and go up through the left exit; walk down the street that's at a 45° angle off of Ligovsky. At the 1st left and look for the big mound with the grass growing out of it. This old bomb shelter has become one of the hottest clubs in the city. Music ranges from jazz to pop to funk; check *Pulse* for listings. Cover 40-70R. Open M and W-Su 6pm-6am.

**Moloko** (Молоко; Milk), Perekupnoy per. 12 (Перекупной; ☎ 274 94 67). M3, 4: Pl. Aleksandra Nevskovo. One room of this small rock club invites drinking and conversation with friendly local students. The other holds a stage where various local bands perform for an appreciative, gyrating audience. Cover 20-40R. Open Th-Su 7-11pm.

**JFC Jazz Club,** Shpalernaya ul. 33 (Шпалерная; ☎ 272 98 50). M1: Chernyshevskaya. Go right for 4 blocks on pr. Chernyshevskovo (Чернышевского), then turn left on Shpalernaya and look for the sign on the left. The best local jazz in a relaxed, expat setting. Arrive early or call ahead for a table. Cover 60-100R. Open daily 7-11pm.

**The Shamrock,** ul. Dekabristov 27 (Декабристов; ☎ 219 46 25). M4: Sadovaya. Across from the Mariinsky in Teatralnaya pl. A shining example of Ireland's 2nd-largest export, this authentic Irish bar is a fun place to down a beer (or eight). Western music and a young but clean-cut crowd. Pint of Guinness or Kilkenny US$3. Live music Th-Su 9pm-midnight, Sa Irish bands. Open daily noon-2am.

## BI-GAY-LESBIAN NIGHTLIFE

**69 Club,** 2-aya Krasnoarmeiskaya 6 (2-ая Красноармейская; ☎ 259 51 63). M1: Tech-nologichesky Institut. Popular with both gay and straight clubbers, although recent man-agement crackdowns have limited the number of straights. Pop and Eurodance with splashes of techno. Tu night male-only. Staff in sailor costumes. Face control. Cover around 100R, but can get as high as 250R for females. Open daily 11pm-4am.

**Jungle,** ul. Blokhina 8 (☎ 238 80 33). M4: Sportivnaya. Gay club on the Petrogradskaya Storona. Admittance based on membership, but foreigners are welcome. Call in advance. Eurodance with some Russian pop. Erotic and drag shows 1:30am. Cover men 30R, women 70R. Bring ID—no one under 17 is allowed, though exceptions are common. Open F-Sa 11-6am.

# ⚡ DAYTRIPS FROM ST. PETERSBURG

Ride the suburban *elektrichka* trains out of St. Petersburg to witness the Russians' love of the countryside. Many residents of the city own or share a *dacha* (summer cottage) outside the city and go there every weekend; families crowd outgoing trains loaded with groceries and pets. The tsars, too, built country houses—if "house" is a proper word for these imperial monoliths. The three palaces at Peter-hof, Tsarskoye Selo, and Pavlovsk stand on what was German territory during the siege of Leningrad from 1942 to 1944. All were burned to the ground during the Nazi retreat, but Soviet authorities provided the staggering sums of money to rebuild these symbols of rich cultural heritage. Today, diligent maintenance has restored the palaces to their original opulence, and they make for wholly worthwhile day-trips from St. Petersburg. Bring a picnic lunch to eat in the idyllic parks, rather than waste rubles on overpriced restaurants. Wear a jacket if you're going to Peterhof—the grounds run up against the Gulf of Finland and the garden can get quite windy.

## PETERHOF (ПЕТЕРГОФ)

*In summer, the meteor (Метеор; hydrofoil) leaves from the quay on Dvortsovaya nab. (Дворцовая) in front of the Hermitage (30min., every 30min. from 9:30am, 200R). The elektrichka runs year-round from Baltiiskaya vokzal (Балтийская; M1: Baltiiskaya; 40min., every 15min., 8R). Buy round-trip tickets from the suburban ticket office (Пригородная касса; prigorodnaya kassa)—ask for "NO-viy Peter-GOFF, too-DAH ee oh-BRAHT-nah" (Новый Петергоф, туда и обратно; New Peterhof, round-trip). Get off at Novy Peterhof. Sit at the front or you might not see the sign for the station until you're pulling away from it.*

Formerly known as Petrodvorets (Петродворец), this is the largest and most thor-oughly restored of the palace complexes. The entire complex at Peterhof is 300 years old, although many of the later tsars added their own personal touches. To get through the gates you must pay an admission fee that includes access to the **Lower Gardens,** a perfect place for a picnic on the shores of the Gulf of Finland. Most of the fountains are reconstructions, as post-war Germany couldn't remember what it did with the stolen originals. *(Gardens open daily 9am-9pm. 120R, students 60R. Foun-tains flow May-Sept. M-F 11am-7:30pm, Sa-Su 11am-6pm.)*

---

**MAGIC BUS** While the extravagant palaces of the tsars may thrill the senses, the real cultural experience lies in making the trip out to them. No sooner has the *electrichka* started than a parade of vendors arrives giving sales pitches in a capi-talist game of show-and-tell. Just as the ice cream man pauses for breath, the tooth-brush vendor behind him starts. If you manage to escape without buying any tape measures or Russian journals, you'll climb on a bus to your ultimate destination. Inev-itably, when your arms are tightly pinned to your sides, a 250 lb. *babushka* will decide she can fit on board—and magically, she does. (That is, at the expense of your breath-ing room.) Just smile and enjoy the camaraderie; the Russians do.

**GRAND PALACE.** (Большой Дворец; Bolshoy Dvorets). Wanting to create his own Versailles, Peter started building the first residence here in 1714, but his daughter, Empress Elizabeth, and later Catherine the Great, greatly expanded and remodeled it. The rooms reflect the conflicting tastes of various tsars and interior fashions from early Baroque to Neoclassical.

Ascend the exquisite main staircase to the 2nd floor rooms, including the **Chesme Gallery,** a room larger than most single-family homes, whose artwork depicts the 1770 Russian victory over the Turks at Chesme Bay. Catherine arranged for a frigate to explode in front of the painter to ensure the images' authenticity. Farther along, two Chinese lobbies flank a picture gallery that contains 368 portraits by the Italian Pietro Rotari; his widow, strapped for cash, sold the whole lot to Catherine the Great. Through the silk-lined opulence of the palace women's rooms lies the last room on the tour—**Peter's study,** lined with elegantly carved oak wood panels and a rest for the eyes after all the splendor. Much of the room, unlike the rest of the grounds, inexplicably survived the Nazi invasion. (☎ 427 9527. Open Tu-Su 10:30am-6pm; kassa closes 5pm. Closed last Tu of the month. English tour 120R. Palace 230R, students 115R. Cameras 80R, video 200R. Handbags must be checked, 2R.)

**HERMITAGE PAVILION.** While walking along the main path from the Great Palace to the quay, pause periodically to look back at the effect created by the terraced foundation, flanked by golden statues. Just before the quay, past the woods to the left, stands the Hermitage Pavilion, which served as a setting for the amusements of the palace residents. Fans of 17th- and 18th-century European art might find the 2nd-floor room "tapestried" with floor-to-ceiling paintings worthwhile. (Open Tu-Su 10:30am-5pm. 86R, students 43R.)

**MONPLAISIR.** On the right side of the path facing the quay, opposite the Pavilion, stands Monplaisir, where Peter actually lived (the large palace was only for special occasions). Smaller and less ostentatious than its neighbors—he was the tsar with good taste—it is graceful and elegant. The place is peaceful even on the busiest Saturdays. (Open M-Tu and Th-Su 10:30am-6pm. Closed last Th of the month. 170R, students 85R.)

**OTHER BUILDINGS.** Next door is the **Catherine Building** (Екатерининский Корпус; Ekaterininsky Korpus), where Catherine the Great lay low while her husband was being overthrown on her orders. Within the same complex, follow the sound of children's happy shrieks to the **"joke fountains,"** which, activated by a misstep, splash their giggling victims. (Open M-W and F-Su 10:30am-6pm. Closed last F of each month. 86R, students 43R. Camera 60R, video 150R.)

Near the end of the central path to the right, a **wax museum** contains likenesses of historical figures ranging from the evil-looking Ivan the Terrible to the equally evil-looking Rasputin. (Wax museum open daily 9am-5pm. 50R, students 25R.)

# TSARSKOYE SELO/PUSHKIN

*The elektrichka runs from Vitebsky vokzal (M1: Pushkinskaya). Ask for "Pushkin" (tickets 6R) and say "too-DAH ee oh-BRAHT-nah" (туда и обратно; round-trip) to get a round-trip ticket. Don't be worried that none of the signs say Pushkin; all trains leaving from platforms 1-3 stop there. It's the first stop outside Petersburg that actually looks like a station, recognizable by the large number of people (30min.). From the station, take bus #371 or 382 to the end (2R; 10min.). Knowing where to get off is tricky; ask the conductor or get off at the stop after spotting the blue-and-white palace through the trees to the right.*

About 25km south of St. Petersburg, Tsarskoye Selo (Царское Село; Tsar's Village) surrounds Catherine the Great's summer residence, a gorgeous azure, white, and gold Baroque palace overlooking sprawling, English-style parks. The area was renamed "Pushkin" during the Soviet era, although the train station, Detskoe Selo (Детское Село; Children's Village) retained part of the old name. Most Russians use "Pushkin" to refer to the town.

**CATHERINE'S PALACE.** (Екатерининский Дворец; Ekaterininskii Dvorets.) Built in 1756 by the architect Rastrelli before he began work on the Winter Palace, this Baroque Palace was remodeled by Charles Cameron on the orders of Catherine the

Great. She had the good taste to remove the gilding from the facade, desiring a modest "cottage" where she could relax. This opulent residence, named after Catherine I, was largely destroyed by the Nazis; each room exhibits a photograph of it in a war-torn condition. The **Amber Room** suffered the most; its walls were stripped and probably lost forever (one rumor places the stolen furnishings somewhere in Paraguay). Even the exorbitant entrance fees haven't sufficed to repair these mansions completely, but many of the salons, especially the huge, glittering **Grand Hall** ballroom, have been returned to their former glory. Elizabeth used to hold costume parties here. Today there is ample space for to bust out a few dance moves in your stylish *tapochki* (museum slippers). The "golden" suites—so named for their lavish Baroque ornamentation—now hold those original furnishings that survived World War II. Latch onto one of the many English-speaking tours. (☎ 465 53 08. Open W-M 10am-5pm. Closed last M of the month. 220R, students 110R.)

**PARKS.** Many visitors choose to bring a picnic and wander through the surrounding parks. The landscaping, designed by Rastrelli, mixes the wild with the well-manicured. Sprinkled throughout both the trimmed hedges and the waist-high weeds are innumerable pavilions and terraces of varying architectural styles. Here Catherine would ramble with her dogs. Some believe she loved Muffy and Fido (or the Russian equivalent) more than her children; the dogs now rest in peace under the Pyramid. In summer it is possible to take a ferry across the **Great Pond** to the Island Pavilion. The Cold Bath Pavilion (one of the few open to the public) stands in front of the palace to the left. Designed by Charles Cameron, it contains the exotically beautiful Agate Rooms. Across the street from Catherine's Palace, the **lycée** schooled a 12-year-old Pushkin, one of the school's first students. His spartan dorm room can still be seen through hordes of awestruck Russians, along with the classrooms, laboratory, and music rooms. (Parks open daily 10am-11pm. Cold Bath Pavilion open M and Th-Su 10am-5pm. Closed last M of the month. Lycée ☎ 476 6411. Open M and W-Su 10:30am-5:30pm; kassa closes 4:30pm. Camera 100R, video 230R. Parks 50R, students 25R; free after 6pm. Pavilion 80R, students 40R. Lycée 20R, students 10R. Camera 25R, video 50R.)

## PAVLOVSK (ПАВЛОВСК)

*Trains leave from platforms #1-3 at Vitebsky vokzal; get off at the elektrichka stop after Tsarskoye Selo/Pushkin. To get to the palace from the train station, take bus #370, 383, or 383A. Or, cross the street in front of the station and walk through the park. To get to Pushkin from Pavlovsk, take bus #370 or 383 from the Great Palace, or bus #473 from Pavlovsk Station (3R). Small garden open 8am-4:30pm. Park open 24hr. 20R, students 12R. Palace open M-Th and Sa-Su 10am-6pm. 180R, students 90R. English tour 150R. Camera 90R, video 180R.*

Catherine the Great gave the park and gardens at Pavlovsk to her son Paul in 1777, perhaps because she wanted to keep an eye on him. The grounds include the largest **park** of all the outlying palaces, where shady paths wind among wild foliage, classical statuary, bridges, and pavilions. The **Three Graces Pavilion,** in the garden behind the palace, is renowned for the beauty of the central sculpture, carved by Paolo Triscorni in 1802 from a single piece of white marble. To the east stands the **Monument to Maria Fyodorovna,** widow of Paul I. Maria retreated to Pavlovsk after her husband's assassination in 1801 and her hand can be seen in the park today.

Paul's **Great Palace** is not as spectacular (or garish, depending on your architectural taste) as his mother's at Tsarskoye Selo, but is nonetheless worth visiting. The marble columns and sculpted ceilings of the Greek Hall are particularly noteworthy, as is the Gala Bedroom. Marie Fyodorovna's apartments are among the few examples of modest royal taste. Plundered, burnt, and mined by the Nazis, the palace was the hardest hit of those near St. Petersburg, making its current restored state all the more remarkable.

## SHLISSELBURG (ШЛИССЕЛЬБУРГ)

*Express bus #575 runs from M4: Ulitsa Dybenko; buy the ticket from the conductor (1hr., every 30min., M-F 12R, Sa-Su 16R). Ride past the "Шлиссельбург" stop to the last stop,*

*"Петрокрепость" (Petrokrepost). From the bus station, walk across the bridge and turn left, heading toward the river. The boat to the island leaves from in front of the statue of Peter the Great. (3min., 7 per day, last ferry back 4:30pm. Round-trip 15R.) Fortress and museums open daily in summer 10am-5pm. 25R, students 10R.*

About 35km east of St. Petersburg, on an island in the estuary of the Neva river, lies the medieval fortress of Shlisselburg. The fortress played a key role during the Swedish campaign of Peter the Great, who named it Shlisselburg, the key-city, but it has fallen into disrepair. The ruins of the fortress still hides both centuries of history and remarkable architecture; absorb it all in a leisurely, tourist-free setting.

The merchants of Novgorod built the original **fortress** in 1323, calling it Oreshek (Орешек; a tough nut) after the island Orekhovy (Ореховый; Nut Island), and used it as a trading outpost. When the pier burned down in 1352, the clever Novgorodians replaced it with a stone structure. Oreshek became a strategic military point in the 15th century, and was therefore rebuilt from scratch as a fortress with six towers and drawbridges. Ultimately, it spent most of the 17th century under Swedish control. October 1702 saw the forces of Peter the Great retake the fortress and rename it Shlisselburg. In a legendary letter, Peter wrote: "Tough was this nut indeed, but luckily we cracked it; our artillery worked true wonders." From that point on, it was the central base for Peter I's expeditions against Sweden.

Like many fortresses, the fortified island later became a prison for intellectuals, writers, revolutionaries, and other political undesirables. After entering the fortress and walking left on the path along the outside wall, an archway leads to a small courtyard and the **Old Prison,** built in 1789. Between 1826 and 1834, the Old Prison held members of the Decembrist group that had attempted to overthrow the tsarist regime in 1825. From 1884 to 1906 it held condemned revolutionaries, including **Aleksandr Ilyich Ulyanov,** elder brother of Lenin. Aleksandr was arrested for plotting the assassination of Tsar Alexander III; he was executed at Shlisselburg on May 8, 1887. His death marked the beginning of Lenin's deep resentment of the tsarist government. Inside the Old Prison, a **museum** details the building's history. The 3rd Cell shows the fine amenities each Decembrist enjoyed, while the even grimmer 4th Cell depicts what later revolutionaries endured. The first prisoners of Shlisselburg were members of the royal family; in the early 18th century, the displeased Peter sent his first wife Evdokiya Lopukhina and his sister Maria Alekseevna here.

Exiting the museum and walking along the wall where the revolutionaries were executed leads to a door that opens onto a magnificent view of **Lake Ladoga.** (If the door is locked, ask the attendant to unlock it.) During the Nazis' 900-day siege of Leningrad, the only road connecting the city with the mainland, known as "The Road to Life," ran across Ladoga. Ships in the summer and trucks in the winter (when Ladoga froze) carried ammunition and food to the besieged city.

Leaving the courtyard and continuing along the outermost path, one comes to the 1884 **New Prison,** darker and danker than even the Old Prison. The New Prison, too, has a **museum** displaying photos and living conditions of inmates. The far right door in the courtyard leads outside the fortress walls. Near the back of the fortress, an Orthodox Cross marks the **communal grave** of soldiers of the Northern War and World War II. Beyond the Overseer's Building, the **Fourth Prison** building, constructed in 1911, held revolutionaries until the Revolution of 1917, when all the prisoners were freed. An **exhibition and monument** to the World War II battle at Shlisselburg, when the Nazis attempted to obliterate the fortress, marks the middle of the yard. Under wraps behind the monument is a fragment of the 14th-century **Novgorodian fortress**—a precious archaeological find excavated in 1969.

# NOVGOROD (НОВГОРОД) ☎(8)1622

Founded in the 9th century by Prince Rurik, Novgorod (pop. 234,400) blossomed during the Middle Ages. In its heyday, it was home to almost twice its current population, victor over the Mongols, and challenger to Moscow for Slavic supremacy. Moscow ultimately won out, and Ivan III and Ivan IV (the Terrible) subjugated the upstart city (see **History,** p. 588). Novgorod lives on as Russia's best-preserved metropolis; many of the 140 churches and 50 monasteries built between 1100 and 1500 are still standing. Bigger and better restored than Pskov, Novgorod makes a good introduction to early Russia.

## ORIENTATION

Novgorod's heart remains its **kremlin,** from which a web of streets spin outward from the **west side** of the river. The **train station, bus station,** and **telephone office** all lie on the outermost street, ul. Oktyabrskaya (Октябрьская). Pr. Karla Marxa (Карла Маркса) runs from the train station to the earthen walls that surround old Novgorod. Follow ul. Lyudogoshchaya (Людогощая) from the walls, through pl. Sophiyskaya (Софийская) to the kremlin. The river's **east side** is home to most of the churches, as well as Yaroslav's court. Purchase a **map** (30R) from a kiosk inside the train station or at any of the major hotels. The names on the map don't always match the older street signs; many of the names changed a few years ago. Locals use the old and new names interchangeably, and two signs often adorn one corner.

## TRANSPORTATION

**Trains:** To: **St. Petersburg** (4½hr., 7 per day, 48R) and **Moscow** (9½hr., 3 per day, 68R). Watch your belongings closely on the Novgorod-Moscow train. *Kassy* open 24hr., but closed for random breaks.

**Buses:** To the right as you face the train station, in a building labeled "Автостанция" (avtostantsia). Station open 5am-10pm. Buses run to: **Moscow** (10hr., 1 per day, 90R); **St. Petersburg** (3½hr., 7 per day); and **Pskov** (4hr., 2 per day, 65.40R).

## PRACTICAL INFORMATION

**Tourist Office: Excursion Office** (Экскурсионный отдел; ekskusionny otdel), ul. Meretskovo 2 (Мерецкого), in the big white building in front of the kremlin. Enter through the courtyard in back. Go to the end of the hall and turn left; the office is the 2nd door on the right. English tours of Novgorod (7.2R) and the kremlin (4.8R), but no maps or brochures. Open M-F 9am-6pm.

**Currency Exchange:** Ul. Velikaya 16 (Великая), inside Gostinitsa Intourist. Exit the kremlin to the right, cross the park, and continue on to the river. Follow Velikaya along the water past the odd-looking theater. Exchanges any hard currency, but only has good rates for dollars. Open M-F 9am-6pm, Sa 9am-5pm. Also at any **"Обмен Валюты"** sign.

**ATM:** Cirrus accepted in the **train station.** Also at any **"Банкомат"** sign.

**Luggage Storage:** In the train station (6.30R 1st day, 10.30R afterward). Open 24hr.

**Telephone Office:** Opposite the bus station on ul. Oktyabrskaya. Phones on the right are for direct calls. Prepay at the *kassa* for a booth number, then get change if you have time left. For international calls either dial direct or pay in advance (the wait for international calls can be 1hr.). Alternatively, call **AT&T Direct** or a similar service in Moscow (see **Essentials: Communication,** p. 604). Local and intercity calls 29R for 150 units.

**Post Office:** B. Sankt Peterburgskaya 9. Open M-F 9am-2pm and 3-7pm, Sa 9am-4pm.

**Postal code:** 173 001.

## ACCOMMODATIONS

Novgorod's accommodations provide a wide range of comforts and prices. **Gostinitsa Sadko** (Гостиница Садко), ul. Fyodorovsky Ruchei 16 (Фёдоровский Ручей, formerly Gagarina), features a friendly staff, spacious rooms with private baths, and a remote location. From the kremlin, cross the footbridge and take the first left onto ul. Bolshaya Moskovskaya. Walk two blocks, then turn right onto Fyodorovsky Ruchei. The hotel is five minutes up on the right. (☎66 30 04; fax 66 30 17; root@sadko.vnov.ru. Singles 330R; doubles 460R. Breakfast included. English spoken. MC/Visa.) **Gostinitsa Turist** (Турист), nab. Aleksandra Nevskovo 19/1

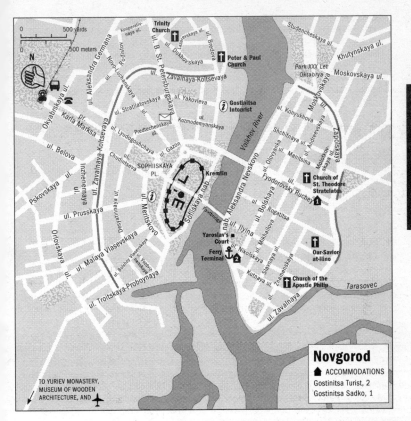

**Novgorod**

⬥ ACCOMMODATIONS

Gostinitsa Turist, 2
Gostinitsa Sadko, 1

(Александра Невского) is sometimes called Hotel Russia. Faded hotel with brusque staff and large rooms with private baths; some have views of the beloved kremlin. From the kremlin, cross the foot bridge and walk past the walls of Yaroslav's court. (☎341 85. Singles 260R; doubles 340R.)

## 🗋 FOOD

The few eateries with any kind of ambience cater to tourists and raise their prices accordingly. If you're short of cash, the kremlin is the perfect place for a picnic; try *shashlyky* and *sloiki* (слойки; a delicious pastry with jam), available at an outdoor stand. The well-stocked **grocery store, Vavilon** (Вавилон), ul. Lydogoshchaya 10, is another alternative to fancy dining in Novgorod. (Open daily 8am-11pm.) There's a **market** on ul. Fyodorovsky Ruchei (formerly Gagarina) that runs from Aleksandra Nevskovo to ul. Bolshaya Moskovskaya. In addition to fruit and vegetables, you'll find clothes, shoes, and toiletries. (Open daily 8am-8pm.)

**Detinets** (Детинец; ☎746 24). Within the walls of the kremlin. Rough brick walls, wooden spoons, and real candles take diners back to the middle ages. Tour groups fill the place; call ahead. The 1st floor bar serves jolly *medovukha* (медовуха; mead), for 14.25R per mug, *golubtsy* (голубцы; stuffed cabbage; 68R), and *shchi* (щи; meaty cabbage soup, 42.50R). Main dishes 65-120R. Open daily 11am-11pm.

**Pri Dvore** (При Дворе; ☎743 43). Outside the kremlin. *Shashlyky* grilled outside (28R). Sandwiches (from 60R) served inside. Open daily 11am-4pm and 6-11pm. For heartier fare go to their **restaurant** at ul. Lyudogoshchaya 3, just past the intersection with ul. Frolovskaya (Фроловская). Main dishes 61-86R. Open daily noon-4pm, 6pm-1am.

**Skazka** (Сказка; Fairy Tale), ul. Meretskovo 13 (☎771 60). To the left of the square in front of the kremlin. Go left through the park about 150m; the restaurant occupies the corner of ul. Meretskovo and ul. Volosova (Волосова), behind the children's playground. Veggie salads 18-35R; glass of wine 20R. Main dishes 45-110R. Open daily noon-midnight. Call ahead. In the less formal **dessert hall,** snack on sandwiches (5-30R), pizza (55-60R), or ice cream (12-16R). Open daily 11am-10pm.

## 👁 SIGHTS

### THE KREMLIN

Sometimes known as *detinets* (a small kremlin), Novgorod's pride and joy is impressive nonetheless. Its walls, 3m thick and 11m high, and nine spiraling towers protect most of the city's sights, which are clustered around a grassy park. To the immediate right of the lakeside entrance, bells are arranged at the base of the **belfry;** at the west gate stands **clock tower** (часовня; chasovnya). The tower's bell used to call citizens to meetings of the city council, until the Ivans did away with both the bell and the council. *(Belfry and clock tower open daily 6am-midnight. Free.)*

**ST. SOPHIA'S CATHEDRAL.** (Софийский Собор; Sofiysky Sobor.) Entering the kremlin from the west side of the river, the golden-spired building to the left is the oldest stone building in Russia. This 11th-century Byzantine cathedral, with intricately carved western doors depicting scenes from the Bible, dominates the complex. A shadowy interior obscures the few remaining icons; most are in the museum. With the exception of the interior of the dome, the frescoes were repainted in the 19th century. The gigantic bronze chandelier was given to the city by Tsar Boris Godunov. *(Open daily 8am-8pm; services 10am and 6pm. Free.)*

**FACETED CHAMBER.** (Грановитая Палата; Granovitaya Palata.) Next to the clock tower sits the Faceted Chamber, a monument to religious devotion with an elaborate collection of golden artifacts. The collection can only be toured with a guide (in Russian). Buy your ticket at the museum and wait in front of the doors until they spot you on the security camera and let you in. *(Open Th-Tu 10am-6pm. Closed last F of the month. 35R, students 19R. Camera 20R, video 100R.)*

**NOVGOROD UNITED MUSEUM.** The exhibits in the Novgorod United Museum, inside the classical structure within the kremlin, lead visitors through the city's history. Architectural finds and birch-bark inscriptions dominate the first few rooms but give way to typical displays of the tsarist era (medals, uniforms, and portraits). The red Soviet rooms are more interesting. The 2nd floor holds famous icons; the city hung one of the Virgin Mary on its gates in 1169 to save itself from the Suzdal. When the icon began to cry, the besieging army fled in terror. The other half of the 2nd floor houses a portrait gallery and the deservedly lesser-known works of 19th- and 20th-century masters. *(Open M and W-Su 10am-6pm. Closed last Th of the month. Museum 35R, students 19R. Camera 20R, video 100R.)*

**RUSSIAN MILLENNIUM.** (Тысячелетие России; Tysyacheletie Rossii.) In the center of the kremlin park, directly in front of the museum, stands the Russian Millennium. It was built in 1852 as one of three identical bell-shaped monuments; the 2nd stands in St. Petersburg, the 3rd in Kiev. Engraved in the bronze are a thousand years of Russian history; the figure kneeling before the angel on top represents the Russian conversion to Christianity in 988. The old favorites—Rurik, Prince Vladimir of Kyiv, and Peter the Great—are all here.

**OUTSIDE THE KREMLIN WALLS.** At the southern edge of the park the **Novgorod Horseman** commemorates the city's longevity, but only by default. Designed for Moscow after World War II, the statue was sent to Novgorod after the capital rejected it. Right in front of it stretches a sizeable **beach** where you can lounge with the locals when you've seen enough history for one day.

## OTHER SIGHTS

**YAROSLAV'S COURT.** (Ярославово Дворище; Yaroslavovo Dvorishche). Across the footbridge from the kremlin lies Yaroslav's Court, the old market center and the original site of the palace of Novgorod princes. It contains what's left of the 17th-century waterfront arcade, several 13th- and 16th-century churches, and the market gatehouse, now a **museum.**

**YURIEV MONASTERY.** (Юрьев Монастырь; Monastyr). Dating from 1030, Yuriev Monastery is one of the three working monasteries around the city. Its white-washed buildings, which stand amid broad, windy marshes, have an almost mysti-cal quality to them. From here you can see Lake Ilmen, the site of Rurik's 9th-century court, from which the state of Russia originated. The twin-domed **St. George's Cathedral** (Георгиевский Собор; Georgievsky Sobor), founded in 1119, houses icons dating from the 12th century, as well as a unique round pulpit (кафедра; kafedra). The church is undergoing extensive reconstruction. *(Take bus #7 (2R) from the stop on Meritskovo between Chudintseva and Prusskaya, on the side across the street from the park. Go past the airport and get off when you see the gold dome of the monastery. Open daily 10am-6pm. 24R, students 12R. Camera 10R, video 30R.)* On the way out note the bright blue cupolas of **Khristovozdvizhensky Sobor** (Христогоздвиженский Собор); golden stars symbolize the monastery's high status.

# PSKOV (ПСКОВ)
☎(8)1122

Pskov made its first foray into the history books in 903 as a flourishing regional trading post. As such, it was a popular target for invaders, including Swedes, Poles, Lithuanians, and Germans. While the invaders never actually took the city, the dam-age they wrought drove the Pskovians to throw themselves into the protective arms of the Russian Empire in 1510. By that time, trade routes had started to shift and eventually Pskov lost its stature as an economic center. Today, with more churches than restaurants and hotels combined, Pskov stands as a spiritual center. Unfortu-nately, most of the religious buildings desperately need repair, but the few that are open to the public serve as spectacular reminders of Pskov's great history.

## ⊞ ORIENTATION

The **bus** and **train stations** are next to each other on ul. Vokzalnaya (Вокзальная). This street intersects with the end of the **Oktyabrskii pr.** (Октябрьский пр.), Pskov's main axis, a couple of blocks to the right as you exit either station. Oktyabrsky pr. is home to Gostinitsa Oktyabrskaya, as well as the **telephone** and **post offices.** In the main square, **Oktyabrskaya pl.** (Октябрьская пл.) intersects with **ul. Sovetskaya** (Советская), which runs up to the kremlin at the town's north end. The **Velikaya** (Великая) and **Pskova** (Пскова) **Rivers** meet at the northernmost corner of the kremlin. Across the Velikaya is Gostinitsa Sputnik, and farther along **Rizhsky pr.** (Рижский) sits Gostinitsa Rizhskaya. The old outer town walls run for 9km along the river and **ul. Sverdlova** (Свердлова), past Pskov's two large parks. City **maps** are usually available at Gostinitsa Oktyabrskaya.

## ▣ TRANSPORTATION

**Trains:** To: **St. Petersburg** (6hr., 5 per day, 60R); **Moscow** (12hr., 2 per day, 103R); **Kaliningrad** (13hr., 1 per 1-2 days, 477R); **Riga, LAT** (6hr., 1 per day, 676R); **Vilnius, LIT** (8hr., every 1-2 days, 508R); and **Minsk, BLR** (15hr., 2 per week, 300R). Ticket office open 24hr.

**Buses:** The best way to and from Pskov, unless you're going to Moscow. To: **Pechory** (1½hr., 8 per day, 17.70R); **Novgorod** (4hr., 2 per day, 65.40R); and **St. Petersburg** (7hr., 5 per day, 75R). Each *kassa* sells tickets for different destinations, indicated to the right of the window. *Kassa* #5 for advance sales. Station open 5am-8pm.

**Local Transportation: Buses** #17 departs from the front of the train station and stops in front of Gostinitsa Oktyabrskaya, between Gostinitsa Turist and Gostinitsa Rizhskaya (see **Accommodations,** below), and at the kremlin. Buy tickets (2.5R) on board.

## ⚡ PRACTICAL INFORMATION

**Tourist Offices: Oktyabrskaya Tourist Bureau** (☎ 16 42 27). In Gostinitsa Oktyabr-skaya. Provides maps and brochures and arranges English tours. A **tourist bureau** (☎ 219 06 and 239 88; fax 72 32 57), on the right just after the entrance to the krem-lin, provides historical pamphlets and arranges English tours. Open M-F 9am-1pm and 2-6pm, Sa-Su 9am-2pm.

**Currency Exchange:** Oktyabrsky pr. 23/25 (☎ 16 19 83). Next to Sberbank (Сбербанк) across the street from Gostinitsa Oktyabrskaya. **Traveler's checks** cashed for a 3% commission. Open M-F 9am-2pm and 3-8pm, Sa 9am-3pm. Better exchange rates at most "Обмен Валюты" signs.

**Luggage Storage:** In the train station (10.50R for a large locker). Open 24hr. In the bus station (3R per bag). Open 8am-8pm.

**Telephones:** ul. Nekrasova 33 (Некрасова). Facing Oktyabrsky pr., in a large gray build-ing opposite the statue of Kirov between ul. Nekrasova (Некрасова) and ul. Gogolya (Гоголя). Prepay for intercity and international calls; you will receive change if there is time left. Open 24hr. **Faxes** at *kassy* 5 and 6. Open daily 7:30am-10:30pm.

**Post Office:** ul. Sovetskaya 7 (Советская; ☎ 227 19). Obscured by trees on the north side of pl. Oktyabrskaya. Open M-F 9am-2pm and 3-7pm, Sa-Su 9am-2pm.

**Postal code:** 180 000.

## 📍 ACCOMMODATIONS

Most hotels offer reasonably priced rooms, but there aren't any incredible values. For slightly higher prices, **HOFA** (see **St. Petersburg: Accommodations,** p. 646) pro-vides homestays (170R per night).

**Gostinitsa Rizhskaya** (Рижская), Rizhsky pr. 25 (☎ 46 22 23). Hop on bus #17 from the train station (2.5R). Tries for Western chic and almost pulls it off. Boasts such luxuries as a posh lobby, elevator, and soft foam mattresses. Private bath, TV, phone, and fridge in every room. Singles 250R; doubles 400R.

**Gostinitsa Oktyabrskaya** (Октябрьская), Oktyabrskaya pr. 36 (☎ 72 12 99). Take bus #11, 14, or 17 from the train station. The hotel is on your right, just before a park with a monument to Pushkin and his nurse. Relatively comfortable rooms with friendly staff and homey, if mismatched, decor. Singles with private bath and shower, TV, and fridge, as well as cheaper rooms without private bath—but take one look at the seatless toilets and curtainless showers (5R) and you may decide to splurge. Singles 75R, with bath 375R; doubles 132R, 690R.

**Gostinitsa Turist** (Турист), ul. Paromenskaya 4 (Пароменская; ☎ 44 51 51). Bus #17 stops just past the bridge. Tucked between Upeniya Paromenya and Velikaya. Typically unspectacular but decent budget hotel close to the kremlin. Singles 61R, with bath 90R; doubles 122R, 180R.

## 🍴 FOOD

Restaurants sell a variety of salty, fatty, potato-based foods. Fortunately, the numerous kiosks sell fresh bread, fruits, and vegetables. Vendors congregate at the **Central Market** (Центральный Рынок; Tsentralny Rynok) on pr. Karla Marxa (Карла Маркса) at the top of Pushkinskaya (Пушкинская). The entrance gate is labeled "РЫНОК" in huge letters. (Opens 8am.) A well-stocked western-style **gro-cery store** (i.e., you pick up your own goods and take them to the register) is both named and located at Oktyabrskya 12. (Open daily 9am-11pm.)

**Uyut** (Уют; Comfort), behind Cafe Cheburechnaya (see below). A Russian cafe with a dark but tidy wooden interior. Upper floor is a disco bar. Salads 14-20R; main dishes 22-46R. Cafe open daily noon-midnight. Bar open Su-Th 10pm-2am, F-Sa 10pm-5am.

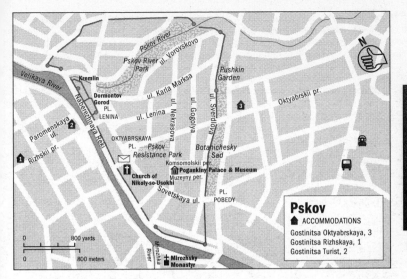

**Pskov**

▲ ACCOMMODATIONS

Gostinitsa Oktyabrskaya, 3
Gostinitsa Rizhskaya, 1
Gostinitsa Turist, 2

RUSSIA

**Aurora** (Аврора), Oktyabrsky pr. 36, connected to Gostinitsa Oktyabrskaya. On the 2nd floor. Strives for elegance with fancy silverware and a stylish bar as the focal point. Standard menu, but less greasy than usual Russian fare. Borscht 17.90R. Main dishes 40-60R. Open M-Th and Su 1pm-midnight, F-Sa 1pm-2am.

**Cafe Cheburechnaya** (Кафе Чебуречная), Oktyabrsky pr. 10A. In an orange clapboard building; enter from behind. Georgian greasy spoon very popular with locals. Old-school Soviet decor (vinyl) surrounds you, from the abacus to the reel-tape player. *Chebureki* (greasy but tasty meat pies) and meaty main dishes 15-30R. Open daily 11am-6pm.

## 👁 SIGHTS

**▩MIROZHSKY MONASTERY.** (Мирожский Монастырь; Monastyr.) Located downriver from the showier kremlin, the monastery walls enclose the **Cathedral of the Transfiguration** (Спасо-Преображенский Собор; Spaso-Preobrazhensky Sobor), which dates from 1156 and features spectacular frescoes typical of the Pskov region. *(Take bus #2 down ul. M. Gorkovo; get off at Krasnoarmeiskaya ul. Cross Krasnoarmeiskaya and follow Yubileinaya across the bridge. Any of the paths through the woods to the left leads to the monastery. Open Tu-Su 11am-6pm. 100R, students 60R.*

**KREMLIN.** With its thick stone walls topped by authentic wooden roofs and spires, the kremlin seems to hold time at bay outside its arched portals. In the courtyard just inside the main gate stands the ruins of Dovmontov's City (Довмонтов Город; Dovmontov Gorod), named for Prince Dovmont, who ruled here from 1266 to 1299. In contrast to the numerous attractions within Novgorod's kremlin, the interior courtyard here has only one building: the golden-domed **Trinity Cathedral** (Троицкий Собор; Troitsky Sobor). Founded in the 10th century by Saint Olga (Russia's first Christian monarch, who married Prince Igor of Kyiv and was later beatified) on her way to nearby Novgorod, this is actually the 4th cathedral to stand on this spot. The current structure, covered with frescoes that exemplify the Pskovian school of icon painting, was built in 1869. Those closest to the ceiling are the oldest. White walls and fresh flowers make the cathedral more inviting than its mustier counterparts. *(From the train station, take bus #17 or any bus going to Pl. Lenina; get off when you spot the kremlin walls. Kremlin open 24hr. Church open 8am until the end of the evening service. Services daily 9-11am and 6-8pm. Free, but donations appreciated.)*

**POGANKIN PALACE AND MUSEUM.** (Поганкины Палаты и Музей; Pogankiny Palaty i Muzey.) The wealth and heritage of Pskov rest in Pogankin Palace and

Museum, originally the home of a 17th-century merchant. Start by climbing to the 2nd floor, which is often populated by students meticulously copying the icons on display. Vaulted ceilings and well-lit cases of coins and jewelry await visitors on the first floor. Next to the main hall is the picture gallery, which houses temporary exhibits. *(On Komsomolsky pr. (Комсомольский), at the intersection with Nekrasova. Enter through the new wing, buy your ticket, and go down the stairs and out through the courtyard to the main house. Open Tu-Su 11am-6pm. Closed last Tu of the month. 45R, students 30R.)*

## ⚡ DAYTRIP FROM PSKOV

### PECHORY MONASTERY

*Buy a ticket to Pechory at the Pskov bus station (17.70R); buy a return ticket as soon as you arrive, unless you want to camp with the monks. Schedules vary, but the last bus leaves at 5:50pm M-F, 7:35pm Sa-Su. Go to the right on Yurevskaya ul. (Юревская). At the fork go left onto Oktyabrskaya; when it ends go right into the courtyard in front of the entrance. ☎ 215 93. Open daily 6am-9pm. English tour 200R; call at least 1 week in advance.*

If you happen to be in Pskov overnight, **Pechory Monastery** (Печоры Монастырь; Monastyr) makes a good excursion for the next day. Founded in 1473, the monastery sheltered more than 200 monks in the 16th century, when it doubled as a fortress. Today the complex is home to approximately 60 monks. Looking straight from the main gate, the golden-domed 1827 **St. Michael Church** (Михайловская Церковь; Mikhaylovskaya Tserkov) stands beyond the "no entrance" (Нет Входа) sign. Through the archway to the left and down the hill stands the yellow and white **Assumption Cathedral** (Успенский Собор; Uspensky Sobor), crowned with gold-starred blue domes. (Services daily 6am and 6pm.) The door on the left leads to the sacred caves, where monks and hermits are sealed in the walls. The caves are generally closed to visitors, but you can try negotiating with the guard. Next to the cathedral stands a whitewashed belfry. A few steps down, the beautiful flower garden surrounds a sacred water fountain, which serves as the site of regular pilgrimages; besides being holy, the water is reputedly potable. Ask the gatekeeper about paying for permission to bring a camera. Women must cover their heads and wear skirts, which can be borrowed at the entrance.

# THE KALININGRAD REGION (КАЛИНИНГРАДСКАЯ ОБЛАСТЬ)

History and fate have conspired to leave the Kaliningrad region (Kaliningradskaya Oblast) part of Russia. The capture of the region, once East Prussia, by the Soviets at the end of World War II marked the end of a 700-year period during which the city was a focal point of German culture. In the decades that followed, the region underwent intense Russification and thousands of ethnic Germans were exiled to Siberia. With the unraveling of the Soviet Union the region found itself an island of armed, bewildered Russians severed from the Motherland by newly sovereign Latvia, Lithuania, and Belarus. Visitors can still enjoy both Kaliningrad's charm and the unspoiled beaches of Svetlogorsk, which few have bothered to explore.

# KALININGRAD (КАЛИНИНГРАД)  ☎(8)0112

Sovietization was carried out so thoroughly after the Red Army's 1945 occupation that a contemporary observer would hardly suspect that Kaliningrad (pop. 419,000) existed as a German city for 700 years. Once home to philosopher Immanuel Kant, the former Königsberg (King's City)—named for its importance to Prussia—was completely razed during World War II. For security reasons, the city, renamed after Stalin's henchman Mikhail Ivanovich Kalinin (who never set foot here), was only opened to tourists in 1991. Kaliningrad remains an island of confusion, edging economically ahead of Russia proper but lagging far behind its Baltic neighbors. The city, even with its flashes of color, shady parks, and friendly residents, isn't picturesque, but it offers a glimpse of Russia without leaving Europe too far behind.

## ORIENTATION

Both the bus and southern train stations lie on **pl. Kalinina** (Калинина). **Leninsky pr.** (Ленинский), the main artery, runs perpendicular to pl. Kalinina north across the **Pregolya River** (Преголя) and **Kneiphof Island**, site of the cathedral. It continues past the hideous House of Soviets to **Tsentralnaya pl.** (Центральная), home to **Gostinitsa Kaliningrad** (Гостиница Калининград; Hotel Kaliningrad), then veers left to its end, **pl. Pobedy** (Победы), where a statue of Lenin presides over an expanse of concrete. Just before the square, **Teatralnaya pr.** (Театральная) splits off to the left, becomes **pr. Mira** (Мира), and heads toward the zoo, while **ul. Chernyakhovskovo** (Черняховского) travels east toward the central market and the amber museum.

## TRANSPORTATION

**Trains: Yuzhny Vokzal** (Южный Вокзал; South Station; ☎49 24 41 and 49 99 91), pl. Kalinina 1, next to the bus station and behind the statue of Kalinin, handles international connections. Open 4am-midnight. International *kassa* upstairs to the right of the exit open 8am-8pm. Local *kassa* left of the exit. To: **Moscow** (23-24hr., 1 per day, *platskartny* 324R); **St. Petersburg** (22hr., 1 per day, *platskartny* 391R); **Gdynia, POL** (5hr., 1 per day, 180R) via **Gdańsk, POL** and **Malbork, POL**; and **Vilnius, LIT** (8hr., 1 per day, 272R). **Severny Vokzal** (Северный Вокзал; North Station; ☎49 26 75), north of pl. Pobedy, in front of the big pink building that once held the local KGB headquarters, sends trains to Baltic Coast cities.

**Buses:** pl. Kalinina, east of Yuzhny Vokzal (☎44 36 35). To: **Gdańsk, POL** (5hr., 2 per day, 135R); **Warsaw, POL** (8-9hr., 2 per day, 250R); **Riga, LAT** (9½hr., 1 per day 225R); and **Hrodna, BLR** (10hr., 1 per day, 245R). *Kassa* open daily 5:30am-2pm and 3-11:30pm.

**Public Transportation:** The transportation system in Kaliningrad is undergoing a massive overhaul. **Buses**, which are now privatized, will speed your journey. Prices (2-3R) are posted in the bus window; pay the conductor if there is one, or the driver when you get off if not. Some lack numbers, so you may have to look for your destination written on the front. Slower public **trams** still traverse the city (1R); trams #2 and 3 run from pl. Kalinina to pl. Pobedy via pl. Tsentralnaya, connecting Yuzhny Vokzal and Severny Vokzal, while tram #1 runs east to west from beyond the zoo toward the market.

**Taxis:** In every major square, especially at the train stations, Gostinitsa Kaliningrad, the zoo, and pl. Pobedy. Agree on a price before setting off; don't pay more than US$2.

## PRACTICAL INFORMATION

**Tourist Office: Noktyurn** (Ноктюрн; ☎/fax 46 95 78), to the left of the lobby of Gostinitsa Kaliningrad. No train tickets. German spoken. Open M-Sa 8am-6pm.

**Currency Exchange: Kiosks** with "Обмен Валюты" (obmen valyuty) signs dot major downtown intersections. **Investbank** (Инвестбанк), Leninsky pr. 28 (☎43 46 62). Facing away from Gostinitsa Kaliningrad (see **Accommodations,** below), it's across the street to the right. Accepts AmEx **traveler's cheques** and gives MC/Visa **cash advances,** both for a 2% commission. There's a 24hr. MC **ATM** outside and a MC/Visa one outside Gostinitsa Kaliningrad. Branch offices are popping up throughout Kaliningrad. Open M-Sa 9:30am-1pm and 2-4pm.

**Luggage storage:** Buy a *zheton* (жетон; token) at one of the bus station *kassy* for 2.60R. Open M-Sa 6am-10pm, Su 6am-6pm.

**Pharmacy:** Apteka (Аптека), Leninsky pr. 67 (☎43 27 83). The best bet for western brands. Open daily 8am-8pm.

**Telephones:** Ul. Leonova 20, next to the post office. **Faxes** available. Open daily 8am-9pm. **International Telephone Center** (☎45 15 15; fax 46 95 90), inside Gostinitsa Kaliningrad, on the left as you enter. Open daily 7:30am-11pm.

**Internet Access: Kiberda Internet Club** (☎51 18 30), Komsomolskaya 87 (Комсомольская), near the post office. Fast connections for 35R per hr., plus food and pool. The **telephone office** (see above) has 2 connections (40R per hour) and the more central **Gostinitsa Kaliningrad** (see below) houses its own cybercafe (40R per hour).

**Post Office:** Out of the way at ul. Leonova 22 (Леонова; ☎21 92 70). A right off pr. Mira, past Gostinitsa Moskva. Open M-F 9am-6pm, Sa 10am-6pm. Poste Restante and **EMS** at window #8, to the left in the main lobby (☎21 16 10). **Branch** at ul. Krasnook-tyabrskaya 6/12 (Краснооктябрьская; ☎44 33 15), to the right of Leninsky pr. before the river. The communication center in Gostinitsa Moskva is more convenient.

**Postal code:** 236 000.

# ⌐ ACCOMMODATIONS

First there was nothing. Then, the Germans came, and they were not pleased. So, Kaliningrad built for the Germans many fine hotels, but the Germans were still not pleased, and the Germans decided to go to Florida. Then the ruble was devalued, and the many fine hotels were not pleased, because they couldn't get much money out of the Russians, their only clientele after the Germans left. But then came you, the budget traveler, and you said, "It is good." You may then complain about the 16R visa registration fee charged by most hotels.

**Gostinitsa Zolotoya Bukhta** (Гостиница Золотая Бухта; Golden Cake Hotel), Khmelnitskovo 53 (Хмельницкого; ☎44 57 77 and 44 58 78). From the bus station, turn left onto Leninsky and take the 3rd right onto Khmelnitskovo. Get in touch with your nautical self in this high-style hotel run by the Baltic Fleet. Posh rooms stocked with a phone, fridge, cable, and even a flask for your convenience. All rooms with bath. Singles US$9; doubles US$13; triples US$16.

**Gostinitsa Ademi** (Адеми), nab. Marshala Bagramyana 34 (наб. Маршала Баграмяна; ☎46 16 62; fax 46 16 41). From Leninsky pr., cross the bridge heading toward Tsentralnaya pl.; the hotel is on the left. Yes, it's on a ship. Good location, upscale facilities, and rock-bottom prices. Sauna, restaurant, bar, business center, and casino on premises. English-speaking reception 24hr. Singles 160R; doubles 180R, with bath 350R; triples with bath 400R.

**Gostinitsa Kaliningrad** (Гостиница Калининград), Leninsky pr. 81 (☎46 94 40; fax 46 95 90; market@hotel.kaliningrad.ru), on the north side of Tsentralnaya pl. The fanciest digs in town, and the interior even looks stylish...compared to the nearby House of Soviets. Also houses a tourist office, exchange office, phone center, and a business center. Reception 24hr. Singles US$28-48; doubles US$50-67. AmEx/MC/Visa.

**Gostinitsa Moskva** (Москва), pr. Mira 19 (☎27 20 89), a few blocks past pl. Pobedy and just past Baltika Stadium on the left, across from the zoo. Take any tram in the direction of "Парк Калинина" (Park Kalinina). Russians from other cities stay here when they're in town. Somewhat musty rooms and iffy hot water. Singles US$7, with shower US$13; doubles US$15, US$25; triples US$17, US$34.

# ◖ FOOD

While eating out in Kaliningrad can be an adventure, especially for non-Cyrillic readers, nice places can be found and new restaurants are slowly appearing. For groceries, head to the **central market** (центральный рынок; tsentralny rynok), originally built for a 1930s trade exhibition, at the intersection of ul. Chernyakhovskovo and ul. Gorkovo. (Open daily 9am-6pm.) Several reasonably well-stocked **supermarkets** lie along Leninsky pr., between Tsentralnaya pl. and pl. Pobedy.

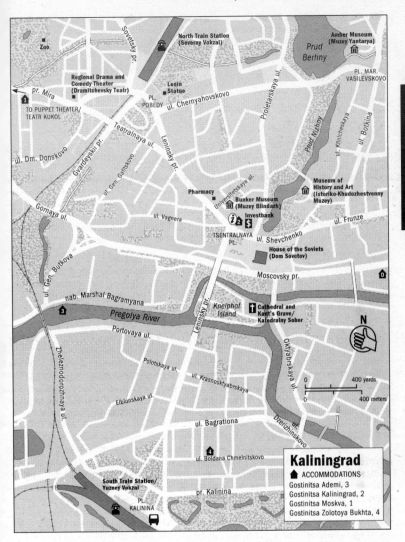

**Chyorny Kot** (Чёрный Кот; Black Cat), Leninsky pr. 111, on the same side of the bridge as the bus station. Follow the stream of ravenous Russians downstairs to sample cheap, fast, delicious Russian dishes and drinks. The staff is happy to oblige foreigners and the menu features pictures. Dinner US$1-3.

**Pri Svechakh** (При Свечах; By Candlelight), pr. Mira 4, on the terrace of the Dramatichesky Teatr (☎21 17 71). The best outdoor cafe in the city. Relax and watch the crowds rush by over a cold *EKU Pils* (10R) and real sandwiches.

**Titanic** (Титаник), Chernyakhovskovo pr. 74 (☎53 67 68), between pl. Pobedy and the central market. Possibly the most unexpected dining experience in the city, this restaurant aims to recreate the blockbuster that recreated the ship that...nevermind. Two-story replica features lifeboats that double as booths. Excellent soup. Main dishes 54-150R.

**Oleg's Uzbek Kitchen,** Staraya Bashnya (Старая Башня; ☎46 17 00), Kiosk #52, in the shadow of the ultra-hideous House of Soviets on ul. Shevchenko. A real sit-down place with real and bountiful Uzbek specialties for US$1-2. Open daily noon-2pm.

## 👁 SIGHTS

### CATHEDRAL

☎ *44 68 68 and 27 25 83. Open daily 9am-5:30pm. 4DM (pay in rubles), students 20R.*

The city's pride and joy during its 700-year stint as Königsberg, the Cathedral ages away on the large Kneiphof Island in the middle of the Pregolya River. It was damaged by fire back in 1944, but funds are now being raised to build a new roof and restore the towers. Meanwhile, the burnt-out shell stands as both a reminder of Kaliningrad's German heritage and a monument to the Russian conquest of the city, while the plastic surgery progresses with the ebb and surge of German tourism. Inside, where Prussian kings were once crowned, you can see the vandalized and eroding tombs lining the cathedral's walls, or climb the mythical steps made famous by German Romantic writer E.T.A. Hoffmann. The **Kaliningrad Symphony** occasionally holds concerts here; inquire within.

**KANT'S GRAVE.** Walk around (outside) to the back of the cathedral to find the immaculately kept grave of Immanuel Kant (1724-1804), the German philosopher who spent his entire life in Königsberg and taught at the local university. Kant's grave is enclosed by pink marble colonnades, probably to protect him from the busloads of German tourists who visit him daily. Other Kant paraphernalia, including a macabre copy of his death mask, are in the museum upstairs in the cathedral.

**JULIUS RUPP MEMORIAL.** Behind the cathedral stands a monument erected in 1991 to Julius Rupp (1809-1884), one of Königsberg's most famous pastors, whose house once stood on this spot. Rupp founded a new, unofficial religious order called *Druzya Sveta* (Друзья Света; Friends of the World), which stood for harmony among all peoples and religions. Though Rupp was frequently chastised for his views in the 19th century, he remained one of Königsberg's most influential thinkers and passed many of his beliefs to his niece, artist Käthe Kollwitz.

### MONUMENTS TO SOVIET GLORY

Since 1255, when Teutonic knights first arrived in this area, a castle has guarded the hill east of what is now Tsentralnaya pl. As part of the effort to turn Königsberg into a truly Soviet city, the original castle was blown up in 1962 and replaced by the **House of Soviets** (Дом Советов; Dom Sovetov), an H-shaped monstrosity that, after 35 years, stands incomplete even as it begins to crumble. Meanwhile, the nearby **Gallery of Artists** (Художественная Галерея; Khudozhestvennaya Galereya), displays local artwork and exhibits on the history of the *oblast. (Moskovsky pr. 60/62.* ☎ *46 71 79. Open Tu-Su 11am-7pm. 10R.)* In the middle of **pl. Pobedy** (Victory Square) stands a 7m **statue of Lenin,** one of the last monuments from the Soviet era still standing. If you liked that, don't miss the genial-looking statue of **Mikhail Ivanovich Kalinin,** waving to the city named after him, which he never saw, from outside Yuzhny Vokzal. Two blocks to the left of Lenin, at Sovetsky pr. 3-5, a glorious pink-and-white Prussian building was once the home of the Kaliningrad **KGB.**

## 🏛 MUSEUMS

**Museum of History and Art** (Историко-Художественный Музей; Istoriko-Khudozhestvenny Muzey), Klinicheskaya 21 (Клиническая; ☎45 38 44). From Tsentralnaya pl., walk up the north side of the House of Soviets along ul. Shevchenko, which becomes ul. Klinicheskaya and snakes around Nizhny Lake. The museum is halfway up the lake. The 2nd floor is devoted to the heroic Soviet army and its 1945 conquest of

RUSSIA

the depraved German city of Königsberg. Another room displays propaganda promoting various communist ideals, featuring such cuddly characters as Lenin and Stalin. English captions. Open Tu-Su 10am-6pm. 20R, students 10R. Camera 30R.

**Amber Museum** (Музей Янтаря; Muzey Yantarya), Vasilevskovo pr. 1 (Василевский; ☎46 15 63). Located in one of Königsberg's 7 remaining city gates, the museum displays amber crowns, jewelry boxes made for Catherine the Great, one of the world's largest single pieces of amber (which weighs in at a hefty 4.28kg), and even the poor insects who met their fate inside the hardening tree sap. Nearly 90% of the world's amber comes from nearby Yantar, much of it smuggled out illegally every year, and these are the best specimens of the lot. The gift shop downstairs sells amber souvenirs, but other vendors offer similar pieces for less. Open Tu-Su 10am-5pm, *kassa* closes at 4pm. 20R, students 10R. Camera 30R.

**Bunker Museum** (Музей Блиндаж; Muzey Blindazh). Off Leninsky pr., on ul. Universitetskaya 2 (Университетская; ☎53 65 93), opposite the garden of the University of Kaliningrad. This underground complex has taken over the rooms from which the Nazis directed their defense of Königsberg before the city was finally conquered by Soviet forces on April 9, 1945. The museum presents the capture of the city in detail; unlucky Room 13 has been left exactly as it was when the commander signed the city over to the Red Army. English captions. Open daily 10am-6pm. 20R, students 10R.

**Museum of the History of the World's Oceans** (Музей Истории Мирого Океана; Muzei Istorii Mirovo Okeana), Bagramyana 1 (Баграмяна; ☎43 63 02). On the Pregolya River near the Hotel Ademi. The submarine is visible from the Leninsky bridge. Check out the glory of the Russian navy and the wonders of the sea. Wander through exhibits on the "Vityaz," which, under German ownership as the "Mars," once helped thousands of Germans flee the area as the invading Red Army closed in on the city. Open M-F 3-6pm, Sa-Su 11am-6pm. 30R.

# ♫ ENTERTAINMENT

A Weimar-era residence houses the beautiful **Dramatichesky Teatr** (Драматический Театр), pr. Mira 4. Ask the friendly director Anatoly Kravtsov for a tour of the building. (☎21 24 22. Open daily 9am-9pm; performances 10-15R.) Kaliningrad's beer/vodka gardens are plentiful and the closest thing to nightspots outside the sketchy casinos. The **stadium** across from the zoo, on pr. Mira near Gostinitsa Moskva, is home to Kaliningrad's beloved soccer team, Baltika. It's worth seeing the team play if you're a soccer fan, but beware the crowd of drunk men.

# ♬ DAYTRIP FROM KALININGRAD

## SVETLOGORSK (СВЕТЛОГОРСК)

*Svetlogorsk is best reached by train. Trains from Kaliningrad (1hr., 12 per day, 12R) stop at both Svetlogorsk 1 and Svetlogorsk 2, which is closer to the center of town. In front of Svetlogorsk 2, ul. Lenina (Ленина) runs parallel to the sea. The impatient can take the chairlift from behind the station directly to the beach. (Daily 10am-8pm. 6R.) Otherwise, a left down ul. Lenina leads to the center of town (5min.).*

Formerly the German town of Rauschen, this seaside resort was used by Soviet officials as a spot for rest and relaxation. Today, German tourists have returned to Svetlogorsk. Those old enough to remember can tell you that much of the old charm is still here—tall pines line quiet streets with lovely old villas perched above the Baltic. The main attraction is the beach, which is quite pleasant. Stroll along the promenade and enjoy the tranquil vistas, at least until you reach the area with vendors hawking amber. At the east end of the promenade sits a **sundial,** purportedly the largest in Europe, with a beautiful multicolored mosaic on its face. At ul. Lenina 5, on the outskirts of town, a small **chapel** stands in memory of the 34 people who died when a Soviet military aircraft crashed into a kindergarten on the site. Among the dead were 23 children. The incident was covered up until 1991, when the Russian Orthodox Church decided to build the chapel.

# NEAR KALININGRAD

## KURSHSKAYA KOSA (КУРШСКАЯ КОСА)

Nearly 80km long and never more than 4km wide, the Kurshskaya Kosa (Curonian Spit) is essentially a giant sandbar. Stunningly beautiful pine forests cover all but the western side, which has been molded by Baltic winds into a series of famous sand dunes. The eastern side faces the calmer waters of the Kurshisky Zaliv (Кушиский Залив; Curonian Lagoon), and is home to a few villages, including tiny Rybachy (Рыбачий), the best base for exploring the Spit.

**⬛ TRANSPORTATION.** Abandon any dreams of cruisin' in a hot-rod rental—non-residents are barred from driving on the spit. Envision instead over-crowded **buses** (50min., every hr., 12R) or the more pleasant **trains** (50min., 6 per day, 12R) from Kaliningrad to **Zelenogradsk** (Зеленоградск). Then hop a **bus** to **Morskoe** or **Klaipėda, LIT** that stops in **Rybachy** (45min., 8 per day, 11R; buy tickets in the train station opposite the buses). Public transportation links the three major settlements along the Russian part of the Spit: **Lesnoe** (Лесное), the forest village, **Rybachy,** the fishing village, and **Morskoe** (Морское), the sea village, near the Lithuanian border.

**◧⬛ ORIENTATION AND PRACTICAL INFORMATION.** From Rybachy's bus-station, take a right onto the main drag, ul. Pobedy (Победы), which ends at the main highway. The road north to Morskoe and Klaipėda lies straight ahead, while Zelenogradsk is to the left. Just down the road toward Zelenogradsk stands a large **map** with English notations. Rybachy's **post** and **telephone office** lies at Pobedy 29. (Open M-Sa 9am-5pm.) For other services, head back inland.

**⬛⬛ ACCOMMODATIONS AND FOOD.** Rybachy boasts one budget place to stay, the **ZRP Rest Home,** which offers sparse but clean rooms with shared baths for 5-10R per person. Some overlook the lagoon, but none have telephones. Many visitors come just to eat at Rybachy's fantastic restaurant, ⬛**Traktir Forosh** (Трактиръ форош), at the end of ul. Pobedy along the highway. Their specialty is locally- caught seafood, including delicious fried eel, but they do meats and salads pretty well too. Everything is served with generous side dishes of veggies, bread, and red caviar. (Main dishes 90-150R. Open daily noon-4am.)

**⬛⬛ SIGHTS AND HIKING.** Tourist infrastructure on the Spit ranges from minimal to nonexistent, so don't expect visitor centers or many hiking trails. There are a few access points to the sea and the lagoon between towns; these usually have a bus stop. Otherwise, scores of unpaved roads and unmarked footpaths crisscross the forest. Most of these, the product of grazing cattle, lead to private homes or nowhere at all. The one **hiking trail** in the area is about 15 minutes from Rybachy down the road toward Zelenogradsk, but it is not to be missed. Look for signs along the road in English for Excursion Route "Island" (Остров); the trailhead is on the right just after the lake on the left. An gentle 3.5km loop, it was built in 1998 by a group of environmentalists. Follow the wooden arrows (some of which are missing, in which case follow the bigger path) to the top of Müller's Hill, the highest point on the spit. Climb the taller of the two observation towers for a view that will make even the most jaded hiker gape in awe. The entire spit is visible, from Lesnoe to Lithuania and from idyllic Rybachy on the lagoon to the shimmering Baltic. From here, the trail descends into a pleasant pine forest whose trees slant to one side from the force of the wind. This part of the trail is poorly maintained, and you may even find yourself forced back the other way to return to town. Once there, take a walk down by the **beach;** head down the road toward Klaipėda and Morskoe. Just after a bend (10min.), a power line crosses the road; turn left here onto the path beneath it. This path continues straight until you reach the vast and empty sands.

# THE TRANS-SIBERIAN RAILROAD

The lifeline that connects the gilded domes and tinted windshields of Moscow with the rest of her proud but crumbling empire, the Trans-Siberian railroad is a trip through Russia in the fullest sense. Over the course of 6½ days, the train rolls through 9289km, two continents, and seven time zones, over endless taiga and titanic rivers. While the exterior journey is certainly spectacular, travelers will likely remember most what goes on inside the train. Whether you find yourself riding with a nightgowned *babushka* and her bucket of berries or middle-aged men who drink vodka before bed and beer for breakfast, the ride is a crash-course in Russian culture. For years, the Trans-Siberian was a mysterious voyage past closed cities and missile silos, attempted by only the most intrepid of travelers. Today, agencies in both Asia and Russia have cracked this tough nut, providing help with tickets and visas. While backpackers and tours have discovered the Trans-Siberian, it remains an exotic, unpolished journey that can't be matched.

**LOGISTICS.** The term "Trans-Siberian" generally doesn't refer to a single train, but to three sets of tracks and the numerous trains that run along them. The **Trans-Siberian** line links Moscow and Vladivostok, the **Trans-Mongolian** connects Moscow with Beijing via Ulaanbaatar, Mongolia, and the **Trans-Manchurian** loops through Manchuria en route to Beijing. Most westerners buy a ticket at one end for the entire trip, but it is possible to travel point-to-point. In addition to the well-known trans-continental trains, there are many shorter (and dirtier) inter-city lines. You'll need **visas** to enter China and Mongolia; the Chinese visa is best obtained in Moscow (see p. 610), while a Mongolian visa can be picked up either in Moscow (see p. 610), Irkutsk (see p. 683), or Ulan Ude. Mongolian consular representatives will need a passport-sized photo to process visas. (No invitation needed for 7-day tourist visa. 1-month tourist visa US$25 for 1-week processing, US$50 overnight. Transit visa requires continuing train ticket and valid Chinese visa. 1-week processing US$15, overnight US$30.)

**COSTS.** The cost of a Trans-Siberian ticket depends on myriad variables, including where and when you buy it, how far you're going, what class you want, whether you're Russian or foreign, and whether the salesperson likes you. Tickets are most expensive in Moscow, but are still cheaper than buying a string of tickets from town to town. Summer prices are always higher than winter prices. If you're only making a few stops, you're best off going through the **Traveler's Guest House** in Moscow (see p. 613) which offers several different types of Trans-Siberian tickets for a US$15 commission. More importantly, they'll explain in excellent English how the railroad works and can help you choose the ticket best suited to your itinerary. Allow at least five days for processing during high season. Routes include: **Beijing via Mongolia** US$187; **Beijing via Manchuria** US$209; **Vladivostok** US$75; and **Ulaanbaatar** US$145. (All prices are for 2nd class tickets during the high season.) If you speak Russian, you can save nearly 30% by buying directly from **Tsentralnoe Zheleznodorozhnoe Agenstvo** (Центральное Железнодорожное Агенство; Central Train Agency) in Moscow (see **Intercity Transportation,** p. 608).

**DEPARTING.** All Trans-Siberian **trains** depart from Moscow's **Yaroslavsky Vokzal** (see p. 608). The better long-distance trains, called *firmeny* (фирменный; quality), offer cleaner facilities but can also cost twice as much as the regular *skory* (скорый; rapid) trains. Local color aboard *skory* makes for an entertaining short trip, but drunks and offensive odors make the *firmeny* worth the money for trips longer than 24hr. From Moscow, the *firmeny* trains are: **train #2** (Rossia; Россия; Russia) departing for **Vladivostok** at 3:26pm on odd days (52½hr.); **train #10** (Байкал; Baikal) to **Irkutsk** and **Lake Baikal,** departing at 9:29pm on odd days (79½hr.); and **train #20** (Russky Poezd; Русский Поезд; the Russian Train)

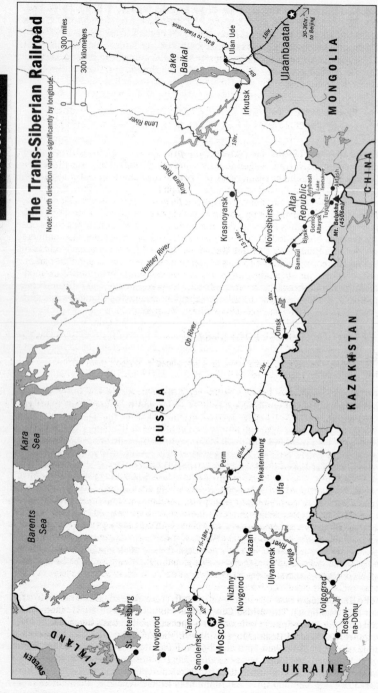

# The Trans-Siberian Railroad

Note: North direction varies significantly by longitude.

to **Beijing** on the Trans-Manchurian, departing Fridays at 10:56pm (145½hr.). Other trains include **train #4** (Kitaisky Poezd; Китайский Поезд; the Chinese Train) to **Beijing** via **Ulaanbaatar,** departing Tuesdays at 11:42pm (131hr. to Beijing) and **train #6** to **Ulaanbaatar,** departing Wednesdays and Thursdays at 11:42pm (99½hr.). *Firmeny* trains usually have a plaque on the side of each car stating the train's name. In all cases, "odd" (нечетный) and "even" (четный) refers to calendar days.

> **TRAIN TIME.** The Trans-Siberian traverses 7 time zones, but all train arrivals and departures are listed in Moscow time at stations as well as in *Let's Go.*

**LIFE ABOARD THE TRAIN.** Two attendants—*provodnik* (male) or *provodnitsa* (female)—sit in each train wagon to make sure all goes smoothly; they offer tea (2R) more cheaply than the restaurant car. Try to avoid the first or last *coupé* in the wagon; these neighbor the toilets and, especially on non-*fermeny* trains, the stench can become unbearable after several days (on *fermeny* trains they're cleaned several times per day). Always carry your own toilet paper. A posted schedule in each wagon lists arrival times for each *stoyanka* (stop; стоянка). When the train stops for longer than 15min., locals come out to hawk food to passengers, but there are other feeding options (see **"I'll Get That To Go,"** below). Your compartment-mates will probably come aboard with lots of sausage and veggies to share; you might want to do the same. Depending on the train, Moscow and Yekaterinburg are separated by about 28½hr. and 23hr. more stand between you and Novosibirsk. From Novosibirsk, it's 32hr. more to Irkutsk. Another 8hr. gets you to Ulan Ude, and it's a mere day from there to Ulaanbaatar, which is 36hr. from Beijing.

# YEKATERINBURG (SVERDLOVSK) ☎ (8)3432

> **TIME CHANGE.** Yekaterinburg is 2hr. ahead of Moscow (GMT +5).

The site of the Romanov family's brutal assassination in 1918 and hometown of Boris Yeltsin, Yekaterinburg, or Sverdlovsk as far as the railroad is concerned, (Екатеринбург/Свердловск; pop. 1.3 million) has lost some appeal since the royal remains took the Trans-Siberian back to St. Petersburg in 1998 for their interment. It might, however, still serve as a welcome respite for those longing to stand on terra firma. From the station, take trolley #1 or 9, or any bus with "пр. Ленина" on it to the main street, **pr. Lenina.** All public transportation costs 3R. Alternatively, it's just a 10-minute walk away from the train station along ul. Yakova Sverdlova (Якова Свердлова), which runs into ul. Karla Libknekhta (Карла Либкнехта).

Heading up ul. Karla Libknekhta toward pr. Lenina, you can't miss the **Church of the Resurrection** (Церковь Воскресение; Tserkov Voskresenye) on your left, which holds the distinction of being the church visited by the Romanovs during their final three months of life. In front of the church, a statue of two proud Soviet workers looks out across the street at an empty lot, once the site of the Ipatiev house, where the Romanovs were kept under house arrest and ultimately shot. The house was bulldozed during the Soviet era, supposedly in order to build an underpass, but as yet no underpass stands on the spot.

The **US Consulate** is at ul. Gogolya 15, 4th fl. (Гоголя; ☎56 46 19 and 56 46 91; open M-F 9am-6pm). The **British Consulate** is next door. (☎56 49 31. Open M-F 11am-7pm, Sa 11am-5pm.) Cash **traveler's checks,** receive **cash advances,** or use the 24hr. **ATM** at **Most Bank** (Мост Банк), ul. Mamina-Sibiryaka 145. (Мамина-Сибиряка. Open M-Th 9am-1pm and 2-4pm, F 9am-1pm and 2-3pm.) **MDM Bank** (МДМ Банк), ul. Pushkina 6 (Пушкина), has the best exchange rate in town. (Open M-Th 9:15am-1pm and 2-4:30pm, F 9:15am-1pm and 2-3:30pm.) Another ATM sits at Yakova Sverdlova 22, 10 minutes from the station. **Pharmacies** line ul. Yakova Sverdlova. If you manage to squeeze through the crowds and bus-

**I'LL GET THAT TO GO** If you ride the Trans-Siberian the way most Russians do, you'll spend most of your time eating. The thought of munching for six days straight might not appeal to the exercise-crazed set, but if you plan properly, it can be six days of bliss. Above all, keep an open mind about trying new things—but stick to the tried-and-true when necessary. At every stop longer than 15min., a flock of *babushki* and little boys will storm the platform hawking water, ice cream, meat pies, and vegetables. Back on board, *firmeny* trains all pull restaurant cars, featuring the ethnic food of whichever region the train is rolling through that day, but many travelers avoid them entirely. The best culinary experiences are more spontaneous. If you're lucky, a Russian family will bring the better half of their vegetable garden aboard and treat the car to a feast. The first course is usually *Baltika #3* and dried fish. Then comes vodka, chased down by a little juice. Finally, the meal: cucumbers, tomatoes, dill, bread (dark, of course), sausage, and roast chicken, all seasoned with a film canister of salt. Eat until the sun goes down, finish the vodka, and hit the sack.

tling kiosks outside the train station, you'll find yourself facing the large **Gostinitsa Sverdlovsk** (Гостиница Свердловск; ☎53 65 74) at ul. Chelyuskintsev 106 (Челюскинцев), on the corner with ul. Yakova Sverlova. Find comfort, privacy, and your own shower in a single for 350R. Yekaterinburg has a busy cafe scene, which picks up in the evening. Cheap meals abound along ul. Lenina. Given enough time, you can have a **shower** at track #1—look for the "Душ" (dush; shower) sign. **Postal code:** 620 101.

# NOVOSIBIRSK (НОВОСИБИРСК) ☎(8)3832

The population of this, the largest city in Siberia, went from zero to 1.5 million in less than 100 years, largely due to Stalin's efforts to build up Soviet heavy industry far from the reach of potential invaders. With uninspired rectilinear architecture and a central square only Big Brother could love, Novosibirsk has left generations of Russians wondering, "Why here?" Still, in typically Russian fashion, the city's residents haven't complained and have managed to take everything very much in stride. Novosibirsk has taken to capitalism far more readily than most Siberian cities and as a result there are more signs of life than decay: the parks don't look like abandoned lots and unfinished buildings make up much less than half of the city.

 **TIME CHANGE.** Novosibirsk is 3hr. ahead of Moscow (GMT+6).

**TRANSPORTATION.** The **train station**, ul. Shamshurina, sends trains to: **Moscow** (48-52hr., 5-6 per day, 900R); **Yekaterinburg** (22hr., 7-8 per day, 500R); and **Krasnoyarsk** (13hr., 5-6 per day, 300R). The following Trans-Siberian services stop in Novosibirsk (in Moscow time): **train #2** to **Vladivostok** (4 days, odd days 4:50pm, 1000R); **train #4** to **Beijing** via **Ulaanbaatar** (Th 9:15pm, 3000R); **train #20** to **Beijing** (Su 8:55pm); and **train #6** to **Ulaanbaatar** (F and Sa 9:15pm, 1700R). Novosibirsk is also a gateway to Central Asia. Trains run to various cities, but the main route, the Turkistan-Siberian railway, goes to **Almaty, KAZ** (35-40hr., daily 2pm, 1030R).

**ORIENTATION AND PRACTICAL INFORMATION.** The **Metro** (3R) connects the city center, **pl. Lenina** (пл. Ленина), to the train station at Garina-Mikhailovskovo (Гарина-Михайловского). From the train station, walk out into the city and then underground where you see the "M." Take the Metro one stop to **Sibirskaya** (Сибирская), then walk upstairs to change stations; one more stop takes you to pl. Lenina. The Sibirskaya Metro is close to the circus, the Ascension Church, the market, and the stadium, but most other sights are near pl. Lenina. **Krasny pr.** (Красный пр.), Novosibirsk's main drag, runs through pl. Lenina. Directly opposite the statue of Lenin, ul. Lenina (ул. Ленина) runs out of the square. Next to ul. Lenina, at the corner of the square, **Vokzalnaya Magistral** (Вокзальная Магистраль) runs down a couple blocks to **pr. Dmitrova** (Димитрова). Buy a Novosibirsk **atlas** (150R) at **Dom Knigi** (Дом Книги), Krasny pr. 31, on the corner of Krasny pr. and Vokzalnaya Magistral. (Open daily 10am-7pm.) **Alfa Bank** (Альфа Банк), Dimitrova 1, across from New York Pizza, has the city's most versatile, sexy **ATM.** (MC/Visa. Open M-Sa 8:30-7:30pm, Su 9am-3pm.) **Store luggage** in the basement of the train station. Follow signs marked "Камера Хранения" (6.30-14.70R). There is a **pharmacy** at ul. Chaplygina 58, on the corner of Krasny pr. and across the street from St. Nicholas's Church. (☎23 32 07. Open daily 8am-8pm.) The **telephone office,** ul. Lenina 5, offers fairly reliable **internet access** inside (20R per hr.; ☎22 02 28; open 24hr.; open daily 9am-9pm). There are internet terminals outside New York Pizza (see below), but you'll have to contend with swarms of teenagers struggling to destroy alien civilizations. (20R per hr. 8am-midnight, 60R midnight-8am.) The **post office** sits at ul. Sovetskaya 33. (☎22 05 83. Open M-F 8am-7pm, Sa-Su 8am-6pm; 8am-1pm on the 4th M of the month.) **Postal code:** 630 099.

**▐▌▐▌ ACCOMMODATIONS AND FOOD.** Novosibirsk has two soulless but adequate hotels that differ mainly in location. **Hotel Novosibirsk** is across from the train station. (Новосибирск. ☎20 11 20; fax 21 65 17. Singles 190R, with bath 570R; doubles with bath 450R. Breakfast included.) **Hotel Tsentralnaya** (Центральная), ul. Lenina 3, is in the center. Take the Metro to Pl. Lenina, then head down ul. Lenina one block. (☎22 72 94; fax 22 76 60. Singles 150R, with bath 450R.)

A large **market** on ul. Krylova (Крылова) covers nearly as much area as the stadium it borders. (Open daily 8am-7pm.) **Gastronom,** Krasny pr. 30, offers indoor shopping. (Open daily 8am-9pm.) For pizza as good as any you'll find in Manhattan (at a third of the price), head to **New York Pizza,** Dimitrova 4. (Slices 15-20R; burritos 12-16R; quesadillas 23-25R. Open 24hr.)

**▣▐▌ SIGHTS AND ENTERTAINMENT.** The **Novosibirsk Picture Gallery** (Новосибирская Картинная Галерея; Novosibirskaya Kartinnaya Galereya), Krasny pr. 5, features a varied collection with works by Surikov and Roerich. (☎22 20 42. Open M and W-Su 10am-6pm. 25R, students 15R.) In the middle of the road, just off pl. Lenina, the gold-domed **St. Nicholas's Chapel** (Часовня во имя Святитиля Николая; Chasovnya vo imya Svyatitilya Nikolaya) supposedly sits in the exact center of Russia. (Open daily noon-5pm.) The larger **Ascension Church** (Храм Вознесения Господня; Khram Vozneseniya Gospodnya), at the intersection of ul. Gogolya (Гоголя) and ul. Sovetskaya, flaunts a heavenly blue ceiling and a dazzling white and gold iconostasis. If you've got some time, **Obskoe More** (Обское Море), a huge lake created by a dam in the Ob River, offers fresh air and swimming. From the main train station, catch a suburban train to "Обское Море."

---

**DOES THAT COME WITH THE ROOM?** True to the communist spirit in which they were built, all large hotels in Siberian cities are created equal. They're all towering concrete blocks with billiard tables, a bar, and elevators that seems very reluctant to carry any weight at all. Once you're been heaved up to the 29th floor, you'll find that your room is invariably equipped with a telephone. This might seem great until you realize you have no friends to call within a 2000-mile radius. The fact is, the phones are meant predominantly for incoming—not outgoing—phone calls. Unless you unplug your phone, you're likely to receive the call around 11pm, asking if you want a prostitute sent to your room. No, reception isn't playing a practical joke: they just do a lousy job of keeping your room number private. Bear this in mind when you lie awake at night, wondering why your mattress feels so well-worn. Just remember: *Let's Go* does not recommend prostitution.

# KRASNOYARSK (КРАСНОЯРСК) ☎(8)3912

Founded as a Cossack fort in the 17th century, Krasnoyarsk straddles the 2km-wide Yenisey River. During the Cold War, the city was closed to foreigners because of its defense industry, but today it's trying to use its history and natural resources to escape Siberian anonymity. The efforts haven't paid huge dividends, but the city does have enough commercial activity and pre-revolutionary architecture to distance it from most other truck-side civilization muscled out of the taiga.

 **TIME CHANGE** Krasnoyarsk is 4hr. ahead of Moscow (GMT+7).

**TRANSPORTATION.** The **train station**, ul. Tridsatovo Iyulia (30-го Июля; ☎29 34 34), on the north bank of the Yenisey just west of the city center, sends trains to: **Novosibirsk** (14hr., 2-6 per day, 180R); **Irkutsk** (19hr., 1-5 per day, 220R); and **Vladivostok** (3 days, 1-3 per day, 820R). The following **Trans-Siberian** trains pass through (in Moscow time): **Moscow** (train #1 even days 4:50am, #3 Sa 3:21am, #5 Th and Su 3:21am; 1106R); **Vladivostok** (train #2 even days 3:48am, from 820R); **Beijing** (train #4 F 10:10am, train #20 M 9:35am; 1500R); and **Ulaanbaatar** (46hr., train #6 Sa-Su 10:10am, from 1000R). International tickets must be purchased at the downtown ticket office, ul. Robespiera 20 (Робеспиера; open M-F 8am-7pm, Sa-Su 9am-6pm).

**ORIENTATION AND PRACTICAL INFORMATION.** Everything of interest, with the exception of the Stolby Nature Reserve, lies on the north bank. Coming straight out of the train station, take bus #55 (3R) from the parking lot on the right to the centrally located Hotel Krasnoyarsk (4 stops). Krasnoyarsk's three main streets, **ul. Lenina** (Ленина), **pr. Mira** (Мира), and **ul. Karla Marxa** (Карла Маркса), all run west-east from the train station, parallel to the river. There's no tourist office, but the folks at **Service-Center Trans-Sib** (Сервис-Центр Транс-Сиб), on the main floor of the train station, reserve domestic train tickets and provide international **telephone** and **fax** services. (☎29 26 92; fax 21 65 71. Open M-F 9am-8pm.) You can snag a **map** (15R) in the lobby of Hotel Krasnoyarsk. **Exchange currency** at **Most Bank** (Мост Банк), in the tower across the street from Hotel Krasnoyarsk. They also give MC and Visa **cash advances** for a 1.5% commission, cash **traveler's checks** for no commission, and house a 24hr. **ATM.** (☎23 69 82. Open M-F 9:30am-6pm, Sa 9:30am-3pm.) **Store luggage** in the basement of the train station—look for signs marked "Камера Хранения." (12R per bag. Open 24hr.) **Internet Cafe MaxSoft**, ul. Uritskovo 61, 4th fl., is all internet and no cafe. (☎65 13 85. 30R per hr. Open M-F 9am-8pm.) The **post office** is at ul. Lenina 62. (☎27 07 48. Open M-Sa 8am-2pm and 3-7pm.) An international **telephone office** is just across the street. **Postal code:** 660 049.

**ACCOMMODATIONS AND FOOD. Hotel Krasnoyarsk**, ul. Uritskovo 94, (Урицкого), on the corner of ul. Venbauma and ul. Karla Marxa, is the most convenient option. Take bus #55 from the train station. (☎27 37 69 and 27 95 07; fax 27 02 36; hotelkrs@online.ru; http://hcom.krs.ru/hotelkrs. Singles 610R; doubles 305R per person. Breakfast included.) Five minutes farther along the waterfront, away from the train station, lies the permanently anchored hotel-ship **Mikhail Godenko.** The idea of lodging on a boat sounds neat, but the experience is marred by small, dirty rooms. (☎29 04 81. Singles 155R; doubles 255R.) Aboard the same boat, **Restauran Volna** has a typical Russian menu with an emphasis on seafood. (☎29 04 81. Salmon *pelmeny* 46R. Sturgeon *shashlik* 84R.) Cheaper options include the **24hr. cafe**, on the 3rd floor of the Hotel Krasnoyarsk, and **Rosso Pizza**, pr. Mira 111. (Slices 18-22R. Open daily 11am-midnight.) Serve yourself at the 24hr. **Gastronom Krasny Yar** (Красный Яр), across from the geological museum (see below) on pr. Mira.

**SIGHTS AND ENTERTAINMENT.** Although he studied in St. Petersburg, 19th-century Russian painter Vasily Ivanovich Surikov was born and raised in Krasnoyarsk, and his estate has now been turned into the **V. I. Surikov Museum-**

**Estate** (Музей-усадьба В. И. Сурикова; Muzey-usadba V. I. Surikov), ul. Lenina 98. Inside the elegant house, ten rooms on two floors showcase Surikov's life and work. (☎27 08 15. Open Tu-Su 11am-7pm. 8R, students 4R.) One block south, the **Central Geological Museum of Siberia** (Музей Геологой Центральной Сибирии; Muzey Geologoy Tsentralnoy Sibirii), pr. Mira 37, is a rock collector's dream, showcasing minerals and stones found nowhere else on earth. The museum displays the riches of the Krasnoyarsky Kray, where 92% of Russia's platinum and the world's second-largest chunk of pure gold have been unearthed. If you want to see the rocks in their natural state, museum director Victor Sovluk can arrange a **backpacking expedition.** (☎27 74 40; director ☎27 62 62; geomuseum@krsk.ru. Open M-F 9am-5pm. Russian tour 7R.) Around the corner, the gold-domed **Russian Orthodox Church** (Покровский Кафедральный Собор; Pokrovsky Kafedralny Sobor), ul. Surikova 26, was built in the late-18th century. (Open daily 8am-7pm.) Farther east, the **Krasnoyarsk Art Museum,** ul. Parizhskoy Kommuny 20 (Парижской Коммуны), at the corner of ul. Karla Marxa, displays work by Surikov and other Siberian artists. (Open Tu-Su 10am-6pm. 10R, students 3R.)

The **Museum-Ship St. Nicholas** (Музей-Пароход Св. Николай; Muzey-Parokhod Sv. Nikolai) sits at the east end of ul. Dubrovinskovo, near the Philharmonic Hall. In 1897, this ship carried Lenin up the Yenisey to his exile in Shushensk. Later it transported Tsar Nicholas II and now the museum features wax figures of both men, as well as a **samovar** exhibit. (☎23 94 03. Open Tu-Su 11am-6pm. 5R, students 2R.)

# IRKUTSK (ИРКУТСК)   ☎(8)3952

A Siberian trading post for three centuries, Irkutsk is one of the few eastern metropoles that sprang up *before* the Trans-Siberian's tracks were laid. Once a bazaar for fur-traders and a den for desperate gold-diggers, the city developed as a feisty mix of high culture and window-smashing brawls. This pit of unchecked capitalism said *"nyet"* to the Revolution in 1917, welcomed the retreating White troops, and didn't turn Red until 1920. Today, Irkutsk is much less of an anomaly, as it stumbles through the same economic malaise as the rest of Russia. Nonetheless, the city's grand (if crumbling) brick facades and the colossal beauty of nearby Lake Baikal have made it the most popular stop for Trans-Siberian travelers.

>  **TIME CHANGE** Irkutsk is 5hr. ahead of Moscow (GMT+8).

**TRANSPORTATION.** The **train station,** on ul. Vokzalnaya (☎43 17 17 and 28 22 87), sends trains to: **Ulan Ude** (8hr., 3 per day, 190R); **Krasnoyarsk** (19hr., 3-4 per day, 360R); and **Moscow** (3½ days, 1-3 per day, 1300R). The following Trans-Siberian trains pass through (in Moscow time): **train #2 to Vladivostok** (even days 9:45am, 1100R); **#4 to Beijing** (Sa 3:46am, 2400R); **#6 to Ulaanbaatar** (Su-M 3:43am, 1100R); and **#20 to Beijing** (Tu 3:36am, 2400R). Foreigners must purchase tickets from *kassa* #6 or 7 (☎28 28 20) in the suburban ticketing hall (with the glass doors). **Irkutsk's bus station,** ul. Oktyabrskoy Revolutsiye 11 (Октябрьской Революцие; ☎27 24 11) lies near the Decembrists' houses (see **Sights and Entertainment,** p. 684).

**ORIENTATION AND PRACTICAL INFORMATION.** The Angara River bisects the town; the old city center and all the sights lie on the right bank, while the train station and some budget accommodations sprawl along the residential left bank. The best place to buy **maps** (60R) and get other info on Irkutsk is the lobby of **Hotel Baikal Irkutsk,** (formerly Hotel Intourist, as the massive sign atop the building will attest) at bul. Gagarina 44 (Гагарина). Crossing the bridge from the train station, go right and follow the waterfront along ul.

Gagarina. The **Mongolian consulate,** ul. Lapina 11 (☎/fax 34 21 45 and 34 24 45), can arrange visas if you have a passport-sized photo ready for them. Only **Vnesh-torg-bank** (Внешторг-Банк), ul. Sverdlova 40, #201, cashes **traveler's checks** (2% commission plus US$0.50 per check). You can also get MC/Visa **cash advances** for a 2% commission. (☎24 39 16. Open M-F 9:30am-1pm and 2-4pm.) There is a MC/Visa **ATM** at Alfabank, Bul. Gagarina 34, two blocks from Hotel Baikal-Irkutsk, heading away from the main bridge. To **store luggage,** exit the train station, go left, and keep going until the other side of the post office to the door marked "Камера Хранения" (14.70R). You can check email at **Internet Klub 38 Net,** ul. Marata 38. Enter through the alley off ul. Sverdlova, opposite the supermarket. (☎24 23 52. 30R per hr. Open daily 9am-8pm.) The **telephone office,** ul. Proletarskaya 12 (Пролетарская), is across from the circus. (Open 24hr.) The main **post office,** ul. Stepana Razina 23 (Степана Разина), holds Poste Restante. (☎33 26 92. Open M-F 8am-8pm, Sa-Su 9am-6pm.) **Postal code:** 664 000.

**▛▟▌ ACCOMMODATIONS AND FOOD.** Finding a place to stay in Irkutsk can be a problem. Most places fill up quickly and don't take bookings from individual travelers. Many of the cheaper accommodations won't accept foreigners, except perhaps for very persistent foreigners. **Baikal Complex** (see **Transportation,** p. 686) is sometimes able to find homestays. (Singles US$17; doubles US$32.) All in all, your best bet is probably **Amerikansky Dom** (Американский Дом), ul. Ostrovsk-ovo 19 (Островского; ☎43 26 89; fax 27 92 77), owned by Lida Sclocchini, the Russian widow of the man from Philadelphia whose early-80s love affair was the basis for the film *From America With Love*. With the train station behind you, follow the tram tracks up the hill to the left and veer to the right when the tracks fork. From there, walk up two blocks, take a right after a cluster of kiosks, and then take the second real left onto ul. Kaiskaya (Каиская). Ul. Ostrovskovo (unmarked) is about 400m ahead on the right, on the street below the main drag at the top of the hill; Amerikansky Dom is 30m down on the right (15-20min.). Alternatively, take a taxi from the station (20-30R). The clean, Western-style house has hot water but only seven beds that fill quickly with Trans-Siberian backpackers; call at least four days ahead. (Laundry US$5. US$20. Breakfast included. Trips to Lake Baikal US$50 for 1-2 people, US$60 for 3.) **Hotel Gornyak** (Горняк), ul. Lenina 21 (☎24 37 54), on the corner of ul. Lenina and ul. Dzerzhin-skovo (Дзержинского), has small doubles with hall bathrooms for 150R. **Gos-tinitsa Rus** (Гостиница Рус), ul. Sverdlova 19 is a good combination of comfort and value, right in the hear of the city. The downside is it's owned by the Regional Administration and often fills up a month in advance. (☎24 27 15 and 25 64 00; fax 24 07 33. Singles 400R; doubles 714R.) If all else fails, try **Hotel Angara,** ul. Sukhe-Batora 7 (Сухэ-Батора), which has overpriced rooms in the center of town. Ask for the 3rd floor—it's the cheapest. (☎25 51 06; fax 25 51 03. Hot water. Singles 1027R; doubles 1340R. Breakfast included.)

A **supermarket, Magazin Okean** (Магазин Океан), at the corner of ul. Sverdlova and Stepana Razina, sells everything from fruit to film. (Open M-F 9am-9pm, Sa 9am-8pm.) The **central market** hawks fresh fruit, veggies, cheese, and meat. (Open daily 8am-8pm.) From the station, walk about 10 minutes along ul. Dzerzhinskovo and take a right on ul Chekhova (Чехова). Any form of transport that reads "рынок" (rynok) will also do. **Cafe Sport Express,** in the stadium, serves killer *pel-meny* (42-50R) and other cheap, delicious dishes. (☎33 48 30. Open daily 11am-1am.) **Cafe Karlson** (Карлсон), ul. Lenina 15, is central and the food isn't bad. (☎33 30 97. Main dishes 40-60R. Open daily 10am-midnight.)

**▣▐ SIGHTS AND ENTERTAINMENT.** Irkutsk's most illustrious residents were the Decembrists (see **History,** p. 591), who arrived as exiles in the 19th century. Two of their houses are open to the public: **Muzey-Dekabrista Volkonskovo** (Музей-Декабриста Волконского), ul. Volkonskovo 10, waits on a dusty side street just off of ul. Timiryazeva (Тимирязева). To get there, take trams #1-4 to Dekabersky Sabitiye and walk around the big domed church. If you had the stamina to read *War and Peace*, this one should be a real treat. (☎27 57 73. Open Tu-Su 10am-6pm; *kassa* closes at 5:30pm. 30R, students 15R.) A block away, the **Prince Sergey Trubetskoy House-Museum** (Музей Трубецкого), ul. Dzerzhinskovo 64, exhibits his books, furniture, tapestried icons, silverware, and photos of his jail cell. (☎27 57 73. Open M and Th-Su 10am-6pm; last admission 5:30pm. 30R, students 15R.) Near the river, the **Regional Museum** (Краеведческий Музей; Kraevedchesky Muzey), in a Victorian building at ul. Karla Marxa 2 (Карла Маркса), exhibits furs, skis, Buddhist masks, drums, woven icons, music shells, and pipes of local Siberian tribes. (☎33 34 49. Open Tu-Su 10am-6pm. 40R, students 20R.) The **Sukachev Art Museum** (Художественный Музей Имени Сукачева; Khudozhestvenny Muzey Imeni Sukacheva), ul. Lenina 5, houses Chinese vases and Siberian paintings of the 16th to 20th centuries. (☎34 42 30. Open M and W-Su 10am-6pm. 40R, students 20R.) The gold-columned iconostasis in **Znamensky Monastery** (Знаменский Монастырь), north of the town center on ul. Angarskaya (Ангарская), is brightened by a chandelier-lit interior. Take trolley #3 or buses #8, 13, or 31 to the first stop past the northern bridge or walk along ul. Frank Kamenetskovo (Франк Каменецкого), bear right at the fork, and cross the street to the blue-green domes. (Open daily 8:30am-8pm. Services daily 8:30 and 11am.)

At dusk, locals head to the obelisk on the river at the end of Karla Marxa to drink and watch the sunset. When it gets dark, the crowd heads across the cove to **Youth Island** (Остров Юности; Ostrov Yunosty) to drink more and dance until morning. (Open Su-Th 7pm-1am, F-Sa 7pm-3am. Cover 10R, weekends 20R.)

# LAKE BAIKAL (ОЗЕРО БАЙКАЛ)

At 1637m, Lake Baikal is the deepest body of fresh water in the world, containing one-fifth of the earth's fresh water. At 23,000 sq. km, its surface is twice as large as that of North America's Lake Superior. At 25 million years old, it is also the world's oldest lake (most aren't older than 100,000 years). Surrounded by snow-capped peaks, its waters teem with some 450 species found nowhere else in the world—translucent shrimp, oversized sturgeon, and deepwater fish that explode when brought to the surface. The *nerpa* freshwater seal lives 3000km from its closest relative, the Arctic seal, and no one knows quite how it got here. One deepwater fish has evolved into a gelatinous blob of fat—so fatty, in fact, that locals stick wicks in its lipidinous lumps and use them as candles.

Baikal's shores are no less fascinating than its waters. Reindeer, polar foxes, wild horses, brown bears, wild boars, and nefarious Siberian weasels hide in the surrounding mountains while glacial lakes melt into ice-cold waterfalls. Buryat *ger* (traditional Buryat tent-homes, also known as *yurts*) communities border the edges. Painted rocks and "wishing" trees strung with colored rags recall the area's shamanistic heritage; the Buryat region to the northeast counts 45 Buddhist monasteries. Deserted gulags (where many unfortunate Buddhist lamas and shamans spent their last days under the atheist Soviet regime) pepper the outskirts.

In recent years, authorities and international organizations have begun initiatives to preserve the region. **Barguzinsky National Reserve** (Баргузинский Заповедник; Barguzinsky Zapovednik), on Baikal's east shore, was Russia's first national

**THE UNDERWATER RAILROAD** In winter, Lake Baikal freezes, and the extraordinarily deep ice enables ferry routes to become roads for trucks. The sturdiness of the ice was first tested during the Russo-Japanese War (1904-05) when the Russian Army—foreshadowing such future Russian engineering brilliance as the draining of the Aral Sea and Chernobyl—built train tracks over the ice in order to get carloads of troops to the front lines faster. Then spring arrived...those tracks now have the distinction of being the deepest underwater railway in the world.

reserve. **Pribaykalsky National Park** (Прибайкальский Национальный Парк) encompasses much of the lake's west coast and is the closest reserve to Irkutsk. When fog doesn't obscure the treetops, views encompass ancient pine forests and crystal-clear water. Some days, visibility is better in the water (30m) than on land. **Olkhon Island,** also part of the park, is a prime spot for seal watching.

**TRANSPORTATION.** Buses and ferries run to different areas of Lake Baikal. Going farther than Listvyanka can be difficult on short notice, as transport to many destinations sells out well in advance. **Buses** run from Irkutsk to **Listvyanka;** return buses leave from the boat dock. (2hr., 4 per day, 37.60R.) There's also a daily bus to **Khuzhir** on **Olkhon Island** (8hr.; 8am, return 9am; 172.10R). Reserve tickets for this bus at least one month in advance. If you don't mind going without a seat for eight hours, show up and try to slip the bus driver a few extra US dollars.

**Ferries** run from June to September and buses are less frequent in winter. Olkhon Island is inaccessible for about a month in spring and fall when there's too much ice for the ferry, but not enough ice for the bus to drive on. Irkutsk's **ferry terminal** (☎ 23 80 53) is on ul. Solnichnaya, south of town. From ul. Lenina in Irkutsk, take bus #16 or trolleybus #5 to the terminal (20min., 2R). Book ferries at least 10 days in advance. A **hydrofoil** runs between Irkutsk and **Listvyanka**, book at least a day in advance. (70min.; Tu-Th 8:30am, F-Sa 8:30am, 2pm, Su 8:30am, noon, 2pm; return Tu-Th noon, F-Sa noon, 4:30pm, Su noon, 4pm, 4:30pm; 28.40R.) The ferry to **Khuzhir** was down for repairs at press time, but should be operational by 2001 (7hr., W 9am, return Th 12:20pm, 230R).

It's possible to see the Baikal region on a **guided tour.** Irkutsk-based **Baikal Complex** (☎/fax 38 92 05 and 43 20 60; travel@irk.ru and baikal@online.ru; www.baikal-complex.irk.ru), run by the remarkably efficient and resourceful Yuri Nemirovsky, can arrange a variety of services to suit any budget.

## LISTVYANKA

The most popular destination for daytrippers is a tourist-friendly town of 2500 where meandering cows battle visitors for control over the one and only real street, ul. Gorkovo (Горького), which runs from the boat dock to the typically concrete Hotel Baikal, three kilometers away. Yeltsin and German Chancellor Helmut Kohl stayed in this hotel during their 1993 trip to Lake Baikal. **St. Nicholas Church,** ul. Kylekova 88, built in gratitude for a miraculous ship rescue, sits in a small valley away from the lake, making for a great stroll. Facing away from the docks, go left and turn right when you see a green spire to the right. Plain white walls and detailed, golden-framed icons wait inside the church. (Open M-F 9am-7pm.)

Hotel Baikal (see above) houses an **exchange office** that gives MC/Visa **cash advances** for a 1.5% commission but won't exchange traveler's checks. (Open daily 8am-2pm and 6pm-midnight.) Take a left out of the boat dock to get to the **post office,** ul. Gorkovo 49. (Open M-F 8:30am-1pm and 3-5:30pm, Sa 8:30am-noon; closed last Thursday of each month.) Get info and **maps** (7-22R) of Lake Baikal and the surrounding area at the national park office at ul. Gorkovo 39, 20m from the ferry dock. They rent doubles upstairs for 105R. **Traktir** (Трактир), ul. Chapaeva 24 (Чапаева), on the first road that heads away from the water, going left and facing away from the dock, provides a cheap place to hang your hat. Comfortable rooms in this elegant wooden house go for 300R. Enjoy the *banya* for 100R per hour, or take a one- to two-hour excursion on the lake for 350R. **Nikolai's** (У Николы), ul. Gornaya 16 (Горная), is housed in a big wooden house on a hill. Facing away from the dock, go left for five to 10 minutes, cross the bridge, and take a right up the hill on the other side of the valley. (☎ 11 25 99. *Banya* 150R per hr. 550R, with lake view 600R.) **Bistro** (Бистро), by the boat docks, sells decent food. (*Pelmeny* 18R. Open daily 10am-10pm.) Peddlers on the docks sell cheap smoked fish.

## OLKHON ISLAND

**Khuzhir,** the main town on Olkhon Island, has as many telephones as paved roads and as many toilets as restaurants (pick a number and multiply it by zero). The rest of the island is undeveloped, but that hasn't kept tourists away. Olkhon, which offers excellent hiking, camping, and relaxation spots, is an ideal destination for those who want to experience the raw beauty of Baikal. Heading north along the shore from Khuzhir, rocky cliffs give way to white sandy beaches. You can pretend you're in Hawaii until you try jumping into the frigid waters. It's also possible to **camp** for free in the hills near the beach.

Buses from Khuzhir leave from in front of **Gostinitsa Svetlana.** To get there, take the first right past the Gastronom heading away from the water, walk to the end of the street, and take a left onto ul. Lesnaya (Лесная). The hotel will be on the right at the end of the road, just before a playing field. Buy bus tickets at least one day in advance at the unmarked house just before Gostinitsa Svetlana. A **post office** sits on ul. Lenina, a few blocks toward the water from Gastronom and to the left.

Khuzhir's tourist industry is monopolized by the affable and incomprehensibly resourceful Nikita Bercharov. ■ **Nikita's "place where you can stay"** (he doesn't want to call it a hotel or *turbaza*), ul. Kirpichnaya 8, is full of friendly faces and blessed with a nightly campfire. Warm, cozy beds and three meals per day will cost you US$15. Nikita can organize a variety of excursions at very short notice, from boat tours to horse treks (US$3-20). Enjoy his *banya* for US$5 per hour for up to four people. From the Gastronom in the center of town, take your first right as you walk down the hill toward the water. Ul. Kirpichnaya is the last left before the edge of town. Nikita's place is an unmarked complex surrounded by a wooden fence, behind a small open space for horses.

The **Gastronom** in the center of town makes a convenient stop for grub. Alternatively, head up the road away from the water for a few minutes to the smaller, but better stocked, **Khoroshy Magazin** (Хороший Магазин; Good Store).

# ULAN UDE (УЛАН УДЭ)  ☎(8)3012

Ulan Ude is where Slavic Russia meets its Asian counterpart and where the world's largest bust of Lenin sits ignored by local Buddhists. The Buryat people roamed the region semi-nomadically long before the Russians arrived. While today most Buryats have adopted the Russian language, native culture, from the ubiquitous *pozy* (traditional meat dumplings) to the local *datsan* (Buddhist monastery), persists.

 **TIME CHANGE** Ulan Ude is 5hr. ahead of Moscow and is in the same time zone as Mongolia and China (GMT+8).

■ **TRANSPORTATION.** Ulan Ude is the last (or first, depending on the direction you're traveling) major Russian city on the Trans-Mongolian line. The station sends trains to: **Irkutsk** (8hr., 4-5 per day, 125R); **Ulaanbaatar, MON** (24hr., 1 per day, 100R); and **Beijing, CHI** (2 per week, 2700R). The following **Trans-Siberian trains** pass through the city (in Moscow time): **train #2** to **Vladivostok** (odd days at 5:18am, 690R); **#6** to **Ulaanbaatar** (Su-M 11:16am); **#4** to **Beijing** (Sa 11:16am, 1810R); and **#20** to **Beijing** (Tu 11:06pm, 2250R). Foreigners must purchase tickets from the Intourist *kassa* on the second floor of the station; look for the door with the "Международные Кассы" sign. (Open daily 9am-noon, 1-7pm, and 2-7am.)

■■ **ORIENTATION AND PRACTICAL INFORMATION.** Ulan Ude's main square, **pl. Sovetov** (Советов), lies 500m south of the **train station** (☎34 25 31), just off Revolutsiye 1905-a goda (Революцие 1905-го года). To reach the square, take bus #10 or 36 (3R) or take a right as you exit the station, then another right under the bridge 400m later. **Exchange currency** in the lobby of **Hotel Buryatiya** (Бурятия), just off ul. Lenina. They also have the city's most convenient **ATM** and sell **maps.** (Open M-Sa 9am-1pm and 2-6pm.) **Store luggage** in the center hall of the train station (small bags 6R; large 14R). A **24hr. pharmacy** sits at ul. Lenina 29. (☎21 24 37. Ring bell midnight-6am.) Take the tram downhill from Hotel Buryatiya to the first stop across the river and the **business center** (бизнес центр), ul. Babushkina 20 (Бабушкина), which provides **internet access** (1R per min.; open daily 9am-1pm and 2-6pm), **fax,** and 24hr. international **phone service. Postal code:** 670 000.

**▉▉ ACCOMMODATIONS AND FOOD.** The best bargain is **Hotel Barguzina** (Баргузина), ul. Sovetskaya 28. Take bus #36 from the train station and ask the driver for the hotel by name, or walk bus #10 to pl. Sovietov, walk two blocks down ul. Lenina, and go right on ul. Sovietskaya. Rooms don't have hot water, but a shower on the second floor does. (☎21 57 46. Singles with bath 153R; doubles 246R.) It's also next to Nirvana, Ulan Ude's hippest nightclub, which can be either a good or a bad thing. The more upscale **Hotel Geser** (Гэсэр), ul. Ranzhurova 11 (Ранжурова) has an English-speaking staff. The cushy rooms make you wonder why you're not paying more. Head up Lenina to the post office and take a left. Geser is 100m off the road, on the right as you walk past the post office. (☎21 61 51. Singles with bath 262R; doubles 430R. Breakfast included.) Both hotels have **24hr. cafes.** Numerous small cafes line ul. Lenina. **King's Burger** (Кинг'с Бургер), ul. Lenina 21, serves a decent hamburger (16-27R), pizza (22-52R), and *Buryat kroket* (крокет), a dumpling filled with potatoes, lettuce, and some meaty stuff called *farsh* (15R; ☎21 52 53; open daily 8am-1am). **Poznaya** (Позная), on the corner of ul. Lenina and ul. Sovetskaya, serves great *pozy* for 5.50R. (Open daily 10am-11pm.)

**▉▉ SIGHTS AND ENTERTAINMENT.** Begin your tour of Ulan Ude at the city's main square, **pl. Sovetov,** which is crowned by an enormous bust of Vladimir Ilyich Lenin—the largest bust in the world. At the southwest corner of the square, on the corner of ul. Lenina, stands the yellow **Buryat State Academic Theater of Opera and Ballet** (Бурятский Государственный Академический Театр Оперы и Балета; Buryatsky Gosudarstvenny Akademichesky Teatr Opery i Baleta), a classical building with two horsemen guarding the entrance; the steps at the rear afford stunning views of the city center and the surrounding mountains. (Season Oct.-May.)

The recently reopened **Museum of Buryat History** (Музей истории Бурятии; Muzey Istorii Buryatii), ul. Profsoyuznaya 29 (Профсоюзная), off ul. Kommunisticheskaya by Hotel Buryatia, was first founded in 1923 but closed down, supposedly for renovation, in 1980. True renovations began only after Ulan Ude celebrated the 250th anniversary of Buddhism in Russia in 1992, and it finally reopened to the public in May 1997. Today the museum includes exhibits on the history of the city and the БАМ (BAM), the costly second Trans-Siberian railway. There's also a huge collection of Buddhist paraphernalia. (☎21 65 87. Open Tu-Su 10am-6pm. 50R.) Follow the tram tracks down ul. Kommunisticheskaya (Коммунистическая) away from pl. Sovetova and take a right at the bottom of the hill, just past some kiosks and umbrellas, to reach the local **Buddhist shrine** (ламрим; lamrim), right next to the hardware store. Walk past the black gate and ask to take a peek inside. The surrounding 18th- and 19th-century **wooden houses** comprise the oldest part of town.

The two most interesting sights lie outside the city limits. The **Ethnographic Museum** (Етнографический Музей; Etnografichesky Muzey), 10km north of the city center, can be reached via bus #8 (every 30min., 5R) from the south end of pl. Sovetov; if you're looking into Lenin's ear, you're in the right place. Ask the driver to stop at "Etnografichesky Muzey," then walk about down the road that veers left from the bus stop (15min.); the museum will appear after the green fence on the right ends. The museum is an open-air complex of reconstructed buildings that depict the traditional way of life in the region. It consists of several *ger* (Buryat tent-homes) and features a copy of a wooden Russian country church. (☎33 57 54. Open M-F 9am-5pm, Sa-Su 10am-6pm; last admission 30min. before closing. 20R.)

The most fascinating building in the Buryat region is in the hamlet of **Ivolga** (Иволга), 28km west of Ulan Ude. Amidst the hills stands **Datsan-Ivolga,** a large Buddhist monastery complete with a yellow curved roof, a white picket fence with Buddhist prayer drums, and a village full of Mongolian-trained Buddhist lamas. (Visit in the morning or early afternoon. Free.) Built very rapidly in 1942—the main temple took only 45 days to complete—the shrine served as the center of Buddhism in the former Soviet Union. While Stalin was sending monks to the gulag, he paradoxically permitted the construction of the *datsan*, which has stood undisturbed ever since. In the main temple are several Buddhist scriptures handwritten in Tibetan and Sanskrit and a display of gifts. Around the edge of the complex are 120 prayer drums, each inscribed with sacred scripture. The lamas' houses are behind the complex. From the bus station in Ulan Ude (two blocks to the left of Hotel Barguzin) buses leave at 7am, noon, and 4pm and stop outside the *datsan* (8R).

# ULAANBAATAR, MONGOLIA ☎ 1

>
> **VISA REQUIREMENTS** Mongolia requires that tourists possess a valid passport and a visa, which can be arranged with little hassle at the Mongolian embassies in Moscow (☎(7-095) 229 67 65; fax 291 61 71; see Embassies and Consulates, p. 610), London (☎(44-0171) 937 01 50; fax 937 11 17), and Washington, D.C. (☎(1-202) 298-7117; fax 298-9227).

| | | |
|---|---|---|
| **CURRENCY** | US$1 = 1083T (TUGRIKS) | 1000T = US$0.92 |
| | CDN$1 = 735T | 1000T = CDN$1.36 |
| | UK£1 = 1580T | 1000T = UK£0.63 |
| | IR£1 = 1236T | 1000T = IR£0.81 |
| | AUS$1 = 624T | 1000T = AUS$1.60 |
| | NZ$1 = 465T | 1000T = NZ$2.15 |
| | SAR1 = 155T | 1000T = SAR6.43 |
| | DM1 = 497T | 1000T = DM2.00 |

Ulaanbaatar ("UB" in hipster parlance) is working very hard at getting rich very quickly. Schools only began teaching English in 1994, but the city is already filled with English signs and Mongols eager to try out their English on tourists. It's a big, noisy mess that throws together country folk in traditional garb, young up-and-comers, a sizeable expat community, and a small army of alcoholics. While UB has some of the best sights and nightlife between Moscow and Beijing, a proper visit requires an exploration of the surrounding countryside— from Lake Khousgol in the north to the Gobi desert in the south—where much of the population still lives in nomadic *ger* communities, unaffected by the cosmopolitan fever of the capital.

**◼️🔋 ORIENTATION AND PRACTICAL INFORMATION.** Map labels and street names are in Mongolian, which usually employs a Cyrillic script, and sometimes in Russian. While English has gained recent favor, Russian remains the most popular second language. The center of town is **Sukhbaatar Square,** marked by a small statue of the patriot for whom it is named. To get there from the train station, take bus #4 (T100). The **train station** is on Teeverchid St. International tickets must be bought at the **International Railway Ticketing Office** (open M-F 9am-1pm and 2-5pm, Sa-Su 9am-2pm); exit the train station, turn left, and walk about two minutes to the yellow building set back from the road on the right. Train schedules are given in UB, not Moscow, time. The bank on the second floor has a **currency exchange** that cashes **traveler's checks** for a 2% commission and gives AmEx/MC/Visa **cash advances** for a 4% commission. (Open M-F 9am-12:45pm and 2-4pm.) For general info and **maps** of the city (T5000), head to **Hotel Ulaanbaatar,** a block past Sukhbaatar Square coming from the train station. The English speakers at **Juulchin Tourist,** Chinghis Khaan

5B (☎32 84 28; fax 32 02 46; jlncorp@magicnet.com; www.mol.mn/juulchin), behind the Bayangol Hotel, arrange trips to the Gobi Desert, the ancient capital of Karakorum, and the lake regions. The **Chinese Embassy** is at Zaluuchuudyn Ave. 5, a block east of the northeast corner of the square. (30-day tourist visa $30 for 7-day processing, $60 for same-day processing. ☎32 09 55. Open M, W, and F 9:30am-noon.) If you're not convinced that UB is an ex-pat haven, just stop by **Scrolls English Bookstore** (☎31 44 74), Khudaldaany St. 22, between the Wrangler Jeans store and Millie's Cafe. The **telephone office** is in the same building. Calls to North America cost T2309; Australia T2430 per min; Europe T2309 per min. (Open 24hr.) **Internet@copycenter,** at the corner of Zaluuchuud Ave. and Baga Toyruu St., offers good rates. (T1000 per hr. Open M-F 10am-11pm, Sa-Su 10am-7pm.) The **post office** is on the corner of Enkh Tayvan Ave. and Sukhbaatar St. (Open M-F 7:30am-9pm, Sa 8am-8pm, Su 9am-8pm.) **Postal code:** 210613. **Mongolia country phone code:** 976.

**■⌂ ACCOMMODATIONS AND FOOD.** Ulaanbaatar has some of the best accommodations on the Trans-Siberian route. Most mid-range hotels in the capital accept major credit cards and the staff generally speak English well. For a truly Mongolian experience, head to ⊠ **Gana's Guest House** (☎/fax 36 73 43; call for pick-up) near the Gandan Hiid monastery. Facing away from the train station, turn right, walk five minutes and take the first hard left. Pass two intersections and ascend a hill; signs on the right side of the road lead the way. The guest house consists of five to six Mongolian *ger* with four to five beds each. The hot shower and outhouses are in back, but the incredibly comfy beds and views more than make up for the inconvenience. (Dorms US$3; *ger* US$5.) For something more socialist, head to **Serge's Guest House,** 50 Enchtaivan St. Follow the directions to Gana's, but turn right at the second major intersection. Serge's is behind the pink door on the right. (☎32 02 67; sergetour@hotmail.com. Laundry T500. 2-bed dorms US$4; 4-bed US$5.)

Many street cafes offer Mongolian fare for less than US$1. For decent pizza (T2200) and Anglophone company, head to the **Khan Brau Restaurant and Pub,** a block up from Sukhbaatar on the left side of Chengis Ave. The place jumps with live music on Friday and Saturday nights. For tasty smoothies (T2200), head to **Millie's Cafe,** on the second floor of the Center Hotel, opposite the Art Museum on Khuldaany Ave. This expat haven has a friendly, English-speaking staff that serves Western food at regrettably Western prices. (☎32 82 64. Sandwiches T2500-3500. Open M-Sa 9am-7pm, Su 10am-3pm; dinners Tu and Th 7-10pm by reservation only.) For a sample of UB's international cuisine, drop by **Taj Mahal,** 50m from the road on Boga Toyruu St. Mongolian women in traditional Indian dress serve a variety of Indian dishes. (☎31 53 86. Tandoori kebabs T3500-4800. Samosas T1900.)

**▣ SIGHTS.** Opposite Sukhbaatar Sq., between Chinghis Khaan Ave. and Marx St., stands the fantastic ⊠ **Monastery-Museum of Choijin Lama,** a complex of five temples made into a museum by the communists in 1942. It now features a collection of treasures, including 108 masks used in ceremonial Tsam dancing.

**MONGOLIAN 101** Mongolian is notoriously difficult. Full of long unpronounceable words and gurgles and hisses that sound like satanic chants played backward, its expressions for "have some more yogurt" and "my grandmother can kick your grandmother's ass" sound remarkably similar to Westerners. Any attempt to speak the local language will consequently be met with enthusiasm from locals. Mongolian can be fun, especially the greetings. Greet someone on an errand with *"Üil bütemjtei bain boltugai,"* literally "may your action be creative." Hail someone in the countryside with *"Süreg mal targan uu?"* which means, "Are your livestock fat and healthy?"

(☎32 47 88. Open daily May-Sept. 10am-6pm; Oct.-Apr. W-Su 10am-5pm. T1700.) The **Gandan Khiid Monastery** is the center of Mongolian Buddhism. Built in 1810, the monastery was partially destroyed in the 1930s and only restored in 1990. The main temple houses a colossal statue of Janraisig, the Buddha of compassion and mercy. Follow the directions to Gana's Guest House, but keep going past the sign. (Monastery open 24hr. Main temple open daily 9am-4pm. T1000.) The elegant home of Mongolia's last king, the **Bogd Khaan Winter Palace Museum** exhibits religious and cultural artifacts from the 17th-20th century, as well as a collection of preserved animals. From the Bayanyol Hotel on Chinghis Ave., take any bus marked "зайсан" (zaisan) two stops (T200). (Open Su-Tu and F-Sa 10am-5pm. US$2.) The **Zanabazar Museum of Fine Arts,** on Khudaldaany St., two blocks west of the main square, is named for the king, painter, linguist, and architect. It exhibits his works, along with a collection that includes both prehistoric works and modern masterpieces. (☎32 60 60. Open in summer daily 9am-6pm; off-season 10am-5pm. T2400, students T1000.) The **Museum of Natural History** sits at the corner of Khuvsgalchid Ave. and Sukhbaatar St. The main thrill here comes from the fully reconstructed dinosaur skeletons, including a large carnivorous Tarbosaurus. (☎31 81 79. Open daily May-Sept. 10am-4:30pm; Oct.-Apr. W-Su 10am-4:30pm. T1700.) The **Naadam Festival,** held annually July 11-13, features competitions in wrestling, archery, and horsemanship. Book accommodations well in advance if you plan to be in town during the festival.

RUSSIA

# SLOVAKIA (SLOVENSKO)

**IF YOU'RE HERE FOR...**

**4-6 DAYS.** Stop in **Banská Bystrica** (p. 708) for a taste of Slovak life and a visit to **Bojnice's** storybook castle (p. 710). Then hit **Liptovský Mikuláš** (p. 713) for spectacular hikes in the **Low Tatras** (p. 712).

**1-2 WEEKS.** Hike your heart out in the **High Tatras** (p. 721), a combination of glitzy resorts and tiny mountain villages offering some of the best hiking and skiing in Europe.

After a history scarred by nomadic invasions, Hungarian domination and 40 years of Soviet industrialization, Slovakia has finally emerged as an independent country. Freedom has introduced new challenges, though, as the older generation reluctantly gives way to their chic offspring. The nation remains in a state of generational flux between industry and agriculture, unable to muster the resources necessary for an easy Westernization and unwilling to return to its past. This leaves a strange mixture of fairy-tale traditionalism and easy-going youth, which combine with low prices to create a haven for budget travelers. From tiny villages to the busy streets of its capital, Slovakia is coming to grips with progress, as the good old days retreat to castle ruins, pastures, and the stunning Tatras above.

## SLOVAKIA AT A GLANCE

**OFFICIAL NAME:** Slovak Republic

**CAPITAL:** Bratislava (pop. 452,000)

**POPULATION:** 5,400,000

**LANGUAGE:** Slovak, Hungarian

**CURRENCY:** 1 koruna (Sk) = 100 halierov

**RELIGION:** 60% Roman Catholic, 10% atheist, 8% Protestant, 22% Other

**LAND AREA:** 48,800km²

**GEOGRAPHY:** Mountainous, with lowlands in the southwest and east

**CLIMATE:** Temperate

**BORDERS:** Austria, Czech Republic, Hungary, Poland, Ukraine

**ECONOMY:** 62% Services, 33% Industry, 5% Agriculture

**GDP:** US$8,300 per capita

**EMERGENCY PHONE NUMBERS:** Ambulance 155, Fire 150, Police 158

**COUNTRY CODE:** 421

**INTERNATIONAL DIALING PREFIX:** 00

# HISTORY

**JUST A SLAV LIKE ONE OF US.** Slovakia's history is that of an embattled border region, susceptible to the whims and invasions of its more powerful neighbors. Though it was occupied by the **Romans** from 6 AD until the fall of the Roman Empire in the 5th century, several ethnic groups battled over the land in the period that followed. Slovakia was almost entirely settled by the **Slavs** by the 6th century. The Slavs' first known political formation was the **Samo Empire,** an empire that gained its independence from the invading Franks and Avars (a nomadic-like tribe from Central Asia) by beating the Frankish Army of King Dagobert near Vogatisburg in 631. Even after this empire fell in 665, the Slavs remained strong enough to contain two invasions from Asian nomadic tribes which would otherwise have raided Western Europe. The next Slav state was formed in 833 when **Prince Mojmír** of Moravia attacked and annexed Nitra.

**CAN'T WE ALL JUST GET ALONG?** The Slavs, despite this unification, were unable to fend off the Franks and Germans, who saw their empire as a target for Christianization and as a rich depository of silver, iron, and copper. The Germans beat the Franks to the chase and established **Prince Ratislav I** as the empire's leader in 853. Rastislav succeeded in both signing a peace treaty with the Franks and securing help from Byzantine Emperor Michael III in Christianizing the Slavs. Michael sent the apostles **Cyril and Methodius**, who instituted the first Slavic alphabet. After Ratislav was taken prisoner by the Franks, Svätopluk ascended to the throne in 872. He was crowned king in 880 by Pope John VIII. After Svätopluk's death in 894, Slavs, Bavarians, and Magyars fought over Slovakia. The independent Slav state began to disappear in 907 as the Magyars triumphed and Slovakia was gradually integrated into the Hungarian Kingdom. True to form, soon the Slovak territories were again plagued by destruction as neighboring countries battled over their riches.

**THOSE HAPPENIN' HABSBURGS.** The bloody Tatar invasions of 1241-43 only served to further weaken the Hungarians, who were finally defeated by the Ottomans at the 1526 **Battle of Mohács.** Hungary was subsequently divided into three territories; Slovakia avoided Turkish rule and was inherited by the **Habsburgs,** who moved the capital north to Bratislava (called "Pressburg" by the Austrians) in 1536. From here, the Habsburgs managed to wrench all of Hungary free from Turkish hands and eventually rebuild the region. They also had some religious spring cleaning to do, replacing Slovakia's **Lutheranism** and **Calvinism** with **Roman Catholicism;** religious wars followed throughout the 17th century. During Habsburg rule (1526-1830), Maria Theresa's reign (1740-80) was particularly jumpin', as she would frequently hold court in Bratislava and invite such musical prodigies as Mozart and Haydn to perform. Freedom from the Turks, however, came at a price, as Slovakia's resources were depleted in defending the Habsburg rule from Turkish invasion.

**POWER HUNGARY.** In the 18th century, a Slovak nationalist movement emerged. Slovaks were becoming increasingly self-aware and restless under Habsburg rule; they yearned for a concrete form of unity. The movement was bolstered by the codification of the Slovak language, completed by **Ľudovít Štúr** in 1846. Despite the persistence of this momentum, Hungarian power continued to grow. With the establishment of the **Austro-Hungarian Dual Monarchy** in 1867, Hungary strengthened its hold on Slovakia. Without their own province, Slovaks lived directly under Hungarian rule. Ignoring the wise advice of intellectuals, the Hungarian government, particularly under **Count István Tisza,** intensified the policy of Magyarization. This forced many Slovaks to leave their homeland and alienated those who stayed.

**CZECHOSAYWHO?** The Slovak national movement continued to blossom through the turn of the century. On October 28, 1918, six days before Austria-Hungary sued for peace in World War I, Slovakia, Bohemia, Moravia, and Sub-Carpathian Ruthenia combined to form **Czechoslovakia,** a new state with its capital at Prague. Fortunately, the new state was able to repel a 1919 invasion of Slovakia by Hungarian Communist **Béla Kun** and secured the withdrawal of Romanian troops from Ruthenia. It became a liberal democracy based on the US model and the only state in Eastern Europe not to fall to fascist, authoritarian, or communist rule.

**WORLD WAR II.** As Adolf Hitler plotted to expand his territory, Czechoslovakia was one of his first targets. Abandoned by Britain and France in the **Munich Agreement** of September 1938, Slovaks clamored for autonomy. A month later, they got their wish, as Slovakia was proclaimed an autonomous unit within a federal Czecho-Slovak state. As Hitler occupied Prague, Slovakia decided to withdraw from the federation; on March 14, 1939, the first independent Slovak Republic was established with Father Jozef Tiso as head of government of the puppet state. Hungary took the opportunity to kick its neighbor while it was down, helping itself to the province of Ruthenia. Between 1942 and 1944 approximately 70,000 Slovak Jews and other "undesirables" were sent to concentration camps. As a culmination of the Partisian resistance against the fascist government, Slovaks staged the two-month **Slovak National Uprising** (Slovenské Národné Povstanie; SNP) against Tiso and the Nazis in August 1944 (see **Banská Bystrica: Sights,** p. 709).

**POST WORLD WAR II.** After World War II, Slovakia again became a part of democratic Czechoslovakia. Unfortunately, things did not go smoothly. Tiso was hanged for treason and cooperation with the Nazis. The new state lost Ruthenia again, this time to the Soviets, and took out its frustrations internally by expelling Slovakia's ethnic Hungarians and Saxons. **Communists,** led by Czech **Klement Gottwald,** won 36% of the vote in 1946 and soon dominated the government. In February 1948, as the Popular Front government fell apart, they mounted a Soviet-backed coup. The 1948 constitution guaranteed equal status for the Czech and Slovak states, but Slovaks were still wary of a Czech-dominated government. Meanwhile, the entire state was still under Soviet domination. It took a Slovak, **Alexander Dubček,** to shake the regime out of its subservience to Moscow. In the 1968 **Prague Spring,** Dubček introduced his "Socialism with a Human Face," a purging technique that was innovative in subjecting the old guard to public disgrace. Soviet tanks immediately rolled into Prague, crushed his allegedly disloyal government, and plunged the country back into totalitarianism. Bratislava was dubbed a "capital city," and rural Slovakia underwent heavy industrial development.

**CZECHOSLOVAKIA.** The communists remained in power until the **Velvet Revolution** of 1989, when Czech dissident and playwright **Václav Havel** was elected president. The government introduced a pluralistic political system and a market economy. In this fertile political environment, Slovak nationalism blossomed into a **Declaration of Independence** from the Czech Republic on January 1, 1993. This bloodless split came to be known as the **Velvet Divorce.** After centuries of conquest and alliance, Slovaks have an independent state to call their own at last.

# POLITICS

The only thing I know about Slovakia is what I learned firsthand from your foreign minister, who came to Texas.

　　—George W. Bush to a Slovak journalist as quoted by Knight-Ridder News Service, June 22, 1999. Bush met with Janez Drnovsek, the prime minister of *Slovenia,* NOT SLOVAKIA.

The constitution adopted by the Slovak National Council on September 1, 1992 provides for a 150 deputy legislature. Deputies are chosen in a general election. The president is head of state and is elected by a 60% majority of the National Council for a five-year term. The president appoints the prime minister, who forms the supreme executive body of the republic.

Coming out of the 1993 Velvet Divorce with only 25% of former Czechoslovakia's industrial capacity and even less of its international reputation, Slovakia has had more trouble adjusting to the post-Eastern Bloc world than its former partner. Relations with Hungary and the Czech Republic are strained. Political instability has isolated Slovakia from the West and potential membership in both the **EU** and **NATO.** The primary instigator of this volatility, **Vladímir Mečiar,** is both the most loved and most hated political figure in Slovakia today. He has thrice been elected prime minister and thrice been removed. During his terms he violated the constitution, cancelled presidential elections and referendums on NATO membership, and even granted amnesty to terrorists suspected of kidnapping the son of former president **Michal Kovac.** Though Mečiar dropped off the political radar after losing power in the September 1998 elections, the damage he wrought is only slowly being repaired. In May 1999, **Rudolf Schuster,** former mayor of Košice, became president. His election, along with the appointment of Prime Minister **Mikuláš Dzurinda,** brought promises of further Westernization and a brighter future.

# CULTURE

## NATIONAL HOLIDAYS IN 2001

**January 1** Origin of the Slovak Republic

**January 6** Epiphany

**April 13** Good Friday

**April 15** Easter

**May 1** Labor Day

**July 5** Sts. Cyril and Methodius Day

**August 29** Anniversary of Slovak National Uprising

**September 1** Constitution Day

**September 15** Our Lady of the 7 Sorrows

**November 1** All Saint's Day

**December 24-26** Christmas

# LITERATURE AND ARTS

Art in Slovakia has had to struggle long and hard to escape the orbit of neighboring traditions. The Slovak tongue, for example, only emerged as a literary language distinct from Czech in the 18th century. Early examples of the Slovak novel, such as **Ignác Bajza's** *René* (1785), were written in a Slovak dialect of Czech, rather than a distinct language. The Slovak literary tradition really got started with the 19th century linguist and nationalist **Ľudovít Štúr,** whose "new" language based on the Central Slovak dialects inspired a string of national poets. Foremost among these was **Andrej Sládkovič,** author of the national epic *Marína* (1846). Sládkovič's contemporary, the poet and revolutionary **Janko Kráľ,** launched an enduring tradition of Slovak Romanticism with his ballads, epics, and lyrics, a tradition followed by the rustic poets **Svetozar Vajansky** and **Pavol Ország Hviezdoslav.** Visual artists of the early 1800s looked abroad for inspiration, but toward the end of the century, painters such as **Mikoláš Aleš** turned their attention back to Slovakia.

In the wake of World War I, Slovak nationalism and literature matured concurrently. More cosmopolitan influences began to appear alongside Romanticism: **E. B. Lukáč** introduced **Symbolism** to the Slovak tradition while **Rudolf Fábry** championed **Surrealism.** The long-established primacy of the lyric began to give way to novels and short stories. As in poetry, rural themes and village life took center stage, often as an object of celebration, but increasingly as the butt of scorn and ridicule. **Janko Jesenký** savaged the regional linchpins of the post-war government in his novel *The Democrats (Demokrati).* Meanwhile, **Andrej Ocenasa** led a prominent generation of composers who blended classical and folk strands in their works.

The Slovak literati reacted to communist rule after World War II. In his 1967 novel *The Taste of Power*, **Ladislav Mnačko** was one of the first writers in Eastern Europe to speak out against Stalinism. Around the same time, **Ján Kadar** directed *The Shop on Main Street*, the best known Slovak contribution to world cinema.

# RELIGION

The **Velvet Revolution** in 1989 marked the end of official atheism and the beginning of widespread religious practice. Today Roman Catholicism is the chief religion, while Protestantism and Orthodoxy claim a large minority.

# FOOD AND DRINK

Slovakia emerged from its 1000-year Hungarian captivity with a taste for paprika, spicy *guláš*, and fine wines. The good news for vegetarians is that the national dish, *bryndžové halušky*, is a plate of dumpling-esque pasta smothered in a thick sauce of sheep or goat cheese; the bad news is that it sometimes comes flecked with bacon. Being vegetarian is easy in cities but difficult otherwise. The Slovaks like their *knedliky* (dumplings) but—unlike in the Czech Republic—it's often possible to escape them and have *zemiaky* (potatoes) or *hranolky* (fries) instead. Slovakia's second-favorite dish is *pirogy*, a pasta-pocket filled with potato or *bryndža* cheese, topped with bacon bits. *Pstruh* (trout), often served whole, is also popular. *Kolačky* (pastry) is baked with cheese, jam or poppy seeds, and honey.

White **wines** are produced northeast of Bratislava in the Small Carpathians, especially around the town of Pezinok. *Riesling* and *Müller-Thurgau* grapes are typically used, and quality varies greatly. *Tokaj* wines (distinct from Hungarian *Tokaj Aszú*) are produced around Košice. Enjoy any of these at a *vináreň* (wine hall). *Pivo* (beer) is served at a *pivnica* or *piváreň* (tavern). The favorite Slovak beer is *Zlatý Bažant*, a light, slightly bitter Tatran brew. Slovakia produces several brandies: *slivovica* (plum), *marhulovica* (apricot), and *borovička* (juniper-berry).

# CUSTOMS AND ETIQUETTE

**Tipping** is common in restaurants; most people round up to a convenient number by refusing change when they pay—an 8-10% tip is generous and marks you as a tourist. Most **museums** close Mondays, and **theaters** take a break during July and August. Slovakia is intensely Roman Catholic, resulting in social mores that are often quite conservative. **Grocery store attendants** will accost you if you don't grab a basket by the entrance. More often than not, restaurant **toilets** will be locked with the key *(kluč)* hanging up by the bar. Most bus and train stations and some restaurants are **nonsmoking,** though most Slovaks do in fact smoke.

# SPORTS

Slovakia's **winter sports** are strong, especially ice hockey and skiing. Slovakia has made a Poprad-Tatry bid for the 2006 Winter Olympics, but due to limited financial guarantees from the government it will likely be turned down.

Although winter sports are more dominant, Slovaks don't neglect **summer sports** either. Slovakia won three medals in the 1996 Atlanta Olympics, and, more recently, Karol Kučera defeated Andre Agassi in the 2000 French Open.

# LANGUAGE

**Slovak,** closely related to **Czech,** is a tricky Slavic language, but any attempt to speak it will be appreciated. **English** is not uncommon among Bratislava youth, but people outside the capital are more likely to speak **German,** and those near the border Polish. You can find English-speakers in most tourist offices and cities. **Russian** is understood, but not always welcome. When speaking Slovak, the two golden rules are to pronounce every letter—nothing is silent and it's all phonetic—and to emphasize the first syllable. Accents on vowels affect length, not stress. Flick the "r" off the top of your mouth. For a collection of commonly used words and phrases, see **Glossary,** p. 698 and **Phrasebook,** p. 699.

# ADDITIONAL READING

Literature on and from Slovakia in English is particularly difficult to find, owing perhaps to the dominance of other states and traditions in the region's history. For one-stop Slovak history, Stanislav Kirschbaum's *A History of Slovakia: The Struggle for Survival* is a well-researched (if somewhat biased) study of the Slovak people through centuries of conquest. Peter Petro's *A History of Slovak Literature*, which explores the literary tradition with a keen eye to its political and cultural interactions, is equally comprehensive.

# TRAVELING ESSENTIALS

Citizens of South Africa and the US can visit Slovakia without a visa for up to 30 days; Australia, Canada, Ireland, New Zealand, and the UK 90 days. To apply for a visa, contact an embassy or consulate in person or by mail; processing takes two business days (single-entry US$20; double-entry US$22; 90-day multiple-entry US$40; 180-day multiple-entry US$62; transit—good for 30 days—US$20). Visa prices vary with exchange rate. Apply to an embassy or consulate in person or by mail; processing takes two days. Submit your passport (which must be valid for eight months from the date of application), company check or money order for the fee, one visa application per planned entry, and two passport photos per application. Visas are not available at the Slovak border and there is no fee for entering or exiting Slovakia. Travelers must register their visas within three days of entering the Slovakia, though hotels will do this automatically. If you intend to stay longer or obtain a visa extension, you must notify the Office of Border and Alien Police in the town where they are staying in the first three business days of their arrival. For a list of Slovak embassies and consulates, see **Essentials: Embassies and Consulates,** p. 18. In general, Slovak customs are quick and painless; a border crossing should add no extra time to your journey. As always, it's easiest to take a direct train or bus from Bratislava to the nearest major city in the neighboring country.

# TRANSPORTATION

**BY PLANE.** Bratislava does have an international airport, but entering the country via air may be inconvenient and expensive as few international carriers fly here. Flying to nearby **Vienna,** Austria, and taking a bus or train from there is much cheaper and takes about the same time.

**BY TRAIN OR BUS.** International bus and rail links connect Slovakia to its neighbors. Large train stations operate **BIJ-Wasteels** offices, which offer 30% discounts on tickets to European cities, except Prague, for those under 26. **EastRail** is valid in Slovakia; **Eurail** is not. As everywhere, you'll pay extra for an *InterCity* or *EuroCity* fast train, and if there's a boxed R on the timetable, a *miestenka* (reservation; 7Sk) is required. If you board the train without a reservation, expect to pay an additional 150Sk fine. International ticket counters have multilingual signs.

**BY LOCAL TRANSPORTATION.** Larger towns have multiple *stanice* (train stations); the *hlavná stanica* is the main one. Smaller towns have only one, and tiny villages usually have just a decaying hut with an illegible schedule. Tickets must be bought before boarding the train, except in the tiniest towns. **ŽSR** is the national train company; every information desk has a copy of **Cestovný poriadok** (58Sk), the master schedule, which is also printed on a large, round board in most stations. In

# GLOSSARY

| ENGLISH | SLOVAK | PRONOUNCE |
|---|---|---|
| one | jeden | YED-en |
| two | dva | dvah |
| three | tri | tree |
| four | štyri | sh-TEE-ree |
| five | päť | peht |
| six | šesť | shest |
| seven | sedem | SE-dem |
| eight | osem | O-sem |
| nine | deväť | DEH-veht |
| ten | desat | DEH-saht |
| twenty | dvadsať | DVAHD-saht |
| thirty | tridsať | TREED-saht |
| forty | štyridsať | SHTIH-rihd-saht |
| fifty | päťdesiat | PEHTY-dehs-ee-aht |
| sixty | šesťdesiat | SHEST-dehs-yat |
| seventy | sedmdesiat | SEHDM-dehs-yat |
| eighty | osemdesiat | OH-sehm-dehs-ee-aht |
| ninety | deväťdesiat | DEH-vehty-dehs-ee-aht |
| one hundred | sto | stoh |
| Monday | pondelok | PO-nde-lok |
| Tuesday | utorok | UH-to-rok |
| Wednesday | streda | SRE-dah |
| Thursday | štvrok | SCHTVR-tok |
| Friday | piatok | PYA-tok |
| Saturday | sobota | SO-bo-tah |
| Sunday | nedeľa | NE-dye-jya |
| a day | deň | dyenh |
| a week | týždeň | TEE-zhde-nh |
| morning | ráno | RAH-no |
| afternoon | poobede | PO-O-beh-de |
| evening | večer | VE-cher |
| today | dnes | dnes |
| tomorrow | zajtra | ZAY-trah |
| spring | jar | yar |
| summer | leto | leh-to |
| fall | jeseň | YE-senh |
| winter | zima | ZI-ma |
| hot | horúco | KHO-ruh-tso |
| cold | chladno | KHLA-dnoh |
| pharmacy | lekáreň | LE-kaa-renh |
| water | voda | VO-da |
| with shower | so sprchou | so spr-kho |

| ENGLISH | SLOVAK | PRONOUNCE |
|---|---|---|
| post office | pošta | PO-shtah |
| stamp | známka | ZNAA-mka |
| airmail | letecká pošta | LE-te-tskaa po-shta |
| departure | odchod | OD-khod |
| arrival | príchod | PREE-khod |
| one-way | jedno směrný | YED-nyo SMER-nye |
| round-trip | spiatočný | SPYAH-toch-nee |
| station | stanica | STAH-nee-tsa |
| ticket | lístok | LEE-stok |
| train | vlak | vlak |
| bus | autobus | AUH-to-bus |
| airport | letisko | LE-ti-skoh |
| grocery | potraviny | PO-tra-vi-nee |
| breakfast | rañajky | RA-nya-ky |
| lunch | obed | O-bet |
| dinner | večera | Ve-che-ra |
| menu | menu | me-nuh |
| sugar | cukor | CU-kor |
| bread | chlieb | chleep |
| vegetables | zelenina | ze-LEH-nee-na |
| beef | hovädzie | KHO-veh-dzye |
| chicken | kura | KUH-rah |
| pork | bravčové | braucove |
| fish | ryba | Ri-bah |
| coffee | káva | KAH-va |
| milk | mlieko | m-LYE-ko |
| beer | pivo | PEE-vo |
| eggs | vajcia | VAY-tsi-ya |
| holiday | sviatok | SVEE-a-tokh |
| open | otvorené | O-tvoh-re-nee |
| closed | zatvorené | ZA-tvoh-re-nee |
| bank | banka | BAN-kah |
| police | policia | PO-lee-tsi-ya |
| exchange | zmenáreň | ZME-naa-renh |
| toilet | toaleta/WC | VEH-TSEH |
| square | námestie | NAH-mes-tye |
| castle | zámok | ZAA-mok |
| church | kostol | KO-stol |
| tower | veža | VE-zha |
| market | trh | trch |
| right | vpravo | fpravo |
| left | vľavo | flyavo |

# PHRASEBOOK

| ENGLISH | SLOVAK | PRONOUNCIATION |
|---|---|---|
| Yes/no | áno/nie | ah-NOH/NEH |
| Please | prosím | PROH-seem |
| Thank you | ďakujem | DAK-oo-yem |
| Hello | Dobrý deň | doh-BREE den |
| Good-bye | Dovidenia | doh-vee-DEN-eea |
| Good morning | Dobré ráno | doh-BREH RAH-no |
| Good evening | Dobrý večer | doh-BREE VE-tcher |
| Good night | Dobrú noc | doh-BROO NOTS |
| Sorry/Excuse me | Prepáčte/Prepáčte mi | PREH-pach-te/PREH-pach-te mee |
| Help! | Pomoc! | pah-MOTS |
| When? | Kedy? | keh-DEE |
| Where is...? | Kde je? | k-DEH yeh |
| How do I get to...? | Ako sa dostanem...? | AH-koh sa doh-STAN-em |
| How much does this cost? | Koľko to stojí...? | KOHL-ko toh STOH-yee |
| Do you have...? | Máte...? | MAH-teh |
| Do you speak English? | Hovoríte po anglicky? | ho-vo-REE-te poh ahng-GLIT-ski |
| I don't understand. | Nerozumiem. | neh-rohz-OOM-ee-em |
| I don't speak (language) | Nehovorím. | NE-kho-vo-reem po... |
| Please write it down. | Prosím napište to. | PRO-seem nah-PEESH-tye toh |
| Speak a little slower, please. | Prosím pomaly. | PRO-seem poh-MAH-le |
| I'd like to order... | Poprosil by som... | khtyel bikh |
| I'd like to pay/We'd like to pay. | Rád by som zaplatil/Radi by sme saplatili | RAAD bih som ZA-plah-tyll |
| I think you made a mistake in the bill. | Myslím, že ste sa pomýlili v úcte. | MEE-sleem zhe steh sa PO-mee-lili v UH-tste |
| Do you have a vacancy? | Máte voľnú izbu? | MAH-te VOL-noo iz-BOO |
| I'd like a room. | Poprosil by som izbu. | PO-pro-sil bih som IZ-buh |
| May I see the room? | Môžem izbu vidiet? | MO-zhem IZ-buh VI-dy-et |
| No, I don't like it. | Nie, nepáči sa mi. | NEH, ne-pah-chi sa mi. |
| Yes, I'll take it. | Áno, vezmem ju. | ANOH, VEZ-mem yu |
| Will you tell me when to get off? | Poviete mi kedy vystúpiť? | PO-vye-teh mi KE-dy VY-stoo-pith |
| Is this the right train/bus to...? | Je toto správny vlak/autobus do...? | Ye toto SPRAA-vnee vlak/auto-bus doh... |
| I want a ticket to... | Chcem listok do... | KH-cem lee-stok doh.. |
| How long does the trip take? | Ako dlho trvá cesta? | AKOH dl-HO TR-vah tse-stah |
| When is the first/next/last train to... | Kedy ide prvý/ďalší/posledný vlak do... | KE-dy ye PR-vee/DYA-lshee/PO-sled-neeh vlak doh... |
| I've lost my... | Stratil som môj... | STRA-til som muoy... |
| Would you like to dance? | Smiem prosiť? | SMYEM PRO-sit? |
| Go away. | Choď preč. | KHOD PRECH |

western Slovakia, *odchody* (departures) and *príchody* (arrivals) are posted on yellow and white signs, respectively, but don't always believe information about platforms—check the station's display board for the right *nástupište* (gate). In eastern Slovakia, ask "*Je to správne nástupište do...?*" ("Is this the right platform for...?") Reservations are sometimes required and generally recommended for *expresný* trains and first-class seats, but are not necessary for *rychlík* (fast), *spešný* (semifast), or *osobný* (local) trains. Both first and second class are safe and relatively comfortable. Station **locker** instructions probably won't be in English. Insert a 5Sk coin, choose a personal code on the *inside*, insert your bag, and try to shut the door. If it does not lock, throw a loud tantrum, and try another locker. Repeat 10 times. If this fails, go to the luggage window. To reclaim your bag, arrange the outer knobs to fit your personal code. Sometimes the aging circuit takes a few seconds to register and open. Left luggage offices (10-20Sk) are easier.

In many hilly regions, **ČSAD** or **SAD buses** are the best and sometimes the only option. Except for very long trips, buy the ticket on the bus. Schedules seem designed to drive foreigners batty with their many footnotes; the most important are as follows: **X** (it actually looks like two crossed hammers), weekdays only; **a,** Saturdays and Sundays only; and **r** and **k,** excluding holidays. **Numbers** refer to the days of the week on which the bus runs—1 is Monday, 2 is Tuesday, and so forth. *"Premava"* means including; *"nepremava"* is except; following those words are often lists of dates (day, then month). In the summer, watch out for July 5, when the entire country shuts down for Sts. Cyril and Methodius Day.

**Taxis** are fairly safe and convenient but can be much more expensive than buses or trams. Though haggling for prices is not widespread, be sure to check the price of the trip before getting in.

**BY THUMB.** *Let's Go* does not recommend hitchhiking. Hitchhiking is not very successful nor common in Slovakia. If you do, use a sign.

**BY BIKE.** The rambling wilds and ruined castles of Slovakia inspire great bike tours. The Slovaks love to ride bicycles, especially in the Tatras, the foothills of West Slovakia, and Šariš. **VKÚ** publishes color maps of most regions (70-80Sk).

# TOURIST SERVICES AND MONEY

| CURRENCY | | |
|---|---|---|
| US$1 = 48SK (SLOVAK KORUNY) | 10SK = US$0.21 | |
| CDN$1 = 32SK | 10SK = CDN$0.31 | |
| UK£1 = 67SK | 10SK = UK£0.14 | |
| IR£1 = 54SK | 10SK = IR£0.18 | |
| AUS$1 = 27SK | 10SK = AUS$0.36 | |
| NZ$1 = 20SK | 10SK = NZ$0.49 | |
| SAR1 = 6.8SK | 10SK = SAR1.46 | |
| DM1 = 22SK | 10SK = DM0.46 | |

The main tourist information offices form a loose conglomeration called **Asociácia Informačných Centier Slovenska (AICS);** look for the green logo. The offices are invariably on or near the town's main square; the nearest one can often be found by dialing 186. English is often—but not always—spoken here; accommodation bookings can usually—but not always—be made; and the staff is usually—but not always—delightful. **SATUR,** the Slovak branch of the old Czechoslovakian Čedok, seems more interested in flying Slovaks abroad on package tours, but may be of some help. **Slovakotourist** can be of assistance when available. Visa and American Express are the most accepted **credit cards,** although credit cards are not necessarily accepted in most places.

After the 1993 Czech-Slovak split, Slovakia hastily designed its own currency, which is now the country's only legal tender. One hundred **halér** make up one Slovak **koruna (Sk).** The currency rates above are those for September, 2000; with inflation around 14%. **Post offices** tend to have better exchange rates than banks. **Všeobecná Úverová Banka (VÚB)** has offices in even the smallest towns and cashes AmEx **traveler's cheques** for a 1% commission; most offices give **MC** cash advances. Many **Slovenská Sporiteľňa** bureaus handle **Visa** cash advances. 24hr. Cirrus/MC/Visa/Plus **ATMs** can be found in all but the smallest towns. They do not accept **AmEx.**

Many banks close at 3:30pm. Shops are usually open 9am-6pm, closed by noon on Saturdays, and closed on Sundays. While tourist agencies are hit-or-miss, tourist offices are on the whole reliable and plentiful. Be wary of vendors and those renting private rooms who don't list prices, as tourists can be a target.

# HEALTH AND SAFETY

**Tap water** varies in quality and appearance but is generally safe. If it comes out of the faucet cloudy, let it sit for five minutes—it's just air bubbles. A reciprocal agreement between Slovakia and the UK entitles Brits to free medical care here. *Drogerie* (drugstore) shelves heave with Western brand names; obtaining supplies shouldn't be hard. Bandages are *obväz*, aspirin *aspirena*, tampons *tampony*, and condoms *kondómy*. Slovakia is friendly toward **lone women travelers,** though they may encounter stares. Although **homosexuality** is legal, a gay couple walking down the street may encounter stares or insults. **Ganymedes,** the national gay organization, runs hotlines, but few employees speak English. There are virtually no minorities in Slovakia except for the Roma, who face much discrimination.

# ACCOMMODATIONS AND CAMPING

Foreigners will often pay up to twice as much as Slovaks for the same room. Finding cheap accommodations in Bratislava before the student dorms open in July is impossible, and without reservations, the outlook in Slovenský Raj and the Tatras can be bleak. Otherwise, it's not difficult to find a bed as long as you call ahead; just don't expect an English-speaker on the other end. The tourist office, **SATUR,** or **Slovakotourist** can usually help. Most hostels provide guests with a towel and a bar of soap. **Juniorhotels (HI),** though uncommon, are a step above the usual hostel. In the mountains, **chaty** (mountain huts/cottages) range from plush quarters for 400Sk per night to a friendly bunk and outhouse for 150Sk. **Hotel** prices fall dramatically outside Bratislava and the High Tatras, and they are rarely full. **Pensions** *(penzióny)* are less expensive than hotels, and often more fun. **Campgrounds** lurk on the outskirts of most towns, and many offer bungalows for travelers without tents. Camping in national parks is illegal.

# KEEPING IN TOUCH

Slovakia has an efficient **mail** service, taking two to three weeks depending on the (international) destination. Mail can be received general delivery through **Poste Restante.** Address envelope as follows: Maxfield (First name) MORANGE (LAST NAME), **Poste Restante,** Horna 1 (Post office address), Banská Bystrica (City) 97400 (Postal code), SLOVAKIA. Almost every post office (pošta) provides **Express Mail Services,** but to send a package abroad, a trip to a *colnice* (customs office) is in order. Even in small towns, **card phones** are common, and although they sometimes refuse your card (150Sk), they're much better than the coin-operated variety. Purchase cards at kiosks and telecommunications offices near some post offices. International access numbers include: **AT&T Direct** ☎ 00 42 700 101; **BT Direct** ☎ 0800 04401; **Canada Direct** ☎ 0800 000 151; **MCI WorldPhone** ☎ 08000 00112; **Sprint** ☎ 0042 187 187. **Internet access** is available in large and some mid-sized cities. Slovakia's only **English-language newspaper** is the weekly *Slovak Spectator* (24Sk), available at the Bratislava and Banská Bystrica Interpress stores. It is geared toward a business audience, but it has some useful entertainment listings and publishes an annual glossy *The Slovak Spectator* brochure (75Sk) for tourists. Other English-language finds are likely to be dreary government propaganda.

# BRATISLAVA ☎(0)7

Perched directly between Vienna and Budapest, Bratislava (pop. 452,053) is experienced most often as a passing blip, a blur of highrises and hills on the way to bigger, more cosmopolitan cities. Soviet-style apartment blocks and polluted roadways are reminders of the city's history of oppressive rulers: Habsburgs, Magyars, Soviets and, some would say, Czechs. While it's tempting to follow suit and pass Bratislava by, the city will surprise those who take the time to discover it. Its cobblestoned

Old Town is full of relaxing cafes, talented street musicians, and stunning Baroque buildings, while the outskirts of town are laced with vineyards and castle ruins. Major renovations in the last five years have improved the city's outlook, and progress shows no sign of stopping. Above all, Bratislava offers a glimpse into the psyche of a nation struggling to redefine itself.

# ✈ ORIENTATION

The **Dunaj** (Danube) runs east-west across Bratislava. The city's southern half consists of little more than a convention center, an amusement park, and miles of postwar high-rises. **Nový Most** (New Bridge), the spaceship-like bridge connecting the two sections, becomes the highway **Staromestská** to the north. The **Bratislavský Hrad** (Bratislava castle) towers on a hill to the west, while the city center sits between **Námestí Slovenského narodneho povstania** (**Námestí SNP;** Slovak National Uprising Square), the administrative center of town, and the river. Don't get off at the **Nové Mesto** train station; it's much farther from the center than **Hlavná stanica** (Main station). From the station, take tram #1 to "Poštová" at Námestí SNP. From the bus station, take trolley bus #215 to the center, or turn right onto Mlynské nivy and walk 10 minutes to Dunajská, which leads to **Kamenné námestí (Stone Square),** the center of town.

# ◪ INTERCITY TRANSPORTATION

**Airplanes: M.R. Štefánik International Airport** (☎48 57 11 11), 8km northeast of the city center. To reach the city center, take bus #61 from the airport to the train station and switch to tram #1, getting off at "Poštová" on Nám. SNP. Flights are very infrequent. It is better to use the much larger airport in nearby Vienna. The following carriers have local offices: **Austrian Airlines** (☎55 41 16 10), **British Airways** (☎52 49 98 01-2), **ČSA** (☎59 26 10 38), **Delta** (☎52 92 09 40), **LOT** (☎52 96 40 07), and **Lufthansa** (☎52 96 78 07).

**Trains: Bratislava Hlavná stanica** (☎50 58 44 84), north of the center. From the center, head up Štefánikova, turn right onto Šancová, and then left up the road that goes past the waiting buses. International tickets at counters #5-13. **Wasteels** office at the front of the station sells discounted international tickets to those under 26. (☎52 49 93 57; wasteels@zutom.sk; open M-F 8:30am-4:30pm.) To: **Vienna, AUS** (1½hr., 3 per day, 248Sk); **Budapest, HUN** (2½-3hr., 7 per day, 660 Sk); **Prague, CZR** (5hr., 7 per day, 300Sk); **Krakow, POL** (8hr., 1 per day, 1080Sk, Wasteels 865Sk); **Warsaw, POL** (8hr., 1 per day, 1400Sk, Wasteels 811Sk); and **Berlin, GER** (10hr., 2 per day, 3600Sk, Wasteels 2534Sk).

**Buses:** Mlynské nivy 31 (☎0984 22 22 22), east of the center. To: **Vienna, AUS** (1½hr., 7 per day, 140Sk); **Prague, CZR** (5hr., 7 per day, 290Sk); **Budapest, HUN** (4hr., 1 per day, 500Sk); **Berlin, GER** (12hr., 1 on Friday, 1600Sk); and **Warsaw, POL** (13hr., 1 on F, 670Sk). More frequent and consistent than trains. Check ticket for bus number (č. aut.), as several different buses may depart from the same stand simultaneously.

**Hydrofoils: Lodná osobná doprava,** Fajnorovo nábr. 2 (☎52 49 35 18; fax 52 93 22 31), along the river. A scenic alternative to trains for Danube destinations. To: **Vienna, AUS** (1½hr., 1 per day, one-way 240AS, round-trip 370AS); **Budapest, HUN** (4hr., 1-2 per day, one-way 700AS, round-trip 1000AS); and **Devín Castle** (2 per day T-Su, one-way 70Sk, round trip 95Sk). Book tickets at least 48hr. in advance and show up at least 30min. early. Major credit cards accepted. May-Oct. 1.

# ▣ LOCAL TRANSPORTATION

**Local Transportation:** All daytime trips on **trams** or **buses** require a ticket for each trip. Tickets are sold at kiosks or the orange *automats* found at most bus stations (6Sk for 10min., 12Sk for 30min., 18Sk for 60min.). **Night buses** marked with black and orange numbers in the 500s require 2 tickets. They run at midnight and 3am. Trams and buses

**Bratislava**

🏠 ACCOMMODATIONS

Pension Gremium, 1
Youth Hostel Bernolak, 2
Youth Hostel, 3

0 ───── 300 yards
0 ───── 300 meters

**SLOVAKIA**

run 4am-11pm. Most trams pass by Námestí SNP while most buses stop at the north base of Nový Most. Joyriding will cost you 1000Sk; authorities *do* check. Tourist passes sold at some kiosks: 24hr. 70Sk, 48hr. 130Sk, 3 days 160Sk, 7 days 240Sk.

**Taxis: Otto Taxi** (☎54 79 33 33), **BP** (☎ 65 42 33 33), or **FunTaxi** (☎54 77 73 77).

**Hitchhiking:** Those hitching to **Vienna, AUS** cross Most SNP and walk down Viedenská cesta. This road also heads to **Hungary** via Győr, though fewer cars head in that direction. A destination sign might help. Hitchers to **Prague, CZR** take bus #121 or 122 from the center to the Patronka stop. Hitching is legal (except on major highways) and common, but not recommended by *Let's Go*.

# 🛈 PRACTICAL INFORMATION

## TOURIST AND FINANCIAL SERVICES

**Tourist Office: Bratislavská informačná služba (BIS),** Klobúčnicka 2 (☎54 43 37 15 and 54 43 43 70; fax 54 43 27 08; bis@bratislava.sk; www.bratislava.sk/bis). Sells **maps** (28Sk), gives **city tours,** and books rooms (50Sk fee; singles 900-2500Sk). Open M-F 8am-7pm, Sa-Su 9am-2pm. **Branch** in the train station annex open 9am-6pm daily.

**Embassies: On the web:** www.foreign.gov.sk. **Canada** (honorary consulate), Mišíkova 28 (☎52 44 21 75; fax 52 49 99 95). Open M-F 8:30am-noon, 1:30-4pm. **UK,** Panská 16 (☎54 41 96 32-3; fax 54 41 00 02). Open M-F 8:30am-12:30pm and 1:30-5pm. Visa section open M-F 9-11am. **US,** Hviezdoslavovo nám. 4 (☎54 43 08 61 or 54 43 33 38; after hours emergency ☎0903 70 36 66; fax 54 41 51 48). Open M-F 8am-4:30pm.

Visa section open M-F 8-11:30am. **Australians, Irish, New Zealanders,** and **South Africans** should contact the British Embassy in an emergency.

**Currency Exchange: VÚB,** Gorkého 9 (☎59 55 79 76; fax 59 55 80 90). Cashes traveler's checks for a 1% commission and handles MC/Visa **cash advances.** Open M-W and F 8am-5pm, Th 8am-noon. A **24hr. currency exchange machine** outside Česko-slovenská Obchodná Barka on the corner of Michalská and Zámočnícka changes US$, DM, UK£, and several other western European currencies into Sk for no commission. **24hr. ATMs** are all over the center and at the train station. Virtually all of them accept Cirrus/Maestro/Plus.

## LOCAL SERVICES AND COMMUNICATION

**Luggage Storage:** Finicky lockers at the train and bus stations (5Sk). Better to use the luggage storage rooms: bus station 10Sk, open M-F 5:30am-10pm, Sa-Su 6am-6pm; train station 20Sk, open daily 6am-6pm.

**English Bookstore: Eurobooks,** Jesenského 5/9 (☎/fax 5441 7959; eurobooks@eurobooks.sk; www.eurobooks@eurobooks.sk), has extensive selection. Open M-F 9am-7pm, Sa 9am-1pm. **Interpress Slovakia** (☎44 87 15 01; interpress@interpress.sk), on the corner of Sedláska and Michalská, carries a wide range of foreign press. Open M-Sa 7am-10pm, Su 10am-10pm.

**Bi-Gay-Lesbian Hotline:** ☎211 54 61.

**Laundromat: INPROKOM,** Laurinská 18 (☎54 13 11 42). Same-day service 10-85Sk per garment; slower service 7-49Sk. Open M-F 11am-6pm.

**Pharmacy:** The most central one is at Námestí SNP 20 (☎54 43 29 52), on the corner of Gorkého and Laurinská. Open M-F 7:30am-7pm, Sa 8am-5pm, Su 9am-5pm.

**Internet Access: Internet Club,** Jesenského 7 (☎0903 96 71 21; icaffe@tatrahome.sk; www.tatrahome.sk). Five quick PCs with helpful English- and German-speaking staff to boot (2Sk per min.). Open M-Sa 9am-6:30pm. **Klub Internet,** Valanského nábr. 2 (☎59 34 91 96; tatrashop@tatrahome.sk). At the back of the National Museum on Múzejná. 7 speed machines (2Sk per min.). Open M-F 9am-9pm, Sa-Su noon-9am.

**Telephones:** On Námestí SNP, Františkánské námestí, behind the National Theater, and all over the place. Most use phone cards, which can be purchased at the post office and kiosks.

**Post Office:** Námestí SNP 35 (☎54 43 51 80). **Poste Restante** at counter #5. Open M-F 7am-8pm, Sa 7am-2pm. **Postal code:** 81000 Bratislava 1.

# ☛ ACCOMMODATIONS

Bratislava's tourist agencies rent out everything but retirement homes and orphanages to the Vienna-bound crowds in the summer. During July and August, several dorms open up as hostels. Until then, good deals are hard to come by. Most cheap beds are near the station on the northeast side of town, a 20-minute walk or five-minute tram ride from the center. Pensions or **private rooms** (900-2500Sk, see **Tourist Office,** above) provide a cheap and comfortable alternative.

**Youth Hostel Bernolak,** Bernolákova 1 (☎52 49 77 24). From the train station, take bus #23, 74, or 218, or tram #3 to "Račianské Mýto." From the bus station, take bus #121 or 122. Here you'll find comfort and peace of mind. All doubles with bath and fridge. Check-out 9am. Open July 1-Sept. 15. 300Sk per person; 10% off with Euro26, HI, and ISIC.

**Youth Hostel,** Wilsonova 6 (☎52 49 77 35). See directions for YH Bernolak—Wilsonova runs parallel to Bernolákova. Remarkable only for the price; you might consider a private room if you stay here. Check-out 9am. Open July-Aug. Shared bath. 2- to 3-bed dorms 200Sk per person; 30% off with Euro26, HI, or ISIC.

**Pension Gremium,** Gorkého 11 (☎54 13 10 26; fax 54 43 06 53). Its central location just off Hviezdoslavovo námestí affords great convenience but comes at the price of raucous street noise. Sparkling private showers, huge fans, a popular cafe, and English-speaking reception make this pension truly agreeable, and prices are buoyed up accordingly. Local phone calls 5Sk. Check-out noon. Only five rooms, so call several days ahead. (One) single 890Sk; doubles 1290Sk; (one) larger double 1600Sk. Light breakfast included. MC/Visa.

**Výskumný ústav zváračský,** Pionierska 17 (☎49 24 67 61; fax 49 24 63 35). Take tram #3 from the train station to "Pionierska." The entrance is 150m up the street on the right. The concrete-box exterior of this lively university dorm houses dozens of modest doubles. Shared bath. No English spoken. Check-out 9am. Curfew midnight. 600Sk; 400Sk June 15-Sept. 1 and on weekends.

**Autocamping Zlaté Piesky,** Senecká cesta 2 (☎44 45 05 92; fax 44 25 73 73), in suburban Trnávka. Take tram #2 or 4 or bus #215 from the train station to the last stop and cross the footbridge. Campground and bungalows down by the lake, 25min. from town. 100Sk per adult, 50Sk per child. Cottage doubles (no bath) 420Sk; bungalow doubles (with bath) 930Sk.

# 🖰 FOOD

Red-canopied cafes abound in the city's old center, but virtually none serve food. A few of Bratislava's restaurants serve the region's spicy meat mixtures with numerous varieties of west Slovakia's celebrated *Modra* wine, a strong-flavored specialty and source of pride among locals. Since establishments in Bratislava come and go at a surprising rate, you can always look around the next corner for something to satiate you. Offering a lull from both cost and confusion is **Tesco Potraviny,** Kamenné námestí 1, a grocery and department store. (Open M-W 8am-7pm, Th 8am-8pm, F 8am-9pm, Sa 8am-6pm, Su 9am-6pm.)

🖼 **Prašná bašta,** Zámočnícka 11 (☎54 43 49 57). Dark alcoves with funky sculptures inside and a leafy terrace outside. Occasional live music. Excellent traditional Slovak dishes 88-185Sk. Open daily 11am-11pm.

**Crepa,** Michalská 22. A little bit of Paris served with Slovak and inventive fillings. You can grab a crepe for the dining room or enjoy it in the nearby Františkánske námestí. (25-140Sk). Open M-Th 8am-11pm, F 8am-midnight, Sa 10am-midnight, Su 10am-11pm.

**Vegetarian jedáleň,** Laurinská 8. Local businessfolk and young Slovak herbivores alike line up at this cafeteria-style lunch spot for the few hours it's open. Menu changes daily and features such dishes as vegetable risotto and sheep's cheese *halušky* (minus the bacon). Prices hover around 50-100Sk. Open M-F 11am-3pm.

**Black Rose,** Michalská 7 (☎54 41 21 94). Tasty pizza and Slovak main dishes (92-200Sk) taste great in this sidewalk cafe or low-ceilinged basement pub. Open M-Sa 11am-1am, Su 11am-midnight.

**Cafe London,** Panská 17 (☎54 43 12 61), in the British Council's courtyard. For those saturated with sheep's cheese, Cafe London offers the comfort of good, old-fashioned sandwiches and other light meals (52-118Sk) that are not particularly British. They also brew a great cappuccino (52-119Sk). Open M-F 9am-9pm.

# 🖰 SIGHTS

Most of the sights in Bratislava are roughly bordered by Námestí SNP, Štúrova, the Dunaj, and Starometská. Our suggested walking tour starts at Námestí SNP and continues through Primaciálne námestí, Hlavné námestí, Hviezdoslavovo námestí, and Námestí Ľudovita Štúra. We orient our listings from these five squares. We also include two additional sights—Bratislava Castle and Devín Castle.

## YOU WANT FRIES WITH THAT?
Just when you thought the hardest challenge in ordering food was comprehending Slovak, you come to a Bratislava burger stand. A *syrový burger* (cheeseburger) costs less than a *hamburger so syrom* (hamburger with cheese) because, as the stand owner will explain with humiliatingly clear logic, a cheeseburger is made of cheese—*only* cheese. A *pressburger*, named after Bratislava's former moniker Pressburg, consists of bologna on a bun, and hamburgers are actually ham. Everything comes boiled except, of course, the cheese.

# DOWNTOWN

**NÁMESTÍ SNP.** This square commemorates the bloody and ultimately unsuccessful Slovak National Uprising against the fascist regime (see **History**, p. 692). Together with the adjoining Kamenné námestí, they comprise the heart of the modern city. If you walk down Suché mýto from Námestí SNP to Kamenné námestí and turn right on Klobučnícka, a short walk will bring you to the **Hummel Museum.** A CD shop serves as the entrance to this museum, which is devoted to the 19th-century Austrian composer and pianist Johann Nepomuk Hummel. *(Open Tu-Su 1-5pm. 15Sk.)* **Although St. Michael's Tower** (Michalská Brána) is actually billed as the **Museum of Arms and Fortifications,** the 13th-century tower above the weapons showcase is the real attraction. Turn right out of Námestí SNP and left on Michalská to get there. St. Michael's Tower is the only preserved gateway from the town's medieval fortifications. After perusing the weapons, trot up to the top for a view of the city. *(Open M and W-F 10am-5pm, Sa-Su 11am-6pm. Last entry ½hr. before closing. 20Sk.)* **Grassalkovich Palác,** Hodžovo námestí 1, is up Poštová from Námestí SNP. Grassalkovich Palác is the grandest of the city's many Hungarian aristocratic residences; so grand, in fact, that former Premier Mečiar turned it into the Presidential Palace. Behind the castle, the Grassalkovich Gardens are open as a park, though the security is a presence.

**PRIMACIÁLNE NÁMESTÍ.** If you cross Šturova from Námestí SNP and head down Uršulinska, you will reach Primaciálne námestí at the intersection of Uršulinska and Klobučinska. The Neoclassical **Primate's Palace** (Primaciálny Palác; Primaciálne námestí 1) on the square dates from 1781 and owes its name to Prince and Primate Emmerich Esterházy, its inhabitants in the 1730s. In 1805, Napoleon and Austrian Emperor Franz I signed the Peace of Pressburg (the German name for Bratislava) here, two weeks after the decisive French victory at Austerlitz. Buy tickets on the second floor and head upstairs to see the Hall of Mirrors (Zrkadlová Sieň), where it all happened, as well as some 17th-century tapestries and a small Baroque church. *(Open Tu-Su 10am-5pm. 20Sk, under 15 free.)*

**HLAVÉ NÁMESTÍ.** To reach Hlavé námestí from Primaciálne námestí, walk down Klobučnícka away from BIS. Klobučnícka ends at Hlavé námestí. This square is a popular spot for tourists perusing souvenir stands and free theatrical performances (weather permitting). In the early evening, it's filled with strolling couples and ice cream-eating teenagers. The **Town History Museum** (Muzeum Histórie Mesta; Hlavné námestí), is in the Old Town Hall Stará Radnica adjacent to Hlavné námestí. It houses an impressive 1:500 scale model of 1945-55 Bratislava that you can admire for free. The rest of the collection includes a battery of untranslated Slovak notices describing the medieval town, a series of galleries illustrating Bratislava's development, and some grisly torture displays. *(☎54 43 46 90. Open Tu-F 10am-5pm, Sa-Su 11am-6pm. 25Sk, students 10Sk.)*

**HVIEZDOSLAVOVO NÁMESTÍ.** If you take Rybárska Brana from Hlavé námestí, the road will end at Hviezdoslavovo námestí. More than a square, Hviezdoslavovo námestí is actually a park surrounded by 19th-century architecture. To get to **St. Martin's Cathedral** (Dóm sv. Martina), take Ventúrska from Hviezdoslavovo námestí, a left on Panská, and a right on Kapitulská. This is a fairly unspectacular Gothic church where the kings of Hungary were crowned for three centuries. It is now undergoing renovations to restore some of its former glory, but is still used frequently for services. **The Museum of Jewish Culture** (Muzeum Židovskej Kultúry; Židovská 17) can be reached from St. Martin's Cathedral by crossing the Starometská freeway via the overpass. This museum preserves valuable fragments of a nearly vanished population: **Schlossberg,** the old Jewish quarter, was bulldozed in the name of "progress." *(☎54 41 85 07. Open M-F and Su 11am-5pm. Last entry 4:30pm. 60Sk, students 40Sk.)* Ballet and opera are performed nearly daily at the 1886 **Slovak National Theater** (Slovenské Národné Divadlo), right off Hviezdoslavovo námestí.

**NÁMESTÍ L'UDOVÍTA ŠTURA.** Taking Mostová from Hviezdoslavovo námestí will bring you to Námestí L'udovita Stúra. This square celebrates L'udoviť Štúr, who codified the Slovak language in the 19th century as distinct from Czech (see **Litera-**

**ture & Arts,** p. 695). The **Slovak National Museum** (Slovenské Národné Muzeum; Vajanského nábr. 2), can be reached by turning left out of Námestí L'udovíta Štúra on Vajanského nábr. and right on Fajnorovo nábr. It houses the region's archaeological finds, including casts of local Neanderthal skeletons. (☎ *59 34 91 11. Open Tu-Su 9am-5pm. 20Sk, students 10Sk. Special exposition tickets 20Sk for 30min.)* To get to the **Slovak National Gallery** (Rázusovo nábr. 2) from Námestí L'udovíta Štúra, turn right on Rázusovo nábr. The gallery displays well-preserved sculpture, frescoes, and paintings from the Gothic and Baroque periods. Its outside courtyard (free) offers bizarre and beautiful modern sculptures and benches for respite. (☎ *54 43 17 03; info@sng.sk; www.sng.sk. Open Tu-Su 10am-6pm. 35Sk, students 10Sk, children under 6 free, family ticket 60Sk.)* The **New Bridge** (Nový Most), whose reins are held by a giant flying saucer, can be reached most directly by continuing down Rázusovo nábr. from the National Gallery. It has nice views and a restaurant to boot. (*10Sk to climb to the top.)*

## BRATISLAVA CASTLE (BRATISLAVSKÝ HRAD)

Visible from the Danube's banks to the center's historic squares, the four-towered Bratislava Castle (Bratislavský Hrad) is the city's defining landmark. The castle's heyday came in the 18th century, when Austrian Empress Maria Theresa held court there. Having been destroyed by fire in 1811 and by bombs during WWII, what is left today is largely communist-era restoration, which *almost* succeeds in capturing the castle's former glory. If you climb the Crown Tower (Korunná veža), at the top you'll get both a view of the Danube winding from Austria to Hungary and a vista of Bratislava. The castle grounds are ideal for picnicking high above the city. The **Historical Museum** (Historické Muzeum) inside displays temporary exhibits from the Slovak National Museum. (*On Zámocká. Take Ventúrska from Hviezdoslavovo nám., turn left on Panská, turn right on Kapitulská, left in front of St. Martin's Cathedral, and cross the Starometská freeway via the overpass. Follow Zámocké schody to the Castle. Open Tu-F 9am-5pm, Sa-Su 10am-6pm. 30Sk, students 15Sk.)*

## DEVÍN CASTLE

Slovakia's best-loved castle ruins perch on a promontory 9km west of downtown Bratislava. The fortress itself overlooks the confluence of the mighty Morava and Dunaj rivers. Fortified by Slavs in the 9th century, this large outcrop fell under the control of Magyars, was fortified in the 15th and 16th centuries, and then destroyed by Napoleon in 1809. Recent excavations have found traces of settlements on the site dating as far back as 5000 BC. Under communist control, the castle grew to symbolize totalitarianism, sheltering sharpshooters who were ordered to fire at anyone walking the beach alongside the Morava, which marks the Austrian border. Paths wind through the rocks and ruins, while a **museum** shows off local archaeological finds. A small amusement park at the castle's base provides a strange contrast. (*Take bus #29 to Devín from below Nový Most and get off at the Strbska stop. Continue on the main road 200m in the same direction, and turn left just before the bridge onto the second, unmarked street by the white stone fence. The parking lot at the end of this street leads to the castle. Museum ☎ 65 73 01 05. Open May-Oct. Tu-Su 10am-5pm, July-Aug. 10am-6pm; last entrance 4:30pm. 40Sk, students, seniors, and children 10Sk.)*

# 🎭 ENTERTAINMENT

For film, concert, and theater (both puppet and dramatic) schedules, get a copy of *Kám v Bratislave* at BIS (see **Tourist Offices,** p. 703). Although it's entirely in Slovak, the info is easy to decipher. **Slovenská filharmonia** (Slovak Philharmonic) plays regularly at Palackého ul. 2; the box office is around the corner on Medená. (☎ 54 43 33 51; open M-Tu and Th-F 1-7pm, W 8am-2pm.) The Filharmonia as well as most theaters vacation in July and August. Tickets to the **Národné divadlo** (National Theater) are sold at the box office at Laurinská 20. (Open M-F noon-6pm. Tickets from 200Sk, 50% discount with student ID.) A dozen **cinemas** are scattered across the city; most show films in the original with Slovak subtitles. In late September and early October, the **Bratislava Music Festival** brings dozens of acts to the city.

# ◩ NIGHTLIFE

**Charlie's Pub,** Špitálka 4 (☎52 92 51 39; www.charlies-pub.sk). Located in the basement of a cinema, Charlie's attracts wilder crowds who feel the need to bust a move. Drink specials and theme parties run rampant. Cover 30Sk. Open Tu-Th 8pm-4am, F-Sa 8pm-5am.

**Dubliner,** Sedlárska 6 (☎54 41 07 06; www.irishpub.sk). Bratislava's *ersatz* Irish pub is hugely popular after dinner, when its mix of patrons spill out to the street. An *Irish Post* from 1939 charts Hitler's grab for Czechoslovakia. Expensive Guinness (85Sk); local brands are also pricey (45Sk). Irish specialty dishes (50-225Sk) and occasional live music. Open M-Sa 9am-1am, Su 11am-midnight.

**Krater,** Vysocá 14 (☎52 92 74 08). An eatery during the week, Krater becomes a thumping disco complete with neon lights, translucent-floored catwalks, and dancing youth over the weekend. Cover 20Sk. Disco open F-Sa 6pm-5am, Su 6pm-2am.

**Alligator Club,** Laurinská 7 (☎54 41 86 11). A mainly 20-something crowd drifts between the club's sidewalk tables and basement bar, sipping beer (17-70Sk) and enjoying frequent live rock and blues performances. Open M-F 10am-midnight, Sa 11am-midnight, Su 4pm-10pm.

# CENTRAL SLOVAKIA

Rail connections are poor but journeys spectacular in the hills of central Slovakia, where medieval miners once dug into the richest gold and silver deposits in Europe. Located between Bratislava and the snow-capped Tatra mountains, the region is now a barely touristed blend of Slovak folk tradition and the endless possibilities for hiking, biking, fishing, hang-gliding, or virtually any other outdoor activity you can imagine. It's tempting to neglect Central Slovakia in favor of her more glamorous neighbors to the northeast, but those who stop to explore the wealth of history and outdoor opportunities will be extravagantly rewarded.

# BANSKÁ BYSTRICA  ☎(0)88

Banská Bystrica (BAN-skaah bis-TREE-tsah) is the perfect mix of cosmopolitan flare and country scenery. The old town center is a lively, car-free square, filled with dozens of outdoor cafes serving surprisingly good coffee, some of the best folk-art boutiques in Slovakia, and mellow locals strolling with ice cream in hand. Just beyond the town, and in view of most of it, lie rolling fields and forested hillsides that make a tremendous playground for biking, hang-gliding, and light hiking. Banská Bystrica maintains an elegant charm and relaxing atmosphere that make it an ideal place to rest up en route to or from the Tatras.

## ◪ ◲ ORIENTATION AND PRACTICAL INFORMATION

You may find yourself spending a fair stretch of time in the gorgeous hills and valleys of Banská Bystrica, as transport connections in the area are less than flawless. The train and bus stations are next to each other (☎0984 23 23 23). Trains leave for **Bratislava** (4hr., 1 per day, 204Sk) and **Košice** (4hr., 1 per day, 204Sk), while many more leave for these destinations from **Zvolen** (½hr., every hr., 16Sk). **Buses** go to **Bratislava** (4hr., 20 per day, 200Sk), **Liptovský Mikuláš** (2hr., 9 per day, 85Sk), and **Košice** (4hr., 7 per day, 200Sk). **24hr. luggage lockers** cost 5Sk. To get to the town center, walk past the gas (petrol) station behind the bus station and cross Cesta K. Smrečine into the gardens. Take the pedestrian underpass under the highway and continue along Cesta K. Smrečine; a left onto Horná at the glass pyramidal bookstore brings you to **Námestí SNP,** the town center (15min.). Alternatively, the city bus (there's only one and it's a minibus) takes people right to the city center. Get off at the "Nám. Š. Moyzesa" stop (5Sk).

**Kultúrne a Informačné Stredisko (KIS),** Námestí Š. Moyzesa 26, between Horná and Námestí SNP, has leaflets about cultural events, maps (18Sk), and info on Banská

Bystrica's accommodations. If asked they will book private rooms at no fee. (☎161 86; fax 415 29 14; pkobb@isternet.sk; www.isternet.sk/pkobb. Open May 15-Sept. 15 M-F 8am-7pm and Sa 9am-7pm; off-season M-F 9am-5pm.) **VÚB**, Námestí Slobody 1 (☎450 56 00) and Dolná 17 (☎412 39 00) off Námestí SNP, **exchanges currency** and cashes **traveler's checks** for a 1% commission. (Open M-W and F 7:30am-4:30pm, Th 7:30am-noon.) There's a 24hr. Cirrus/Plus **ATM** outside the tourist office. **Interpress Slovakia**, Dolná 19, sells English-language journals and newspapers. (Open M-F 7am-8pm, Sa 8am-2pm, Su 11am-4pm.) The **laundromat CITO**, Kapitulská 15, offers three-day service. (☎415 12 28. Open M-F 8am-6pm, Sa 9am-noon.) Several **pharmacies** operate around Námestí SNP; try **Lekáreň pod Bránom** at Námestí SNP 14. (Open M-F 7:30am-6pm, Sa 8am-noon.) **Internet Club**, Horná Strieborná 8, has internet access. (☎415 50 40; uniplus@netax.sk. Open M-F 9am-8pm, Sa 10am-1pm. 25Sk per 15min.) The **post office** is at Horná 1, just off Nám. SNP next to the tourist office. (☎415 26 37. Open M-F 8am-8pm, Sa 8am-noon.) A card **phone** stands outside; coin-operated phones are inside the building. **Postal code:** 97401.

## ACCOMMODATIONS AND FOOD

Summer visitors should ask **KIS** (see above) about temporary **hostel** arrangements. The best option is to get them to book **private rooms**, which are often comfortable and affordable (around 200Sk). Failing this, **Turistic Hotel Milvar**, Školská 9 (☎413 87 73), rents out basic singles with shared baths and lots of natural light. From Námestí SNP, turn right through the arch across from clocktower to Horná Strieborná and follow the road as it angles left to become Strieborna. Once over the river, take a right on J.G. Tajovského and follow it under the highway. The first right and then the first left on Školská will bring you there (25min.; 300Sk per person). **Hotel Národný dom**, Národná 11, off Námestí SNP, is admirably central and has common areas on each floor. Rooms are well-lit and spacious, but showers are rather rusty. The cafe downstairs and opera house next door keep the place lively at night as well as noisy. (☎412 37 37; fax 412 57 86. Singles 700Sk, doubles 1080Sk, triples (with toilet) 1380Sk.) If you're in an absolute bind, head farther up J.G. Tajovského from Turistic Hotel Milvar to **Hotel Turist ATC**, J.G. Tajovského 68, a year-round hostel with a common room and central bathroom. No curfew. (☎412 45 10. Doubles with sinks 200Sk.)

Tops for food is ■ **Slovenská pivnica**, on Lazovná 18 off Nám. SNP, which is located in a cozy underground bunker and serves traditional Slovak food. (☎415 50 36. Dishes 48-129Sk. Open M-Sa 11am-10pm.) **Copaline Baguette**, Dolná 1, which stuffs fresh French bread with ham, cheese, eggs, shrimp, salmon, and anything else they can think up—just point at the *sendvič* you want (42-92Sk), while you're at it, try the tasty chocolate *pudink* (16Sk) for dessert. (☎412 58 68. Open M-F 6:30am-midnight, Sa-Su 8am-midnight.) Look for groceries at **Prior** on the corner of Horná and Cesta K. Smrečine, by the pyramidal bookstore. (Open M-F 8am-7pm, Sa 8am-1pm. MC/Visa.)

## SIGHTS

A cluster of the town's oldest buildings stands on Námestí Š. Moyzesa. The tourist office is on the ground floor of the **barbakan** fortification in the middle of the square; next door, the restored **Pretórium**—once the town hall, now the **Galéria**—displays three floors of local avant-garde art. (☎412 48 64. Open Tu-F 9am-6pm, Sa-Su 10am-4pm. 20Sk, students 10Sk.) The Galéria is not to be confused with the **Galleria,** on the other side of the barbikan, which also displays local art, but with a greater emphasis on sculpture. (Open Tu-F 9am-5pm, Sa-Su 10am-4pm.) The large church behind the Galéria and the fortification is the Romanesque **Church of the Virgin Mary** (Kostol Panny Márie), which sports a fine Baroque ceiling and an even finer Gothic altarpiece by Majstr Pavel of Levoča (see **Levoča**, p. 717). Wandering onto **Nám. SNP** from the tourist office, the **Museum of Central Slovakia** (Stredoslovenské Múzeum), Nám. SNP 4, has a historical collection well-presented in a restored Renaissance house. (Open M-F 9am-noon and 1-5pm, Su 1-5pm. 15Sk, students 8Sk. English language pamphlet 3Sk.)

Heading left from the tourist office on Horná 55 is **Skuteckého dom,** the restored 18th-century neo-Renaissance villa of local artist Dominik Skutecký (1848-1921) that now displays the state's collection of his work. A dogged realist in the age of Impressionism, Skutecký focused throughout his life on social and folk scenes. (☎412 54 50. Open Tu-Su 10am-5pm. 10Sk, students 4Sk, children 2Sk. Ask to borrow the glossy English catalog.)

The ▓ **Museum of the Slovak National Uprising** (Múzeum Slovenského národného povstania) looks like a cracked flying saucer that landed in the gardens of Kapitulská. Banská Bystrica was the rebels' headquarters during the eight weeks of fighting that began when Nazi forces entered puppet ally Slovakia's territory on August 29, 1944 (see **History,** p. 692). The museum charts the course of the failed insurrection and the grim Nazi reprisals that followed, and sets the SNP in the wider context of World War II, the "independent" Slovak state of Josef Tiso, and the deportation of the Slovak Jews organized by his regime. No written English help is given, but any knowledge of the war helps make sense of the exhibits. Turn right from the tourist office into Nám. SNP, then an immediate left onto Kapitulská. (Open Tu-Su 9am-6pm. 50Sk, students 10Sk.)

## ♫ ENTERTAINMENT

**Cinemas** are the primary evening entertainment in Banská Bystrica. Almost all show Hollywood flicks and almost all are subtitled in Slovak—look for *titulky* on the cinema's posters around town to verify subtitling. The two main cinemas are **Kino Hviezda,** Skuteckého 3 (☎412 35 15 and 414 20 74; cinema.web.sk/kino), and **Art Kino,** Nám. Slobody 3 (☎415 24 66). Tickets are 35-60Sk depending on popularity and date of release. Otherwise, **Piváreň Perla,** Horná 52, is a lively local favorite where copper vats of *Perla* bubble right behind the bar while locals chain-smoke in front of it. Both barflies and businessfolk enjoy the quality microbrew (12Sk) on communal tables and benches. Ignore the stares; don't be shy about scooting right in. (Open M-Sa 8am-11:30pm.) The town's well-known **Rázcesti puppet theater,** Kollárova 18, offers popular Slovak shows. (☎412 41 93. Box office open Sept.-June M-F 2-4pm. Tickets 30-50Sk.)

## ⚑ OUTDOORS

For more active entertainment, Banská Bystrica offers ample outdoor adventures, including bike rental, hiking, horseback riding, and rock climbing. To reach **Spedik-Jahn,** a travel agent in the village Tajov that rents bikes, take the city bus from the bus station to **Tajov** (☎419 73 80. 2hr. 60Sk, 4hr. 40Sk, 8hr. 30Sk, 1wk. 900Sk). The bus runs hourly during the week and every two hours on weekends (7km, 10Sk). Popular hiking trails run from **Donovaly,** the ski area accessible by bus from Banská Bystrica (25km, 20Sk). **Škola Paragliding Donovaly,** Mistriky 230 (☎419 97 32), runs a paragliding school for around 2400Sk, as does **Pegas Paragliding,** na Uhlisten 26 (☎411 36 84; 3300Sk; 10% student discount). Call ahead for both. **Pony Farma-Suchý Urch,** Jazdiareň Uhlisko (☎415 45 90), offers horseback riding for all levels.

## ⚑ DAYTRIP FROM BANSKÁ BYSTRICA

### BOJNICE

*To get to Bojnice, take the bus to Prievidza from Banská Bystrica (1-2hr., 12 per day, 77Sk) or Bratislava (2½hr., 12 per day, 120Sk). Facing ul. A. Hlinku from the Prievidza bus station, take local bus #3 from the "Bojnice-Čajka" stop on the right side of the street (8Sk, 15min. to the castle). Castle open Apr. Tu-Su 10am-4pm; May-Sept. Tu-Su 9am-5pm; Oct.-Mar. 10am-3pm. 120 Sk, children 60Sk. Tour included. Cameras 30Sk. Excellent English guidebook 30Sk.*

Although many of Slovakia's castles survive today only in ruins or as recon-structions, the ◼ **castle** at Bojnice remains a real-life fairy tale minus the dragon. Originally a 12th-century wooden fortress for a Benedictine monastery, it was traded between nobles for 500 years until the Pálffy family gained posses-sion of it in 1644 and held on to it until 1908. The last of the noble line was Jan Pálffy, whose lifelong effort was to "remodel" the palace in the romantic style of a Loire-valley chateau. The castle today is the result of his efforts, and easily outdoes any other in Slovakia in both opulence and splendor. The guided tour visits galleries, gardens, hunting rooms, bedrooms, a citadel, a chapel, a crypt, a cave, medieval washrooms, and the magnificent Oriental and Golden Halls. If you're not mesmerized by costumed noblewomen who haunt the hallways and turrets, then you will be by the stunning rooms and vistas of the basin region. If you prefer real ghosts, come in late April or early May for the **International Festi-val of Ghosts and Spirits,** when the castle is overtaken by spirits of its past inhab-itants and is host to special events.

# MALÁ FATRA MOUNTAINS

The Malá Fatra mountain range is an exhilarating melange of alpine meadows, steep ravines, and limestone peaks. Whether you're out for a day hike or planning on staying at a *chaty* (huts) along the way, there are hikes here of all difficulty lev-els and durations. Žilina, a nearby town, is an ideal place to make your base.

## ŽILINA ☎(0)89

Its location on a major railway makes Žilina (ZHI-li-na; pop. 87,000) a great head-quarters for adventures in the nearby Malá Fatra mountains, although Žilina itself is a rather boring town. The **train station** sits on ul. Hviezdoslava. Trains run to **Brat-islava** (2½hr., 17 per day, 188Sk) and **Košice** (3-4hr., 21 per day, 222Sk). The **bus sta-tion** is almost opposite the train station on the corner of ul. Hviezdoslava and ul. 1. Maja. Buses head to **Bratislava** (3½hr., 4 per day, 186Sk); **Banská Bystrica** (2hr., 17 per day, 84Sk); and **Liptovský Mikuláš** (2hr., 14 per day, 84Sk). To get to the town center, walk straight out of the train station and through the underpass; ul. Nar-odná stretches up from the underpass to the new town square, Nám. A. Hlinku. Go straight through the square, head up the stairs to Farská ul., and you'll arrive in Mariánske nám., the old town square. **Selinan,** a travel agency-cum-tourist office, Burianova Medzierka 4, is on a small street parallel and to the left of Farská ul. from Nám. A. Hlinku. They sell **hiking maps** of the nearby mountains. (☎562 14 78; fax 562 31 71. Open May 15-July M-F 8am-6pm; Aug. M-F 8am-5pm; Sept.-May 14 M-F 8am-4:30pm.) **VÚB,** on the corner of Nám. A. Hlinku and ul. Narodná, **exchanges currency** and cashes **traveler's checks** for a 1% commission. (Open M-W and F 8am-noon and 1-4pm, Th 8am-noon.) A 24-hour Cirrus/Plus **ATM** operates outside the main entrance of the huge Tesco on Nám. A. Hlinku.

Cheap beds are hard to come by in Žilina, but you can find them at the **hostel** by the hospital on ul. Vojtecha Spanyola 43. From the train station, turn left onto ul. Hviezdoslava and right onto ul. 1. Maja at the bus station. After ul. 1. Maja turns onto Veľká Okružná ul., turn left onto ul. Vojtecha Spanyola. Walk 50m past the concrete walkway to the main hospital and take a left after the bus stop onto a small path that leads to the hostel. The name on the door is Slobodáreň NSP. (15min.) Spacious singles with balcony and bath are a meagre 300Sk. (☎511 06 71. Check-out 10am. Curfew 10pm.) For eats, ◼ **Zábavné centrum,** Sládk-ovičova ul 164, features terrific service and an English menu with pictures so you always know what you're getting. The kitchen offers a wide range of main dishes (85-180Sk) and scrumptious desserts (35-85Sk). You can also top off dinner with some light gambling. (☎562 64 16. Open daily 9am-4am.) For trail food, **Tesco** on Nám. A. Hlinku has groceries on the ground floor. (☎562 22 61. Open M-F 8am-8pm, Sa 8am-6pm, Su 8am-2pm.)

SLOVAKIA

**EVERY KILO COUNTS** *Chatas* are mountain huts where weary hikers or skiers spend the night and warm before a fire. Most *chatas* also have a menu of warm meals and a beverage list, which rivals that of many restaurants. The food they serve doesn't grow on any summit, however, and each hut has a crew that's responsible for lugging every tomato, onion, and bottle of beer up the 1000 or more meters. These powerful porters get paid by the kilogram, and with crowns at stake, the loads pile up. Standard beer trips mean 70kg (154lbs) while gas for cooking doesn't weigh less than a crushing 90kg (198lbs). During peak periods, workers make several trips every day, and a few individuals have staked out names as *chata* legends, carrying up to 230kg (506lbs) with no assistance.

## HIKING IN MALÁ FATRA

If you choose to stay at the *chaty* on the mountains, you will find that beds are less than 150Sk. Dress warmly for all hikes, as the wind above tree level is cold and gusty, and don't leave Žilina without VKÚ map 110 from Selinan (72Sk).

**MOUNT VEL'KÝ ROZSUTEC.** It is not the highest mountain in the range, but Vel'ký Rozsutec (1610m), whose massive bald crown rises a steep 400m from the field at its shoulder, boasts the most exciting slopes. The ■ **best hike** in the region begins in **Štefanová**. Take the Terchova-Vrátna bus from platform #10 in Žilina to Štefanová (31Sk) and follow the yellow trail to **sedlo Vrchpodžiar**. A right onto the blue trail just after the saddle goes straight up a tumbling mass of waterfalls and rapids known as **Horne diery** (Upper Hole). Ladders and chains make several nearly vertical—and breathtaking—sections possible, but the ascent is not for the fainthearted. Continue along the blue trail to **sedlo Medzirozsutce;** a right onto the red trail leads to the summit. Descend by continuing on the red trail until it intersects with the green trail near **sedlo Medziholie.** A right onto the green leads back down to Štefanova (round trip 5½hr.). For a less vigorous trip in the same area, take the blue trail from sedlo Medzirozsutce around the mountain's summit until it meets the green trail near sedlo Medziholie. A right here will take you across a sweeping field of wildflowers and back down to Štefanova (as above).

**MOUNT VEL'KÝ KRIVÁN.** At 1708 meters, **Veľký Kriván** is the highest peak in the range. Take the bus from platform #10 in Žilina to **Terchová, Vrátna** (31Sk) and get off at **Chata Vrátna** at the end of the road. The green trail will take you straight up to **Snilovské sedlo;** from there, a right on the red brings you to the summit (3hr.). It's much more pleasant, however, to take the **chairlift** from Chata Vrátna to Snilovské Sedlo and connect with the red trail there. (Operates daily June-Sept. 8:30am-4:15pm. 90Sk, children 50Sk). The red trail travels the entire ridge. One runs along 4km of beautiful vistas on the ridge line to **Poludňový grúň** (1460m); from the green trail at Snilovské Sedlo, turn left onto the red trail. Once at Poludňový grúň, take a left onto the yellow trail to descend back to Chata Vrátna (round-trip 6½hr.)

# NÍZKE TATRY (LOW TATRAS)

To the south of Liptovský Mikuláš are the Nízke Tatry, or Low Tatras, whose name is meaningful only in comparison to their taller Carpathian cousins to the north. These mountains are not to be underestimated: many peaks tower above the treeline, making this an excellent place for hiking. Liptovský Mikuláš is a good base for hiking, and buses from the town will take you near any number of trailheads. With the VKÚ maps, available at Informačné Centrum (see **Liptovský Mikuláš**, below), it's possible to compose endless hikes in the Low Tatras; all of the trails are well-marked and easy to follow.

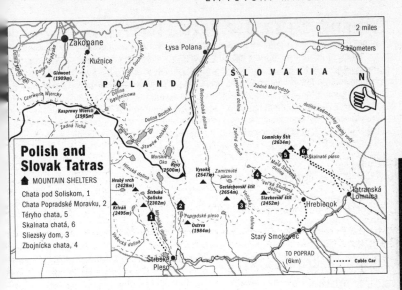

**Polish and Slovak Tatras**

🔺 MOUNTAIN SHELTERS

Chata pod Soliskom, 1
Chata Popradské Moravku, 2
Téryho chata, 5
Skalnata chatá, 6
Sliezsky dom, 3
Zbojnícka chata, 4

## LIPTOVSKÝ MIKULÁŠ ☎ (0)849

Famed as the place where Slovak folk hero and outlawed champion of the poor Juraj Jánošík was caught and stuck on a spike for stealing from the rich in 1713, Liptovský Mikuláš (LIP-tov-skee MEE-koo-lash; pop. 33,000) is a quiet town with little to see but the mountain ranges around it. These, however, are quite magnificent, and the town's proximity to the Nízké Tatry, makes it a perfect place to stay when hiking in that region.

The **train station** (☎552 28 42) lies on Štefánikova, and the **bus station** (☎552 36 38) is the asphalt lot directly outside. **Trains** run to: **Poprad** (1hr., 7 per day, 50Sk); **Košice** (2hr., 7 per day, 150Sk); and **Bratislava** (4hr., 9 per day, 252Sk). **Buses** run to: **Poprad** (1-2hr., 5 per day, 46Sk); **Košice** (3-4hr., 2 per day, 140Sk); and **Bratislava** (4hr., 4 per day, 250Sk). The **town center** is an easy 10-minute walk from the bus and train terminals. Follow Štefánikova toward the gas station at the bus station's far end, then turn right onto Hodžu. **VÚB**, Štúrova 19, **exchanges currency**, cashes **traveler's checks** for a 1% commission and has a Cirrus/EC 24-hour **ATM**. (☎552 23 57. Open M-W and F 7:30am-4:30pm, Th 7:30am-noon.) **Postal code:** 03101.

The tourist office, **Informačné Centrum**, Nám. Mieru 1, on the northern side of the square in the Dom Služieb complex, sells local hiking maps, including the indispensable VKÚ sheets 122 (79Sk) and 123 (68Sk). They will also book private rooms (180-400Sk) in town for a 20% deposit. You can also secure recreational information; ask for info on watersports, paragliding, horseback riding, and rock climbing in Demänovská valley. Also ask for the green (not pink) Orava Litpov Horehronie, a hiking and cycling **map** and guide book (125Sk; ☎552 24 18; fax 55 14 48; infolm@trynet.sk; open June 15-Sept. 15 and Dec. 15-Mar. 31 M-F 8am-7pm, Sa 8am-2pm, and Su noon-6pm; Sept. 16-Dec. 14 and Apr.-June 14 M-F 9am-6pm, Sa 8am-noon). **Rent bikes** from Cycloturistika (1hr. 60Sk, 4hr. 220Sk, 1 day 300Sk; 4hr. personal guide 500Sk). Boating, canoeing, and swimming are available at **Autocamping Liptovský Trnovec**, (☎/fax 559 73 00), 6km from Liptovský Mikuláš on Liptovský Mara lake. The tourist office can provide more details.

Finding a bed shouldn't be hard. If you want to skip the private rooms, try the central **Hotel Kriváň**, Štúrova 5, directly across the square from the tourist office. The rooms are tiny but feature fluffy beds. (☎552 24 14; fax 551 47 48. Checkout

**WHERE'S JURAJ'S EPIC FILM?** A cross between Robin Hood and William Wallace, Juraj Jánošík (1688-1713) is legendary throughout the former Czechoslovakia. Juraj's saga began when his father was beaten to death by their landowner for taking time off to properly bury his wife. This horror prompted Jánošík to take to the hills as a champion of the people. For two years, Jánošík and his loyal followers stole from the rich and gave to the poor, until he was caught by a nobleman in 1713. He was sentenced to death by hanging—from a hook through his rib cage—in the central square of Liptovský Mikuláš. Terchová, Jánošík's birthplace, is on the way from Žilina to Vrátna Dolina. As the bus turns toward the mountains you'll see a huge aluminum statue of the hero overlooking the town.

2pm. Singles 300Sk, with bath or shower 420Sk; doubles 470Sk, 620Sk; triples with bath and TV 930Sk.) Restaurants dot the town's streets; for large, hot sandwiches (32-37Sk) and quick service, try **Honey's Bistro,** Nám. Osloboditel'ov. (Open M-Th 9am-9pm, F-Sa 9am-midnight, Su 4pm-10pm.) Stock up on provisions for hiking trips at the **Supermarket Delvita** in the Prior building on Nám. Mieru. (Open M-F 8am-7pm, Sa 8am-1pm.)

## HIKING IN NÍZKE TATRY

**MOUNT ĎUMBIER AND CHOPOK.** To get to the top of the range, Mt. Ďumbier (2043m), catch an early bus from platform #11 at the Liptovský Mikuláš bus station to **Liptovský Ján** (25min., every hr., 12Sk) and hike the blue trail up the Štiavnica river and onto the Ďumbierske Sedlo by Chata generála M.R. Štefanika (5hr.). Then follow the red trail to the ridge, which leads to the summit (1½hr.). Going back down the ridge and following the red sign leads to the neighboring peak, Chopok (2024m, the second-highest in the range), and another hut, where *Martiner* beer is on tap (30Sk), beds are plentiful (80Sk), and capuccino is as frothy as ever (25Sk). From Chopok, it's a mellow walk down the blue trail to the bus stop at **Otupné,** just behind Hotel Grand (1¾hr.).

**DEMÄNOVSKÁ JASKYŇA SLOBODY.** (Demänov Cave of Liberty.) For a shorter hike, catch a bus from platform #3 at Liptovský Mikuláš to the "Demänovská jaskyňa slobody" stop (20min., every hr., 10Sk) and walk past the cave itself on the blue trail to Pusté sedlo Machate (1½hr.). To get back, either backtrack on the blue trail or take the local green trail back to the road and turn right to walk back to the Cave of Liberty (round-trip 3½hr.).

**DEMÄNOVSKÁ L'ADOVÁ JASKYŇA.** This is a spectacular ice cave midway between Liptovský Mikuláš and Jasná is well worth a visit. Take the bus from Liptovský Mikuláš to Jasná. Get off at the "Kamenná chata" stop (15min.) and follow signs up the hill to a valley view and the cave entrance (25min.). The cave features the bones of prehistoric bears and the signatures of 18th- and 19th-century visitors. The last part of the tour brings visitors to a frozen waterfall draped beneath bleached stone. Be sure to bring a sweater—it is an *ice* cave, after all. (Open Sept.-May Tu-Su 9am-2pm; June-Aug. 9am-4pm. 40-minute tours leave every 1-2hr. 80Sk, students 60Sk. English tour 50Sk.)

# SPIŠ

Most tourists know Spiš (SPISH) only as a neighbor of the Tatras and the home of Kežmarok. To the east, flatter land leads to tiny towns where villagers walk their cows and the lawnmower has not yet replaced the scythe. In the minds of romantics, the white sprawling ruins of Spišský Castle rule the region, and Levoča, home of the world's tallest Gothic altar, bustles with the wealthy merchants who placed it there. For centuries an autonomous province of Hungary with a large Saxon population, Spiš made its last bid for independence in 1918, before being folded up into Czechoslovakia until the Velvet Revolution in 1993. Today, the region boasts one of Slovakia's most exhilarating national parks, Slovak Paradise (Slovenský Raj), and a collection of churches and ruins that merit exploration.

# KEŽMAROK ☎(0)968

Prosperous Kežmarok (KEZH-ma-rok; pop. 18,000) was named a free royal city in 1380 but was soon conquered by the Taborites. It changed hands countless times until 1702, when the persecuted townsfolk finally managed to buy their freedom from monarchical control. Once they had it, the people were loathe to relinquish autonomy and proclaimed their own republic even as late as 1918, when they were incorporated into the Czechoslovak state. Today Kežmarok's finest buildings—remarkable churches and the old castle—add charm to the already pleasant city. Cheap accommodations and a train line to Poprad also make it a good base for exploring the nearby peaks of the Vysoké Tatry (High Tatras).

**⌐ TRANSPORTATION. Trains** run to and from **Poprad** (20-30min., 12 per day, 13Sk) from the stately, bright yellow station, across the river at the junction of Toporcerova and Michalská (☎452 32 98). **Buses** leave from under blue and yellow canopies opposite the trains for: **Poprad** (20-30min., 2 per hr., 14Sk); **Tatranská Lomnica** (30min., 27 per day, 18Sk); **Starý Smokovec** (40min., 17 per day, 24Sk); and **Levoča** (1hr., 10 per day, 38Sk).

**◪ ORIENTATION AND PRACTICAL INFORMATION.** To get to the center, cross the footbridge on the left (*not* the main transport bridge) at the base of the train station and follow Dr. Alexandra to the main Hlavné nám., where the Baroque tower of the town hall (*radnica*) rises above two-story dwellings. Hiding in an alcove at Hlavné nám. 46, the tourist office **Kežmarská Informačná Agentura** sells a handy **map** (12Sk) of town and books private rooms and pensions for 250-300Sk. (☎/fax 452 40 47; infokk@sinet.sk. Open June-Sept. M-F 8:30am-5pm, Sa-Su 9am-2pm; Oct.-May M-F 8:30am-5pm, Sa 9am-2pm.) **Slovenská Sporiteľňa**, Dr. Alexandra 41, **exchanges currency** for no commission and cashes AmEx/MC/Visa **traveler's checks** for a 2% commission. (☎452 30 41. Open M and F 7:30am-4pm, Tu 7:30am-1pm, W 7:30am-5pm, Th 7:30am-2pm.) An MC/Visa **ATM** stands outside. The pharmacy **Lekáreň Na Námestí** sits at Hlavné nám. 58. (Open M-F 7:30am-5pm, Sa 8am-noon.) The **post office,** Mučeníkov 2 (☎452 28 22), lies where Hviezdoslavova becomes Mučeníkov. (Open M-F 8am-noon and 1-7pm, Sa 8-10am.) **Postal code:** 06001.

**▮▮▮ ACCOMMODATIONS AND FOOD.** Except for the 2nd weekend in July, when Kežmarok hosts a European folk arts festival, there shouldn't be a problem finding cheap accommodations, and the tourist office (see above) is always there to help. ▨ **Penzión No. 1,** Michalská 1, is run by the most congenial of couples who have a cellar den and a two-hole backyard green they'll encourage you to use. Turn left out of the station; it's the first building you reach. Ring the bell upon arrival. (☎452 46 00. Divine breakfast 120Sk. Check-out 10am. Reserve well in advance. Doubles and triples 200Sk per person.) Reception is sporadic at the ski-lodge **Hotel Štart,** off Pod lesom behind the castle, but rooms are decent. From the train station, turn left and walk 10 minutes down Michalská. Turn right at the bridge onto Nižná brána, and take the first left onto Pod lesom. The hotel is to the left, up a hill after the intersection with Sverná. (☎452 29 15; fax 452 29 16. Check-out 8am. Up-to-4-person rooms 200Sk per person, with bath 270Sk.)

It's not glamorous, but for a good, cheap Slovak meal, try **Restaurant Tiffany,** Hlavné nám. 40, which features a beer garden and a rare nonsmoking area out back. (Main dishes 47-84Sk; beer 15Sk. Open M-Sa 8am-10pm, Su 9am-9pm.) **Barónka Restaurant,** Hlavné nám. 46, behind the tourist office, has a slightly classier atmosphere with shaded lamps and potted plants. (☎452 45 01. Slovak standards 58-120Sk. Open M-F 10am-11pm, Sa-Su noon-10pm.) A **grocery,** Dr. Alexandra 35, stocks basic foods. (Open M-Sa 7am-10pm, Su 8am-10pm.)

🔎📺 **SIGHTS AND ENTERTAINMENT.** From the main Hlavné nám., a walk down Hviezdoslavova leads to Kežmarok's highlight, the ▨ **Wooden Articulated Church** (Dreverý Atikulárny Kostol). Three anti-Protestant regulations governed its construction in 1717—the church had to be built outside the town walls, hence the location; it could not have a foundation, hence the sinking sensation; and it had to be financed with parish funds alone, hence the decision to build it entirely out of wood. Constructed in the shape of a Greek cross, the church and its astonishing Baroque interior of yew and lime bursts with imagination and resourcefulness; the porthole-shaped windows are the mark of the Swedish sailors who helped build it. You may have to wait outside while a tour is finishing, but it's well worth it. Be sure to get the English pamphlet describing its construction. Although the church is still used for services, some local Protestants felt more secure with a solid foundation and so erected the colossal **New Evangelical Church** (Nový Evanjelický Kostol), which blended Romanesque, Byzantine, Renaissance, and middle-eastern styles. The facade is more impressive than the sparse interior. The Kežmarok-born Imre Thököly, exiled to Turkey for fighting the Habsburgs, now rests peacefully in his own private vault. (Both churches open June-Sept. daily 9am-noon and 2-5pm; Oct.-May Tu and Th 10am-noon; no tours during services Su 9-10:15am. Slovak tour 20Sk, students 10Sk.) The last of the town's three churches, the **Basilica of the Holy Cross** (Kostol sv. Križa) stands in the middle of Staré Mesto, dominating Nám. Požiarnikov. From Hlavné nám. walk down Dr. Alexandra and turn right onto Nám. Požiarnikov. Several 15th-century Gothic altars, two organs, and some fine frescoes decorate the interior. (Open M-F 9am-6pm. 10Sk.)

Hlavné nám. and Nová meet at the impressive **Kežmarok Castle,** Hradné nám. 42. Owned by the powerful Habsburgs, Thurzos, and Thökölys, the castle rarely stayed in one family's possession longer than a generation or two, and its owners were often at war with the town. The 15th-century fortification fashionably defies stylistic categorization; Renaissance decor hangs from its stocky Gothic frame and its courtyard contains the foundations of a 13th-century Saxon church. The tour, run by the **Kežmarok Museum,** is greatly improved by the English guidebook sold at the ticket office (6Sk). Among the stops is an exhibit on Dr. Vojtech Alexander (see **"I Proclaim it Highly Unsafe!"** below), a radiology pioneer. (☎452 26 18. Open Tu-F 9am-4:30pm, Sa-Su 9am-4pm. Tours every 30-60min. 35Sk, students 15Sk.)

The **Castellan Club,** underneath the castle on Starý trh, carries on the noble tradition of raucous revelry. One smoky room sports disco lights and rhythm, while the bar sits under a large tree. (☎452 27 80. *Tatran* 25Sk. Open Su-Th 3pm-3am, F-Sa 8pm-3am.) **Kino Iskra,** Hlavné nám. 3, in the Poľnobank building, shows standard Hollywood flicks (50-55Sk; ☎452 25 41).

---

# I PROCLAIM IT HIGHLY UNSAFE!

Dr. Vojtech Alexander, a pioneer in the field of radiology, was born in Kežmarok in 1857. He is famous for owning and using the first X-ray machine in Hungary, now on display at the Kežmarok Museum. One of his most important tasks was testing the safety of his ground-breaking machine; Dr. Alexander, one of the bright lights of his day, decided to make his determination by photographing his own unborn son. After undergoing constant exposure to a primitive X-ray machine during crucial stages of development, the child was born with severe mental defects. Some speculate it was the effects of the machine; others simply say that he took after his old man.

# LEVOČA

☎(0)966

Levoča (LEH-vo-cha; pop. 13,500) attracts tourists with its picturesque walled medieval center, its laid-back atmosphere, and the serenity of the gently rolling fields of wheat that surround the town. These aren't what brought the former capital of Špiš to its glorious state, however. This success is owed instead to the "Law of Storage," a 16th-century imperial concession that forced merchants passing through to sell their goods at wholesale prices for 15 days. Quick to capitalize on its opportunities, the town grew wealthy and fostered a burgeoning network of craft guilds led in reknown by Master Pavol. Pavol's workshop added artistic distinction to the town's commercial prosperity in pioneering an expressive style of wood-carving and erecting the world's tallest Gothic altar. Today people aren't forced to sell their belongings when they visit, but they stay voluntarily, especially when the annual Festival of Marian Devotion attracts Catholic pilgrims in early July.

**TRANSPORTATION.** Levoča can only be reached by bus. The **bus station** (☎451 22 30) rarely opens its info booth, but departure times are listed on a large billboard. **Buses** run to: **Poprad** (30min., 2 per hr., 26Sk); **Prešov** (1¼ hr., 14 per day, 60Sk); and **Košice** (2hr., 3 per day, 100Sk).

**PRACTICAL INFORMATION.** To get to the center, turn right out of the station and walk 100m to the intersection with the main road, **Probstnerová cesta.** Walk straight through, then continue on the footpath to the right, uphill, past Jesus and to the right onto Nová. Nová leads directly to the main square, **Nám. Majstra Pavla** (15min.). There's an infrequent **local bus** (6Sk) that covers the same distance more circuitously; to catch it, turn left from the station and walk up the small road behind it to the red and white bus stop sign. The helpful **tourist office,** Nám. Majstra Pavla 58, books *penzióny* and private rooms for 300Sk per person. (☎161 86; fax 451 37 63; tiklevoc@nextra.sk; www.levoca.sk. Open May-Sept. M-F 9am-5pm, Sa-Su 9:30am-2pm; Oct.-Apr. M-F 9:30am-4:30pm.) **Slovenská Sporiteľňa,** Nám. Majstra Pavla 56, gives MC/Visa **cash advances** and cashes **traveler's checks** for a 1% comission. (Open M, Th, and F 7:35am-3pm, Tu 7:35am-1pm, W 7:35am-4pm.) It also has a Cirrus/MC/Plus/Visa **ATM** outside. The **pharmacy,** Nám. Majstra Pavla 13, posts a list of other pharmacies open on weekends in its window. (☎451 24 56. Open M-F 7:30am-5pm.) Slow but steady **internet access** is available at **Internet Cafe,** Nová 79. (45Sk per 30min. Open M-F 9am-4pm.) The **post office** is at Nám. Majstra Pavla 42. (☎451 24 89. Open M-F 8am-noon and 1-4:30pm, Sa 8-10:30am.) **Postal code:** 05401.

**ACCOMMODATIONS AND FOOD.** Finding accommodations is not terribly difficult except during the first weekend of July, when 600,000 pilgrims invade the town. The tourist office (see **Practical Information,** above) can point you toward **private rooms** and nearby **campsites.** Most of the cheaper accommodations lie just outside the medieval center. One option in the center is the family-run gem ■ **Penzión Šuňavský,** Nová 59. Follow the directions above to the center; the pension is on Nová on the left. The proprietors speak English and the rooms are comfortable and clean. If adventures in Spiš tire you out, you can always settle for watching the fish in the garden pond. (☎451 45 26; mobile ☎090 531 89 90. Call at least 2 days ahead. June-Sept. 350Sk per person, off-season 300Sk. Breakfast included.)

There's a **grocery** at Nám. Majstra Pavla 45. (Open M-Th 6:45am-6:30pm, F 6:45am-7pm, Sa 6:45am-noon, Su 9am-noon.) The light and airy **U 3 Apoštolov,** Nám. Majstra Pavla 11, has windows that open to the street. It serves vegetarian dishes (20-66Sk) in addition to traditional Slovak food (94-189Sk; ☎451 23 52; open daily 9am-10pm). The cafeteria-style **Vegetarián,** Uhoľná 3, is a cheaper and healthier alternative that serves five dishes each day (38-47Sk), soups (7-9Sk), and salads (8-10Sk). It also doubles as a health-food store, selling tofu, muesli bars, and soy milk. (☎451 45 76. Open M-F 10am-3pm.)

**■ SIGHTS.** Levoča's star attraction is the 14th-century **St. Jacob's Church** (Chrám sv. Jakuba), home to the world's tallest Gothic altar (a staggering 18.62m) carved by Majster Pavol from 1507-1517. At the base of the altar is a fantastic and comical relief carving of the Last Supper, and, above it, a triptych with figures of St. Jacob, St. John, and the Virgin Mary with Jesus. All are close to 2.5m tall and extremely detailed. To the left of the altar, a medieval mural depicts the seven deeds of bodily mercy and the seven deadly sins. Another mural presents the sad tale of St. Dorothy. Thrust into a pagan land, she was given the choice of heathenry with a rich husband or chaste Christianity with a torturous death. What could she do? She was a saint, after all. Putting 5Sk into the automatic info box yields commentary on the sculptures in English or Hungarian. (Open summer M 11am-5pm, Tu-F 9am-5pm, Sa 9am-noon, Su 1-2:30pm; off-season M 11am-4pm, Tu-Sa 9am-4pm, Su 1-4pm. 40Sk, students 20Sk. No sleeveless shirts.)

Three branches of the **Spišské Museum** dot Nám. Majstra Pavla. By far the best is **Dom Majstra Pavla** at #20, with an exhibition on the master's work that contains high-quality facsimiles of much of his best stuff and allows you to get much closer to the Last Supper than you can in the church itself. The museum staff shows a 20-minute video about Levoča's history; it's in English and just might persuade you that the town is more than a one-majster show. The **town hall** *(radnica)*, in the middle of the square, is aesthetically and architecturally appealing and houses a few relics of Levoča's past. According to legend, the white lady now painted on one of the doors betrayed the town by giving the city's keys to her lover—an officer in the invading Hungarian army. The **Cage of Shame** (Klietka Hanby), the oversized birdcage in the square, is where women of supposedly loose morals were pilloried in the 16th century. The **3rd branch** at #40, is a less-than-thrilling display consisting largely of portraits. (All open May-Oct. Tu-Su 9am-5pm; Nov.-Apr. Tu-Su 8am-4pm. Each 20Sk, students 10Sk.) The neo-Gothic **Basilica of the Virgin Mary** (Bazilika Panny Marie), separated from Levoča by 3km of wheat fields and visible from town, stands on top of Mariánská hora. It attracts 600,000 pilgrims the first weekend in July for the **Festival of Marian Devotion.** The festival, which began in the 13th century, culminates in a Sunday 10am mass, which the Pope led himself in 1995.

# NEAR LEVOČA

### SPIŠSKÉ PODHRADIE AND ŽEHRA

*Buses come from Levoča (20min., every 30min. until 9:30pm, 14Sk); Poprad (1hr., every 30min. until 9pm, 52Sk); and Prešov (1½hr., every hr. until 7pm, 52Sk).*

There's nothing to see in Spišské Podhradie (SPISH-skay POD-hra-dyeh) itself, but two of Slovakia's finest monuments lie in hills above the valley. West of town, walled **Spišska Kapitula,** the region's religious capital, contains **St. Martin's Cathedral** (Katedrála sv. Martina) and some pretty stained-glass windows. The clergy were driven out by scientific socialists in 1948, but have since regrouped. From the bus stop, walk left through the gardens and over the river; the main road here winds up and around to the cathedral (15min.). Get tickets from the info building 10m from the church. *(Open daily May-Oct. 10am-5pm. 30Sk, students 20Sk. No sleeveless shirts.)* The formidable mass and grandeur of **Spišský Castle** (Spišský hrad), Central Europe's largest, sprawls over the opposite mountain. There's been a fortified settlement here for two millennia, but the present ruins are the remains of the 13th- to 17th-century Hungarian castle that dominated the Spiš region until it burned down in 1780. Many paths lead there (check the info map at the castle end of the main square), but the most satisfying is the grassy 2km trek from the left side of the town's cemetery. With your back to the departing-times board at the bus stop, head right to the main square. Follow it left out of town; the cemetery will be on your left over a bridge. Watch out for cow patties. Much of the better-preserved section is roped off, but the grounds, walls, and especially the central turret, provide terrific views. *(Open daily 8:30am-6pm; last admission 5:15pm. 50Sk, students 30Sk; after 6pm for exploring ruins 25Sk, 15Sk. Cameras 10Sk.)*

A beautiful, if long, walk from the castle brings you to **Žehra,** home of the **Church of the Holy Spirit** (Kostol Svätého Ducha), which is about 3km away but not to be missed if you have the energy. Its interior is plastered with remarkable 14th-century frescoes uncovered in the 1950s. From the castle entrance, descend to the closer parking lot and hike the yellow trail from the back end, past the limestone crags and down into the wide valley. The church's onion-domed tower is easy to spot. If you stay as close to the castle as possible, it's about 6km along the road back to Spišské Podhradie. *(Open M-Sa 9:30am-4pm, Su 2-4pm. 20Sk, students 10Sk.)* **Groceries** line Marianské nám. **VÚB,** Marianské nám. 34, cashes **traveler's checks.** *(☎ 454 11 49. Open M-W and F 8am-noon and 1-4:30pm, Th 8:30am-2pm.)*

# SLOVENSKÝ RAJ NATIONAL PARK ☎(0)942

The Slovenský Raj (Slovak Paradise) National Park, southeast of the Nízke Tatry, has an entirely different feel from Slovakia's more mountainous parks. Instead of heavily-touristed peaks, it encompasses forested hills and deep limestone ravines carved by fast-flowing streams. Life moves at a slightly slower pace in the tiny villages and grassy meadows, and hikers and skiers have left a legacy in the trails connecting these towns cut off from the rest of Slovakia.

**TRANSPORTATION.** Nestled in a gorge on the shores of manmade lake Palčmanská Maša, **Dedinky** (pop. 400) is the largest town on Slovenský Raj's southern border. The road to paradise is rocky; the best way to negotiate it is to catch the **bus** from **Poprad** (dir. Rožňava; 1hr., 6 per day, 38Sk). The bus stops first at the Dobšinská ľadová jaskyňa, then at the village Stratená, and finally at a junction 2km south of Dedinky. Watch for the huge blue road sign at the intersection just before the bus stop. From here you're in for a hike. From the intersection, walk down the road that the bus didn't take, which curves down into the basin and comes to an intersection. Turn right and find the Dedinky railway station and a big dam. Cross the dam, turn left and walk 10 minutes to Dedinky. Or, take the slightly steeper yellow trail that branches off to the right 200m from the intersection. When you reach the road at the bottom, turn left and the dam will be on your right. This way is about 5-10 minutes quicker, or 15 minutes if you want to roll down the hills.

**PRACTICAL INFORMATION.** Pick a copy of **VKÚ sheet #124,** one of the excellent green hiking maps (79-85Sk), before entering the region or at Hotel Priehrada (see below). A **chairlift** runs from Hotel Priehrada up to Chata Geravy (see below; July-Aug. M 9am-3pm, Tu-Su 9am-4:30pm; May-June M 9am-3pm, Tu-Su 9am-4pm; daily Sept. 9am-2:45pm. 60Sk, round-trip 100Sk). **Tókóly Tours,** along the town's only road 200m from Hotel Priehrada, rents **boats** and **bikes.** (☎(0)965 449 33 10. Bikes 20Sk per hr.; 4-person rowboats 50Sk per hr.; 2-person paddle boats 60Sk per hr. Open daily in summer 9am-7pm.) Dedinky's small **post office** is behind the wooden tower near the bus stop in the center of town. (Open M-F 8am-10pm and 12:30-3pm.) **Postal code:** 04973.

**ACCOMMODATIONS AND FOOD.** It's wise to book ahead in January, July, and August. In Dedinky, **Hotel Priehrada** rents dated but comfortable rooms with shared baths and lake views and simple *chaty* with private baths. Priehrada also has a preposterously cheap **campsite** on the shore of the lake.

## IS IT JUST ME OR IS IT COLD IN HERE?

Though the existence of Dobšinská ľadová jaskyňa was known for several centuries, it wasn't until 1870 that brave mining academy graduate Eugen Ruffiny was lowered into the cave by his peers to explore it. He discovered the 23km of caverns that make up the Stratenská cave system, with a vertical span of up to 194m. Within a year the cave was open to the public, with wooden walkways winding through a small number of the many caverns. Soon thereafter the ice was used for skating, and in 1890 the first concert ever given in an ice hall took place, paying tribute to Carl Luis Habsburg. These entertainments began, as one might expect, to take their toll on the caves, and in 1953 Turist National Enterprise took over management and curtailed all sporting and musical events. Today the caves remain a tourist attraction not to be missed.

(☎798 12 12; fax 798 12 21. Reception 24hr. Check-out 10am in hotel, 9am in *chaty*. Rooms and *chaty* 250Sk per person high season; Sept. to mid-Dec. and Apr.-June rooms 120Sk, *chaty* 80Sk. 25Sk per person; tents 25Sk.) **Penzión Pastierňa**, Dedinky 42, has good rooms with shared bath. Facing Hotel Priehrada from the town center, turn left and then right at the 2nd turn. (☎981 75. Reception until 10pm. Rooms 250Sk per person.) The chairlift behind Hotel Priehrada will take you to **Chata Geravy**, situated at a trailhead, and their small rooms with homey beds. (Reception until 11pm. 150Sk; check for vacancies with Hotel Priehrada before going up.)

You can get groceries at **Delika**, near the bus stop (open M-F 7:30am-9pm, Sa 7am-5pm, Su 9am-5pm) or at the store at the base of the ice-cave trail (see below; open M and Th 7-10am and 1-2pm, Tu 10am-3pm, F 8am-3pm, Sa 7am-noon). Restaurants are scarce. If pressed, try the one in **Hotel Priehrada**. (Main dishes 31-142Sk. Open 7am-10pm.) The **restaurant** in Penzión Pastierňa serves Slovak standards (73-155Sk) along with a few vegetarian dishes (37-49Sk) and wine (25Sk; open daily 8am-10pm). **Ľadová Jaskyňa** restaurant sits at the bottom of the ice caves. (Main dishes 128-214Sk. Open daily 9am-5:30pm.)

🎫 **SIGHTS.** Some 110,000 cubic meters of water are still frozen from the last Ice Age in the form of a giant underground glacier in the ■ **Dobšinská Ice Caves** (Dobšinská ľadová jaskyňa), a 23km stretch of ice. The 30-minute tour covers only 475m of the cave, but that's awe-inspiring enough, with hall after hall of frozen columns, gigantic ice walls, and hardened waterfalls. Bring a sweater—the cave temperature hovers between -3.8° and +0.5°C year-round. To get here from Dedinky, take the 7:15am, 10:56am, or 2:39pm **train** for two stops (9Sk, 15min.). The one road from the cave train station leads 100m out to the main road. Turn left—the cave parking lot is 250m ahead. From there, the blue trail leads up a steep incline to the cave (20min.). Alternatively, a **bus** (14Sk) leaves from outside Hotel Priehrada at 10am and drops you at the aforementioned parking lot. (Open May 15-June and Sept. Tu-Su 9:30am-2pm; July-Aug. 9am-4pm. English tours 140Sk, students 110Sk. 20-person minimum. Cameras 100Sk.)

🏔 **HIKING.** As this is a national park, camping and fires are prohibited. Cascade trails are one-way—you can go up, but not down. Most trails are closed November to June to those without certified guides.

**Biele vody** (White Waters; 1¾hr.). The hike up one of the park's many rapids, featured in most tourism pictures, involves a ladder and is one-way. From Hotel Priehrada in Dedinky, take the red trail to Biele Vody. The blue cascade trail will be on the left. Chata Geravy (see above) waits at the top, and the green trail leads back down. Or, ride the rollercoaster chairlift. Watch your footing on slippery rocks, wooden ladders, and bridges.

**Havrania skala** (Crow's Cliff; 3hr.): This hike is remarkable mainly for the views from the top and the 2 cliffside caves the trail passes. From the Stratená bus stop, the green trail leads up the hill to the underwhelming Občasný prameň spring (1hr.); from Chata Geravy, it's 1½hr. along the yellow trail. From the spring, it's a 30min. climb up the steep, earthy yellow trail to the top of Havrania skala and a gorgeous view. The trail continues downhill steeply for 1hr. to meet the road just west of Stratená—turn left at the tarmac.

**Veľký sokol** (Big Falcon; 8hr.): A more demanding hike into the heart of Slovenský Raj and up its deepest gorge. Follow the road west from Stratená or east out of the ice caves (facing the road, take a right). At the head of the big U-bend, take the green trail north, over the Sedlo Kopanec (987m), and along the stream. Turn right onto the road and take the red path to the bottom of the gorge. The one-way yellow trail leads up the ravine, criss-crossing the mountain stream. Your feet will get wet and muddy, the logs are slippery, and some of the walkways inspire belief in a Supreme Being. From the top, the red path returns to Chata Geravy and the descent to Dedinky. Those who don't like wet feet can follow the red trail from the bottom of the gorge to the top around the northern edge (30min. longer).

# VYSOKÉ TATRY (HIGH TATRAS)

The High Tatras are mesmerizing. Spanning the border between Slovakia and Poland, the jagged mountains are home to hundreds of addictive hiking and skiing trails along the highest peaks in the Carpathian range (2650m). Millions of visitors pack the slopes and trails each year—the trains are always crowded and the trails overrun with scampering tots (who knew 4-year-olds made good mountaineers?). Budget accommodations, however, are still easy to find—cheap beds abound in the mountain *chaty* (huts). After reaching the Tatras via Poprad, hikers usually stay in Starý Smokovec, better for transportation and hiking, or Tatranská Lomnica, a cheaper and more peaceful place to stay.

The Tatras are a wonderful place for a hike, but in winter a guide is almost always necessary. Snowfall in the Tatras is very high and avalanches are common. Each year, dozens of winter hikers in the area die, often on "easy" trails. Even in summer many hikes are extremely demanding and require a good deal of experience. Make sure you have a map and information about the trail before beginning. Updated trail condition and weather information is available at www.tarap.sk. Check with a mountain rescue team, a local outdoors store, or a tourist office before going anywhere without an escort.

# POPRAD                                       ☎ (0)92

Poprad (pop. 53,000) was born when Czechoslovakia linked four sleepy mountain villages with drab apartment blocks. It's not a pretty place, but it does boast superb transport lines to the High Tatras and the towns of the Spiš region. Aside from this transport convenience, Poprad has little to offer the traveler. Most stop here only long enough to change trains on the way to the Tatras, which, when they aren't shrouded in clouds, cast their jagged shadow over the town and nearby villages.

**TRANSPORTATION. Trains** (☎ 716 84 84) arrive at the north edge of town from **Košice** (1¼hr., 15 per day, 108Sk) and **Bratislava** (5hr., 10 per day, 294Sk). *Tatranská elektrická železnica* (TEŽ; electric train) connects Poprad with the **Tatran resorts** (every hr., up to 26Sk), but **buses** are generally quicker and more frequent. Buses (☎ 772 35 65; info window open M-F 7am-3pm), stop near the train station at the corner of Wolkerova and Alžbetina, on the way to: **Tatran resorts** (16-26Sk); **Košice** (2hr., 9 per day, 220Sk); **Banská Bystrica** (2½hr., 17 per day, 150Sk); and **Zakopane, POL** (2hr., 2 per day July-Aug. and Dec.-Mar.; 130Sk).

**⊞⊠ ORIENTATION AND PRACTICAL INFORMATION.** To get to the center, walk up Alžbetina, which runs between the bus and train stations. Take the first left onto Hviezdoslavova, then the first right onto Mnoheľova. This leads to Nám sv. Egída. To reach the old square from the train station, walk up Alžbetina, then turn left onto Štefánikova. When it intersects with Továrenska turn left and stay straight until you enter Sobotské nám. At **Popradská Informačná Agentúra,** Nám. sv. Egídia 114, the English-speaking staff sells **VKÚ sheet #113** of the High Tatras (79Sk) and has accommodations and recreation info. (☎161 86 and 72 17 00; infopp@pp.psg.sk. Open M-F 8:30am-5pm, Sa 9am-1pm.) **VÚB,** Mnoheľova 9, cashes AmEx and Visa **traveler's checks** for a 1% commission. (☎605 11 11. Open M-W and F 8am-5pm, Th 8am-noon.) 24hr. Cirrus/Plus **ATMs** are all over town. **Store luggage** at the train station. (5Sk; 10-20Sk per day at the office. Open 24hr.) To get to **Hotel Garni,** Karpatská 11, walk down Alžbetina away from the train station toward the bus station, then go right onto Karpatská. (☎776 38 77; fax 630 77. Breakfast 60Sk. Check-out 2pm. Singles with bath 320Sk; doubles 400Sk, with bath 440Sk; triples 600Sk.) There's a **supermarket** on the top floor of **Prior** at Mnoheľova and Nám. sv. Egídia. (Open M-F 8am-8pm, Sa 8am-7pm, Su 10am-4pm.) **Egídius,** Mnoheľova 18, has a beer garden, Slovak restaurant, and candle-lit cafe. (☎772 28 98. Main dishes 50-210Sk. Open daily 11am-11:30pm.) At night head to the old square and slam one down at **Vináreň sv. Juraj,** Sobotské nám. 29. (☎776 95 58. *Tatran* 25Sk. Open Su-Th 11am-11pm, F-Sa 11am-5am. Disco open 9pm-5am.) **Postal code:** 05801.

# STARÝ SMOKOVEC ☎(0)969

Starý Smokovec (STAH-ree SMO-ko-vets) is the High Tatras' most central resort and, founded in the 17th century, one of the oldest. Cheap accommodations down the road in Horný Smokovec make it easily accessible to the budget traveler. The town itself has developed with tourists in mind and is comprised of little more than hotels and restaurants, but the mountain trails are nothing short of spectacular.

**⊟ TRANSPORTATION.** TEŽ **trains** go to **Poprad** (30min., every hr., 14Sk) and **Tatranská Lomnica** (15min., every 30min., 10Sk) from the trains station at the town's lowest point, below the central road. **Buses** to many Tatran resorts stop in a parking lot to the right, facing uphill, of the train station. A **funicular** runs to **Hrebienok** (see below; every 30-40min; 1am-1:30pm; up 70Sk, down 40Sk, round-trip 80Sk.)

**⊠ PRACTICAL INFORMATION.** There are no street names, but signs point to hotels, restaurants, and services. Head uphill on the road that runs just left of the train station, then cross the main road, veering left. The friendly staff of **Tatranská Informačná Kancelária,** in Dom Služieb, provides weather info and sells hiking **maps,** including the crucial **VKÚ sheet #113** (79Sk) of the High Tatras (Open M-F 8am-5:30pm, Sa 8am-1pm). **Slovenská Sporiteľňa,** also in Dom Služieb, cashes **traveler's checks** for a 1% commission and gives MC/Visa **cash advances.** A 24hr. Cirrus/Plus **ATM** is just outside. (☎442 24 70; fax 442 32 53. Open M 7:30am-noon and 12:30-3:30pm, Tu 7:30am-1pm, W 7:30am-noon and 12:30-5pm, Th-F 7:30am-noon and 12:30-3pm.) There's a pharmacy, **Lekáreň U Zlatej Sovy,** on the 2nd floor of Dom Služieb. (☎442 21 65. Open M-F 8am-noon and 12:30-4:30pm, Sa 8am-noon.) The **post office** is near the train station. (☎442 24 71. Open M-F 7:30am-4pm, Sa 8-10am.) **Postal code:** 06201.

**⌐⌐⌐ ACCOMMODATIONS AND FOOD.** Up the road from the train station on the way to Dom Služieb, an **InfoPanel** displays info on hotels, pensions, and hostels in the greater Smokovec area and has a free phone for reservations. Most budget options are in the hamlet of **Horný Smokovec.** Turn right on the main road from the train or bus stations and walk 10 minutes to **Hotel Šport.** It combines with the nearby Hotel Bellevue to offer a restaurant, cafe, sauna, swimming pool, and massage parlor. (☎442 23 61; fax 442 27 19. Breakfast 70Sk. Reception 24hr. Check-out 10am. Book at least 1 week ahead. Singles 405Sk; doubles 710Sk; triples 1005Sk.) Another 15 minutes along the road (or two stops from Starý Smokovec on the TEŽ toward Tatranská Lomnica) and across the train tracks down a short path through the trees is **Hotel Junior,** with compact rooms, shared baths, a disco, and air hockey. (☎442 26 61; fax 442 24 93. Check-out 10am. Book 1 week ahead. Doubles 360Sk; triples 490Sk; quads 560Sk; with ISIC 200Sk per person including breakfast.) If you're intent on staying in Starý Smokovec, **Hotel Smokovec,** directly up the hill from the train station, offers pricey but beautiful rooms. (☎442 51 91; fax 442 51 94; www.slovakia.net/smokovec. Reception 24hr. Check-out 10am. Doubles 760Sk high season, 590Sk offseason; triples 710Sk, 540Sk; quads 670Sk, 500Sk.)

**Grocers** clutter Starý Smokovec, with five on the main road just above the bus and train stations. The largest is the *potraviny* in the shopping block above the bus station. (Open M-F 7:45am-6pm, Sa 8am-12:30pm, Su 9am-12:30pm.) Decent restaurants, however, are sparse. **Restaurant Koliba** (☎/fax 442 22 04 22 04) breaks the trend. Facing downhill, head into the parking lot to the right of the train station and across the tracks. Try the infamous flaming *Tatranský čaj* (Tatran tea, 40Sk), but don't singe your eyebrows! (Main dishes 99-190Sk;. Open daily 5pm-midnight.) **Bistro Tatra,** just up the steps from the bus station, is for those who like their Slovak fare served extra-fast. (Main dishes 52-105Sk. Open daily 10am-7pm.)

🏔 **OUTDOOR ACTIVITIES AND HIKING. T-ski,** in the funicular station, offers everything from ski classes to river-rafting trips, and rents sleds, skis, and mountain guides. (☎442 32 00. Sleds 50Sk per day; skis 190-390Sk per day; guides from 4000Sk per day. Open daily 9am-6pm.) Mountain bikes can be rented for 299Sk per day at **Tatrasport,** up the hill from the bus lot. (☎442 52 41. Open daily 8am-6pm.)

The funicular to **Hrebienok** (1285m) carries loads of people daily to the crossroads of numerous trails. It's a 35-minute hike up the green rail from behind Hotel Grand, but the road next to the trail detracts from the experience. More a hotel than a mountain shelter, the deluxe **Bilíkova Chata,** just beyond the funicular station on the green trail, has steaming food, warm beds, and a terrific view from its terrace. (☎442 24 39. 750Sk per person.) Another 20 minutes from Hrebienok, the green trail leads north to the foaming **Volopády studeného potoka** (Cold Stream Waterfalls). The incline is small; the hike through trees and the waterfall well worth it. The eastward blue trail descends gradually from the waterfall through the towering pines to Tatranská Lomnica (1¾hr.), while the yellow trail plunges sharply down along the river to Tatranská Lesná (1¾hr.). A TEŽ train can whisk you from Tatranská Lomnica and Tatranská Lesná back to Starý Smokovec. The long, red Tatranská magistrála trail travels west from Hrebienok along the side of mountains and hits **Sliezsky dom** (2¼hr.; 1670m; ☎442 52 61; 400Sk per person), then zig-zags down to **Chata Popradské Pleso** on the shore of the lake Popradské Pleso (1500m; 5½hr.; ☎449 21 77; 350Sk per person in summer, 270Sk off-season). From here, the red trail continues to **Štrbské Pleso** (7hr. from Hrebienok; see below). Before Popradské Pleso there are three trails back to civilization; two lead to Tatranská Polianka and one to Vyšné Hágy (2hr. each). A more daunting blue trail branches north from the *magistrála* 20 minutes west of Hrebienok to climb one of the highest Tatran peaks, the stony **Slavkovský Štít** (2452m; 8hr. round-trip from Hrebienok; for advanced hikers).

The *magistrála* also heads north from Hrebienok to the lake **Skalnaté Pleso** and its nearby *chata* (2¼hr.). The hike to **Malá studená dolina** (Little Cold Valley) is fairly relaxed; take the red trail from Hrebienok to **Zamkovského Chata** (1475m; ☎442 26 36; 260Sk per person) and onto the green trail. This leads to **Téryho Chata** (2015m; 4hr.; ☎442 52 45; 270Sk per person; breakfast included), which goes above tree-line to a high lake.

**SLOVAKIA**

> **WHAT'S NEXT, EQUALITY?** A display in Kežmarok castle
> (see **Sights and Entertainment**, p. 716) tells the tales of the first climbers to conquer
> the high Tatras, a group that included many men and one extraordinary woman. Beata
> Laška demanded to be a part of the expedition, then successfully kept up with the men
> around her as they reached the summit. Rather than praising Beata for the difficulties
> she overcame, though, her husband Albert (17 years her junior) declared her "insubor-
> dinate" and "brash," imprisoned her, and enjoyed the fruits of her fortune for the rest
> of his days. Beata spent the final six years of her life going mad in the castle dungeon.

An extremely difficult but rewarding hike traverses the immense **Veľká studená dolina** (Big Cold Valley) to **Zbojnícka Chata**. From Sliezsky Dom (see above), take the green trail to **Zamrznuté Pleso** (Cold Lake; 2047m), turn right onto the blue trail at the lake, and follow the crashing **Veľký studený potok** (Big Cold Stream), to **Studeného vodopády** (waterfalls), via Zbojnicka Chata. From here, the green trail returns to Hrebienok, running above tree-line most of the day. (8hr. round-trip to Hrebienok; for advanced hikers only. All trails open July-Sept.; many closed Nov.1-June 15. All of the *chaty* double as restaurants, but they're the only restaurants, so pack plenty of carbs.)

# NEAR STARÝ SMOKOVEC: ŠTRBSKÉ PLESO

The hotels and ski jump towers that clutter placid **Štrbské Pleso** (Štrbské Lake; SHTERB-skay PLEH-soh) seem to be trying to recapture the spirit of the 1975 "Interski" Championship, while hordes of tourists walk the streets. Distractions aside, Štrbské Pleso maintains peace and quiet in certain places, and you can imagine what the area was like before tourism caught Štrbské Pleso by surprise.

**⌘ TRANSPORTATION AND PRACTICAL INFORMATION.** TEŽ **trains** arrive from **Starý Smokovec** (30min., every hr., 18Sk); **Tatranská Lomnica** (55min., every hr., 26Sk); and **Poprad** (1¼hr., every hr., 26Sk). Budget travelers should leave the town before dusk, since hotel prices are higher than the elevation. Cheap beds are a short train ride away in Starý Smokovec and Tatranská Lomnica. Before you go, buy groceries at the *potraviny* up the hill from the train station. (Open daily 7am-7pm.)

**◢ HIKING.** Several beautiful hikes begin from town. A lift runs in summer, hoisting visitors to **Chata pod Soliskom** (1840m), which overlooks the lake and the expansive plains behind Štrbské Pleso. The lift is 10 minutes up the road from the trains; follow the signs or the yellow trail. (Runs June 25-Sept. 9 8:30am-4pm. July-Aug. one-way 100Sk, round-trip 150Sk; June and Sept. 70Sk, 100Sk.) A small restaurant under the top lift station, **Bivak Club**, offers tea (20Sk), Tatran fast food (35-55Sk), and, of course, beer (30Sk). Once at the top, hike the red trail to the peak of **Predné Solisko** (2093m); to get down, take the steep blue trail or turn left onto the yellow trail and left again when it hits the red one. The red trail returns to town (2¾hr.).

Two magnificent day hikes start from Štrbské Pleso, both involving stretches with chains. For both, dress warmly and bring plenty of food and water. The yellow route heads from the east side of the lake (follow the signs to Hotel Patria) out along **Mlynická dolina** to mountain lakes and **Vodopády Skok** (Waterfalls). It then crosses **Bystré Sedlo** (saddle; 2314m) and circles **Štrbské Solisko** (2302m) before returning to Štrbské Pleso (8-9hr.). The route includes some steep ascents and descents that take you well above the tree-line. Turn left where the yellow trail ends at the red trail, 30 minutes from Štrbské Pleso, to get back to town.

The second hike takes you to the top of **Rysy** (2499m) on the Polish-Slovak border, Poland's highest peak and the highest Tatra scalable without a guide.

From Štrbské Pleso, follow the *magistrála* to **Chata Popradské Pleso** (1500m; ☎ 449 21 77; 350Sk per person). From here, take the blue trail up the side of the valley and turn right onto the red trail after 30 minutes to tackle Rysy. Go past the lake **Zabie Plesá** to the remains of Chata pod Rysmi (2250m), a solemn reminder of the power of winter storms in the mountains. Rysy is 40 minutes from the *chata*; allow 8-9 hours for the trip there and back. This hike is for advanced hikers and should be attempted only in good weather. The stretch from Štrbské Pleso to Chata Popradské Pleso (1¼hr.) is part of the *magistrála* and attracts people with its views of the valley. A green trail branches off after 30 minutes and rolls by the **Hincov potok** (stream) to the *chata* and its lake.

From the *chata*, the 15-minute yellow trail (open July-Oct.) leads south to the **Symbolic Cemetery** (Symbolický cintorín; 1525m). Built between 1936 and 1940 by painter Otakar Štafl, the field of painted crosses, metal plaques, and broken propeller blades serves as "a memorial to the dead, and a warning for the living," for those who have died and those who are still climbing in the Tatras. The trail ends at a paved blue path. The weary can descend the blue trail to the Popradské Pleso TEŽ stop (45min.), but backtracking to Štrbské Pleso is far more interesting. The *magistrála* continues from the *chata* for hours along scenic ridges to **Hrebienok** (see **Starý Smokovec: Hiking**, p. 723). There's a steep climb up the face of **Ostrva** (1984m) to the **Sedlo pod Ostrvou** (Ostrva saddle; 1966m), but it levels off after that.

# TATRANSKÁ LOMNICA ☎ (0)969

Of the Tatran resorts, peaceful Tatranská Lomnica (TA-tran-ska LOM-nee-tsa) is by far the best place to stay. It's only 7km from Starý Smokovec, but what a difference 7km makes—even the tourists are relaxed. The snow is deep and the sleeps are cheap. In summer, few trails lead directly from town; the ear-popping lift to Lomnický Štít is the town's main attraction. Thanks to frequent TEŽ trains, however, all of hiking country is close by.

**⌐ TRANSPORTATION.** TEŽ **trains** run to **Starý Smokovec** and **Štrbské Pleso. Buses,** however, are the best way to get to **Poprad** (30min., every hr., 19Sk). Pay for tickets at the machines at the stations, lest ye face serious penalties (up to 600Sk).

**⁊ PRACTICAL INFORMATION.** With nameless streets and scattered buildings, the village can be confusing, but excellent signs to restaurants, hotels, and services are everywhere and almost everything is within spitting distance of the train station. The **information board** halfway between the train stop and Hotel Lomnica, away from the tracks, displays the location of hotels, pensions, and restaurants. You can amuse yourself with the free phone to call for reservations and neat buttons that light up if rooms are available. **Currency exchanges** are around town. **Slovenská Sporiteľňa,** in the woods behind the train station, cashes **traveler's checks** and has a 24hr. Cirrus/Plus **ATM.** (☎ 96 72 59; fax 96 76 67. Open M 7:30am-3pm, Tu 7:30am-1pm, W 7:30-11:30am and noon-5pm, Th-F 7:30-11:30am and noon-3pm.) **Poľnobank,** along the track across from the railroad station, has another Cirrus/Plus ATM. **Sport & Moda,** between the main road and the train station, rents **skis** with accessories (290Sk per day). The **post office** lies behind the train station. (☎ 44 68 25 34. Open M-F 8:30-noon and 1-3:30pm, Sa 8-10am.) **Postal code:** 05960.

**⌐⌐ ACCOMMODATIONS AND FOOD.** If you don't have a tent, don't fret—virtually all of the hotels and pensions in town are remarkably cheap. **Penzión Bělin,** in the center of town, is by far one of the best. The friendly, English-speaking staff rents out warm rooms in their giant yellow house for bargain prices. There are kitchens and satellite TVs in the common room on each floor. Follow the sign from the info board into the gardens. At the 2nd path junction

(50m), take the left one that heads up to the road. Turn right to find Bělín. (☎446 77 78. Check-out 9am. 2- and 4-person rooms 250Sk high season, 230Sk off-season. Discounts for longer stays.) For camping, take the main road away from town. Turn right at the first intersection to get to the campsites on the edge of the national park. The second facility, the colossal **Eurocamp FICC,** 4km from town, has its own train stop (every hr., 6Sk). It rents 118 spacious bungalows with spotless showers. (☎446 77 41; fax 446 73 46. Tents 90Sk, plus 120Sk per person. 2-person bungalows with bath 1000Sk, quads 1800Sk.) A sports store rents **bikes** (250Sk per day), and **in-line skates** (200Sk per day; open daily 8am-8pm). There is also a grocery store, disco, restaurant, and bar on the premises. From Eurocamp, head 10 minutes. away from the mountains to reach **Športcamp** and its tiny, shiny 14- to 20-bed dorms with shared showers and tent sites. (☎/fax 446 72 88. Reception 7am-10pm. 80Sk per person; tents 70Sk. Dorms 200Sk. Showers 12Sk after first night.)

There's a **supermarket** just behind the main train station building. (Open M-F 7:45am-7pm, Sa 7:45am-3pm, Su 8am-3pm.) Restaurants line the train tracks and the main road, but most are insufferably touristy. ■ **Reštaurácia Júlia,** 200m below the station (follow the sign), somehow manages to transcend the pervasive kitsch with its Slovak specialties. (☎446 79 47. Main dishes 55-170Sk. Open daily 12:30pm until the last guest leaves.)

**⊞⚠ SIGHTS AND HIKING.** Get tickets early for the remarkable lift up to **Lomnický Štít** (2634m), the Tatras' second-highest peak. Follow the signs around town to the *lanová draha* **mini-cabins** that ride up to the glacial lake of **Skalnaté Pleso** (1751m). The 4-person lift runs continuously if there's demand, or every hr. otherwise, from behind Hotel Horec. (Open 8:30am-7pm; last ascent 6:30pm. Round-trip 300Sk.) From the lake, a larger mini-cabin ascends to the summit while a chairlift plows to **Lomnické Sedlo.** (Mini-cabin 400Sk round-trip; chairlift 150Sk round-trip.) A 550Sk day ticket can be obtained for skiing the excellent trails from Skalnatá Chata to Tatranská Lomnica. On a clear day, the peak offers a staggering view of just about everywhere. The craggy mountain peak has good picnic spots; at the lake, **Skalnatá Chata** is an admirable refreshment stop. Dress warmly—it snows up here even in July.

Hiking is generally better from Starý Smokovec or Štrbské Pleso, but a few full-day hikes are accessible from Tatranská Lomnica's lift. The red *Magistrála* trail heading southwest from **Skalnaté Pleso** toward **Lomnická vyhliadka** (1524m) and then to **Zamkovského Chata** (2hr.) is challenging but well worth the view (see **Hiking: Starý Smokovec,** p. 723). The blue trail from the info board in town to **Vodopády studeného potoka** (Cold Stream Waterfalls) and back to Tatranská Lesná is gentler (4½hr.).

**⊡ ENTERTAINMENT.** While most people in Tatranská Lomnica are too exhausted from skiing and hiking to function beyond 8pm, there are a few options for night action. **Kino Tatry,** in the Tatranské Kulturne Centrum, probably requires the least energy, with the usual mindless Hollywood films in all their Anglophone splendor. From the bus or train station, turn right onto the main road and then right again at the Muzeum Tanaf signs. (☎446 72 19. Centrum open M-F 8am-noon and 1-5pm, Sa 8am-3pm. 20Sk. Shows at 4:45 and 7pm. 40-56Sk.) **Oaza Disco Bar,** in the same building, features 1960s rock, laser lights, and gaudy wallpaper. (Open Su-Th 4pm-1am, F 4pm-2am, Sa 4pm-3am).

# ŠARIŠ

Tucked away in the green hills of east Slovakia, Šariš is still struggling to deal with many of the political events of the last 80 years. A long-time buffer against Turkish invasions, the region and its sleepy towns still stand behind bastions built to repel the Sultan. Amidst the backdrop of folk tales and chiming bells stand two giant Campbell's soup cans, beckoning you to a shrine to native son Andy Warhol in the miniscule town of Medzilaborce.

# KOŠICE

☎(0)95

Slovakia's second largest city, Košice (KO-shih-tseh; pop. 241,000), combines the laid-back feel of a country town with the culture and convenience of a larger metropolis. The political and economic changes in the region's recent history have left their mark, however, and the sight of the row upon row of highrises surrounding the inner city is quite a shock in contrast to the painstakingly renovated and preserved Old Town. While the medieval gold craftsmen who founded the town would wince at Košice's recently-closed steel foundries, they would smile at the city center's dancing wrought iron fountains and Glockenspiel bells.

## ORIENTATION

Košice's **Staré Mesto** (Old Town) lies close to the **train station**. To get to the central **Hlavná** and the tourist office, exit the station and follow the "Centrum" signs across the park that lies just in front and to the right of the train station. You'll arrive at **Mlynská**, which intersects Hlavná at the cathedral.

## TRANSPORTATION

**Trains:** On Predstaničné nám. (☎613 21 75). To: **Bratislava** (6hr., 15 per day, 366Sk); **Budapest, HUN** (5hr., 6 per day, 800Sk); **Kraków, POL** (6hr., 1 per day, 690Sk); **Lviv, UKR** (6hr., 1 per day, 1900Sk); **Prague, CZR** (10hr., 7 per day, 620Sk); and **Kyiv, UKR** (12hr., 1 per day, 2800Sk).

**Buses:** ☎680 73 06. Next to the train station. More expensive than trains, but sometimes faster and more scenic for local trips. To: **Bratislava** (5hr., 10 per day, 380Sk).

**Public Transportation: Trams** and **buses** traverse the city and its suburbs. Tickets 10Sk from kiosks and little orange boxes at bus stops.

**Taxis: Rádio Taxi** (☎163 33), **Classic Taxi** (☎622 22 44), and **CTC** (☎43 34 33).

## PRACTICAL INFORMATION

**Tourist Offices: Mestské Informačna Centrum,** Hlavná 8 (☎625 88 88). Dispenses info on hotels and cultural happenings. Open M-F 9am-6pm, Sa 9am-1pm. **Tatratour,** Alžbetina 6 (☎622 23 98), near the cathedral, cashes **traveler's checks** for a 1% commission and arranges pensions for 600Sk per person. Open M-F 9am-5:30pm.

**Currency Exchange: VÚB** branches are liberally sprinkled throughout the city; the one at Hlavná 8 (☎622 62 50) cashes **traveler's checks** and **exchanges currency** for a 1% commission and gives MC **cash advances.** Open M-W and F 7:30am-5pm, Th 7:30am-noon. 24hr. Cirrus/MC/Visa **ATMs** magically spit cash in front of many VÚB branches.

**Luggage Storage:** At the train station. 10Sk per bag under 15kg.; heavier bags 20Sk. Small lockers 5Sk. Open 24hr.

**International Bookstore: SFA,** Hlavná 97 (☎623 36 76). Through the arch and up the stairs. Small selection. Open M-F 10am-6pm.

**Pharmacy: Lekáreň Pri Dóme,** Mylinská 1. Open M-F 7:30am-6:30pm, Sa 8am-noon.

**Telephones:** Around Hlavná and outside the post office (see below).

**Internet Access:** At the central tourist office, Hlavná 8 (see above). 10Sk per 10min., 50Sk per hr. **Internet café 115,** Hlavná 115. 50Sk per hr.; coffee included. Open daily 8am-4pm.

**Post Office:** Poštová 20 (☎622 26 37). Open M-F 7am-7pm, Sa 7am-2pm.

**Postal code:** 04001.

## ACCOMMODATIONS

Keep in mind that some larger hotels are much cheaper than *penzióny;* the cheapest of both are a short way outside the center. The tourist office can help you locate

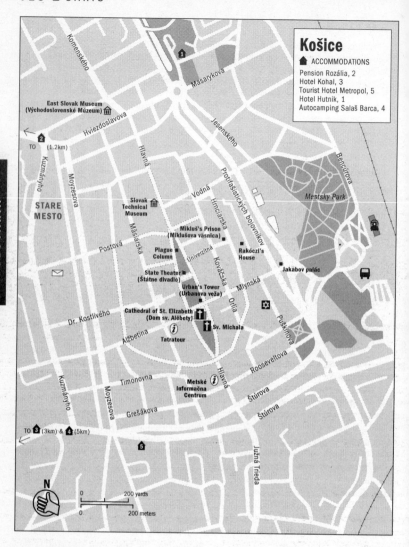

Košice

**ACCOMMODATIONS**

Pension Rozália, 2
Hotel Kohal, 3
Tourist Hotel Metropol, 5
Hotel Hutnik, 1
Autocamping Salaš Barca, 4

a bed. **Student dorms** are the cheapest option (about 150Sk per night) in July and August, but are very far from the center.

**Tourist Hotel Metropol,** Štúrova 32 (☎ 625 59 48). Small, basic rooms and a friendly staff. Three stops away on tram #6 or bus #11, 16, or 30 from the train/bus station, or a 20min. walk. Follow directions to Hlavná (see above) and turn left, then right onto Štúrova. You'll see a sign for Metropol on your left; walk through the gate into a flower-filled yard with a fountain. Turn left and go upstairs for the reception (24hr.). Massages (4Sk per min.) and restaurant. Check-out 10am. Triples and quads 300Sk per person.

**Hotel Hutnik,** Tyršovo nábrežie 1 (☎ 633 7511 ext. 15; fax 633 77 80). From the train/bus station, cross the bridge en route to the center and take 1st right onto ul. Protifašistických bojovníkov. Walk 15min. and the hotel will appear on the right after a rotary. A large, comfortable hotel with a bus stop just outside. Reception 24hr. Check-out noon. Singles and doubles with shared toilets 600Sk, 800Sk.

**Hotel Kohal,** Trieda SNP 61 (☎642 55 72). Take tram #6 in front of the train/bus station to a roundabout at Toryská and Trieda SNP. Get off at the Ferrocentrum stop, after the tram turns right onto Trieda SNP. Kohal will be to your right, large, with basic comforts. Breakfast 90Sk. Shared bath. Reception 24hr. Check-out 2pm. Hostel singles 210Sk; doubles 400Sk. AmEx/MC/Visa.

**Penzión Rozália,** Oravská 14 (☎633 97 14). From the train station, take tram #6 to Amfitáter (20min.) and walk up Stará spišská cesta with the park and amphitheater on the left. After 10min., Oravská appears on the right; there's no sign, but ring the bell at #14. Small rooms overlooking a garden. Call ahead. Singles 250Sk, with bath 600Sk; doubles 500Sk, 800Sk.

**Autocamping Salaš Barca,** (☎623 33 97). From the train/bus station, take tram #6 to the "Ferrocentrum" stop and switch to tram #9. Get off at the "Verejny Cintorín" stop and continue on foot for 200m; turn right at the sign. Reception 24hr. 2- and 5-person bungalows 400Sk per person; (one) quint 900Sk.

# ◖ FOOD

With restaurants on roof-top terraces, tucked away under arches, and on the central square itself, Košice is a gastronomic paradise. Vegetarians need look no further, and connoisseurs of Slovak cuisine will find enough *knedle* (dumpling) to keep them happy for months. For **groceries,** try the **Tesco** at Hlavná 109. (☎670 48 10. Open M-F 8am-8pm, Sa 8am-6pm, Su 8am-5pm.)

**Ajvega,** Orlia 10 (☎622 04 52), off Mlynská. Veggie pastas, pizzas, soups, and salads with a Mexican twist. The extensive menu presents many tasty options. Main dishes 45-89Sk. Up the winding staircase, **Restaurant Veža** (the tower), with a more elegant decor and a roof-top terrace, offers the same menu. Open daily 11am-10pm.

**Reštaurácia Vevericka** (Squirrel Restaurant), Hlavná 97 (☎622 33 60). Look for the pair of squirrels over the dark wood. Outdoor seating with hearty Slovak fare 34-142Sk. Open daily 9am-10pm.

**Pizzeria Venezia,** Mlynská 20 (☎622 44 44). People-watch on the patio and eat hefty pizza (88-110Sk). Open daily in summer 9am-midnight; off-season 10am-midnight.

**Cukráreň Aida,** Hlavná 80. Tables and booths extend nearly as far as the eye can see. The crowds come for gourmet sweets (9-58Sk) and fabulous ice cream (5Sk per scoop). Open daily 8am-10pm.

# ◖ SIGHTS

**◪ CATHEDRAL OF ST. ELIZABETH.** (Dom sv. Alžbety.) The cathedral is the centerpiece of Bulbous **Hlavná,** which marks the heart of historic Košice at its widest point. Begun in 1378 as a high-Gothic monument, the cathedral has undergone repeated confused renovations; it now stands as a conglomeration of almost every style known to Western architecture. In 1900, restorers built a crypt under the cathedral's north nave. Transported from Turkey in 1906, Košice's revolutionary hero, **Ferenc Rakóczi II,** has proven to be less rebellious in a sarcophagus. The cathedral's little brother next door, the **Chapel of St. Michael** (Kaplnka sv. Michala), serves as a mortuary. (Under renovation in summer 2000.) Outside, a relief of St. Michael weighs the souls of the dead. On the other side of the cathedral, the barren facade of **Urban's Tower** (Urbanova veža) seems almost two-dimensional next to the ornaments of St. Elizabeth's. A closer look, however, reveals 36 tombstones lining the exterior, one of which dates from the 4th century. Across the park from St. Michael's, stairs lead down to a free **underground museum,** home to the ruins of the town's fortifications. *(Open daily July-Sept. 15 11am-7pm. Tours every 30min.)*

**AROUND JACOB'S PALACE.** (Jakubov palác.) Walking down Mlynská from the cathedral toward the train station leads to the 19th-century **Jacob's Palace**, built of stones discarded from the cathedral. Currently occupied by the British Council, the palace served as a temporary home to Czechoslovakia's president in the spring of 1945. Backtrack to the center and head left down Puškinova to the closed **synagogue**. Behind the cathedral on Hlavná, on the far side of the fountain (which dances to music afternoons and evenings), stands the neo-Baroque **State Theater** (Štátne divadlo), built the end of the 19th century. Past the theater on Hlavná, the **Plague Column** (Morový sloup) commemorates the devastating outbreak of 1711.

**EAST SLOVAK MUSEUM.** (Východnoslovenské Múzeum.) Running right from Hlavná between the Column and the theater, Univerzitná leads to two branches of the East Slovak Museum: **Mikluš's Prison** (Miklušova väznica) and **Rakóczi's House.** Housed in the former city jail, Mikluš's prison details life behind bars from the 17th to the 19th century, including prisoner graffiti, death sentences, and torture instruments. The tour covers reconstructed prison chambers, many with unflattering sketches of the executioners, and photo collections depicting various methods of torture. Rakóczi's House is a shrine to Ferenc Rakóczi II, Hungary's anti-Habsburg national hero, but is dull if you don't speak Slovak. (Hrnčiarska 7. Open Tu-Sa 9am-5pm, Su 9am-1pm. Ticket office behind the gate at Hrnčiarska. Tours every hr. 20Sk, students 10Sk.)

At the farthest end of Hlavná from the cathedral stands the archeological branch of the East Slovak Museum. Exhibits of finds from near Košice and about the region's military history and castles. The museum's pride, however, awaits downstairs behind a two-ton door. In 1935, while laying foundations for new finance headquarters at Hlavná 68, workers discovered a copper bowl filled with 2920 gold *tholars* and a gold Renaissance chain over 2m long. Both are on display in the vault. (Hviezdoslavova 2. ☎622 30 61. Open Tu-Sa 9am-5pm, Su 9am-1pm. 20Sk, students 10Sk.)

## 🎵 ENTERTAINMENT

Fans of high and low culture alike will not be disappointed by Košice. Information about Košice's **philharmonic** and four **theaters** is available at the tourist office, Hlavná 8. Beer and wine halls are plentiful in the town center.

**Jazz Club,** Kovača 39 (☎622 42 37). Jazz only comes around a few times a week, but large crowds enjoy the disco, oldies, and salsa that fill the gaps. Cover 40Sk, plus 50Sk for live music. Open daily 4pm-3am.

**Country Club Diera** (The Hole), through the arch at Poštová 14 (☎622 05 51). Quenches the Slovak thirst for Bluegrass. Tequila shots and 7 types of whiskey await in this spirited bastion of the Wild Wild West. Open M-Tu and Th 11am-1am, W 11am-2am, F-Sa 11am-3am, Su 3pm-midnight.

**Da Gama,** Marskiarska 9 (☎623 32 05). A compact pub where locals fill the tables nightly. Sit right down and call for a *Gambrinus* (23Sk). Open M-F noon-midnight, Sa-Su 3pm-midnight.

**Bar u Slona** (At the Elephant), Hlavná 37 (☎622 62 31), in a quiet courtyard concealed by a short passageway. Enter at the brass elephant on a leg and a trunk. Pizza 48-58Sk. *Heineken* 68Sk, *Plzeň* 33Sk. Open M-Sa 10am-11pm, Su 2-11pm.

# PREŠOV
☎(0)91

More than a millennium ago, the first Slavic agricultural estates were already in place where Prešov (preh-SHUV; pop. 100,000), Slovakia's third-largest city, now stands. The atmosphere today is cosmopolitan, but the historic buildings and monuments attest to rural roots and a time gone by.

**🚆 TRANSPORTATION. Trains** (☎ 773 10 43) travel to: **Košice** (50min., 17 per day, 30Sk); **Bratislava** via **Kysak** (4½hr., 9 per day, 366Sk); and **Kraków, POL** (5½hr., 3 per day, 500Sk). **Buses** (☎773 13 47), opposite the train station, travel to: **Košice** (30-45min., 3 per hr., 31Sk) and **Poprad** (1½hr., every hr., 84Sk).

**🗺 ORIENTATION AND PRACTICAL INFORMATION.** Prešov's stem, **Košická,** sprouts straight from the train station, becoming **Masarykova,** then **Hlavná,** home of the Church of St. Nicholas. **Buses** and **trolleys** (all except #19 and 31) traveling left from the train station go to the center; take the walkway under Masarykova and purchase an 8Sk ticket from the orange *automats* at major stops, or from kiosks. Otherwise, the center is a 20-minute walk left from the train station along Košická or a 70Sk taxi ride away. **Mestské Informačné Centrum,** Hlavná 67, provides info on the town and hotels. (☎186 and ☎/fax 73 11 13. Open May-Oct. M-F 8:30am-5:30pm, Sa 9am-noon; Nov.-Apr. M-F 8am-4:30pm.) **Exchange currency** at **Istrobanka,** Hlavná 75, which has good rates and a 24hr. Cirrus/MC/Visa **ATM.** The bank also cashes **traveler's checks** for no commission. (☎758 04 18; fax 772 31 65. Open M-F 8am-5pm.) There is another Cirrus/MC/Visa ATM at the bus station opposite stand #11. A **24hr. pharmacy** sits at Sabinovská 15 (☎771 94 05). Walk up Hlavná away from the train station towards the center; Sabinovská is just past the major intersection on the left. Surf the internet at **Arcadia Internet Club,** Slovenská 46. (☎771 26 34. M-F 40Sk per hr., Sa-Su 35Sk per hr. Open daily 10am-10pm.) The **post office,** Masarykova 2, sits just south of the city center. (☎773 45 24. Open M-F 8am-7pm, Sa 8am-1pm.) **Telephones** are outside. **Postal code:** 08001.

**🏠🍴 ACCOMMODATIONS AND FOOD.** Prešov doesn't have many cheap beds, but the tourist office can help you if you're in a pinch. To get to **Turistická Ubytovňa Sen,** Vajanského 65, take a bus toward the center. Get off at "Na Hlanéj," at the entrance to the main square. Follow the departing trolley and take the first right onto Metodova. Vajanského is five minutes up; turn left and the hostel is on the right. It rents 27 beds, has one shower, and is close to the center. (☎773 31 70. Reception 24hr. Check-out 10am. Approx. 200Sk.) **Penzión Lineas,** Budovatelská 14, is closer to the train station than to the center. From the station, walk toward the town center, take the first left on Škultétýho, and another left onto Budovatelská. (☎772 33 25 ext. 28; fax 772 32 06. Pets allowed. Reception 24hr. Check-out 11am. Doubles with bath 450Sk.) **Penzión Andreas,** on Jarková, rents six cushy rooms in the center of town for less than equivalent hotels. Follow the bus directions for Turistická Ubytovňa Sen, then follow the tram to Florianova. Turn left here and left again onto Jarková. The pension is on the left. (☎772 32 25. Reception 11am-11pm. Check-out 8am. Call 1 week ahead. Singles 400Sk; doubles 800-1000Sk.)

What it may lack in accommodations, Prešov makes up for in dining. For do-it-yourself-ers, there's a **Tesco** supermarket, Legionarova 1, where Hlavná becomes Masarykova. (Open M-F 8am-8pm, Sa 8am-5pm, Su 8am-3pm.) **Florianka,** Baštová 32, sits through the archway next to Slovakia's best hotel and restaurant management school, which has made this former firehouse its training ground. Dine outside if the blazing red interior is too much for you; just don't try to ride the pushcart firetruck. The student chefs and waitresses serve with class. (☎773 40 83. Main dishes 41-119Sk. Open M-F 11am-9pm.) **Senator,** Hlavná 67, overlooking Staré Mesto, caters to all appetites with vegetarian dishes (55-100Sk) and meatier Slovak fare. (☎773 11 86. Main dishes 70-270Sk. Open M-F 10am-10pm, Sa-Su 11am-10pm). A beer hall is attached. (Open daily 3pm-midnight.) **Bagetéria,** Hlavná 36, serves baguette sandwiches (30-51Sk) with and without meat. (☎773 26 02. Open M-Th 6:30am-9pm, F 6:30am-10pm, Sa 8am-10pm, Su 8:30am-9pm.) Down the street from Bagetéria, **Veliovič Cukráreň,** Hlavná 28, is more than an ice cream shop with sweets (6-12Sk), hefty desserts (banana splits 45Sk), and cappuccino (20Sk; open M-F 8am-9pm, Sa-Su 9am-9pm).

**NEW YORK, PARIS, PREŠOV** At first glance, it may seem that one of these places is "not like the others." Prešov's residents proudly broadcast, however, that the 49th parallel runs right through the city's Hlavná ul., placing it on a direct line with the City That Never Sleeps and the City of Light. Souvenirs and advertising pair New York with the Statue of Liberty, Paris with the Eiffel Tower, and Prešov with a bottle of beer. It seems, however, that the person who dreamed up this bit of geographical trivia might have had a few too many of those bottles of beer: while Prešov and Paris are indeed in cosmic alignment, New York hovers around the *41st* parallel.

■ **SIGHTS.** Hlavná's Renaissance houses stand back in deference to the town's older **Church of St. Nicholas** (Kostol sv. Mikuláša). The Gothic church's distinctive turrets attest to Saxon influence in Prešov during the late Middle Ages. The church opens its doors only irregularly other than for services; long-sleeved shirts will spare you glares. Near the church is the **Wine Museum**, Floriánova ul. This cellar drinking establishment showcases more than 1000 varieties of wines, many of which you can sample for 10-100Sk. If you're looking for more than a sample, bottles range from 60Sk for more common local vintages to 20,000Sk for a 1942 Argentinian wine, the pride of their international collection. (☎773 31 08. Open M-F 8am-noon and 12:30-7pm, Sa 8am-noon. 40Sk; 20Sk per person for groups of 5 or more.)

Also near the church is the 16th-century **Rákoczi Palace**, Hlavná 86, with its attic gable of plants and saints, houses the **Regional Museum** (Krajské múzeum). The exhibition on fire moves from making it in the Stone Age to fighting it in more recent eras, concluding with old fire trucks parked out back. A new exhibit upstairs is dedicated to another element: moving photographs from a 1998 flood that ravaged a nearby village. (☎773 47 08. Open Tu-F 9am-noon and 12:30-5pm, Sa 9am-1pm, Su 1-5pm. 20Sk, students 10Sk.) Amble down to the Greek Orthodox **St. John's Cathedral** (Katedrálny chrám sv. Jána Krstiteľa), at the base of Hlavná, to peek at the breathtaking altar. On the west side of Hlavná, the restored Gothic **Šarišská Gallery**, Hlavná 51, features local Slovak art. (☎772 54 23. Open Tu-W, F 8am-5pm, Th 8am-6pm, Sa 9am-1pm, Su 2-6pm. 10Sk, students 5Sk; Su free.)

Heading left from the town hall on Hlavná, the narrow, medieval Floriánova leads to **St. Florian's Gate** (Brána sv. Floriána), a remnant of Prešov's early Renaissance fortifications and a tribute to Prešov's patron saint. A left onto Ku Kumštu after the church of St. Nicholas leads to Švermova and a courtyard at #56. Inside is a **synagogue**, with an ornate interior and a 1991 monument to Prešov's 6000 victims of the Holocaust and the Tiso regime. If the doors are closed, you can still see the interior via the **Judaica Museum**, on the upper balcony. (☎773 16 38. Open Tu-W 11am-4pm, Th 3-6pm, F 10am-1pm, Su 1-5pm. 60Sk, students 10Sk.)

■ **NIGHTLIFE.** There's a surprising amount of nightlife in this placid town—see for yourself at any of Prešov's numerous pubs, *vinareň*, and nightclubs. **Piváreň Smädný Mních Victoria**, Svátoplukova 1, on a side passage, features the "Thirsty Monk" (20Sk) and many happy locals. (☎570 27. Open Su-F 9am-10pm.) The foot-tapping live folk music (Tu and Th 5-9pm) at **Vináreň Neptun**, Hlavná 62, provides a refreshing break from Abba and friends. Head through the arch; the entrance is on the right. (☎773 25 38. Open M-Th 5-10pm, F 5pm-2am, Sa disco 8pm-3am.) If it's Abba you want, the red-lighted **Alfa**, Kováčska 3, is the place to be. Dress up and dress tight. (☎772 52 52. Open F-Sa 8:30pm-4:30am, W-Th and Su 8pm-4am.)

# NEAR PREŠOV

## MEDZILABORCE                                         ☎(0)939

*Catch a train from Prešov to Humenné (1¾hr., 6 per day) and then switch trains to Medzilaborce (50min., 8 per day). The whole trip costs 96Sk. If you catch the 8:03am train to Humenné, you can make this a daytrip.*

While Medzilaborce (pop. 6,500) is not especially spectacular, it can claim one peculiar attraction: its **Museum of Modern Art** (Múzeum Moderného Umenia), on A. Warhola street. From the train station, turn left onto Dobranského, which becomes A. Warhola; look for the two Campbell's soup cans guarding the entrance. The museum was established in 1991 by John Warhol, brother of Andy, in memory of his sibling and parents. The location is not as random as it might initially seem—the Warhol family migrated to the US after World War II from the tiny village of Miková near Medzilaborce. Andy (or Andrej, as his birth certificate would have it) was born two years later and never got to see the homeland his family remembered. The museum displays 17 Warhol originals, as well as possessions important to Warhol and his family's history, such as the dress worn by the Warhol boys for their Baptism. The biographical information on Warhol—emphasizing his humble beginnings and shy demeanor—is particularly interesting in light of the very high profile he kept after achieving stardom. Also on display are works by his brother Paul, which range from experiments with the screenprinting Andy made famous to decorative pieces painted with colored eggs, and works by Paul's son James. (☎732 10 59; fax 732 10 69. Open Tu-F 9am-noon and 1-4pm, Sa-Su 10am-noon and 1-4pm. 100Sk, students 50Sk. Cameras 100Sk, video 300Sk.)

If you're not an early riser (and what aspiring pop artist is?) and miss the 8:03am train, you can crash at **Športklub,** Mierova 20. From the museum, A. Warhola continues over the river and becomes Mierova. The hotel is on the left just after the rail crossing. Basic rooms with a funky smell and 1970s style. If no one is at the reception desk, call the phone number for help. (☎732 32 18 55. 4-bed dorms with hot water and shared bath 150Sk.)

# BARDEJOV ☎(0)935

Bardejov (bar-day-YOV; pop. 38,000) and its nearby healing springs have been a site of both great prosperity and terrible disaster since the town was officially settled some 800 years ago. Positioned on a trade route to Poland and Kyivan Rus, Bardejov profited handsomely from each caravan that passed by, but all the wealth in the world coudn't stop the earthquakes, Turkish armies, and fires that have rolled through in the last 500 years. Neither plague nor natural disaster could keep the town in ruins, however, and the last reconstruction effort won Bardejov a 1986 UNESCO heritage gold medal.

**█ TRANSPORTATION. Trains** (☎472 36 05) go to: **Prešov** (1¼hr., 8 per day, 38Sk); **Košice** (1¾-2¼hr., 7 per day, 66Sk); and **Kraków, POL** (7hr., 3 per day, 716Sk). The quickest way to and from Bardejov is by **bus** (☎474 82 70). To: **Prešov** (50min., 15 per day, 48Sk); **Košice** (1¾hr., 12 per day, 77Sk); and **Poprad** (2 hr., 12 per day, 92Sk).

**█ ORIENTATION AND PRACTICAL INFORMATION.** From the train station, turn left and cross the road. Take the stone path to the right through the ruined, lower gate of **Staré Mesto** (Old Town) onto Stöcklova. Follow Stöcklova around to the left and turn right onto Paštová to reach Radničné nám., the main square. **Globtour Bratislava,** the tourist office on Radničné nám. 21, sells **maps** of Bardejov and Bardejovské Kúpele (10Sk; ☎/fax 472 62 73; open June 15-Sept. 15 M-F 9am-6pm, Sa-Su 10am-noon and 1:30-4pm; Sept. 16-June 14 M-F 9am-4:30pm). **Exchange currency,** get MC/Visa **cash advances,** or cash AmEx/Visa **traveler's checks** for a 1% commission at **VÚB,** Kellerova 1. There is also a Cirrus/MC **ATM** inside. (☎472 26 71. Open M-W and F 8am-5pm, Th 8am-noon. ATM open daily 6am-10pm.) Another Cirrus/MC ATM sits on Poštová. A **pharmacy** lies at Radničné nám. 43. (☎472 75 62. Open M-F 8:30am-noon and 1-4:30pm.) The **post office** is at Dlhý rad 14. (☎472 40 62. Open M-F 7:30am-6pm, Sa 8-11:30am.) The outer foyer sells phone cards. (Open M-F 7:30am-6pm, Sa 7:30-11:30am.) **Telephones** stand outside. **Postal code:** 08501.

SLOVAKIA

**▗▖ ACCOMMODATIONS AND FOOD.** More accommodations are available outside of town, but options are limited without a car. **Športhotel,** Katuzovovo 31, 15 minutes from the train station, is popular with a younger crowd. Turn right from the station and follow Slovenská; take the first left onto Kúpelná, and, after 200m, a right on Kellerova (not well-marked, but you'll see a bridge when you turn). Take the first left after the bridge and the hotel will appear on the right. (☎472 49 49; fax 472 82 08. All rooms with bath. Hot water 4-10pm. Reception until 10pm. Check-out 10am. Call ahead. Doubles 500Sk; triples 700Sk; quads 800Sk.) For slightly less rowdy neighbors, call **Penzión Semafór,** Kellerova 13 (mobile ☎0905 83 09 84), which rents three plush doubles with bath. Follow directions to Športhotel, but turn left on Kellerova and look for the green fence on your right. (450Sk per person.)

Most restaurants in Bardejov are inexpensive, but few rise above the rabble of snack bars and drab beer halls. **U Zlatá Koruny,** Radničné nám. 41, stands out from the rest, serving a variety of wines and elegant dishes (55-150Sk). They also have nine vegetarian options (32-61Sk; ☎472 53 10; open M-F 9am-10pm, Sa-Su 9am-11pm). **Reštaurácia Na Bráne,** Jiráskova 3, at the end of Hviezdoslavova, serves up a fair amount of grease with their meals (30-85Sk), but the dishes are quite tasty. (☎472 23 48. Open M-F 8am-8pm, Sa-Su 8am-7:30pm.) Next to the natural science chapter of the Bardejov museum sits **Bagetária U Paliho,** Rhodýho 4. Design your own sandwich or salad from well-displayed greens, cheeses, and breads (14-80Sk; open Su-Th 10am-11pm, F-Sa 10am-midnight).

**▣ SIGHTS.** Bardejov may be the only town in Šariš where the square's centerpiece isn't a church. The maple tree at the south end is a gift from the US, brought in 1991 by former vice president Dan Quayle. The **town hall** (*radnica;* ☎474 60 38), Radničné nám. 48, now serves as one of the town's museums, displaying historic trinkets. Among them is the key to the city, which the mayor's wife passed to her treacherous Turkish lover in 1697; she was later executed for her deceit. The **ikony** exhibition, Radničné nám. 27 (☎472 20 09), houses a huge collection of Orthodox icons. The aptly-named "Nature of Northeastern Slovakia" display in the **Prírodopisné Múzeum,** on Rhodýho 4, will tickle the taxidermist in you. (☎472 26 30. All museums open daily May-Oct. 15 8:30am-noon and 12:30-5pm; Oct. 16-Apr. Tu-Su 8am-noon and 12:30-4pm. 25Sk, students 10Sk.)

The **Church of St. Aegidius** (Kostol sv. Egídia), at the downhill end of Radničné nám., contains 11 Gothic wing altars crafted between 1450 and 1510. The biggest and most valuable is the 15th-century **Nativity Altar.** (Open M-F 10am-4pm, Sa 10am-2pm. 25Sk, students 15Sk; to ascend the tower: 40Sk, 20Sk.) A walk down Veterna, over the main road and left up Pod lipken leads to the **Church of the Holy Cross** (Kostol sv. Kríža), which stands watch over Bardejov's cemetery. A forest path leads past 14 stark Stations of the Cross before reaching the weed-filled graveyard. A full panorama of Bardejov's valley stretches below, but watch out for the stinging nettles. Veterna ends at one of Bardejov's 12 (of 23 original) extant **bastions,** which first served as a crossroads beacon and later as the local beheading stock. The tourist office has pamphlets on **walking tours** around Bardejov and its 14th-century towers. One focuses on the history of Bardejov's Jewish quarter at ul. Mlynská, west of the city center, where there is a closed **synagogue** and a memorial plaque to the more than 7,000 Bardejov Jews who perished during the Holocaust.

During the last weekend of August, the town square comes alive for an annual market in celebration of **St. Aegidius.** The 3rd week of July brings exhibition and traditional dancing to the town square in honor of **Roland,** Bardejov's patron saint.

# NEAR BARDEJOV

## BARDEJOVSKÉ KÚPELE

*Take bus #12 to the end of the line from the front of the train station in Bardejov (20min., 7Sk). Skansen (☎ 472 27 20) open daily May-Sept. 9am-noon and 12:30-5pm; Oct.-Apr. 8:30am-noon and 12:30-3:30pm. On weekends, walk 10m past the museum in order to be let in. 20Sk, students 10Sk.*

About 5km from Bardejov, the Bardejovské Kúpele (Bardejov Baths) work wonders with its springs and country air. Actual curing stations are off-limits, but several free fountains spurt with the spa's acidic water. The complex is a collection of 18th- and 19th-century buildings and ugly hotels, built more recently and in need of much more work than their historic counterparts. The spa reached its zenith in the late 18th and early 19th centuries with such clients as Alexander I of Russia, Emperor Joseph II of Austria-Hungary, and the wives of Austrian Emperor Franz Joseph and Napoleon, but World War I and the fall of the empire cut the spa off from Hungarian aristocrats. On the resort's outskirts, Slovakia's oldest folklore exhibition sits in a hectare replica of Šariš village life. In summer, the **skansen** (or Múzeum Ľudovej Kultúry; Museum of Folk Culture), which exhibits ethnographic objects, religious icons, and relics from casino days, hosts regular folk festivals and craft days.

SLOVAKIA

# SLOVENIA
# (SLOVENIJA)

**IF YOU'RE HERE FOR...**

**2-3 DAYS.** Take in a gallery by day and a cafe by night, making sure to enjoy the music festivals that come and go during the summer months in **Ljubljana** (p. 743).

**1 WEEK.** After a couple of days in **Ljubljana** (p. 743), hikers should head to **Lake Bohinj** (p. 752) and those looking to unwind to the coastal **Piran** (p. 756). **Bled** p. 749), with its castle set in the Julian Alps, is an ideal endpoint for any trip.

Slovenia, the most prosperous of Yugoslavia's breakaway republics, revels in its newfound independence, modernizing rapidly while turning a hungry eye toward the West. It has quickly separated itself from its neighbors, using liberal politics and a high GDP to gain entrance into highly sought-after trade and security alliances. For a country half Switzerland's size, Slovenia, on the "sunny side of the Alps," is also extraordinarily diverse: in a day, you can breakfast on an Alpine peak, lunch under the Mediterranean sun, and dine in a vineyard on the Pannonian plains.

**SLOVENIA AT A GLANCE**

**OFFICIAL NAME:** Republic of Slovenia

**CAPITAL:** Ljubljana (pop. 270,000)

**POPULATION:** 2 million

**LANGUAGE:** Slovenian

**CURRENCY:** 1 tolar (SIT) = 100 stotins

**RELIGION:** 71% Roman Catholic, 4% atheist, 25% other

**LAND AREA:** 20,256 km²

**GEOGRAPHY:** Mountains, valleys, and plateaus

**CLIMATE:** Mediterranean and continental

**BORDERS:** Austria, Croatia, Hungary, and Italy

**ECONOMY:** 60% Services, 35% Industry, 5% Agriculture

**GDP:** US$10,300 per capita

**EMERGENCY PHONE NUMBERS:** Ambulance 112, Fire 112, Police 113

**COUNTRY CODE:** 386

**INTERNATIONAL DIALING PREFIX:** 00

# HISTORY

**THE EARLY YEARS.** Originally inhabited by Celts and Illyrians, Slovenia was taken by the Roman Empire in the the first century BC. The **Alpine Slavs**, predecessors of the Slovenes, migrated to the Eastern Alps in the 6th century, absorbing the existing cultures. A Slavic kingdom emerged under **Samo** (623-658) but fell to the Franks after 748. Though the Slavs were assimilated by invading Magyar and Bulgarian tribes, the tribal duchy of **Carinthia**—precursor to modern Slovenia—survived.

**GERMANS AND HABSBURGS AND FRENCH, OH MY!** Following the fall of the Frankish Empire in the 10th century, Slovene lands were given to the Germans, and the Slovenes were reduced to serfdom. The kingdom was not secure, however, and the territory occupied by Slovene speakers changed hands frequently, falling briefly under Slavic rule in the 13th century when **Otakar II** of Bohemia tried to establish a Slavic empire. Between 1278 and 1335, all but Istria (nabbed by Venice), fell to the **Habsburgs.** The Habsburg rule, while stifling, spared Slovenes Turkish invasion, per-

Slovenia

mitting them to reach high levels of literacy and technological development, and to begin develop a market economy. It was also during this time that the Slovenes were introduced to Roman Catholicism. Habsburg rule lasted for several centuries, although in the early 1800s some of the Slovene lands were overrun by Napolean I's armies. This period, during which the French supported such ideas as making Slovene the official language, contributed to the growing hunger for a national identity in the latter half of the century. This desire for a voice was marked by the formation of the first Slovene political parties and the codification of the Slovene language.

**FIGHTING FOR FREEDOM.** After the collapse of the Austro-Hungarian Dual Monarchy (see **Hungary: History**, p. 309), Slovenia agreed to join the newly formed Kingdom of Serbs, Croats, and Slovenes (renamed **Yugoslavia**—Land of the South Slavs—in 1929). The new state was too weak, however, to withstand the attacks of Hitler's armed forces during **World War II.** When Yugoslavia fell in 1941, Slovenia was partitioned among Germany, Italy, and Hungary. Slovene resistance groups were formed and united under the **Slovene National Liberation Front**, which soon joined the Yugoslav partisan army of **Josip Broz Tito**. Led by the Communist party, the army was eventually recognized by the British and Americans as an ally.

**GAINING A VOICE.** By the end of World War II, partisans had occupied all of Yugoslavia, and once again a unified state emerged as the Communist nation of Yugoslavia (1945), of which Slovenia became a republic. Tito liquidated Slovene politicians and leaders who failed to cooperate with the Communists; tens of thousands of Slovene patriots were murdered at **Kočevje.** (The 50th anniversary of this mass murder was commemorated in 1995, ending five decades of silence.) Slovenia's economy, politics, and society adhered to the Stalinist model, but after a rift formed between Tito and Stalin in 1948, Yugoslavia began to introduce a market economy. Slovenia was soon acknowledged as the economically strongest and most Westernized of the Yugoslav republics.

Political dissent built up in the 1970s and 80s though, as long-stifled ethnic conflicts were increasingly recognized. As a result, in April 1990 Slovenia held the first contested elections in Yugoslavia since before the war, empowering a center-right coalition that called for independence. On June 25, 1991, Slovenia seceded from the federation, and in 1992 Slovenia was recognized by the European Community.

# POLITICS

Under the December 1991 constitution, the country is headed by a popularly-elected **president**, who serves a five-year term; **Milan Kučan** won re-election in February 1997. In addition to commanding the armed forces, the president nominates the **executive**, which consists of a **prime minister** and cabinet ministers. The **legislative assembly** is comprised of 90 elected delegates, including an Italian and a Hungarian speaker. The assembly is advised by a 40-member non-partisan state council.

In April 2000 Slovenia's prime minister **Janez Drnovsek**, of the **Liberal Democratic Party** (made up of former Communists), lost the majority in a confidence vote after his conservative coalition partner, the **People's Party**, decided to leave the government. The People's Party merged with the Christian Democrats to form **SLS & SKD Slovenian People's Party**. The country was without a government until June 7, when parliament approved the center-right cabinet proposed by Prime Minister-designate **Andrej Bajukin**. On June 8, Bajukin announced that the three goals of his cabinet are to hasten Slovenia's entrance to the EU, to clear up any remaining issues with other countries from World War II, and to boost the confidence of Slovenes.

In addition to its anticipated membership in the EU, Slovenia has gained membership in international organizations such as the Council of Europe, the IMF, the World Bank, the World Trade Organization, and the Central Europe Free Trade Area. In 1999, Slovenia served as the non-permanent member of the UN Security Council. While NATO disappointed Slovenia by denying it membership in the organization's first round of expansion, the nation is preening itself for inclusion in the upcoming second round.

# CULTURE

| NATIONAL HOLIDAYS IN 2001 | |
| --- | --- |
| **January 1-2** New Year | **June 25** National Day |
| **February 8** Culture Day (Prešeren Day) | **August 15** Assumption |
| **April 15-16** Easter | **October 31** Reformation Day |
| **April 27** National Resistance Day (WWII) | **November 1** Remembrance Day |
| **May 1-2** Labor Day | **December 25** Christmas |
| **June 3** Pentecost | **December 26** Independence Day |

# LITERATURE AND ARTS

Slovenian literature and art dates back to the 11th century—most early works were purely devotional and religious. In the 19th century, however, Slovene literature emerged as an important national art form with the codification of the language by **Jernej Kopitar** in 1843 and the writings of the Romantic poet **France Prešeren** (see **Ljubljana: Sights,** p. 746). Prešeren was instrumental in revitalizing Slovene literature through his use of Western European literary models in his patriotic poems. Throughout the later **Realist** period (1848-1899), writers such as **Fran Eriaveć** focused on folkloric themes with a patriotic flavor; the first Slovene novel, *The Tenth Brother (Deseti brat)*, by **Josip Jurčič**, was published in 1866.Č

In the first half of the 20th century, **Modernist** prose flowered in **Ivan Čankar's** 1904 *The Ward of Our Lady of Mercy (Hisa Marije pomocnice)*, while **Expressionism** showed the social and spiritual tensions brought on by World War I in the poetry of **Tone Seliskar, Miran Jarc,** and **Anton Vodnik,** and in the plays of **Slavko Grum.** Coincident with the Modernist and Expressionist movements in Slovene literature, architect **Jože Plečnik** was a major figure in the development of **Art Deco.** While he designed buildings in both Vienna and Prague, his masterpiece was his transformation of his hometown, Ljubljana, from a provincial city to a cosmopolitan capital (see **Ljubljana: Sights,** p. 746).

SLOVENIA

The advent of Soviet **Socialist Realism** crushed many of the modern and avant-garde trends that had diversified the Slovene literary movement. At the end of the 1970s, a number of Slovenian writers, including **Vitomis Zupan**, **Igor Torkar**, and **Jože Snoj**, wrote books dealing with Stalinism in Slovenia. The Postmodern trend of the 1980s showed up in the so-called **"Young Slovenian Prose"** movement, which had its strongest representation in short prose pieces. Today, two prominent authors in international literature include poet **Tomaž Šalamun** and Ljubljana-based cultural critic and essayist **Slavoj Žižek**.

# FOOD AND DRINK

For mouth-watering homestyle cooking, try a *gostilna* or *gostišče* (interchangeable words for a restaurant with a country flavor, although a *gostišče* usually also rents rooms). Start with *jota*, a soup with potatos, beans and sauerkraut. *Svinjska pečenka* (roast pork) is tasty, but **vegetarians** should look for *štruklji*—large, slightly sweet dumplings eaten as a main dish. In a pinch, vegetarians can always rely on the abundant pizzerias for meatless dishes. Slovenes savor their desserts; one of their favorites is *potica*, which consists of a sheet of pastry that is spread with a rich filling and rolled up. The most popular filling is made from walnuts.

The country's **winemaking** tradition dates from antiquity. *Renski Rizling* and *Šipon* are popular whites. Slovenia produces many unique red wines, including the light *Cviček*, from the central region, and the potent *Teran*, from the coast. The art of brewing is centuries old here as well; good beers include *Laško* and *Union*. For something stronger, try *žganje*, a strong fruit brandy. The most enchanting alcoholic concoction is *Viljamovka*, distilled by monks who know the secret of getting a full pear inside the bottle. **Tap water** is drinkable everywhere.

# CUSTOMS AND ETIQUETTE

In general, **business hours** are Monday to Friday 8am-5pm, Saturday 8am-noon. Slovenians welcome foreigners to their country with open kitchens. If you are fortunate enough to be invited into someone's home, remember to bring an odd number of **flowers** for a lady. At restaurants and cafes, the bill is never split; one person pays for everything, and any payment redistribution can be attended to later. **Tipping** is not expected, although rounding up will be appreciated; 10% is sufficient for good service. **Homosexuality** is legal and supported by student groups, but is still not common and may elicit unsure or unfriendly reactions from middle-aged or elderly Slovenes. Slovenes dress well; **clothing** is expensive except for a period during the summer when some stores are forced to have sales according to government regulation. Topless bathing is not uncommon but nude bathing is. **Smoking** is accepted.

When **hiking**, there are a few strictly Slovenian rules of the road that everyone should know. Trails throughout Slovenia are marked with a white circle inside a red one; look for the blazing sign on trees and rocks. A bend in the trail may be marked by a bent red line. When trails separate, a sign usually indicates which one is headed where. In Slovenia, hikers always greet each other on the path. As old-timers will remind you, the person ascending the path should speak up first; respect belongs to those who have already seen the summit.

# LANGUAGE

**Slovene**, a Slavic language, employs the Latin alphabet. Most young people speak at least some **English**, but the older generation (especially in the Alps) is more likely to understand **German** (in the north) or **Italian** (along the Adriatic). You also might find some **Hungarian** in the East. Many cities along the Italian border are officially bilingual. The tourist industry is generally geared toward Germans, though most tourist office employees speak English.

When speaking Slovene, "č" is pronounced "ch," "š" is "sh," and "ž" is pronounced is "zh." "R" is at times a vowel (pronounced "er"), while "v" and "l" turn silent at the strangest times. Phrases essential to winning the natives over include *"dober dan"* ("good day"), *"prosim"* ("please"), and *"hvala lepa"* ("thank you very much.") The words most frequently used in this chapter are *"Stari Grad"* ("Old Town"), *"Trg"* ("square"), *"cesta"* ("road"), *"cerkev"* ("church"), *"most"* ("bridge"), and *"lekarna"* ("pharmacy").

| ENGLISH | SLOVENIAN | PRONOUNCIATION |
|---|---|---|
| Yes/no | Ja/Ne | yah/neh |
| Please | Prosim | PROH-seem |
| Thank you | Hvala | HVAA-lah |
| Hello | Zdravo | ze-drah-voh |
| Good-bye | Na svidenje | nah SVEE-den-yeh |
| *Sorry*/Excuse me | Oprostite | oh-proh-stee-teh |
| Help! | Na pomoč! | nah poh-MOHCH |
| How much does this cost? | Koliko to stane? | koh-lee-koh toh stah-neh |
| Do you have...? | Ali imate...? | AA-li i-MAA-te |
| Do you speak English? | Govorite angleško? | go-vo-REE-teh ang-LEH-shko |
| I don't understand | Ne razumem. | neh rah-ZOO-mehm |
| May I see the room? | Lahko vidim sobo? | lah-KOH VEE-dihm SOH-boh |
| Will you tell me when to get off? | Mi lahko prosim poveste, kdaj moram izstopiti? | mih lah-KOH PROH-sihm poh-VEH-steh kdaay MOH-rahm EES-toh-pih-tih |
| I want a ticket to... | Rad(a) bi vozovnico za... | rat (RAA-dah) bih voh-ZOW-nih-tsoh zah |
| Where is the *bathroom*/nearest *telephone booth* public phone/ center of town? | Kje je najbližja telefonska go vorilnica/center mesta? | kyeh ye nay-BLEEZH-yah teh-leh-FOHN-skah/TSEHN-tehrr MEH-sta |

# ADDITIONAL READING

Jill Benderly's *Independent Slovenia: Origins, Movements, Prospects*, a volume of essays explores the peaceful transition to Slovenian independence with writings from economic theorists, Slovenia's foreign minister, punk sociologists, and radical feminists. Native Slovene Roman Latković's travelogue *Bewitching Istria: A Never-Ending Story* delivers a more sensual approach to Slovenia. Of course, no reading about Slovenia is complete without a foray into the wacky yet brilliant world of cultural critic Slavoj Žižek. *The Žižek Reader* offers an entertaining introduction to the work of this flamboyant essayist.

# TRAVELING ESSENTIALS

Australian, Canadian, Irish, New Zealand, UK, and US citizens can visit visa-free for up to 90 days. South Africans need visas (3-month single-entry or 5-day transit US$26; 3-month multiple entry US$52). Apply by mail or in person in your home country (see **Essentials: Embassies and Consulates,** p. 18); call the embassy in your country for an application. Processing takes four business few days and requires your passport, fee in the form of a money order, and a self-addressed, stamped (certified mail) envelope. Visas cannot be purchased at any border crossing. There is no entry fee required at the border. The easiest way to enter or exit Slovenia is to take a direct bus or train from Ljubljana to the capital city of the neighboring country.

# TRANSPORTATION

**BY PLANE.** There are three international airports, but commercial flights all arrive at **Ljubljana Airport,** which has regular bus service to Ljubljana 23km away. The national carrier **Adria Airways** (☎ (386) 61 136 2499; fax 61 323 356) flies to European capitals. Flying into the country is the best option if you are traveling a long distance; otherwise, trains are better for connecting from other major cities.

**BY TRAIN.** When entering the country, you might consider flying to **Vienna** and taking a train to Ljubljana if time is not an issue, as flights to Vienna tend to be cheaper than those to Ljubljana. Trains from Vienna to Ljubljana are infrequent and the trip lasts 6½ hours and tickets cost around US$50 one-way. Otherwise, trains are cheap, clean, and reliable. You can usually find a seat on local trains, though it's best to avoid peak commuting hours near Ljubljana. Round-trip tickets are 20% cheaper than two one-way tickets. For most international destinations, travelers under 26 can get a 20% discount; check at the Ljubljana station (look for the **BIJ-Wasteels** logo). First and second class do not differ much; save your money and opt for the latter. ISIC holders get 30% off domestic tickets. In both cases ask for a *"popust"* (discount). *"Vlak"* means train, *"prihodi vlakov"* means arrivals, and *"odhodi vlakov"* means departures. Schedules usually list trains by direction; look for trains that run *dnevno* (daily).

**BY BUS.** Buses are roughly 25% more expensive than trains, but run to some otherwise inaccessible places in the mountains. Tickets are sold at the station or on board; put your luggage in the passenger compartment if it's not too crowded. All large backpacks cost 220Sit extra.

**BY CAR, BOAT, THUMB, OR BIKE.** For those traveling by car, the **Automobile Association of Slovenia's** emergency telephone number is 987. A regular **hydrofoil** service also runs between **Venice** and **Portorož.** *Let's Go* does not recommend **hitchhiking,** which is extremely uncommon in Slovenia. If not traveling by bus or train, most Slovenes transport themselves by bike. Nearly every town has a bike rental office.

# TOURIST SERVICES AND MONEY

| CURRENCY | | |
|---|---|---|
| US$1 = 233SIT (SLOVENIAN TOLARS) | | 100SIT = US$0.43 |
| CDN$1 = 158SIT | | 100SIT = CDN$0.63 |
| UK£1 = 341SIT | | 100SIT = UK£0.29 |
| IR£1 = 266SIT | | 100SIT = IR£0.38 |
| AUS$1 = 134SIT | | 100SIT = AUS$0.74 |
| NZ$1 = 100SIT | | 100SIT = NZ$1.00 |
| SAR1 = 33.5SIT | | 100SIT = SAR2.98 |
| DM1 = 107SIT | | 100SIT = DM0.93 |

**Tourist offices** are located in most major cities and tourist spots. The staff are generally helpful, speak English and German, provide basic information, and assist in finding accommodations. The main tourist organization in Slovenia is **Kompas.**

The national currency is the Slovenian **tolar** (Sit). Currency prices tend to be stable and are set in Deutschmarks (DM) rather than dollars (US$). The currency rates above are those for September 2000; Slovenian **inflation** is around 6% so expect some change in prices over the next year. **Banks** are usually open Monday-Friday 8am-5pm and Saturday 8-11am. Rates vary, but tend to be better in major cities. Some establishments charge no commission, a fact reflected by worse rates; post offices have the worst of all. Most **exchange offices,** which can be quicker and easier, offer fair rates. Almost everyone—from restaurants and shops to train stations—accepts major **credit cards,** including AmEx, but the most widely endorsed is Mastercard, followed by Visa. AmEx **traveler's cheques** and **Eurocheques** are accepted most places. There's a 20% **value-added tax,** but for purchases over 9000Sit, it is refundable at the border (ask the store salesperson for a tax-free check). There are many 24hr. **ATMs** around the country, though some may not accept foreign bank cards. You can, fortunately, withdraw money from bank tellers. Two major Slovenian banks are **Ljubljanska Banka** and **Gorenjska Banka.**

# HEALTH AND SAFETY

Slovenia's **climate** varies by region: Mediterranean near the Adriatic, Alpine in the mountains, moderately continental on the eastern plains, and pleasant everywhere in summer, though snow may strew the Alps as late as June. A Slovene proverb says that if it doesn't rain on May 15, it will rain for 40 days afterwards, but don't use this as a reason to avoid spring visits—even the groundhog isn't always right.

   **Crime** rates, especially for violent crime, are very low in Slovenia. Even in the largest cities, friendly drunks and bad drivers are the greatest public menace. The occasional unwanted ogles and pick-up lines do occur. **Medical facilities** are of high quality, and most have English-speaking doctors. There is also a hospital for foreigners in Ljubljana (see **Ljubljana: Practical Information,** p. 743). UK citizens receive free medical care with a valid passport; other foreigners must pay cash. **Pharmacies** are also stocked to Western standards, although brand names will be different; ask for *obliž* (band-aids), *tamponi* (tampons), and *vložki* (sanitary-pads) in Slovenian. **Gay hotlines** include **Galfon** (☎ 132 40 89; open daily 7-10pm) and **Lesebitra** (minus26@hotmail.com). A hotline for **women and minorities** is ☎ 133 05 89 (answered M-F 4-6pm, Th 10am-noon).

# ACCOMMODATIONS AND CAMPING

At the height of tourist season prices are steep, service slow, and rooms scarce. The seaside, packed as early as June, is claustrophobic in July and August. Tourists also tend to swarm to the mountains during these months. **Youth hostels** and **student dormitories** are cheap, but are generally open only in summer (June 25-Aug. 30). While hostels are often the cheapest (2500-3000Sit) and most fun option, **private rooms** are the only cheap option on the coast and at Lake Bohinj. Prices for private rooms vary according to location, but rarely exceed US$30, and most rooms are good. Inquire at the tourist office or look for *Zimmer frei* or *Sobe* signs on the street. *Pensions* are pricey. **Hotels** fall into five categories (L (deluxe), A, B, C, and D) and are expensive. **Campgrounds** can be crowded, but are in excellent condition. Bungalows are rare. **Reserve** all accommodations at least three days in advance.

# KEEPING IN TOUCH

**Mail** is the cheapest means of communication. **Post offices** are usually open Monday to Friday 8am-7pm and Saturday 8am-noon, with night and Sunday service in larger cities. To send letters via airmail, ask for *letalsko*. Air mail takes 1-2 weeks to reach North America, Australia, New Zealand, and South Africa. To the US, letters cost 105Sit and postcards cost 95Sit; to the UK 100Sit for letters, 90Sit for postcards; to Australia and New Zealand 110Sit and 100Sit. Mail can be received general delivery through **Poste Restante.** Address envelope as follows: Andrea (First name) VOLFOVÁ (LAST NAME), POSTE RESTANTE, Ljubljanska 4 (Post office address), Bled (City) 4260 (Postal code), SLOVENIA. While at the post office, purchase a magnetic **phone card** (750Sit per 50 impulses, which yields 1½min. to the US). Cards are also available at kiosks and gas stations. Dial 901 for English-speaking operator-assisted collect calls. If you want to call collect from a post office, say *"P.O. pogovor."* Calling the US is expensive (over US$6 per min.). If you must, try the phones at the post office and pay when you're finished.

**PHONE CHANGES.** Slovenia is in the process of changing all of its phone numbers. Although we've accounted for as many as possible, many will continue to change through 2001, and therefore some of the numbers we list will be wrong. When you call a changed number, a voice will tell you in both English and Slovenian what the new number is.

# LJUBLJANA ☎(0)1

Though you can walk from one end to the other in under 30 minutes, Ljubljana (pop. 276,000) is lively capital city. An earthquake in 1895 leveled everything but a few Roman walls, and the city has been rebuilding with considerable vigor ever since. The beautifully organized city center, with columns and pyramidal structures, was designed by Slovenia's very own Josip Plečnik (see **Literature and Arts,** p. 738), who weaved into it his entire architectonic genius. With students comprising 10% of the city's population, you won't have to go very far for nightlife, though clubbing fans might find more to do on the coast. Ljubljana's entertainment scene focuses more on its many lively cafes and summer music and arts festivals. To truly enjoy the city, slow your step a bit and watch people stroll along the green Ljubljanica River as it ambles along.

## ■ ORIENTATION

The curvy **Ljubljanica River** is enveloped by Central Ljubljana, with the picturesque **Stare Miasto** (Old Town) on one bank and 19th- and 20th-century buildings on the other. After a half-mile from either bank the rich historic area turns into a concrete business district. The **train** and **bus stations** are on **Trg Osvobodilne Fronte (Trg O.F. or O.F. Square).** To get to the city center, stand with your back to the train station, turn right and then left onto **Miklošiceva cesta** and follow it to **Prešernov Trg,** the main square. After crossing the **Tromostovje** (Triple Bridge), you'll see Stare Miasto at the castle hill's base; the **tourist office** is on the left at the corner of Stritarjeva and Adamič-Lundrovo nabr. To reach **Slovenska,** walk up **Čopova** from Prešernov Trg.

## ▐ TRANSPORTATION

**Flights:** A **shuttle** (mobile ☎(0)4 087 77 66) goes from major hotels to the **airport** (mobile ☎(0)4 202 27 00), 23km away in Brnik. Reservations, made through hotels, are required. 3500Sit, round-trip 4000Sit. You can also take the **public bus** from the #28 stop (1hr., 510Sit). Buses depart M-F every hr. 6:10am-8:10pm, Sa-Su at 6:10am and then every hr. 9:10am-7:10pm. **Adria Airways,** Gosposvetska 6 (☎231 33 12; fax 232 16 68); **Austrian Airlines,** Dunajska 107 (☎436 12 83; fax 436 12 82); **Lufthansa,** Gosposvetska 6 (☎232 66 69; fax 232 66 72); **Swissair,** Dunajska 156 (☎569 10 10; fax 569 10 00); **British Airways,** Slovenska 56 (☎300 10 00; fax 300 10 39).

**Trains:** Trg O.F. 6 (☎291 33 32 and 291 33 80). To: **Zagreb, CRO** (2½hr., 7 per day, 2400Sit); **Trieste, ITA** (3hr., 3 per day, 4000Sit); **Vienna, AUS** (5-6hr., 2 per day, 10,500Sit); **Venice, ITA** (6hr., 3 per day, 6000Sit); **Munich, GER** (6-7hr., 3per day, 11,700Sit); and **Budapest, HUN** (9¼hr., 2 per day, 9000Sit).

**Buses:** Trg O.F. 4 (☎234 46 06), in front of the trains. To: **Rijeka, CRO** (3hr., 3 per day, 2680Sit) and **Zagreb, CRO** (3hr., 3 per day, 2570Sit).

**Public Transportation:** Buses run until midnight. Drop 140Sit in change in the box beside the driver, or buy 100Sit tokens (*žetoni*) at post offices or kiosks. Daily (350Sit) and weekly (1650Sit) **passes** are sold at **Ljubljanski potniški promet,** Trdinova 3.

**Taxis:** ☎97 00 through 97 09, or catch one on the street. About 130Sit per km.

**Car Rental: Kompas Hertz,** Miklošiceva 11 (☎231 12 41). Open M-F 7am-8pm, Sa 7am-2pm.

**Bike Rental:** Popreil (☎306 12 05 and mobile ☎ (0)4 169 65 15) is a man who rents bikes via the **Cutty Sark Pub,** Knafljiev prehod 1, through the arch on Wolfova (☎125 14 77; open daily 9am-8pm) and **Maček Pub,** Krojaška 5 (☎125 37 91; open daily 9am-8pm) for 500Sit per hr., 2500Sit per day.

## ▐ PRACTICAL INFORMATION

**Tourist Office: Tourist Information Center (TIC),** Stritarjeva 1 (☎306 12 35 and 306 12 15; fax 306 12 04; pcl.tic-lj@ljubljana.si). Offers free **maps** and excellent brochures—including the useful *Ljubljana from A to Z* and *Events* (free)—and arranges accommodations. Open June-Sept. M-F 8am-8pm, Sa-Su 10am-6pm; Oct.-May M-F 8am-6pm, Sa-Su 10am-6pm. The **branch** at the train station (☎133 94 75) is open daily June-Sept. 8am-9pm; and Oct. M-F 10am-6pm.

**Budget Travel: Erazem,** Trubarjeva cesta 7 (☎433 10 76; fax 433 20 84). Student-oriented. Open June-Sept. M-F 10am-5pm, Sa 10am-1pm; Oct.-May M-F noon-5pm.

**Embassies and Consulates: Australia,** Trg Republike 3 (☎125 42 52). Open M-F 9am-1pm. **UK,** Trg Republike 3 (☎200 39 10; fax 125 01 74). Open M-F 9am-noon. **US,** Prešernova cesta (☎200 55 99; fax 200 55 55). Open M-F 9am-noon and 2-4pm.

**Currency Exchange:** *Menjalnice* abound. **Ljubljanska banka** has branches all over the city that **exchange currency** and cash **traveler's checks** for decent rates and no commission.

**ATMs:** Somewhat finicky 24hr. ATMs are all over the city, but the cards accepted vary widely. Maestro/Cirrus/MC machines are common, while Visa/Plus machines are slightly scarcer.

**American Express:** Trubarjeva 50 (☎433 20 28). Open M-F 8am-8pm.

**Luggage storage:** At the train station. Look for *"garderoba"* signs. 220Sit per day. 24hr.

**International Bookstore: MK-Knjigarna Konzorcij,** Slovenska 29 (☎241 06 50). Extensive selection of English-language books, as well as international magazines and newspapers. Open M-F 9am-7:30pm, Sa 9am-1pm.

**Laundromat: Tic,** Student Campus, Cesta 27. Aprila 31, Building 9 (☎257 43 97). Self-service. 1017Sit per 5kg load. Open M-F 8am-2pm and 4-7pm, Sa 8am-2pm.

**Hotlines:** For **women** (☎133 05 89; M-F 4-6pm and Th 10am-noon.) **Bisexual/Gay/ Lesbian, Galfon** (☎132 40 89; daily 7am-10pm).

**24hr. Pharmacy:** Miklošičeva 24 (☎31 45 58).

**Medical Assistance:** In an emergency, call **Bohoričeva Medical Centre,** Bohoričeva 4 (☎232 30 60), or **Klinični center,** Zaloška 7 (☎433 62 36 and 431 31 13).

**Telephones:** Around the post office and all over town. Magnetic phone cards available in post office and at newsstands (100 impulses for 1700Sit). There are 24hr. phones in the post office on Trg O.F., to the right of the train station.

**Internet Access: Cybercafe Podhod,** Plečnikov Podhod (☎121 41 00), between Maximarket and Kongresni Trg 2. Computers in the back; ask at the bar. 7Sit per min., 400Sit per hr. Open daily July-Aug. 7am-10pm, Sept.-June 7am-2pm. Also at **K-4** (see **Nightlife,** p. 748).

**Post Office:** Slovenska 32. **Poste Restante** held for 1 month at the counter labeled *"poštno ležeče pošiljke."* Open M-F 7am-8pm, Sa 7am-1pm.

**Postal code:** 1101.

# ACCOMMODATIONS

Ljubljana is not heavily touristed by backpackers, and therefore lacks true budget accommodations. On top of that, there is a nightly **tourist tax** (187Sit). Finding cheap accommodations is easier in July and August, when high school dormitories open their doors to tourists. The **TIC** (see **Tourist Office,** above) will help you find **private rooms.** (Singles 2200-3500Sit; doubles 4000-5500Sit.)

■ **Dijaški Dom Tabor (HI),** Vidovdanska 7 (☎31 60 69 and 32 10 67; fax 32 10 60). Clean, with a friendly staff. Popular with backpackers. 180 beds in doubles and triples with shared bath. Laundry 1000Sit. Free Internet access 6am-10pm at reception. Luggage storage. Reception 24hr. Check-out 11am. Open June 25-Aug. 28. 2263Sit with student ID. Generous breakfast included.

**Dijaški Dom Bežigrad,** Kardeljeva pl. 28 (☎34 28 67; fax 34 28 64). From the train station, cross the street and turn right. Walk to the intersection with Slovenska and take bus #6 (Čmuče) or #8 (Ježica) and get off at "Stadion" (5min.). Walk 1 block to the crossroads; there you'll see a sign for reception. Buildings are ugly, rooms are snug but clean and comfortable. Reception 24hr. Negotiable check-out 8am. Open July 1-Aug. 25. Singles 2813Sit, with shower 3313Sit; doubles 1813Sit, 2813Sit; triples 1813Sit, 2213Sit.

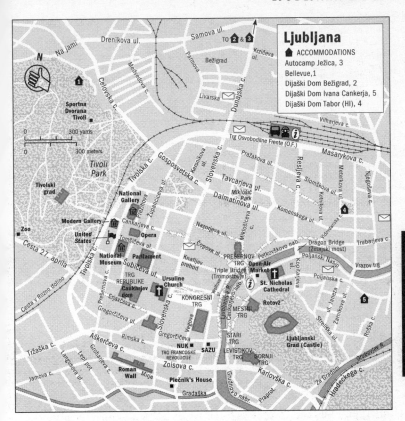

**Dijaški Dom Ivana Cankarja,** Poljanska 26-28 (☎474 86 00; fax 432 03 69). Turn right and go into the courtyard. Reception is on the other side of the complex; pretty good location with decent dorm accommodations. Reception 24hr. Relaxed check-out 11am. Open June 25-Aug. 30. Singles 3213Sit; doubles 2613Sit per person; triples 2413Sit. Students 10% off. Breakfast included.

**Bellevue,** Pod gozdom 12 (☎133 40 49; fax 133 40 57). From the train station, turn right and follow Trg O.F. to the crossroads. Cross the street, continue on Tivolska, then take a right onto Celovska. Walk along the park on the left side of the street to the parking lot; from there, follow the curving street uphill (20min.). Gloomy but nicely situated in Tivoli Park. Shared bath. Reception 24hr. Reservations recommended. Singles 4113Sit; doubles 7113Sit; triples 10,813Sit. Breakfast included.

**Autocamp Ježica,** Dunajska 270 (☎568 39 13; fax 568 3912; acjezica@siol.net). Follow directions to Dijaški dom Bežigrad (see above), but get off at "Ježica," where you'll see a turnaround on the left. Reception 24hr. Relaxed check-out 1pm. Reservations recommended. 637Sit per adult with tent. Bungalow singles 5407Sit; doubles 8507Sit; triples 12,807Sit.

# 🍴 FOOD

The cheapest places to eat are **cafeterias,** where university students cash in their government-subsidized *studentske bone* (student tickets), but many good restaurants and pizzerias are also at hand in the Old Town. Traditional Slovenian food is typically a mix of Austrian fare and Italian pasta, and several good establishments

feature this eclectic taste. The largest **grocery store** in town is located in the basement of the Maximarket on Trg Republike. (Open M-F 9am-8pm, Sa 8am-5pm.)
There's a huge **outdoor market** at Vodnikov Trg next to the cathedral. (Open M-Sa
9am-6pm, Su 9am-2pm.) Fast food stands abound, featuring such favorites as the
*burek*—fried dough filled with meat *(mesni)*, cheese *(sirov)*, or a pizza mixture—
and the rare but present horseburger *(konji burger)*, made out of, yes, horse meat.

**Pizzeria Foculus,** Gregorčičeva 3 (☎21 56 43), between Slovenska and the river. Tons
of huge pizzas with both vegetarian and carnivorous combinations; if you're brave try
the Hawaiian pizza, with chocolate and whipped cream. 660-1170Sit. Open M-F 10am-
midnight, Sa-Su noon-midnight.

**Gostilna Pri Pavli,** Stari Trg 21. Serves a mean *Ljubljanski zrzek* (steak Ljubljana style,
1200Sit), spaghetti with mushrooms (650Sit), and "natural steak" (which is actually
chicken; 1000Sit), in a boxy front room. Open M-F 7am-10pm, Sa 7am-3pm.

**Kitajska Restavracija Šanghaj,** Poljanska 14 (☎433 80 54). This is good Chinese food
in a land without many establishments of its kind. Soups 300-350Sit, main dishes 980-
1100Sit. Open daily 11am-11pm.

**Cafeteria Maximart,** Trg Republike, in the same building as Maximart. Excellent food in
a friendly, dirt-cheap, student-only place. Salad, soup, main dish, and dessert all for
1200Sit. Open M-F 9am-7pm, Sa 9am-4pm.

**Samsara,** Petkovško nab. A huge array of ice cream concoctions (100-800Sit) and
mixed drinks (500-750Sit), as well as half-sandwiches (400-450Sit) in a fun outdoor
setting by the river. Summer weekends are livened by nighttime musical performances.
Open daily Apr. 15-Oct. 10 9am-midnight.

## ◎ SIGHTS

One way to see the city is to meet in front of the city hall *(rotovž)*, Mestni Trg 1, for
the 2½ hour **walking tour** in English and Slovene. (Daily June-Sept. 5pm; Oct.-May Su
11am. 700Sit, students 500Sit. Buy tickets from the guide.) In front of the city hall sits
a fantastic **fountain,** wrought by local master Francesco Robba in 1751 and embellished with allegorical sculptures of three rivers—the Ljubljanica, Sava, and Krka.

**PREŠEREN SQUARE.** A short walk from the city hall down Stritarjeva and across
the Triple Bridge leads to the main square, Prešernov Trg. The square was named
for celebrated Slovenian poet France Prešeren, whose statue stands here (see **Literature and Arts,** p. 738 and **Model Indecency,** below). The square is dominated by the
Neoclassical **Franciscan Church** (Frančiškanska cerkev) built in the 17th century
*(closed 12:30-3pm).* Robba also crafted the impressive altar inside.

---

**MODEL INDECENCY** After an earthquake in 1895, Ljubljana hur-
ried to rebuild itself. Then-mayor Ivan Hribar, responsible for much of the present city's
appearance, ordered the large statue of Prešeren and his (nude) muse that now
adorns Prešeren Trg erected around the turn of the 19th century. Upon seeing the muse
in all her naked splendor, the bishop of St. Nicholas was horrified and commanded
that the statue wear a tarp to cover her breasts and preserve her decency. After two
years, Ivan won, and the breasts again saw the light of day.

---

**TRIPLE BRIDGE.** (Tromostovje.) This bridge is an attraction in itself. It dates
from the 1930s, when revered architect Josip Plečnik (see **Literature & Arts,** p. 738)
modernized the old Špitalski most by supplementing the stone construction with
two footbridges. They now provide a majestic entrance to Old Ljubljana.

**ST. NICHOLAS CATHEDRAL.** Cross the bridge back to the Old Town and take a
left along the water to walk by the gorgeous arcades, also designed by Plečnik, that
form part of the nearby market. On your right, the cathedral *(stolnica)* occupies
the site of an old Romanesque church. Its location was originally where fishermen

and townsfolk threw garbage into the Ljubljanica. When the litterers were forced by law to live on the very banks they had defiled, they built a small chapel dedicated to their patron, St. Nicholas. Today's cathedral dates from the early 18th century; little original artwork remains, but visitors can still admire the 15th-century Gothic *Pietà*, the impressive triple organ, and the gold leaf trim. *(Closed noon-3pm.)*

**DRAGON BRIDGE.** (Zmajski most.) At the end of Vodnikov trg, the Dragon Bridge spans the Ljubljanica with a pleasant view of the flowered banks and the Triple Bridge. Built in 1901 to replace the old "Butcher's Bridge," it was originally named after Emperor Franz Jozef, but the locals never accepted it as such; the dragons of Ljubljana's coat of arms, which adorn the bridge, gave it its current name.

**LJUBLJANA CASTLE.** (Ljubljanski Grad.) On the opposite side of Vodnikov trg, the narrow path Studentovska leads uphill to Ljubljana Castle. The castle dates from at least 1144, but was almost entirely destroyed by an earthquake in 1511; the present buildings date from the 16th and 17th centuries, but the concrete slabs used in restoration significantly dampen the overall effect. Aside from the great view offered by the castle's tower, the structure looks more majestic from the Old Town and from the grounds surrounding it. *(Open June-Sept. 10am until dark; Oct.-May 10am-5pm. Free temporary exhibit June-Sept. Tu-Su 11am-7pm. Tower 200Sit, students 150 Sit.)*

**OTHER SIGHTS.** Back and across the bridge on Prešernov trg, turn left on Wolfova and continue as it becomes Gosposka to reach the gray and orange **National University Library** (Narodna in Univerzitetna Knjižnica), built by the omnipresent Plečnik, and connected to the ruins of a Roman wall on **French Revolution Square** (Trg Francoske Revolucije). The square and its environs were once occupied by the Teutonic Knights; the neighborhood **Križanke,** the Slovene translation of their name, still commemorates them. In the square, the Knights set up a monastery, which was abandoned in the 18th century. It was restored under Plečnik's guidance, and now hosts music, theater, and dance performances for the **Ljubljana International Summer Festival.** *(Mid-July-Sept.; see Entertainment, below.)*

Behind the Ursuline Church on Slovenska is **Trg Republike,** home to the Parliament, the colossal Maximarket, and the even-bigger **Cankarjev dom,** the city's cultural center, which has the excellent **Galerija CD,** featuring both local Slovenian artists and Western masters. *(Open Tu-Su 10am-7pm, Su 10am-2pm. 500Sit, students 300Sit.)* Nearby, on the corner of Cankarjeva and Prešernova, stands one of Ljubljana's most notable structures: The **Church of Cyril and Methodius** (Crkva Ciril in Metodja), the only Serbian Orthodox church in the country. *(Open Tu-Su 2-6pm. Free.)*

# 🏛 MUSEUMS

Most of Ljubljana's museums cluster around the Slovenian Parliament near Trg Republike. All are closed on Monday.

**▨ The Plečnik Collection** (Plečnikova zbrika), Karunova 4 (☎283 50 67; fax 283 50 66). Part of the Architectural Museum (Architekturni muzej). Walk up Slovenska, turn left on Zoisova, then right onto Emonska. Cross the bridge; the museum lies behind the church. In a house that Plečnik built for himself, this museum chronicles the ascetic life and work of this genius. Open Tu and Th 10am-2pm or by appointment 1 week in advance. Guided tours only; available in English. 600Sit, students 300Sit.

**National Museum** (Narodni Muzej), Muzejska 1 (☎214 44 72). Detailed temporary exhibits on archaeology, culture, and Slovenian history dating back to Roman times. The Museum of Natural History upstairs showcases a collection of birds and geology exhibits. Open Tu-W and F-Su 10am-6pm, Th 10am-8pm. Temporary exhibits 700Sit, students 500Sit. Natural History Museum 300Sit, students 300Sit; Su free.

**Modern Gallery** (Moderna Galerija), Cankarjeva 15 (☎251 41 01). A good-sized collection of 20th-century experimental Slovenian paintings and sculptures. Open June-Aug. Tu-Sa 11am-7pm, Su 3-7pm; Sept.-May Tu-Sa 10am-6pm. 1200Sit, students 600Sit.

SLOVENIA

**National Gallery** (Narodna Galerija), Cankarjeva 20 (☎241 54 34). Houses portraits and impressionist paintings from the 17th and 18th centuries as well as carved religious icons from as far back as 1270. Open Tu-Su 10am-6pm. 700Sit, students 500Sit; Sa afternoons free.

**Tivoli Castle** (Tivolski Grad), Pod turnom 3 (☎22 56 32). From Cankerjeva, follow Jakopičevo sprehajališče in Tivoli Park. Home to the International Center of Graphic Art, the castle features temporary exhibits and hosts the International Biennial of Graphic Art. Open Tu-Sa 10am-6pm, Su 10am-1pm. 200Sit, students 100Sit.

## ♫ ✾ ENTERTAINMENT AND FESTIVALS

Just as neighboring Zagreb's calendar is full of fairs, Ljubljana's is packed with festivals, including the **International Jazz Festival** in early June; the vaguely titled **International Summer Festival** in July and August, a conglomeration of musical, operatic, and theatrical performances; and the **Ljubljana International Film Festival** (LIFF) in November. **Slovene Music Days** gets it all started in mid-April. Most festivals take place in **Cankarjev dom**, Prešernova 10 (☎425 81 21), the major concert and congress hall, or the outdoor **Križanke Summer Theatre, Festival Ljubljana**, Trg Francoske revolucije 1 (☎426 43 40).

Cankarjev dom also hosts the **Slovene Symphony Orchestra.** (Oct.-June. Box office in the basement of Maximarket. Tickets 1000-3000Sit.) The **opera house**, Župančičeva 1, hosts performances from September to June. (☎426 45 49. Tickets 1000-3000Sit.) **Tivoli Hall**, a sports arena in the center of Tivoli Park, hosts basketball, hockey, and rock concerts. Inquire about these and all other events at TIC (see **Tourist Office,** p. 743) or Festival Ljubljana (see above).

## ⬧ NIGHTLIFE

If Ljubljana's cultural options don't suit your fancy, join its large student population at the cafes or bars on **Trubarjeva, Stari Trg,** and **Mestni Trg.**

■ **Casa del Papa,** Celovška 54a (☎134 31 58). A "clean, well-lighted place" that pays homage to Hemingway with its decor as well as the Spanish beats from the club downstairs. Too highbrow for the student crowd. Beer (0.25L 280Sit), coffee (140Sit), and sandwiches (400-600Sit). Open daily 8pm-5am.

■ **Joe Peñas Cantina Y Bar,** Cankarjeva 6 (☎121 58 00). Fourteen *tequilas de la casa* adorn the mantle behind the bar, including banana and coffee. The frozen strawberry *margaritas* will keep you looking for your parrot all night long (750Sit). Open M-Th 10am-1am, F-Sa 10am-2am, Su noon-11pm.

■ **Le Petit Café,** Trg Francoske revolucije 4 (☎12 64 88). Strategically located next to the university library, this Francophile cafe is *the* student hangout in Ljubljana. Parisian music, of course, and quiet nights. The house specialty, white coffee *Le Petit* (250Sit), is superb. Cakes 400Sit. Open M-F 7:30am-11pm, Sa 9am-11pm, Su noon-11pm.

**K-4,** Kersnikova 4 (☎431 70 10). Student-run cafe/bar/club/cyber hangout. DJ or live music nightly. Remodeled annually and always hip. Sunday is gay night. Cover 200-1000Sit, students 40% off. Open Oct.-June daily 9am-4am; clubbing starts at 9pm.

## ⬧ DAYTRIPS FROM LJUBLJANA

### ŠKOCJANSKE CAVES ☎(0)67

*Trains run from Ljubljana to Divača en route to the coast (1½hr., 19 per day, 1300Sit). Signs from the station lead to the ticket booth (45min.). ☎63 28 40. Tours daily June-Sept. 10am-5pm; Oct-May 10am, 1pm, and 3pm. 1500Sit, students 700Sit.*

Far less crowded than other caves in the region, Škocjanske, UNESCO-protected since 1986, is an amazing system of caverns said to have inspired such literary greats as Dante Alighieri. The Silent Cave features enormous karst (limestone) formations including stalactites, stalagmites, and rock curtains. This impressive hall pales in comparison to120m-tall gorge the Reca River has carved underground.

**WHAT A WAY TO GO** In 1483 German knight Erazem Lueger stepped across the border between what were then the Hungarian and German empires, thereby disrespecting Friedrich III, the German emperor. As the legend goes he was outlawed, arrested, and sentenced to death. Miraculously, he escaped and holed up in Predjama Castle, an impenetrable fortress. Friedrich III sent his entire army after the errant knight, but the rocky fortress proved strong and the siege lasted longer than a year. What Friedrich didn't know was that Erazem had a secret escape tunnel by which he could obtain supplies. In fact, it looked like the besieged might even outlast his besiegers, who were growing weary of their encampment and were running low on food themselves. One of Erazem's servants, however, plotted to betray him. As the outhouse was separate from the castle, the deceitful servant agreed to light a candle when his lord answered nature's call that night. With a single catapult round, Friedrich won his revenge on the rebel knight, who died in the least honorable of positions.

## POSTOJNA CAVES ☎(0)67

*From Ljubljana, trains (1hr.10min., 19 per day, 740Sit) and buses (1hr., every 30min., 900Sit) go to Postojna on the way to Istria. The walk from the train station to the cave is 45min. Turn right on Kolodvorska cesta and follow its curves to the intersection with Ljubljanska cesta. Turn left and follow it to the center of town. Follow signs out of town to the cave. Open daily May-Sept. 9am-6pm, Oct.-Apr. 10am-4pm. Tours leave May-Sept. every hr., Oct.-Apr. every even hr. 2100Sit, students 1050Sit. English tours available.*

A single chamber of the 2 million-year-old Postojna Cave (Postojnska Jama) would warrant a trip here. The constant and abundant flow of tourists, however, has turned the caverns into more of an amusement park than anything else. If you can forget the large crowds, you'll be blown away by the astonishing array of plant-like stalagmites, alabaster curtains, gorges, rivers, and multi-colored stalactites. The obligatory tour covers only 20% of the cave's 27km and lasts an hour and a half; part is on foot and part on a train. The final "hall" of the tour has amazing acoustics and used to host occasional musical performances by Slovenian groups until the negative effects on the cave became apparent. Bring a jacket or rent a cloak for 300Sit; the temperature in the cave is a constant 8°C.

■ **Predjama Castle** (Predjamski grad), 9km from Postojna, is nearly impossible to reach but definitely worth the try. Carved into the face of a huge cliff, the former home of the robber baron Erazem is, as the brochure calls it, "almost arrogant in its simplicity." (☎751 52 60. Open daily June-Aug. 9am-7pm; May and Sept. 9am-6pm; Mar.-Apr. and Oct. 10am-5pm; Jan.-Feb. and Nov.-Dec. Tu-F 10am-4pm, Sa-Su 10am-5pm. 700Sit, students 350Sit.) On the last Sunday in August, a colorful **knights' tournament** takes place outside the castle. During the school year, two school buses go to **Bukovje**, 2km from the castle (15min., M-F, 300Sit). You can also walk from Postojna, and although hitchhikers may be accommodated, passing cars are rare. *Let's Go* does not recommend hitchhiking.

# THE JULIAN ALPS (JULIJSKE ALPE)

Arnold Rikli, founder of the Climatic Health Resort in Bled, declared that "water of course is good, air is even better, and light is the best." Covering northwest Slovenia, the Julian Alps fuse all three elements perfectly. Although they are not as high as their Austrian or Swiss cousins, they are no less stunning. Whether you're looking for wilderness near Lake Bohinj, authentic cultural festivities in Kranjska Gora, or the well-groomed spas in Bled, the Julian Alps offers something for every taste.

## BLED ☎(0)4

Bled (pop. 6000) has all the beauty and exquisite stillness of a postcard: green Alpine hills, snow-covered backdrop peaks, a translucent blue-green lake, and a stately castle poised above the panorama. People have been coming here for centu-

S L O V E N I A

ries to recuperate in spas or to lose themselves in the splendor of a warm summer evening. This internationally known resort is a paradise, but unlike other spas and resorts, is one where locals and vacationers mix, lending the nearly too-manicured surroundings an air of reality.

**⊡ TRANSPORTATION. Trains** arrive from Ljubljana (☎ 74 11 13, 1hr., 500Sit) on their way to **Salzburg, AUS** and **Munich, GER.** From there, take one of the frequent commuter buses (10min., 210Sit) to Bled. These stop on Ljubljanska and at the main **bus station** at Cesta Svobode 4 (☎ 74 11 14), closer to the hostel and the castle. **Buses** arrive from **Ljubljana** (1½hr., every hr., 980Sit). **Kompas Hertz,** Ljubljanska 7, **rents cars.** (☎/fax 574 15 19. Open June-Aug. M-F 7am-noon and 6-8pm, Sa 7am-1pm; Oct.-May M-F 7am-noon and 5-7pm, Sa 7am-1pm.)

**◪◪ ORIENTATION AND PRACTICAL INFORMATION.** Bled is spread around the lake, with most buildings clustered along the eastern shore. **Ljubljanska,** the main street, leads straight to the water. For tourist info, visit **Turističko društvo,** Cesta Svobode 15, where you can pick up a copy of the illustrated *Bled Tourist News* (500Sit) and a **map** of Bled. (☎574 11 22; fax 574 15 55. Open July-Aug. M-Sa 8am-10pm, Su 10am-10pm; June and Sept. M-Sa 8am-8pm, Su 10am-6pm; Nov.-Dec. 20 and Jan. 6-Feb. M-Sa 9am-5pm, Su 9am-2pm; Mar.-May, Oct., and Dec. 20-Jan. 5 M-Sa 8am-7pm, Su 9am-5pm.) **Gorenjska Banka,** Cesta Svobode 15, **exchanges currency,** cashes **traveler's checks,** and gives MC **cash advances.** (☎74 13 00. Open July-Aug. M-F 8am-6pm, Sa 8am-noon; Sept.-June M-F 9-11:30am and 2-5pm, Sa 8-11am.) **SKB Banka,** Ljubljanska 4, gives Visa **cash advances.** (Open M-F 8:30am-noon and 2-5pm.) A 24hr. Cirrus/Maestro/MC **ATM** sits outside Gorenjska Banka. An all-purpose **shopping center** is at Ljubljanska 4. In an **emergency,** call ☎575 40 00. There's a **pharmacy** at Prešernova 36. (☎74 15 22. Open M-F 7am-7:30pm, Sa 7am-1pm.) **Internet access** is available at the library, Ljubljanska 10. (☎575 16 00. 1000Sit per hr. Open M, Tu, and Th 8am-2pm, W 8am-7pm, F 2-7pm.) The **post office** is at Ljubljanska 10. (☎74 80 20. Open July-Aug. M-F 7am-8pm, Sa 7am-1pm; Sept.-June M-F 7am-7pm, Sa 7am-noon.) **Postal code:** 4260.

**⊓ ACCOMMODATIONS. Globtour,** Ljubljanska 7, can arrange **private rooms.** (☎74 18 21; fax 74 71 85; globtour.bled@g-kabel.si. July-Aug. singles 2600Sit; doubles 2000Sit per person. Sept.-Dec. 20 and Jan. 3-Apr. 15 2300Sit; 1700Sit. Apr. 16-June 20 2100Sit; 1500Sit. Tourist tax 154Sit per night. Stays under 3 nights 30% more.) You can also find a private room on your own; look for *Sobe* signs, particularly on Prešernova cesta and Ljubljanska. The newly renovated ▨ **Bledec Youth Hostel,** Grajska cesta 17, is a bright supernova in the backpacker's dark sky. Everything from the stylish wooden furniture to the private bathrooms and showers is brand new and squeaky clean. Facing away from the bus station, turn left and walk the steep street all the way to the top, bearing left at the fork. (☎74 52 50; fax 74 52 51. Sheets 400Sit. Breakfast 600Sit. Laundry 500Sit per 5kg. Reception in summer 7am-8pm; off-season 7am-7pm. Check-out 10am. Book 1 day in advance. 2200Sit; 10% off with ISIC, FIYTO, IYTC, or PZS-IYHF. Tourist tax 154Sit; 77Sit with student ID.) **Camping Zaka-Bled,** Kidričeva 10c, sits in a beautiful valley on the opposite side of the lake. Walk around the bus station and go downhill on Cesta Svobode. At the lake, turn left and walk 25 minutes to reach the camp. Bike rental (500Sit per hr., 1100Sit per 4hr., 1700Sit per day), sand volleyball, tennis and basketball courts, a store, a restaurant, and a beach are all available. (☎575 20 00; fax 575 20 02. Reception 24hr. Check-out 3pm. Open Apr.-Oct. 1400Sit per person. 10% off with student ID. Tourist tax 77Sit.)

**◳ FOOD.** Restaurant prices get higher the closer you move to the lake. **Gostilna pri Planincu,** Grajska cesta 8, near the bus station, gets packed around 9pm. The service is mediocre but the food rocks. (☎574 16 13. Main dishes 900-1800Sit; huge pizzas 650-870Sit. Open daily 9am-11pm.) **'P'hram,** Cesta Svobode 19a, serves Slovenian main courses for 550-1250Sit, including the delicious *kranjska klobasa* (Carolinian sausage; 700Sit). It's dark, but you can sit outside with a distant view of the lake. (☎79 12 80. Open daily 9am-11pm.) **Franci Šmon**, Grajska cesta 3, serves sweets and good coffee at plush booths or marble tabletops on the terrace. (☎74 16 16. Tortes 80-300Sit; coffee 120Sit. Open Th 8am-10pm, F-W 7:30am-10pm.) The path around Lake Bled has many benches and is perfect for picnicking. For **groceries,** go to **Žiliva Kranj** in the shopping complex on Ljubljanska cesta 13. (Open daily 6am-midnight.)

🖾 **SIGHTS.** A stroll around the lake's 6km perimeter should take about two hours. On the **island** in the center of the lake stands the stunning **Church of the Assumption** (Cerkev Marijinega Vnebovzetja). Today's structure dates from the 17th century, though a unique pre-Romanesque apse remains. There are many ways to approach the island. At the managed swimming area below the castle, you can rent a **boat.** (3-person 1000Sit per hr., 5-person 1500Sit; 1000Sit deposit.) You can also travel via gondola-style boats called **plentas** from various points along the shore. *Plentas* depart when they are full and the church opens when they arrive. (Round-trip 1½hr., 1500Sit.) Swimming to the island is permissible, but dripping in the church is not. Dive in from the beaches and docks on the side of the lake opposite Bled. The concrete swimming area has a waterslide. The water is warm in summer but becomes a massive ice-skating rink in winter. (Open daily 7am-7pm. 600Sit per day, students 500Sit; after noon 500Sit, 400Sit. Lockers 300Sit. Chair rental 200Sit.)

The 16th-century **Bled Castle** (Blejski grad) rises 100m above the water. The official path to the castle is on Grajska cesta, although there are several more pleasant hikes through the forest. From the lake, go to St. Martin's Church (Cerkev sv. Martin) on Kidričeva cesta and follow the path uphill. Another route begins behind the swimming area; follow blazes marked with a number "1" up the hill. Included in the entrance fee is the castle's splendid museum of the history of the Bled region with furniture, weapons, and the skeleton of an Alpine Slav woman from a nearby excavation site. (Castle open daily 8am-8pm. Museum open daily Mar.-Nov. 8am-8pm, Dec.-Feb. 9am-4pm. 600sit; students 500Sit.)

🖾 **ENTERTAINMENT.** From mid-June to September, **concerts** and traditional **cultural activities** take place on the island, on the promenade, and in the hotels. The tourist office carries a free monthly brochure filled with events from folklore shows to children's entertainment programs. The nightlife in Bled centers more around gambling and hotel lounges. The adolescent crowd at the **Brooklyn Club,** on the ground floor of the shopping complex on Ljubljanska cesta, occasionally takes a break from the bar to boogie. (1 free drink with 1000Sit cover. Open daily 9pm-4am.) A slightly older, local crowd gathers at the imaginatively named **Pub,** Cesta Svobode 8a, under Hotel Jelovica. (☎574 22 17. 0.3L Union 220Sit, 0.3L Guinness 400Sit. Open M-F 7am-midnight, Sa-Su noon-midnight.)

🖾 **OUTDOORS.** Numerous **hiking paths** snake from the lake into the neighboring hills. The **Bled-Rafting** booth, near the tourist office, rents **mountain bikes** and offers **whitewater rafting.** (Bikes 500Sit per hr., 1100Sit per half-day, 1700Sit per full day; rafting 3500sit per person, 2pm daily. Open daily 8am-7pm.) 🖾 **Blejski Vintgar,** a 1.6km gorge traced by the waterfalls, green pools, and rapids of the Radovna River, carves through the rocks of the **Triglav National Park** (Triglavski Narodni). A series of bridges wind through the gorge, leading to the 16m **Šum Waterfall,** which is unfortunately difficult to see from any vantage point on the hike. The walk through the gorge borders on paradise and the fresh air leaves you with a sense of euphoria. From Bled, go over the hill on Grajska cesta and turn right at the bottom. After 100m, turn left and follow the signs for Vintgar. You can also take one of the frequent buses to Podhom (200Sit) and follow the well-marked 1.5km route. From July to September, Alpetour runs a special bus. (☎574 11 14, 9:30am, 250Sit.) Once at the waterfall, either return the same way or follow the signs to Sv. Katarina-Bled. (Round-trip 6km. 1hr. Admission 400Sit; students 300Sit.)

# LAKE BOHINJ (BOHINJSKO JEZERO)    ☎(0)4

Although it's only 30km southwest of Bled, Bohinjsko Jezero's (BOH-heen-sko YEH-zeh-roh) natural character makes it seem worlds away. Protected by the borders of Triglav National Park, this glacial lake—together with its surrounding wildflowers, waterfalls, and windy peaks—is arguably the best place in all of Slovenia for alpine fun. Some travel here for the water sports, but most come to ascend the heights and experience mountain hospitality on their return.

**⎗ TRANSPORTATION.** The nearest town is **Bohinjska Bistrica** 6km to the east. The lake itself is surrounded by three villages: Ribčev Laz, Stara Fužina, and Ukanc. **Trains** arrive in Bohinjska Bistrica from **Ljubljana** (2½hr., 8 per day, 1200Sit) via **Jesenice** (you may need to change). It's easier to take a direct **bus** from **Ljubljana** (2hr., every hr., 1400Sit) via **Bled** (35min., 510Sit) and **Bohinjska Bistrica** (10min., 250Sit). These take you either to Hotel Jezero in Ribčev Laz, or all the way to Hotel Zlatorog, in Ukanc on the other side of the lake.

**✴⎙ ORIENTATION AND PRACTICAL INFORMATION.** You should find everything you need in **Ribčev Laz**, on the water's edge—just ask at the **tourist office,** Ribčev Laz 48. They also **exchange currency** and cash **traveler's checks** for a 3% commission. (☎572 33 70; fax 572 33 30; tdbohinj@bohinj.si. Open July-Aug. M-Sa 8am-6pm, Su 9am-3pm.) **Alpinsport,** Ribčev Laz 53, near the bridge, rents **mountain bikes, kayaks, canoes,** and offers **canyoning** in nearby gorges. (☎572 34 86 and 65 00 36. Bikes 700Sit per hr., 1900Sit per 3hr., 2900Sit per day; kayaks 700Sit, 1800Sit, 3000Sit; canoes 700Sit, 2000Sit, 3600Sit; canyoning 7900Sit per 2-3hr., 9900Sit per 4hr. Open daily Sept.-June 10am-5pm; July-Aug. 9am-8pm.) The lake has **no pharmacy;** the closest is in Bohinjska Bistrica at Triglavska 15. (☎572 16 30. Open M-F 8am-7:30pm.) The nearest bank, **Gorenjska Banka,** Trg. Svobode 26, is also in Bohinjska Bistrica, and **exchanges currency** and cashes **traveler's checks** for no commission. (☎572 16 10. Open daily 9-11:30am and 2-5pm.) In town, the **post office,** Ribčev Laz 47, has terrible rates but exchanges currency for no commission and cashes traveler's checks for a 2% commission. (Open July-Aug. M-F 8am-7pm, Sa 8am-noon; Sept.-June M-F 8am-6pm, Sa 8am-noon.) **Postal code:** 4265.

**⌂⍒ ACCOMMODATIONS AND FOOD.** You can find a **private room** by looking for the *Sobe* (room) signs around town. Alternatively, the tourist office (see above) arranges private rooms and hotels for all three villages. (Private rooms July 8-Aug. 26 1600Sit per person; Aug. 27-July 7 1300Sit. Tourist tax 154Sit per night. 30% more for stays under 3 nights. 20% more for a single. 2-star hotels 1600Sit; 2500Sit. 3-star hotels 1300Sit; 2200Sit.) **AvtoCamp Zlatorog,** Ukanc 2, is close to the Savica Waterfall and many trailheads. Take a bus to the Hotel Zlatorog (see above) and backtrack for a few minutes. It's on the west side of the lake and usually has spaces available. (☎572 34 82; fax 572 34 46. Reception July-Aug. 24hr.; off-season 8am-noon and 4-8pm. Check-out noon. Open May-Sept. July-Aug. 1600Sit per person; May-June and Sept. 1000Sit. Tourist tax 84Sit per night.) The tourist office operates **Camping Danica,** Bohinjska Bistrica 4264, just outside of town. Get off the bus or train in Bohinjska Bistrica and continue in the direction of the bus; the campground will be on the right. (☎572 10 55 and 574 60 10; fax 572 33 30. Open May-Sept. July-Aug. 1100Sit per person; May-June and Sept. 800Sit. Tourist tax 100Sit.)

The smell of sizzling fresh fish entices visitors into excellent, but pricey, local restaurants. Hit **Restavracija Center,** Ribčev Laz 50, for dinner. They serve a great "tourist menu" that includes soup, salad, and a main dish (100Sit), as well as spaghetti (850Sit) and ham omelettes (650Sit; ☎72 31 70; open daily 8am-11pm). **Gostišče Kramar,** Stara Fužina 3, is slung low over the lake; its wood-burning stove and über-comfy wicker chairs hover scarcely a meter above the water. Better for coffee and the astounding view of the lake than for food, this place makes a good after-dinner stop. Follow the dirt path on the left after the stone bridge for 10 minutes. (☎72 36 97. Coffee 150Sit. 0.5L *Laško* 300Sit. Milkshakes 350Sit. Grilled octopus 1100Sit. Open Su-Th 10am-midnight, F-Sa 10am-1am.) At **Planšar,** Stara Fužina 179, across the street from the Alpine Highlander Museum (see p. 753), homemade curd pies (800Sit) and plates of mixed cheese (800Sit) await. (☎ 76 72 54. Open same hours as museum.) The **Mercator Supermarket,** Ribčev Laz 49, is by the tourist office. (Open M-F 7am-8pm, Sa 7am-5pm.)

**⚠ BIKING AND HIKING. Mountain bikes** are not allowed on the trails, but they can be fun on the forest roads (gozdna pot) and specially marked rough dirt roads (poljska pot). Stick to the southern side of the lake (a left at the fork in Ribčev Laz) because the other sides are for hiking only. See **Essentials: Camping and the Outdoors,** p. 37, for general information about hiking and safety.

Any number of trips can be made from the shores of Bohinj, from the casual to the nearly impossible. Several good **maps** are available; the ones that cover the most area without losing too much detail are *Triglavski Narodni Park* and *Triglav* (both 1300Sit), available at the tourist office. The most popular and accessible destination is **Savica Waterfall** (Slap Savica), source of the Bohinj River. Take a bus from Ribčev Laz to "Bohinj-Zlatorog," get off at Hotel Zlatorog, and follow the signs uphill to Savica Waterfall (1hr. to the beginning of the trailhead at Koča pri Savici, then 20min. to the waterfall). If you forego the bus, turn left at the lake in Ribčev Laz and follow the unexciting road along the lake past Ukanc (3hr.). Highlights along the way include the **Church of the Holy Ghost,** built in 1743, and the sobering **Austro-Hungarian World War I Cemetery.** Once at the entrance to the powerful 60m waterfall, there's a 300Sit fee (students 200Sit) to continue. Adventurers can return along a different trail that skirts the north side of Lake Bohinj. Look for its entrance at Koča pri Savici, and keep to the westbound trail on the left (3hr.).

If, instead of turning back at the waterfall, you follow the signs toward **Black Lake** (Črno Jezero), you'll leave the valley behind and be at the base of the gigantic **Julian Peaks** (1½hr.). The hiking is very steep here; be extremely cautious. Shortly after reaching the ridge line, a trail to the right (Dol Pod Stadorjem) leads to Mt. Viševnik. Turn south from this peak to **Pršivec** (1761m; 2½hr.), where the view of the lake is breathtaking. Return the way you came or follow the trail east to return along the ridge via **Stara Fužina** and **Ribčev Laz** (2½hr.). If you opt for the latter route, be advised that the sun can be brutal and there's no shade.

The more traditional (but equally difficult) way to reach Pršivec is from Stara Fužina. Cross the bridge in Ribčev Laz and follow the road to the next village, Stara Fužina. Walk straight through town to Pension Rabič (20min.). Once there, you'll have to pass through a closed gate, which is perfectly legal unless you're behind a steering wheel. After **Devil's Bridge** (Hudičev most), built by an Italian named Diavollo, Mr. Devil himself, follow the leftmost road at the fork (*not* the trails along the river pointing toward Korita Mostnice). Continue along the marked carriage path that leads into the woods on the left. This will take you to the road; follow it for 50m and then turn left at the crucifix. From here, signs lead to **Vogar** (1hr.) and Pršivec (4hr.). The path to Vogar winds steeply through a forest and is paved with rocks.

While resting between hikes, you can take in a bit of Alpine culture. The 15th-century **Church of John the Baptist,** across the stone bridge, has colorful frescoes and an ornate altar. (Open June-Sept. 15 9am-noon and 3-6pm. 100Sit.) The **Alpine Highlander Museum,** 1.5km north in Stara Fužina, exhibits objects from the life of a 19th-century highlander. (Open July-Aug. Tu-Su 11am-7pm; Sept.-Oct. and Dec. 25-June Tu-Su 10am-noon and 4-6pm. 300Sit, students 200Sit.)

**🎵 ENTERTAINMENT. Amor Club,** Ribčev Laz 50, next to the tourist office, is the only nightspot in town, but even so, it only draws a crowd on weekends. (☎ 72 31 70. Open daily 9pm-4am. 500Sit cover F and Sa.) Lake Bohinj hosts several festivals during the summer months. **Kresna Noč** (Midsummer Night) in mid-August is the most spectacular, with candles and fireworks decorating the night sky. The **Peasant's Wedding Day** at the end of July is a continuation of tradition; it's an elaborate (and real) wedding ceremony, more for locals than tourists. The mid-September **Kravji bal** (Cow Ball) in Ukanc is a huge dance held on the day the bovines are brought out of their alpine pastures for the winter. For further information, visit the tourist office (see above).

> **COMING TO A HEAD...OR THREE** Slovenia's highest peak, Mt. Triglav (2864m), may not seem like much of an ascent until you realize that, on a clear day, the sea is visible from the summit. Originally worshipped by pre-Christian Slovenes, "3 Heads" was first conquered in 1778 and has since become a symbol of the country's identity. The 3-peaked contour was the symbol of the Liberation Front when Slovenia was occupied during World War II and today has a place on the national flag and coat of arms; politicians make the hike to show off their national spirit. If you reach the summit, you will be treated like a hero on your return: it's the one way of truly becoming a Slovene. Don't forget to leave your name in the book at the top. A good route up Mt. Triglav begins in Stara Fužina. Some have done it in a day, but two days provide for a safer and more enjoyable journey. There is an abundance of mountain huts along the way, but bring your wallet because higher altitude means more expensive supplies and beds. For 500Sit, *How to Climb Triglav* details all the options.

# KRANJSKA GORA ☎(0)4

Kranjska Gora (pop. 2000) is so close to the Austrian and Italian borders that most people are trilingual. This tiny mountain village, however, still maintains a distinctly Slovenian flavor. Home to jagged peaks, fields of yellow grass, and a curious museum of traditional folk fashion, Kranjska Gora offers a happy combination of nature and culture.

**TRANSPORTATION.** **Buses** run to and from **Bled's** train station (45min., every hr., 700Sit) and **Ljubljana** (2¼hr., every hr., 1500Sit).

**ORIENTATION AND PRACTICAL INFORMATION.** The entire village is spread along **Borovška cesta**. To get there from the **bus stop** on Koroška cesta, walk in the same direction as the bus and take the first left onto **Kolodvorska cesta,** continuing to the end of the street. A right turn on Borovška leads past a church and into the center of town. The tourist information center, **Turistično društvo Kranjska Gora,** Tičarjeva 2, is in the center of town on the corner of Tičarjeva and Borovška. The staff arranges private rooms, cashes **traveler's checks** for a 3% commission, and sells **maps.** (☎588 17 68; fax 588 11 25; turisticno.drustvo.kg@siol.net. Open daily July-Aug. 8am-2pm and 3-8pm; Sept.-June 8am-3pm.) There is a **pharmacy, Lekarna Kranjska Gora,** at Naselje Slavka Černeta 34. (☎588 17 85. Open M-W and F 7:30am-3pm, Th noon-7pm, Sa 8am-1pm.) A better option is **SKB Banka,** Borovška cesta 99a, which cashes AmEx **traveler's cheques** for a 500Sit commission, **exchanges currency** for no commission, and has a 24hr. Cirrus/Maestro/MC/Plus/Visa **ATM** and currency exchange machine. (☎588 20 06; fax 588 19 69. Open M-F 8:30am-noon and 2-5pm.) You can rent **mountain bikes** and **skis** at **Aval,** Borovška 88a, to explore Kranjska Gora's hills. (☎588 10 39; fax 574 50 40. Bikes 500Sit per hr., 1200Sit per half-day, 1800Sit per day; skis 1200Sit per day, boots and poles 600Sit each. Open daily 8am-6pm.) **Telephones** are in the post office. **Internet access** is available on two slow machines in **Gostilna Frida,** Koroška 4a. (8Sit per min. Open daily 10am-11pm.) The **post office,** Borovška 92, exchanges currency for no commission but at bad rates. (☎588 17 70; fax 588 14 67. Open July 15-Sept. 15 M-Sa 8am-8pm; Sept. 16-July 14 M-F 8am-7pm, Sa 8am-noon.) **Postal code:** 4280.

**ACCOMMODATIONS AND FOOD.** To secure a **private room,** look for the *Sobe* (room) signs around town or go to the tourist office. (Breakfast 800Sit. July 17-Aug. 20 1700Sit; Apr.-July 17 and Aug. 21-Dec. 24 1500Sit; Jan.-Mar. 1400Sit. 1000Sit extra for a single; 300Sit more for 2-star hotels; 700Sit more for for 3-star. Tourist tax 154Sit. 20% more for stays under 3 nights.) There are neither budget hotels nor camping. The **Emona Merkur Market,** Borovška 92, is a sure bet for **groceries.** (Open M-F 7am-8pm, Sa 7am-7pm, Su 8am-noon.) The buffet-style **Bife,** in the market, provides inexpensive food under the penetrating stare of a bright yellow bird in a baseball cap. (Goulash 450Sit; risotto 450Sit. Open daily 7am-7pm.) **Gostilna pri Martinu**, Borovška 61, has huge portions served by friendly waiters. The menu changes daily but is always 1100Sit. (☎582 03 00. Open daily 10am-11pm.)

**🔳🔳 HIKING AND ENTERTAINMENT.** All the hiking information that you could possibly need is available at **Agencija Julijana**, near the parking lot on Borovška cesta. They can also tell you about the many **ski lifts** near town. (☎/fax 588 13 25. Open daily 8am-noon and 3-8pm.) Hiking and walking **maps** of the area are available from the tourist information center (1200Sit). Look for the village of **Podkoren**, 3km from Kranjska Gora toward the Austrian border, known for its well-preserved folk architecture. It also harbors the natural reserve **Zelenci**, which is the source of the Sava Dolinka River. **Rateče**, a small village with alpine houses 7km from Kranjska Gora, sits below **Pec** (1510m) and near the three-way border with Austria and Italy. One of the most interesting hikes in the area runs through the **Planica Valley** to the mountain of **Tamar**. From town, follow the abandoned railroad westward. After passing the ski lifts that dominate the view to the left, you'll reach the old railroad station in Rateče. Turn left into the Planica valley to enjoy an amazing view of the **Mojstrovka, Travnik**, and **Šit Mountains.** Continue past the ski ramps for 30 minutes to reach the mountain home **Tamar**, from which **Jalovec**, the symbol of Slovenian mountaineers and among the most beautiful of the peaks, can be seen.

The village's nightlife consists largely of sleeping. During summer, however, it wakes up for three months of festivities including concerts, fashion shows, farm markets, and sports events. Consult the tourist information center (see above) for a free seasonal booklet. **Hotel Prišank**, Borovška 93, has an entertainment room with billiards (150Sit) and foosball (60Sit). The tiny **Caffe Pinki**, Borovška 91, is the best place to wet your whistle. (☎88 17 66. 0.5L Union 270Sit. Open daily 9am-11pm.)

# ISTRIA

Though Slovenia claims only 40km of the Adriatic coast, this stretch of green bays and old coastal towns has developed its own Italian flavor, with palm trees, vineyards, and fishing boats dotting the shore. Koper, with its extensive transport, facilitates jaunts between Venetian-tinged Piran, where the light from Venice can actually be seen, and the beachside (if sandless) fun of Portorož.

## KOPER                                    ☎(0)66

With no beaches, too much industry, and plenty of trains, Koper (pop. 20,000) serves primarily as the accommodation and transportation hub for Slovenian Istria.

**▐ TRANSPORTATION. Trains** from **Ljubljana** are less frequent than buses but are cheaper. (2¼hr., 5 per day, 1220-1440Sit.) The **bus** (☎639 52 69) and **train** (☎639 52 63) **station** is at Kolodvorska 11. Direct **buses** arrive from **Piran** (40min., every 20min. until 11pm, 420Sit) via **Portorož** (35min., 380Sit); **Ljubljana** (2½hr., 13 per day, 1900Sit); **Trieste, ITA** (45min., 16 per day, 460Sit); **Poreč, CRO** (2hr., 5 per day, 1140Sit); and **Pula, CRO** (3¼hr., 2 per day, 2000Sit).

**🔳🔳 PRACTICAL INFORMATION. ATMs** are abundant in the city center. **Dijaški Dom Koper**, Cankarjeva 5, is one of two youth hostels in all of Slovenian Istria. From the train/bus station, turn right and follow Kolodvorska cesta toward the city center. After passing straight through a rotary and then Kosovelov Trg., walk up Manesiceva to Trg Brolo and take a right onto Cankarjeva (1km). It's large, clean, and centrally located. (☎27 32 50; fax 27 31 82. Check-in after noon. Check-out 10am. Open June 15-Aug 21. 380 beds, most in triples. 2570Sit for stays under 3 nights. 2380Sit with ISIC or IH, breakfast included. Tourist tax 77Sit.) Just a short walk to the town center leads to **Gostišče Istrska Klet**, Župančičeva 39, which serves both traditional Slovenian dishes and specialties from the sea. (*Kranjska klobasa* 700Sit; seafood risotto 700Sit. Open M-Sa 6:30am-9pm.)

# PORTOROŽ
☎(0)5

If Slovenian Istria were condensed into one town, with Koper as the bus station and Piran the museum, Portorož (port-oh-ROZH; pop. 9000) would provide the entertainment. Portorož consists of a mere street, but the beach and its diversions are the major draw. While it is the most heavily touristed of the three cities, the grassy beach, seaside restaurants, holiday feel, and deep blue tide make it worth battling the crowds: the exuberance of Portorož almost eclipses its plastic feel.

**⊟ TRANSPORTATION.** A **bus** connects Portorož to **Koper** (35min., every 20min. until 11pm, 380Sit) and **Ljubljana** via **Postojna** (2¾hr., 9 per day, 2000Sit from Ljubljana). Thomas Mann wrote that Venice should be entered only by sea; accordingly, a **catamaran** makes the **Portorož-Venice** trip. (June 20-Sept. 12 Tu and Sa, Apr.-Nov. Sa, Apr. 7-June 16 and Sept. 15-Nov. 5 also F and Su; 8am; 2½hr.; 11,000Sit.) Ask the tourist office for more info. For **taxis** call ☎674 55 55 or 673 07 00.

**⁊ ORIENTATION AND PRACTICAL INFORMATION.** Most streets start from **Obala**, the waterfront boulevard, and head uphill. The main bus stop is just a little way up the road across from the **tourist office**, Obala 16, which hands out free **maps**. (☎674 02 31 and 674 82 60; fax 674 82 61. Open daily July-Aug. 9am-1:30pm and 3-9:30pm; Sept.-June Th-Tu 10am-5pm, W 10am-3pm.) Better rates are available at numerous small **exchange offices** on Obala. There is a 24hr. Cirrus/Maestro/MC **ATM** at Obala 53. **Atlas Express**, Obala 55, rents **mountain bikes, road bikes,** and **scooters**, offers made-to-order excursions, sells tickets for organized trips, and **exchanges currency**. (☎74 88 21; fax 74 88 20; atlas.portoroz@siol.net. Mountain bikes 1500Sit per 2hr., 2200Sit per 6hr., 3500Sit per day. Road bikes 1200Sit, 1800Sit, 3000Sit. Scooters 4000Sit, 7000Sit, 8000Sit. Open daily July-Sept. 8am-8pm; Oct.-June M-Sa 8am-7pm.) There is a **pharmacy**, **Lekarna Portorož**, at Obala 41. Walk down Obala, turn right into the Hotel Palace Courtyard, and follow the sign. (☎674 86 70. Open M-F 8:30am-7pm, Sa 8:30am-1pm.) **Internet access** is available about 1km away in the direction of Piran at Obala 11. (800Sit per hr. Open M-F 1-9pm, Sa-Su 3-9pm.) The **post office** is at K Stari cesti 1. They exchange currency and cash traveler's checks for a small commission. (☎674 67 57. Open M-Sa 8am-9pm.) **Postal code:** 6320.

**⌂⌂ ACCOMMODATIONS AND FOOD.** As a rule, hotels and *pensions* are expensive and crowded, although prices drop dramatically in the off-season. **Palma**, upstairs from the tourist office, arranges private **accommodations**. (☎74 90 10; fax 74 67 73. Open July-Aug. M-Sa 8am-9pm, Su 10am-5pm; Sept.-June M-F 8am-5pm, Sa 8am-1pm. July-Aug. singles 3700Sit; doubles 4600Sit; triples 6400Sit. Rooms much cheaper in the off-season. 50% more for stays under 3 nights. Tourist tax 300Sit.) To find a room on your own, look for *Sobe* or *Zimmer frei* signs along Obala. **Lucija**, Seča 204, a nearby campground, is accessible by bus from the station (every 15min., 210Sit). It offers rowing, sailing, swimming, and waterskiing facilities. (☎/fax 677 10 27. Reception 24hr. July-Aug. 1500Sit per person. May-June and Sept. 1300Sit. Tourist tax 100Sit.) Faceless **restaurants** line the coastal side of Obala. Locals deny the existence of budget eats, but there is a large supermarket, **Mercator Degro**, on Obala next to the bus station. (Open M-Sa 7am-8pm, Su 9-11am.)

# PIRAN
☎(0)5

Piran's central buildings form an oval around a statue of native-born violinist and composer Giuseppe Tartini, whose serene composure reflects the town's feel. Medieval Venice, under whose rule Piran flourished, seems to sigh through the richly colored shutters. With only 5000 inhabitants, the town occupies no more than a tiny peninsula, but its beauty far surpasses that of its larger neighbors.

**⊟ TRANSPORTATION.** Buses arrive in Piran from **Ljubljana** via **Koper** (40min., every 20min., 420Sit) and **Trieste, ITA** (1½hr., 6 per day, 800Sit).

**◪ PRACTICAL INFORMATION.** Facing the sea, take a right from the bus stop along the quay to the marina, then to the central **Tartinijev Trg**. The **tourist office**, Tartinijev Trg. 2, provides info on Piran and Slovenian Istria. They also organize tours of Slovenian Istria in English for 3000-8000Sit. (☎673 02 20; fax 673 02 21. Open July-Aug. M-F, Su 9am-1:30pm and 3-9:30pm, Sa 9am-10pm.) There is a **pharmacy** at Tartinijev Trg. 4. (☎673 01 50. Open M-F 8am-8pm, Sa 8am-1pm.) **Banka Koper**, Tartinijev Trg. 12, **exchanges currency** and cashes **traveler's checks**. (☎673 32 00. Open M-F 8:30am-noon and 3-5pm, Sa 8:30-noon.) **Cyber Point**, Županičeva 14, has **internet access**. (800Sit per hr. Open M-F 1-9pm, Sa-Su 3-9pm.) **Telephones** are at the post office and card phones are at the corner of Zelenjavni Trg. The **post office**, Leninova 1, **exchanges currency** and cashes **traveler's checks** for no commission. (☎673 26 77. Open M-F 8am-8pm, Sa 8am-noon.) **Postal code:** 6330.

**▛▟ ACCOMMODATIONS AND FOOD.** To book a private room, visit **Maona**, Cankarjeva nabrežie 7. Walking toward the marina from the bus station, it's on the right. (☎/fax 673 12 90; maona@siol.net; www.maona.si. July-Aug. singles 2800Sit; doubles 4400-4900Sit; triples 6500-6900Sit. Much cheaper May-June and Sept.-Oct. 50% more for stays under 3 nights. Tourist tax 200Sit. Open M-F 9am-8pm, Sa 10am-1pm and 5-8pm, Su 9am-noon and 5-8pm.) Mr. Val of **Val Piran (HI)**, Gregorčičeva 38a, runs a great little hostel near the lighthouse. To get there from the bus, just keep walking toward the tip of the peninsula; the sign is on the right. (☎673 25 55; fax 673 25 56. Reception 24hr. Check-out 11am. June 15-Sept. 15 3300Sit per person, Sept. 16-June 14 3000Sit. Stays under 3 nights in high season 10% more. 10% off with ISIC.) Mr. Val also runs a **restaurant** outside the *pension*, offering a tourist menu (1300Sit) and pasta (from 700Sit; open daily 10am-10pm). To avoid the high-priced waterfront restaurants, try **Pizzeria Surf**, Županičeva ul. 21. (☎673 11 75. Pizza 700-1550Sit. Big salads 600Sit. Open daily 10am-11pm.) Interchangeable restaurants line the shore. **Supermarket Kras** is at Zelenjavni Trg. 1, with an **outdoor market** out front. (Open M-F 7am-7pm, Sa 7am-2pm, Su 8am-noon.)

**☎ SIGHTS.** Although you'll be tempted to jump in the sea anywhere along the peninsula, waiting until after you stroll along Piran's streets is worth it. The Gothic **Church of St. George** (Crkva sv. Jurja), built in the 14th century, is a short walk uphill from Tartinijev Trg. Piran's most prominent church, it has a magnificent interior and terraces with breathtaking views of the sea. Next door is the 1609 **St. George Tower**. If you climb all 146 stairs you'll be rewarded with equally impressive views of Piran and the Adriatic. (Open daily 10am-10pm. 100Sit.) A walk along the quay brings you to the **lighthouse** at the end of the peninsula. The **aquarium**, Tomažičeva 4, on the water opposite the marina, has an enormous variety of marine life in 25 tanks. (Open daily June-Sept. 9am-10pm. 350Sit.)

**SLOVENIA**

# UKRAINE
# (УКРАЇНА)

## IF YOU'RE HERE FOR...

**3-5 DAYS.** Discover the poplar-crowned and golden-domed **Kyiv** (p. 766), the country's proud capital.

**1-2 WEEKS.** Frolic in **Crimea's** (p. 780) many resorts and explore the former-USSR party-town **Odessa** (p. 790).

**2-3 WEEKS.** Head to Transcarpathia; **Lviv** (p. 797) really is an undiscovered jewel.

Translated literally, the word "Ukraina" (Україна) means "borderland," and it is this precariously balanced position that the country has occupied for most of its history. Vast, fertile, and perpetually tempting to its invaders, newly independent Ukraine still oscillates between nostalgic and overbearing Russia on one side, and a bloc of *nouveau riche* on the other. Historic Kyiv, the cradle of Slavic Orthodox culture, now finds itself besieged by Western Ukraine with its uniate congregations in lavish cathedrals, its bold rhetoric of Ukrainian nationalism, and its traditional affinity for Europe; on the other side is Crimea, whose predominantly Russian population longs for the days of Soviet stability and tourist industry. Ukraine's citizens—from the ubiquitous old *babushki* to the cell-phone-sporting *biznesmeni*, from the village boys to the urban-high-heeled women—live in a world of past splendor and current corruption. Traveling through Ukraine's landscape is an absolutely unique experience; with no beaten path from which to stray, the challenges of exploration reward with a genuine and intriguing look into Ukrainian life. As if in a time warp, Ukraine offers fascinating but unfrequented museums and theatres, wonderful but undeveloped castles, and magnificent Black Sea coast that remains spirited and lively even after years of Soviet order and post-Soviet chaos. This country, whose idealism swirls and sometimes clashes with reality, offers many treasures—they just wait to be discovered.

## UKRAINE AT A GLANCE

**OFFICIAL NAME:** Ukraine

**CAPITAL:** Kyiv (2.6 million)

**POPULATION:** 49,811,174 (73% Ukrainian, 22% Russian, 1% Jewish)

**LANGUAGE:** Ukrainian, Russian

**CURRENCY:** 1 hryvna=100 kopiykas

**RELIGION:** 29% Ukrainian Orthodox, 7% Uniate, 4% Protestant

**LAND AREA:** 603,700 km²

**GEOGRAPHY:** Mountains; plains near the Hungarian border

**CLIMATE:** Temperate continental

**GEOGRAPHY:** Plains

**BORDERS:** Belarus, Hungary, Moldova, Poland, Romania, Russia, Slovakia

**ECONOMY:** 56% Services, 30% Industry, 14% Agriculture

**GDP:** $2,200 per capita

**EMERGENCY PHONE NUMBERS:** Fire 01, Police 02, Emergency 03

**COUNTRY CODE:** 380

**INTERNATIONAL DIALING PREFIX:** 810

# HISTORY

**KYIVAN RUS.** Recorded Ukrainian history dates from the **Kyivan Rus** dynasty that sprang from the infiltrations of Viking (Varangian) warrior-traders into the Dnieper

River region in 882. They grew wealthy from the new north-south fur trade among Constantinople, Novgorod, and Baltic trade organizations. Kyivan aristocracy, though of Varangian stock, quickly became Slavicized, adopting Christianity and the Cyrillic alphabet. Prince **Volodymyr the Great** welcomed missionaries from **Constantinople** and was baptized in 988. With Christianity came a flow of Byzantine thought and culture of which Kyivan Rus grew so enamored that it tried to conquer its southern neighbors three times. Volodymyr's son **Yaroslav** promoted architecture, art, music, and the development of written Old Church Slavonic (see p. 776). Unfortunately, Yaroslav's rule marked the high before the crash, as changes in trade routes and squabbling over succession left the empire a target for invaders.

**MONGOL INVASION.** Invasion is exactly what **Genghis Khan** had in mind when he moved into Ukraine in the 1230s; grandson Batu sacked Kyiv in 1240. Batu's death halted the **Golden Horde's** march into Europe but not Mongol rule in Ukraine, which persisted as late as 1783 in the Crimea. By the mid-14th century, Ukraine proper was ruled by the Horde and the Grand Duchy of Lithuania (including present-day Poland), while serfdom and Roman Catholicism slowly were working their way in from the West. Meanwhile, eastern Ukrainian **Cossack** bands, composed of independent Tartar groups joined by peasants fleeing serfdom, came under the employ of the Polish-Lithuanian government as soldiers against Constantinople and Muscovy. In 1648, a legendary rebellion led by a Cossack *hetman* (commander-in-chief) **Bohdan Khmelnitsky** defeated the Poles and won Kyiv and Lviv. A 1654 agreement with Moscow brought an ally into the war with Poland, but Khmelnitsky's death left confusion that led to decline known as **"the Ruin."** By 1667, the nation was forced to

> **THE ARTIFICIAL FAMINE** In 1930, the first of the USSR's 5-year plans collectivized agriculture and set state quotas for agricultural production. In Ukraine the policies were met with fierce opposition and farmers destroyed their livestock in protest. Stalin, in order to break the resistance, raised grain quotas for the Crimea, the Caucasus, the lower Volga, and part of Belarus to impossible levels. Exit visas for the region were prohibited and taking from the harvest before the state had its "share" was punishable by death. The effects were devastating: the most conservative estimates put the death toll from starvation from winter 1932 to summer 1933 at 4.8million, not including the atrocities committed by the thousands of troops sent to enforce collectivization. Stalin himself confessed to "ten of millions" of deaths in a conversation with Winston Churchill in August 1942. Historians, pouring over what Soviet records they could find, put the official number at 6-8 million.

accept a treaty cutting Ukraine along the Dnieper River. Russia won the east (Left Bank), including Kyiv and Odessa, and the west went to Poland. Under the **Russian Empire,** most of Ukraine was reorganized into provinces. Jews were restricted to the Polish-controlled Right Bank, which became known as the **Pale of Settlement,** with Odessa growing into a large metropolis and Jewish center. Native culture was given a freer reign in Western Ukraine and its capital city, Lviv, which fell into Austro-Hungarian hands after the **First Partition of Poland** in 1772.

**THE MODERN UKRAINE.** The 19th century saw Ukraine become a more vital part of the Russian empire, as Odessa society under Governor **Mikhail Vorontsov** hosted Pushkin for part of his exile (see **Alupka,** p. 788). Ukrainian nationalism also resurfaced, led by the poet and painter **Taras Shevchenko,** who sought to revitalize the Ukrainian language and establish a free and democratic state. Shevchenko was arrested and exiled to Central Asia. Ukraine declared its independence in 1918, but the **Bolsheviks** set up a rival government in Kharkiv and seized complete power during the Civil War (1918-20); the Poles retook Lviv and Western Ukraine only to lose them again in 1940. The next 70 years saw one tragedy after another, as this "bread basket of Russia" bore the brunt of Stalin's murderous collectivization of agriculture, Nazi invasion, a long-standing ban against Ukrainian in Soviet schools, and the 1986 meltdown at the **Chernobyl** nuclear power plant.

Ukraine pulled out of the Soviet Union on December 1, 1991, following an overwhelming vote by 93% of its population for complete **independence.** But the Soviet legacy has not been so easily shed: ownership of the Black Sea Fleet at Sevastopol is in dispute, as is the status of the Crimea. Today Ukrainian has been restored as the official language, except in the predominantly Russian Crimea. The **Crimean Tartars**, deported to Uzbekistan in 1944, have begun to return to the region.

# POLITICS

Ukraine is in pretty bad shape. GDP initially shrunk 72% after the nation declared independence, and fell an additional 0.4% in 1999. Ukraine's trade surplus, however, rebounded to $2.34 billion from $351 million in 1998, and GDP is expected to grow 1% in the coming year. The new **hryvna** has gone sour as the nation's creditors, most notably the **IMF,** have grown sick of the lack of financial reform. Corruption is endemic, with an estimated four of five Ukrainian banks controlled by organized crime and 6.5% of all business income spent in bribes to government officials. Total graft in the Ukraine was estimated at $91 million in 1999, and grew by more than a third in the first quarter of 2000.

Factories stand still, agriculture tries to rid itself of Communist collectivization, and technological industries try to cope with "brain drain" to Moscow and Israel. Perhaps most devastating, however, is the communist work ethic—the old joke, "they pretend to pay us, and we pretend to work" still rings true.

Democracy only begun to arrive, though its stepsister capitalism can be spotted in parts of Kyiv and Odessa. **President Leonid Kuchma** won a second five-year term in

October 1999, despite his dismal record of economic stagnation and political repression. Kuchma has used tax and libel laws to shut down media outlets critical of his regime, and 38 Ukrainian journalists have been murdered since 1991. Opposition to the president remains strong, particularly on the left.

# CULTURE

## NATIONAL HOLIDAYS IN 2001

**January 1** New Year's

**January 7** Orthodox Christmas

**March 8** International Women's Day

**April 13** Good Friday

**April 15** Easter

**May 1-2** Labor Day

**May 9** Victory Day

**June 4** Holy Trinity

**June 28** Constitution Day

**August 24** Independence Day

## LITERATURE AND ARTS

Ukraine's written tradition shares its roots with those of Russia and Belarus in the histories and sermons of the Kyivan Rus. Religious works in **Old Church Slavonic** gave way to original works, characterized by their stylized writing and exuberant praise of the empire. Perhaps the most important literary endeavor of this era was the 12th century *Song of Igor's Campaign (Slavo o polku Ihorevi)*, a largely symbolic epic unsurpassed in the courtly tradition. (**Vladimir Nabokov** rendered the epic in English in 1960.) The **visual arts** developed also, with Byzantine influences on architecture, manuscripture, and iconography. Further artistic progress was quashed, however, when the Lithuanian-Polish alliance swallowed Ukraine.

After a long dormancy, Ukrainian literature re-emerged in the 17th and 18th centuries. The most accomplished author of the period, **Ivan Kotliarevsky,** virtually created the Ukrainian vernacular with his comic travesty of Virgil's *Aeneid*, the *Eneïda*. In 1830s Kyiv, **Mykola Kostomarov, Panteleymon Kulish,** and **Taras Shevchenko** (see **Kyiv: Sights,** p. 775) joined the **Brotherhood of Sts. Cyril and Methodius,** devoted to increasing Ukrainian national consciousness. Shevchenko's brilliantly crafted poems, which sometimes resemble folk songs, speak of Ukrainian autonomy and idealize the Cossack period. He was also a painter; his work straddles Classicism and an emerging Realism. Composer Mykola Lysenko dominated secular music with output such as an opera of Nikolai Gogol's *Taras Bulba*.

The early 20th century saw a dramatic outburst of artistic activity. Major literary movements overtook one another rapidly: the Modernism of **Lesya Ukrainka** (the country's foremost female poet) gave way to decadent Realism in prose and Symbolism in verse. Another, newly developed movement, Futurism, gave Ukraine one of its greatest poets of the century, **Mykola Bazhan.** In the visual arts, **Monumentalism** dominated painting while **Neo-Baroque** dominated in the graphic arts. Communist-imposed **Social Realism** rained on the artistic parade, with mass censorship and Stalinist purges of dissenting writers. Under communism, creativity lay dormant until Nikita Kruschev's thaw of the early 1960s, when it burst forth in expressionistic paintings of communist horrors, and in the works of aptly-named **Writers of the Sixties,** Vasyl Stus, Lina Kostenko, and others, who wrote just enough to warrant even tougher repression in the coming decades. The result was a coma that the arts—at least among non-exiles—are just beginning to awaken from.

## RELIGION

In Western Ukraine, centuries of Polish influence have made Uniate Catholicism the dominant religion. The eastern portion of the country is dominated by the Ukrainian Orthodox Church, and Jews represent a tiny minority.

# FOOD AND DRINK

New, fancy restaurants are popping up to accommodate tourists and the few Ukrainians who can afford them. There are few choices between these and the *stolovayas* (cafeterias), dying bastions of cheap, hot food. There is usually a choice of two soups, two main dishes, and some *kompot* (a homemade fruit drink). Non-fresh *stolovaya* food can knock you out of commission for hours, while a good *stolovaya* meal is a triumph of the human spirit. **Vegetarians** will have to create their own meals from potatoes, mushrooms, and cabbage. Most Ukrainian restaurants do not include side dishes with their main dishes.

Fruits and veggies are sold at **markets;** bring your own bag. Markets are open daily. **State food stores** are classified by content: *hastronom* (гастроном) packaged goods; *moloko* (молоко) milk products; *ovochi-frukty* (овочі-фрукты) fruits and vegetables; *myaso* (мясо) meat; *hlib* (хліб) bread; *kolbasy* (колбаси) sausage; and *ryba* (риба) fish. In the suburbs, there is one store per designated region, simply labeled *mahazyn* (магазин; store). Kiosks often have the same products as expensive Western stores at much lower prices. Drinking **tea** is a national ritual.

**Liquor** is cheap and available. A half-liter bottle of *Stolichnaya* costs about 3hv and is generally tastier than the moonshine *(samohonka)* Ukrainians might offer you in their homes. *Obolon* (оболонь) is the most popular beer, but Lviv's *Zoloty kolos* (Золотий Колос) and *Lvivske* (Львівське) are of higher quality. Few eateries carry water and those that do charge more for it than juice.

**JUST FOR THE TASTE** When the sun is high and the steppe is hotter than a Saharan parking lot, Aussies thirst for a *Fosters,* Czechs a *Pilsner,* and Yankees a *Bud,* but a true Ukrainian won't have anything other than a ladle of **kvas** (квас). In Kyiv you'll see it served from siphons, in the provinces from rusty cisterns. The taste—kind of like beer without the hops—varies depending on the container, but it all comes down to acidic bread bubbles; the drink is based on a sourdough solution that rushes tingling into your bloodstream. It's so addictive that Kyiv drinks *kvas* all summer, even in the rain, when groups of young tots, middle-aged shoppers, and love-struck teenagers huddle around toothless tap-masters, all under one leaky umbrella.

# CUSTOMS AND ETIQUETTE

Arrive at parties bearing flowers, vodka, or pastries for the hosts, and expect chitchat to soon evolve into political discussion. Unless you know the situation in Ukraine well, confine your comments to the beauty of the countryside and the hospitality of its people. Topics such as abortion and **homosexuality,** although not taboo, provoke a negative reaction. Dinners can last long into the evening; if you try to leave early, you may offend your hosts. Not eating your food is equally insulting. Although locals don't usually leave **tips,** most expats give 10%. Backpacks give away your foreignness (wear a plastic bag like everyone else), as does sloppy dress. Women and girls are often dressed up, or rather, hardly dressed; shorts, if worn at all, are fancy and normally accompanied by formal shoes. In restaurants, it is unheard of for women to pay.

# SPORTS

Football (soccer) is the national craze, with seven-time national champions **Dynamo Kyiv** crowned again this past season and **Shaktar Donetsk** in second place. Dynamo has performed well in past years against such top European teams as Juventus. The national team performed well in the qualifying for the 1998 world cup, only to lose to eventual number three Croatia. Hockey is also very popular. Ukraine did manage to field a strong team at the 1998 Winter Olympics, its first winter games since independence, placing well in biathalon, freestyle ski jumping and figure skating.

# LANGUAGE

It's extremely difficult to travel without knowing some **Ukrainian** or **Russian.** In Kyiv, Odessa, and Crimea, Russian is more common than Ukrainian (although all official signs are in Ukrainian). In Transcarpathia, Ukrainian is preferred—people will speak Russian with you only if they know you are not Russian. *Let's Go* uses Ukrainian names in Kyiv and Western Ukraine, and Russian in Crimea and Odeshchina.

The Ukrainian alphabet resembles Russian, but with a few character and pronunciation differences. The most notable additions are the "і" (*ee* sound) and the "ї" (*yee* sound)—the "и" is closest to "s*i*t." The rarely used "є" sounds like "ye" in "yep!" The "ґ" (hard "g") has been reintroduced since independence but is not yet widely used, and the "г," pronounced "g" in Russian, comes out like an "h." Roll your "r"s, but not too flamboyantly. Words that appear frequently in this chapter include: *apteka* (аптека; pharmacy); *avtovokzal* (автовокзал; bus station); *hastronom* (гастроном; supermarket); *hostinitsa* (гостініца; hotel or guest house); *kostyol* (костьол; church); *rynok* (ринок; market); and *sobor* (собор; cathedral). The Ukrainian alphabet resembles Russian (see **The Cyrillic Alphabet,** p. 15), but with a few differences. The most notable additions are the "і" (*ee* sound) and the "ї" (*yee* sound)—the "и" is closest to "s*i*t." The rarely used "є" sounds like "ye" in "yep!" The "ґ" (hard "g") has been reintroduced since independence but is not yet widely used, and the "г," pronounced "g" in Russian, comes out like an "h."

# ADDITIONAL READING

For an overview of Ukrainian history pick up *Borderland: A Journey through the History of Ukraine* by *Economist* journalist Anna Reid. For more depth, Miron Dolot offers a riveting memoir of Stalin's forced collectivization of agriculture, bleakly titled *Execution by Hunger: The Hidden Holocaust.* Author Glenn Cheney captured a more recent national tragedy in his travelogue *Journey to Chernobyl: Encounters in a Radioactive Zone.* Finally, if chasing radiation isn't your game, cozy up with the country's best young poets and prose writers in *From Three Worlds: New Ukrainian Writing,* edited by Ed Hogan.

# TRAVELING ESSENTIALS

Travelers from Australia, Canada, Ireland, New Zealand, the UK and the US arriving in Ukraine must have a **visa,** which requires an **invitation** from a citizen or official organization, or a tourist voucher from a travel agency. Regular single-entry visa processing for Americans at a Ukrainian embassy or consulate (see **Essentials: Embassies and Consulates,** p. 18)—with invitation in hand—ordinarily takes up to nine days (mailing time not included; enclose pre-paid FedEx envelope to speed the return). Single-entry visas US$30; double-entry US$60 and multiple-entry US$120, and transit US$15, not including the US$45 processing fee. Three-day rush service costs US$60 (double-entry US$120) and same or next-day service costs US$100, not including the US$45 processing fee. Submit a completed visa application, an invitation or confirmation from a hotel in Ukraine, your passport, two passport-size photos, and payment by money order or cashier's check. For transit visas no invitation is required, instead submit either a visa from the next country to which you are travelling or a ticket indicating the next country to which you are travelling. See **Russia: Essentials,** p. 588, for organizations that arrange **invitations** and visas. **Diane Sadovnikov,** a former missionary living and working in Ukraine, also arranges invitations. Together with her husband Yuri, she arranges accommodations, airport drop-off/pick-up (US$20-30), invitations (US$40), phone calls, and faxes. It's best to fax Diane a month in advance (US ☎(757) 463-6906, fax (757) 463-5526, UKR ☎/fax 044 516 2433; travel-ims@attglobal.net). **Janna Belovsova,** of Eugenia Travel in Odessa, can also help with visa invitations. (☎482 21 85 83; ☎/fax 482 22 05 54; janna@eugen.intes.odessa.ua.)

UKRAINE

When proceeding through **customs** you will be required to declare all valuables and foreign currency above US$1000 (including traveler's checks). It is illegal to bring Ukrainian currency into Ukraine—if you have any *hrvyny*, don't say it. Foreigners arriving at Kyiv's Borispol airport must purchase a $23 per week health-insurance policy for their stay in Ukraine; bring exact change. The policy is essentially an entry tax; it doesn't provide access to any health care services.

Upon arrival, check into a hotel, where the staff will register your visa for you, or register with the hall of nightmares that is the **Office of Visas and Registration** (UVIR; OBИP), in Kyiv at blv. Tarasa Shevchenka 34 (Тараса Шевченка), or at police stations in smaller cities, within your first three days in the country. Visas may also be extended here. If you do not get your visa registered, you may get hassled or fined when trying to leave. **Do not lose the paper given to you when entering the country to supplement your visa;** it is required to leave and begging the immigration officials to kick you out of the country will do no good. Once you depart Ukraine, your visa becomes invalid. If you have a double-entry visa, you'll be given a re-entry slip (*vyezd;* въезд) when you arrive.

# TRANSPORTATION

**BY PLANE. Air Ukraine** flies to Kyiv, Lviv, and Odessa from a number of European capitals. Air France, ČSA, Lufthansa, LOT, Malév, SAS, and Swissair also fly to Kyiv, generally once or twice a week.

**BY TRAIN.** Trains run frequently from all of Ukraine's neighbors, and are the most popular way of entering the country and for traveling overnight and for long distances. When coming from a non-ex-Soviet country, expect a two-hour stop at the border while the wagons get their wheels changed.

On most trains within Ukraine there are two **classes:** *platzkart*, where you'll be crammed in with *babushki* and their baskets of strawberries, and *coupé*, a more private 4-person compartment but still with disgusting bathrooms. Unless you are determined to live local, pay the extra two dollars for *coupé;* it can make the difference between dreading and tolerating a long trip. The ticket sales people will sell you a *coupé* seat unless you say otherwise. Except in Kyiv, where **platform** numbers are posted on the electronic board, the only way to figure out which platform your train leaves from is by listening to the distorted announcement. In large cities, trains arrive well before they are scheduled to depart, so you'll have a few minutes to show your ticket to cashiers or fellow passengers, look helpless, and say "платформа?" (plaht-FORM-ah?) For some stellar advice on post-Soviet train travel, see **Russia: Transportation,** p. 602.

**BY BUS. Buses** are cheaper and more frequent than trains and provide the best means to travel around the country. Bus schedules are generally reliable, but low demand sometimes causes cancellations. Buy tickets at the *kassa* (box office); if they're sold out, go directly to the driver, who will magically find a seat and pocket the money.

**BY FERRY.** Ferries across the Black Sea are limited to a few routes from Odessa and Yalta to **Istanbul.**

**BY TAXI.** Taxi drivers love to rip off foreigners, so set the price before the ride.

**BY THUMB.** Or by "sign"—hitchhikers are common on Ukrainian roads, holding signs with the desired destination. *Let's Go* does not recommend hitchhiking.

# TOURIST SERVICES AND MONEY

There is no state-run tourist office. Remains of Soviet **Intourist** have offices in hotels and provide tourist-related information, though usually not in English. They're used to dealing with groups, to whom they sell "excursion" packages to nearby sights, rather than individuals.

| CURRENCY | | |
|---|---|---|
| US$1 = 5.56HV (UKRAINIAN HRYVNY) | | 1HV = US$0.18 |
| CDN$1 = 3.71HV | | 1HV = CDN$0.27 |
| UK£1 = 8.00HV | | 1HV = UK£0.13 |
| IR£1 = 6.24HV | | 1HV = IR£0.16 |
| AUS$1 = 3.15HV | | 1HV = AUS$0.32 |
| NZ$1 = 2.35HV | | 1HV = NZ$0.43 |
| SAR1 = 0.79HV | | 1HV = SAR1.27 |
| DM1 = 2.51HV | | 1HV = DM0.40 |

In September 1996, Ukraine decided to wipe the extraneous zeros off most prices by replacing the **karbovanets** (Krb; a.k.a. **kupon**) with a new currency, the **hryvnia** (гривна; hv; plural *hryvny*); each *hryvnia* is worth 100,000 karbovantsi. The exchange rates above are those for September 2000; with Ukrainian **inflation** around 20%, expect rates and prices quoted in *hryviny* to change significantly over the next year. **Exchanging** US dollars and Deutschmarks is simple, as Ukrainians frequently use the two currencies themselves; *Obmin Valyut* (Обмін Валют) kiosks in the center of most cities offer the best rates; other currencies pose difficulties. **Traveler's checks** can be changed into dollars for small commissions in many cities. **Western Union** is everywhere. Most banks will give MC/Visa cash advances for a high commission. The lobbies of fancier hotels usually exchange US dollars at lousy rates. **Private money changers** lurk near legitimate kiosks, ready with brilliant schemes for ripping you off. **Do not** exchange money with them; it's illegal. **ATMs** abound in cities.

# HEALTH AND SAFETY

While Ukraine is neither violent nor politically volatile, it is poor and its people desperate. Keep your foreign profile low, watch your belongings, and don't make easy acquaintances, especially on the street. Don't be afraid to initiate contact; people who don't go out of their way to approach you can generally be trusted. The risk of **crime,** though made much of, isn't much greater than in the rest of Eastern Europe. It's a wise idea to **register** with your embassy once you get to Ukraine. For more information, see **Safety and Security,** p. 25.

**Water** is bad and hard to find in the bottled version; it's best to boil it or learn to love brushing your teeth with soda. Fruits and vegetables from open **markets** are generally safe, although storage conditions and pesticides make thorough washing imperative. Meat purchased at public markets should be checked very carefully and cooked thoroughly; refrigeration is a foreign concept and insects run rampant. Don't trust the tasty-looking hunks of meat for sale out of buckets on the Kyiv subway—they are not safe. Embassy officials declare that Chernobyl-related **radiation** poses minimal risk to short-term travelers, but the region should be given a wide berth. Public restrooms range from yucky to scary. Pay **toilets** (платній; platnyi) are cleaner and (gasp!) might provide toilet paper, but bring your own anyway.

**Pharmacies** are quite common and carry Western products. Aspirin is the only painkiller on hand, but plenty of cold remedies and bandages are available. **Sanitary napkins** (гігієнічні пакети; hihienchni paketi), **condoms** (презервативи; prezervativy, and **tampons** (прокладки; prokladki) are intermittently sold at kiosks.

**Women** traveling alone *will* be addressed by men on the streets, in restaurants and pretty much anywhere they go. Ukrainian women never go to restaurants alone, so expect to feel conspicuous if you do, even in the middle of the day. There is not much **racial diversity** in Ukraine. Although non-Caucasians may experience discrimination at stores, restaurants, and hotels, the biggest problems come from the militia, which frequently stops people whom they suspect to be non-Slavic.

UKRAINE

## ACCOMMODATIONS AND CAMPING

Not all hotels accept foreigners, and those that do often charge them many times more than what a Ukrainian would pay. Though room prices in Kyiv are astronomical, singles run anywhere from 5hv to 90hv in the rest of the country. The phrase "самое дешёвое место" (samoe deshovoe miesto) means "the cheapest place." More expensive hotels aren't necessarily nicer, and in some hotels, women lodging alone may be mistaken for prostitutes. Most cities have cheap hotels above the train stations—these are usually seedy and unsafe. Standard hotel rooms include a TV, phone, and a refrigerator. You will be given a *vizitka* (визитка; hotel card) to show to the hall monitor (дежурная; dezhurnaya) to get a key; surrender it on leaving the building. **Valuables** should never be left unattended; ask at the desk if there's a safe. **Hot water** is a rarity—always ask before checking in. **Private rooms** can be arranged through overseas agencies or bargained for at the train station. Most cities have a **campground,** which is a remote hotel with trailers for buildings. The old Soviet complexes can be quite posh (and quite expensive), with saunas and restaurants. Free camping is illegal, and enforcement is merciless.

## KEEPING IN TOUCH

**Mail** is cheap and quite reliable (approx. 10 days to the US). The easiest way to mail letters is to buy pre-stamped envelopes at the post office. Mail can be received general delivery through **Poste Restante** (До Востребования in Russian, До Запитание in Ukrainian). Address envelopes as follows: Michal (First name), ENGELMAN (LAST NAME), POSTE RESTANTE, Ul. Sadovaya 10 (Post office street address), 270 015 (Postal code) Odessa (City), UKRAINE.

**Telephones** are stumbling toward modernity, as a few central telephone centers spiff themselves up. The easiest way to make international call with a calling card or collect is with **Utel** (Ukraine telephone). Buy a Utel phonecard (sold at most Utel phone locations) and dial the number of your international operator (counted as a local call): **AT&T** ☎ (8) 100 11—wait for another tone after the 8; **BT Direct** ☎ (8) 10 04 41; **Canada Direct** ☎ (8)100 17; **MCI** ☎ (8) 100 13; and **Sprint** ☎ (8) 100 15. Alternatively, call at the central telephone office—estimate how long your call will take, pay at the counter, and they'll direct you to a booth. Dial 810, followed by country code, city code, and number. Calling is expensive: to Eastern Europe $0.06 per min.;

---

**CALLING À LA UKRAINE** may be challenging at first. To make an intercity call **within** Ukraine, dial 8 + area code + phone number. To place an international call **from** Ukraine, dial 810 + country code + area code + phone number. Finally, to call **to** Ukraine from outside the country, dial 380 + area code without the zero + phone number.

---

Western Europe $1.50; North America $2.50 per min. There's no need to dial a country code when calling Moldova. For **intercity calls** inside Ukraine, dial 8, then city code and number. Local calls from gray payphones generally cost 10-30hv. For an English-language operator, dial 8-192. **Email** is the easiest and cheapest way of communicating with the outside world.

# KYIV (КИЇВ)                                    ☎ (8)044

> Most often of all I soothe my aged imagination with pictures of gold-domed,
> garden-cloaked and poplar-crowned Kyiv.
> ——Taras Shevchenko (from exile)

Straddling the wide Dnieper River layered with hills and indulging in greenery, Kyiv (pop. 2,600,000) is a becoming place, although it still hasn't quite figured out how to become a thriving capital(ist) metropolis. Once the USSR's third largest city, the simultaneously eastern and western Kyiv has been adjusting to its new role (and newly spelled name) as the capital of an independent and nationalistic Ukraine. Slow development has left the city with a provincial air and a relative lack of tourists. As Ukraine's center for everything, Kyiv should share the vibrancy and vivacity that other newly liberated Eastern European cities possess. In many ways it does, with rich sights and fashionable youth. Nonetheless, its sights and museums often stand empty, locals still prefer to store their money under the pillows, and *babushki* fill the streets in colorful scarfs and orthopedic shoes. Extensive construction and remodeling projects, however, speak to the city's commitment to stumble all the way to the 21st century.

# ✴ ORIENTATION

Kyiv straddles the **Dnieper River** (Дніпро; Dnipro), but almost all of its attractions and services lie on the right (west) bank. The **Metro's** (Metropoliten) three intersecting lines—blue (MB), green (MG), and red (MR)—cover the city center but leave most of the outskirts to trolleys and trams. The **train station** lies at MR: Vokzalna (Вокзальна). Two stops away is the **Khreshchatyk** (Хрещатик) stop and its corresponding street, Kyiv's main thoroughfare, which runs from Bessarabska Square to European Square. It contains the heart of Kyiv, **Maydan Nezalezhnosti** (Майдан Незалежності; Independence Plaza), a fountain-filled fun spot next to the post office. Up the hill, Khreshchatyk turns into the stately, tree-lined vul. Volodymyrska (Володимирьська). To the west of these lies Kyiv's Upper City, home to some of its best-known churches. To the east, along the west bank of the Dnieper, **Khreshchatyk Park** covers the slope that runs from the city center to the water's edge. Blv. Shevchenka (Шевченка) and vul. Khmelnytskoho (Хмельніцького) run perpendicular to Khreshchatyk, leading to the western edge of the central Starokyivsky (Old Kyiv) District. You can buy **maps** (3-5hv) in kiosks.

# ☒ INTERCITY TRANSPORTATION

**Flights: Kyiv-Boryspil Airport** (Київ-Бориспіль; ☎ 296 72 43), 30min. drive southeast of the capital. Cash-only currency exchange (Обмин Валют; Obmin Valyut). Representatives of tourist agencies wait near the exit, offering city tours and transportation services. Among them, **Autolux shuttles** (Автолюкс) take the newly arrived anywhere in the city. (☎ 296 74 84. Every 30min. $10.) A private **taxi** (Таксис; taksys; ☎ 295 95 08) costs around 70hv to the center. The **city bus** (політ; polit) or a **marshrutne taksi** (маршрутне таксі)—a faster, privately owned bus with a small surcharge—leaves every 20min. (or whenever it fills up), and dumps passengers off at MR: Livoberezhna (Лівобережна; 10-20hv). Buy your ticket on the bus. Airline offices:

**Air Ukraine,** pr. Peremohy 14 (☎ 216 70 40 or 276 70 59; fax 216 76 09). Open M-F 10am-5pm.

**Air France,** Velyka Zhytomyrska 6/11 (☎ 464 10 10). Open M-F 9am-5pm.

**Austrian Airlines/Swissair,** vul. Chervonoarmiska 9/2 (☎ 244 35 40 or 244 35 41). Open M-F 10am-5pm.

**British Airways,** vul. Yaroslaviv Val. 5 (☎ 490 60 60). Open M-F 9am-6pm, Sa 10am-2pm.

**ČSA,** vul. Ivana Franka 36 (☎ 246 56 28). Open M-F 9am-5pm.

**Delta Airlines,** blv. Tarasa Shevchenka 10 (☎ 246 56 56 or 246 38 48). Open M-F 9am-6pm.

**KLM,** vul. Ivana Franka 29 #2 (☎ 246 55 85). Open M-F 10am-5pm.

**LOT,** next to ČSA (☎ 246 56 20). Open M-F 9am-5pm, Sa 10am-2pm.

**Lufthansa,** vul. Khmelnytskoho 52 (☎ 238 61 01; fax 238 61 02). Open M-F 9am-5:30pm.

**Malév,** vul. Hospitalnaya 12 (☎ 247 86 72; fax 247 86 72). Open M-F 10am-5pm.

**Trains: Kyiv-Passazhyrsky** (Київ-Пассажирський; schedule info ☎ 005), Vokzalna pl. MR: Vokzalna. In the main ticketing room on the ground floor, arrivals are listed on the left and departures on the right. **Tickets** can be purchased on the ground floor, after standing in the long lines of hall 4, or at the Intourist window on the 2nd floor. Open daily 8am-1pm, 2-7pm, and 8pm-7am. There are **Advanced-Ticket Offices** at blv. Shevchenka 38, straight up vul. Kominternu from the train station, or at MR: Universytet

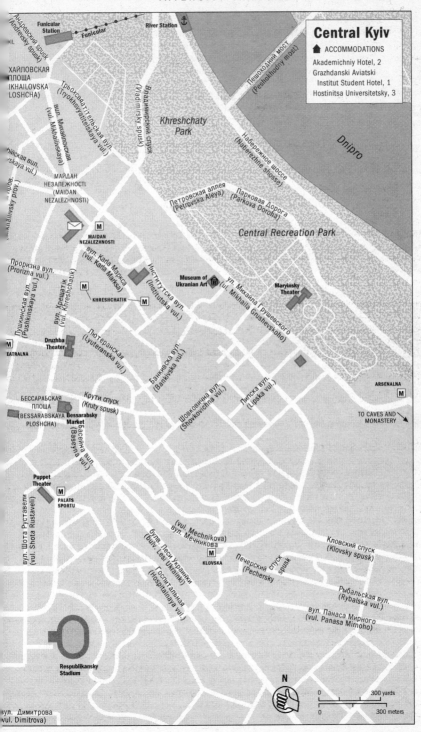

Central Kyiv

Funicular Station
Funicular
River Station

**Central Kyiv**

🏠 ACCOMMODATIONS

Akademichniy Hotel, 2
Grazhdanski Aviatski
Institut Student Hotel, 1
Hostinitsa Universitetsky, 3

Андрьвскй спуск
(Andreivsky spusk)
ИЛ

ХАЙЛОВСКА
ПЛОЩА
ИКХАILOVSKA
LOSHCHA)

Трьохсвятітельская вул.
(Tryohsvyatitelskaya vul.)

вул. Михайловская
(vul. Mikhailovskaya)

Владимирский спуск
(Vladimirsky spusk)

Khreshchaty Park

Dnipro

Набережное шоссе
(Naberezhne shosse)

Пешоходни мост
(Peshokhodny most)

айская вул,
rskaya vul.)

МАЙДАН
НЕЗАЛЕЖНОСТІ
(MAIDAN
NEZALEZHNOSTI)

Петровская аллея
(Petrovska Aleya)

Парковая Дорога
(Parkova Doroha)

*Central Recreation Park*

ailovsky prov.)

✉ MAIDAN NEZALEZHNOSTI

вул. Карла Маркса
(vul. Karla Marksa)

Інститутска вул.
(Institutska vul.)

Museum of Ukranian Art 🏛

ул. Михаила Грушевского
(ul. Mikhaila Grushevskoho)

Maryinsky Theater

Прорізна вул.
(Prorizna vul.)

Пушкінская вул.
(Pushkinskaya vul.)

вул. Хрещатик
(vul. Khreshchatik)

Ⓜ KHRESHCHATIK

Ⓜ
EATRALNA

Druzhba Theater

Лютеранская
(Lyuteranska vul.)

Банкивска вул.
(Bankivska vul.)

Шовковична вул.
(Shovkovichna vul.)

Липска вул.
(Lipska vul.)

ARSENALNA
Ⓜ

TO CAVES AND MONASTERY ➤

БЕССАРАБСКАЯ
ПЛОЩА
(BESSARABSKAYA
PLOSHCHA)

Крути спуск
(Kruty spusk)

Bessarabsky Market

Басейна вул.
(Baseyna vul.)

Puppet Theater

Ⓜ PALATS SPORTU

вул. Шота Руставели
(vul. Shota Rustaveli)

(vul. Mechnikova)
вул. Мечникова

б'лв. Леси Украинки
(bulv. Lesi Ukrainki)

Госпітальная
(Hospitalnaya vul.)

Ⓜ KLOVSKA

Печерский спуск
(Pechersky spusk)

Кловский спуск
(Klovsky spusk)

Рыбальская вул.
(Rybalska vul.)

вул. Панаса Мирного
(vul. Panasa Mirnoho)

Respublikansky Stadium

N

0   300 yards
0   300 meters

ул. Димитрова
(vul. Dimitrova)

(Університет). Cross and go left down Shevchenka. No passport required to buy domestic tickets. Offices open M-F 8am-8pm, Sa-Su 9am-6pm. Scalpers add 4-6hv to the price, but may have some tickets that are otherwise unavailable. Ask a clerk to check if the ticket is valid before paying by saying *"Pro-VER-teh, po-ZHA-lus-tah, EH-tot bee-LYET"* (Проверте пожалуйста этот білет; Please, check this ticket"). If Intourist or the *kasa* claim not to have tickets, try again both 6 and 2 hr. before the train leaves. Trains are better than buses for long-distance travel. To: **Kamyanets-Podilsky** (11hr., 1 per day, 17hv, *coupé* 26hv); **Odessa** (11hr., 5 per day, 24hv, *coupé* 40hv); **Lviv** (12hr., 6 per day, 24hv, *coupé* 50hv); **Ivano-Frankivsk** (16hr., 2 per day, 15hv, *coupé* 36hv); **Simferopol** (18hr., 5 per day, 27hv, *coupé* 60hv); and **Uzhhorod** (19½hr., 4 per day, 16hv, *coupé* 25hv). For **international tickets,** you will need to present your passport so they can charge you a higher price. To: **Minsk, BLR** (12-13hr., 1 per day, 70hv); **Warsaw, POL** (15hr., 2 per day, 190hv); **Moscow, RUS** (15-17hr., 15 per day, 60-95hv); **Bratislava, SLK** (18hr., 1 per day, 500hv); **Budapest, HUN** (25hr., 1 per day, 440hv); and **Prague, CZR** (34hr., 1 per day, 650hv).

**Buses: Tsentralny Avtovokzal** (Центральний Автовокзал), Moskovska pl. 3 (Московська; ☎265 05 30). A 10min. walk from Libidska, the last stop on the MG line. Take a right and then a left out of the Metro, and look for bus #4. If it isn't there, walk 100m to the big highway, then take a right and follow it for 300m. Long-distance destinations: **Chişinău, MOL** (Kishinev; 12hr., 2 per day, 47hv); **Dniepropetrovsk** (8hr., 2 per day, 40hv); **Kharkiv** (7.5hr., 5 per day, 35.20hv); **Minsk, BLR** (2 per day, 21hv); **Odessa** (10hr., 6 per day, 55hv); **Moscow, RUS** (21hr., 2 per day, 75.50hv); and **Prague, CZR** (30 hr., 2 per day, 330hv). Private **Darnytsa** (Дарница), pr. Gagarina (Гагаріна; ☎559 46 18), sends buses to **Dnieperpetrovsk** (9hr., 18hv).

# ⊏ LOCAL TRANSPORTATION

**Public Transportation:** Kyiv's **Metropoliten** is efficient in covering the city center, but its 3 intersecting lines (MB, blue; MG, green; MR, red) leave large areas between stops and do not reach most residential areas. Buy your blue token (житон; zhiton) at the *Kasa* (Каса) for 0.50hv. If you're in Kyiv for a while, invest in a metro pass (2-week 12hv, 1-month 25hv). Special passes (2-week 29hv; 1-month 57hv) are good on all public transportation, including buses, trolleys, and trams. Slide your card through the slot on top of the turnstile at the metro, or show it upon request to the conductor on the bus. Be sure to punch your ticket on board. The stations' signs are all in Cyrillic—consult your handy *Let's Go* subway map. "Перехід" (perekhid) indicates a walkway to another station, "вихід у місто" (vykhid u misto) an exit onto the street, "вхід" (vkhid) an entrance to the Metro, and "нема вхіду" (nema vkhidu) no entrance. Trolleys, buses, and *marshrutke taksi* (private vans that are labeled exactly as buses are and travel along identical routes) don't announce their stops. **Buses** will stop at each station, but you should request stops from *marshrutke* drivers. Buy *marshrutke* tickets (0.75hv) on board, and bus tickets (individually or in packets) at kiosks or from badge-wearing conductors. **Trolleys** and buses with identical numbers may have very different routes; a route map is a good investment. Public transport runs 6am-midnight, but some buses travel later. In general, for late-night travel, taxis are the only option.

**Taxis:** Avoid taxis when you can, as they overcharge foreigners. If you can't, give the driver an address *near* your hotel; he won't assume so quickly that you're a businessman on an expense account. Ordering a **state taxi** (☎058; identified by the checkered sign on top) is always cheaper than hailing a cab on the street. In the city-center, cabs are often available at Maydan Nezalezhnosti. Cab rides in the city center cost approximately US$2 (US$5 in the suburbs). The private company **Taksys** (Таксис; ☎295 95 08) charges 0.40hv per min. 6am-11pm, and 0.44hv per min. 11pm-6am. 60hv to the airport. Owners of **private cars** often act as taxi drivers. These rides are usually the cheapest, but set the price before getting in. Hold your arm down at a 45°angle to hail a ride. It is not advisable to get in a private car with more than one person already in it. Let's Go does *not* recommend private rides.

**Car Rental: Avis,** Hospitalna 4, #404 (☎294 21 04; rus@avis.relc.com). English-speaking operator. $40 per day.

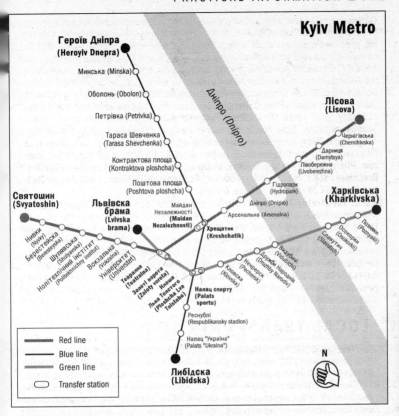

**Kyiv Metro**

Героїв Дніпра
(Heroyiv Dnepra)

Минська (Minska)

Оболонь (Obolon)

Петрівка (Petrivka)

Тараса Шевченка
(Tarasa Shevchenka)

Контрактова площа
(Kontraktova ploshcha)

Поштова площа
(Poshtova ploshcha)

Святошин
(Svyatoshin)

Львівська
брама
(Lvivska
brama)

Майдан
Незалежності
(Maidan
Nezalezhnosti)

Хрещатик
(Kreshchatik)

Нивки (Nyvky)
Берестейска (Beresteyska)
Шулявська (Shulyavska)
Політехнічний інститут (Politekhnichny institut)
Вокзальна (Vokzalna)
Університет (Universitet)

Театральна (Teatralna)
Золоті ворота (Zoloty vorota)
Площа Льва Толстого (Ploshcha Lva Tolstoho)

Палац спорту
(Palats
sportu)

Республіки
(Respublikansky stadion)

Клоеска (Klovska)
Дружби Народів (Druzhby Narodiv)
Печерск (Pechersk)
Видубичі (Vidubichi)

Палац "Україна"
(Palats "Ukraina")

Либідска
(Libidska)

Дніпро (Дніпро)

Гідропарк
(Hydropark)

Дніпро (Dnipro)

Арсенальна (Arsenalna)

Лісова
(Lisova)

Чернігівська
(Chernihivska)

Дарниця
(Darnytsya)

Лівобережна
(Livoberezhna)

Харківська
(Kharkivska)

Позняки (Poznyaki)
Червоний хутір (Radzyaki)
Оскорки (Osokorki)
Славутич (Slavuich)

Red line
Blue line
Green line
Transfer station

N

# ⁊ PRACTICAL INFORMATION

## TOURIST & FINANCIAL SERVICES

**Tourist Offices:** Kyiv still lacks official tourist services, because, like everything else here, the industry is still in the process of developing. Representatives of various agencies at the airport offer vouchers (for those without visas or invitations), excursion packages, hotel arrangements, and other services. All of them have offices in the city: **Tourist Office** (Туристичне бюро; Turistichne byuro), vul. Khmelnytskoho 13 (Хмельницького), ☎226 21 96 or 224 85 42. Open M-F 9am-5pm. **Yana** (Яна), vul. Saksahanskoho 42 (Саксаганського; ☎443 84 39). Open M-F 9am-5pm. **Advanced-Ticket Office,** blv. Tarasa Shevchenka 38, has a tourist office with occasional English translator. Open M-F 9am-5pm.

**Embassies: Australia,** vul. Kominternu 18/137 (Комінтерну; ☎235 75 86). Open 10am-1pm. **Belarus,** vul. Yanvarskoho Vossttanaya 6 (Январского Восстания; ☎290 02 01). Open M-F 10am-5pm. **Canada,** vul. Yaroslaviv Val 31 (Ярославів Вал; ☎464 11 44). Open M-Tu and Th-F 8:30am-noon. **Latvia,** vul. Desyatynia 4/6 (Десятинна; ☎229 27 45). Open M-F 10am-5pm. **Moldova,** vul. Sichnevoho Postannya 6 (Січневого Постання; ☎290 06 10; fax 290 77 21). Open M-F 9am-1pm and 3-6pm. MR: Arsenalna. **Russia,** Povitroflotsky pr. (Повітрофлотський; ☎244 09 63; fax 246 34 69). Open M-Th 9am-6pm, F 9am-5pm. **UK,** vul. Desyatynia 6 (☎462 00 11; fax 462 79 47). Open M-F 9am-5:30pm. **US,** vul. Pimonenko 6 (Пімоненко; ☎246 80 48 and 246 92 83; after hours emergency ☎216 38 05; fax 236 482; www.usemb.kyiv.ua). From the corner of Maydan Nezalezhnosti and Sofiyivska, take trolley #16 or 18 for 4 stops. Continue on vul. Artema (Артема), turn right before the post office, then left on Pimonenko. The embassy is tucked away behind the gates.

UKRAINE

**Currency Exchange:** *Obmin-Valyut* (Обмін-Валют) windows are everywhere, and often take only US$ and DM. Rates tend to be good, as they are primarily for locals who keep their money in dollars. New booths that cash traveler's checks and give MC/Visa advances usually have bad rates or high commissions. Try **Legbank** (Легбанк), vul. Shota Rustaveli 12 (Шота Руставелі). From MB/G: Palats sportu (Палац спорту), go northwest on vul. Rohnydinska (Рогнидінська) and turn right on Rustaveli. 3% commission for MC/Visa, 2% for traveler's checks if over US$250, otherwise flat US$5. Open M-F 9am-7pm, Sa 9am-6pm. Bank Ukrupspilka (Укрупспілка), the **National Bank of Ukraine,** on the corner of Institutska and Khreshchatyk, does everything for a 3.5% commission. They also offer **Western Union** services. Open daily 9am-1pm and 2-8pm.

**ATMs:** Cirrus/MC/Maestro/Visa machines are inside the TSUM Department Store at vul. Khreshchatyk 38, at the post office, and at various banks and fancy hotels. Look for Банкомат (Bankomat) signs. **Hostinitsa Bratislava** on vul. Malishka 1 (Малішка; MR: Darnitsya; Дарніця) has a 24hr. Western Union and a SWIFT money transfer service.

## LOCAL SERVICES, EMERGENCY & COMMUNICATIONS

**Luggage Storage:** At the train station. Look for Камери Схову (kamery skhovu), down the stairs outside the main entrance (2hv). Open daily 8am-noon, 1-7:30pm, 8pm-midnight, and 1-7:30am. Most major hotels have lockers for non-guests that might more secure. Try **Hotel Rus,** Hospitalna 4. 3hv per bag per night. Open 24hr.

**English Bookstores: Znaniya** (Знанія), blv. Khreshchatyk 44 (☎224 82 19), has the best selection, which isn't saying much. Open M-F 10am-2pm and 3-7pm. **Dinternal Ltd.,** vul. Museyny Provulok 2 (☎228 63 14; dinter@public.ua.net), opposite Dynamo Stadium, also has English books. Two English weeklies, the newspaper *Kyiv Post* and the magazine *What's On,* are available for free in bars and expensive restaurants.

**24hr. Pharmacy: Apteka,** vul. Ivana Franka 25/40 (Івана Франка; ☎224 29 88), the purple building on the corner with vul. Khmelnytskoho, sparkles with sanitized cleanliness and carries high-quality products. Ring the bell 8pm-8am.

**Medical Assistance:** Check with the **US Embassy** (see above) for a list of safe hospitals. **Emergency Care Center,** vul. Mechnikova 1 (☎227 92 30), also has a **dental clinic** (☎227 42 40). The **American Medical Center,** vul. Berdicherska 1 (☎211 65 55; fax 211 65 57), will cost you dearly. **Ukrainian Medical Services** (☎440 63 44) has a 24-hr. English staff.

**Telephones: Myzhmisky Perehovorny Punkt** (Мижміський Переговорний Пункт), at the post office (see below), or **Telefon-Telefaks** (Телефон-Телефакс), around the corner (entry on Khreshchatyk). Both offices open 24hr. **Public telephones** (Таксофон; Taksofon) work only with a phone card, which can be purchased at any post office (5.40hv for 90 units, 7.20hv for 120 units). For information on how to call outside of the country, see **Keeping in Touch,** p. 766. **English operator** ☎8-192. Long distance phone services are operated by Utel (Ukrainian Telecommunications). Window #3 at the telephone office puts calls through to North America. State the number of minutes you want and pay up front. They insist they can't dial AT&T or MCI operators, but yellow-framed Utel phones will do the trick. When making an international call from a private phone, dial 8, wait for a tone, then dial 10, country code, city code, and number. Not as widespread as Taksofon, **Utel phone cards** are available in denominations of 10hv, 20hv, and 40hv at the post office and upscale hotels. Utel phones can be found in the post office, the train station, hotels, fancy restaurants, and Dom Ukrainsky (Дом Український), across from Hotel Dnieper.

**Internet Access: Kiber Kafe** (Кібер Кафе; Cyber Cafe), Prorizna 21 (Прорізна; ☎228 05 48). Smoky but centrally located and often packed during evenings with Ukrainians playing computerized cards and expats checking email on one of 14 speedy computers. 10hv per hr. Open daily 10am-2am.

**Post Office:** At vul. Khreshchatyk 22 (☎228 00 68; fax 228 33 82), next to Maydan Nezalezhnosti. **Poste Restante** at counters #29-30. Pre-stamped airmail envelopes (3.52hv at counter #1) are the easiest way to send international mail. To mail packages, enter on the Maydan Nezalezhnosti side. Also houses a full-service copy/fax/ photo center. Open M-Sa 8am-9pm, Su 9am-7pm.

**Postal Code:** 252 001.

# ACCOMMODATIONS

Accommodations in Kyiv suffer from an unfortunate combination of capitalist prices and socialist quality. Unless you have money to spare, be prepared to stay in a Soviet subdivision like the rest of the city. Hotels are geared toward high-paying customers, and foreigners pay rates that are often twice those paid by Ukrainians. Check-out is generally by noon. People offer private rooms at the train station.

**Grazhdanski Aviatski Institut Student Hotel,** vul. Nizhinska 29E (Ніжіньська; ☎484 90 59). From behind MR: Vokzalna, turn right into the passageway leading to the trams. Ride 6 or 7 stops on tram #1K or 7 to "Граматна" (Hramatna); get off at the "Індустраільна" (Industrailna) stop. Backtrack 1½ blocks, turn right onto vul. Nizhinska, cross at the 1st intersection with a trolleybus, then follow the path into the complex. Keep the 1st building on your right as you walk diagonally to block "Д." After passing Д on the right, look for the "Гостиница ФПК" (Gostinitsa FPK) sign above the entrance (50min.). Their clean rooms are the best deal around if you don't mind the trek. *Lux* rooms (comprise a double and a single with TV and fridge and a shared bathroom) singles 45.50hv; doubles 55.44hv; barer rooms 10hv.

**Akademichniy Hotel** (Академічний), vul. Perovskoyi Sofiy 6/11 (Перовської Софії; ☎/ fax 446 90 31). MR: Shuliavska (Шулявська). Turn right out of the Metro and head down Prospekt Peremohy (Перемоги). Take the 2nd right to vul. Perovskoyi; the hotel will be the distinguished-looking building on your right. Reservations required, and rooms fill up during conference times, so call ahead. Singles with bath and phone US$30; doubles US$45.

**Hostinitsa Universitetsky** (Университетский), vul. Lomonosova 81 (Ломоносова; ☎261 74 54). MB: Libidska (Лібідска). Go right, then left through the Metro tunnels to bus #38. Take it to the end at "Ковалевської" (Kovalevskoy), then go a little farther to the two 9-story buildings (45min. from center). *Avtosvit* (австосвіт) minibuses won't stop unless you flag them down (0.75hv), but are worth the trouble for direct transport. Primarily for Ukrainian students, but if you call the director beforehand and ask for him when you show up, you can get a room (director's ☎266 55 09). Check-in noon. Spacious doubles with shower, kitchen, and balcony 57.60hv, with TV and fridge 84hv; lone double 28hv.

# FOOD

Babushki on the street, merchants in the *rynki* (ринкі; markets) and kiosks, and restaurant owners want nothing more than to feed you their myriad colorful products. Many restaurants are pricey and cater almost exclusively to foreigners and the few Ukrainians who can afford them. Check out the *Kyiv Post* and *What's On* for ads and reviews. Yellow and red signs mark the Ukrainian fast food chain "Shvidko" (Швидко; quickly). If you don't mind the tab, **Arizona, Bombay Palace** (especially good for vegetarians), and the outrageously priced **San Tori** are among the most popular. Expats hang out at **Uncle Sam's** (☎227 20 00), **Tequila House** (☎417 03 68), and **O'Brien's Irish Pub** (☎229 15 84). Those looking for kosher food can try out **Haifa** (Хайфа), vul. Konstantinovskaya (Константиновская; ☎417 25 12). Locals choose Kyiv's specialty drinks over munchies—vendors sell *Stolichnaya* vodka, *kava po-skhidnomu* (кава по-східному; Turkish coffee), and good old *kvas* (квас; 0.5L 0.30hv in the most touristed areas). For those on a tight budget, the best option is a trip to one of Kyiv's *rynki*. The ubiquitous *hastronomy* (supermarkets; гастрономи) usually close around 7pm. Their Western equivalents have sprung up in the center; though they can be good for refrigerated meat and other rarities, many of the same items can be found at *hastronomy* for much lower prices. As the name backwardly suggests, **7/24** on vul. Baseyna 1/2 (Басейна; ☎221 58 57), behind Bessarabsky Rynok, is always open. MC/Visa.

UKRAINE

## RESTAURANTS

**Pantagruel** (Пантагруель), vul. Lysenko 1 (Лисенко; ☎228 81 42), right next to MG: Zoloty Vorota. Authentic Italian food prepared by an authentic Italian chef in an authentic Italian cellar. Outdoor seating in the summer. Main dishes 25-40hv. Live music F-Sa 8-10pm. English-language papers. Open M-Th and Su 11am-11pm, F-Sa 11am-2am.

**Cafe Jepsen** (Кафе Джепсен), Lvivska Ploshcha 8 (Львівська Пл.; ☎212 51 06). The aviation maps and model planes that hang from the ceiling lend credibility to the rumor that Cafe Jepsen is the hangout of Kyiv's pilots. Large portions of Ukrainian specialties. Main dishes 20-50hv. Open 11am-11pm.

**Pizza Lola** (Піцца Лола), vul. Lva Tolstoho 8 (Льва Толстого; ☎224 74 23). MB: Ploshcha Lva Tolstoho. Follow the street for 2min.; Lola's is in the basement on the left. These Ukrainian pizzas put Italy to shame. To avoid fighting for a table, have them put your personal circle of joy in a box and walk a block up the street to eat in the park. Main dishes 13.50-27hv. 1-person cheese pizza 13.50hv, with 2 toppings 19hv. 0.5L beer 3.50hv. Open daily 11am-9pm, in summer until 10pm (kitchen closes at 9:30pm).

## CAFES

🖼 **Cafe Panorama** (Кафе Панорама; ☎417 74 89). Walk down Andraivesky uzviz, 25m past St. Andrew's Church and up the steep wooden steps on the right. Quiet outdoor seating and glorious views of Podil from its perch above Kyiv. Simple beef or chicken *shashlik* 15hv. Main dishes 12-19hv. 0.5L *Obolon* 5hv. Open daily 11am-11pm.

**Kavyarnya Svitoch** (Кавярня Світоч; Cafe Svitoch), vul. Velyka Zhytomyrksa 8a (☎264 08 09). On the right as you follow the street (and the smell of chocolate) from Mikhailivska pl. A famous Lviv confectioner opened a Kyiv outlet in 1995; the cafe, popular among students, is next door. The place for black coffee (2hv) and dark chocolate (0.20-2hv). Hot drinks from around the world. Open daily 9am-9pm.

## MARKETS

Ukraine has a European passion for fresh food, but so do the occasional swarms of flies. *Babushki*, *dyevotchki* (girls), and others lay out their products—anything from fruits, vegetables and meat to dresses and laundry detergent in a picturesque fashion. Small markets are everywhere, larger ones are at major locations.

**Bessarabsky Rynok** (Бессарабский Ринок; ☎224 89 34), at the intersection of vul. Khreshchatyk and blv. Shevchenka. No mere gaggle of *babushki* selling berries. On the edge of Kyiv's most chic neighborhood, Bessarabsky offers the best meat, fruit, and vegetables of the Ukrainian countryside, all in a classical yellow structure.

**Volodymyrsky-Kolhospny Rynok** (Володимирский-Колгоспний Ринок), vul. Telmana (Тельмана), between vul. Chervonoarmiska and blv. Horkoho (Бул Горкого). MB/G: Palats Ukraina (Палац Україна). Even larger than the Bessarabsky. Plenty of food, flowers, clothes, tapes, and unhappily caged animals. Open daily 10am-7pm.

# 🔾 SIGHTS

The seat of Kyivan Rus (see **History**, p. 758) and for a millennium Ukraine's capital, Kyiv boasts sights almost as numerous as its lush-green parks. Church domes and monuments to religious and national figures mix with Soviet architecture, all overlooking the vast and tranquil Dnieper River. Many of the city's older monuments are currently being renovated, but a glance out of an upper-story window will quickly remind one of Shevchenko's favorite green and gold city.

## VUL. KHRESHCHATYK AND ENVIRONS

**KHRESHCHATYK STREET.** (Вул. Хрещатик; Vulitza Khreshchatyk.) Kyiv centers around this broad commercial avenue, built after World War II—its size testifies to Soviet bombast, although the surrounding buildings have retained a tremendous amount of character. On weekends, the street is closed to traffic as Kyivans come out to shop, stroll, and even ride horses. Khreshchatyk begins at the intersection with blv. Shevchenka, where **Lenin,** surrounded by inspirational sayings, still gazes off into the future. At #2 is the central department store **TSUM** (ЦУМ), which sells everything from guitars to lawn chairs to coffee cake. Don't let the fancy new facade fool you; it's still run like a state store. *(Open M-Sa 9am-8pm. MC/Visa.)* An archway on Khreshchatyk leads to the *passazh*, Kyiv's most cosmopolitan area with elegant, high-priced cafes and bars. *(MR, MB: Khreshchatyk.)*

**INDEPENDENCE PLAZA.** (Майдан Незалежності; Maydan Nezalezhnosti; formerly October Revolution Square). Book vendors, musicians, hipsters, and those gathering to talk away the evening over tankards of beer or *kvas* fill the terrace around the large fountains. Right-wing, left-wing, and tourist propaganda is sold along the fountain walls while the occasional street performer pleases crowds. At night, the Metro stop underneath shelters Kyiv's best street musicians. The square saw revolution in 1905 and later, the execution of Nazi war criminals. The **statue of Archangel Michael** was unveiled in 1996 and displays on its base the distances from Kyiv to all the capitals of the world. *(MR, MB: Khreshchatyk.)*

**OTHER SIGHTS.** Just past the Independence Plaza to the right is vul. Institutska (Інститутська), another facade-filled promenade. Uphill to the left glows the bright-yellow **Palace of Culture** (Палац Культурни; Palats Kulturny), one of Kyiv's largest concert halls and a Neoclassical rival to the Rococo **National Bank of Ukraine** (Національний Банк України; Natsionalny Bank Ukrainy), also on the right.

# KHRESHCHATYK PARK

*Vul. Khreshchatyk continues up into Evropeyska Ploshcha (Европейска пл.; European Sq.), where it meets the stately Volodymyrsky uzviz that runs through Kyiv's vast Khreshchatyk Park. The park is enormous, with each monument tucked away in its own corner; you'll do best to just wander to the birds' songs.*

**ARCH OF BROTHERHOOD.** Referred to by locals as the "Yoke," this silver croquet wicket towers over the park and is a monument to the 1654 Russian-Ukrainian Pereyaslav union (see **History**, p. 759). It now serves as a popular meeting spot for couples, who come here for a romantic view of the Dnieper River below. Go right at the arch and into the park for the monument to **brave soccer players** (see below).

**PRINCE VOLODYMYR STATUE.** Brandishing a cross, Prince Volodymyr is overlooking the river in which he had the whole city baptized in 988—despite freezing temperatures—making Orthodox Christianity the official religion of Kyivan Rus. *(Statue is to the left across Volodymyrsky uzviz.)*

**MARIYINSKY PALACE.** Built by Francesco Rastrelli, who also designed Kyiv's St. Andrew's Church and much of St. Petersburg, the palace was ordered for Tsaritsa Elizabeth's visit in the 1750s. It began to be called Mariyinsky in honor of Maria Alexandrovna, consort of Russian Czar Alexander II. Today the palace is used for formal state receptions. *(Atop the hill from Prince Volodymyr Statue on the right. ☎ 293 49 09. Organized tours through the Museum of the History of Kyiv only.)*

# TARAS SHEVCHENKO BOULEVARD

*Perpendicular to vul. Khreshchatyk from the park, beginning at the Lenin statue.*

The boulevard (Булв. Тараса Шевченка; Blv. Tarasa Shevchenka) is dedicated to Taras Shevchenko, whose poetry reinvented the Ukrainian language in the mid-

**KYIV 3, NAZIS 0** Following the devastating Nazi invasion of Kyiv in September 1941, a German soldier discovered that one of his prisoners was a member of the city's *Dynamo Kyiv* soccer team. Officers quickly rounded up the other players, and arranged a "death match" between them and the German army team. Despite the Dynamos' weakened condition and a referee dressed in a Gestapo uniform, they won the game 3-0. Shortly thereafter the entire team was thrown into a concentration camp, where most of them perished in front of a firing squad. Their memory—and Kyiv's pride—lives on in a monument overlooking Khreshchaty Park.

UKRAINE

19th century (see **Literature & Arts**, p. 761), and whose paintings depict vivid scenes of traditional Ukrainian festivals and country life. Banished in 1847, he never returned to Kyiv. The **Taras Shevchenko University**, which still leads independent thought in Ukraine, stands on the boulevard. The university's students and old men gather around the park benches nearby; the young to contemplate some Taras, the old to play chess. Farther on, at #20, stands the many-domed ochre **Volodymyrsky Cathedral,** built to mark 900 years of Christianity in Kyiv. Its interior features examples of Byzantine and Art Nouveau styles. People stop to pray and light a candle in front of the many icons. A **botanical garden** offers some shade across from the cathedral. *(0.30hv, students 0.10hv. Open 9am-9pm.)*

## ST. SOPHIA AND ENVIRONS

*MG: Zoloty Vorota, or trolley #16 from Maydan Nezalezhnasti.*

**GOLDEN GATE.** (Золоти Ворота; Zoloty Vorota). Actually made of wood and stone, the gate has marked the entrance to the city since 1037. As legend has it, its strength saved Kyiv from the Tatars during the reign of **Yaroslav the Wise,** whose statue stands nearby (see **History,** p. 758). A **museum** devoted to the gate is inside, but is closed for renovation. *(300m down Volodymyrska vul. from St. Sophia.)*

**ST. SOPHIA MONASTERY COMPLEX.** Enormous and elaborate, St. Sophia Monastery is what many tourists come to Kyiv to see: golden onion domes, decorated facades, and exquisite Byzantine icons from the 11th century. The interior mosaics are not to be missed, though not all of them have been restored. The monastery was the cultural center of Kyivan Rus and is still the focal point of the increasingly complex question of Ukrainian nationalism. In July 1995, the government denied the Uniate Church's desire to bury its patriarch here. When the funeral procession, led by the Ukrainian nationalist militia, attempted entry into the complex, they were violently rerouted by the police. By the entrance to St. Sophia lies pl. Khmelnytskoho, supervised by the statue of hetman Bohdan Khmelnytsky (see **History,** p. 759). *(Volodymyrska vul. 24. Open M-Tu and F-Su 10am-5:30pm, W 10am-4:30pm. 10hv, museum and exhibitions 2hv more. 1hr. tours 10hv. English tours available. Cameras 10hv.)*

**MIKHAILIVSKYI ZOLOTOVERKHY MONASTERY.** (Михайлівский Золотоверхий Монастир; Monastir). The freshly painted blue and gold-domed monastery now draws many tourists who unknowingly appreciate the failure of the 1934 Soviet plan to demolish all religious sights in Kyiv. *(At the top of Mikhaylivska pl. Open 9am-9pm. Free.)* A **museum** in the bell tower leads up to the actual chamber of the bells. *(Open Tu-Su 11am-5pm. 2hv, students 1hv.)* To the right of the monastery, vul. Tryokhsvyatytelska passes a series of smaller churches as it winds its way down to the park **Volodymyrska Hirka** (Володимирска Гірка), full of tiny pavilions and sculptures by folk artists. The park is also rumored to be a **gay cruising spot.**

**MIKHAILIVSKA SQUARE.** (Михайлівська пл.). The recent renovations of this square included a new statue of **Princess Olga,** grandmother of Volodymyr I and perhaps the first Christian in Kyivan Rus. She is surrounded by St. Cyril, St. Methodius (see **What's in a name?,** p. 14), and St. Andrew the Apostle, who is believed to have blessed these lands centuries before the founding of Kyiv. Behind the princess and to her left stands the monumental **Ministry of Foreign Affairs,** which we've measured to be 90% pillar, 10% building. In the summer of 2000, the square hosted the festivities accompanying US President Bill Clinton's visit to Ukraine. *(Vul. Volodomyrska.)*

## ANDRIVSKY PATH AND THE PODIL DISTRICT

*A **funicular** goes up Andrivsky from MB: Poshtova. (Every 5min., daily 6:30am-11pm. 0.50hv.) Alternatively, walk down from Mikhailivska Square.*

The easiest way to see the cobblestone **Andrivsky path** (Андрівські узвіз; Andrivsky Uzviz), a winding road lined with cafes, souvenir vendors and galleries, is to ride up and walk down. As you walk down, look for signs offering "Виставка" (vistavka; exhibition) of local artists' work. Next to the entrepreneurs selling real Ukrainian pipes and Soviet Army hats, independent galleries show the newest and boldest

## GOD OR VODKA?

Kyiv has almost as many churches as trees. Despite a 13th century Mongol burning-spree and the destructive Soviet "socialist reconstruction," pear-shaped domes tower everywhere. Since the end of the Communist ban on religious practices, Pravoslav Orthodoxy, with all its sacramental bells and whistles, has flourished in Kyiv. It has every reason to—as the capital of Kyivan Rus, the first great civilization of the Eastern Slavs, Kyiv was the birthplace of Pravoslavism. While Princess Olga had been privately baptized in the mid-900s, it wasn't until her grandson Volodymyr (folk hero and saint to Ukrainians and Russians alike) ascended to the throne that Christianity caught on among the Slavs. After an unpromising beginning that included paganism and well-documented promiscuity, Volodymyr decided that an up-and-coming empire needed an advanced religion. He first considered Islam, but the ban on alcohol was too much for the prince to handle. "Drinking is the joy of the Russes," he was recorded to have said, "and we cannot exist without that pleasure." Among the remaining options, Volodymyr and his Kyivan entourage chose Eastern Orthodoxy, after a visit to Byzantium's Constantinople convinced them that nothing can beat well-spaced golden domes. Orthodoxy was officially proclaimed the imperial religion, and the residents of Kyiv were herded into the Dnieper for baptism in 988.

work Ukrainian visual artists have to offer, though most just sell touristy paintings of the **St. Andrew's Cathedral** (closed for renovations). After passing Bulgakov's house, Andrivsky uzviz spills out onto **Kontraktova Sq.** (Контрактова пл.), the center of **Podil**, Kyiv's oldest district and the city center in the 10th and 11th centuries. This pleasant neighborhood is home to a wealth of small **churches.**

**TITHE CHURCH.** (Desatinia Tserkva; Десатиниа Церква). Ruins are the only remnant of the oldest stone church of Kyivan Rus (c. 989-96), which converted pagan Kyivans to Christianity in the 10th century. It endured for centuries, only to be deliberately destroyed by the Soviet "Socialist Reconstruction" program in 1937. *(Walk up the gray steps at the corner of Andrivsky uzviz, Desatynia, and Volodymyrska.)*

## BABYN YAR AND ST. CYRIL'S

*Take trolley #27 for 8 stops from MB: Petrivka, or trolley #16 from Maydan Nezalezhnosti for about 10 stops. The monument—a large group of interlocking figures—stands in the park near the TV tower, at the intersection of vul. Oleny Telihy and vul. Melnykova.*

**BABYN YAR.** (Бабин Яр.) The World War II monument at Babyn Yar marks the graves of the first victims in Ukraine, buried in September 1941. Although the plaques state that 100,000 Kyivans died here, current estimates double that figure. Many of the victims—most of them Jews—were buried alive. On an incline above the grass-covered pit, the statue shows the victims falling to their deaths.

## KYIV-PECHERY MONASTERY

*MR: Arsenalna. Turn left as you exit and walk 20min. down vul. Sichnevoho Povstaniya. Trolleybus #20 can also take you here (2 stops going left from the Metro toward the river). Open daily 9:30am-7pm, in winter until 6pm. Monastery 16hv, students 8hv. Museum 3hv, students 1hv. Russian tours free; private tours in English 80hv.*

Kyiv's oldest and holiest religious site, the mysterious Kyiv-Pechery Monastery (Києво-Печерська Лавра; Kyivo-Pecherska Lavra) deserves a full day of exploration. Most of the sights are undergoing a much-needed renovation that should soon have the monastery sparkling, but which meanwhile makes navigation and museum access difficult. The 12th-century **Holy Trinity Church** (Троїцка надзрамна церква; Troitska Nadzramna Tserkva) serves as the entrance to the monastery. The church's interior (take a left upon entering) contains some beautiful frescoes, a 600kg censer, and the ruins of an ancient church. Be sure to step into the functioning **Refractory Church,** home to one of the longest and most decorated domes in the complex. The 18th-century Great Cave Bell Tower (Велика лаврська дзвіниця;

UKRAINE

Velyka lavrska dzvinytsya) offers fantastic views of the river and apartment blocks mingled with golden domes. *(Open daily 9:30am-8pm. 2.50hv, students 1hv.)*

**MONASTERY'S MUSEUMS.** The monastery is surrounded by patriotic museums dedicated to the history of Ukraine. The **Museum of Books and Bookmaking** (Музей книги и книгопечатанія; Muzey Knigi i Knigopechataniya) details the history of book and printing development in Ukraine, while the **Museum of Historical Treasures** (Музей Історіческих драгоценностей; Muzey Istoricheskikh Dragotsennostey) displays precious stones and metals, both ancient and modern. The ticket shows a map of the complex, but the labels are in Cyrillic only. *(Open M and W-Su 9:30am-4pm.)*

■ **CAVES.** After death the monastery's monks were mummified and entombed in the dark caves—the most interesting part of the complex. Buy a candle (0.50-1hv) as you enter if you want to see anything. Women should cover their heads and shoulders; men should wear pants. People offer unofficial tours of the underground as you enter the complex for around US$10, but the icon-filled caves are pretty self-explanatory. *(Open M and W-Su 9-11:30am and 1-4pm.)*

**MOTHERLAND STATUE.** Looking toward the monastery's domes, the metal motherland figure celebrates the World War II victory and was designed by the wife of the sculptor of the Volgograd Motherland statue. Plans to tear down the tin mama and replace her with a monument to the victims of Chernobyl have not yet come to fruition, but the statue might fall of its own accord. *(At the end of Sichnevoho Povstaniya.)*

# 🏛 MUSEUMS

■ **Chernobyl Museum,** Provulok Zhorevii 1 (☎417 54 22). At the lower end of Adrivsky uzviz, pass through Kontraktova Sq. Powerful imagery conveys the magnitude of the disaster and explains why the Soviet Union fell apart. Ask about the video, usually shown during tours, that shows the explosion. Open M-Sa 10am-6pm. Closed last M of the month. Free.

**National Museum of Ukrainian History** (Національний Музей Історії України; Natsionalny Muzey Istorii Ukrainy), vul. Volodymyrska 2 (☎228 65 45), up the stairway at the crossroad with Andrivsky uzviz. Houses exhibits from the Stone Age to the present. Open M-Tu and Th-Su 10am-6pm. Closed last Th of the month. 4.80hv, students 2.40hv. Tours available in Ukrainian and German.

**Museum of Ukrainian Literature** (Музей Літератури України; Muzey Literatury Ukrainy), vul. Khmelnytskoho 11. Highly nationalistic, the museum traces Ukrainian literature from its inception to the present, quoting Ivan Franko and Taras Shevchenko the entire way. English-speaking guides are available only through Intourist for an exorbitant rate. Open M-Sa 9am-5pm. 1.20hv, students 0.60hv.

**Taras Shevchenko Museum,** Blv. Tarasa Shevchenka 12 (☎224 25 56). One of the largest and most beautiful museums in the former USSR, the museum contains a huge collection of Shevchenko's sketches, paintings, and prints, as well as some of his correspondence and poetry. Open Tu-Su 10am-5pm; closed last F of the month. 1hv, students 0.30hv. English tours 20hv, students 10hv.

**Bulgakov's House,** Andrivsky uzviz 13 (☎416 31 88), next to the National Museum of Ukrainian History. All you ever wanted to know about Mikhail Bulgakov's *White Guard* (see **Russia: Literature and Arts,** p. 761), a sympathetic look at a White Army family in Kyiv during the Civil War. Confusing if you haven't read the book. Open M-Tu and Th-Su 10am-6pm. 2hv, students 1hv. 45min. English tour 10hv.

# 🎭 ENTERTAINMENT

Be sure to check the *Kyiv Post* and *What's On* (www.whatson-kyiv.com), for listings of all entertainment. The daily and weekend **bazaars** in the summer at Respublikansky Stadion and Vokzalny are experiences in themselves, even if you don't buy any of the myriad sodas and cigarettes hauled in from all over the former Soviet Union. The festival **Kyiv Days** takes place the last weekend in May, when Maydan Nezalezhnosti is packed with *shashlik* stands, orchestras, and craftspeople.

## SPORTS AND THE OUTDOORS

During the soccer season (late spring to fall), don't miss **Dynamo Kyiv,** one of the top teams in Europe. Check with the *kasa* at the Respublikansky Stadium on vul. Chervonoarmiska. (MB: Respublikansky stadion. *Kassa* open daily 10am-6pm. 3-5hv.)

On hot summer days, locals head out to ◪ **Hydropark** (Гідропарк), an **amusement park** and **beach** on an island in the Dnieper. (MR: Hidropark.) Tucked in a corner near the bridge, the Venice Beach of Ukraine hosts young buffs lifting spare automobile parts to keep in shape. The beach has showers, toilets, and changing booths, and no one seems to charge admission. **Rent boats** at **Otdykh na vode—Fregat** (Отдых на воде—Фрегат), on the east shore of Hidropark, near the Metro bridge. (Boat or waterbike 5hv per hr. Open daily 9am-8pm, last rental 6pm.) **Spike Bowling Club,** on the beach at Peremohy 84, hosts Kyiv's pin-topplers. (☎442 64 64. Open M-Th 5pm-3am, F 2pm-4am, Sa 11am-4am, Su 1pm-3am.)

## PERFORMANCES

Every March, international troupes come for a two-week multilingual **theater festival. Kinopanorama,** S. Rustaveli 19 (☎227 11 35), and the new **Kino Palats,** vul. Institutska 1, right across from Maydan Nezalezhnosti, show the last movie of the night in English, after all the Ukrainians are in bed. **UIA Ticket Sales** and reservations, Prosp. Peremohy 14 (☎221 83 80) can provide tickets and information.

**Philharmonic,** Volodymyrsky uzviz 2 (☎229 62 51). Classic and classical. *Kassa* open M 3-7pm, Tu-F noon-7pm.

**Shevchenko Opera and Ballet Theater,** Volodymyrska vul. 50 (☎224 71 65 or 229 11 69). MR: Teatralna. Several shows each week at noon and 7pm. Ticket office open M 3-7pm, Tu-Su 11am-2pm and 3-7:30pm.

# ◪ NIGHTLIFE

Perhaps it is the many cathedrals looming overhead, or the fact that by midnight many people are too drunk to walk, but when it comes to nightlife Kyivans are often content to spend their twilight hours sipping an *Obolon* beer outdoors. Kyiv's most popular discos pale next to the shining stars of Moscow, but keep your ears open for occasional raves. **Al Capone,** Kostyantynivska 26, in a converted cinema, is the boss of late boogying. Disco **New York,** Perova 2 (☎558 25 45), near Park Peremchy, has a loyal following.

## BARS

**Rock Cafe** (Рок Кафе), vul. Horodetskoho 10 (☎228 36 38). MG: Maydan Nezalezhnosti. Walk 300m along the street to the right of the giant steps; the cafe is on your right, at the left corner of a plaza full of similarly relaxing outdoor late-night cafes. This easygoing coffeeshop, where unpretentious expats hang with their local acquaintants, evolves into a busy bar at night. Coffee or half-glass of sparkling water 3hv. Outdoor seating. Pool 4hv per game. 0.5L *Obolon* 5hv. Open daily 11am-3am.

**O'Brien's Pub,** vul. Mikhailyska 17a (Міхайлівська; ☎229 15 84), off Maidan Nezalezhnosti. The new Irish cellar in town, full of British expats, and perhaps the most relaxed drinking atmosphere outside Khreshchatyk Park. Open daily 8am-2am.

**Miami Blues,** vul. Chervonoarmiska 114 (Червоноармійська; ☎252 89 98). Expensive but fascinating look at Ukrainian yuppie culture. Live jazz M and Th-F and an adventurous drink menu: try the fruity *lemon fleep* or the local favorite *BMW*. Outdoor seating. Open 24hr., but dies out around 1am.

**The Cowboy Bar,** vul. Khreshchatyk 15 (☎228 17 17), at the far end of the *passazh*. A piece of Ukraine-generated America on Kyiv's Euro-trash street. Raw, unpainted wood, cigarette smoke, and live blues, jazz, and country music nightly after 9:30pm (10:30pm in summer). Behind the bar, a "Wanted" poster promises a reward for the capture of "Robber Boss Wild Bill." *Obolon* 6hv. Cover 10hv, women free. Open daily 6pm-6am.

## GAY AND LESBIAN ENTERTAINMENT

In the eyes of many Ukrainians, homosexuality is simply not acceptable. Discrimination and homophobia are widespread, and thus the gay scene in Ukraine has failed to take off the same way it has in Moscow. Gay nightlife, previously limited to private parties and irregular club venues, is slowly developing, however. In the summer, the scene is revived substantially, thanks to Hydropark; follow the mob to **Youth Beach** (Molodizhny Plyazh). There, buy a 1hv boat ride to the beach opposite, where the crowd is mixed and clothes are optional. There's also an all-gay beach nearby, but it's muddy. **The Cage,** Kutzova 3 (☎573 88 47) is a nightclub where the gay scene is reportedly becoming established, but things of this sort of change quickly here. Consult the *Kyiv Post* (or call the entertainment editor) for updated information. The **lesbian** scene is still very much underground.

# CRIMEA (КРЫМ)

Thanks to its position on the Black Sea Coast, the Crimea has been a trading thoroughfare since antiquity. The much-sought-after peninsula was annexed by Russians in 1783 and officially given to Ukraine in 1954. Russian-speaking and proud-spirited, Crimea has reacted rebelliously to the collapse of the USSR: street signs retain their Soviet name and locals still call their currency "rubles." Despite the restrictions on electricity and hot water and the staggering economy, the rocky shores to which Tsars, Mongols, and Soviet workers flocked retain their appeal. From Simferopol, redeemed only by its rail connections and the splendor of nearby Bakhchisarai, travelers can reach the sandy shores of Feodosia or the maritime history of Sevastopol. Others rave the month of August away atop the nuclear reactor at Kazantip. Then there's Yalta, where *literati* once vacationed, but only the ghost of Chekhov remains. Livadia, where Roosevelt, Churchill, and Stalin divided up the post-World War II world, and Alupka, a testament to the decadence of empire, await exploration just off the coast.

**WHO OWNS CRIMEA?** In the 5th century BC, Herodotus first recorded that Scythians and Greeks dwelled in Crimea, but invaders such as Slavs and Romans have been joining the beach party ever since. Many Mongols settled and, over the next 500 years, became the indigenous Crimean Tatars.

Crimea was part of the Mongol Horde and later held semi-independent status under Ottoman protection. Catherine the Great annexed Crimea in 1783 and refurbished it as a Russian beach resort extraordinaire. During the several Russo-Turkish wars in the 19th century, the Tatars emigrated to escape Tsarist rule. The 1854 Crimean War saw France and Britain clash with Russia over the city of Sevastopol. The Russians evacuated, leaving the Tatars to revive their national heritage, language, and culture. In 1917, the Tatars declared autonomy against the will of the Bolsheviks. Russia soon regained control and paid its citizens to settle in the city. On the night of May 18, 1944, Stalin had the entire Crimean Tatar population shipped to Uzbekistan.

In 1954 Khrushchev gave Crimea to Ukraine as a "gift" to celebrate 300 years of union between Russia and Ukraine—Crimeans still believe he must have been drunk. Russian-speaking Crimeans have always identified with Russian rule and culture and are unenthusiastic about being part of Ukraine. In 1991 Crimeans voted largely in favor of preserving the Soviet Union, and since the collapse "of the big Ma" its citizens have made several attempts at independence. Crimea is currently an autonomous republic within Ukraine, but on paper only. The Tatars have been returning *en masse* since 1989 to demand the return of their land. Amidst the turmoil, Crimea's future remains unclear; the only certainty is that the peninsula's lucrative tourist industry is bound to attract even more heated claims to the region.

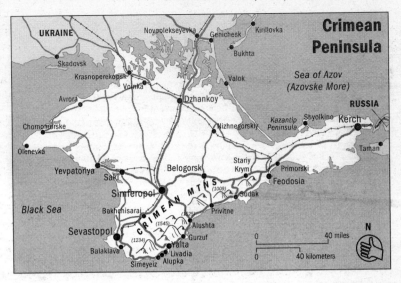

**Crimean Peninsula**

UKRAINE
Novoolekseyevka
Genichesk
Kirillovka
Skadovsk
Bukhta
Krasnoperekopsk
Voinka
Valok
Avrora
Dzhankoy
**RUSSIA**
Chornomorske
Nizhnegorskiy
Kazantip Peninsula
Shyolkino
Kerch
Olenevka
Taman
Stariy Krym
Belogorsk
Yevpatoriya
Saki
Primorski
Simferopol
CRIMEAN MTNS *(1009)*
Feodosia
**Black Sea**
Bakhchisarai
Sudak
*(825)*
Privitne
*(1545)*
Alushta
Sevastopol
Gurzuf
*(1234)*
Yalta
Balaklava
Livadia
Simeyeiz
Alupka

*Sea of Azov (Azovske More)*

0 — 40 miles
0 — 40 kilometers

N

# SIMFEROPOL (СІМФЕРОПОЛЬ)  ☎ (8)0652

UKRAINE

God made Crimea, and all Simferopol (sim-fer-ROH-pul) got was a train station and proximity to Bakhchisarai (see below). Visit it only as a means to a southward end.

**▣ TRANSPORTATION.** The **train station** (*vokzal*) at ul. Gagarina (Гагарина; ☎ 005), sends buses to: **Odessa** (14hr., 1 per day, 36hv); **Kyiv** (19hr., 5 per day, 72hv); **Moscow** (28hr., 4 per day, 96.50hv); **Lviv** (32hr., 2 per day, 71hv); and **Minsk** (35hr., 1 per week, 86hv). Tickets for the *elektrichka* (electric train) are sold behind the main station building. These head to **Sevastopol** (2½hr., 8 per day, 2.10hv) via **Bakh-chisarai** (45min., 1hv). **Buses** are in high demand; be sure to buy tickets in advance. They head to: **Bakhchisarai** (1hr., 5 per day, 2.20-3hv); **Feodosia** (2hr., every hr. 7am-7pm, 7.76hv); **Sevastopol** (2hr., 9 per day, 6.50hv); **Kazantip** (4hr., 2 per day, 20.50hv) and **Rostov-na-Donu** (14hr., 1 per day, 49hv). **Buses, trolleys,** and **service-taxis** to **Yalta** leave from the train station, next to the McDonald's (2hr., every 20min., buses 5hv., trolleys 5.60hv, taxis 10hv.) All other buses leave from the station at ul. Kyivskaya 4; to get here, take bus #2 or 4 from the train station and #4 from the center.

**▨ PRACTICAL INFORMATION.** **Ukrsotzbank,** ul. Kirova 26, exchanges currency, offers **Western Union** services, cashes traveler's checks, and gives MC/Visa cash advances for a 2.5% commission. (Exchange services daily 8am-4pm. Branch at ul. Gorkovo 2 open daily 4-6pm). If you're staying overnight before catching the next train, hop on bus #5 for three stops to **Gostinitsa Ukraina,** ul. Rozy Lyuksemburg 7-9 (Люксембург; ☎ 51 01 65). Unlike the rest of the town, the hotel has a constant sup-ply of electricity. (Singles 37.50hv, with bath 90hv; doubles 57hv, 127hv; triples 78hv.) The **post office** (open M-F 8am-7pm, Sa-Su 9am-4pm) and the **telephone office** (open 24hr.) are next to Gostinitsa Ukraina. Not much goes on in the dimly lit streets after dark, but you can find a few cafes along ul. Pushkina, the only street that makes a real attempt at nightlife. **Café Anulia** (Ануля) at #6 offers Ukrainian and American dishes to the accompaniment of a strobe light. (Main dishes 2-7hv. Open 10am-10pm.) **Billiard** (Бильярд), in the park across from Gostinitsa Ukraina, has a pool table, beer (4hv), and music every night after 8:30pm.

# NEAR SIMFEROPOL

## BAKHCHISARAI (БАХЧИСАРАЙ)

*The elektrichka is the cheapest and fastest transport (45min., 8 per day, 1hv); several daily buses also make the trip (1hr., 5 per day, 2.20hv) from the Simferopol bus station.*

Amidst the dry, solemn cliffs of the Central Crimean steppe, the ancient Tartar town of Bakhchisarai buzzes of historical and architectural excitement. The local specialty, *moloko*, which consists of cannabis boiled in goat's milk, is regrettably illegal and not found in restaurants. Discretion is your friend if you try to procure some of this magic potion.

An outpost of the Byzantine Empire at the end of the 6th century and subsequently the seat of Tatar power, the town now leads a casual rural life around three of Crimea's most evocative monuments, the rose-speckled Khan's Palace, the Saint Assumption Monastery and the excavated Jews' Fortress. All three lie along the same main road, but a round-trip hike to all three means over two hours in the merciless summer sun. Bring good hiking shoes, a hat, and water.

**SAINT ASSUMPTION MONASTERY.** (Свято-Успенский Печерний Монастир; Sviato-Uspensky Pecherny Monastir.) Carved out of a cliff in the 15th century, the monastery commands one of the best views in all of the central steppes. The monastery was central to religious life in the times when Orthodox Christianity competed with the Tatars' Islam. *(Give yourself a head start on the trip: marshrutke taksi 0.30hv, regular taxi 5hv. Services daily 3pm.)*

**JEWS' FORTRESS.** (Чуфут-кале; Chufut-kale.) The settlement received its current name when the capital of the Crimean Khanka moved to what is now Bakhchisarai some time in the 16th century, leaving only Jews and Armenians to occupy the old fort. Forged entirely by nature, it remains an impressive stronghold. The first structures worthy of exploration inside the fortress are the two *kenassi* (кенасси; prayer houses). The one to the left was built in the 14th century from the cliff stones, while the red-pillared *kenassa* on the right dates back to the 18th century and includes a Hebrew inscription commending Bakhchisarai. Up the road lie the ruins of a 1346 **mosque** and, further along, the domes of a 1437 **mausoleum** built for Dzhanike Khan. Nearby is a small wishing-tree, where you can add your piece of cloth to the others hanging in the wind. Beyond the Byzantine wall stands a 15th-century **cave complex,** with two stories, a central pillar, and hollows for wine production and storage. *(From the monastery, walk up the road for 800m, then bear left.)*

**KHAN'S PALACE.** (Ханський Палац; Khansky Palats.) It was built in the early 16th century by the second Crimean Khan, though much of what remains was added piecemeal over the centuries. Most delightful are the courtyards and fountains; the Khan used one of the former to confine his black-market harem. In the Fountain Courtyard the 1733 **Golden Fountain** and the famous 1764 **Fountain of Tears**, supposedly built by a disconsolate khan who had fallen in love with a dying slave, still flow today. Two roses collect the fountains tears. Pushkin re-immortalized the fountain in his poem *Bakhchisarai Fountain* (Бахчисарайский Фонтан; Bakhchisaraisky Fontan). *(From the Chufut-kale, walk back down the road past the monastery and mosque. Open daily 9am-4:30pm, closed last day of the month. 14hv, students 7hv.)*

## FEODOSIYA (ФЕОДОСИЯ) ☎(8)06562

Feodosiya sits on the blue shores of the Black Sea but is also delightfully close to the green sea of Azov. Founded as the ancient slave-trading town of Theodosia, the 16km stretch of bronze sand has attracted vacationers for centuries. From the **bus station,** head past the little church, turn right on ul. Fedko (Федко), and cross the bridge over the tracks to reach the **beach.** Beaches with toilets and shower cost 1hv; free beaches without amenities are farther out to your left. To reach the city center, face the sea, keeping ul. Fedko to your right, turn left across the park, and then right on pr. Lenina. City **buses** #2 and 4 run along ul. Fedko. The beachfront pr. Lenina turns into ul. Gorkovo; follow it uphill and turn left into a residential area to see a 1348 **Genoese fortress** and a pair of diminutive but appealing **Armenian churches**.

**Buses** connect Feodosia with **Simferopol** (3hr., 11 per day, 8.66hv) and **Yalta** (3hr., 12 per day, 14hv). Many buses on the Simferopol-Kerch route (11 per day, 9hv) pass through Feodosia. The **post office** (open M-F 8am-8pm, Sa-Su 8am-6pm) and **telephone office** (open 24hr.) are at ul. Galereyna 9. On the beachfront, the ▧ **Gostinitsa Astoriya** (Гостинитса Астория), pr. Lenina 9, has clean and relatively affordable rooms. (☎323 16, reservations ☎323 27. Hall shower 3hv. Call ahead in summer. Some English spoken. Singles with sink and TV 18.75hv, with toilet 25hv, with bath 49hv; doubles 29hv, 39.75hv, 56hv.) A *Kvartirnoe Byuro* (housing office) at the bus station arranges **private rooms**. (Open daily 8am-noon and 2-6pm. 3hv, with bath and other amenities 10hv.) For affordable fare away from the beach, there's the **Cafe Assol** (Ассоль) at the intersection of ul. Liebknechta (Либнехта) and ul. Galereyna, one block up from the water, which serves kebabs (5hv) and other dishes (2-7hv. Open daily 9am-11pm.) Feodosiya is on 24 hours a day, and the cafe-bars and discos that line the beachfront keep the music pumping. At night, every cafe offers live music, and dancing to Russian pop lasts until the morning. The **fountain of light and music** enlivens the walk up pr. Lenina. Back at the southern end, a **Luna-Park** (amusement park) entertains for 3-5hv per ride. **Aqua-Dance** (look for the blue waterslide to the left) turns into a happening disco club after dark. (Cover 5hv.)

## NEAR FEODOSIYA: THE KAZANTIP PENINSULA ☎(8)06557 (КАЗАНТИП)

If you thought Moscow's clubs were overpriced and Kyiv's discos weren't disco enough, head to the Kazantip Peninsula on the Azov Sea when August rolls around. In Aug. 10-25, the hippest Eastern European DJs congregate here and mix up a unique barrage of techno beats. The rave has been gaining momentum, and last year nearly 10,000 ravers came to celebrate the end of the summer. For two weeks the sleepy town of **Shyolkino** (Шёлкино) plays host as festival-goers play watersports in the daytime. Come night, DJs mix on or near the beach, and endless dancing and swimming ensue, all in the shadow of a looming, never-used **nuclear reactor**.

**Buses** from **Simferopol** (4hr., 2 per day, 20.50hv) and **Feodosiya** (1hr., 3 per day, 5hv) arrive in **Shyolkino**, but other buses travel more frequently to the nearby **Lenina**, from where you can get a taxi to Shyolkino for 2hv. During the rave festival many people sleep on the beach (if they sleep at all), where it's free to pitch a tent. *Let's Go* does not recommend sleeping on beaches. The **post office** (open M-F 8am-1pm and 2-6pm, Sa 8am-1pm) is on the main road and the **telephone office** (open 24hr.) is just around the corner. The main road leading from the town center to the beach is Leninsky (Ленинський). At #1/2 near the top (behind the bus station and to the left past the post office) is **Gostinitsa Briz** (Бриз; ☎685 20 and 687 08), which offers bare singles for US$3 and doubles with shower and breakfast for US$8. A number of inexpensive cafes lie around the bus stop and the beach, including the **Tantsuyushchi Delfin** (Танцующий Делфин; Dancing Dolphin; main dishes 4-8hv). All beachfront establishments are open 24hr. during the festival. **Postal code:** 334 640.

## YALTA (ЯЛТА) ☎(8)0654

Bigger and better known than Feodosiya, Yalta is no more exciting. On a bright summer day, the narrow tree-lined streets, cloud-topped mountains, and the sparkling sea give visitors to Yalta the momentary illusion of being in the city that inspired Chekhov, Rachmaninov, and Tolstoy. Come evening, the power outages, quiet waterfront, and *babushki* selling the last of their fruits and vegetables serve as a reminder that this is not quite paradise on earth. The palaces of Alupka and Livadia and the picturesque Swallow's Nest are only a short boat ride away, and the streets display proud reminders of the artists who found their muse in Yalta.

## ✦ ORIENTATION

Yalta sprawls along the Black Sea and is centered around the pedestrian **Lenina** (Ленина). It runs most of the length of the waterfront *(naberezhnaya)* from Lenina Square, where a statue of Vladimir Ilyich towers over the palms. From the bus and trolley stations, take trolleybus #1 toward the center. The trolley runs down **ul. Moskovskaya** (Московськая) past the circus and market to **Sovetskaya pl.** (Советськая), where ul. Moskovskaya converges with **ul. Kyivskaya** (Києвськая). You can get off here and walk two blocks to the sea to nab. Lenina, with its seaside restaurants and street performers. A left turn leads to the old quarter and the cheaper hotels. The pedestrian **ul. Pushkinskaya** (Пушкинськая) and the parallel **ul. Gogolya** (Гоголя) veer inland off nab. Lenina to Kinoteatr Spartak, also a major stop on trolleybus #1. **Maps** are 3-5hv at newsstands, but the tourist office sells better ones (see below).

## ▐ TRANSPORTATION

**Buses:** Moskovskaya ul. 57 (☎34 20 92). To: **Simferopol** (2hr., every 30min., 5.60hv); **Sevastopol** (2½hr., 4 per day, 6.25hv); and **Feodosia** (5hr., 3 per day, 13.50hv). Advance tickets available above and behind the ordinary ticket *kassa*.

**Water Shuttles:** To **Alupka** (1hr., 8 per day, 7hv) via **Swallow's Nest** (45min., 5hv) and **Livadia** (15min., 2hv). Tickets in front of Casino Diana. 25% off before 10am.

**Trolleys:** The **trolleybus station** is across the street from the bus station, through the underpass. Sends slow but comfortable trolleys to **Simferopol** (2½hr., every 20min., 4.08hv). **Local trolleys** (0.30hv) run throughout the city; #1 covers most of the central area. It travels from the bus station to Kinoteatr Spartak. From there, #8 goes to Poliana Skazok and Chekhov's house. 3hv fine for riding ticketless.

## 🛈 PRACTICAL INFORMATION

**Tourist Office: Intourist**, ul. Drazhinskovo 50, in the Hotel Yalta, gears its pricey English-language tours to large groups but has good city **maps** (5hv). Open daily 9am-5pm. **Eugenia Travel,** ul. Roosevelta 5 (☎32 81 40), at the sea terminal, is a great resource on Ukraine. English spoken. See **Odessa: Tourist Office,** p. 792, for more info.

**Currency exchange:** Everywhere, and are all part of a cartel offering uniformly bad rates. A few near the post office charge 0.5% less. A window in the central telephone office offers **Western Union** (open daily 8:30am-4pm) and gives MC/Visa **cash advances** for a 3% commission. **Ukreksimbank,** Moskovskaya ul. 31a, to the left of the circus at the Tsirk (Цирк; circus) stop, cashes **traveler's checks** for a 2.5% commission.

**ATM:** *Bankomat* (Банкомат) next to window #1 at the post office. Also offers **Western Union** services.

**Luggage Storage:** At the bus station. Look for "Камера-хранения" (kamera khranenya) to the left of the station, before the underpass. 0.90hv for 24hr. Open daily 8am-noon and 1-8pm.

**24-hr. Pharmacy:** Botkinskaya ul. 1 (Боткинская). At night (Su-F 6pm-8am, Sa 5pm-11am), knock at the *dezhurnaya*'s door, Botkinskaya 3.

**Telephones:** Moskovskaya ul. 9, down the alleyway past a flower market. Buy tokens for local (0.20hv per min.) or intercity calls (0.75hv). To the US 11.10hv per min. Fax 0.25hv per page. Telephones open 24hr.; fax open daily 8am-noon and 1-7:30pm.

**Internet Access: Internet Club Yalta,** ul. Marshaka 9 (Маршака), on the corner with Pushkinaya. Turn right behind Kinoteatr Spartak and walk up the stairs. Frustratingly slow connection and lots of children playing Quake. 4hv per hr. Open 10am-11pm.

**Post Office:** pl. Lenina. **Poste Restante** (До востребования; do vostrebovanya) is at window #4. Fax and copy center. Open M-F 7:30am-9pm, Sa-Su 8am-8pm.

**Postal code:** 986 00.

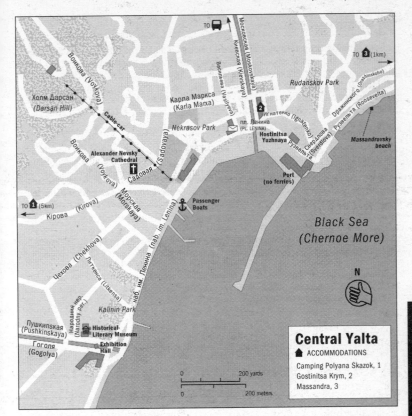

**Central Yalta**

▲ ACCOMMODATIONS

Camping Polyana Skazok, 1
Gostinitsa Krym, 2
Massandra, 3

UKRAINE

## ACCOMMODATIONS

The prices at Yalta's hotels have increased dramatically and may continue to do so. Lone travelers will have difficulty getting a place in a double, so book ahead. Bus station *babushki* often offer unbeatable deals on **private rooms.** A good rate is 20-30hv, but expect to pay more as you get closer to the waterfront. A *kvartirnoe byuro* (квартирное бюро; housing office) near the trolley-bus *kassa* offers rooms with bath starting at 30hv. (☎34 26 79. Open M-Sa 8am-6pm, Su 9am-5pm.)

**Gostinitsa Krym** (Крым), Moskovskaya ul. 1/6 (☎32 60 01; reservations ☎32 78 73). Clean rooms in a conveniently central location. 3 stops on trolley #1 from bus station. Hot water usually 7-11pm. Hall shower 3.25hv. Registration 1.35hv. Call ahead. Singles 33hv; doubles 50hv; triples 65hv. Cheaper after 1st night.

**Massandra** (Массандра), ul. Drazhinskovo 48 (Дражинского; ☎35 25 91), a 15min. trudge from the town center but not far from the beach. Walk up Drazhinskovo and turn left at Avalon Cafe (Авалон), or take *marshrutke taxi* #34 up the hill. All doubles; if you come alone they'll give you a roommate. Small but attractive rooms. 40hv per person, with bath, TV, fridge, and toilet 50hv. Prices higher in July.

**Motel-Camping Polyana Skazok** (Поляна Сказок), ul. Kirova 167 (Кірова; ☎39 74 39). Take bus #11, 26, or 27 from the bus station or bus #8 from the center to "Polyana Skazok" (Поляна Сказок; Fairy Tale Meadow), then head uphill along a busy but otherwise pretty country road (20min.). They don't allow tents, but it's cheap (cheaper with a caravan) and in a nice spot. 2-person bungalow US$5 (shared showers and toilets); motel doubles US$10. Prices higher in July.

## FOOD

Many restaurants along **nab. Lenina** serve food and liquor for high prices but offer a reasonable selection of good food. The city's **cafeterias** (stolovaya) are the last bastions against the hot dog and pizza epidemic plaguing the former USSR. A well-stocked **Gastronom** (Гастроном), nab. Lenina 4, sells delicious bread for pennies. (Open daily 8am-3pm and 4-8pm.) The open-air **market** across from the circus, accessible by trolleybus #1, has bountiful fruit and vegetable. (Open 8am-8pm.)

**Russkye Bliny**, ul. Morskaya 4/2, a block above the waterfront. Popular for a quick meal. *Bliny* (Ukrainian take on French crepes) with jam 1.60hv. Main dishes 4-8hv. Open daily 8am-11pm.

**Yalos** (Ялос), on nab. Lenina across from the Amusement Park; look for a large green sign. Ukrainian, Crimean, American, and Italian cuisine, the latter with several successful vegetarian choices. Main dishes 5-19hv. Live music at night. Open daily noon until the last customer leaves.

**Pizzeria** (Пиццерия) on nab. Lenina, halfway through the *passazh* to ul. Sadovaya. Extensive menu heavy on meat and alcohol, but with a few appealing fish and vegetarian options. Blue tablecloths add some class despite the plastic chairs. Main dishes 5-14hv. Open daily 10am-5am.

## SIGHTS

**ON THE WATERFRONT.** For a panoramic view of the city, take the chair-lift (канатная дорога; kanatnaya doroga) from behind Casino Diana on nab. Lenina to a gaudy **mock Greek temple.** There, you'll find an irreverent statue of **Zeus**, unperturbed that the only idol worshipped here is Coca-Cola. *(Open daily June-Oct. 10am-3am. Round-trip 8hv.)* Yalta's shady **parks** provide an intermediate level of cool between the bracing sea and scorching sun.

**ANTON CHEKHOV LEGACY.** If Anton Chekhov is your deity of choice (see **Russia: Literature & Arts,** p. 593), Yalta is your Mecca, or at the very least Medina. The author lived here for the last five years of his life, fighting off tuberculosis, and you can very nearly retrace his every step in monuments and plaques. On nab. Lenina at the entrance of Gurman, you can see where he once slept, and on ul. Litkensa (Литкенса) you'll find the **school** where he taught. At ul. Kirova 112, explore the **white dacha** he built, the garden he planted, and the **museum** his sister dedicated to him, all remarkably well-preserved. The museum displays manuscripts, old editions, and the room where the author entertained such luminaries as Rachmaninov and Tolstoy. *(Take bus #8 from Kinoteatr Spartak on ul. Pushkinskaya (every 40min.). Alternatively, take the much more frequent trolleybus #1 to Pionerskaya (Пионерская), cross the street and walk up the hill.* ☎ *39 49 47. Open Tu-Su 10am-5:15pm. 10hv, students 5hv.)*

**OTHER SIGHTS.** The kitschy ■ **Fairy-Tale Meadow** (Поляна Сказок; Polyana Skazok) is dotted with wooden sculptures of characters from Russian and Ukrainian fairy tales, including Snow White (Belaya Snegichka). *(Take bus #8 a few stops past the Chekhov Museum. Open in summer 9am-6pm; off-season 9am-5pm. 4hv.)* To get to the **Uchan Su Waterfall,** keep going up the road to Polyana Skazok past the campground. Turn right up the hill after the bridge, follow the sign to Detsky Lager Isary (Детский Лагерь Исары), and promptly turn right onto one of the footpaths uphill. Stay on the bluffs with the stream below to your right and climb. At some point, the trail will cross the stream. There are lots of unmarked trails, but it's hard to get lost: down leads to civilization, up to cliffs. The waterfall itself—more of a water-trickle—is not nearly as interesting as the hike there. Many a newlywed has left a tatter of clothing on the wishing trees under the falls. Wooden steps take you partway up the cliff for a fair view.

# 🏛 MUSEUMS

Vendors sell Crimean landscapes along with jewelry and other local novelties across the waterfront. To check out more recent trends in Russo-Ukrainian art, drop by the **Art Exhibition Hall** (Выставнный зал; Vistavny zal) or on ul. Gogolya 2, which straddles the waterway with monthly exhibits. (☎ 23 38 35. Open Tu-Su 9am-9pm. 4hv.) Up the street to the right, the **Yalta Historical-Literary Museum**, ul. Pushkinskaya 5a, presents random, esoteric displays that rotate annually. (Open Tu-Su 11am-7pm. 5hv, students 3hv.) If this collection stretches the limits of your eclecticism, you'll be relieved to find the **Museum of Lesya Ukrainka** on ul. Ekaterinskaya 8 (Екатеринская). It pays tribute to the famous Ukrainian writer who lived here briefly in 1897 (see **Literature and Arts**, p. 761; ☎ 32 16 34; open Tu-Su 10am-6pm; closed last day of the month; 1.50hv, students 1hv.)

# 🎵📺 ENTERTAINMENT AND NIGHTLIFE

Yalta has many **beaches**; follow the seashore either way from the harbor. City beaches cost 1.50hv, commercial beaches 3hv, and some are free after 6pm. Most are crowded and all lack sand. If boredom strikes, try out **jet-ski** or **hydroplanes** (6hv per min.), or the more reasonable **carousel** (1hv per 5min.). **Inflatable mattresses** cost 2hv per hr. The evening **amusement park** (lunapark) on nab. Lenina offers spinning rides and bumper cars (2-7hv per ride).

Nightlife in Yalta tends to be sedate. People chat, stroll, and enjoy the night air around Pl. Lenina and the *naberezhnaya*, especially if the electricity is out. When it's on, many of the beachfront restaurants have live music and dancing. During the summer tourist season, the **Marino Wine Shop** at the corner of nab. Lenina and ul. Morskaya holds wine tasting of famous Crimean wines. (Every 1-2hr., 3-9pm.) Bars along the beach stay open as long as there are customers, and at **Guinness**, ul. Sverdlova 7, you can get a pint for 8hv. If the beat of the nostalgic and celebratory Russian songs on the waterfront doesn't make you tick, try **Discoclub Saturn** on Sovetskaya pl., or the hipper **Kaktus** (Кактус) in the white-columned hall on the western tip of the harbor, across from Pl. Lenina. (Cover 10hv.)

# 🔳 DAYTRIPS FROM YALTA

## LIVADIA (ЛІВАДИЯ)

*Buses #26 and 27 arrive from Yalta (10min., every 30-40min., 0.65hv).* ***Minibuses*** *(marshrutky) labelled "Лівадія" arrive from throughout Yalta for slightly higher prices. If possible, take the* ***water shuttle*** *(15min., every 1½hr., 2hv). From the dock in Livadia, head left a few hundred meters; tell them you're going to the "leeft" (лифт; lift) if they try to charge you entry to the beach. Turn right into the cool passage, then take the elevator up to the palace. (Daily 7am-1pm and 4-6pm. 0.50hv.)*

Only an hour's hike or a 15-minute boat ride away, Livadia hosted the imprecisely named **Yalta Conference** of 1945. Churchill, Roosevelt, and Stalin met for a week in February at Tsar Nicholas II's summer palace to hash out postwar territorial claims. Secretly, the Russians committed to enter the war against Japan after the German defeat, which Stalin did two months after the German surrender, and after the atomic bomb on Hiroshima had decided things. In return, Roosevelt and Churchill agreed to return all Soviet prisoners of war. Some considered the conference a great cave-in on the Anglo-American side, especially because of the subsequent Soviet influence in Eastern Europe. A second school of thought, represented by the ideologically confused tour guides, thinks the conference guaranteed "50 years of peace."

The **Great Palace** (Великий Дворец; Veliky Dvorets), an Italian-style villa with with an exquisite marble and wood interior and a tiled Arab Courtyard, was built in 1911 and is worth the visit. The view from Nicholas' windows reminds that it was good to be tsar. (That is, until the masses revolted.) The lower level commemorates

UKRAINE

the conference, while the upper level houses the sentimentally royalist **Nicholas II Museum.** The guides will make you don felt slippers inside, which will stay on your feet about as well as Roosevelt, Churchill, and Stalin stuck to the agreement. (Open daily in summer 10am-6pm; off-season Th-Tu 10am-4pm. 8hv, students 6hv.)

## ALUPKA (АЛУПКА)

*Take the* **water shuttle** *(1hr., every 1½ hr., 7hv), or* **bus #27** *(1½ hr., every 40min., 1.95hv) from Yalta. On your way back, walk past the cable car to Miskhor (Мисхор), and return to Yalta from there (ferry 6.50hv).*

The fishing village of Alupka is home to the most extravagant *dacha* in Greater Yalta. **Vorontsov Palace** (Дворец Воронцова; Dvorets Vorontsova) is a still-active compound built by the wealthiest governor-general of Odessa, Count Mikhail Vorontsov (see **History,** p. 758). Construction of the palace took over 30 years, finishing in 1841. The interior is full of Romantic English landscapes and portraits of renowned figures, including Catherine the Great and her Crimea-hungry advisor Potemkin. *(Open May-Sept. daily 9am-5pm; Oct.-Apr. Tu-Th and Sa-Su 9am-5pm. 6hv, students 3hv.)* From the palace door, walk through the park 1km back up the coast toward Yalta to a **cable car** (канантная дорога; kanatnaya doroga), which ascends 1200m to the Ay-Petra Plateau, a breathtaking and popular spot for a picnic. Be sure to dress warmly. *(Cable car runs M-W and F-Su 9am-6:30pm. Round-trip 16hv.)* At the bottom of the cable-car station, **Cafe Khashta Bash** (Хашта Баш; ☎ 72 12 85), whose most exotic feature is its Tatar name, serves a reasonable selection of non-hot-dog, non-*shashlyk* dishes, with an emphasis on seafood. (Main dishes 8-15hv.)

En route to Alupka, **Lastochkino Gnezdo** (Ласточкино Гнездо; Swallow's Nest) is Crimea's most photogenic, or at least most photographed, site. The tiny castle, perched on a cliff, has starred in postcards since its construction in 1912. You can use the short ferry stop-over to take in the view and take a picture of your own. If you do bother to get off, the entrance fee is 1hv.

# SEVASTOPOL (СЕВАСТОПОЛЬ)    ☎ (8)0692

Sevastopol is positioned so ideally it couldn't help but become a focal point in world history. It first achieved international significance in the Crimean War (1854-55) and later in World War II, when its tragic losses placed it among the ranks of the Soviet "Hero Cities." Rebuilt before ornament had become taboo in Soviet circles, central Sevastopol, unlike its Crimean counterparts, is elegant and formal. Monuments and memorials dot its landscape. Russia and Ukraine still quarrel over the ownership of the Sevastopol's Black Sea Fleet, and uniformed sailors from both countries fill the streets. The city's ban on foreigners was lifted in 1996, and with it went Sevastopol's shroud of secrecy. With a story to tell on every corner, it maintains an independence of spirit that's proud even for Crimea.

## ◆ ORIENTATION

Greater Sevastopol is impossibly complicated, with poorly marked streets on several peninsulas jutting into the harbor in every possible direction. Happily, the center of town is confined to a single peninsula on the southwestern tip of Crimea, right below the Sevastopol harbor. **Ul. Lenina** (Ленина) runs north to south along Yuzhnaya Bay (Южная) at the right edge of the center. At **pl. Ushakova** (Ушакова), it converges with **ul. Bolshaya Morskaya** (Болшая Морская), which runs parallel to it in the interior of the peninsula. **Pr. Nakhimova** (Нахимова) intersects both to the north, below Artilleriyskaya Bay (Артиллерийская) and turns into **ul. Generala Petrova** (Генерала Петрова) at **pl. Lazaryova** (Лазарёва). **Ul. Admirala Oktyabrskova** (Адмирала Октябрьского) intersects ul. Bolshaya Morskaya up the road from pl. Ushakova and heads west. **Primorsky blv.** (Приморский) and **nab. Kornilova** (Корнилова) are the promenades across Artilleriyskaya Bay, northwest of pr. Nakhimova. The city center is ill-defined, but pl. Lazaryova, up the street from **Gostinitsa Sevastopol,** is a good starting location. **Maps** (5-6hv; in Russian only) are available from the pavement book dealers and **Soyuzpechat** (Союзпечать) kiosks.

## ⌐ TRANSPORTATION

**Trains: Vokzal** (вокзал; ☎52 30 77 and 36 60 74). To: **Kyiv** (19hr., 2 per day, 30hv); **Moscow** (28hr., 1 per day, 97hv); and **St. Petersburg** (37hr., 1 per day, 120hv). *Elektrichka* (commuter rail) runs to **Simferopol** (3hr., 7 per day, 2.10hv), where you can connect to other destinations. *Elektrichka* tickets sold behind the train station to the left. Open daily 6am-midnight. Entrance to the train station 2hv midnight-4am.

**Buses:** Pl. Revyakina 3 (☎46 16 32). Across a few tracks behind the train station or 1 stop on trolleybus #7. To: **Simferopol** (2hr., 7 per day, 5.60hv); **Yalta** (2hr., 8 per day, 6.25hv); **Feodosiya** (7hr., 2 per day, 22.20hv); and **Rostov-na-Donu** (14hr., 1 per day, 55hv). Open daily 6am-6pm.

**Local Transportation: Trolleybuses** (0.30hv; pay on board) are efficient and convenient. #12 runs up ul. Bolshaya Morskaya. #7 and 9 circle the center, stopping at the train station. #5 goes up ul. Admirala Oktyabrskova to the west of the peninsula. **Ferries** leave from Artilleriyskaya Bay behind Gostinitsa Sevastopol for the north shore (Severnaya Storona), landing near pl. Zakharova (20min., every hr., 1.50hv). A passenger boat leaves from a nearby dock for **Uchkuyuvka Beach,** on the open sea north of town (20min., every 40min., 2.50hv).

## ⁊ PRACTICAL INFORMATION

**Tourist Offices:** Excursion offices abound on Primorsky blv., offering pricey, but convenient guided tours of Crimean sites and of the city and boat tours of the harbor (20-30hv). There are 2 tourist agencies in Gostinitsa Sevastopol at Nakhimova 8.

**Visa Registration: OVIR,** ul. Pushkina 12. Between the upper part of ul. Lenina and the sea. Register here if Sevastopol is your point of entry into Ukraine. Open M and F 10am-noon and 2-4pm, Tu 2-4pm.

**Currency Exchange:** Everywhere, with the best rates in Crimea. Only banks have Western currency or rubles. **Bank Aval,** ul. Suvorova 39 (☎46 05 75 and 46 01 75), near the intersection of ul. Bolshaya Morskaya and ul. Admirala Oktyabrskova; head upstairs and through the arched door. Gives MC/Visa **cash advances** for a 3% commission and cashes AmEx and Thomas Cook traveler's checks for a 2.5% commission. **Western Union** available here and at the **post office.** Open M-F 9am-noon and 1-3pm.

**ATM:** In the lobby of Gostinitsa Sevastopol (see **Accommodations,** p. 789).

**Luggage Storage:** In the train station's back entrance, on the 2nd floor. 1.50hv for 24hr. Open daily 8-11am and noon-8pm.

**Pharmacy: Apteka** (Аптека), ul. Admirala Oktyabrskova 2 (☎45 56 86), at the intersection with ul. Bolshaya Morskaya. Open daily 8am-8pm.

**Telephones:** In the post office, on the ground floor and to the left. To: North America 9hv per min.; western Europe 6.50hv per min.; Australia 9.10hv per min. Open 24hr.

**Post Office:** ul. Bolshaya Morskaya 21. Copy center. **Western Union** available. Open M-F 8am-7pm, Sa-Su 9am-6pm.

**Postal code:** 99011.

## ⌐ ACCOMMODATIONS

For an extended summertime stay, it's hard to beat the **private rooms** aggressively advertised by *babushki* in the train station for 10-20hv per day.

**Gostinitsa Sevastopol,** pl. Nakhimova 8 (☎52 36 82). 5 stops from the bus station on trolleybus #1, 3, 7, or 9. Comfortable rooms in a centrally located luxurious hotel. Hot showers 2.50hv for 30min. Singles with toilet and sink 51hv, with bath, phone, and fridge 87hv; doubles 95hv, 135hv; triples 120hv, 155hv.

**Gostinitsa Krym** (Крым), ul. 6 Bastionnaya 46 (Бастионная; ☎52 22 53), up ul. Admirala Oktyabrskova from ul. Bolshaya Morskaya. Also on trolleybus line #5, 6, or 10. A 14-story monument to Soviet design. Hot water 7-10pm. Singles with bath 70hv; doubles 90hv; triples 72hv.

## 🜚 FOOD

The central **outdoor market** lies downhill from pl. Lazaryova at the intersection of ul. Partizanskaya (Партизанская) and ul. Odesskaya (Одесская). (Open Tu-Su 8am-5pm.) An elegant and well-stocked **Hastronom** grocery store sits at pr. Nakhimova 5. (Open M-Sa 8am-2pm and 3-8pm, Su 8am-3pm.)

■ **Restoran Nikita-klub** (Ресторан Никита-клуб), Shestakova spusk 1a (Шестакова; ☎24 98 13), diagonally uphill from pl. Lazaryova. World cuisine and a charming hilltop view. Slightly upscale, but definitely worth the price—chairs have buttons to call waiters! Main dishes 8-13hv. Open daily 11am-midnight.

**Kafe-Bistro Dialog** (Диалог), ul. Bolshaya Morskaya 19, next to the post office on the intersection with ul. Sergeyeva Tsenskovo. An old-school *stolovaya* (cafeteria) repackaged as a slick new cafe. Main dishes 3-8hv; salads 1-7hv. Open daily 9am-10pm.

**Medzhik Burger** (Меджик Бургер; Magic Burger), ul. Bolshaya Morskaya 15 and Aizovskovo 5. Look for the revolving chef sign. Russo-Ukrainian-American fast food, take it or leave it. Pizza 10hv; *pelmeni* 3hv; burger 4hv. Open daily 9am-10pm.

## 👁🎵 SIGHTS AND ENTERTAINMENT

Sevastopol lives and breathes military history. The rotunda of the ■ **Panorama Museum of the Defense of Sevastopol** (Панорама Оборона Севастополь; Panorama Oborona Sevastopola), at the end of Istorichesky blv. (Исторический), was built in 1905 to commemorate the 50th anniversary of the siege on the city; it's an impressive 3D, 360° image that thrusts you in the midst of battle. (☎52 21 46. Open daily in summer 9am-6pm; off-season Tu-Su 9am-5pm. Mandatory 40min. tour 6hv, students 4hv.) A nearby **amusement park** has bumper cars (2hv), a "chamber of fear" (2hv), and other attractions. To get there, take the #12 trolley to Pl. Ushakova, then walk uphill through the park. (3hv. Open daily 9am-8pm.)

Much of the rest of Sevastopol is maritime-oriented. The **Museum of the Black Sea Fleet** (Музей Чёрноморского Флота; Muzey Chornomorskovo Flota), ul. Lenina 11, founded in 1869, displays model ships, naval paintings, and personal effects of notable sea dogs. (☎52 22 89 and 52 03 92. Open daily in summer 10am-5pm; off-season W-Su 10am-5pm. Closed last F of the month. 8hv, students 4hv.) The pseudo-Byzantine **St. Vladimir's Cathedral** (Владимирский Собор; Vladimirsky Sobor), on the crest of the peninsula near ul. Marata (Марата), is the resting place of Orthodox admirals. (30min. visits 2hv.)

To get to the **beach,** head out of town, away from the dirty harbor. Take the boat or trolleybus #10 to its terminus, **Plyazh Omega** (Пляж Омега), a vaguely horseshoe-shaped bay ringed by mixed rocks and sand. (Boats 8hv per hr.; pedal boats 6hv per hr.; catamarans 12hv per hr.; or windsurfing gear 6hv per hr. Open daily 9am-9pm; windsurfing 10am-6pm.) Beachfront bars are largely interchangeable; most charge 4-6hv for domestic beer. For the best nightlife, there's **Bunker** (Бункер), ul. Marata 5 (Марата). Look for the orange sign down the alley near ul. Lenina 32 and head down tunnel after strangely painted tunnel. The club itself, safe from nuclear holocaust 37m underground, hosts rock groups from all over Russia and Ukraine. (Bottle of wine 2.20hv; beer 3-7hv. Cover 5hv. Best to visit 8pm-midnight.)

# ODESSA (ОДЕССА)      ☎(8)0482

Since its 1794 founding by Catherine the Great, intriguing Odessa (pop. 1,000,000), with its limestone buildings and classical facades has been an important port blessed by prosperity and cursed by corruption. With French, British Turkish, Greek, Italian, Russian, and Jewish influences, life in the port town has always been entertaining. A place for intellectuals as well as thieves and *mafiosi*, Odessa has inspired and served as background from Pushkin to the more modern Isaac Babel. Today, the splendor endures, but post-Soviet chaos has left many former sights in ruin. Not surprisingly, Odessa has taken to post-Soviet crime like a duck to water, becoming one of the parent cities of the Russian mafia. With the shell of past greatness cracking under its own unused weight, the party town of the former USSR still hums, but at a lower frequency.

# ■ ORIENTATION

Odessa's center is bounded by the **train station** to the north and the **port** to the south. All streets have been recently renamed and labeled in both Ukrainian and Russian; *Let's Go* lists Russian names. Numbering of streets begins at the sea and increases inland. From the train station, walk across the park to the stop opposite **Spartak stadium** (Спартак) and take trolley #5 or 9 to central **pl. Grecheskaya** (Греческая), right off Odessa's most famous street, **ul. Deribasovskaya** (Дерибасовская). Ul. Deribasovskaya can also be reached by tram #2, 3, or 12 from the station. The tree-lined promenade of **Primorsky blv.** (Приморский) is separated from the sea and the sea terminal by the famous **Potemkin Stairs,** where you may be able to find a simple English **map** (1hv) of the city center. Odessa's **beaches** stretch for miles east of the center and may be reached via trolleybus #5 or 9 from pl. Grecheskaya. More detailed maps are available throughout the city (3-5hv) from newspaper kiosks and pavement book merchants.

Like other places in Eastern Europe, Odessa changed its street names following the collapse of communism to remove many a Stalin or Lenin from its street signs. Unlike in other places, though, the confused (or sentimental?) Odessites still refer to many streets by their old name, making navigation potentially confusing. Use your handy *Let's Go* guide to decipher Odessaspeak:

| NOW | THEN |
| --- | --- |
| Yekaterininskaya | Karla Marksa |
| Rishelyevskaya | Lenina |
| Frantsuzky bld. | Proletariat |
| Polskaya | Garibaldi |
| Armenskaya | Leninskovo Battaliona |
| Grecheskaya | Libknechta |
| Yevreyskaya | Babelya |

# ■ INTERCITY TRANSPORTATION

**Trains: Vokzal** (Вокзал), pl. Privokzalnaya (Привокзальная; ☎005 or 27 42 42), at the north end of ul. Pushkinskaya. International (non-former USSR) and advance tickets (usually not necessary) in the Mizhnarodny Zal (window #19; Мижнародный Зал; International hall), to your left as you enter the building. Open daily 8am-noon and 1-7pm. Tickets also available at the **Central Ticket Bureau,** ul. Srednefontanskaya (Среднефонтанская). Take bus #136 or 146 or the more frequent trams #17 or 18 from across the park to Sredni Fontan (Central Fountain) and look for the "Центральные Железнодорожные Кассы" (Tsentralne zheleznodorozhnye kassy) sign. To: **Chişinău, MOL** (6hr., 3 per day, 27hv); **Kyiv** (12hr., 2 per day, 38hv); **Simferopol** (13hr., 1 per day, 34hv); **Kharkiv** (15½hr., 2 per day, 45hv); **Lviv** (16hr., daily, 45hv); **Dnipropetrovsk** (17hv, 1 per day, 32 hv); **Minsk, BLR** (19hr., 1 per day, 107hv); **Moscow, RUS** (26hr., 3 per day, 121hv); **St. Petersburg, RUS** (35hr., 1 per day, 112hv); and **Rīga, LAT** (49hr., 95hv).

**Buses:** Ul. Dzerzhinskovo 58 (Дзержинского; ☎004 or 32 56 93). Take tram #5 from the train station or #15 from the city center. Both stop 4 blocks north of the station. Buses around Ukraine are more efficient and cheaper than trains. Get tickets at least the night before, or you'll be standing the entire ride. To: **Chişinău, MOL** (5hr., every 1hr., 18hv); **Simferopol** (8hr., 2 per day, 26hv); and **Kyiv** (12hr., 4 per day, 39hv).

**Ferries: Morskoy Vokzal** (Морской Вокзал; Sea Terminal), ul. Suvorov 12 (Суворов; ☎22 32 11). To: **Istanbul, TUR** (1-2 days, 4 per week, 250hv) and **Haifa, ISR** (2-3 days, 2 per month, 413hv). Open M-F 9am-5pm, Sa-Su 10am-2pm. Very few ferries leave Odessa on regular schedules. **Eugenia Travel** (see **Tourist Office**, p. 792) at the left corner of the terminal, arranges occasional cruises to **Yalta**.

# ⊡ LOCAL TRANSPORTATION

**Public Transportation:** The train station and pl. Grecheskaya are main end points. Info desk inside the train station (in Russian; 1hv per question). **Trams** and **trolleybuses** cost 0.50hv and run almost everywhere 7am-midnight. **Buses** (0.60hv) are confusing, but locals can point you to the one you need. On the trolleys, buy your tickets from the badge-wearing *konduktor*. On buses, pay as you exit.

**Taxis:** Speedy **marshrutke** (fast private minibuses that copy trolleybus routes, but without regular stops); tell them where you're going. Numbers indicate which trolleybus route they are taking (1hv). If you're desperate, new **yellow taxis** are on the expensive side, so haggle away. Don't pay more than 4hv from pl. Grecheskaya to the train station. **Unofficial cabs,** hailed by holding out your palm while facing traffic, are cheaper. Always set the price before the ride.

# ⊠ PRACTICAL INFORMATION

## TOURIST AND FINANCIAL SERVICES

**Tourist Office: Eugenia Travel,** ul. Primorskaya 6 (☎21 85 81; fax 22 40 47; janna@eugen.intes.odessa.ua) in Morskoy Vokzal offers tours of the catacombs, the city, and the rest of Ukraine. Expensive, but worth it. Call the director Janna Belovsova (☎22 05 54), who speaks perfect English, for special tours. Open daily 9am-6pm.

**Visa Registration:** **OVIR** (ОВИР), ul. Bunina 38 (Бунина; ☎28 28 22). If you have already registered in Ukraine, you needn't register here, but check to be safe. Keep the registration card to avoid a heavy "fine" at the border.

**Tourist Police: Kantselyariya dlya inostrantsev** (Канцелярия для иностранцев; Office for Foreigners), ul. Preobrazhenskaya 44 (☎28 28 17). Deals with crimes by and against foreigners, but don't expect knights in shining armor.

**Currency Exchange: Obmin Valyut** (Обмен Валют) are on every corner. Worst rates are at the airport and at the train and bus stations. **Bank Aval,** ul. Sadovaya 9 (Садовая) cashes **travelers checks** and gives **cash advances** for a 2% commission. Bank Porto-Franko (Порто-Франко), ul. Pushkinskaya 10 (☎21 70 13) does the same for a 1% commission (US$5 minimum charge).

**ATM:** Cirrus/MC/Visa ATMs can be found in the lobby of Hotel Londonskaya, Primorsky blv. 11, in Mick O'Neil's (see **Nightlife**, p. 779), the sea terminal, and the post office.

## EMERGENCY AND COMMUNICATIONS

**24hr. Pharmacy: Apteka #16,** ☎28 70 71. In the train station.

**Medical Assistance:** Information ☎23 63 87. Neighborhood **Polykliniks** treat foreigners registered in Ukraine. Call ☎03 to find out which one to go to. Students free.

**Telephones:** At the post office, to the left as you enter. Pay ahead. Open 24hr. Local calls require phone cards, sold at the post office and used in blue or yellow booths around town. **Utel** cards and phones for international calls are sold at the sea terminal and Mick O'Neil's (see **Nightlife**, p. 796). **Fax:** 0.50hv to receive plus 1.50hv per min.

**Internet Access: Komputer-Klub,** ul. Preobrazhenskaya 38 (☎37 27 14), on the corner with Grecheskaya (Греческая). Fast. 4.50hv per hr., after 11pm 4hv. Open 24hr.

**Post Office:** Ul. Sadovaya 10 (Садовая). **Poste Restante** (до востребования; do vostrobovaniya) at counters #15 and 16; pre-stamped airmail envelopes (конверт с марками; konvert s markami) and packages in the small room to the left of the central hall. **Western Union.** Open M-Sa 8am-8pm, Su 8am-6pm.

**Postal code:** 65 000.

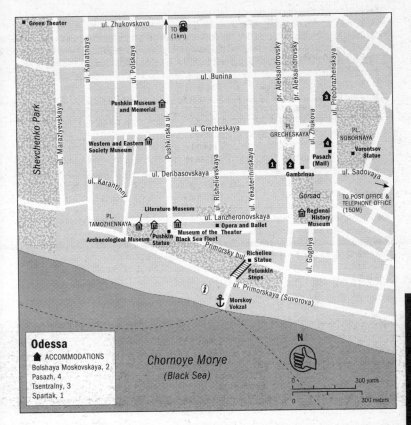

**Odessa**

**⌂ ACCOMMODATIONS**
Bolshaya Moskovskaya, 2
Pasazh, 4
Tsentralny, 3
Spartak, 1

*Chornoye Morye*
*(Black Sea)*

# ⌂ ACCOMMODATIONS

**Private rooms** are the cheapest option (from US$5 per person), but you'll be lucky to get anything near the center. Train station hawkers hold signs—some variation on "Сдаю комнату" (Sdayu komnatu; room to rent). Ask *"Skolko?"* (Сколько; how much). The *babushki* will start at US$10; haggle down and don't pay until you see the room. A deposit is often required for keys in summer.

Prices are inconsistent in the downtown **hotels**—make sure a ghost television or refrigerator isn't added to your bill. Truly budget-minded travelers request *"samoye deshovoye mesto"* (самое дешёвое место; the cheapest place), which lands you in a triple or quad. Most hotels overcharge foreigners and have infrequent hot water; the city turns water off from midnight to 6am. Take tram #3 or 12 from the train station to the downtown hotels, all near noisy pl. Grecheskaya and ul. Deribasovskaya (Дерибасовская). Get a room away from the street.

**Passazh** (Пассаж), ul. Preobrazhenskaya 34 (☎20 48 49). From Pl. Grecheskaya, head towards Pl. Sobonaya (Собоная) and turn right onto Preobrazhenskaya. This fairly charming hotel is next to the Passazh. Pleasant, boxy little rooms. Hall shower with occasional hot water 1.50hv. Call ahead in summer. Singles with sink 59hv, with toilet and shower 107hv; doubles 92hv, 135hv; triples 114hv.

**Bolshaya Moskovskaya** (Большая Московская), ul. Deribasovskaya 29 (☎22 40 16). The highly ornamented front hides a less elegant interior, but the rooms are clean and prices good. Singles 32hv, with bath 73hv; doubles 42hv, 104hv; triples 53hv, 150hv.

**Odessa State University Dormitories,** ul. Dovzhenko 9b (Довженко; ☎21 87 60, reservations ☎63 04 67; fax 63 32 66). From the left side of the train station, take trolley #7. From pl. Grecheskaya, take trolley #5 or 9. Go down ul. Mevchenko (Мевченко), then down ul. Dovzhenko, take a right directly after #7, and zig-zag around the tan-tiled building on the right. Call Irina Kolegaeva, the university dean, before you come and she will make sure they have a room ready for you. If you can't reach her by phone, stop by her office at ul. Mayakovskaya 7 (Маяковская). Clean rooms with kitchen and shared shower. 10min. from the beach. Restaurant downstairs for cheap eats. Open July-Aug. Dorms 10hv.

**Camping "Delfin"** (Кемпинг "Дельфин"), dor. Kotovskovo 307 (Котовского; ☎55 50 52 or 55 30 42). From the train station, take trolley #4 or 10 and transfer to tram #7; get off 20min. later at "Лузанивка" (Luzanivka) and continue 500m. Or take bus #130 or 170 from pl. Grecheskaya. Remote even for a campground, but the friendly staff, cheap restaurant, sauna, bar, and private beach may appeal to the most budget of budget travelers. Infrequent hot water. English spoken. Bungalows 20hv per person.

# 🍴 FOOD

Odessa is blessed with good restaurants, markets, and more cafes than any other city in Ukraine. Ul. Deribasovskaya is packed with classy and interchangeable cafes that all serve great food and open and close at will. The **Privoz mega-market** (Привоз), Privoznaya ul. (Привозная), across the street to the right of the train station, sells mega-fruit, mega-vegetables, and mega-dairy products amidst clothing and hardware. Keep a hand on your wallet—pickpocketing is rampant. (Open daily 8am-6pm.)

**Steakhouse** (Стейкхаус), ul. Deribasovksaya 20 (☎28 77 75). Enjoy a prime slice of meat and a casual atmosphere in a country setting. Outdoor seating is perfect for people-watching. Soups and pasta 6-9hv. Veal, chicken, beef, or fish 21-50hv. MC/Visa.

**Klarabara** (Кларабара), ul. Preobrazhenskaya 28 (☎20 03 31), in the Gorsad. This "restoranchik" offers its main dishes (19-36hv) against the background of a fireplace in winter and the lively outdoors in summer. Beer 7-12hv. Menu in English. Jazz band nightly 7:30-11:30pm.

**Café Piknik** (Пикник) ul. Yekaterininskaya 23 (☎24 13 18). Caucasian specialties minutes away from Odessa's cosmopolitan center. Shashlik and other main dishes 6-18hv. Open 11am-midnight.

# 👁 SIGHTS

■ **CATACOMBS.** When Catherine the Great decided to build up Odessa, the material for the construction—limestone—was mined from below, leaving behind a series of dark and intertwining catacombs that is the longest such network in the world. During World War II, Odessa's resistance fighters, men, women, and children alike, hid in these tunnels for 73 days, surfacing only for raids against the Nazis. The accessible portion of catacombs lies under the village of Neribaiskoye, where the city has set up an outstanding subterranean **museum.** The catacombs are only accessible through one entrance, and with a tour guide. Lantern in hand, your guide will explain the re-created resistance camp: the well, bathrooms, and sitting room (with a picture of Stalin torn down repeatedly during *perestroika*), the makeshift weapons factory and shooting range. At Guard Point #1, soldiers had to sit for two-hour shifts in complete darkness to wait for German attackers. Graffitied rocks have been transported from the original site; one declares "Blood for blood; death for death." This understated and haunting complex is now one of the most moving World War II memorials in the former USSR. *(30min. car ride from Odessa. Eugenia Travel (see **Tourist Office**, p. 792) provides rides and guided tours. 3hr. English tour $45. Excursion times and prices vary depending on demand.)*

**411TH BATTALION MONUMENT.** Far from the busy commercial center lies the Memorial Complex of the 411th Battalion, one of Odessa's more entertaining monuments. The typical armaments of the Soviet forces are here in all their glory, spread over a large park. You'll think the guns and torpedoes are impressive until you get to the other end of the park and see the tanks (the turrets even move), the bomber, a tractor disguised as a tank, and—yes—the battleship, carried here in pieces via tractor-trailer. They're all free for you to climb on, in, and around, but you'll have to share the fun with dozens of little boys and girls making "ratt-ta-tatt-tatt" noises as they aim the big, bad guns. There is a small museum by the battleship. The cliffs along the rocky coast are a short walk from behind the bus stop. At high tide, the sea provides its own violent spectacle. *(The complex is on ul. Amundsena (Амундсена), take bus #108 or 127 or tram #26 from the train station (30-40min.). Museum open Sa-Th 10am-6pm. 2hv.)*

**UL. DERIBASOVSKAYA.** The center of Odessa's street culture, ul. Deribasovskaya is where jazz musicians play, mimes tailor their performances to the wishes of the most generous donors, and *biznesmeni* swagger with their cell phones. On the east end of the street is the captivating Gorsad (Горсад), where artists sell jewelry, landscape painting, and the traditional *matrioshka* dolls. Beyond the Gorsad, Deribasovskaya ends at the intersection with ul. Preobrazhenskaya. Cross the street to see the **statue of Mikhail Vorontsov,** Odessa's powerful governor during the 1820s. The statue is swell, but it's a poor substitute for the cathedral that used to stand here. It was destroyed in 1936 in an effort to quell the ecclesiastical agitation threatening Soviet rule. The square is still called **Cathedral Square** (Пл. Соборная; Pl. Sobornaya). A block to the left on ul. Preobrazhenskaya is the aromatic **flower market,** where old women advise suitors about the best flowers to buy. One block south of Deribasovskaya is museum-lined ul. Lanzheronovskaya.

**UL. PUSHKINSKAYA.** With cobblestones and charming street lamps, this avenue is a favorite among locals and quite possibly Odessa's most beautiful street. Ul. Push-kinskaya's namesake poet lived at #13 during his exile; his house is now a museum (see **Museums,** p. 778). At #17, the **Filarmoniya** (Филармония), built from 1894 to 1899, looks out sternly from the corner with ul. Bunina (Бунина). It's one of only two surviving opera houses constructed with special 19th-century acoustics (the other is Milan's La Scala). A bit farther down, the large, gray **Brodsky Synagogue** used to be the center of Odessa's large Jewish community; today it contains an archive. A left at the Filarmoniya leads toward **Park Shevchenko,** a vast stretch of greenery that separates the city from the sea; at the entrance stands a **monument** to the poet Taras Shevchenko (see **Literature & Arts,** p. 761). Within are the remainders of the **Khadjibei Fortress** and, overlooking the harbor, a spiked memorial and eternal flame to the **Unknown Seaman.** *(From Deribasovskaya, turn right onto ul. Pushkinskaya.)*

**PRIMORSKY BLV. AND THE POTEMKIN STAIRS.** (Потёмкинская Лестница; Potomkinskaya Lestnitsa.) Primorsky blv. is a shady promenade, with some of the finest facades in Odessa, and a prime people-watching spot. The statue of **Aleksandr Pushkin** turns its back unceremoniously to the City Hall, which refused to help fund its construction. On either side of the City Hall are Odessa's two symbols: **Fortuna,** goddess of fate, and **Mercury,** god of trade (also, fittingly for Odessa, the god of thieves). From Primorsky blv. the 192 steps of the **Potemkin Stairs** stretch to ul. Suvorova and the Sea Terminal. Director Sergei Eisenstein used them in his 1925 silent epic *Battleship Potemkin,* and the name stuck. A concrete statue of the **Duc de Richelieu,** the city's first governor, stares down the steps toward the port. Past the bridge to the left is the long, white **Mother-in-Law Bridge,** built, they say, so an elderly lady could more easily visit her son-in-law, a high-ranking Communist official. More beautiful buildings, including the **House of Scientists,** a club for the intelligentsia, lie farther down ul. Gogolskaya. *(Runs parallel to the waterfront and ul. Primorskaya.)*

# 🏛 MUSEUMS

▨ **Literature Museum** (Литературный Музей; Literaturny muzey), Lanzheronovskaya 2 (☎22 32 13). A fascinating look at the city's rich intellectual and cultural heritage through its books, prints, and photos, with an emphasis on Pushkin and Gogol. The collection includes the famous letter from Vorontsov to the Tsar asking that Pushkin be sent out of Odessa "for his own development," because he "is getting the notion into his head that he's a great writer." Labels only in Russian. Open Tu-Su 10am-5pm. 6hv.

**Archaeological Museum** (Археологический музей; Arkheologichesky muzey), Lanzheronovskaya 4. Ancient Greek and Roman artifacts found in the Black Sea region, including a notable collection of gold coins stored in a basement vault. Open W-Su 10am-5pm. 6hv, students 3hv. English booklet 5hv.

**Museum of the Black Sea Fleet** (Музей чорного морского флоту; Muzey chornovo morskovo flotu), ul. Lanzheronovskaya 6 (Ланжероновская; ☎24 05 09), near the Opera and Ballet Theater. Boasts a unique collection of models of old ships in what was once a luxury club for 19th-century dandies. A few WWII cannons are included for good measure. Open M-W and F-Su 11am-5pm. 2hv.

**Pushkin Museum and Memorial** (Литературно-мемориальный музей Пушкина; Literaturno-memorialny muzey Pushkina), ul. Pushkinskaya 13 (☎24 92 55). The 1821 building was Pushkin's residence during his brief exile here from the St. Petersburg nightlife (see **Literature & Arts**, p. 761). Better than other Pushkin museums. Open daily 9am-4pm. 4hv, students 2hv.

# ⚄ ENTERTAINMENT

⚄**BEACHES.** The farther from the center you go, the cleaner the beaches are, but none of them hold a candle to the ones in Crimea. Most can be reached either by public transportation or on foot. **Arkadiya** (Аркадия), the city's most popular beach on summer nights, is the last stop on trolley #5. Bus #129 stops here as well. The shoreline from Park Shevchenko up to Arkadiya makes a good path for an early-morning jog. **Zolotoy Bereg** (Золотой Берег; Golden Shore) is farther away, but boasts the most impressive sea and surf. Trams #17 and 18 stop here and at the **Chayka** (Чайка) and **Kurortny** (Курортный) beaches. **Chornomorska** (Чёрноморска), the beach of the proletariat, lies just outside a high-rise monstrosity of a neighborhood. Take tram #29 to the last stop and keep going. Tram #5 stops at **Lanzheron** (Ланжерон), the beach closest to central Odessa, and at **Otrada** (Отрада).

**SHOWS AND CONCERTS.** The **Teatr Opery i Baleta** (Театр Оперы и Балета), pr. Chaikovskovo 3 (Чайковского; ☎29 13 29), at the end of ul. Rishelevskaya, has shows nightly. Odessa's elite arrive in their most dashing attire. Sunday matinees begin at noon, and evening performances (W-Su) start at 6pm. Buy tickets a day in advance, or at least that morning, from the ticket office to the right of the theater. (Open M-F 10:30am-5pm, Sa-Su 10:30am-4pm. Normally 15-25hv, US$3-35 when a major act comes to town.) The **Filarmoniya ticket office** is in the Filarmoniya, ul. Bunina 15 (☎25 69 03). Schedules are as unpredicatable as the economy. (Season Sept.-June. Open 11am-7pm. 5-15hv.)

# ⚄ NIGHTLIFE

Odessa never sleeps. The restaurants, cafes, and bars on **ul. Deribasovskaya** hop all night with beer, vodka, and music ranging from Euro-techno to Slavic folk. For younger and more light-footed entertainment, the concentration of discos in **Arkadia** (see **Beaches** above), attracts Odessa's hippest crowds as soon as the summer nights grow warm. Dance the night away in the open air of **Kontiki,** among the pseudo-classical columns of **Itaka,** or by the wooden posts of **Pago Pago. Club Assol** is open year-round. (Cover 10-20hv, drinks 3-7hv.)

⚄ **Gambrinus** (Гамбринус), Deribasovskaya 31 (☎22 51 51), at the intersection with ul. Zhukova (Жукова). The dark, spacious interior resembles a beer hall, with tables made of beer vats. Two old men play Slavic folk tunes on violins while you drink draft beer (0.5L 5-8hv) and munch on excellent snacks. A historical landmark that was the center of Odessa's cultural scene before the Revolution, it can still sustain hours of drunken literary talk. Open daily 10am-11pm.

**Mick O'Neil's,** a.k.a. Irish Pub, Deribasovskaya 52. Odessa's elite gather here to get noticed as they talk on cell phones and drink imported beer (0.33L 8-10hv) or fancy fruit shakes (12hv). Mick's has gobbled up Odessa's night scene with its sparkling interior, satellite TV, decent food, and groovin' live music (8-11pm). The clientele consists almost exclusively of foreigners and local *biznesmeni*. English menu. Open 10am-2am.

**Fidel** (Фидел), Deribasovskaya 23. Live music weekends, but popular on weeknights as well. Beer and 4-15hv. Wine, French or Georgian, 1hv. Open daily until 3am.

# TRANSCARPATHIA (ЗАКАРПАТТЯ)

Between east and west, poor but rich in historical significance and ardently patriotic, Western Ukraine is trying to strengthen the country's national identity and move closer to capitalist Europe while breaking away from the Russian grip. The lovely Habsburg city of Lviv proudly leads the region in championing the distinct Ukrainian language, culture, and the Uniate faith. Farther south, tucked in the Carpathian mountains, pragmatic Uzhhorod is home to people who peacefully host a melange of ethnic and cultural influences. Cobblestoned and sprinkled with architectural gems, Western Ukraine and Trans-Carpathia offer a captivating combination of provincial culture and a new urban sophistication.

## LVIV (ЛЬВІВ)                    ☎ (8)0322

Dear Abby,
Divorced from Poland in 1945 after 600 years of ups and downs, I just went through a breakup with the USSR, for whom I had cooked and slaved for over 45 years. I'm living with my old mother Kyiv now, but we don't even speak the same language! In spite of my age, I feel ready to be conquered by the world. My Polish half-sister, Kraków, tells me that living with tourists creates all sorts of ills, but I just want to be loved, admired, and remembered. My steeple-filled city center teems with energy that can't be found anywhere else in Ukraine, and, if I do say so myself, I'm fun! Why won't anyone enter my gates?

   Worthy and waiting, Lviv.

## ✴ ORIENTATION

The center of town is **pl. Rynok** (Ринок), the old market square. Around it, a grid of streets forms the **Old Town,** which holds most of the sights. A few blocks back toward the train station, the broad and stately **pr. Svobody** (Свободи) runs from the Opera House to **pl. Mitskevycha** (Міцкевича), the old town's center of commerce. **Prospekt Shevchenka** (Шевченка) extends to the right of pl. Mitskevycha. Tram #1 runs from the main train station to the Old Town's center, tram #6 to the north end of pr. Svobody. Tram #9 goes from the Old Town to the station; otherwise, it's a 40-minute walk. Ukrainian dominates all official communication, but Russian is understood. Unless stated otherwise, assume that English is not spoken anywhere.

## ▣ TRANSPORTATION

**Airport:** Southwest of the city, at vul. Lyubinska (Любінська). ☎ 69 21 12, 69 21 13, 69 21 14, and 69 22 00.

**Trains:** pl. Vokzalna (Вокзальна; ☎ 748 20 68; info ☎ 005). **Tickets** at Intourist windows #23-25 on the 2nd floor. To: **Uzhhorod** (8hr., 1 per day, 30hv); **Kyiv** (12hr.; 8 per day; *platzkart* 28hv, *coupé* 50hv); **Odessa** (14hr., 3 per day, *platzkart* 35hv, *coupé* 50hv); **Przemyśl, POL** (3½hr., 3 per day, 45hv); **Kraków, POL** (8hr., 1 per day, 95hv); **Warsaw, POL** (13hr., 1 per day, 100hv); **Budapest, HUN** (14hr., 1 per day, 217hv); **Bratislava, SLK** (18hr., 1 per day, 320hv); **Prague, CZR** (21hr., 1 per day, 350hv); and **Moscow, RUS** (29hr., 4 per day, 135hv).

**Buses:** The **main station,** vul. Stryska (Стрийська; ☎ 63 24 73 and 63 25 31). From town, take trolley #5 or bus #71. Bus #18 goes to the train station, where trams into town are frequent. Schedules differ on Su. To: **Przemyśl, POL** (4hr., 14 per day, 29-

50hv); **Kraków, POL** (8hr., 1 per day, 74hv); and **Warsaw, POL** (10hr., 4 per day, 83hv). Lviv also has a series of smaller **regional stations.** The one at vul. Khmelnytskoho 225 (Хмельницького; ☎52 17 40), can be reached by bus #4 from vul. Shevchenka (Шевченка). Buses to **Brest, BLR,** leave from here on odd-numbered days (8hr., 2 per day, 27hv), and from the **train station** on even-numbered days. For long-distance destinations, buy tickets a day in advance from the bus station or the **Avtokasa,** Teatralna 26 (Театральна; ☎72 76 43). Open daily 9am-2pm and 3-6pm. Buy advance tickets to Poland at window #1; same-day at window #2.

**Public Transportation: Maps** available at the international bookstore (see below) include public transit: **trams** in pink, **trolleys** in red, and **buses** in blue. Buy tickets (0.30hv for trams and trolleys, 0.50hv for buses) on board from the badge-wearing *konduktor.* 5hv fine for riding ticketless. **Marshrutke** (private minibuses) 0.80hv. In the Old Town, pl. Halitska (Галицька) is a hub for buses.

# ▮ PRACTICAL INFORMATION

**Tourist Offices: Lviv Intourist** (☎72 67 40; fax 97 12 87), in Hotel George (Готель Жорж), pl. Mitskevycha 1, has expensive guided **tours** in English and info about the city. Take tram #1 from the train station to "Дорошенка" (Doroshenka). Walk another block and head right at the park; the hotel is the big pink building at the end. Open M-F 9am-5pm. For other questions, the friendly staff at the service desk of the **Grand Hotel** speak English and might be of help.

**Currency Exchange:** The exchange in **Hotel George** (see **Tourist Offices,** above) doesn't have great rates, but cashes **traveler's checks** and gives MC/Visa **cash advances** for 3% commission. Open daily 9am-5pm. **Avalbank** (Авальбанк), vul. Slovatskoho 1 (Словацького; ☎ 97 18 17), in the post office, cashes AmEx/Thomas Cook **traveler's checks** and provides MC/Visa **cash advances** for 4% commission. Open M-F 9am-12:30pm and 2-5:30pm. **Prominvestbank** (Промінвестбанк), vul. Hnatyuka 2 (Гнатюка) does the same for 3% commission. Open M-F 9am-4pm.

**ATM:** Cirrus/Visa/MC ATMs are at pr. Svobody 19, on the 1st floor of the post office, and next to the McDonald's on pr. Shevchenka.

**Western Union: X-Change Points,** on the 2nd floor of the post office. Open M-F 9:30am-5pm, Sa 9:30am-2pm. Also at **Natsionalny Bank Ukraina** (Національний Банк Україна) on Kopernika 4 (Коперника). Open M-F 9am-5pm.

**Luggage Storage:** At the **Hotel George** (see **Tourist Offices,** above), 1hv per bag per day. At the train station, 2hv.

**International Bookstore:** pl. Mitskevycha 8 (Міцкевича). A small international selection. Also sells a great city **map** for 2-3hv. Open M-F 10am-6pm, Sa 10am-4pm.

**Ambulance:** ☎056 (US$10).

**24hr. Pharmacy: Apteka #24** (Аптека) on Kopernika 1 (Коперника) or **Apteka #28,** vul. Zelena 33 (Зелена; ☎75 37 63).

**Telephones:** vul. Doroshenka 39, behind an unmarked door around the corner from the post office (see below). Open daily 7am-midnight. Blue phones marked "Таксофон" (taksofon) are operated by phone cards available at the post office and some kiosks. **Utel** cards at the telephone center, the post office, and hotels George, Sputnyk, Lviv, and Karpaty.

**Internet Access: Internet Cafe,** vul. Zelena 14 (Зелена). From Hotel George (see **Tourist Offices,** above), turn right and walk down pr. Shevchenka to the monument. Turn left and follow the street to vul. Ivana Franka (Ивана Франка), turn right, and walk until you see vul. Zelena; it's behind the busy Pizzeria San Remo. Fast connection 1hv per 15min.

**Post Office:** vul. Slovatskoho 1 (☎72 39 43), a block from Park Ivana Franka, to the right as you face the university. **Poste Restante** on the 2nd floor, window #3. Open M-F 8am-8pm, Sa 8am-6pm, Su 8am-2pm.

**Postal code:** 79 000.

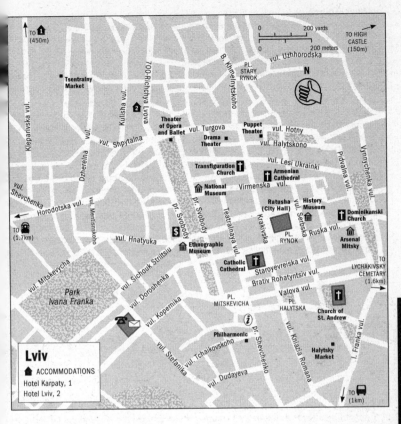

**Lviv**
♠ ACCOMMODATIONS
Hotel Karpaty, 1
Hotel Lviv, 2

UKRAINE

## ACCOMMODATIONS

The Grand Hotel opened its gleaming salons to the public, but not to the budget traveler (US$250 per room)—although you might want to exploit its downstairs bathroom. Prices are rising, though the city is still much more affordable than Kyiv. Some student dorms open up in July and August—the best way to get in is to go through Hotel George's service office (see Tourist Offices, above; call in advance).

**Hotel Lviv,** vul. 700-Richya Lvova 7 (700-Річия Львова, ☎79 22 70, 72 47 93, and 74 33 65), at the northern tip of pr. Svobody. Take tram #6 from the train station to the 1st stop after you see the Opera House on your right. Walk back to the Opera House; the hotel is 1 block behind it on the left. A bit noisy, but central. Hot water 24hr. Spartan singles with TV 37hv, with bath 67hv; doubles 23hv, 52hv.

**Hotel Karpaty** (Карпати), vul. Kleparivska 30 (Клепарівська; ☎33 34 27). From the Opera House, walk straight, bear right onto Shevchenka when the road splits, then take a right onto vul. Kleparivska. Continue straight past Krakivsky Rynok until you see the hotel on your right (20min.). Tram #4 from vul. 700-Richya Lvova (700-Річия Львова) also stops near the hotel. Clean rooms. Hot water for 90min. in morning and afternoon and 1hr. at night. Singles 35.10hv, with bath 80.50hv; doubles 38.90hv, 94.80hv.

## FOOD

**Pl. Rynok** is the restaurant and cafe center of Lviv. The most convenient **market** is **Halytsky Rynok** (Галицький Ринок), behind the flower stands across from St.

Andrew's Church and one block from Hotel George. Fresh berries, honey, and vegetables line the path to the market. (Open in summer daily 7am-6pm.) A little farther out is the cheaper and bigger **Tsentralny Rynok** (Центральний), called **Krakivsky Rynok** (Краківський) by locals. (Open M-Sa 6am-9pm.) There are several 24hr. grocery stores; **Mini Market,** vul. Doroshenka 6, is a block from the Grand Hotel. Lviv is also famous for its "Svitoch" confectionery. The main kiosk with sweets is at the intersection of pr. Svobody (Свободи) and vul. Horodotska (Городоцька).

> **U Pani Stefi** (У Пані Стефи), pr. Svobody 8. Traditional Ukrainian food, carved wooden tables, Ukrainian music, and waitresses in colorful, traditional garb. A little tourist-geared but worth the experience. Main dishes 10-15hv. Open daily 10am-10pm.

> **Videnska Kavyarnya** (Віденська Кавярня), pl. Svobody 12 (☎72 20 21). Lviv's trendiest place to have dessert, but they serve a great dinner as well. English menu. Main dishes 6-20hv. Open daily 9am-11pm.

> **Pizza Chelentano** (Челентано), pr. Svobody 24, behind the Opera to the left. Popular with the after-theater and student crowds alike, this colorful pizzeria is also a favorite among expats. Pizza 4-30hv, toppings 2hv. Open daily 10am-11pm.

> **Mediviya** (Медівія), vul. Krakivska 17 (Краківська, ☎72 91 41), not far from pl. Rynok. The wooden picnic tables in this small room are often packed. Fresh, cheap traditional food cooked by Ukrainians for Ukrainians. Salads and appetizers for less than 1hv, main dishes 1.50-4hv. Open daily 10am-10pm.

## ■ CAFES

Lviv is so reknowned for its cafe culture there are even songs about it. Maybe it's the Viennese atmosphere, but the little elegant cafes always attract a crowd of locals happy to have a cup of strong, black, warm liquid with friends.

▨ **Italiysky Dvoryk** (Італійський Дворик), pl. Rynok 6. Here, Lviv's hippest sip coffee among Renaissance statues and arches in the courtyard of a 16th-century merchant's house. A museum upstairs contains his most fashionable belongings. Unpretentious crowd of intellectuals and art-lovers. Coffee 1.20hv. Open daily 10am-8pm.

▨ **Svit Kavi** (Світ Кави), pl. Katedralna 6 (Катедральна). The exotic coffees at this shop have quickly become famous. An international selection for 1.50-4hv per cup. Open daily 9am-9pm.

## ◉ SIGHTS

Lviv's churches, squares, and ancient tenements create a city as splendid as Prague or St. Petersburg. With a heavy Polish and Austrian influence on the architecture, the city has an air more western and European than that of the rest of Ukraine. If you are specifically interested in seeing churches, the best time is between 5 and 7pm, when doors open for the faithful.

### OUTSIDE THE OLD TOWN

**HIGH CASTLE HILL.** (Высокий Замок; Vysoky Zamok.) Introduce yourself to Lviv by climbing High Castle Hill, the former site of the Galician king's palace. Now a Ukrainian flag and the hideous TV tower hover above the magnificent panoramic view. *(Follow vul. Krivonoca (Кривоноса) from its intersection with Hotny and Halytskono. Go until you pass #39, then take a left down the long dirt road and begin to wind your way up around the hill counter-clockwise.)*

**LICHAKIVSKY CEMETERY.** (Личаківський Цвинтар; Lychakivsky Tsvyntar.) The paths of Lviv's famous necropolis provide a pleasant strolling ground. For the most instructive visit, follow Mechnykova down past the empty space to the main gate. Upon entering, follow the path to the right to visit the graves of famous Ukrainian artists. On the left, a hammer-armed Stakhanovite decorates the eternal bed of **Ivan Franko** (Іван Франко), poet, socialist activist, and a celebrated national hero. *(From vul. Lychakivska (Личаківська), head down vul. Mechnykova to the Cemetery; tram #7 stops right out front. Open daily 9am-9pm. 1hv, students 0.50hv.)*

## OLD TOWN

**PL. RYNOK.** The heart of the city is pl. Rynok, the historic market square, surrounded by a collage of richly decorated merchant homes dating from the 16th to 18th centuries. The **town hall** (ратуша; ratusha) is a 19th-century addition.

**BOYM'S CHAPEL.** (Каплиця Боїмів; Kaplytsya Boimiv.) The Renaissance Boym's Chapel is the only example of Lviv's religious architecture that's more a tourist attraction than a house of worship. It was commissioned by a rich Hungarian merchant, Boim, and contains the remains of 14 members of his family. *(Open Tu-Sa 10am-5pm. 1hv, students 0.50hv.)*

**OTHER SIGHTS.** The massive **Assumption Church** (Успенська Церква; Uspenska Tserkva) lies just up vul. Pidvalna (Підвальна); enter through the archway. Next to the church, **Kornyakt's Tower** (Башта Корнякта; Bashta Kornyakta) hoists a bell 60m above ground. A stroll up vul. Federova, then left on vul. Virmenska, lands you at the barricaded **Armenian Cathedral** (Вірменський Собор; Virmensky Sobor). It seems so out of place that one would never guess it has stood here since the 14th century. Next to it is the **Armenian Quarter,** with old inscriptions still intact.

## PROSPEKT SVOBODY (FREEDOM BOULEVARD)

From the dazzling **Theater of Opera and Ballet** (Театр Опери а Балету; Teatr Opery a Baletu; see **Entertainment,** p. 802) walk down the boulevard's right side past shops and hotels, lodged in the facades of old Polish apartments. The promenade that runs through the center of the boulevard is popular for early-evening ice-cream strolling and intense chess matches. In the middle of pr. Svobody, a monument to the celebrated national poet **Taras Shevchenko** looks over patriotic parades and other high-energy gatherings. At the end of pr. Svobody, the **Mickiewicz statue** honors the Polish poet and patriot and serves as the site of concerts, heated political discussions, and the occasional Hare Krishna sing-along.

## IVAN FRANK PARK

From pr. Svobody, head down Hnatyuka, then take a left on Sichovka Stritsiv to **Ivan Franko Park** (Парк ім. Ивана Франка; Park im. Ivana Franka), which faces the grand columned facade of **Lviv University.** Franko looks down to the right on the students. Walk all the way uphill through the park to be rewarded by **St. Yura's Cathedral** (Собор св. Юра; Sobor sv. Yura). The interior of this 18th-century wonder houses an elaborate altar. Outside, note the equestrian dragon-slayer Yura (George) perched over the entrance. *(Open daily 7am-1pm and 3-8pm.)* Toward the train off vul. Horodetska is **St. Elizabeth's Cathedral.** Constructed by Poles when they first settled in Lviv, its spires purposefully reach higher than St. Yura's domes to assert the dominance of Polish Catholicism over Ukrainian Orthodoxy. Now, both churches have become Uniate, the predominent religion of the region.

## 🏛 MUSEUMS

More frequented than the lonely museums of other Ukrainian cities, Lviv's museums can provide you with enough intellectual fodder for years; just take your pick.

**History Museum** (Історичний Музей; Istorychny Muzey), pl. Rynok #4, 6, and 24. The museum at #4 recounts the history of Lviv during the World Wars. The adjoining Italian Courtyard, #6, presents military clothing, paintings, and other household treasures of the Italian *mascalzone* (rascals) who lived here in the 16th century. #24 has 3 floors of various medieval artifacts. Open Th-Tu 10am-5pm. Each 0.50-1hv.

**Museum of National Architecture** (Музей Народної Архітектури та Побуту у Львові; Muzey Narodnoi Architektury ta Pobutu u Lvovi) at Shevchenkivsky Hay (Шевченківський Гай). From vul. Doroshenka (Дорошенка), take tram #2 or 7 to Mechnikova, or walk along vul. Lychakivska to vul. Krulyarska and head all the way up the hill, bearing right at the top to reach the outdoor museum. This open-air ethnographic museum features a collection of wooden houses (скансен; skansen) from all around Western Ukraine, one of which is now an active church. Open Tu-Su 11am-7pm. 1hv.

**Ethnographic Museum** (Музей Этнографії; Muzey Etnohrafii), pr. Svobody #15. At the corner of vul. Hnatyuka. Harbors an excellent exhibit of Ukrainian dress, archaeological artifacts, painted eggs, and musical instruments. Open W-Su 10am-6pm. Tours 3hv, students 1.50hv; exhibitions 1hv, 0.50hv.

## 🎵 ENTERTAINMENT

Pr. Svobody fills up after lunch with colorful characters singing wartime and harvest tunes to accordion accompaniment. By 8pm, the sounds of light jazz from sidewalk cafes fill the avenue, coffeehouses cloud up with smoke and reverberate with political discussion, and auditoria echo with arias or tragic monologues.

Opera, experimental drama, cheap tickets, and an artistic population make Lviv's performance halls the second most frequented institutions after cafes. Purchase tickets at the *teatralny kasy* (театральни каси; box offices), pr. Svobody 37. (Open M-Sa 10am-1pm and 2:30-5pm.)

**Teatr Opery Ta Baletu** (Театр Опери Та Балету), pr. Svobody 1 (☎ 72 88 60). You don't have to love opera and you don't even need a tux; you just have to go. Great space, great voices, great set. Hear Verdi, Puccini, or Mozart from the front row for 6-10hv.

**Philarmonia** (Філармонія), vul. Tchaikovskoho 7 (☎ 75 21 01), around the corner from Hotel George. Less frequent performances than the Opera, but with many renowned guest performers. Ticket office open 11am-2pm and 4-8pm. Tickets 2-5hv.

## 🍸 NIGHTLIFE

After spending the day singing in the streets and lounging in the java houses, at night Lviv sits down for a final cup. Check for event notices in the basement of the Puppet Theater.

**Club-Cafe Lyalka** (Клуб-Кафе Лялька), vul. Halytskoho 1 (Галицького), below the Teatr Lyalok (Puppet Theater). Downstairs, artsiness fights artfulness for supremacy. Shabbily dressed starving artists do shots while arguing with sophisticated black-clad wine-sippers. A wall of posters advertises past and future concerts; speakers play soft Italian rock or Australian pop; graffitied bedsheets hang from the ceiling. A little slow on weeknights, but the place to be when the disco ball turns. Wine 2.50hv; coffee 1hv. Cover 5hv disco nights. W Jazz. Open M-F 1-11pm, Sa-Su 11am-1am.

**Club-Cafe za Kulisamy** (Клуб-Кафе за Кулісами), vul. Tchaikovshoho 7, on the 2nd floor of the Philharmonic. Entrance to the left, but not well marked. The kind of place that people find out about from friends, this intimate cafe is full of well-acquainted groups. Sounds of practicing Philharmonic artists leak in. Hard liquors and suds available, but they somehow seem out of place—it's coffee and Marlboro all the way. Beyond mellow. Coffee 1hv. Open daily noon-midnight.

**Zoloty Kolos** (Золотий Колос), vul. Kleparivska 18 (Клепарівська; ☎ 33 04 89). The ex-USSR's best brewery continues to brew the ex-USSR's best beer. (Bottles 1.30hv.) Descend into the spacious, cobblestone-walled cellar to enjoy hops'n'malt (0.5L 1.80hv). When *Zoloty Kolos* is unavailable, the weaker but equally tasty *Lvivske Pivo* foams. Open daily 10am-11pm.

**Picasso** (Пікасо), vul. Zelena 88 (Зелена). An older and somewhat wealthier local crowd fills this dance club with artistic pretense. Cover 5hv weeknights; weekends men 10hv, women 7hv. Men 20+.

## UZHHOROD (УЖГОРОД)                    ☎ (8)03122

Uzhhorod is a small town that plays the role of a big city to the tiny villages nearby. It did not escape Soviet urban planning unscathed, but its colorful facades remind visitors of the times when Austro-Hungary and Czechoslovakia ruled here; its streets along the Uzh offer pleasant views and strolls. Uzhhorod's three main tourist attractions are conveniently situated right next to one another. To reach the majestic **Kafedralny Cathedral** (Кафедральний собор; Kafedralny Sobor), take a right from the base of the pedestrian bridge facing the Hotel Koruna, then take a left up the stairs at the Philharmonia building. Come out of the alley and head to the left. Follow the road in front of the cathedral to reach a small **castle** (замок; zamok) featuring statues and a museum. The castle was involved in the predictably unsuccessful 1704 Trans-Carpathian revolt against the Habsburgs. The museum exhibits traditional Carpathian clothing. (Open Tu-Su 9am-5pm. 1.50hv, students 0.50hv.) Across the way, the **Folk Architecture and Life Museum** (Музей Народної Архітектури і Побуту; Muzey Narodnoi Arkhitektury i Pobutu), an open-air display at vul. Kapitulna 33-33a (Капітульна), consists of a dozen original wood and stone huts typical of the region and a wooden church built without nails. (Open W-M 9am-5pm. 1hv, students 0.50hv.)

Most international connections go through the town of **Chop:** get there by "Електичка" (elektrichka; every 30min., 2hv). Domestic **trains** run to Lviv (7hr., 3 per day, 16hv, *coupé* 24hv) and **Kyiv** (18hr., 2 per day, 31hv, *coupé* 49hv). **Buses** go to: **Lviv** (7hr., 1 per day, *platzkart* 15hv, *coupé* 20hv); **Bratislava, SLK** (2 per day, 92hv); and **Prague, CZR** (1 per day, 140hv). Many buses (1hr., 2.75hv) and trains (2hr., 3.50hv) run daily to **Mukachevo** (Мукачево), with additional international connections. International train tickets can be bought at the **Zaliznichni Kvytkovi Kasa** (Залізнічні Квиткові Каса), vul. Lva Tolstoha 33 (Льва Толстога; open daily 8am-5pm), but for routes originating in Mukachevo, call **Intourist** (☎ 938 29 58). Uzhhorod straddles the **Uzh** (Уж) River. The train and bus stations are a two-minute walk apart. To reach the center of town, turn right out of the train station and head down vul. Pidhradska two blocks to vul. Mukachivska. Go left and head through the square at the end of the street; take a final right and cross the pedestrian bridge. Store **luggage** in the building to the right of the train station. (2hv per day. Open M-Sa 9am-7pm.) Near the pedestrian bridge, **Ukraine Export-Import Bank**, pl. Petefi, 19 (Петефі), cashes **traveler's checks** for 2% commission. (☎ 122 62. Open M-Th 9am-12:45pm and 2-4pm, F 9am-12:45pm and 2-3pm.) An immediate left after the bridge leads to the **post office**, nab. Nezalezhnosti 9. (Open M-F 7am-6pm, Sa 7am-5pm.) The **telephone office** in the same building is open 24hr. **Postal code:** 294 000. For accommodations, head to **Turbaza Svitanok** (Турбаза Світанок), vul. Koshytska 30 (Кошицька). From the pedestrian bridge, go left at the Hotel Koruna, then a right and another left. Follow this street as it bears right and uphill into Zhulanatska (Жуланацька). Turn left at the next major intersection and go straight until you come to vul. Sobranetska (Собранецька). Take a right and walk five minutes uphill. Alternatively, take a cab from the train station for 4hv. The Turbaza is also the main **tourist office** for treks into the Carpathians. (☎ 343 09. Hot water 2hr. per day. Bare singles 16hv, with bath 44hv; doubles with bath 30hv per person.) The **cafeteria** next door to Turbaza Svitanok could put a Ukrainian grandmother to shame. (Meals 1-2hv. Open 8:30-9:30am, 1:30-3pm, and 6:30-8pm.)

# GATEWAY CITIES

## BERLIN, GERMANY ☎ (0)3

**PHONE CODES**  Country code: **49**. International dialing prefix: **00**.

Berlin's ability to flourish in times of adversity has always made it a remarkable city. Raised in the shadow of global conflict, post-World War II Berliners responded with a storm of cultural activity and the sort of free-for-all nightlife you might expect from a population with its back against the Wall. The fall of the physical and psychological division between East and West in 1989 symbolized the end of the Cold War, and Berlin was officially reunited to widespread celebration on October 3, 1990. The task of uniting Berlin's twin cities, though, has proven no easier than that of stitching together both halves of the country; it seems that Eastern and Western Berliners don't really like each other as much as they once imagined they would. But as Karl Zuckmayer once wrote, "Berlin tasted of the future, and for that one happily accepted the dirt and the coldness as part of the bargain."

**VISAS** EU citizens may visit, study, and work in Germany without a visa. Citizens of Australia, Canada, New Zealand, and the US do not need a visa for stays of up to 90 days within six months. Citizens of South Africa need a visa to enter Germany; contact the nearest German Consulate General.

**CURRENCY**

| | |
|---|---|
| US$1 = DM2.18 (DEUTSCHMARKS) | DM1 = US$0.46 |
| CDN$1 = DM1.47 | DM1 = CDN$0.68 |
| UK£1 = DM3.23 | DM1 = UK£0.31 |
| IR£1 = DM2.48 | DM1 = IR£0.40 |
| AUS$1 = DM1.27 | DM1 = AUS$0.79 |
| NZ$1 = DM0.97 | DM1 = NZ$1.04 |
| SAR1 = DM0.31 | DM1 = SAR3.20 |

## ✴ ORIENTATION

Berlin is an immense conglomeration—eight times the size of Paris—of two once-separate cities: the former East, which contains most of Berlin's landmarks, historic sites, and concrete socialist architectural monsters, and the former West, which functioned for decades as an isolated Allied protectorate.

The commercial heart of the united city lies in West Berlin, southwest of the **Tiergarten,** centered around **Bahnhof Zoo** and **Kurfürstendamm (Ku'damm).** Southeast of Ku'damm, **Schöneberg** is the nexus of the city's gay and lesbian community. North of Ku'damm, **Charlottenburg** is home to countless cafes, restaurants, and *pensionen.* **Strasse des 17. Juni** runs east from Charlottenburg through the Tiergarten to the triumphant **Brandenburg Gate** on the other side, opening onto **Unter den Linden,** Berlin's most famous boulevard. The broad, tree-lined throughway cuts through **Mitte** and empties into **Alexanderplatz,** the commercial center of Eastern Berlin. The west-east Spree River splits between Mitte and Alexanderpl., forming the **Museumsinsel** (Museum Island), Eastern Berlin's cultural epicenter. Heading south from the Brandenburg Gate and the **Reichstag,** Ebertstrasse runs haphazardly through construction sites to **Potsdamer Platz.** Southeast of Potsdamer Pl. lies **Kreuzberg,** home to radical leftists, Turks, punks, and homosexuals. Northeast of the city center, **Prenzlauer Berg,** a former working-class-suburb-turned-squatter's-paradise, rumbles

# Central Berlin

GATEWAY CITIES

1/2 mile
1/2 kilometer

N

ROSA-LUXEMBURG-PLATZ

ALEXANDER PLATZ

Fernsehturm

Marienkirche

Berliner Dom

Alte Synagoge

HACKESCHER MARKT

Bodemuseum

Pergamon Museum

Alte Nationalgalerie

Zeughaus

ORANIEN-BURGER TOR

Humboldt Universität

Staatsoper

BEBEL PLATZ

GENDARMEN-MARKT

Bahnhof Friedrichstr.

FRIEDRICHSTR.

Checkpoint Charlie

former Berlin Wall

KOCHSTR.

Unter den Linden

MITTE

MOHREN-STR.

STADT MITTE

Brandenburger Tor

PARISER PLATZ

POTSDAMER PLATZ

Martin-Gropius-Bau

Reichstag

Soviet Army Memorial

Kongresshalle

Str. des 17 Juni

Philharmonie

Kunstgewerbemuseum

Neue Nationalgalerie

Schloß Bellevue

GROSSER STERN

Siegessäule

TIERGARTEN

LEHRTER STADTBAHNHOF

TO ZOOLOGISCHER GARTEN, KUDAMM

River Spree

Heinrich-Heine-Str.

MÄRK. MUS.

SPITTEL MARKT

Lindenstr.

Hofjäger-Allee

Entlastungsstr.

John-Foster-Dulles-Allee

Str. des 17 Juni

Moltkestr.

Wilhelmstr.

with as-yet-unrestored pre-war structures and sublime cafes. Southeast of Mitte, **Friedrichshain** is emerging as the center of Berlin's counterculture.

For visits of more than a few days, the blue-and-yellow **Falk Plan** (DM11) can be useful. Dozens of streets and subway stations in Eastern Berlin have been renamed in a purge only recently completed; be sure your map is up-to-date.

## ⬛ TRANSPORTATION

> **!** Although Berlin is by far the most tolerant city in Germany, economic chaos has unleashed a new wave of right-wing extremism, particularly in the outer boroughs of Eastern Berlin. While it's unlikely that you'll encounter neo-Nazi skinheads, it is important for members of ethnic minorities as well as gays and lesbians to take precautions when traveling in suburban East Berlin or on the S-Bahn late at night.

**Airplanes:** ☎(0180) 500 01 86 for all airports. **Flughafen Tegel** is Western Berlin's main airport. Take express bus X9 from Bahnhof Zoo, bus 109 from U6 Jakob-Kaiser-Platz, or bus 128 from U6: Kurt-Schumacher-Platz. **Flughafen Tempelhof** handles domestic and European flights. U6: Platz der Luftbrücke. **Flughafen Schönefeld,** southeast of Berlin, handles intercontinental flights and those to the former USSR. Take S9 or 45 to Flughafen Berlin Schönefeld, or bus 171 from U7: Rudow.

**Trains:** ☎(0180) 599 66 33. Most trains stop at both **Zoologischer Garten (Bahnhof Zoo)** and **Ostbahnhof.** To: **Prague, CZR** (5hr., 4 per day, DM127); **Warsaw, POL** (6hr., 4 per day, DM49); and **Kraków, POL** (10½hr., 4 per day, DM51).

**Buses:** ZOB (Central Bus Station; ☎301 80 28), by the *Funkturm* near Kaiserdamm. U2: Kaiserdamm or S4, 45, or 46: Witzleben. Buses are often cheaper than trains.

**Public Transportation:** BVG (Berliner Verkehrsbetriebe; ☎194 49), in the bus parking lot outside Bahnhof Zoo (☎25 62 25 62). The **bus, Strassenbahn** (streetcar), **U-Bahn** (subway), and **S-Bahn** (surface rail) systems are extensive and efficient. Berlin is divided into 3 transit zones: **Zone A** (downtown Berlin); **Zone B** (almost everywhere else); and **Zone C** (outlying areas including Potsdam and Oranienburg). The **Liniennetz** map is free at any tourist office or subway station. U- and S-Bahn lines generally do not run 1-4am, although most S-Bahn lines run hourly on weekend nights and the U9 and 12 run 24hr. F-Sa. **Night buses** (designated "N") run every 20-30min.; pick up the free *Nachtliniennetz* map at the BVG.

**Tickets:** A single ticket (2-zone *Langstrecke,* AB or BC, DM3.90; 3-zone *Ganzstrecke* DM4.20) is good for 2hr., but passes are usually better values. A **Tageskarte** (AB DM7.80, ABC DM8.50) is valid until 3am the next day. A **Gruppentageskarte** (AB DM20, ABC DM22.50) allows up to 5 people to travel together on the same ticket. The **WelcomeCard** (DM32) is valid on all lines for 72hr. The **7-Tage-Karte** (AB DM40, ABC DM48) is good for 7 days. Buy tickets from *Automaten* (machines), bus drivers, or ticket windows in U- and S-Bahn stations. **Validate tickets** in the box marked *"hier entwerten"* before boarding, or face a DM60 fine.

**Hitchhiking:** *Let's Go* does not recommend hitchhiking. It's illegal to hitch at rest stops or on the highway. **Mitfahrzentralen: City Netz,** Joachimstaler Str. 17 (☎194 44), arranges **ride-sharing.** U9, 15: Kurfürstendamm. Open M-F 9am-8pm, Sa-Su 9am-7pm.

**Taxis:** ☎26 10 26, 21 02 02, and 690 22. Call at least 15min. in advance. Women may request a female driver. Trips within the city usually cost less than DM40.

## ⬛ PRACTICAL INFORMATION

### TOURIST AND FINANCIAL SERVICES

**Tourist Offices:** www.berlin.de. Most sell city maps (DM1) and book same-day hotel rooms (from DM50, plus DM5 fee). **Euraide,** in Bahnhof Zoo, to the left and down the passage on the right as you face the *Reisezentrum.* Open daily 8am-noon and 1-6pm.

**Tours: Berlin Walks** (☎301 91 94) offers a range of English-language walking tours, including **Infamous Third Reich Sites, Jewish Life in Berlin,** and the **Discover Berlin**

GATEWAY CITIES

**Walk** (3-7hr.). All tours depart 10am from the taxi stand in front of Bahnhof Zoo; Discover Berlin Walk in summer also 2:30pm (DM18, under 26 DM14). **Insider Tour** provides a thorough historical narrative and hits all the major sights (3½hr.). Departs from the McDonald's by Bahnhof Zoo daily Mar.-Nov. 10am and 2:30pm. DM15.

**Budget Travel: STA,** Goethestr. 73 (☎311 09 50). U2: Ernst-Reuter-Platz. Open M-W and F 10am-6pm, Th 10am-8pm. **Kilroy Travels,** Hardenbergstr. 9 (☎310 00 40), 2 blocks northwest of Bahnhof Zoo. Open M-F 10am-6pm, Sa 11am-3pm.

**Embassies:** The locations of embassies remain in flux; for the most up-to-date info, call 20 18 60. **Australia,** Friedrichstr. 200 (☎880 08 80). U2, 6: Stadtmitte. Open M-F 9am-noon. **Canada,** Friedrichstr. 95 (☎20 31 20; fax 20 31 25 90), on the 12th fl. of the International Trade Center. S1, 2, 3, 5, 7, 9, 25, 75, or U6: Friedrichstr. Open M-F 9am-noon. Appointments at 2pm. **Ireland,** Friedrichstr. 200 (☎22 07 20). Open M-F 9:30am-noon, 2:30-4:45pm. **New Zealand,** Friedrichstr. 60. (☎20 62 10). Open M-F 9am-1pm, 2-5:30pm; F until 4:30pm. **South Africa,** Friedrichstr. 60 (☎22 07 30). **UK,** Unter den Linden 32-34 (☎20 18 40; fax 20 18 41 58). S1, 2, 3, 5, 7, 9, 25, 75, or U6: Friedrichstr. Open M-F 9am-4pm. **US Citizens' Service,** Clayallee 170 (☎832 92 33; fax 831 49 26). U1: Oskar-Helene-Heim. Open M-F 8:30am-noon. **US Consulate,** Neustädtische Kirchstr. 4-5 (☎238 51 74; fax 238 62 90). S1, 2, 3, 5, 7, 9, 25, 75, or U6: Friedrichstr. Open 8:30am-5:30pm, by appointment only.

**Currency Exchange: Wechselstube,** Joachimstaler Str. 1-3, near Bahnhof Zoo. Good rates and no commission. Open M-F 8am-8pm, Sa 9am-3pm. **ATMs** are ubiquitous.

**American Express:** Bayreuther Str. 23 (☎21 49 83 63). U1, 2, or 15: Wittenbergpl. Open M-F 9am-6pm, Sa 10am-1pm.

## EMERGENCY AND COMMUNICATIONS

**Emergency: Police,** ☎110. **Ambulance** and **fire,** ☎112.

**Crisis Lines:** English spoken at most crisis lines. **American Hotline,** ☎(0177) 814 15 10. Crisis and referral service. **Sexual Assault Hotline,** ☎251 28 28. Open Tu, Th 6-9pm, Su noon-2pm. **Schwules Überfall,** for victims of gay bashing, ☎216 33 36. Hotline and legal help. Open daily 6-9pm.

**Pharmacies: Europa-Apotheke,** Tauentzienstr. 9-12 (☎261 41 42), near Bahnhof Zoo. Open M-F 9am-8pm, Sa 9am-4pm. For info about **late-night pharmacies,** call 011 89.

**Medical Assistance:** The American and British Embassies have a list of English-speaking doctors. **Emergency Doctor** (☎31 00 31) and **Emergency Dentist** (☎89 00 43 33).

**Internet Access: Alpha,** Dunckerstr. 72 (☎447 90 67), in Prenzlauer Berg. U2: Eberswalder Str. DM12 per hr. Open daily 3pm-midnight. **Cyberb@r,** Joachimstaler Str. 5-6, near Bahnhof Zoo on the 2nd floor of Karstadt Sport department store. DM5 per 30min.

**Post Office:** Budapester Str. 42, opposite the Europa-Center near Bahnhof Zoo. Open M-Sa 8am-midnight, Su 10am-midnight.

## ACCOMMODATIONS

Same-day accommodations aren't impossible to find even in summer, although it's best to call ahead. If arriving on a weekend or during the Love Parade (mid-July), book ahead. For DM5, **tourist offices** find rooms in hostels, *Pensionen*, and hotels, but be prepared to pay DM70 for singles, DM100 for doubles.

**Circus,** Rosa-Luxemburg-Str. 39-41 (☎28 39 14 33; fax 28 39 14 84; circus@mind.de), near Alexanderpl. U2: Rosa-Luxemburg-Platz. A heroic effort at hostel hipness, with internet and a disco ball in the lobby. Sheets DM4. Bikes DM12 per day. Reserve ahead and reconfirm a day before. 5- to 6-person dorms DM25; singles DM45; doubles DM40; triples DM35; quads DM40.

**Clubhouse Hostel,** Johannisstr. 2 (☎28 09 79 79). S1, 2, or 25: Oranienburger Str., or U6: Oranienburger Tor. Great location in the center of the Oranienburger Str. club and bar scene. Breakfast DM7. Internet DM1 per 5min. Call 2-3 days ahead. 8- to 10-person dorms DM25; 5- to 7-bed DM30; doubles DM40.

**Mitte's Backpacker Hostel,** Chausseestr. 102 (☎262 51 40; fax 28 39 09 35; backpacker@snafu.de; www.backpacker.de). U6: Zinnowitzer Str. An English-speaking haven filled with whirlwind tourers. Eager staff with tips on sightseeing and nightlife. Sheets DM5. Laundry DM5. Bikes DM10-12 per day. Internet access. Reception 7am-9:30pm. 5- to 6-person dorms DM27-29; doubles DM38; triples DM33; quads DM31.

**Hotel-Pension Cortina,** Kantstr. 140 (☎313 90 59; fax 31 73 96). S3, 5, 7, 9, or 75: Savignyplatz. Bright, convenient, and hospitable. Breakfast included. Dorms DM35-60; singles DM60-90; doubles DM90-150.

**Pension Berolina,** Stuttgarter Pl. 17 (☎32 70 90 72; fax 32 70 90 73). S3, 5, 7, 9, 75: Charlottenburg or U7: Wilmersdorfer Str. Simple, spartan rooms. Shared bathrooms. Breakfast DM8. Reservations recommended. Singles DM60; doubles DM80; triples DM90; quads DM100; quints DM110.

## ☕ FOOD

The most typical Berlin food is Turkish; every street has its own Turkish *Imbiss* or restaurant. The *Döner Kebab*, a ground-lamb and salad sandwich, has cornered the fast-food market, with falafel running a close second (each DM3-5). **Aldi, Plus, Edeka,** and **Penny Markt** are the cheapest supermarket chains; most are open Monday to Friday 9am to 6pm and Saturday 9am to 4pm. At Bahnhof Zoo, **Ullrich am Zoo,** below the SBahn tracks, and **Nimm's Mit,** near the *Reisezentrum*, have longer hours. (Both open daily 6am-10pm.) The best **open-air market** fires up Saturday mornings on Winterfeldtplatz. For cheap vegetables, check out the **Turkish market** in Kreuzberg, along Maybachufer on Fridays (U8: Schönleinstr.). **Mensas,** student dining halls, offer cheap meals for students.

**Mensa TU,** Hardenbergstr. 34 (☎311 22 53). 10min. from Bahnhof Zoo. Meals DM4-5 for students, others DM6-7. Cafeteria downstairs has longer hours and slightly higher prices. *Mensa* open M-F 11:15am-2:30pm. Cafeteria open M-F 8am-7:45pm.

**Mensa der Humboldt-Universität,** Unter den Linden 6, in the back of the university's main building. The cheapest *Mensa* in Berlin, conveniently located for sight-seeing in Eastern Berlin. Full meals DM2.50-4. Student ID required. Open M-F 11:30am-2:30pm.

**Baharat Falafel,** Winterfeldtstr. 37. U1, 2, 4, or 15: Nollendorfplatz. The best falafel in Berlin (DM6-7). Open daily 11am-2am. Closed last week in July.

**Die Krähe,** Kollwitzstr. 84 (☎442 82 91), off Kollwitzpl. U2: Senefelderplatz. Changing weekly menu. Breakfasts under DM10; crunchy salads DM12; Sunday buffet DM13.50. Open M-Th 5:30pm-2am, F-Sa 5:30pm-3am, Su 10:30am-2am.

**Café Hardenberg,** Hardenbergstr. 10 (☎312 33 30), opposite the TU *Mensa,* but with more atmosphere. Order sizzling breakfasts (DM5-12) day or night. Salads and pasta DM5-13. Open M-F 9am-1am, Sa-Su 9am-2am.

## ◉ SIGHTS

Many major sights lie along the route of **bus 100,** which travels from Bahnhof Zoo to Prenzlauer Berg via the Siegessäule, Brandenburg Gate, Unter den Linden, Berliner Dom, and Alexanderplatz (day pass DM7.80, 7-day pass DM40).

### CENTRAL BERLIN

For decades a barricaded gateway to nowhere, the reopened **Brandenburg Gate** (Brandenburger Tor) symbolizes reunited Berlin, connecting Unter den Linden on the east with the Tiergarten park and Strasse des 17. Juni on the west. Built during the reign of Friedrich Wilhelm II as an emblem of peace, the locked gate embedded in the Berlin Wall was a symbol of Cold War division. The **Berlin Wall** itself is a dinosaur, with only fossil remains. Fenced overnight on August 13, 1961, the 165km wall separated families and friends, sometimes even running through homes. Portions are preserved near the *Ostbahnhof* and by Potsdamer Platz; the longest remaining bit is the brightly painted **East Side Gallery** (S3, 7, 9: Ostbahnhof). **Potsdamer Platz,** cut off by the wall, was once a major Berlin transportation hub, designed under Friedrich Wilhelm I to approximate Parisian boulevards; the surrounding area is

**GATEWAY CITIES**

now the world's largest construction site. Just south of Potsdamer Platz stands the **Martin-Gropius-Bau**, Stresemanstr. 110, designed by Martin Gropius, a pupil of Schinkel and uncle of *Bauhaus* architect Walter Gropius. The popular **Haus am Checkpoint Charlie**, a museum on the site of the famous border crossing point, is a mixture of Western tourist kitsch and Eastern earnestness. *(Friedrichstr. 44. U6: Kochstr. or bus #129. ☎ 251 10 31. Open daily 9am-10pm. DM8, students DM5.)*

## WEST BERLIN

Just north of the Brandenburg Gate sits the imposing, stone-gray **Reichstag**, former seat of the parliaments of the German Empire and the Weimar Republic, and as of 1999, home to the German parliament, the *Bundestag*. Shortly after Hitler became Chancellor in 1933, a mysterious fire in the Reichstag provided a pretext to declare a state of emergency, giving the Nazis broad powers to arrest opponents. In the heart of **Tiergarten**, in the center of old Berlin, the 70m **victory column** (Siegessäule), topped by a gilded statue of winged victory, commemorates Prussia's 1870 triumph over France. Climb 285 steps for a panoramic view. *(Bus #100, 187, or 341 to Grosser Stern. Open Apr.-Nov. M 1-6pm, Tu-Su 9am-6pm. DM2, students DM1.)*

**Charlottenburg Castle** (Schloss Charlottenburg), the vast Baroque palace built by Friedrich I for his second wife, Sophie-Charlotte, presides over a carefully landscaped park. Seek out the **Palace Gardens**, with their lakes, footbridges, fountains, and carefully planted rows of trees surrounding the **Royal Mausoleum**. *(U7: Richard-Wagner-Platz or bus #145 from Bahnhof Zoo to Luisenpl./Schloss Charlottenburg. ☎ 32 09 11. Castle open Tu-F 9am-5pm, Sa-Su 10am-5pm; mausoleum open Apr.-Oct. Tu-Su 10am-noon and 1-5pm; garden open Tu-Su 6am-9pm. Entire palace complex Tageskarte DM15, students DM10.)*

## EAST BERLIN

The Brandenburg Gate opens east onto **Unter den Linden**, once one of Europe's best-known boulevards and the spine of pre-war Berlin. At the intersection of Friedrichstr. and Unter den Linden rises the stately **German State Library** (Deutsche Staatsbibliothek); the shady, ivy-covered courtyard houses a pleasant cafe. Beyond the library is **Humboldt University**, whose halls have been trodden by the likes of Einstein, Hegel, and Marx. Next door, the Neoclassical **New Guard House** (Neue Wache) was designed by Schinkel. Buried inside are urns full of earth from the Buchenwald and Mauthausen concentration camps, as well as the battlefields of Stalingrad, El Alamein, and Normandy. Across the way is **Bebelplatz**, where on May 10, 1933, Nazi students burned nearly 20,000 books by "subversive" authors.

Berlin's most impressive ensemble of 19th-century buildings is a few blocks south of Unter den Linden at **Gendarmenmarkt**. The twin cathedrals, **Deutscher Dom** and **Französischer Dom**, grace opposite ends of the square; in between lies the Neoclassical **Schauspielhaus**, Berlin's most elegant concert space. After crossing the Schlossbrücke over the Spree, Unter den Linden passes by **Museum Island** (Museumsinsel), home of four major museums (see **Museums**, below) and the **Berliner Dom**. The beautifully bulky cathedral was severely damaged by bombs in 1944; it has emerged from a 20-year restoration with a stunning interior. *(S3, 5, 7, 9, 75: Hackescher Markt. Open daily 9am-7:30pm. DM5, students DM3.)* To the left stands the pillared **Altes Museum**. The **Lustgarten** in front, normally a pleasant collection of trees and benches, will be completely overhauled in the next few years to look as it did in the 19th century. Across the street, the Lustgarten turns into Marx-Engels-Pl. under the amber-colored **Palace of the Republic** (Palast der Republik), where the GDR parliament met. Crossing the Liebknecht-Brücke leads you to a small park on the right-hand side of the street, which used to be collectively known as the **Marx-Engels Forum**; the park has not been renamed, but the street is now called Rathausstr. On the other side of Museum Island, Unter den Linden becomes Karl-Liebknecht Str., and leads into the monolithic **Alexanderplatz**. The undisputed landmark of the district is the **television tower** (Fernsehturm), the city's tallest structure. *(Open daily Mar.-Oct. 9am-1am; Nov.-Feb. 10am-midnight. DM10.)*

##  MUSEUMS

Berlin is one of the world's great museum cities. The **Staatliche Museen Preussischer Kulturbesitz (SMPK)** runs the four major museum complexes: **Museum Island** (S3, 5, 7, 9, 75: Hackescher Markt; bus #100: Lustgarden); **Tiergarten-Kulturforum,** on Matthäikirchplatz (walk up Potsdamer Str. from S1, 2, 25, or U2: Potsdamer Platz); **Charlottenburg** (U7: Richard-Wagner-Platz, or bus #145 from Bahnhof Zoo to Luisenpl./Schloss Charlottenburg); and **Dahlem** (U2: Dahlemdorf). All cost DM4, students DM2. A one-day *Tageskarte* (DM8, students DM4) is valid for all SMPK museums on the day of purchase; a *Wochenkarte* (DM25, students DM12.50) is valid for an entire week. The first Sunday of the month is free.

- **Painting Gallery** (Gemäldegalerie; ☎20 90 55 55), Tiergarten-Kulturinform. Rightly one of Germany's most famous museums. Stunning and enormous collection by Dutch, Flemish, German, and Italian masters, including works by Rembrandt, Breughel, Vermeer, Raphael, Titian, Botticelli, and Dürer. Open Tu-Su 10am-6pm. SMPK prices.
- **Pergamonmuseum** (☎203 55 00), on Museum Island. One of the world's great ancient history museums, thanks to Heinrich Schliemann, who traversed the world, pillaged the debris of ancient civilizations, and reassembled it at home. Mind-boggling exhibits: the entire Babylonian Ishtar Gate, the Roman Market Gate of Miletus, and the Pergamon Altar of Zeus. Open Tu-Su 9am-6pm. *Tageskarte* required. Free audio tours.

##  NIGHTLIFE

Berlin's nightlife is absolute madness, a teeming cauldron of debauchery. Bars, clubs, and cafes jam until at least 3am and often stay open until daylight; on weekends, you can dance non-stop from Friday night until Monday morning. If at all possible, try to hit Berlin during the **Love Parade**, usually held in the second weekend of July, when all of Berlin just says "yes" to everything. The best nightlife areas in Berlin include: **Kreuzberg, Potsdamer Platz,** Mitte's **Oranienburger Str.,** and its intersection with **Friedrichstr.** The social nexus of **gay and lesbian** nightlife centers around **Nollendorfplatz** and the gay neighborhood (Schwuler Kiez) of **Schöneberg.** For up-to-date events listings, pick up a copy of the amazingly comprehensive *Siegessäule* (free), named after the phallic monument.

- **Tresor/Globus,** Leipziger Str. 126a (☎229 06 11), in Mitte. U2, or S1, 2, 25, or bus N-5, N-29 or N-52 to Potsdamer Platz. Globus chills with house; Tresor thumps to techno. Cover W DM5, F DM10, Sa DM15-20. Open W and F-Sa 11pm-6am.
- **SO36,** Oranienstrasse 190 (☎61 40 13 06; www.SO36.de), in Kreuzberg. U1, 12, 15: Görlitzer Bahnhof; bus N29: Heinrichplatz. Berlin's only truly mixed club, with a clientele of hip heteros, gays, and lesbians grooving to a mish-mash of wild genres. Monday trance; Thursday hip-hop/reggae/punk/ska; weekends run the gamut from techno to live concerts. Cover varies. Open daily after 11pm.

# HELSINKI, FINLAND  ☎09

| PHONE CODES | Country code: **358**. International dialing prefix: **00**. |
| --- | --- |

Helsinki's broad avenues, grand architecture, and green parks make it a model of 19th-century city planning. The city distinguishes itself with a multicultural flair: Lutheran and Russian Orthodox cathedrals stand almost face-to-face, and youthful energy mingles with old world charm.

 **VISAS** EU citizens do not require visas to visit, study, or work in Finland. Citizens of Australia, New Zealand, Canada, and the US can visit for up to 90 days without a visa. South Africans need a visa to enter as short-stay tourists.

| | |
|---|---|
| US$1 = 5.61MK (MARKKA, FIM) | 1MK = US$0.18 |
| CDN$1 = 3.79MK | 1MK = CDN$0.26 |
| UK£1 = 9.18MK | 1MK = UK£0.11 |
| IR£1 = 7.55MK | 1MK = IR£0.13 |
| AUS$1 = 3.67MK | 1MK = AUS$0.27 |
| NZ$1 = 2.99MK | 1MK = NZ$0.33 |
| SAR1 = 0.97MK | 1MK = SAR1.04 |

(CURRENCY)

## TRANSPORTATION AND PRACTICAL INFORMATION

Sea surrounds Helsinki on the east and west, and the city center is bisected by two lakes. Helsinki's main street, **Mannerheimintie**, passes between the bus and train stations on its way to the city center, eventually crossing **Esplanadi**. This tree-lined promenade leads east to **Kauppatori** (Market Square) and the beautiful South Harbor. Both Finnish and Swedish are used on all street signs and maps. *Let's Go* uses the Finnish names in all listings and maps.

**Flights: Helsinki-Vantaa Airport** (☎96 00 81 00; 3.40mk per min.) **Buses** #615 (more direct) and 616 run frequently between the airport and the train station square (15mk). A **Finnair bus** shuttles between the airport and the Finnair building at Asemaaukio 3, next to the train station (35min., every 20min. 5am-midnight, 27mk).

**Trains:** (☎707 57 06, and 03 02 72 09 00.) To: **St. Petersburg, RUS** (7hr., 2 per day, 284mk); and **Moscow, RUS** (15hr., daily at 5:34pm, 485mk). Lockers 10mk per day.

**Buses:** (☎02 00 40 10.) The station is between Salomonkatu and Simonkatu; from the Mannerheimintie side of the train station, head down Postikatu past the statue of Mannerheim. Cross Mannerheimintie onto Salomonkatu and the station will be to your left.

**Ferries: Silja Line,** Mannerheimintie 2 (☎980 07 45 52 or 091 80 41). Take tram #3B or 3T from the city center to the Olympic terminal. **Viking Line,** Mannerheimintie 14 (☎12 35 77). **Tallink,** Erottajankatu 19 (☎22 82 12 77). Viking Line and **Finnjet** (contact Silja Line) depart from Katajanokka Island, east of Kauppatori (take tram #2 or 4). Silja Line sails from South Harbor, south of Kauppatori (take tram #3T).

**Public Transportation:** (☎010 01 11; 2mk per call.) The **metro, trams,** and **buses** run 5:30am-11pm. Some tram and bus lines, including tram #3T, continue until 1:30am. Night buses, marked "N," run after 1:30am. Buy single-fare tickets on buses and trams or from machines at the metro station (15mk); 10-trip tickets (120mk) are available at R-kiosks and at the **City Transport** office in M: Rautatientori (open M-Th 7:30am-6pm, F 7:30am-4pm; closes 1hr. later in winter). Tickets are valid for 1hr. (transfers free); punch your ticket on board. The **Tourist Ticket,** available at City Transport and tourist offices, provides unlimited local transit (1-day 25mk, 3-day 50mk, 5-day 75mk).

## PRACTICAL INFORMATION

**Tourist Offices: City Tourist Office,** Pohjoisesplanadi 19 (☎169 37 57; fax 169 38 39; www.hel.fi). From the train station, walk 2 blocks south on Keskuskatu and turn left on Pohjoisesplanadi. Open May-Sept. M-F 9am-7pm, Sa-Su 9am-3pm; Oct.-Apr. M-F 9am-5pm, Sa 9am-3pm. **Hotellikeskus** (Hotel Booking Center; ☎22 88 14 00; fax 22 88 14 99), in the train station, books rooms (30mk in person, free by phone or email). Open June-Aug. M-F 9am-7pm, Sa-Su 10am-6pm; Sept.-May M-F 9am-5pm. **Helsinki Card,** sold at the tourist office, Hotellikeskus, central R-kiosks, and most hotels, provides museum discounts and unlimited local transport (1-day 130mk, 3-day 190mk).

**Budget Travel: Kilroy Travels,** Kaivokatu 10 (☎02 03 54 57 69), sells domestic and international tickets. Open M 10am-8pm, Tu-F 10am-6pm, Sa 10am-4pm.

**Embassies: Canada,** Pohjoisesplanadi 25B (☎17 11 41). Open M-F 8:30am-noon and 1-4:30pm. **Estonia,** Itäinen Puistotie 10 (☎622 02 88). **Ireland,** Erottajankatu 7A (☎64 60 06). **Latvia,** Armfeltintie 10 (☎476 47 20). **Lithuania,** Rauhankatu 13A (☎60 82 10). **Poland,** Armas Lindgrenintie 21 (☎684 80 77). **Russia,** Tehtaankatu 1B (☎66 18 76). **South Africa,** Rahapajankatu 1A 5 (☎68 60 31 00). **UK,** Itäinen Puistotie 17 (☎22 86 51 00). Also handles diplomatic matters for **Australia** and **New Zealand.** Open M-F 8:30am-5pm. **US,** Itäinen Puistotie 14A (☎17 19 31).

**Currency Exchange: Exchange,** Kaivokatu 6, across from the train station. Cash exchange free; 30mk for up to 6 traveler's checks. Open M-F 8am-8pm, Sa 10am-4pm. **ATMS** are commonplace.

**Emergencies:** ☎112. **Police,** ☎100 22.

**Pharmacy: Yliopiston Apteekki,** Mannerheimintie 96 (☎41 78 03 00). Open 24hr.

**Medical Assistance: Aleksin lääkäriasema,** Mannerheimintie 8 (☎77 50 84 00).

**Internet Access: Cable Book Library,** Mannerheimintie 22-24, in the Lasipalatsi mall directly across from the bus station. Open M-Th 10am-8pm, Su noon-6pm.

**Post Office:** Mannerheiminaukio 1A (☎195 51 17). Open M-F 7am-9pm, Sa 9am-6pm, Su 11am-9pm.

# ⌕ ACCOMMODATIONS

Make reservations during June and July.

**Hotel Erottanjanpuisto (HI),** Uudenmaankatu 9 (☎64 21 69; fax 680 27 57). Turn right from the train station, left onto Mannerheimintie, and right onto Erottajankatu; Uuden-maankatu is on the right. Posh but pricey. Breakfast 25-35mk. Laundry 40mk. Reception 24hr. Check-in 10pm. Check-out 1pm. In summer, dorms 145mk, singles 260mk, doubles 320mk; off-season 140mk, 250mk, 300mk; nonmembers 15mk more.

**Eurohostel (HI),** Linnankatu 9, Katajanokka (☎622 04 70; fax 65 50 44; euroh@icon.fi; www.eurohostel.fi). 200m from the Viking Line/Finnjet ferry terminal. From the train station, head right to Mannerheimintie, and take tram #2 to Mastokatu; or tram #4 to Munkkiniemi (both dir.: Katajanokka). From Uspensky Cathedral, head down Kana-vankatu, turn left on Pikku Satamankatu, and bear right on Linnankatu. Finland's largest hostel, with bright rooms, non-smoking floors, and sauna. Singles 180mk; doubles 210mk; triples 315mk. Nonmembers 15-17mk more. Student discounts in winter.

**Finnapartments Fenno,** Franzeninkatu 26 (☎773 16 61; fax 701 68 89). From the train station, turn left, follow Kaisaniemenkatu, and bear left onto Unioninkatu (which becomes Siltasaarenkatu); or catch the metro to Hakaniemi. Then head right on Porthaninkatu, left onto Fleminginkatu, then left again. Economy singles with radio, sink and fridge 180 mk; regular singles 270mk; doubles 350mk.

# ⌕ FOOD

Escape pricey restaurants at **Alepa supermarket,** under the train station (open M-F 7:30-am-10pm, Sa 9am-10pm, Su 10am-10pm) or at **open-air markets** at **Kauppatori,** by the port (open June-Aug. M-Sa 7am-2pm and 4-8pm; Sept.-May M-F 7am-2pm) or the nearby **Vanha Kauppahalli** (Old Market Hall; open M-F 8am-8pm, Sa 8am-3pm).

**Zetor,** Kaivokatu 10, in Kaivopiha, the mall directly opposite the train station. Food, dancing, and tractors. Sit on a log stump to enjoy tiny fried fish. Main dishes 40-100mk. Open Su-M 3pm-1am, Tu-Th 3pm-3am, F 3pm-4am, and Sa 1pm-4 am.

**Café Engel,** Aleksanterinkatu 26, in Senate Square. Light fare for the budding intellec-tual crowd. Try the variety of coffees (from 12mk) and cakes (from 25mk). Open M-F 7:45am-midnight, Sa 9:30am-midnight, Su 11am-midnight.

**Golden Rax Pizza Buffet,** in the Forum, opposite the post office. All-you-can-eat pasta and pizza bargain extravaganza (43mk). Open M-Sa 11am-9pm, and Su 12am-9pm.

# ⌕ SIGHTS

**Tram #3T** circles past the major attractions in an hour, offering the city's cheapest tour. Better yet, walk—most sights are within 2km of the train station. Pick up a copy of the booklet *See Helsinki on Foot* before you go. The famed architect Alvar Aalto once said of Finland, "Architecture is our form of expression because our lan-guage is so impossible," and the bold 20th-century creations amid slick Neoclassi-

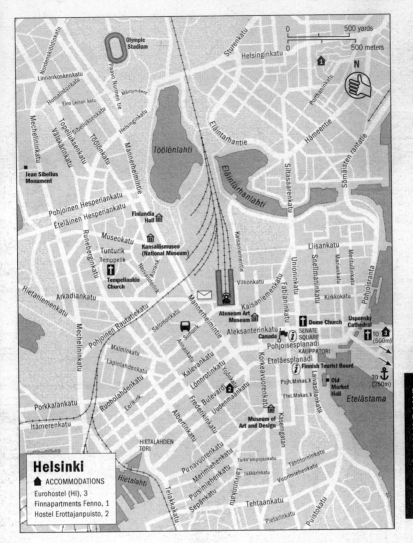

Helsinki

▲ ACCOMMODATIONS
Eurohostel (HI), 3
Finnapartments Fenno, 1
Hostel Erottajanpuisto, 2

GATEWAY CITIES

cal works that suffuse the region prove him right. Much of the layout and architecture of the old center, however, is the brainchild of a German: Carl Engel. After Helsinki became the capital of the Grand Duchy of Finland in 1812, Engel was chosen to design an appropriately grand city. In **Senate Square** (Senaatin Tori), on the corner of Unioninkatu and Aleksanterinkatu, his work is well represented by the **Dome Church** (Tuomiokirkko), completed in 1852. After marveling at the Neoclassical exterior, the austere interior of the Lutheran cathedral comes as quite a contrast. (Open June-Aug. M-Sa 9am-6pm, Su noon-8pm; Sept.-May Su-F 10am-4pm, Sa 10am-6pm.) A few blocks to the east, on Katajanokka island, the **Uspensky Orthodox Cathedral** (Uspenskinkatedraadi) guards the island with its red and gold cupolas. (Open M and W-F 9:30am-4pm, Tu 9:30am-6pm, Sa 9am-4pm, Su noon-3pm.)

Across from the train station stands Finland's largest art museum, the **Ateneum Taidemuseo**, Kaivokatu 2, with predominantly Finnish art from the 1700s to the

1960s. (Open Tu and F 9am-6pm, W-Th 9am-8pm, Sa-Su 11am-5pm. 15mk, students 10mk; special exhibits 30-35mk.) Aptly named for the crossing over stage in mitosis, **Kiasma,** Mannerheiminaukio 2, houses great modern art from Finnish and international artists in a funky silver building. (Open Tu 9am-5pm, W-Su 10am-10pm. 25mk, students 20mk.) Across the street, **Finlandia Talo,** Mannerheimintie 13E, stands as a testament to Alvar Aalto, who designed both the building and the interior and furnishings. (Guided tours 25mk, children 15mk.) Parks burst with beauty every summer, especially the promenade along lilac-covered **Töölönlahti** and **Tahti-torninvuori** (Observatory Park), overlooking Uspensky Cathedral.

##  ENTERTAINMENT AND NIGHTLIFE

Sway to afternoon music in **Esplanadi** (the park between Pohjoiesplanadi and Eteläesplanadi) or party with a younger crowd at **Kaivopuisto park** (on the corner of Puistokatu and Ehrenstromintie in the southern part of town) or **Hietaniemi beach.** (From Mannerheimintie, head down Hesperiankatu to the western shore.) The free English-language papers *Helsinki This Week, Helsinki Happens,* and *City* list popular cafes, bars, nightclubs, and events. Many clubs have an age 22 minimum. Bouncers and cover charges usually relax on weeknights; speaking English may help. With the exception of licensed restaurants and bars, the state-run liquor store **Alko** has a monopoly on sales of alcohol more potent than light beer. (Branch at Mannerheimintie 1, in Kaivopiha across from the train station. Open M-F 9am-8pm, Sa 9am-6pm.) Euro-pop at **Fennia,** Mikonkatu 17, opposite the train station. (22+. Cover 30mk. Open M-F 11pm-4am, Sa-Su 8pm-4am.) Sip 80-proof on the terrace at **Vanha** (Old Students' House), Mannerheimintie 3. The wide selection includes 130 beers. (Beer from 25mk. Cover up to 150mk for live bands. Open M-F 10am-2am, Sa 10am-4am, Su noon-midnight.) **Storyville,** Museokatu 8, near the National Museum, has live jazz and blues after 10pm. (Jazz club open 8pm-4am. Bar upstairs open M-Su 7pm-4am.) **DTM** (Don't Tell Mama), Annankatu 32, has a gay and mixed crowd. (20+. Open Su-Th 10pm-4am, F-Sa 9pm-4am.) **Decadenz,** a shop in the Forum, stocks flyers with rave info. Open M-F 10am-9pm, Sa 9am-6pm, Su 2pm-8pm.

# İSTANBUL, TURKEY ☎ (212,216)

**PHONE CODES** | Country code: **90.** International dialing prefix: **00.**

Straddling two continents and almost three millennia of history, İstanbul exists on an incomprehensible scale. The city unfolds against a densely historic landscape of Ottoman mosques, Byzantine mosaics, and Roman masonry. In its current incarnation, İstanbul is the most crowded and cosmopolitan city in the Turkish Republic. This urban supernova explodes out into the surrounding countryside behind an ever-expanding front of new construction sites, but no crane or cement truck could possibly hope to keep up with the pace of İstanbulian life.

**VISAS** Canadians and New Zealanders can stay for up to three months without a visa; South Africans are permitted to stay visa-free for one month. Citizens of Australia, Ireland, the UK, and the US require visas; it is most convenient to get them upon arrival in Turkey. A three-month visa costs AUS$30 for Australians, UK£10 for British citizens, IR£13 for Irish citizens, and US$45 for US citizens.

## ⬛ TRANSPORTATION

**Flights:** İstanbul's airport, **Atatürk Havaalanı,** is 30km from the city. The domestic and international terminals are connected by a **bus** (every 20min. 6am-10pm). To get to **Sultanahmet,** take a Havaş shuttle bus from either terminal to Aksaray (every 30min.

| | US$1 = 650,00 TL (TURKISH LIRA) | 100,000 TL = US$0.15 |
|---|---|---|
| C U R R E N C Y | CDN$1 = 440,000 TL | 100,000 TL = CDN$0.23 |
| | UK£1 = 960,000 TL | 100,000 TL = UK£0.10 |
| | IR£1 = 740,000 TL | 100,000 TL = IR£0.13 |
| | AUS$1 = 370,000 TL | 100,000 TL = AUS$0.27 |
| | NZ$1 = 281,391 TL | 100,000 TL = NZ$0.35 |
| | SAR1=93,756 TL | 100,000 TL = SAR1.07 |

6am-9pm, $7). From there, take an Eminönü-bound **tram** to Sultanahmet (walk uphill along the overpass to the Lâleli tram stop). You can also take a **taxi** ($4) to the Yeşilköy train station and take the commuter rail *(tren)* to the end of the line in Sirkeci. A direct taxi to Sultanahmet costs $17-20. To **Taksim,** take the Havaş shuttle bus to the end of the line (every 30min. 6am-9pm, $6). To get to the airport, have a private service such as **Karasu** (☎638 66 01) or **Zorlu** pick you up from your hostel ($5.50), or take the Havaş airport shuttle from the Taksim McDonald's (45min., every 30min., $6).

**Trains:** It's better to take the bus to and from İstanbul. **Sirkeci Garı** (☎(212) 527 00 50/ 1), in Eminönü sends trains to Europe via: **Bucharest, ROM** (17½hr., 1 per day, $30); **Athens, GRE** (24hr., 1 per day, $60); and **Budapest, HUN** (40hr., 1 per day, $90).

**Intercity Buses: Esenler Otobüs Terminal** (☎658 00 36). Take the tram to Yusufpaşa ($0.50), walk to the Aksaray Metro, and take it to the *otogar* (15min., $0.50). Most companies have courtesy buses, called *servis,* that run to the *otogar* from Eminönü, Taksim, and other city points (free with bus ticket). From İstanbul, buses travel to every city in Turkey. **Kamil Koç** (☎658 20 00 or 658 20 02) runs to **Ankara** (6hr.; every hr.; $22, students $20). **Pamukkale** runs to **Pamukkale** (10hr.; 7 per day; $21, students $19). Unlicensed **international** companies have been known to offer discounts on trips to Western European destinations and then ditch their passengers in Eastern Europe.

**Local Buses:** Run 5am-midnight, less frequently after 10:30pm, arriving every 10min. to most stops. Hubs are **Eminönü, Aksaray** (Yusufpaşa tram stop), **Beyazıt, Taksim, Beşiktaş,** and **Üsküdar.** Signs on the front indicate destination, and signs on the right-hand side list major stops. **Dolmuş** (private minibuses running a particular route) are more comfortable but less frequent than buses. Most *dolmuş* gather on the side streets north of Taksim Sq.

**Public Transportation: AKBİL** is an electronic ticket system that lets you save 15-50% on fares for municipal ferries, buses, trams, seabuses, and the subway (but not *dolmuş*). After an initial deposit of $5, add money in 1,000,000TL increments from any of the white IETT public bus booths that have the sign "AKBİL *satılır*."

**Trams:** The **tramvay** runs from Eminönü to Zeytinburnu ($0.50 per ride). A ramshackle **commuter rail** (known locally as *tren*) runs between Sirkeci Gar and the far western suburbs. A 2-stop **metro** runs from the Karaköy side of Galata Bridge to Tünel, where an old-fashioned trolley car continues along İstiklâl Cad. to Taksim.

**Taxis:** Little. Yellow. Fiats. Better? Not really; taxi drivers are even more reckless and speed-crazed than other İstanbul drivers. 1 light on the meter means day rate; 2 mean night rate. Rides within the city shouldn't cost more than $5.

## ✳ ORIENTATION

Waterways divide İstanbul into three sections. The **Bosphorus Strait** (Boğaz) separates Asia from Europe. Turks call the European side Avrupa and the Asian side Asya. The **Golden Horn,** a sizeable inlet, splits Avrupa into northern and southern parts. Directions in İstanbul are usually further specified by district. Most of the sights and tourist facilities are in Sultanahmet, south of the Golden Horn and towards the eastern end of the peninsula, which is framed by the Horn and the **Sea of Marmara.** The other half of Avrupa is focused on **Taksim Square,** the commercial and social center of the northern bank. Two main arteries radiate from it: **İstiklâl Caddesi,** the main downtown shopping street, and **Cumhuriyet Caddesi.** The Asian side of İstanbul is primarily residential, but offers plenty of strolling and a more relaxed pace.

# 🔢 PRACTICAL INFORMATION

**Tourist Office:** 3 Divan Yolu (☎/fax 518 87 54), at the north end of the Hippodrome in Sultanahmet. Open daily 9am-5pm. Branches in Taksim's **Hilton Hotel Arcade** on Cumhuriyet Cad., **Sirkeci train station, Atatürk Airport,** and **Karaköy Maritime Station.**

**Budget Travel: Indigo Tourism and Travel Agency,** 24 Akbıyık Cad. (☎517 72 66; fax 518 53 33; www.indigo-tour.com), in Sultanahmet's hotel cluster. IYTC cards $10. Also sells bus, plane, and ferry tickets, arranges airport shuttle service, tours, and holds mail. Open in summer daily 8:30am-7:30pm; off-season M-Sa 9:30am-6pm.

**Consulates: Australia,** 58 Tepecik Yolu, Etiler (☎257 70 52; fax 257 70 54); visas 10am-noon. **Canada,** 107/3 Büyükdere Cad., Gayrettepe (☎272 51 74; fax 272 34 27). **Ireland** (honorary), 25/A Cumhuriyet Cad., Mobil Altı, Elmadağ (☎246 60 25); visas 9:30-11:30am. **New Zealand,** 100-102 Maya Akar Center, Büyükdere Cad., Esentepe (☎211 11 14; fax 211 04 73). **South Africa,** 106/15 Büyükdere Cad., Esentepe (☎275 47 93; fax 288 76 42). Open M-F 9am-noon. **UK,** 34 Meşrutiyet Cad., Beyoğlu/Tepebaşı (☎293 75 40; fax 245 49 89). Open M-F 8:30am-noon. **US,** 104-108 Meşrutiyet Cad., Tepebaşı (☎251 36 02; fax 251 32 18). Open M-F 8:30-11am.

**Currency Exchange:** *Bureaux de change* around the city open M-F 8:30am-noon and 1:30-5pm. Most don't charge commission. **ATMs** generally accept all international cards. Most banks exchange **traveler's checks.** Exchanges in Sultanahmet have poor rates and a 2% commission, but are open late and on the weekends.

**American Express: Türk Express,** 47/1 Cumhuriyet Cad., 3rd fl. (☎235 95 00), uphill from Taksim Sq. Open M-F 9am-6pm. **Branch** in Hilton Hotel, Cumhuriyet Cad. (☎241 02 48). Open daily 8:30am-8pm. Neither gives cash advances or accepts wired money.

**Emergencies: Police,** ☎155. **Ambulance,** ☎112.

**Tourist Police:** In Sultanahmet, at the beginning of Yerebatan Cad. (24hr. hotline ☎527 45 03 or 528 53 69; fax 512 76 76). They speak the best English of all local cops, and their mere presence causes hawkers and postcard-selling kids to scatter.

**Hospitals: American Hospital,** Admiral Bristol Hastanesi, 20 Güzelbahçe Sok., Nişantaşı (☎231 40 50), applauded by İstanbul natives and tourists and has many English-speaking doctors. **German Hospital,** 119 Sıraselviler Cad., Taksim (☎251 71 00), also has a multilingual staff and is conveniently located for Sultanahmet hostelers.

**Post Office (PTT):** Main branch in Sirkeci, 25 Büyük Postane Sok. Stamp and currency exchange services open 8:30am-7pm. 24hr. phones. The **branch** off Taksim Sq. at the mouth of Cumhuriyet Cad. is convenient for mailing packages or making calls. 24hr. international phone office. No collect calls allowed. Open M-F 8am-8pm, Sa 8am-6pm. Phonecards available 30, 60, or 100 *kontür* (credits); 1 credit lasts 2-10 seconds during international calls. **Sirkeci postal code:** 5270050 and 5270051.

**Telephone Code:** ☎212 for the European side, ☎216 for the Asian side.

# 🔺 ACCOMMODATIONS

Budget accommodations are concentrated in **Sultanahmet** (a.k.a. Türist Şeğntral), bounded by Aya Sofia, the Blue Mosque, and the walls of the Topkapı Palace. The side streets around **Sirkeci** railway station and **Aksaray** have dozens of dirt-cheap and pretty dirty hotels. Hotels in **Lâleli** are the center of prostitution in İstanbul and should be avoided. Rates sometimes rise by 20% in July and August. All accommodations listed below are in Sultanahmet.

🏠 **İstanbul Hostel,** 35 Kutlugün Sok. (☎516 93 80; fax 516 93 84; email info@valide.com), down the hill from the Four Seasons Hotel. Cleanest bathrooms in town, and all the major amenities. Internet $2 per hr. Happy hour 6:30-9:30pm (beer $2). Breakfast $2. Dorms $7; doubles $16. Traveler's checks and cash only.

🏠 **Orient Youth Hostel,** 13 Akbıyık Cad. (☎517 94 93; fax 518 38 94; email orienthostel@superonline.com; www.hostels.com/orienthostel), 2 blocks south of Aya Sofia, on the backpacker strip. It's happy hour daily till 10pm. At night, the fun moves

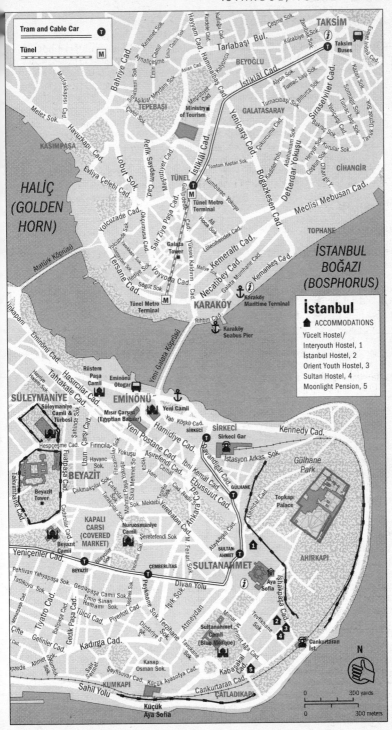

**İstanbul**

🏠 **ACCOMMODATIONS**
Yücelt Hostel/
Interyouth Hostel, 1
İstanbul Hostel, 2
Orient Youth Hostel, 3
Sultan Hostel, 4
Moonlight Pension, 5

to the bar (see **Entertainment,** p. 820). Belly dancing M, W, F 10pm. Breakfast included. Dorms $5; doubles $17; deluxe with TV and bath $35; quads $112.

■ **Moonlight Pension,** 87 Akbıyık Cad. (☎517 54 29 or 518 85 36; fax 516 24 80). Far from the madding backpacker scene. Rooftop views. Kitchen. Moonlights as a laundromat and internet cafe. Breakfast $2. Dorms $5; doubles $16; triples $21. MC/Visa.

**Yücelt Hostel/Interyouth Hostel,** 6/1 Caferiye Cad. (☎13 61 50 or 513 61 51; fax 512 76 28; email info@backpackersturkey.com; www.yucelthostel.com). A 3-building complex with amenities up the wazoo and a friendly staff make this a backpacker favorite. Breakfast $3. Dinner $3. Dorms $7-9; singles $18; doubles $18; triples $27. MC/Visa.

**Side Pension/Hotel Side,** 20 Utangaç Sok. (☎/fax 517 65 90), near the entrance of the Four Seasons Hotel. Look for the giant bearded heads on the street. This hotel/pension occupies the 2 buildings by the corner of Tevfikhane Sok. and Utangaç Sok. Pension singles $20; doubles $25; triples $35. Add $10 for clean, modern bath. Hotel singles $40; doubles $50; triples $60. Prices 20% less in winter. MC/Visa.

# ░ FOOD

İstanbul's restaurants, like its clubs and bars, often stick by the golden rule that if it's well advertised or easy to find, it's not worth doing. Great meals can be found on İstiklâl Cad. and around Taksim. Small Bosphorus suburbs such as **Arnavutköy** and **Sarıyer** (on the European side) and **Çengelköy** (on the Asian side) are the best places for fresh fish. **Vişne suyu** (sour cherry juice) is sold by vendors in Ottoman costume wearing big steel teapots on their backs ($.20-30). The best open-air market is the daily one in **Beşiktaş,** near Barbaros Cad.

■ **Doy-Doy,** 13 Şifa Hamamı Sok. (☎517 15 88). From the south end of the Hippodrome, walk down the hill around the edge of the Blue Mosque and look for the blue and yellow sign in the trees. The best-best and cheapest-cheapest of Sultanahmet's cheap eats, the 3-story Doy-Doy keeps locals and backpackers coming back for more-more. Tasty *kebap* and salads ($3.50 and under). Open daily 8:30am-late.

■ **Naregatsi Cafe.** Upstairs at the mouth of Sakezağacı Cad., across from the Ağa Camii. Perhaps the weirdest spot in the Taksim area, Naregatsi serves gourmet cafe fare in the midst of a galactic, high-speed collision of kitsch and concept art. Warhol would feel right at home. 4 flavors of cappuccino $3.50. Open daily noon-11:30pm.

**Dârüzziyâfe** (☎511 84 14/5; fax 526 18 91), behind the Sultanahmet Camii on the Hippodrome. Mellow atmosphere and attentive service. The specialty, *Süleymaniye çorbası* (meat and veggie soup; $2), is a must, as is the *çilek keşkül* (strawberry pudding; $1.50). No alcohol—they serve rosehip nectar instead. Open daily noon-11pm.

**Cennet,** 90 Divan Yolu Cad. (☎513 14 16), on the right side of the road as you walk from Sultanahmet toward Aksaray. Watch women make *gözleme* (Anatolian pancakes), particularly divine with cheese ($1). Live Turkish music and dancing nightly. $1 service charge added per person. Open daily 10am-midnight.

# ▣ SIGHTS

**HAGIA SOPHIA.** (Aya Sofia.) Built in AD 537 under the Justinian the Great, flush from reconquering Italy, as the main cathedral of a resurgent Byzantine Empire, the Aya Sofia was for 900 years the largest church in the world. When Constantinople fell to the Ottomans in 1453, it was converted into a mosque—indeed, its domed shape became the template for mosques all over the Ottoman Empire. Its religious life came to a close in 1932, when Atatürk declared it a museum. The **nave** is overshadowed by a gold-leaf mosaic **dome** lined with hundreds of circular windows. The **mihrab,** the calligraphy-adorned portal pointing towards Mecca, stands in the **apse,** which housed the altar of the Christian cathedral. The marble square on the floor marks the spot where Byzantine emperors were crowned. The **minbar,** the platform used by imams to address the crowd, is the stairway right of the *mihrab.* The **gallery** contains Byzantine mosaics as well as the famed **sweating pillar,** sheathed in bronze. (*Museum open Tu-Su 9:30am-4:30pm. Gallery open Tu-Su 9:30am-4pm. $6.50.*)

**BLUE MOSQUE.** (Sultanahmet Camii.) Located between the Hippodrome and Hagia Sofia, the six-minareted, multi-domed structure is the Blue Mosque. Completed in 1617, it was Sultan Ahmet's response to the architectural challenge of Hagia Sofia. (Open Tu-Sa 8:30am-12:30pm, 1:45-3:45pm, and 5:30-6:30pm. Dress modestly and remove your shoes. Women should cover their heads.)

**THE HIPPODROME.** (At Meydanı.) Few sights in Sultanahmet conjure images of the glory of Byzantine Constantinople like the Hippodrome. Built by the Roman Emperor Septimus Severus in AD 200, it served as a place for chariot races and public executions. The politically opposed **Hippodrome Factions** arose out of the Hippodrome's seating plan, which was determined by social standing. In AD 532, a tax protest turned into the full-out Nika Revolt. The city was ravaged in the ensuing melée. The tall, northernmost column with hieroglyphics is the **Dikili Taş,** an Egyptian obelisk erected by the Pharaoh Thutmosis III in 1500 BC and brought to Constantinople in the 4th century by Emperor Theodosius I. Farther south, the subterranean bronze stump is all that remains of the **Serpentine Column,** originally placed at the Oracle of Delphi. The southernmost column is the **Column of Constantine.** On the east side along Atmeydan Sok. is İbrahim Paşa Sarayı, the **Museum of Turkish and Islamic Art.** (Behind the Blue Mosque. Open Tu-Su 9:30am-4:30pm. US$2.)

**UNDERGROUND CISTERN.** (Yerebatan Sarayi.) Sultanahmet's most mysterious attraction is the oft-overlooked Underground Cistern. This palace is actually an underground cavern whose shallow water eerily reflects the images of its 336 supporting columns, all illuminated by colored lighting. Underground walkways originally linked the cistern to Topkapı Palace, but were blocked to curb rampant trafficking in stolen goods and abducted women. (As you stand with your back to Aya Sofia, the entrance lies 175m from the mosque in the small stone kiosk on the left side of Yerebatan Cad. Open daily 9:30am-5:30pm. $4, students $3.25.)

**TOPKAPI PALACE.** (Topkapı Sarayi.) Towering from the high ground at the tip of the old city and hidden behind walls up to 12m high, the palace was the nerve center of the Ottoman Empire. Topkapı offers unparalleled insights into the wealth, excess, cruelty, and artistic vitality that characterized the Ottoman Empire at its peak. Built by Mehmet the Conqueror between 1458 and 1465, it became an imperial residence during the reign of Süleyman the Magnificent. The palace is divided into a series of courts, all surrounded by the palace walls. The general public was permitted entrance to the **first courtyard** through the **Imperial Gate** to watch executions, trade, and view the nexus of the Empire's glory. At the end of the first courtyard, the **Gate of Greeting** (Bab üs-Selam) marks the entrance to the **second court.** To the right, the **Imperial kitchens** house collections of porcelain and silver. The last set of doors of the narrow alley lead to the palaces' Chinese and Japanese **porcelain collections.** The **Inner Treasury,** next door, is where various instruments of cutting, bludgeoning, and hacking are kept. The third court, officially known as **Enderun** (inside), is accessible through the inappropriately named **Gate of Felicity** (Eunuch's gate). Moving along down the colonnade brings you to the **Palace Treasury.** One of the highlights is the legendary **Topkapı dagger** (essentially three giant emeralds with a knife sprouting out of them), a gift Sultan Mahmut I intended to present to Nadir Shah of Iran in return for the solid gold throne displayed elsewhere in the treasury. Wrestle your way to the front of the line leading up to all 86 karats of the Pigot Diamond, better known as the **Spoonmaker's Diamond** because it was traded to a spoonmaker in exchange for three spoons. The **Pavilion of Holy Relics,** just on the other side of the courtyard, is leagues ahead in beauty and elegance. It holds the booty taken from Egypt by Selim the Grim as well as relics from Mecca, including the **staff of Moses** and hairs from **Mohammad's beard.**

The highlight of the **fourth courtyard** is the **Circumcision Room.** The **Harem's** 400-plus rooms housed the sultan, his immediate family, and an entourage of servants, eunuchs and general assistants. The mandatory tour begins at the **Black Eunuchs' Dormitory.** Next is the women's section of the harem, including the lavish chambers of the **Valide Sultan,** the sultan's mother and the most powerful woman in the Harem. Surrounding the room of the queen mum are the chambers of the **concu-**

**bines,** the women who put the slut back in sultanate. *(Open Tu-Su 9am-4:30pm. Each day's open galleries are posted next to the ticket window. Palace $6.50. Harem closes at 4pm. Mandatory tours of the Harem leave every 30min. 9:30am-3:30pm. Harem $4.)*

**GRAND BAZAAR.** Consisting of over 4000 shops, several banks, mosques, police stations, and restaurants, the enormous Grand Bazaar could be a city unto itself. It forms the entrance to the massive mercantile sprawl that starts at **Çemberlitaş** and covers the hill down to Eminönü, ending at the **Egyptian Spice Bazaar** (Mısır Çarşısı) and the Golden Horn waterfront. *(From Sultanahmet, follow the tram tracks toward Aksaray for 5min. until you see the mosque on your right. Enter the mosque's side gate, and walk with the park on your left to the entrance. Open M-Sa 9am-7pm.)*

## 🛁 TURKISH BATHS

Most İstanbul baths *(hamams)* have separate women's sections or women's hours, but not all have designated female attendants.

▓ **Çemberlitaş Hamamı,** 8 Verzirhan Cad. (☎522 79 74), just a soap-slide away from the Çemberlitaş tram stop. One of the cleanest and most beautiful *hamams* in İstanbul, built by Sinan in 1584. Both the men's and women's sections have marble interiors under large domes. Vigorous "towel service" after the bath requires a tip of $1.50-3. Bath $14, with massage $18; students $8, $12. Open daily 6am-midnight.

▓ **Çinli Hamamı,** in Fatih, near the butcher shops at the end of Itfaiye Cad. Built for the pirate Barbarossa, this excellent authentic bath still has a few of its original İznik and Kütahya tiles. Bath $5; massage $6. Both sections open 8am-8pm.

## 🎭 NIGHTLIFE

Nightlife is centered around **Taksim** and **İstiklâl Cad.** In **Sultanahmet,** all pubs are within 100m of another and have standardized beer prices ($1-1.25). The Beşiktaş end of **Ortaköy** is a maze of upscale hangouts; along the coastal road toward Arnavutköy are a string of open-air clubs. Cover charges are high ($18-45), and bouncers highly selective, but wander between **Ortaköy** and **Bebek** and try your luck.

▓ **Mordi Cafe Bar,** 47 Akbıyık Cad., down the street from the Orient Hostel in Sultanahmet. Leagues above the other backpacker bars in cleanliness and ambiance, this spot was formerly a private residence. Extraordinarily friendly staff. Happy hour until 10pm.

▓ **Jazz Stop,** at the end of Büyük Parmakkapı Sok in Taksim. Live bands lay the funk, blues, and jazz on thick as a mixed group of music lovers looks on. Beer $3; liquor from $6. Live music nightly from 11pm. Sept.-May F-Sa cover $10. Open 11am-4am.

**Peyote,** İmam Adnan Sok. (☎293 32 62), next to Leman Kültür, in Taksim. This humble spot is one of the area's cheapest venues for live music, popular with artists. F-Sa cover $7.50; 1 drink included. Live music Tu-Sa at 11:30pm. Open M-Sa 6pm-4am.

# BEIJING (北京), CHINA ☎(0)10

| PHONE CODE | Country code: **86.** International: **00.** |
| --- | --- |

China's forefathers have cultivated the nation's dreams of grandeur for as long as the Chinese have grown rice. Born of these visions of greatness, Beijing's Forbidden City, its Summer Palace, and the nearby Great Wall testify to a long history of imperial ostentation. Today, modern skyscrapers tell of capitalism's encroachment, the latest grand-scale revolution in Beijing's tumultuous history; life for most Beijing residents is quickly changing. Whether the national capital is your first or last stop on a Trans-Siberian itinerary, take a moment to enjoy Beijing, the enigmatic gateway to the People's Republic of China.

**VISAS** Visas are required of all travelers to China. Travelers arriving on the Trans-Siberian railroad should get a visa from the Chinese Embassy in **Moscow** (p. 605) before their departure.

<table>
<tr><td>US$1 = Y8.27 (RENMINBI)</td><td>Y10 = US$1.20</td></tr>
<tr><td>CDN$1 = Y5.61</td><td>Y10 = CDN$1.90</td></tr>
<tr><td>UK£1 = Y12.45</td><td>Y10 = UK£0.80</td></tr>
<tr><td>IR£ = Y9.99</td><td>Y10 = IR£1.00</td></tr>
<tr><td>AUS$1 = Y4.85</td><td>Y10 = AUS$2.00</td></tr>
<tr><td>NZ$1 = Y3.88</td><td>Y10 = NZ$2.60</td></tr>
<tr><td>6OSAR1 = Y1.18</td><td>Y10 = SAR8.50</td></tr>
</table>

CURRENCY

## ORIENTATION

Beijing is vast. Sprawling. Immense. Really, really big. Everything in Beijing is far away from everything else, and most of the budget accommodations are littered around the city's perimeters. The **Forbidden City** and **Tiananmen Square** form the city center on either side of **Changan Jie** (长安街), the main downtown east-west thoroughfare. **Dazhalan** and **Wangfujing,** southwest and northeast of Tiananmen Square, respectively, are full of shopping options. To the northeast is **Gongren Tiyuchang Bei Lu** (工人体育场北路), commonly known as Gongti Bei Lu, which leads to **Sanlitun,** one of the city's embassy compounds. Many older neighborhoods and *hutongs* (Beijing alleyways) are preserved in the **Drum Tower** and **Lama Temple** sectors to the north. To the far northwest is the zoo, the silicon district, Beijing and Qinghua Universities, and farther out, the **Summer Palace** and **Old Summer Palace.**

## TRANSPORTATION AND PRACTICAL INFORMATION

**Flights: Capital Airport** (shǒudū jīchǎng; 首都机场; š6456 2580), 1hr. outside the city by taxi (at least Y80; more to book in advance). **Civil Aviation Administration of China (CAAC;** zhōngguó mínháng; 中国民航), has several offices, but is headquartered in the Aviation Bldg. on 15 Xi Changan Jie (☎6601 7755; 24hr. domestic inquiry ☎6256 7811; international inquiry daily 8am-5pm ☎6256 6783).

**Trains:** Foreigners enter and exit through the **Beijing Main Station** (běijīng huǒchē zhàn; 北京火车站; ☎6512 9525 or 6563 3242) or **Beijing West Station** (běijīng xī zhàn; 北京西站;☎6321 6253), on Lianhuachi Dong Lu near Lianhuachi Park (bus #52).

**Travel Agencies:** There is a **tourist information service** in Beijing (☎6513 0828), but no actual tourist bureau. **China International Travel Service (CITS;** zhōngguǒ guójì lǚxíng shè; 中国国际旅行社), in the west lobby of the Beijing International Hotel, 9 Jianguomennei Dajie (☎6512 0507; fax 6512 0503). Open M-F 8:30am-noon and 1:30-5pm. **Branch** in the World Trade Tower, 1 Jianguomenwai Dajie, Ste. L100A (☎6505 3775 or 6505 2288, ext. 8110; fax 6505 3105). Open M-F 9am-noon and 1-5pm, Sa 9am-noon. CITS also has an English-language information hotline (☎6505 2266). **Tianhua International Travel Service** (tiānhuá guójì lǚxíng shè; 天华国际旅行社;☎8727 5387; fax 8727 5389) sits to the left of the business center and lobby of Jinghua Hotel. Arranges Mongolian, Russian, and Kazakh visas, railway tickets, cheap accommodations in Mongolia, and tours to the Gobi and other tourist spots. Open daily 8:30am-5pm.

**Embassies:** Beijing has two huge embassy compounds. One is at **Jianguomenwai,** near the Friendship Store, and the other is at **Sanlitun,** home to dozens of expat bars. **Australia,** 21 Dongzhimenwai Dajie, Sanlitun (☎(010) 6532 2331; fax 6532 4349). **Canada,** 19 Dongzhimenwai Dajie, Sanlitun (☎6532 3536; fax 6532 4072). **Ireland,** 3 Ritan Dong Lu, Jianguomenwai (☎6532 2914; fax 6532 6857). **Mongolia,** 2 Xiushui Bei Jie, Jianguomenwai (☎6532 1203; fax 6532 5045). **New Zealand,** 1 Donger Jie, Ritan Lu (☎6532 2731; fax 6532 3424). **Russia,** 4 Dongzhimennei, Beizhong Jie

GATEWAY CITIES

(embassy ☎6532 2051, visa ☎6532 1267; fax 6532 4853), is near, but not in, San-litun. **South Africa,** 50 Liangmaqiao Lu, Lufthansa Center, C801 (☎6465 1941). **UK,** 11 Guanghua Lu, Jianguomenwai (☎6532 1961; fax 6532 1939). **USS,** 2 Xiushui Dong Jie, Jianguomenwai (☎6532 3831; fax 6532 6057).

**Currency Exchange:** Almost every hotel and hostel as well as the **Bank of China** can exchange traveler's checks and US dollars. To cash traveler's checks into US dollars, head to **CITS** or the **Bank of China Head Office** (☎6601 6688), 410 Fuchengmennei Dajie, 2nd Fl., Counter 1 or 2.

**ATMs:** Nearly all accept AmEx, Cirrus, MC, Plus, and Visa. Locations include: **Bank of China,** 8 Yabao Lu, Chaoyang; **Palace Hotel,** 8 Jinyu Hutong, Dongdan Bei Dajie; **Landmark Towers,** 8 Dongsanhuan Bei Lu, Chaoyang; **Central Garden Hotel,** 18 Gaoliang-qiao Lu, Haidian; **Capital Airport; Friendship Store,** 17 Jianguomenwai Dajie; **Everbright China,** Changan Bldg., 7 Jianguomennei Dajie; **SCITECH Shopping Center,** 22 Jianguomenwai Dajie; or the **China World Hotel,** 1 Jianguomenwai Dajie.

**Emergency: Police, ☎**110. **Fire, ☎**119. **Ambulance, ☎**120.

**Police: Public Security Bureau** (gōngān jú; 公安局), 85 Beichizi Dajie (☎6524 2063; foreigners section ☎6404 7799, ext 2061; visa administrative dept. ☎6512 8871 2860), east of the Forbidden City.

**Telephones:** Almost all accommodations have telephones for international (IDD) calls. **Directory Assistance: ☎**114. **International Directory Assistance: ☎**115.

# ACCOMMODATIONS

In Beijing, budget typically means poor location around the city's southern periphery. The hostels and hotels along the mid-stretch of **Nansanhuan Lu**, between **Yangqiao** and **Muxiyuan** exits, teem with backpackers. These outposts provide dirtcheap dorms, bike rental, ticket and tour booking, and internet access. As with the rest of Beijing, the state of budget travel is in constant flux, so budget and location are beginning to merge, even for foreigners—**Beijing International Youth Hostel** and **Zhaolong International Youth Hostel** are two shining examples.

■ **Beijing International Youth Hostel** (bêijīng guójì qīngnián læshè; 北京国际青年旅舍), Beijing International Hotel, 9 Jianguomennei Dajie, Bldg. 2, 10th Fl. (☎6512 6688, ext. 6145 or 6146; fax 6522 9494), at the end of the road leading north from the main train station. Or take the subway or any bus to Beijing Zhankou or Beijing Zhan; the airport bus stops outside, too. Spankin' new. Reservations recommended. Dorms with A/C Y50, for nonmembers Y60.

■ **Zhaolong International Youth Hostel** (zhàolóng qīngnián læshè; 兆龙青年旅舍), 2 Gongren Tiyuguan Bei Lu (☎6597 2299; fax 6597 2288), at Sanhuan Lu, just behind the Zhaolong Hotel. Take bus #3, 43, or 300 to Baijiazhuang; it's a 5min. walk north. A backpacker's heaven. Sparkling rooms with A/C and shared showers positively glisten. 3- to 6-person dorms Y50, 2-person Y60; nonmembers Y60, Y70.

■ **Jinghua Youth Hostel** (jīnghuá fàndiàn; 京华饭店), Xiluoyuan Nanli, Yongdingmenwai Dajie, Fengtai (☎6722 2211 ext. 3359; fax 6721 1455), east of the smelly canal from McDonald's. Take bus #66 from Qianmen to Yangqiao. With a pool, 24hr. bar, co-ed dorms, and an unending flow of travelers, the Jinghua is a cauldron of carousal, arousal, and extra-spousal scandal. Deposit Y50. 30-person dorm Y25; doubles with bath Y140 and up; triples with bath Y180-35.

**Fangyuan Hotel** (fāngyuán bīnguǎn; 芳园宾馆), 36 Dengshikou Xi Jie (☎6525 6331), near Wangfujing Dajie and a 20min. walk from Tiananmen Square. Accessible by buses #103, 104, 108, and 111. Large, clean, slightly musty rooms in a terrific area. Deposit based on room rate. Reservations morning of arrival only. Singles Y126; doubles Y177-267, triples Y342. Breakfast included.

# FOOD

The streets of Beijing burst with food options. The *hutongs* (alleyways) overflow with stalls that vary in quality but are consistently low in price; special attention

GATEWAY CITIES

should be paid to the areas around **Qianmen** and **Wangfujing**, and **Tiantan, Ritan**, and **Beihai Parks.** Some great, not-too-expensive restaurants can be found around **Liang-maqiao**, as well as in a gray building with hanging eaves called **Hualong Jie** on Nan-heyan Dajie, a 5min. walk west from Wangfujing Dajie. An absolute must-see, the night food market at **Donganmen**, off Wangfujing Dajie, serves treats like fried ice cream and more exotic fare like whole-sparrows-on-a-stick nightly from dusk to 9:30pm. For an easy sit-down meal, just head into any restaurant that advertises *jiachangcai* (everyday family food; 家常菜). Tasty, filling meals are about Y10-20 per person, but foreigners are sometimes ripped off, so be careful.

**Beijing duck** is as intrinsic to the capital's history as *jingiu* and the Forbidden City. Food fit for kings, at prices budget travelers can stomach, is available at **Qian-men Quanjude Roast Duck Restaurant** (qiánmén quánjùdé kǎoyā diàn; 前门全聚德烤鸭店), 32 Qianmen Dajie. Founded in 1864, the Qianmen location is the oldest of the 15 branches. A pictorial menu helps walk tourists through a first-time Beijing duck experience. Meals Y75-100, carving extra. (☎6511 2418 or 6701 1379. "Fancier" part open daily 11am-1:30pm and 4:30-8:30pm; "less fancy" part 10am-9pm.)

## 👁 SIGHTS

**TIANANMEN SQUARE.** (Tiānānmén guǎngchǎng; 天安门广场.) As one of the largest and most notorious public meeting spaces in the world, Tiananmen Square has created enough historical and political fodder to last a lifetime. The political epicenter of popular protest in modern China, the square has witnessed May 4th anti-imperialist demonstrations, anti-Japanese protests, Mao Zedong's proclamation of the People's Republic of China, Red Guard rallies of the Cultural Revolution, politically charged outpourings of grief for Zhou Enlai, and pro-democracy protests. For most Chinese, Tiananmen Square remains an ideological mecca, a field of cement where they pay tribute to the heroes and victims of China's tumultuous history. Vivid images of the bloody events of 1989 may at times surface, but for now, the square seems rooted in a celebratory atmosphere, a prime kite-flying and picture taking site. On the north side of the square, the **Monument to the People's Heroes,** an angular slab of granite erected in 1958, depicts heroic, revolutionary events from recent Chinese history. At its southern end, Mao rests peacefully in the stately **Chairman Mao Mausoleum** (máo zhǔxí jìniàn táng; 毛主席纪念堂). *(Between Changan Dajie and Qianmen Dajie. Subway: Qianmen. Buses #1, 4, 10, and 20 stop along Changan Jie to the north, while #5, 9, 17, 22, 47, 53, 54, 59, and 307 reach Qianmen to the south. Bus #116 runs along the side of the square. Mausoleum open M-Sa 8:30-11:30am.)*

**FORBIDDEN CITY.** (Zǐjìn chéng; 紫禁城) During the palace's 500-year history, only 24 emperors and their most intimate attendants could have known every part of its 800 buildings and 9000 chambers. The Forbidden City, so named because commonfolk were barred from entry, was opened to the public in 1949. Now referred to as the **Imperial Palace** (gù gōng; 故宫), the complex is the largest and most impressive example of ancient architecture in China.

Construction of the Forbidden City was completed in 1406, the 4th year of Ming Emperor Yongle's reign. It was based on a principle of work before play; the administrative offices and temples are in the front, while the markets are in the back. The Son of Heaven conducted his stately affairs in the **ceremonial halls** of Taihedian, Zhonghedian, and Baohedian. The first hall is also the hall of the imperial throne. Past the **imperial living quarters**, Qianqinggong, Jiaotaidian, and Kunninggong (now voyeur-friendly peering halls), is the **Imperial Garden** and an impressive artificial **Mountain of Piled Excellence** topped with a pagoda. *(Take any bus to Tiananmen Square. Open daily 8:30am-5pm; last admission 3:30pm. English translations. Audio tours (narrated by Roger Moore) Y30, Y200 deposit. Palace Museum Y30, all-inclusive admission Y50. Students half-price, groups of more than 10 Y45, children under 1.2m free.)*

**SUMMER PALACE** (yìhé yuán; 颐和园). Constructed in 1750, the Summer Palace is the largest imperial palace and garden complex in China. Scattered across the emperors' enormous summertime playground are over 3000 halls, pavilions, towers, courtyards, and even a re-creation of the southern Chinese city of Suzhou where empresses could go "shopping" for fine silk. **Suzhou Jie** (苏州街) is the one area far enough off the beaten path to not to make it onto the mapped walking tour; it is a must-see all the same. Cool green water laps the sidewalks, stylized gondolas idle beside dumpling restaurants, and stone walkways wind between water on one side, and shops, snack stands, and street artists on the other.

Other sights include Empress Dowager Ci Xi's infamous **Marble Boat** (built in 1888 courtesy of embezzled funds), the **Seventeen Arch Bridge** topped with 544 stone lions, the **Pavilion for Listening to Orioles,** and the **Porcelain Pagoda.** A stroll along the stunning 728m **Long Corridor** (cháng láng; 长廊) winds past 8000 paintings and around most of the sights. *(The quickest way to the Summer Palace is to take minibus #375 from Xizhimen station. Bus #332 from the zoo stops there. From Qianmen, the Palace is 1½-2hr. away by bicycle. Open daily 8:30am-5pm. Map 10Y. All 3 main parks Y25-33.)*

**BADALING GREAT WALL** (bādálíng cháng chéng; 八达岭长城). Badaling is the part of the wall to visit if you want to take pictures and have admirers back home recognize them as the Great Wall. The government has taken great pains to restore this part to its "original" condition. Every tower and turret stands just as it did when the Mongols overran the country 700 years ago, give or take a few souvenir shops. Guard rails and a cable car (Y40, round-trip Y50) make Badaling the best, almost easy, way to see the Great Wall. You'll get to rub elbows with tourists from all around the world. *(Take bus #5 or 44 from Qianmen to Deshengmen, then walk over the nearby overpass, and hop on bus #919 from in front of a monstrous circular building. Badaling is the next stop (1½hr., Y5.5). Official tour buses #1, 2, and 4 (Y36) leave for Badaling Great Wall and the Ming Tombs from the northeast corner of Qianmen (6-10am), Beijing Train Station (6-10am), and the zoo (6-11am). Hotel services and tour guides are the most expensive means. Open daily 8am-8pm. Y30, students Y17.5.)*

**OTHER GREAT WALL SIGHTS.** Badaling isn't the only stop along the Great Wall. More difficult to access, but slightly more satisfying experiences (read: less tourist kitsch) await visitors at **Mutianyu** (慕田峪长城), **Simatai** (司马台长城), and **Huanghua** (黄花长城). Jinghua Hotel (see p. 822) runs tours and arranges other means of transportation to these sections.

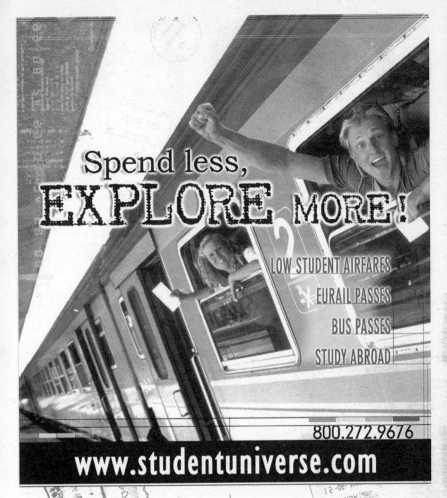
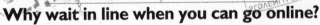

# INDEX

## A

accommodations 35
  dorms 36
  home exchange 36
  hostels 35
Acmeism 594
aerogrammes 40
Aggtelek, HUN 379
AIDS/HIV 32
air travel 45
Akhmatova, Anna 594, 656
Aladzha Monastery, BUL 135
Albright, Madeleine 207
alcohol 3, 28
  *becherovka* 209
  *bevanda* 150
  *borovička* 696
  *Borsodi* 367
  *krupnik* 459
  *kvas* 596, 762, 773, 775
  *marhulovica* 696
  *miód* 459
  *nalewka na porzeczce* 459
  *obolon* 774
  *pálinka*
    *barack pálinka* 312, 371
    *szilcapálinka* 312
    *unicum* 312
  *rakiya* 106, 437
  *rose brandy* 130
  *slivovica* 696
  *slivovice* 209
  *vodka* 773
  *Zubrówka* 459
Aleksandr Column 650
Alexander II. See tsars.
Alexander the Great 434, 446
Alexander, Dr. Vojtech 716
Alexandrescu, Grigore 554
Alighieri, Dante 748

Alupka, UKR 788
American Express 24, 25
American Express offices
  Berlin, GER 807
  Brno, CZK 268
  Bucharest, ROM 565
  Istanbul, TUR 816
  Kraków, POL 483
  Moscow, RUS 611
  Opatija, CRO 172
  Prague, CZR 222
  Pula, CRO 165
  Rīga, LAT 393
  Sofia, BUL 115
  Split, CRO 186
  Tallinn, EST 286
  Vienna, AUS 66
  Warsaw, POL 469
  Zagreb, CRO 158
Andreevski, Petre 436
Andropov, Yuri 592, 619
Antonescu, Gen. 553
appeasement 206
April Laws 309
Archabbey of Pannonhalma, HUN 344
archaeological sites
  Pliska, BUL 144
  Veliki Preslav, BUL 144
Schöenberg, Arnold 61
Asen, Ivan and Peter 103
Asparukh 102
Augustus 166
Aurelius, Marcus 60
Auschwitz-Birkenau, POL 489–490
**AUSTRIA** 58–75
  accommodations and camping 63
  additional reading 62
  at a glance 58
  culture 60
  customs and etiquette 62
  food and drink 61
  history 58

  keeping in touch 63
  literature 60
  music 61
  national holidays 60
  politics 60
  tourist services and money 63
  transportation 62
  traveling essentials 62
  visual arts and architecture 61
Austro-Hungarian Empire 9, 309, 693
Axis powers in Bulgaria 435

## B

Bach, Johann Sebastian 250
Bachkovo Monastery, BUL 124
Badascony, HUN 360
Baden bei Wien, AUS 73
Bagryana, Elisaveta 105
Bakhchisarai, UKR 782
Bakuriani, Abazii and Grigorii 124
Balchik, BUL 134
Balkan War 435
Banská Bystrica, SLK 708–710
Bansko, BUL 125–127
Bardejov, SLK 733–734
Bardejovské Kúpele, SLK 735
Bartók, Béla 311
Baryshnikov, Mikhail 396, 654, 658
Baška, CRO 174
baths
  Budapest, HUN 335

INDEX

# MAP INDEX

# ABOUT LET'S GO

## FORTY YEARS OF WISDOM

As a new millennium arrives, *Let's Go: Europe*, now in its 41st edition and translated into seven languages, reigns as the world's bestselling international travel guide. For over four decades, travelers criss-crossing the Continent have relied on *Let's Go* for inside information on the hippest backstreet cafes, the most pristine secluded beaches, and the best routes from border to border. In the last 20 years, our rugged researchers have stretched the frontiers of backpacking and expanded our coverage into Asia, Africa, Australia, and the Americas. This year, we've introduced a new city guide series with titles to San Francisco and our hometown, Boston. Now, our seven city guides feature sharp photos, more maps, and an overall more user-friendly design. We've also returned to our roots with the inaugural edition of *Let's Go: Western Europe*.

It all started in 1960 when a handful of well-traveled students at Harvard University handed out a 20-page mimeographed pamphlet offering a collection of their tips on budget travel to passengers on student charter flights to Europe. The following year, in response to the instant popularity of the first volume, students traveling to Europe researched the first full-fledged edition of *Let's Go: Europe*, a pocket-sized book featuring honest, practical advice, witty writing, and a decidedly youthful slant on the world. Throughout the 60s and 70s, our guides reflected the times. In 1969 we taught travelers how to get from Paris to Prague on "no dollars a day" by singing in the street. In the 80s and 90s, we looked beyond Europe and North America and set off to all corners of the earth. Meanwhile, we focused in on the world's most exciting urban areas to produce in-depth, fold-out map guides. Our new guides bring the total number of titles to 51, each infused with the spirit of adventure and voice of opinion that travelers around the world have come to count on. But some things never change: our guides are still researched, written, and produced entirely by students who know first-hand how to see the world on the cheap.

## HOW WE DO IT

Each guide is completely revised and thoroughly updated every year by a well-traveled set of nearly 300 students. Every spring, we recruit over 200 researchers and 90 editors to overhaul every book. After several months of training, researcher-writers hit the road for seven weeks of exploration, from Anchorage to Adelaide, Estonia to El Salvador, Iceland to Indonesia. Hired for their rare combination of budget travel sense, writing ability, stamina, and courage, these adventurous travelers know that train strikes, stolen luggage, food poisoning, and marriage proposals are all part of a day's work. Back at our offices, editors work from spring to fall, massaging copy written on Himalayan bus rides into witty, informative prose. A student staff of typesetters, cartographers, publicists, and managers keeps our lively team together. In September, the collected efforts of the summer are delivered to our printer, who turns them into books in record time, so that you have the most up-to-date information available for your vacation. Even as you read this, work on next year's editions is well underway.

## WHY WE DO IT

We don't think of budget travel as the last recourse of the destitute; we believe that it's the only way to travel. Living cheaply and simply brings you closer to the people and places you've been saving up to visit. Our books will ease your anxieties and answer your questions about the basics—so you can get off the beaten track and explore. Once you learn the ropes, we encourage you to put *Let's Go* down now and then to strike out on your own. You know as well as we that the best discoveries are often those you make yourself. When you find something worth sharing, please drop us a line. We're Let's Go Publications, 67 Mount Auburn St., Cambridge, MA 02138, USA (email: feedback@letsgo.com). For more info, visit our website, www.letsgo.com.

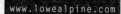

www.lowealpine.com

# If I had my life to live over again,

I would relax. I would limber up. I would take more chances.

## I would take more trips.

I would climb more mountains, swim more rivers, and watch more sunsets.

I would go places and do things and travel lighter than I have.

## I would ride more merry-go-rounds.

Excerpt from Nadine Stair, 85 years old / photo> John Norris

technical packs & apparel

Will you have enough stories to tell your grandchildren?

Yahoo! Travel

Do You YAHOO!?

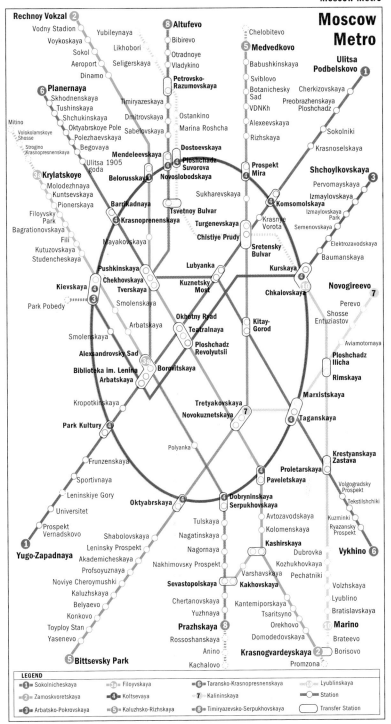

# Moscow

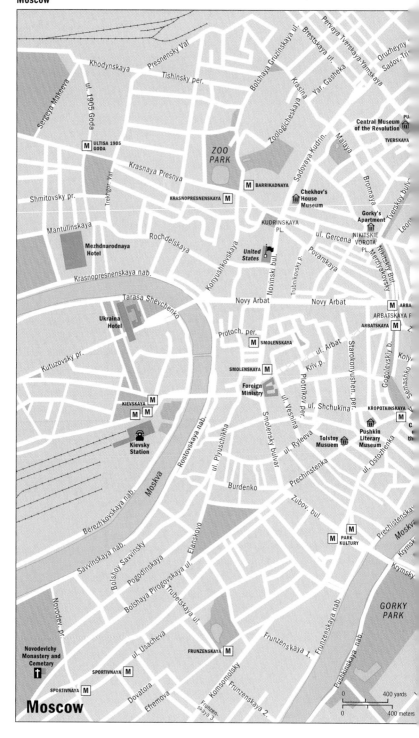

Khodynskaya
Presnensky Val
Tishinsky per.
Sergera Makeeva
ul. 1905 Goda
Pervaya Tverskaya-Yamskaya
Bolshaya Gruzinskaya ul.
Brestskaya ul.
Krasina
Yar. Gasheka
Oruzheyny
Sadov. Tri

**M** ULTISA 1905 GODA

Central Museum of the Revolution
PU
TVERSKAYA

Zoologicheskaya
Malaya

Krasnaya Presnya

**ZOO PARK**

Sadovaya-Kudrin.
Bromaya
Tverskoy bulv.

Shmitovsky pr.

**M** BARRIKADNAYA

Chekhov's House Museum

**KRASNOPRESNENSKAYA** **M**

Gorky's Apartment
Leon

Mantulinskaya

Rochdelskaya

KUDRINSKAYA PL.
ul. Gercena
NIKITSKIE VOROTA PL.
Nikitsky bulv.
Merzlyakovsky

Mezhdnarodnaya Hotel

Konyushkovskaya
United States
Novinsky bul.
Povarskaya
Trubnikovsky p.

Krasnopresnenskaya nab.

Tarasa Shevchenko

Novy Arbat
Novy Arbat
**M** ARBA
ARBATSKAYA F

Ukraina Hotel

Protoch. per.
**M** SMOLENSKAYA
ARBATSKAYA **M**

Kutuzovsky pr.

**SMOLENSKAYA** **M**

Foreign Ministry

ul. Arbat
Kriv. p.
Plotnikov per.
ul. Veshna
Starokonyushen. per.
ul. Shchukina
Gogolevsky b.
Koly
Semashk

**KROPOTKINSKAYA**

**KIEVSKAYA** **M**
**M** **M**

Rostovskaya nab.
ul. Plyuschikha
Smolensky bulvar
ul. Ryleeva
Tolstoy Musuem
Pushkin Literary Museum
**M** C
th
ul. Ostozhenka

Kievsky Station

Moskva

Berezhkovskaya nab.
Burdenko
Prechinstenka
Prechistenskay
Moskv

Savvinskaya nab.
Bolshov Savvinsky
Pogodinskaya
Elanskovo
Zubov. bul.
**M** PARK KULTURY
Krymsk
Krymsky

Novodev. pr.
Bolshaya Pirogovskaya ul.
Bolshaya Trubetskaya ul.
**GORKY PARK**

Novodevichy Monastery and Cemetary

ul. Usacheva
**FRUNZENSKAYA** **M**
Frunzenskaya 1.
Frunzenskaya nab.
Pushkinskaya nab.

**SPORTIVNAYA** **M**
**SPORTIVNAYA** **M**
Dovatora
Efremova
Frunzen-skaya 3.
Komsomolsky
Frunzenskaya 2.

| 0 | | 400 yards |
|---|---|---|
| 0 | | 400 meters |

# Moscow

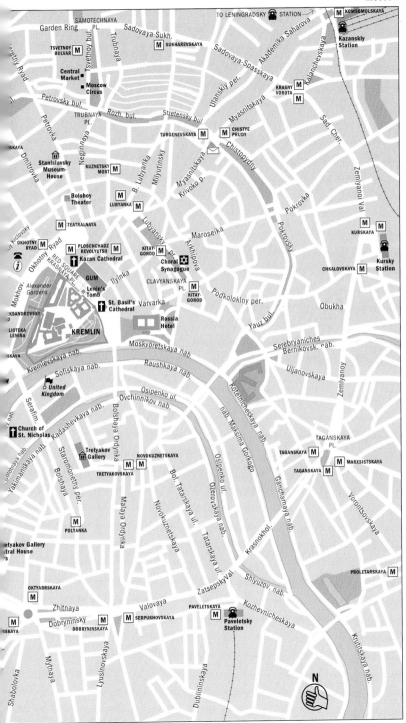

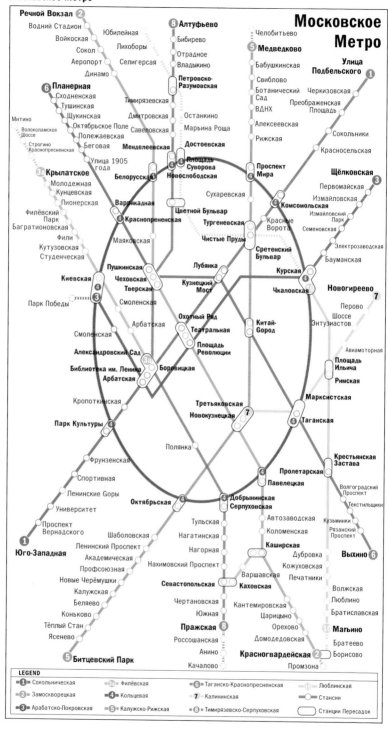

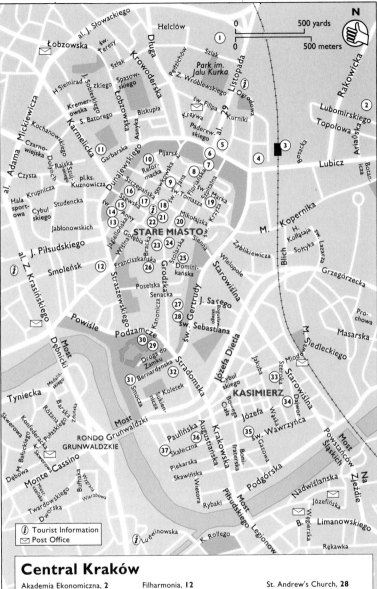

## Central Kraków

Akademia Ekonomiczna, 2
Almatur Office, 24
Barbican, 6
Bernardine Church, 32
Bus Station, 4
Carmelite Church, 11
Cartoon Gallery, 9
City Historical Museum, 17
Collegium Maius, 14
Corpus Christi Church, 35
Czartoryski Art Museum, 8
Dominican Church, 25
Dragon Statue, 31

Filharmonia, 12
Franciscan Church, 26
Grunwald Memorial, 5
Jewish Cemetery, 33
Jewish Museum, 34
Kraków Głowny Station, 3
Monastery of the
    Reformed Franciscans, 10
Muzeum Historii Fotografii, 23
Orbis Office, 19
Pauline Church, 37
Police Station, 18
Politechnika Krakowska, 1

St. Andrew's Church, 28
St. Anne's Church, 15
St. Catherine's Church, 36
St. Florian's Gate, 7
St. Mary's Church, 20
St. Peter and Paul Church, 27
Stary Teatr (Old Theater), 16
Sukiennice (Cloth Hall), 21
Town Hall, 22
University Museum, 13
Wawel Castle, 29
Wawel Cathedral, 30

*(i)* Tourist Information
✉ Post Office

Prague

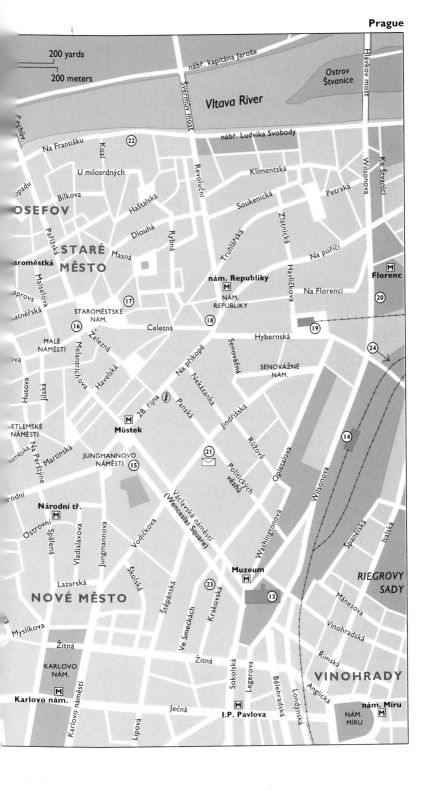

Prague

**Central Budapest**

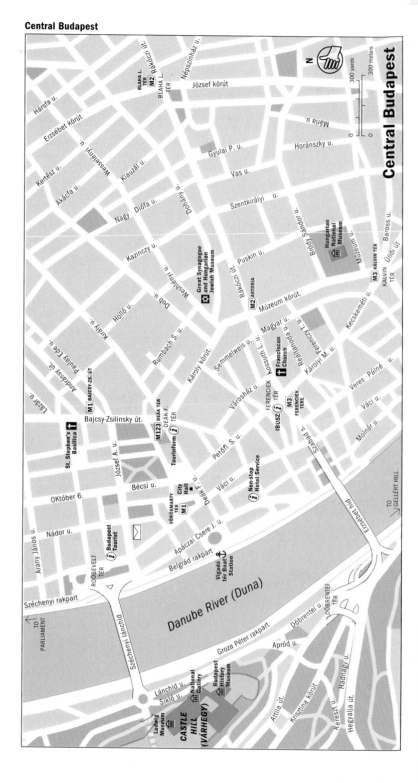

Central Budapest